Financial Services

Financial Services

Thummuluri Siddaiah
Professor of Management and Dean
Sri Venkateswara University, Tirupati

Pearson

The publishers are grateful to the organizations and individuals who have allowed the use of their copyrighted material. Each source is acknowledged in the appropriate place in the text. While every effort has been made to trace the owners, the publishers apologize for any inadvertent errors or omissions and would welcome corrections to be incorporated into the next edition or reprint of the book.

Assistant Acquisitions Editor: Maran A.
Senior Development Editor: Shabnam Dohutia
Assistant Production Editor: Barun Kumar Sarkar
Compositor: Glyph International
Printer: India Binding House, Noida

ISBN: 978-81-317-3159-8

First Impression, 2021
Eleventh Impression, 2023
Twelfth Impression

Published by Pearson India Education Services Pvt Ltd, CIN: U72200TN2005PTC057128.

Head Office: 1st Floor, Berger Tower, Plot No. C-001A/2, Sector 16B, Noida – 201 301, Uttar Pradesh, India.

Registered Office: Featherlite, 'The Address' 5th Floor, Survey No 203/10B, 200 Ft MMRD Road, Zamin Pallavaram, Chennai - 600044
Website: in.pearson.com, Email: companysecretary.india@pearson.com

Printed in India by: Rakmo Press Pvt. Ltd., New Delhi

In memory of
my late parents,
Thummuluri Nagamma and
Thummuluri Narayana,
and
my late daughter Haritha

About the Author

Thummuluri Siddaiah is a professor of management at Sri Venkateswara University, Tirupati, Andhra Pradesh. He received master's degrees in commerce and economics from Sri Venkateswara University, and went on to receive an M.Phil. from the Delhi School of Economics. He received his Ph.D. in the area of banking in 1984.

Professor Siddaiah's academic interests include finance and information systems. He has taught courses in finance and information systems at the master's level for over 30 years, and has over 20 years' experience in teaching financial services to MBA students. He has been a visiting faculty at management institutes across the country.

Besides teaching and research, Professor Siddaiah is involved in executive development programmes and various administrative and advisory roles. He is the principal of Sri Venkateswara University College of Commerce, Management and Computer Science, Tirupati, and the dean of the faculty. He has also served as the registrar of Sri Venkateswara University. Professor Siddaiah has been a member of the Expert Committee of the All India Council for Technical Education (AICTE) and the chairperson of the Peer Team of the National Assessment and Accreditation Council (NAAC). Professor Siddaiah is associated with the Institute of Chartered Accountants of India (ICAI) as an examiner, and was the vice president of the Indian Association for Management Development. Professor Siddaiah has presented papers on contemporary issues in finance in several seminars and conferences. His columns have appeared in newspapers, magazines and journals. He is the author of *International Financial Management*, published by Pearson Education.

Brief Contents

Contents

Preface

Financial institutions are a vital part of an economy. Their primary function is to mobilize savings and allocate them to those in need of funds. Financial institutions encourage a higher level of savings and investment, leading to economic growth. Each type of financial institution has a special role as these institutions are conceived to provide specialized services. Failure to provide these services can be costly to the economy as efficient financial services are a necessary condition for sustainable economic growth.

Financial markets facilitate the mobilization of savings and help in allocating funds to different sectors of the economy. The savings in an economy are mobilized for investment by issuing different kinds of financial instruments, known as *securities*. Financial institutions, financial markets and financial instruments together form the financial system of an economy.

The world of finance has been changing in size, structure and scope at a rate never imagined or expected by economists. In many countries—particularly in developed economies like the United States, the United Kingdom and Japan—the contribution of the financial sector to the GDP has increased from less than 2 per cent in the 1940s to more than 8 per cent in the twenty-first century. The innovations in finance have increased the efficiency of the global financial system tremendously. For instance, the innovations in risk management techniques and methods have facilitated the widening and deepening of the global financial markets. The number of new financial products and services has expanded dramatically. New classes of financial institutions, such as asset management companies, special-purpose vehicles, private equity firms, depositories and custodians, have emerged. Securitization, the process of pooling and converting assets into tradable securities, now pervades financial markets across the globe. Financial markets are increasingly swayed by credit default swaps, the villain of the global recession of 2007.

Globalization of national economies in tandem with financial liberalization has stimulated the demand for cross-border finance and fostered the creation of an internationally mobile pool of capital. The advancements in computing and communication technology have also spurred the growth of cross-border capital movements. Such developments in the world economy have brought about many changes in the size, structure and scope of the financial services industry. A major change that has taken place in the world of finance is financial disintermediation. The deficit units (users of finance) have directly established relationships with the providers of finance (savers), bypassing intermediate institutions like banks. Companies and other borrowers now tend to rely more and more on money and capital markets, so the competition among the providers of financial services has increased. Non-banking financial companies are competing aggressively with banks for household savings and corporate finance. They are garnering a rising share of savings as households bypass bank deposits to hold their funds in higher-return instruments such as mutual funds. Mutual funds, which are better able to diversify risk and take advantage of economies of scale, have grown dramatically, in size as well as in sophistication. The expansion of non-banking financial intermediaries has forced commercial banks to seek innovative ways to expand and diversify their operations in order to maintain their competitiveness and profitability. As a consequence, distinctions between commercial banks and other financial institutions are getting blurred. The competition among the providers of financial services has also led to the deepening and broadening of financial markets.

Financial services encompass several financial products and services that are delivered by various kinds of financial institutions or agencies. The intense competition in the financial services industry requires every provider of financial services to be more efficient and effective. The growing aspirations and expectations of the users of financial services constantly challenge the providers of financial services. To meet such challenges, many kinds of new financial products and services have been developed with new delivery mechanisms. Alongside, new regulations governing the various kinds of financial products and services have come into being. With time, the whole gamut of financial services has become more complex.

Financial Services aims to make the complex nature of financial products and services simple and easy to comprehend. The book provides the analytical framework for a range of financial products and services offered by various financial institutions and agencies. The simplified presentation of regulatory and legislative frameworks is an important characteristic of this book. The book explains concepts with the help of real-life examples, box items, questions and cases. The content of this book has been class-tested with the students of MBA in different institutions over the last 20 years.

Organization

The book is divided into 23 chapters. A brief outline of each chapter is presented here.

Chapter 1, "Financial Services: An Overview", presents a bird's eye view of the financial services industry. The interrelationship between different components of the financial system is the highlight of this chapter.

Chapter 2, "Stock Exchanges in India", deals with the origin and development of stock exchanges in India. The two major stock exchanges—the Bombay Stock Exchange and the National Stock Exchange—are described with a focus on their trading systems.

Chapter 3, "Financial Instruments", describes the various types of financial instruments that are in use. The regulatory framework for issuing different kinds of securities is also discussed in this chapter.

Chapter 4, "Management of Capital Issues", presents the procedural aspects involved in the issue of various types of financial securities. The description of offer documents is a key aspect of this chapter.

Chapter 5, "Pricing of Capital Issues", discusses the pricing of capital issues. The various methods of pricing capital issues along with the regulatory framework are discussed. The book-building process is also dealt with in this chapter.

Chapter 6, "Settlement of Stock Market Transactions", presents the various issues involved in the settlement of stock market transactions. The concepts of *badla* and rolling settlement are clearly explained.

Chapter 7, "Merchant Banking", presents the evolution of the concept of merchant banking and the functions of a merchant banker. The SEBI guidelines with regard to merchant banking are also discussed in this chapter.

Chapter 8, "Intermediaries in Capital Issues", describes the roles of various intermediaries involved in capital issues within the framework of SEBI regulations.

Chapter 9, "Financial Derivatives", explains the trading of different kinds of financial derivatives. The origin and development of derivatives trading in India are also highlighted in this chapter.

Chapter 10, "Depository and Custodial Services", describes the depository system in India. The SEBI regulations with regard to depository and custodial services are also discussed.

Chapter 11, "Insider Trading", explains the concept and ramifications of insider trading. The SEBI regulations to control insider trading and some real-life cases of insider trading are also presented in this chapter.

Chapter 12, "Credit Rating Services", deals with credit rating issues, including the importance and methodology of credit rating. The profiles of major credit rating agencies are also discussed along with SEBI regulations.

Chapter 13, "Mutual Funds", traces the origin of mutual funds and presents the structure of mutual funds in India. The performance evaluation models are also highlighted in this chapter.

Chapter 14, "Insurance Services", presents the origin and development of the insurance industry in India. The role of the Insurance Regulatory and Development Agency is discussed along with the regulatory framework of the insurance business.

Chapter 15, "Venture Capital Financing", explains the concept and special features of venture capital. The structure of venture capital funds in India is also discussed along with SEBI guidelines.

Chapter 16, "Securitization", describes the process of securitization and discusses the benefits and the legal framework of securitization.

Chapter 17, "Corporate Restructuring", describes different forms of corporate restructuring. The takeover code of SEBI, the process of buy-back of shares, and the SEBI guidelines for acquisitions and takeovers are also discussed in this chapter.

Chapter 18, "Leasing and Hire Purchase", traces the origin of leasing in India. Different lease evaluation methods and the special features of hire purchase are also described in this chapter.

Chapter 19, "Non-banking Finance Companies", explains the special features of NBFCs and presents the prudential norms governing them. Corporate governance is also explained with respect to NBFCs.

Chapter 20, "Chit Funds", traces the origin of chit funds in India. The modus operandi of chit fund operations is explained along with the legal framework.

Chapter 21, "Nidhis", presents an overall idea of the functioning of Nidhis. The legislative measures governing the functioning of Nidhis are also discussed in this chapter.

Chapter 22, "Housing Finance", describes the importance of housing finance in India. The housing policy initiatives of the Government of India are discussed along with the directives of RBI and NHB.

Chapter 23, "Factoring and Forfaiting Services", discusses the importance of factoring and the process of factoring.

Features

Financial Services uses a number of pedagogical tools to help explain the complexities of financial products and services:

Learning Objectives: Each chapter starts with learning objectives that identify the key topics discussed in the chapter.

LEARNING OBJECTIVES

After studying this chapter, you should be able to:

- Understand the concept of capital formation.
- Discuss the relationship between savings and investment.
- Understand the nature of savings and the role of savings in economic development.
- Highlight the importance of investment.
- Understand the concept of a financial system.
- Describe the constituents of a financial system.
- Develop a bird's-eye view of global financial services.

Margin Notes: The margin notes facilitate the learning process by highlighting important definitions and facts.

Free-float capitalization refers to the value of that proportion of total shares of a company that are readily available for trading in the market.

shares of a company that are readily available for trading in the market. Free-float stock generally excludes promoters' holding, government holding, holdings by persons/bodies with controlling interest, holdings through the FDI route, strategic stakes by private corporate bodies/individuals, equity held by associate/group companies (cross holdings), equity held by employee welfare trusts and other locked-in shares that do not come to the market for trading in the normal course. Thus, the market capitalization of each company in the index is reduced to the extent of its readily available shares for trading in the market.

The BSE keeps a close watch on the events that might affect the index on a regular basis. It makes adjustments for rights, bonus and other issues. If no adjustment is made, a discon-

Solved Examples: Solved examples illustrate how numerical problems can be approached. These examples are designed to help students apply the concepts discussed in the chapter.

Example 18.3

Ramco Ceramics Limited is contemplating investing in equipment costing INR 20 million. The company can purchase the equipment by raising additional debt at a simple interest rate of 10 per cent per annum. The equipment has an effective life of five years with zero salvage value. The company follows the straight-line method of depreciation and is in the 30 per cent tax bracket. Alternatively, the company can take the equipment on a finance lease with a five-year primary period at INR 5 million payable annually in arrears. Should the company lease the asset?

Solution

Table 18.2 shows the cash flows of lease financing.

Table 18.2 Cash flows of lease financing (figures in INR million)

	Year 0	*Year 1*	*Year 2*	*Year 3*	*Year 4*	*Year 5*
1. Purchase price avoided	20	—	—	—	—	—
2. Depreciation	—	(4)	(4)	(4)	(4)	(4)

Boxes: The chapters are interspersed with boxes that provide interesting facts related to the topic discussed in the chapter. These additional bits of information help retain the students' interest and provide them insights into real-world events.

Box 2.1 Stock Exchanges in India

Bombay Stock Exchange Ltd, National Stock Exchange of India Ltd, and Over-the-Counter Exchange of India (OTCEI) are the major stock exchanges in India. Besides these, there are several regional stock exchanges in the country:

- Ahmedabad Stock Exchange
- Bangalore Stock Exchange
- Bhubaneshwar Stock Exchange
- Calcutta Stock Exchange
- Cochin Stock Exchange
- Coimbatore Stock Exchange
- Delhi Stock Exchange
- Guwahati Stock Exchange
- Hyderabad Stock Exchange*
- Jaipur Stock Exchange
- Ludhiana Stock Exchange
- Madhya Pradesh Stock Exchange
- Madras Stock Exchange
- Magadh Stock Exchange*
- Mangalore Stock Exchange*
- Meerut Stock Exchange
- Pune Stock Exchange
- Saurashtra Kutch Stock Exchange*
- Uttar Pradesh Stock Exchange
- Vadodara Stock Exchange

* 4 exchanges have been since derecognized

Real-world Data: Information from sources such as SEBI, RBI, NSE, and various financial service organizations help students understand the applications of various concepts in the real world.

Table 2.3 The Indian stock market: A comparison with international markets (end December 2007)

Particulars	*USA*	*UK*	*Japan*	*Singapore*	*India*
Number of listed companies	5130	2588	3844	472	4887*
Market capitalization (USD billion)	19947	3859	4453	353	1819
Market capitalization ratio (per cent)	149.1	157.13	90.25	274.41	200.09
Turnover (USD billion)	42613	10324	6497	384	1108
Turnover ratio (per cent)	216.5	270.1	141.6	122.0	84

* Companies listed on the BSE
Market capitalization is computed as a percentage of gross national income 2006.
Source: NSE, Indian Securities Market— A Review (2008)

Questions and Problems: Each chapter has end-of-chapter questions that test the students' understanding of the chapter. The problems at the end of relevant chapters are designed to help students practice numerical problems discussed in the chapter.

Questions and Problems

1. What are the different forms of corporate restructuring? What purpose(s) do they serve?
2. Discuss merger motives.
3. What are the different types of mergers? Give examples of each type.
4. What do you understand by acquisitions? When does an acquisition become a takeover? Discuss the reasons for takeovers.
5. What is the role of price-earnings ratio in stock swapping? Illustrate your answer.
6. Discuss different methods of financing mergers and acquisitions.

Based on the above data, determine: (i) the pre-merger market price of a share of each company; and (ii) the maximum exchange ratio *ABC* can offer without dilution of EPS and market price per share.

18. A summary balance sheet of M/S Srinivas Enterprises is provided in Table 17.16.

Table 17.16 Summary balance sheet of M/S Srinivas Enterprises (INR million)

Liabilities		*Assets*	
Paid-up equity share capital (10 million shares at INR 10	100	Net fixed assets	150

Case Studies: The case studies at the end of relevant chapters provide real as well as hypothetical data to help students analyse the concepts discussed.

Case Study

Stock scams have become a common phenomenon in many economies. As soon as a scam is discovered and follow-up action initiated, another scam manifests itself in a different form. The series of scams in the Indian stock markets have resulted in the near-collapse of the trading and settlement system in the stock exchanges. The following scams have had a lot of publicity because of the magnitude of the funds involved.

The Harshad Mehta Phenomenon

The major securities scam with far-reaching implications occurred in India in 1992. The stock scam, which came to be known as the Harshad Mehta phenomenon, threw the functioning of the money market and stock market out of gear. The scam was really a diversion of funds from the banking system, in particular the inter-bank market in government securities, to brokers for financing their operations in the stock market. When the new government at the Centre accelerated the process of economic liberalization in 1991, the stock market started booming. The BSE Sensex, the barometer of the Indian economy, rose from below 2000 in early 1991 to 4,467.30 in March 1992. Thus, there was an enormous requirement of funds to support the stock market

Summaries: The summaries at the end of each chapter present a quick recapitulation of the key concepts in the chapter. This helps the students revise the main topics in the chapter.

Summary

1. Capital formation is the net addition to the capital stock or to the value of the amount of increase of the capital stock, which is required for producing goods and services.
2. Saving is any income that is not spent on current consumption (that is, the excess of income over present consumption). Savings may be private savings or public savings.
3. It is estimated that the household savings in financial assets have increased from INR 6,504,120 million in 2006–07 to INR 7,468,650 million in 2008–09. Much of the financial savings are in the form of bank deposits.
7. A financial system is a set of financial institutions, financial instruments and financial markets that facilitate the transfer of savings from savers to those who can put the savings to use with the objective of achieving economic development.
8. Financial intermediaries mobilize the savings from the savings-surplus units by issuing claims against themselves and lend those funds to those who are in need of them.
9. Financial markets act as conduit through which the funds are transferred from the savers to the users.

The Teaching and Learning Package

The teaching and learning package includes an instructors' manual and PowerPoint lecture slides, which can be downloaded from www.pearsoned.co.in/thummulurisiddaiah, the book's companion Web site.

The instructors' manual provides chapter overviews and hints to relevant chapter-end problems. The PowerPoint lecture slides are designed to provide an overview of the important points discussed in each chapter.

A Note on the Terms and the Currency System Used in this Book

- The ISO 4217 code for currencies has been used in this book. So, readers will find that INR has been used in place of Rs, GBP in place of £, USD in place of $, and JPY in place of ¥.

- As far as possible, million and billion have been used to represent large numbers in place of lakh and crore, which are commonly used in Indian books. However, where the primary data was available in lakh and crore (most of the RBI and SEBI data, for instance), the information has been retained in the original style. The following table will help readers convert amounts in lakh/crore to amounts in million/billion in the same currency:

Amount in lakh/crore	*Amount in Figures*	*Amount in million/billion*
1 lakh	100,000	100 thousand
10 lakh	1,000,000	1 million
1 crore	10,000,000	10 million
10 crore	100,000,000	100 million
100 crore	1,000,000,000	1 billion

Acknowledgements

I thank my family members, Ms Usha Rani, Dr Harini, Dr Mruthyunjaya, Dr Alekhya, and Ch Guru Sai, for their endurance through the years that I spent in writing this book. Special thanks are due to my daughter, Dr Alekhya, who has helped me in keying in the manuscript and in formatting the equations, charts, and tables in this book. She spared many hours on this work despite the fact that, as an MBBS student, she had her own load of assignments to deal with.

I would like to thank the editorial team at Pearson Education for their support. I have gained the knowledge and skills required for writing this book by reading the works of many great authors and through interactions with my students. I owe a great deal to them.

Thummuluri Siddaiah

Chapter 1

Financial Services: An Overview

LEARNING OBJECTIVES

After studying this chapter, you should be able to:

- Understand the concept of capital formation.
- Discuss the relationship between savings and investment.
- Understand the nature of savings and the role of savings in economic development.
- Highlight the importance of investment.
- Understand the concept of a financial system.
- Describe the constituents of a financial system.
- Develop a bird's-eye view of global financial services.

1.1 Introduction

Capital is one of the most important factors of production, particularly in a developing country like India. Capital formation is one of the major determinants of a country's ability to produce goods and services. **Capital formation** refers to the transfer of savings from the savers to the users of capital. It is also defined as the net addition to the capital stock or to the value of the amount of increase of the capital stock that is required for producing goods and services. *Capital stock* is the total quantity of a country's capital goods consisting of machinery, equipment, buildings and intermediate goods not consumed directly. Capital stock also includes intangible assets (for example, computer software). The higher the rate of capital formation, the faster the growth of the gross domestic product (GDP) in the country. Without getting into a debate on whether the rising level of income is the cause or effect of capital formation, it may be stated that income and capital move hand in hand and capital formation is essential for the economic development of any country.

__Capital formation__ is defined as the net addition to the capital stock or to the value of the amount of increase of the capital stock that is required for producing goods and services.

In capital formation, one can identify three major sub-processes. They are saving, financing and investment. *Saving* is a process by which the claims to resources are set aside and they are available for other purposes. *Financing* is the process by which the savings are pooled and made available for investment. *Investment* is the process by which the savings are actually committed to production of goods and services required by the people to satisfy their needs and wants.

The __GDP__ of a country is the country's aggregate production of final goods and services during a specified period.

The **GDP** of a country is the country's aggregate production of final goods and services during a specified period. The process of production in a country generates not only goods and services but also income for those participating in the process. Thus, the GDP of a country can also be stated as the aggregate real income in the country. The aggregate income can also be represented as a sum of consumption and savings. Saving plays a very important role in any economy since it is savings that gives rise to new investment and, thus, economic growth.

__Saving__ is defined as the activity by which claims to resources that might be put to current consumption are set aside and so become available for other purposes.

1.2 Savings

People and organizations might spend a part of their income on goods and services of current consumption and save the rest, which represents a claim on the society for goods and services in future. **Saving** is thus defined as the activity by which claims to resources that might be put to current consumption are set aside and so become available for other purposes. In other words, saving is any income that is not spent on current consumption, or the excess of income over present consumption. Saving and the rate of saving in an economy depend on income levels (since individual income should be high enough to permit savings) in that economy, the willingness of the income earners to postpone consumption (that is, forgo some consumption today for more consumption in future), and the presence of an effective institutional mechanism to mobilize the savings and facilitate the investment of those savings in productive activities. The savings in an economy are also governed by tastes, habits and social environment.

1.2.1 Types of Savings

Savings may be private or public. The savings of the government through normal budgetary channels and the savings of public sector enterprises are known as *public savings*. All other savings (saving by households and business enterprises) are known as *private savings*. Savings of private sector enterprises are known as *corporate savings*. Corporate saving is nothing but the retained earnings (that is, the earnings after tax minus payment of dividend and interest). If the government sector is in deficit, then the government is dissaving and contributing negatively to aggregate domestic savings. To sustain domestic investment, the government may supplement the domestic savings with the flow of foreign capital. In other words, to fill the gap between national savings and national investment, it is necessary to draw on the savings of foreigners. Institutional savings mostly depend on the profitability of the enterprises or firms and corporate policies. Examples of this are dividend and investment policies. Government policy (monetary and fiscal) also determines the level of institutional savings in a country.

1.2.2 Savings Rate and Pattern

As Table 1.1 indicates, household savings as a percentage of GDP in India increased from 24.1 per cent in 2005–06 to 24.3 per cent in 2007–08. But in 1950–51, the savings rate in India was a mere 10.2 per cent. Therefore, there has been a significant increase in the rate of savings by households in India since 1950–51. Household savings in physical assets are higher than the household savings in financial assets. The household savings account for the bulk of domestic savings, the contribution of the public sector and the private corporate sector being relatively small. It can be further observed from the table that gross domestic savings as a percentage of GDP increased from 34.21 per cent in 2005–06 to 37.7 per cent in 2007–08. The gross capital formation has also increased from 34.8 per cent in 2005–06 to 38.7 per cent in 2007–08.

The different forms of financial savings of the household sector in India are presented in Table 1.2. It is estimated that household savings in financial assets have increased from INR 6,50,412 crore in 2006–07 to INR 7,46,865 crore in 2008–09. Most of it is in the form of bank deposits. As given in the table, in 2008–09, bank deposits constituted about 55 per cent of the total financial assets of the household sector. Therefore, commercial banks play a dominant role in mobilizing household savings. In recent years, shares and debentures have also become attractive, although their share in the total financial assets of the household sector is very low — about 12 per cent in 2007–08. Mutual funds have been increasingly attracting the household sector. The share of mutual funds in the total financial assets of the household sector was about 4.9 per cent in 2007–08. The proportion of insurance funds in total financial assets has also increased over time. The proportion of provident and pension funds and the share of claims on the government in the total financial assets of the household sector have shown a decreasing trend. Thus, there has been a remarkable rise in the institutionalization of savings as evidenced by increasing ownership of financial assets in the economy. The share of banks and other financial institutions taken together in the total financial claims has increased gradually over the years.

The rapid growth of household savings in the form of financial assets has been brought about by diversified growth of the financial system. There has been a widening and a deepening of the financial structure over time. This has helped to channelize the growing volume of household savings in the form of financial assets into diverse productive activities in the public and private sectors. Specialized financial institutions such as development financial institutions, insurance companies, non-banking finance companies (NBFCs) and mutual funds have helped both the public sector and the private corporate sector to bridge their resource gap to a considerable extent.

Table 1.1 Gross domestic saving and investment in India

Item	Per cent of GDP (at current market prices)				Amount (in INR crore)		
	Average 1999–2000 to 2007–08	*2005–06*	*2006–07*	*2007–08**	*2005–06*	*2006–07*	*2007–08**
1	**2**	**3**	**4**	**5**	**6**	**7**	**8**
1. Household saving *of which:*	23.0	24.1	24.1	24.3	8,64,653	9,94,898	11,50,135
a) Financial assets	11.0	11.7	11.7	11.7	4,20,974	4,82,822	5,53,289
b) Physical assets	12.1	12.4	12.4	12.6	4,43,679	5,12,076	5,96,846
2. Private corporate sector	5.8	7.7	8.3	8.8	2,76,550	3,42,284	4,16,936
3. Public sector	0.9	2.4	3.3	4.5	86,823	1,37,926	2,12,543
4. Gross domestic saving	29.7	34.2	35.7	37.7	12,28,026	14,75,108	17,79,614
5. Net capital inflow	0.2	1.2	1.1	1.4	44,604	46,698	65,899
6. Gross domestic capital formation	29.9	35.5	36.9	39.1	12,72,630	15,21,806	18,45,513
7. Errors and omissions	0.2	0.7	0.5	0.3	23,741	19,297	16,167
8. Gross capital formation *of which:*	29.8	34.8	36.4	38.7	12,48,889	15,02,508	18,29,346
a) Public sector	7.2	7.6	8.0	9.1	2,71,835	3,29,679	4,29,014
b) Private corporate sector	9.5	13.7	14.8	15.9	4,91,983	6,11,044	7,49,894
c) Household sector	12.1	12.4	12.4	12.6	4,43,679	5,12,076	5,96,846
d) Valuables	0.9	1.2	1.2	1.1	41,392	49,709	53,591

Source: Reserve Bank of India, Annual Report 2008–09.

Table 1.2 Financial savings of the household sector (gross)

Item	Per cent of total financial saving (in INR crore)					
	2006–07	2007–08 (P)	2008–09	2006–07	2007–08 (P)	2008–09
1	**2**	**3**	**4**	**5**	**6**	**7**
Financial saving (gross)	**100.0**	**100.0**	**100.0**	**6,50,412**	**7,15,994**	**7,46,865**
a) Currency	10.2	11.4	12.5	66,274	81,278	93,056
b) Deposits	49.1	52.2	58.5	3,19,385	3,74,088	4,36,710
i) With banks	47.8	50.4	54.9	3,11,215	3,60,727	4,09,678
ii) With non-banking companies	0.2	0.5	1.8	1,516	3,751	13,453
iii) With cooperative banks and societies	0.0	0.0	0.0	131	266	133
iv) Trade debt (net)	1.0	1.3	1.8	6,523	9,345	13,446
c) Share and debentures	9.0	12.4	2.6	58,598	89,134	19,349
i) Private corporate business	3.7	4.4	4.2	23,755	31,565	31,124
ii) Banking	0.0	0.1	0.1	206	766	995
iii) Units of Unit Trust of India	0.0	0.0	−0.4	−310	−324	−2,737
iv) Bonds of public sector undertakings	0.0	0.0	0.1	237	328	446
v) Mutual funds (other than UTI)	5.3	7.9	−1.4	34,709	56,799	−10,478
d) Claims on government	3.0	−4.0	−3.1	19,198	−28,315	−23,479
i) Investment in government securities	0.3	−2.1	−4.5	1,654	−14,714	−33,879
ii) Investment in small savings, etc.	2.7	−1.9	1.4	17,544	−13,601	10,400
e) Insurance funds	17.7	18.0	20.1	1,14,851	1,28,930	1,50,337
i) Life insurance funds	17.1	17.4	19.5	1,10,965	1,24,422	1,45,876
ii) Postal insurance	0.3	0.4	0.3	2,200	2,729	2,594
iii) State insurance	0.3	0.2	0.3	1,686	1,779	1,868
f) Provident and pension funds	11.1	9.9	9.5	72,106	70,878	70,891
GDP at current market prices				41,29,173	47,23,400	53,21,753

P: Provisional. #: Preliminary estimates.
Note: Components may not add up to the totals due to rounding off.
Source: Reserve Bank of India, Annual Report 2008-09.

Financial deepening is measured by the size of the financial assets in relation to the size of the economy, and financial widening is measured by the number and variety of participants and financial instruments in a financial system.

1.2.3 Financial Deepening and Widening

The nature, composition and growth of financial assets along with the number of participants in the financial system reflect the sophistication, development and growth of the financial system in an economy. It is in this context that two terms—financial deepening and financial broadening—are discussed. *Financial deepening* is measured by the size of financial assets in relation to the size of the economy, or the GDP. Financial assets, which include bank deposits, loans, stock market trades, insured and pension assets, reflect the future expectation of the economy whereas the GDP is the current economic size of the country. The ratio between the financial assets and the GDP is the factor by which one can measure the relationship between financial assets and GDP. The higher this ratio, the deeper is the financial system. *Financial widening* refers to the number and variety of participants and financial instruments in a financial system. Financial widening indicates how diverse the financial system is. The more the number of banks, insurance companies, savers, investors, borrowers, stocks listed and financial instruments, the wider the economy is financially. Developed economies have highly developed financial systems that broaden access to funds. This means that they provide both savers and investors more choices for investing savings and raising capital. Conversely, in underdeveloped economies, since access to institutional funds is limited, businesses or savings-deficit units may resort to high-cost informal sources such as moneylenders. Limited access to institutional funds and higher cost of funds would reduce the economic activities in the economy and thus lower the resulting economic growth. Thus, a well-diversified array of financial instruments along with well-regulated and developed financial institutions and markets facilitate the institutionalization of domestic savings. The wide array of financial instruments can meet the varying risk/reward preferences of both savers and investors.

To conclude, the savings rate in India is very high, and could be mobilized for productive investment. But a large part of the savings is wasted or left idle or used unproductively. In such circumstances, savings may fail to contribute to capital formation. A country's economic development depends more on where and how savings are used rather than on the absolute quantity of savings.

1.3 Investment

Investments are broadly of two kinds—financial investment and real investment. *Financial investment* refers to investment in financial assets such as shares, debentures, bank deposits and bonds. Financial assets represent the claims on a stream of income and/or assets of organizations, whether private sector firms or public sector undertakings or governments, which issue those assets in the form of securities such as equity shares, debentures and bonds. Financial assets can also be described as the store of purchasing power that can be used by their owners according to their wish.

Investments in financial assets are of no use either for consumption or production. On the other hand, **real investment** is investment in real assets that can be used for producing goods and services meant for ultimate consumption. Thus, what matters in the development of the economy is real investment. The more the investment, the higher the production of goods and services in the economy. But the level of investment in a country depends not only on the savings but also on factors such as government policies, expectations about the return on investment and existence of an entrepreneurial class. Investment, therefore, implies the existence of savers and their willingness to entrust their savings with others in return for income in the form of interest and dividend, and also the existence of entrepreneurs willing to obtain the savings of others for a price. Investment involves saving income and taking a risk in using that saving in some productive effort. Thus, it is savings that lead to capital formation or investment and it is investment that leads to economic growth. The transformation of savings into investment causes economic growth. The higher the savings, the larger is the investment and the higher is the economic growth, other factors remaining the same.

> ***Real investment*** *is investment in real assets that can be used for producing goods and services meant for ultimate consumption.*

In every economy, there are savings-surplus units, savings-deficit units and neutral units. *Savings-surplus units* are those individuals or organizations whose savings are in excess of their investments. *Savings-deficit units* are the individuals or organizations whose savings are less than their investments. *Neutral units* have investments equivalent to their savings. In the earlier days of the capitalist economy, the entrepreneur or the businessman was an individual who invested his own savings in the business, which he managed himself. But the entrepreneur of modern times has brought into existence large-scale business units with finance raised from others. The modern entrepreneur organizes all production facilities including labour and finance. Thus, in the current capitalist economy, a part of the investment is carried out directly by those who save and another part of the investment results from the transfer of savings from those who save to those who invest. In other words, saving and real investment are not undertaken by the same individuals or organization. Therefore, the transfer of investible funds from their owners to entrepreneurs is inevitable. This transfer takes places through a system called the *financial system*. One possibility is that the expenditure on investment may exceed the current savings in the economy. This deficit is filled by past savings (accumulated) and/or money newly created by the banking system. There is also a possibility that the investment expenditure may fall short of savings. The excess savings may remain as idle funds either in the hands of the actual savers or with financial institutions on behalf of the actual savers. But with globalization, the funds move across countries and, therefore, savings and investments get equalized at the global level.

1.4 The Financial System

To meet the growing needs of the economy, there must be an institutional mechanism or a system to mobilize savings and transfer them from those who save to those who are prepared to invest or take up productive activities. But the savers and investors may require certain safeguards before transferring savings to others or investing them in productive activities. They may require institutions and instruments to facilitate the transfer of rights and interests along with adequate laws and enforcement agencies. Thus, there is a need for an effective financial system which can mobilize and channelize savings for capital formation. The efficiency of a financial system depends primarily on its ability to facilitate the flow of savings into the most productive investment. Although there are arguments and counterarguments on whether financial development spurs economic growth or economic growth generates demand for financial products, many research studies support the view that the development of the financial system contributes to economic growth. A well-developed financial system could channelize financial resources to the most productive use. A vibrant and efficient financial system encourages a higher level of savings and investment and ultimately a higher rate of economic growth.

1.4.1 What Is a Financial System?

A *system* is defined as a set of elements that are interrelated and interactive. The elements operate together to accomplish a stated purpose, goal or objective. It is the common purpose, goal or objective which makes the elements belong together. A **financial system** consists broadly of financial institutions, financial markets and financial instruments or securities as elements, as shown in Figure 1.1. The common goal of all these elements is to transform financial savings into real investment. Thus, a financial system is a set of financial institutions, financial instruments and financial markets which facilitate the transfer of savings from savers (surplus units) to those who can put the savings into use (deficit units) with the objective of achieving economic development. Regulatory and development agencies such as the RBI and SEBI can also be considered an integral part of the financial system.

*A **financial system** is a set of financial institutions, financial instruments and financial markets, which facilitate the transfer of savings from the savers to those who can put the savings to use with the objective of achieving economic development.*

The financial system has the following functions:

1. Establishes a bridge between savers and investors in order to transform entrepreneurial ideas into reality.
2. Increases the saving as well as the investment rate.
3. Makes the allocation and utilization of savings optimal and efficient.
4. Influences directly as well as indirectly the volume of funds to be made available for productive activities.

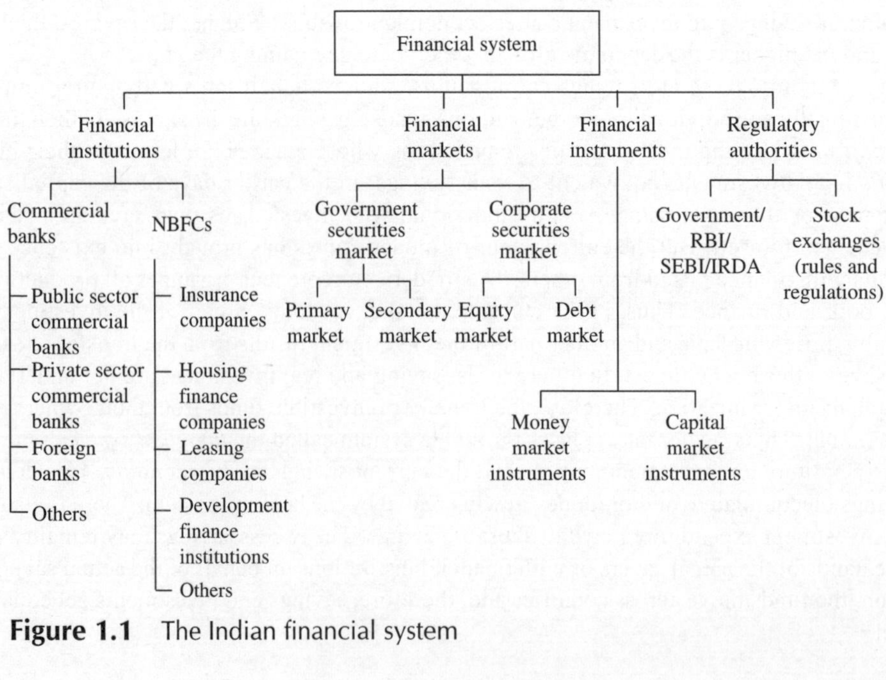

Figure 1.1 The Indian financial system

The various services that are created and delivered by the financial system are known as **financial services.** Financial services are the services required for mobilizing savings and channelling them to productive activities for producing final goods and services.

The various services that are created and delivered by the financial system are known as ***financial services.***

1.4.2 Financial Institutions

Financial institutions are the main constituent of a financial system. Financial institutions are also known as financial intermediaries because they intermediate between savers and the investors, particularly real investors. Real investors are those entities that create and use productive assets to produce goods and services for the ultimate consumers. The financial intermediaries mobilize the savings from the savings-surplus units by issuing claims against themselves and lend those funds to those who are in need of them. The financial intermediaries issue different kinds of claims, which may be called securities, to the savers in order to satisfy their requirements. On the other hand, they accept the claims or the securities of a different nature issued by the users of the funds. The claims or securities issued by the financial institutions are more liquid than the claims or securities these financial institutions buy from the investors, who are the ultimate users of the funds. Even the maturity period and size of claims issued to the savers of funds by financial institutions are different from those issued by the users of funds. In other words, financial institutions, particularly banks, provide liquidity, maturity and size intermediation. Thus, financial institutions can be termed asset transformers.

Financial institutions are known as financial intermediaries because they intermediate between savers and investors, particularly real investors.

In recent years, a new trend called financial disintermediation has set in. The new phenomenon is that corporations have begun bypassing banking channels and accessing funds directly from the savers by issuing securities suitable for the investors.

It may be noted that the financial intermediaries do not directly add to the real capital formation in a country. But they are a necessary link between the savers and the real investors. By providing safety, profitability and liquidity for the funds saved by the savers, the financial intermediaries facilitate or encourage savings in the economy. Most of the savers in a country like India are small and geographically scattered. These small savings are effectively mobilized and made available to the industrial units in bigger lots by the financial institutions. If the industrial units have to mobilize funds directly from the small savers, it would become difficult and burdensome. Moreover, it is not cost effective. The presence of financial institutions is also an assurance to the entrepreneurs that the funds will be made available at a reasonable price. Therefore, the entrepreneurs do not have to bother about the funds and can concentrate on productive activities. In this way, the financial institutions facilitate the process of investment in a country. Another notable aspect is that financial institutions follow directives from the Reserve bank of India, which is the regulatory authority, and accordingly ensure the allocation of scarce resources in the country among various sectors in consonance with national priorities.

1.4.3 Types of Financial Institutions

Financial institutions are of different kinds, such as commercial banks, cooperative banks, and non-banking finance institutions. Different institutions provide specialized services to the economy. For example, banks, as the providers of banking services, are the mechanism through which the monetary policy of the government is implemented. Similarly, mutual funds provide a mechanism for collecting small savings and pooling them into large capital meant for users of the funds. Thus, each kind of financial institution has a special role to play in the economy.

Financial institutions are of different kinds, such as commercial banks, cooperative banks and non-banking finance institutions.

Commercial banks mobilize, pool and channelize savings into productive activities, thereby contributing to the economic growth of the country. The commercial banking sector comprises public sector banks, private banks and foreign banks. Public sector banks comprise the State Bank of India and its seven associate banks and 19 other banks owned by the Government of India, and account for almost three-fourths of the banking sector. The Government of India has majority shareholdings in these public sector banks.

Banks collect savings from individuals and organizations, primarily in the form of deposits, and deploy them as credit to various sectors of the economy such as agriculture and industry. Service sector units are also beneficiaries of the benevolence of banks. Banks offer different types of deposit schemes to suit the needs of the depositor-customers and thereby attract deposits in large measure. Banks also provide finance to the savings-deficit units by subscribing to different types of industrial securities. The commercial banks in India have recorded phenomenal progress since nationalization of 14 major commercial banks in 1969. The unprecedented expansion of the branch network, mobilization of savings and reorientation of credit flows to benefiting the hitherto neglected sectors of the economy are the major achievements of the banking system in India.

The traditional functions of commercial banks are taking deposits and balance-sheet lending. But with the growth and expansion of NBFCs, competition in the banking industry has become intense. In this scenario, the commercial banks have had to expand and diversify their operations in order to maintain their competitiveness and profitability. The commercial banks have successfully diversified into non-traditional financial activities such as leasing, insurance, underwriting and issue management. The deepening and broadening of the financial system have created new opportunities for commercial banks as well.

For many years, banks have dominated the Indian financial system. A large chunk of household savings took the form of bank deposits, while the banks were the chief source of funds for corporations in the form of short-term and long-term loans. But in recent years, non-banking financial companies and other financial avenues including mutual funds and insurance have come on the scene to compete aggressively with banks for household savings. As households show an interest in high-return instruments, the non-banking financial agencies have garnered a rising share of household savings. Institutions such as mutual funds and pension funds have grown in size and sophistication by diversifying risk and taking advantage of economies of scale.

The Indian financial system has a two-tier structure of development finance institutions: all-India financial institutions and institutions at the state level. The all-India financial institutions such as the Industrial Development Bank of India (IDBI), the Industrial Finance Corporation of India (IFCI) and the Industrial Credit and Investment Corporation of India (ICICI) were set up in the post-independence era to finance the industrial development of the country along the desired direction. They are also known as term-lending institutions or *development banks*. They have gained in size and stature over time and emerged as significant players wielding considerable influence in determining the quantum, structure and direction of corporate financing in the country. While lending to corporations, they prioritize projects as projects coming up in backward regions, projects coming up in the small-scale sector, projects promoted by new and technical entrepreneurs, projects producing goods of mass consumption and projects in the nature of export promotion and import-substituting industrial units. When availability of finance from normal channels to certain types of industries—industries which deserve special attention on economic and social grounds—is deficient, the development banks step in to fill the gap. Hence, development banks are known as gap fillers. At the state level, the State Financial Institutions and State Industrial Development Corporations were created to provide project finance, equipment leasing, corporate loans, short-term loans and bill discounting facilities to business organizations. The government holds the majority of shareholdings in these financial institutions. Thus, development finance institutions direct their efforts to specific development objectives, which include growth of broad-based entrepreneurship.

Specialized finance institutions like the Export-Import Bank of India (Exim Bank), the Infrastructure Development Finance Company, Small Industries Development Bank of India (SIDBI), National Housing Bank, National Bank for Agriculture and Rural Development (NABARD), mutual funds and a host of insurance companies including the Life Insurance Corporation of India and General Insurance Corporation of India are also part of the Indian financial system. As key players in the Indian financial market, they too foster the development of the economy.

The insurance sector in India has traditionally been dominated by the state-owned Life Insurance Corporation of India and the General Insurance Corporation and its four subsidiaries. But with a new government policy, a number of new joint venture private companies have entered the life and general insurance sectors. A new set of financial institutions such merchant banks, hedge funds and private equity have come on the scene in a big way. They have also become an integral part of the financial system of the country.

For many years since India's independence in 1947, banking facilities were, in effect, not available to the bulk of the Indian population. At that time, indigenous banks and money-lenders dominated credit deployment in the country. As the years passed, it was realized that credit flow from the organized banking system was highly concentrated, catering only to a small segment of the population. The government, therefore, decided to take on ownership and direct control of the banking system. The culmination of this was the nationalization of many commercial banks and the establishment of a host of other banking institutions such as regional rural banks, NABARD and SIDBI.

1.4.4 Financial Markets

Financial markets are another significant component of the Indian financial system. They act as a conduit through which funds are transferred from the savers to the users. Financial markets facilitate the buying and selling of financial instruments, also called financial assets or financial securities. That is, financial markets provide a mechanism for the trading of industrial securities. The interaction of buyers and sellers in the financial markets also leads to price discovery. Financial markets also provide liquidity. In the absence of liquidity in the market, the owners of financial instruments should hold their securities till their maturity or till they are liquidated by the issuer(s). The functions of financial markets also include separation, distribution, diversification and reduction of risk. A financial market is said to be perfect when it has a large number of participants, there is a free flow of information and the participants are rational and have homogeneous expectations. In reality, financial markets are characterized by many imperfections. A financial market attains equilibrium when the expected demand for funds matches the planned supply of funds. The supply of funds is generated from saving and credit creation. Banks can create credit subject to statutory reserve requirements.

__Capital market__ is a market for long-term funds and the securities traded in the capital market are equity shares, preference shares, debentures and bonds. The money market deals in securities that are of a short duration.

Now, let us discuss the classification of financial markets. The *financial market* may be classified as government securities market and corporate securities market. The *government securities market* in India has two segments—the primary market and secondary market. The *primary market* consists of the issuers of securities—the central and state government—while the buyers include commercial banks, primary dealers, financial institutions and insurance companies. The *secondary market* includes commercial banks, financial institutions, insurance companies, provident funds, trusts, mutual funds and the Reserve Bank of India.

On the basis of the type of instruments traded, the financial market for corporate securities may be classified as capital market and money market. The **capital market** is a market for long-term funds and the securities traded in the capital market are equity shares, preference shares, debentures and bonds. Capital markets play an important role in the transfer and allocation of resources to various investment units. They can facilitate changes in corporate ownership structure.

The primary market provides direct finance to savings-deficit economic units and the secondary market is a market for the existing securities.

The capital market is divided into primary and secondary markets. The *primary market* is the market for primary issues, i.e., the securities issued by the corporate sector, including finance or banking companies, for the first time. The primary market provides funds to the enterprises for starting new organization(s) or for their expansion/diversification. The methods by which the primary issues are made include public issue through a prospectus, offer for sale, private placement and the rights issue. Thus, the primary market provides direct finance to the savings-deficit economic units. The *secondary market* is a market for existing securities. It is also known as stock market or stock exchange, and provides an institutional mechanism for the purchase and sale of securities that have already been issued. Thus, the stock market provides liquidity and marketability for industrial securities, which may be equity securities or debt securities.

If the securities traded in a financial market are short-term securities, such a financial market is known as *money market*. A financial market for long-term securities is called *capital market*. The traditional cut-off rule for the short term and the long term is one year. The call money market and commercial bill market are examples of money market. Corporate financial instruments traded in the money market are commercial papers, certificates of deposits and commercial bills. The main participants in the money market are the Reserve Bank of India, commercial banks, mutual funds, the Discount and Finance House of India, and NBFCs.

The financial market that provides a mechanism or a system for the trading of securities such as equity shares already issued is called __stock market.__

The financial markets for corporate securities can also be classified as debt and stock markets. A *debt market* is a financial market for debt securities such as debentures, bonds and commercial paper. The debt instruments may be traded either in a money market or in a capital market depending on whether they are short-term or long-term.

The financial market that provides a mechanism or a system for trading long-term securities such as equity shares which have been already issued is called the **stock market.** In India, there are 23 recognized stock exchanges that operate under government-approved rules, bylaws and regulations. The Indian stock market is almost wholly dominated by two major stock exchanges—the

National Stock Exchange of India Ltd. (NSE) and Bombay Stock Exchange (BSE). The benchmark indices of the two exchanges—Nifty of NSE and Sensex of BSE—are closely followed. The two exchanges also have an F&O (futures and options) segment for trading in equity derivatives including the indices. The major players in the Indian stock market are mutual funds, financial institutions and Foreign Institutional Investors (FIIs) representing mainly venture capital funds and private equity funds. Under the process of de-mutualization, stock exchanges have been converted into companies, in which brokers hold only minority shareholding.

The financial market that facilitates the fresh issue of financial securities is known as *primary market* or the new issues market. In other words, the primary market is a market for new capital issues, whether they are equity or debt securities, or short-term or long-term securities. Although organizationally the primary market is distinct from the stock market, the two markets are susceptible to common influence and are also the cause and effect of each other. Price movements on the stock market and the volume of activity in the primary market are directly and closely related. The new capital issues tend to increase when stock prices are rising and decrease when stock prices are declining. The stock markets are usually the first to absorb the changes in the economic environment, but the effect is quickly transmitted to the primary market. So the stock market sets the tone and tenor of the financial market as a whole. Thus, the flow of savings into real investment is profoundly influenced by stock market behaviour.

The financial markets may also be classified as organized markets and unorganized (informal) markets. The *organised markets* are the markets governed by certain explicit rules, regulations and statutes (for example, the stock market). The *unorganized markets* are those that are not governed by prescribed rules and regulations (for example, the grey market). Transactions in the unorganized markets take place according to conventions, practices and understanding.

1.4.5 Financial Securities

Financial securities are financial assets representing claims to the payment of money in future; it may be the repayment of the principal and/or payment in the form of interest or dividend. A variety of securities are created and marketed in order to satisfy the variegated requirements of both the suppliers and users of the funds. The securities may be direct securities (primary) or indirect securities (secondary). *Direct securities* are those issued by the users of the funds directly to the suppliers of funds. The various securities issued by the corporate sector are direct securities (for example, shares and debentures); whereas the financial claims created by financial intermediaries are *indirect securities* (for example, bank deposits and insurance policies).

> ***Financial securities*** *are financial assets representing claims to the payment of money in future.*

Financial securities may be broadly classified into corporate securities and government securities. *Government securities* are securities issued by the government for raising a public loan or as notified in the official gazette. These securities are treasury bills or dated securities, which include promissory notes and bonds. Besides the Union government, state governments also issue securities to raise funds to meet their expenditure commitments. Government undertakings also issue securities to raise funds for their own business commitments. The government securities market plays a vital role in the Indian economy as it provides the benchmark for determining the level of interest rates in the country through the yields on the government securities, which are treated as the risk-free rate of return.

Corporations may issue many types of instruments to finance their growth. In general, financing instruments fall into one of two categories: debt and equity. Although there are exceptions, *debt instruments* (e.g., debentures) generally represent fixed obligations to repay a specific amount at a specified date in the future, together with interest. *Equity instruments* (e.g., equity shares) generally represent ownership interests entitled to dividend payments, when declared, but with no specific right to a return on capital. Within these two categories, there is a wide variety of rights, privileges and limitations that may be established by the issuing company.

Each type of security has its own return and risk characteristics. Equity securities tend to have a higher expected return with more risk as well. In addition to conventional securities such as equity shares, bonds and debentures, there are other types of securities such as derivative securities. *Derivative securities* are those whose values are derived from the values of underlying assets. The derivative securities are traded in a market known as the *derivative market*. Commercial paper and certificates of deposits are the short-term securities traded in the money market. A new set of financial instruments such as GDRs/ADRs, euro bonds, flexi bonds, indexed bonds and participatory notes (PN) has also made its appearance in the financial markets. The financial securities have certain basic characteristics, which include liquidity, divisibility, marketability, reversibility and transferability.

1.5 The Regulatory Authority

The Indian financial system has independent regulators in the sectors of banking, insurance and capital markets. The role of the regulatory authority is to ensure that the participants in the financial system conduct their activities according to the guidelines and directives of the government. In the financial sector, the government plays the role of regulator through statutory bodies such as the RBI and SEBI. The RBI was established in 1935 as the central bank and a regulator for the financial and banking system. It formulates the monetary policy and prescribes exchange control norms. The Banking Regulation Act, 1949, and the Reserve Bank of India Act, 1934, authorize the RBI to regulate the banking sector in India. The Insurance Regulatory and Development Authority (IRDA) is the regulatory authority in the insurance sector under the Insurance Regulatory and Development Authority Act, 1999.

The main objectives of SEBI are to protect the interests of investors in securities trading and promote the development of securities markets in the country.

SEBI, established under the Securities and Exchange Board of India Act, 1992, is the regulatory authority for capital markets in India. The main objectives of SEBI are to protect the interests of investors in securities trading and promote the development and regulation of the securities market. The trading of securities and other operations of stock exchanges are governed by the provisions of the Securities Contracts (Regulation) Act, 1956, and the Companies Act, 1956. Besides, each stock exchange has its own rules and by-laws to govern trading of securities on the stock exchanges.

1.6 Globalization of Financial Services

The globalization of financial services refers to the integration of providers of financial services throughout the world into an international provider of financial services. The providers of financial services may include financial markets and financial institutions. With globalization, the activities of the providers of financial services need not be limited to their country of origin and operation. Nor are the seekers of financial services in a country limited to the financial services provided in their country. For example, before economic liberalization, corporations in India mainly depended on banks and financial institutions operating in India and, of course, some corporations would have raised funds by issuing securities in the domestic financial market. The present situation is very different from what it was before liberalization of the economy (i.e., before the 1990s). Now a business house has many options for its financing. It can shop around the globe for a loan with a lower interest rate and more convenient terms and conditions, or it can raise funds by issuing appropriate securities in the international financial market. It can also hedge against possible risks by choosing from a variety of derivative products available in the global derivative markets.

There are several forces that have driven the globalization of financial services. All such forces may be classified as advancements in computing and communication technology, globalization of national economies, and liberalization of several restrictions placed on cross-border trade and investments. The rules and regulations governing cross-border capital movements and entry of foreign financial institutions into domestic financial markets have been liberalized. In other words, globalization is taking place through the integration of national economies. As a result, the real economic activity of a company has been dispersed over different countries or regions. Alongside, financial services have also dispersed. The conventional multinational or trans-national companies have been transformed and new companies have been created to produce and distribute goods and services through networks that span the globe. The components of a passenger car, for example, are produced in one country, assembled in another country, and the final product is sold throughout the world. The integration of national economies became possible because countries reduced the barriers to international trade and allowed cross-border investments.

Due to technological advancements and financial liberalization, competition between the providers of financial services has intensified. With easy access to information, facilitated by the revolutionary changes in information technology, the financial awareness of people has increased. Further, a new class of investors, called FIIs, and high net worth individuals have emerged as major market participants. Together with private equity, hedge funds and pension funds, they hold the financial levers of many countries. The participation of this new class of investors in the financial markets would have implications for financial innovation, risk management and quality of intermediation. Thus, institutional investors have emerged as the driving force behind many of the changes and innovations taking place in the financial markets. For example, screen-based trading, demutualization of stock exchanges, emergence of depositories and custodians, introduction of derivatives and launching of euro-issues are largely in response to the needs and demands of institutional investors, particularly the FIIs and PEs in India. Financial innovations have brought about revolutionary changes in financial instruments and processes. The deregulation of the financial services industry and intense competition have undoubtedly placed an increased emphasis on the need to design new products, develop better processes and implement more effective solutions to increasingly complex financial problems.

With the advancements in communication and computing technology, investors are now able to analyse, monitor and manage risks associated with different kinds of investments. As there is a wider choice of available financial services, the users are migrating from less efficient service providers to value-added providers. The globalization process has transformed the financial services industry by shifting the advantage from the providers of financial services to the users. Thus, the nature and scope of financial services have undergone a thorough change. A new financial system, a new class of service providers and a totally new set of paradigms have emerged to meet the changing requirements of the service seekers.

In the changing environment, conventional financial institutions have found new ways of intermediating funds. Financial globalization has also deepened and widened the financial markets, creating new sources of business for these institutions. Thus, financial institutions, like commercial banks, have expanded beyond their conventional business of deposit-taking and credit deployment to enter investment banking, asset management and insurance sectors. In other words, the conventional financial institutions, including commercial banks, have diversified their sources of income and business risk by entering new lines of business like financial services.

To sum up, in the last 20 to 25 years, there have been several developments in the financial system across the world. The volume of activity in the financial system has risen sharply and its functioning has increasingly diversified. Thus, the recent past has witnessed the financial system growing in strength and diversity.

Summary

1. Capital formation is the net addition to the capital stock or to the value of the amount of increase of the capital stock, which is required for producing goods and services.
2. Saving is any income that is not spent on current consumption (that is, the excess of income over present consumption). Savings may be private savings or public savings.
3. It is estimated that the household savings in financial assets have increased from INR 6,50,412 crore in 2006–07 to INR 7,46,865 crore in 2008–09. Much of the financial savings are in the form of bank deposits.
4. The rapid growth of household savings in the form of financial assets has been brought about by the diversified growth of the financial system. There has been both a widening and a deepening of the financial structure over time.
5. The nature, composition and growth of financial assets along with the number of participants in the financial system reflect the sophistication, development and growth of the financial system in an economy.
6. Investment implies the existence of savers and their willingness to entrust their savings to others in return for income in the form of interest and dividend.
7. A financial system is a set of financial institutions, financial instruments and financial markets that facilitate the transfer of savings from savers to those who can put the savings to use with the objective of achieving economic development.
8. Financial intermediaries mobilize the savings from the savings-surplus units by issuing claims against themselves and lend those funds to those who are in need of them.
9. Financial markets act as conduit through which the funds are transferred from the savers to the users.
10. A variety of financial securities are created and marketed in order to satisfy the variegated requirements of both the suppliers and users of the funds.
11. The role of the regulatory authority is to ensure that participants in the financial system conduct their activities according to the guidelines and directives of the government.
12. The deregulation of the financial services industry has placed an increased emphasis on the need to design new financial products, develop better processes and implement more effective solutions to increasingly complex financial problems.

Questions

1. How do you define capital formation? Establish the relationship between capital formation and the economic development of a country.
2. What do you understand by saving? Elucidate the factors that influence savings in a country.
3. How is the relationship between savings and investments brought about by financial institutions?
4. Critically comment on the savings pattern in India.
5. What factors influence investments in a country?
6. What is a financial system? Discuss the role of each of the constituents of the financial system.
7. How has globalization brought about changes in the financial services industry? What are the challenges of the financial services industry?

Chapter 2

Stock Exchanges in India

LEARNING OBJECTIVE

After studying this chapter, you should be able to:

- Explain the functions of stock markets and their role in the economy.
- Present a historical perspective of stock exchanges in India.
- Highlight stock market reforms.
- Present an overview of stock exchanges in India.
- Compare Indian stock markets with other stock markets in the world.

2.1 Introduction

There is a universal clamour in economies around the world for accelerated economic growth and development. Increasing real per capita income and equitable distribution of income and wealth are the major objectives of the government. These involve balanced development of all sectors of the economy—agriculture, industry and services. The development of agriculture and industry presupposes the development of infrastructure like transport, communication, power, irrigation and education. All these sectors require a large resource base, which underdeveloped economies especially lack. In other words, domestic capital as compared to the investment needed is inadequate in developing economies like India. Moreover, there is a wide disparity in income and wealth distribution among individuals in the developing countries. The inequalities are apparent in India, too, with a significant proportion of the population living at or below the subsistence level and a sizeable proportion in the very rich category, with some even figuring in the list of the world's top billionaires. Despite the skewed distribution of income and wealth, a huge savings potential exists, particularly among the middle-income and top-income groups. Thus, there is a greater possibility of mobilization of sufficiently large amounts of savings even in developing countries. The savings of some sections of society may be small at the individual level but, when mobilized, can make a significant contribution to the economic development of a country. If the country lacks suitable institutional machinery to mobilize and invest the available savings, a significant proportion of the savings tends to be misdirected into unproductive channels. The savings might even be frittered away and not accumulate at all. Thus, the importance of mobilizing savings and channelizing them into productive activities cannot be overemphasized.

Business enterprises, especially the corporate form of businesses, can directly access the savings of individuals and utilize them for productive purposes. By offering different kinds of securities, such as equity shares, preference shares, bonds, debentures and other hybrid securities with varying rights and degrees of risk to suit the capacity and requirements of different kinds of investors, corporate enterprises can mobilize savings from a wide range of people and thus make much-needed investment avenues available to them. However, the efforts of corporate enterprises to mobilize savings can be successful only with adequate marketability and liquidity of the investments made by the public. It is in this context that stock exchanges come into the picture.

2.1.1 The Role of Stock Markets in the Economy

In the development of corporate enterprises and thus the economy, stock markets have a special and an important role to play. Well-organized stock exchanges provide liquidity and marketability for the securities issued by corporate enterprises. The development of the stock market is the barometer of the performance of the economy of a country.

The secondary market for capital issues is known as stock market.

A stock exchange, commonly known as stock market, is a secondary market for capital issues such as equity shares. A stock market can be considered as a system that includes procedures, rules, regulations and infrastructure for trading of securities that are already issued. The major functions of stock markets are:

1. Stock markets impart sufficient liquidity to industrial securities by providing a ready and continuous market. Adequate liquidity for investments enables investors to withdraw their capital from investments as and when required without any loss of the investment.
2. Stock markets determine the economic value of the securities that are traded. Such price fixing from time to time is useful for investors as well as others, including policymakers.
3. Stock markets provide marketability for industrial securities, without which investors cannot trade in the securities. This facilitates mobilization of savings for investment. Without stock markets, much of the savings of the people would either remain idle or be used for unproductive activities.
4. Stock markets also provide safety and transparency in dealings in securities because their working is governed by a set of rules and regulations.
5. Stock markets facilitate mobilization of savings and channelize them into productive activities or priority areas. The price differences and changes in prices of securities of different companies indicate the gradation in the profitability of the companies. The prices of securities depend on the profit potential or economic value of the companies. Thus, stock exchanges direct the flow of savings into productive areas of the economy by attracting investors to the securities that command high economic value. A higher price of a security means that the company which has issued that security has greater profit potential or economic value.
6. Stock markets promote an equity cult among the investing public, and thereby facilitate the formation of risk capital. Without risk capital, no economy can register faster growth. All the innovations in the real market (i.e., market for goods and services) are born out of risk capital investment. In other words, stock exchanges facilitate risk capital formation by initiating the investors into risk-taking.
7. Stock markets are efficient and enable investors to buy or sell securities quickly at prices close to their intrinsic values.
8. Stock markets provide educative value to investors by making available various kinds of information.
9. Stock markets indicate the actual value of the firm through securities price, which helps participants in mergers and acquisitions to arrive at the best bargaining price.

Although stock exchanges are markets, they differ from ordinary commodity markets in many respects. Most commodities are abundant and widespread in their supplies, especially in these days of globalization, and, therefore, there is large scope for mutual substitution. However, stock exchanges trade securities that are issued by firms. As each firm is unique, the supplies of each firm's securities are limited. There is large scope for a single individual or a group of individuals to manipulate the securities market to one's advantage. Therefore, market manipulation, price rigging and other kinds of fraud are easier in stock markets.

2.2 Listing and Delisting of Securities

Listing of securities on a stock exchange means the admission of the securities of a company to trading privileges on the stock exchange. There is no statutory obligation that every company must get its shares listed on a recognized stock exchange. Listing of securities is voluntary. However, if a company declares in the prospectus that it would seek listing of securities, then it is bound by the Companies Act, 1956, to seek listing from the stock exchange(s) concerned by fulfilling all the listing formalities. The government is also empowered to compel a company, when it is so necessary or expedient in the interests of the investing public, to get the securities listed. Section 73 of the Companies Act, 1956, makes it obligatory for companies seeking to offer securities to the public for subscription through a prospectus to make an application in one or more recognized stock exchanges for permission to deal in the securities offered in such stock exchanges.

__Listing__ means the admission of securities of a company for trading on the stock exchange.

The main purpose of listing is to have provision for liquidity, marketability and free negotiability of the securities.

Listing provides liquidity, marketability and free negotiability for the listed securities. Liquidity means that the investor who wants to withdraw a particular investment can easily do so without any loss of time. Marketability enables the investor to buy or sell the security to his best advantage at any time. Negotiability enables the investor to pledge the securities as collateral for any loan to be taken by him. Specifically, the listed securities can enjoy the following advantages:

- Provide ready marketability to the securities.
- Impart liquidity to the securities.
- Provide free negotiability to the securities.
- Provide proper control and supervision of trading of securities and thereby protect the interests of shareholders and the general investing public.
- Provide a much higher collateral value for bank credit and other purposes.
- Provide tax relief.
- Enhance the image and status of the company, which would fetch several benefits for the company.
- Presuppose full disclosure of information. This enables the investors to take informed decisions.
- Listing of securities allows efficient allocation of capital among competing uses/projects.
- Enable capital to flow into the priority areas of investment.
- The shareholders of listed companies enjoy a privileged position in society. When securities are listed on a stock exchange, it gives an impression that the company is economically a sound concern.

The process of listing securities is not free from demerits. Some of them are:

1. May give scope for price rigging and market manipulation, which leads to misallocation of capital in the country.
2. Rampant speculation in the stock market might affect market sentiment and thereby spoil the equity cult among the investing public.
3. Might facilitate hostile takeovers, which will have a deleterious effect on the corporate management.
4. Fulfilment of listing requirements may expose the company to severe competition.

Despite such disadvantages, companies generally prefer listing of securities as the advantages of doing so outweigh the disadvantages. Liquidity, marketability and price continuity of the securities provided by the stock exchanges have a salutary effect on the investment climate and allocation of capital in the country.

2.2.1 The Listing Agreement

The listing agreement *is an agreement between a company and the stock exchange entered on the listing of securities on the stock exchange.*

A company that wants to get its securities listed on a stock exchange is required to enter into an agreement with the stock exchange. Such an agreement is called **the listing agreement.** Once the listing agreement is signed by the company, it shall abide by the rules and regulations of the stock exchange.

There are many clauses in the listing agreement and companies are required to comply with all of them. For example, one of the clauses states that a company has to complete the allotment of securities offered to the public within 30 days of the date of closure of the subscription list and approach the designated stock exchange for approval of the basis of allotment, failing which interest at the rate of 15 per cent shall be paid to the investors. Further, the company has to provide facilities for prompt transfer, registration, subdivision and consolidation of securities. The company is also required to give proper notice of closure of transfer of books and record dates, and forward annual reports, balance sheets and profit and loss accounts to the stock exchange.

The listing agreement is governed by guidelines issued by the Securities and Exchange Board of India (SEBI) from time to time. For example, in April 2008, SEBI modified Clause 49 of the Listing Agreement. It says that at least half of the board of directors of a listed company should consist of independent directors if the non-executive chairman of the company is related to the promoters or persons occupying managerial positions. The minimum age for independent directors is fixed at 21 years. Further, SEBI modified the listing agreement in April 2009. According to it, the companies shall hold all unclaimed shares in public issues in a separate demat suspense account opened by the issuer with one of the depository participants. Any corporate benefit accruing on unclaimed shares such as bonus shares or a split shall also be credited to this account. The listed companies are required to declare their dividend on per share basis only. The companies should disclose the details of each class of security separately.

Under Clause 40 A (i) of the listing agreement, a company must have the minimum non-promoter holding at the level of public shareholding as required at the time of listing on a continuous basis. If the non-promoter holding is less than the limit of public shareholding as required at the time of initial listing, the company will have to increase the non-promoter holding to at least 10 per cent within one year. If the company fails to do so, then it is required to make an offer to buy the remaining shareholding as provided in the SEBI Takeover Code.

2.2.2 Delisting of Securities

Delisting of securities means permanent removal of securities of a listed company from a stock exchange. Delisting is different from suspension or withdrawal of admission to dealings of listed securities, which stock exchanges may resort to for a limited period. Delisting implies that the company whose shares are being delisted will become a closely held company, although it may continue to be a public limited company. The investors will lose the opportunity to trade in these securities. In other words, consequent to delisting of securities, the investors will lose liquidity of their holdings. In such a case, the investors may not have any exit route.

> ***Delisting of securities** means permanent removal of securities from trading on a stock exchange.*

Delisting is not an issue in many countries and stock exchanges do not impose any restriction on delisting, provided there is an exit offer for investors. As a matter of fact, the decisions on listing and delisting are based on commercial considerations. One argument is that in a free economy or a market-driven economy, there should not be any entry and exit barriers. If the shareholders approve and the minority shareholders are adequately compensated, there is no problem in delisting. But a problem arises if delisting is detrimental to the interests of the shareholders, particularly minority shareholders. Delisting goes against the shareholders when the exit mechanism and the exit price offered to the minority shareholders inadequately compensates them for the total loss of investment opportunity.

Routes of delisting

There are different routes of delisting, which can be categorized as routes of voluntary delisting and routes of compulsory delisting. A brief description of each of them follows.

> *Delisting may be voluntary or compulsory.*

Voluntary delisting In voluntary delisting, the company may seek delisting of its shares from all the recognized stock exchanges where they are listed. To do so, the company has to obtain a special resolution from the shareholders of the company. To pass the special resolution, at least 75 per cent of the shareholders who are present at the general meeting must vote in favour of the resolution. Further, the shareholders have to be provided an exit route by the promoters or those who are in control of the management.

Companies seek voluntary delisting for various reasons. Some of them are as follows:

- Since the National Stock Exchange of India Ltd. (NSE) and Bombay Stock Exchange of India (BSE) offer nationwide trading facilities with a geographical spread of online trading terminals, companies may feel it is an unnecessary burden to maintain the listing of their securities on regional stock exchanges. Hence they go in for delisting of their securities from regional stock exchanges.
- Some companies may become private in order to do away with public scrutiny. They do this by resorting to acquisition of shares in the open market or by exercising the buy-back option. So a company might gradually reduce the floating stock through open market acquisition or through buy-back, and then go in for delisting. In such a situation, even if the offer price is not a fair price, the shareholders have to tender their shares. Otherwise, they could end up with shares without liquidity in case the securities are delisted. Therefore, the residual (minority) shareholders are left with no option upon a proposal of delisting of securities.

Compulsory delisting In compulsory delisting, the stock exchanges themselves can, under certain circumstances, compulsorily delist the securities of a listed company subject to certain procedures.

- If a company fails to pay the listing fee or does not comply with the rules of the stock exchange/SEBI guidelines, or unfair trading practices are followed by the promoters/management, the stock exchange may resort to compulsory delisting. In such cases, there is no exit route for shareholders. However, the stock exchange may allow trading in such securities under a permitted category for a period of one year after delisting. If the actions (omissions and commissions) of the management or promoters of the company have caused compulsory delisting, they would be liable to compensate the shareholders by acquiring the shares from them at a fair value.

- Mergers and amalgamations and schemes of arrangements under court directives may also result in delisting. The management of the restructured company may seek delisting of shares in order to convert the company into a closely held company. According to the SEBI Substantial Acquisitions of Shares and Takeovers Regulations, 1997, if the public shareholding slides to 10 per cent or less of the voting capital of a company consequent on substantial acquisition of shares, or if the public offer is in respect of a company where the public shareholding is already less than 10 per cent, the acquirer who has made the public offer has an option to buy the outstanding shares from the remaining shareholders at the same offer price.
- By operation of law on account of directives under the Bureau for Industrial and Financial Reconstruction (BIFR), companies, particularly sick companies, can be delisted.

According to a study by *The Economic Times* (December 6, 2009), BSE and the NSE have delisted as many as 1,450 companies since 1996 for violation of listing norms. The percentage of suspended companies in the BSE works out to around 25 per cent of the companies listed, whereas it is 8 per cent in the NSE. The money blocked in these securities was estimated to be over INR 580,000 million. But the promoters of most of the companies sold their shares in the open market before delisting and consequently their shareholding came down to below 5 per cent and, in some cases, their stake went down to below 1 per cent.

In just six months (the first half of 2004), the BSE delisted 992 companies for non-compliance of the terms of the listing agreement. These companies were defaulters for more than three years. Moreover, many of these companies were not available at their addresses. However, among these 992 companies, some were profit-making and some had healthy book value per share.

SEBI (Delisting of Equity Shares) Regulations, 2009

As delisting of shares has become a major issue for financial regulators, SEBI appointed a 12-member committee under the convenorship of Pratip Kar, the executive director of SEBI, to examine and review the present conditions for delisting of securities of companies and suggest related norms and procedures. The committee felt that in a free market economy, there should not be any selective restriction or discrimination against any class of companies for delisting. Keeping in view the larger interests of investors, the committee made a wide range of recommendations. Based on these recommendations, SEBI, in a notification dated October 10, 2009, issued regulations classified as SEBI (Delisting of Equity Shares) Regulations, 2009. It is expected that these regulations will make the process of delisting more transparent while protecting the interests of investors, particularly minority shareholders. The salient features of these regulations are as follows:

1. No company shall apply for and no recognized stock exchange shall permit the delisting of equity shares of a company—(a) pursuant to a buy-back of equity shares by the company, or pursuant to a preferential allotment made by the company; or (b) unless a period of three years has elapsed since the listing of that class of equity shares on any recognized stock exchange; or (c) if any instruments issued by the company, which are convertible into the same class of equity shares that are sought to be delisted, are outstanding.
2. A company may delist its equity shares from all recognized stock exchanges where they are listed or from the only recognized stock exchange where they are listed, provided all public shareholders holding equity shares of the class that are sought to be delisted are given an exit opportunity.
3. A company may delist its equity shares from one or more recognized stock exchanges where they are listed and continue their listing on one or more other recognized stock exchanges subject to fulfilment of the following:
   (a) if after the proposed delisting from any one or more recognized stock exchanges, the equity shares would remain listed on any recognized stock exchange which has nationwide trading terminals, no exit opportunity is required to be given to the public shareholders; and
   (b) if after the proposed delisting, the equity shares would not remain listed on any recognized stock exchange having nationwide trading terminals, an exit opportunity shall be given to all public shareholders holding the equity shares that are sought to be delisted.

4. The promoters of the company shall, upon receipt of in-principle approval for delisting from the recognized stock exchange, make a public announcement. The public announcement shall contain all material information. Before making the public announcement, the promoter shall open an escrow account and deposit the total estimated amount of consideration calculated on the basis of the floor price and number of equity shares outstanding with public shareholders in the account.
5. The promoter shall despatch the letter of offer to the public shareholders of equity shares, not later than 45 working days from the date of the public announcement. The letter of offer shall be accompanied with a bidding form for public shareholders and a form to be used by them for tendering shares. The offer shall remain open for a minimum of three working days and a maximum of five working days, during which the public shareholders may tender their bids.
6. All public shareholders of the equity shares that are sought to be delisted shall be entitled to participate in the book-building process. A promoter or a person acting in concert with any of the promoters shall not make a bid in the offer and the merchant banker shall take necessary steps to ensure compliance with this sub-regulation. Any holder of depository receipts issued on the basis of underlying shares held by a custodian and any such custodian shall not be entitled to participate in the offer.
7. The offer price shall be determined through book building, after fixing the floor price and disclosure of the same in the public announcement and the letter of offer.
8. The floor price shall not be less than: (a) where the equity shares are frequently traded in all the recognized stock exchanges where they are listed, the average of the weekly high and low of the closing prices of the equity shares of the company during the 26 weeks or 2 weeks preceding the date on which the recognized stock exchanges were notified of the board meeting in which the delisting proposal was considered, whichever is higher, as quoted on the recognized stock exchange where the equity shares of the company are most frequently traded, (b) where the equity shares of the company are infrequently traded in all the recognized stock exchanges where they are listed, the floor price shall be determined by the promoter and the merchant banker taking into account certain parameters stated in the regulations.
9. An offer made under these regulations shall be deemed successful if post offer, the shareholding of the promoter (along with the persons acting in concert) taken together with the shares accepted through eligible bids at the determined final price exceeds (a) 90 per cent of the total issued shares of that class excluding the shares held by a custodian and against which depository receipts have been issued overseas, or (b) the aggregate percentage of pre-offer promoter shareholding and 50 per cent of the offer size.
10. Where the offer fails, the equity shares deposited or pledged by a shareholder shall be returned or released to him within 10 working days from the end of the bidding period, and no final application shall be made to the stock exchange for delisting of the equity shares.
11. A recognized stock exchange may, by order, delist any equity shares of a company on any ground prescribed in the rules made under Section 21A of the Securities Contracts (Regulation) Act, 1956. However, no order shall be made unless the company concerned has been given a reasonable opportunity of being heard.
12. The promoter of the company shall acquire delisted equity shares from the public shareholders by paying them the value determined by the valuer. No promoter shall directly or indirectly employ the funds of the company to finance an exit opportunity or acquisition of shares.

2.3 Speculation

A speculator is one who takes a calculated risk with the hope of getting a correspondingly greater return and the process is called ***speculation****.*

Speculation is often considered gambling. However, the two are different. A gambler depends on the chance of a successful outcome, whereas the speculator makes a rational calculation of success in a transaction. In other words, a gambler takes a chance on an unknown event with the hope of receiving a very large reward, whereas a speculator takes a calculated risk with the hope of getting a correspondingly greater return. The positive side of speculation is that it provides liquidity, mobility and price continuity, which are essential for any market.

All investments are based on expectations of profit-earning potentiality of the company, the prospects of the industry, trends of currency and banking policies, trends of interest rates and political and non-political considerations, to name a few factors. Speculators in general study all such factors and accordingly take positions in the stock market. Speculators are thus the pathfinders of the stock market.

But speculation, more often than not, is abused and misused. A person who has neither money nor knowledge may also speculate in the market. As a result, the market may witness violent and sudden fluctuations in stock prices. In earlier days, when the traditional carry-forward system was in vogue, speculation in the stock market was operationally facilitated by blank transfers and the carry-forward system. A blank transfer involves the transfer of a security from the owner without mentioning the name of the transferee on the transfer deed. Such a blank transfer facilitates negotiability of the security and reduces the cost of transfer since there is no payment of stamp duty. As a result, there would be higher negotiability of the security, facilitated by carry forward and *badla* financing. The carry forward of transactions from one settlement to another also encourages unhealthy speculation.

2.4 Stock Exchanges in India: A Historical Perspective

The origin of stock exchanges in India can be traced back to the eighteenth century. But a perceptible volume of trading in securities is noticeable from the 1830s. There were only a few brokers who were recognized by the business community, among them Premchand Roychand, a significant figure in the financial history of Mumbai. A broker is expected to buy securities at the lowest price or sell them at the highest price obtainable, offer his expert advice and guidance in matters of investment according to the temper and inclinations of his clients, and establish and maintain a lasting relationship with his clients as their ever-present well-wisher. Admission to the Bombay Stock Exchange as a member used to be preceded by an inquiry into the character of the applicant by the managing committee of the stock exchange. The price of the admission card was originally fixed at INR 51. But by 1909, the price of the card touched INR 2,500 and INR 7,000 in 1917. The number of members in the Bombay Stock Exchange was about 300 in 1877 and increased to 478 in 1921. Till 1938, an admission card was treated very much like a wedding invitation, since it was extended only to relatives of the existing brokers and authorized clerks. A member could act as a broker or jobber. As a broker, he worked as an agent of a client and as a jobber he worked as a principal. Of course, difficulties arose when the same member was allowed to act in both capacities.

With the enactment of Companies Act in 1850, many joint stock companies came up and trading in securities got a fillip. The number of share brokers also increased. The brokers in Bombay gathered for their business in a street in Bombay, which has come to be known as Dalal Street. The brokers founded the Native Stock and Share Brokers' Association in 1877. The main aims of the association were to protect the interests of the broking community and promote healthy trading practices. The development of the cotton textile industry in Ahmedabad and the consequent increase in the volume of business in shares led to the establishment of the Ahmedabad Share and Stock Brokers' Association in 1894. The brokers used to congregate and trade in an open area. The development of jute and tea industries in eastern India led to the establishment of the Calcutta Stock Exchange Association in 1908. In the post-World War I period, stock trading became a lucrative business due to the industrial boom. This encouraged many people to invest in stocks, leading to the enlargement of the scope and operations of the stock exchanges.

In Bombay, another stock exchange called the Bombay Stock Exchange Limited was formed in 1917, followed by the establishment of the Gujarat Share and Stock Exchange in Ahmedabad in 1920. Although the Madras Stock Exchange was formed around that time, it could not withstand the fatal blow of the depression and ceased to exist in 1923. In order to protect the interests of the investing public, the Securities Contracts Control Act was enacted by the government of Bombay in 1925. Under this act, all contracts on a stock exchange other than ready delivery contracts were declared void unless they had complied with the rules as approved by the government. In 1929, the crisis on Wall Street also influenced trading in Indian bourses. Share prices crashed in all the stock exchanges in the country and investors suffered huge losses. Forward dealings were suspended temporarily in order to avoid a serious crisis in the stock markets. But in the 1930s, the stock markets recovered and share dealings increased with the floating of new companies, particularly textile mills and plantation companies. The Madras Stock Exchange Association Private Limited was established in 1937 to meet the needs of investors in south India. The Punjab Stock Exchange Limited was established in 1936, followed by the formation of the Bengal Share and Stock Exchange Limited in 1937.

The year 1945 saw hectic activity in the stock markets because of the Second World War and the resultant economic boom. During this period, many new stock exchanges came up in different parts of the country. In

Table 2.1 Ownership of shares and stocks (1944–45)

Name of the company (paid up capital in INR per share)	*Range assumed for small and middle sized holdings*	*Percentage of number of small and middle sized holders to total number of holders*	*Percentage shares held by small and middle sized holders to total shares*
Tata Iron & Steel (75)	1 to 50	92	–
Apollo Mills (2)	1 to 2000	98.5	58.6
ACC (100)	1 to 50	82	25.4
Belapur Sugar (50)	1 to 50	93	40.0
Scindia Steam (15)	1 to 300	90	45.6
Central Bank (25)	1 to 200	96	46.9
New India Ins. (15)	1 to 100	97.5	54.1
Tata Hydro (100)	1 to 50	92	36.5

Source: S. K. Muranjan, *Modern Banking in India,* (Bombay: Kamala Publishing House, 1952), pp. 379–380.

1944–45, there were more than 13,000 companies with a paid-up capital of more than INR 3,600 million. Of these companies, about a thousand with a paid-up capital of more than INR 2,600 million had their shares quoted on different stock exchanges in the country. At the war-inflated values of that year, these quoted stocks and shares were estimated to have a value of INR 10,000 million. Table 2.1 shows the ownership pattern of shares and stocks in 1944–45. It is evident from the table that, on the whole, a very small percentage of shareholders were holding a very large proportion of shares.

The post-war boom prompted the government to undertake an inquiry through the directors of monetary research into the working conditions of the different stock exchanges in the country to see how far speculation had contributed to inflation and devise measures to regulate the working conditions of the stock exchanges. This work was subsequently taken over by the economic adviser to the ministry of finance, who submitted the report in July 1947. In 1948, a committee was appointed by the government to consider the recommendations contained in the report and submit detailed proposals for legislation. The committee indicated the broad lines for framing legislation. Again in 1951, the government appointed another committee under the chairmanship of A.D. Gorwala. The committee submitted its report along with a draft bill in July 1951. The government, after taking the opinions of the stock exchanges and other interested associations and individuals, prepared a bill known as the Securities Contracts (Regulation) Bill and got it enacted in September 1956. Thus, under the new constitution, the Government of India enacted the Securities Contracts (Regulation) Act, 1956, to regulate the working of stock exchanges in the country.

According to this act, a stock exchange would have to get permission from the government in order to conduct trading in securities. The stock exchanges were, thus, subject to government control and supervision. The act gave wide powers to the government to regulate and control the establishment and functioning of stock exchanges. This applied to all dealings in securities. Contracts for the sale or purchase of any security could be prohibited by the government under the act in order to prevent undesirable speculation. The act envisaged that no person could conduct the business of dealing in securities in any state or area except under the authority of a licence granted by the central government. The government was also empowered to license dealers in securities. Options dealings were prohibited. The government could also withdraw recognition granted to a stock exchange and direct recognized stock exchanges to make rules or amend any rules already made in respect of the by-laws or the constitution of the stock exchange. The act also empowered the government to declare that in any notified state or area, all contracts in securities (other than spot delivery contract—which were not entered into through, with or between members of recognized stock exchanges—would be illegal and punishable with a fine or imprisonment or both. Thus, the new act was a legislative measure that provided the government a flexible apparatus for the regulation of stock exchanges in the country. Further, in 1959, the government set up a Directorate of Stock Exchanges with the headquarters in Bombay and branch offices in Calcutta and Delhi to ensure proper administration of the regulatory provisions of the Securities Contract (Regulation) Act, 1956.

In terms of the Securities Contract (Regulation) Act, 1956, the government recognized stock exchanges in Bombay, Calcutta, Madras, Ahmedabad, Delhi, Hyderabad, Indore and Bangalore. In all these cities, only

Box 2.1 Stock Exchanges in India

Bombay Stock Exchange Ltd, National Stock Exchange of India Ltd, and Over-the-Counter Exchange of India (OTCEI) are the major stock exchanges in India. Besides these, there are several regional stock exchanges in the country:

- Ahmedabad Stock Exchange
- Bangalore Stock Exchange
- Bhubaneshwar Stock Exchange
- Calcutta Stock Exchange
- Cochin Stock Exchange
- Coimbatore Stock Exchange
- Delhi Stock Exchange
- Guwahati Stock Exchange
- Hyderabad Stock Exchange*
- Jaipur Stock Exchange
- Ludhiana Stock Exchange
- Madhya Pradesh Stock Exchange
- Madras Stock Exchange
- Magadh Stock Exchange*
- Mangalore Stock Exchange*
- Meerut Stock Exchange
- Pune Stock Exchange
- Saurashtra Kutch Stock Exchange*
- Uttar Pradesh Stock Exchange
- Vadodara Stock Exchange

* 4 exchanges have been since derecognized

one stock exchange was recognized. Wherever more than one exchange existed, the active members of the non-recognized stock exchanges were admitted to the recognized one under concessional terms of membership. The constitutions of the recognized stock exchanges were modified to conform to the act. However, there was a certain amount of diversity in the organization of the various stock exchanges. For example, the Bombay, Ahmedabad and Indore exchanges were in the nature of private clubs while the others were companies limited by guarantee or public limited companies incorporated under the Companies Act.

In order to meet the growing interest in securities trading, many stock exchanges across the country have been set up over time. Box 2.1 lists the stock exchanges functioning in India.

A circular of the Ministry of Finance vide F. No. 14(2) SE/85 dated August 23,1985, stipulated that all existing listed companies were also required to be listed on the stock exchanges located in the state or area in which the registered office or the main works/fixed assets of the company were located. The idea behind this circular was that stock exchanges should cater to the need of regional investors and that of the industry for mobilization and regional allocation of capital and resources. The listing of securities on more than one stock exchange enabled investors to trade in shares at the exchange closest to them.

However, in recent years, one can see structural changes in the Indian stock markets. For example, the two major stock exchanges, the Bombay Stock Exchange and the National Stock Exchange, have introduced online trading of securities and provided a nationwide trading platform. With the geographical spread of online trading terminals of these two exchanges, the regional stock exchanges have lost their business. Companies also started feeling that it was an unnecessary burden to continue listing their securities on regional stock exchanges when national-level stock exchanges had extended their reach across the country. This has resulted in the regional stock exchanges becoming dormant.

2.5 Indian Stock Market Reforms

Globalization of the Indian economy has given rise to the need for improving market efficiency, enhancing transparency, preventing unfair trade practices and thereby bringing the Indian securities markets on a par with the best markets in the world. The Government of India has introduced certain reforms through appropriate bodies to the securities markets in the recent past. The important ones are as follows:

1. The reforms started with the establishment of the Securities and Exchange Board of India (SEBI in 1992 by an act of Parliament. The main objectives of SEBI are: (a) to protect the interests of investors; (b) to promote the development of the securities market; and (c) to regulate the securities market in the country.
2. In consonance with its objectives, SEBI has issued certain regulations covering the following aspects.

(a) Eligibility norms for companies issuing securities
(b) Pricing by companies issuing securities
(c) Promoters' contribution and lock-in requirements
(d) Pre-issue obligations
(e) Contents of offer document
(f) Post-issue obligations
(g) Advertisements
(h) Issue of debt instruments
(i) Book building
(j) Initial public offers through the online system
(k) Issue of capital by designated financial institutions
(l) Shelf prospectus
(m) Preferential issues
(n) Qualified institutions placement
(o) OTCEI issues
(p) Bonus issues
(q) Miscellaneous aspects

3. With the repeal of the Capital Issues (Control) Act in 1992, the government's control over the pricing of capital issues ceased. The pricing of capital issues is now entirely left to market forces. However, to protect the interests of the investors, particularly small investors, SEBI has issued guidelines to govern the pricing of capital issues.
4. Earlier, trading on stock exchanges would take place through an open outcry system. The major problem with this system was that it did not allow immediate matching of bids and recording of transactions. Lack of transparency and efficiency also characterised the outcry system. In order to bring the stock exchanges up to international standards, SEBI directed that all stock exchanges in the country go online. Accordingly, all the Indian stock exchanges have introduced online fully automated screen-based trading systems. Indian stock exchanges are also permitted to set up trading terminals abroad. Besides, the trading platform of Indian stock exchanges is now accessed through the Internet, which means that the Indian stock markets have gone global. This enables investors to participate in large numbers in the trading of Indian securities, and thereby improve the depth and liquidity of the market.
5. For a very long time, stock markets were bogged down with the *badla* system, which had in-built speculative characteristics. The *badla* system allowed market participants to buy or sell securities without being in possession of either the requisite money or the share certificates. This led to rampant speculation and manipulation in the stock markets. In other words, the *badla* system was a deterrent to the orderly growth of stock markets in the country. It was in this context that the rolling settlement on a T+5 (i.e., trading day + 5 days) basis was introduced in the Indian stock markets in 2001. Subsequently, the settlement period has been reduced progressively from T+5 to T+3 and then to T+2. It is heartening to note that the Indian stock markets moved from the account period settlement (weekly) to T+5, then to T+3 and to T+2 in just 21 months despite initial resistance from the member-brokers and others.
6. Another milestone in stock market reforms is derivative trading. In order to enable market participants to hedge their price risks, trading in derivatives took off in the Indian stock markets in June 2000.
7. Historically, the settlement of trades and transfer of ownership of securities involved the physical movement of papers or certificates. This, besides being time consuming, gave rise to different kinds of risk including bad deliveries. To prevent these problems, the Depositories Act was passed in 1996 to provide for the establishment of depositories in securities and allow trading and recording of securities in electronic (demat) form.
8. The ownership and management of stock exchanges were initially vested in the hands of members who were none other than the broking community. The dominance of broker-members in the management of the stock exchanges caused a lot of problems to investors and regulators as well. In order to improve the governance of stock exchanges and protect

Corporatization and demutualization of stock exchanges is a process by which ownership, management and trading are separated.

the interests of investors, corporatization and demutualization of stock exchanges were made mandatory. Corporatization and demutualization of stock exchanges is a process by which ownership, management and trading are separated.

9. In order to avoid risks in the trading of securities, a comprehensive risk management system was introduced. Accordingly, certain norms with regard to capital adequacy for members of stock exchanges, margin requirements, limits on exposure and turnover, indemnity insurance, online position monitoring and automatic disablement are prescribed.
10. The primary concern of regulators is investor protection. SEBI has initiated several measures for this, which include the setting up of investor grievance cells for redressal of grievances and launching of the securities market awareness campaign. The Government of India has also instituted a fund called the Investor Education and Promotion Fund in October 2001 for the promotion of investors' awareness and protection of their interests. Stock exchanges have also initiated investor education programmes like seminars, workshops and conferences. SEBI's disclosure and investor protection guidelines are primarily aimed at the protection of investors' interests.

2.5.1 Indian Stock Markets in Terms of International Markets

Following economic reform measures, particularly financial reforms, the stock markets in India have registered phenomenal development. There is no denying the fact that even before the economic reforms were initiated, the Indian stock markets had a long history and played a significant role in the industrial development of the country. Although all the stock market indicators show a declining trend in 2008–09 compared to the previous year in view of the global economic downturn, in an absolute sense the stock markets in India are on a sound footing. In terms of P/E ratio, price-book value ratio and market capitalization-to-GDP ratio (vide Table 2.2) the Indian stock markets are comparable to that of any country. As can be seen from Table 2.3, Indian stock markets rank second in terms of the number of listed companies. In terms of the

Table 2.2 Indian stock market indicators

	BSE		*NSE*	
Indicator	*2007-08*	*2008-09*	*2007-08*	*2008-09*
1	**2**	**3**	**4**	**5**
1. BSE Sensex / S&P CNX Nifty				
(i) End-period	15644	9709	4735	3021
(ii) Average	16569	12366	4897	3731
2. Coefficient of variation	13.7	24.2	14.4	23.2
3. Price-earning ratio (end-period)	20.1	13.7	20.6	14.3
4. Price-book value ratio (end-period)	5.2	2.7	5.1	2.5
5. Yield (per cent per annum) (end-period)	1.1	1.8	1.1	1.9
6. Listed companies	4,867	4,929	1,381	1,432
7. Cash segment turnover (INR crore)	14,67,865	11,00,074	35,51,038	27,52,023
8. Derivative segment turnover (INR crore)	2,42,308	12,268	1,30,90,478	28,96,194
9. Market capitalization (INR crore) (end-period)	51,38,015	30,86,076	48,58,122	1,10,10,482
10. Market capitalization to GDP ratio (per cent)	108.8	52.8	102.9	100.3

Source: RBI Macroeconomic and Monetary Developments: First Quarter Review 2008–09.

Table 2.3 The Indian stock market: A comparison with international markets (end December 2007)

Particulars	*USA*	*UK*	*Japan*	*Singapore*	*India*
Number of listed companies	5130	2588	3844	472	4887*
Market capitalization (USD billion)	19947	3859	4453	353	1819
Market capitalization ratio (per cent)	149.1	157.13	90.25	274.41	200.09
Turnover (USD billion)	42613	10324	6497	384	1108
Turnover ratio (per cent)	216.5	270.1	141.6	122.0	84

* Companies listed on the BSE
Market capitalization is computed as a percentage of gross national income 2006.
Source: NSE, Indian Securities Market— A Review (2008)

market-capitalization ratio, India is far ahead of the USA, UK and Japan. However, in terms of market capitalization and turnover ratio, India lags behind many countries.

2.6 Bombay Stock Exchange Limited (BSE)

Bombay Stock Exchange Limited, popularly known as the BSE, is the oldest stock exchange in Asia. It was established in 1875 as the Native Share and Stock Brokers Association (Association of Persons). It was the first stock exchange in India to obtain permanent recognition from the Government of India under the Securities Contract (Regulations) Act, 1956. It has been demutualized and corporatized according to the provisions of the Companies Act, 1956, under the BSE (Corporatization and Demutualization) Scheme, 2005. With demutualization, the trading rights and ownership rights in BSE have been delinked. As a corporatized entity, the BSE is professionally managed under the overall direction of the board of directors comprising eminent professionals and representatives of trading members. Thus, the BSE has been transformed from a non-profit association of brokers into a for-profit corporate entity.

2.6.1 Listing of Securities on the BSE

BSE has a separate listing department to grant approval of listing of securities of public limited companies, central or state government securities. The approval for listing is granted in accordance with the provisions of the Securities Contracts (Regulation) Act, 1956, the Securities Contracts (Regulation) Rules, 1957, the Companies Act, 1956, guidelines issued by SEBI and rules, by-laws and regulations of the BSE. As per Section 73 of the Companies Act, 1956, a company seeking the listing of its securities is required to submit a letter of application to the stock exchange where it proposes to have its securities listed before filing the prospectus with the Registrar of Companies. An organization intending to get its securities listed on the BSE has to comply with the listing requirements prescribed by it. Some of the requirements are as follows:

*A **large cap company** is a company with a minimum issue size of INR 100 million and market capitalization of not less than INR 250 million. A **small cap company** is a company other than a large cap company.*

1. Companies have been classified as large cap companies and small cap companies for listing purposes. A **large cap company** is a company with a minimum issue size of INR 100 million and market capitalization of not less than INR 250 million. A **small cap company** is a company other than a large cap company.
   (a) For large cap companies:
      (i) The minimum post-issue paid-up capital of the applicant company shall be INR 30 million;
      (ii) The minimum issue size shall be INR 100 million; and
      (iii) The minimum market capitalization of the company shall be INR 250 million. Market capitalization shall be calculated by multiplying the post-issue paid-up number of equity shares with the issue price.
   (b) For small cap companies:
      (i) The minimum post-issue paid-up capital of the company shall be INR 30 million;
      (ii) The minimum issue size shall be INR 30 million;
      (iii) The minimum market capitalization of the company shall be INR 50 million;

(iv) The minimum income/turnover of the company should be INR 30 million in the preceding 12-month period;

(v) The minimum number of public shareholders after the issue shall be 1,000; and

(vi) A due diligence study may be conducted by an independent team of chartered accountants or merchant bankers appointed by the BSE. The requirement of a due diligence study may be waived if a financial institution or a scheduled commercial bank has appraised the project in the preceding 12 months.

2. All companies listed on the BSE are required to pay to the BSE the annual listing fee by 30 April of every financial year, as per the schedule of listing fees prescribed from time to time.
3. Companies making public/rights issues are required to deposit 1 per cent of the issue amount with the designated stock exchange before the issue opens. This amount is liable to be forfeited in the event of the company not resolving the complaints of investors regarding delay in sending refund orders/share certificates and non-payment to underwriters and brokers.
4. Companies delisted by the BSE and seeking relisting are required to make a fresh public offer and comply with the extant guidelines of SEBI and BSE regarding initial public offerings.

Likewise, the BSE has prescribed the minimum listing requirements for companies listed on other stock exchanges and for companies delisted by the BSE seeking relisting on the BSE. It has also prescribed norms for permission to use the name of the BSE in an issuer company's prospectus.

2.6.2 The BSE's Online Trading System (BOLT)

The BSE provides an efficient and transparent market for trading in equity shares, debt instruments and derivatives. The online trading system of the BSE, popularly known as BOLT, is a proprietary system and BS 7799-2-2002 certified. The BSE has a nationwide reach with a presence in more than 400 cities and towns in India, leading to a significant increase in volumes and liquidity.

Trading on the BOLT system is conducted from Monday to Friday between 9.55 a.m. and 3.30 p.m. The scrips traded on the BSE have been classified into "A", "B", "B2", "T", "S", "TS", "F", "G" and "Z" groups based on certain qualitative and quantitative parameters.

The "F" group represents fixed income securities and the "T" group represents scrips that are settled on a trade-to-trade basis as a surveillance measure. The "S" group represents scrips forming part of the "BSE-Indonext" segment. The "TS" group consists of scrips in the "BSE-Indonext" segment, which are settled on a trade-to-trade basis as a surveillance measure. The "G" group represents government securities. The 'Z' group consists of scrips of companies that have failed to comply with the listing requirements of the BSE and/or have failed to resolve investor complaints or have not made arrangements with the depositories.

The BSE also provides a facility to market participants for online trading of odd-lot securities in physical form in all the groups of securities. The scrips of the companies that are in demat form can be traded in the market lot of one but the securities of companies that are still in physical form are traded on the BSE usually in the market lot of either 50 or 100. Investors who possess quantities of securities less than the market lot are required to sell them as "odd-lots". The facility of trading in odd-lots of securities not only offers an exit route to investors to dispose of their odd lots of securities but also provides them an opportunity to consolidate their securities into market lots. The facility of selling physical shares in compulsory demat scrips is called the Exit Route Scheme. This facility may be used by small investors for selling up to 500 shares in physical form in respect of scrips of companies in which trades are required to be compulsorily settled by all investors in demat mode.

In order to facilitate trade in securities of companies that are actively traded at other regional exchanges but not listed on the BSE, it permits trading in "Permitted Securities", provided they meet the relevant norms specified by the BSE.

*A **tick size** is the minimum difference in prices between two orders on the same side, i.e., buy or sell entered on the system for a particular scrip.*

2.6.3 Tick Size

A **tick size** is the minimum difference in prices between two orders on the same side, i.e., buy or sell entered on the system for particular scrip. Trading in scrips listed on the BSE is done with a tick size of INR 0.05. However, in order to increase liquidity and enable market participants to place orders at finer rates, the BSE has reduced the tick size from INR 0.05 to INR 0.01 in case of units of mutual funds, securities traded in the "F" group and equity shares with closing price up to INR 15 on the last trading day of the calendar month. Accordingly, the tick size in various scrips quoting up to INR 15 is revised to INR 0.01 on the first trading day of the month. The tick size that is revised in this way on the first trading day of the month remains unchanged during the month even if the prices of scrips change.

2.6.4 Basket Trading System (BTS)

The BSE has a facility of the Basket Trading System (BTS), which enables investors to create Sensex-linked portfolios and a linkage of market prices of the underlying securities of the Sensex in the cash segment and futures on the Sensex. In the BTS, investors can buy or sell all 30 scrips of the Sensex in one transaction in the proportion of their respective weights in the Sensex. The investors need not calculate the quantity of Sensex scrips to be bought or sold for creating Sensex-linked portfolios as this function is performed by the system. However, investors can create their own baskets by deleting certain scrips from the 30 scrips in the Sensex. The investors can also change the weights of securities in such profiled baskets and enter their own weights. They can also select less than 100 per cent weightage to reduce the value of the basket according to their own requirements. In order to participate in the BTS, the members need to indicate the number of Sensex baskets to be bought or sold. The value of one Sensex basket is calculated by the system by multiplying INR 50 to the prevailing Sensex value. The minimum value of shares to be bought or sold is INR 50,000 for each order. The BTS provides the arbitrageurs an opportunity to take advantage of price differences in the underlying Sensex and futures on the Sensex by simultaneous buying and selling of baskets comprising the Sensex scrips in the cash segment and Sensex futures.

2.6.5 Trading and Settlement Cycle

The order in the trading and settlement cycle for scrips under compulsory rolling settlement in the Bombay Stock Exchange is stated in Table 2.4.

Settlement of a trade means the payment of money and delivery of securities. Settlement of a trade can be done by a member-broker on his own account or on behalf of his client. In case the delivery or payment in respect of a transaction executed by a member-broker is to be given or taken by a registered custodian, then the latter has to confirm the trade done by a member-broker on the BOLT system through a 6A/7A entry. For this purpose, custodians have been given connectivity to the BOLT system and admitted as a clearing member of the clearing house. In case the transaction done by a member-broker is not confirmed by a registered custodian within the time permitted, the liability for pay-in of funds or securities in respect of the same devolves on the concerned member-broker.

Table 2.4 The trading and settlement cycle

Day	*Activity*
T	Trading on exchange and daily downloading of statements showing details of transactions and margins at the end of each trading day. Downloading of provisional securities and funds obligation statements by member-brokers. 6A/7A* entry by the member-brokers/confirmation by the custodian.
T + 1	Confirmation of 6A/7A data by the custodian up to 11.00 a.m. Downloading of final securities and funds obligation statements by members.
T + 2	Pay-in of funds and securities by 11.00 a.m. and payout of funds and securities by 1.30 p.m. The member-brokers are required to submit the pay-in instructions for funds and securities to banks and depositories respectively by 10.30 a.m.
T + 3	Auction on exchange at 11.00 a.m.
T + 4	Auction pay-in and pay-out of funds and securities by 12 noon and 1.30 p.m., respectively.

Note: *6A/7A is a mechanism whereby the obligation of settling the transactions done by a member-broker on behalf of a client is passed on to a custodian based on confirmation from the latter. The custodian can confirm online the trades done by the members and up to 11.00 a.m. the next trading day. Late confirmation of transactions by the custodian after 11.00 a.m. and up to 12.15 p.m. on the next trading day is, however, permitted subject to payment of charges for late confirmation, at 0.01 per cent of the value of confirmed trades or INR 10,000, whichever is less.

2.6.6 Bulk and Block Deals

Bulk deal refers to a single transaction or set of transactions in which the traded volume bought or sold under any single client code is more than 0.5 per cent of the number of equity shares of a listed company. The member-brokers are required to make a disclosure of a single trade immediately upon the execution of the order. Member-brokers are also required to disclose, within one hour of the closure of trading hours, when the cumulative quantity traded under any single client code on that day either bought or sold is more than 0.5 per cent of the number of equity shares of a listed company.

According to SEBI, a *block deal* is a trade with a minimum quantity of 0.5 million shares or a minimum value of INR 50 million, executed through a single transaction and through a separate window of a stock exchange. As per SEBI guidelines, a separate trading window should be kept open for a limited period of 35 minutes from the beginning of trading hours of the stock exchange. Orders should be placed at a price not exceeding ±1 per cent from the ruling market price or previous day's closing. Every trade executed must result in delivery and shall not be squared off or reversed.

2.6.7 BSE Indices

The Bombay Stock Exchange came out with a stock index called Sensex, which has subsequently become the barometer of the Indian stock market. The BSE Sensitive Index (BSE-SENSEX) was first compiled in 1986 on a market capitalization-weighted methodology of 30 component stocks representing a sample of large, well-established and financially sound companies. The base year of the Sensex was 1978–79. In January 1989, the BSE introduced the BSE National Index (base: 1983–84 = 100) with 100 stocks listed at five major stock exchanges in India—Bombay, Calcutta, Delhi, Ahmedabad and Madras. The BSE national index was renamed the BSE-100 index on October 14, 1996, and since then it has been calculated taking into consideration only the prices of stocks listed at the BSE. To provide a better representation of the increased number of listed companies, increased market capitalization and the industry groups, the BSE constructed two new index series—BSE-200 and DOLLEX 200—in May 1994. In order to fulfil the need of the market participants for still broader, segment-specific and sector-specific indices, the BSE launched the BSE-500 index and five sectoral indices in 1999. In 2001, the BSE started the BSE-PSU index, DOLLEX-30, and BSE TECK Index. The BSE shifted all its indices to a free-float methodology (except BSE-PSU index) in a phased manner. The values of all BSE indices are updated every 15 seconds during market hours and displayed through the BOLT system, the BSE Web site and news agencies. All BSE indices are reviewed periodically by the Index Committee of the BSE. The committee frames broad policy guidelines for the development and maintenance of all BSE indices.

Indices are calculated using the *free-float market capitalization methodology*. This involves calculation of the index by taking into consideration the free-float market value of the concerned stock. The free-float market value is known as free-float capitalization, which refers to the value of that proportion of total shares of a company that are readily available for trading in the market. Free-float stock generally excludes promoters' holding, government holding, holdings by persons/bodies with controlling interest, holdings through the FDI route, strategic stakes by private corporate bodies/individuals, equity held by associate/group companies (cross holdings), equity held by employee welfare trusts and other locked-in shares that do not come to the market for trading in the normal course. Thus, the market capitalization of each company in the index is reduced to the extent of its readily available shares for trading in the market.

Free-float capitalization refers to the value of that proportion of total shares of a company that are readily available for trading in the market.

The BSE keeps a close watch on the events that might affect the index on a regular basis. It makes adjustments for rights, bonus and other issues. If no adjustment is made, a discontinuity would arise between the current value of the index and its previous value despite the non-occurrence of any economic activity of substance. When a company included in the compilation of the index issues rights shares, the free-float market capitalization of the company increases by the number of additional shares issued based on theoretical (ex-rights) prices. So the base market capitalization is recast as follows:

$$\text{New base market capitalization} = \text{Old base market capitalization} \times \frac{\text{New market capitalization}}{\text{Old market capitalization}}$$

When a company included in the compilation of the index issues bonus shares, the market capitalization of the company does not undergo any change. Therefore, there is no change in the base market capitalization. But the number of shares in the formula is updated. Base market capitalization adjustment is required when new shares are issued by way of conversion of debentures, mergers and spin-offs or when the equity is reduced by way of buy-back of shares and corporate restructuring.

2.7 The Pherwani Committee

The Indian stock market witnessed phenomenal growth in the 1980s.The number of listed companies, market capitalization and trading volume increased substantially. However, it was observed that the servicing of investors had been very poor, and small investors were not able to participate in stock market trading effectively. It was in this context that the Government of India appointed a high-powered study group, popularly known as the Pherwani Committee, in 1991. The committee first reviewed the functioning of the existing stock exchanges in the country, and recommended the establishment of an integrated national stock market system. However, for such a nation-wide system to be effective, several support agencies would be required to provide a uniform and high-quality trading, settlement, clearing and depository services. The committee recommended the establishment of the following institutions:

(i) the National Clearing and Settlement System to administer the clearing and settlement functions at a national level, and arrange for payment against delivery as a counter guarantor to participating members.

(ii) the Central Depository Trust to usher in scripless trading.

(iii) the Securities Facilities Support Corporation, which would be entrusted with the task of establishing and maintaining the network.

The committee also recommended the creation of a three-tier stock market system as follows:

(i) Principal stock exchanges would comprise the five major exchanges currently functioning in the metropolitan centres of Mumbai, Delhi, Kolkata, Chennai and Ahmedabad.

(ii) Regional stock exchanges would comprise exchanges established in smaller metros and urban centres and would, in the first instance, comprise all other existing stock exchanges.

(iii) Additional trading floors would be created as third-tier in the National Stock Market System.

The committee recommended that a new stock exchange be promoted immediately as a model exchange. The new exchange, to be called the National Stock Exchange, would provide access to investors from across the country on an equal footing, and work as an integral part of the National Stock Market System. The NSE would have a separate trading ring and create an active secondary market for debt instruments. Listing of companies on the NSE should be restricted to medium-sized companies so that the focus would be reoriented on the issues of smaller companies.

2.8 National Stock Exchange of India Ltd (NSE)

Following the recommendations of the study group on the establishment of new stock exchanges, National Stock Exchange of India Limited (NSE) was established in November 1992 with the following objectives:

- Establishing a nationwide trading facility for equities, debt instruments and hybrids;
- Ensuring equal access to investors from across the country through an appropriate communication network;
- Providing a fair, efficient and transparent securities market to investors using electronic trading systems;
- Enabling shorter settlement cycles and book entry settlements systems; and
- Meeting the current international standards of securities markets.

The NSE, promoted by leading organizations such as the Industrial Development Bank of India Limited, Industrial Finance Corporation of India Limited, Life Insurance Corporation of India, State Bank of India,

ICICI Bank Limited, is a de-mutualized stock exchange where the ownership and management of the exchange are completely divorced from the right to trade on it. Its board of directors comprises senior executives from promoter institutions, eminent professionals in the fields of law, accountancy, economics, finance and taxation, public representatives, nominees of SEBI and full-time executives of the NSE. While the board deals with broad policy issues, decisions relating to market operations are delegated by the board to various committees constituted by it. Such committees include representatives from trading members, professionals, the public and the management. The day-to-day management of the NSE is delegated to the managing director, who is supported by a team of professional staff.

The NSE commenced its operations soon after its recognition as a stock exchange in April 1993 under the Securities Contracts (Regulation) Act, 1956. The NSE has three main segments—the Wholesale Debt Market (WDM) segment, which commenced operations in June 1994, the Capital Market (Equities) segment, which started functioning in November 1994, and the Derivatives segment, which commenced operations in June 2000.

2.8.1 Listing Requirements

The main eligibility criteria for listing initial public offerings (IPOs) on the NSE are as follows:

1. The paid-up equity capital of the company shall not be less than INR 100 million and the capitalization of the applicant's equity shall not be less than INR 250 million. For this purpose, the post-issue paid-up equity capital for which listing is sought shall be taken into account.
2. Either the applicant seeking listing or the promoters/promoting company incorporated in or outside India shall have at least three years' track record.
3. The project/activity plan of the applicant must have been appraised by a financial institution established under Section 4A of the Companies Act, 1956, or a state finance corporation or a scheduled commercial bank with a paid-up capital exceeding INR 500 million or category-I merchant bankers with a net worth of at least INR 100 million or a venture capital fund with a net worth of at least INR 500 million. Alternatively, the applicant should have working capital arrangements with a bank having a net worth of not less than INR 500 million. This clause shall not be applicable for listing of equity shares and securities convertible into equity issued by a banking company or an infrastructure company. This clause shall also not be applicable for securities other than equity shares or securities convertible into equity shares at a later date issued by government companies, public sector undertakings, financial institutions, nationalized banks, statutory corporations, banking companies and subsidiaries of scheduled commercial banks.
4. The issuer shall have adhered to conditions precedent to listing as emerging inter-alia from the Securities Contracts (Regulations) Act, 1956, the Companies Act, 1956, the Securities and Exchange Board of India Act, 1992, any rules and/or regulations framed under foregoing statutes and any circular, clarifications or guidelines issued by the appropriate authority under the foregoing statutes.
5. No disciplinary action has been taken by other stock exchanges and regulatory authorities on the company in the past three years.
6. The promoting company (if any) has not defaulted on payment of listing fees to any stock exchange in the last three years or has not been delisted or suspended in the past and has not been proceeded against by SEBI or other regulatory authorities in connection with investor related issues or otherwise.
7. The promoting company's (if any) track record in redressal of investor grievances or promoting company's arrangements envisaged are in place for servicing its investor.
8. The promoting company's (if any) shareholding pattern on March 31 of the preceding three years separately showing promoters and other groups' shareholding pattern should be as per regulatory requirements.
9. The promoting company's (if any) litigation record, the nature of the litigation and status of litigation during the preceding three years need to be clarified to the exchange.

The NSE has also prescribed minimum requirements for listing of existing companies listed on other stock exchanges. The requirements for listing of the securities of an existing company are largely the same as prescribed for the IPOs. In addition, the applicant has to have paid dividend in at least two of the last three financial years immediately preceding the year in which the listing application has been made, or the applicant has to have distributable profits in at least two of the last three financial years or the net worth of the applicant should be at least INR 500 million.

2.8.2 Listing Fee

The NSE has fixed the initial listing fee at INR 7,500 and the annual listing fee at different levels ranging from INR 4,200 to INR 70,000, depending on the company's paid-up share capital. The larger the paid-up share capital, the higher the annual listing fee.

Reverse book-building *is a mechanism provided for capturing sell orders on an online basis from the shareholders through respective book-running lead managers.*

2.8.3 Reverse Book-building

Reverse book-building is a mechanism provided for capturing sell orders on an online basis from the shareholders through respective book-running lead managers. It can be used by companies intending to delist their shares through a buy-back process. The reverse book-building system (a fully automated screen-based bidding system) of the NSE provides a fair, efficient and transparent method of collecting offers from the shareholders.

2.8.4 NSE Indices

The main indices offered by the NSE are S&P CNX Nifty, CNX Nifty Junior and S&P CNX 500. The S&P CNX Nifty, popularly known as Nifty 50, is the leading index for large companies listed on the NSE. It is owned and managed by India Index Services and Products Ltd (IISL), which is a joint venture between the NSE and CRISIL. In fact, IISL is the first specialized company that focuses on the index as a core product and it has a consulting and licensing agreement with Standard & Poor (S&P), the world leader in index services. The term CNX stands for CRISIL NSE Indices, which reflects the identities of both the promoters. It is a well-diversified 50-stock index accounting for 22 sectors of the economy. The base is defined as 1,000 at the price level of November 3, 1995, when the total capitalization was INR 2,060,000 million. It is used for a variety of purposes such as benchmarking fund portfolios, index-based derivatives and index funds.

The S&P CNX 500 is India's first broad-based stock market index, representing about 96 per cent of the total market capitalization and about 93 per cent of the total turnover on the NSE. The S&P CNX 500 companies are disaggregated into 72 industry indices (S&P CNX industry indices). Industry weights in the index reflect the industry weights in the market. For example, if the automobile sector has a 2 per cent weightage in the universe of stocks traded on the NSE, the automobile stocks in the index would also have an approximate representation of 2 per cent in the index.

The CNX Nifty Junior is an index for companies listed on the NSE. It consists of 50 companies representing approximately 10 per cent of the traded value of all stocks on the NSE. It is also owned and operated by India Index Services and Products Ltd. The CNX Nifty Junior and the S&P CNX Nifty represent the 100 most liquid stocks traded on the NSE. However, no one company can be listed on both indices simultaneously.

2.8.5 Settlement System

The National Stock Exchange offers a rolling settlement on a T+2 basis. In a typical situation, trades taking place on Monday are settled on Wednesday, the trades made on Tuesday are settled on Thursday, and so on. For arriving at the settlement day, all intervening holidays including bank holidays, NSE holidays, Saturdays and Sundays are excluded. The rolling settlement cycle in the NSE is described in Table 2.5.

Table 2.5 The rolling settlement cycle of the NSE

Activity	*Days*
Rolling settlement trading	T
Custodial confirmation	T + 1 working days
Delivery generation	T + 1 working days
Securities and funds pay-in	T + 2 working days
Securities and funds pay-out	T + 2 working days
Valuation debit	T + 2 working days
Auction	T + 3 working days
Bad delivery reporting	T + 4 working days
Auction settlement	T + 5 working days
Rectified bad delivery pay-in and pay-out	T + 6 working days
Re-bad delivery reporting and pickup	T + 8 working days
Close out of re-bad delivery and funds pay-in and pay-out	T + 9 working days

In order to protect the interests of investors in financial markets and, more importantly, for minimizing risk of loss arising from deficient understanding of markets and instruments, the National Stock Exchange introduced a facility for testing and certification by launching the NSE Certification in Financial Markets in 1998. This is an online testing system, which tests the practical knowledge and skills required to operate in financial markets in a secure and unbiased manner and awards certificates based on relative merit. The testing ensures that the calibre of persons entering this field remains high in the best interests of a mature and vibrant market.

2.9 National Securities Clearing Corporation Ltd (NSCCL)

The NSCCL carries out the clearing and settlement of trades executed on the stock exchange.

National Securities Clearing Corporation Ltd (NSCCL), a wholly owned subsidiary of the National Stock Exchange, was established in August 1995. It was incorporated as a company under the Companies Act, 1956. The main objectives of the NSCCL are to bring and sustain confidence in clearing and settlement of trading in securities, promote and maintain consistent settlement cycles, provide counterparty guarantee against risk and operate a tight risk-containment system. The NSCCL carries out the clearing and settlement of trades executed in the equities and derivatives segments and operates a subsidiary general ledger for settlement of trades in government securities. It aggregates trades over a trading period, nets the positions to determine the liabilities of members and ensures movement of funds and securities to meet respective liabilities. It has empanelled 12 clearing banks to provide banking services to trading members and established connectivity with both the depositories for electronic settlement of securities.

The NSCCL is also the clearing and settlement agency for all deals executed in the retail debt market. The settlement schedule for the retail debt market (government securities) is listed in Table 2.6.

Funds settlement and securities settlement shall be through existing clearing banks and depositories of the NSCCL, in a manner similar to the capital market segment. In case of short deliveries, unsettled positions shall be closed out. The close-out would be done at zero-coupon yield curve valuation for prices plus a 5 per cent penalty factor. The buyer shall be eligible for the highest traded price from the trade date to the date of

Table 2.6 Settlement schedule for the NSCCL

Day	*Description*
T	Trade date
T + 1	Custodial confirmation
T + 2	Securities and funds pay-in
T + 2	Securities and funds pay-out

close-out or closing price of the security on the close-out data plus interest calculated at the rate of overnight FIMMDA-NSE MIBOR for the close-out data, whichever is higher, and the balance shall be credited to the investor protection fund.

The NSCCL has put in place a comprehensive risk management system, which is constantly upgraded to pre-empt market failures. The risk containment measures include capital adequacy requirements of members, monitoring of member performance and track record, stringent margin requirements, position limits based on capital, online monitoring of member positions and automatic disablement from trading when limits are breached. The clearing members of capital market and trading members of the wholesale debt market of the NSE are allowed to participate in clearing and settlement of trades done in government securities, subject to a minimum net worth of INR 10 million. An initial contribution to the Settlement Guarantee Fund of this market by way of an interest free security deposit of INR 0.5 million is required to be kept with the NSCCL. A member desiring to participate in this segment might opt to set aside a contribution of INR 0.5 million from his additional base capital available on the capital market segment and/or futures and options segment(s) towards the interest-free security deposit. Mark-to-market margins are applicable on all-open positions in government securities and shall be calculated on the basis of zero-coupon yield curve prices. This margin shall be payable on T + 1 day. Institutions that are permitted under the relevant regulations to transact only on the basis of giving and taking delivery will operate through the custodial mechanism and shall be exempt from margin as in the case of equities. Custodial trades on behalf of provident funds transacting through SGL II accounts shall also be eligible for margin exemption. The gross exposure in respect of these securities shall not exceed 20 times the interest-free security deposit. Any member seeking a higher exposure shall be required to bring in additional base capital as in capital market segment.

2.10 The Over-the-Counter Exchange of India (OTCEI)

Small investors across the country used to face problems of access, liquidity, delays in payment and delivery and uncertainty regarding prices at which their shares were bought or sold. Prohibitive issue costs, restricted access to the markets and administered pricing of their shares were the main problems faced by companies, particularly small and medium enterprises. The key issue for these companies was raising timely, cost-effective and long-term capital to sustain their operations and enhance their growth. It was in this backdrop that the OTC Exchange of India was incorporated as a public limited company in 1990 under the provisions of the Companies Act, 1956. It was promoted by UTI, ICICI, IDBI, IFCI, SBI Capital Markets, Canbank Financial Services, General Insurance Corporation of India and the subsidiaries of GIC. The OCTEI aims to help entrepreneurs raise finance for new projects in a cost-effective way and provide investors with a transparent and efficient mode of trading of securities. It is a recognized stock exchange under the Securities Contract (Regulations) Act. Many feel the OTCEI is the Indian version of the National Association of Securities Dealers – Automated Quotations (NASDAQ). It is an exchange without a specified trading floor. In other words, it is a ringless screen-based stock exchange with state-of-the-art telecommunications networking and software systems. The listing of securities is national listing right from day one. The companies thus have the benefit of nationwide listing and trading of their scrips by listing at just one exchange, i.e., the OTCEI.

The Over-the-Counter Exchange of India (OTCEI) was the first exchange to introduce a totally transparent screen-based trading system and depository-based trading and rolling settlement system in India.

A company which has issued capital of at least INR 3 million can be listed on the OTCEI, if it is not listed on any other stock exchange and is not engaged in the business of finance, leasing and amusement parks. That is, the minimum issued equity share capital of a company for eligibility for listing on the OTCEI is INR 3 million. The OCTEI is the only exchange to offer listing to companies with paid-up capital of below INR 30 million. It is ideally suited for start-up enterprises as a three-year track record is not mandatory. Any company listed on the exchange, besides meeting all SEBI requirements, needs to be sponsored on the exchange by one of its members. Vasundhara Rasayans was the first company to be listed on the OTCEI on July 28, 1992.

2.10.1 Intermediaries

The OTCEI has three types of intermediaries—members, dealers and sponsors. Members and dealers may carry out the activities of trading, underwriting, market making and participation in bought-out deals. But dealers cannot sponsor an issue for listing. The sponsors can perform the function of sponsorship of issues, but are not permitted to participate in secondary market activities. The members and dealers are required to register with SEBI as stockbrokers.

Only corporate entities with a minimum net worth of INR 10,000,000 are eligible for membership. Individuals are not eligible to become the members of the OTCEI. The corporate entity that seeks membership should be incorporated under the Companies Act, 1956, and have at least two directors with a minimum of two years' experience in capital market/stock-broking/portfolio management/investment consultancy. Whole-time directors of the corporate entity should at least be graduates. The functions of the members include appraisal and evaluation of project proposals, valuation of shares for the valued companies, participation in bought-out deals, stockbroking, and market-making.

Individuals and corporate entities can become dealers. Individuals must be at least a graduate and have a net worth of at least INR 1.5 million to be eligible to become dealers. They should also have a minimum of two years' experience in capital markets/stock-broking/portfolio management/investment consultancy. Organizations incorporated under the Companies Act, 1956, with a net worth of at least INR 2 million can become dealers, provided they fulfil certain other conditions. The Organizations should have at least two whole-time directors with a minimum of two years' experience in capital market/stock broking/portfolio management/ investment consultancy. It should also have at least two whole-time directors who are at least graduates. The functions of dealers include stockbroking, market-making, investors' services and participation in bought-out deals as co-investors.

The dealers may act as market-makers, that is, they offer two-way quotes for scrips. There are three types of market-makers—compulsory market-makers, additional market-makers and voluntary market-makers. While compulsory market-makers have to make the market (offer buy and sell quotes) in a scrip for a minimum period of 18 months, additional market-makers have the responsibility for 12 months and voluntary market-makers for 3 months. Compulsory market-makers and additional market-makers are appointed at the time of the public issue/offer for sale itself. Voluntary market-makers are dealers or members of the OTCEI who also want to make the market in the scrip along with compulsory market-makers and additional market-makers, after the scrip is listed.

A company wishing to list securities on the OTCEI must appoint one of the members of OTCEI as its sponsors. For the purpose of obtaining the listing, the sponsor has to appraise the project and/or the company and certify to the OTCEI that having examined the technical, managerial, commercial, economic and financial aspects of the project and/or the company, and having been satisfied that the company has or will have the necessary infrastructure as regards land, manpower, raw material supplies, power, water, spares and market necessary for its operations, the project and/or company is viable and investment worthy. After appraising the project, the sponsor determines the price at which the shares of the company will be offered to the public/ members and dealers of the OTCEI. Listing will be granted only on the issue being fully subscribed. In the event of the issue not being fully subscribed by the public, the sponsor will be responsible for subscribing to the unsubscribed portion on the terms envisaged by the sponsor and the company. The sponsor gives an undertaking to the OTCEI that it will compulsorily and continuously make the market by offering two-way quotes for buying and selling of the security. The sponsor arranges with one other member or dealer of the OTCEI for making market compulsorily in the security for a period of one year from the date of commencement of public trading.

2.10.2 Trading of Securities

A company may offer its shares to the public either directly or indirectly. Under direct offer, a company can offer its shares directly to the public after getting it sponsored by a sponsor. But under the indirect offer, the company may allot its shares first to the sponsor, who along with the company can at a later and convenient time make a public offer.

Earlier, what was traded on the OTCEI was not the share certificate but the counter receipt (CR). The CR is a tradable document containing the name of the investor, name of the company, number of shares, name and address of the registrar, price, commission, investor's signature and name and signature of the issuing counter. Anyone who would like to have a share certificate either for sentimental reasons or obtaining loans had to deposit the CR with the registrar and collect the share certificates. However, from March 1, 1999, the OTCEI stopped trading in CRs and asked the companies to convert CRs into share certificates. In other words, the OTCEI has shifted trading from counter receipts to share certificates.

Thus, the OTCEI was the first exchange to introduce a totally transparent screen-based trading system, and depository based trading and rolling settlement system in India. It has tied up with the NSCCL for clearing. The other special features of the OTCEI include compulsory market-making and sponsorship-based listing of companies. The OTCEI is the first and only stock exchange in the country to have an organized form of market-making with strict regulations governing the same. The sponsorship and market-making ensures liquidity and better valuation for the securities.

The OTCEI has an online monitoring and surveillance system, through which the exposure of members and dealers is monitored on a real-time basis. The system is also capable of continuously marking positions to market and relate mark-to-market losses to the available base capital and margins. The base minimum capital is taken as security for due performance and fulfilment by the members of their operations and obligations towards the OTCEI. The minimum base capital is INR 0.4 million. The members may opt for the base minimum capital by way of cash, FDRs, bank guarantee or securities.

The OTCEI collects the margins (daily margin, mark-to-margin and value-at-risk margin) from the members/dealers depending on their positions/exposures and market volatility, in line with SEBI requirements. Members and dealers contribute to the Settlement Fund of which the Brokers' Contingency Fund forms a part. The Brokers' Contingency Fund helps to complete the financial settlement in the unlikely event of a broker defaulting in payment of funds. This virtually eliminates the counterparty risk of trading on the OTCEI.

The OTCEI became the first stock exchange in 1993 to open investor grievance cells in four metros in the country. These cells handle complaints/queries from investors against brokers and/or companies listed on the OTCEI. The investor grievances are broadly classified as company-related and broker-related. Company-related grievances include non-receipt of securities sent for transfer, non-receipt of corporate benefits (for example, dividends, bonus and rights), and non-receipt of share certificates in exchange for counter receipts. Broker-related grievances include non-rectification of documents returned as bad delivery by the broker and non-receipt of funds/securities on sale/purchase. The OTCEI has set up the Investor Compensation Fund to address and compensate the claims of investors and protect them in case of default or loss of security. The Investor Compensation Committee of the OTCEI decides on the claims filed by the investors.

With its advanced trading systems and market-friendly trading procedures, the OTCEI provides a good exit route for venture capitalists and private equity funds for their investments. The market structure is such that venture capitalists would have an attractive alternative market to offload their holdings to a wide range of financial intermediaries. Although the preferred route for an exit can be through the IPO mechanism, the unlisted securities market of OTCEI does help the venture capitalists.

2.11 S.A. Dave Committee Recommendations

SEBI appointed a committee under the chairmanship of S.A. Dave on April 17, 1996, to review the working and operations of the OTCEI. The committee observed that the OTCEI had certain special features like compulsory market-making, rolling settlement, sponsorship, depository-based trading and ringless trading, which other stock exchanges did not have. The committee was of the opinion that while retaining the exclusive and unique features of the exchange, the OTCEI trading system needed to be strengthened in the interest of healthy development of the Indian capital market. The following are the major recommendations of the committee:

1. SEBI may remove the upper limit of INR 250 million and allow all companies, irrespective of their size, to be listed on the OTCEI, on the same lines as other stock exchanges.
2. All companies which do not fulfil the minimum shareholding criteria and thus face devolvement of their issues should either refund monies to the shareholders or may be given the option of seeking listing on the OTCEI, provided they undertake to fulfil the conditions of sponsorship and market-making.
3. The sponsors on the OTCEI should be permitted to give their appraised future projections in the issue document in cases where they are undertaking the market-making responsibility
4. All the bought-out-deals undertaken in the past as well as future that may not fulfil the three-year dividend paying record or the financial institution appraisal and funding criteria should also be allowed the facility of an offer for sale, listing and trading only on the OTCEI.
5. In the larger interests of investors, all such companies that are otherwise de-listed from other exchanges may seek listing in the separate listed scrips category of the OTCEI.

6. In order to provide greater depth and liquidity to the market and to increase trading volumes, instruments like futures and options on stocks along with stock lending may be encouraged on the OTCEI.
7. A shift from the T + 3 to T + 5 settlement system where the pay-in takes place on the fifth day and pay-out on the sixth day is essential. However, the OTCEI should revert to a T + 3 system at a later date when the banking system in India is geared to support such a system.
8. Only issues with a paid-up capital of up to INR 100 million will attract mandatory market-making provisions on a graded basis. Companies with an initial market capitalization of up to INR 50 million at the time of issue (first or subsequent as the case may be) will require an initial market-making inventory of 5 per cent of the issue. Companies with a market capitalization between INR 50 million and INR 100 million will require an initial market-making inventory of 2 per cent.

2.12 Listing on US Stock Exchanges

Leading software firm Infosys Technologies Ltd listed its shares on the NASDAQ stock exchange on March 11, 1999, and became the first Indian company to offer its shares on any US bourse. Later, many companies were successfully listed on the New York Stock Exchange (the world's largest in market capital) and NASDAQ. The Indian companies listed on US stock exchanges include Satyam Infoway, rediff.com, ICICI Bank, Wipro Technologies, VSNL, Dr Reddy's Lab, Satyam Computers, HDFC Bank, MTNL and Tata Motors. Global visibility is the main factor driving Indian companies to be listed on the US stock exchanges. Listing abroad also helps build familiarity about Indian companies among foreign investors, making it easier to attract more retail investors. The companies may also get more funds and better corporate governance. They also benefit the US investors, who get greater liquidity and more opportunities to participate in economic growth outside the USA. But listing on US stock exchanges is not easy. In order to be listed, a company must make its accounts compatible with the accepted American accounting principles. As Indian companies follow accounting practices that are significantly different from American standards, it may take months, sometimes years, to fulfil the US accounting standards. In fact, the stringent accounting norms have hampered the plans of many Indian companies to offer their stocks on the US bourses. But adhering to one of the most stringent accounting norms in the world improves corporate discipline and brings many benefits to all the stakeholders of the company.

2.13 Risk Management Framework

The online trading system in stock exchanges has significantly increased the volume of trades, and consequently increased the risk of default (in meeting payment or delivery obligations) by the market participants. To control the default risk, the stock exchanges have initiated a number of measures. One such measure is the introduction of the rolling settlement system, particularly the T+2 settlement cycle. The rolling settlement has substantially lowered the default risk in stock trading. Further, stock exchanges have also introduced a host of prudential and supervisory measures for brokers. These include capital adequacy requirement, margin requirements, limits on exposure and trading, online position monitoring and automatic disablement. A new initiative to allot a unique identification code to each broker, aimed at tracking his activity across exchanges, has also been launched. Even if there is any default in payment or delivery of shares by the counterparty, the risk is borne by the clearing corporation, which acts as a counterparty to every transaction that takes place on the stock exchanges. All these measures are supposed to protect the trading system from risk.

In order to address the risks involved in stock market transactions, SEBI has issued a comprehensive risk management framework which contains the various risk management measures. The core of the risk management system is the liquid assets (cash, bank fixed deposits, bank guarantee and securities of the central government) to be deposited by members with the stock exchange/clearing corporation. This rule ensures that the broker or dealer is able to maintain operations and does not adversely affect the capital market even if he has a large amount of bad debt. The liquid assets shall cover the following four requirements at all points of time.

1. MTM (mark-to-market) losses
2. Value-at-risk (VaR) margins
3. Extreme loss margins
4. Base minimum capital

Table 2.7 VaR margins for stocks

Liquid categorization	*One-day VaR*	*Scaling factor for illiquidity*	*The VaR margin*
Liquid securities (Group I)	Scrip VaR	1.00	Scrip VaR
Less liquid securities (Group II)	Higher of scrip VaR and three times index VaR	1.73 (square root of 3.00)	Higher of 1.73 time Scrip VaR and 5.20 times index VaR
Illiquid securities (Group III)	Five times index	1.73 (square root of 3.00)	8.66 times index VaR

The mark-to-market margins are determined by the net notional loss suffered by the broker on his outstanding position in various scrips. The stock exchanges shall collect the mark-to-market margin from the member or broker before the start of trading of the next day. The MTM margin shall also be collected/adjusted from/against the cash/cash equivalent component of the liquid net worth deposited with the exchange. The MTM margin shall be collected on the gross open position of the member. There would be no netting off the positions and set off against MTM profits across two rolling settlements, i.e., T day and T-1 day. The margin so collected shall be released along with the pay-in, including early pay-in of securities.

The VaR margin is a margin intended to cover the largest loss that can be encountered on 99 per cent of the days (99 per cent value at risk). It is considered to be the best margining system in the world. This margining system is applicable on a broker's outstanding positions in specific scrips, which are divided into three categories on the basis of their traded volume and frequency of trades. The VaR margins for different groups of stocks are as listed in Table 2.7.

For liquid stocks, the margin covers one-day losses, and for illiquid stocks it covers three-day losses so as to allow the clearing corporation to liquidate the position over three days. This leads to a scaling factor of $\sqrt{3}$ for illiquid stocks. For liquid stocks, the VaR margins are based only on the volatility of the stock while for other stocks, the volatility of the market index is also used in the computation.

The VaR margin shall be collected on an upfront basis by adjusting against the total liquid assets of the member at the time of trade. It shall be collected on the gross open position of the member. The gross open position for this purpose would mean the gross of all net positions across all the clients of a member including his proprietary position.

The impact cost shall be the percentage price movement caused by an order size of INR 0.1 million from the average of the best bid and offer price in the order book snapshot.

The categorization of securities on the basis of their liquidity is shown in Table 2.8.

The extreme loss margin covers the expected loss in situations that go beyond those envisaged in the 99 per cent value at risk estimates used in the VaR margin. The extreme loss margin for any stock shall be the value that is the higher of 5 per cent and 1.5 per cent times the standard deviation of daily logarithmic returns of the stock price in the last six months. This computation shall be done at the end of each month by taking the price data on a rolling basis for the past six months and the resulting value shall be applicable for the next month. The extreme loss margin shall be collected on the gross open position of a member (i.e., gross of all net positions across all the clients of a member including his proprietary position).

Table 2.8 Categorization of securities

Group	*Trading frequency (over the previous six months)*	*Impact cost (over the previous six months)*
Liquid securities (Group I)	At least 80% of the days	Less than or equal to 1%
Less liquid securities (Group II)	At least 80% of the days	More than 1%
Illiquid securities (Group III)	Less than 80% of the days	Not applicable

Table 2.9 Top stock exchanges in terms of the number of companies listed (2008)

Sl. No.	*Exchange*	*Total companies*	*Domestic companies*	*Foreign companies*
1	BSE	4921	4921	0
2	TSX Group	3841	3755	86
3	BME Spanish Exchanges	3576	3536	40
4	LSE	3096	2415	681
5	NYSE Euronext (US)	3011	2596	415
6	NASDAQ OMX	2952	2616	336
7	Tokyo SE Group	2390	2374	16
8	Australian SE	2009	1924	85
9	Korea Exchange	1793	1789	4
10	NSE	1406	1406	0
11	Hong Kong Exchanges	1261	1251	10
12	NYSE Euronext (Europe)	1002	1002	0

Source: World Federation of Exchanges

The brokers, besides being subject to individual by-laws of the stock exchanges, shall maintain a base minimum capital stated as follows:

- BSE, the NSE, and Calcutta Stock Exchange: INR 1 million
- Ahmedabad Stock Exchange and Delhi Stock Exchange: INR 0.7 million
- Other stock exchanges: INR 0.4 million

The exchanges may maintain the base minimum capital at INR 0.1 million if the average daily turnover is less than INR 10 million for any three consecutive months. The excess of the base minimum capital over INR 0.1 million may be refunded to the members of the exchange subject to certain conditions. Thus, the amount of base minimum capital determines a broker's intra-day trading limit and gross exposure limit. These limits can be increased only by a corresponding increase in the minimum capital requirement.

In case of any shortfall in margins, the terminals of the broker shall be immediately deactivated. However, the transactions done by institutional investors (for example, FIIs, mutual funds, banks and public financial institutions) shall be exempted from margin payments.

The stock exchanges or clearing corporations have the right to impose additional risk containment measures over and above the risk containment system mandated by SEBI. The members of the stock exchange should have a prudent system of risk management to protect themselves from client default.

2.14 World's Top Stock Exchanges

The world's top 12 stock exchanges in terms of the number of companies listed (2008) are shown in Table 2.9. As can be observed from the table, the BSE ranks first with 4,921 companies listed on it, followed by the Toronto Stock Exchange (3,841), BME Spanish Exchanges (3576) and London Stock Exchange (3096). As can be further observed from the table, most of the stock exchanges are international stock exchanges since they have foreign companies listed on them. It is only the Indian bourses which do not have foreign companies listed on them.

2.15 Turnover Velocity

Stock turnover velocity is the ratio of traded turnover to market capitalization. The turnover velocity may be an indicator of the breadth of activity and liquidity in the market. The higher the stock turnover ratio, the better the liquidity and more widespread the activity in the market. Investors are attracted to markets with high share turnover velocity since it means lower impact costs (the cost of entering and exiting a stock).

Table 2.10 Turnover velocity of domestic shares

Sl. No.	*Exchange*	*2008 (Percentage)*	*2007 (Percentage)*
1	BSE	29	29.4
2	TSX Group	103.8	83.7
3	BME Spanish Exchanges	171.4	191.9
4	LSE	152.7	154.2
5	NYSE Euronext (US)	240.2	166.9
6	NASDAQ OMX	1026.5	625.2
7	Tokyo SE Group	151.2	138.4
8	Australian SE	113.0	101.6
9	Korea Exchange	196.3	192.6
10	NSE	75.7	67.7
11	Hong Kong Exchanges	86	94.1
12	NYSE Euronext (Europe)	141.8	136.9

Source: World Federation of Exchanges

The turnover velocity of domestic shares on prominent stock exchanges in the world is shown in Table 2.10. As can be seen from the table, in contrast to the global trend, the share turnover velocity in India is very low. The share turnover velocity on the BSE was 29 per cent in 2008 while on the NSE it was 75.7 per cent in 2008. In 2007, these figures were 29.4 per cent and 67.7 per cent, respectively. The share turnover velocity in stock exchanges like NASDAQ, NYSE, London Stock Exchange, BME Spanish and Tokyo Stock Exchange are very high—over 100 per cent.

The low share turnover velocity in India may be attributed to concentration of trading in few stocks and high promoter holding in companies. For example, though the BSE has the largest number of shares listed on it, the top 5 per cent companies in terms of market capitalization account for over 80 per cent of the trading volume. In fact, the big traders in the Indian stock markets do not look beyond the top 100 companies. Also, promoter shareholding in India is over 50 per cent as against 10-15 per cent in developed countries. Thus, trading in Indian stock exchanges is highly concentrated, leading to many attendant problems.

2.16 Stock Market Concentration

Market concentration in general refers to the extent or degree to which a few firms account for a relatively a large percentage of the trades. Stock market concentration is the extent to which a stock market is dominated by only a few companies. There are two measures of stock market concentration: (i) percentage of market capitalization of the largest 5 per cent of all firms and (ii) percentage value traded by the largest 5 per cent of all firms. As shown in Table 2.11, Indian stock markets are as highly concentrated as other leading stock markets in the world. The BSE accounts for a concentration rate of 77.9 per cent in terms of market value and 88.6 per cent in terms of trading value. The NSE records a little less than the BSE as far as market concentration rates are concerned. It may be noted that the higher the market concentration, the lower the liquidity in the market. In other words, market concentration and liquidity in the market are negatively correlated. However, some research studies have found a positive correlation between volatility of the market and market concentration. Thus, high market concentration is not desirable for a stock market.

2.17 Stock Market Volatility and Return

The Research Bureau of *The Economic Times* conducted a study in 2007 on stock market volatility and return. According to the study, the United States registered least volatility (12.6 per cent) and least return (11.5 per cent). Countries like Argentina, Brazil, Russia and Turkey have recorded more than 30 per cent volatility. The stock market volatility of India and China was at 24.2 per cent and 22.2 per cent, respectively. European and

Table 2.11 Market concentration (2008)

Sl. no.	*Exchange*	*5% market value*	*5% trading value*	*Number of companies*
1	BSE	77.9 %	88.6%	246
2	TSX Group	75.37%	86.3%	79
3	BME Spanish Exchanges	NA	NA	NA
4	LSE	88.8%	84.4%	121
5	NYSE Euronext (US)	54.8%	30.3%	85
6	NASDAQ OMX	69.1%	33.1%	136
7	Tokyo SE Group	60.3%	66%	118
8	Australian SE	85.3%	76.4%	96
9	Korea Exchange	63.1%	58%	89
10	NSE	74.8%	79.3%	71
11	Hong Kong Exchanges	79.5%	80.9%	63
12	NYSE Euronext (Europe)	69.3%	63.3%	44

Source: World Federation of Exchanges

Asian markets are not as volatile as Latin American markets, the study observed. Though there appears to be no systematic relationship between volatility and return, the emerging markets have high volatility and high returns, with a few exceptions. Brazil, China and India have registered a stock market return of more than 50 per cent. However, the volatility in these countries is not as high as their return. It was further observed that the underdeveloped economies experienced more volatility than the developed economies due to several reasons. Normally, developing economies may not have enough capacity to absorb huge inflows of funds. Moreover, price discovery is also not efficient in developing markets. All such factors contribute to stock market volatility. Countries with economic credibility and political stability can manage even high volatility and thereby avoid turmoil in the stock markets. In fact, some would see volatility as an opportunity for investors to enter stock markets.

Summary

1. Stock exchanges are secondary markets for the securities already issued by businesses. In other words, stock exchanges provide liquidity and marketability for the securities issued by the companies and, thereby, play a significant role in the economic development of a country.
2. The listing of securities on a stock exchange has both merits and demerits. Although listing provides liquidity, marketability and free negotiability of securities, it may also give scope for price rigging and market manipulation, leading to misallocation of capital in the economy.
3. The Securities Contract (Regulation) Act, 1956, has given a fillip to the development of stock markets in India. In order to meet the growing needs of the investing public, the number of stock exchanges in the country has increased to 23. Among them, BSE is the largest, followed by the NSE.
4. The securities markets in India have undergone many reforms in recent years. Particularly after the establishment of SEBI in 1992, the very complexion of the Indian securities markets has changed. SEBI has prescribed many guidelines which have far-reaching implications for the protection of investors' interests as well as for orderly development of securities markets.
5. The online trading, rolling settlement, depository system, demutualization of stock exchanges and derivatives trading are considered to be highly significant reform measures initiated by SEBI.
6. The Bombay Stock Exchange (BSE) is the oldest stock exchange in Asia. It is the largest stock exchange in the world in terms of the number of companies listed. It provides an efficient and transparent market for trading in equity shares, debt instruments and derivatives. It offers a rolling settlement on a T+2 basis.
7. The BSE Sensex is one of the most popular stock market indices in the world. It was first compiled in 1986 on market capitalization-weighted methodology of 30 component stocks representing a sample of large, well-established and financially sound companies.
8. The National Stock Exchange was established in 1992 on the recommendations of the Pherwani Committee. It

provides a nationwide trading facility for equities, debt instruments and hybrids. The S&P CNX Nifty, popularly known as Nifty, is the leading stock market index for companies listed on the NSE. The NSE also offers rolling settlement on a T+2 basis.

9. The NSCCL, a wholly owned subsidiary of the NSE, provides clearing and settlement facilities for securities traded on the NSE. It has put in place a comprehensive risk management system, which is constantly upgraded to pre-empt market failures.
10. The OTCEI was established in 1990 to help entrepreneurs, especially small entrepreneurs, to raise funds for new projects in a cost-effective way and to provide investors with a transparent and efficient mode of trading in securities. It was the first stock exchange in India to introduce totally transparent screen-based trading, depository-based trading and the rolling settlement system.
11. SEBI has also introduced a comprehensive risk-management framework with various risk containment measures. The margins prescribed in this regard are market-to-market margins, value at risk margins and extreme loss margins. The base minimum capital is also insisted upon by SEBI.
12. The stock turnover velocity is the ratio of the traded turnover to market capitalization. In contrast to the global trend, the share turnover velocity in Indian stock markets is very low. The share turnover velocity on the BSE was as low as 28 per cent, while on the NSE it was 59 per cent in June 2007. In the stock exchanges in the developed world, the share turnover velocity is very high. In many a case, it exceeds 100 per cent.

Questions

1. What is the role of the securities markets in the economic development of a country?
2. Discuss the functions of a stock market.
3. What do you understand by listing of securities? Discuss the advantages and disadvantages of listing.
4. Distinguish between speculation and investment.
5. Trace the origin of stock markets in India. Also state the chronological developments in the stock markets.
6. Discuss the reforms in securities markets. Do you feel they are adequate?
7. State the major recommendations of the Pherwani Committee.
8. Trace the origin of the BSE.
9. Explain BOLT and BTS.
10. What do you understand by a stock market index? Why are there so many indices? What purpose(s) do they serve?
11. Explain the salient features of the BSE Sensex.
12. Discuss the eligibility criteria for the listing of securities on the BSE.
13. What are the objectives of the National Stock Exchange (NSE)?
14. Discuss the eligibility criteria for listing initial public offerings on the NSE.
15. Explain the structure of the NSE.
16. Explain the various NSE indices.
17. Explain the salient features of rolling settlement.
18. Give a brief account of the NSCCL.
19. Explain the special features of the OTCEI.
20. What are the major recommendations of the S.A. Dave Committee?
21. Explain the risk management framework as suggested by SEBI.
22. What is stock turnover velocity? Explain the major reasons for low stock turnover velocity in India.

Case Study

Stock scams have become a common phenomenon in many economies. As soon as a scam is discovered and follow-up action initiated, another scam manifests itself in a different form. The series of scams in the Indian stock markets have resulted in the near-collapse of the trading and settlement system in the stock exchanges. The following scams have had a lot of publicity because of the magnitude of the funds involved.

The Harshad Mehta Phenomenon

The major securities scam with far-reaching implications occurred in India in 1992. The stock scam, which came to be known as the Harshad Mehta phenomenon, threw the functioning of the money market and stock market out of gear. The scam was really a diversion of funds from the banking system, in particular the inter-bank market in government securities, to brokers for financing their operations in the stock market. When the new government at the Centre accelerated the process of economic liberalization in 1991, the stock market started booming. The BSE Sensex, the barometer of the Indian economy, rose from below 2000 in early 1991 to 4,467.30 in March 1992. Thus, there was an enormous requirement of funds to support the stock market operations. Heavy margins imposed by the stock exchange on settlement trading added to the funds requirement.

Harshad Mehta was once an assistant with the New India Assurance Company. He had a talent for winning the confidence of senior bankers, fund managers and the key men who mattered in securities trading. He had a good grasp of the regulations governing the financial market and, more importantly, the loopholes that he could exploit to maximum advantage.

The scandal was about the diversion of massive bank funds for stock market operations. Mehta, a leading broker who had earned the title of big bull, used over INR 6,220 million of SBI funds and INR 3,500 million of NHB funds for his stock market operations. Many other banks, domestic as well as foreign, were also reported to have participated in the scam. Thus, Mehta channelled hundreds of millions of rupees from the money market to fund his amazing run on the stock market. Following the discovery of the scam, in less than two months the stock index came down to 3,086.40, registering a fall of nearly 30 per cent from the peak level. Thousands of middle-class investors suffered huge losses. It also wiped out the market value of shares to the tune of more than INR 1,000,000 million.

Ready forward deals came in handy for the diversion of funds from the money market to the stock market. In a ready forward deal, one bank sells government securities to another bank and buys them back at the end of a certain period (typically 15 days) at a slightly higher price. The price difference represents the margin to the bank which buys the securities. It is a form of secured short-term loan from one bank to another against government securities. The ready forward deal is also known as repo or repurchase agreement. It is very popular throughout the world and an important tool in the hands of the banks to manage their statutory liquidity ratio (SLR) requirements.

In order to make quick money, many banks indulged in speculative dealings by entering into double ready forward delivery deals. These deals essentially involved selling securities which would fall steeply when an interest hike was expected and switch the funds to those securities which would record a smaller drop. After the fall in prices, the bank/broker would offload the holdings and buy more of the original securities, leaving the player with the same securities he had started with. Normally, such transactions, which reach a peak around the time of a coupon rate (the interest rate of the securities themselves), peter out a short while later. But when the last hike was announced on March 17, 1992, from 12 to 12.5 per cent, the market experienced an abnormally high level of activity—and this was what led to the uncovering of the stock scam, which was unprecedented in the history of the Indian stock market.

The normal settlement process in government securities is that the banks involved in securities transactions make payments and deliver the securities directly to each other. However, a broker may get involved in the transactions only to bring the buyer and the seller together and help them negotiate the terms, for which he earns a commission from both parties. In other words, the broker does not handle either the cash or the securities. However, during the time of the scam, some banks adopted an alternative settlement process, according to which the deliveries of securities and payments were made through the broker. In this settlement process, the buyer and the seller of the government securities may not even know with whom they have traded. But the broker knows both the parties. When the cheques were issued in favour of another bank, the broker, who was intermediating, found a way of crediting the account payee cheque to his account. Moreover, some banks were persuaded to part with cheques without actually receiving securities in return.

In buying and selling of government securities, there is no physical transfer of the securities. A record of the deals is maintained by the public debt office of the RBI in a Securities General Ledger (SGL). What actually changes hands is a banker's receipt, which is evidence that the issuer has the securities. A bank receipt acts as a receipt for the money received by the selling bank. Hence the name bank receipt. A bank receipt implies that the issuer actually has the securities and holds them in trust for the buyer. But, in reality, the issuer of a bank receipt may not have the securities at all. In other words, a bank may issue a bank receipt (BR) which is not backed by actual securities. During the scam, fake BRs were also created to replace the actual securities. Further, even the securities themselves were forged.

Brokers used the fake BRs to obtain unsecured loans from the banking system. Also, the cheques issued in favour of some banks were credited to the brokers' accounts. There were also instances of the same broker selling the same security on the same day to different banks at different prices. Thus, the funds were misappropriated from the banking system and perhaps invested in the stock market. There was a powerful bear cartel operating in the market with money misappropriated from the banking system. When the stock prices rose steeply, it was most likely that a considerable part of the money misappropriated by this group would have been spent on financing the losses in the stock market. The monitoring and surveillance systems in the banking system were very poor. That also facilitated the scam.

The Ketan Parekh Scam

Another scam in the Indian stock market happened in 2001 when Mumbai broker Ketan Parekh used bank funds to prop up scrips in the stock market. Parekh formed a network of brokers from smaller stock exchanges in the country, bought shares of some companies when they were trading at low prices, and saw the prices go up while continuously trading. He focussed primarily on the shares of 10 companies for his dealings. When the prices of those shares were high enough, he pledged those shares with banks as collateral for funds. It was found that Parekh rigged the prices of scrips of Global Trust Bank, Zee Telefilms, HFCL, Lupin Laboratories, Aftek Infosys and Padmni Palymer. As long as the share prices were rising, there was no problem. But when the stock markets around the world started crashing in March 2000, the values of stocks held by Parekh and his network of brokers also declined. They were asked by the banks to either pledge more shares as collateral or return some of the money borrowed. That eventually led to payment problems in the stock markets. By February 2001, the stocks held by Parekh and his associates lost heavily in terms of value. That worsened the payment problems, particularly in the Calcutta Stock Exchange. Many brokers, including the top brokers of the Calcutta Stock Exchange, defaulted on their payment. In the process, many people, including some leading banks, lost a lot of money.

Parekh had heavy cash dealings with Madhavapura Mercantile Cooperative Bank (MMCB), a small Ahmedabad-based bank. He issued cheques to MMCB drawn on Bank of India, against which MMCB issued pay orders. The pay orders were discounted at Bank of India, State Bank of India and Punjab National Bank. He discounted about 250 pay orders worth about INR 24 billion between January and March 2001. In the process, Bank of India lost about INR 1.2 billion and other banks also lost a good amount of money in the scam.

Parekh and different companies owned by him also borrowed funds directly from MMCB. MMCB released funds to Parekh without proper collateral security and even crossed its capital market exposure limits. The Global Trust Bank also issued loans to Parekh and its exposure to the capital market was above prescribed limits. Parekh and his associates held a significant stake in Global Trust Bank and rigged the prices of the scrip of Global Trust Bank before its proposed merger with UTI Bank. The Parekh scandal ultimately resulted in the busting of the Global Trust Bank and Madhavapura Mercantile Cooperative Bank.

SEBI made an investigation into the stocks of Himachal Futuristic Communications, Zee Telefilms, Adani Exports, Global Tele-Systems, Ranbaxy Laboratories, Shri Adhikari Brothers Television Network, Shonkh Technologies International, Padmini Technologies and Aftek Infosys, which were traded during the period between October 1999 and March 2001. The investigation revealed that Parekh and 17 other entities, which were directly or indirectly related to or associated with him, were involved in market manipulation in these stocks. The modus operandi of all the entities to manipulate various scrips was, by and large, the same. Parekh was found to be the mastermind behind all the acts of omissions or commissions by the entities. Therefore, SEBI issued fresh orders on November 13, 2007, restraining Parekh and the 17 other entities from accessing the stock market for 14 years. The latest order ran concurrently with the earlier order served to Parekh and some other entities on December 12, 2003, that also restrained him, among others, from accessing the equity market for 14 years.

The entities that have been barred from accessing the stock market for 14 years include Kartik Parekh, Classic Credit, Panther Fincap and Management Services, Luminant Investment, Chitrakut Computers, Saimangal Investrade, Classic Infin, Panther Investrade, Goldfish Computers and Nakashtra Software. SEBI has also restrained Triumph International Finance India, Triumph Securities and NH Securities from accessing the stock market for five years.

The IPO Scam of 2005

There are two categories—high net worth individual (HNI) category and retail individual investor category—under which an individual can invest in an initial public offer (IPO). An HNI is one who invests over INR 100,000 in a public issue, while those who invest a lesser amount fall in the category of retail investors. According to SEBI guidelines for public issues through book-building, 35 per cent is reserved for retail individual investors and 15 per cent for HNIs. Thus, there is a large chunk of the issue available for retail investors. As the total number of retail investors is large, each may get a small quantity of shares. So if a single large application amount is split into smaller applications, which fall into the retail category, there is a greater chance that on the whole, such an investor may end up with more number of shares. Within the retail investor category, there are different ratios for each level of applied shares. For example, those who have applied for 400 shares may be allotted 100 shares, those who have applied for 200 shares may get 50 shares, and so on. This also leads investors to formulate different strategies to give themselves a better chance of allotment.

Roopalben Nareshbhai Panchal based in Ahmedabad, Purushottam Budhwani in Mumbai and some others masterminded the IPO scam in 2006. They opened thousands of fictitious/*benami* bank accounts under different names. The people who lent their names and identities for the purpose were even paid money up-front. In some cases, accounts were opened on the same day with the same branch of Bharat Overseas Bank. The addresses were similar in most cases, as were the names, with minor variations. The bank accounts were used to secure the IPO finance and open demat accounts with depository participants. Multiple demat accounts and multiple bank accounts were opened to ensure that the investors could make multiple applications under the retail category. Then the scamsters applied for the IPOs. The application forms carried identical addresses and serial numbers were in perfect sequence. The Bharat Overseas Bank was also made to lend to these dummy IPO applicants. After the allotment, but before listing, thousands of fictitious entities transferred their shares to demat accounts controlled by Panchal, Budhwani and others in off-market transactions. These individuals, in turn, sold the shares to other entities or, in some cases, directly in the market. Since most of the IPOs opened at a premium, considerable profit was made even after clearing the loan from Bharat Overseas Bank. Thus, these individuals managed to corner a sizeable chunk of allotment in the retail category through this process, shoving aside many small investors.

It was discovered that some investors had used false identities and bank accounts to buy more shares in the IPOs of Yes Bank and IDFC. SEBI was reported to have discovered a single investor with 6,500 demat accounts and another with around 1,315 demat accounts. Following an initial probe,

SEBI banned four stockbrokers and 35 investors from trading in the IPOs.

Scandals like forging share certificates, irregular transactions through *havala* purchases, issuing of excess duplicate share certificates, price rigging, insider trading and other market manipulations have become common phenomena in stock markets. These happenings have not gone unnoticed. But the efforts to plug loopholes in the system of trading and settlement and thereby prevent such market manipulations have not yielded the desired results. This is one of the reasons why small investors are shying away from stock markets in India.

Question

Analyse the scams presented in this case study and identify the systemic failures.

Chapter 3

Financial Instruments

LEARNING OBJECTIVES

After studying this chapter, you should be able to:

- Describe equity-linked securities.
- Present fixed-interest rate securities.
- Examine the feasibility of investing in floating-rate securities.
- Highlight short-term securities.
- Discuss regulations pertaining to the issue of different kinds of securities.

3.1 Introduction

Financial instruments, also known as financial products, are the vehicles through which investments are made. Hence, they are investment vehicles. People, particularly the investing public, always look for new financial products to satisfy their evolving financial needs. The investors always aim at maximizing the return on their investment with minimum risk. They seek financial products that will provide them with increasing yield with the least risk. This does not mean that investors do not accept risky products; they do accept risky products provided there is a return commensurate with the risk. The investors always make a trade-off between the return and the risk while buying any financial product, whether it is an industrial security or an insurance product. The more the number of financial products available, the better it is for the investors, because they can choose the best product(s) to fulfil their investment objectives. It is in this context the financial engineering plays a role. *Financial engineering* refers to the process of designing, developing and implementing innovative financial instruments, processes or solutions to problems in finance. Thus, one of the major objectives of financial engineering is to come up with innovations in financial instruments. The variegated financial instruments that are available in the financial markets today are born out of financial engineering. Financial engineers structure the cash flows of a financial product in such a way that both parties—the issuer of the financial instrument and the investor—would be satisfied in terms of the risk as well as the return. Since risk-return characteristics are different for different investors and different issuers, and they are evolving, there is always a need for new financial instruments.

With the deregulation of the financial services industry, a variety of new financial instruments have captured the attention of the investors. The financial markets are full of innovative instruments vying with competitive rates of return and incentives for increasing yield. Since most people do not know what these securities entail, the average investor makes investment decisions based on a vague idea of the returns and goes along with the market sentiment. This chapter is aimed at describing the various financial instruments that are popular, especially in India.

3.2 Equity Shares

*An **equity share** is a certificate representing the ownership of a company, and the equity shareholder is a part owner of the company with certain rights and responsibilities.*

The most popular alternative method for long-term capital funding of a company has been equity shares. Like debt securities, equity shares are issued by companies to raise long-term funds. While the holder of debt securities becomes a creditor, the owner of equity shares becomes the owner of the company. Thus, an **equity share** is a certificate representing the ownership of a company. The equity shareholder is thus a part owner of the company, with certain rights and responsibilities.

The company that issues the equity shares may not buy these shares from the shareholders, except in special circumstances. But the shareholders can sell the equity shares in the secondary market to those who want to buy those shares. Therefore, an investor can buy the equity shares either directly from the company (primary market) or from the existing shareholders of the company (secondary market). The primary capital market enables the investors to buy the shares from the company, whereas the secondary market, known as the stock market, provides liquidity for investors who have already purchased the shares.

As owners of the company, the equity shareholders share the company's success and failure. If the company performs well or prospers, the equity shareholders can receive high rates of return. But the equity shareholders will lose money if the company does not do well or goes bankrupt. On liquidation, the company sells its assets and pays off all its creditors first. The equity shareholders may receive what is left after the creditors, including preference shareholders and others, are paid off. The success or failure of a company is the success or failure of the investment in equity shares. Therefore, investment in equity shares is considered to be relatively risky compared with investment in debt securities. However, the equity shareholders have certain rights, which the other investors of the company such as creditors and preference shareholders do not have. As the owners of the company, the equity shareholders are the highest authority in the organization and decide all the key matters concerning the company. They have voting rights which they may exercise during the election of the board of directors that forms the top-level management of the company. Further, the liability of the equity shareholders is limited to their equity capital contribution. Investors, in general, prefer equities as they outperform other investments like debentures and bonds over a long period of time. Investment in equities also provides a diversification benefit to the investors as they are not perfectly correlated with other investments. Investment in equities is a long-term asset which can be a good match against long-term liabilities.

Equity shares are of two types—voting rights shares and non-voting rights shares.

Notwithstanding certain benefits associated with investment in equity shares, companies might find it difficult to access long-term fund requirements through equity, primarily due to difficult market conditions. Even though equities are very high-return-yielding assets, many investors keep away from stock markets because equities are also high-risk assets. Investors also need expertise to select the equities that can meet their return-risk characteristics.

3.2.1 Non-voting Rights Shares

The concept of non-voting rights shares has generated considerable interest among investors and companies. The idea was conceived in the 1980s by the Institute of International Economics, Washington, and thereafter it became quite popular all over the world, particularly in the United States. In India, non-voting rights shares were first mooted by the working group of the Planning Commission, which was set up to study the development of the capital market in India.

The equity shares of a company may be classified as those with voting rights and those without voting rights. The holders of shares with voting rights have a say in all major corporate matters, including the appointment of the board of directors. The holders of shares without voting rights do not have the right to participate in corporate decision-making. But non-voting shareholders are entitled to dividends if they are declared by the company. Companies that have a good track record but are apprehensive of losing control of the management will find non-voting shares ideal to raise funds. By issuing non-voting shares, these companies can raise equity capital without diluting control of the company.

3.2.2 Voting Rights Shares

Shares with voting rights are also classified as shares with one vote per share and those with more than one vote per share. The equity shares with more than one vote per share are known as *super voting shares*. Voting rights enable the shareholders to participate in the decision-making process of the company so that they can insulate themselves from the consequences of bad decisions. The non-voting shares can protect a company from unwanted takeover bids because the existing management of the company controls the voting shares and would not allow a takeover bid to occur. This ensures the stability of the management, particularly of the board of directors. Non-voting shares give greater flexibility to the companies to raise capital. They also attract investment from non-resident Indians and foreign investors. By issuing non-voting shares, a company can reduce its debt–equity ratio.

Non-voting shares have more liquidity than voting shares since the holders of voting shares are generally not willing to sell their shareholdings. Therefore, voting shares usually have a large premium relative to non-voting shares. Moreover, the bid–ask spread for voting shares is also usually larger because of less liquidity.

A large number of small investors are usually not very interested in participating in the policy matters of the company. Realistically speaking, these investors have little chances of influencing the company through their vote. If the chance to vote is realistically less for a minor retail investor, then it makes little sense to buy voting shares at a higher cost. Therefore, they are more interested in receiving good dividends and capital appreciation. Non-voting rights shares might carry a higher rate of dividend to compensate for the loss of voting rights. But non-voting shareholders would be entitled to bonus and rights issues. Moreover, if a company fails to pay dividend for two consecutive years, non-voting shareholders would be entitled to exercise voting rights on a pro-rata basis till the company resumes the payment of dividend. Ultimately, by owning non-voting shares, the investors place a bet on the management of the company to make the right decisions to ensure long-term profitability of the company.

3.3 Preference Shares

***Preference shares** possess the characteristics of equity as well as debt.*

Preference shares have some of the characteristics of equity and some of the characteristics of debt. Like debt security holders, preference shareholders receive dividend at a fixed percentage from the company on their investment. The company has the discretion to pay dividend to the preference shareholders. The preference shares may be issued with a clause stating that if the company fails to pay the specified percentage of dividend in any particular year(s) due to loss, then in a future year, when it makes a profit, the company will pay the dividend of that year and of the years in which it did not pay. Thus, the unpaid dividends of preference shares may cumulate and be paid to the preference shareholders before any dividend is paid to the equity shareholders. Such preference shares are known as cumulative preference shares. There are also non-cumulative preference shares on which the issuing company pays dividend only when it earns profits sufficient to pay dividend. The preference shareholders get preference over the equity shareholders at the time of payment of dividend. But the preference shareholders cannot participate in the profits of the company beyond the specified percentage of dividend. Although there is no legal requirement for the company to pay dividend on the preference share capital, the non-payment of preference dividend has credit implications. The interest on debt securities is a tax-deductible expense, whereas the payment of preference dividend is not a tax-deductible expense for the company. Therefore, debt is cheaper than preference share capital for the company.

3.3.1 Cumulative Convertible Preference Shares

***Cumulative convertible preference (CCP) shares** have all the positive attributes of convertible debentures by providing flexibility and options to the investor.*

Cumulative convertible preference (CCP) shares are on a par with convertible debentures and provide flexibility and options to the investor. The concept of CCP shares came about in 1985 to meet the requirements of the corporate sector and investors in India. The main object of CCP shares is to enable new entrepreneurs to meet a part of their financial requirements in such a way that the investors are protected from risk in the early stages of the project and later given a share in the profitability of the company.

The Controller of Capital Issues (CCI) issued guidelines on August 19, 1985, under the Capital Issues (Control) Act, 1947, for the issue of the CCP shares. The salient features of these guidelines are as follows:

1. The objectives of the issue of CCP shares would be: (a) setting up new projects; (b) expansion or diversification of existing projects; (c) normal capital expenditure for modernization; and (d) working capital requirements.
2. The amount of CCP shares to be issued will be to the extent that the company would be offering equity shares to the public for subscription. In case the projects are assisted by financial institutions, the quantum of the issue would be approved by the financial institutions/banks.
3. The CCP shares would be deemed to be an equity issue for the purpose of calculation of the debt–equity ratio.

4. The entire issue of CCP shares would be convertible into equity shares between the end of three and five years, as may be decided by the company and approved by the CCI.
5. The conversion of the CCP shares into equity would be deemed as being one resulting from the process of redemption of preference shares out of the proceeds of a fresh issue of shares made for the purpose of redemption.
6. The rate of preference dividend payable on CCP shares would be 10 per cent.
7. On conversion of the preference shares into equity shares, the right to receive arrears of the dividend, if any, on the preference shares up to the date of conversion shall devolve on the holder of the equity shares on such a conversion. The holder of the equity shares shall be entitled to receive the arrears of the dividend as and when the company makes a profit and is able to declare such a dividend.
8. The CCP shares would have voting rights as applicable to preference shares under the Companies Act, 1956. The CCP shareholders, under Section 87 (2)(a) of the Companies Act would have the right to vote only on resolutions which directly affect their rights and under Section 87 (2)(b)(i) on every resolution if the dividend has remained unpaid for an aggregate period of not less than two years preceding the date of meeting.
9. The conversion of the CCP shares into equity shares would be compulsory at the end of five years and the aforesaid preference shares would not be redeemable at any stage.
10. The face value of CCP shares will ordinarily be INR 100 each and the instrument shall be listed on one or more stock exchanges in the country.
11. The company shall meet the legal requirements such as incorporation with the articles of association and passing special resolutions in this regard under Section 81(1A) of the Companies Act, 1956.

Thus, CCP shares contain all the positive features of equity and preference shares as well as convertible debentures. The new instrument not only helps new entrepreneurs but at the same time protects investors from erosion of their capital by investing in new ventures. New companies undertaking capital-intensive projects of long gestation periods cannot attract equity investment in the beginning. Such companies can issue CCP shares with a deferred interest liability and avoid cash outflows in the initial stages when there are no earnings. Later, when the project becomes profitable, the CCP shares can be converted into equity and the dividend declared.

According to the guidelines, CCP shares give an assured return of 10 per cent per annum, even during the gestation period, which may not be available in the case of equity shares. Even if the profits are inadequate in the initial stage, the dividend payable accumulates, and the entire amount is paid before any dividend is paid to the equity shareholders. There will be an appreciation in the share price conversion if the project is economically viable and the company starts paying dividend. However, the main disadvantage of CCP shares is that if the company performance is poor, CCP shares would be quoted at below par value and on compulsory conversion, the CCP shareholders will have to take the low quoted equity shares and run the risk of heavy capital loss.

3.3.2 Rights Issue to Preference Shareholders

According to the statutes, it is only the equity shareholders who have the pre-emptive right to maintain their proportionate ownership in the company. However, a blue-chip pharmaceutical company, Cipla, made a rights issue in 1991 to its preference shareholders at the ratio of one equity share for every preference share held. It was a unique issue. The equity shares were offered at par (INR 100) when the current book value of the equity stock was INR 2,119 and the market value was around INR 4,500. When it became a controversial issue, the company defended its decision by stating that over the years, preference shareholders had been getting a small fixed rate of dividend while the real value of their shares had deteriorated drastically because of inflation. On the other hand, the equity shareholders had been raking in money through healthy dividends and three bonus issues during the 1980s. The equity shareholders of the company accused Cipla of defrauding them. They said that the rights issue would put preference shareholders, who by definition have made relatively safe investments, on a par with the equity shareholders who had taken a risk while investing in equity stock.

Box 3.1 illustrates the cumulative convertible preference shares (CCPS) scheme of Tata Steel.

Box 3.1 Tata Steel Issues CCPS of INR 54810 Million

The committee of directors of Tata Steel, at a meeting held on October 5, 2007, approved the following:

(a) The company would issue cumulative convertible preference shares (CCPS) of INR 54810 million to its existing equity shareholders on a rights basis in the ratio of 9:10.

(b) Six CCPS of a face value of INR 100 would be compulsorily and automatically converted into one equity share fully paid up of INR 10 each at a premium of INR 590.

(c) The CCPS would be compulsorily and automatically converted into equity shares fully paid up on September 1, 2009 without any application or any further act on the part of the CCPS holders.

(d) There shall be no redemption of the CCPS.

On conversion of the CCPS into equity shares, the equity share capital of the company would stand increased to 822.10 million shares of INR 10 each.

Source: Based on "Tata Steel Issues CCPS of Rs. 5,481 Crore," Newswing, accessed at http://newswing.com/?p=1098, September 2010.

3.4 Fixed-income Securities

Organizations are flooding the market with issues of fixed-income paper of various types. Competition in the financial markets and the need to reduce the cost of capital have forced them to develop innovative financial products within the given legal framework. Let us look briefly at various conventional and new financial instruments that have been in vogue.

3.4.1 Debentures

*A **debenture** is a debt security issued by a company acknowledging its obligation to repay the principal with interest at the specified rate as per the indenture.*

A **debenture** is a debt security issued by a company acknowledging its obligation to repay the sum as well as the interest at the specified rate of interest as per the indenture. The indenture is a contract between the issuer and the debenture holders and contains the rights of the debenture holder's and the issuer's legal requirements.

Debentures are usually unsecured and as such they do not have any lien against specific property of the issuer as security for the obligation. In other words, debenture holders are general creditors whose claims are protected by the property of the issuer not otherwise pledged. In the case of subordinated debentures, the debenture holders will have claims on assets of the company only after a senior debt has been paid off in the event of bankruptcy of the company. The debentures may be subordinated either to a particular kind of loan or to all other debt.

Debenture holders have the right to receive interest at the rate specified in the debenture certificate before any dividend is paid to the shareholders. Even if the company makes a loss, it has to pay interest on the debentures. If a company fails in its business, the debenture holders will be preferential creditors and they will be entitled to the repayment of their principal plus interest, if any, before the shareholders are paid anything.

As per Section 117 B of the Companies Act 1956, any company making a public or rights issue of debentures should appoint one or more debenture trustees before issuing the prospectus or the letter of offer and obtain their consent which shall be mentioned in the offer document. The debenture trustees shall not:

(a) Beneficially hold shares in a company;
(b) Be beneficially entitled to monies which are to be paid by the company to the debenture trustees; and
(c) Enter into any guarantee in respect of principal debt secured by the debentures or interest thereon.

A debenture trustee can be a scheduled bank, an insurance company, a body corporate or a public financial institution. The functions of debenture trustees include the following:

(i) To protect the interests of the debenture holders by addressing their grievances;
(ii) To ensure that the assets of the company issuing debentures are sufficient to discharge the principal amount; and
(iii) To ensure that the company does not commit any breach of the provisions of the trust deed.

Thus, a debenture trustee ensures that all the indenture provisions are met, including the timely payment of interest and principal.

In order to prevent default in redemption of debentures, Section 117C of the Companies Act, 1956, prescribes that "where a company issues debentures, it shall create a debenture redemption reserve for the redemption of such debentures, to which adequate amounts shall be credited out of its profits every year until such debentures are redeemed". It is clarified further that:

(a) For non-banking financial companies (NBFCs) registered with the RBI under Section 45-1A of the RBI (Amendment) Act, 1997, the adequacy of the debenture redemption reserve will be 50 per cent of the value of debentures issued through public issue and no debenture redemption reserve is required in the case of privately placed debentures.

(b) For manufacturing and infrastructure companies, the adequacy of debenture redemption reserve will be 50 per cent of the value of debentures issued through public issue and 25 per cent for privately placed debentures.

(c) No debenture redemption reserve is required for debentures issued by all-India financial institutions and banks regulated by the RBI for both public issues as well as privately placed debentures.

The plain vanilla debentures are intrinsically long-term in nature and are not attractive when interest rates are on the rise. Obviously, no investor wants to park his funds for a long time at pre-determined coupon rates when he can expect to get a better return in future. But in recent years, particularly during the economic downturn, debentures have become more attractive. Many companies have issued debentures, particularly non-convertible debentures (NCDs), to raise long-term funds. Companies have found that NCDs are a cheaper source of funds compared to bank credit. While the benchmark prime lending rate (PLR) hovered around 12.5 per cent, the actual cost of corporate borrowings was as high as 1.5–2.5 per cent above PLR. But companies could raise long-term debt at marginally cheaper rates (10–11 per cent including distribution cost) through NCDs. At these rates, NCDs are also attractive to investors because they are able to get higher rates of return compared to bank deposits. Moreover, NCD issuance is an easy way of raising funds from the capital market. NCDs are unsecuritized lending and not directly linked to the company balance sheet.

Short-term debentures with tenure of less than 18 months with high coupon rates and often with additional upfront incentives are also popular. The debentures that are rated and over 18 months may provide investors with a put option after a certain period, say one year. This means the investor can withdraw his funds after the expiry of the one-year period.

3.4.2 Convertible Debentures

> ***Convertible debentures*** *are unsecured debt instruments that can be converted into equity shares of the issuing company at the option of their holder(s).*

If an option is given to debenture holders to convert their debentures into equity shares at a specified rate of exchange after a specified period, such debentures are called **convertible debentures**. Convertible debentures are unsecured debt instruments that can be converted into equity shares of the issuing company at the option of their holder(s). The right to convert the debt security into equity shares is granted by the issuing company to the investor. SEBI restricts the conversion period to 36 months and credit rating is mandatory if the conversion is made after 18 months. Conversion beyond 36 months is permissible only if the conversion is made optional with the put and call option.

For a long time, debentures have been used as a source of long-term finance by many companies in India. But it was only in the early 1980s that some companies in India (TELCO for example) made pioneering use of the new financial instrument called convertible debentures. For some time thereafter, there was a lull in the convertible debenture market as many companies did not evince any interest in the instrument. The main reason was that the equity market was not doing well as the market prices of many companies' shares were not very much above the par value. Unless the price at which debentures are to be converted into equity shares is sufficiently lower than the market price, the debenture holder does not benefit. Therefore, only a few companies whose shares commanded a decent premium in the stock market could think of issuing convertible debentures. But there was a boom in the Indian stock market in 1985, with the market prices of shares of many companies rising significantly. That gave a fillip to the use of convertible debentures as a method of long-term finance by a number of companies.

There are many advantages of convertible debentures. The investor gets the opportunity to convert his investment partly or fully into shares at a price much lower than the market price. This gives him a chance to sell the shares at a profit soon after conversion, even if there is a slight drop in the market price. The gain made in this way often works out to be a higher percentage of return on investment. The non-convertible portions of partly convertible debentures also offer an attractive long-term investment avenue for the investor. Many have found this to be a very stable source of current income. The main advantage for the company issuing convertible debentures is that the debentures get converted into shares at a substantial premium in most cases. When a company converts debentures into shares at a hefty premium, its obligation to service the share capital will be much less compared to the cost of servicing the share capital if the entire amount had been raised through an equity issue at par.

3.4.3 Call Money-linked NCDs

__Call money-linked NCDs__ are non-convertible debentures on which interest is calculated as per the call money rates.

The call money market is an integral part of the money market. In the call money market, funds are borrowed and lent on an overnight basis, but generally the funds are transacted for a period not exceeding 14 days. Banks and financial institutions including mutual funds and insurance companies are major participants in the call money market. It is a market for matching short-term surplus funds with short-term requirement of funds. Financial institutions, particularly commercial banks, borrow in the call money market to meet statutory requirements such as the cash reserve ratio (CRR) and Statutory Liquidity Ratio (SLR). The interest rates are determined by the demand and supply of funds at that moment of time.

GE Capital Services India (GE Caps) launched the country's first call money-linked floating rate NCDs in May 1998. The INR 500 million issue was priced at a spread of 400 basis points over the Reuters Mumbai Inter-bank Overnight Average Rate (MIBOR). The debentures would have a tenor of three years with a put and call option at the end of one and two years, respectively. Interest would be calculated by compounding the rate of MIBOR plus 4 per cent on a daily basis. The interest would be paid monthly on the tenth day of the succeeding month. On May 4, 1998, MIBOR stood at 5.97 per cent. With MIBOR averaging around 6 per cent, the return on this paper worked out to 10 per cent.

MIBOR is the weighted average of call money rates of 17 institutions including banks, primary dealers and financial institutions. The weights are assigned to four groups of players—nationalized banks, foreign banks, private banks and financial institutions. Within the groups, each player is weighted, based on balance sheet size. Thus, MIBOR is a fairly accurate indicator of overnight money rates and a good benchmark for pricing financial instruments. The spread over MIBOR reflects all the risks associated with the tenor, issuer and market.

Subsequently, Reliance Industries Limited (RIL), Infrastructure Leasing and Financial Services (IL&FS) and Larsen & Toubro (L&T) issued call-linked bonds with private placements offering 225 basis points above MIBOR. These bonds, however, came with a cap and a floor. That is, the bond offered floating interest rates within a band of 15.5 per cent and 9.5 per cent. Thus, if call rates fall below 7 per cent, the investors are protected as the bond would continue to yield 9.5 per cent. On the other hand, if call rates rise to over 13 per cent, the borrowers are protected as they would not have to shell out more than 15.5 per cent.

3.4.4 Bonds

A __bond__ is a promissory note that is issued by a borrower for the repayment of the principal amount with interest to the lender.

Bonds are long-term debt securities packaged in a convenient form for sale to individuals and institutions. It is a promissory note issued by a borrower for the repayment of the principal amount with interest to the lender. Specifically, the issuer of the bond agrees to pay a fixed amount of interest periodically and repays the principal amount at the date of maturity or at the stated date. A typical bond carries coupons which the lender (investor) clips off and mails to the issuer of the bond to claim interest payment. It is the usual practice to pay interest semi-annually, although some bond issues promise to pay interest in intervals as short as a month or as long as a year. A bond may have a single maturity date or a series of maturity dates. The principal amount involved in a bond is called par value, which may be different from the market value of the bond. The market value of the bond changes depending on market conditions, particularly the prevailing market rate of interest. If the market interest rate changes to a rate that is higher than the coupon rate of the bond, the bond sells at a discount to par value. If the market rate of interest is below the coupon rate, the bond sells at a premium. However, when the bond matures, the issuer of the bond repays the par or face value of the bond to the bond holder. Thus, a bond may be sold at a discount or at a premium, or at par, but the repayment will be the bond's par value or face value.

There are different classifications of bonds. According to one classification, bonds may be government bonds or corporate bonds. *Government bonds* are those issued by the Union government, state government or local bodies like municipalities. Government bonds are viewed as one of the safest of all investments. Therefore, the interest rates on investment in government bonds are generally lower than those of bonds issued by other bodies. Some government bonds offer tax-free interest. For example, the Government of India issued 10 per cent tax-free relief bonds in 1995. These bonds had a maturity period of 5 years. The minimum investment was INR 1,000 and in multiples thereof. There was no upper limit on investment. Interest was payable half-yearly by post-dated interest warrants. Interest earned on the bonds was totally free from income tax. There was wealth tax exemption without any limit and gift tax exemption up to an overall limit of INR 0.5 million in value in the aggregate for various issues of relief.

Corporate bonds are debt securities issued by companies. They are considered to be riskier than government bonds. Corporate bonds may be long-term bonds or medium-term bonds. *Medium-term bonds* have maturities ranging from 1 to 10 years and are known as notes. *Long-term bonds* may have different maturities of even up to 50 years. For example, RIL issued Yankee bonds with a maturity period of 50 years.

Another way to classify bonds is to categorize them as international bonds and foreign bonds. *International bonds* are issued within a market that is foreign to the issuer's home market. They may be issued in a currency other than that of the country in which the bonds are issued (for example, Eurobonds). *Foreign bonds* are denominated in the currency of the country in which a foreign company issues the bonds. For example, Samurai Bonds are bonds denominated in Japanese Yen and issued in Japan by an American company. An Indian example is the five-year Resurgent India Bonds issued by the State Bank of India in August 1998. These bonds were aimed at non-resident Indians (NRIs), Overseas Corporate Bodies (OCBs) and banks acting in a fiduciary capacity on behalf of NRIs and OCBs. The banks and institutional investors cannot buy these bonds on their own. The amount would be raised in three currencies with interest rates being 7.75 per cent on US dollars (USD), 8 per cent on British pounds (GBP) and 6.75 per on deutsche marks (DEM). The interest payments would be half-yearly or on a cumulative basis. The interest and the principal would be fully repatriable for non-resident holders. The minimum subscription was USD 2,000, GBP 1,000 and DEM 3,000. The interest and principal amount are exempted from income tax, wealth tax and gift tax in India. The bonds can be gifted to Indian residents. They were easily transferable between NRIs/OCBs. There was a facility of premature encashment without penalty after six months in non-repatriable Indian rupees.

Bonds may also be classified as callable bonds and puttable bonds. *Callable bonds* give the bond issuer a right, but not the obligation, to redeem the bonds at a predetermined price before maturity. On the other hand, *puttable bonds* give the investor the right, but not the obligation, to sell the bonds back to the issuer at a predetermined price and date. The call and put features of the bond give protection to the issuers as well as the investors from interest rate risk. That is, the call feature of the bond gives protection to the issuer from decreasing interest rates in the economy and the put feature of the bond protects the investor from increasing interest rates. But the protection comes at a cost. As the call feature of the bond favours the issuer, the interest rate on the callable bond is higher. So the cost of the option is the higher interest rate.

The put feature of the bond favours the investor and, therefore, the interest rate on the put bond is lower. The interest lost is the cost of the option. Thus, the option comes at the expense of one of the parties—the issuer or the investor. In other words, only one of the parties profits from the bonds with the option feature.

Issuing different kinds of bonds in different brand names to meet different requirements of investors is not new to the Indian capital market. The following example illustrates this point.

The Industrial Credit and Investment Corporation of India Limited (ICICI) came out with four kinds of bonds in April 1996. They were Ashirwad (deep discount bonds), Akshay (monthly income bond), Shubh Laabh (money-back plus bond) and Suvidha (regular return bond). As per the terms of the Ashirwad deep discount bond, an investment of INR 5,200 becomes INR 0.2 million in 25 years. In the Akshay monthly income bond, an investment of INR 8,000 gets a steady income of INR 100 to INR 965 per month and INR 8,000 to INR 77,000 at the end of 20 years depending on the choice-of-wait period. In the Shubh Laabh money-back plus bond, an investment of INR 6,000 comes back to the investor after three years. In addition, the investor would get INR 10,000 after 10 years. In the Suvidha regular return bond, an investment of INR 5,000 earns 16 per cent per annum half-yearly for a maximum of 5 years.

3.4.5 Zero-coupon Bonds or Deep Discount Bonds

*A **zero-coupon bond** is a fixed-income security that pays interest at maturity instead of periodically during the life of the bond.*

A **zero-coupon bond** is a fixed-income security, the interest on which is paid at maturity instead of periodically during the life of the bond. Zero-coupon bonds are also known as *deep discount bonds*. Generally, they are issued at a discount to par or face value and over time the interest compounds, which results in par value at maturity. The difference between the issue price and the face value is the amount of discount that the investor gets by way of return. The investor profits from the bond going up in value. The zero-coupon bonds/deep discount bonds are perceived to be riskier than similar bonds and thus priced accordingly. As these are long-term bonds, they may be issued with call provisions. If a bond issue is given public security status, the government and private trusts can also invest in the issue. Some examples of deep-discount bonds/zero-coupon bonds are stated as follows.

1. ICICI issued deep discount bonds in the name of Ashirwad in April 1996. An investment of INR 5,200 becomes INR 200,000 in 25 years. Alternatively, at the option of the investor, he can receive INR 40,000 each year at the end of 23, 24, 25, 26, and 27 years. There was an early redemption option at the end of 5, 10, 15 and 20 years, both for the investor and the issuer.
2. TATA Steel issued deep discount bonds in September 1996. An investor, by investing INR 5,100 (for a set of three bonds), can receive INR 25,000 in three instalments of INR 7,500, INR 7,500 and INR 10,000 at the end of 9, 10 and 11 years, respectively. The investor as well as the company may exercise the option of early redemption at INR 11,250 at the end of 5 years.
3. Larsen and Toubro Limited issued deep discount bonds in September 1996. An investor who invests INR 6,100 can receive INR 30,000 in three instalments of INR 9,000, INR 10,000 and INR 11,000 at the end of 9, 10 and 11 years, respectively. Early redemption options are available for both parties at the end of five and seven years. It is also stated that the difference between the issue price and the face value/deemed face value paid by the company on redemption/early redemption would be in the nature of interest.
4. A zero-coupon bond is a relatively new financial instrument in the Indian capital market. Mahindra & Mahindra (M&M) was the first company in India to come out with an issue of zero-coupon bonds in the early 1990s. The company offered investors a choice between two types of debentures: (a) 12.5 per cent debentures of INR 110, each fully convertible into two shares of INR 10 each at a premium of INR 45 per share after the expiry of 18 months, and (b) zero-coupon bonds of INR 90, each fully convertible into two shares of INR 10 each at a premium of INR 35 per share after the expiry of 18 months. Thus, the investor in zero-coupon bonds was offered conversion into equity shares at a reduced premium such that the difference in premium is roughly equivalent to the interest he would have otherwise earned during this 18-month period. However, the major attraction for the investor lies in the tax concessions available for capital gains. If an individual investor sells the shares after the expiry of 12 months from the date of conversion, the profit on the sale becomes a long-term capital gain, which would be concessionally treated for tax purposes.

The advantages of zero-coupon or deep discount bonds are as follows:

- The investor may get more tax advantages on receiving a capital gain rather than interest income.
- There may not be a reinvestment risk for the investor. Reinvestment risk refers to the probability that the interest rates in the economy would fall in the future.
- The investment in a zero-coupon bond is a leveraged investment since the bonds being purchased at a discount result in a relatively small upfront payment, which gives the investor an opportunity to access a larger amount.

Thus, zero-coupon bonds/deep discount bonds are highly suitable for those who plan for retirement or for children's education and settlement.

Tax-free bonds *are a debt security whose interest income is totally exempted from income tax; in certain cases the amount invested in these bonds may also be exempted from wealth tax.*

3.4.6 Tax-free Bonds

Tax-free bonds are issued by some organizations, particularly public sector organizations. The interest income from tax-free bonds is totally exempted from income tax, and in certain cases the amount invested in these bonds may also be exempted from wealth tax. Such bonds are very attractive to investors, particularly those who are in high tax brackets, because the pre-tax effective yield to maturity would be very high with tax exemption. Some examples of tax-free bonds are as follows:

1. Konkan Railways issued 10.5 per cent tax-free bonds in December 1996. The issue was rated "AAA (so)" by Credit Rating Information Services of India Ltd (CRISIL). The interest on the bonds was exempted from income tax without any limit and the investment in the bonds was exempted from wealth tax. A rebate of income tax under Section 88 for investment up to INR 70,000 to individual investors was available if they had not transferred/sold the bonds for three years. There was an upfront discount of 5 per cent. The pre-tax effective yield to maturity with Section 88 benefits for individuals was 23.91 per cent for people in the 40 per cent tax bracket, 20.79 per cent for people in the 30 per cent tax bracket and 17.52 per cent for people in the 15 per cent tax bracket.
2. The Indian Railway Finance Corporation Limited issued 2.5 million secured redeemable non-convertible tax-free bonds in March 1996. The bonds were in denominations of INR 1,000 and were offered at a discount of 5 per cent. They would be redeemed at par after seven years. The issue was rated "AAA (so)" by CRISIL and "LAAA (so)" by ICRA Limited (formerly known as Investment Information and Credit Rating Agency of India Ltd). The interest on these bonds was exempted from income tax without any limit and the investment in the bonds was also totally exempted from wealth tax. The issue had a buyback option after two years from the date of allotment from individual bondholders up to a face value of INR 40,000, provided the bonds had been held for a continuous period of one year. However, the buyback was limited to INR 20 million per year on a first-come-first-served basis.
3. The Industrial Bank of India Limited (IDBI) made a public issue of IDBI Flexibonds-23 for tapping the retail bond market. The issue was opened for subscription on March 21, 2005. The issue had a target amount of INR 4,000 million with a greenshoe option to retain an additional amount of INR 4,116.40 million. The issue was rated "AA+ (stable)" by CRISIL, "AA+ (Ind.) (outlook on rating is stable)" by Fitch Ratings and "LAA+" by ICRA. The issue offered one instrument—IDBI Infrastructure (Tax Saving) Bond—with two options, an annual interest option and a cumulative option. Under the annual interest option, the investor can choose to receive interest at 5.80 per cent per annum, payable annually for five years, while under the cumulative option, an initial investment of INR 5,000 becomes INR 6,630 after five years. The minimum investment in the bonds is one bond of INR 5,000. Investment in these bonds would be eligible for tax benefits under Section 88 of the Income-tax Act, 1961, up to an investment amount of INR 0.1 million, subject to the bonds being held for a minimum period of three years from the date of allotment.

3.4.7 Fifty-year Yankee Bonds

Reliance India Limited issued 50-year Yankee bonds, the longest ever maturity offering by any sovereign or corporate body with a "Baa3" rating from Moody's, in 1996. The bonds also had a Standard and Poor rating of BB+. Thus, it was placed on par with the country's sovereign rating. This was the first Asian offer with this maturity. Merrill Lynch was the sole lead manager of the USD 100 million Yankee bonds issue. The Yankee bonds are due for redemption on August 6, 2046, and have put and call options after 30 years on August 6, 2026. The coupon rate was fixed at 10.50 per cent. It was expected that the inflation rate all over the industrialized world would come down to the range of 0–2 per cent and, therefore, the real interest rate on these bonds would work out to over 8 per cent. With such an expectation, the issue was fully subscribed solely through screen deals and phone calls without spending any money on road shows. That also reflects the increasing interest of foreign investors in Indian securities.

3.4.8 Junk Bonds

Junk bonds are high yield bonds with speculative grade or below-investment grade. This means that the probability of default with junk bonds is higher than with other bonds. Junk bonds have become popular all over the world, more so in the United States. They are not really worthless pieces of paper as the name suggests. In fact, junk bonds are very high-yield bonds with high risk. They are issued by companies whose credit rating is below the safest investment grade. In other words, the risk associated with junk bonds is very high but so are the yields. Historically, average yields on junk bonds have been between four and six percentage points above those on comparable US treasuries. Junk bonds are high-interest bonds whose value remains high even with low interest rates in the economy. But when the general interest rates rise, the value of these bonds is bound to fall and their comparative advantage is lessened. Thus, investing in junk bonds requires a high degree of analytical skill and knowledge of specialized credit. Junk bonds are mainly used to finance leveraged buyouts, mergers and takeovers.

> ***Junk bonds** are high-yield bonds with a speculative grade or below-investment grade.*

One example is the Drexel Burnham Lambert Investment Bank, which was the Wall Street firm that pioneered the concept of selling high-risk, high-yielding bonds to US investors. Michael Milken, the head of the firm's bond trading operations, was the brain behind the junk bonds. In the late 1980s, US investors were very interested in junk bonds and Drexel cashed in on the situation and earned a record pre-tax profit of USD 1.1 billion in 1986 while Milken became the most talked about multi-millionaire. Of course, Drexel and Milken met their downfall very soon. Drexel was fined USD 650 million in 1989 for various securities law violations and forced into bankruptcy in 1990. Milken was indicted in 1990 on charges of fraud. Another popular name associated with junk bonds is Ivan Boesky.

Originally, junk bonds were the bonds issued by organizations that were at one time investment grade (bonds considered to have an acceptable risk of default are investment grade). Subsequently, due to one reason or another, these companies became fallen angels. Since many companies met this fate, shrewd investors searched through the heap of so-called junk for low-priced bonds of companies with the potential of being restored to investment grade. When they found them, they earned substantial profits on these bonds by buying them cheap and disposing them when their price appreciated.

Although junk bonds originated in the United States in the 1970s, they became popular in many countries by the 1980s. Junk bonds have been instrumental in mobilizing a large pool of loan capital for many enterprises, particularly for innovative enterprises in the United States. Over the years, even established companies have issued junk bonds. The biggest investors in the junk bonds market are mutual funds and insurance companies, followed by provident funds and savings and loan associations. It is observed that the risk-adjusted returns for portfolios of junk bonds are quite high. This means that the credit risk of these bonds is more than compensated for by their higher yields.

Junk bonds provide an instrument through which investors can get a high return with full knowledge of the risks involved. The borrowers can also get the loan capital they require on terms they can afford. In recent years, the default rate on junk bonds is also reduced by their shorter life span with the issuers redeeming the junk bonds earlier than higher grade debt due to their higher cost. It may be noted that if the companies had to rely only on the highly rated securities and borrowings, many enterprises with potentially good prospects would have never taken off. However, there are some who are sceptical about the future of junk bonds. They feel that the future of junk bonds is very bleak since the default rate is very high due to the nature of such bonds. Such apprehensions can be erased if appropriate regulations are framed and implemented for the protection of investors. This will help in sustaining the momentum of junk bonds. Junk bond investment can rely on credit analysis, which involves analysis of the issuer's fundamentals.

3.4.9 Secured Premium Notes (SPNs)

Secured premium notes are a variant of zero-coupon bonds. TISCO was the first company in India to issue SPN in July 1992. The details of the TISCO issue are as follows: The face value of SPN was INR 300. It involved a cash down payment of INR 150 and the remaining INR 150 on the first call, which was to be made after six months of allotment. Each SPN was accompanied by a warrant for subscribing to one ordinary share of TISCO between one and one-and-a-half years from the date of allotment. This required full payment of

INR 80 per share at the time of exercising the right under the warrant. No interest or repayment of principal would be due or accrue on the SPN during the first three years. Thereafter, the investor would receive four equal annual installments of INR 300 each (INR 150 towards the principal plus INR 150 towards interest) from the end of the fourth year onwards till the end of the seventh year. The SPN floated by TISCO has been assigned the "AAA" rating by CRISIL, which indicates the highest degree of safety regarding the timely payment of interest and the principal.

3.4.10 Treasury Bills

Treasury bills are short-term financial instruments issued by the government to enable people to invest their surplus funds while avoiding default risk.

Treasury bills, popularly known as T-bills, are short-term financial instruments issued by the government to enable people to invest their surplus funds while avoiding default risk. They are also the instruments by which governments can borrow for their short-term expenditure needs. Any entity, including individuals, firms, corporate bodies, trusts, research institutions, mutual funds, foreign institutional investors (FIIs) and provident funds, can bid for and purchase T-bills. In India, they are sold by the RBI through fortnightly or monthly auctions (by calling bids from investors) at varying discount rates depending on the bids. They are issued at a discount to the face value. But they are repaid at par on the expiry of their tenure at the office of the RBI. The rate of discount and the corresponding issue price are determined at each auction. Thus, the return on investment in T-bills is the difference between the maturity value and the issue price.

Although there are different kinds of T-bills such as ad-hoc T-bills, 91-day T-bills, 182-day T-bills and 364-day T-bills, the most popular T-bills are the 91-day T-bills and 364-day T-bills. They are issued in the form of a promissory note or by credit to the subsidiary general ledger (SGL) account or gilt account in a dematerialized form. T-bills are available for a minimum amount of face value of INR 25,000 and in multiples thereafter. T-bills also have a secondary market. Besides, the Discount and Finance House of India (DFHI) is the market maker, which provides two-way quotes daily. Thus, T-bills are highly liquid financial instruments.

The major advantages of T-bills are that they are approved assets for SLR purpose. Because they are sovereign paper, there is no default risk. There is no uncertainty of return as the return is locked in at the time of investment itself. There is transparency in buying and selling of T-bills, and the process involved in buying and selling is simplified. T-bills are considered the most liquid money market instrument. Further, there is no tax deduction at source. Due to these reasons, T-bills provide better returns, especially in the short-term, though the returns are determined by market forces. Since banks do not pay any interest on deposits of less than 15 days, or balances maintained in current accounts, T-bills are the best investment avenue for any number of days. In other words, T-bills help in deployment of idle funds for a very short period as well. Further, one can buy T-bills of different maturities to match the respective maturity of funds outflow. T-Bills are also avenues to invest surplus funds depending on staggered funds requirements.

3.4.11 Commercial Paper (CP)

*A **commercial paper** (CP) is a short-term debt security issued by companies to raise funds for their short-term requirements.*

A **commercial paper** (CP) is a short-term debt security issued by companies to raise funds to meet their working capital needs. Commercial paper originated in the United States in the early nineteenth century to enable industrial and commercial firms to raise short-term funds, particularly from outside the state. This was necessary because US banking laws generally restricted banks' activities to the state where they were established. The development of consumer finance companies in the 1920s and the high cost of bank credit resulting from the incidence of compulsory reserve requirements also contributed to the popularity of CP in the United States. CP entered other countries in the twentieth century and the CP market of the United States became the model for most emerging markets. Canada is the second most important CP market in the world.

Although the basic objective of a CP is to provide a flexible and viable alternative to bank credit, there are different rules and regulations regarding the issue of CP across countries. For example, in countries like Australia, Canada, the Netherlands and Norway, there are no restrictions as to who can and cannot issue a CP. But in other countries there are certain restrictions. In most countries, the average maturity period of a

CP is about 30 days. However, in Canada, the CP is generally issued for a term ranging from 30 days to 365 days, though terms as short as overnight are also available. The CP issued in Canada is generally secured by the pledge of assets. In many countries, there are no prospectus requirements. The rating of a CP is also compulsory in some countries. In France, the United Kingdom and Norway, the size of the minimum issue is fixed. In Spain, a CP is guaranteed by banks and, therefore, they are subject to reserve requirements. Thus, many variations exist among different markets across the world due to local market situations. Notwithstanding such variations, the CP has emerged as an important short-term financial instrument among the wave of innovations sweeping the world.

In India, the CP came as a solution to the problem of inflexibility underlying the old cash credit system. Following the recommendations of the Committee to Review the Working of the Monetary System (chaired by Sukhamoy Chakravarty) and the Working Group on the Money Market (chaired by N. Vaghul), the commercial paper as a money market instrument was introduced on January 1, 1990. The main aim of launching a CP in India was to enable or facilitate highly rated corporate borrowers to diversify their sources of short-term borrowings and provide an additional instrument to investors. Raising funds through CP is used when banks are reluctant to lend short-term funds. For example, in 2009, banks in India showed a reluctance to lend freely because of sluggish economic conditions. Therefore, companies like HPCL, ONGC, SAIL and Sundaram Finance turned to commercial papers to raise funds for their working capital needs. Of course, the CP issue turned out to be a cheaper option—an average discount on a CP ranged between 5–6 per cent while the benchmark prime lending rates of commercial banks ranged between 10–16 per cent.

The Reserve Bank of India issued detailed guidelines through the Non-Banking Companies (Acceptance of Deposits through Commercial Paper) Direction in 1989. According to these guidelines, only highly rated businesses with a tangible net worth of not less than INR 100 million are allowed to issue CPs with maturity between three to six months. It is also stipulated that a CP could be issued in multiples of INR 2.5 million and the amount to be invested by a single investor should not be less than INR 10 million. The aggregate amount to be raised by the issue of commercial paper is limited to 20 per cent of the company's working capital (fund based) limit. In other words, the issuance of the CP has to be carved out of the working capital (fund based) limit. The intention is that a commercial paper would help reduce the cost of borrowing but not result in any increase in overall resources. The CP should be in the form of usance promissory note, negotiable by endorsement and delivery, and issued at a discount to reflect the interest rate. The discount rate is to be freely determined by the issuer. The issuer should bear the expenses of the issue, including stamp duty, dealer's fee and the rating agency fee. The CP can be issued to any person or business including banks. A non-resident Indian can also invest, but on a non-repatriable basis, and such a CP will not be transferable. The issue of a CP cannot be underwritten or co-accepted in any manner. Further, a company issuing a CP is free to request its bankers to provide standby facility for an amount not exceeding that of the issue for meeting the liability of commercial paper on maturity. It is also stipulated that a company issuing a CP should ensure that the relevant provisions of the various statutes such as the Companies Act, Income Tax Act and Negotiable Instruments Act are followed.

Advantages of commercial paper

The main advantage of a commercial paper lies in its simplicity as there is hardly any documentation between the issuer of a CP and the investor. There is also flexibility with regard to the maturity of the CP; the CP provides the issuer company the flexibility in matching the amount and maturity of its debt to its working capital requirement. A company can also diversify its sources of funds by issuing a CP.

A company can raise short-term funds by issuing a CP at a cheaper rate than a loan from the bank. In other words, the cost of funds raised through a CP is less than that of other sources of funds. At the same time, the investors can get higher return on investment in a CP compared to what is obtainable from banks on time deposits. Another major advantage of a CP is its liquidity. The investors can have high liquidity for their investment in a CP as there is a continuous market for it.

Companies can easily raise funds by issuing a CP in the inter-corporate market. Between public deposits (PDs) and a CP, the cost of administration of public deposits is higher. Finally, the CP market brings the short-term borrower (deficit units) into direct contact with investors (surplus units), thereby disintermediating the role of banks. Thus, the launching of CP in the Indian money market was a step in the right direction towards a mature money market catering to the varied needs of companies and investors.

Guidelines for Issue of Commercial Paper (July 2006)

The CP, as a privately placed instrument, was introduced in India in 1990 to enable highly rated corporate borrowers to diversify their sources of short-term borrowings and provide an additional instrument to investors. Subsequently, primary dealers, satellite dealers (the system of satellite dealers has been discontinued with effect from June 1, 2002) and all-India financial institutions were also permitted to issue CP to enable them to meet short-term funding requirements for their operations. The Reserve Bank of India reviews the CP guidelines from time to time and issues Master Circulars. The latest Master Circular was issued by the Reserve Bank of India on July 1, 2009, incorporating all the existing guidelines/instructions/directives on the subject. The salient features of these guidelines are presented here.

- **Eligibility to issue:** Companies, primary dealers and all-India financial institutions (FIs) can issue CP to raise short-term resources under the umbrella limit fixed by the RBI. Companies are eligible to issue CP provided: (a) the tangible net worth of the company, as per the latest audited balance sheet, is not less than INR 40 million; (b) the company has been sanctioned working capital limit by banks or FIs; and (c) the borrowal account of the company is classified as a standard asset by the financing bank(s)/FIs.
- **Rating requirement:** All eligible participants shall obtain the credit rating for issuance of commercial paper from either CRISIL or ICRA or Credit Analysis and Research Ltd (CARE) or Fitch Ratings India Pvt. Ltd, or such other credit rating agencies as may be specified by the Reserve Bank of India from time to time, for the purpose. The minimum credit rating shall be P-2 of CRISIL or an equivalent rating by other agencies. The issuers shall ensure at the time of issuance of the CP that the rating so obtained is current and is not due for review.
- **Maturity:** The CP can be issued for maturities between a minimum of seven days and a maximum of one year from the date of issue. The maturity date of the CP should not go beyond the date up to which the credit rating of the issuer is valid.
- **Denominations:** The CP can be issued in denominations of INR 0.5 million or multiples of it. The amount invested by a single investor should not be less than INR 0.5 million (face value).
- **Limits and the amount of issue of CP:** The CP can be issued as a "stand alone" product. The aggregate amount of CP from an issuer shall be within the limit as approved by its board of directors or the quantum indicated by the credit rating agency for the specified rating, whichever is lower. Banks and FIs will, however, have the flexibility to fix working capital limits duly taking into account the resource pattern of company financing including CP.

  A financial institution can issue a CP within the overall umbrella limit fixed by the RBI, that is, issue of CP together with other instruments—term money borrowings, term deposits, certificates of deposit (CDs) and inter-corporate deposits should not exceed 100 per cent of its net owned funds, as per the latest audited balance sheet.

  The total amount of the CP proposed to be issued should be raised within a period of two weeks from the date on which the issuer opens the issue for subscription. The CP may be issued on a single date or in parts on different dates provided that in the latter case, each CP shall have the same maturity date. Every issue of CP, including renewal, should be treated as a fresh issue.
- **Issuing and paying agent (IPA):** Only a scheduled bank can act as an IPA for issuance of CP.
- **Investment in CP:** The CP may be issued to and held by individuals, banking companies, other corporate bodies, NRIs and FIIs. However, investment by FIIs would be within the limits set for their investments by SEBI.
- **Mode of issuance:** The CP can be issued either in the form of a promissory note (Schedule I) or in a dematerialized form through any of the depositories approved by and registered with SEBI.

  The CP will be issued at a discount to face value as may be determined by the issuer. No issuer shall have the issue of a CP underwritten or co-accepted. While the option is available to both issuers and subscribers to issue/hold CP in dematerialized or physical form, issuers and subscribers are encouraged to prefer exclusive reliance on the dematerialized form of issue/holding. However, with effect from June 30, 2001, banks, FIs and PDs are required to make fresh investments and hold a CP only in dematerialized form.

- **Payment of CP:** The initial investor in a CP shall pay the discounted value of the CP by means of a crossed account payee cheque to the account of the issuer through an IPA. On maturity of the CP, when it is held in physical form, the holder of the CP shall present the instrument for payment to the issuer through the IPA. However, when the CP is held in demat form, the holder will have to get it redeemed through the depository and receive payment from the IPA.
- **Stand-by facility:** In view of a CP being a "stand alone" product, it would not be obligatory in any manner on the part of the banks and FIs to provide stand-by facility to the issuers of a CP. The banks and FIs have, however, the flexibility to provide for a CP issue, credit enhancement by way of stand-by assistance/credit, back-stop facility and so on, based on their commercial judgement, subject to prudential norms as applicable and with specific approval of their boards.

  Non-bank entities including corporate organizations may also provide unconditional and irrevocable guarantee for credit enhancement for a CP issue provided:

  (i) The issuer fulfils the eligibility criteria prescribed for issuance of the CP;

  (ii) The guarantor has a credit rating at least one notch higher than the issuer given by an approved credit rating agency; and

  (iii) The offer document for the CP properly discloses the net worth of the guarantor company, the names of the companies to which the guarantor has issued similar guarantees, the extent of the guarantees offered by the guarantor company and the conditions under which the guarantee will be invoked.
- **Procedure for issuance:** Every issuer must appoint an IPA for issuance of a CP. The issuer should disclose to the potential investors its financial position as per the standard market practice. After the exchange of deal confirmation between the investor and the issuer, the issuing company shall issue physical certificates to the investor or arrange for crediting the CP to the investor's account with a depository. Investors shall be given a copy of the IPA certificate to the effect that the issuer has a valid agreement with the IPA and documents are in order.

Roles and responsibilities

The roles and responsibilities of the issuer, IPA and credit rating agency (CRA) are as follows:

(a) Issuer

With the simplification of procedures for CP issuance, issuers will now have more flexibility. The issuers would, however, have to ensure that the guidelines and procedures laid down for the CP issuance are strictly adhered to.

(b) Issuing and Paying Agent (IPA)

(i) The IPA will ensure that the issuer has the minimum credit rating as stipulated by the RBI and the amount mobilized through the issuance of a CP is within the quantum indicated by the CRA for the specified rating or as approved by its board of directors, whichever is lower.

(ii) The IPA has to verify all the documents submitted by the issuer, viz., copy of the board resolution, signatures of authorized executants (when the CP is in physical form), and issue a certificate that documents are in order. It should also certify that it has a valid agreement with the issuer.

(iii) Certified copies of original documents verified by the IPA should be held in the custody of the IPA.

(iv) Every CP issue should be reported to the Reserve Bank of India.

(v) IPAs, which are NDS members, should report the details of the CP issue on the NDS platform within two days of the date of completion of the issue.

(vi) Further, all scheduled banks acting as an IPA will continue to report CP issuance details as hitherto within three days of the date of completion of the issue, incorporating details till the NDS reporting stabilizes to the satisfaction of the RBI.

(c) Credit Rating Agency (CRA)

(i) The code of conduct prescribed by SEBI for CRAs for undertaking rating of capital market instruments shall be applicable to the CRAs for rating a CP.

(ii) Further, the credit rating agency would henceforth have the discretion to determine the validity period of the rating depending on its perception of the strength of the issuer. Accordingly, the CRA shall, at the time of rating, clearly indicate the date when the rating is due for review.

(iii) While the CRAs can decide the validity period of credit rating, they would have to closely monitor the rating assigned to issuers vis-à-vis their track record at regular intervals and be required to make their revision in the ratings public through their publications and website.

Documentation procedure

The Fixed Income Money Market and Derivatives Association of India (FIMMDA) may prescribe, in consultation with the RBI, for operational flexibility and smooth functioning of the CP market, any standardized procedure and documentation to be followed by the participants in consonance with international best practices. Issuers/IPAs may refer to the detailed guidelines issued by the FIMMDA in this regard on July 5, 2001. Violation of these guidelines will attract penalties and may include debarring of the entity from the CP market.

Defaults in the CP market

In order to monitor defaults in the redemption of a CP, scheduled banks that act as IPAs are advised to immediately report, on occurrence, the full particulars of defaults in repayment of CPs to the RBI.

Non-applicability of certain other directions

Nothing contained in the Non-Banking Financial Companies Acceptance of Public Deposits (Reserve Bank) Directions, 1998, shall apply to any NBFC insofar as it relates to acceptance of deposit by issuance of a CP, in accordance with the guidelines.

It may be mentioned that the CP has become a very popular short-term financial instruments. It has successfully replaced bank credit for working capital requirements of corporate organizations, particularly top companies. Banks and financial institutions are picking up the commercial paper to invest their liquid funds. Mutual funds also find it lucrative to park their funds in short-term instruments like commercial paper. The P1 rated companies are able to raise funds at 4 to 5 per cent.

3.4.12 Certificate of Deposit (CD)

> ***Certificate of deposit*** *is a negotiable money market instrument issued by financial institutions and commercial banks acknowledging the receipt of deposits.*

Certificate of deposit (CD) is a negotiable money market instrument issued in dematerialized form or in material form as a usance promissory note in exchange for funds deposited at a bank or other eligible financial institutions for a specified time period. Investors are paid a set rate of interest. In other words, CDs are fixed income-bearing securities which offer a guaranteed interest paid at regular intervals or at redemption. They generally offer a higher interest rate than normal bank savings accounts including time deposits. The maturity of CDs ranges from a few weeks to several years.

CDs were introduced in India in 1989 to further widen the range of money market instruments and give investors greater flexibility in deployment of their short-term surplus funds. Initially, CDs issued by a bank and outstanding at any point of time could not exceed 1 per cent of fortnightly average aggregate deposits during the previous year. Subsequently the limit has been raised. As such, CDs are quite similar to time deposits mobilized by banks in which individuals, corporations, companies, trusts, funds and so on can invest. The banks have the freedom to issue CDs at a discount on face value. Initial guidelines prescribed that CDs could be issued only by commercial banks excluding the RRBs. The denomination of CDs should be in multiples of INR 0.5 million subject to a minimum issue size of INR 2.5 million. The maturity period of CDs should not be less than three months and not more than one year. The CDs are freely transferable by endorsement and delivery but only after 45 days of the date of issue. The banks cannot buy back their own CDs before maturity and they cannot grant loans against CDs. The issuers have to maintain CRR and SLR on the issue price of CDs.

Guidelines for issue of CD

A Master Circular issued by the Reserve Bank of India on July 1, 2009, consolidates and updates all the instructions/guidelines contained in the circulars insofar as they relate to guidelines for issue of CDs. The guidelines incorporating all the amendments issued till date are as follows:

- **Eligible issuers:** The CDs can be issued by scheduled commercial banks excluding regional rural banks and local area banks, and select all-India financial institutions that have been permitted by the RBI to raise short-term resources within the umbrella limit fixed by the RBI (i.e., term money, term deposits, commercial papers and inter-corporate deposits should not exceed 100 per cent of net owned funds as per the latest audited balance sheet).
- **Minimum size:** The minimum deposit that can be accepted from a single subscriber should not be less than INR 0.1 million and in the multiples of INR 100,000 thereafter.
- **Subscribers:** Individuals, corporations, companies, trusts, funds, and associations can subscribe to CDs. NRIs may also subscribe to CDs but only on a non-repatriable basis. Such CDs cannot be endorsed to another NRI in the secondary market.
- **Maturity:** The maturity period of CDs issued by banks should not be less than 7 days and not more than one year. FIs can issue CDs for a period of not less than 1 year and not exceeding 3 years from the date of issue.
- **Discount/Coupon rate:** The CDs may be issued at a discount on face value. Banks/FIs are also allowed to issue CDs on a floating rate basis, provided the methodology of compiling the floating rate is objective, transparent and market-based. The issuing bank/FI is free to determine the discount/coupon rate. The interest rate on floating rate CDs would have to be reset periodically in accordance with a pre-determined formula that indicates the spread over a transparent benchmark.
- **Reserve requirements:** The banks have to maintain the appropriate reserve requirements, that is, the CRR and SLR, on the issue price of the CDs.
- **Transferability:** Physical CDs are freely transferable by endorsement and delivery. Dematerialized CDs can be transferred as per the procedure applicable to other demat securities. There is no lock-in period for the CDs.
- **Loans/Buy-backs:** The banks/FIs cannot grant loans against CDs. Further, they cannot buy back their own CDs before maturity.
- **Format of CDs:** The banks/FIs should issue CDs only in the dematerialized form. However, according to the Depositories Act, 1996, investors have the option to seek the certificates in physical form. Accordingly, if an investor insists on a physical certificate, the bank/FI may inform the Reserve Bank of India about such instances separately. Further, issuance of CDs will attract stamp duty. There will be no grace period for repayment of CDs. If the maturity date happens to be a holiday, the issuing bank should make the payment on the immediate preceding working day. Banks/FIs may, therefore, so fix the period of deposit that the maturity date does not coincide with a holiday to avoid loss of discount/interest rate.
- **Security:** Since physical CDs are freely transferable by endorsement and delivery, it will be necessary for banks to see that the certificates are printed on good quality security paper and take necessary precautions to guard against tampering with the document. They should be signed by two or more authorized signatories.
- **Payment of certificate:** Since CDs are transferable, the physical certificate may be presented for payment by the last holder. The holders of dematerialized CDs will approach their respective depository participants (DPs) and have to give transfer/delivery instructions to transfer the demat security represented by the specific ISIN to the "CD Redemption Account" maintained by the issuer. The holder should also communicate to the issuer by a letter/fax enclosing the copy of the delivery instruction it had given to its DP and intimate the place at which the payment is requested to facilitate prompt payment. Upon receipt of the demat credit of CDs in the "CD Redemption Account", the issuer, on maturity date, would arrange to repay to holder/transferor by way of banker's cheque/high value cheque, and so on.
- **Accounting:** The banks/FIs may account the issue price under the head "CDs issued" and show it under deposits. Accounting entries towards discount will be made as in the case of "cash certificates". The banks/FIs should maintain a register of CDs issued with complete particulars.
- **Standardized market practices and documentation:** The Fixed Income Money Market and Derivatives Association of India may prescribe, in consultation with the RBI, for operational flexibility and smooth functioning of the CD market, any standardized procedure and documentation that are to be

followed by the participants in consonance with international best practices. The banks/FIs may refer to the detailed guidelines issued by the FIMMDA in this regard on June 20, 2002.

- **Reporting:** The banks should include the amount of CDs in the fortnightly return under Section 42 of the Reserve Bank of India Act, 1934, and separately indicate the amount so included by way of a footnote in the return. Further, banks/FIs should submit a fortnightly return as per the format of the Reserve Bank of India within 10 days from the end of the fortnight date.

For an overall evaluation, CDs have been successfully launched in the Indian financial market. The success of the CDs clearly shows that there is need for such an instrument, since sufficient short-term idle funds are available with companies and other corporate bodies. Many banks and financial institutions have found CDs a useful financial instrument to mobilize deposits fast, even if at a high price. Although the effective interest rate on CDs for the banks which issue CDs works out to be higher than that paid on time deposits, the CDs are still cheaper than call and short money rates. The subscribers to CDs also find that holding of CDs till maturity is highly rewarding.

3.5 Floating-rate Bonds

> ***Floating-rate bonds*** *are the debt securities whose interest varies as per the respective reference rate.*

Some debt securities, instead of carrying a fixed interest rate over the life of the security, carry a variable interest rate that is linked to a benchmark rate. **Floating-rate bonds** offer interest rates that can float with some short-term rate, such as the London Inter-Bank Offered Rate (LIBOR), MIBOR, T-bill rate and so on. The main aim of floating-rate bonds is to reduce the risk of volatile interest rates in the economy. For example, the Government of India issued floating rate bonds in 2009 for an aggregate amount of INR 30,000 million (nominal) by auction. The bonds had a tenure of eight years and were issued at par (i.e., at INR 100). The bonds carried an interest rate, which was calculated by adding a spread to a variable base rate. The spread was decided in the auction conducted by the Reserve Bank of India and remained unchanged during the currency of the bond. The variable base rate was the average rate of the implicit yields at cut-off prices emerging in the immediate previous six auctions of the 364-day treasury bills held prior to the relative half-year coupon period. The interest would be paid every half year. The base rate for calculation of interest for the first coupon period commencing from December 6, 2001 to June 5, 2002, as per the aforesaid formula was 6.99 per cent. The base rate for the subsequent half-yearly coupon periods, worked out as per the aforesaid formula, would be announced by the RBI on or before the commencement of the respective coupon period.

In the event of the 364-day treasury bill auctions being discontinued during the currency of the floating rate bonds, the applicable variable base rate would be the average of the yield to maturity (YTM) rate prevailing for one year Government of India security as on the last six reporting Fridays prior to the commencement of the relative half-yearly coupon period, worked out in consultation with the FIMMDA. This rate would be announced by the RBI on or before the commencement of the relative half-yearly coupon period. There would be no floor or cap on the interest rate on the floating rate bonds. The bonds will be repaid at par on December 6, 2009.

Another example is floating rate notes issued by ICICI in March 1997. ICICI launched USD 100 million subordinated floating rate notes (FRN) issue with a coupon of 80 basis points over the six-month LIBOR. The FRN had a 10-year final maturity, with a call option for ICICI after five years. The notes were be listed on the Luxembourg stock exchange.

3.5.1 Indexed Bonds

> *An* ***indexed bond*** *is a financial instrument the return for which is benchmarked to an index or some other standard.*

An **indexed bond**, as the name suggests, is a financial instrument the return for which is benchmarked to an index or some other standard. This could be an equity index, interest rate on a sovereign security, the wholesale price index or even the rate of inflation. In case of equity-based indexation, the funds raised through the bond are invested in the portfolio comprising the index in the same proportion as their weight in the index. The returns are, therefore, the same as those from the equity index. Thus, equity-index bonds are by nature equity investments.

An inflation-indexed bond links the interest rate of the bond to changes in some specified price index. The basic objective of price indexation is to insulate contractually created claims on the bond from the effects of changes in the purchasing power of money. In an inflation-indexed bond, the principal amount is adjusted against inflation periodically and the interest is calculated on the inflation-adjusted principal. For example, a company issues a 10-year bond with 6 per cent coupon on January 5, 2009. An investor purchases the bond by paying the principal amount of INR 5,000. The interest payment becomes due on July 5, 2009. During that period, the inflation rate in the country rises by 5 per cent. So the inflation-adjusted principal on July 5, 2009, becomes INR 5,250 and, accordingly, the interest payment is calculated on INR 5,250 at 6 per cent per annum. The investor's return is thus protected against rising inflation. In other words, inflation-indexed bonds provide the hedge only against the principal and not the coupon. Equally hedged is the bond holder's principal amount from deflation as it comes with a guarantee that the bond value will not fall below par. The Reserve Bank of India issued inflation-indexed bonds in 1997 for five years, called the 6 per cent Capital Indexed Bond 2002. Many countries, including the United States, the United Kingdom, Canada and Australia, have issued inflation-indexed bonds at different times. The countries generally issue such bonds when faced with high inflation rates.

3.5.2 Equity-linked Notes (ELN)

***Equity-linked notes** are structured financial products that offer part of the upside potential return from owning certain equity stocks but limit nominal losses if held until maturity.*

Equity-linked notes (ELN) are structured financial products that offer part of the upside potential return from owning certain equity stocks but limit nominal losses if held until maturity. They are listed on stock exchanges and also traded over the counter (OTC). The maturity periods of ELN vary from one to 10 years but no payment of interest or dividend is made during the period. On maturity, the principal amount plus an additional amount depending on the value of the underlying equity (i.e., stock, basket of stocks, index or basket of indices, or a mix of these) is paid to the holder of these securities.

ELN may have protected or unprotected principal payment. An unprotected ELN is similar to a direct investment in equity. The investor participates in all market moves. Thus, the investor runs the risk of losing some of his initial investment. In a protected ELN, the investor participates in favourable moves only and is guaranteed full repayment of the initial investment. This structure is similar to a direct investment in equity with long put option.

A typical ELN is a package of a call option and a zero-coupon bond. The discount to the face value of the bond is used to purchase the call option on the underlying equity. For example, the 10-year zero-coupon treasury bond yields 5 per cent per annum. So the present value of a zero-coupon bond (face value of INR 10,000) is INR 6,140. In an ELN of INR 10,000, the principal component is INR 6,140 and the interest component is INR 3,860, which is used to buy equity options. In other words, the forgone coupons (the bond being zero-coupon) worth INR 3,860 are used to buy call options on equity. Thus, the ELN consists of principal amount with attached equity options. Accordingly, the payoff on the ELN is the redemption of the principal (INR 6,140) at the end plus the value, if any, of the equity call options.

On maturity of the ELN, the coupon is equal to either (a) zero, if the underlying equity has depreciated from the strike level (i.e., a certain threshold), or (b) the participation times the percentage change in the underlying equity times the par amount of ELN, if the underlying equity appreciates. The participation rate is the rate at which the investor participates in the appreciation of the underlying equity. For example, a participation rate of 60 per cent implies that a 10 per cent increase in the underlying equity will result in a coupon of 6 per cent. Thus, the zero-coupon bond provides the buyer of ELN with principal protection while the call option provides the ELN buyer with exposure to the underlying equity.

The redemption amount at maturity is equal to the original principal amount plus an index payment, which is determined as follows:

$$\text{Participation rate} \times \frac{(\text{Index}_1 - \text{Index}_0)}{\text{Index}_0} \times \text{Principal amount}$$

Where

Index_1 = Index level at maturity

Index_0 = Initial index level, specified at the issue of the ELN

It may be noted that the investor may set Index 0 as equal to the market level at issue or another desired level. For example, an investor has purchased 10-year 100 per cent principal protected ELN with 100 per cent participation in the upside of the Sensex for INR 10,000 when the index level is 12,000. At maturity, if the Sensex is at 15,000, then the coupon would be as follows:

$$100 \times [(15{,}000 - 12{,}000)/12{,}000] \times \text{INR } 10{,}000 = \text{INR } 2{,}500$$

The total payoff would be INR 12,500. If the Sensex is below 12,000 at maturity, the final payoff to the investor will be INR 10,000 (the principal amount).

The coupon of an ELN can be below or above the market yield of a similar borrowing by the same issuer with a normal fixed principal repayment. As far as the pricing of an ELN is concerned, the structure of the note as well as market factors enter into the pricing of an ELN. Generally, the investor specifies either the coupon level or the participation rate, and the other will be determined accordingly. For example, when the coupon in a protected ELN note is below market, the difference between the market yield and the lower coupon offsets the cost to the issuer of linking the principal repayment to a protected equity index. A lower coupon rate, therefore, results in a higher participation in the performance of the index. Zero-coupon notes have the highest possible participation rate. The lower the floor level, the higher the coupon will be. The lower the index volatility and the longer the tenor, the higher is the participation rate. The participation rate also depends on the issuer of the security and its corresponding credit quality.

3.5.3 Participatory Notes (PN)

***Participatory notes** are a kind of offshore derivative instrument used by overseas investors to park their funds.*

Participatory notes (PNs), a kind of offshore derivative instrument, are investment vehicles used by overseas investors. The participatory notes may have either stocks or equity derivatives or a stock market index as the underlying asset. In other words, the return on the participatory notes may be directly related to the appreciation in prices of the underlying asset or security. The underlying securities may be stocks, basket of stocks, index, basket of indices or a mix of these. Like any derivative instrument, the value of PNs fluctuates depending on the price of the underlying asset or security.

In the Indian context, PNs are derivative instruments issued to foreign-based companies or individuals by an FII or its sub-accounts against the holding of shares in India. That is, PNs are issued by registered foreign institutional investors to overseas investors who wish to invest in the Indian stock market without registering themselves in India. The foreign institutional investors usually buy securities including derivatives in the Indian stock market and then issue PNs to foreign investors. Any dividends or capital gains derived from the underlying securities are also remitted to the original investors.

According to SEBI guidelines, the FIIs are not allowed to issue participatory notes to Indian nationals, persons of Indian origin and overseas corporate bodies which are majority-owned or controlled by NRIs. The PNs can be issued only to regulated entities and the issuers of PNs are responsible for exercising due diligence on their clients, based on "know your client" principles. Further, a regular reporting requirement is put in place to monitor PNs.

The foreign institutional investors issue PNs to investors abroad with details of scrips that can be bought and expected returns over a specific period of time. If the client agrees, it deposits the funds with the overseas branch of the FII and the Indian arm of that FII proceeds with the transaction, buying the scrips in the Indian market and settling it on its own account. The details of the investors are not revealed at all in India. In other words, it is difficult to establish the beneficial ownership of the ultimate investor(s). It is feared that participatory notes have become handy for Indian money launderers who first take funds out of the country through the *hawala* route, and then get that money back using PNs. This route is also used for round tripping, that is, bringing back unaccounted money stashed away in foreign bank accounts. Further, PNs are largely blamed for volatility in stock prices. The overseas investors, particularly hedge funds, have to locate markets where they can get better returns for longer periods. In their search, they may find that the Indian capital market is more attractive compared to developed markets. But the Indian government's policy restricts international access to the Indian capital market. Therefore, the overseas investors have found a way in PNs to enter the Indian capital market by circumventing the government policy.

***Depository receipts** are negotiable financial instruments representing a foreign company's shares and traded on local stock exchange(s).*

3.6 Global Depository Receipts (GDRs) and American Depository Receipts (ADRs)

Depository receipts (DRs) are negotiable financial instruments representing a foreign company's shares. They are traded on local stock exchange(s). DRs are certificates that allow investors to hold shares of a foreign listed company. Although a DR can also represent a debt instrument, in reality it rarely does. DRs trade freely in the overseas financial markets like any other foreign currency-denominated security. The DRs take the form of GDRs to reflect the fact that they are marketed globally rather than in a specific country or market. If the DRs are denominated in U.S. dollars and marketed in the United States only, then the DRs may take the form of American Depository Receipts (ADRs). The DRs denominated in Indian rupee are known as Indian Depository Receipts and they are listed on Indian stock exchange(s). Except for the place of listing, GDRs, ADRs and IDRs are broadly similar from the legal, operational, technical and administrative standpoint. GDRs are usually listed on an exchange in Europe, often Luxembourg, but London is also used. The DRs are mainly issued because of complexities involved in buying and trading of foreign currency-denominated shares. Listing of shares on a foreign stock exchange like the NYSE and NASDAQ is a complex process. Listing requirements are very stringent in many countries. For example, to get their shares listed on the New York Stock Exchange, Indian companies have to prepare their accounts as per the Generally Accepted Accounting Principles (GAAP). In such situations, the shares can be listed on foreign stock exchanges indirectly by using GDRs, ADRs and so on. Thus, DRs are good means of investment for foreign investors. Foreign investors can easily invest in Indian companies by buying the GDRs/ADRs issued by Indian companies.

The process of issuing DRs is as follows:

1. A depository buys a certain number of shares of a foreign listed company through its foreign branch or through a local custodian.
2. Based on the shares purchased, the depository issues DRs in a pre-determined ratio. In other words, each DR represents a fixed number of shares as underlying.
3. Then the DRs are sold to the investors and listed on the local stock exchange(s) for trading. The DRs are traded freely in the overseas market like any other local currency-denominated securities.

The special features of DRs are as follows:

1. The holder of DRs has an option to convert DRs and hold the equity shares instead.
2. The DRs do not entitle the holder to any voting rights and, therefore, there is no fear of loss of management control.
3. DRs are fungible. The holder of DRs is given the option to cancel his DRs with the depository and recover the proceeds by selling the underlying shares. The companies are also given the option to convert the shares so released into DRs.
4. An investor who wants to cancel his DRs may do so by advising the depositary to request the custodian to release his underlying shares and relinquishing his DRs in lieu of shares held by the custodian. The depositary will instruct the custodian about cancellation of the DRs and to release the corresponding shares, collect the sales proceeds and remit the same to the investor. The DRs can be cancelled only after a cooling period of 45 days.
5. Dividend payments are made by the company in its local currency, which the depository converts into a foreign currency and pays to the investor after deducting a withholding tax, if any.
6. As far as pricing of DRs is concerned, in the road shows the relevant presentations are made to potential investors and an indication of the investor response is obtained. The issuer fixes the range of the issue price and finally decides on the issue price after assessing the investor response at the road shows.
7. The cost of floating DRs is quite high and is only justifiable if the amount of finance to be raised is quite large

There are many advantages of DRs. The company issuing DRs can get greater exposure and raise funds in the international capital market. This will also add to the prestige of company, resulting in brisk trading of its shares in the local market. The company, by issuing DRs, encourages foreign investment that will have several benefits for the country's economy as a whole. The proceeds of DR issues are collected in a foreign currency, which would help the issuer to utilize the same for meeting the foreign exchange component of project cost, repayment of foreign currency loans, meeting overseas commitments and for other similar purposes. Further, the company whose shares are converted into DRs does not take on any foreign exchange risk as the dividend outgoes are made in local currency, though it does get the foreign currency by way of issue proceeds. Thus, the foreign exchange risk or currency risk is placed totally on the investor. The holders of DRs automatically become international investors and get the benefits arising from international diversification of investment.

Notwithstanding these advantages, issuing of DRs is a time-consuming and complex process. For example, to raise funds by issuing ADRs, a company has to prepare its accounts as per the Generally Accepted Accounting Principles. There are three levels of ADRs depending on their adherence to GAAP. For a Level-I ADR, the receipts issued in the US are registered with the Securities and Exchange Commission (SEC), but the underlying shares held in the depositary bank are not registered with the SEC. They must partially adhere to GAAP used in the United States. Level-II ADRs are those in which both the ADRs and the underlying shares (that already trade in the foreign company's domestic market) are registered with the SEC. They must also partially adhere to GAAP. Level-III ADRs must adhere fully to GAAP and the underlying shares held at the depositary bank are typically new shares and not those already trading in the foreign company's domestic currency.

In India, RIL was the first company to raise funds through a GDR issue. Initially, companies issued GDRs at a discount to the Indian market price, but later they offered favourable conversion rates from GDRs to equity or warrants instead of a discount. Towards the end of 1993, investment interest in India built up to a near frenzy, and GDR issues were placed at a premium to Indian market prices. Infosys Technologies was the first Indian company to use the ADR route.

3.7 Sponsored Secondary ADRs

The Reserve Bank of India allowed Indian companies to offer their local investors the option of converting their shares into ADRs vide its circular dated November 23, 2002. The RBI issued operative guidelines for the disinvestment of shares by Indian companies in the overseas market through the issue of ADRs/GDRs. Accordingly, an Indian company may sponsor an issue of ADRs/GDRs with an overseas depository against shares held by its shareholders at a price to be determined by the lead manager of the issue. That is, a company may sponsor a secondary ADR offering against the block of shares to be divested by their shareholders. This is in contrast to a normal ADR offer in which fresh shares are issued and cash flows of the company are augmented. The company that sponsors the secondary ADR offer will not receive any proceeds of this offering and the net proceeds after the offering expenses will be distributed to the selling shareholders. Then why do companies sponsor the secondary ADR offering? They do so to enhance liquidity of their shares and to become more globalized. The benefit for the shareholders is that they get an opportunity to sell their holdings at a premium to the market price. That is, the sponsored secondary ADRs enable the shareholders of the company to encash their holdings at a higher price than that prevailing on the local stock exchange(s). A company that wants to offer sponsored secondary ADRs may follow the procedure below.

(i) Seek the approval of two-thirds of its shareholders for launching the sponsored secondary ADRs programme.
(ii) Appoint lead manager(s) for the issue.
(iii) File the offer document with the SEC to seek regulatory approvals.
(iv) Make an open offer to its shareholders to tender their shares.
(v) If the number of shares offered for conversion is more than the maximum issue size as decided by the company, they will be accepted on a pro-rata basis as per the guidelines issued by the Reserve Bank of India.
(vi) Shares are kept in escrow account till ADRs issue is concluded.
(vii) Lead managers follow the book-building process to offer the ADRs to overseas investors.
(viii) After completing the book-building process, the proceeds of the ADRs issue net of issue expenses will be proportionately paid to the shareholders who have tendered their shares.

Infosys Technologies Limited, commonly known as Infosys, was the first company to take advantage of the Sponsored Secondary ADR Program. Infosys, the second largest software exporter in India, made three sponsored secondary ADR offerings, one in July 2003, the second in May 2005 and the third in November 2006. The main aim of Infosys was to be the first Indian company to enter the NASDAQ 100 index by increasing its profile with global investors. To mention one offering, in November 2006, Infosys offered USD 1.6 billion worth ADRs at a price of USD 53.50—a 3.2 per cent discount on the ADR trading price on NASDAQ. This was the largest international offering from India. Since then, many Indian companies have issued depository receipts. In 2005, there were 41 depository receipt issuances but that number declined toll in 2009. In 2009, the ADR issue by Sterlite Industries, India's largest copper producer, was very prominent. Sterlite Industries came up with an ADR issue of USD 1.5 billion in July 2009 to fund its power generation and acquisition plans. It sold 123.5 million shares at USD 12.15 apiece. Each ADR represents one equity share of the company. It was the biggest equity sale in the US by an Indian company since ICICI Bank raised USD 2.46 billion in June 2007. Earlier (June 2007), Sterlite Industries had also raised about USD 2 billion in an ADR offering.

3.7.1 Regulations to Issue GDRs/ADRs

Indian companies can issue GDRs or ADRs in accordance with the Foreign Currency Convertible Bonds and Ordinary Shares (Through Depository Receipt Mechanism) Scheme, 1993, and guidelines issued by SEBI from time to time. As per the existing guidelines, an Indian company can issue GDRs/ADRs if it is eligible to issue shares to foreigners including NRIs under the FDI scheme. Unlisted companies that have not yet accessed the GDRs/ADRs route for raising capital would require prior or simultaneous listing of their shares on the domestic stock exchange(s). The proceeds raised through GDRs/ADRs have to be kept abroad till actually required in India. Pending repatriation or utilization of the proceeds, the Indian company can invest the funds only in specified securities. There are no end use restrictions except for a ban on deployment of such funds in the real estate or stock market. There is no monetary limit up to which an Indian company can raise funds through the GDRs/ADRs route. Voting rights on underlying shares shall be as per the provisions of the Companies Act, 1956, and the voting rights can be exercised only in a manner incorporated in the terms of the GDRs/ADRs. The pricing of ADRs/GDRs shall be made at a price not less than the higher of the following two averages: (a) the average of the weekly high and low of the closing prices of the underlying shares quoted on the stock exchange during the six months preceding the relevant date, and (b) the average of the weekly high and low of the closing prices of the related shares quoted on a stock exchange during the two weeks preceding the relevant date.

Till 2001, the GDRs/ADRs used to be fungible one way, that is, foreign investors could convert their GDRs/ADRs into underlying shares and sell them in the local market. However, they were not permitted to reconvert shares bought on the local exchange into ADRs/GDRs. Since 2002, two-way fungibility has been permitted. Accordingly, reissuance of depository receipts is permitted to the extent to which they have been redeemed into underlying shares and sold in the domestic market.

The issue-related expenses (covering fixed expenses like underwriting commissions, lead manager charges, and legal expenses as well as other reimbursable expenses) shall be subject to a ceiling of 4 per cent in the case of GDRs and 7 per cent in the case of ADRs. Issue expenses beyond the said ceiling would need prior approval of the Reserve Bank. Any income by way of dividends distributed, declared or paid by any Indian company is exempt from tax and is not taxable in the hands of the investor. All transaction of trading of depository receipts outside India, among non-resident investors, will be free from any liability to income tax in India on capital gains therefrom. If any capital gains arise on the transfer of the underlying shares in India to the non-resident investor, he or she is liable to income tax under the provisions of the Income Tax Act, 1961. The Indian company issuing depository receipts is required to pay a stamp duty of 0.1 per cent on the value of each underlying share. A transfer of depository receipts is not subject to Indian stamp duty. However, upon the acquisition of equity shares from the depositary in exchange for depository receipts, the non-resident holder will be liable for Indian stamp duty at the rate of 0.25 per cent of the market value of the depository receipts or equity shares exchanged. A sale of equity shares by a non-resident holder will also be subject to Indian stamp duty at the rate of 0.25 per cent of the market value of the equity shares on the trade date.

Summary

1. Financial instruments are the means by which investments are made. They are investment vehicles.
2. An equity share is a certificate representing the ownership of a company and an equity shareholder is a part owner of the company with certain rights and responsibilities.
3. The equity shares of a company may be classified as those with voting rights and those without voting rights.
4. Preference shares have some of the characteristics of equity and some of the characteristics of debt.

5. CCP shares have all the positive attributes of convertible debentures, besides providing more fllexibility and options to the investor.
6. A debenture is a debt security issued by a company acknowledging its obligation to repay the sum as well as the interest at a specified rate of interest as per the indenture.
7. If an option is given to debenture holders to convert their debentures into equity shares at a specified rate of exchange after a specified period, such debentures are called convertible debentures.
8. A bond is a promissory note issued by a borrower to repay the principal amount with interest to the lender. Zero-coupon bonds are fixed-income securities that pay interest at maturity instead of periodically. SPNs are a variant of zero-coupon bonds.
9. Junk bonds are high-yield bonds with a speculative or below investment grade.
10. Treasury bills, popularly known as T-bills, are short-term financial instruments issued by the government to enable people to invest their surplus funds while avoiding default risk.
11. PNs, a kind of offshore derivative instrument, are investment vehicles used by overseas investors. Participatory notes may have either stocks or equity derivatives or the stock market index as the underlying asset.
12. Commercial paper and CDs are money market instruments. A commercial paper is issued by businesses, while CDs are issued by banks.
13. Depository receipts are negotiable financial instruments representing a foreign company's shares but are traded on local stock exchange(s).

Questions

1. Discuss the important features of equity shares.
2. What are the advantages and disadvantages of cumulative convertible preference shares?
3. How are convertible debentures superior to non-convertible debentures?
4. What could be the motives for subscribing to floating rate bonds?
5. What category of investors could prefer zero-coupon bonds?
6. Analyse the secured premium notes that are issued by Tata Steel.
7. Bring out the important features of T-bills.
8. Critically examine the guidelines for issuing commercial paper.
9. How would commercial banks mobilize deposits through the CDs route?
10. Explain the process of issuing GDRs/ADRs.

Chapter 4

Management of Capital Issues

LEARNING OBJECTIVES

After studying this chapter, you should be able to:

- Present the activities involved in issue management.
- Understand the eligibility conditions for public issues.
- Focus on norms for the allotment of securities as well as promoters' contribution.
- Present norms for sweat equity and employee stock option scheme (ESOS) and employee stock purchase scheme (ESPS).
- Understand the concepts of bonus issues, rights issues, and Euro issues.
- Describe the features of the prospectus for public issues.

4.1 Introduction

Issue management refers to the management of various kinds of issues of securities, which include public and rights issues and offers for sale. A *public issue* refers to an invitation by a company to the public to subscribe to the securities offered through a prospectus. A *rights issue* is an issue of capital offered to the existing shareholders through a letter of offer. An *offer of sale* is an offer of securities by the existing shareholders, particularly the promoters of the company, to a select few through private negotiation.

Issue management *refers to the management of various kinds of issues of securities, which include public issues, rights issues and offer for sale.*

Among the various kinds of issues, public issues attract a lot of attention since they involve a series of complex activities with a wide range of implications. The major activities involved in a public issue are as follows:

(a) The company should pass the necessary resolutions under Section 81(1) (a) and Section 293 (1) (d) of the Companies Act, 1956.
(b) Finalize the type of securities to be issued.
(c) Appoint the lead manager(s) to the issue.
(d) Decide the stock exchange(s) where the securities are to be listed.
(e) Submit a copy of the memorandum of association and articles of association to stock exchanges.
(f) Make appraisal arrangements with the merchant bankers and banks, among others.
(g) Structure the public issue.
(h) Select and appoint the intermediaries (underwriters, bankers, brokers, printers, registrars, advertising agency and so on) in consultation with the lead manager(s).
(i) Finalize underwriting arrangement.
(j) Finalize the trustees if issuing debt securities.
(k) Prepare the draft prospectus and discuss the draft prospectus with all the concerned parties.
(l) File the offer document with the Securities and Exchange Board of India (SEBI) and the concerned stock exchanges along with due diligence certificate.
(m) Obtain the necessary clearance from SEBI.
(n) Design the marketing strategy, particularly the promotion strategy (advertisements, press conferences, road shows) and distribution strategy.
(o) File the prospectus with the necessary documents as required U/S 60 of the Companies Act, 1956, with the registrar of companies.

(p) Make arrangements for opening and closing the issue.
(q) Follow up with registrars.
(r) Complete the post-issue formalities including allotment.
(s) Dispatch allotment letters/refund orders and share certificates.
(t) Make arrangements for listing the securities on the selected stock exchanges.

Thus, issuing securities through a public offer involves a different kind of management with practical knowledge and professional skills.

4.1.1 Going Public: Benefits and Limitations

Going public has both advantages and disadvantages. As advantages outweigh disadvantages, many companies prefer going public.

Going public offers a company the following advantages:

- The company has access to a vast source of funding. So the company can mobilize the funds freely and with less cost of capital.
- Going public attracts the attention of several people. The media, including the electronic media, plays a vital role in this regard. The company can cash in on the wide publicity and use it for building its image in the long run as well as to market its products or services.
- It helps the company forge relationship with suppliers, distributors, creditors and others.
- Once a company has gone public, it becomes easy to access the capital market again and again through subsequent equity/debt offerings.
- The valuation of a company that has gone public is easy compared to a company that has not gone public.
- Going public enables the company to have access to a wider distribution of its shareholdings.

Thus, going public offers a lot of opportunities to a company for growth of business and development of brand equity. However, going public puts a lot of responsibility on the company's management as well.

- A company has to comply with several pre-issue and post-issue regulatory and statutory requirements if it has to go public. Non-fulfilment of any of the requirements may cost the company dearly.
- Periodic financial reporting by the company is necessary under law. This may result in revealing or disclosing certain information which would have otherwise been considered confidential.
- When the company goes public, the number of shareholders increases. This makes the strategic business decision-making process difficult.

In view of such disadvantages in going public, many entrepreneurs do not offer securities to the public.

4.1.2 Rule 19(2) (b) of the Securities Contracts (Regulation) Rules, 1957

All listed companies with certain exceptions are required to ensure a minimum level of public shareholding at 25 per cent of the total number of issued shares of a class or kind for the purpose of continuous listing.

As per rule 19(2) (b) the of Securities Contracts (Regulations) Rules, 1957, all listed companies are required to ensure a minimum level of public shareholding at 25 per cent of the total number of issued shares of a class or kind for the purpose of continuous listing. There are a couple of exceptions to this. These are:

(a) Companies which, at the time of initial listing, had offered less than 25 per cent but not less than 10 per cent of the total number of issued shares of a class or kind, in terms of Rule 19 (2) (b) of the Securities Contract (Regulation) Rules, 1957, or companies that desire to list their shares by making an initial public offering (IPO) of at least 10 per cent in terms of the same rule.

(b) Companies that have, irrespective of the percentage of their shares with the public at the time of initial listing, reached a size of 20 million or more in terms of the number of listed shares and INR 10,000 million or more in terms of market capitalization.

The companies falling under (a) and (b) categories are required to maintain the minimum level of public shareholding at 10 per cent of the total number of issued shares of a class or kind for the purpose of continuous listing.

However, this requirement of maintaining the minimum level of public shareholding on a continuous basis is not applicable to government companies (as defined under Section 617 of the Companies Act, 1956), infrastructure companies [as defined under clause 1.2.1 (xv) of the SEBI Disclosure and Investor Protection (DIP) Guidelines, 2000] and companies referred to the Board for Industrial and Financial Reconstruction (BIFR).

The public shareholding for the purpose of continuous listing will continue to comprise shares held by entities other than promoters and the promoter group and shares held by custodians against which depository receipts (DRs) are issued overseas.

As per the Rule 19 (2) (b), the shareholding pattern shall be reported under three categories—shares held by the promoter and promoter group, shares held by the public and shares held by custodians against which DRs have been issued. Further, details such as the number of shareholders, the number and percentage of shares held and the number of shares held in dematerialized form shall be provided for all the three categories. The percentage of public shareholding shall be computed as "shares held by the public" as a percentage of the total number of shares held by promoters, the promoter group and the public.

4.2 SEBI (Issue of Capital and Disclosure Requirements) Regulations, 2009

SEBI has issued new regulations that are more comprehensive than the existing guidelines with regard to capital issues. The salient features of the new regulations are as follows:

No issuer shall make a public issue or rights issue of specified securities:

(a) If the issuer, any of its promoters, promoter group or directors or persons in control of the issuer is debarred from accessing the capital market by SEBI;

(b) If any of the promoters, directors or persons in control of the issuer was or also is a promoter, director or person in control of any other company which is debarred from accessing the capital market under any order or directives by SEBI;

(c) If the issuer of convertible debt instruments is in the list of wilful defaulters published by the RBI or has defaulted on payment of interest or repayment of principal amount in respect of debt instruments issued by it to the public, if any, for a period of more than six months;

(d) Unless it has made an application to one or more recognized stock exchanges for the listing of specified securities on such stock exchanges and has chosen one of them as the designated stock exchange. Provided that in case of an initial public offer, the issuer shall make an application for listing of the specified securities in at least one recognized stock exchange with nationwide trading terminals.

(e) Unless it has entered into an agreement with a depository for dematerialization of specified securities already issued or proposed to be issued;

(f) Unless all the existing partly paid-up equity shares of the issuer have either been fully paid-up or forfeited;

(g) Unless firm arrangements for finance through verifiable means towards 75 per cent of the stated means for it, excluding the amount to be raised through the proposed public issue or rights issue or through existing identifiable internal accruals, have been made.

4.2.1 Eligibility Requirements

An issuer can make an initial public offer if:

(a) It has net tangible assets of at least INR 30 million in each of the preceding three full years, of which not more than 50 per cent is held in monetary assets. If more than 50 per cent of the net tangible assets is held in monetary assets, the issuer has made firm commitments to utilize the excess monetary assets in its business or project;

(b) It has a track record of distributable profits (excluding extraordinary items) for at least three out of the immediately preceding five years;

(c) It has a net worth of at least INR 10 million in each of the preceding three full years;

(d) The aggregate of the proposed issue and all the previous issues made in the same financial year in terms of the issue size does not exceed five times its pre-issue net worth;

(e) If it has changed its name within the last one year, at least 50 per cent of the revenue for the preceding year has been earned by it from the activity indicated by the new name.

An issuer not satisfying any of these conditions can make an initial public offer if:

(a) (i) The issue is made through the book-building process and the issuer undertakes to allot at least 50 per cent of the net offer to qualified institutional buyers and refund full subscription monies, if it fails to make an allotment to the qualified institutional buyers; or

(ii) At least 15 per cent of the cost of the project is contributed by scheduled commercial banks or public financial institutions, of which not less than 10 per cent shall come from the appraisers, and the issuer undertakes to allot at least 10 per cent of the net offer to the public to qualified institutional buyers and to refund full subscription monies if it fails to make the allotment to the qualified institutional buyers;

(b) (i) The minimum post-issue face value capital of the issuer is INR 100 million; or

(ii) The issuer undertakes to provide market-making for at least two years from the date of listing of the specified securities, subject to the following:

(A) The market makers offer buy and sell quotes for a minimum depth of 300 specified securities and ensure that the bid-ask spread for their quotes does not, at any time, exceed 10 per cent;

(B) The inventory of market makers, as on the date of allotment of the specified securities, shall be at least 5 per cent of the proposed issue.

An issuer may make an initial public offer of convertible debt instruments without making a prior public issue of its equity shares and listing. An issuer shall not make an allotment pursuant to a public issue if the number of prospective allottees is less than 1,000. No issuer shall make an initial public issue if there are any outstanding convertible securities of any other right which would entitle any person any option to receive equity shares after the initial public offer (certain exceptions are also given in this regard). Further, no issuer shall make an initial public offer unless as on the date of the registering prospectus or red herring prospectus with the Registrar of Companies, the issuer has obtained grading for the initial public offer from at least one credit rating agency registered with SEBI.

For further public offer, the following conditions are applicable:

(a) The aggregate of the proposed issue and all previous issues made in the same financial year in terms of issue size does not exceed five times its pre-issue net worth;

(b) If it has changed its name within the last one year, at least 50 per cent of the revenue for the preceding one full year has been earned by it from the activity indicated by the new name.

4.2.2 Minimum Promoters' Contribution

The promoters of the issuer shall contribute not less than 20 per cent of the post-issue capital in case of an initial public offer, and 20 per cent of the proposed issue size or the extent of 20 per cent of the post-issue capital in case of a further public offer. In case of a composite issue, the promoters should contribute either to the extent of 20 per cent of the proposed issue size or to the extent of 20 per cent of the post-issue capital excluding the rights issue component. Where the minimum promoters' contribution is more than INR 1,000 million, the promoters shall bring in at least INR 1,000 million before the date of opening of the issue and the remaining amount may be brought on pro-rata basis before the calls are made to the public.

The requirements of minimum promoters' contribution shall not apply in the following cases.

1. An issuer that does not have any identifiable promoter; or
2. In case of a further public offer where the equity shares of the same class are proposed to be allotted pursuant to conversion or exchange of convertible securities offered through the offer or proposed to be allotted in the offer have been listed and are frequently traded in a recognized stock exchange for a

period of at least three years and the issuer has a track record of dividend payment for at least immediately preceding three years.

4.2.3 Lock-in of Securities

The minimum promoters' contribution shall be locked in for a period of three years from the date of commencement of commercial production or the date of allotment in the public issue, whichever is later. The promoters' contribution that is in excess of the minimum shall be locked in for a period of one year.

In the case of an initial public offer, the entire pre-issue capital held by persons other than promoters shall be locked in for a period of one year. But this is not applicable to the equity shares allotted to employees under an employee stock option or the employee stock purchase scheme of the issuer prior to the initial public offer, if the issuer has made full disclosures with respect to such options or scheme. It is also not applicable to equity shares held by a venture capital fund or a foreign venture capital investor for a period of at least one year prior to the date of filing the draft prospectus with SEBI.

4.2.4 Minimum Offer to Public

The net offer to the public in case of an initial public issue shall be at least 10 per cent or 25 per cent of the post-issue capital, as the case may be. In case of a further public offer, the net offer to the public shall be at least 10 or 25 per cent of the issue size, as the case may be. This regulation shall not apply if the issuer is a government company or statutory authority or corporation or any special-purpose vehicle set up and controlled by any one or more of them, which is engaged in the infrastructure sector.

4.2.5 Reservation on Competitive Basis

In case of an issue made through the book-building process, the issuer may make reservation on competitive basis out of the issue size excluding promoters' contribution and the net offer to the public in favour of the following categories of persons.

(a) Employees of the issuer including employees of the promoting companies in case of a new issue;

(b) Shareholders (other than promoters) of:

(i) listed promoting companies, in case of a new issuer, and

(ii) listed group companies, in case of an existing issuer.

(c) Persons who, as on the date of filing the draft offer document with SEBI, are associated with the issuer as depositors, bondholders or subscribers to services of the issuer making an initial public offer. The issuer shall not make the reservation to the issue management team, syndicate members, their promoters, directors and employees and for the group or associate companies of the issue management team and syndicate members and their promoters, directors and employees.

In the case of an issue made other than through the book-building process, the issuer may make a reservation on the competitive basis out of the issue size excluding promoters' contribution and the net offer to the public in favour of the following categories of persons:

(a) Employees of the issuer, including employees of the promoting companies in case of a new issuer;

(b) Shareholders (other than promoters) of:

(i) listed promoting companies, in case of a new issue, and

(ii) listed group companies, in case of an existing issuer

In case of a further public offer (not being a composite issue), the issuer may make reservations on competitive basis out of the issue size, excluding the promoter's contribution and net offer to the public in favour of retail individual shareholders of the issue.

The reservation on a competitive basis shall be subject to the following conditions:

(a) The aggregate of reservations for employees shall not exceed 10 per cent of the issue size;

(b) Reservation for shareholders shall not exceed 10 per cent of the issue size;

(c) Reservations for persons who as on the date of filing the draft offer document with SEBI have business associations as depositors, bondholders and subscribers to services with the issuer making an initial public offer shall not exceed 5 per cent of the issue size;

(d) No further application for the subscription in the net offer to the public category shall be entertained from any person (except an employee and retail individual shareholder) in favour of whom reservation is made on a competitive basis;

(e) Any unsubscribed portion in any reserved category may be added to any other reserved category and the unsubscribed portion, if any, after such *inter-se* adjustments among the reserved categories shall be added to the net offer to the public category;

(f) In case of under-subscription in the net offer to the public category, a spill-over to the extent of under-subscription shall be permitted from the reserved category to the net public offer category.

Reservation on a competitive basis means reservation wherein specified securities are allotted in the same proportion as the ratio of the number of specified securities applied for in a particular reserved category to the number of specified securities reserved for that category.

4.2.6 Allocation in Net Offer to Public

In an issue made through the book-building process, the allocation in the net offer to the public category shall be made as follows:

(a) Not less than 35 per cent to retail individual investors;

(b) Not less than 15 per cent to non-institutional investors;

(c) Not more than 50 per cent to qualified institutional buyers, 5 per cent of which shall be allocated to mutual funds. Where the issuer is required to allocate 60 per cent of the net offer to the public to qualified institutional buyers in terms of the provisions of sub-clause (b) of clause (2) of Rule 19 of the Securities Contracts (Regulations) Rules, 1957, allocation to retail individual investors and non-institutional investors shall be 30 per cent and 10 per cent, respectively. In addition to the 5 per cent allocation available, mutual funds shall be eligible for allocation under the balance available for qualified institutional buyers.

In an issue made through the book-building process, the issuer may allocate up to 30 per cent of the portion available for allocation to qualified institutional buyers to an anchor investor in accordance with certain conditions.

In an issue made through the book-building process, allocation in the net offer to the public category shall be made as follows:

(a) Minimum 50 per cent to retail individual investors; and

(b) The remaining to:

(i) individual applicants other than retail individual investors, and

(ii) other investors including corporate bodies or institutions, irrespective of the number of specified securities applied for;

(c) Unsubscribed portion in either of the categories specified in (a) or (b) may be allocated to applicants in the other category.

4.2.7 Minimum Subscription and Oversubscription

The minimum subscription to be received in an issue shall not be less than 90 per cent of the offer through an offer document. In the event of non-receipt of the minimum subscription, all the received money shall be refunded to the applicants forthwith, but not later than 15 days of the closure of the issue in case of a non-underwritten issue and 70 days of the closure of the issue in case of an underwritten issue, where the minimum subscription including devolvement obligations paid by the underwriters is not received within 60 days of the closure of the issue. However, this regulation is not applicable to the offer for sale of specified securities and also to public issues by infrastructure companies if the disclosures regarding the alternate source of funding of the objects of the issue have been made in the offer document.

Minimum subscription to be received in a public issue shall not be less than 90 per cent of the offer through the offer document.

No allotment shall be made by the issuer in excess of the specified securities offered through the offer document. However, in case of oversubscription, an allotment of not more than 10 per cent of the net offer to the public may be made for the purpose of making allotment in minimum lots.

4.2.8 Period of Subscription and Application Value

The minimum period for which a public issue has to be kept open is three working days and the maximum is 10 working days. The minimum period for a rights issue is 15 working days and the maximum is 60 working days. The issuer shall mention in the offer document the minimum application size in terms of the number of specified securities, which shall fall within the range of minimum application value of INR 5,000 to INR 7,000. The issuer shall invite applications in multiples of the minimum application value. The minimum sum payable on application shall not be less than 25 per cent of the issue price. In case of an offer for sale, the issue price payable for each specified security shall be brought in at the time of application. The allotment of specified securities to applicants other than anchor investors shall be within the specified investor categories and on a proportionate basis and the number of securities allotted shall be rounded off to the nearest integer, subject to the minimum allotment being equal to the minimum application size, as determined and disclosed by the issuer.

4.2.9 Conditions for Convertible Debt Instruments

In addition to the relevant requirements as applicable to equity issues, an issuer making a public issue or rights issue of convertible debt instruments shall comply with the following major conditions:

Convertible securities are those that may be converted into equity shares of the issuer as per specified terms and conditions.

(a) Obtain credit rating from one or more credit rating agencies;
(b) Appoint one or more debenture trustees;
(c) Create debenture redemption reserve;
(d) Ensure in case the issuer proposes to create a charge or security on its assets in respect of secured convertible debt instruments that:

 (i) such assets are sufficient to discharge the principal amount at all times,
 (ii) such assets are free from any encumbrance.

The non-convertible portion of partly convertible debt instruments issued by a listed company, the value of which exceeds INR 5 million, may be rolled over without change in the interest rate subject to the following conditions:

(a) Seventy-five per cent of the holders of the convertible debt instruments of the issuer have, through a resolution, approved the rollover through postal ballot;
(b) The issuer has undertaken to redeem the non-convertible portion of the partly convertible debt instruments of all the holders of the convertible debt instruments who have not agreed to the resolution;
(c) Credit rating has been obtained from at least one credit rating agency within a period of six months prior to the due date of redemption and has been communicated to the holders of the convertible debt instruments before the rollover.

An issuer shall not convert its optionally convertible debt instruments into equity shares unless the holders of such convertible debt instruments have sent their positive consent to the issuer. The non-receipt of reply to any notice sent by the issuer for this purpose shall not be construed as consent for conversion of any convertible debt instruments. Where the value of the convertible portion of any convertible debt instruments issued by an issuer exceeds INR 5 million and the issuer has not determined the conversion price of such convertible debt instruments at the time of making the issue, the holders of such instruments shall be given the option of not converting the convertible portion into equity shares.

If one or more holders of convertible debt securities do not exercise the option to convert the instruments into equity share capital at a price determined at the general meeting of the shareholders, the issuer shall redeem that part of the instruments within one month from the last date by which the option is to be exercised, at a price that shall not be less than its face value.

In case of an initial public offer of convertible debt instruments without a prior public issue of equity shares, the promoters shall bring in a contribution of at least 20 per cent of the project cost in the form of equity shares, subject to contributing at least 20 per cent of the issue size from their own funds in the form of equity shares. The promoters' contribution in case of any issue of convertible securities shall not be at a price lower than the weighted average price of the equity shares arising out of the conversion of such securities.

No issuer shall issue convertible debt instruments for financing replenishment of funds or for providing loan to or for acquiring shares of any person who is part of the same group or who is under the same management. However, an issuer may issue fully convertible debt instruments for these purposes if the period of conversion of such debt instruments is less than 18 months from the date of issue of such debt instruments. A model of a public issue is given in Box 4.1.

__Rights__ are an option given to existing shareholders of a company to purchase additional shares of the company at a stated price on or before a stated date.

4.3 Rights Issues

Whenever a company issues additional equity capital, it has to be offered in the first instance to the existing shareholders on a pro-rata basis as per Section 81 of the Companies Act, 1956. The shareholders may forfeit this right partially or fully by a special resolution. This will enable the company to issue additional capital to the public, or it can pass a simple resolution and take permission of the central government.

Box 4.1 Pipavav Shipyard Limited: IPO Details

Issue open: September 16, 2009
Issue close: September 18, 2009
Price band: INR 55–INR 60 per equity share
Minimum bid size: 110 equity shares
Issue size: 85,450,225 equity shares of INR 10 (including anchor investor portion up to 15,273,040 equity shares)
Issue size (INR million): 4699.8–5127
Face value: INR 10 per equity share
Issue type: 100 per cent book built issue IPO
Listing at: BSE, NSE
Maximum subscription amount for retail investor: INR 100,000
Book running lead managers: JM Financial Consultants Private Limited, Citigroup Global Markets India Private Limited, Enam Securities Private Limited and SBI Capital Markets Limited.

Pipavav Shipyard Limited

Promoted by SKL Infrastructure Limited, Grevek Investments and Finance Pvt Limited and Punj Lloyd Limited, Pipavav Shipyard Limited was incorporated in 1997. It is currently constructing the Pipavav Shipyard, located on the west coast of India adjacent to major sea lanes between the Persian Gulf and Asia. On completion of construction, the Pipavav Shipyard will be capable of ship construction and repairs for a range of vessels of different sizes and types, as well as fabrication and construction of products such as offshore platforms, rigs, jackets and vessels (but excluding subsea pipelines) for oil and gas companies.

The issue is for less than 25 per cent of the post-issue share capital of the company, and at least 60 per cent of the net issue shall be allotted to qualified institutional buyers (QIBs), out of which 5 per cent shall be available for allocation on a proportionate basis to mutual funds only and the remainder shall be available for allocation on a proportional basis to all QIBs, including mutual funds, subject to valid bids being received at or above the issue price. The QIB portion includes the anchor investor and the company may consider participation by anchor investors in the net issue for up to 15,273,040 equity shares in accordance with the SEBI regulations. Further, up to 600,000 equity shares shall be available for allocation on a proportionate basis to employees, subject to valid bids being received at or above the issue price.

Pipavav Shipyard Limited IPO Grading/Rating

Credit Analysis & Research Limited (CARE) has assigned an IPO Grade 3 to the Pipavav Shipyard Limited IPO. This means that as per CARE, the company has average fundamentals. CARE assigns IPO grading on a scale of 5 to 1, with Grade 5 indicating strong fundamentals and Grade 1 indicating poor fundamentals.

Thus, when a company wishes to raise capital by issuing additional securities, it shall give the existing shareholders the opportunity, ahead of the general public, to buy the new issue in the proportion of the number of shares already owned by them. That privilege, extended to the existing equity shareholders, is called a **right**. This pre-emptive right entitles the existing shareholders to maintain their share of ownership in the company. The additional shares are normally offered below the current market price and rights have to be exercised within a relatively short period. The rights can be exercised by the shareholders or they can be allowed to expire, or they can be sold in the market. When the rights are not exercised or sold, such shares shall be allotted to shareholders who have applied for additional shares on a pro-rata basis. This method of raising finance is similar to a private placement and it primarily reduces the cost of financing substantially. Existing shareholders are already familiar with the company and therefore have basic information about the issuer company. However, they are updated about the major developments in the company through letters of offer.

No issuer shall make a rights issue of equity shares if it has outstanding fully or partly convertible debt instruments at the time of making the rights issue, unless it has made a reservation of equity shares of the same class in favour of the holders of such outstanding convertible debt instruments in proportion to the convertible part. The equity shares reserved for the holders of fully or partially convertible debt instruments shall be issued at the time of conversion of such convertible debt instruments on the same terms as the shares offered in the rights issue.

The abridged letter of offer, along with the application, shall be dispatched to all the existing shareholders at least three days before the date of opening of the issue. The shareholders who have not received the application form may apply in writing on plain paper, along with the requisite application money. Where any shareholder makes an application on the application form as well as on plain paper, the application is liable to be rejected at the option of the issuer. The issue price shall be decided before determining the record date, which shall be determined in consultation with the designated stock exchange. A rights issue shall be open for subscription for a minimum period of 15 days and a maximum period of 30 days.

4.4 Bonus Issues

> ***Bonus shares*** *are equity shares issued by a company to its existing shareholders free of cost.*

Bonus shares are equity shares issued by a company free of cost to its existing shareholders. No new funds are raised with a bonus issue. The number of shares for each shareholder depends on the number of shares the shareholder already owns and the ratio of bonus shares decided by the company. If an investor holds 100 shares of a company and a 1:1 bonus offer is declared, the investor would get 100 free bonus shares. So the total shareholding of the investor in the company will now be 200 instead of 100 at no cost to the investor. Thus, bonus issues increase the number of outstanding shares of the company. If the profits remain the same, the earnings per share (EPS) will decline as the earnings of the company will have to be divided by the number of shares outstanding. Thus, the stock price will decrease proportionately to the number of new shares. But in reality, this may not happen due to other market forces.

Bonus shares are issued by the company by capitalizing its free reserves that is, converting the reserves into share capital. It means that the net worth of the company does not increase with the issue of bonus shares as the bonus issue is made by merely transferring funds from reserves and surplus account to the paid-up share capital account of the company. For a shareholder, the total number of shares owned by him increases but the proportion of his shareholdings in the total shares outstanding of the company remains constant. In other words, there is no dilution of ownership of the company as the bonus shares are issued to the shareholders in proportion to their existing shareholding in the company. The value of investment of a shareholder also remains the same, though the number of shares owned by him increases after the bonus issue.

It may be noted that free reserves are built by ploughing back the profits over the years. In other words, free reserves are the accumulated undistributed profits. So the bonus shares are issued out of the funds of the shareholders. Moreover, the distribution of stock dividend (bonus shares) does not entail the release of assets of the company. The company and the shareholders both benefit by bonus issues.

4.4.1 Benefits to Shareholders

1. The main advantage of bonus issues is that the shareholders would get more cash dividend in future if the company maintains the pre-bonus dividend rate. But this depends on the profit-earning capacity of the company. If the earnings of the company do not increase in future, the rate of dividend in future will be lower because earnings per share of the stock will drop in proportion to the new issue and consequently the dividend per share will come down. As a result, the market price of the shares will come down because the market price adjusts according to the number of bonus shares issued. On the other hand, if the company is able to maintain the current rate of dividend even after the bonus issue, the shares of the company would be quoted at a much higher price. If the total cash dividend to be received by a shareholder after a bonus issue is protected or it marginally increases, the market price of the shares may not be affected.
2. Generally, a company announces bonus issue when its share price goes up to a respectable level and the management sees bright prospects for profitability of the company. Thus, a bonus issue is a signal that the company will have increasing profits and dividends to service its larger equity in the future. This creates a positive sentiment in the market, leading to better market prices for the shareholders of the company.

4.4.2 Benefits to the Company

1. A company that goes in for a bonus issue can conserve cash. The bonus issue allows the company to declare dividend on equity shares without using up the cash. The cash thus conserved may be used to finance profitable investment opportunities or increase its liquidity position.
2. When a company faces a stringent cash difficulty (liquidity crunch), it cannot distribute dividend in cash. Further, the company may also face certain restrictions, especially from its creditors to pay dividend in cash. In such cases, the only way to satisfy the shareholders or to maintain the confidence of the shareholders is to issue bonus shares.
3. A company may issue bonus shares to reduce the market price of its shares and thereby increase its shareholder base. The lower market price may attract even small investors as the shares will be affordable to the small investors. Thus, bonus issues could enable wider distribution of shareholdings of the company. This will also increase trading activity in the shares of the company, resulting in a better value for the shareholders.

Notwithstanding the benefits both for the company as well as the shareholders, bonus issues are also prone to misuse by the company promoters. They may use the bonus issue as a speculative tool to earn higher profits for themselves in the short run. If the company fails to earn increasing profits after the bonus issue, the market price of the share may show a downward trend, which may affect the reputation and goodwill of the company. All these may become detrimental to the interests of the shareholders.

4.4.3 Legal Framework

The issue of bonus shares is governed by the relevant provisions in the Companies Act, 1956, and the guidelines issued by SEBI from time to time. SEBI has issued guidelines for bonus issues, which are contained in Chapter XV of the SEBI (Disclosure and Investor Protection) Guidelines, 2000. A company issuing bonus shares should ensure that the issue is in conformity with these guidelines. The salient features of these guidelines are as follows.

1. No issuer shall make a bonus issue of equity shares if it has outstanding fully or partly convertible debt instruments at the time of making the bonus issue, unless it has reserved equity shares of the same class in favour of the holders of such outstanding convertible debt instruments in proportion to the convertible part.
2. The equity shares reserved for the holders of fully or partly convertible debt instruments shall be issued at the time of conversion of such convertible debt instruments on the same terms or the same proportion on which the bonus shares were issued.
3. The bonus issue shall be made out of the free reserves built out of the genuine profits or securities premium collected only in cash.

4. The reserves created by the revaluation of the fixed assets shall not be capitalized for the purpose of issuing bonus shares.
5. The bonus shares shall not be issued in lieu of dividend.
6. An issuer announcing a bonus issue after the approval of its board of directors and not requiring shareholders' approval for capitalization of profits or reserves for making the bonus issue shall implement the bonus issue within 15 days from the date of approval of the issue by its board of directors.
7. Where the issuer is required to seek the shareholders' approval for capitalization of profits or reserves for making the bonus issue, the bonus issue shall be implemented within two months from the date of meeting of its board of directors wherein the decision to announce the bonus issue was taken subject to the shareholders' approval.
8. Once the decision to make a bonus issue is announced, the issue cannot be withdrawn.
9. Bonus shares can be issued by a company only if the articles of association of the company authorize a bonus issue. Where there is no provision in this regard in the articles, they must be amended by passing a special resolution at the general body meeting of the company.
10. If the subscribed and paid-up capital of the company exceeds the authorized capital consequent on the issue of bonus shares, a resolution shall be passed by the company at its general meeting for increasing its authorised share capital. The authorized capital can be increased only by an amendment to the capital clause of the memorandum of association.
11. If the company has availed itself of any loan from the financial institutions, prior permission is to be obtained from such institutions for issue of bonus shares.
12. If the company is listed on the stock exchange, the stock exchange must be informed of the decision of the board to issue bonus shares immediately after the board meeting.
13. Where the bonus shares are to be issued to non-resident members, prior consent of the Reserve Bank of India should be obtained.

4.5 Indian Depository Receipts (IDRs)

In order to enable foreign companies to directly access the Indian capital market, **Indian Depository Receipts (IDRs)** were introduced on the lines of global depository receipts (GDRs) and American depository receipts (ADRs) in 2004. Initially, the norms for companies seeking to issue IDRs were stringent. But over time, the norms have been relaxed. As per the latest regulations of SEBI, a company making an issue of IDR shall satisfy the following conditions:

***Indian depository receipts (IDRs)** are DRs issued by a foreign company in Indian currency.*

(a) The issuing company is listed in its home country;
(b) The issuing company is not prohibited from issuing securities by any regulatory body; and
(c) The issuing company has a track record of compliance with securities market regulations in its home country,

An issue of IDR shall be subject to the following conditions:

(a) The issue size shall not be less than INR 500 million;
(b) The procedure to be followed by each class of applicants for applying shall be mentioned in the prospectus;
(c) The minimum application amount shall be INR 20,000
(d) At least 50 per cent of the IDR issued shall be allotted to qualified institutional buyers on a proportionate basis and the balance 50 per cent may be allocated among the categories of non-institutional investors and retail individual investors including employees at the discretion of the issuer, and the manner of allocation shall be disclosed in the prospectus.

IDRs shall not be automatically fungible into underlying equity shares of the issuing company. The issuing company shall enter into an agreement with a merchant banker. Through a merchant banker, the issuing company shall file a draft prospectus with SEBI. The stock exchange where the IDRs are proposed to be listed, along with the post-issue lead merchant bankers and registrars to the issue, shall ensure that the basis of allotment is finalized in a fair and proper manner in accordance with the allotment procedure.

4.6 Preferential Issues

***Preferential issues** entail allotment of securities to a select group of people on a private placement basis.*

There are many methods of raising capital by companies and preferential issue is one of them. **Preferential issue** refers to the issue of equity shares/fully convertible debentures (FCDs)/partly convertible debentures (PCDs) or any other security which would be converted into or exchanged with equity shares at a later date, by the listed companies to any select group of persons U/S 81 (1A) of the Companies Act, 1956, (in the United States under Rule 144A of the U.S. Securities Act) on a private placement basis. The select set of people could be promoters, their friends and relatives, or institutional investors. Retail investors are not invited to participate in such issues.

The main advantage of raising funds through a preferential issue is that it helps save costs and time compared to a public issue. Further, if the company is not doing well at that point of time but requires funds, then retail investors may not want to participate in such an issue. Even in such instances, some institutions could view the company's troubles as temporary and feel that an injection of capital could help it out of the trough. In fact, a company needs such investors in times when market sentiment is weak and a public issue might fail.

The promoters use preferential allotments to increase their stake in their companies. However, there are some promoters who misuse this facility by initially selling their existing holdings at a higher price in the secondary market and then build up their stakes through preferential allotment at a lower price. In other words, the promoters may enrich themselves in an unfair manner to the detriment of the company and smaller shareholders. The merits and demerits of preferential issues are discussed in greater detail in Section 5.3.1, Chapter 5. In order to prevent unfair practices, SEBI has framed certain guidelines, which are described in the following paragraphs.

The issuer shall not make a preferential issue of specified securities to any person who has sold any equity shares of the issuer during the six months preceding the relevant date. However, in respect of the preferential issue of equity shares and compulsorily convertible debt instruments, whether fully or partly, SEBI may grant relaxation from the requirement.

The specified securities allotted on a preferential basis to a promoter or promoter group and the equity shares allotted pursuant to the exercise of options attached to warrants issued on a preferential basis to the promoter or promoter group shall be locked in for a period of three years from the date of allotment of the specified securities or equity shares allotted pursuant, as the case may be, to the exercise of the option attached to the warrant. However, not more than 20 per cent of the total capital of the issuer shall be locked in for three years from the date of allotment. Further, equity shares allotted in excess of 20 per cent shall be locked in for one year from the date of their allotment pursuant to exercise of options or otherwise, as the case may be. The specified securities allotted on a preferential basis to persons other than the promoter and promoter group and the equity shares allotted pursuant to the exercise of options attached to warrants issued on a preferential basis to such persons shall be locked in for a period of one year from the date of their allotment. The lock-in of equity shares allotted pursuant to conversion of convertible securities other than warrants issued on a preferential basis shall be reduced to the extent by which the convertible securities have already been locked in. The entire pre-preferential allotment shareholding of the allottees, if any, shall be locked in from the relevant date up to a period of six months from the date of preferential allotment.

4.7 Qualified Institutional Placement (QIP)

***Qualified institutional placement (QIP)** refers to the allotment of securities by a company to select institutional investors on a preferential basis.*

Qualified institutional placement (QIP) refers to the allotment of securities by a company to select institutional investors on a preferential basis. A listed issuer may make a qualified institutions placement if it satisfies the following conditions:

(a) A special resolution approving the qualified institutions placement is passed by its shareholders,

(b) The equity shares of the same class, which are proposed to be allotted through QIP or pursuant to conversion or exchange of eligible securities offered through QIP, are listed on a recognized stock exchange with nationwide trading terminals for a period of at least one year prior to the date of issuance of notice to its shareholders for convening the meeting to pass the special resolution,

(c) It is in compliance with the requirement of minimum public shareholding specified in the listing agreement with the stock exchange.

Allotment under QIP shall be made subject to the following conditions:

(a) A minimum of 10 per cent eligible securities shall be allotted to mutual funds. If the mutual funds do not subscribe to the said minimum percentage or any part thereof, such a minimum portion or a part thereof may be allotted to other qualified institutional buyers.

(b) No allotment shall be made, either directly or indirectly, to any qualified institutional buyer who is a promoter, or to any person related to promoters of the issuer company.

In qualified institutional placement of non-convertible debt instruments along with warrants, an investor can subscribe to the combined offering of non-convertible debt instruments with warrants or to the individual securities, that is, either non-convertible debt instruments or warrants.

The minimum number of allottees for each placement of eligible securities made under QIP shall not be less than:

(a) Two, where the issue size is less than or equal to INR 2,500 million;

(b) Five, where the issue size is greater than INR 2,500 million.

No single allottee shall be allotted more than 50 per cent of the issue size. The qualified institutional buyers belonging to the same group or who are under the same control shall be deemed to be a single allottee. The aggregate of the proposed QIP and all previous QIPs made by the issuer in the same financial year shall not exceed five times the net worth of the issuer as per the audited balance sheet of the previous financial year. The tenure of the convertible or exchangeable securities issued through QIP shall not exceed 60 months from the date of allotment.

4.8 Green Shoe Option

*The **green shoe option** refers to the option of allocating shares in excess of the shares included in the public issue to stabilize the post-listing price.*

The **green shoe option** is an option of allocating shares in excess of the shares included in the public issue and operating a post-listing price stabilizing mechanism in accordance with certain guidelines. A company making a public issue of equity shares may avail itself of the green shoe option and, as per SEBI regulations, it can appoint one of the merchant bankers or book runners as the stabilizing agent who will be responsible for the price stabilization process. The stabilizing agent shall enter into an agreement with the issuer company prior to the filing of the offer document with SEBI. The agreement contains all the terms and conditions including fees charged or the expenses to be incurred by the stabilizing agent for this purpose. The stabilizing agent shall also enter into an agreement with the promoter(s) or pre-issue shareholders who will lend their shares, specifying the maximum number of shares that may be borrowed from the promoters or the shareholders, which shall not be in excess of 15 per cent of the total issue size. The details of the agreements shall be disclosed in the prospectus.

In case of an initial public offer by an unlisted company, the promoters and pre-issue shareholders, and in case of a public issue by a listed company, the promoters and pre-issue shareholders holding more than 5 per cent shares, may lend the shares. The lead manager or lead book runner in consultation with the stabilizing agent shall determine the number of shares to be over-allotted with the public issue, subject to the maximum number specified earlier. The allocation of these shares shall be on a pro rata basis for all the applicants. Thus, *over-allotment* refers to an allotment of shares in excess of the size of a public issue, made by the stabilizing agent out of the shares borrowed from the promoters or the pre-issue shareholders or both.

The stabilizing agent shall borrow shares (in dematerialized form only) from the promoters or the pre-issue shareholders or both, to the extent of the proposed over-allotment. The stabilization mechanism shall be available for the period disclosed by the company in the prospectus, which shall not exceed 30 days from the date when trading permission was given by the stock exchange(s).

The stabilizing agent shall open a special account with a bank and a special account for securities with a depository participant. The money received from the applicants against the over-allotment in the green shoe option shall be kept in the special bank account and be used for the purpose of buying shares from the market during the stabilization period. The shares bought from the market by the stabilizing agent, if any, during the stabilization period shall be credited to the special demat account. The shares bought from the market and lying in the special demat account shall be returned to the promoters immediately, in any case not later than two working days after the close of the stabilization period.

As it is the responsibility of the stabilizing agent to stabilize the post-listing price of the shares, the stabilizing agent determines the timing of buying the shares, the quantity to be bought and the price at which the shares are to be bought.

On the expiry of the stabilization period, if the stabilizing agent does not buy shares to the extent of the shares over-allotted from the market, the issuer company shall allot new shares to the extent of the shortfall in a dematerialized form to the special demat account within five days of the closure of the stabilization period. These shares shall be returned to the promoters by the stabilizing agent in lieu of the shares borrowed from them and the special demat account shall be closed after that. The company shall make a final listing application in respect of these shares to all the stock exchanges where the shares allotted in the public issue are listed.

The stabilizing agent shall remit an amount (equal to further shares allotted by the issuer to the demat account as multiplied by the issue price) to the issuer company from the special bank account. The amount left in this account, if any, after this remittance and deduction of expenses incurred by the stabilizing agent for the stabilization mechanism shall be transferred to the investor protection fund of the stock exchanges where the shares of the issuer company are listed.

4.9 Sweat Equity

Sweat equity shares *are shares issued by a company to a select group of its employees and promoters on very favourable terms in recognition of their services to the company.*

A company may issue equity shares to its employees and promoters on very favourable terms in recognition of their services to the company. Such equity shares are known as sweat equity. According to the Companies Act, 1956, **sweat equity shares** are equity shares issued by a company to its employees or directors at a discount or for considerations other than cash for providing knowhow or making available rights in the nature of intellectual property rights or value additions, by whatever name it is called. In order to avoid the misuse of the provisions of the Companies Act, 1956, and to protect the interests of all the stakeholders of the company, SEBI issued certain regulations in this regard.

4.9.1 SEBI (Issue of Sweat Equity) Regulations, 2002

SEBI issued certain regulations to govern the issue of sweat equity shares. These regulations are called the SEBI (Issue of Sweat Equity) Regulations, 2002. The highlights of these regulations are as follows:

A listed company can issue sweat equity shares to its employees and directors by passing a special resolution under clause (a) of sub-section (1) of Section 79A of the Companies Act, 1956. The explanatory statement to the notice and the resolution proposed to be passed in the general meeting for approving the issuance of the sweat equity shall contain information regarding the total number of shares to be issued as sweat equity, the current market price of the shares, the value of the intellectual property rights or technical knowhow or other value additions to be received from the employee or director along with the valuation report/basis of valuation, the consideration to be paid for the sweat equity, the names of the employees or directors or promoters to whom the sweat equity shares shall be issued and their relationship with the company and the price at which the sweat equity shall be issued.

The regulations state that the price of sweat equity shares shall not be less than the higher of: (i) the average of the weekly high and low of the closing prices of the related equity shares during the last six months preceding the relevant date, or (ii) the average of the weekly high and low of the closing prices of the related equity shares during the two weeks preceding the relevant date. The relevant date here is 30 days prior to the date on which the meeting of the general body of the shareholders is convened.

The amount of sweat equity shares issued shall be treated as part of the managerial remuneration for the purposes of Sections 198, 309, 310, 311 and 387 of the Companies Act, 1956, if the following conditions are fulfilled:

(i) The sweat equity shares are issued to any director or manager; and
(ii) They are issued for non-cash consideration, which does not take the form of an asset that can be carried to the balance sheet of the company in accordance with the relevant accounting standards.

The sweat equity shares shall be locked in for a period of three years from the date of their allotment. If a company makes a public issue after it has issued sweat equity, the SEBI Regulations on Public Issues in terms of lock-in and computation of promoters' contribution shall apply.

The regulations have also prescribed the accounting treatment of the issue of sweat equity shares, action against intermediaries, penalties and procedure and the powers of SEBI in this regard, among other things.

4.9.2 Unlisted Companies (Issue of Sweat Equity Shares) Rules, 2003

SEBI issued certain rules for unlisted companies with regard to issue of sweat equity shares. According to these rules, a company shall obtain the approval of shareholders by way of a separate resolution in the general body meeting in case of grant of shares to identified employees and promoters during any one year, equal to or exceeding 1 per cent of the issued capital of the company at the time of grant of the sweat equity shares.

A company shall not issue sweat equity shares for more than 15 per cent of the total paid-up equity share capital in a year or shares of the value of INR 5 crore, whichever is higher, except with the prior approval of the central government. The price of sweat equity shares to be issued to employees and directors shall be on a fair price calculated by an independent valuer.

The amount of sweat equity shares issued shall be treated as part of the managerial remuneration for the purposes of Sections 198, 309, 310, 311 and 387 of the Companies Act, 1956, if the following conditions are fulfilled:

(i) The sweat equity shares are issued to any director or manager

(ii) They are issued on non-cash considerations, which do not take the form of assets that can be carried to the balance sheet of the company in accordance with the relevant accounting standards.

Sweat equity shares issued to employees or directors shall be locked in for a period of three years from the date of allotment.

Where a company proposes to issue sweat equity shares for considerations other than cash, it shall comply with the following major requirements:

(i) The valuation of the intellectual property or of the knowhow provided or other value addition to the consideration for which sweat equity capital is issued shall be carried out by a valuer;

(ii) The valuer shall consult such experts as he may deem fit with regard to the nature of the industry and property or the value addition;

(iii) The valuer shall submit a valuation report to the company giving the justification for the valuation;

(iv) The company shall give the justification for the issue of the sweat shares for considerations other than cash, which shall form part of the notice sent for the general body meeting.

The rules have also prescribed the disclosure in the director's report, certificate from auditors and accounting policies.

4.10 SEBI (Employee Stock Option Scheme and Employee Stock Purchase Scheme) Guidelines, 1999 (Updated till September 2009)

*The **employee stock option scheme** envisages a contract between a company and its employees that gives the employees the right to buy a specific number of the company's shares at a fixed price within a certain period of time. The **employee stock purchase scheme** allows employees to purchase employer's equity shares, usually at a discount on its market price.*

Employee stock option schemes and employee stock purchase schemes have gained popularity as incentive schemes aimed at improving the performance of employees in an organization. They are also expected to enhance employee motivation. Many companies use such incentive plans or schemes to compensate, retain and attract employees. These schemes are particularly useful in attracting talented, highly valued professionals or scarce skills to the company. It is expected that such schemes will foster employee commitment and a feeling of ownership and instill a sense of belonging to the company.

The **employee stock option scheme** envisages a contract between a company and its employees that gives the employees the right to buy a specific number of the company's shares at a fixed price within a certain period of time. Employees who are granted stock options hope to profit by exercising their options at a price which is lower than the current market price. The employee stock option scheme is different from the *employee stock ownership plan*, which is a retirement plan. Here is an example to explain the employee stock option scheme. A company grants its employees the option to purchase 500 shares of the company's stock at the current market price of INR 1,500. This price is known as the *grant price*. The employee can exercise his option on or before, say, June 30, 2015. The employees may also be allowed to exercise their option when the company's stock reaches a certain price. Suppose the price of the stock increases to INR 1,800.

The employee may exercise his option to buy 500 shares at INR 1,500 and sell the stock at the current market price of INR 1,800. Companies sometimes revalue the price at which the options can be exercised. This may happen, for example, when a company's stock price has fallen below the original exercise price. Companies revalue the exercise price as a way to retain their employees. A model of the employee stock option scheme is presented in Appendix 4.2.

SEBI has issued certain guidelines for companies offering equity shares to their employees. According to the guidelines, an employee is defined as a permanent employee of the company working in India or outside India; or a director of the company, whether whole-time director or not; or a permanent employee or director of a subsidiary company or holding company in India or outside India. SEBI has also prescribed certain conditions for the director nominated by an organization as its representative on the board of directors of the company to be eligible to participate in the ESOS of the company. An employee who is a promoter or belongs to the promoter group shall not be eligible to participate in the ESOS. A director who either by himself or through his relative or through any body corporate directly or indirectly holds more than 10 per cent of the outstanding equity shares of the company shall not be eligible to participate in the ESOS. A promoter is defined as a person or persons who are in overall control of the company; or the person or persons who are instrumental in the formation of the company or programme pursuant to which the shares were offered to the public; or the person or persons named in the offer document as promoter(s). Where a promoter of a company is a body corporate, the promoters of that body corporate shall also be deemed to be promoters of the company.

There are two schemes in this regard: the ESOS, under which a company grants employees stock options, and the ESPS, under which a company offers shares to its employees as part of its public issue or otherwise. The employee stock option is defined as the option given to whole-time directors, officers or employees of a company which gives such directors, officers or employees the benefit or right to purchase or subscribe at a future date the securities offered by the company at a predetermined price.

No ESOS shall be offered unless the company constitutes a compensation committee for administration and superintendence of the ESOS. The compensation committee shall be a committee of the board of directors consisting of a majority of independent directors. Besides other responsibilities, the committee shall frame suitable policies and systems to ensure there is no violation of SEBI regulations. Before offering ESOS, the company must get the approval of its shareholders in the form of a special resolution at the general body meeting. The explanatory statement to the notice and the resolution proposed to be passed in the general body meeting for the ESOS should contain information such as the total number of options to be granted, identification of the classes of employees entitled to participate in the ESOS, the maximum period within which the options shall be vested, exercise price or pricing formula, exercise period and process of exercise, the appraisal process for determining the eligibility of employees for the ESOS, the maximum number of options to be issued per employee and in aggregate, the method the company shall use to value its options, whether fair value or intrinsic value, and requirements of vesting and the period of vesting.

Vesting is defined in this regard as the process by which an employee is given the right to apply for shares of the company against the option granted to him in pursuance of the ESOS. The *vesting period* is the period during which the vesting of the option granted to the employee in pursuance of the ESOS takes place. *Intrinsic value* is the excess of the market price of the share under the ESOS over the exercise price of the option.

The companies granting options to their employees pursuant to the ESOS will have the freedom to determine the exercise price subject to accounting policies as specified in Schedule-I. There shall be a minimum period of one year between the grant of options and vesting of options. The company shall have the freedom to specify the lock-in period for the shares issued pursuant to the exercise of the option. However, the employee will not have the right to receive any dividend or to vote or in any manner enjoy the benefits of a shareholder in respect of the option granted to him till the shares are issued on the exercise of the option.

The amount payable by the employee, if any, at the time of grant of the option may be forfeited by the company if the option is not exercised by the employee within the exercise period or the amount may be refunded to the employee if the option is not vested due to non-fulfilment of conditions relating to vesting of the option as per the ESOS.

Options granted to an employee shall not be transferable to any person and no person other than that employee shall be entitled to exercise the option. Further, the option granted to the employee shall not be pledged, hypothecated, mortgaged or otherwise alienated in any other manner.

The director's report shall contain all the particulars with regard to the ESOS If any options granted to employees in pursuance of pre-IPO ESOS are outstanding at the time of IPO, the IPO document of the company shall disclose all the information specified.

The ESPS is different in operation, though its objectives are the same as that of the ESOP. In the **employee stock purchase scheme**, the employees use their own funds to purchase their employer's stock, usually at a discount on its market price. The ESPS may involve regular payroll deductions for employees electing to participate. A model of an ESPS is presented in Appendix 4.3.

SEBI has prescribed the following guidelines with regard to the employee stock purchase scheme. According to the guidelines, an employee who is a promoter or belongs to the promoter group and a director who either by himself or through his relatives or through any body corporate directly or indirectly holds more than 10 per cent of the outstanding equity shares of the company shall not be eligible to participate in the ESPS.

No company can offer the ESPS to its employees unless the shareholders of the company approve it by passing a special resolution at the meeting of the general body of the shareholders. The explanatory statement to the notice and the resolution proposed to be passed by the shareholders shall contain all the relevant information about the offer. Approval of shareholders by way of a separate resolution at the general meeting shall be obtained by the company in case of allotment of shares to employees of a subsidiary or holding company and to employees, during any one year, equal to or exceeding 1 per cent of the issued capital of the company at the time of allotment of shares.

The company shall have the freedom to determine the price of the shares to be issued under an ESPS, provided it conforms to the accounting policies. The shares issued under an ESPS shall be locked in for a minimum period of one year from the date of allotment. However, if the ESPS is part of a public issue and the shares are issued to employees at the same price as in the public issue, the shares issued to employees pursuant to the ESPS shall not be subject to any lock-in. The shares issued under the ESOS/ESPS to promoters prior to the IPO shall be subject to lock-in as per the provisions of SEBI (Disclosure and Investor Protection) Guidelines.

The director's report or annexure thereto shall contain the various details of the ESPS. It should also contain the employee-wise details of the shares issued to senior managerial personnel, any other employee who is issued shares in any one year amounting to 5 per cent or more shares issued during that year, and identified employees who were issued shares during any one year equal to or exceeding 1 per cent of the issued capital of the company at the time of issuance. The diluted EPS pursuant to the issuance of shares under the ESPS and consideration received against the issuance of shares under the ESPS should also form part of the director's report.

The shares issued pursuant to an ESOS/ESPS shall be listed immediately upon exercise in any recognized stock exchange where the securities of the company are listed. No listed company shall make any fresh grant of options under any ESOS framed prior to its IPO and prior to the listing of its equity shares unless such a pre-IPO scheme is in conformity with these guidelines and the pre-IPO scheme is ratified by its shareholders in the general meeting subsequent to the IPO. For listing of shares issued pursuant to the ESOS or ESPS, the company shall make an application to the Central Listing Authority as per SEBI Regulations and obtain the in-principle approval from stock exchanges where it proposes to list the said shares. Box 4.2 gives examples of ESOP offers by companies.

Box 4.2 Examples of ESOPs

ESOPs are used by companies to reward employees for their performance. As the price of ESOPs is decided by the company, the employees are at liberty to exercise the options granted to them.

The value of ESOPs depends on how the stock market performs and how the underlying stocks perform in the market. For example, when the stock market fell from a high of 21,000 in January 2008 to a low of 8,047 in March 2009, employees of several companies found that their ESOPs had "gone underwater", a term used when the option price falls below the market price, making the option useless for the employee. More specifically, Reliance Industries Limited (RIL) issued ESOPs to some of its employees at the rate of INR 1,250 per share in 2008. After a few months (in October 2008), the share price dropped to a low of INR 930. However, in September 2009 it crossed the INR 2,100 mark. The employees of HDFC Bank too were allotted ESOPs under ESOS X, ESOS XI and ESOS XII. Options were offered to employees at INR 1,098.70. Here too the stock price slipped to a low of INR 823 in November 2008 but rose above INR 1,495 in September 2009. Other organizations like IDFC, Yes Bank, and Motilal Oswal Financial Services offer this benefit too. The employees of these companies have had immense profits from ESOPs following the rally in the stock markets.

4.11 Euro Issues

***Euro issues** are capital issues priced in foreign currency and offered to overseas investors.*

In the early 1990s, a series of events and incidents led to the depletion of India's foreign exchange reserves. International credit rating agencies downgraded India's credit rating to a level below "investment grade". The financial agencies were not enthusiastic in meeting Indian companies' long-term foreign currency requirements. Therefore, companies started exploring alternative sources of foreign currency funds, leading to Indian euro issues. **Euro issues** are capital issues priced in foreign currency and offered to overseas investors. The first euro issue was RIL's GDR issue of USD 150 million in May 1992. Euro-issues may take the form of GDRs, ADRs or euro-convertible bonds.

A depository receipt is basically a negotiable certificate, denominated mostly in U.S. dollars, that represents a non-U.S. company's publicly traded local currency equity shares. Although a DR can also represent a debt instrument, in reality it rarely does. DRs are created when the equity shares (denominated in local currency) are delivered to the depository's local custodian bank against which the depository bank issues DRs in U.S. dollars. These DRs may trade freely in the overseas financial markets like any other dollar-denominated security. Indian issues of DRs have taken the form of GDRs to reflect the fact that they are marketed globally rather than in a specific country or market. If the DRs are denominated in U.S. dollars and marketed in the United States only, then the DRs may take the form of ADRs.

Foreign currency convertible bonds (FCCBs) are low-yield bonds, usually with tenure of five years. At maturity, the bondholders can either redeem their principal or convert the bonds into equity at a predetermined exchange rate. He may also have the option to retain it as a bond. Depending on the agreement, the bondholders can even convert the bonds into equity midway through the life of the FCCBs. Thus, FCCBs offer investors the option of conversion into equity and the benefit of capital appreciation on its sale. The investor's downside is protected as he continues to earn a fixed interest on the bonds. For companies, there is an added attraction of a delayed dilution of controlling interest at least till such time as the loans are converted into equity. Companies with low-debt equity ratios and large foreign exchange earnings potential typically opt for the FCCB route. Further, the conversion feature in the FCCB offers the issuer a lower interest cost than that of a similar non-convertible issue or borrowing. The FCCBs allow the company to avoid any current dilution in EPS that a further issuance of equity would cause while still offering a security to the investor that is traded and priced according to its underlying equity value. The FCCBs typically carry less restrictive covenants besides being easier to market. In the second half of 1993, a number of companies in India opted for the euro-convertible route. It started in July 1993 with a company called Essar Gujarat accessing the ECB market for a USD 75 million FCCB issue.

4.11.1 FCCBs and Ordinary Shares (Through DR Mechanism) Scheme, 1993

The Government of India notified the Issue of FCCBs and Ordinary Shares (Through DR Mechanism) Scheme, 1993, for facilitating the issue of FCCBs and DRs by Indian companies. The salient features of this scheme are stated in the following paragraphs:

1. A company wishing to raise capital from abroad by issuing FCCBs or equity shares through GDRs / ADRs is required to obtain prior permission from the Government of India.
2. A company seeking permission shall have a consistent track record of good performance (financial or otherwise) for a minimum period of three years, on the basis of which an approval for finalising the issue structure would be issued to the company by the government.
3. The issuing company shall deliver the securities to a domestic custodian bank which will, in terms of the agreement, instruct the overseas depository bank to issue GDRs or certificates to non-resident investors against the shares or bonds held by the domestic custodian bank.
4. A GDR may be issued for one or more underlying shares or bonds held with the domestic custodian bank.
5. The FCCBs and GDRs may be denominated in any freely convertible foreign currency. However, the shares underlying the GDRs and the shares issued upon conversion of the FCCBs shall be denominated only in Indian rupee.
6. The pricing should not be less than the higher of the following two averages.

   (a) The average of the weekly high and low of the closing prices of the related shares quoted on the stock exchange during the six months preceding the relevant date;

   (b) The average of the weekly high and low of the closing prices of the related shares quoted on a stock exchange during the two weeks preceding the relevant date.

The relevant date is the date 30 days prior to the date on which the meeting of the general body of shareholders is held in terms of Section 81 (1A) of the Companies Act, 1956, to consider the proposed issue.

7. All FCCBs shall be subject to the following maximum spreads over six months LIBOR for the respective currency in which the loan is being raised or the applicable benchmark(s), as the case may be.

Type of project	*All-in-cost*
Normal projects	150
Infrastructure	250
Long-term	300

8. The FCCBs for meeting rupee expenditure under the automatic route shall be hedged unless there is a natural hedge in the form of uncovered foreign exchange receivables, which will be ensured by authorized dealers.
9. The FCCBs exceeding USD 50 million would be permitted only for financing import of equipment and for foreign exchange needs of infrastructure projects.
10. No financial intermediary shall be allowed access to FCCBs or to provide guarantees.
11. The FCCBs pending utilization would need to be parked overseas.
12. An Indian company that is not eligible to raise funds from the Indian capital market, including a company that has been restrained from accessing the securities market by SEBI, will not be eligible to issue FCCBs and GDRs.
13. Unlisted Indian companies issuing FCCBs/GDRs shall be required to simultaneously get listed on the Indian stock exchange(s). In the case of unlisted companies, the pricing should be in accordance with the RBI notified under the Foreign Exchange Management Act, 1999.
14. Indian companies engaged in IT software and IT services are eligible to offer to their non-resident/resident permanent employees, including Indian and overseas working directors, GDRs against the issue of ordinary shares subject to the operational guidelines issued from time to time by the government.
15. Indian companies registered in India and engaged in the following sectors/areas where 80 per cent of the turnover is from these sectors/areas of the operation/business of the company in the three previous financial years are eligible to offer GDRs against the issue of ordinary shares to their non-resident/resident permanent employees (including Indian and overseas working directors) and also of their subsidiary companies, incorporated in India or abroad, subject to the eligibility conditions and operation guidelines.

    (i) Information technology and entertainment software,
    (ii) Pharmaceuticals,
    (iii) Biotechnology,
    (iv) Any other activities within the knowledge-based sector as notified by the government from time to time.

    These norms would also be available for multi-product diversified companies that do not conform to the criteria of 80 per cent turnover but having average annual export earnings of INR 1,000 million from the sectors mentioned above in the three previous financial years.

16. The GDRs may be listed on any of the overseas stock exchanges or over-the-counter exchanges or through bank entry transfer systems prevalent abroad and such receipts may be purchased, processed and freely transferable by a person who is a non-resident.
17. A non-resident holder of the GDRs may transfer those receipts or ask the overseas depository bank to redeem the receipts.
18. In the case of redemption, the overseas depository bank shall request the domestic custodian bank to get the corresponding underlying shares released in favour of the non-resident investor for being sold directly on behalf of the non-resident or being transferred in the books of account of the issuing company in the name of the non-resident.

19. The GDRs redeemed and underlying shares sold may be re-issued to the extent of such redemption and sale made in the domestic market.
20. On redemption, the cost of acquisition of the shares underlying the GDRs shall be considered as the cost on the date on which the overseas depository bank advises the domestic custodian bank for redemption.
21. The price of the ordinary shares of the issuing company prevailing in the NSE or BSE on the date of the advice of redemption shall be taken as the cost of acquisition of the underlying ordinary shares.
22. For the purposes of conversions of FCCBs, the cost of acquisition in the hands of the non-resident investors would be the conversion price determined on the basis of the price of the shares at the NSE or BSE on the date of conversion of FCCBs.

4.12 Initial Public Offers Through the Stock Exchange Online System (E-IPOs)

***E-IPOs** are public capital issues offered online.*

A company can also make a public issue of securities through the online system of a stock exchange. In such a case, the issuer company shall comply with the following requirements as per SEBI regulations.

1. For making a public issue of securities, at the first instance the company shall enter into an agreement with the merchant banker, stock exchange(s), brokers and registrars. The intermediaries shall have electronic connectivity with the stock exchange(s) through which the securities are offered under the system.
2. The company shall make an issue advertisement which, in addition to other required information, contains the date of opening and closing of the issue, the method and process of application and allotment and the details of stockbrokers.
3. When the issue is open to the public for subscription, investors may approach the brokers of the stock exchange(s) through which the securities are offered under the online system to place an order for subscribing to the securities; or the investors may directly send the application form along with the cheque/demand draft for the sum payable towards application money to the registrar to the issue, or place the order to subscribe through a stockbroker under the online system.
4. The broker shall enter the buy order in the system, on behalf of the clients, with the necessary details and give an order number/order confirmation slip to the applicant.
5. The broker may collect the full amount of the application money as margin money from the clients before he places an order on their behalf.
6. The broker shall open a separate bank account (escrow account) with the clearing house bank for primary market issues and the amount collected by the broker from his clients as margin money shall be deposited in this account.
7. While the issue is open for subscription, the broker shall at the end of each day forward the order data to the registrar to the issue.
8. On the date of closure of the issue, the final status of the order received shall be sent to the registrar/company.
9. After the closure of the issue, the designated stock exchange(s), lead manager and registrar shall finalize the basis of allocation.
10. The stock exchange(s) shall process and make allocation of securities. The details of allocation are sent to the brokers, who in turn intimate the fact of allocation to their clients/applicants.
11. The brokers shall hand over the application forms of the successful applicants to the stock exchange(s), which shall submit the same to the registrar to the issue and the issuer company.
12. On the pay-in day, the broker shall deposit the amount collected from the clients in the separate bank account opened for primary issues with the clearing house bank.
13. The clearing house bank shall debit the primary issue account of each broker and credit the amount so collected from each broker to the "issue account".
14. On payment and receipt of the sum payable on application for the amount towards minimum subscription, the company shall allot the shares to the applicants.

15. If the minimum subscription as disclosed in the prospectus is not received, the issue proceeds shall be refunded to the applicants.
16. The subscriber shall have an option to receive the security certificates or hold the securities in dematerialized form.
17. The brokers and other intermediaries engaged in the process of offering shares through the online system shall maintain the relevant records for a period of five years for inspection by SEBI.

The main advantages of the online IPO system are: (i) the investor parts with money only after the allotment, (ii) it eliminates refunds except in the case of direct applications and (iii) it reduces the time taken to process the issue.

4.13 Private Placement

*Offering shares directly to a select group of investors is known as **private placement.***

Private placement refers to the direct sale by a company of its securities to a select group of investors, usually to big investors such as banks, financial institutions, mutual funds and high net worth individuals. There is no requirement of filing a prospectus with SEBI or other authorities as the subscribers are a few sophisticated and experienced investors. The financial instruments offered in the private placement market include equity shares, preference shares and convertible and non-convertible debentures.

Companies, particularly private limited companies and closely held companies, opt for private placement of their issues and avoid public issues for the following reasons:

(i) Fear of takeover;
(ii) The public issue market is costly due to various issue expenses such as brokerage, underwriting commission, listing expenses, printing expenses, mailing expenses, legal expenses and advertising expenses; and
(iii) Public issues involve long-drawn process and, therefore, the time frame required to mobilize funds usually ranges from six months to one year.

As per the Companies Act, 1956, an offer of securities to more than 50 persons is deemed to be a public issue. In India, mostly debt securities are privately placed though there are instances of private placements of equity shares. Unlike public issues of bonds, it is not mandatory for corporate houses issuing bonds in the private placement market to obtain and disclose credit rating from an approved credit rating agency. Rating is, however, required for listing.

4.14 Bought-out Deals

*A **bought-out deal** is a deal in which the entire equity or any security issue is bought in full or in lots by an institution with the intention of offloading it later in the market.*

A company can also raise capital through bought-out deals. A **bought-out deal** is a deal in which the entire equity or any security issue is bought in full or in lots by an institution with the intention of offloading it later in the market. The bought-out deals can be undertaken in the case of equity shares, debentures and bonds. A company that chooses the bought-out deal route first approaches an institution or institutions (for example, a bank or a financial institution). The institution then appraises the proposal and a negotiated deal is reached between the company and the institution for the price and the volume and modalities of placement. Once the agreement is signed, the institution passes the consideration money to the company and in turn gets the securities duly transferred to it. Depending on the market situation, the securities will be disinvested to the public through an offer and the securities may also be listed on the stock exchange(s). Thus, the bought-out deals obviate direct retailing of securities by the company; allowing the company to save time and issue expenses. A company need not wait for months to utilize the issue proceeds as it can get the funds upfront through a bought-out deal. The credibility of the issue also increases with the involvement of a reputed bank, financial institution or a merchant banker in the deal.

4.15 Fast-track Issues

SEBI introduced fast-track issues to provide a faster and cost-effective method of raising capital by companies that are listed on a recognized stock exchange for at least three years and have an average free float market capitalization of INR 100,000 million or more. The companies should have an excellent track record in redressing investor grievances, compliance with the listing agreement and promoter group stake in dematerialized form. Fast-track issues help big companies raise capital very quickly, in addition to reducing the issue costs.

4.16 Anchor Investors

***Anchor investors** are investors who are required, as per the regulations of SEBI, to invest a minimum of INR 100 million and bring in 25 per cent of the margin on application and the remaining 75 per cent within two days of the closure of the issue.*

In June 2009, SEBI approved the concept of anchor investor who can subscribe up to 30 per cent of the quota reserved for qualified institutional buyers in an issue. **Anchor investors** are required to invest a minimum of INR 100 million and bring in 25 per cent of the margin on application and the remaining 75 per cent within two days of the closure of the issue. The lock-in period for anchor investors is 30 days. Generally, allotment of securities to anchor investors takes place through competitive bidding a day before the public issue opens. The anchor investor cannot be related to promoters, the promoter group and book-running lead managers. The main advantage for the issuer is that it can attract high-quality investors besides avoiding volatility in prices of securities on listing.

4.17 Application Supported by Blocked Amount (ASBA)

***ASBA** envisages blocking the application money in a bank account till the allotment of securities is made.*

In the process of streamlining public issues, SEBI introduced the concept of **ASBA**, according to which the applicants of public issues can block the application money in a bank account. The investor submits an ASBA physically or electronically through the Internet banking facility to the self-certified syndicate bank (SCSB) with whom the bank account to be blocked is maintained. The SCSB then blocks the application money in the bank account specified in the ASBA. The application money remains blocked in the bank account till the finalization of the basis of allotment in the issue. After finalization of allotment, the registrar to the issue sends an appropriate request to the SCSB for unblocking the relevant bank account and for transferring the requisite amount to the issuer's account. The SCSB can also unblock the account in case of withdrawal/failure of the issue. In case of a rights issue, the application money is debited from the bank account of the applicant after the receipt of instruction from the registrar. As per the SEBI regulations, the issuer shall provide the ASBA facility in all public issues made through the book-building route and also in rights issues. Note that a SCSB is a bank which offers the facility of applying through the ASBA process. A bank seeking to offer the ASBA facility shall submit a certificate to SEBI in the prescribed format.

The conditions for ASBA are as follows.

In a public issue, the applicant shall be:

(i) A resident retail individual investor;
(ii) Bidding at cut-off, with a single option as to the number of shares bid for;
(iii) Applying through blocking of funds in a bank account with the SCSBs;
(iv) Agreeing not to revise his bid;
(v) Not bidding under any of the reserved categories.

In a rights issue, the applicant shall:

(i) Hold the shares of the issuer in dematerialized form as on the record date and apply for entitlements and/or additional equity shares in dematerialized form;
(ii) Not renounce his entitlements in full or in part;
(iii) Apply through blocking of funds in a bank account with the SCSB.

4.18 Offer Documents

As per SEBI regulations, no issuer shall make a public issue or a rights issue where the aggregate value of the specified securities offered is INR 5 million or more unless a draft offer document has been filed with SEBI through a lead merchant banker at least 30 days prior to registering the prospectus, a red herring prospectus or a shelf prospectus with the registrar of companies or filing the letter of offer with the designated stock exchange, as the case may be. SEBI may specify changes or issue observations, if any, on the draft offer document within 30 days. The draft offer document filed with SEBI shall be made public for comments, if any, for a period of at least 21 days from the date of such filing by hosting it on the websites of SEBI, recognized stock exchanges where specified securities are proposed to be listed and merchant bankers associated with the issue. The lead merchant bankers shall, after expiry of the period, file with SEBI a statement giving information on the comments received by them or the issuer on the draft offer document during that period and the consequent changes, if any, to be made in the draft offer document.

Offer document refers to the prospectus in the case of a public issue or offer for sale and letter of offer in the case of a rights issue, which is filed with the registrar of companies and stock exchanges. An offer document covers all the relevant information to help an investor to make his/her investment decision.

For fast-track issues, filing of the offer document is not mandatory if the issuer satisfies the following conditions.

(a) The equity shares of the issuer have been listed on any recognized stock exchange having nationwide trading terminals for a period of at least three years immediately preceding the reference date;

(b) The average market capitalization of public shareholding of the issuer is at least INR 100,000 million;

(c) The annualized trading turnover of the equity shares of the issuer during the six calendar months immediately preceding the month of the reference date has been at least two per cent of the weighted average number of equity shares listed during such a six-month period;

(d) The issuer has readdressed at least 95 per cent of the complaints received from the investors till the end of the quarter immediately preceding the month of the reference date;

(e) The issuer has been in compliance with the equity listing agreement for a period of at least three years immediately preceding the reference date;

(f) The entire shareholding of the promoter group of the issuer is held in dematerialized form on the reference date.

The **offer document** in this context is the prospectus in the case of a public issue or offer for sale and a letter of offer in the case of a rights issue, which is filed with the registrar of companies and stock exchanges. An offer document covers all the relevant information to help an investor to make his/her investment decision. A draft offer document is the offer document in the draft stage. A red herring prospectus is a preliminary registration statement that describes the issuer and the issue. It is updated many a time before it is made into a prospectus. It does not have details of the price, the number of shares being offered or the amount of issue. But it does mention the upper and lower price bands. It is called a red herring prospectus because it contains a passage in red that states that the company is not attempting to sell its shares before the registration is approved by SEBI.

4.18.1 Prospectus

According to Section 2(36) of the Companies Act, 1956, "a prospectus means any document described or issued as a prospectus and includes any notice, circular, advertisement, or other document inviting deposits from the public, or inviting offers from the public, or inviting offers from the public for the subscription of shares or debentures of a body corporate".

The prospectus is a legally binding document and is to be compulsorily issued. It also serves the purpose of providing information to the investing public to help them take informed decisions. The **prospectus** is the primary document that helps investors learn about the company in its different dimensions. Knowledge of the details of the company, which include the management, products and financial performance, enable the investing public to assess the pros and cons of investing in the company.

*The **prospectus** is the primary document that helps investors learn about the company in its different dimensions.*

Matters to be specified in the prospectus and reports to be set out therein are clearly stated in Schedule II (Sections 44(2) (a) and 56) of the Companies Act, 1956. The prospectus provides for greater disclosure of information regarding the company, its management, the projects proposed to be undertaken by the company, its financial performance for the last five years and the management's perception of risk factors so as to enable the investors to take informed investment decisions. According to Section 370 (1B) of the Companies Act, 1956, the prospectus must also contain particulars with regard to other listed companies under the same management which have made any capital issue during the last three years. At the end, a declaration has to be given by the directors of the company that all the relevant provisions of the Companies Act, 1956, and the guidelines issued by the government have been complied with and no statement made in prospectus is contrary to the provisions of Companies Act and rules made thereunder. The details of the prospectus are presented in Appendix 4.1.

4.18.2 Shelf Prospectus

Public sector banks, scheduled commercial banks and public financial institutions shall issue a shelf prospectus in terms of Section 60A of the Companies Act, 1956, for issues of debt securities. All the provisions of the SEBI guidelines shall apply as if it were a draft prospectus. The eligible institutions shall file the shelf prospectus after incorporating updates in terms of information memorandum in respect of the second or any subsequent offer of securities with SEBI. They shall open the particular stage of offer of securities after filing the information memorandum/shelf prospectus as updated with the registrar of companies and with SEBI.

4.19 Funds Raised in the Primary Market

The funds mobilized by companies in India, both in the private and public sector, from the primary market through public issues are shown in Table 4.1. As the table shows, very large amounts of funds were mobilized through private placements in 2007–08 and 2008–09. As usual, private sector companies have dominated the public sector companies in the issuance of securities. The proportion of IPOs in the total public issues in terms of the number of issues and amounts mobilized declined in 2008–09 because of the slump in the secondary markets. Except for the year 2008–09, funds raised through GDRs/ADRs are also quite substantial.

The amount raised through IPOs increased very significantly from INR 285,040 million in 2006–07 to INR 425,950 million in 2007–08 (vide Table 4.2). The amounts raised through further capital issues also increased substantially from INR 50,040 million in 2006–07 to INR 444,340 million in 2007–08. The proportion of funds raised through rights issues is much greater than that of public issues. As can be observed from Table 4.3, the proportion of equity funds was greater than that of debt funds since 2003–04. In 2005–06 and 2006–07, there were no public debt issues. Even in 2007–08, the proportion of debt funds raised through public issues was much lower.

Table 4.1 Mobilization of resources from the primary market

	2007–08		*2008–09*	
Description of item	*No. of issues*	*Amount (INR crore)*	*No. of issues*	*Amount (INR crore)*
A. Prospectus and rights issues:				
1. Private sector	115	63,638	45	14,671
a. Financial	11	14,676	2	466
b. Non-financial	104	48,962	43	14,205
2. Public sector	4	20,069	–	–
a. PSU	–	–	–	–
b. Government companies	2	2,516	–	–
c. Banks/FIs	2	17,553	–	–
Total (1+2)	119	83,707	45	14,671
Of which:				
i. Equity	116	82,398	45	14,671
ii. Debt	3	1,309	–	–
B. Private placement				
1. Private sector	1,616	1,29,677	1,053	93,036
a. Financial	905	88,291	683	60,246
b. Non-financial	711	41,386	370	32,790
2. Public sector	199	83,048	228	1,09,709
a. Financial	132	56,185	123	64,608
b. Non-financial	67	26,863	105	45,101
Total (1+2)	1,815	2,12,7252	1,281	2,02,745
Of which:				
i. Equity	2	1,410	8	960
ii. Debt	1,813	2,11,315	1,273	2,01,785
C. Euro issues (ADRs and GDRs)		**26 26,556**		**13 4,788**

Source: RBI Annual Report, 2008–09

Table 4.2 Fund mobilization by public equity issues

Issue	*2006–07* Number	*2006–07* Amount (INR million)	*2007–08* Number	*2007–08* Amount (INR million)
IPOs	77	285,040	85	425,950
Issues by listed companies	**47**	**50,040**	**39**	**444,340**
Public issues	8	12,930	7	119,160
Rights issues	39	37,110	32	325,180
Total	124	335,080	124	870,290

Source: NSE, Indian Securities Market: A Review, 2008

Table 4.3 Fund mobilization through debt and equity (public issues)

Year	*Percentage share* Equity	*Percentage share* Debt
1995–96	72.39	27.61
1996–97	55.99	44.01
1997–98	41.17	58.83
1998–99	15.34	84.66
1999–2000	58.41	41.59
2000–01	52.79	47.21
2001–02	16.88	83.12
2002–03	18.00	82.00
2003–04	80.47	19.53
2004–05	83.96	16.04
2005–06	100.00	0.00
2006–07	100.00	0.00
2007–08	98.12	1.88

Source: NSE, Indian Securities Market: A Review, 2008

Summary

1. Issue management refers to the management of various kinds of issues of securities, including public issues, rights issues and offers for sale.
2. SEBI has prescribed eligibility conditions separately for public issues by unlisted companies and listed companies. However, certain companies such as banking and infrastructure companies are exempted from eligibility norms.
3. A company is free to fix the price for public issues and make reservations and/or firm allotment of securities to various categories of persons subject to certain conditions.
4. A green shoe option is an option of allocating shares in excess of the shares included in the public issue and operating a post-listing price stabilizing mechanism in accordance with certain guidelines.
5. In a public issue by an unlisted company, the promoters shall contribute not less than 20 per cent of the post-issue capital. In the case of a public issue by listed companies, the promoters shall contribute either to the extent of 20 per cent of the proposed issue or ensure post-issue shareholding to the extent of 20 per cent of the post-issue capital.
6. Sweat equity shares are equity shares issued by a company to its employees or directors at a discount or for considerations other than cash for providing knowhow or making available the rights in the nature of intellectual property or value additions, whatever the name.
7. Employee stock option refers to the option given to whole-time directors, officers or employees of a company that gives such directors, officers or employees

the benefit or right to purchase, or subscribe at a future date, the securities offered by the company at a predetermined price. Under the employee stock option scheme, a company offers shares to its employees as part of a public issue or otherwise.

8. Preferential issue refers to the issue of securities to any select group of persons U/S 81 (1A) of the Companies Act, 1956, on private placement basis.
9. Euro issues refer to issues of FCCBs, GDRs or ADRs.
10. A prospectus is any document described or issued as a prospectus and includes any notice, circular, advertisement or other document inviting deposits from the public or inviting offers from the public for the subscription of shares or debentures of a body corporate.
11. The prospectus provides for greater disclosure of information regarding the company, its management, the projects proposed to be undertaken by the company, the financial performance of the company and management perception of risk factors, to name a few components, so as to enable the investors to take informed investment decisions.

Questions

1. Discuss the activities involved in a public issue.
2. What are the eligibility conditions for public issues?
3. What are the conditions to be satisfied for making a public issue of debt securities?
4. Discuss the basis of allotment of public issues.
5. What is green shoe option?
6. Why should promoters contribute to the share capital of a company? What are the SEBI regulations in this regard?
7. Discuss the SEBI regulations governing sweat equity.
8. Explain ESPS and ESOS and discuss the implications of the SEBI regulations.
9. What are the motives for preferential issues?
10. Define qualified institutions placement.
11. Discuss the trends in euro issues.
12. What are the features of GDRs/ADRs?
13. Define a prospectus. What purpose(s) does it serve?
14. Discuss the main points of a prospectus. Do you feel they are all necessary for an investor?
15. Discuss the trends in funds raised in the primary market.

Appendix 4.1

The Prospectus

A prospectus shall have three parts, Part–I, Part–II and Part–III. A brief description of each part of the prospectus is given here.

Part –I

A. General information:

(a) Name and address of the registered office of the company.

(b) Consent of the Government of India for the present issue and letter of intent/industrial licence.

(c) Names of regional stock exchange and other stock exchanges where application is made for listing of the present issue.

(d) Provisions of sub-section (1) of Section 68A of the Companies Act, 1956, which deals with punishment for fictitious applications.

(e) Statement or declaration about refund of the issue if minimum subscription of 90 per cent is not received within 90 days from the date of closure of the issue.

(f) Declaration about the issue of allotment letters/ refunds within the stipulated period and interest in case of any delay in refund at the prescribed rate.

(g) Date of opening of the issue, date of closing of the issue, date of earliest closing of the issue.

(h) Name and address of auditors and lead managers.

(i) Name and address of trustee under debenture trust deed (in case of debenture issue).

(j) Whether rating from any rating agency has been obtained for the proposed issue.

(k) Underwriting of the issue (details about the underwriters and their amounts of commitment) and the declaration by the board of directors that the underwriters have sufficient resources to discharge their respective obligations.

B. Capital structure of company

(a) Authorized, issued, subscribed and paid-up capital.

(b) Size of present issue, separately giving reservation for preferential allotment to promoters and others.

(c) Paid-up capital after the present issue or after conversion of debentures (if applicable).

C. Procedure for application and mode of payment

(a) Terms of payments.

(b) Rights of the instrument holders.

(c) Availability of forms, prospectus, mode of payment, etc.

(d) Tax benefits, if any, for the company and its shareholders.

D. Particulars of the issue

(a) Objects.

(b) Project cost.

(c) Means of financing (including contribution of promoters).

E. Company, management and project

(a) History and main objects and present business of the company.

(b) Promoters and their backgrounds.

(c) Names and address of the company directors.

(d) Location of the project.

(e) Plant and machinery, technology, process.

(f) Collaborations, if any.

(g) Availability of infrastructure facilities.

(h) Schedule of implementation of the project and progress so far.

(i) Details about the products (nature of the product(s), marketing setup, export possibilities).

(j) Future prospects (capacity utilization, cash profits, net profits).

(k) Subsidiary(ies) of the company, if any.

F. Particulars in regard to the companies under the same management that made any capital issue during the last three years (issue(s) details need to be furnished).

G. (a) Outstanding litigation, if any, pertaining to matters likely to affect operation and finances of the company, and criminal prosecution launched against the company and the directors for alleged offences.

(b) Particulars of default, if any, in meeting statutory dues, institutional dues, etc.

(c) Any material development after the date of the latest balance sheet and its impact on performance and prospects of the company.

H. Management perception of risk factors (such as sensitivity to foreign exchange rate fluctuations, difficulty in availability of raw materials or in marketing of products, cost/time overruns).

Part –II

General information

i. Consent of directors, auditors, solicitors, managers to the issue, registrar of the issue, bankers to the issue, etc.

ii. Changes, if any, in directors and auditors during the last three years and reasons thereof.

iii. Authority of the issue and details of resolution passed for the issue.

iv. Procedure and time schedule for allotment and issue of certificates.

v. Names and addresses of the company secretary, legal adviser(s), lead manager(s), co-manager(s), auditor(s), banker(s), broker(s), etc.

Financial information

i. A report by the auditors of the company with respect to:

(a) profits and losses and assets and liabilities in accordance with sub-clause (2) or (3) of this clause, as the case may require; and (b) the rates of dividends, if any, paid by the company in respect of each class of shares in the company for each of the five financial years immediately preceding the issue of the prospectus, giving particulars of each class of shares on which such dividends have been paid and particulars of the cases in which no dividends have been paid in respect of any class of shares for any of those years.

ii. If the company has no subsidiaries, the report shall:

(a) deal with the profits or losses of the company (distinguishing items of a non- recurring nature) for each of the five financial years immediately preceding the issue of the prospectus; and (b) deal with the assets and liabilities of the company at the last date to which the accounts of the company were made up.

iii. If the company has subsidiaries, the report shall:

(a) deal separately with the company's profits or losses as provided by sub-clause (2) and, in addition, deal either:

(i) as a whole with the combined profits or losses of its subsidiaries so far as they concern members of the company; or

(ii) individually with the profits or losses of each subsidiary so far as they concern members of the company;

or instead of dealing separately with the company's profits or losses, deal as a whole with the profits or losses of the company and, so far as they concern members of the company, with the combined profits or losses of its subsidiaries;

and

(b) deal separately with the company's assets and liabilities and, in addition, deal either:

(i) as a whole with the combined assets and liabilities of its subsidiaries, with or without the company's assets and liabilities, or

(ii) individually with the assets and liabilities of each subsidiary, and shall indicate in respect of assets and liabilities of the subsidiaries the allowance to be made for persons other than members of the company.

iv. If the proceeds or any part of the proceeds of the issue of the shares or debentures are to be applied directly or indirectly:

(i) in the purchase of any business; or

(ii) in the purchase of an interest in any business and by reason of that purchase or anything to be done in consequence thereof, or in connection therewith, the company will become entitled to an interest with respect to either the capital or profits and losses or both, in such business exceeding 50 per cent thereof, a report made by accountants upon:

(a) the profits or losses of the business for each of the five financial years immediately preceding the issue of the prospectus; and

(b) the assets and liabilities of the business at the last date to which the accounts of the business were made up, being a date not more than 120 days before the date of issue of the prospectus.

v. (i) If the proceeds or any part of the proceeds of the issue of the shares or debentures are to be applied directly or indirectly in any manner resulting in the acquisition by the company of shares in any other body corporate; and

(ii) If by reason of that acquisition or anything to be done in consequence thereof or in connection therewith, that body corporate will become a subsidiary of the company;

A report made by accountants upon:

(a) the profits or losses of the other body corporate for each of the five financial years immediately preceding the issue of the prospectus; and

(b) the assets and liabilities of the other body corporate at the last date to which its accounts were made up.

The said report shall (a) indicate how the profits or losses of the other body corporate dealt with by the report would, in respect of the shares to be acquired, have concerned members of the company and what allowance would have fallen to be made, in relation to assets and liabilities so dealt with for holders of other shares, if the company had at all material times held the shares to be acquired; and (b) where the other body corporate has subsidiaries, dealt with the profits or losses and the assets and liabilities of the body corporate and its subsidiaries in the manner provided by sub-clause (2) above in relation to the company and its subsidiaries.

vi. Principal terms of loans and assets charged as security.

Statutory and other information

i. Minimum subscription.

ii. Expenses of the issue (item-wise).

iii. Underwriting commission and brokerage.

iv. Details of previous public or rights issue if any (during last five years).
v. Commission or brokerage on previous issue.
vi. Issue of shares otherwise than for cash.
vii. Debentures and redeemable preference shares and other instruments issued by the company outstanding as on the date of prospectus and terms of issue.
viii. Option to subscribe.
ix. Details of the property purchased by the company.
x. Details of directors, proposed directors, whole-time directors, their remuneration, appointment and remuneration of managing directors, interests of directors, their borrowing powers and qualifications shares.
xi. Rights of members regarding voting, dividend, lien on shares and the process for modification of such rights and forfeiture of shares.
xii. Restrictions, if any, on transfer and transmission of shares/debentures and on their consolidation/splitting.
xiii. Revaluation of assets, if any, during last five years.
xiv. Material contracts and documents. Time and place at which the contracts together with documents will be available for inspection from the date of prospectus until the date of closing of the subscription list.

Part III of Schedule II of the Companies Act, 1956, specifies the provisions applying to Part-I and Part-II of the Schedule.

DECLARATION: All the relevant provisions of the Companies Act, 1956, and the guidelines issued by the government have been complied with and no statement made in the prospectus is contrary to the provisions of the Companies Act, 1956, and rules thereunder.

Place:
Date:

Finding the disclosures specified in Schedule II of the Companies Act, 1956, inadequate, SEBI has specified certain other aspects to be incorporated in the prospectus. SEBI has also elaborated on the disclosures specified in Schedule II of the Companies Act. The important aspects to be incorporated in the prospectus as per the SEBI (Disclosure and Investor Protection) Guidelines are specified here.

1. Disclaimer clause:

(A) A prospectus shall contain the following disclaimer clause in bold capital letters.

"It is to be distinctly understood that the submission of the Offer Document to SEBI should not, in any way, be deemed or construed that the same has been cleared or vetted by SEBI. The SEBI does not take any responsibility either for the financial soundness of any scheme or project for which the issue is proposed to be made or for the correctness of statements made or opinions expressed in the Offer Document. The Lead Manager to the issue (specify name) has certified that the disclosures made in the preliminary Offer Document are generally adequate and are in conformity with SEBI Guidelines for Disclosure and Investor Protection for the time being in force. This requirement is to facilitate investors to take an informed decision for making investment in the proposed issue. It should also be clearly understood that while the issuer is primarily responsible for the correctness, adequacy and disclosure of all relevant information in the Offer Document, the Lead Manager is expected to exercise due diligence to ensure that the company discharges its responsibility adequately in this behalf and towards this purpose, the Lead Manager has to furnish to SEBI a Due Diligence Certificate dated—which reads as follows.

i. We have examined various documents including those relating to litigations like commercial disputes, patent disputes, disputes with collaborators, etc and other materials in connection with the finalization of the Offer Document pertaining to the said issue;

ii. On the basis of such examinations and the discussions with the company, its directors and other officers, other agencies, independent verification of the statements concerning the objects of the issue, projected profitability, price justification and contents of the documents mentioned in the Annexure and other papers furnished by the company.

We confirm that:

(a) the draft Offer Document forwarded to SEBI is in conformity with the documents, materials and papers relevant to the issue;

(b) all the legal requirements connected with the said issue as also the guidelines, instructions, etc issued by SEBI, the Government and any other authority in this behalf have been duly complied with; and

(c) the disclosures made in the draft Offer Document are true, fair and adequate to enable the investors to make a well informed decision as to the investment in the proposed issue.

iii. We confirm that besides ourselves, all the intermediaries named in the Offer Document are registered with SEBI and that till date such registration is valid.

iv. We have satisfied ourselves about the worth of the underwriters to fulfil their underwriting commitments.

The filing of offer document does not, however, absolve the company from any liabilities under Section 63 or

68 of the Companies Act, 1956, or from the requirement of obtaining such statutory or other clearances as may be required for the purpose of the proposed issue. SEBI further reserves the right to take up, at any point of time, with the lead merchant banker(s) any irregularities or lapses in offer document".

(B) A prospectus shall also contain the following disclaimer statement from the issuer and the lead manager.

"The issuer company and the Lead Manager accepts no responsibility for statements made otherwise than in the prospectus or in the advertisement or any other material issued by or at the instance of the issuer and that any one placing reliance on any other source of information would be doing so at his own risk".

(C) Disclaimer clause of SEBI: The following must be incorporated in the Prospectus:

"SEBI only gives its observations on the Offer Documents and this does not constitute approval of either the issue or the Offer Document."

(D) Disclaimer clause of the designated stock exchange: The following must be incorporated in the prospectus.

"It is to be distinctly understood that the permission given by the stock exchange (name specified) should not in any way be deemed or construed that the Red Herring Prospectus has been cleared or approved by the stock exchange (name specified) nor does it certify the correctness or completeness of any of the content of the Red Herring Prospectus."

(E) Disclaimer clause of the Reserve Bank of India (if applicable).

(F) Disclaimer in respect of jurisdiction.

2. The following clause on general risk shall be incorporated in the prospectus.

"Investment in equity and equity related securities involve a degree of risk and investors should not invest any funds in this offer unless they can afford to take the risk of losing their investment. Investors are advised to read the risk factors carefully before taking an investment decision in this offering. For taking an investment decision, investors must rely on their own examination of the issuer and the offer including the risk involved. The securities have not been recommended or approved by SEBI nor does SEBI guarantee the accuracy or adequacy of this document".

3. The following matter on the issuer's absolute responsibility shall also be incorporated in the prospectus.

"The issuer, having made all reasonable inquiries, accepts responsibility for and confirms that this offer document contains all information with regard to the issuer and the issue, which is material in the context of the issue, that the information contained in the offer document is true and correct in all material aspects and is not misleading in any material respect, that the opinions and intentions expressed herein are honestly held and that there are no other facts, the omission of which make this document as a whole or any of such information or the expression of any such opinions or intentions misleading in any material respect".

4. Minimum subscription.

(a) For non-underwritten public issues, the following statement shall appear in the prospectus.

"If the company does not receive the minimum subscription of 90 per cent of the issued amount on the date of closure of the issue, or if the subscription level falls below 90 per cent after the closure of issue on account of cheques having been returned unpaid or withdrawal of application, the company shall forthwith refund the entire subscription amount received. If there is a delay beyond 8 days after the company becomes liable to pay the amount, the company shall pay interest as per section 73 of the Companies Act, 1956".

(b) For underwriting public issues, the following statement shall appear in the prospectus.

"If the company does not receive the minimum subscription of 90 per cent of the net offer to the public including devolvement of underwriters within 60 days from the date of closure of the issue, the company shall forthwith refund the entire subscription amount received. If there is a delay beyond 8 days after the company becomes liable to pay the amount, the company shall pay interest prescribed under section 73 of the Companies Act, 1956".

5. Utilization of issue proceeds.

(A) The prospectus shall contain a statement of the board of directors of the issuer company to the effect that:

(i) All monies received out of the issue of shares or debentures to the public shall be transferred to a separate bank account other than the bank account referred to in sub-section (3) of Section 73 of the Companies Act, 1956.

(ii) Details of all monies utilized out of the issue referred to in sub-item (i) shall be disclosed under an appropriate head in the balance sheet of the issuer company indicating the purpose for which such monies had been utilized; and

(iii) Details of all unutilized monies out of the issue of shares or debentures, if any, referred to in sub-item (i) shall be disclosed under an appropriate separate head in the balance sheet of the issuer company indicating the form in which such unutilized monies have been invested.

(B) The prospectus shall also contain a statement of the board of directors of the issuing company to the effect that:

(i) The utilization of monies received under promoters' contribution and from firm allotments and reservations shall be disclosed under an appropriate head in the balance sheet of the issuer company indicating the purpose for which such monies have been utilized; and

(ii) The details of all unutilized monies out of the funds received under promoters' contribution and from firm allotments and reservations shall be disclosed under a separate head in the balance sheet of the issuer company indicating the form in which such unutilized monies have been invested.

6. Basis for issue price.

The basis for issue price/floor price/price band shall be disclosed and justified on the basis of the following information, which shall also be disclosed separately:

(i) Earnings per share (pre-issue) for the last three years as adjusted for changes in capital.

(ii) P/E pre-issue.

(iii) Average return on net worth in the last three years.

(iv) Minimum return on increased net worth required maintaining pre-issue EPS.

(v) Net asset value per share based on last balance sheet.

(vi) Net asset value per share after issue and comparison thereof with the issue price.

(vii) An illustrative format of disclosure in respect of basis for issue price.

(viii) Comparison of all the accounting ratios of the issuer company as mentioned above with the industry average and with the accounting ratios of the peer group.

(ix) The face value of shares (including the statement about the issue price/floor price/price band being 'X' times the face value) provided that the projected earnings shall not be used as a justification for the issue price in the prospectus and provided further that the accounting ratios disclosed in the prospectus in support of basis of the issue price shall be calculated after giving effect to the consequent increase in capital on account of compulsory conversions outstanding, as well as on the assumption that the options outstanding, if any, to subscribe for additional capital will be exercised.

SEBI has also specified the contents of the abridged prospectus, letter of offer, abridged letter of offer, prospectus for IDRs and abridged prospectus for IDRs. In all these offer documents, the nature of information is more or less the same but the format and details differ.

Appendix 4.2

Jindal Steel and Power Limited: Employees Stock Option Scheme, 2005

The shareholders of the Company have, in their meeting held on July 25, 2005, approved issuing of Stock Options to the eligible employees of the Company and it subsidiaries. The Stock Option Scheme (ESOS-2005) is given here:

1. Title, extent and commencement

The Scheme shall be called the "Employees Stock Option Scheme-2005" or "ESOS-2005". It applies only to the eligible employees and all subsidiaries whether now or hereafter existing, who are in permanent employment and whole time Directors of such Company.

2. Objects

- **i.** To foster employee commitment and a feeling of ownership.
- **ii.** To retain employees or specific skill groups amongst them.
- **iii.** To attract talented / highly valued professionals or scarce skills.
- **iv.** To instill a sense of belonging to the Company

3. Definition

In this Scheme, unless the context otherwise requires,

(a) "Board" means the Board of Directors for the time being of the Company.

(b) "Company" means JINDAL STEEL & POWER LIMITED or JSPL.

(c) "Compensation Committee" means the Compensation Committee constituted by the Board under clause 5 of SEBI (Employees Stock Option Scheme and Employees Stock Purchase Scheme) Guidelines, 1999.

(d) "Director" means a member of Board of the Company.

(e) "Permanent Incapacity" shall mean "permanent total disability" as defined in the Workmen's Compensation Act, 1923.

(f) "Eligible Employee" means an employee who qualifies for issue of Options under this Scheme and who fulfills the minimum conditions of service and other conditions as decided in the appraisal process by the Compensation Committee. An Employee who is a promoter or belongs to the promoter group shall not be eligible for participation in the Scheme. A director who either by himself or through his relative/s or through any body corporate, directly or indirectly holds more than 10 per cent of the outstanding equity shares of the Company shall not be eligible to participate in the ESOS- 2005.

(g) "Employee" means

(a) a permanent employee of the Company working in India or out of India; or

(b) A whole time Director of the Company; or

(c) An employee as defined in (a) or (b) of the subsidiary in India or out of India.

(h) "Employee Compensation" means the total cost incurred by the Company towards Employee Compensation including basic salary, dearness allowance, other allowances, bonus and commissions including the value of perquisites provided, but does not include (a) the fair value of the Options granted under ESOS-2005 (b) the discount at which shares are issued under Employee Stock Purchase Scheme, if any.

(i) "Exercise" means making of an application by the employee to the Company for issue of shares against Option vested in him in pursuance of ESOS-2005.

(j) "Exercise Period" means the time period after vesting within which the employee should exercise his rights to apply for shares against Options vested in him in pursuance of ESOS-2005.

(k) "Exercise Price" means the price determined by the Compensation Committee and payable by the Optionee to the Company for issue of shares against Options vested in him in pursuance of the ESOS-2005

(l) "Grant "means issue of Option to eligible employees under ESOS-2005.

(m) "Fair Value of an Option" means the fair value calculated in accordance with Schedule III to SEBI (Employees Stock Option Scheme and Employees Stock Purchase Scheme) Guidelines, 1999.

(n) "Option" means a Stock Option comprising of a right, but not an obligation granted to an employee under the ESOS-2005 to apply for shares of the Company at the Exercise Price, subject to the requirements of vesting.

(o) "Optionee" means the holder of an Option granted pursuant to ESOS- 2005.

(p) "Promoter" means;

(a) the person or persons who are in over all control of the Company;

(b) the person or persons who are instrumental in the formation of the Company or programme pursuant to which the shares were offered to the public;

(c) the person or persons named in the offer document as promoter(s)

Provided that a director or officer of the Company, if they are acting as such only in their professional capacity will not be deemed to be promoter.

[**Explanation:** where a promoter of a Company is a body corporate, the promoters of that body corporate shall also be deemed to be promoters of the Company.]

(q) "Promoter group" means

(a) an immediate relative of the Promoter (i.e., Spouse of that person or any parent, brother, sister or child of a person or of the spouse);

(b) persons whose shareholding is aggregated for the purpose of disclosing in the offer document under the head "Shareholding of promoter group".

(r) "Shares" mean the equity shares of the Company and securities convertible into equity shares, if any.

(s) "Subsidiary" means a subsidiary of the Company, whether now or hereafter existing as defined under section 4 of the Companies Act, 1956.

(t) "Vesting" means the process by which the employee is given the right to apply for shares of the Company against the Options granted to him in pursuance of ESOS-2005.

(u) "Vesting Period" means the period during which the vesting of Option granted to the employee in pursuance of ESOS-2005 takes place.

All other expression unless defined herein shall have the same meaning as have been assigned to them under the SEBI (Employees Stock Option Scheme and Employees Stock Purchase Scheme) Guidelines, 1999; the SEBI Act, 1992, the Securities Contracts (Regulation) Act, 1956, SEBI (Disclosures and Investors Protection) Guidelines, 2000, the Companies Act, 1956 and all statutory modifications or re- enactments thereof as the case a may be.

4. Number of shares within the scope of the Scheme

Subject to provisions of ESOS-2005, the aggregate number of shares, which may be granted to employees or whole time Directors of the Company or its subsidiary shall not exceed 11,00,000. Forfeited/lapsed stock options under this scheme can be reissued by the compensation committee at its absolute discretion.

5. Administration of ESOS-2005

(a) The Compensation Committee appointed by the Board in its meeting held on 12.05.05 or as may be constituted/ reconstituted by the Board from time to time will monitor the administration and superintendence of ESOS- 2005.

(b) Subject to the provisions of the Scheme and subject to the approval/s of relevant authorities, if any Compensation Committee shall have the absolute authority and discretion, to administer the ESOS-2005 and among other things to:

1. To decide the quantum of options to be granted to any employee.
2. To decide the conditions under which the options granted to employees may lapse
3. To determine Exercise Price of the options granted under ESOS-2005;
4. To select the employees to whom Options may, from time to time be granted;
5. To determine the Vesting period and the Exercise Period.
6. To dispose of, at its sole discretion and in the interest of the Company, the options not applied for, by the employees offered under the Scheme.
7. To determine the terms and conditions, not inconsistent with the terms of the Scheme of any Option;
8. To prescribe, amend and rescind rules and regulations relating to the Scheme;
9. To decide the procedure for making fair and reasonable adjustment to the number of Options and to the exercise price in case of Right Issue / Bonus Issue, other corporate actions or other wise.
10. To construe and interpret the terms of the Scheme and Options granted pursuant to the Scheme.
11. Any other related or incidental matter.

(c) All decisions, determinations and interpretations of the Compensation Committee shall be final and binding on all Optionees.

6. Appraisal of eligible employees

The appraisal process and the criteria to be followed in respect of grant of Options shall be such as may be decided by the Compensation Committee.

7. Grant of Options

(a) Options may be granted to all the eligible employees, existing on the date of grant of Options for number to be decided by the Compensation Committee. Employees joining after this date shall also be considered for grant of Options.

(b) The Compensation Committee may, in one or more tranches and on such dates and after such period as it shall determine grant options to such eligible employees as it may, in its absolute discretion identify on such terms and conditions and for such consideration as it may decide.

(c) The date of grant of Option shall, for all purposes, be the date on which the Compensation Committee makes the determination for granting such Options or such other date as is determined by the Compensation Committee. Notice of the determination shall be given to each employee to whom Option is so granted within a reasonable time after the date of such grant.

8. Vesting of Options

The Option granted under this Scheme shall vest with the eligible employees in the following manner:

1. 50 per cent of entitlement on expiry of two years after the grant of Option
2. 25 per cent of entitlement on expiry of three years after the grant of Option
3. 25 per cent of entitlement on expiry of four years after the grant of Option

9. Individual limits for grant of Options

No employee shall be granted Option(s) to purchase more than 5,000 shares.

10. Entitlement of shares

Each Option shall entitle the Optionee to apply for and seek allotment of one equity share of INR 5 ranking pari passu in all respect including dividend with the existing equity shares of the Company.

11. Exercise price

The Compensation Committee shall determine the exercise price of the shares arising on exercise of Option based on the price per share equivalent to 75 per cent of the average of the daily closing price of equity shares of the Company during 30 days preceding the date of grant of Options as quoted on BSE or the NSE wherever the trading volume of equity shares in aggregate during the said period is more.

12. Exercise period

The Optionees may apply for and seek allotment of shares against Options vested in them in whole or part, as the case may be, within a period as may be decided by the Compensation Committee. Applications duly filled and signed by the Optionees along with the exercise price should be sent to the Company for allotment of shares against Options. In case of resignation of any employee, the Vested Options shall be exercised within one month of the resignation, otherwise the Options will lapse.

13. Exercise of option and rights as shareholders

(a) Any Options granted hereunder shall be exercisable according to such terms and conditions as may be determined by the Compensation Committee.

(b) As Option shall be deemed exercised when the Company receives: (a) written application for exercise of Option from the Optionee and (b) full payment for the shares with respect to which the Option is exercised.

(c) Shares issued upon exercise of Option shall be in the name of the Optionee/Nominee, as the case may be. Until the shares are issued, no rights to vote or receive dividends or any other rights as a shareholder shall exist with respect to the shares notwithstanding the exercise of Option. The Company shall issue (or cause to be issued) such shares within reasonable time after the Option is exercised.

14. Non-transferability of options

The Options granted to the employees under ESOS-2005 shall not be pledged, hypothecated, mortgaged or otherwise alienated in any other manner. In case option granted to an employee is pledged, hypothecated, mortgaged or otherwise alienated in any other manner, no shares shall be allotted against such option.

15. Terms and conditions of the shares

(a) All shares allotted on exercise of Options will rank pari-passu with all other equity shares of the Company for the time being including dividend that may be declared for the year in which the share is issued.

(b) There shall be no lock in period of the shares allotted under the Scheme.

16. Amendment and termination of the Scheme

(a) The Compensation Committee may at any time, amend, alter, suspend or terminate the scheme, provided that the Company obtains shareholder's approval for any amendment to the extent required.

(b) No amendment, alteration, suspension or termination of the Scheme shall impair the existing rights of any Optionee, unless mutually agreed otherwise between the Optionee and the Compensation Committee, which agreement must be in writing and signed by the Optionee and the Company. Termination of the Scheme shall not affect the Compensation Committee's ability to exercise the power given to it with respect to Options granted under this Scheme prior to the date of such termination.

17. Accounting policy

The Company shall comply with the accounting policies specified in the SEBI (Employees Stock Option Scheme and Employees Stock Purchase Scheme) Guidelines, 1999 or any other policy as may be prescribed under the law in respect of the accounting for such Options.

18. Adjustments in case of corporate actions such as rights/ bonus issues, merger and sale of division etc

The Compensation Committee will make a fair and reasonable adjustment in the manner as provided in the SEBI (Employees Stock Option Scheme and Employees Stock Purchase Scheme) Guidelines, 1999 to the number of Options and to the exercise price at the time of corporate actions such as the rights/ bonus issue, merger, sale of division etc by the Company between the date of grant of option and exercise of the Options.

19. Valuation of options

The Company shall use intrinsic value method as defined in the SEBI (Employees Stock Option Scheme and Employees Stock Purchase Scheme) Guidelines, 1999 to value its options or by any other method as may be decided by the Compensation Committee as per SEBI Guidelines.

20. Employees compensation cost

The Company shall calculate the employee compensation cost using the intrinsic value of the Stock Options or by any other method as may be decided by the Compensation Committee within the SEBI Guidelines. The difference between the employee compensation cost so computed and the employee compensation cost that shall have been recognized if it had used the fair value of the Options, shall be disclosed in the directors' report and also the impact of this difference on profits and on EPS of the Company shall also be disclosed in the directors' report.

21. General

(a) The Scheme shall not form part of any contract of employment between the Company and the Employee. The rights and obligations of any individual under the terms of his office or employment with the Company shall not be affected by his participation in this Scheme or any right which he may have to participate in it and nothing in this Scheme shall be construed as affording such an individual any additional rights as to compensation or damages in consequence of the termination of such office or employment for any reason.

(b) This Scheme shall not confer on any person any legal or equitable rights (other than that to which he would be entitled as an ordinary member of the Company) against the Company either directly or indirectly or give rise to any cause of action in law or in equity against the Company.

(c) Employee Stock Option Plan to be formulated by the Compensation Committee in terms of clause 5 (b) of this scheme will form an integral part of this scheme and shall always be read with this scheme.

Source: http://www.jsteelpower.com/files/esos%202005.pdf

Appendix 4.3

Nalwa Sons Investment Limited: Employee Stock Purchase Scheme 2005

Chapter 1
Title

This Scheme shall be called the Nalwa Sons Investment Limited – Employees Stock Purchase Scheme 2005.

Chapter 2
Authority and effective date

This Scheme is in accordance with the provisions of the Companies Act, 1956, as amended read with the SEBI (Employee Stock Option Scheme and Employee Stock Purchase Scheme) Guidelines, 1999, as amended and all other regulations and provisions of law for the time being in force, and shall be subject to any modifications or amendments thereof effected from time to time by way of an ordinance or legislative enactment. This Scheme shall be deemed to be effective as of the date it is approved by the members of the Company at a General meeting.

Chapter 3
Objectives

1. To provide means to enable the Company to attract and retain appropriate human talent in the employment of the Company;
2. To motivate the employees of the Company with incentives and reward opportunities;
3. To achieve sustained growth of the Company and the creation of shareholder value by aligning the interests of the employees with the long term interests of the Company; and
4. To create a sense of ownership and participation amongst the employees.

Chapter 4
Definitions and interpretation

In this Scheme the following expressions, including their grammatical variations and cognate expressions shall, unless repugnant to the context or meaning thereof, have the meaning assigned to them respectively hereunder:

1. "Act" means the Companies Act, 1956 (1 of 1956) or any statutory modification or re-enactment thereof.
2. "Board of Directors" or "Board" means the Board of Directors for the time being of the Company or any Committee thereof.
3. "Company" means Nalwa Sons Investment Limited, a company incorporated under the Act and having its registered office at Delhi Road, Hisar – 125 005.
4. "Employee" means
   (a) a permanent employee of the Company working in India or out of India; or
   (b) a director of the Company, whether a whole time director or not, holding directly or indirectly less than 10 per cent of the outstanding Shares of the Company; or
   (c) an Employee as defined in sub-clauses (a) and (b) of a subsidiary of the Company, in India or out of India.
5. "Employee Compensation" shall mean the total cost incurred by the Company towards employee compensation including basic salary, dearness allowance, other allowances, bonus and commission including the value of all perquisites provided, but does not include discount at which shares are issued under this Scheme.
6. "Offer of Shares" means and includes a letter in writing from the Company communicating, among other things, the number of equity Shares to which an Employee is entitled to apply for and seek allotment thereof.
7. "Promoter" shall have the meaning ascribed to it under the SEBI Guidelines.
8. "Promoter Group" shall have the meaning ascribed to it under the SEBI Guidelines
9. "SEBI Guidelines" shall mean the SEBI (Employee Stock Option Scheme and Employee Stock Purchase Scheme) Guidelines, 1999, as amended.
10. "Share" means equity shares of the Company
11. "Share Price" means the price per share to be paid by the Employees for the purchase of the Shares pursuant to the Offer of Shares.

   All other expressions unless defined herein shall have the same meaning as have been assigned to them under the SEBI (Employee Stock Option Scheme and Employee Stock Purchase Scheme) Guidelines, 1999; the SEBI Act, 1992; and the Securities Contracts (Regulation) Act, 1956.

   SEBI (Disclosure and investor protection) Guidelines or any statutory modifications or reenactments thereof as the case may be.

Chapter 5
Eligibility

1. Except as prohibited in Clauses 2 and 3 hereinafter, all Employees as defined in Clause 4 of Chapter 4 shall be eligible to participate in this Scheme ("Eligible Employees").
2. An Employee who is a Promoter or belongs to the Promoter Group shall not be eligible to participate in the Scheme.

3. A director who either by himself or through his relative or through any body corporate, directly or indirectly holds more than 10 per cent of the outstanding Shares of the Company shall not be eligible to participate in the Scheme.
4. The Board shall, within the parameters set out above, determine and decide the date and criteria for determining Eligible Employees for the purpose of entitlement to shares offered under the prevalent practices in the industry, overall industry scenario and the conditions of the capital market.
5. The Board shall, based on the various criteria, including one or more of the following but not limited to:
   (i) future performance potential of the Eligible Employee;
   (ii) grade and merit of the Eligible Employee;
   (iii) the criticality of the Eligible Employee in furthering Company's interests, decide on which of the Eligible Employees should be offered Shares under this Scheme. Accordingly the Board shall make an offer, in writing, to such Employees detailing the number of shares and the price as which the offer is made under the terms and conditions of the Scheme. The Board of Directors may in its absolute discretion vary or modify such criteria and/or selection and/or the terms and conditions.

Chapter 6
Entitlement to shares

The maximum number of shares to which each category (grade wise) of Eligible Employees is entitled is given hereunder:

Sl. No. Category Maximum No. of Shares Entitlements

1. Sr. Executive: 45,000
2. Executive: 42,000
3. Jr. Executive: 41,000
4. Employees of Subsidiary: 41,000

Notwithstanding anything herein contained, the total number of equity shares that may be issued under the Scheme will not be more than 7,70,424 equity shares.

Chapter 7
Pricing of shares

The price of the Shares to be allotted under the Scheme to the Eligible Employees of the Company shall be INR 10 per Share.

Chapter 8
Mode of applying for shares

1. The Employees to whom Shares are offered under the Scheme shall make an application to the Company in the prescribed Application Form along with payment of the total amount of the Share Price for up to the maximum number of Shares for which the offer has been made.
2. The payment shall be made by way of demand draft / local cheques drawn in favour of the Company, i.e., Nalwa Sons Investments Limited or in favour of such trust or other entity as the Board may specify while making the offer and payable at Hisar / Delhi or by cash.
3. The period within which the application for seeking allotment (for the purpose of the Scheme, the term "allotment" to include transfer) of shares under this Scheme should be submitted by the Employees shall be decided by the Board.
4. The Board shall have, in its absolute discretion, the right to reject any application which is not complete in all respects. The application money received, if any, in respect of such rejected applications shall be refunded to the Employees within a period of 5 days after the date of rejection of the application.

Chapter 9
Allotment of shares

On receipt of application(s) complete in all respects as stated above, the Board shall make an allotment of Shares either directly from the Company or through a trust or any other mechanism as permissible under law. The Employees shall have the option to hold the Shares in physical form by way of share certificates or in electronic form with any of the depositories registered with the SEBI.

Chapter 10
Listing of the shares

If not already listed, the Shares to be allotted under this Scheme shall be listed immediately upon allotment on the stock exchange(s) where the Shares of the Company are listed. As and when applicable, the Company shall make an application to the appropriate authorities and obtain the approval in-principle from the stock exchanges where it proposes to list the Shares allotted under this Scheme.

Chapter 11
Rights of the shareholders

Upon allotment of shares, the applicant Employees shall become members of the Company and shall be entitled to all the rights of a member including with respect to voting rights, receipt of dividend, etc. The Shares to be allotted shall rank pari-passu in all respects with the outstanding Shares of the Company.

Chapter 12
Lock-in of shares

The Shares allotted in terms of this Scheme to the Employees shall not be transferred for a period of one (1) year from the date of allotment thereof.

Chapter 13
Cessation of employment

On cessation of the employment of an Employee on account of resignation, termination, death or for any other reason after an application has been made for allotment of Shares under this

Scheme, but prior to allotment of such Shares by the Company, the Employee shall not be entitled to any Shares. The application made for allotment of Shares shall be rejected on occurrence of any of the aforesaid events and the application money shall be refunded to the Employee.

Chapter 14
Disclosure and accounting policies

In the implementation of the Scheme, the Company shall conform to the disclosure and accounting polices specified under the SEBI Guidelines, as may be applicable.

Chapter 15
Loan facility

The Board may, at its discretion, decide to grant loans to the Employees for subscribing to Shares under this Scheme in accordance with the provisions of the Act and other applicable law.

The Board may also decide to grant loans or any other form of financial assistance to a trust or any other entity to acquire, purchase or subscribe to the Shares (in case the Scheme is administered through the trust or any other entity) in accordance with the provisions of the Act and other applicable law.

Chapter 16
Shareholders' approval

As soon as may be possible the Company shall seek the approval of the shareholders to issue shares to Employees under this Scheme, by way of special resolution(s) by calling an extraordinary general meeting (EGM)/annual general meeting (AGM) of the members of the Company, as required under applicable laws.

Chapter 17
No employment rights conferred

Nothing contained herein shall give or confer upon any Employee the right to continuation of any employment with the Company or interfere in any way with the right of the Company to terminate the employment of such Employee at any time and for any reason whatsoever.

Chapter 18
Amendment or termination of the scheme

The Board in its absolute discretion may from time to time amend, alter or terminate the Scheme or the terms and conditions thereof. Provided that the Board shall not, without the approval of the shareholders of the Company, amend the Scheme to increase the aggregate number of Shares which may be issued pursuant to the provisions of the Scheme, except as otherwise stated elsewhere in this Scheme. Without prejudice to the above, the Board may without any reference to or consent of the Employee concerned, amend the Scheme to comply with any statute, regulation or guideline, which is or may hereinafter, become applicable to this Scheme.

Chapter 19
New schemes

Nothing contained in the Scheme shall be construed to prevent the Company directly or through any trust settled by the Company, from implementing any other new scheme for granting stock options and/or share purchase rights, which is deemed by the Company to be appropriate or in the best interests of its employees, whether or not such other action would have any adverse impact on this Scheme. No Employee or other person shall have any claim against the Company and/or any trust as a result of such action.

Chapter 20
Governing law

The Scheme shall by construed in accordance with the laws of India. All disputes arising out of or in connection with the Scheme shall be referred to arbitration in accordance with the provisions of the Arbitration and Conciliation Act, 1996. The venue of arbitration shall be Hisar, Haryana, India.

Source: http://www.nalwasons.com/esps-scheme.pdf

Chapter 5

Pricing of Capital Issues

LEARNING OBJECTIVES

After studying this chapter, you should be able to:

- Review the method of pricing of capital issues under the Controller of Capital Issues (CCI) regime.
- Introduce the concepts of net asset value (NAV), profit-earning capacity value (PECV) and market value (MV).
- Discuss the CCI guidelines with respect to pricing of capital issues.
- Present SEBI regulations with regard to the pricing of capital issues.
- Explain the book-building process.
- Discuss the implications of the price-earnings (P/E) ratio.

5.1 Introduction

Capital issues control was first introduced in India under Defence of India Rule 94 A, which was promulgated on May 17, 1943, under the Defence of India Act, 1939. Until that time, raising of capital was free from controls. During the Second World War, the main aim of the capital issues control was to prevent the establishment of industries that did not assist in the production of essential war or consumption goods. The government wanted resources to be used mainly for war purposes, and accordingly companies were allowed to tap household savings sparingly. Capital issues control was retained after the Second World War, and Defence Rule 94A was replaced by the Capital Issues (Continuance of Control) Act, 1947. The main objectives of the act were to modulate and channel investments in desired directions and protect the interests of the investors. Another way to view this act was that the government wanted to use it as a means to ensure balanced investment of the country's resources in industry, agriculture and social services. The act was intended to be temporary and, therefore, it was renewed periodically. However, it was made permanent in 1956 and placed on the statute book as the Capital Issues (Control) Act, 1947.

The objectives of the Capital Issues (Control) Act, 1947, were:

- to ensure that investment does not take place contrary to the objectives of the five-year plans or flow into unproductive or wasteful channels;
- to further the growth of joint stock companies with sound capital structure and promote a rational and healthy expansion of the joint stock companies in the general public interest; and
- to direct and distribute appeals for public subscription to new issues of capital to avoid any undue concentration or overcrowding in a particular period or part of the year.

To administer the act, the Government of India created an institutional set-up called the Controller of Capital Issues (CCI) as a part of the Ministry of Finance. Under the provisions of the act, companies in India were required to obtain approval from the CCI for raising capital. There were also tight controls on rights issues and bonus issues as well. All these were done as per the industrial policy of the government. The Indian government's policy then was to give a predominant position to the public sector enterprises in the economy. As part of this policy, various industries were nationalized and certain sectors of the economy were reserved for the public sector. Private sector enterprises were restricted and access to equity markets was highly regulated.

As per the CCI guidelines, all new companies can issue shares only at par. Only existing companies with substantial reserves can issue shares at a premium, which has to be calculated in accordance with CCI norms. A company was deemed eligible for exemption from the consent of the CCI if the securities were proposed to be issued at par and not at a premium or discount. In special cases, a premium was allowed to the extent that the issue price with a premium is not unreasonable in the context of the break-up value of the shares and the profit-earning capacity of the company. The factors considered in determining the premium on the equity issue were the break-up value of the shares, the value of the shares on the basis of the company's profit-earning capacity, the assessment of its future growth prospects, the dividend record and resources position of the company and the extent of foreign participation in the company's capital.

The CCI claimed that the methods used to determine the premium were objective. But the actual methods of the CCI in working out the premium on new issues of shares were unknown. To clear the doubts in the minds of the investing public on the methods by which the premium on capital issues was calculated or to lend greater transparency to the valuation process, the CCI issued Valuation Guidelines to the public in July 1990. But it was stated that these guidelines were only for internal official use and therefore not to be quoted, cited or published as official guidelines. The Valuation Guidelines were applicable to the valuation of equity shares of companies (private and public limited), Indian business/net assets of the sterling tea companies and Indian business/net assets of branches of foreign companies.

5.2 Determination of Share Premium

According to the CCI guidelines, the best reasonable judgement of the value is referred to as the **fair value**. The difference between the fair value and the face value of the securities is the **premium**. The fair value can be calculated on the basis of the following.

*The best reasonable judgement of the value is referred to as **fair value**. The difference between the fair and the face value of securities is the **premium**.*

a. NAV
b. PECV
c. MV, in the case of listed shares.

5.2.1 Net Asset Value (NAV)

The NAV represents the true net worth of a business after making a provision for all the present and potential liabilities. It is calculated on the basis of the figures in the latest audited balance sheet. The calculation is as follows:

*The **NAV** represents the true net worth of a business after making a provision for all the present and contingent liabilities.*

1. Equity capital
2. Add free reserves
3. Total (1 + 2)
4. Contingent liabilities
5. Net worth (3 − 4)
6. Fresh capital issue (face value)
7. Total net worth (5 + 6)
8. Number of shares (existing and fresh)
9. NAV per share (7/8)

The CCI guidelines state that in calculating the NAV, the following points are also to be kept in view.

a. Intangible assets like goodwill, patents, trademarks and copyrights should not be taken into account in calculating the assets.
b. Revaluation of fixed assets, if any, is ordinarily not taken into account. However, if the revaluation had taken place long ago, say nearly 15 years back, it may not be reasonable to deduct it from the total assets.
c. Any reserve which has not been created out of genuine profits or out of cash (for example, the amalgamation reserve) will not be taken into account.
d. Provision for gratuity based on the actuarial valuation net of taxes as well as provision for any other terminal benefits due to the employees should be deducted.
e. Arrears of preference dividend, unclaimed dividend and dividend not provided for separately but proposed to be paid out of reserves, arrears of depreciation, provision not made for bad and doubtful debts and miscellaneous expenditure not written off will be deducted.

f. In the case of contingent liabilities, a judgement must be made of the liabilities that are likely to impair the net worth of the company and it should be provided for on the liabilities side of the balance sheet.

g. In the matter of provision for depreciation, the following approach should be adopted.

(i) Straight line method, if consistently followed by the company.

(ii) Written down value (WDV) method, as claimed by the company for income-tax purposes if company has switched over from the WDV method to straight line method during the last five years.

Where the company follows the straight line method for new assets and the WDV method for old assets, the depreciation charged in books will be accepted.

5.2.2 The Profit-earning Capacity Value (PECV)

The PECV is calculated by capitalizing the average of the after-tax profits.

As per the CCI guidelines, the PECV is calculated by capitalizing the average of the after-tax profits at the following rates:

a. 15 per cent in the case of manufacturing companies
b. 20 per cent in the case of trading companies
c. 17.5 per cent in the case of intermediate companies (companies whose turnover from the trading activity is more than 40 per cent but less than 60 per cent of their total turnover.

In exceptional cases the capitalization rate for manufacturing companies may have to be liberalized in order to ensure a fair and equitable valuation. Such cases are illustrated here:

- Where, in the case of a listed share, the average of the NAV and the profit- earning capacity value based on the 15 per cent capitalization rate is less than the average market price by a substantial margin, say over 20 per cent, and the company has a track record of high and consistent dividend payments and bonus issues and the established position as a market leader in its field. The characteristics would be reflected in the market price of the share.
- Where the company has a high profitability rate as revealed by the percentage of after-tax profits to the equity capital of the company.
- Where the company has diversified its activities and is a multi-unit company as a result of which it would be in a position to sustain its overall profits even if any one part of its operations runs into difficulties. In such cases, the capitalization rate could be liberalized suitably up to a maximum of 12 per cent with a view to arrive at a fair and equitable valuation.

In accordance with the CCI guidelines, the provision for taxation is to be dealt with in the following manner:

- In the case of widely held companies, the provision for tax is assumed at the current tax rate under the Income Tax Act. If, however, the actual tax liability is higher than the tax liability at the current tax rate, then the actual will be taken into account. The actual tax liability is the average of the tax liability (in percentage points) for the preceding three years or the actual tax liability in the latest accounting year, whichever is higher.
- In the case of private limited companies and closely held companies, the provision for taxation is the actual tax liability, subject to a minimum of the current tax rate. If the private limited is being converted into a public limited company, the actual tax provision will be restricted to a maximum of 70 per cent.

For the computation of average profits, the CCI guidelines prescribed the following approach:

1. It should broadly be checked that the profits shown in the audited accounts of the company are true profits and that there has been no attempt at window dressing of the accounts to inflate the profits. It is important to exclude the non-recurring miscellaneous income of an abnormal nature or magnitude and the writing back of provisions.
2. Ordinarily, the averaging of profits will be done for the latest three years for which the audited accounts are available. But in appropriate cases it would be advisable to take into account the profits of the latest five years in order to arrive at a fair and realistic estimate of the future maintainable earnings.

3. If the year-to-year variation in the profits of the last three years can be considered to be normal, the average may be calculated on the basis of simple arithmetic average. But if the profits are rising consistently from year to year at a steady rate and there are reasons to believe that the rising trend will be maintained, the average may be calculated on a weighted basis, giving a weightage of three for the latest year, two for the middle year and one for the oldest year.
4. If a business has sustained losses in all the three years or even in the latest two years, the PECV will have to be regarded as nil. But if the business has sustained a loss in only one of the three years and there are reasons to believe that the loss in that year was a freak loss and does not represent the true earning potential of the business, it would be open to exclude the freak year and work out an average based on the working results of the remaining four of the latest five years. If that average is more than the profits of the latest year, the profits of the latest year are considered.

In the case of fresh capital to be raised to finance a new or an expansion project for which the company holds a letter of intent or an industrial license, or if the expansion or new project is on the ground and tangible progress has been made in implementing the project, then the forecast of future profits from the projects must be taken into consideration. It is assumed that the fresh capital would contribute to the profits up to a maximum of 50 per cent of the existing rate of profitability, and the profitability rate is calculated as shown in Equation 5.1.

$$\text{Profitability rate} = \frac{0.5 \times \text{Fresh capital (face value)} \times \text{Average PAT}}{\text{Existing net worth}} \tag{5.1}$$

Here, PAT = Profit after tax.

By keeping these points in view, the PECV is calculated as follows:

1. Average profit before tax (PBT)
2. Tax at statutory rate
3. Average PAT (1 – 2)
4. Preference dividend
5. Net PAT (3 – 4)
6. Contribution to PAT by fresh issue, if any
7. Total PAT (5 + 6)
8. Number of equity shares
9. Earnings per share (EPS)
10. PECV at 15 per cent
11. Fair value per share (average of NAV and PECV)
12. Premium per share (fair value – face value)

5.2.3 Market Value

The CCI guidelines stated the following procedure regarding determination of market value:

1. The average market price is determined by taking into consideration the stock market quotations in the preceding three years (after making appropriate adjustments for bonus issues and dividend payments) as follows.

   d. The high and low of the preceding two years; and

   e. The high and low of each month in the preceding 12 months.

2. The average market price is kept in the background as a relevant factor while settling the fair value unless there are reasons to believe that the market price is vitiated by speculative transactions or manipulative practices.
3. The reasonableness of the fair value is checked against the average market price on the following lines.

   a. If the average of the NAV and PECV on the 15 per cent capitalization basis is less than the average MV by only about 20 per cent, then the average MV will be taken as the fair value.

Table 5.1 Computation of net asset value (NAV)

Sl. No.	*Items*	*Amount (INR million)*
1	Equity capital	1500
2	Free Reserves	1200
3	Total (1 + 2)	2700
4	Contingent liabilities	50
5	Net worth (3 – 4)	2650
6	Fresh capital issue (Face value at INR 100)	500
7	Total net worth (5 + 6)	3150
8	Number of shares (existing + fresh) (in million)	15 +5 = 20
9	Net asset value per share (INR)	**157.5**

b. If the average of the NAV and PECV is less than the average market value, say by more than 20 per cent, then the PECV will be recalculated by liberalizing the capitalization rate of 15 per cent suitably. This is done in the following manner.

If the average market price is more than 20 per cent to 50 per cent of the fair value, the capitalization rate will be 12 per cent.

If the average market price is more than 50 per cent to 75 per cent of the fair value, the capitalization will be 10 per cent.

If the average market price is more than 75 per cent and above the fair value, the capitalization rate will be 8 per cent.

The fair value is determined on the basis of the average of the NAV and the recalculated PECV. As a matter of prudence, it may be desirable to deduct at least one year's dividend per share from the average of the NAV and the PECV to arrive at the fair value. A cushion of this order may be required as a safeguard against future uncertainties.

Tables 5.1–5.3 throw light on the concepts of NAV and profit earning capacity value.

Many stock market experts found that the CCI guidelines were inadequate and inconsistent. They felt that pricing of the capital issues as per the CCI guidelines was conservative. Their apprehensions were confirmed with heavy oversubscription of public issues. Because of the CCI's conservative pricing policy, the investors were in many cases rewarded handsomely as the post-issue prices were more than the issue prices.

Therefore, the method of pricing as per the CCI guidelines was found wanting and experts favoured deregulation to the extent of allowing the issuers total freedom in pricing their issues. At the same time, others argued that in the present condition of the Indian stock market, with its inefficiency, lack of transparency and prevalence of malpractices, totally unregulated freedom for issuers to price their issues would place investors at considerable risk. It was at this juncture that the Pherwani Study Group was appointed by the government. The group examined several aspects of pricing of public issues and favoured a market-based approach to pricing.

On the other hand, in the 1980s, the Government of India initiated the process of economic liberalization. The economy was opened up for foreign companies and the role of the private sector was much appreciated. These initiatives also made the capital market buoyant. Many companies tapped the primary market to raise funds and the response of retail investors to the public issues was overwhelming. The total capital raised from the primary market increased from INR 1.96 billion in 1979–80 to INR 65 billion in 1989–90.

Table 5.2 Year-wise profits

Year	*Profit before tax (INR million)*	*Profit after tax (INR million)*
2005 – 06	3000	2040
2006 – 07	3200	2176
2007 – 08	3500	2380
Total	9700	6596

Table 5.3 Profit-earning capacity value (PECV)

Sl. No.	*Items*	*Profit after tax (INR million)*
1	Average PAT (INR million)	2198
2	Preference dividend	34.7
3	PAT after preference dividend (INR million)	2163
4	Contribution to PAT by fresh issue*	204
5	Total PAT (5 + 6)	2367
6	Number of equity shares (million)	20
7	EPS (INR)	118,35
8	PECV at 15 per cent (i.e. EPS × 10.2)	1207
9	Fair value per share (INR)	108.9
10	Calculated premium per share (INR) or (Fair value – Face value of INR 100 per share)	8.9 or 9

*Calculated as per Equation 5.1

With the increasing interest of retail investors, many dubious companies that did not have any real projects raised money by issuing shares, only to vanish later. Stock market frauds and manipulations also multiplied. It was in this context that the Government of India established the Securities and Exchange Board of India (SEBI) on April 12, 1988, through an administrative order. But the board was given statutory status with the enactment of the Securities and Exchange Board of India Act in 1992. The preamble to the Securities and Exchange Board of India describes the basic functions of SEBI as "... to protect the interests of investors in securities and to promote the development of, and to regulate the securities market and for matters connected therewith or incidental thereto".

Immediately after gaining statutory powers, SEBI issued a consultative paper on free-market pricing of capital issues for public debate and invited views by April 1, 1992. The various issues involved in the free market pricing of securities offered to the public or existing shareholders by different companies under different situations were discussed.

For the first issue of new companies, two options were suggested. According to the first option, a new company, that is, a company without a track record of profitability set up either by a first-generation entrepreneur or an established promoter with a track record, may be allowed to freely price its first issue and list the securities on the main stock exchanges. Option two allows the new companies to go to the market with public issues at par.

For the first issues by existing private companies with a track record of profitability, there could be three options. The first allows these companies to price their first issues freely and list the securities on the main stock exchanges. Option two permits the companies to go to the market only at par. Under option three, the OTC exchange may also provide an option and the issuers may make a public issue on this exchange depending on the size of the issues. The OTC exchange can provide these issuers with listing conditions different from those of the other exchanges, which would include a lower requirement for the minimum issue capital and the minimum public offer compared to the other stock exchanges, the sponsorship of the determination of the price of the shares offered to the public members and dealers of the OTC, compulsory market-making by the sponsor and another member dealer for one year, and an undertaking by the sponsor to offer and allot the securities to the public in a fair manner. The disclosure and investor protection angles would be taken care of by the OTC exchange.

Existing listed companies could be allowed to raise fresh capital by pricing their issues subject to their conforming to certain guidelines. These guidelines would not be for prior clearance or approval but only for disclosure and investor protection. The determination of the price should be left to the lead managers and principal underwriters in consultation with the issuers themselves. This would call for a greater degree of responsibility, high standards of diligence and competence of the merchant bankers and underwriters. They should take into account the realities of the Indian stock market, interests of the issuer, interests of the investors and interests of the others concerned.

As far as composite issues are concerned, there is a case for allowing the existing shareholder the benefit of having stayed with the company and giving him shares at a price lower than the public issue price. The public issue could be at a market price.

The concept paper evoked a lot of discussion and gave way to new guidelines to be issued by SEBI. As per the new guidelines, the pricing of capital issues was freed from the requirements of prior approval from any regulatory authority. The free pricing of capital issues brought about sweeping changes in the capital market. Many companies took advantage of the new pricing policy and issued shares at a hefty premium. Some companies even charged an unrealistically heavy premium, which turned out to be a raw deal for the investors. In many cases the post-issue prices came down to half or even less than half of the pre-issue price. As the post-issue prices started falling, investors started becoming cautious. As a result, the subsequent capital issues received very poor response. There were many issue failures, going by the number of under-subscriptions. After burning their fingers, the issuers started adopting a realistic methodology to price their new issues. SEBI also directed the issuers to indicate the premium they would have obtained based on the CCI formula, so as to enable the investors to judge capital issues based on their price as per the conservative norms of the CCI.

Notwithstanding such reactions in the capital market, SEBI went ahead with the implementation of new guidelines. The guidelines primarily aimed at ensuring proper disclosure and investor protection. However, they have been revised many a time in tune with the needs of the day. The latest guidelines of SEBI are briefly presented in the following sections.

5.3 SEBI (Issue of Capital and Disclosure Requirements) Regulations, 2009

According to the latest SEBI regulations, the issuer may determine the price of the specified securities or the coupon rate and conversion price of convertible securities in consultation with the lead merchant banker or through the book-building process. An issuer may offer specified securities at different prices subject to the following conditions:

a. Retail individual investors or retail individual shareholders may be offered specified securities at a price lower than the price at which the net offer is made to other categories of applicants. However, such a difference shall not be more than 10 per cent of the price at which the specified securities are offered to the other categories of applicants.
b. In case of a book-built issue, the price of the specified securities offered to an anchor investor shall not be lower than the price offered to other applicants.
c. In case of a composite issue, the price of the specified securities offered in the public issue may be different from the price offered in the rights issue and the justification for such a price difference shall be given in the offer document.

The issuer may mention a price or price band in the draft prospectus (in the case of a fixed price issue) and the floor price or price band in the red herring prospectus (in the case of a book-built issue) and determine the price at a later date before registering the prospectus with the registrar of companies. However, the prospectus registered with the registrar of companies shall contain only one price or the specific coupon rate, as the case may be. If the floor price or price band is not mentioned in the red herring prospectus, the issuer shall announce the floor price or the price band at least two working days before the opening of the bid (in the case of an initial public offer) and at least one working day before the opening of the bid (in the case of a further public offer) in all newspapers in which the pre-issue advertisement was released. The cap on the price band shall be less than or equal to 120 per cent of the floor price. The cap on the price band includes a cap on the coupon rate in the case of convertible debt instruments. The floor price or the final price shall not be less than the face value of the specified securities.

An issuer making an initial public offer may determine the face value of the equity shares in the following manner.

(a) If the issue price per equity share is INR 500 or more, the issuer shall have the option to determine the face value at less than INR 10 per share. However, the face value shall not be less than INR 1 per equity share.
(b) If the issue price per equity share is less than INR 500, the face value of the equity shares shall be INR 10 per equity share. However, this regulation is not applicable to the initial public offer made by any government company, statutory authority or corporation or any special purpose vehicle set up by any of them which is engaged in the infrastructure sector.

The disclosure about the face value of equity shares shall be made in the advertisement, offer document and application form in identical font size as that of the issue price or price band.

5.3.1 Pricing of Preferential Issues

Preferential issues refer to the allotment of corporate securities to a select set of people such as promoters, relatives of promoters and institutional investors on a private placement basis. According to Section 81 (1A) of the Companies Act, 1956, a private placement is neither a rights issue nor a public issue as the retail investors or existing shareholders are not invited to participate. It is faster route through which listed companies can infuse fresh capital into their business in a cost-effective manner. The securities that form preferential issues are equity shares, cumulative convertible preference shares, optionally convertible preference shares and warrants, with equity share options. Companies such as Hotel Leela Ventures, Kotak Mahindra Bank, Pantaloon Retail, Max India and Mysore Cement are examples of companies that have issued equity shares through preferential offers in the recent past.

Preferential issues have merits as well as demerits. As far as merits are concerned, preferential offers save time and cost. Raising capital through a public issue or rights issues is a time-consuming process as many formalities have to be fulfilled. The public issues or rights issues are also expensive as money has to be spent on various items including advertising, printing of issue material, commission and brokerage. When a company is doing well or the capital market is passing through a slump (i.e., the market sentiment is weak), preferential issues are the best option available to the company to raise fresh capital. While subscribing to the preferential issue, the promoters or institutional investors may feel that the market sentiment or troubles of the company are temporary and an injection of capital could help the company come out of the trough. When the company is raising capital through preferential issue, particularly when the market sentiment is weak or when the company is passing through a troubled time, it is a good sign of the confidence the promoters or institutional investors have in the prospects of the company. The fact that the promoters wish to increase their stake is a signal that the company has the potential to grow. Preferential offers are also used to ward off the risk of a takeover. If the shares are issued to the public, there is a chance that the public may sell the shares in the future to a firm that has an intention to take over the issuer company. Instead, in a private placement, especially to the promoters of the company, such a takeover risk can be avoided.

However, preferential offers are misused more often than not. Promoters may secure the shares at a low price to consolidate their holdings in the company. There is a possibility of insider trading. To cash in on the buoyancy in the stock market, the promoters may offload their existing holdings at ruling high market prices and replenish their holdings through preferential offers by paying less than the fair price. Thus, the promoters can profit from the bull run in the market without losing their controlling interest in the company. It is a reality that promoters use preferential allotments as a means for raising their stake in their companies. It is also observed that a group of people, particularly the promoters of the company, enrich themselves in an unfair manner to the detriment of the company and smaller shareholders. Therefore, the government (SEBI) has taken a serious view of the misuse of preferential issues and issued regulations or guidelines. These regulations or guidelines have been revised from time to time keeping in view the ingenuity of people in misusing preferential offers. The SEBI regulations with regard to pricing of preferential issues are discussed here.

If the equity shares of the issuer have been listed on a recognized stock exchange for a period of six months or more as on the relevant date, the equity shares shall be allotted at a price not less than higher of the following.

(a) The average of the weekly high and low of the closing prices of the related equity shares quoted on the recognized stock exchanges during the six months preceding the relevant date; or

(b) The average of the weekly high and low of the closing prices of the related equity shares quoted on a recognized stock exchange during the two weeks preceding the relevant date.

If the equity shares of the issuer have been listed on a recognized stock exchange for a period of less than six months as on the relevant date, the equity shares shall be allotted at a price not less than the higher of the following.

(a) The price at which the equity shares were issued by the issuer in its initial public offer or the value per share calculated in a scheme of arrangement under Section 391 to 394 of the Companies Act, 1956, pursuant to which the equity shares of the issuer were listed, as the case may be; or

(b) The average of the weekly high and low of the closing prices of the related equity shares quoted on the recognized stock exchange during the period shares have been listed preceding the relevant date; or

(c) The average of the weekly high and low of the closing prices of the related equity shares quoted on a recognized stock exchange during the two weeks preceding the relevant date.

Any preferential issue of specified securities to qualified institutional buyers not exceeding five in number shall be made at a price not less than the average of the weekly high and low of the closing prices of the related equity shares quoted on a recognized stock exchange during the two weeks preceding the relevant date.

5.4 Book-building

Book-building *is a process in which the price of new securities is determined on the basis of real-time feedback of investors.*

Book-building is a process in which the price of new securities is determined on the basis of real-time feedback from potential investors. Put differently, book-building is a process by which the demand for the proposed public issue is elicited and built up, and accordingly the price of a security is determined. It is an alternative to the predetermined fixed pricing of securities. In the book-building process, the demand for an issue of securities is assessed based on the bids received at various prices from the investors and then the price of the securities is discovered. Thus, it can be said that book-building is the process of market-based price discovery and price determination. It is a transparent and flexible pricing system that aims at ascertaining the highest market-clearing price.

SEBI initially issued guidelines for book-building in 1995. According to these guidelines, the companies that raised a capital at least INR 1,000 million have the option to appoint one of the merchant bankers as the book-runner. A preliminary prospectus is filed with SEBI without mentioning the price. The book-runner circulates a copy of this red herring prospectus to the institutional buyers who are eligible for firm allotment and to the underwriters, indicating the feasible price band. After the offers are received, the book is closed and in consultation with the issuer the merchant banker determines the best price. The net public issue is priced at the price arrived at through the book-building process. Thus, the book-building facility is available only as an alternative to firm allotment and available only to the extent of the percentage reserved for firm allotment. In other words, a company can either reserve the securities for firm allotment or issue them via the book-building process. If the book-building option is used, underwriting is mandatory to the extent of the net offer to the public. According to the SEBI (Disclosure and Investor Protection) Guidelines, 2000, an issuer company may make an issue of securities to the public through a prospectus in a manner of 100 per cent of the net offer to the public through the book-building process or 75 per cent of the net offer to the public through the book-building process, or 25 per cent at the price determined through book-building. But in the latest regulations issued by SEBI in August 2009, the division of a 75 per cent book-building and 25 per cent fixed price issue is done away with. The issuer can offer specified securities at different prices, subject to certain conditions. But the book-building process is the main highlight of the new regulations issued by SEBI.

5.4.1 The Pure Auction Method of Book-building

In the ***pure auction method*** *of book-building, the issuer mentions a floor price and the investors are free to bid at any price above the floor price.*

In order to allow investors to decide the price rather than the issuer, SEBI announced on November 9, 2009, a **pure auction method** of book-building for follow-on public offerings (FPOs). Initially, this method was applicable only to FPOs, and that too, to the portion reserved for institutional investors. According to this method, the issuer mentions a floor price and the investors are free to bid at any price above the floor price. The shares are allotted on a top-down basis, starting from the highest bidder. But as per the SEBI announcement, retail investors are allotted the shares at the floor price only.

The pure auction method is in contrast to the usual book-building process. In the typical book-building as it is in vogue, the issuer mentions the price band within which the investors have to bid. The investors can bid within that band only. Further, the investors have to factor in oversubscription while applying for the securities. Suppose one wants to be allotted 10,000 shares. He has to bid for many times that quantity since the allotment is done on a pro-rata basis. But that is not required in the pure auction method. The investor can bid only for the exact quantity that he intends to buy. But he must quote a price which can ensure him the desired quantity, since the investor who bids conservatively may lose out in the pure auction method. The pure auction method is particularly useful to investors who bid aggressively in order to make a quick buck within a few days of listing of an issue. But what SEBI intended was that by allowing the investors rather than the issuers to decide the price, it would make the price discovery process practical. In other words, real price discovery is possible when there is no price indication from the issuer and the price is freely determined through an auction.

In this connection, a mention may be made of the Dutch auction method, which is a method by which investors bid for the number of shares at the price at which they want to buy them. But the allotment of shares is made only at the last successful bid price. Say an issuer has fixed the floor price at INR 100 and the lowest bid received by the issuer is at INR 120. The investors who have bid above INR 120 will be allotted shares only at INR 120 and not at the price which they quoted in their bids.

5.4.2 Benefits of Book-building

There are several benefits of book-building and some of them are briefly stated here.

1. Book-building leads to price discovery and helps in finding the intrinsic value of the security being offered.
2. The price of the security is determined in a more realistic way by taking into consideration the demand for the security.
3. The issuer gets a maximum price for the security.
4. As the issue is pre-sold, there is no uncertainty about the success of the issue.
5. The book-building process results in lower cost of the issue. Specifically, book-building helps the issuer save a lot of money on advertisements and brokerage. So the net funds to be received by the issuer will be very high.
6. The book-building process involves many syndicate members, which enhances the credibility of the issue.
7. The issuer has greater flexibility with regard to price determination and size of the issue.
8. There is greater transparency in the allotment of securities to the investors.
9. As many intermediaries are associated with the book-building process, the investors will have more confidence in the issue.
10. As the price of the security is market determined, there is very little possibility that the market price of the security would fall below the issue price. Therefore, investors are less likely to suffer from erosion of their investment on listing.
11. The issuing company can choose quality investors.
12. There is very little time lag between the date of opening of the issue and the allotment of the securities. Thus, the issuer can have quick access to the funds. Since the investors pay at the end of the pricing process, there is no upfront payment like application money. So the investors need not lock up their funds in the issue for a long time. Book-building also eliminates the arbitrage opportunity.
13. Every offer involves an issue cost, whether successful or not. Further, there is a stipulation of a minimum subscription. This puts the issuer at risk, which can be avoided in a book-building exercise. If there is not enough demand for the issue, which is known before launching the issue, the issuer can simply withdraw from the market and thereby avoid a large amount of issue costs.
14. The book-building process with its inherent characteristics creates liquidity and buoyancy in the capital market.

5.4.3 Limitations of Book-building

Book-building also suffers from certain dangers. Some of them are mentioned here.

- A few institutional investors may form a cartel and corner a large chunk of shares by quoting a lower bid to the issue.
- Awareness about the book-building concept is still very low among retail individual investors and, therefore, their participation in the book-building process is minimal. So many retail individual investors are not able to reap the benefits of book-building.

- The book-building process in the present format does not lead to real price discovery. In the fixed pricing format, the promoter or merchant banker in consultation with the management of the company fixes a single price. In the book-building format, too, he sets the issue price, though within a band. Practically speaking, there is no price discovery by the market.

Despite certain limitations and with comprehensive SEBI regulations in place, book-building is very beneficial and advantageous to both the issuer company and the investors.

5.5 The Price-Earnings Ratio (P/E Multiple)

Price-earnings multiple *is the ratio of the current market price of a stock to the EPS.*

The P/E multiple is widely used in inter-firm, inter-industry and inter-market comparisons. Particularly in the free pricing environment, issuers and merchant bankers need to value their proposed issue on a scientific basis before fixing the actual price. The price-earnings multiple is a widely used parameter in the valuation of equity issues. The price-earnings multiple is the ratio of the current market price of a stock to EPS.

There are different ways of looking at a P/E multiple. It is often used as a measure to judge whether a particular stock is fairly priced, underpriced or overpriced. A P/E multiple also represents the number of years it would take for the EPS at the present rate to equal the price being paid. The P/E ratio can also be considered as the amount paid for INR 1 of the EPS. For example, if a stock has a P/E ratio of 20, it means that for every one rupee of net earnings, the price paid is INR 20.

The share value is the EPS times the P/E multiple. For example, a firm has an EPS of INR 4 and its stock price is INR 100. So the P/E multiple is 25. Suppose the firm expects its EPS to be INR 5 next year. Then the expected share value will be INR 125 (INR 5 × 25 = INR 125). Thus, the share value is the expected EPS divided by the reciprocal of the P/E multiple (INR 5 ÷ 1/25). Thus, the higher the P/E multiple, the higher the value of the stock.

Theoretically, the price (market value) of a share is the present value of the cash flows to be received by the shareholder from the company. The shareholders would receive dividend from the company only as long as the company exists. In other words, the shareholders would receive an infinite stream of dividend from the company. Further, the dividend per share is expected to grow when the company ploughs back its profits. The growth in dividend is the company's internal rate of return times the retention ratio. Thus,

$$P_0 = \frac{D_1}{(K_e - g)}$$

In terms of EPS, the market value of a share can be stated as follows:

$$P_0 = \frac{EPS(1-b)}{(K_e - rb)}$$

$$\gg \frac{P_0}{EPS} = \frac{(1-b)}{(K_e - rb)}$$

$$\frac{P}{E} = \frac{\text{Dividened payout ratio}}{\text{Requried rate of return on equity} - \text{Expected growth rate in dividends}}$$

The growth rate of dividends depends on the retention ratio as well as the rate of return on assets. The required rate of return on equity (ROE) is given as follows:

$$ROE = R_f + R_p$$

$$= \text{Risk free return} + (\text{Beta of equity} \times \text{Market price of risk})$$

Where

D_1 = Dividend per share in year 1; b = Retention ratio; r = Return on assets; K_e = Cost of equity or equity capitalization rate or required rate of ROE; g = Growth rate (rb); D_1 / EPS_1 = Payout ratio; b = 1 – Payout ratio

As the dividend payout ratio increases, the P/E multiple also increases. So the company's payout ratio has a positive effect on the P/E multiple. But increase in the payout ratio lowers the expected growth rate in dividends which, in turn, leads to a decrease in the P/E multiple. Thus, the effect of increase in the payout ratio may neutralize the effect of the decrease in growth rate.

The major determinants of the value of a stock are future cash receipts (dividends) and the equity capitalization rate (the required rate of return). It is thus logical that the higher the expected future returns from a stock, the higher the P/E multiple. In contrast, the higher the discount factor (the required rate of return), the lower the P/E multiple. If the investors of a company feel insecure about the future returns from their stock-holdings, then they require a higher return on their investment. In other words, the higher the risk involved in the investment, the higher the required rate of return (the discount rate) and the lower the P/E multiple. By discounting the future earnings, the investor places the future in the present perspective.

5.5.1 Determinants of the P/E Multiple

The P/E multiple is calculated for a stock, an industry or a market. Although several factors influence P/E multiples, it is essentially the earnings potential of a firm, an industry or market and the degree of uncertainty of those earnings that determine the P/E multiple. Thus, the firms, industries or markets that have no expectation of high growth in future earnings tend to have a low P/E ratio. On the other hand, a high expectation of future growth in earnings may command a higher P/E ratio. For example, economic liberalization in a country may raise expectations of future growth in corporate earnings. As a result, a rise in the P/E multiple for the market as a whole is not unexpected.

The risk involved in the equity investment also influences the P/E multiple. For example, a firm with highly fluctuating demand for its product may have a high discount factor and a low P/E ratio for its stock. The higher the risk, the greater the required rate of return and hence, the lower the P/E multiple. Some companies with poor current earnings or accumulated losses may have a very high P/E multiple. This might be because of high expectation of future earnings of these companies and at the same time, the investors may not have any fears or insecurity about the earning capacity of these companies.

Stock prices are influenced by the interest rates in an economy. As the interest rates fall, the stock prices rise and vice versa. With the rise (or fall) in stock prices, the P/E multiple will increase (or decrease). Thus, there is an inverse relationship between the interest rate in an economy and the P/E multiple of the market.

Investors may pay a higher price for a stock which has high marketability and liquidity. So the stocks that are highly marketable and liquid may have a high P/E multiple. The size of the company, popularity of the company, brand image and track record and the reputation of the management all matter in the determination of the P/E multiple of a stock.

The P/E multiple is largely influenced by the company policy on the matters like dividend distribution, bonus issue, premium on capital issues and financial leverage since they have a significant bearing on the earnings potential of the company. Thus, any change in the company policy on such matters will result in changes in the P/E multiple.

The equity stocks in a market often differ in their P/E multiples. There are certain stocks trading at a very low P/E ratio and certain others trading at a very high P/E ratio. As a result, the common investor is confused about what constitutes a desirable P/E for a particular stock, industry or market. Fortunately or unfortunately, there is no fixed number for any stock, industry or market as the ideal P/E multiple.

However, there are certain conventions according to which (1) if the price-earnings to growth ratio exceeds one, it implies that the stock is overvalued; (2) if it is less than one, the stock is undervalued; and (3) if the ratio equals one, the stock is fairly valued. Further, the P/E multiple for the market as a whole would be the inverse of the real rate of return required by the investors. Note that the real rate of return is the nominal rate of return adjusted for inflation in the economy.

5.5.2 Limitations of the P/E Multiple

The P/E multiple is the most abused and misused parameter in financial analysis. While using this parameter in stock value judgement, one should keep in mind its limitations and how it has been computed. Specifically, the errors in the computation of the EPS and the manipulation or rigging of stock prices need to be checked. The loose ends in the accounting system are used by some firms to exaggerate PAT and, accordingly, the EPS. This gives rise to the wrong P/E multiple. Further, if the EPS remains not adjusted suitably for the mid-year changes in the number of shares consequent on a bonus issue, rights issue or convertible securities issue, the resultant P/E multiple will be erroneous. Similarly, the price manipulations or rigging in a stock market may also distort the P/E multiple.

5.6 Listing Price

> The **listing price** is the market price on the first day after the listing of securities on the stock exchange.

The **listing price** is the market price on the first day after the listing of securities on the stock exchange. The correctness of the IPO pricing may be reflected in the list price. Of course, the list price of a stock depends on several factors including the premium in the grey market. There may be underperformers as well as over-performers. The performance of a sample of stocks is given in Table 5.4. As can be observed from the table, some stocks have done extremely well on listing. A study conducted by *The Economic Times* on July 12, 2007 reveals that listing gains reached an all-time high of 51 per cent in 2003 and fell to 30 per cent in 2006 and just 2 per cent in the first half of 2007. In 2001 and 2002, the listing gains were negative. Of the 159 book-built IPOs between 2000 and 2007, two-thirds saw listing gains. A listing gain is defined as the return on the IPO scrip at the close of the listing day over the allotment price. It may be noted that the underpriced issues would lead to noticeable listing gains. In other words, aggressive pricing strategy may erode listing gains. The listing gains are governed by many factors. For example, if the primary market is buoyant, the issuers generally fix a competitive price which may not result in listing gains. The listing gain has a strong positive correlation with the market capitalization or the size of the issue. Underpricing is more pronounced in the case of smaller issue sizes. Further, new companies may generally have the least listing gain, but the listing gains may go up along with the age of the company. Therefore, the age (operational history) of the issuer reflects the level of maturity of the firm, which is a factor to be reckoned in the pricing of the issue.

Listing gains indicate that the issues are underpriced. Then the question arises: Why are public issues under-priced? There are many reasons for this. Underpricing is done deliberately in order to attract a wide variety of investors so that the share ownership is widely distributed. This enables the company to possess adequate liquidity for the shares in the stock market. This, in turn, also helps the company in raising capital in future on favourable terms. In fact, pricing of public issues depends on several factors. The reputation of intermediaries such as brokers, underwriters and lead managers is also an important factor in determining the price of public issues. The extent of institutional participation in capital issues also influences the pricing of issues. Obviously, the reputation or quality of the promoter(s) of the firm making the public issue also influences the pricing of issues. Information asymmetry may also cause incorrect pricing of capital issues.

Although it is essential to expand the investor base and channelize household savings into the capital market, the policies of the government have edged out the small investors from the primary market over the years. Over time, public issue as a percentage of a company's equity capital has been brought down, in steps, from 75 per cent to 60 per cent to 40 per cent to 25 per cent (in most cases now even to 10 per cent). Out of the public issue, only 25 per cent has been reserved for small investors. It is only in recent years that the reservation for retail investors has been increased to 35 per cent. This means that when a company offloads 10 per cent, the retail investors would get only 3.5 per cent. Therefore, the need of the hour is to bring a large proportion of the retail investors into the equity market so that the benefits of growth of the corporate sector are shared by all.

Table 5.4 Performance of select public issues

Company	*Date of listing*	*Issue price (INR)*	*Close price on first day of trading (INR)*
Orbit Corporation Ltd	April 12, 2007	110	128.20
ICRA Limited	April 13, 2007	330	803.25
MIC Electronics Ltd	May 30, 2007	150	338.15
Time Technoplast Ltd	June 13, 2007	315	480.90
Fortis Healthcare Ltd	May 9, 2007	108	100.15
Allied Digital Services Ltd	July 25, 2007	190	330.15
Gammon Infrastructure Projects Ltd	April 3, 2008	167	158.15
Sita Shree Food Products Ltd	April 7, 2008	30	43.70
V-Guard Industries Ltd	Mar 13, 2008	82	75.95
Reliance Power Ltd	Feb 11, 2008	450	372.30

Source: NSE, Indian Securities Market—A Review, 2008

Table 5.5 Meltdown of IPOs

Company	*Date of listing*	*Issue price (INR)*	*Close price at end of March 2008 (INR)*
Insecticides (India) Ltd	May 30, 2007	115	46.85
Nelcast Limited	Jun 27, 2007	219	97.30
Roman Tarmat Ltd	July 9, 2007	175	72.75
Empee Distelleries Ltd	Nov 26, 2007	400	153.10
Renaissance Jewellery Ltd	Dec 12, 2007	150	71.80
Brigade Enterprises Ltd	Dec 31, 2007	390	168.55
KNR Constructions Ltd	Feb 18, 2008	170	84.60
Bang Overseas Ltd	Feb 20, 2008	207	122.60
Future Capital Holdings Ltd	Feb 1, 2008	765	639.55
Shriram EPC Ltd	Feb 20, 2008	300	238

Source: NSE, Indian Securities Market—A Review 2008

The share prices that reach dizzy heights on listing, driven by hype, may subsequently witness a sharp downtrend. A sample of companies that have witnessed a sharp downtrend is presented in Table 5.5. As can be observed from the table, some shares were quoted at a heavy discount of more than 50 per cent. The meltdown in IPOs could be the fallout of the aggressive pricing done by the issuers to take maximum advantage of the bullish market prevailing at the time of the issue. The slump in the stock market following the listing may also deal a severe blow to the IPOs.

5.7 The Grey Market

*The unofficial market where the trading of shares in forthcoming IPOs is conducted is called the **grey market**.*

The unofficial market where the trading of shares in forthcoming IPOs is conducted is called the **grey market**. Trades in securities done in the grey market are settled on the day of the listing of the securities on the stock exchange(s). As one of the common strategies is to sell the shares on the first day of the listing and book profits, the traders short sell in the grey market in the anticipation that the securities will list at a price lower than that expected by most market players. In other words, the short sellers feel that the premium on the IPO is unwarranted. But the buyers in the grey market expect that the listing price will be higher than the issue price. It is a fact that the grey market exists whenever there is a strong response for a public issue.

The grey market consists of various types of players. Investors who want a certain number of shares of a company but expect that they are unlikely to be allotted that number of shares in the public issue because of the strong demand turn to the grey market. Some other investors may be ready to offload the shares at the decided price. There may be others who want to speculate and make quick money without much effort. Thus, all these parties conduct the deals outside the system before the shares actually hit the market. In reality, a few brokers in cities like Kolkata, Ahmedabad and Rajkot usually deal in the grey market exclusively. These brokers often work hand-in-hand with promoters and in the process also control the prices at which the issues are listed.

Although the price quoted in the grey market is often used as a benchmark for the market's expectations regarding a particular stock issue, it does not guarantee that when the stock is actually listed and starts trading on the exchange, it will attain the same price immediately. It is often said that the premium in the grey market is an indicator of the price at which the stock is expected to list. But it may not be so in all cases. For example, the shares of National Hydroelectric Power Corporation (NHPC) were trading at a premium of INR 7 in the grey market but never rose to that price on listing. The NHPC went public in August 2009 with an issue of 1680 million shares to mobilize INR 60,480 million, the price band being INR 30 to 36. This is an example of the fact that the grey market price may change from time to time depending on the expectations in the market conditions in the post-issue period. Another example, the premium (grey market) on Oil India shares fell from INR 100 to INR 40 after the poor performance of NHPC on listing. Oil India went public in September 2009 with 26.4 million shares at a price band of INR 950 to INR 1,050.

Since the SEBI rules do not permit shares to be transferred before the day of listing, the execution of the deals made in the grey market would take place once the listing of securities on the stock exchange is done, or they may be settled without any transfer of shares with the settlement being done in cash. According to the convention, once a trade is done at a stipulated price, the seller of the securities has to deliver the securities after they have been allotted to him by the company. If the seller falls short in receiving the exact number of shares that he has sold in anticipation, then he will have to buy the shares from the market once the shares get listed to honour his commitment. Thus, grey market operations also influence the listing price of securities. Though grey market operations are illegal, they continue to thrive.

Summary

1. The main aims of capital issues control were to prevent the establishment of those industries that did not assist in the production of essential war or consumption goods and to restrict the growth of mushroom companies with little chance of survival in normal times.
2. According to the CCI guidelines, the most reasonable judgement of the value is referred to as the fair value. The difference between the fair and the face value of the securities is the premium.
3. The NAV represents the true net worth of the business after making a provision for all the present and potential liabilities.
4. According to the latest SEBI regulations, the issuer may determine the price of specified securities or the coupon rate and conversion price of convertible securities in consultation with the lead merchant banker or through the book-building process.
5. Book building is a process in which the price of new securities is determined on the basis of real-time feedback of investors. It is an alternative to the predetermined fixed pricing of securities.
6. The piece-earnings multiple is the ratio of the current market price of a stock to the EPS.
7. The grey market is an unofficial market where trading of shares in forthcoming IPOs is conducted. Trades in securities done in the grey market are settled on the day of the listing of the securities on the stock exchange(s).

Questions

1. Discuss the CCI guidelines on the valuation of securities.
2. Differentiate between NAV and PECV.
3. How do you calculate the NAV as per the CCI norms?
4. What are the steps involved in computation of the PECV as per the CCI norms?
5. How is the market value determined as per the CCI norms?
6. What are the salient features of consultative paper issued by SEBI in 1992?
7. Critically evaluate SEBI regulations of 2009 with regard to pricing of capital issues.
8. What are the SEBI guidelines for the pricing of preferential issues?
9. Explain the book-building process. What are the limitations of the existing form of the book-building process? How they can be avoided?
10. What are the implications and limitations of the P/E ratio?
11. What do you understand by the grey market? What would the grey market indicate? Should the grey market be banned?

Case Study

Thinksoft Global Services Ltd IPO

Thinksoft Global Services Limited was incorporated on June 8, 1998, as Relliant Global Services (India) Private Limited in Bangalore, Karnataka.

Thinksoft is a banking, financial services and insurance (BFSI) focused software-testing enterprise. Thinksoft operates as a specialist and niche player in the financial and insurance software-testing space. The company's service in the area of testing and business requirements assurance includes functional testing, performance testing, test automation and requirement documentation services.

ICRA has assigned an IPO Grade 2 to Thinksoft Global Services Ltd IPO, indicating below average fundamentals. ICRA assigns IPO grading on a scale of 5 to 1, with 5 indicating strong fundamentals and 1 indicating poor fundamentals.

Issue open: September 22, 2009
Issue close: October 1, 2009
Price band: INR 115 to INR 125 per equity share
Minimum bid size: 50 equity shares
Issue size: 3,646,000 equity shares of INR 10 each; fresh issue of 13,50,000 equity shares and offer for sale of 22,96,000 equity shares

Issue size (INR million): 455.7
Issue price: INR 125 per share
Face value: INR 10 per equity share
Issue type:100 per cent book built issue IPO
Listing at: BSE, NSE
Maximum subscription amount for retail investor: INR 100000
Book running lead managers: Karvy Investor Services Limited

Standard Chartered PLC: Public Issue and Listing of Indian Depository Receipts

Standard Chartered PLC is a leading international bank, listed on the London and Hong Kong stock exchanges. It has operated for over 150 years in some of the world's most dynamic markets and earns around 90 per cent of its income and profits in Asia, Africa and the Middle East. This geographic focus and commitment to developing deep relationships with clients and customers has driven the bank's growth in recent years.

With approximately 1,700 branches and outlets in more than 70 markets, Standard Chartered offers exciting and challenging international career opportunities for more than 75,000 staff. The bank is committed to building a sustainable business in the long run and aims for the highest standards of corporate governance, social responsibility, environmental protection and employee diversity. This heritage and these values are expressed in its brand promise, "Here for good".

Standard Chartered PLC announced during the last week of May 2010 the issue of 240,000,000 Indian depository receipts at a price band of INR 100 to INR 115 per IDR. Every 10 IDRs represent one ordinary share of Standard Chartered PLC, having a nominal value of USD 0.50. Bids can be made for a minimum of 200 IDRs and in multiples of 200 IDRs thereafter.

The 24,000,000 new Standard Chartered ordinary shares which will be issued in connection with the IDR issue will be allotted on or around June 7, 2010, with each new ordinary share having a nominal value of USD 0.50.

The IDRs are expected to be listed on Bombay Stock Exchange Limited (BSE) and National Stock Exchange of India Limited (NSE) by 11 June.

The company has appointed the following financial advisers in relation to the issue of the IDRs: UBS Securities India Private Limited and Goldman Sachs (India) Securities Private Limited (as global coordinators); JM Financial Consultants Private Limited, DSP Merrill Lynch Limited, Kotak Mahindra Capital Company Limited and SBI Capital Markets Limited (as book running lead managers). The company has appointed Standard Chartered–STCI Capital Markets Limited as a co-book running lead manager. As corporate brokers to the company, J.P.Morgan Cazenove and UBS Investment Bank will provide additional advice and guidance in connection with the proposed issue.

The Red Herring Prospectus is available on the website of SEBI at www.sebi.gov.in and the respective websites of the book running lead managers at www.ubs.com/indian-dr, www2.goldmansachs.com/worldwide/india, www.jmfinancial.in, www.dspml.com, www.kotak.com, www.sbicaps.com and co-book running lead manager at www.standardchartered-wealthmanagers.co.in. Investors should note that investment in IDRs involves risk and for details relating to the same, see the section titled "Risk Factors" of the Red Herring Prospectus.

Source: http://investors.standardchartered.com/releasedetail.cfm?ReleaseID=474792

Question

How do you justify the price band fixed by the two companies? You may visit the website of the respective companies if further information is required.

Chapter 6

Settlement of Stock Market Transactions

LEARNING OBJECTIVES

After studying this chapter, you should be able to:

- Present a historical perspective of the settlement system in stock exchanges.
- Explain the concept of *badla* and its implications.
- Present government initiatives with regard to settlement of stock market transactions.
- Discuss the developments in the settlement system in India.
- Explain the rolling settlement system.
- Deal with the concept of margin trading.
- Discuss the securities lending scheme.

6.1 Introduction

A stock market is a trading platform through which investors can buy and sell listed securities that may be equity shares or debt securities like bonds and debentures. Only registered brokers and sub-brokers are allowed to do business or make transactions on the stock exchange. Therefore, an investor who wants to buy or sell securities through a stock exchange needs to register himself/herself with one of the brokers or sub-brokers by signing an agreement. The investor may also be required to deposit some money with the broker or sub-broker, which is known as the *margin*. Depending on the margin, the broker will have exposure in terms of the trading of securities on behalf of the investor.

Settlement is the process through which the buyer of the securities makes the payment and the seller delivers the securities. This settlement process ensures that the seller delivers the securities and receives the sale proceeds minus the brokerage amount, stamp duty and securities transaction tax, and that the buyer pays the purchase price plus other incidental expenses like the brokerage, stamp duty and securities transaction tax and receives the securities.

***Settlement** is the process through which the buyer of the securities makes the payment and the seller delivers the securities.*

The period within which buyers receive their shares and sellers receive their money is called a **settlement cycle**. The market participants buy and sell the same company shares within a settlement cycle and settle only their net outstanding positions at the end of the cycle. The entire process of settlement of securities and money is managed by the stock exchange. This chapter focuses on the changes in the settlement process.

*The period within which buyers receive their shares and sellers receive their money is called a **settlement cycle**.*

6.2 The Traditional Perspective

Historically, as per the bylaws and regulations of stock exchanges, transactions in stock markets could result in one of the following:

a. Spot delivery: Delivery and payment on the same day as the date of the contract or on the next day.

b. Hand delivery: Delivery and payment within the time or on the stipulated date when entering into the contract. This time or date shall not be more than 14 days following the date of the contract.

c. Special delivery: Delivery and payment within any time exceeding 14 days following the date of the contract as may be stipulated when entering into the contract and permitted by the stock exchange concerned.

d. Clearing of the account: Clearance and settlement through the clearing house of the stock exchange.

The buying and selling of stocks for spot delivery or hand delivery could be done in cleared as well as non-cleared securities, but buying and selling transactions for the clearing could be done only in cleared securities.

The contracts for special delivery could be entered into for cleared or non-cleared securities after obtaining permission from the concerned stock exchange.

Thus, shares listed on the stock exchanges were classified into two categories—(i) the *cleared list* and (ii) the *non-cleared (cash) list*. Only shares included in the cleared list enjoyed the facility of forward trading, and the transactions in the non-cleared shares took the form of contracts for spot delivery, which meant that the shares were delivered and the price for them generally paid on the day after the transaction.

Buying and selling of stocks for spot delivery or hand delivery are done in cleared as well as non-cleared securities, but buying and selling transactions for the clearing could only be done in cleared securities.

6.2.1 Cleared Securities

Cleared securities are securities for which transactions are settled through the clearing house of the stock exchange. The buying and selling transactions for the clearing are for the account or fortnightly settlement. The transactions for clearing generally commence in the afternoon session on a Friday and end a fortnight later in the afternoon session of the third Friday. Any purchase or sale made during a clearing cycle may be offset by a subsequent sale or purchase during the same clearing cycle. All outstanding transactions (purchases or sales) have to be settled by delivery and payment on the prescribed clearing day(s) unless they are to be carried over to the next clearing cycle. After the last business day of each clearing cycle, deliveries and payments are made through the clearing house. The system thus eliminates all intermediaries and brings the buyer and seller together.

__Cleared securities__ are securities for which transactions are settled through the clearing house or clearing corporation of the stock exchange.

Although the proportion of securities on the cleared list is very small, the volume of trading in the cleared securities is very large. For example, for the three years from 1966 to 1968, about 97–98 per cent of the annual trading volume on the stock exchanges was accounted for through cleared securities alone, which formed just about one-third of all listed equities in terms of market value. Another way of looking at this is that the shares of non-cleared securities in the total trading volume was only 2–3 per cent, even though they represented about two-thirds of the aggregate market value of all listed equities.[1]

6.2.2 Forward Trading

Forward trading is the trading of securities that involves delivery and payment to be made on a specified date in future. Stock exchanges had a system of fortnightly settlement periods for forward transactions. All forward transactions that take place during a particular fortnight are settled through a system of clearing on the settlement day. Forward trading facilitates the buying and selling a large quantity of securities without paying money for the purchase or delivering the securities immediately. Market operators can also enter into offsetting transactions before the settlement date so that they ultimately pay only the difference in prices. That is, the real transfer of securities between the buyer and the seller rarely happens in forward trading. Such transactions are usually backed by speculation. It may be noted that the lower the proportion of stocks delivered in the total number of stocks traded, the greater is the extent of speculation. Moreover, the stock trading system that exists in the stock markets also provided a facility to "carry forward" the outstanding transactions from one settlement to another for an indefinite period.

__Forward trading__ is the trading of securities that involves future delivery and payment.

6.2.3 Carry Forward

In general, if a person wants to buy an asset, whether it is a real asset or a financial asset, he can do so with one of two options. He can use his own money to buy the asset. In this case, he gives up the opportunity cost (the return he could have earned otherwise) of the money utilized for making the down payment for the asset purchased. Alternatively, he can borrow money on interest and buy the asset. Of course, there is also the possibility of using both the owned and borrowed money to buy the asset. However, when dealing with stock markets, there is another provision that enables the buyers to buy the stock without using their own money and without having to borrow money. That is, one can go long (buy the stock without any down payment) and carry one's transaction forward under the carry forward mechanism and pay contango charges (interest).

The amount paid (interest) by the buyer of the securities for carrying his transaction forward under the carry forward mechanism is known as __contango__.

[1]U.L. Gupta, "Speculation at the Indian Stock Exchanges," *Business Analyst,* Sept-Dec 1969, pp. 241–242.

Thus, the buyer of securities, for example, can take delivery of the securities and pay for the same on the settlement date if he has not already offset his forward purchase. Alternatively, the buyer can carry forward his purchase position to the next settlement by reversing his purchase position in the current settlement with a sale transaction at the making-up price and creating a fresh purchase position in the next settlement. The *making-up price* is fixed by the stock exchange, which is usually the rounded-up figure of the closing quotation of the security on the last trading day of the settlement. In the process, the buyer of the securities may have to pay or receive, as the case may be, the difference between his original purchase price (contract price) and the making-up price.

Similarly, a seller, if he has not already offset his sale contract by a purchase contract, can either give delivery of shares and receive payment for the sale or alternatively can carry forward his sale position in the current settlement to the next settlement. The carry forward of the sale position is done by reversing the sale position in the current settlement by a purchase position at the making-up price and creating a fresh sale transaction in the next settlement. In the process, the seller would receive or pay, as the case may be, the difference between his contract price and the making-up price.

When a buyer (bull) of shares wants to carry forward his purchase position, particularly when stock prices are falling, but the seller would like to give delivery of the shares, the *badliwalla* or financier comes on the scene. The financier takes delivery of the shares (purchases) in the current settlement from the seller on behalf of the purchaser who does not want to take delivery but wants to carry forward his purchase to the next settlement, and simultaneously enters into a contract with that purchaser to sell the same shares to him in the next settlement. This type of transaction is known as the *vyaj badla.* The difference between the purchase price in the current settlement and the sale price in the next settlement is the interest earned by the financier. The interest amount thus paid by the purchaser (bull) to the financier or the short seller is called **contango**, popularly known as the *badla* rate. The *badla* rates are determined by market forces but vary from settlement to settlement and from scrip to scrip. The *badla* rates are high in a bull run, but generally the rates reflect interest rates in the economy. The contango charges can also be viewed in a different perspective. The bull pays the contango charges to buy the upside potential of security price and the bear (short seller) is compensated for giving up the upside potential.

In times of oversold position (that is, rising prices), the seller (bear) of the shares may have to pay the buyer for carrying over the transaction to the next settlement. The charges paid by the seller to the buyer to carry forward his position are known as *backwardation.* Where there are more short sales than long positions, there is a need for securities to be lent in the market to meet the shortfall. Thus, the stock lender steps in to meet the shortfall but he needs to be paid by the short seller.

The rationale for providing the facility to carry forward the transaction from one settlement period of 14 days to another is that it provides liquidity and breadth to the market. Without a carry forward facility, all purchases outstanding at the end of a settlement are required to be paid with the delivery of the relevant securities. Similarly, all sales outstanding at the end of the settlement have to result in the delivery with the receipt of the consideration amount. This would lead to a narrow market and low turnover of business, with attendant problems of illiquidity of securities and sharp changes in prices. Thus, the carry forward system can increase the volume of trade and add liquidity to the market but it was also seen as a conduit for rampant speculation. A study conducted by L.C. Gupta on 47 shares on the forward trading list revealed that in two of the 47 cases, the trading volume was over 100 times the volume of transfers registered with the respective companies; in nine other cases it was over 20 times, in six cases between 10 and 20 times and in seven cases between five and 10 times. The study concluded that the percentage of equity capital changing hands between the investors, as evidenced by transfers registered with companies, was below 8 per cent in a large majority of companies.[2]

__Badla__ is a penalty interest that a party who expects a rise in prices or a party who expects a fall in prices has to pay to the other party for the carry-over of a transaction from one settlement to another.

6.2.4 Badla

Badla is a penalty interest that the bull (a party who expects a rise in prices) or the bear (a party who expects a fall in prices) has to pay to the counterparty for the carry-over of a transaction from one settlement to another. When a bear has sold more shares than he can deliver at the settlement date, the bull will have the chance to demand delivery and thus force the bear to either cover with an offsetting transaction, which eventually leads to further rise in prices, or pay the *badla* at market rates. The bear agrees to pay the *badla* and carry over the transaction if he is confident that

[2]L.C. Gupta, "Review of Management," *Economic and Political Weekly* 8, no. 34, August 25, 1973, pp. 85–96.

forthcoming events will cause a fall in prices. On the other hand, when a bull has bought more shares than he has money with which to take delivery, the bear gets his chance of offering delivery of securities. This forces the bull either to sell out, that is, pay the difference, which must cause a fall in prices, or pay the reverse *badla*. It may be noted that the threat on the part of the bull to take delivery or on the part of the bear to offer delivery is, of course, a bluff. In reality, the bull has no money to pay and take delivery of the stock and the bear has no scrip to deliver. The actual position of the market is stage-managed or manipulated in favour of either bulls or bears. The confidence of the party who is at the disadvantageous position will ultimately decide the level of the *badla* rates.

The *badla* rates that are determined by market forces vary from settlement to settlement and from scrip to scrip in the same settlement. The *badla* rates generally depend on a varying set of factors including the extent of outstanding position, floating stocks, returns available in alternative investments, ready availability of finance and the extent of short sales. Thus, there exists a relationship between the *badla* rates in the stock market and the return from alternative investments. In other words, there is a close integration between the return from *badla* finance on the one hand and the returns from other avenues of investment on the other hand.

The *badla* system of trading was permitted in only four of the 22 stock exchanges in India, namely Bombay, Calcutta, Delhi and Ahmedabad. The other 18 stock exchanges had weekly settlement systems without the carry forward facility (that is, without a *badla* system). The market participants in these stock exchanges were either forced to indulge in intra-settlement speculation or resort to covert *badla* operations outside the confines of the exchanges-sponsored settlement system. It was found that the intra-settlement mechanism had caused distortions in market prices, and the covert *badla* operations exposed the market participants as well as the investor–traders to unregulated and personal risks.

Within the regulatory framework of the self-regulatory stock markets, the *badla* system virtually dominated the Indian stock markets for a long time and became a haven for the speculators. The speculators in the stock markets either square off their transactions within the settlement period or carry forward their outstanding positions to the next settlement through the *badla* system. Thus, the *badla* system enables the speculators to be more aggressive in their speculative operations since it provides a kind of safety net.

The advantages of the *badla* system are:

1. Since there is no transfer of ownership of securities and stamp duty, the transaction costs of trading are lower. The market participants can avoid the stamp duty on share transfers applicable to the cash market transactions. These lower transaction costs generate a high volume of trade, resulting in more liquidity in the market. The large trading volume also drives down jobbing spreads, which also adds to the liquidity of the market.
2. The capital necessary to assume a position (buy or sell) through *badla* trading is lower than that in the cash market.
3. In a highly liquid market, the share prices reflect the information available to market participants more quickly. So the share market is more efficient and less volatile with *badla* trading than without it. This increases the investors' confidence in the stock market.

The disadvantages of the *badla* system are:

1. The *badla* system makes share prices more volatile than they would be otherwise. Due to the *badla* system, the market participants, particularly the speculators, form syndicates known as bulls and bears. Each of these seeks to drive prices in its favour by using all sorts of methods. Thus, bouts of boom and depression in the stock markets are not caused as much by economic events as they are by speculative activities.
2. The *badla* system of yesteryears facilitates many market abuses including price rigging and insider trading.
3. It also causes a distortion of the market system by making the trading largely concentrated in a small group of shares while neglecting the rest. This creates an artificial financial advantage for some companies, particularly the large companies, and puts the smaller companies at a corresponding financial disadvantage.
4. The *badla* system is a deterrent to the orderly growth of the stock markets in the country.
5. The *badla* system provides almost unlimited leverage to operators, causing a high risk in the market.
6. The essential problem with *badla* is its non-transparent and double-edged leverage.

It was also observed by many stock market pundits that the *badla* system and its inherent speculative element had done more harm than good to the markets. It allowed for mindless and reckless speculation. An impression was created in market circles that the *badla* system existed only to facilitate speculation. The stock scam of 1992 was attributed to the *badla* system that existed at that time. The leverage embedded in *badla* caused a steady stream of payment crises in the stock markets. Thus, the *badla* or a carry forward system that had existed in the Indian stock markets resulted in systemic risk and market manipulation.

6.2.5 The Positive Role of Speculation in the Stock Market

Members of stock exchanges in India may be categorized as *jobbers* and *speculators*. *Jobbers* offer bids and present rates for a scrip, and are ready to buy and sell the scrip depending on demand and supply positions of the scrip in the market. Jobbers absorb the excess in the demand side as well as in the supply side of a security. On the other hand, **speculators** are those who buy and sell securities without the intention of taking or giving delivery of the securities. Their intention is always to make windfall gains by speculating on the price changes. They may also resort to market manipulations in the process of making a quick buck. Speculation in the Indian stock markets was facilitated by the provision for a blank transfer in the Companies Act, 1956, and the facility of carry forward of deals from one settlement to another provided by the stock exchanges.

> ***Speculators** are those who buy and sell securities without the intention of taking or giving delivery of securities.*

It is generally accepted that there is a need for speculation in the market, whether it is a stock market or a commodity market. The main advantage with speculation is that it improves the liquidity of the shares or commodities dealt in the market. When there is sufficient liquidity in the market, investors can easily convert their investment in shares into cash with the least possible loss at any time. Speculation also ensures a continuous market for the shares, which is essential for price discovery in the market.

A market with a speculative fervour is believed to have a cushion against price fluctuations. During a period of falling prices, the fall takes more time as there are support levels at every stage of the fall. The same scenario holds true during an upswing in the prices of stocks. Thus, speculation plays a positive role in stabilizing the prices in the stock market. As speculation is a double-edged weapon, there is disagreement regarding the degree of speculation that is required for a market.

6.3 Government Initiatives

There was a steep rise of prices in the stock markets in the first half of 1969 due to the investment interest stimulated by the Union budget of 1969–1970 and the improved performance of major sectors of the economy—industry and agriculture. The share price index of the Reserve Bank of India rose from 80.7 at the end of 1968 to 99.8 in mid-June 1969. It was at this time that the Government of India imposed a ban on the "trading of contracts for clearing", technically known as *badla* trading, under the bylaws of stock exchanges in order to curb unhealthy trends and prevent undesirable speculation. With contracts for the clearing trades officially banned, *badla* trading continued to be conducted in the name of hand delivery contracts in specified shares. A *hand delivery contract* is a contract for delivery and payment within the time or on the dates stipulated when entering into a contract. That date or time shall not be more than 14 days following the date of the contract. However, it was stated that in the case of such shares as may be designated by the governing board of the stock exchange as specified shares, the delivery and payment may be extended or postponed by further periods of 14 days each, so that the overall period does not exceed 90 days from the date of the contract. But in reality, this 90-day period was commonly exceeded. The proviso was officially recognized by the Government of India in July 1983. But SEBI imposed a ban on such trading in the existing form on December 13, 1993, and suggested an alternative system. The main features of the alternative system are as follows:

1. At the end of a settlement, all brokers are required to pay/deliver their net positions. Consistent with this, a carry forward mechanism will enable the buyers who are short of money to finance their transactions through a financier and the sellers who are short of shares to effect delivery by obtaining shares. *Badla* charges may be paid by the buyer to the financier and by the short seller to the lender of securities.
2. On the pay-in day, the clearing house receives all securities sold and the payment for all securities bought. The transactions between the financier and the long buyer and the broker lending the shares

and the short seller will be carried forward to the next settlement but shall not form part of the transactions in the next or any subsequent settlement. Such transactions shall not be allowed to be squared off but will be settled by delivery and payment. Such transactions shall be subject to an initial carry over margin of 30 per cent and an additional margin of 15 per cent shall be payable for each subsequent carry forward. However, in no case will a transaction be allowed to be carried forward beyond a period of 90 days.

3. Brokers will be required to pay margins on a gross basis and not on a net basis. The margins for carry forward transactions shall be payable on the basis of making-up prices.
4. Squaring up is allowed during the same settlement but will not be allowed between carry forward transactions and the current transactions of the settlement either for the financier (or lender of securities) or the purchasers (or the sellers).
5. Stock exchanges will have to make provisions to see that the shares are actually delivered to the clearing house and no delivery outside should be allowed. The money adjustment through exchange of *kapalis* (credit notes) and delivery through delivery advices should be strictly disallowed in the clearing mechanism.
6. The jobbers may be provided with necessary funds so that they may maintain adequate securities in which they are jobbing. But such facilities can be offered only on the condition that they also undertake the basic obligations, namely to provide two-way quotes for buying and selling and that the spread in these prices are reasonable, depending upon the scrip position. The jobbers are also required to buy and sell a minimum number of shares at quoted prices.
7. The prudential norms for limiting the carry forward position in aggregates will be in the range of 20–25 per cent of the total net outstanding position in the market at the end of the settlement. To administer this effectively, this norm will be made applicable broker-wise. Similar norms for scrip-wise positions would also have to be laid down. Proposals from exchanges are welcome in this regard. If in any settlement the carry forward position exceeds the laid down norms, the exchange will have to enforce the delivery and payment for the outstanding net position. This will act as a circuit breaker.

The alternative system suggested by SEBI was essentially aimed at the settlement of transactions through payment by buyers and delivery by sellers. It did not permit squaring up of carry forward transactions, which need to be settled only by delivery and payment. Also, the new system did not allow for a transaction to be carried forward beyond a period of 90 days. Buyers who are short of funds to finance their purchases can avail themselves of *badla* finance, and sellers who are short of shares to effect deliveries can borrow shares from lenders of securities. The buyers would be required to pay for *badla* finance and sellers to pay for borrowing securities. But the earlier *badla* system benefited short sellers, who were rewarded with contango (*badla*) charges despite having sold shares without possessing them.

The alternative system suggested by SEBI was not accepted by the bourses. The main arguments put forth by the market operators were as follows:

1. The alternative system does not allow for squaring up of carried over transactions in the second and subsequent settlements. This exposes the market operators to unpredictable risks. Moreover, the denial of squaring up of transactions does not provide any speculative incentives to the operators and hence restricts trading.
2. The carry over is subjected to a margin of 30 per cent initially and a further margin of 15 per cent in each subsequent settlement. Such margins were felt to be too high. Under these norms, many brokers would not be able to transact large business. The financiers feel that this margin requirement was an additional charge on their profits.

The abolition of the *badla* system resulted in a considerable shrinkage in the volume of business. It also led to the widening of spreads between buying and selling prices and marred liquidity in the market. But SEBI was confident that with the globalization of the economy, the inflow of large foreign funds, entry of foreign stock-broking firms and expansion of private sector mutual funds, overall business was bound to grow by leaps and bounds. It strongly felt that the traditional *badla* system was faulty and a deterrent to the orderly growth of the markets when they were going global.

6.3.1 G.S. Patel Committee

In the midst of heated debate on the carry-forward system, SEBI appointed the G.S. Patel Committee which submitted its report in March 1995. The highlights of the committee's recommendations are as follows:

1. Daily margins of 15 per cent on gross position shall be imposed against the earlier proposal of excessive margins of 30 per cent of the first settlement and climbing to 90 per cent by the fifth settlement.
2. The margin is to be charged on prices marked-to-the-market on a weekly basis.
3. Twenty-five per cent of the profit earned by the broker on the carry forward of position shall be impounded.
4. Squaring up shall be permitted between the second and sixth settlement unlike the earlier SEBI stand of carry forward transactions of delivery or payment as the case may be.
5. Capital adequacy norms shall be enforced effectively.
6. Resumption of trading in specified shares is to be preceded by screen-based trading.
7. A strong monitoring system is to be put in place. Stock exchanges have to fix responsibility on executive directors for surveillance, audit and reporting.
8. There shall be a uniform settlement period for all stock exchanges.
9. SEBI may permit the restoration of the carry forward system with prudential precautions.
10. The indigenous system of *badla* should not be revived.
11. SEBI should permit the continuance of individual carry forward transactions for a period of 90 days.
12. Each transaction carried over from a settlement should be identified by a transaction number, which will be continued in every carry over to ensure that no transaction is carried beyond 90 days.
13. This safeguard could be implemented by a monthly auditor's report certifying that a broker has not carried forward any transaction beyond 90 days.
14. The resumption of trading in specified shares should, as far as possible, be preceded by the facility of screen-based trading to ensure greater transparency.
15. At the end of each trading day, members should be made to demarcate all transactions as those meant for delivery, jobbing, carry forward and trading on own account, and report on these separately. However, trading for transactions meant for delivery need not be conducted separately.
16. Shares issued by *vyaj badla* financiers should be deposited and kept in the safe custody of the stock exchange. This is intended to prevent these shares being traded until the financier has been paid.
17. Brokers should maintain separate accounts of *vyaj badla* financiers and their own sources of finance.
18. Payment of contango charges to short sellers should be permitted as they also perform a useful function in moderating excesses in the market.

Thus, the G.S. Patel Committee sought to retain the good elements of the traditional *badla* system while eliminating the malpractices.

Based on the recommendations of the G.S. Patel Committee, SEBI permitted the stock exchanges to resume carry forward trading in shares. The revised carry forward system (RCFS) announced by SEBI on July 28, 1995, was largely based on the recommendations of the G.S. Patel Committee. However, the system announced by SEBI was more stringent as it aimed at restricting the quantum of forward business. The revised system stipulated that carry forward transactions should not exceed 25 per cent of a broker's total transactions on that day. Also, the rate of daily margins stipulated by SEBI was higher than those proposed by the Patel committee. It was also stated that the stock exchanges need to seek prior permission from SEBI for commencing forward trading in securities. This permission would, however, be granted only if the stock exchanges had a screen-based trading system and an effective monitoring and surveillance system. SEBI also said that the exchanges must introduce the twin-track system, which would provide for segregation of transactions into carry forward and cash. The margin on carry forward transactions would be imposed on a gross basis varying from 20 per cent in the first settlement period to 50 per cent in the fifth settlement. The sixth settlement would be a delivery/payment period. The financiers funding the carry forward transactions are the lenders of funds and therefore should not be permitted under any circumstances to square up their positions till repayment of the loan and shares received by such financiers against those transactions is deposited and kept in the safe custody of the clearing house of the stock exchanges. Every member would be required to keep a record of the source of finance and maintain separate accounts of finance with sub-accounts at the clearing house. The carry forward position shall be disclosed to the market scrip-wise and broker-wise by the stock exchanges at the beginning of the carry forward session.

The following four features in the new carry forward system were considered to be an improvement on the old *badla* system:

1. As trading in the new carry forward system has to be screen-based, there will be greater transparency. Non-computerized exchanges would not be permitted to have the carry forward system. Screen-based trading is far more transparent and allows for better control systems. It allows for immediate intermediation in case of any problem at the initial stages.
2. Transactions would be demarcated right from the beginning and the transactions would be separate for delivery, jobbing and carry forward.
3. Financiers involved in carry forward operations would not be permitted to square up their positions, and the shares received by them against financing would be kept in safe custody. Financiers would thus remain only financiers and not be allowed to become players too. In the case of *badla*, the lender would receive collateral in the form of securities. He would therefore become a player apart from being a financier. Most of the problems with the *badla* system arose on this account. Now, the collateral would have to be deposited in the stock exchange and there is no chance of the *badla* financier playing the market himself. Consequently, all related problems would also disappear. This is a major difference between the *badla* system and the new system.
4. Mark-to-market concept, with losses being collected and profits being withheld, would be brought into operation initially on a weekly basis and later on a daily basis. This system, which was not there in *badla*, would impart safety to the market.

The stock market players, however, were not happy with SEBI's modified forward trading system. They said that conditions like quantitative restrictions on carry forward transactions and steeper daily margins made the new system unworkable. The stipulation that only 25 per cent of the transactions could be carried forward was not practical. This would go against the very nature of the carry forward system—which is to enhance liquidity, particularly during "tight money periods" when the delivery market is down. The scrip-wise disclosure of outstanding positions for each broker would distort the pricing process as well.

6.3.2 J.R. Varma Committee

The J.R. Varma Committee set up by SEBI to review the RCFS submitted its report in August 1997. The major recommendations of the committee are as follows:

1. Abolish the twin-track system of segregating carry forward trades and delivery trades.
2. A uniform margin of 10 per cent on gross positions with daily marking-to-market should be applied to both types of transactions.
3. In the case of *vyaj badla*, the financier should be allowed to take custody of the shares with two safeguards. The first safeguard is that the financier would be required to return the same distinctive numbers of shares that he has taken as collateral. This would prevent the financier from trading in these shares. The second condition is that the *vyaj badla* financier would be subject to mark-to-market, like any other seller, on the shares withdrawn by him. This would deal with the issue of the counterparty risk faced by borrowers in cases where the financier defaults in returning the shares if the value increases.
4. The committee recommended elimination of:

   a. The limit of 90 days for carried forward transactions,

   b. Settlement only by delivery after the seventy-fifth day,

   c. A limit of INR 100 million on financier funding, and

   d. The overall limits, sub-limits on purchase and sale, scrip-wise limits on carry forward transactions and on overall transactions.

5. The committee emphasized some of the existing safeguards:
   a. Capital adequacy and other prudential safeguards should be strictly enforced.
   b. The stock exchanges should ensure that the scrips have sufficient floating stock and high liquidity while choosing scrips for carry forward.
   c. Exchanges should have adequate monitoring and surveillance systems to enable the timely use of the various powers vested in them to regulate the market. These powers include suspending the carry forward facility whenever the aggregate outstanding position in any security exceeds pre-announced limits, imposition of price corrective measures, fixing of differential rates of making-up prices, prohibiting short sales and long purchases, suspending buying-in and selling-out provisions, ordering contraction of outstanding carry forward position, imposition of limits on purchases and sales for speculative business, imposing additional limits on price fluctuations, suspending off-the-floor transactions, fixing maximum and minimum prices and regulating carry forward charges.

These recommendations were aimed at modifying the RCFS and bringing in a new system called the modified carry forward system (MCFS).

In order to introduce rolling settlement in the stock exchanges in a phased manner, SEBI reconvened the J.R. Varma Committee. The terms of reference of the committee were to consider the proposal of the Bombay Stock Exchange (BSE) for the introduction of the carry forward mechanism in rolling settlement, to suggest adequate safeguards in this regard and to consider revisions in the existing carry forward system. The committee held three meetings in November and December 1999.

The committee felt that the proposal for daily carry forward under rolling settlement (CFRS) did not present any new conceptual issues. The carry forward period shrank from two weeks to one week when weekly settlements were introduced; it could shrink to a day when daily (rolling) settlements are introduced. The fundamental characteristics of the instrument would not change and the risk-mitigating mechanisms would not be materially different.

The committee recommended that the weekly carry forward system under the rolling settlement system be introduced as a carry forward product to make it easier for the market to understand and use the product. Exchanges must be allowed to introduce futures contract in individual stocks directly, without first creating a carry forward product and then migrating it to a futures contract. The committee was of the view that the two products—weekly CFRSs and futures contract on individual stocks—can coexist. The committee was also of the opinion that daily carry forward and weekly carry forward be permitted and the stock exchanges should be free to decide whether to introduce either of the two or both or neither. The choice should be left to the individual stock exchanges.

In the process of implementing the rolling settlement system, SEBI constituted a group, with J.R. Varma as the chairman, in April 2001 to examine the need for having deferral products like CFRS and continuous net settlement (CNS) in rolling settlement. The group was of the view that with the modernization of the stock market over the last few years, particularly with dematerialization and the introduction of derivative markets, it was possible to have a clear segregation of the cash and derivative markets in stocks. The introduction of large-scale rolling settlement provides the natural opportunity to carry out this transformation. The group, therefore, recommended that from July 2, 2001, the cash market must be a pure rolling settlement market without any deferral products and simultaneously a complete set of derivative products on the index and on individual stocks should be introduced in the derivative markets.

6.4 Settlement Cycle

When a sale transaction is made the buyer of the securities should receive the securities purchased and the seller of the securities should get the money for the securities sold. After sale of securities through a stock exchange how quickly one gets the money/securities depends on the settlement cycle. The period, within which the settlement is made, i.e., the period within which buyers receive their shares and sellers receive their money is called the settlement cycle. Settlement as such is the process whereby the securities are delivered by the seller and payment is made by the buyer. During any particular settlement cycle one can trade in securities (buying and selling) many a time but settlement is made on net outstanding positions at the end of the cycle only. For example, during a particular settlement cycle one has made the following transactions:

- Bought 100 shares of Reliance Industries Limited
- Sold 50 shares of Reliance Industries Limited
- Bought 100 shares of Tata Steel
- Bought 50 shares of Tata Motors
- Sold 150 shares of Tata Motors

Then, at the end of the settlement cycle, he/she will receive 50 shares of Reliance Industries Limited and 100 of Tata Steel and receive money for selling a net 100 shares of Tata Motors. In other words, all purchase and sale transactions made by a member of the stock exchange within a settlement cycle are settled on a net basis at the end of the settlement cycle.

The account period settlement implies that all trades executed in a given account period are netted to form a single position per security per member and then settled at one time. Rolling settlement implies that all the trades scheduled for settlement will have the same number of days after the trade date.

The settlement periods can be categorized as account period settlement and rolling settlement. The account period settlement implies that all trades executed in a given account period are netted to form a single position per security per member and then settled at one time. On the other hand, rolling settlement implies that all the trades scheduled for settlement will have the same number of days after the trade date. That is, in a rolling settlement, each trading day is considered as a trading period and trades executed during the day are settled based on the net outstandings for the day.

Though all the principal stock exchanges in India had been following the account period settlement method, the duration of the account period and time lag for final settlement was not uniform in all the exchanges. For example, BSE, the Calcutta Stock Exchange, and the Ahmedabad Stock Exchange had 14 days account period, whereas the Delhi Stock Exchange had 7 days and the Madras Stock Exchange had two settlements in a week. Whatever the duration, the settlement used to take a long elapsed time because of the extensive effort involved in collection, segregation, and distribution of share certificates and also cheque clearing. Almost 14 days were required for the receipt of shares, sorting of shares, delivery of shares, and clearing of cheques.

This practice of having different settlement cycles enabled the traders' shifting of positions from one exchange to another, resulting in excessive speculation. That also gave ample scope for rampant speculation and diverse manipulations such as insider trading and price rigging. It may be noted that the stock market scam of 1992 was driven by the loopholes in the trading and settlement systems in the Indian stock markets. Many stock market pundits were of the opinion that the stock exchanges in the country should have a shorter settlement period which can be a panacea for many ills of the stock markets. Arthur Andersen & Associates, an international consultancy firm, conducted a study on behalf of BSE and submitted its report in August 2002. One of the aspects studied by the consultancy firm was the settlement periods. The study pointed out that non-uniformity in the settlement cycles resulted in many disadvantages. The non-uniformity in settlement cycles provides settlement arbitrage opportunities. Selling in a market with a shorter cycle and buying in a market with a longer settlement cycle would lead to an imbalance of buy and sell orders. Further, the dates fixed by the individual stock exchanges for the pricing of ex-dividend or bonus or rights for scrip might also be different across stock exchanges in the country. This could result in further price differentials and arbitrage opportunities. Therefore, the study recommended that all stock exchanges in the country should have a uniform settlement period of five days and the carry-forward of transactions from one settlement to another should be dispensed with. The uniform settlement cycle makes all markets equally attractive to various participants and ensures minimal price differentials and arbitrage opportunities. This also results in higher operational efficiency as members have only one settlement position.

Arthur Andersen preferred the rolling settlement to the account period settlement because of the following benefits of rolling settlement.

1. It limits the number of outstanding clearances at any one time and thus reduces the overall market exposure.
2. It avoids trade processing congestion as trades are settled daily and therefore results in improved operational efficiency and reduced risk.
3. It would ensure that all share and money settlement work is completed on the same settlement day.
4. It would also be in line with international trends as most of the leading countries in the world are under rolling settlement.

To implement the rolling settlement, the consultancy firm listed the following requirements.

a. Depositories should be established, which allows book entry transfer of shares.
b. Automated links should be established between the clearing house, the clearing bank, and the depository within a principal exchange. They, in turn, should be linked to the national clearing facility. Delivery versus payment can only be accomplished if mechanisms for electronic cash and share transfers are implemented.

Since settlement occurs on every business day for a given trade day under a rolling settlement, these requirements are must.

6.4.1 Rolling Settlement

Long settlement periods and carry forward of transactions were the major factors behind the rampant speculation and malpractices in the Indian stock markets. Although there were repeated demands from many quarters for a shorter settlement period, there had been little progress on this front for a long time. It was only in 2000 that SEBI made an attempt to reduce the settlement period by introducing the rolling settlement system in leading stocks on a T (trade day) + 5 basis. It was also made mandatory for all exchanges to follow a uniform weekly trading cycle in respect of scrips not under rolling settlement. All these developments had resulted in a steep fall in trading volumes at the stock exchanges. The trading volumes in most stocks fell by nearly 90 per cent after a shift to the new settlement cycle. The devastating impact of rolling settlement, however, did not deter SEBI from going ahead with stock market reforms. In line with the economic reforms taking place in India, SEBI announced that all the stock exchanges in the country would uniformly follow rolling settlement with effect from December 2001. Subsequently, the settlement period has been reduced progressively from $T + 5$ to $T + 3$ days. From April 1, 2003, the Indian stock markets moved to the $T + 2$ rolling settlement. This brought the Indian stock market on a par with emerging markets such as South Korea and Taiwan. However, most of the developed markets such as in the United Kingdom, United States, Japan and Europe still work on the $T + 3$ rolling settlement. The Indian stock markets have moved from the account period settlement (weekly) to $T + 5$ to $T + 3$ to $T + 2$ in just 21 months despite initial resistance from the stockbrokers.

Under rolling settlement, the trades done on a particular day are settled after a given number of business days. In the case of $T + 2$ settlement cycle, the final settlement of transactions done on T (the trade day) by exchange of monies and securities between the buyers and sellers takes place on the second business day. Thus, the pay-in and pay-out of both funds and securities are completed on the second day of the transaction.

The transactions in securities of companies that have made arrangements for dematerialization of their securities are settled only in the demat mode on $T + 2$ on a net basis, that is, the buy and sell positions of a member-broker in the same scrip are netted and the net quantity and value are required to be settled. However, transactions in securities of companies that are in the "Z" group or that have been placed under trade to trade by the exchange as a surveillance measure are settled only on a gross basis and the facility of netting of buy and sell transactions in such scrips is not available.

The trading and settlement process is summarized as follows:

1. Investors place orders with their brokers or sub-brokers.
2. Brokers validate the orders and route them to the stock exchange through their computer terminals.
3. Order matching is done at the stock exchange.
4. Investors are informed of trade confirmation through the brokers.
5. Trade details are then sent to the clearing corporation or clearing house of the exchange.
6. The clearing corporation determines each one's obligation and instructs the clearing banks to make funds available by pay-in-time.
7. The clearing corporation instructs the depositories to make securities available by pay-in-time.
8. The clearing corporation asks clearing banks to debit the account of clearing members/custodians and credit its account.
9. The clearing corporation asks the depository to credit the securities to the account of clearing members/custodians.

10. The clearing corporation asks the clearing banks to credit the account of custodians/clearing members and debit its account.
11. The depository informs custodians/clearing members through depository participants about the pay-in and pay-out of securities.
12. In case of a buy order, clearing members instruct their DP to credit the client's account and debit its account.
13. In case of a sell order, the clearing members instruct their DP to debit the client's account and credit its account. The money will be credited to the client's account.

The time schedule for implementation of $T + 2$ rolling settlements is as follows:

$T + 1$

By 11.00 a.m.—Confirmation of all trades

By 1.30 p.m.—Processing and downloading of files to brokers/custodians

$T + 2$

By 11.00 a.m.—Pay-in of securities and funds

By 1.30 p.m.—Pay-out of securities and funds

Thus, if an investor sells shares, the money is received by the broker of the seller on the third day. If an investor buys shares, the broker of the seller gets the shares on the third day. Usually, the investor will get his money or his stocks from his broker on the day after the broker receives them.

The stock markets have reacted sharply to the new settlement system. The volume of trade fell drastically in reaction to the rolling settlement system. For example, the average daily trading volume of Global Trust Bank slipped from 0.55 million before the introduction of the rolling system to a mere 20,000 immediately after the rolling system was introduced. The average daily trading volume of Essar Steel fell from 0.2 million before the rolling system to just about 5000 after the rolling system was introduced. The same is the case with scrips such as PentaSoft, Orchid Chemicals, KLG System, Kotak Mahindra, BFL Software and Blue Star. This is only an illustrative list of companies whose shares have fallen so drastically immediately after the introduction of the rolling settlement system in Indian bourses.

6.5 Broking Services

Broking services play an important role in stock market operations. Brokers are classified into two categories—full service brokers and discount brokers. **Full service brokers** offer a wide variety of financial services. They keep their clients informed and updated about stock performances, market trends and tax laws among other things. They give advice and investment recommendations to their clients. They offer guidance on which stocks to buy and which stocks to sell. They maintain research facilities that they use to analyse market trends and predict future price movements of stocks. Thus, they help their clients in all respects to make their investment decisions as per their financial goals. On the other hand, **discount brokers** do not offer any personalized service to their clients other than executing trade instructions given by their clients. They charge less commission than full service brokers. The services provided by full service brokers are expensive. Discount brokers are ideal for those investors who can make their own investment decisions.

*Brokers are classified into two categories—full service brokers and discount brokers. **Full service brokers** offer a wide variety of financial services but the **discount brokers** do not offer any personalized service for their clients other than executing the trade instructions given by their clients.*

While engaging the services of a broker, the investor has to open an account, which may be a cash account or a margin account. In a *cash account*, the client has to deposit the full amount of the price of the securities that he wants to buy through the broker. In a *margin account*, the investor is given the opportunity to buy the securities "on margin", which means that the investor can buy the securities with less cash in his account than the cost of the securities. The investors can place different types of orders with the brokers such as market order, stop order or limit order. If the investor asks his broker to buy or sell the securities at the current market price, the order is known as a *market order*. In a *stop order*, the investor asks the broker to trade the securities at a specified price, while a *limit order* instructs the broker to trade the specified securities at a specified or better price. The orders can also be good till cancelled or can be a day order. A *good till cancelled* order will remain in effect until it is cancelled by the investor. A *day order* remains in effect only till the end of the current trading day.

6.6 Leverage and Margin Trading

***Leverage** in the context of stock market trading refers to buying shares using borrowed money.*

Leverage, a potential tool in financing and investment, refers to buying shares using borrowed money. A highly leveraged position would be one where a person with funds of say INR 10,000 is able to own an asset worth INR 1,000,000. Consequently, a small percentage change in the price of a security could result in a large percentage change in the fortunes of the investor. For example, a 2 per cent rise in the price of a security may yield a profit of 200 per cent on the initial investment to the buyer of the security. However, a price drop of 2 per cent would result in a loss of 200 per cent for him. That is, the leverage could generate bankruptcy leading to a payment crisis in the market. Leverage also comes in handy for market manipulators. If a leverage of 10 times is available, a small amount of INR 0.1 million may enable manipulators to have the positions of INR 10 million in the market, which might move the prices of stocks accordingly.

Every investor has to deposit a certain amount of money either in the form of cash or in the form of securities as approved with his broker while buying the securities. Such deposits of money are known as *margins* and they are held in an account called the margin account. The main objectives of margins are to ensure default-free trading in the stock market and minimize market aberrations (volatility). But while fixing the margins, it should be ensured that liquidity in the market is not affected adversely.

Margins are of two types—initial margin and maintenance margin. The margin paid at the time of purchase of securities is called the *initial margin*. After the purchase of securities on the margin, there is a *maintenance margin* below which the margin is not allowed to fall. If the margin falls below the maintenance margin, the broker calls for additional cash from the investor. If the investor fails to pay the money within the specified time, the broker may sell the securities purchased for the investor.

Margin trading is trading in securities by paying small margins, as determined by the stock exchanges. An investor can buy the securities by either paying the purchase price in full or by using the margin account. In the latter case, a margin of say INR 1,000 may give access to INR 10,000 if the margin requirement is 10 per cent. In other words, the investor pays a portion of the purchase price and the broker lends the difference at a specified rate of interest. For collateral, the broker holds on to the purchased securities. The percentage of margin funding may range between 50 to 90 per cent depending on the investor and his relationship with his broker. To take an example, Mr X buys a stock at INR 1,000 and subsequently the price rises to INR 1,250. If Mr X purchases the stock by paying the amount in full, he earns a 25 per cent return on his investment. But if Mr X purchases the stock on margin by paying only INR 500 in cash, he earns a 50 per cent return on the money he invested. Of course, Mr X still owes INR 500 plus interest to his broker. The downside of using a margin account is that if the stock price decreases, substantial losses can mount. In this example, if the stock price falls to INR 750, the investor will lose 25 per cent of his investment in case of full payment for the stock. But if the investor has purchased on margin, the investor will lose 50 per cent. Still, the investor owes INR 500 plus interest to his broker. Thus in rising markets, trading on margin yields very good profits for the investor. It allows the investor to gain exposure to a larger volume of business than he would otherwise have got. Thus, profits are highly leveraged. But losses are equally leveraged, too.

6.6.1 SEBI Guidelines for Margin Trading

1. SEBI has categorized securities into Group 1, Group 2 and Group 3. The securities with mean impact cost of less than or equal to 1 and having traded on at least 80 per cent (±5 per cent) of the days for the previous 18 months are categorized as Group 1. In addition to the securities categorized as Group 1, all the securities which are offered in IPOs and which meet the conditions for inclusion in the derivative segment of the stock exchanges are eligible for margin trading facility.
2. Only corporate brokers with a net worth of at least INR 30 million are eligible to offer margin trading facility to their clients. The net worth for this purpose would mean capital excluding preference share capital plus free reserves less non-allowable assets—fixed assets, pledged securities, member's card, non-allowable securities, bad deliveries, doubtful debts and advances, pre-paid expenses, intangible assets and 30 per cent of marketable securities.
3. For the purpose of providing the margin trading facility, a broker may use his own funds or borrow from scheduled commercial banks and/or NBFCs regulated by the RBI. A broker shall not be permitted to borrow funds from any other source.

4. The broker shall not use the funds of any client for providing the margin trading facility to another client, even if the same is authorized by the client.
5. At any time, the total indebtedness of a broker for the purpose of margin trading shall not exceed five times his net worth.
6. The total exposure of the broker towards the margin trading facility shall be within the self-imposed prudential limits and shall not, in any case, exceed the borrowed funds and 50 per cent of his net worth. The term *total exposure* would mean the aggregate outstanding margin trading amount in the books of the broker for all his clients.
7. In any case, the exposure to any single client at any point of time shall not exceed 10 per cent of the total exposure of the broker.
8. The initial and maintenance margin for the client shall be a minimum of 50 per cent and 40 per cent, respectively, to be paid in cash. For this purpose, the initial margin would mean the minimum amount, calculated as a percentage of the transaction value, to be placed by the client with the broker before the actual purchase. The broker may advance the balance amount to meet full settlement obligations. The maintenance margin would mean the minimum amount, calculated as a percentage of the market value of the securities, calculated with respect to the last trading day's closing price, to be maintained by the client with the broker. Fixed deposits with banks and bank guarantees shall be treated as cash equivalent and be considered as an acceptable form of initial and maintenance margins.
9. When the balance deposit in client's margin account falls below the required maintenance margin, the broker shall promptly make margin calls. However, no further exposure can be granted to the client on the basis of any increase in the market value of the securities.
10. The exchange/broker shall have the discretion to increase the margins. In such a case, the margin call shall be made as and when required.
11. The broker may liquidate the securities if the client fails to meet the margin call made by the broker or fails to deposit the cheques on the day following the day on which the margin call has been made or where the cheque deposited by the client has been dishonoured.
12. The broker may also liquidate the securities in case the client's deposit in the margin account (after adjustment for mark to market losses) falls to 30 per cent or less of the latest market value of the securities in the interregnum between the making of the margin call and receipt of payment from the client.
13. The broker shall maintain separate client-wise accounts of the securities purchased on margin trading with depositories and shall enable the client to observe the movement of securities from his account (through the Internet). The broker shall also maintain a separate record of details (including the sources) of funds used for the purpose of margin trading.
14. SEBI and the stock exchange(s) shall have the right to inspect the books of account and/or any other documents maintained by the broker with respect to the margin trading.
15. The stock exchange(s) shall disclose the scrip-wise gross outstanding in margin accounts with all brokers to the market. Such disclosure regarding margin trading done on any day shall be made available after the trading hours on the following day, through its website.
16. The stock exchanges shall also put in place a suitable mechanism to capture and maintain all relevant details including member-wise, client-wise, scrip-wise information and source of funds of the members pertaining to margin trading on their exchange, both on a daily as well as on a cumulative basis.
17. The brokers wishing to extend the facility of margin trading to their clients would be required to obtain prior permission from the exchange(s) where the margin trading facility is proposed to be provided. The exchange shall have the right to withdraw this permission at a later date, after giving the reasons for the same.
18. A broker should take adequate care and exercise due diligence before providing margin trading facility to any client.
19. A client will be allowed to obtain the margin trading facility from one broker per exchange for buying securities in that exchange. To ensure this, it shall be obligatory on the part of every broker to obtain a declaration from his client whether he has availed himself of any margin trading facility from any broker in any exchange, or whether his request for margin trading with any broker was rejected and, if so, in both the cases obtain the name of the broker and his registration number.

20. Before providing the margin trading facility to a client who has already availed himself of the margin trading facility from another broker in the same exchange, the broker shall obtain a no-objection certificate in writing from the other broker. The other broker shall be required to convey his objection, if any, in writing within a period of 21 days from the date of receipt of the query from the broker, failing which the broker would be free to proceed with providing the margin trading facility to the client.

6.6.2 Cross Margining

In order to free up funds for market participants, SEBI decided on December 3, 2008, to extend the facility of cross margining across cash and derivative segments to all categories of market participants. To understand cross margining, suppose an investor wants to buy 500 shares of RIL and already holds a short position of 400 shares of RIL in the futures segment of the stock exchange. Any loss due to an intra-day fall in the price of RIL shares will be neutralized by gains on the corresponding short positions held by the investor in the RIL stock futures. The value of the transaction that faces risk is only of those 100 shares that do not have a corresponding short position. As per SEBI guidelines, the stock exchange will levy a margin only on 100 shares. Earlier, derivative and cash market trades were treated as separate transactions. This would help the market participants reduce their margin requirements. However, positions in cash and derivative segments will be available for cross margining to the extent they offset each other. SEBI has also imposed a spread margin of 25 per cent of the total applicable margin on the eligible offsetting positions in the respective cash and derivative segments. Cross margining benefits would be computed at the client level on an online real-time basis and provided to the trading member/clearing member/custodian, as the case may be, who in turn will pass on the benefit to the client. For institutional investors, the cross margining benefit will be provided after confirmation of trades. Further, to avail of the facility of cross margining, a client would have to maintain two accounts. However, positions across the two accounts shall be taken together for the purpose of compliance.

6.7 Short Selling

Short selling refers to the sale of a stock that the seller does not own at the time of sale. The B.D. Shah Committee appointed by SEBI in 1996 defined a short sale as "selling of the shares without having the physical possession of the shares unless it is either for squaring up of an earlier purchase in the same settlement of the same stock exchange or against the pending deliveries from the same stock exchange pertaining to previous settlements". Thus, short selling is the sale of securities and subsequent purchase of the same securities at a lower price, thereby resulting in a gain. The short seller expects a fall in the securities' prices. It is feared that unfettered short selling could be a means to hammer down prices by bear cartels and that short selling implicitly encourages manipulation of stock prices. The counter argument is that buyers generally inflate prices and cause distortion in the securities' prices, but the short sellers correct such distortion and bring the prices to the correct level.

There has been a serious debate over the implications of short selling. Some consider short selling as an important mover of stock markets. It helps liquidity in the market besides providing efficient price discovery. But opponents argue that short selling has inherent potential risks and even destabilizes the market. Notwithstanding the conflicting schools of thought, SEBI has recognized short selling as an investment activity that needs to be governed by certain guidelines or regulations. Therefore, based on the recommendations of the B.D. Shah Committee and also the Secondary Market Advisory Committee, SEBI has framed and issued guidelines to regulate short selling in stock markets. The salient features of these guidelines are as follows:

1. All classes of investors—retail and institutional investors—are permitted to short sell.
2. Naked short selling shall not be permitted and, accordingly, all investors would be required to honour their obligations of delivering the securities at the time of settlement.
3. No institutional investor shall be allowed to do day-trading, that is square-off their transactions intra-day. All transactions would be grossed for institutional investors at the custodians' level and the institutions would be required to fulfil their obligations on a gross basis. The custodians, however, would continue to settle their deliveries on a net basis with the stock exchanges.
4. The stock exchanges shall frame necessary uniform deterrent provisions and take appropriate action against the brokers for failure to deliver securities at the time of settlement, which shall act as a sufficient deterrent against failure to deliver.

5. The securities traded in the futures and options segment shall be eligible for short selling. SEBI may review the list of stocks that are eligible for short selling transactions from time to time.
6. Institutional investors shall disclose upfront at the time of placement of the order whether the transaction is a short sale. However, retail investors would be permitted to make a similar disclosure by the end of the trading hours on the transaction day.
7. The brokers shall be mandated to collect the details on scrip-wise short sell positions, collate the data and upload it on the stock exchanges before the commencement of trading the following trading day. The stock exchanges shall then consolidate such information and disseminate the same on their websites for the benefit of the public on a weekly basis.

It was realized that short selling cannot take place unless a system of securities borrowing and lending is in place. Therefore, in order to provide necessary impetus to short selling, SEBI introduced a scheme called the securities lending scheme.

6.8 Securities Lending Scheme 1997

SEBI formulated a scheme for securities lending and borrowing (SLB) under which certain intermediaries approved by SEBI could provide the SLB facility. The salient features of the scheme are as follows:

1. The entities desirous of offering the facility of SLB may seek registration with SEBI for the same under the scheme.
2. The clearing corporation/clearing house would require to be registered as an approved intermediary with SEBI for SLB for handling settlement shortages. Only the clearing corporation/house of the stock exchanges shall be permitted to act as approved intermediaries (AI).
3. The clearing corporation/house may borrow, on behalf of the members, securities for the purpose of meeting shortfalls, if any, in the settlement, subject to the following.
   (i) The clearing corporation/house shall borrow the required securities to meet the shortfall on the day of settlement, for a maximum period of seven trading days excluding the day of borrowing.
   (ii) The defaulter selling broker may make the delivery within three trading days from the due date, i.e., the settlement date, subject to the charges for late delivery as may be prescribed by the stock exchanges.
   (iii) In the event of the defaulted selling broker failing to make the delivery within the aforesaid three trading days, the clearing corporation/house shall buy the securities from the open market and return the same to the lender within seven trading days.
   (iv) The cost, if any, incurred by the clearing corporation/house in this regard shall be recovered from the defaulted selling broker. This would be in addition to other penal charges.
   (v) The return of the borrowed securities by the clearing corporation/house shall be independent of the normal settlement.
4. In order to enable lending of idle securities by investors, the clearing corporation/house may borrow securities from any person through his account with the depository participant and select the borrower on a random basis.
5. The clearing corporation/house of the stock exchanges shall work out a mechanism to borrow securities at a market determined rate.
6. In case of the inability of the clearing corporation/house to borrow the securities fully or partly for the purpose of meeting the shortfall in the settlement, the outstanding transaction shall be closed out.
7. The exchanges and the clearing corporation/house shall closely monitor the shortages in securities in every exchange at the time of delivery in the settlement and shall take appropriate punitive action against any member who is found to be defaulting frequently in the delivery of securities.

Within the overall framework of the securities lending scheme, the stock exchanges are required to put in place a full-fledged SLB scheme. The SLB scheme shall be operated through a clearing corporation/house of stock exchanges having nationwide terminals.

The broad framework for SLB is as follows:

1. Securities lending and borrowing shall take place on an automated, screen-based, order-matching platform that will be provided by the AIs. This platform shall be independent of the other trading platforms.
2. All categories of investors including retail and institutional ones are permitted to borrow and lend securities. The borrowers and lenders shall access the platform set up by the AIs through the clearing members including banks and custodians who are authorized by the AIs.
3. The AIs, clearing members and clients shall enter into an agreement that specifies the rights, responsibilities and obligations of the parties. There would be one master agreement with two individual parts. The first part of the agreement is between the AIs and clearing members and the second part is between the clearing members and the clients.
4. The settlement cycle for SLB transactions shall be on a $T + 1$ basis and the transactions shall be independent of normal market settlement. The settlement of the lending and borrowing transactions shall be done on a gross basis at the level of clients. This means that there is no netting of transactions at any level.
5. Approved intermediaries shall frame suitable risk management systems to guarantee delivery of securities to the borrower and return of securities to the lender.
6. Position limits at the level of the market, clearing members and the client shall be decided from time to time by AIs in consultation with SEBI.
7. There shall be no lending and borrowing activity during the periods of corporate action in the security and this shall be disclosed by AIs to the market.
8. The AIs shall disseminate the details of SLB transactions executed on the platform provided by them and the outstanding positions on a weekly basis in a public domain.

Summary

1. Settlement is a process whereby payment is made by the buyer of the shares and delivery of the shares is made by the seller of the shares.
2. It is the obligation of the stock exchange to ensure that the buyers who have paid for the shares purchased receive the shares, and sellers who have delivered the shares receive payment for the same.
3. The period within which buyers receive their shares and sellers receive their money is called a settlement cycle.
4. Historically, transactions in stock markets may be for spot delivery, hand delivery, clearing or special delivery.
5. The transactions for spot delivery or hand delivery can be done in cleared as well as non-cleared securities, but transactions for the clearing can be done in cleared securities only.
6. A *vyaj badla* transaction takes place when a buyer of securities wants to carry forward his purchase position and the seller would like to give delivery of the securities.
7. The economic rationale behind the *badla* system is market liquidity. But it enables the speculators to be more aggressive in their speculative operations as it provides a kind of safety net.
8. Speculators buy and sell securities without the intention of taking or giving delivery of securities.
9. The main advantage of speculation is that it improves liquidity for the shares or commodities dealt in the market.
10. The Government of India imposed a ban on the "trading of contracts for clearing" (*badla* trading) in the late 1960s to curb unhealthy trends in the markets and prevent undesirable speculation.
11. The government has changed its stance many a time and permitted the *badla* system in other forms. A RCFS, based on the recommendations of the G.S. Patel Committee, was introduced on July 28, 1995. Finally, SEBI introduced a rolling settlement system in 2001.
12. Most of the developed markets are still working on the $T + 3$ rolling settlement. But Indian stock markets have moved from the account period settlement (weekly) to $T + 5$ to $T + 3$ to $T + 2$ in just 21 months.
13. In the case of $T + 2$ settlement cycle, the final settlement of transactions done on T (trade day) by exchange of monies and securities between buyers and sellers respectively takes place on the second business day.
14. Brokers are classified into two categories—full service brokers and discount brokers. Full service brokers offer a wide variety of financial services but the discount brokers do not offer any personalized service to their clients other than executing the trade instructions given by their clients.

15. Margin trading is trading in securities by paying small margins as determined by the stock exchanges.
16. Margin trading is trading in securities by paying a small margin as determined by the stock exchanges.
17. SEBI formulated a scheme for SLB, under which certain intermediaries approved by SEBI could provide the SLB facility.

Questions

1. Explain the different types of deliveries that used to take place in stock markets. What are their deficiencies?
2. What is carry forward? Explain its implications for stock trading.
3. Describe *badla* and discuss its merits and demerits.
4. How does *badla* lead to excessive speculation in stock markets?
5. Discuss the government initiatives to curb excessive speculation and malpractices in stock markets.
6. Discuss the salient features of the recommendations of the G.S. Patel Committee.
7. What were the objectives of the J.R. Varma Committee? What are its major recommendations?
8. What is a trading cycle?
9. Differentiate between account period settlement and rolling settlement.
10. What advantages can one perceive with the rolling settlement?
11. What could be the disadvantages of the $T + 2$ settlement system?
12. Comment on broking services.
13. What is margin trading? Evaluate the SEBI guidelines with regard to margin trading.
14. Discuss the securities lending scheme of SEBI.

Chapter 7

Merchant Banking

LEARNING OBJECTIVES

After studying this chapter, you should be able to:

- Trace the origin of merchant banking.
- Present the services of merchant banks.
- Discuss the Securities and Exchange Board of India (SEBI) rules and regulations with regard to merchant banking.
- Understand the concept of due diligence.

7.1 Introduction

The origin of merchant banking can be traced back to the period when people used to deposit their money and other valuables with grain merchants in their locality for safe custody before going on a trip. On returning from their sojourn, they would collect their belongings from the merchants. There were no charges for the safekeeping. With the passage of time, the merchants realized that the money deposited with them could be used for lending. Thus, the merchants started lending to the needy in the area and charged them interest on that amount. Some merchants even shared their interest income with the depositors. As time passed, even people who were not going out of town started depositing their money with the merchants for interest. The merchants, in turn, used that money for lending on a regular basis and, thereby, made profits. Some merchants who were trading overseas had a large business that focused on money transactions. They even financed kings, emperors and some governments. Kings used to borrow funds from merchants to fight wars. Such merchants were also requested by the lesser known merchants to guarantee the bills to be accepted by them. This was how merchants became involved in the business of banking and became merchant bankers. Merchant bankers were thus involved in banking along with commercial activities of sale and purchase of commodities. As they were also engaged as agents, these merchant bankers were also called commission agents. The main objective of merchant bankers was to maximize their profit by providing different kinds of financial services. Thus, the term **merchant bank** stems from leading merchants who evolved into bankers when they had built up a sufficient reputation for soundness, reliability and the wealth needed to earn the trust of the people.

*The term **merchant bank** stems from leading merchants who transitioned from the merchandize business to banking.*

Merchant banking got a fillip with the industrial revolution in England. As industrial activities expanded, the business of merchant banking grew at a brisk pace. Even with the expansion of banking activities, merchant bankers continued both their banking and trading activities and spread their business all over the world. Some of the prominent merchant banks were Baring Brothers, Rothschild, Warburg, Schroder, Horstman & Co, Kleinwort Sons & Co, Ruffer & Sons, Brown Shipley & Co, Blackstone, ChinaVest, Goldman Sachs and Antony Gibbs.

As the years passed, the original merchant bankers divested themselves of their traditional merchandising business and concentrated on providing financial services. Further, as the business of merchant banking became lucrative, many players entered the field and the merchant banking business became more competitive. In order to survive, merchant bankers diversified into new lines of business, which included discounting of bills, managing issues of corporate securities and arranging finance for projects located abroad. Merchant bankers further diversified into new lines of services relating to mergers, takeovers and capital restructuring.

After the Second World War, industrial activity picked up and development activities accelerated in many countries, including some underdeveloped countries. This provided many opportunities for merchant banks to move into new financial activities. They also started specializing in activities such as issue management, bill acceptance, trustee business, agency business, corporate restructuring, mergers and takeovers, project management and corporate counselling. The organizational structure of merchant banks also changed from being family-owned businesses to professionally managed businesses. Thus, merchant banking became a specialized and professional financial services business. In the process of expanding their business and making their services available to various clientele, merchant banks also entered into new lines of business and established branches. The new lines of services included leasing, corporate counselling, portfolio management and venture capital. Another major development was when commercial and investment banks entered the merchant banking field. They did this either by annexing merchant banking activities to their traditional businesses or by undertaking core merchant banking services through their subsidiaries established exclusively for the purpose. Thus, the role of merchant banks evolved when the leading merchant firms became heavily involved in advising as well as financing their clients.

7.2 The Special Role of Merchant Banks

Merchant banks, investment banks, development banks and commercial banks are fraternal organizations and the dividing line between them is superfluous or thin.

Merchant banks, development banks, commercial banks and investment banks are fraternal organizations and the dividing line between them is very thin as their functions mostly overlap. The primary function of **investment banks** is to canalize savings into investments by helping firms and industrial organizations raise funds from the financial market. They provide a gamut of financial services including the management of corporate mergers and acquisitions. **Development banks** are the financial institutions that directly participate in the economic development of the country by undertaking promotional activities and providing long-term finance to business units. **Commercial banks** accept deposits of various types and maturities and provide different kinds of credit to organizations and individuals. They also offer facilities like withdrawal of money by cheque, discounting of bills, issuing of drafts and many other banking services including home banking.

Merchant banks, on the other hand, offer a package of services ancillary to the promotion and development of industry. These services are mostly fee-based services such as credit syndication, portfolio management and management of public issues. Merchant banks provide their clients with financial analysis, industry expertise and advice on strong industry relationships. Their fund-based functions include investment in private equity, structured equity and bridge financing. They generally invest in private or public companies to finance growth, acquisitions and management/leveraged buyouts (LBOs) and recapitalizations. They may also provide their clients with working capital financing for a particular project or provide credit to their clients to enable them to tide over liquidity problems, if any. Merchant banks may focus on a particular country or they may stretch their operations to other countries.

7.3 Merchant Banking in India

Merchant banking started in India in the nineteenth century with the establishment of agency houses of London-based merchant banks. The agency houses were primarily engaged in overseas trade and commerce. But they also provided financial services like bill discounting. East India House was a popular agency house in India during this time. The managing agency system gave a big boost to merchant banking activities in India. The entire Indian industry was virtually under the control of the managing agency system in the pre-Independence period. A managing agency was a group of persons or a syndicate or a firm. There were many managing agencies in the pre-Independence period. They played the role of promoters and became pioneers in industrial development. Managing agencies thus floated many companies, especially in the pre-independence period.

The development of the corporate form of business organizations owes much to the pioneering efforts of the managing agency system. As promoters of companies, managing agencies took all the responsibilities and risks of business. The absence of an investing class and organized capital market forced the managing agencies to be the suppliers of industrial finance. The paucity of managerial talent in the country also made the managing agencies take up the responsibility of managing the companies promoted by them. Thus, the managing agencies acted as promoters and suppliers of capital and eventually became responsible for managing the organizations promoted by them. These services made the managing agency system indispensable to the industrial development of India. The hallmark of the managing agency system was the group management of companies floated by a managing agent. Group management led to administrative integration, which resulted in several benefits for the companies. But many problems with the managing agency system surfaced with the passage of time. It was observed that the system favoured the concentration of economic power in the hands of a small number of business houses. As there was rampant misuse of power by the managing agency system, there was widespread demand for its abolition. Eventually, it was abolished in January 1972. However, many of the services of managing agencies and merchant banks could not be separated as they were overlapping. The merchant banks were also engaged in the promotion of industrial units as the managing agencies.

After the Second World War, industrial activity picked up in India as well. Companies floated different kinds of securities to raise capital, which gave further fillip to the development of merchant banking. Merchant banks could also find good business in stock broking and underwriting of public issues. In the post-Independence period, the Government of India established financial institutions such as the Industrial Financial Corporation of India (IFCI) and Industrial Development Bank of India (IDBI) to provide development finance to industry. ICICI was also established in 1955 with the support of some financial institutions and banks. The establishment of Life Insurance Corporation (LIC) and Unit Trust of India (UTI) gave a further boost to capital market activity. All these institutions actively participated in the promotion and development of the Indian industry. They took up many merchant banking activities including underwriting of public issues. In fact, the development finance institutions became instrumental in the orderly development of the capital market in India.

Merchant banking as a specialized business started in India with the establishment of the merchant banking division of National & Grindlays Bank in 1969. The First National City Bank also opened a management consultant division in 1969 to take up merchant banking activities. But these units concentrated more on new issue management. When these two foreign banks made inroads into the traditional business of indigenous banks and broking firms, the nationalized commercial banks started exploring the possibility of entering into the merchant banking business. At the same time, the Banking Commission (1972) examined the need for setting up merchant banking institutions and acceptance and discount houses. The commission observed that the merchant banking institutions could help in the growth of the Indian economy. Accordingly, the commission recommended establishing new institutions to offer various financial services. The recommendations of the commission came in handy for the commercial banks to enter the merchant banking business. The State Bank of India, which had already been providing underwriting services, opened its merchant banking division in 1972–73 at its head office. Other commercial banks also took up merchant banking activities on the lines of the State Bank of India. Term lending institutions like ICICI, state financial corporations, IFCI and IDBI also entered the merchant banking business. With the entry of commercial banks and financial institutions into the merchant banking business, the number of public issues, particularly equity issues, and the amount mobilized thereby increased substantially.

During 1971–72, only about 60 companies had gone public. But in 1985–86, about 760 companies went public and most of these issues were oversubscribed many a time. Along with the increasing number of companies going public, many merchant banking firms mushroomed. Private firms including DSP Financial Consultants, Twentieth Century Finance Corporation and Credit Capital Finance Corporation also entered the merchant banking business. Some professional broking houses also set up merchant banking firms. Due to their long association with the capital markets, they wielded considerable influence on the business of merchant banking. In order to take up merchant banking activities more vigorously, some of the public sector commercial banks established full-fledged subsidiaries. For example, the State Bank of India established SBI Capital Markets in July 1986, which took over the merchant banking division of the SBI. The Bank of Baroda and Punjab National Bank also established wholly owned subsidiaries. As many institutions, in the private sector as well as the public sector, mushroomed, competition intensified and merchant banking became a highly competitive business. At the same time, industrial development was subdued. All these factors led to the failure of some merchant banks.

The Indian economy saw progressive liberalization in the 1980s. The government initiatives of liberalization and deregulations resulted in a conducive environment for industrial growth. Funds raised through capital markets during the 1970s were to the tune of INR 1,000 million on an average per year. But in the 1980s, barring the year 1987, the amount raised was of the order of INR 50,000 million on an average per year. All this reflects the increasing role of merchant banks. To meet the increasing demands of the industry, merchant banks designed and developed a variety of financial services. It was at that juncture that the Government of India established SEBI as a development and regulatory body for orderly growth and development of the securities market in the country.

7.4 The Concept of Merchant Banking

There is no particular definition of a merchant bank or merchant banking. According to SEBI, "a merchant banker is a corporate body which is engaged in the business of issue management either by making arrangements regarding selling, buying or subscribing to securities or acting as manager, consultant, adviser or rendering corporate advisory service in relation to such issue management". The meaning of merchant banking given by SEBI is very narrow but serves the regulatory purpose of SEBI.

The reason there is no particular definition of a merchant bank or merchant banking is because they provide variegated services that are subject to change over time. Further, there is no uniformity in the services being provided by different merchant bankers. In general, **merchant banking** can be viewed as the operations that provide the support, knowledge and resources to individuals and organizations for starting, improving, expanding and sustaining their business and investments.

Merchant banking *can be viewed as operations that provide support, knowledge and resources to individuals and organizations for starting, improving, expanding and sustaining their business and investments.*

7.5 Merchant Banking Services

Merchant banks are now engaged in providing a wide spectrum of financial and related services to their clientele. The scope of such services is not delineated. Today, merchant banks provide all types of financial services and management services as well. Some merchant banks provide individual and corporate investors with services that enable them to participate in global financial markets and tap opportunities for co-investment. All merchant bankers do not provide every service. Each merchant bank endeavours to provide one or a few services to the satisfaction of its clientele. The most popular services offered by merchant banks all over the world are as follows:

1. Project counselling services
2. Corporate advisory services
3. Corporate restructuring services
4. Capital restructuring services
5. Credit management services
6. Issue management services
7. Portfolio management services
8. Private equity services
9. Mezzanine financing services
10. Structured products services

A brief description of each of these services is given in the following sections.

7.5.1 Project Counselling Services

Projects are specific time-bound schemes or programmes undertaken with a profit or development motive. They can be short-term projects or long-term projects, depending on the goals. *Project counselling* involves extending technical advice to entrepreneurs on various aspects of projects. A project may have different stages such as planning, analysis, selection, implementation and review. Planning involves generation and screening of project ideas. Corporate analysis consists of market and demand analysis, technical analysis and financial analysis. Project selection involves the consideration of risk and return aspects of the projects. The major aspects involved in project implementation are project implementation planning, monitoring and control. The project review consists mainly of project performance evaluation and abandonment analysis. All these different aspects of project management are technical and demand expert knowledge and skills. Merchant banks have developed expertise in different areas of project management. For example, a particular merchant bank may have expertise in conducting feasibility studies and preparing project reports. Another merchant bank may have expertise in project implementation. Some merchant banks have also established technical consultancy divisions for preparing project reports and conducting market surveys. So different merchant banks are specialized in different aspects of project management and, accordingly, they offer those services to their clientele.

7.5.2 Corporate Advisory Services

Earlier, business houses used to rely on mostly in-house advisory services. As competition intensified in the economy and opportunities abounded, they began to seek the services of experts and professionals. Corporate advisory services are highly specialized in nature and offer real value addition to the clientele. Merchant banks provide a wide variety of corporate advisory services to enable their clientele to do their businesses efficiently at their maximum potential through effective management of their resources. They offer advisory services on issues like diversification of products and product lines, strengthening the existing product lines, revival of sick units, monitoring of rehabilitation schemes and takeovers of sick units. More specifically, merchant banks provide advisory services on various business aspects such as location of plants, scale of operations, market surveys, demand forecasting, new product development, pricing of products, product diversification, brand management, logistics, competitive strategies, cost analysis and cost reduction, raising of funds, allocation of resources and legal formalities.

In India, family-owned businesses are very common. But such businesses are prone to disputes due to personal and professional differences among family members. Merchant banks are recognized as good mediators or effective dispute settlers in cases of differences within the family. A split in a family group may involve distributing different units of business among the disputing family members. While extending services for smooth distribution of the units among the family members, the merchant bank also keeps the interests of other shareholders of the company in view.

Merchant banks are also involved in finalizing business deals. Gone are the days when a single person or a small group of people used to be involved in structuring the deals. Now, with competition intensifying and processes becoming complex in general, professional services are sought to negotiate the deals and react quickly when faced with a deadlock or stalemate during negotiations. The role or importance of the merchant bank depends on the nature of the deal. The trickier and more strategic the deal, the greater the importance or role of the merchant bank.

7.5.3 Corporate Restructuring Services

In the era of liberalization and globalization, every industry is preparing itself to face global challenges. Business organizations are on a restructuring spree in order to meet the challenges and are cashing in on the opportunities arising from globalization of economies. Industry groups shedding companies and companies dropping divisions have become a common practice. Thus, strategic consolidation has become a necessity in order to survive and grow in the fast-changing competitive environment.

Corporate restructuring refers to changes to be brought about in the operations or assets or ownership of a firm. The main aim of capital restructuring is to maximize the value of the firm or shareholders' value. Corporate restructuring may take the form of mergers, acquisitions, takeovers, spin-offs, leveraged buy-outs, buy-back of shares and capital restructuring. The specific goals of corporate restructuring may be to limit competition, effectively use underutilized resources, gain economies of scale, accelerate business growth, circumvent statutory regulations, reduce tax liability and provide better customer service.

Corporate restructuring in any form does not take place spontaneously, nor can it be carried out overnight. Corporate restructuring is a long-term strategy to achieve corporate goals. It involves a continuous search for the right opportunities and putting in serious efforts to materialize the identified opportunities. For example, for a company to acquire another business, the company should first identify a business that can be acquired. Then proper evaluation of the financial implications of the acquisition has to be done, followed by negotiation and execution of the deal. Further, a sound strategy has to be designed and followed to integrate the business thus acquired with the existing business of the company. In this context, the role of the merchant bank cannot be overemphasized. It advises its clientele on various aspects of corporate restructuring. Merchant banks identify the firms with matching characteristics and assist in preparation of restructuring proposals. They may also assist the companies in compliance with legal requirements and in obtaining consent from the concerned authorities. They also coordinate the work of several parties like solicitors and accountants involved in the restructuring task. Merchant banks may also guide and assist their clientele in takeover bids, which include both defence against takeover bids and making takeover bids.

Merchant banks may also assist clients in negotiating the mergers. They may recommend suitable merger strategies after careful examination of both financial and non-financial aspects. The balance sheets of both the companies involved in the merger are thoroughly analysed to arrive at a fair value of consideration. Besides determining the quantum of consideration to be paid in the merger, merchant banks determine the nature of consideration (for example, cash or shares) to be paid in the case of mergers or acquisitions. Company laws, SEBI guidelines, and other rules and regulations pertaining to corporate mergers are scrupulously examined by merchant banks to avoid any legal complications in the matter.

7.5.4 Capital Restructuring Services

Merchant banks may formulate financial restructuring schemes and monitor the implementation of the schemes. A firm can finance its assets either by equity or a combination of equity and debt. Financial structure refers to the various means of financing the assets of the company. Capital structure is a variant of financial structure that refers to the proportionate relationship between debt and equity. Capital structure decisions are significant managerial decisions, which influence the shareholders' return and risk. Whenever a firm wants to raise funds to finance its investments, it has to take a capital structure decision. The decision is basically one that is taken with regard to the quantity and method of financing. It involves the analysis of various factors that influence the capital structure of the firm.

A capital structure decision is evaluated in terms of its impact on the value of the firm. The firm should take a decision that would maximize the value of the firm. The use of debt in the capital structure may result in the lower cost of capital since the interest paid on debt is a tax deductible expense. That is, the interest tax shield creates value for the shareholders. But the tax benefit of the debt may be offset by other factors like financial distress. Therefore, the firm should weigh the costs and benefits associated with employing debt in the capital structure and take a decision that maximizes the value of the firm so that it has an optimum proportion of debt in its capital structure. Any demand for additional capital envisages a new capital structure. Put differently, any change in the quantity and forms of financing would amount to capital restructuring. The new financing decision of the firm may influence the debt–equity relationship, which, in turn, has implications for the value of the firm.

Merchant banks also offer their services for capital restructuring. They undertake the responsibility of designing the capital structure of their clientele. While designing the corporate structure of a firm, they analyse various factors that govern the capital structure. The factors include profitability, liquidity, control, nature of industry, timing, taxes, legal framework and company characteristics. Capital restructuring may also involve mergers and takeovers. Merchant banks may use their expertise and advise companies, including sick companies, on how to maintain optimum capital structure.

7.5.5 Credit Syndication Services

Sometimes, it may not be possible for a single financial agency to satisfy the entire financial needs of a firm. In such cases, the firm's entire requirement of external funds may be met by a group of financial agencies as a syndicate. The process of providing credit by a syndicate of credit institutions or agencies is known as **credit syndication.** Credit syndication involves estimating the total funds requirement of a firm, drawing a financial plan for the entire credit requirement, negotiating with the credit institutions, selecting the banks/financial agencies for participation in financing, preparing the application for financial assistance from the selected banks/financial agencies, following up on the loan application and obtaining the sanction of the proportionate share of funds from each participating institution, and the completion of other formalities including the legal documentation for drawing the amounts sanctioned. Credit syndication may also cover the working capital finance and bridge loans for the firms.

Credit syndication *refers to the process of providing credit for a project by a group of credit institutions.*

Merchant banks play a very active role in credit syndication. Their services range from identifying and assessing the funds requirements of the client firm to completing the formalities for the withdrawal of the sanctioned loan amounts. Merchant banks work in close collaboration with the client on the one hand and credit agencies on the other. The banks may also arrange foreign currency loans by getting foreign banks or foreign financial agencies into the credit syndicate for a particular firm.

7.5.6 Issue Management Services

Merchant banks are also actively involved in management of public issues. In order to meet their investment needs, firms issue different kinds of securities like equity shares, preference shares, debentures and bonds to raise funds from the primary market. The major activities in issue management are preparation of the action plan and the budget for the issue, preparation of the application to SEBI, drafting of the prospectus or offer document, selection of intermediaries like underwriters, brokers and bankers, obtaining approval from SEBI and other organizations, coordinating with all the intermediaries of the issue, and placing of the issue.

It is mandatory that every issue should have lead managers and the number of lead managers for an issue depends on the size of the issue. Depending on the category, merchant banks can act as lead managers, advisors, consultants, co-managers and underwriters. Thus, merchant banks play a very significant role in issue management. As lead managers, they assume almost the entire responsibility of the public issue.

7.5.7 Portfolio Management Services

__Portfolio management__ refers to management of investment portfolios for others by professionals in investment management.

Portfolio management refers to management of investment portfolios for others by professionals in investment management. Investors may find it difficult to take investment decisions when they do not have adequate knowledge and the skills to buy or sell securities. Some investors may not find the time to constantly keep track of the developments in the capital market. Therefore, they cannot make wise investment decisions on their own. They may also find it difficult to maintain all the documents relating to their investments and receive the interest or dividends from the companies. The investors may also not be in a position to keep track of the payment of interest or dividend on their investments and may thus lose their income.

Merchant banks, being professionals in investment management, offer solutions to such problems of investors through portfolio management. These banks invest and manage the funds on behalf of the clients by keeping in view the investment objectives of the client, the tax bracket of the client and such other factors, which the client may ask the merchant bank to consider.

7.5.8 Private Equity Services

Equity investment in a company that is not publicly traded is __private equity,__ and a firm that trades in private equity is called a __private equity firm.__

Private equity refers to an investment, usually a very large investment, made in a closely held company (unlisted company) by a fund (firm) instituted by high net worth individuals and institutional investors. Private equity may also be understood as the large amounts of money raised directly from high net worth individuals and institutions, pooled into a fund that invests in a range of business ventures. Thus, equity investment in a company that is not publicly traded is a private equity, and a firm that trades in private equity is called a **private equity firm.**

Private equity is a very good source of funds for companies, especially when they are in danger of bankruptcy. It provides companies access to a great deal of capital very quickly. It is a common practice that these private equity funds acquire private companies, nurture them and fuel their growth. Later, they either sell these companies to other investors or make them public. Private equity firms may also buy out publicly traded companies, make them private, undertake the restructuring process and then relist the shares on the stock market. Some private equity firms conduct LBOs, in which the large amounts of debt are used to fund a large purchase. As private equity is used to fund new technologies, make acquisitions or strengthen a company's balance sheet, it is known as a long-term source of funds. Private equity firms may also specialize in a particular type of investment. The most common private equity investment strategies include venture capital, LBOs, distressed investments, growth capital and mezzanine capital. Merchant banks play an important role in arranging private equity or participating in private equity.

7.5.9 Mezzanine Financing Services

In __mezzanine financing,__ the debt holder (the provider of mezzanine financing) is given the right to convert his debt into equity if the debt is not repaid as per the terms of the loan agreement.

Mezzanine financing is basically debt capital but it is considered a hybrid of debt and equity because in this type of financing, the debt holder (the provider of the finance) is given the right to convert his debt into equity if the debt is not repaid as per the terms of the loan agreement. The debt holder may reserve the right to take over an ownership interest in the borrower company if the loan is not paid on time and in full. Mezzanine financing is provided very quickly with little due diligence on the part of the lender. Further, as it is provided on a second or even third mortgage basis (no collateral for the debt), mezzanine financing involves a high interest rate. Although it is generally provided in emergency situations, such as a cash crunch which prevents the company from securing a conventional loan, buying an asset or property quickly before bank lending can be arranged, it is also used for LBOs. Mezzanine financing also makes it easier for the borrowers to obtain further loans from other sources. As mezzanine financing is treated like equity on a company's balance sheet, the borrower will have further debt capacity to obtain standard bank financing. But the borrower company should have a good track record including a history of profitability and genuine business expansion plans to attract mezzanine financing. Merchant banks may play an active role in arranging mezzanine financing for their clientele.

7.5.10 Structured Product Services

***Structured products** are a special kind of financial instrument designed to possess different combinations of risk–return characteristics.*

Structured products are a special kind of financial instrument designed to possess different combinations of risk–return characteristics. These financial instruments are different from conventional securities such as equity shares, debentures and bonds with respect to return and risk profiles, and have embedded features of options, swaps, forwards or futures. Structured products are customized products designed to suit the needs of specific objectives and risk profiles of investors. For example, investors who do not want to have equity share price fluctuations and at the same time are not content with the interest rate on bonds may be ready to take higher risks provided the principal amount at least is safe. For such investors, a structured product such as an equity-linked note is a more suitable investment avenue. The equity-linked note is designed in such a way that a portion of the investment is put into risk-less bonds and the rest is used to buy equity stock. The portion of investment in safe bonds will fetch interest at a specified rate. The investment in bonds is designed in such a way that the maturity amount of the bond and the interest, if any, will ensure that the investor receives the original principal amount that he has put in the equity-linked note. The portion that is invested in a risky asset such as equity stock provides the potential for higher returns but bears the brunt of price fluctuations and possible losses.

Like equity-linked notes, there are many customized structured products. To structure a product, expertise in economics, accountancy, legal aspects and marketing is required. The process of quantification of risk and the pricing of the financial product is known as financial engineering. It is in this context that merchant banks play an important role, not only in designing the structured products but also in marketing them. Earlier, investors had the option of investing only in equity shares, bonds, debentures, bullion, or real estate. These investments had constraints with regard to return, risk, liquidity and marketability. The structured products now offer a wide variety of investment opportunities for the investors to choose according to their individual return–risk profile.

7.6 SEBI (Merchant Bankers) Rules and Regulations

SEBI first issued certain rules and regulations in 1992 to regulate the activities of merchant banks. These rules have been revised many a time to suit the changing situations. The SEBI's latest regulations applicable to merchant bankers are presented in this section. As per the regulations, no institution can act as a merchant banker unless it holds a certificate granted by SEBI. SEBI may grant or renew a certificate to a merchant bank subject to certain conditions. The important conditions are:

- it shall abide by the rules and regulations made under the SEBI Act, 1992, with respect to the activities carried on by it as the merchant banker;
- it shall pay the amount of fee for registration or renewal, as the case may be, in the manner provided in the regulations; and
- it shall take adequate steps for the redressal of grievances of the investors within one month of date of receipt of the complaint. The certificate of registration or its renewal is valid for a period of three years from the date of its issue.

An institution that wants to act as merchant banker should apply to SEBI for the grant of registration. The applicant institution should be a corporate body other than a non-banking finance company, as defined under the RBI Act, 1934. While granting the certificate of registration, SEBI verifies whether the applicant has the necessary infrastructure like adequate office space, equipment and manpower to effectively discharge its activities.

Table 7.1 Categories of merchant bankers

Type of merchant banker	*Minimum net worth*
Category I	INR 50,000,000
Category II	INR 5,000,000
Category III	INR 2,000,000
Category IV	Nil

7.6.1 Categories of Merchant Bankers and Capital Adequacy Requirement

Merchant bankers are classified into four categories on the basis of the net worth to be maintained as per SEBI norms.

Merchant bankers are classified into four categories. Each category is required to maintain a net worth (paid-up share capital plus free reserves) of at least the amount as specified in Table 7.1.

A merchant bank of Category I can carry on any activity of issue management, which consists of the preparation of prospectus and other information relating to the issue, determining financial structure, the tie-up of financiers and final allotment and refund of the subscriptions. It can also act as the adviser, consultant, manager, underwriter or portfolio manager.

A merchant bank of Category II can act as the adviser, consultant, co-manager, underwriter or portfolio manager.

A merchant bank belonging to Category III can act as an underwriter, adviser or consultant to an issue.

A merchant bank of Category IV can act only as adviser or consultant to an issue.

Every merchant bank has to keep and maintain the following books of accounts, records and documents.

i. A copy of the balance sheet as at the end of each accounting period;
ii. A copy of profit and loss account for that period;
iii. A copy of the auditor's report on the accounts for that period; and
iv. A statement of the financial position.

Merchant banks are required to preserve these books of accounts and other records for a minimum period of five years.

7.6.2 Suspension/Cancellation of Registration

The certificate of registration issued to a merchant bank may be suspended when:

- the merchant bank violates the provisions of the SEBI Act, rules or regulations;
- the merchant bank fails to furnish any information relating to its activities, as required by SEBI, and furnishes wrong or false information;
- the merchant bank fails to maintain the capital adequacy requirement; or
- the merchant bank fails to pay the prescribed fees.

The certificate of registration may be cancelled when:

- the merchant bank indulges in deliberate manipulation or price rigging or cornering activities affecting the securities market and the investors' interests;
- the merchant bank is guilty of fraud or is convicted of a criminal offence; or
- the financial position of a merchant bank deteriorates to such an extent that its continuance as a merchant bank is not in the interest of the investors.

7.6.3 Code of Conduct

The following are some of the aspects of the code of conduct, as prescribed by SEBI for merchant bankers.

- A merchant bank should not associate with any business other than that of the securities market.
- A merchant bank should observe high standards of integrity and fairness in all its dealings.

- A merchant bank should render at all times high standards of service, exercise due diligence, ensure proper care and exercise independent professional judgement.
- A merchant bank should not make any exaggerated statements.
- A merchant bank should not be party to price rigging and manipulation.
- A merchant bank should not divulge to other clients, press or any other party any confidential information about their clients.
- A merchant bank should ensure that the investors are provided with true and adequate information and any complaints from investors are dealt with adequately.
- A merchant bank should also ensure that all professional dealings are carried out in a prompt, efficient and cost-effective manner.
- A merchant bank should ensure that good corporate policies and corporate governance practices are in place.
- A merchant bank should always endeavour to render the best possible advice to the clients keeping their needs as the first priority.

7.6.4 Defaults and Penalties

If a merchant bank violates any of the provisions of the SEBI regulations, penalty points may be imposed. The defaults of merchant banks are classified into four categories—general, minor, major and serious. Each default attracts penalty points of 1, 2, 3 and 4, respectively. For example, unethical conduct and non-cooperation with SEBI in furnishing explanatory documents would attract four penalty points. A merchant bank that attracts four or more penalty points may be restrained from associating with or managing any issues for a certain period. However, imposition of penalty points is not a necessary condition for initiation of proceedings against a merchant bank. SEBI may initiate action against any merchant bank under the relevant SEBI regulations, whether any penalty point is imposed or not.

7.6.5 Role of Merchant Banks in Issue Management

A merchant bank, as a lead manager of an issue, is obliged to undertake a number of activities, some of which are pre-issue activities while others are post-issue activities.

As per the SEBI regulations, a merchant bank of Category I can act as a lead manager of an issue. As lead manager of an issue, the merchant bank is obliged to undertake a number of activities, some of which are pre-issue activities while others are post-issue activities. SEBI has categorized them as pre-issue obligations and post-issue obligations.

The main pre-issue obligations are as follows:

- The lead manager of an issue is responsible for drafting the offer document.
- The lead manager shall exercise due diligence. That means it shall satisfy itself about all the aspects of the offering, and veracity and adequacy of disclosure in the offer document. Section 62 of the Companies Act, 1956, places civil liability on every responsible person of the company and makes them liable for compensation for loss due to misstatements in the prospectus. Further, Section 63 of the Companies Act, 1956, places criminal liability on every responsible person of the company and makes them liable for imprisonment and fine for misstatements in the prospectus.
- The lead manager shall file the offer document with SEBI along with the due diligence certificate and requisite fee.
- The lead manager shall enter into a memorandum of understanding (MOU) with the issuer company. The MOU specifies their mutual rights, liabilities and obligations relating to the issue.
- In case a public or rights issue is managed by more than one merchant banker, the rights, obligations and responsibilities of each merchant banker shall be demarcated.
- Before advising the issuer on the appointment of other intermediaries, the lead manager shall independently assess the capability and capacity of the various intermediaries to carry out assignments.
- The lead manager shall ensure that the other intermediaries being appointed are duly registered with SEBI, wherever applicable.

- The lead manager shall, while filing the draft offer document with SEBI, also file the draft offer document with the stock exchanges where the securities are proposed to be listed. The draft offer document is also made available to the public.
- The lead manager shall obtain and furnish to SEBI an in-principle approval of the stock exchanges for listing of the securities within 15 days of filing of draft offer document with the stock exchanges.
- The lead manager shall ensure that for public issues, offer documents and other issue materials are dispatched to the various stock exchanges, brokers, underwriters, bankers to the issue, investors associations, etc., in advance as agreed upon. In the case of rights issues, the lead merchant banker shall ensure that the abridged letters of offer are dispatched to all shareholders at least one week before the date of opening of the issue.
- After a period of 21 days from the date the draft offer document was made public, the lead manager shall file a statement with SEBI giving a list of complaints received by it, stating whether it proposes to amend the draft offer document, and if so, highlighting the amendments.
- The lead manager shall ensure that the matters in the abridged prospectus are not extraneous to the contents of the prospectus.
- The lead manager shall ensure that every application form distributed by the issuer company or anyone else is accompanied by a copy of the abridged prospectus.
- The lead manager shall ensure that the issuer company has entered into agreements with all the depositories for dematerialization of securities.

As per the SEBI regulations, the following are the post-issue obligations of a lead manager of an issue:

- The lead manager shall ensure the submission of the post-issue monitoring reports as per prescribed formats within three working days from the due dates.
- The lead manager shall actively associate itself with post-issue activities, namely, allotment, refund and dispatch, and shall regularly monitor redressal of investor grievances arising thereof.
- If the issue is proposed to be closed at the earliest closing date, the lead manager shall satisfy itself that the issue is fully subscribed before announcing the closure of the issue.
- In case there is a devolvement on underwriters, the lead manager shall ensure that the underwriters honour their commitments within 60 days from the date of the closure of the issue. In case of unsubscribed issues, the lead manager shall furnish information in respect of underwriters who have failed to meet their underwriting devolvement to SEBI.
- The lead manager shall ensure that monies received pursuant to the issue and kept in a separate bank as per the provisions of Section 73 (3) of the Companies Act, 1956, is released by the said bank only after the listing permission under the said section has been obtained from all the stock exchanges where the securities were proposed to be listed as per the offer document.
- The lead manager shall ensure that in all issues, the advertisement giving details relating to oversubscription, basis of allotment, number, value and percentage of applications, number, value and percentage of successful allottees, date of completion of dispatch of refund orders, date of dispatch of certificates and date of filing of listing application is released within 10 days from the date of completion of the various activities.
- In a public issue of securities, the executive director/managing director of the designated stock exchange along with the lead manager and the registrars to the issue shall be responsible for ensuring that the basis of allotment is finalized in a fair and proper manner in accordance with SEBI guidelines.
- The lead manager shall continue to be responsible for post-issue activities till the subscribers have received the shares/debenture certificates or refund of application money and the listing agreement is entered into by the issuer company with the stock exchange and listing/trading permission is obtained.

7.7 Due Diligence

Due diligence is a process of verifying the truth of the claims made by a person or an organization. It is also understood as a process of research analysis conducted to determine the exact value by considering the strengths and weaknesses of a person or an organization or any subject. Due diligence unearths information, thereby reducing the uncertainty in, say, investment proposals. For example, due diligence helps an acquirer to know whether there are any legal and regulatory issues involving the target company. Due diligence is performed in different contexts. It can be conducted by financial institutions, including commercial banks, before sanctioning credit to a business organization. It is conducted by some agencies to provide the investors with sufficient, relevant and timely information to help them take informed investment decisions. Similarly, the seller of a business may conduct due diligence to be assured of the ability of the buyer to complete the sale transaction. Specifically, the seller may examine whether the buyer has the resources to carry out the sale transaction. In the same way, the buyer may also conduct due diligence to know whether the seller has the rights (intellectual property rights, for instance) to sell the business.

Due diligence *is a process of verifying the truth of the claims made by a person or an organization.*

The subjects that may come up for scrutiny under due diligence may be legal, financial, technical or marketing-based. The focus areas in due diligence may be business plans, marketing, competition, investment opportunities, technology, management team, manufacturing processes, infrastructure, manpower resources, sources of raw materials, relations with suppliers and other agencies including government agencies, environmental issues, customer relations, accounting system, audit system, organizational structure, organizational culture and legal and regulatory issues.

As per SEBI regulations, the merchant bank as a lead manager of a public issue has to exercise due diligence and a certificate to that effect should be submitted to SEBI along with the draft offer document. To issue such a certificate, the merchant bank shall satisfy itself about all the aspects of the offering, and veracity and adequacy of disclosure in the offer document. Thus, the merchant bank has to examine various documents including those relating to litigation like commercial disputes, patent disputes, and disputes with collaborators and confirm that the draft prospectus/letter of offer forwarded to SEBI is in conformity with the documents, materials and papers relevant to the issue. By due diligence, the merchant bank should also confirm that the disclosures made in the draft prospectus/letter of offer are true, fair and adequate to enable the investors to make a well-informed decision as to investment in the proposed issue.

The variety of merchant banking services provided by two of the major commercial banks in India is presented in Box 7.1 and Box 7.2.

Box 7.1 Canara Bank—Merchant Banking Services

Canara Bank is one of the leading merchant bankers in India, offering services to banks, PSUs, state-owned corporations, local statutory bodies and the corporate sector. It is a SEBI-registered Category I merchant banker/underwriter that undertakes issue management (public/rights/private placement issues), underwriting, consultancy and corporate advisory services, among other services. It also holds the SEBI registration certificate to act as "bankers to an issue" with a network of exclusive capital market service branches to handle "capital market"–related assignments. It undertakes "project appraisals" with resource raising plans from the capital market/debt markets and facilitates tie-ups with banks/financial institutions and potential investors. It extends services under a single window concept covering the following areas:

1. Merchant banking
2. Commercial banking
3. Investments
4. Bankers to issue—escrow bankers
5. Underwriting
6. Loan syndication

It has been associated with issues ranging from INR 10 million to INR 15,000 million, involving various types of industries, banks and other organizations. It has an edge in handling private placement issues.

The range of services it covers includes equity issue (public/rights) management and debt issue management, private placements, project appraisals, monitoring agency assignments, IPO funding, security trustee services, agriculture consultancy and services corporate advisory services.

It also offers issue management services such as project appraisal, capital structuring, preparation of offer document and tie-ups (placement).

Finally, it offers a marketing edge/products to retail investors in the form of constant updates of the list of potential investors—institutions, provident, pension and gratuity funds, high net worth individuals and others—and continuously assesses their investment appetites and helps issuers in the effective marketing of the products.

Source: Canara Bank, http://www.canarabank.com

Another example is that of the Punjab National Bank, as described in Box 7.2.

Box 7.2 Punjab National Bank—Merchant Banking Services

Punjab National Bank, established in 1895, serves over 35 million customers through 4,520 branches and 439 extension counters and is the largest among nationalized banks. The bank has recently been ranked twenty-first among the top 500 Indian companies and ninth among the top 50 brands by *The Economic Times*. According to the Forbes annual list of 2000 global giants Punjab National Bank tops the list of nationalized banks with a global ranking of 695. All the branches of the bank have been computerized. The bank has a motto of "Any Time, Anywhere Banking" through the introduction of centralized banking solution (CBS), and more than 2,511 offices have already been brought under its ambit.

The bank is registered with SEBI as a Category I merchant banker for providing all the major merchant banking services. The gamut of merchant banking services includes:

- Issue management services—to act as book running lead manager/lead manager for IPOs/FPOs/rights issues/debt issues
- Project appraisal
- Corporate advisory services
- Underwriting of equity issues
- Banker to the issue/paying banker
- Refund banker
- Monitoring agency
- Debenture trustee
- Marketing of the issue through a strong network of QIBs/HNIEs/corporate bodies and retail investors. The bank itself is one of the major investors in the market with a treasury of INR 450,000 million.

The software for handling the refund banker is one of the best systems in the industry. Its unique features provide online payment of the instrument by 2,470 branches in 733 centres, the online status of paid instruments and 100 per cent reconciliation at any point of time. The bank has an exclusive and specialized capital market service branch in New Delhi for providing merchant banking services to corporate organizations.

It also offers depository services to its clients and has designated a large network of branches to cater to their demat requirements through the depository participant of NSDL and CDSL depositories. It offers e-facility to demat account holders to submit their delivery instructions through the Internet and has launched "online securities trading facility" in strategic alliance with IDBI Capital Market Services Ltd.

Source: Punjab National Bank, http://pnbindia.in

Summary

1. The term merchant bank stems from leading merchants who transitioned from the merchant business to banking when they had built up a sufficient reputation for soundness, reliability and wealth to earn the trust of the people.
2. Merchant banking got a fillip with the industrial revolution in England. As the industrial activities expanded, the business of merchant banking grew at a brisk pace.
3. As against the commercial banks providing different kinds of credit to various organizations and individuals, merchant banks offer a package of services ancillary to the promotion and development of the industry. The services provided by merchant banks are mostly fee-based financial services.
4. According to SEBI, a merchant banker is a body corporate that is engaged in the business of issue management either by making arrangements regarding selling, buying or subscribing to securities or acting as manager, consultant, adviser or rendering corporate advisory services in relation to such issue management.
5. The most popular services offered by merchant banks all over the world are project counselling services, corporate advisory services, corporate restructuring services, capital restructuring services, credit management services, issue management services, portfolio management services, private equity services, mezzanine financing services and structured products services.
6. The SEBI rules as applicable to merchant banking clearly state that no institution can act as a merchant banker unless it holds a certificate granted by SEBI. SEBI may grant or renew a certificate to a merchant banker subject to certain conditions.
7. Merchant banks are classified into four categories. These four categories are required to maintain a net worth

(paid-up share capital plus free reserves) of not less than the amount specified.

8. A merchant bank as a lead manager of an issue is obliged to undertake a number of activities, some of them pre-issue activities and others post-issue. SEBI has conveniently categorized them as pre-issue obligations and post-issue obligations.

9. Due diligence is a process of research analysis conducted to determine the exact value by considering the strengths and weaknesses of a person or organization or any subject.

Questions

1. Trace the origin of merchant banking.
2. Explain the nature and meaning of merchant banking.
3. Describe the various services of merchant banks.
4. Discuss the role of merchant banks in the promotion and development of industry in a country.
5. Critically evaluate the SEBI guidelines with regard to merchant banking.
6. What are the pre-issue and post-issue obligations of lead managers?
7. What do you understand by structured products? Explain the role of merchant banks in designing structured products.
8. What role can merchant banks play in corporate restructuring?
9. What is the importance of capital restructuring? How can merchant banking services be put to effective use in capital restructuring?
10. Explain the concept of due diligence.

Chapter 8

Intermediaries in Capital Issues

LEARNING OBJECTIVES

After studying this chapter, you should be able to:

- Highlight the role of underwriters in issue management.
- Evaluate SEBI regulations for underwriters.
- Describe the role of the registrar and the share transfer agent in issue management and the SEBI regulations.
- Present the SEBI regulations pertaining to stockbrokers and sub-brokers.
- Describe the role of bankers in issue management and SEBI regulations with regard to the bankers for an issue.
- Highlight the importance of debenture trustees and mention the SEBI regulations pertaining to debenture trustees.

8.1 Introduction

*A **capital issue** is an offer of sale of industrial securities to the public or to the existing holders of securities.*

A **capital issue** is an offer of sale of corporate securities such as equity shares, bonds and debentures by any financial corporation to the public or the holders of the securities. Savings and investments are brought together or synchronized through capital issues. *Capital issue management* is a process involving a number of activities. The success of issue management depends on how well these various activities are carried out. In order to perform the issue management activities effectively and efficiently, they are assigned to professionals called *intermediaries*. These intermediaries include the lead managers, underwriters, brokers, registrars, bankers and trustees. Although there are many intermediaries involved in capital issues, this chapter attempts to discuss the roles and responsibilities of the major and important intermediaries. The regulatory framework pertaining to the intermediaries is also presented in this chapter.

Although the role of every intermediary is important for the success of a capital issue, it is the lead manager's role that is pivotal. The lead manager is involved in pre-issue as well as post-issue activities. Of the pre-issue activities, the lead manager mainly takes care of due diligence of the issuer's operations, management, business plans and other aspects. It is also the responsibility of the lead manager to get offer documents such as the prospectus approved by the appropriate authorities (for example, SEBI). The lead manager is involved in appointing other intermediaries such as the registrar, brokers, printers and advertising agencies. The lead manager should coordinate the activities of all other intermediaries and monitor their performance on a continuous basis. As discussed in Chapter 7, Category-I merchant bankers can act as the lead manager of a capital issue.

8.2 Underwriters

Investment banks and brokerage firms have unique opportunities to make money by underwriting public offerings of securities such as equity shares, bonds and debentures. When a company organizes a public issue, it often looks to underwriters to sell and promote its offering. The underwriters, in turn, receive a percentage of each security sale as commission.

__Underwriting__ is an agreement with or without conditions to subscribe to the unsubscribed portion of capital issues.

Underwriting is an insurance term that originated from English merchant banking. Underwriting may be defined as an agreement between the issuer of securities and the counterparty, called the underwriter (either a person or an institution), to the effect that in the event of the public not taking up the whole of the securities issued or the number mentioned in the agreement, the underwriter will, for an agreed commission, take an allotment of the part of the securities for which the public has not applied. Simply stated, underwriting refers to an agreement with or without conditions to subscribe to the unsubscribed portion of capital issues when they are offered to the investing public.

According to Section 69 of the Companies Act, 1956, no allotment shall be made of any share capital of a company offered to the public for subscription unless the amount stated in the prospectus as the minimum amount to be subscribed has been received by the company. If the minimum subscription mentioned in the prospectus is not subscribed, all monies received on application must be refunded forthwith without any interest. If any such money is not repaid within 130 days of the date of issue of the prospectus, the directors of the company shall be liable to repay the monies with interest. This is as per Section 73 of the Companies Act, 1956. In other words, a company will face serious problems if it fails to raise the minimum subscription. Hence, there arises a need for underwriting, which provides insurance against the under-subscription of an issue.

The reasons identified for the under-subscription of capital issues are many. If the stock market in a country is passing through a phase of depression, public issues may not attract the attention of the investing public. A less-developed investment habit of the public and uncertainty about the profit-earning capacity of industrial concerns may also be the reasons for under-subscription of capital issues. The demand for new capital issues is always highly selective and concentrated on issues that have a chance of immediate capital appreciation.

The main advantages of underwriting are that the issuer of securities need not wait for the ultimate sale of its securities to start its operations since there is certainty that the issue will be subscribed either by the public or the underwriter(s); and the very fact that the securities are underwritten by a reputed institution enhances the marketability of the issue. It may be noted that a high premium is placed on issues backed by well-known underwriters.

8.2.1 Underwriting: A Historical Perspective

Before the Second World War, underwriting in India was occasional and mostly in the nature of share-pushing. It was done by certain individuals, groups of people or stockbrokers simply to take advantage of the rising stock market. Public capital issues were underwritten without regard to the real merits of the issues. There was no regular and institutional mechanism to underwrite the public issues in India until 1955. The underwriting scenario in India changed with the establishment of the Industrial Credit and Investment Corporation of India Limited (ICICI) in 1955. One of the primary objectives of ICICI was to provide underwriting facilities to new capital issues. Subsequently, institutions like Industrial Finance Corporation of India, Life Insurance Corporation of India, Industrial Development Bank of India and Unit Trust of India were established and they also began to play a progressive role in the underwriting of public issues. State-level financial institutions such as state financial corporations and state industrial infrastructure development corporations have also assumed the role of underwriters for public issues, although they were established primarily to provide risk capital and other promotional and development assistance to the industrial undertakings. The State Bank of India, which is a leading public sector bank, did not engage in the underwriting business as it was statutorily prohibited from purchasing or underwriting shares of companies. However, it was permitted to buy or underwrite debentures. Thus, the emergence of development finance institutions including LIC has given a fillip to institutional underwriting in India.

The approach of institutions in underwriting public capital issues is entirely objective and the decision is based on the long-term viability of the industrial project rather than on the immediate saleability of the public issue. Therefore, institutional agencies examine various aspects of the project as if they were considering the project for a long-term institutional loan. The main objective of institutional underwriting is to fill the gap when the market is unable to fully subscribe to new capital issues.

Financial institutions support new capital issues at all times, whether the stock markets are booming or busting. This helps to maintain the flow of new capital issues at all times. Some institutions like the Life Insurance Corporation of India align their underwriting policy with their investment policy. Accordingly, they restrict underwriting to public issues and to such amounts as they would like to hold in their portfolio of investments. In other words, institutions are not interested simply in the earning of underwriting commission.

Stockbrokers and commercial banks also play an important role in underwriting of capital issues. But the approach of private sector commercial banks and stock brokers is highly selective. They generally back issues of strong ownership companies. For them, especially for stockbrokers, a successful flotation of the issue is more important than a sound project. The general tendency of stockbrokers is to underwrite an issue only if they regard the issue as a good one and, therefore, readily saleable. Further, stockbrokers limit their participation in underwriting to amounts that are considered to be within their distributive capacity. The underwriting business is quite lucrative if the public response to the public issues is encouraging. But a poor public response can cause devolvement to become very large, resulting in underwriters losing their money and some of them going bankrupt. Some of the underwriters may also back out of their commitments.

After the 1970s, the underwriting business in India has undergone changes. The institutions, particularly the all-India development finance institutions, have increasingly participated in the underwriting of new capital issues. An interesting development in the 1970s was the formation of larger underwriting groups meant for the underwriting of individual issues and adoption of consortium approach. Some commercial banks, particularly the State Bank of India and the National and Grindlays Bank, set up merchant banking divisions to provide various types of services, including underwriting services, to industrial units.

Underwriting activity increased phenomenally as the industrial development of the country picked up momentum. The number of underwriters also increased and many new categories of institutions have taken to the underwriting business. Apart from equity shares, debentures and preference issues are also underwritten. In earlier years, underwriting was compulsory in India for public issues at par and those at premium of less than 25 per cent of par value. But since October 1994, SEBI has made underwriting of public issues optional in order to reduce issue expenditure.

8.2.2 The Underwriting Agreement

The underwriter and the company that issues the securities for public subscription enter into an agreement after negotiations and concurrence on terms and conditions. The agreement covers the amount of the public issue agreed to be underwritten by the underwriter(s) and the commission payable for such an undertaking. The agreement may also provide the procedure for the computation of the underwriter's obligation and the effecting/discharging of underwriting obligations. In the case of syndicate underwriting or group underwriting, the agreement mentions each participant's obligation in the total underwriting commitment. The agreement may also incorporate other terms and conditions, if any, agreed on by the parties—the issuer of the securities and the underwriter.

8.2.3 Forms of Underwriting

Underwriting may take any of the following forms.

(i) The underwriter agrees to buy the unsubscribed part of the public issue within a prescribed time. Thus, the underwriter gives a firm commitment to subscribe to the unsubscribed portion of the issue. This is the most common type of underwriting.

(ii) The underwriter may purchase outright the public capital issue with a view to reselling instead of being the backer behind the public offering.

(iii) The underwriting may take the form of a joint underwriting arrangement, which is called an underwriting syndicate, in which many individuals or institutions participate in the underwriting of a particular issue. The capital issues may be too large for one underwriter to manage effectively. Thus, the investment banker, also known as the underwriting manager, invites other institutions or individuals to participate in a joint distribution of the offering. The group of underwriters is known as the syndicate. Members of the syndicate usually make a firm commitment to distribute a certain percentage of the entire offering and are held financially responsible for any unsold portions.

8.2.4 SEBI (Underwriter) Rules and Regulations, 1993

SEBI has issued certain rules and regulations for the governance of underwriters. The highlights of these rules are as follows:

1. No person shall act as an underwriter unless he holds a certificate granted by SEBI under the regulations. However, a stockbroker or merchant banker holding a valid certificate of registration shall be entitled to act as an underwriter without obtaining a separate certificate for underwriting activities. The certificate of registration or its renewal, as the case may be, shall be valid for a period of three years from the date of its issue to the underwriter.

2. The capital adequacy requirement shall not be less than a net worth of INR 2 million. Notwithstanding this regulation, every stockbroker who acts as an underwriter shall fulfil the capital adequacy requirements specified by the stock exchange of which he is a member.
3. Every underwriter shall enter into an agreement with each organization on whose behalf he is acting as the underwriter and the said agreement shall contain the period for which the agreement shall be in force, the amount of underwriting obligations, the period within which the underwriter has to subscribe to the issue after being intimated by or on behalf of such an organization, the amount of commission or brokerage payable to the underwriter and details of arrangements, if any, made by the underwriter for fulfilling the underwriting obligations.
4. The underwriter shall not derive any direct or indirect benefit from underwriting the issue other than the commission or brokerage payable under an agreement for underwriting.
5. The total underwriting obligations under all the agreements shall not exceed 20 times the net worth.
6. Every underwriter, in the event of being called upon to subscribe to securities of an organization pursuant to an agreement, shall subscribe to such securities within 45 days of the receipt of such intimation from such an organization.
7. Every underwriter shall keep and maintain the relevant books of account and documents.
8. Every underwriter shall, after the close of each financial year and as soon as possible but not later than six months from the close of the said period, furnish to SEBI, if so required, copies of the balance sheet, profit and loss account, statement of capital adequacy requirement and such other documents as may be required by SEBI.
9. Every underwriter shall preserve the books of account and other records and documents for a minimum period of five years.
10. Every underwriter shall appoint a compliance officer who shall be responsible for monitoring the compliance of the act, rules and regulations, notifications, guidelines and instructions issued by SEBI or the Government of India and for the redressal of investors' grievances.
11. Where it appears necessary, SEBI may appoint one or more persons as the inspecting authority. The inspecting authority shall undertake the inspection of the books of account, other records and documents of the underwriter to ensure that the books of account and other records and documents are being maintained in the required manner. The inspecting authority shall also investigate the complaints received from investors, other underwriters or any other person or any matter having a bearing on the activities of the underwriter and to investigate *suo motu* the affairs of the underwriter in the interest of the securities business or investors' interests. It shall be the duty of every director, proprietor, partner, officer and employee of the underwriter, who is being inspected, to produce to the inspecting authority such books, accounts and other documents in his custody or control and furnish the inspector with the statements and information relating to an underwriter within such time as the inspecting authority may require.
12. An underwriter who fails to comply with any conditions subject to which the certificate has been granted or contravenes any of the provisions of the act, rules or regulations shall be dealt with in the manner provided under the SEBI (Procedure for Holding Enquiry by Enquiry Officer and Imposing Penalty) Regulations, 2002.

Every underwriter shall at all times abide by the code of conduct, the salient features of which are as follows.

- An underwriter shall make all efforts to protect the interests of its clients.
- An underwriter shall maintain high standards of integrity, dignity and fairness in the conduct of its business.
- The underwriter shall at all times render high standards of service, exercise due diligence, ensure proper care and exercise independent professional judgement.
- An underwriter shall not divulge to other issuers, press or any party any confidential information about its issuer company that has come to its knowledge and deal in securities of any issuer company without making a disclosure to SEBI as required and also to the board of directors of the issuer company.
- An underwriter or any of its employees shall not render, directly or indirectly any investment advice about any security in the publicly accessible media, whether real-time or non-real time, unless the

disclosure of his interest, including its long or short position in the said security, has been made while rendering such advice.

- An underwriter or any of its directors, partners or manager having the management of the whole or substantially the whole of the affairs of the business, shall not either through its account or their respective accounts or through their associates or family members, relatives or friends indulge in any insider trading.
- An underwriter shall not indulge in any unfair competition that is likely to be harmful to the interest of other underwriters carrying on the business of underwriting or likely to place such other underwriters in a disadvantageous position in relation to the underwriter while competing for or carrying out any assignment.
- An underwriter shall have internal control procedures and financial and operational capabilities which can be reasonably expected to protect its operations, clients and other registered entities from financial loss arising from theft, fraud and other dishonest acts, professional misconduct or omissions.
- An underwriter shall not be party to or instrumental in creation of a false market, price rigging or manipulation or the passing of unpublished price-sensitive information in respect of securities which are listed and proposed to be listed in any stock exchange to any person or intermediary.
- An underwriter shall not make any untrue statement or suppress any material fact in any documents, reports, papers or information furnished to SEBI.
- An underwriter or any of its employees shall not render, directly or indirectly, any investment advice about any security in the publicly accessible media, whether real-time or non-real time, unless a disclosure of his interest including its long or short position in the said security has been made, while rendering such advice.
- An underwriter shall ensure that any person it employs or appoints to conduct business is fit and proper and otherwise qualified to act in the capacity so employed or appointed, including having relevant professional training or experience.

Sub-underwriting

Underwriters can reduce their commitment by getting a capital issue sub-underwritten by others. That is, an underwriter can arrange for the sub-underwriting of its underwriting obligation on their own account with any person or persons on terms to be agreed upon between them. However, the underwriter shall be primarily responsible for sub-underwriting and any failure or default on the part of the sub-underwriters to discharge their respective sub-underwriting obligations shall not exempt or discharge the underwriter of its underwriting obligations under this agreement.

Computation of underwriter's obligation

If an issue is undersubscribed, the underwriting obligation shall be determined in the manner set out as follows, provided that under no circumstances shall the underwriter's obligation to subscribe/procure subscription to the securities exceed the amount mentioned in the agreement.

The following applications for securities shall be treated as *pro tanto in* or towards the satisfaction of the underwriter's obligations under the agreement.

- Applications that have been accepted excluding those withdrawn before allotment; and
- Applications received from the underwriter or any of its sub-underwriters including those applications bearing the stamp of the underwriter or any of the sub-underwriters.

After making these adjustments, the underwriting obligation of an underwriter and other underwriters shall be subject to following further adjustments.

- The application received from the public independently, that is, those applications not discussed, shall be apportioned among all the underwriters. To the extent where underwriting obligations have not been fully satisfied after adjustments in the proportion of their respective underwriting obligations, their respective underwriting obligation shall stand reduced.
- If after the adjustments have been carried out, it is found that the securities available for adjustment are in excess of the securities required to be subscribed in fulfilment of the underwriting obligations of

one or more individual underwriters, then the excess amount required to meet the underwriting obligations of any underwriter shall be further apportioned among such other underwriters whose underwriting obligations have not been fully discharged in proportion to their underwriting obligations.

After determining the underwriting obligations, the company shall communicate in writing to the underwriter the total number of shares/debentures remaining unsubscribed and the number of shares/debentures required to be taken up by the underwriter or the subscription to be procured therefore by the underwriter within 30 days after the date of closure of the subscription list. The underwriter, on being satisfied about the extent of devolvement of the underwriting obligation, shall immediately and in any case not later than 30 days after the receipt of the communication make or procure the applications to subscribe to the shares/debentures and submit the same along with the application money to the company. In the event of failure of the underwriter to make the application to subscribe to the shares, the company shall be free to make arrangements with one or more persons to subscribe to such shares. This will be without prejudice to the rights of the company to take such measures and proceedings as may be available to it against the underwriter including the right to claim damages for any loss suffered by the company due to the failure on the part of the underwriter to subscribe to the shares. The company is free to quantify the damages as a multiple of the value of the shares/debentures not subscribed to by the underwriter.

The underwriting commission

In consideration of the underwriter's agreeing to underwrite the securities, the company shall pay to the underwriter a commission at the rates agreed upon between the company and the underwriter. The rates so agreed upon shall be subject to the provisions of Section 76 of the Companies Act, 1956. The underwriting commission shall be payable by the company within 15 days from the date of finalization of allotment. The obligation to pay the underwriting commission shall arise only on the underwriter fulfilling his underwriting obligation and duly subscribing to the securities, if any, devolved on him. It may be noted that the commission is paid to the underwriter for the risk he/it has assumed whether or not an underwriter is called upon to take up any shares

The company's obligation

The company shall, immediately after the closure of the subscription list, take expeditious steps for processing the applications and complete the allotment within the time limit prescribed under the Companies Act, 1956, and comply with the listing requirements. If the company fails to receive 90 per cent of the issue, including the amount received from the underwriters towards devolvement, within 60 days from the date of closure of the subscription list, the company shall refund the amount paid by the underwriter in fulfilment of his underwriting obligations.

Right of termination

The underwriter shall have an option to be exercised by him at any time prior to the opening of the issue as notified in the prospectus of terminating this agreement under any or all of the following circumstances.

- If any of the representations/statements made by the company to the underwriter and/or in the application forms, negotiations, correspondence, the prospectus or in the letter of offer are found to be incorrect;
- A complete breakdown or dislocation of business in a major financial markets occurs;
- War is declared or an insurrection occurs or a civil commotion or any other serious or sustained financial, political or industrial emergency or disturbance affecting the major financial markets in the country arises.

8.2.5 Criteria for Selecting the Underwriter

The underwriter plays an important role in the success of any public issue. Therefore, the company (issuer of securities), while selecting an individual or institution as the underwriter, should examine several aspects in order to judge the strengths and weaknesses of the individual or institution. The main criteria for selection of underwriter(s) are stated as follows.

- Certificate of registration issued by SEBI.
- Necessary infrastructure like adequate office space, equipment and manpower needed for effective discharge of the activities.
- Adequacy of financial and manpower resources.

- Previous performance with respect to the amount procured by the underwriter in issues of various sizes.
- Previous performance of the underwriter with regard to type of issues it has handled.
- Network of individuals or institutions.
- In the case of (previous) undersubscribed issues, the amount of devolvement and the way the underwriter responded to or managed such devolvement.
- Region of the underwriter's operation in relation to the region of operation of the company.
- Number of issues the underwriter is handling at present.
- Compliance with SEBI rules and regulations.
- Adherence to the code of conduct prescribed by SEBI.
- Record of violations of the provisions of any acts, penalties and punishments.
- Values, attitudes and perceptions of the underwriter.
- General reputation or image of the underwriter.

Above all, the potential issuer (company) should consider the placement power of the underwriter, that is, the ability to ensure the success of the issue, given the price and other market conditions.

8.2.6 Underwriter's Considerations

Even as companies (issuers) consider several aspects for the selection of the underwriter(s), the underwriter also examines several factors before committing to an issue. Primarily, the underwriter makes a thorough study of the project for which the funds are to be raised. The response of the investing public to a capital issue depends largely on the project for which the funds are being raised. The issuer's track record with regard to public issues and the general reputation and public image of the company are also considered. As the success of the issue also depends on the intermediaries, the professional competence of various intermediaries such as the lead manager(s), brokers and sub-brokers, registrars, bankers, printers and advertising agencies are also assessed by the underwriter(s). The price fixed or proposed to be fixed for the security may also be considered to gauge the likely public response to the issue. The market situation is also a factor to be studied for its favourableness to the proposed issue. The potential competition for the issue is specifically analysed to determine the likely success of the issue. The primary and secondary markets for securities are closely related. So it is necessary to observe stock market movements and forecast the likely trend at the time the proposed capital issue will be made public. The regulator's (for example, SEBI's) attitude towards the issuer as well as the proposed issue may also be considered by the underwriter. All other environmental factors may also be analysed for their influence on the proposed issue. By considering all the relevant factors, the underwriter estimates the quantum of risk involved in the proposed issue and based on such assessment of risk, it may commit to the issue. If it decides to underwrite the issue, the underwriting commission is negotiated.

8.3 Registrar and Share Transfer Agent

__Registrars__ and __share transfer agents__ are engaged in keeping the investors' account on behalf of a body corporate. Their services include effecting the transfer of ownership of securities.

One of the intermediaries in securities market transactions is the registrar. According to SEBI, a **registrar** is a person appointed by a body corporate or any person or group of persons to carry on the following activities.

- Collecting applications from investors in respect of a capital issue;
- Keeping a proper record of applications and monies received from investors or paid to the seller of the securities; and
- Assisting organizations or persons or a group of persons in determining the basis of allotment of securities in consultation with the stock exchange, finalizing the list of persons entitled to the allotment of securities and processing and despatching of allotment letters, refund orders or certificates and other related documents in respect of the capital issue.

SEBI defines a **share transfer agent** as any person who on behalf of any organization, department or division of an organization maintains the records of holders of securities issued by such an organization and deals with all matters connected with the transfer and redemption of securities.

8.3.1 SEBI (Registrars to an Issue and Share Transfer Agents) Rules, 1993

No person or organization can act as a registrar or share transfer agent without holding a certificate of registration granted by SEBI. The application for the registration may be for any of the following categories.

(a) Category I: To carry on the activities as a registrar to a capital issue and share transfer agent.
(b) Category II: To carry on the activities either as a registrar to an issue or as a share transfer agent.

For Category I, the capital adequacy requirement is INR 0.6 million (net worth) and for Category II it is INR 0.3 million (net worth). The capital adequacy requirement shall not be applicable for a department or division of a body corporate performing the activities of registrar or share transfer agent. Net worth means:

(a) In the case of an applicant being a proprietary concern or a firm or an association of persons or any body of individuals, the value of capital contributed to such business by the applicant and the free reserves of any kind belonging to the business of the applicant, and
(b) In the case of an organization, the value of the paid-up capital and the free reserves as disclosed in the books of account of the applicant at the time of making the application.

SEBI, on being satisfied that the applicant is eligible, shall send this information to the applicant mentioning the category for which the applicant has been found eligible for the grant of certificate, subject to the payment of the fee prescribed. When a registrar to an issue or share transfer agent fails to pay the prescribed fee, SEBI may suspend the certificate, whereupon the registrar to an issue or share transfer agent shall cease to carry on any of his activities as a registrar to an issue or share transfer agent.

General obligations and responsibilities

Every registrar to an issue and share transfer agent holding a certificate shall at all times abide by the code of conduct as specified by SEBI. No registrar to an issue shall act as the registrar for any issue of securities in case he or it is an associate of the body corporate issuing the securities. A registrar to an issue shall be deemed to be an associate of the other organization where he or it controls directly not less than 10 per cent of the voting power of the body corporate, or he or any of his relatives is a director of the organization. Every registrar to an issue and share transfer agent being an organization shall keep and maintain certain books of accounts (for example, the balance sheet, profit and loss account) and documents (for example, the statement of capital adequacy). The registrar to an issue and the share transfer agent shall keep and maintain the books of accounts relating to all sums of money received and expended by them and the matters in respect of which the receipt and expenditure take place, their assets and liabilities and a statement of capital adequacy requirements for each quarter.

Every share transfer agent shall maintain the following records for the organization on whose behalf he is carrying on the activities of the share transfer agent.

(a) List of holders of securities of such an organization
(b) The names of the transferor and transferee and the dates of transfer of securities
(c) Other records as may be specified by SEBI for carrying out activities as share transfer agents.

It shall be the duty of every director, proprietor, partner, officer and employee of the registrar to an issue or the share transfer agent, being inspected, to produce to the inspecting authority such books, accounts and other documents in his custody or control and furnish the authority with the statements and information relating to the transactions in the securities market within such time as the said officer may require.

Every registrar to an issue or share transfer agent shall enter into a legally valid agreement with the issuer of securities or the organization. In the case of a large issue, the issuer may decide to appoint or associate more than one registrar. In such a case, the agreement shall be executed by all the registrars and the lead manager shall be a confirming party. The agreement shall be valid at least until the expiry of one year from the date of closing of the issue. In the case of an agreement entered into by a share transfer agent with an organization, it shall be valid for a minimum period of one year's renewal if the circumstances require.

Code of conduct

A registrar to an issue and the share transfer agent shall observe a certain code of conduct prescribed by SEBI, the salient features of which are as follows.

- A registrar to an issue and the share transfer agent shall maintain high standards of integrity in the conduct of its business.
- A registrar to an issue and the share transfer agent shall fulfil its obligations in a prompt, ethical and professional manner.
- A registrar to an issue and the share transfer agent shall at all times exercise due diligence, ensure proper care and exercise independent professional judgement.
- A registrar to an issue and the share transfer agent shall make appropriate disclosure to the client of its possible source or potential areas of conflict of duties and interest, which would impair its ability to render fair, objective and unbiased services.
- A registrar to an issue and the share transfer agent shall not divulge to other clients, press or any other person any confidential information about its clients that has come to their knowledge, except with the approval/authorization of the clients or when it is required to disclose the information under the law in force at that time.
- A registrar to an issue and share transfer agent shall not, for any dealings in securities, be party to or instrumental for the creation of false market, price rigging or manipulation or passing of unpublished price-sensitive information with respect to the securities that are listed and proposed to be listed in any stock exchange to any person or intermediary.

The nature of services offered by RCMC Share Registry (P) Ltd is given in Box 8.1. The case discussed in the box will illustrate the practical aspects of the services of a registrar and share transfer agent.

8.3.2 Criteria for Registrar and Share Transfer Agent Selection

Registrars and share transfer agents play an important role in the success of any corporate issue. In brief,

- They are responsible for receiving applications for securities from various collection centres through the branches of the bankers to the issue.
- They prepare the basis of allotment of securities to the applicants.
- They arrange the despatch of allotment letters, share certificates and refund orders.
- They prepare a register of members.
- They facilitate the transfer of securities.

Box 8.1 Registrar and Share Transfer Agent Services: A Case of RCMC Share Registry (P) Ltd

RCMC Share Registry (P) Ltd was established in 1984 as a registrar and share transfer agent. We are registered with SEBI vide Registration No. INR000000429 as a "Registrar to an Issue and Share Transfer Agent" in Category I.

Emphasizing the interests and benefits of the shareholders as well as the stakeholders, the company offers consultancy services regarding the registrar and share transfer, depository connectivity, registrar to IPO, fixed deposit accounting, share accounting, mutual fund processing and others. Apart from these, it also provides electronic connectivity with the National Securities Depository Ltd. (NSDL) and the Central Depository Services Ltd. (CDSL) through leased line connections.

The company provides services in the areas of issue management, investor services and others and maintains the entire record of shareholders along with replying to queries/complaints/enquiries from the investors. Its clients include Rural Electrification Corporation Ltd, Steel Authority of India Ltd, Ballarpur Industries Ltd and Jindal Saw.

Highlights of its services include:

- Web-based online enquiry module: This enables customers to view all shareholders/ management enquiries/reports regarding the up-to-date status of transfers/dividends. A user name and password is provided and access to the information is possible only after verification of the user name and password.
- Customized reports to meet the requirements for both physical and electronic mode of activities.
- A full-time investor service cell to answer all queries.

- They maintain an updated list of securities holders.
- They send dividend/interest warrants.
- They handle investor complaints.

In view of the many responsibilities they undertake, a company would base its selection of an organization as the registrar and share transfer agent based on certain criteria. The key ones are as follows:

- SEBI registration.
- Track record of the organization in matters relating to registrar and share transfer agent services.
- Availability of infrastructure, including the necessary systems.
- Ranking of the registrar by a prime public issue monitor.
- Cost of the services.
- Reliability and trustworthiness of the registrar regarding confidential matters.
- Contacts with other agencies like bankers and brokers.
- Previous experience of the company with the registrar.
- Number of issues the registrar is handling at the time of selection.

8.4 Stockbroker and Sub-broker

Financial securities can be purchased or sold by anyone who has money or securities. However, people who have knowledge about market trends are likely to be more successful in their investments. A **stockbroker** is one who acts as an agent for buying and selling stocks and bonds, besides undertaking other services. According to SEBI, a stockbroker is one who is a member of a stock exchange. A **sub-broker** is any person who is not a member of a stock exchange but acts on behalf of a stockbroker as an agent or otherwise for assisting investors in buying, selling or dealing in securities through such stockbrokers.

*A **stockbroker** is one who acts as an agent for buying and selling of corporate securities. A **sub-broker** acts on behalf of the stockbroker.*

8.4.1 SEBI (Stockbroker and Sub-broker) Regulations, 1992

No stockbroker or sub-broker shall buy, sell or deal in securities unless he holds a certificate granted by SEBI. An application by a stockbroker for the granting of a certificate shall be made through the stock exchange of which he is a member. SEBI may require the applicant to furnish all the information required for the grant of a certificate of registration. SEBI shall take into account all matters relating to the buying, selling or dealing in securities while granting the certificate of registration. SEBI shall consider whether the applicant:

- Is eligible to be admitted as a member of a stock exchange;
- Has the necessary infrastructure like adequate office space, equipment and manpower to effectively discharge his activities;
- Has past experience in the business of buying, selling or dealing in securities;
- Is subjected to disciplinary proceedings under the rules, regulations and by-laws of a stock exchange with respect to his business as a stockbroker involving either himself or any of his partners, directors or employees; and
- Is a fit and proper person.

A broker shall have an absolute minimum of INR 0.5 million as deposit with the stock exchanges at Mumbai and Kolkata or INR 0.35 million as a deposit with the stock exchanges at Delhi and Ahmedabad or INR 0.2 million in the case of stock exchanges at other places. The security deposit kept by the members in the exchanges shall form part of the base minimum capital. The additional or optional capital required of a member at any point of time should be such that together with the base minimum capital, it is not less than 8 per cent of the gross outstanding business in the exchange. The gross outstanding business would mean the aggregate of up-to-date sales and purchases by a member broker in all securities put together at any point of time during the current settlement.

The corporate broker

A company seeking registration as a corporate broker (member) of any stock exchange shall have a minimum paid-up capital stated as follows:

a. INR 3 million for stock exchanges at Mumbai and Kolkata
b. INR 2 million for stock exchanges at Delhi, Ahmedabad and Chennai
c. INR 1 million for other stock exchanges

In addition, a corporate member shall at all times maintain a net worth, i.e., the aggregate of paid-up capital and free reserves, which shall conform to the capital adequacy norms as specified by SEBI. If a corporate member seeks to become a member of more than one stock exchange, the requirements as stated earlier shall be fulfilled in respect of each of the stock exchanges. Separate and segregated accounts in respect of each of the stock exchanges of which he is a member shall be maintained.

SEBI, on being satisfied that the stock broker is eligible, shall grant a certificate of registration. The stockbroker holding a certificate shall at all times abide by the code of conduct.

Sub-broker

The eligibility criteria for registration as a sub-broker shall be as follows.

(i) In the case of an individual:

(a) The applicant is not less than 21 years of age;
(b) The applicant has not been convicted of any offence involving fraud or dishonesty;
(c) The applicant has at least passed the twelfth-standard equivalent examination from an institution recognized by the government.
(d) The applicant is a fit and proper person.

(ii) In the case of a partnership firm or a body corporate, the partners or directors, as the case may be, shall comply with the requirements contained in clauses (a) to (c).

(iii) The applicant has the necessary infrastructure like adequate office space, equipment and manpower to effectively discharge his activities.

(iv) The applicant shall be a person recognized by the stock exchange as a sub-broker affiliated to a member broker of the stock exchange.

SEBI, on being satisfied that the sub-broker is eligible, shall grant a certificate of registration subject to certain terms and conditions. The sub-broker shall pay the fees as specified, abide by the code of conduct, enter into an agreement with the stockbroker for specifying the scope of his authority and responsibilities, comply with the rules, regulations and by-laws of the stock exchange and not be affiliated to more than one stockbroker of one stock exchange.

The sub-broker seeking registration shall be recognized by the stock exchange before the application is recommended to SEBI for registration as a sub-broker. Similarly, the applications for the cancellation the sub-broker's registration must be forwarded to SEBI only after the sub-broker seeking cancellation is de-recognized by the stock exchange.

General obligations and responsibilities

The general obligations and responsibilities of a stockbroker are as follows.

1. Every stockbroker shall keep and maintain the following books of account, records and documents:
   - Register of transactions
   - Client's ledger
   - General ledger
   - Journals
   - Cash book
   - Bank passbook
   - Member's contract books

- Margin deposit book
- Registers of accounts of sub-brokers
- Agreement with the sub-broker and with the client of the sub-broker
- Documents register containing particulars of securities received and delivered in physical form and the statement of account and other records relating to receipt and delivery of securities provided by the depository participants in respect of dematerialized securities.

Every stockbroker shall, after the close of each accounting period, furnish to SEBI, if so required, as soon as possible but not later than six months from the close of the said period a copy of the audited balance sheet and profit and loss account at the end of the said accounting period.

2. There shall be an agreement between the stockbroker and the client. In the agreement, the parties have to agree to terms and conditions as specified by SEBI.
3. There shall be a tripartite agreement between the stockbroker, sub-broker and client. They shall agree to terms and conditions as specified by SEBI.
4. In the agreement with the client, the stockbroker shall declare that he has brought the contents of the risk disclosure document to the notice of the client and made him aware of the significance of the said document.
5. There shall be a separate agreement between the stockbroker and the sub-broker. The agreement will state that the sub-broker is affiliated to the stockbroker and that the sub-broker shall within the scope of the authority act as a sub-broker within the meaning and subject to SEBI regulations.
6. The stockbroker, sub-broker and the client shall be entitled to terminate the agreement without giving any reasons to the other party after giving notice in writing of not less than one month to the other party.

A stockbroker or a sub-broker who contravenes any of the provisions of the relevant framed act, rules or regulations shall be liable one or more of the following actions.

- Monetary penalty
- Penalty
- Prosecution

A stockbroker or a sub-broker shall be liable for monetary penalty for the following violations.

- Failure to file any return or report with SEBI;
- Failure to furnish any information, books or other documents within 15 days of the issue of notice by SEBI;
- Charging brokerage that is in excess of the brokerage specified in the regulations or the by-laws of the stock exchange;
- Failure to maintain books of accounts or records as per the act and the rules or regulations framed under it;
- Failure to readdress the grievances of investors within 30 days of receipts of notice from SEBI;
- Indulging in fraudulent and unfair trade practices relating to securities;
- Execution of trade without entering into an agreement with the client;
- Failure to segregate his own funds or securities from the client's funds or securities or using the securities or funds of the client for his own purpose or for purposes of any other client;
- Acting as an unregistered sub-broker or dealing with unregistered sub-brokers;
- Failure to exercise due skill, care and diligence.

A stockbroker or a sub-broker shall be liable for any action including suspension or cancellation of his certificate of registration as a stockbroker or a sub-broker, as the case may be, if he ceases to be a member of a stock exchange, he has been declared defaulter by a stock exchange and not re-admitted as a member within a period of six months, surrenders his certificate of registration to SEBI or he has been declared insolvent or an order for winding up has been passed in the case of a broker or sub-broker being a company registered under the Companies Act, 1956.

A stockbroker or a sub-broker shall be liable for prosecution for any of the following violations.

- Dealing in securities without obtaining a certificate of registration as a stockbroker or a sub-broker from SEBI.
- Market manipulation of securities or index.
- Indulging in insider trading in violation of SEBI regulations.
- Failure to pay penalty imposed by the adjudicating officer or failure to comply with any of his directives or orders.

Transactions between the client and stockbroker/stockbroker and clearing member

1. It shall be compulsory for all brokers as members of a stock exchange to keep the client's money in a separate account and their own money in a separate account. No payment for transactions in which the member broker is taking a position as a principal will be allowed to be made from the client's account.
2. Every member broker shall keep such books of account as will be necessary to show and distinguish in connection with his business as a member or the moneys received from or on account of and moneys paid to or on account of each of his clients as well as the money received and the money paid on the member's own account.
3. Member brokers shall issue the contract note for purchase/sale of securities to a client within 24 hours of the execution of the contract.
4. In case of purchases on behalf of clients, member brokers shall be at liberty to close out the transactions by selling the securities in case the client fails to make the full payment to the member broker for the execution of the contract within the prescribed period.
5. In case of sales on behalf of clients, member brokers shall be at liberty to close out the contract by effecting purchases if the client fails to deliver the securities sold with valid transfer documents within the prescribed period.
6. It is expected that the member brokers of stock exchanges know their clients through a proper introductory procedure and exercise due precaution while dealing with the clients.
7. All payments shall be received/made by the brokers from/to the clients strictly by account payee crossed cheque/demand drafts or by way of direct credit into the bank account through electronic fund transfer (EFT) or any other mode allowed by RBI. For their transactions, the brokers shall accept cheques drawn only by the clients and issue cheques only in favour of the clients. However, in exceptional circumstances, the broker or sub-broker may receive the amount in cash to the extent that it is not in violation of the income-tax requirements as may be in force from time to time.
8. In the case of securities giving/taking delivery of securities in the demat mode should be directly to/from the beneficiary accounts of the clients except delivery of securities to a recognized entity under the approved scheme of the stock exchange and/or SEBI.
9. A stockbroker or sub-broker of an exchange cannot deal with brokers/sub-brokers of the same exchange either for proprietary trading or for trading on behalf of clients, except with the prior permission of the stock exchange.
10. The clearing member and trading member shall enter into an agreement that should clearly state the nature of the relationship between the two and specify the duties, responsibilities, obligations and code of conduct of the concerned parties.
11. The clearing member shall enter into a separate agreement with each of the trading members on whose behalf he will be clearing trades. The agreement shall include the exposure limit details applicable to the trading member. Such limits may be decided by the clearing member, subject to the requirements prescribed by the relevant authority from time to time.
12. The clearing member shall collect margins from the trading member as prescribed by the relevant authority from time to time. However, if the clearing member finds it necessary, he shall be authorized to levy and collect an additional margin over and above those imposed by the stock exchange/clearing corporation and the trading member shall be liable to pay the margins within the stipulated time.
13. The clearing member shall ensure that the trading member collects margins from his clients on a gross basis.

14. In the event of a default of the trading member on his own account, the client money shall remain safe and shall not be utilized to meet the trading member's liabilities. In such cases, the client's positions shall be transferred to the clearing member or another trading member.

Foreign broker

A *foreign broker* shall be allowed to assist and operate only on behalf of registered foreign institutional investors. The foreign broker only transmits orders to a member of an Indian stock exchange and the orders are executed on the stock exchanges only by members of the stock exchanges. The registration of the foreign brokers is done by SEBI on a specific application made by a foreign broker. The registration is subject to an express undertaking by the foreign broker that it would be operating only on behalf of the registered FIIs and not act on its own account as a principal. Necessary permission may be given by the RBI to a foreign broker to open a foreign currency denominated bank account and a rupee account with a designated bank branch. The RBI may also give permission to the foreign broker to open custodian accounts with each custodian of the registered FII on whose behalf he would be operating. The securities delivered to the foreign broker by the member of the Indian stock exchange against the purchases of the FIIs are passed on to the custodian of the FII within 48 hours after due verification. Similarly, securities received for delivery from the custodian of the FII against sale transactions are routed through the foreign broker's custodian to the member of the stock exchange within 48 hours.

8.4.2 Criteria for Selection of a Stockbroker

Stockbrokers play a significant role in the success of any corporate issue. Therefore, a company selecting brokers for its capital issue should keep in view the following aspects with regard to the brokers.

- SEBI registration.
- Previous performance with respect to the amount procured by the broker in issues of various sizes.
- Ranking of the broker by a prime public issue monitor in terms of the number of issues and the size of issues handled by him.
- Network of its sub-brokers.
- Close rapport with other agencies involved in the capital issue.
- Region of its operation.
- Number of capital issues the broker is handling at the time of selection.

8.5 Banker to an Issue

A banker to a public issue carries out all the activities involved in the collection of funds from the applicants to the public issue, issuing refunds to those applicants who have not been allotted the securities and transferring funds to the concerned issuer. The banker makes all the arrangements to receive the applications from the investors at the collection centres. He also makes quick estimates of collections and accordingly advises the issuer about the closure of the issue. It may be noted that any lapse on the part of the banker may also result in a poor show of the public issue.

*A **banker to an issue** carries out all the activities involved in the transfer of funds from the investors (who have subscribed to a capital issue) to the issuer.*

8.5.1 SEBI (Bankers to an Issue) Regulations, 1994

As per the SEBI (Bankers to an Issue) Regulations, 1994, a banker to an issue means a scheduled bank carrying on all or any of the following activities:

- Acceptance of application and application monies.
- Acceptance of allotment or call monies.
- Refund of application monies.
- Payment of dividend and interest warrants.

No person shall carry on any activity as a banker to an issue unless he holds a certificate granted by SEBI, as specified under the regulations. An application by the scheduled bank for the grant of a certificate as the banker to an issue shall be made to SEBI in the prescribed form. SEBI shall take into account the following aspects for considering the grant of a certificate.

- The applicant has the necessary infrastructure, communication and data-processing facilities and manpower to effectively discharge its activities,
- The applicant or any of its directors is not involved in any litigation connected with the securities market and that has an adverse bearing on the business of the applicant or has not been convicted of any economic offence,
- The applicant is a scheduled bank,
- The applicant is a fit and proper person,
- The granting of the certificate to the applicant is in the interest of investors.

SEBI, on being satisfied that the applicant is eligible, shall grant the certificate of registration. On the granting of a certificate, the applicant shall be liable to pay the fees. Where the applicant fails to pay the prescribed fees, SEBI may suspend the registration certificate, whereupon the applicant shall cease to carry on any activity as a banker to an issue for the period during which the suspension subsists.

General obligations and responsibilities

As per the SEBI regulations, every banker to an issue shall maintain the following records with respect to:

- The number of applications received, the names of the investors, the dates on which the applications were received and the amount so received from the investors,
- The time within which the applications received from the investors were forwarded to the body corporate or registrar to an issue as the case may be,
- The dates and amount of refund monies paid to the investors.

Every banker to an issue shall enter into an agreement with the organization that it is representing. The agreement shall contain the following.

(a) The number of centres at which the applications and application monies of an issue of a body corporate will be collected from the investors,

(b) The time within which the statement regarding the applications and application monies received from the investors investing in an issue of a body corporate will be forwarded to the registrar to an issue or the body corporate as the case may be,

(c) That a daily statement will be sent by the designated controlling branch of the bankers to the issue to the registrar to an issue indicating the number of applications received on the date from the investors investing in the issue of a body corporate and the amount of application money received.

Every banker to an issue shall inform SEBI forthwith if any disciplinary action is taken by the RBI against the banker to an issue. Provided that if as a result of any such action, the banker to an issue is prohibited from carrying on the activities, the certificate of registration shall be deemed to have been suspended or cancelled as the case may be. Every banker to an issue shall abide by the code of conduct as prescribed by SEBI. Further, every banker to an issue shall appoint a compliance officer who shall be responsible for monitoring the compliance of the rules and regulations issued by SEBI or the Government of India.

Inspection of books

SEBI may request the RBI to undertake the inspection of the books of accounts, records and documents of the banker to an issue for any of the following purposes.

- To ensure that the books of accounts are being maintained in the required manner,
- To check hat the provisions of the act, rules and regulations are being followed,
- To investigate the complaints received from investors, the body corporate or any other person on any matter having a bearing on the activities of the banker to an issue,
- To investigate such matters as may be required by SEBI.

It shall be the duty of every director, proprietor, partner, officer and employee of the banker to an issue who is being inspected, to produce to the inspecting authority such books, accounts and other documents in his custody or control and furnish it with the statements and information relating to his activities as a banker to an issue within such time as the RBI may require.

8.5.2 Criteria for Banker Selection

The banker plays an important role in the success of any corporate issue. Hence, the following aspects need to be considered while selecting a banker for a capital issue.

- SEBI registration.
- Efficiency of service rendered by the banker in past issues.
- Experience of the lead manager(s) with the banker.
- Network of branches and their locations.
- Region of concentration of operations of the bank.
- Ranking by a prime public issue monitor.
- Banker's willingness to bear part of the issue expenses.

8.6 Debenture Trustee

*A **debenture trustee** is a trustee for securing any issue of debentures of an organization or any private placement of debentures made by a listed company that are proposed to be listed.*

A debenture is a financial instrument of debt issued by a company acknowledging its obligation or commitment to repay the amount with interest according to the terms and conditions specified in it. The debentures shall not carry any voting rights. Sections 117 to 123 of the Companies Act, 1956, regulate the provisions relating to debentures, appointment of debenture trustees and their duties, the creation of indenture, the redemption of a reserve account and the liability of trustees.

When debentures are issued to the public, there are a large number of debenture holders on the register of the company. As such, it may not be feasible to create charge in favour of each of the debenture holders. Therefore, a trust is created by a trust deed in favour of all the debenture holders. The trust enables the property to be held by a person or persons for the benefit of some other person known as the beneficiary. The trust deed may grant the trustees a fixed charge over the freehold and leasehold property while a floating charge may be created over other assets. As per Section 125 (4) of the Companies Act, 1956, the registration of a charge for the purpose of issue of debentures is mandatory. Section 128 stipulates that where a company issues a series of debentures secured by charge, the benefit will be available to all debenture holders *pari passu*.

In terms of Section 117B of the Companies Act, 1956, it is mandatory for any company making a public/rights issue of debentures to appoint one or more debenture trustees before issuing the prospectus or letter of offer and obtain their consent, which shall be mentioned in the offer document. But as per the SEBI regulations, the appointment of debenture trustees is compulsory only in the case of debentures with a maturity of 18 months or more. The debenture trustee shall not beneficially hold shares in a company, be beneficially entitled to monies that are to be paid by the company to the debenture trustees, and enter into any guarantee in respect of the principal debt secured by the debentures or interest thereon.

Section 117C of the Companies Act, 1956, casts an obligation on the company to create a debenture redemption reserve out of the proceeds from the profits of the company every year till redemption of the debentures.

According to Section 117B of Companies Act, 1956, no company shall issue a prospectus or a letter of offer to the public for subscription of its debentures unless the company has, before such issue, appointed one or more debenture trustees for such debentures and, on the face of the prospectus or the letter of offer, stated that the debenture trustee or trustees have given their consent to the company to be so appointed. Provided that no person shall be appointed as a debenture trustee if he:

- Beneficially holds shares in the company,
- Is beneficially entitled to money that is to be paid by the company to the debenture trustee or
- Has entered into any guarantee in respect of principal debts secured by the debentures or interest thereon.

Subject to the provisions of the Companies Act, 1956, the functions of the debenture trustees shall generally be to protect the interest of the holders of debentures (including the creation of securities within the stipulated time) and redress the grievances of the holders of the debentures effectively. The main functions of the debenture trustee are:

- To ensure that the assets of the company issuing debentures and each of the guarantors are sufficient to discharge the principal amount at all times,
- To satisfy himself that the prospectus or the letter of offer does not contain any matter that is inconsistent with the terms of the debentures or the trust deed,
- To ensure that the company does not commit any breach of covenants and provisions of the trust deed,
- To take such reasonable steps that will remedy any breach of the covenants of the trust deed or the terms of issue of debentures,
- To take steps to call a meeting of holders of the debentures as and when such a meeting is required to be held.

8.6.1 SEBI (Debenture Trustee) Regulations, 1993

According to SEBI, a debenture trustee is a trustee by a trust deed for securing any issue of debentures of a body corporate or any private placement of debentures made by a listed company that are proposed to be listed. The SEBI (Debenture Trustees) Regulations, 1993, stipulates that no person shall act as a debenture trustee unless he holds a certificate granted by SEBI under the regulations. An application by a debenture trustee for grant of a certificate shall be made to SEBI in the prescribed form. For considering the grant of a certificate, SEBI shall verify whether:

- the applicant has the necessary infrastructure like adequate office space, equipment and manpower to effectively discharge his activities,
- the applicant has any past experience as a debenture trustee or has in his employment a minimum of two persons who have experience in matters that are relevant to a debenture trustee,
- any person directly or indirectly connected with the applicant has not been granted registration by SEBI under the act,
- the applicant has in his employment at least one person who possesses professional qualifications in law from an institution recognized by the government,
- any of the directors or principal officers of the applicant at any time has been convicted for any offence involving moral turpitude or found guilty of any economic offence,
- the applicant is a fit and proper person, and
- the applicant fulfils the capital adequacy requirements as specified by SEBI.

No institution shall be entitled to act as a debenture trustee unless it is either a scheduled bank carrying on commercial activity, a public financial institution within the meaning of the Companies Act, 1956, an insurance company or a body corporate. The capital adequacy requirement shall not be less than a net worth of INR 10 million. No debenture trustee shall act as such for any issue of debentures in case it is an associate of the body corporate or it has lent and the loan is not yet fully repaid or is proposing to lend money to the body corporate.

Responsibilities and obligations

No debenture trustee who has been granted a certificate shall act as such in respect of each issue of debentures unless he enters into a written agreement with the body corporate before the opening of the subscription list for the issue of debentures. It shall be the duty of the debenture trustee to:

- call for periodical reports from the body corporate,
- take possession of the trust property in accordance with the provisions of the trust deed,
- enforce security in the interest of the debenture holders,
- complete such acts as are necessary in the event the security becomes enforceable, and
- carry out such acts as are necessary for the protection of the debenture holders and do all things necessary to resolve the grievances of the debenture holders.

The debenture trustee shall ascertain and satisfy itself that:

(a) in case the allotment letter has been issued and the debenture certificate is to be issued after registration of charge, the debenture certificates have been despatched by the body corporate to the debenture holders within 30 days of the registration of the charge with the registrar of companies.

(b) debenture certificates have been despatched to the debenture holders in accordance with the provisions of the Companies Act, 1956.

(c) interest warrants for interest due on the debentures have been despatched to the debenture holders on or before the due dates.

(d) debenture holders have been paid the monies due to them on the date of redemption of the debentures.

The debenture trustee shall also ensure on a continuous basis that the property charged to the debentures is available and adequate at all times to discharge the interest and principal amount payable in respect of the debentures and that such property is free from any other encumbrances except those that are specifically agreed on by the debenture trustee. It is also the responsibility of the debenture trustee to exercise due diligence to ensure compliance by the body corporate with the provisions of the Companies Act, 1956, the listing agreement of the stock exchange or the trust deed.

The debenture trustee shall appoint a nominee director on the board of the body corporate in the event of:

(a) two consecutive defaults in payment of interest to the debenture holders,

(b) default in creation of security for debentures, or

(c) default in redemption of debentures.

The debenture trustee shall communicate to the debenture holders on a half-yearly basis regarding compliance with the terms of the issue by the body corporate, defaults, if any, in payment of interest or redemption of debentures and action taken thereof. The debenture trustee shall call or ensure that the body corporate calls a meeting of all the debenture holders on:

(a) a requisition in writing signed by at least one-tenth of the debenture holders in value for the time being outstanding or

(b) the happening of any event, which constitutes a default or which in the opinion of the debenture trustees affects the interest of the debenture holders.

No debenture trustee shall relinquish its assignments as a debenture trustee in respect of the debenture issue of any body corporate unless and until another debenture trustee is appointed in its place by the body corporate. The debenture trustee may inspect books of account, records, registers of the body corporate and the trust property to the extent necessary for discharging its obligations.

Inspection

Whenever necessary, SEBI may appoint one or more persons as the inspecting authority to undertake inspection of the books of account, other records and documents of the debenture trustee for any purposes as specified by SEBI. It shall be the duty of every director, officer and employee of the debenture trustee who is being inspected to produce such books and other documents as present in their custody or control to the inspecting authority and furnish it with statements and information relating to the debenture trustee within such time as the inspecting authority may require.

Summary

1. A capital issue is an offer of sale of corporate securities to the public or to existing holders of securities. Savings and investments are brought together or synchronized through capital issues.
2. Underwriting refers to an agreement with or without conditions to subscribe to the unsubscribed portion of capital issues when they are offered to the investing public.
3. No person shall act as an underwriter unless he holds a certificate granted by SEBI under the regulations.
4. Registrars and share transfer agent are engaged in keeping the investors' account on behalf of an organization. Their services include effecting the transfer of ownership of securities.

5. A stockbroker is one who acts as an agent for the buying and selling of corporate securities and a sub-broker acts on behalf of the stockbroker.
6. No stockbroker or sub-broker shall buy, sell or deal in securities unless he holds a certificate granted by SEBI.
7. A banker to a public issue carries out all the activities involved in the collection of funds from the applicants to the public issue, issuing refunds to those applicants who have not been allotted the securities and transferring funds to the concerned issuer.
8. All scheduled commercial banks are eligible to act as banker to an issue as per SEBI regulations.
9. A debenture trustee is a trustee by a trust deed for securing any issue of debentures of a body corporate or any private placement of debentures made by a listed company that are proposed to be listed.

Questions

1. Critically evaluate SEBI regulations with regard to underwriting.
2. What are the different forms of underwriting? What are the implications of each of them for the issuer of securities?
3. What could be the reasons for failure (under-subscription) of public issues?
4. What are a company's considerations in selecting underwriters?
5. What is the role of a registrar and a share transfer agent in capital issue management?
6. Bring out the important features of SEBI regulations with regard to the registrar and share transfer agent.
7. What are the services of stockbrokers? How would SEBI regulations facilitate effective functioning of stockbrokers and sub-brokers?
8. Can the services of stockbrokers be dispensed?
9. Critically evaluate the role of bankers in the success of a capital issue. Also comment on SEBI regulations with regard to bankers to an issue.
10. What is the necessity of a debenture trustee? Evaluate the legal and regulatory framework for a debenture trustee.

Chapter 9

Financial Derivatives

LEARNING OBJECTIVES

After studying this chapter, you should be able to:

- Explain the concept of derivatives.
- Discuss the different kinds of financial derivative products such as forwards, futures, options and credit default swaps.
- Present the salient features of the L.C. Gupta Committee recommendations.
- Highlight SEBI guidelines for derivatives trading.
- Provide a brief account of the derivative products in Indian stock markets.

9.1 Introduction

Derivatives involving agricultural commodities and precious metals like gold and silver have been in existence for a very long time, perhaps for centuries. It is said that derivatives, particularly forwards, have been around as long as there has been commerce that involves business risk. However, organized commodities exchanges, on which derivatives are traded, came into existence in the beginning of the eighteenth century. The Chicago Board of Trade (CBOT) was started sometime in the middle of the nineteenth century and is now the largest derivatives exchange in the world. Financial derivatives with underlying financial assets such as equities, debt instruments and currencies, have been in vogue for only the last thirty to forty years. Following the collapse of the Bretton Woods System in the early 1970s, financial markets in the world witnessed a high degree of volatility. The instability in foreign exchange rates and volatile interest rates, which have direct implications for prices of many financial securities, particularly equities, have necessitated the development of financial derivatives markets across the globe. It is worth noting that the Chicago Mercantile Exchange (CME) and the London International Financial Futures and Options Exchange (LIFFE) are the biggest financial derivatives exchanges in the world. In India, financial derivatives trading started in June 2000 with the launch of stock index futures by the National Stock Exchange (NSE) of India and Bombay Stock Exchange (BSE). Subsequently, many financial derivative products have been introduced in the Indian markets.

The market for derivatives has witnessed a phenomenal rise in the trading of derivative products, especially in recent years, because of the increasing risk aversion of investors and also the increasing trading activity in capital markets. This phenomenon has been witnessed all over the world. The total number of futures and options contracts traded on the 69 exchanges in the world (tracked by the Futures Industry Association) increased from 938.22 million in 1992 to 15,526.63 million in 2007 to 17,652.70 million in 2008 (see Tables 9.1 and 9.2). The number of options is always more than the number of futures. On the whole, the number of derivatives traded globally increased by 13.7 per cent in 2008 over 2007.

Derivatives trading initially started with commodity derivatives, which became very popular over time. But it was only in the 1970s that financial derivatives came into prominence with increasing activity in capital markets. Although financial derivatives are late entrants, they account for two-thirds of total derivatives trading. As can be observed from Table 9.3, the derivatives on equity indices alone account for more than one-third of the total derivatives contracts in 2008, followed by derivatives on individual equities. All the financial derivatives put together account for more than 88 per cent of the total derivatives traded in 2008. Region-wise analysis (Table 9.4) indicates that North America accounts for about 40 per cent of the total global trading in derivatives, followed by Asia Pacific, which accounts for 28 per cent.

Table 9.1 Global derivatives trading (in terms of contracts)

Year	*Number of contracts (in million)*
1992	938.22
2000	2,989.45
2001	4,347.32
2002	6,217.28
2003	8,162.54
2004	8,864.71
2005	9,973.67
2006	11,862.21
2007	15,526.63

Source: FI Magazine, March/April 2008

Table 9.2 Global derivatives volume

Type	*Jan–Dec 2008*	*Jan–Dec 2007*	*Percentage change*
Futures	8,291,625,474	7,217,729,477	14.9
Options	9,361,078,147	8,308,902,627	12.7
Total Volume	**17,652,703,621**	**15,526,632,104**	**13.7**

Source: FI Magazine, March/April 2009

Table 9.3 Global derivatives volume (by category)

Category	*Jan–Dec 2008*	*Jan–Dec 2007*	*Percentage change*
Equity index	6,488,620,434	5,499,833,555	18.0
Individual equity	5,511,194,380	4,400,437,854	25.2
Interest rates	3,204,838,617	3,745,176,350	– 14.4
Agricultural	888,828,194	640,683,907	38.7
Energy	580,404,789	496,770,566	16.8
Currency	577,156,982	459,752,816	25.5
Precious metals	180,370,074	150,976,113	19.5
Non-precious metals	175,788,341	106,859,969	64.5
Others	45,501,810	26,140,974	74.1
Total	**17,652,703,621**	**15,526,632,104**	**13.7**

Source: FI Magazine, March/April 2009

Table 9.4 Global derivatives volume (by region)

Region	*Jan–Dec 2008*	*Jan–Dec 2007*	*Percentage change*
Asia Pacific	4,974,727,462	4,289,600,329	16.0
Europe	4,167,116,664	3,592,095,161	16.0
North America	6,995,493,016	6,137,204,923	14.0
Latin America	854,405,219	1,048,627,318	– 18.5
Others	660,961,260	459,104,373	44.0
Global total	**17,652,703,621**	**15,526,632,104**	**13.7**

Source: FI Magazine, March/April 2009

Financial derivatives trading has increased tremendously not only in terms of turnover but also in terms of variety of products. Although financial derivatives are primarily meant for hedging against fluctuations in prices of financial products such as equity shares, a lot of speculative activity is witnessed in the derivatives market as well.

9.1.1 The Concept of Derivatives

As the name indicates, a **derivative** is a financial instrument that derives its value from the price of its underlying asset, commodity, security, or other such items. A derivative has no independent value as such. According to the L.C. Gupta Committee, "a derivative means forwards, futures or option contracts of pre-determined fixed duration, linked for the purpose of contract fulfilment to the value of the specified real or financial asset or to index of securities". In terms of this definition, derivatives mainly include forwards, futures and options. A combination of two or more of these derivative instruments can also be used to create new instruments. For example, forwards and options are two basic derivative instruments, which can be innovatively combined to create a wide range of new derivatives. The actual design of any derivative instrument depends on its purpose. Derivatives are mostly customized or tailor-made as per the requirements of the investors, so many derivative products are highly complex in design.

*A **derivative** is a financial instrument that has no value of its own but derives its value from the price of its underlying asset, commodity, security or other such items.*

9.1.2 Functions of the Derivatives Market

The primary function of the derivatives market is to enable investors to manage their risks by hedging or insuring themselves against adverse price movements in volatile markets. For example, a person may wish to sell his shares at a price that he considers safe at a future date. But a fall in the price of these shares would prevent him from receiving the price he was expecting. To hedge such a risk, he can enter into a forward contract and any loss caused by the fall in the cash price of the shares will then be offset by the profits on the forward contract. This hedging of risk is the equivalent of insurance against the risk of market-price variations. Speculators, who are very important organs of any market, can also participate in derivatives trading. It may be noted that no market can exist without speculators. It is the speculator who is the counterparty to every contract the hedger initiates. Speculators provide liquidity and help maintain price stability in the financial market.

The primary function of the derivatives market is to enable investors to manage their price risks by hedging or insuring themselves against adverse price movements.

The functions of the derivatives market are as follows:

- To facilitate the transfer of risk from risk-averse investors (hedgers) to risk-takers (speculators).
- To help in discovering prices of derivatives as well as of underlying assets.
- To increase the volume of trade in the cash market.
- To make the capital market vibrant and thereby help business units raise funds at ease and on favourable terms.
- To increase the savings and investments in the economy.

9.1.3 Types of Derivatives

There are many kinds of derivative products in the market. Broadly, they are classified as financial derivatives, commodity derivatives and currency derivatives. Derivatives may also be classified as over-the-counter (OTC) derivatives and exchange-traded derivatives, or as forward contracts, futures and options.

Over-the-counter derivatives, also known as OTC derivatives, are bilaterally negotiated contracts between two parties. The important feature of OTC derivatives is that they are customized contracts that suit the specific requirements of the parties. Since they are private contracts, they are prone to credit risk. That is, a counterparty may fail to honour his commitment to the contract. OTC derivatives are also characterized by information asymmetry and lack of transparency. OTC derivatives have been legally permitted in the Indian market only recently, but are still limited to those derivatives in which at least one of the parties is the RBI, a scheduled commercial bank or similar agency falling under the purview of the RBI under certain acts.

***Over-the-counter (OTC) derivatives** are customized financial derivative contracts that suit the specific requirements of the parties.*

Exchange-traded derivatives *are standardized contracts traded on recognized exchanges; the prices of these are determined by the interplay of demand and supply forces in the market.*

Exchange-traded derivatives are standardized contracts traded on recognized exchanges; the prices of these are determined by the interplay of demand and supply forces in the market. There is virtually no credit risk in exchange-traded derivatives as the performance of the contracts is guaranteed by the clearing house or clearing corporation of the exchange. Margin requirements and marking-to-market are the hallmarks of exchange-traded derivatives.

9.2 Financial Forward Contracts

A ***forward contract*** *is a financial contract to buy or sell a certain quantity of a financial product at a price determined at the time of entering the contract on a specified future date.*

A financial **forward contract** is a financial contract to buy or sell on a specified future date a certain quantity of a financial product (for example, shares, bonds, currency) at a price determined at the time of the contract. A forward contract locks the price of the underlying security. Whatever the price of the underlying security on the date of maturity of the forward contract, the contract is executed on the date of maturity at the agreed-upon price. The forward contract price is generally different from the spot price. The *spot price* is the current price at which the financial instruments are traded for immediate delivery. A forward contract has no value at origination as no party to a contract is required to pay any amount to the other at that time. However, it may become valuable as the forward price or the spot price of the underlying asset changes over time.

9.2.1 Zero-sum Game

A forward contract is a zero-sum game, as the gain of one party is the loss of the counterparty. As the spot price of the underlying asset changes over time, the price of a forward contract would change, though the original forward price (delivery price) remains unchanged. But on the date of maturity of the contract, which is the delivery date, the profit or loss is actually realized by each party. If the spot price of the underlying security is greater (less) than the original forward price, the buyer (party that is long) of the forward contract realizes the actual profit (or loss) and the seller (party that is short) of the forward contract books the same amount of loss (or profit). Before the maturity date of the contract, one party could book a profit and at the same time another party makes a loss with the change in the forward price or spot price of the underlying asset.

For example, suppose the equity shares of Reliance Industries Limited (RIL) are currently selling at INR 1,000. Based on their own perception, X and Y have entered into a forward contract. X agrees to deliver 100 shares of RIL at INR 1,050 on September 30, and Y consents to take delivery of the shares by paying the agreed price. After some days of entering into the forward contract, the market price of the share increases to INR 1,070. If this price stays at the delivery date, Y (long position) would stand to gain and X (short position) would lose. With an increase in the market price of the underlying security, the long position will be profitable, while the short position will be profitable with a decrease in the market price of the underlying security. Thus, the profit of one party is the loss for another party and, therefore, forward trading is a zero-sum game. It may be noted that the party (either the long position or short position) who no longer wants to continue with the contract may sell the forward contract to anyone at any time at a negotiated price, which may be different from the delivery price of the contract.

The forward price generally depends on the expectation of the spot price on the delivery date. As expectations about the future spot price of the underlying asset change, the forward price may also change. The forward price also varies with the maturity of the forward contract—the longer the maturity period of the contract, the higher the forward price. The price of a one-month forward contract is typically different from that of a three-month forward contract. Let us now look at the details of the settlement mechanism of forward contracts.

9.2.2 Cash Settlement

Forward contracts are privately arranged agreements between two parties, one of which agrees to buy the underlying financial product (takes a long position in a forward contract) while the other agrees to sell the same financial product (takes a short position in the same forward contract). The quantity of the financial product and maturity period of the forward contract are designed according to the requirements of the contracting parties. In other words, forward contracts are customized or tailor-made contracts. The normal practice is that no money changes hands when forward contracts are finalized. On the date of maturity of the contract, the party taking the long position in the forward should purchase the underlying asset on the delivery date and the party taking short position commits to delivering the underlying asset on the same date. But in practice, forward contracts are cash settled, which means that the party with the profitable position receives the difference between the spot rate and the original forward price from the other party.

9.2.3 Default Risk

Although forward contracts are hedging tools (means of avoiding price risk), they themselves entail risk to the extent that they are exposed to default risk by the counterparty. Forwards are not traded on organized exchanges and, therefore, there is no one to guarantee the fulfilment of the contract by the counterparty. If the trading is done through organized exchanges, the clearing corporation of the exchange interposes between the buyer and seller, thereby guaranteeing the payment of money and delivery of securities.

Further, forward contracts suffer from inadequate liquidity in the market, which means that the parties cannot quickly buy and sell the forward contracts at fair prices. Rampant speculation may also be seen in the forward market as the trading activities in the forward market are not regulated and there are no margin requirements and position limits.

9.3 Financial Futures

Although forwards and futures in commodities have existed for centuries, financial futures are a recent phenomenon. Financial futures include currency futures, interest rate futures and stock index futures. Among financial futures, currency futures first emerged in 1972 in the United States. It was only in the 1980s that the interest rate futures and stock index futures came into being.

Financial futures are standardized, legally enforceable forward contracts traded on designated exchanges called futures exchanges. Futures are standardized with regard to the contract size and also the maturity period of the contract. In order to avoid default risk, futures contracts entail the depositing of margins. The margin requirements, daily settlement and delivery procedure are all standardized. Although the price of the futures is negotiable between the parties, it is regulated by the futures exchange. Futures price movements are regulated by imposing certain limits to avoid speculative excesses. Position limits are also prescribed in order to avoid undue influence on the market prices by any single party.

> ***Financial futures*** *are standardized, legally enforceable forward contracts traded on designated exchanges called futures exchanges.*

Once a futures contract is finalized by both the buyer and the seller, the clearing house of the futures exchange interposes itself in every contract. It becomes the seller of the contract for the long position and the buyer of the contract for the short position. The clearing house of a futures exchange is committed to delivering the asset to the long position and the payment to the short position. It is also a common practice that the counterparties close out their positions before the maturity of the contract by entering into an equal and opposite transaction and taking gain or loss thereon. This is called *reversing trade*. By reversing trade, one can net out the long and short positions.

At the maturity of the contract, the profit or loss to the buyer/seller of futures is typically the difference between the spot price of the underlying financial asset at the time of maturity and the futures price fixed at the time of entering the original contract. Depending on the spot price of the asset at the time of delivery, the gain or loss on a futures contract would arise. It may be noted in this context that trading in futures offers the opportunity to profit from any potential economic situation (boom or depression).

9.3.1 Marking-to-Market

Forward contracts and futures are usually taken as one and the same by the common person because the basic mechanism of futures and forwards is the same. But, in reality, futures and forwards differ in the way they are maintained and executed. In case of a forward contract, the settlement takes place on the date of the maturity of the contract. No payment of cash takes place before the settlement or at the time of initiation of the contract. On the other hand, in a futures contract, an amount called the margin money has to be deposited with the clearing house or clearing corporation at the time of initiation of the contract. Because it guarantees the performance of the counterparty, the clearing house needs to protect itself from default by the counterparty. Therefore, it imposes margin requirements through a process known as marking-to-market.

Table 9.5 Example of futures price

Day	*Futures price (INR)*
1	1215
2	1220
3	1217
4	1215
5	1220
6	1230
7	1225

***Marking-to-market** is the process of scaling up or scaling down of the futures contract to the current market level.*

Marking-to-market is the process of scaling up or down of the futures contract to the current market level. Accordingly, the two parties involved in a futures contract are required to pay the margin on a regular basis as per the marking-to-market factor. The process of marking-to-market is explained in the following example.

Suppose the current futures price of shares of Tata Motors for delivery seven days from now is INR 1210. The futures price over the next five days is as given in Table 9.5.

The convergence principle implies that the spot price of the share in the cash market must equal the futures price on the delivery date. The daily settlement on the basis of mark-to-market is as given in Table 9.6. It may be observed from Tables 9.5 and 9.6 that the sum of all the daily profit/loss equals the difference in the current futures price and the price on the date of maturity of the futures contract.

Thus, marking-to-market involves the daily settlement of futures. This makes the futures more attractive than forwards because the holder of futures may receive cash on a daily basis. For example, a long futures position makes an immediate gain when the spot price rises. If the interest rates increase along with the spot price, the buyer of the futures contract will have immediate cash flows through the withdrawal of money (the excess of balance over the initial margin) from his margin account, which can be invested at a higher rate of interest for the remaining period of the futures contract. Let us now look at the details of the types of margins and settlement mechanisms in futures.

9.3.2 Types of Margins

The clearing house or clearing corporation of a futures exchange would insist that the deposit of funds in the margin account be maintained by the members of the futures exchange, particularly the seller and the buyer of the futures. The amount to be deposited by the parties at the time of the contract is known as *initial margin.* At the end of each trading day, the margin account is adjusted with the gain or loss, as shown in Table 9.6. When there is any decrease in the futures price, the buyer of the futures would incur a loss and the seller would gain. Therefore, the margin account of a long position (buyer) is debited by the amount of loss and simultaneously the margin account of a short position is credited by the same amount. On the contrary, if

Table 9.6 Daily settlement for a futures example

Day	*Gain or loss for one share (INR)*
1	1215 – 1210 = 5
2	1220 – 1215 = 5
3	1217 – 1220 = (–) 3
4	1215 – 1217 = (–) 2
5	1220 – 1215 = 5
6	1230 – 1220 = 10
7	1225 – 1230 = (–) 5
	Sum: 15

there is any increase in the futures price, the buyer will gain and the seller will lose. So the margin account of a long position is credited by the amount of profit and simultaneously the margin account of a short position is debited by the same amount.

The parties to the futures contract are entitled to withdraw any balance from their respective margin account whenever the balance amount is in excess of the initial margin. The clearing house may also set another kind of margin known as *maintenance margin* for each margin account of a member that is lower than the initial margin. The clearing house of the exchange always ensures that the balance in the margin account never falls below the maintenance margin. If the balance in the margin account falls below the maintenance margin, the party is asked to top up the margin account to the initial margin level by depositing the extra amount.

9.3.3 Cash and Physical Settlement

Futures are always cash settled whereas forwards mostly involve physical settlement. Cash settlement means there is no physical delivery of the underlying securities on the date of maturity of the contract. To distinguish between these two, let us take an example. A trader, for instance, has taken a long position in 500 shares of a company at INR 100 in the futures market. By the end of the contract period, the price has gone up to INR 110. Therefore, the futures exchange will pay the trader INR 5,000 as the settlement value. Suppose, the price has gone down to INR 95 per share. The trader would then have to pay INR 2,500 to the futures exchange. This is called cash settlement. Now suppose it is a forward contract which should be physically settled. Then, the trader will pay INR 50,000 to the counterparty and in return the counterparty will deliver 500 shares to the trader at the maturity of the forward contract. Despite the decline of the price, the trader still has to pay INR 50,000.

Some financial futures do have securities as their underlying assets. But there are also financial futures such as stock index futures that represent only a hypothetical portfolio of the constituent stocks. Such futures cannot be settled by physical delivery of the underlying stocks and, therefore, must be cash settled. The cash payment equals the difference between the spot price and delivery price.

9.3.4 Types of Financial Futures

Financial futures are of different kinds such as stock futures, stock index futures and currency futures. Let us discuss these in detail.

Stock futures

A **stock futures contract** is a futures contract that involves trading of equity shares of a company. For example, an investor wants to buy 300 shares of RIL but he will have money for this purpose only after three months. The current market price of the RIL shares is INR 1,150. He fears the price will go up in the next three months. Therefore, he buys three-month RIL futures (market lot of 300 shares) at INR 1,160 per share. Suppose after three months the market price of the shares is INR 1,200. The investor has thus locked the price at INR 2,150, which is lower than the spot price after three months. If the spot price after three months is lower than the futures price, the investor would have incurred a loss on the futures trading. It may be noted that one party's gain is another party's loss and, therefore, a futures contract is always a zero sum game.

*A **stock futures contract** refers to a futures contract that involves trading of equity shares of a company.*

Stock index futures

Stock index futures are a type of contract that involves a stock index as an underlying asset. Similar to other financial futures, a stock index futures contract involves the buying and selling of standardized units of a particular index at a predetermined price and at a fixed date in the future. In index futures, the underlying asset is the index and it derives its value from the value of the underlying index. An index, in turn, derives its value from the prices of securities that constitute the index. That is, an increase in the value of the stock index is equal to the increase in the total value of the stocks comprising the stock index. Thus, the stock index measures the changes in the value of a portfolio of stocks traded on a particular stock exchange over a period of time. The BSE Sensex, S&P CNX Nifty, NASDAQ 100 and S&P 500 are examples of stock indices.

__Stock index futures__ refer to a contract that involves a stock index as an underlying asset.

A typical stock index futures contract specifies the underlying index, contract size, daily price movement limits and tick size. Stock index futures are traded in terms of the number of contracts, where each contract is to buy or sell a fixed value of the index. The value of the index is the value of the index multiplied by the contract size. The contract size is the permitted lot size, which varies from exchange to exchange and from time to time. In the case of S&P CNX Nifty futures, the permitted market lot size is 100 at present. Therefore, for every one point increase in futures price, the party who holds the long position would gain INR 100 × 1, or INR 100, and that will be the loss for the short position holder.

The value of one futures contract is given as:

Market lot × Value of S&P CNX Nifty

Suppose the S&P CNX Nifty futures for May has closed at 3,473. The value of one futures contract is then INR 347,300 (i.e., 100 × 3473).

The traders in index futures take a particular view on the way the index will move. By taking a position in index futures, the traders buy or sell the group of securities (portfolio) that constitute the index. A buy position on a stock index amounts to a buy position on all the stocks that constitute the index. Although these two positions appear to be similar, they are not equivalent. If one wants to buy the stock, he may have to pay the entire price of the stock immediately. On the other hand, if he buys the stock index futures, he is required to pay only a fraction of the price as margin and on that he may even get some interest. Thus, buying stock involves opportunity cost, that is, foregoing interest on the money (price of the stock) paid on the stock. The theoretical price of stock index futures is determined as follows.

$$F_t = S_t e^{(r-d)(T-t)}$$

Where

F_t = Index futures price at time t

S_t = Spot price of index at time t

r = Risk-free rate of interest per annum

d = Dividend yield (annualized) on the portfolio of securities constituting the index

$(T-t)$ = Time gap in years between the time when the futures contract matures and the current time.

In case a specific dividend is not expected on the underlying equity stocks (portfolio) during the period of the futures contract, the formula has to be modified as follows.

$$F_t = S_t e^{(r)(T-t)}$$

Where

$e^{(r)(T-t)}$ = Cost of carry (i.e., the interest on the value of the portfolio underlying the futures)

If the portfolio underlying the stock index futures provides an excess return over the risk-free rate of return, then

$$F_t = S_t e^{(R-d)(T-t)}$$

Where

R = Return provided by the portfolio underlying the index. The excess return $(R - r)$ can be considered as the growth rate of the futures price.

Stock index futures are always cash settled. What is delivered at the termination of the contract is the money difference between the price at the time of the contract and the price at the termination of the contract.

Example 9.1

The current value of S&P CNX Nifty is 3,380. The stocks that constitute the index provide a dividend yield of 2 per cent per annum (i.e., the average dividend yield of those companies for which the ex-dividend date is during the life of the futures contract). The risk-free rate of interest is 6 per cent per annum. What is the three-month futures contract on S&P CNX Nifty?

Solution

$F_t = 3{,}380 \times e^{(0.06 - 0.02)(0.25)} = 3413.97$

Stock index futures are the most popular form of equity derivatives internationally. Stock index-based derivatives such as stock index futures and stock index options are more cost effective than derivatives based on individual stocks. They are more suited to institutional investors, particularly for portfolio hedging. Stock-index based derivatives are more popular and, therefore, more liquid than other types of equity derivatives.

Currency futures

A **currency futures contract** is a type of contract that involves exchanging one currency against another currency at a specified exchange rate and on a specified date in the future. For example, suppose an Indian firm has purchased goods worth USD 10 million from a U.S. supplier. The payment can be made in 90 days. The spot rate is USD/INR 48. During the next 90 days, the USD might rise against the INR. To guard against such a risk, the Indian firm enters a futures contract, according to which the counterparty will deliver USD 10 million in 90 days and in return the firm would pay INR 480.50 million (at the futures price of USD/INR 48.50). Here, the Indian firm has offset a short underlying position in USD by going long in the futures market, which means buying USD for future delivery. By entering into a futures contract, the firm has eliminated the foreign exchange risk on the transaction of buying goods on credit.

*A **currency futures contract** is a type of contract that involves buying or selling of one currency against another currency at a specified exchange rate and on a specified date in the future.*

Currency futures can be used for speculative purpose as well. For example, a market participant expects that the GBP would appreciate against INR in the future. The spot rate is GBP/INR 78. He thus purchases 30-day futures on GBP at GBP/INR 78.50 for GBP 1 million. At the end of the 30-day period, the spot rate is, say, GBP/INR 80.00. So on each GBP of the contract amount, he would make a profit of INR 1.50. Of course, if expectations go wrong, the speculator would incur a loss.

Interest rate futures

The volatility of interest rates causes interest rate risk. For example, a firm has borrowed at a floating rate interest. Any increase in interest rates in the economy will lead to an increase in the firm's interest cost, and lower profits. Similarly, investors who own fixed interest-bearing securities will experience a decline in the value of their assets if interest rates rise. On the contrary, a decline in interest rates will reduce the interest income for a floating rate lender. All types of holders of debt securities, whether short-term debt instruments such as commercial paper or long-term debt securities such as floating-rate bonds, are prone to interest rate risk. Financial institutions including banks that have made floating rate loans and financed them with fixed interest rate sources of capital are also exposed to interest rate risk.

Thus, the holders of debt securities are exposed to considerable interest rate risk because of unexpected changes in interest rates in the market. The yield-to-maturity (YTM), which is the internal rate of return of the cash flows of a bond, has a direct relation with the price of the bond. As the interest rates change, the YTM also changes. Further, as the YTM increases, the bond price decreases and vice versa. In other words, as the interest rates in the market fall, the prices of outstanding bond issues rise. In all these cases, interest rate derivatives can serve to hedge the unexpected changes in interest rates.

Interest rate futures involve assets for which the prices depend on the level of interest rates in the economy. As per the Reserve Bank of India, **interest rate futures** are a type of standardized interest rate derivative contract traded on recognized stock exchanges to buy or sell a notional security or any other interest-bearing instrument or an index of such instruments or interest rates on a specified future date at a price determined at the time of the contract. Globally, interest rate futures account for more than 70 per cent of the total derivative transactions. Although interest rate futures are available on underlying securities of multiple maturities, most of the global markets trade futures on two underlying securities—one the long-term securities (maturities of 10 years or more) and another the short-term securities (maturity up to one year). The interest rate futures on Eurodollars, treasury bills and treasury bonds are widely used.

__Interest rate futures__ are a type of standardized interest rate derivative contract traded on recognized stock exchanges to buy or sell a notional security or any other interest-bearing instrument or an index of such instruments or interest rates at a specified future date at a price determined at the time of the contract.

The following example illustrates the use of interest rate futures. In February, a firm expects interest rates to come down in March. So it purchases a T-bill futures contract at INR 950 (5 per cent discount) in February. The price of T-bills with March settlement date is, say, INR 960 (4 per cent discount rate). As expected, the interest rates have declined. So the firm accepts the delivery of the T-bills and sells them for more than what it has paid for them, making a profit. If the interest rates have risen over this period, the price of T-bills as of the March settlement would be less than INR 950 and the firm would have incurred a loss. If the firm had anticipated that the interest rates would rise, it would have sold a T-bill futures contract with a March settlement date.

9.3.5 Uses of Forwards and Futures

Forwards and futures are used for hedging, speculation or arbitrage. A brief description of each of them is given here.

Hedging

***Hedging** is the process of transferring price risk by a person or organization to others who are willing to bear the risk for windfall gains.*

Hedgers use futures for protection against adverse future price movements of the underlying asset. The primary purpose of **hedging** is to transfer the price risk faced by a person or organization to others who are willing to bear the risk for windfall gains. Thus, hedgers seek to eliminate the price risk they face in their regular business activities. They are often business organizations or individuals who have a genuine transaction in the underlying asset. Hedging may be short or long. In a *short hedge*, the trader or investor anticipates a fall in the price of a commodity, stock or asset that he owns and, therefore, sells that commodity, stock or asset at a specified price to be delivered on a specified date in future. For example, an investor wants to protect the value of his portfolio of equity stock worth INR 10 million against fluctuations in the stock prices. Therefore, the investor may protect the value of the portfolio by taking a short position in the stock index futures such as S&P CNX Nifty futures. Assuming that the portfolio has a beta of 0.9, the investor has to sell Nifty futures worth INR 9 million (i.e., 0.90 × INR 10 million). *Beta* is a measure of the relative riskiness of the portfolio as compared to the index. A beta of 0.9 indicates that for every one per cent change in the value of the index, there will be a 0.9 per cent change in the value of the portfolio. This means the volatility of the portfolio is less than that of the index. It is further assumed that the closing price of the May Nifty futures is 3,484. So the firm has to sell 26 futures [i.e., INR 9 million / (100 × 3484)]. At the maturity of the futures contract, the futures price will equal the spot price of the index. The gain or loss on the portfolio holdings are almost offset by the loss or gain on the 26 futures held short.

In a *long hedge*, the trader or investor wishes to buy a commodity, stock or asset sometime in the future. But the investor fears that the price of that commodity, stock or asset will rise in the days to come. Therefore, the investor buys it now at a specified price, but the delivery and payment will take place on a certain date in the future. For example, a firm wishes to buy 3,000 shares of Tata Steel at INR 520 per share after three months. It anticipates that the price of the Tata Steel shares will go up in the future. So it enters a three-month forward contract, according to which the firm is obliged to buy 3,000 shares of Tata Steel at the end of three months at INR 520 per share. The forward contract will be performed regardless of the spot rate of the Tata Steel shares on the date of maturity of the forward contract. Both the short and long hedges help the trader or investor avoid the risk arising from fluctuations in prices.

Speculation

Compared to hedgers who perform regular business activities in which they face risk, speculators do not perform such activities. In other words, speculators do not have risk requiring derivatives. But they seek risk or assume risk in the hope of making windfall gains or supernormal profits. Speculators normally go long expecting rise in prices and go short when they expect a fall in the prices. In the process, they may gain or lose depending on whether their expectations are correct or wrong. For example, the closing price of April Nifty index futures is 3,474. Suppose a speculator anticipates that an index will increase in value and accordingly purchases 10 Nifty futures contracts. If the index value increases to 3,480, the speculator will gain INR 600 (INR 6 × market lot of 100) per contract. If the expectation of the speculator goes wrong, he will incur a loss. It may be noted that futures are highly leveraged investments since one can put up a small fraction of the value of the contract as margin and ride on the full value of the contract as it moves up or down.

Arbitrage

Arbitrage refers to the simultaneous buying and selling of a security or commodity to make a profit on the differences in the prices prevailing in two markets (i.e., cash and derivative markets). Such profit is known as *arbitrage profit*. For example, the Nifty index is at 3,450, risk-free interest rate is 6 per cent and the average dividend yield on the stocks that constitute the Nifty is 3 per cent. Therefore, the theoretical value of the futures is INR 3,475.97. Against this, the actual futures price is INR 3,480. As the higher futures price gives arbitrage opportunity, the astute investor can short (sell) the overpriced futures (one market lot of 100) and buy the stocks that constitute the underlying index. Suppose the arbitrageur borrows INR 345,000 for three months at the interest rate of 6 per annum and uses the amount to purchase stocks. After three months the arbitrageur has to pay INR 3,50,100 inclusive of interest towards the loan. Meanwhile, the arbitrageur gets a dividend of INR 2,588. After three months, the futures that he has sold short would fetch him INR 348,000. So his cash flows after three months would be as follows.

***Arbitrage** refers to the simultaneous buying and selling of a security or commodity to make a profit on the differences in the prices prevailing in different markets.*

	All values in INR
Loan repayment	(−)350,100
Dividend	(+)2,588
Futures (sold short)	(+)348,000
Net cash flows	488

It can be observed from this example that one can make a profit of INR 488 by trading in index futures without any initial investment of one's own and without any risk. But, of course, this arbitrage profit would disappear when all the investors try to cash in on the arbitrage opportunity. In general, if the futures price is less than the spot price plus the cost of carry or if the futures price is greater than the spot price plus the cost of carry, arbitrage opportunities exist. It may be noted that when a person trades in futures, he does not actually buy or own anything. He actually speculates on the future direction of the price of the underlying asset. Investors would buy the futures if they expect that the price of the underlying asset will go up in the future and sell futures if they expect that the price of the underlying asset will go down in the future.

9.4 Pricing of Forwards and Futures

The price of a forward contract or futures is governed by interest rates in the economy. Accordingly, the theoretical futures price is given as follows.

$$F_t = S_0 \times e^{(rt)}$$

Where

S_0 = Spot price of a futures

e = Base of the natural logarithm, which has a value of 2.71828

r = Interest rate

t = Period of the futures

The above equation can also mean that an investor can borrow S_0 rupees for a period t at the risk-free interest rate to buy the underlying security and take a short position in the forward /futures. An investor may take a long position in the forward/futures and short in the underlying security. The short position may lead to a cash inflow of S_0 rupees to be invested at rate r.

If the underlying asset produces any income for its owner, this calculation has to be modified. For example, if the underlying asset is the common stock which earns a dividend yield, say d, the interest rate is to be reduced to $r - d$. It may be mentioned that the longer the period of the futures, the greater the value of the futures.

The relationship between the futures price and the spot price is based on the *cost of carry*. The cost of carry is a concept used in the context of commodity futures. It refers to different kinds of costs such as storage cost, insurance cost, transportation cost and financing cost, which are incurred for carrying a commodity forward in time. In the case of futures on equity securities or stock indices, the cost of carry is the cost of financing minus dividend returns. If the dividends are assumed to be zero, the cost of financing is the cost of carry.

To explain with an example, suppose a forward contract has a six-month period. The spot price of the underlying share is, say, INR 100 and the interest rate (r) in the economy is 8 per cent per annum. The theoretical forward price (F_{90}) is given as:

$$F_{90} = 100 \times e^{(0.08 \times 0.50)} = \text{INR } 104$$

The period of the forward contract is six months and therefore it is taken as 0.50 (i.e., half of one year). If the market price of the futures contract is not the theoretically determined price, the arbitrage process comes into effect. For example, the actual forward price is, say, INR 110. A market participant can sell the forward contract at INR 110. Simultaneously, he borrows INR 104 at an interest rate of 8 per cent per annum for six months and uses that amount to buy the underlying share. After six months, the market participant delivers the share and receives INR 110 as per the terms of the forward contract. He will repay the loan of INR 104 with an interest of INR 4 and make a risk-less profit of INR 2. But the actual forward price will soon come to the theoretical level as more and more participants sell the forward contract and buy the underlying asset at the spot price.

9.5 Implied Interest Rate and Open Interest

The *implied interest rate* is the annualized percentage difference between the futures and spot price by taking into account the unexpired period of the futures contract.

The **implied interest rate** is the annualized percentage difference between the futures price and spot price, as computed by taking into account the number of days remaining for the expiry of the contract. The implied interest rate is compared with the existing interest rate to measure the relative profitability of futures. **Open interest** refers to the number of outstanding contracts at a given time or at the end of each trading day. It shows how much interest is present in a particular derivative product. The higher the open interest, the greater the interest of the market participants in that derivative product. Further, increasing the open interest means that fresh funds are being infused into the market and decreasing the open interest means that the market is liquidating.

Open interest refers to the number of outstanding contracts at a given time or at the end of each trading day.

9.6 Basis Risk

The basic expectation while trading in forwards and futures is that as the spot price of the underlying asset changes, so too will the price of the forward or futures that is based on that asset. It is implicitly assumed that the spot price of the underlying asset and forward or futures price would change in a predictable way relative to one another. For example, consider that an investor has purchased 1,000 shares of RIL at INR 1,025. Fearing that the price of the RIL shares will decline, the firm has taken a short position in futures. If the price of the RIL shares falls, the total value of the shares declines. But the price of the futures will also decline by the same amount. So, the gain on the short position in futures will offset the loss on the value of the underlying shares.

The *basis* is the difference between the spot price of an underlying asset and the price of the futures price at any time. The unpredictability of movement of the spot price of the underlying asset and the price of the futures contract is the *basis risk.*

The spot price of the underlying asset and the price of the futures price may differ at any point of time. This difference is known as the **basis**. On the date when the futures contract is finalized, the market participant knows both the spot price of the underlying asset and the price of the futures. On the date of the maturity of the futures contract, the price of the futures would converge with the spot price of the underlying asset. Thus, the basis becomes zero on the maturity date of the futures contract. This is because as the maturity of the futures contract draws nearer, the cost of carry keeps coming down till it becomes zero on the date of maturity.

By taking a long or short position in futures, one can avoid price risk. The market participant is also exposed to another kind of risk called the **basis risk**, which is explained in the following lines. If the underlying asset and futures are held until maturity, the investor bears no risk since the spot price of the underlying asset and futures price become equal on the date of maturity of the futures contract. The gain or loss on the underlying asset is offset by the loss or gain on the futures contract. But after the date of entering into the futures contract and before the date of maturity, the movement of the spot price of the underlying asset and the price of the futures contract is unpredictable. Thus, the hedger cannot predict how the spot price of the underlying asset and the price of the futures contract would move before the maturity date of the futures contract. Such unpredictability or uncertainty of prices is the source of the basis risk. A hedger who wants to liquidate the futures contract at any time before the maturity of the futures contract will face the basis risk.

For example, a person has 1,000 shares of Tata Steel. He has entered a short position to deliver these 1,000 shares in the future. The spot price of the share is INR 500 and the futures price for April delivery is INR 520. The basis is currently INR 20. Suppose the spot price of the share has increased to INR 505, while the futures price has increased to INR 522. So the basis is INR 17. The investor has gained INR 5 per share but lost INR 2 per share on the short futures position. So the net gain is INR 3 per share. Due to uncertainty about the interest rate changes and the asset's yield in the future, the spot price of the underlying asset and futures price do not move in perfect unison at all times. Hence the basis risk arises. If the spot price increases by more than the futures price, the basis is said to have strengthened. If the futures price increases by more than the spot price, the basis is said to have weakened.

An *option* is a contract that gives the holder the right but not the obligation to buy or sell the underlying assets or securities at a predetermined price within or at the end of a specified period.

9.7 Options

Options and futures have many similarities and serve similar purposes but the risk profile of an option is asymmetric. An **option** is a contract that gives the holder the right but not the obligation to buy or sell the underlying asset or security at a predetermined price within or at the end of a specified period. The price at which the option is to be exercised is called the *strike price* or the *exercise price*. Since the right to buy or sell a security is valuable, the purchaser of an option pays an upfront price called the *option premium* to the party who has sold the option.

Options are traded both on exchanges and over the counter. Exchange-traded options are standardized with regard to market lot, trading cycle, expiration date and strike price. On the other hand, the options traded over the counter are private and customized contracts to meet the specific needs of the counterparties. That is, OTC options are tailored to meet the needs of both the buyer and the seller of the options. For example, for OTC (private) options, the expiration date for an option can be fixed by the counterparties according to their requirements. In contrast, the expiration date for exchange-traded options is standardized.

On exchanges, options are traded in cycles such as the January, February, or March cycle. The January cycle consists of the months January, April, July and October. The February cycle consists of the months February, May, August and November. The March cycle consists of the months March, June, September and December. Initially, the options trade with expiration dates in the current month, the following month and the next two months in its cycle. Once the expiration date of the current month has passed, options trade with expiration dates in the next month, the next-but-one-month and the next two months of the expiration cycle. Let us take an example. Suppose a particular stock is on a January cycle. At the beginning of January, options trade with expiration dates in January, February, April and July. At the end of January, options trade with expiration dates in February, March, April and July. It is the same procedure for other cycles. The rule is that when one option reaches expiration, trading begins in another. In the case of exchange-traded options, the strike prices are also determined by the exchanges according to certain rules. A particular stock may have different expiration dates and different strike prices. Thus, there may be many different option contracts trading for a given stock at any point of time. All the options contracts with the same expiration date and strike price are considered as one option series.

Options are of two types—call option and put option. A *call option* gives its owner a right to buy the underlying asset or security and the *put option* gives its owner a right to sell the underlying asset or security. Options are also classified as American and European. **American options** are exercisable at any time prior to the expiration date while **European options** can be exercised only at the expiration date. As such, American options have more value than the corresponding European options.

> ***American options*** *are exercisable at any time prior to the expiration date of the option while* ***European options*** *can be exercised only at the expiration date of the option.*

Suppose an investor has purchased a call option (American type) maturing in June on equity stock of Tata Steel. The exercise price is INR 560. If at any time on or before the maturity date of the call option, the Tata Steel price goes beyond INR 560, the investor exercises the option and buys the underlying stock at the strike price, which is lower than the spot price, and thus makes a profit. On the other hand, if the price of the Tata Steel stock is quoted at INR 560 or less, the investor would not exercise the call option. But the writer or seller of the call option is obliged to sell the shares, if called upon, to the investor at the strike price.

In case the option is a put option, the investor has the right to sell the underlying stock at the strike price. For example, an investor has purchased a put option (American type) maturing in March on RIL stock at a strike price of INR 1,050. If at any time on or before the maturity date of the put option, the RIL price goes below INR 1,050, the investor exercises the option and sells the underlying stock to the option writer at the strike price, which is higher than the spot price, and thus makes a profit. On the other hand, if the price of the RIL stock is quoted in the cash market at INR 1,050 or more, the investor would not exercise the put option. But the writer or seller of the put option is obliged to buy the shares, if called upon, from the investor at the strike price.

A call option holder exercises his option only if the price of the underlying securities rises above the exercise price and the put option holder only if the price falls below the exercise price. Thus, a call option becomes more valuable if the price of the underlying security rises and a put option becomes more valuable if the price of the underlying security falls. The buyer of an option can lose only the option premium paid by him if the price of the underlying asset or security does not move in his favour. But his possible gains are unbounded. On the other hand, the option writer's possible loss is unbounded but his maximum gain is limited to the option premium received by him from the option buyer.

An option may be in-the-money, at-the-money, or out-of-the-money at any time before maturity of the option. At any point in time, if the exercise of the option leads to positive cash flows to the option holder, such an option is considered to be *in-the-money*; if the exercise of the option leads to negative cash flows, the option is *out-of-the-money*; and if the exercise of the option leads to zero cash, flows the option is said to be *at-the-money*.

The major differences between options and futures are as follows.

- Both the parties to a futures contract have the obligation to perform the contract and buy/sell the underlying asset as per the terms of the contract. In an option contract, the writer of the option should always perform the contract and the buyer of the option has the right but not the obligation to buy or sell the underlying asset. The option holder can even allow the contract to expire. There is no compulsion on the part of the option buyer to buy or sell the underlying asset.
- An option entails the payment of the premium by the buyer of the option to the writer of the option. But there is no such premium in the case of futures.
- In the case of futures, both the buyer and seller need to maintain a margin account with the futures exchange. But in the case of options, only the seller of the option needs to pay the margin to the exchange.

9.7.1 Types of Options

Financial options may also be classified as equity options, stock index options and currency options.

Equity options

Equity options are options on the common stock of companies. These options are traded on the exchanges and OTC worldwide. There are many reasons for the trading of options. For instance, an investor has some information that the stock of Hindustan Unilever Limited (HUL) would rise in the near future. But he does not have enough money to buy the stock outright. So he purchases a call option by paying an option premium of INR 200. The call option gives him the right to buy 200 shares of HUL at INR 250 per share on or before November 30. Thus, the investor has got control over INR 50,000 worth of shares by paying just INR 200. If the expectation of the investor goes wrong, the maximum amount that could be lost on the purchase of 200 shares is only INR 200. The investor knows for sure how much his maximum loss could be if his expectations go wrong. However, his profit potential is unlimited if the stock price rises as per his expectation.

Similarly, an investor can buy a put option on the equity if he expects a company's equity stock price would fall in the near future. The value of the put option increases as the price of the underlying stock declines. If the stock price increases against his wishes, the maximum loss will be the price (premium) paid on the put option.

Just as there are many reasons for buying the options, there are many reasons for selling the options. The general expectation of the option writer is that the options that he has sold will not be exercised and, therefore, he will make a profit from the received premium without encumbering any capital. To give an example, an investor has purchased 1,000 shares of Dabur India at INR 105 per share. At present, the price is INR 110. But he wants INR 2 more on each share. So he has sold call options on these shares and received a premium of INR 2 per share. Let us suppose the price of the share declines, and the option holder does not exercise the option. In such a case, the option writer has the premium and still owns the stock. On the other hand, if an investor wants to buy the equity stock of a company, he can write puts on the equity stock of the company. If the price declines, the option holder will exercise the option. So each share would cost him the exercise price minus the premium.

Stock index options

An option with a stock index as an underlying asset is known as an *index option*. Index options are generally European style, that is, they can be exercised or assigned only on the expiry date. Unlike index futures, the buyer of the index option has only the right but not the obligation to buy or sell the underlying index on expiry.

By its very nature, an index cannot be delivered on the maturity of the index futures or index option contract. If an option on a stock is exercised, that stock can be delivered. But in the case of stock index options, delivering all the stocks that make up the index is not possible. Therefore, stock index options are always cash settled. When an option is exercised, the option writer pays cash to the option buyer. If it is a call option, the option holder receives an amount equivalent to the value of the index minus the strike price. If it is a put option, the option holder receives an amount equivalent to the strike price minus the value of the index. For example, the strike price of a call option on S&P CNX Nifty is 3,440. On the day of maturity of the option, the index is at 3,500. The market lot is 100. So the holder of the option would receive $(3{,}500-3{,}440) \times 100 =$ INR 6,000 in cash from the option writer.

Stock options are used to take advantage of the anticipated price movement of individual stocks. They can also be used to protect current or anticipated positions in individual stocks. For example, an institutional investor holds a portfolio consisting of a number of stocks. To protect it against adverse price movements, the institutional investor must buy a put option on every stock in the portfolio, which would be costly. Alternatively, the institutional investor with a diversified portfolio can protect itself against adverse price movements by taking an appropriate position in a suitable stock index option. An institutional investor can obtain downside protection using options at a cost equal to the option price, but preserve the upside potential.

Currency options

A *currency option* gives the right to buy or sell one currency for another currency at a specified exchange rate. Currency call options are used to lock in a maximum price to be paid for a currency in future. In contrast, a currency put option makes known the minimum price at which the option holder can sell one currency against another currency in the future. Currency options can be used both for hedging and speculation. For example, an Indian firm has exported goods to a firm in the United States. At the request of the customer, it is invoiced in U.S. dollars. The Indian firm anticipates that the U.S. dollar will depreciate over time. To insulate itself against possible depreciation of the U.S. dollar, the Indian firm purchases put options on the U.S. dollars, which entitle the firm to sell the dollars at the strike price. Thus, the Indian firm has locked in the minimum rate at which it can exchange U.S. dollars for the Indian currency over a specified period of time. Much against the expectation of the Indian firm, if the USD appreciates over the period of the option, the Indian firm can let the put option expire and sell the U.S. dollars it receives at the spot rate.

Taking another example, a U.S. firm wants to buy equipment from a London-based firm three months from now. But it anticipates an appreciation of the GBP in the three-month period. So the U.S. firm has purchased call options on the GBP, which will hedge the U.S. firm against the potential appreciation of the GBP by the time it purchases the equipment. The U.S. firm lets the call options expire if the spot rate of the GBP exceeds the strike price.

9.7.2 Option Strategies

There are many option strategies that can be adopted by market participants depending on their purpose of trading. Some of the popular option strategies are the bull spread, bear spread, butterfly spread, calendar spread, straddle and strangle.

An investor may adopt a *bull spread* strategy in a situation where the underlying index or stock will go up somewhat or is at least more likely to rise than fall. A call option can be bought with a lower strike price and another call option sold with a higher strike price, with both options having the same expiration date. Alternatively, a put option can be bought with a lower strike price and another put sold with a higher strike price, with both options having the same expiration date. Suppose an investor holds shares of a company and feels that the market will go up. To hedge his position from any steep correction, he may enter into a bull spread. He can sell his positions in the cash market at, say, INR 1,210 (the current market price) and buy an INR 1,250 call, which is available at INR 20 (being the call premium) and sell an INR 1,275 call for INR 12 (call premium). This spread would cost him INR 8 (INR 20 – 12), which would be his maximum loss in case the market falls. On the other hand, he can gain a maximum of INR 17 (the difference between the two strike prices minus the cost of entering the bull spread) if the market continues to go up. It may be noted that the bull spread strategy limits the profit potential as well as the downside risk.

In contrast to a bull spread, there is a strategy called *bear spread* according to which an investor buys a call option with one strike price and sells a call option with another strike price. The strike price of the call option purchased is greater than the strike price of the call option sold. The bear spread can also be created with put options. One can buy a put option with a higher strike price and sell a put option with a lower strike price. The bear spread also limits the profit potential and downside risk for the investor.

Options with three different strike prices can be combined to create a *butterfly spread*. A butterfly spread can be created as follows:

(a) Buy a call/put option with a relatively low strike price
(b) Buy a call/put option with a relatively high strike price
(c) Sell two call/put options with a strike price halfway between call options (a) and (b)

Butterfly spreads can also be shorted by following the reverse strategy as discussed earlier.

Another option strategy is the *calendar spread*, which can be created by selling a call option with a certain strike price and buying a longer maturity call option with the same strike price. A calendar spread can also be created by buying a long maturity put option and selling a short maturity put option.

Two other important option strategies are straddle and strangles. A *straddle* involves buying a call option and a put option with the same strike price and expiration date. A *strangle* consists of buying a call option and a put option with different strike prices but the same expiration date. There are many other strategies by which options can be combined to produce different payoffs.

9.7.3 The Black and Scholes Model

The most popular model for valuation of options is the Black and Scholes Model, named after the authors Fisher Black and Myron Scholes. According to the model, the value of a call option and put option is as follows.

$$C = S_0 N(d_1) - Xe^{-rt} N(d_2)$$

$$P = C + Xe^{-rt} - S_0$$

Where

$$d_1 = \frac{\ln(S_0 / X) + (r + 0.5\sigma^2)t}{\sigma\sqrt{t}}$$

and

$$d_2 = \frac{\ln(S_0 / X) + (r - 0.5\sigma^2)t}{\sigma\sqrt{t}}$$

or

$$d_2 = d_1 - \sigma\sqrt{t}$$

C = Value of the call option
P = Value of put option
r = Risk-free rate of interest
X = Exercise or strike price of the option
t = Time remaining before the expiration date (expressed as a fractions of the year)
σ = Standard deviation of the continuously compounded annual rate of return
ln = Natural logarithm
$N(d)$ = Value of the cumulative normal distribution at d

Example 9.2

Obtain the value of the call option and put option by using the following date. Apply the Black and Scholes model.

Current market price RIL = INR 2,000
Strike price of the option = INR 2,100
Time period to expiration = 3 months (i.e., t = 0.25 years)
Standard deviation of rates of return = 4
Risk- free annual rate of return = 6 per cent

Solution:

$$d_1 = \frac{\ln(2000/2100) + (0.06 + 0.5 \times 4^2)0.25}{4\sqrt{0.25}}$$

$$d_2 = \frac{\ln(2000/2100) + (0.06 - 0.5 \times 4^2)0.25}{4\sqrt{0.25}}$$

$$C = 2000 \times 0.3365 - 2100\, e^{(-)0.06(0.25)} \times 0.1539$$
$$= \text{INR } 355.00$$
$$P = 355 + 2100\, e^{(-)0.06(0.25)} - 2000$$
$$= \text{INR } 423.50$$

9.7.4 Implied Volatility

Volatility refers to the rate and magnitude of the change of prices (up or down) of a security or commodity or any asset. Volatility is of two kinds—historical volatility and implied volatility. Historical volatility is also known as actual volatility or realized volatility. As the name indicates, *historical volatility* measures the price movements based on historical (past) prices. The calculation of historical volatility may involve the following steps.

Volatility refers to the rate and magnitude of the change of prices of a security or commodity or any asset.

1. Measure the percentage price change of a stock. For this, the natural log of the ratio of a stock's price from the current day to the previous day may be calculated.
2. Find the average of day-to-day percentage changes over a certain period of time.
3. Calculate the standard deviation of the price changes that gives the historical volatility of the stock.
4. The historical volatility may also be stated in annual percentage by multiplying the standard deviation with the square root of the average number of trading days in a year.

The price of an option on a stock is generally determined by strike price, expiration date, current stock price, dividend to be paid on the stock, risk-free interest rate and implied volatility. The Black and Scholes option pricing model is composed of all such variables. If the price of an option is known along with all the variables except volatility, then one can estimate the volatility. The volatility thus estimated is known as *implied volatility*. To put it simply, implied volatility is the volatility of a stock as estimated by its option price. Any change in the given variables results in a different implied volatility. Thus, options with different strike prices and/or expiration dates will have different implied volatility. It may be noted that except implied volatility, all the variables in an option pricing model are directly observable. This means that the price of an option can be ascertained through implied volatility. A change in the option price can be understood as a change in the implied volatility. A small implied volatility means that the stock price is expected to move by a small measure in either direction. Implied volatility tends to be higher for out-of-the money options compared to at-the-money options. As the option gets closer to expiration, implied volatility falls. This is because changes in volatility become less significant with fewer trading days.

The implied volatility is the market's perception of the changes in the price of the underlying security. Regardless of actual changes in prices of the underlying security, the implied volatility can change in either direction. When implied volatility is higher, the market participants usually buy options rather than sell.

9.8 Credit Default Swap (CDS)

A **credit default swap** is a credit derivative that provides protection against a credit risk. In a credit default swap, one party (buyer) contracts to make a payment to the other party (seller) in exchange for the pay-off if an underlying financial instrument has exposure to default during a certain period of time. For example, a firm owns INR 10 million worth of corporate bonds issued by an MNC. To hedge against the credit risk, the firm buys a CDS for INR 10 million (value of the CDS) from a bank by agreeing to pay INR 300,000 every year for the duration of the bonds. In case of default by the MNC, the bank pays the difference between the value of the CDS (i.e., INR 10 million) and the market value of the bonds to the firm. The market value of the bonds underlying the CDS depends on the prospects of the issuer of the security, and the market value of the position changes depending on the market value of the underlying security. If the probability of default increases, the CDS is worth more for the protection buyer and worth less for the protection seller. It is the opposite if the probability of default decreases. If there is no default, the seller gains the yearly payments made by the buyer. The periodic payments made by the firm are also known as *protection fee* (or premium) and they are analogous to insurance premium. The issuer of the bond or the credit which underlies the CDS is known as the *reference entity* and a default on the bond is known as a *credit event*. The underlying securities in CDS may be asset-backed securities, corporate debt, collateralized debt or indexes of companies.

A **credit default swap** is a credit derivative that provides protection against a credit risk.

A CDS is also called protection as it provides the buyer with protection against default, credit rating downgrade or another negative credit event. The seller of CDS is called the protection seller since he assumes the credit risk and, therefore, is obligated to pay if a negative credit event occurs. Thus, the buyer of the CDS shifts the credit risk to the seller by buying protection. It is important to note that the protection buyer need not necessarily own the debt security or be exposed to the credit risk to take a credit default swap. The protection buyer shorts the credit, while the protection seller is long. For example, a firm buys protection for a company's bonds of INR 1 million. But the firm does not own the bonds. In the event of a default, the firm buys these bonds in the secondary market at a huge discount, then sells them to the protection seller at par and thereby receives a large sum of money.

The CDS can also be used to replicate the exposure of a bond or portfolio of bonds. That is, the counterparty can create a synthetic portfolio of debt securities in CDS. For example, an investor wants to subscribe to a particular bond but it is difficult for him to obtain that bond in the market. By using CDS, the investor can create a synthetic bond that has the same characteristics (i.e., credit exposure and payoffs).

It may be noted that the amount of periodical payments (premium) made by the protection buyer depends on the quality of the underlying security. The riskier the security, the higher the premium that will be required. In fact, the protection buyer and protection seller bet on the prospects of the firm (reference entity). Thus, the CDS indicates the credit worthiness or risk of the reference entity. The protection buyer takes a negative view of the creditworthiness of the reference entity and the protection seller takes a positive view on the credit quality.

The CDS are negotiated privately and traded over the counter. The counterparty can also exit a contract by selling his interest to another party. For example, one party sells protection to another party, which will then resell the same protection to a different party, and so on. As the buying and selling can take place many times for the same CDS, sometimes in a circle, it is hardly known who stands at each end of a transaction. Although the counterparties may post a collateral to guarantee the fulfilment of their commitments or obligations, it is uncertain whether the protection seller can really pay in the event of a negative credit event. For example, Washington Mutual purchased bonds in 2005 and hedged the exposure by buying CDS from Lehman Brothers. When Lehman Brothers went bankrupt, Washington Mutual lost the protection. Introduced in the 1990s by JP Morgan, CDS have come a long way. The CDS market grew rapidly and its value was estimated to be between USD 45 trillion and USD 60 trillion in 2008, over twice the size of the U.S. stock market. But because a lot of speculation is involved in CDS, it poses a great threat to financial markets around the world. However, it is felt that the availability of CDS is one of the important prerequisites for developing a healthy corporate bond market.

9.9 Government Initiatives

The Indian financial market had been largely sheltered till the early 1990s. The economic reforms initiated at the beginning of 1990s not only created a plethora of opportunities but also exposed the investors and institutions to new risks. The integration of financial markets and the cross-country mobility of capital have thrown open several opportunities for investors but with new kinds of challenges or risks. This has brought risk management to the centre stage of financial management.

There is no denying the fact that financial derivatives representing financial innovation have definite uses. As hedging tools as well as means of speculation, they make financial markets more vibrant and efficient. However, trading in derivatives inherently involves high leverage. Traders with little capital, who can be considered as inadequately capitalized traders or speculators, may be induced to do risky business in the derivatives market. Speculation is necessary for every market, but excess speculation is always dangerous. Moreover, some market participants may not fully understand derivatives and fail to use them appropriately. Therefore, there is a need for a vibrant regulatory system to minimize these dangers. Accordingly, the government has initiated several measures and the important ones are brought out in the following sections.

9.9.1 The L.C. Gupta Committee

Lifting the prohibition on trading in options on securities in 1995 marked the launch of derivatives in the Indian stock market. As a follow-up, SEBI appointed a 24-member committee under the chairmanship of L.C. Gupta in November 1996 to develop an appropriate regulatory framework for derivatives trading in India. The committee examined several aspects of derivatives trading and made far-reaching recommendations.

The committee conducted a survey to assess the nature of the need and interest in various types of financial derivatives among potential market participants. According to the survey, stock index futures ranked as the most popular and preferred type of equity derivative, followed by stock index options and options on individual stocks. Individual stock futures contracts were favoured much less. Of course, only a few countries in the world have futures on individual stocks.

According to the committee, any stock index is much less volatile than individual stock prices. Therefore, lower capital adequacy and margins are required in the case of stock index futures than compared to futures on individual stocks.

The committee was of the opinion that stock index futures would be the best starting point for equity derivatives in India. It favoured the introduction of other types of equity derivatives such as options on stock index and options on individual stocks as the derivatives market in India grew and the market players acquired familiarity with its operations.

The committee made the following recommendations on the regulatory framework.

From the purely regulatory angle, a separate exchange for futures trading seems to be a better arrangement. However, in view of certain infrastructural constraints, the existing stock exchanges with cash trading may be permitted to trade derivatives, provided they meet the following minimum eligibility conditions:

- Trading should take place through an online screen-based trading system, which also has a disaster recovery site.
- The clearing of the derivatives market should be done by an independent clearing corporation that satisfies the conditions laid down by the committee.
- The exchange must have online surveillance capability that monitors positions, prices and volumes in real time so as to deter market manipulation. Price and position limits should be used for improving market quality.
- Information about trades, quantities and quotes should be disseminated by the exchange in real time over at least two information vending networks that are accessible to investors across the country.
- The exchange should have at least 50 members to start derivatives trading.
- If derivatives trading is to take place at an existing cash market, it should be done in a separate segment with a separate membership.
- The derivatives market should have a separate governing council.
- The chairman of the governing council of the derivatives division/exchange shall be a member of the governing council.
- The exchange should have an arbitration and investor grievances redressal mechanism operative from all the four areas/regions of the country.
- The exchange should have adequate inspection capability.
- No trading/clearing member should be allowed to be on the governing council of both the derivatives market and the cash market simultaneously.
- If already existing, the exchange should have a satisfactory record of monitoring its members, handling investor complaints and preventing irregularities in trading.

The committee further stated that the regulatory framework for derivatives trading shall consist of (i) the derivatives exchange's own operational rules and regulations and (ii) SEBI rules and regulations with which the exchange and its members must comply. The exchange level regulations should pertain to entry of traders/members, derivatives contracts, broker-client relationship, trading and reporting procedures, internal risk control systems, margining, clearing, settlement and dispute resolution. The derivative exchanges should necessarily get their rules, by-laws and regulations approved by SEBI before commencement of trading. As far as SEBI is concerned, the committee made the following recommendations.

- SEBI should immediately create a special derivatives cell because derivatives demand special knowledge.
- A derivatives advisory council may also be created to tap outside expertise for independent advice on many problems that are bound to arise from time to time with regard to derivatives.
- SEBI should urgently consider the creation of an economic research wing.

For other major aspects of the subject, the committee made the following observations and recommendations.

1. The committee felt that the derivatives market will have to be subjected to more stringent requirements than is the case with present cash markets.
2. For effectively ensuring capital adequacy, principal reliance has to be placed on the capital and margins actually deposited by the brokers/dealers with the exchange.

3. The clearing members of the derivatives exchange should have a minimum net worth of INR 30 million as per SEBI's definition and shall make a deposit of INR 5 million with the exchange/clearing corporation in the form of liquid assets such as cash and fixed deposits pledged in the name of the exchange or other securities.
4. The broker-members, salespersons/dealers in the derivatives market must have passed a certification programme that is considered adequate by SEBI.
5. Brokers/dealers of the derivatives exchange/division should be required to be registered as such with SEBI.
6. The clearing mechanism should be organized as a separate and independent entity, preferably in the form of a clearing corporation.
7. The clearing corporation will collect the initial (i.e., upfront) margin to which the exposure limits of the broker/dealer would be linked. The clearing corporation will enforce the mark-to-market margin system.
8. The requirements for capital adequacy and upfront margin should be set taking into account the volatility of the underlying market.
9. Since market volatility changes over time, the clearing corporation should continuously analyze this problem and may modify the margin requirements to safeguard the market.
10. The clearing corporation should be an independent corporation. Its governing board should be immune to any interference or direct/indirect pressure by trading interests.
11. Ideally, an independent centralized clearing corporation for the stock exchanges would be the most effective arrangement. The committee urged SEBI to take initiatives with potential promoters to set up a national-level clearing corporation.
12. Apart from the minimum net worth requirement, there should be a maximum exposure limit computed on a gross basis for each broker/dealer.
13. Even the system of mark-to-market margins on a daily basis will not be adequate for safeguarding the market's integrity unless the margins are actually collected before the start of the next day's trading. Even a day's delay in actual collection of the mark-to-market margin can pose a serious threat to the market's integrity. Therefore, the aim should be to collect mark-to-market margins before the next day's trading starts. The capital adequacy requirement for derivatives trading should be finally decided after taking into account both the extent of volatility and the time taken for funds transfer from dealers/members to the exchange.
14. The collection of initial and mark-to-market margins by brokers from their clients should be insisted on in the case of derivatives trading. Margin collection from clients should not be left to the discretion of brokers/dealers.
15. The clearing corporation should segregate the upfront/initial margins deposited by clearing members for trades on their own account from the margins deposited with it on the client account.
16. The clearing corporation must have SEBI approval for its functioning.
17. Derivatives brokers/dealers are expected to know their clients and exercise care to ensure that the derivative product being sold by them to a particular client is suitable to his understanding and financial capabilities.
18. The SEBI (Mutual Fund) Regulations prohibited the use of derivatives by mutual funds. The committee was of the opinion that mutual funds needed the hedging facility. They would be among the most important users of equity hedging through stock index derivatives. Hence, the regulatory prohibition should be removed.
19. Mutual funds should be allowed to use financial derivatives for hedging purposes (including anticipated hedging) and portfolio re-balancing within a policy framework and rules laid down by their board of trustees who should specify what derivatives are allowed to be used, within what limits, for what purposes, for which schemes and the authorization procedure.

According to the committee, risk and complexity among derivative products vary. While some derivatives are relatively simple, many others, especially options, could be highly complex and would require additional safeguards from the investors' viewpoint. In due course, a derivatives exchange may decide to introduce options on stock indexes or individual stocks. Options are a more complex derivative product than index futures because evaluating the fairness of option premium, which is not apparent, is a complex matter.

9.9.2 SEBI Guidelines for Derivatives Trading

SEBI accepted the recommendations of the L. C. Gupta Committee in May 1998 and approved the phased introduction of derivatives trading in India, beginning with stock index futures. Based on the recommendations of the committee, SEBI has framed certain guidelines, the highlights of which are presented in the following sections.

Eligibility for exchanges and clearing house

SEBI has laid down the following eligibility conditions for a derivative exchange/segment and its clearing corporation/house.

1. Derivatives trading shall take place through an online screen-based trading system.
2. The derivatives exchange/segment shall have online surveillance capability to monitor positions, prices and volumes on a real time basis so as to deter market manipulation.
3. The derivatives exchange/segment shall have arrangements for dissemination of information about trades, quantities and quotes on a real time basis through at least two information vending networks, which are easily accessible to investors across the country.
4. The derivatives exchange/segment shall have a satisfactory system of monitoring investor complaints and preventing irregularities in trading.
5. The clearing corporation shall have the capacity to monitor the overall position of members across both the derivatives market and the underlying securities market for those members who are participating in both.
6. The clearing corporation shall have capabilities to segregate initial margins deposited by clearing members for trades on their own account and on account of his client. The clearing corporation/house shall hold the client's margin money in trust for the client's purposes only and not allow its diversion for any other purpose.
7. The clearing corporation/house shall have a separate trade guarantee fund for trades executed on the derivative exchange/segment.

The exchanges that fulfil the eligibility criteria may seek approval from SEBI to start derivatives trading. The derivatives exchange/segment shall have a separate governing council and representation of trading/clearing members shall be limited to a maximum of 40 per cent of the total members of the governing council. The clearing and settlement of derivatives trades shall be through a SEBI-approved clearing corporation/house. Derivatives brokers/dealers and clearing members shall also seek registration from SEBI. This shall be in addition to their registration as brokers of existing stock exchanges. The minimum net worth for clearing members of the derivatives clearing corporation/house shall be INR 30 million. The minimum contract value shall not be less than INR 0.1 million.

Membership and requirements

The following are different types of membership in the derivatives market.

1. *Trading member*: A trading member is a member of a derivatives exchange who can trade on his own behalf and on behalf of his clients.
2. *Clearing member*: A clearing member is permitted to settle his own trades as well as the trades of other non-clearing members known as trading members who have agreed to settle the trades through the clearing member.
3. *Self-clearing member*: A self-clearing member can clear and settle only his own trades.

Every clearing member is required to maintain a net worth of INR 30 million. The clearing members shall furnish an auditor's certificate for the net worth every six months to the exchange. The net worth requirement is INR 10 million for a self-clearing member. Every clearing member, including self-clearing members, shall maintain at least INR 5 million as the liquid net worth with the exchange/clearing corporation.

The liquid net worth for this purpose is defined as the total liquid assets deposited with the clearing corporation towards initial margin and capital adequacy, less initial margin applicable to the total gross open positions at any given point of time on all trades to be cleared through the clearing member. Liquid assets would include cash, fixed deposits, bank guarantees, T-bills and government securities or dematerialized securities pledged in favour of the clearing corporation or bank guarantee. At least 50 per cent of the total liquid assets shall be in the form of cash equivalents, that is, cash, bank guarantees, fixed deposits, T-bills and dated government securities.

The members are required to pass the certification programme approved by SEBI. Further, every trading member is required to appoint at least two approved users who have passed the certification programme. Only the approved users are permitted to operate the derivatives trading terminal.

Eligibility for stocks and indices

SEBI in its circular dated December 2, 2002, stated the following eligibility criteria (revised) for stocks and indices.

1. The stock shall be chosen from among the top 500 stocks in terms of average daily market capitalization and average daily traded value in the prescribed month on a rolling basis.
2. The stock's median quarter sigma order size over the last six months shall be not less than INR 0.1 million. For this purpose, a stock's quarter-sigma order size shall mean the order size (in value terms) required to cause a change in the stock price equal to one-quarter of a standard deviation.
3. The market-wide position limit in the stock shall not be less than INR 50 million. Since the market-wide position limit for a stock is computed at the end of every month, the exchange shall ensure that stocks comply with this criterion before the introduction of new contracts. Further, the market-wide position limit (which is in number of shares) shall be valued taking the closing prices of stocks in the underlying cash market on the date of expiry of the contract in the month.

A stock can be included for derivatives trading as soon as it becomes eligible. However, if the stock does not fulfil the eligibility criteria for three consecutive months after being admitted to derivatives trading, then derivatives contracts on such a stock would be discontinued.

Derivatives contracts may be permitted on an index if 80 per cent of the index constituents are individually eligible for derivatives trading. However, no single ineligible stock in the index shall have a weightage of more than 5 per cent in the index. The index is required to fulfil the eligibility criteria even after trading in derivatives on the index has begun. If the index does not fulfil the criteria for three consecutive months, then derivative contracts on such an index would be discontinued.

Contract size and lot size

SEBI originally prescribed that the value of a derivative contract shall not be less than INR 0.2 million at the time of introducing the contract in the market. For stock-based derivative contracts, the lot size will be in multiples of 100 and the fractions, if any, shall be rounded off to the next higher multiple of 100. Subsequently, SEBI in February 2004 revised the rule position with regard to derivatives contract size. Accordingly, for derivative contracts with contract size/value of INR 0.4 million and above, the lot size/multiplier shall be reduced to half of the existing lot size/multiplier. For derivative contracts with contract size/value of INR 0.8 million and above, the lot size/multiplier shall be reduced to one-fourth of the existing lot size/multiplier. Similarly, where the contract size of the derivative contracts is less than INR 0.2 million, for the sake of standardization, the existing lot size/multiplier shall be increased so as to bring the size to INR 0.2 million. The increase shall be carried out by increasing the lot size/multiplier in multiples of 2. To facilitate the above measures, the stipulation that the lot size/multiplier should be in multiples of 100 stands revoked.

Lot size refers to the number of underlying securities in one contract. The lot size is determined keeping in view the minimum contract size requirement at the time of introduction of derivative contracts on a particular underlying. For example, if shares of a company are quoted at INR 1,000 each and the minimum contract size is INR 0.2 million, then the lot size for that particular scrip stands to be 200,000/1,000 = 200 shares.

Structure of derivatives market

Trading in derivatives may take place either on a separate and independent derivatives exchange or on a separate segment of an existing stock exchange. Derivatives exchanges/segments function as self-regulatory organizations. The clearing and settlement of all trades shall be through a clearing corporation/house that is independent in governance and membership from the derivatives exchange/segment. SEBI provides overall supervision and guidance to the derivatives exchanges/segments and acts as the regulator of the last resort.

Margining system

The margining methodology specified is consistent with the managing system used in developed financial markets worldwide. The derivatives exchanges/segments are given the freedom to either develop their own margin computation system or adapt the systems available internationally to the requirements of SEBI. SEBI has also prescribed risk containment measures for the stock index futures market based on the recommendations of the J.R. Varma Committee. SEBI has asked all the derivatives exchanges/derivatives segments of the exchanges and the clearing corporations of exchanges for index futures trading and settlement to implement the risk containment measures.

Risk containment measures

A portfolio-based margining approach shall be adopted, which takes an integrated view of the risk involved in the portfolio of each individual client comprising his positions in all derivative contracts—index futures, index options, stock options and single stock futures. The parameters for such a model shall include the following.

The initial margin requirements are based on worst-scenario loss of a portfolio of an individual client to cover 99 per cent VaR over a one-day horizon across various scenarios of price changes and volatility shifts. For index products, the price scan range is specified at three standard deviation (3σ) and the volatility scan range at 4 per cent. For stock option contracts, the price scan range is specified at three and a half standard deviation (3.5σ) and the volatility scan range at 10 per cent. There is also a minimum margin requirement. For index futures contracts, it is specified that in no case shall the initial margin be less than 5 per cent of the value of the contract. For index options, a short option minimum charge of 3 per cent of the notional value of all short index options is prescribed and in the case of stock option contracts, a short option minimum charge of 7.5 per cent of the notional value of all short stock option contracts is prescribed. In the case of single stock futures, the initial margin is computed as the worst-scenario loss of a portfolio comprising all the positions of a client in all the futures and options contracts.

Exchange-traded options and futures on indices

SEBI set up a technical group headed by J.R. Varma to formulate risk containment measures for options on index. Based on the recommendations of the group, SEBI has prescribed the following risk containment measures to be adopted by the derivative exchange/segment and the clearing house/corporation for trading and settlement of both index futures and index option contracts.

1. The index option contracts to be traded on the derivative exchanges/segments shall have prior approval of SEBI.
2. Initially the exchanges shall introduce premium-style index options and European-style index options, which shall be settled in cash.
3. The index option contracts shall have a minimum contract size of INR 0.2 million at the time of introduction in the market and they shall have maximum maturity of 12 months and a minimum of three strikes (in the money, near the money and out of the money).
4. The initial margin requirement shall be based on worst-case loss of a portfolio of an individual client to cover a 99 per cent VaR over a one-day horizon. The initial margin requirement shall be netted at the level of the individual client and it shall be on a gross basis at the level of the trading/clearing member. The initial margin requirement for the proprietary position of a trading/clearing member shall also be on net basis.
5. A portfolio-based margining approach shall be adopted, which will take an integrated view of the risk involved in the portfolio of each individual client comprising his positions in index futures and index options contracts.
6. The margin for a calendar spread would be the same as specified for index futures. However, the margin shall be calculated on the basis of delta of the portfolio in each month. Further, as in the index futures market, a calendar spread would be treated as a naked position in the far month contract as the near month contract approaches expiry.

7. The short option minimum margin equal to 3 per cent of the notional value of all short index options shall be charged if the sum of the worst-scenario loss and the calendar spread margin is lower than the short option minimum margin.
8. The net option value shall be calculated as the current market value of the option times the number of options (positive for long options and negative for short options) in the portfolio. This net option value shall be added to the liquid net worth of the clearing member. This means that the current market value of short options will be deducted from the liquid net worth and the market value of long options will be added thereto. Thus, mark-to-market gains and losses on option positions will get adjusted against the available liquid net worth. Since the options are premium style, mark-to-market gains and losses will not be settled in cash for option positions.
9. For options positions, the premium shall be paid in by the buyers in cash and paid out to the sellers in cash on T + 1 day.
10. Until the buyer pays the premium, the premium due shall be deducted from the available liquid net worth on a real time basis.
11. The mark-to-market gains/losses for the index futures position shall continue to be settled in cash.
12. The existing position limits in the index futures market shall be applicable to index options also on the basis of notional value.
13. The computation of worst-scenario loss has two components. The first is the valuation of each option contract under 16 scenarios using an appropriate option pricing model. The second is the application of these scenario contract values to the actual positions in a portfolio to compute the portfolio values and the worst-scenario loss. For computational ease, exchanges are permitted to update the scenario contract value only at discrete points of time every day. However, the latest available scenario contract values would be applied to member/client portfolios on a real time basis.

Single stock futures

SEBI constituted an advisory committee on derivatives under the chairmanship of J.R. Varma to work out the modalities for the introduction of single-stock futures in Indian stock markets. SEBI considered the recommendations of the committee and granted in-principle approval in September 2001 for the introduction of single-stock futures on 31 stocks, in which options contracts had been permitted on BSE and the NSE. Single-stock futures shall be permitted up to a maximum maturity of 12 months. Initially, a single-stock futures contract shall have maturity of three months and at the time of its introduction, three contracts of maturity of one month, two months and three months would be introduced simultaneously. Therefore, at any point in time, at least three single-stock futures contracts on a particular underlying would be available for trading. The exchanges shall initially introduce single-stock futures contracts, which shall be settled in cash.

Exchange-traded options on stocks

On the recommendations of the technical group headed by J.R. Varma, SEBI introduced exchange-traded options on stocks and prescribed the following risk containment measures to be adopted by the derivatives exchange/segment and the clearing house/corporation.

1. The stock option contracts to be traded on the derivative exchange/segment shall have prior approval of SEBI.
2. The exchanges shall introduce premium-settled American-style stock options, which shall be settled in cash at exercise for an initial period of six months; thereafter the stock options, at exercise, shall be settled by delivery.
3. The stock option contract shall have a minimum contract size of INR 0.2 million at the time of its introduction in the market.
4. The stock option contract shall have a maximum maturity of 12 months and a minimum of three strikes.
5. The initial margin requirements shall be based on worst-case loss of a portfolio of an individual client to cover 99 per cent VaR over a one-day horizon. The initial margin requirement shall be netted at the level of the individual client and on gross basis at the level of the trading/clearing member. The initial margin requirement for the proprietary position of the trading/clearing member shall also be on net basis.

6. A portfolio-based margining approach shall be adopted, which would take an integrated view of the risk involved in the portfolio of each individual client comprising his positions in derivative contracts.

Position limits

For index-based products, there is a disclosure requirement for clients whose position exceeds 15 per cent of the open interest of the market in index products. For stock-specific products, the gross open position across all derivative contracts on a particular underlying of a customer/client shall not exceed the higher of 1 per cent of the free float market capitalization (in terms of number of shares) or 5 per cent of the open interest in the derivative contracts on a particular underlying stock (in terms of number of contracts).

These position limits are applicable on the combined position in all derivative contracts on an underlying stock at an exchange. The exchanges are required to achieve client level position monitoring in stages. The client level position limit for interest rate futures contracts is specified at INR 1000 million or 15 per cent of the open interest, whichever is higher.

The trading member position limits for index options are INR 2500 million or 15 per cent of the total open interest in index options, whichever is higher, and for index futures the limits are INR 2500 million or 15 per cent of the total open interest in index futures, whichever is higher. For stock-specific products, the trading member position limit is 20 per cent of the market-wide limit subject to a ceiling of INR 500 million. It is also specified that once a member reaches the position limit in a particular underlying security, the member shall be permitted to take only offsetting positions (which result in lowering the open position of the member) in derivative contracts on that underlying security. In the event the position limit is breached due to the reduction in the overall open interest in the market, the members are required to take only offsetting positions (which result in lowering the open position of the member) in a derivative contract in that underlying and fresh positions shall not be permitted. The position limit at the trading member level is required to be computed on a gross basis across all clients of the trading member.

There are no market-wide limits for index products. For stock-specific products, the market-wide limit of open positions (in terms of the number of underlying securities) on an option and futures contract on a particular underlying stock would be less than 30 times the average number of shares traded daily during the previous calendar month in the cash segment of the exchange or 20 per cent of the number of shares held by non-promoters, that is, 20 per cent of the free float in terms of number of shares of a company.

Participation of FIIs in exchange traded derivative contracts

The Reserve Bank of India has permitted foreign institutional investors to trade in exchange-traded index futures contracts on the derivative segment of BSE and the F&O segment of the NSE, provided the overall open interest of the FII does not exceed 100 per cent of the market value of the concerned FII's total investment. SEBI has permitted FIIs to trade in all exchange-traded derivatives and laid down position limits for trading by the FIIs and their sub-accounts..

RBI in its circular dated September 1, 2003, specified that FIIs may trade in all exchange-traded derivative contracts approved by SEBI from time to time subject to the limits prescribed by SEBI. The position limits for FIIs in equity index derivatives shall be as follows.

1. The FII position limit in all index options contracts on a particular underlying index shall be INR 2500 million or 15 per cent of the total open interest of the market in index options, whichever is higher, per exchange. This limit would be applicable on open positions in all futures contracts on a particular underlying index.
2. The FII position limit in all index futures contracts on a particular underlying index shall be INR 2500 million or 15 per cent of the total open interest of the market in index futures, whichever is higher, per exchange. This limit would be applicable on open positions in all futures contracts on a particular underlying index.

In addition to the above, FIIs shall take exposure in equity index derivatives subject to the following limits.

1. Short positions in index derivatives (short futures, short calls and long puts) not exceeding (in notional value) the FII's holding of stocks.
2. Long positions in index derivatives (long futures, long calls and short puts) not exceeding (in notional value) the FII's holding of cash, government securities, T-bills and similar instruments.

The position limits for stock-based derivatives in case of a trading member/FIIs/mutual funds are as follows.

1. For stocks with an applicable market-wise position limit of INR 5000 million or more, the combined futures and options position limit shall be 20 per cent of an applicable market-wise position limit, or INR 3000 million, whichever is lower and within which the stock futures position cannot exceed 10 per cent of the applicable market-wise position limit or INR 1500 million, whichever is lower.
2. For stocks with an applicable market-wise position limit less than INR 5000 million, the combined futures and option position limit would be 20 per cent of an applicable market-wise position limit or INR 500 million, whichever is lower.

NRIs are also permitted to invest in exchange-traded derivatives contracts subject to the margin and other requirements that are in place for other investors. In addition, NRIs are subject to the following position limits.

For index-based contracts, a disclosure requirement for any person or persons acting in concert who together own 15 per cent or more of the open interest of all derivatives contracts on a particular underlying index. For stock option and single stock futures contracts, the gross open position across all derivatives contracts on a particular underlying stock of an NRI shall not exceed the higher of 1 per cent of the free float market capitalization (in terms of number of shares) or 5 per cent of the open interest in the derivative contracts on a particular underlying stock (in terms of number of contracts).

Adjustment of corporate actions for stock options

The companies may take certain decisions that result in stock benefits and cash benefits. The various stock benefits include bonus, rights, merger/demerger, splits, consolidation, hive-off and warrants. They are all known as *corporate actions*. Therefore, adjustment for corporate actions is essential in order to maintain the value of the position of the market participants on cum and ex-date. This facilitates retaining the relative status of positions, viz. in the money, at the money and out of money. According to SEBI, any adjustment for corporate actions shall be carried out on the last day on which a security is traded on cum basis in the underlying cash market. Adjustments shall refer to modifications in positions and/or contract specifications (strike price, position and market lot/multiplier) so that the basic premise of adjustment is satisfied.

The methodology proposed for adjustment of various corporate actions is as follows.

Adjustment factor

Bonus:

Ratio–A: B; adjustment factor: $\frac{(A+B)}{B}$

Stock splits and consolidations:

Ratio–A: B; adjustment factor: $\frac{B}{A}$

Rights:

Ratio–A: B

Premium: C; face value: D; existing strike price: X

The new strike price shall be arrived at by dividing the old strike price by the adjustment factor, which is as follows.

$$\frac{[(B \times X) + A(C+D)]}{(A+B)}$$

The new market lot/multiplier shall be arrived at by multiplying the old market lot by the adjustment factor.

Existing market lot/multiplier/position: Y

$$\text{New issue size: } \frac{Y(A+B)}{B}$$

The new position shall be arrived at by multiplying the old position by the adjustment factor.

Dividends that are below 10 per cent of the market value of the underlying stock would be deemed to be ordinary dividends and no adjustment in the strike price would be made for ordinary dividends. For extraordinary dividends above 10 per cent of the market value of the underlying stock, the strike price would be adjusted.

9.10 Derivative Products in Indian Stock Markets

Financial derivatives were introduced in Indian stock markets in a phased manner. Index futures were introduced in June 2000, index options in June 2001, stock options in July 2001, stock futures in November 2001 and interest rate futures in June 2003. On June 9, 2000, the Bombay Stock Exchange introduced India's first derivative instrument, BSE (Sensex) index futures. It was introduced with a three-month trading cycle, the near month (one), the next month (two) and the far month (three). A few days later, the National Stock Exchange of India launched S&P CNX Nifty index futures. Sectoral indices were permitted to trade derivatives in December 2002. Interest rate futures were introduced in June 2003. The exchange-traded interest rate futures on a notional bond priced off a basket of government securities were permitted for trading in January 2004. Thus, only two exchanges in India—BSE and the NSE—have been permitted to trade in derivatives products. Of these two exchanges, the NSE accounts for more than 98 per cent of the total turnover in the derivatives market in India.

The options on the indices Nifty and Sensex are European options, while the options on individual stocks in Indian stock markets are American options. The market lot for options on the Nifty is 200, while that for the Sensex and individual stocks is 100. The options created on any day can have three expiry dates—at the NSE the last Thursday and at BSE the last Friday of the current and the next two months. On any day, up to five new options may be created on a security—two in the money, two out of money and one (close to) at the money. For example, suppose a share closes at a price of INR 510. The options that may be created the next day would have exercise prices of INR 520, INR 540, INR 480, INR 460 and INR 500. In the case of call options, the first two would be out of money, the next two in the money and the last one (close to) at the money. In the case of put options, the first two would be in the money, the next two out of money and the last one at the money.

Currency futures trading was introduced in Indian markets in August 2008. According to the Currency Futures (Reserve Bank) Directions, 2008, currency futures are a standardized foreign exchange derivative contract traded on a recognized stock exchange to buy or sell one currency against another on a specified future date at a price specified on the date of the contract, but does not include a forward contract. Currency futures are permitted in USD–INR or any other currency pair as may be approved by the RBI from time to time. Only persons resident in India may purchase or sell currency futures to hedge an exposure to foreign exchange rate risk or otherwise. The size of each contract shall be USD 1,000 and the contracts shall be quoted and settled in INR. The maturity of the contracts shall not exceed 12 months. The settlement price shall be the RBI's reference rate on the last trading day.

The Securities Contract (Regulations) Act, 1956, was amended in 1999 to include derivatives within the scope of securities. The amendment grants legality to exchange-traded derivatives but not to OTC derivatives. It allows derivatives trading either on a separate and independent derivative exchange or on a separate segment of an existing stock exchange. The derivatives exchange has to function as a self-regulatory organization and SEBI acts as its regulator. The responsibility of clearing and settlement of all trades on the exchange is given to the clearing house, which is governed independently.

9.10.1 BSE Derivative Products

BSE launched the first exchange-traded index derivative contract, futures, on the BSE Sensex on June 9, 2000. Later, it introduced index options on the Sensex on June 1, 2001. Stock options were introduced on 31 stocks on July 9, 2001, and single-stock index futures on November 9, 2002. BSE launched weekly options, that is, weekly contracts in options on the shares of four leading companies—Reliance Industries Limited, Satyam Computer Services Limited, State Bank of India, and Tata Steel Limited.

Equity futures and options were introduced with a maximum life of three months. These options expire on the last Thursday of the expiring month. Because of the need for options of shorter maturity, BSE launched weekly options. The weekly options have the same characteristics as those of monthly stock options, except that they are settled on the Friday of every week. These options are introduced on the Monday of every week and have a maturity of two weeks, expiring on the Friday of the expiring week.

Derivatives trading at BSE takes place through a fully automated screen-based trading platform called the derivatives trading and settlement system (DTSS). The DTSS is designed to enable trading on a real-time basis. The derivatives market is order driven. Traders can place orders only through the computer system. The order types have characteristics similar to the ones in the cash market. There are no maximum and minimum prices ranges for futures and options contracts. However, to avoid erroneous order entry, dummy price bands have been introduced in the derivatives segment.

9.10.2 NSE Derivative Products

The NSE launched trading in index futures on June 12, 2000. The index futures contracts are based on the popular market benchmark S&P CNX Nifty index. The futures contracts have a maximum of 3-month trading cycle—the near month (one), the next month (two) and the far month (three). A new contract is introduced on the trading day following the expiry of the near month contract. The new contract will be introduced for a three-month duration. This way, at any point of time, there will be three contracts available for trading in the market—one of near month duration, one of next month duration and one with far month duration. The S&P CNX Nifty futures contracts expire on the last Thursday of the expiry month. If the last Thursday is a trading holiday, the contracts expire on the previous trading day.

The value of the futures contracts on Nifty may not be less than INR 0.2 million at the time of introduction. The permitted lot size for futures and options contracts shall be the same for a given underlying or such lot size as may be stipulated by the exchange from time to time. The price step in respect of S&P CNX Nifty futures contracts is INR 0.05. The base price of S&P CNX Nifty futures contracts on the first day of trading would be a theoretical futures price. The base price of the contracts on subsequent trading days would be the daily settlement price of the futures contracts. There are no day minimum/maximum price ranges applicable for futures contracts. However, in order to prevent erroneous order entry by trading members, operating ranges are kept at ±10 per cent. For orders that have come under price freeze, members would be required to confirm to the exchange that there is no inadvertent error in the order entry and that the order is genuine. On such confirmation, the exchange may approve such orders. Orders that may come to the exchange as a quantity freeze shall be based on the notional value of a contract of around INR 50 million. Quantity freeze is calculated for each underlying on the last trading day of each calendar month and is applicable through the next calendar month.

The NSE introduced trading in index options on June 4, 2001. The options contracts are European-style and cash settled. They are based on the market benchmark S&P CNX Nifty index. The S&P CNX Nifty options contracts have a maximum three-month trading cycle—the near month (one), the next month (two) and the far month (three). On the expiry of the near month contract, new contracts are introduced at new strike prices for both call and put options on the trading day following the expiry of the near month contract. New contracts with new strike prices for the existing expiration date are introduced for trading on the next working day based on the previous day's closing Nifty values as and when required. In order to decide the at-the-money strike price, the Nifty closing value is rounded off to the nearest 10. The in-the-money strike price and the out-of-the-money strike price are based on the at-the-money strike price interval. The base price of the options contracts, on introduction of new contracts, would be the theoretical value of the options contract arrived at based on the Black–Scholes model. The base price of the contracts on subsequent trading days will be the daily close price of the options contracts. If the contract is not traded for the day, the base price of the contract for the next trading day shall be the theoretical price of the options contract arrived at based on the Black–Scholes model.

The specifications of the S&P CNX Nifty index futures are given in Box 9.1. The other derivative products of the NSE are listed in Box 9.2. All these derivative products are patterned on the lines of S&P CNX Nifty futures and S&P CNX Nifty options. In addition to these products, the NSE offers interest rate futures for trading, an outline of which is given in subsequent paragraphs.

All scheduled commercial banks, the Export–Import Bank of India, NABARD and National Housing Bank are eligible to become members of the derivatives exchange/segment. They can act as a member only for their proprietary dealings, to act on their own account, in the interest rate derivatives market. In other words, they cannot act as a member or an agent for any other person, client or customer in any segment of the exchange.

The futures and options trading system of the NSE is called Nationwide Fully Automated Screen-based Trading Arrangement for Nifty Futures and Options (NEAT–F&O). The system is an anonymous and transparent order-driven market that operates on a strict price–time priority basis. The system can be accessed by two types of users—trading members and clearing members. The National Stock Exchange Clearing Corporation Limited (NSCL) clears and settles all the deals executed on the F&O segment of the NSE. It acts as a legal counterparty to all deals and thereby guarantees settlement.

9.10.3 Interest Rate Futures in Indian Markets

Interest rates in India were deregulated in the 1990s as part of economic liberalization. As a result, the interest rates in the market became more volatile, leading to interest rate risk. Therefore, there arose a need to introduce

Box 9.1 S&P CNX Nifty Index Futures

Contract specifications

The security descriptor for the S&P CNX Nifty futures contracts is:

- Market type: N
- Instrument Type: FUTIDX
- Underlying: NIFTY
- Expiry date: Date of contract expiry

Instrument type represents the instrument, i.e., futures on Index.
Underlying symbol denotes the underlying index, which is S&P CNX Nifty
Expiry date identifies the date of expiry of the contract

Underlying instrument

The underlying index is S&P CNX NIFTY

Trading cycle

S&P CNX Nifty futures contracts have a maximum three-month trading cycle— the near month (one), the next month (two) and the far month (three). A new contract is introduced on the trading day following the expiry of the near month contract. The new contract will be introduced for a three-month duration. This way, at any point of time, there will be three contracts available for trading in the market, i.e., one of near month duration, one of mid-month duration and one of far-month duration.

Expiry day

S&P CNX Nifty futures contracts expire on the last Thursday of the expiry month. If the last Thursday is a trading holiday, the contracts expire on the previous trading day.

Trading parameters

- **Contract size:** The permitted lot size of S&P CNX Nifty futures contracts is 200 and multiples thereof.
- **Price steps:** The price step in respect of S&P CNX Nifty futures contracts is INR 0.05.
- **Base prices:** The base price of S&P CNX Nifty futures contracts on the first day of trading would be the theoretical futures price. The base price of the contracts on subsequent trading days would be the daily settlement price of the futures contracts.
- **Price bands:** There are no day minimum/maximum price ranges applicable for S&P CNX Nifty futures contracts. However, in order to prevent erroneous order entry by trading members, operating ranges are kept at ± 10 per cent.
- **Quantity freeze:** Quantity freeze for S&P CNX Nifty futures contracts would be 20,000 units or greater.
- **Order type/order book/order attribute:**
  - Regular lot order
  - Stop loss order
  - Immediate or cancel
  - Good till day
  - Good till cancelled (GTC)*
  - Good till date
  - Spread order

* GTC orders are cancelled at the end of the period of seven calendar days from the date of entering an order

Box 9.2 Derivatives Products of the NSE

CNX Nifty junior futures
CNX Nifty junior options
CNXIT futures
CNXIT options
CNX 100 futures
CNX 100 options
Bank Nifty futures
Bank Nifty options
Futures on individual Securities
Options on individual securities
Interest rate futures on notional 91-day T-bill and notional 10-year bond

hedging instruments to manage interest rate risk. Accordingly, in 1999, the RBI took the initiative to introduce OTC interest rate derivatives such as interest rate swaps (IRS) and forward rate agreements (FRAs).

In November 2002, the RBI constituted a working group under the chairmanship of Jaspal Bindra to review the working of the interest rate futures market. Based on the recommendations of the group, the RBI launched exchange-traded interest rate derivatives (ETIRD) with the following three types of contracts with maturities of up to one year on the NSE.

- Futures on 10-year notional Government of India securities with 6 per cent coupon rate.
- Futures on 10-year notional zero-coupon Government of India securities.
- Futures on 91-day T-bills.

The interest rate futures contracts have a maturity period of one year, with three months' continuous contracts for the first three months and fixed quarterly contracts for the entire year. New contracts are introduced on the trading day following the expiry of the near month contract. The interest rate futures contracts expire on the last Thursday of the expiry month. If the last Thursday is a trading holiday, the contracts expire on the previous trading day. The permitted lot size of the interest rate futures contract is 2,000 and the minimum value of interest rate futures contracts is INR 0.2 million at the time of introduction. The price steps with respect to all interest rate futures contracts is INR 0.01. The futures contracts with face value of INR 100 on notional 10-year coupon-bearing bonds and notional 10-year zero-coupon bonds are based on price quotation, and the futures contracts with face value of INR 100 on notional 91-days treasury bills are based on INR 100 minus yield.

The base price of the interest rate futures on introduction of new contracts is the theoretical futures price computed based on the previous day's closing price of the notional underlying security. The base price of the contracts on subsequent trading days will be the closing price of the futures contracts. However, on those days when the contracts are not traded, the base price is the daily settlement price of the futures contracts. There is no day minimum/maximum price ranges applicable for the futures contracts. However, in order to prevent or take care of erroneous order entry, the operating range for interest rate futures contract is kept at ±2 per cent of the base price. The orders that may come to the exchange as quantity freeze shall be 2,500 contracts amounting to INR 5,000,000, which works out, on the day of introduction, to approximately INR 500 million. For such orders that have come under quantity freeze, the member shall be required to confirm to the exchange that the order is genuine.

Although OTC products have had a good reception in Indian markets, the ETIRD failed to take off for various reasons. Therefore, the RBI appointed another working group under the chairmanship of V.K. Sharma to suggest measures to activate interest rate futures in Indian markets. Based on the group's recommendations, the RBI issued a notification on August 28, 2009, called the Interest Rate Futures (Reserve Bank of India) Directions, 2009, permitting interest rate futures on Indian stock markets.

The features of the standardized interest rate futures are as follows:

- Interest rate futures are permitted on a notional coupon bearing Government of India security (or any other product as may be approved by the RBI from time to time) maturing in at least 7.5 years but not more than 15 years from the first day of the delivery month with a minimum total outstanding stock of INR 100,000 million.
- The notional coupon shall be 7 per cent per annum with semi-annual compounding.
- The contracts shall be settled by physical delivery of deliverable grade securities using the electronic book entry system of the depositories.

Interest rate futures shall be traded on the currency derivative segment of a recognized stock exchange. Persons resident in India may purchase or sell interest rate futures to hedge an exposure to interest rate risk or otherwise. Foreign institutional investors may purchase or sell interest rate futures subject to the condition that the total gross long position in cash and interest rate futures markets taken together do not exceed their individual permissible limit for investment in government securities and the total gross short position, for the purpose of hedging only, does not exceed their long position in the government securities and in interest rate futures at any point of time. No scheduled bank or such other agency shall participate in interest rate futures trading without permission from the respective regulatory department of the RBI.

The surveillance and disclosures of transactions in the interest rate futures market shall be carried out in accordance with SEBI guidelines. The position limits for various classes of participants in the interest rate futures trading shall also be subject to the guidelines issued by SEBI.

Summary

1. A derivative is a financial instrument that derives its value from the price of its underlying asset or security.
2. The primary function of derivative instruments is to enable investors to manage their risks by hedging or insuring themselves against adverse price movements in volatile markets.
3. Financial forwards are customized contracts to buy or sell the underlying securities on a stated date in the future at a predetermined price.
4. Financial futures are standardized, legally enforceable forward contacts to buy or sell a pre-specified financial product at a predetermined price on a specified date or during a specified period.
5. Financial futures include currency futures, interest rate futures and stock index futures.
6. An option is a contract that gives the holder the right but not the obligation to buy or sell the underlying asset or security at a predetermined price during or at the end of a specified period.
7. Options and futures have many similarities and serve similar purposes but the risk profile of an option contract is asymmetric.
8. Stock index futures, stock index options and options on individual stocks are popular forms of equity derivatives.
9. In a credit default swap, one party (buyer) contracts to make a payment to the other party (seller) in exchange for a payoff if an underlying financial instrument is exposed to default during a certain period of time.
10. SEBI appointed the L.C. Gupta Committee to develop an appropriate regulatory framework for derivatives trading in India. The committee examined several aspects and made far-reaching recommendations for derivatives trading in Indian stock markets.
11. Based on the recommendations of the L.C. Gupta Committee, SEBI authorized BSE and the NSE to launch derivatives trading. Accordingly, financial derivatives have been introduced in the Indian stock markets in a phased manner.
12. On June 9, 2000, BSE introduced India's first derivative instrument—BSE (Sensex) index futures. A few days later, the NSE launched the S&P CNX Nifty index futures. Sectoral indices were permitted derivatives trading in December 2002. Interest rate futures were introduced in June 2003. Exchange-traded interest rate futures on a notional bond priced off a basket of government securities were permitted for trading in January 2004.
13. The RBI has permitted FIIs to trade in exchange-traded index futures contracts on the derivative segment of BSE and the F&O segment of the NSE, provided the overall open interest of the FII does not exceed 100 per cent of the market value of the concerned FII's total investment.
14. SEBI has permitted FIIs to trade in all exchange-traded derivatives and laid down the position limits for trading by the FIIs and their sub-accounts.

Questions

1. What do you understand by derivatives? Trace the origin of derivatives. What purpose(s) do they serve?
2. Distinguish between forwards and futures, and futures and options.
3. Explain the mechanics of trading in stock index–based futures and options. How are index-based options different from individual stock-based options?
4. Discuss the main recommendations of the L.C. Gupta Committee.
5. Critically evaluate the SEBI guidelines for derivatives trading in Indian stock markets.
6. Explain the risk containment measures for stock index futures.
7. What are the position limits for trading of derivatives by FIIs?
8. Explain the methodology for adjustment of corporate actions.
9. State the salient features of the scheme for introduction of interest rate futures.
10. How have derivatives become more acceptable to Indian investors?
11. What is the role of speculators in the derivatives market?
12. The current market price of a share of ITC is INR 200. The futures to expire three months from now are quoted at INR 210. The risk-free interest rate is 6 per cent. Is there any arbitrage opportunity? If yes, how can an arbitrageur make use of the situation?
13. Mr Rajesh is appointed as financial adviser to Synthetic Portfolio Ltd, which is a mutual fund. The fund can commence its actual business operations three months from now. Meanwhile, Mr Rajesh wants to do some actual business. What can he do? Will financial derivatives be of any use to him in this regard?
14. Discuss the features of credit default swaps.

Case Study

The following (Table 9.7) is an extract from the records of the National Stock Exchange:

Table 9.7 Extract of records from NSE

Month	*Expiry date of near month contract*	*Closing futures price (INR)*	*Closing spot price (INR)*
Apr 2007	May 31, 2007	4090.25	4087.90
May 2007	May 31, 2007	4290.05	4295.80
Jun 2007	Jul 26, 2007	4293.40	4318.30
Jul 2007	Aug 30, 2007	4508.15	4528.85
Aug 2007	Sep 27, 2007	4429.15	4464.00
Sept 2007	Oct 25, 2007	5037.60	5021.35
Oct 2007	Nov 29, 2007	5907.35	5900.65
Nov 2007	Dec 27, 2007	5803.50	5762.75
Dec 2007	Jan 31, 2008	6162.95	6138.60
Jan 2008	Jan 31, 2008	5133.25	5137.45
Feb 2008	Mar 27, 2008	5181.10	5223.50
Mar 2008	Apr 24, 2008	4732.30	4734.50
April 2008	May 29, 2008	5188.80	5165.90
May 2008	Jun 26, 2008	4850.10	4870.10
Jun 2008	July 24, 2008	3972.75	4040.55

Source: NSE, Indian Securities Market—A Review (2008)

Question

Calculate the implied interest rate. Also determine the relative cost of the futures' market price. How one can make arbitrage profit in the given situation?

Appendix 9.1

In a circular dated July 28, 1999, SEBI gave the following numerical example for a clear understanding of capital adequacy, exposure limits and initial margin requirements.

Suppose the position at the beginning of Day 1 is as follows:

- Member's liquid assets: Cash equivalent deposits INR 3,500,000 and securities deposits (net of haircut) INR 4,000,000
- Member's open position: 200 contracts long in the three-month contract.
- Futures prices: Three-month contract is INR 100,000 and one-month contract is INR 98,000
- Initial margin: 5 per cent
- Days to expiry: Fifth day before expiry of one-month contract

The margin and capital adequacy calculations are as follows:

Initial margin: 5% × 200 × 100,000 = INR 1,000,000

Total open position = INR 20,000,000

Total liquid assets will be treated as INR 7,000,000 only, since at least 50 per cent of total liquid assets must be in cash equivalents

Liquid net worth = INR 7,000,000 − INR 1,000,000
= INR 6,000,000

Thus, both conditions of net worth and exposure limit are satisfied as follows:

INR 6,000,000 > INR 5,000,000

INR 6,000,000 × 33⅓ = (200,00,000) > 20,000,000

Initiation of spread trade on Day 1

Suppose the member does a calendar spread by buying 300 contracts of three-month futures and selling 300 contracts of one-month futures. Since the near-month contract of the spread is five days to expiry, the member will have the full benefit of spread margining.

Margin on spread = 1% × 300 × 100,000
= 300,000

Spread open position = 300 × 100,000 × 1/3
= 10,000,000

Adding the figures for the earlier long position,

Total open position = 20,000,000 + 10,000,000
= 30,000,000

Liquid net worth = 7,000,000 − 1,000,000 − 300,000
= 5,700,000

Thus, both the conditions (as prescribed by SEBI) are satisfied as:

15,700,000 > 5,000,000

25,700,000 × 33⅓ = 190,000,000 > 30,000,000

Margin and capital adequacy calculations on Day 2

Suppose that on Day 2, the member does not initiate any new trades, but prices move up so that the situation is as follows:

- Member's liquid assets: Cash equivalent deposits INR 3,500,000
- Securities deposits (net of haircut): INR 4,000,000
- Member's open position: 200 contracts long in the three-month contract
- 300 contracts spread position (long in three-month contract and short in near-month contract)
- Futures prices: Three-month contracts is INR 101,000
- One-month contract is INR 99,000
- Initial margin: 5 per cent
- Days to expiry: Fourth day before expiry of one-month contract

The margins and exposures for the 200-contract long position would be:

Open position = 200 × 101,000 = 20,200,000

Initial margin = 5% × 200 × 101,000 = 1,010,000

The spread open position for exposure purposes would be INR 14,140,000 as calculated below since the near contract is four days to expiry:

20 per cent of far month = 20% × 300 × 101,000
= INR 6,060,000

Plus

80 per cent of spread = 80% × 1/3 × 300 × 101,000
= 8,080,000

The initial margin on spread would be 545,000 as shown in the following calculations:

20 per cent of far month = 20% × 5% × 300 × 101,000
= 303,000

80 per cent of spread = 80% × 1% × 300 × 101,000
= 242,000

The margin exposure and liquid net worth of the member would be as follows:

Total open position = 20,200,000 + 14,140,000
= INR 34,340,000

Total initial margin = 1,010,000 + 545,400
= 1,555,400

Liquid net worth = 7,000,000 − 1,555,400
= INR 5,444,600

Both conditions are satisfied as shown in the following:

5,444,600 > 5,000,000

25,444,600 × 33 ⅓ (181,486,667) > 34,340,000

Worst-scenario loss

The worst-case loss of a portfolio will be calculated by valuing the portfolio under several scenarios of changes in the index and the volatility of the index. The scenario to be used for this purpose will be as follows:

Risk scenario number	*Price move in multiples of price range*	*Volatility move in multiples of volatility range*	*Fraction of loss to be considered*
1	0	+1	100%
2	0	−1	100%
3	$+\frac{1}{3}$	+1	100%
4	$+\frac{1}{3}$	−1	100%
5	$-\frac{1}{3}$	+1	100%
6	$\frac{1}{3}$	−1	100%
7	$+\frac{2}{3}$	+1	100%
8	$+\frac{2}{3}$	−1	100%
9	$-\frac{2}{3}$	+1	100%
10	$-\frac{2}{3}$	−1	100%
11	+1	+1	100%
12	+1	−1	100%
13	−1	+1	100%
14	−1	−1	100%
15	+2	0	100%
16	−2	0	100%

The price range is defined to be three standard deviations as calculated for VaR purposes in the index futures market for the near-month contract. The volatility range will be taken at 4 per cent for an initial period of six months, after which it shall be reviewed. While computing the worst-scenario loss, it shall be assumed that the prices of futures of all maturities on the same underlying index move up or down by the same amount. For the purpose of calculation of option values, the exchange may use any of the standard option pricing models, namely Black–Scholes, Binomial, Merton and Adesi–Whaley.

The maximum loss under any of the scenarios is referred to as the worst-scenario loss. Subject to additions and adjustments, the worst-scenario loss is the margin requirement for the portfolio.

I. Summary of Parameters Specified for Initial Margin Computation (SEBI Regulations)

Index options	*Index futures*	*Stock options*	*Stock futures*	*Interest rate futures*	*Price scan range*
3 σ	3 σ	3.5 σ	For order size of INR 5 lakh, if mean value of impact cost > 1%, the price scan range be scaled up by $\sqrt{3}$(in addition to look ahead days)	3.5 σ for order size of INR 5 lakh, if mean value of impact cost >1%, the price scan range be scaled up by $\sqrt{3}$(in addition to look ahead days). For long bond futures, 3.5 σ and for notional T-bill futures, 3.5 σ	
Volatility scan range	4%		10%		
Minimum margin requirement		5%		7.5%	For long bond futures, minimum margin is 2%. For notional T-bill, futures minimum margin is 0.2%.

Short option minimum charge	3%	7.5%
Calendar spread	0.5% per month on the far month contract (min 1% and max 3%)	
Mark to market	Net option value (positive for long positions and negative for short positions) to be adjusted from the liquid net worth on a real time basis. The daily closing price of futures contract for mark to market settlement would be calculated on the basis of the last half an hour weighted average price of the contract.	

II. A. Position Limits (SEBI Regulations)

	Index options	*Index futures*	*Stock options*	*Stock futures*	*Interest rate futures*
Client level	Disclosure requirement for any person or persons acting in concert holding 15% or more of the open interest of all derivative contracts on a particular underlying index.	Disclosure requirement for any person or persons acting in concert holding 15% or more of the open interest of all derivative contracts on a particular underlying index.	1% of free float or 5% of open interest, whichever is higher.	1% of free float or 5% of open interest, whichever is higher.	INR 100 crore or 15% of the open interest, whichever is higher.
Trading member level	15% of the total open interest of the market or INR 250 crore, whichever is higher.	15% of the total Open Interest of the market or INR 250 crore, whichever is higher	20% of market-wide Limit subject to a ceiling of INR 50 crore.	20% of market-wide limit subject to a ceiling of INR 50 crore.	INR 500 crore or 15% of open interest, whichever is higher.
Market-wide			30 times the average number of shares traded daily, during the previous calendar month, in the relevant underlying security in the underlying segment or – 20% of the number of shares held by non-promoters in the relevant underlying security, whichever is lower.	30 times the average number of shares traded daily, during the previous calendar month, in the relevant underlying security in the underlying segment or – 20% of the number of shares held by non-promoters in the relevant underlying security, whichever is lower.	

II. B. Position Limits (SEBI Regulations)

	Index options	*Index futures*	*Stock options*	*Single-stock futures*	*Interest rate futures*
FII level	INR 250 crore or 15% of the OI in index options, whichever is higher. In addition, hedge positions are permitted.	INR 250 crore or 15% of the OI in index futures, whichever is higher. In addition, hedge positions are permitted.	20% of market-wide limit subject to a ceiling of INR 50 crore.	20% of market-wide limit subject to a ceiling of INR 50 crore.	USD 100 million. In addition to the above, the FII may take exposure in exchange traded in interest rate derivative contracts to the extent of the book value of their cash market exposure in government securities.
Sub-account level	Disclosure requirement for any person or persons acting in concert holding 15% or more of the open interest of all derivative contracts on a particular underlying index.	Disclosure requirement for any person or persons acting in concert holding 15% or more of the open interest of all derivative contracts on a particular underlying index.	1% of free float market capitalization or 5% of open interest on a particular underlying, whichever is higher.	1% of free float market capitalization or 5% of open interest on a particular underlying, whichever is higher.	INR 100 crore or 15% of total open interest in the market in exchange-traded interest rate derivative contracts, whichever is higher.

II. C. Position Limits (SEBI Regulations)

	Index options	*Index futures*	*Stock options*	*Single-stock futures*	*Interest rate futures*
NRI level	Disclosure requirement for any person or persons acting in concert holding 15% or more of the open interest of all derivative contracts on a particular underlying index.	Disclosure requirement for any person or persons acting in concert holding 15% or more of the open interest of all derivative contracts on a particular underlying index.	1% of free float market capitalization or 5% of open interest on a particular underlying, whichever is higher.	1% of free float market capitalization or 5% of open interest on a particular underlying, whichever is higher.	INR 100 crore or 15% of total open interest in the market in exchange-traded interest rate derivative contracts, whichever is higher.

Chapter 10

Depository and Custodial Services

LEARNING OBJECTIVES

After studying this chapter, you should be able to:

- State the importance of the depository system.
- Review the trading and settlement system in the physical environment.
- Describe the depository system.
- Present the functions of the depository system.
- List the advantages of the depository system.
- Present SEBI regulations pertaining to the depository system.
- Introduce the concept of custodial services and present SHCIL.
- Present SEBI regulations with regard to custodial services.

10.1 Introduction

The Indian capital market has undergone many changes, both qualitative and quantitative, especially over the last two decades. As part of economic reforms in tune with global trends, several controls have been eased or lifted and various procedures streamlined. As a result, there was an unprecedented surge in investment activity in the country. There have been a large number of capital issues every year, accompanied by an unprecedented growth in the stock market turnover. But, as a side effect, many systemic issues surfaced. The 1992 stock scam, said to be the result of systemic failure, exposed many loopholes in stock market trading and operations. The major problems with securities trading in the physical environment, or dealings in physical certificates of securities, were identified as delays in the transfer of ownership of securities, bad deliveries and irregular settlements.

In this context, many initiatives were taken place to improve the system. The major ones include the screen-based trading of securities and the depository system. The securities trading system got a fillip when the NSE launched an online electronic trading system in 1994. A year later, BSE also launched the Bombay Online Trading (BOLT) system. Nevertheless, the settlement and delivery system continued to be subdued as the securities remained in physical form. It was realized that as long as the securities were in material form, screen-based trading could not yield the desired result. Therefore, the depository system was thought of as the inevitable answer to the problems resulting from handling growing volumes of securities being traded. Simultaneously, it addressed the problems associated with the holding and trading of securities in paper form. Without the depository system, every share transfer is required to be accomplished by the physical movement of share certificates. The following steps are used in the trading and settlement system when the securities are in physical form.

(i) The seller places orders with his broker to sell a certain number of securities at a particular price or at the price left to the discretion of the broker.

(ii) The buyer places orders with his broker to purchase a certain number of securities at a particular price or at the price left to the discretion of the brokers.

(iii) The sale and purchase bids are entered by the brokers in the screen-based trading system (BOLT, for example).

(iv) As and when the sale and purchase bids match, the transaction takes place.

(v) Before the pay-in day, the seller of the securities is required to physically hand over the respective certificates along with a transfer deed duly signed by him as a transferor to his broker, and the buyer is required to pay the relevant amount for the securities purchased by him to his broker.

(vi) The broker of the seller and the broker of the buyer, in turn, need to lodge the relevant securities/amounts with the clearing corporation of the stock exchange.

(vii) After the clearing, on the pay-out day, the broker of the seller would get the relevant amount and the broker of the buyer would get the relevant securities, which they would in turn deliver to their respective customers or clients.

(viii) After receiving the securities, the buyer would send them to the concerned company for registering the transfer of ownership of securities in his favour. The securities need to be accompanied by the transfer form duly signed by both the buyer and the seller of the securities and with the relevant stamps affixed. Sometimes, the buyer may resell the securities using a blank transfer form.

(ix) The company having received the transfer form along with the certificates of securities would check the veracity of the transfer forms and certificates. If satisfied in all respects, the company would transfer the ownership of the securities and return the certificates to the transferee duly endorsed.

In the process of the transfer of ownership of securities along these lines, both the buyer and seller of securities may face the following difficulties.

- In many cases, the transfer of ownership is rejected on various technical grounds like mismatch of signatures. This might be the case when the original signature, which is on the records of the company, and the signature on the transfer deed being executed are compared. Other reasons could be the transfer form getting damaged or not duly executed or stamp duty not being adequately affixed.
- If the transfer of ownership is rejected for technical reasons, it has to be returned by the transferee to his broker from whom he had purchased the securities within a stipulated time so that the buying broker can replace the securities along with the transfer forms. In case the rejected transfer deeds are not returned to the buying broker in the stipulated time, the replacement of securities may take a substantial amount of time.
- When the company declares certain benefits such as dividend, bonus shares and rights shares to the shareholders who are on record, the transferee may lose out on such benefits while the transfer of ownership is pending. The transferee may have to make a substantial effort to get such benefits from the actual owner (transferor) whose name still appears on the records of the company.
- The transferee may lose the blank transfer deed along with the certificates of securities. In such a case, it is difficult for the transferee to get duplicate certificates, which are issued in favour of the original transferor, transferred in his favour.
- The securities could be lost in transit either at the time they are sent to the issuer for transfer or while they are sent back by the company after they are transferred.

Thus, the process of settlement of trades and transfer of ownership often involve long delays and a significant portion of transactions ends up as "bad delivery" due to faulty completion of paperwork or differences in signature with the specimens on record with the companies or for other procedural lapses. Investors are also subjected to considerable difficulties in the case of loss of certificates of securities. The significant amount of time lost in effecting ownership changes also impounds a substantial volume of securities at any given time, leading to lower trading volumes on the exchanges and incorrect pricing of securities.

To obviate the hassles and problems associated with the physical handling of securities, the government introduced the depository system under the Depositories Act, 1996, to enable holding and dealing of shares and securities in electronic form. In fact, the depository system was a long-felt need of the investing public for reliable and efficient dealings in the securities market.

*The **Depositories Act, 1996,** enables the setting up of multiple depositories in the country and all the operations of the depositories are governed by regulations as framed by SEBI.*

10.2 The Depositories Act, 1996

The depository system was introduced in India under the 1995 Depository Ordinance, which subsequently became the **Depositories Act** in 1996. The act primarily provides for:

i. A multi-depository system
ii. Dematerialization of securities
iii. Appointment of depository participants

The Depositories Act, 1996, enables the setting up of multiple depositories in the country and all the operations of the depositories are governed by regulations as framed from time to time with reference to the provisions of the Depositories Act. The act envisages the transfer of ownership of securities electronically by book-entry without making the securities move from person to person. The act has made industrial securities freely transferable by restricting the issuer's right to use discretion in effecting the transfer of securities. The transfer deed and other procedural requirements under the Companies Act, 1956, are also dispensed with. The stamp duty on transfer of dematerialization (demat) securities is also waived.

10.3 Constituents of the Depository System

The depository system has the following main constituents.

(i) The depository
(ii) The depository participant (DP)
(iii) The issuer/its registrar and transfer agent (RTA) and
(iv) The clearing house or clearing corporation

10.3.1 The Depository

In the words of the Bank for International Settlements, "a depository is a facility for holding securities, which enables securities transaction to be processed by book entry. Physical securities may be immobilized by the depository or securities may be dematerialized so that they exist only as electronic records". According to the Depositories Act, 1996, a **depository** is a company formed and registered under the Companies Act, 1956, and one that has been granted a certificate of registration under the SEBI Act, 1992. Simply put, a depository is an institution similar to a bank, not for funds but for securities. When an investor deposits securities with a depository, the investor account, popularly known as the *demat account*, with the depository, is credited and securities are sent to the issuer of the certificates of securities for transfer in the name of the depository. Thereafter, the beneficial ownership of securities will be with the investor but legal ownership will be with the depository. That is, a depository is the registered owner of securities held by it on behalf of various investors. The depository's name is entered in the register of the issuer of securities but it has no voting rights or any other rights with respect to the securities held by it. However, the depository as a deemed registered owner has the right to effect the transfer of ownership of securities held by it on behalf of the beneficial owners. The investor, being the beneficial owner, gets all the corporate benefits like interest, dividend, rights shares, bonus shares and voting rights. But it is to be noted that the functions of the depository are carried out through another kind of institution called *depository participants*. The basic functions of the depository are dematerialization and rematerialization of certificates of securities such as shares, bonds, debentures, government securities, commercial paper, certificates of deposits, units of mutual funds and warehouse receipts.

*A **depository** is a company formed and registered under the Companies Act, 1956, that has been granted a certificate of registration under the SEBI Act, 1992.*

According to the Depositories Act, the depository is responsible to every individual investor holding an account with the depository. The depository operates on a two-tier structure, where it maintains the accounts of the DPs, who in turn maintain the investors' or clients' accounts. The online software provided by the depository to the DPs gives it access to each account maintained by the DPs so that their functioning can be monitored and controlled. The depository also maintains online connectivity with the registrars and transfer agents and performs a daily reconciliation of all the account balances to ensure that the number of securities issued and dematerialized in the depository tallies.

The first depository in India was the National Securities Depository Limited (NSDL). It was established in November 1996 by the NSE along with IDBI and UTI. The NSDL facilitates trading and settlement of securities in dematerialized form, which normally obviates all the risks and hassles associated with transacting in physical certificates. India's second depository, the Central Depository Services Limited (CDSL), was established in February 1999 by BSE jointly with some leading commercial banks in the country to provide a system for efficient and instantaneous transfer of securities.

10.3.2 The Depository Participant (DP)

*The **depository participant** (DP) is an intermediary (the first point of contact in the depository system) created under the provisions of the Depositories Act to interact with investors directly.*

The **depository participant** (DP) is an intermediary created under the provisions of the Depositories Act to interact with investors directly. The DP is the first point of contact in the depository system. A broker, a bank, a financial institution or a company can register with SEBI as a depository participant. Every depository shall have to prescribe by-laws, which *inter alia* provide for the eligibility criteria for the admission and removal of securities in the depository system, the eligibility criteria for admission of any person/body as a depository participant and the manner and procedure of dematerialization of securities. As the depository system is always operated electronically, the DP should always have adequate infrastructure including automatic data processing systems, adequate and competent staff, effective procedures and risk management systems.

10.3.3 Registrar and Transfer Agent (RTA)

Registrar and transfer agents (RTAs) provide services such as maintaining ledger records of all the security holders of a company. They affect the real transfer of ownership of securities arising on trades made by the sellers and buyers of the securities of the company. The RTAs can also undertake the processing of interest and dividend warrants, processing of rights and bonus issues and despatch of notices and annual reports among other functions. As the services provided by RTAs are specialized, companies often go in for outsourcing. The business of RTAs is governed by the regulations and guidelines issued by SEBI from time to time.

10.3.4 The Clearing Corporation/Clearing House

The *clearing corporation* or *clearing house* of a stock exchange coordinates between the exchange (for executed trades), the clearing members and custodians (for bringing in necessary funds and securities to be settled), the clearing banks (for funds settlement) and the depository (for securities settlement). The clearing corporation of the stock exchange ascertains the pay-in or pay-out of brokers who have traded the securities on the stock exchange. In the depository system, the actual delivery of securities to the clearing corporation by the selling broker and the actual delivery of securities by the clearing corporation to the buying broker are done by the depository through its electronic linkage with the clearing corporation.

10.4 Functions of Depository

The depository has many functions since it provides several services not only for the investors but also for many others who are concerned with securities trading and settlement. The key functions are described briefly.

10.4.1 Dematerialization

***Dematerialization** is the process by which physical certificates of securities are converted into electronic form.*

Dematerialization is the process by which an investor can get his securities, which are actual certificates, converted into electronic form. An investor who wants to get his securities converted into electronic form should open an account with a depository participant. The investor should surrender the securities he wants to get dematerialized to the depository participant along with the completed dematerialization request form (DRF). Before submission of the certificates, the investor has to write 'Surrendered for Dematerialization' on the form. The DP verifies the form and the certificates of the securities. If they are found to be in order, the DP issues an acknowledgement slip to the investor. The details of the certificates are then entered into the software, which then forwards the details to the depository. Further, the DP despatches the defaced certificates along with the request form to the issuer of the certificates or to the registrar and transfer agent. If no objection is received from the issuer or its RTA, the software at the depository level creates the appropriate credit balance in the investor's account. No credit of any securities to the accounts of any investor shall be made unless the depository receives intimation from the issuer or its RTA.

Thus, the sequence of steps involved in the dematerialization process can be stated as follows.

- The investor submits the DRF to the DP along with the certificates of securities to be dematerialized.
- If everything (certificates and DRF) is in order, the DP issues an acknowledgement slip to the (investor) client.
- The DP enters the details of the DRF in the software provided for the purpose. This generates a number called the dematerialization request number.
- The DRF is then forwarded to the depository electronically.
- The depository forwards the DRF to the issuer of the securities or its RTA electronically.
- The DP despatches the certificates along with the DRF to the issuer of securities or its RTA.
- The issuer or its RTA authorizes the depository to create the appropriate credit balance in the client's account.
- The DP informs the client of the credit entry made in his account.

10.4.2 Rematerialization

Rematerialization is the process by which an investor can get his electronically held securities converted into physical certificates. In case the investor wants to rematerialize his securities, he will have to submit a rematerialization request to the DP with which he has an account. If there is sufficient balance in the investor's account, the DP enters the request in its computer system, which blocks the investor's holdings to that extent. The DP then forwards the same to the depository and simultaneously sends the request form to the issuer of the certificates or the RTA. The issuer/RTA prints the certificates and despatches them to the investor. Simultaneously, the depository in informed so that the investor's demat account is debited by the number of securities that are rematerialized.

***Rematerialization** is the process by which electronically held securities are converted into physical certificates.*

Thus, the sequence of steps involved in the rematerialization process is as follows.

- The client submits the rematerialization request form (RRF) to the DP.
- If everything is in order, the DP accepts the RRF and blocks the balance of the client to the extent of the rematerialization quantity.
- The DP enters the details of the RRF in the computer software provided for the purpose.
- The RRF is electronically forwarded to the depository.
- The depository blocks the balance of the DP to the extent of the rematerialization quantity in the depository system.
- The depository intimates the issuer of securities or its RTA about the rematerialization electronically.
- The DP despatches the RRF to the issuer of securities or the RTA.
- The issuer or its RTA despatches the certificates of securities arising out of the rematerialization to the investor and this is informed to the depository.
- The depository removes the balances from the respective DP's account and the DP removes the balance from the respective client's account.

10.4.3 Transfer of Securities

The depository causes the transfer of securities resulting from the settlement of trades between beneficial owners of securities by recording entries in the respective accounts of the beneficial owners. It may be noted that the transfer of beneficial ownership of securities occurs merely by making book entries in the electronic records of the depository. As the ownership of securities is registered in the name of the depository, the transfer of ownership becomes a smooth affair at the level of the company that has issued the securities.

10.4.4 Pledge and Hypothecation

Securities held in demat form can be used as collateral to secure loans and other credit by the investors. If the certificates are in physical form, the investors may have to deliver the securities physically to the lender whenever they want to borrow money from banks or other institutions. These securities are subject to a lot of scrutiny at the level of the lender and they have to be registered as collateral to the loan. This involves considerable time and money. But the depository system makes the process simple and cost effective. If the client of the depository wishes to create a pledge on the securities owned by him, he can do so by making an application in the specified form. The pledger and the pledgee must have an account in the depository to create a pledge. However, the pledger and the pledgee may hold an account with two different depository participants. The DP, after being satisfied that the securities are eligible for the pledge, shall make a note in its records and forward the application to the depository. The depository shall create and record the pledge and send this information to the DPs of the pledger and pledgee within 15 days. If the depository does not create the pledge, it shall send this information to the DPs along with the reasons. The pledger or pledgee may cancel the pledge by requesting a cancellation to the depository through the DP. The pledgee may invoke the pledge subject to the provisions of the pledge document. If the client intends to create a hypothecation on the securities owned by him, he may do so in accordance with the rules. No transfer of security with respect to which a notice or entry of a pledge or hypothecation is in force shall be caused by the depository participant without the prior concurrence of the pledgee or the hypothecatee as the case may be.

10.4.5 Transmission of Securities

The depository shall make the transmission of demat balances of any client due to death, lunacy, bankruptcy and insolvency. In the case where the deceased was one of joint holders of a demat account, the surviving client(s) shall be the person(s) recognized by the depository as the one(s) with any title to the demat balances in the joint account. In the case where the deceased was the sole holder of the client demat account, his legal heir(s) or the legal representative(s) shall be the only person(s) recognized by the depository as possessing the title to the demat balances in that sole account. The client may nominate any person to whom his securities shall vest in the event of his death in the manner prescribed. The securities held in such a demat account will automatically be transferred in the name of the nominee upon the death of the nominating person. The client may substitute or cancel a nomination at any time.

10.4.6 Freezing of Account

The depository system has a provision according to which a DP can freeze the demat account maintained with the DP. The DP shall freeze the demat account of the investor on the written instructions received from the depository pursuant to the orders of the government, SEBI or a court, tribunal or any other statutory authority. Similarly, the depository shall freeze the account of a DP to the extent of the securities held in the DP's name on the orders of the government, SEBI or any court, tribunal or other statutory authority. The frozen account shall be released on instructions from the relevant authority. The DP's account shall also be frozen on disciplinary grounds or if the DP becomes insolvent, bankrupt or a body corporate is being wound up. If the DP goes bankrupt, the creditors of the DP shall have no access to the holdings in the name of the clients of the DP because the depository holds the investors' accounts on trust. The clients of the DP that is bankrupt or facing liquidation can then either rematerialize their holdings or transfer them to a different demat account with another DP.

10.5 Opening and Closing of the Demat Account

In the depository system, securities are held in depository accounts, which is more or less similar to holding funds in a bank account. The investor who wishes to avail himself the services of a depository shall open an account, popularly known as a demat account, with the depository through a depository participant by applying in the format specified for this purpose. The investor is also required to enter into an agreement with the depository participant. Once the application has been accepted by the depository participant, the investor will be issued a client account number. The client wanting to close his account shall apply in the specified format. A client may close his account if no balances are standing to his credit in the account. In case any balance exists, the account may be closed by the rematerialization of the existing balances in its account and/or by transferring his balances to his other accounts either with the same depository participant or with a different participant.

10.6 Transaction Settlements Under the Depository System

The procedure involved in the buying/selling of securities in the depository system is as follows.

(i) The investor places an order with his broker for the sale/purchase at a particular price or at a price to be decided by the broker.

(ii) The broker enters the bids in the screen-based trading system under the dematerialized platform.

(iii) As the bids match, the transaction of sale/purchase is materialized. These transactions are recorded online in the electronic records of the clearing corporation of the stock exchange.

(iv) In the case of sale of securities, instead of delivering the physical shares or certificates and transfer form to his broker, the investor gives an authorization letter. According to this authorization letter, the demat account of the seller of the securities is debited by the relevant number of securities sold and the corresponding credit entry is made in the broker's depository account through whom the investor has sold the securities with the relevant number of securities.

(v) In the case of purchase of securities, the purchaser gives the relevant amount to his broker before the pay-in day.

(vi) Based on the electronic information received from the clearing corporation of the stock exchange regarding the purchase or sale done by the brokers, the brokers' accounts with the clearing bank (for money transactions) and the brokers' accounts with DPs (for shares transactions) are debited or credited, as the case may be.

(vii) After the pay-out date, the broker pays the money to his client for whom he has sold securities. Similarly, the broker who has purchased the securities for his client ensures the credit of the relevant number of securities to the client's depository account.

Thus, it may be observed that the buyer and seller of the securities are free from all the risks and hassles associated with dealing of securities in material form. The buyer gets instant credit for the relevant number of securities in his depository account from his broker and the seller gets instant credit in his bank account for the money he has to receive from his broker on the sale of his securities.

10.7 Advantages of the Depository System

As mentioned earlier, under the depository system, certificates with respect to the securities are dematerialized and destroyed and credit for the relevant number of securities is given in the depository account of the concerned holder of the securities. Thereafter, the transactions in the dematerialized form are done by way of book entries. In other words, the depository system provides for the conversion of physical securities into the electronic form through a process called dematerialization (demat) of share certificates and facilitates share transactions and transfers electronically without involving any share certificates or share transfer deeds. In the depository system, the securities are held in the name of the depository but the securities holder will continue to be the beneficial owner of the securities in all respects. The system also provides for converting securities from the electronic form to physical form (paper form) through the rematerialization (remat) process.

There are several benefits of the depository system. The key ones are as follows.

- Bad deliveries are common when securities in physical form are being processed for transfer of ownership. This may result in high trading and settlement costs and waste of time. Invalid transfer deeds, forgery of signatures, fake certificates or any other defects in the certificates of securities or in the transfer deed may result in a bad delivery. The depository system does away with all such reasons for objecting to the transfer of ownership of securities. The question of bad delivery does not arise in the depository environment.
- The depository system reduces paperwork and thereby reduces cost and time involved in transfer of securities.
- It eliminates all the risks associated with physical securities such as the loss, theft, mutilation and destruction of securities.
- No stamp duty on transfer of shares is payable on transactions through the depository. This saves of a large amount of money, particularly for big investors and institutional investors.

- The depository system facilitates faster settlement and greater liquidity in the market, which enhances the marketability of securities. In fact, the current rolling settlement cycle being followed in the stock exchanges is made possible only by the depository system.
- Since the shares are in demat mode, it is much easier for the investor to keep records.
- Once an investor opens an account with a DP, the same demat account can be utilized by the investor for trading in securities of other companies that are a part of the depository system.
- The depository system facilitates the trading of even a single share. Therefore, it eliminates the concept of odd lots and the hassles associated with odd lots.
- If an investor wants to pledge or hypothecate the securities, it is easy to do so in the demat mode. Money-lending institutions also extend easy and more credit against securities that are dematerialized. The interest rate may also be low on such bank credit. This is because the demat securities that are pledged or hypothecated can be transferred easily and quickly in the name of the credit institution in case the borrower fails to repay the loan amount as per the terms and conditions of the loan.
- The facility for freezing or locking of an investor's demat account is made available by the depository system. This enables certain authorities and even the investors to make the accounts non-operational, providing complete safety to the investor.
- From the point of view of the brokers, transactions in demat mode reduce the office work from their side. This enables them to service more clients and expand their businesses and diversify into more markets and segments. They can also provide additional value-added services.
- Trading in dematerialized securities may involve less margin payments by the investors as they may be able to deliver securities well before the pay-in day.
- Without the depository system, a lot of physical space may be required to store the certificates of securities. But when they are in electronic form, there is no need to store large numbers of certificates. This results in savings on vault charges and custodian charges.
- In the depository system, there is easy trading and instantaneous settlement of trades. The investors can enter and exit from the trade easily and quickly. This enables the investors, particularly institutional investors, to trade more frequently, leading to increased volume of trade. Thus, the investors can make more profit with their increased business.
- In the depository system, the investors are assured of receiving funds faster on the sale of securities. They can also get immediately registered securities on purchase. Thus, they do not miss out on corporate benefits such as dividends and rights.
- The system makes it easier and faster to provide corporate entitlements like dividends, rights and bonus to the investors when their securities are dematerialized. The securities issued as bonus or on allotment of public issue/rights issue/split are directly credited to the investor's demat account.
- Brokerage charges for the investors are less when the securities are dematerialized because dealings in dematerialized securities reduces the back office cost of handling paper certificates to a great extent.
- DPs need to send reports to their clients on their holdings and transactions periodically. This helps the investors monitor and control their portfolios.
- There is a wide network of DPs operating across the country, which makes the depository services available at the doorsteps of investors. This fosters an equity cult among the investing public, which is essential for faster development of the economy.
- The depository system offers an insurance cover to the investors in the event of a loss suffered by the investor due to negligence at the depository level.

10.8 SEBI (Depositories and Participants) Regulations, 1996

In accordance with the Depositories Act, 1996, there are certain regulations governing the registration of a depository, the certificate of commencement of business, registration of a participant, rights and obligations of various constituents of the depository system and inspection. The salient features of these regulations are as follows:

10.8.1 Registration of Depository

Every depository needs to obtain a certificate of registration as well as a certificate of commencement of business from SEBI by fulfilling certain conditions. SEBI shall not consider an application for registration unless the sponsor belongs to one of the following categories.

- A public financial institution
- A scheduled bank
- A foreign bank operating in India with the approval of the RBI
- A recognized stock exchange
- A body corporate engaged in providing financial services where not less than 75 percent of the equity capital is held by any of the institutions mentioned earlier, jointly or severally
- A body corporate constituted or recognized under any law in force in a foreign country at that time for providing custodial, clearing or settlement services in the securities market and approved by the Government of India
- An institution engaged in providing financial services established outside India and approved by the Government of India
- An applicant is a fit and proper person

The sponsor shall, at all times, hold at least 51 per cent of the equity capital of the depository and the balance of the equity capital of the depository shall be held by its participants. No participant shall at any time hold more than 5 per cent of the equity capital of the depository. However, no foreign entity individually or collectively, either as a sponsor or as a participant or as both sponsor and participant, shall hold more than 20 per cent of the equity capital of a depository. A foreign entity shall mean a body corporate or an entity where more than 51 per cent of its equity is held by persons who are not citizens of India.

10.8.2 Conditions for Registration

A depository shall have a net worth of not less than INR 1,000 million and it shall get its by-laws approved by the depository. It shall have automatic data processing systems, which are protected against unauthorized access, alteration, destruction, disclosure or dissemination of records and data. The network through which continuous electronic means of communications is established between the depository, participants, issuers and issuers' agents must be secure against unauthorized entry or access. The depository shall make adequate arrangements, including insurance, for indemnifying the beneficial owners for any loss that may be caused to such owners by a wrongful act, negligence or default of the depository or its participants or of any employee of the depository or participant.

10.8.3 Registration of the DP

As per the SEBI regulations, the registration of a depository participant with SEBI is also required. An application for the grant of a certificate of registration as a participant shall be made to SEBI in the prescribed form through each depository in which the applicant proposes to act as a participant. The applicant shall belong to one of the following categories.

- A public financial institution
- A scheduled commercial bank
- A foreign bank operating in India with the approval of the RBI
- A state financial corporation
- An institution engaged in providing financial services, promoted by any of the institutions mentioned in Section 10.8.1, jointly or severally
- A custodian of securities who has been granted a certificate of registration by SEBI
- A clearing corporation or a clearing house of a stock exchange
- A stockbroker who has been granted a certificate of registration by SEBI, provided that the stockbroker has a minimum net worth of INR 5 million and the aggregate value of the portfolio of securities of

the beneficial owners held in dematerialized form in a depository through him does not exceed 100 times the net worth of the stockbroker. If the stockbroker seeks to act as a participant in more than one depository, he shall comply with the specified criteria separately for each such depository. Further, when the stockbroker has a minimum net worth of INR 100 million, the limits on the aggregate value of the portfolio of securities of the beneficial owners held in dematerialized form in a depository through him shall not be applicable

- A non-banking finance company with net worth of not less than INR 5 million, provided that such a company shall act as a participant only on behalf of itself and not on behalf of any other person. Further, a non-banking finance company may act as a participant on behalf of any other person if it has a net worth of INR 500 million in addition to the net worth specified by any other authority
- A registrar to an issue or share transfer agent who has a minimum net worth of INR 100 million and who has been granted a certificate of registration by SEBI.

10.8.4 Eligible Securities for Dematerialization

The following securities shall be eligible for being held in dematerialized form in a depository.

- Shares, scripts, stocks, bonds, debentures, debenture stock or other marketable securities of similar nature in or of any incorporated company or other body corporate
- Units of mutual funds, rights under collective investment schemes and venture capital funds, commercial paper, certificates of deposit, securitized debt, money market instruments, government securities and unlisted securities
- Any other security as may be specified by SEBI from time to time.

10.8.5 Other Conditions

Separate accounts shall be opened by every participant in the name of each of the beneficial owners and the securities of each beneficial owner shall be segregated and shall not be mixed up with the securities of other beneficial owners or with the participant's own securities. A participant shall register the transfer of securities to or from a beneficial owner's account only on receipt of instructions from the beneficial owner and thereafter confirm this to the beneficial owner in a manner specified by the depository in its by-laws. Every entry in the beneficial owner's account shall be supported by electronic instructions or any other mode of instruction received from the beneficial owner in accordance with the agreement with the beneficial owner.

Every issuer whose securities have been declared eligible for dematerialization in a depository shall give information to the depository about book closures, record dates, dates for the payment of interest or dividend, dates for annual general meetings and other meetings, dates for redemption of debentures, dates for conversion of debentures and warrants, call money dates and other such information at the time and in the manner specified by the depository in its by-laws or agreement. However, no such information would be required to be given to the depository where the state or the central government is the issuer of government securities.

SEBI has made it mandatory for all newly issued securities to be compulsorily traded in dematerialized form. The admission to a depository for dematerialization of securities has been made a prerequisite for making a public or rights issue or an offer for sale. It has also been made compulsory for public limited companies going for an IPO of any security for INR 100 million or more only in dematerialized form.

10.9 National Securities Depository Limited (NSDL)

*The **National Securities Depository Limited (NSDL)**, promoted by IDBI and others, was the first depository in India.*

The **National Securities Depository Limited (NSDL)** was the first depository in India, established in August 1996. The major promoters of the NSDL were the Industrial Development of India, Unit Trust of India and the National Stock Exchange of India. The main objective of the NSDL is to provide settlement solutions for Indian securities markets. Specifically, it aims at removing the difficulties arising from the use of physical (paper) certificates for the settlement of trades on stock exchanges and improving settlement efficiency.

The basic services provided by the NSDL include account maintenance, dematerialization, rematerialization and settlement of trades. It also provides value-added services like pledge, hypothecation of securities, automatic delivery of securities to clearing corporations, distribution of cash and non-cash corporate benefits such as bonus, rights, stock lending and demat of warehouse receipts and Internet-based services such as SPEED-e and IDeAS. The NSDL has also launched a facility called STEADY (Securities Trading-Information Easy Access and Delivery) to digitally transmit signed encrypted trade information across market participants through the Internet. As on October 31, 2009, the NSDL had 9.68 million investor accounts, more than 10,000 DP service centres and a demat custody value of INR 48,435,260 million.

10.9.1 Dematerialization of Warehouse Receipts

Warehouse receipts are title documents issued by the warehouse authority to depositors against the commodities deposited in the warehouse. These documents are transferred by endorsement and delivery. In the commodity futures market, the futures contract can be settled either by cash or by delivery of the commodity depending on the terms of trade. If a trade is to be settled by delivery of the commodity, the clearing house of the commodity exchange will receive warehouse receipts from the seller instead of actual commodities and transmit these warehouse receipts to the counterparty of the futures contract. If the warehouse receipts are in physical form, they have to be delivered to the buyer who is in a different part of the country. This may lead to systemic inefficiencies. Thus, warehouse receipts in physical form share all the disadvantages of title documents in paper form.

> ***Warehouse receipts*** *are title documents issued by the warehouse authority to depositors against the commodities deposited in the warehouse.*

With the increase in activity in the commodity futures market and the establishment of national, screen-based multi-commodity exchanges, the need for an efficient settlement system was felt. Drawing lessons from the depository system for securities, the NSDL and national multi-commodity exchanges worked out a scheme to extend depository services for settling trades in commodity futures. Investors trading in commodity futures may avail themselves of depository services for receiving and delivering warehouse receipts. Thus, dematerialization of warehouse receipts is one of the functions of the NSDL.

10.9.2 The Dividend Distribution Scheme

Another value-added service offered by the NSDL is the dividend distribution scheme. Under this scheme, the NSDL facilitates the distribution of cash dividend to shareholders. A company that participates in this scheme executes an agreement with the NSDL for the purpose of dividend distribution and furnishes details of dividend payment. The company also provides the NSDL with a downloadable file of shareholders who are eligible to receive the dividend. Then the company gives the NSDL a single cheque for the whole amount of the dividend payable to the shareholders holding shares in dematerialized form with the NSDL. The NSDL directly credits the dividend amount into the accounts of the shareholders with the help of a bank. The major advantage of the scheme is the resulting savings in the administrative cost of dividend distribution. Loss of dividend warrants in transit and fraudulent encashment of dividend warrants can be totally eliminated when dividend distribution takes place through the electronic mode.

10.10 Central Depository Services Limited (CDSL)

The **Central Depository Services Limited** (CDSL) was established in 1999. The chief promoters of the CDSL include the Bombay Stock Exchange Limited, Bank of India, State Bank of India, HDFC Bank Limited and Standard Chartered Bank. The CDSL has a wide network of DPs operating from more than 6,000 sites across the country. The DPs are directly connected to the CDSL, which provides investors to an online and efficient depository service. Equity shares (listed or unlisted), bonds, units of mutual funds, government securities, commercial paper, certificates of deposits and warehouse receipts are eligible for dematerilization. The DPs that register themselves with the CDSL for Internet access can, in turn, provide demat account holders access to their account on the Internet. The DPs can also provide online depository services with the latest status of the investor's account. Different types of accounts can be maintained with the CDSL. The accounts that can be maintained by the clearing corporation or clearing house with the CDSL are called Settlement Default (CH Pool) Account and CH/CC House Account (to be opened for any specific purpose in relation to settlements). Similarly, the depository participants can open and maintain certain accounts with the CDSL. These include

> *The* ***Central Depository Services Limited*** *(CDSL) was the second depository in India, promoted by BSE and others.*

BO Accounts, CM Principal Account, CM Unified Settlement Account, CM Clearing Account, CM Investors' Securities Account and Margin Trading Account. As on November 3, 2009, the CDSL had 487 depository participants, 6,469 DP service centres and 6.12 million investor accounts. The total value of securities in demat custody of the CDSL was INR 8,219,760 million.

10.11 Custodial Services

Custodial services play an important role in the development of financial markets. With the rapid growth of the investing public, the demand for custodial services has increased enormously over time, particularly over the past decade. The investors, mainly institutional investors, seek certain services in relation to their securities from professional bodies like the Stock Holding Corporation of India Limited (SHCIL). The important **custodial services** include safekeeping (plain vanilla custody), settlement of trades, income collection, processing corporate entitlements such as rights and bonus, reporting corporate bodies' performance, multicurrency accounting, tax reporting, cash management, portfolio reporting, proxy voting and foreign exchange management. The custodians may also undertake services of securities lending to their clients. *Securities lending* allows a customer to make additional income by lending his securities to approved borrowers on a short-term basis. Other value-added services provided by custodians include risk measurement, performance measurement and compliance monitoring. Many institutions, including some commercial banks, have entered the arena of custodial services. Each custodial services provider specializes in certain services. For example, a global custodian provides custodial services for cross-border securities. In addition to core custodial services, a global custodian provides services such as executing foreign exchange transactions and processing tax reclaims. A global custodian maintains a sub-custodian or agent bank in each country to help provide custodial services in the foreign countries. The demand for global custodial services has increased enormously in recent years as investors have showed an interest in foreign investment opportunities.

Custodial services *in relation to securities include safekeeping of the securities of a client and other incidental services.*

The custodial services offered by Kotak Mahindra Bank Limited (KMBL) are presented in Box 10.1.

Box 10.1 Kotak Mahindra Bank: Custody Services

Key features and offerings:

- Custody and settlement services
- Depository receipts
- Broker back office
- Escrow accounts
- Foreign direct investment
- Internet interface for clients

The Kotak group has launched custody services as part of its diversified services portfolio in the capital markets industry.

This division delivers securities services to institutional investors—both foreign and domestic—who invest in debt and equity instruments, derivatives, depository receipts and mutual fund units. A dedicated account manager partners clients to meet their needs.

The custodial services offered by Kotak Mahindra Bank include:

- **Account opening:** Kotak Mahindra Bank assists clients in custody account opening documentation requirements and helps them during the SEBI registration process. This includes:
    - Clarification on existing guidelines
    - Providing assistance during the application process, including vetting of application forms
    - Liaison with SEBI and feedback to client on application status
- **Transaction settlement:** As a clearing member with the clearing houses of leading Indian stock exchanges (the NSE and BSE), it performs clearing and settlement of cash and securities on behalf of clients.
- **Securities safekeeping:** Provides safekeeping services for securities—in electronic as well as physical forms.

(Continued)

- **Corporate actions:** It tracks corporate actions and performs corporate actions processing for both voluntary and involuntary events on behalf of its clients. This involves applications made to issuers on behalf of the clients, income collection and following up on corporate action events like dividend, interest, redemption, bonus and rights.
- **Standardized and customized reporting:** Investors need meaningful information that offers an insight into their investment portfolios. Apart from the very comprehensive standard suite of reports, it provides customized reports to clients at various frequencies to enable the clients to efficiently manage their securities portfolio and cash balances and take more informed investment decisions.
- **Compliance monitoring and regulatory reporting:** It monitors compliance by investors with existing guidelines and facilitates reporting to regulators and local authorities on behalf of the clients.
- **Foreign exchange services:** It has a dedicated foreign exchange desk that takes care of clients' needs for currency conversion and risk management products.
- **Proxy services:** It acts on client instructions and participates and votes on their behalf in shareholders' meetings of companies.

Depository receipts: KMBL coordinates with local custodians to ensure prompt receipt of underlying securities against cancelled depository receipts and reports the same to clients on a priority basis.

DP back office for brokers: KMBL manages the pay-in and pay-out of securities to/from clearing houses of stock exchanges on behalf of trading member brokers and undertakes depository transfers of securities on behalf of trading members.

Escrow accounts: KMBL has expertise in customized solutions for escrow arrangements.

Foreign direct investment: It facilitates in the following manner FDI transactions undertaken by clients:

- Close co-ordination between company/counter-party and client for the date of transaction and movement of funds and shares on the transaction date
- Compliance of transaction with regulations
- Follow up with company for filing of necessary documents with regulators

Internet interface for clients: It combines technology and a deep understanding of the investment process to transform data into information that clients need to make investment decisions. KMBL provides a one-of-its-kind Web-enabled interface to its clients. The Web interface delivery system provides different types of information that clients need and in a manner that is most efficient. The interface provides the following functionalities to its clients:

- Instruction input for market transactions
- Instruction input for voluntary corporate actions
- Online generation of various standard reports and ad hoc reports
- Online monitoring of cash and security balances

Source: http://corporatebanking.kotak.com/custody-service/

10.11.1 The Stock Holding Corporation of India Ltd (SHCIL)

The Stock Holding Corporation of India Ltd (SHCIL) was established in 1988 under the Companies Act, 1956. It was promoted by leading financial institutions in the country such as IDBI, ICICI, IFCI, LIC, GIC, UTI and IRBI. Headquartered in Mumbai, the SHCIL has a pan-India presence with more than 170 offices. The SHCIL aims at providing infrastructure facilities for post-trading services such as clearing, depository and other support services. It is a market leader in custodial services with a market share greater than 50 per cent.

The SHCIL is India's first and largest custodian of securities and has a wealth of human resources, technology and infrastructure befitting its position as a pioneer and market leader. The SHCIL mainly offers custodial services, clearing and settlement services, electronic and physical safekeeping services, asset servicing, data bank and client reporting. It has been providing first-rate custodial services to leading financial institutions, insurance companies, mutual funds, foreign institutional investors, banks, Indian and foreign venture capital companies, PF trusts and corporate organizations for over two decades. It is a professional clearing member of BSE and the NSE and facilitates smooth straight through processing (STP) systems with a choice of two reputed service providers enabling the competitive advantage of an efficient settlement. It also facilitates seamless monitoring and constant updates on failed trades, if any, on a T + 2 basis, daily verification of settlements, efficient fund transfer and effortless handling of residual trades. The electronic and physical safekeeping services of the SHCIL include operations on both depositories (the National Securities Depository Limited and Central Securities Depository

Limited) and comprehensive document tracking and storage systems that enable instant tracking of any securities in physical custody. Asset servicing includes a dedicated corporate actions team to ensure the timely forecast of all corporate actions and benefits accruing on client holdings and the handling of all instrument types listed on both exchanges (BSE and the NSE). The SHCIL offers an exhaustive cross-country database of corporate events, book closures, R&T agents, depositories, stock exchanges and other industry-related information. The database caters to all instruments issued in the Indian market such equity, corporate debt, preferred equity, floating rate instruments, CPs, CDs, and pass through certificates (PTCs). It offers customized reporting to provide maximum value for the clients, daily saleable holding reports, timely put/call intimations and forecasts of redemptions and corporate actions. It is a clearing member on the futures and options segment of both the NSE and BSE. It has an extensive audit and risk management systems in place. It offers various types of audits, such as the internal audit of various processes, statutory audit and systems audit. Besides, audits are conducted by clients with respect to their assets. There is also a yearly audit conducted as per SEBI norms with regard to internal controls put in place by the company. The depositories—NSDL and CDSL—also conduct their audit for electronic depository services. A committee has been constituted at the board level to look at any deviations arising from these audit reports.

10.11.2 SEBI (Custodian of Securities) Regulations, 1996

Custodians are an integral part of the securities market that provide services to investors, particularly institutional investors. In order to streamline their interaction and interface with stock exchanges, clearing corporations/houses, stockbrokers, registrars and investors, SEBI has framed certain regulations. The main aspects of these regulations are as follows.

Custodial services in relation to securities include safekeeping of securities of a client and providing services incidental thereto—maintaining accounts of securities of a client, collecting the benefits or rights accruing to the client with respect to the securities, keeping the client informed of the actions taken or to be taken by the issuer of securities which will have a bearing on the benefits or rights accruing to the client and maintaining and reconciling records of the said services. SEBI amended the regulations in 2006. Accordingly, custodial services in relation to securities of a client or gold or gold-related instruments held by a mutual fund means safekeeping of such securities or gold and gold-related instruments and providing services incidental thereto, including maintaining accounts of the securities or gold or gold-related instruments of a client, collecting the benefits or rights accruing to the client with respect to the securities or gold or gold-related instruments, keeping the client informed of the actions taken or to be taken by the issuer of securities which will have a bearing on the benefits or rights accruing to the client and maintaining and reconciling records of the said services.

Any person proposing to provide custodial services shall obtain a certificate of registration by applying to SEBI along with the necessary documents and fee. Before granting registration, SEBI shall take into account the following aspects.

(i) Whether the applicant fulfils the capital requirement, which shall be a net worth of not less than INR 500 million
(ii) Whether the applicant has the necessary infrastructure, including adequate office space, vaults for safe custody of securities and computer systems capability required to effectively discharge his activities as custodian of securities
(iii) Whether the applicant has in his employment adequate and competent persons who have the experience, capacity and ability of managing the business of the custodian of securities.

If satisfied with the application with reference to these criteria, SEBI shall grant a certificate of registration. SEBI may restrict the certificate of registration to provide custodial services either in respect of securities or in respect of gold or gold-related instruments of a client.

Every custodian of securities shall open a separate custody account for each client, in the name of the client whose securities are in its custody, and the assets of one client shall not be mixed with those of another client. Further, every custodian of securities shall enter into an agreement with each client on whose behalf it is acting as custodian of securities and every such agreement shall provide for the following.

(a) The circumstances under which the custodian of securities will accept or release securities from the custody account
(b) The circumstances under which the custodian of securities will accept or release monies from the custody account

(c) The circumstances under which the custodian of securities will receive rights or entitlements on the securities of the client
(d) The circumstances and manner of registration of securities in respect of each client
(e) Details of the insurance, if any, to be provided for by the custodian of securities.

The custodian of securities shall maintain the highest standards of integrity, fairness and professionalism in the discharge of his duties. The custodian shall be prompt in distributing dividends, interest or any such accruals of income received or collected by him on behalf of his clients on the securities in custody. The custodian shall maintain client confidentiality with respect to the client's affairs. The custodian shall also extend to other custodial entities, depositories and clearing organizations all cooperation that may be necessary for conducting business in the areas of inter-custodial settlements, transfer of securities and transfer of funds. A custodian of securities or any of his employees shall not render, directly or indirectly, any investment advice about any security in the publicly accessible media, whether real time or non-real time, unless a disclosure of his interest including long or short position in the said security has been made while rendering such advice. In case an employee of the custodian of securities is rendering such advice, he shall also disclose the interest of his dependent family members and employer including their long or short position in the said security while rendering such advice.

Every custodian of securities shall have adequate internal controls to prevent any manipulation of records and documents. He shall also preserve the following records and documents for a minimum period of five years.

(a) Records containing details of securities received and released on behalf of each client
(b) Records containing details of monies received and released on behalf of each client
(c) Records containing details of rights or entitlements of each client arising from the securities held on behalf of the client
(d) Records containing details of registration of securities with respect to each client
(e) Ledger for each client
(f) Records containing details of instructions received from and sent to clients
(g) Records of all reports submitted to SEBI.

SEBI may appoint one or more persons as inspecting officer(s) to undertake inspection of books of account, records and documents of the custodians. It shall be the duty of the custodian of securities whose affairs are being inspected, and of every director, officer and employee thereof, to produce to the inspecting officer such books, securities, accounts, records and other documents in its custody or control. A custodian of securities who contravenes any of the provisions of the SEBI Act, 1992, the rules framed thereunder or the relevant regulations shall be dealt with in the manner prescribed under the SEBI (Procedure for Holding Enquiry by Enquiry Officer and Imposing Penalty) Regulations, 2002.

Summary

1. The major problems in securities trading in the physical environment were delays in transfer of ownership of securities, bad deliveries and irregular settlements.
2. Bad delivery arises due to faulty completion of paperwork or signature differences with the specimens on record with the companies, or for other procedural lapses.
3. The Depositories Act, 1996, enables the setting up of multiple depositories in the country and all the operations of the depositories are governed by the regulations as framed from time to time with reference to the provisions of the Depositories Act.
4. The basic functions of a depository are dematerialization and rematerialization of certificates of securities such as shares, bonds, debentures, government securities, commercial paper, certificates of deposits, units of mutual funds and warehouse receipts.
5. The DP is an intermediary created under the provisions of the Depositories Act to interact with investors directly.
6. Dematerialization is the process by which an investor can get his securities, which are in physical form as certificates, converted into electronic form.
7. Rematerialization is the process by which an investor can get his electronically held securities converted into physical certificates.
8. The depository system primarily avoids all such objections to the transfer of ownership of securities. It reduces paperwork and, thereby the cost and time, involved in transfer of securities.
9. Promoted by IDBI, UTI and NSE, the NSDL was the first depository established in India in August 1996.

10. The second depository in the country was the Central Depository Services Limited (CDSL) promoted by the Bombay Stock Exchange Limited, Bank of India, State Bank of India, HDFC Bank Limited and Standard Chartered Bank.
11. In accordance with the Depositories Act, 1996, SEBI has made certain regulations governing the registration of a depository, certificate of commencement of business, registration of participant, rights and obligations of various constituents of the depository system and inspection.
12. Important custodial services include safekeeping (plain-vanilla custody), settlement of trades, income collection, process corporate entitlements such as rights and bonus, reporting corporate bodies' performance, multicurrency accounting, tax reporting, cash management, portfolio reporting, proxy voting and foreign exchange management.
13. Any person proposing to provide custodial services shall get a certificate of registration by applying to SEBI along with the necessary documents and fee.
14. The custodian of securities shall maintain the highest standards of integrity, fairness and professionalism in the discharge of his duties.

Questions

1. Discuss the major inadequacies of trading and settlement in the traditional system (physical environment).
2. Explain the role of the major constituents of the depository system.
3. Examine the functions of the depository system.
4. Explain the processes of dematerialization and rematerialization.
5. What are the advantages of the depository system?
6. Critically examine the SEBI regulations with regard to the depository system.
7. What do you understand by custodial services? How do they help the development of the financial market in the country?
8. Bring out the salient features of SEBI regulations with regard to custodial services.

Chapter 11

Insider Trading

LEARNING OBJECTIVES

After reading this chapter, you will be able to:

- Bring out the relationship between market price and intrinsic value.
- Define an efficient market and describe its features.
- Define insider trading in different manifestations.
- Present SEBI regulations on insider trading.
- Cite cases of insider trading.

11.1 Introduction

An *efficient market* is one in which the prices of securities are equal to their respective intrinsic values at all times. The **intrinsic value** of a security is defined as the present value of all cash flows that the owner of the security expects to receive in future. Investors attempt to forecast the timing and size of the cash flows associated with a security and then convert them into present values by using an appropriate discount rate. Thus, the investors have to forecast not only the cash flows that are to be generated by the asset or security throughout its lifetime but also the appropriate discount rate. The *discount rate* is the required rate of return on the investment. The purpose of equity research is to identify the intrinsic value of an asset or security.

*The **intrinsic value** of any asset is the present value of all the cash flows that the asset can generate over its lifetime.*

11.1.1 Market Price Versus Intrinsic Value

While making an investment decision, investors make a comparison of the current market price of the security with its intrinsic value. The securities for which the current market price is less than their intrinsic value are known as underpriced or *undervalued securities* and the securities for which the current market price is more than their intrinsic value are known as overpriced or *overvalued securities*. Undervalued securities signal buy decisions and overvalued securities signal sell decisions. Both undervalued securities and overvalued securities can also be called *mispriced securities*. When the current market price of a security equals the intrinsic value of the security, the price of the security is at *equilibrium*. Markets become efficient when the price of a security is at equilibrium. Any difference between the current market price and the intrinsic value signifies market inefficiency. When the prices are at equilibrium, the investors can get only normal profits or normal returns on their investments.

Markets become efficient when the price of a security is at equilibrium, that is, when the market price is equivalent to the intrinsic value.

There are several factors that influence or determine the intrinsic value. These factors are grouped as general economic factors (for example, the gross domestic product [GDP], inflation, interest rates, budget deficit and government policy, among others); industry factors (such as the industry life cycle and industry structure and performance, among others) and specific company factors (such as management policy, competition, cost structure). As these factors change, the intrinsic value of a security changes too. In essence, the intrinsic value of a security may not remain constant over time.

11.1.2 Market Efficiency

An **efficient market** is one in which all the market participants have the same information and no participant can influence stock prices.

A perfectly competitive market is an **efficient market** since all the market participants have the same information and no participant can influence stock prices. In an efficient market, the security prices reflect all the information about the security. Further, no market participant in an efficient market can get supernormal profits or supernormal returns on his investment. The market price of a security will move only on the information that the factors that influence the prospects a company have changed. These factors, as mentioned earlier, first alter the intrinsic value by influencing the cash flows and discount rate associated with the security. When such information percolates down to the market participants, the stock price will move to reach the new intrinsic value. In the efficient market, the adjustment of the stock price to the new intrinsic value takes place instantaneously, which means that all the information about the intrinsic value changes is reflected in the stock price immediately. Any further change in the stock price will be the result of a new piece of information about the change of the intrinsic value of the security. For example, consider that a company announces it is merging with another company. As this event alters the intrinsic value of the business, the stock price will change. Similarly, the stock price instantaneously responds to corporate actions such as dividend declaration and bonus announcement. Thus, the stock price moves to a new equilibrium level based on the availability of new information.

The current market price will not be equal to intrinsic value when all the information that relates to the intrinsic value is not available to every market participant. The disparity between the market price of a security and the intrinsic value may also be the result of different investors evaluating the available information differently or due to different investors having different expectations about the future of the company. Thus, a security is underpriced or overpriced because of an imperfect market. The underpriced securities create pressure for prices to increase due to increased demand to buy, and overpriced securities create pressure for prices to decrease due to the increased supply to sell. Thus, the prices of all securities do not always reflect intrinsic values all the time, and opportunities for obtaining abnormal profits do arise when the stock markets become inefficient.

As the markets become more developed and efficient, it becomes extremely difficult to make abnormal profits by the buying and selling of the securities in these markets. However, markets differ in their degree of efficiency. Markets in developed countries are more efficient than their counterparts in developing countries. The reason for this is that in the developed countries, the disclosure requirements are more rigorous whereas in less developed countries, they are less rigorous. The degree of efficiency also differs across the stocks in a market. Some of the stocks in a market may be efficiently priced while others may be less efficiently priced. This creates a scope for making supernormal profits on investments in less efficiently priced securities.

11.2 The Concept of Insider Trading

***Insider trading** can be considered as a lawful activity when insiders buy or sell securities of their own companies within the confines of company policy and the regulations governing this trading.*

The term **insider trading** has different connotations. It encompasses both legal and prohibited activity. Insider trading can be considered as a lawful activity when insiders—those privileged with price-sensitive information, such as directors, executives or employees—buy or sell securities of their own companies within the confines of company policy and the regulations governing this trade. But insider trading becomes unlawful when the insider, who is supposed to maintain the confidentiality of the information, uses such price-sensitive information to his or her personal advantage (making profits or avoiding losses on securities trading) to the detriment of other investors who buy or sell their securities without the advantage of such information. The "tipping" price, which is sensitive information, when revealed to other traders by an insider, is also considered unlawful insider trading. Price-sensitive information includes periodical financial results of a company; intended declarations of dividend; the issue or buyback of securities; amalgamations, mergers, or takeovers; spin-offs and sell-offs; and any major expansion plans or execution of new projects, among others.

Some examples of insider trading are as follows:

- The directors, executives, officers or employees of a company may trade in the securities of their own company after learning significant and confidential corporate developments.
- The directors, executives, officers or employees may tip off their friends, family members and business associates. The persons who receive these tips may trade in the securities and make substantial gains or reduce their losses.

- The employees of banking, brokerage and consultancy firms, who are given information to provide services to a company, may take advantage of such information and buy or sell the securities of the company.
- Government employees who learn of confidential information by virtue of their position in the government may also deal in the securities of companies.

11.2.1 The Modus Operandi of Insider Trading

The price of the security tends to change with the availability of new information. If the market is not perfectly competitive, some market participants receive such information before others and become the initiators of price change. As the information gradually spreads among the other market participants, the price changes gain momentum until the new information is completely reflected in the stock price. This lag between the initial price reaction to the information and the time that it is fully reflected in the stock price creates scope for market participants who receive the information earlier to make a profit. Thus, in the inefficient market, there are those who are in the know, and those who get the news late. In other words, the information awareness of the market participants is asymmetrical. The disparities in the market prices and intrinsic values are noted by alert analysts and astute investors and they take advantage of their discoveries. By the time the naive or common investors are able to make decisions, security price adjustments might already have occurred, leaving such investors high and dry.

The modus operandi of insider trading is discussed here.

The insiders may act as initiators of price change by receiving the information much earlier than others. An insider buys the stock of a company at the prevailing market price or perhaps he might also already own the stock. He then reveals some price-sensitive information to a select group of people close to him. These people also buy the stock and further spread the information. This results in an increase in sales volumes and prices of the stock. Thus, the inside information becomes known to a larger group of people, which further pushes up the sales volumes and prices of the stock. After a certain price is reached, the insider sells his holdings as do the ones close to him before others do the same. As many people attempt to sell the stock, the price of the stock falls. When the information is available to everyone, the stock goes back to its realistic price level, which makes common investors lose heavily.

11.2.2 Implications of Insider Trading

Those investors who have inside information may make supernormal profits while the ordinary retail investors end up holding dud stock as the "tip" reaches them only when the stock price is already volatile. The insider may also have information that leads to a fall in the stock price. So he would become alert and sell the stock, which he might already own, before others do so. Thus, the retail investor tends to buy the overvalued stock and sell the undervalued stock due to imbalance in the information flow. The small investor, on the other hand, always gets on the bandwagon rather late since he is away from the real source of information. In other words, those investors who are not in the know will always be left high and dry. Further, the insiders as well as those trading on the basis of insider information have an opportunity to enter and exit at the right time. But the naive investor, with little information, is stuck with the stock at a price that is not favourable to him.

When investors put their money in securities, they trust that the securities markets are efficient and the transactions would take place in a free, fair and transparent trading environment. But insider trading vitiates the market environment and causes distortion in pricing of securities. The insiders may buy or sell the securities of their own companies in breach of a fiduciary duty or other relationship of trust and confidence while in possession of material and unpublished information about the company.

The impact of insider trading on stock markets is negative. As insider trading is not fair play, the other investors may suffer heavy losses in their trade. Besides losing money because of insider trading, the investors, particularly small investors, may also lose their confidence in the stock markets. Thus, insider trading is extremely detrimental to the growth of a healthy capital market where all participants, big and small, can step in with confidence of fair play. Even a small quantity of securities traded by insiders harms the integrity of the markets.

On the other side of the coin, insider trading does have certain positive features. The insiders are privileged to have price-sensitive unpublished information. With such information, they attempt to forecast the return and risk of the investment in the securities of their company. They may correctly perceive the market price of the security to be high or low, and accordingly they may buy or sell the securities. Thus, the insiders feed their information into the market price. As a result, the market price comes closer to the intrinsic value of the security. Since the trades by the insiders are the result of their informed decisions, it would help market efficiency if the insider information is rapidly made public. That is, insider trading enhances market efficiency and price discovery.

If the markets are inefficient, financial analysts attempt to find out something about which the others are unaware. But the dividing line between legitimate research and illegitimate insider trading is thin. Seeking information from all possible sources, including investors who may be senior executives in business firms, sometimes aggressively, is the lifeblood of financial analysts.

Practically, it is difficult to distinguish between genuine trading and insider trading as there are various ways in which information is circulated. In the case of institutional trading, it becomes very difficult to define insider trading as the institutions may deal with different kinds of customers simultaneously. While dealing with different kinds of customers, an institution might have conflicting obligations. For example, consider a bank that has an investment banking division which keeps the material information of a client (issuer of securities) confidential. It also has a broking division, which plans to buy the securities on behalf of another client, and for that it needs material information about the issue. This situation gives rise to conflicting obligations for the bank.

To summarize, although insider trading is not always unlawful, it is difficult to discern the extent of its legitimacy. Therefore, insider trading is generally considered as an unlawful activity.

11.3 Initiatives to Regulate Insider Trading

The U.S. Securities Act, 1933, and the Securities Exchange Act, 1934, were the initial enactments to address insider trading.

The primary aim of any regulation and policy is to foster market efficiency. At the international level, following the stock market crash in 1929, the U.S. government enacted the Securities Act, 1933, and the Securities Exchange Act, 1934. The Securities Exchange Act addresses insider trading directly through Section 16(b) and indirectly through Section 10 (b). Section 16(b) "prohibits short-swing profits (profits realized in any period less than six months) by corporate insiders in their own corporation's stock, except in very limited circumstances. It applies only to directors or officers of the corporation and those holding greater than 10 per cent of the stock and is designed to prevent insider trading by those most likely to be privy to important corporate information". Section 10(b) makes it "unlawful for any person to use or employ, in connection with the purchase or sale of any security registered on a national securities exchange or any security not so registered, any manipulative or deceptive device or contrivance in contravention of such rules and regulations as the SEC may prescribe".

Over the years, the U.S. Securities and Exchange Commission (SEC) has cracked down heavily on insider trading. It has prosecuted many people, including Dennis Levine of Drexel Burnham Lambert and Ivan Boesky (a Wall Street arbitrageur) under the act. A recent and sensational insider trading case is the USD 20-million hedge fund insider trading scam in 2009. The case, popularly known as the Galleon case, created a sensation in the United States. The SEC has entered into arrangements with foreign counterparts for information sharing and cooperation in the investigation and prosecution of the violators of the regulations. The Insider Trading and Securities Fraud Enforcement Act, 1988, expanded the powers of the SEC to provide assistance to foreign regulators. The SEC can use its powers to compel testimony and production of documents at the request of a foreign securities authority.

Even as the U.S. government prohibited it, insider trading was virtually unregulated in the rest of the world, with a few exceptions, until the 1980s. The first effort outside the United States to prohibit insider trading was the European Community Directive Coordinating Regulations on Insider Trading, adopted on November 13, 1989. Insider information was defined as information of a precise nature about a security or an issuer that has not been made public and which, if it was made public, would likely have a significant effect on the price of the security. The directive clearly prohibits insiders from taking advantage of inside information. It also prohibits insiders from tipping off or using others to take advantage of inside information. It is also stated that members may enact laws more stringent than those set out in the directive. Insider trading often crosses borders. Instances of foreign nationals engaging in insider trading in the domestic market or domestic nationals effecting insider trading through foreign accounts have become common. Successful investigations and prosecutions of insider trading cases require international cooperation.

Thus, the European Community Directive requires members to cooperate with each other for the purpose of carrying out their duties.

As far as India is concerned, the Indian government initiated certain measures to curb insider trading. The Companies Act, 1956, and the Securities Contracts (Regulation) Act, 1956, have certain provisions to check the practice. As these were found to be inadequate, the Securities and Exchange Board of India (SEBI) issued certain guidelines as disclosure norms aimed at controlling insider trading. In the recent past, SEBI has tightened insider trading norms. These stricter regulations are aimed at curbing the misuse of price-sensitive information.

11.3.1 SEBI (Prohibition of Insider Trading) Regulations, 1992

SEBI has issued certain regulations for prohibition of insider trading. Originally issued in 1992, the regulations have been updated from time to time. According to SEBI, an **insider** is a person who is or was connected with the company or is deemed to have been connected with the company, and who is reasonably expected to have access to unpublished price-sensitive information with respect to the securities of a company, or who has received or has had access to such unpublished price-sensitive information. The connected person may be a director of the company or a person who occupies a position as an officer or an employee of the company or holds a position involving a professional or business relationship between himself and the company and who may reasonably be expected to have access to unpublished price-sensitive information in relation to that company.

*According to SEBI, an **insider** is a person who is or was connected with the company or is deemed to have been connected with the company, and who is reasonably expected to have access to unpublished price-sensitive information with respect to the securities of a company, or who has received or has had access to such unpublished price-sensitive information.*

Salient features of SEBI regulations on insider trading

1 (a) No insider shall (i) either on his own behalf or on behalf of any other person deal in securities of a company listed on any stock exchange when in possession of any unpublished price-sensitive information; or (ii) communicate, counsel or procure directly or indirectly any unpublished price-sensitive information to any person who while in possession of such unpublished price-sensitive information shall not deal in securities.

1 (b) No company shall deal in the securities of another company or associate of that other company while in possession of any unpublished price-sensitive information.

2. Any insider who deals in securities in contravention of the provisions of the regulations shall be guilty of insider trading.
3. If SEBI suspects that any person has violated any provision of these regulations, it may make inquiries with such persons, or any other person as deemed fit, to form a *prima facie* opinion as to whether there is any violation of the regulations. Before undertaking any investigation, SEBI shall give a reasonable notice to the insider for that purpose. It shall be the duty of every insider, who is being investigated, or any other person to produce to the investigating authority such books, accounts and other documents in his custody or control and furnish the authority with the statements and information relating to the transactions in the securities market within such time as the said authority may require.
4. SEBI may without prejudice to its right to initiate criminal prosecution to protect the interests of investor and in the interests of the securities market and for due compliance with the provisions of the SEBI Act and regulations made thereunder, issue any or all of the following orders.
   - Direct the insider or such person not to deal in securities in any particular manner
   - Prohibit the insider or such person from disposing of any of the securities acquired in violation of these regulations
   - Restrain the insider from communicating or counselling any person to deal in securities
   - Declare the transaction(s) in securities as null and void
   - Direct the person who acquired the securities in violation of these regulations to deliver the securities back to the seller. In case the buyer is not in a position to deliver such securities, the market price prevailing at the time of issuing of such directions or at the time of the transactions, whichever is higher, shall be paid to the seller
   - Direct the person who has dealt in securities in violation of these regulations to transfer an amount or proceeds equivalent to the cost price or market price of securities, whichever is higher, to the investor protection fund of a recognized stock exchange.

5. All listed companies and organizations associated with securities markets shall frame a code of internal procedures and conduct as near thereto the Model Code specified in these regulations.

6 (a) Any person who holds more than 5 per cent shares or voting rights in any listed company shall disclose to the company the number of shares or voting rights held by such a person, on becoming such a holder, within four working days of the receipt of intimation of allotment of shares, or the acquisition of shares or voting rights, as the case may be.

6 (b) Any person who is a director or officer of a listed company shall disclose to the company the number of shares or voting rights held by such a person within four working days of becoming a director or officer of the company.

6 (c) Any person who holds more than 5 per cent shares or voting rights in any listed company shall disclose to the company the number of shares or voting rights held and change in shareholding or voting rights, even if such change results in shareholding falling below 5 per cent, if there has been a change in such holdings from the last disclosure made and such change exceeds 2 per cent of the total shareholding or voting rights in the company.

6 (d) Any person who is a director or officer of a listed company shall disclose to the company the total number of shares or voting rights held and the change in shareholding or voting rights if there has been a change in such holdings from the last disclosure made and the change exceeds INR 5 lakh in value or 25,000 shares or 1 per cent of the total shareholding or voting rights, whichever is lower.

Model code of conduct for prevention of insider trading for listed companies

The following are the main points that constitute the model code of conduct for listed companies.

1. The compliance officer, who is appointed by the listed company, shall be responsible for setting forth policies, procedures, monitoring adherence to the rules for the preservation of price-sensitive information, pre-clearing of designated employees' and their dependents' trades (directly or through respective department heads as decided by the company), monitoring of trades and the implementation of the code of conduct under the overall supervision of the board of directors of the listed company.
2. Employees/directors shall maintain confidentiality of all price-sensitive information. Employees/directors shall not pass on such information to any person directly or indirectly by way of making a recommendation for the purchase or sale of securities. Price-sensitive information is to be handled on a "need-to-know" basis. That is, the price-sensitive information should be disclosed only to those within the company who need the information to discharge their duty.
3. All directors/officers and designated employees of the company shall be subject to trading restrictions as stated below.
    - The company shall specify a trading period, to be called "trading window", for trading in the company's securities.
    - When the trading window is closed, the employees/directors shall not trade in the company's securities in such a period. The trading window shall be closed at the time of declaration of financial results, declaration of dividend, issue of securities, any major expansion plans or execution of new projects, amalgamation, mergers, takeovers and buy-back, disposal of the whole or a substantial whole of the undertaking and any changes in policies, plans or operations of the company. The time for commencement of closing of the trading window shall be decided by the company.
    - The trading window shall be opened 24 hours after the information stated in the previous point is made public. All directors/officers/designated employees of the company shall conduct all their dealings in the securities of the company only in a valid trading window and shall not deal in any transaction involving the purchase or sale of the company's securities during periods when the trading window is closed or during any other period as may be specified by the company from time to time.
4. All directors/officers/designated employees of the company who intend to deal in the securities of the company (above a minimum threshold limit to be decided by the company) should pre-clear the transaction as per the pre-dealing procedure.
5. All directors/officers/designated employees shall hold their investments in securities for a minimum period of 30 days in order to be considered as being held for investment purposes. The holding period

shall also apply to subscription in the primary market. In case the sale of securities is necessitated by personal emergency, the holding period may be waived by the compliance officer after recording in writing his/her reasons in this regard.

6. All directors/officers/designated employees of the listed company shall be required to forward the following details of their securities transactions, including the statement of dependent family members, to the compliance officer.
    - All holdings in securities by directors/officers/designated employees/partners at the time of joining the organization;
    - Periodic statement of any transactions in securities; and
    - Annual statement of all holdings in securities.
7. Any employee/officer/director who trades in securities or communicates any information for trading in securities in contravention of the code of conduct may be penalized and appropriate action may be taken by the company.

How the model code of conduct is given due importance by the companies can be assessed with the case of ITC, as presented in Box 11.1.

Box 11.1 ITC Code of Conduct for Prevention of Insider Trading

The Securities and Exchange Board of India (Prohibition of Insider Trading) Regulations, 1992, has been amended from time to time in terms of which the Company is required to frame a Code of Conduct for prevention of insider trading by employees of the Company, including the Directors, in relation to the securities of the Company.

In line with the said Regulations, a Code of Conduct was adopted by the Board of Directors of the Company at its meeting held on March 27, 2002 and thereafter amended from time to time with the approval of the Board. The Code, as revised with effect from 19 January 2009, is as follows:

1. Prohibition on buying / selling securities of the company by employees including directors

Employees, including Directors, when in possession of any unpublished price sensitive information, as defined in the Regulations, pertaining to the Company, shall not:

- Buy / sell securities of the Company, either on their own behalf or on behalf of any other person.
- Communicate, counsel or procure any unpublished price sensitive information to / from any person.

2. Restriction on buying / selling securities by designated employees and / or their dependants

2.1 Designated employees shall not enter into derivative transaction(s) at any time with respect to the securities of the Company.

2.2 Designated employees shall not buy / sell securities of the Company during Closure of the "trading window", or the period during which trading in the securities of the Company is prohibited.

The trading window shall be closed during the following periods:

a. From 1 April up to twenty-four hours after communication of the annual / fourth quarter financial results to the stock exchanges*.
b. From 1 July up to twenty-four hours after communication of the first quarter financial results to the stock exchanges.
c. From 1 October up to twenty-four hours after communication of the second quarter and half-yearly financial results to the stock exchanges.
d. From 1 January up to twenty-four hours after communication of the third quarter financial results to the stock exchanges.
e. From the date of circulation of the agenda for the meeting of the Board of Directors, in which any material, price sensitive and unpublished event, including the following, are proposed. The closure of the trading window for these events will be advised by the Compliance Officer appointed by the Board of Directors for the purpose of this Code:
    - Proposal in respect of interim / final dividend;
    - Proposal in respect of issue of securities by way of public/ rights/ bonus etc.;

(Continued)

- Proposal in respect of significant expansion plans or execution of new large projects;
- Proposal in respect of amalgamation, mergers, takeovers;
- Proposal in respect of disposal of whole or substantially the whole of the undertaking.

The trading window shall open 24 hours after communication of the decision of the Board of Directors in respect of the above events to the stock exchanges where the Company's securities are listed.

2.3 Designated employees shall require prior clearance, as specified in Clause 2.6, for purchase of securities of the Company, exceeding 50,000 shares in a calendar month (either in one transaction or in a series of transactions). Exercise of options under the ITC Employee Stock Option Schemes (ITC ESOS) shall not require any such clearance. Such prior clearance shall be required also for sale of securities of the Company in a calendar month (either in one transaction or in a series of transactions) exceeding 50 percent of the shares acquired under ITC ESOS and held or 50,000 shares, whichever is higher.

Dependants of designated employees shall require such prior clearance for purchase / sale of securities of the Company, exceeding 50,000 shares in a calendar month (either in one transaction or in a series of transactions).

2.4 Designated employees shall hold the shares allotted upon exercise of options under ITC ESOS for a minimum period of 30 days from the date of allotment thereof ("minimum holding period"). In case of personal emergency, prior clearance shall be required as specified in Clause 2.6, for relaxation of the provision relating to the minimum holding period.

2.5 Designated employees who buy or sell any number of shares of the Company shall not enter into an opposite transaction, i.e., sell or buy any number of shares within 6 months following a prior transaction. It is clarified that exercise of options under ITC ESOS will not be covered under such restriction. However on sale of shares allotted on exercise of options, any subsequent purchase will be subject to the aforesaid restriction on entering into opposite transaction.

In case of personal emergency, prior clearance shall be required as specified in Clause 2.6, for relaxation of the provision relating to sale of shares.

2.6 Prior clearance, referred to in Clauses 2.3 to 2.5, is required to be taken by Designated Employees from the Compliance Officer and a Director. In respect of the Compliance Officer, prior clearance is required to be taken from the Chairman of the Company.

2.7 Purchase / sale transactions for which prior clearance has been obtained by designated employees shall be executed within seven days of such clearance, failing which fresh sanction will be required to be taken, as specified in Clause 2.6.

3. Disclosures

Designated employees shall make the following disclosures of shares and other securities held in the Company by them and their Dependants, to the Compliance Officer:

3.1 Annual disclosure of number of shares and other securities held as on 31 March each year, including details of purchase / sale of shares and other securities during the financial year. This disclosure shall be made within 30 days from the close of each financial year.

3.2 Changes in shareholding of Directors and Company Secretary and their Dependants, when such change exceeds INR 5 lakh in value or 25,000 shares or 1 percent of the total shares of the Company, or such other limit as may be prescribed under the Regulations. This disclosure shall be made within 2 working days of such change to the Company and to the Stock Exchanges where the Company's securities are listed.

Changes in shareholding of designated employees (other than Directors or Company Secretary), when such change exceeds 50,000 shares.

This disclosure shall be made to the Company within 4 working days of such change.

3.3 Disclosure shall be required to be made to the Company by persons upon becoming Directors or Company Secretary within 2 working days in respect of:

- their shareholding in the Company and that of their Dependants.
- their own and their Dependants' position in derivatives with respect to the securities of the Company.

Disclosure shall also be required to be made to the Company by persons, upon becoming Designated Employees (other than Directors or Company Secretary), of the number of shares and other securities held in the Company, within 4 working days of becoming Designated Employees.

(Continued)

4. Penalties for contravention
Violation of this Code will invite severe disciplinary action. Such disciplinary action will be irrespective of action that may be taken by SEBI under the Regulations.

5. General
Employees are advised to peruse the Regulations carefully and acquaint themselves with all the provisions contained therein. Clarification / assistance as necessary may be sought from the Compliance Officer.

Source: http://www.itcportal.com/careers_with_itc/code-intrade.html

Model code of conduct for prevention of insider trading for other entities

The following are the main points of the model code of conduct for entities other than listed companies, as set by SEBI.

1. The compliance officer who is appointed by the organization/firm shall be responsible for setting forth policies, procedures, monitoring adherence to the rules for the preservation of price-sensitive information, pre-clearing of designated employees' and their dependents' trades (directly or through respective department heads as decided by the organization/firm), monitoring of trades and the implementation of the code of conduct under the overall supervision of the partners/proprietors.
2. Employees/directors/partners shall maintain the confidentiality of all price-sensitive information. Employees/directors/partners shall not pass on such information to any person directly or indirectly by way of making a recommendation for the purchase or sale of securities. Price-sensitive information is to be handled on a "need-to-know" basis. That is, the price-sensitive information should be disclosed only to those within the organization/firm who need the information to discharge their duty and whose possession of such information will not give rise to a conflict of interest or appearance of misuse of the information.
3. To prevent the misuse of confidential information, the organization/firm shall adopt a "Chinese Wall" policy that separates those areas of the organization/firm which routinely have access to confidential information, considered "inside areas", from those areas which deal with sales/marketing/investment advice or other departments providing support services, considered "public areas". The employees in the inside area shall not communicate any price-sensitive information to anyone in the public area. The employees in the inside area may be physically segregated from the employees in the public area. In exceptional circumstances, employees from the public areas may be brought "over the wall" and given confidential information on the basis of "need-to-know" criteria under intimation of the compliance officer.
4. Employees/directors/partners shall not use price-sensitive information to buy or sell securities of any sort, whether for their own account, their relative's account or the organization/firm's account or a client's account.
5. All directors/officers/designated employees of the company who intend to deal in the securities of the company (above a minimum threshold limit to be decided by the company) should pre-clear the transaction as per the pre-dealing procedure.
6. In order to monitor Chinese wall procedures and trading in client securities based on inside information, the organization/firm shall restrict trading in certain securities and designate such a list as the restricted/grey list. A security of a listed company shall be put on the restricted/grey list if the organization/firm is handling any assignment for the listed company or preparing an appraisal report or handling a credit rating assignment and is privy to price-sensitive information. Any security which is being purchased or sold or is being considered for purchase or sale by the organization/firm on behalf of its clients or schemes of mutual funds, etc shall be put on the restricted/grey list. As the restricted list itself is highly confidential information, it shall not be communicated directly or indirectly to anyone outside the organization/firm.
7. All directors/officers/designated employees/partners shall hold their investments in securities for a minimum period of 30 days in order to be considered as being held for investment purposes. The holding period shall also apply to subscription in the primary market. In case the sale of securities is necessitated by personal emergency, the holding period may be waived by the compliance officer after recording in writing his/her reasons in this regard. Analysts, if any, employed with the organization/

firm while preparing research reports of a client company shall disclose their shareholdings/interest in such a company to the compliance officer.

8. All directors/designated employees/partners of the organization/firm shall be required to forward the following details of their securities transactions, including the statement of dependent family members, to the compliance officer.
   - All holdings in securities by directors/officers/designated employees/partners at the time of joining the organization;
   - Periodic statement of any transactions in securities; and
   - Annual statement of all holdings in securities.
9. Any employee/officer/director/partner who trades in securities or communicates any information for trading in securities in contravention of the code of conduct may be penalized and appropriate action may be taken by the company.

Code of corporate disclosure practices for prevention of insider trading

To ensure timely and adequate disclosure of price-sensitive information, the following SEBI norms shall be followed by listed companies.

1. Price-sensitive information shall be given by listed companies to stock exchanges and disseminated on a continuous and immediate basis. Listed companies may also consider ways of supplementing the information released to stock exchanges by improving investor access to their public announcements. A senior official, designated as compliance officer by the company, shall be responsible for ensuring that the company complies with continuous disclosure requirements. Disclosure of shareholdings/ownership by major shareholders and disclosure of changes in ownership and the listing agreement shall be made in a timely and adequate manner.
2. Listed companies should follow the guidelines given below while dealing with analysts and institutional investors.
   - Listed companies shall provide only public information to the analyst/research persons/large investors like institutions. Alternatively, the information given to the analyst should be simultaneously made public at the earliest.
   - In order to avoid misquoting or misrepresentation, it is desirable that at least two company representatives be present at meetings with analysts, brokers or institutional investors, and the discussion should preferably be recorded.
   - A listed company should be careful when dealing with analysts' questions that raise issues outside the intended scope of discussion. Unanticipated questions may be taken on notice and a considered response given later. If the answer includes price-sensitive information, a public announcement should be made before responding.
   - When a company organizes meetings with analysts, the company shall make a press release or post relevant information on its website after every such meet. The company may also consider live webcasting of analyst meets.
3. Disclosure/dissemination of information may be done through various media so as to achieve maximum reach and quick dissemination.
4. The disclosures made to stock exchanges may be disseminated by the exchanges to investors in a quick and efficient manner through the stock exchange network as well as through stock exchange websites.

11.4 Recent Cases of Insider Trading

The most well-known of all the cases of insider trading at the global level is the Galleon Hedge Fund case. Founded in January 1997, the Galleon Group manages a series of funds that specialize in the technology and healthcare industries. The Galleon is among the 10 largest hedge funds in the world, and it managed USD 7 billion at its peak in 2008. Galleon's USD 1.2-billion diversified fund has climbed 21.5 per cent a year, on average, since 1992 compared with 7.6 per cent for the Standard & Poor's 500 Index of the largest U.S. companies. The founder of the Galleon Group, Raj Rajaratnam, is the 559th richest person in the world with a net worth of USD 1.3 billion, as per *Forbes* magazine. However, he has been charged along with some others in a case related to the USD 20-million hedge fund insider trading scam, the largest insider trading case in the history of the United States. About 20 people, including four Indians, were charged. Rajaratnam was arrested on October 16, 2009, at his home in Manhattan's Sutton Place and charged with using inside information to trade shares including those of Google Inc, Polycom Inc, Hilton Hotels Corp and Advanced Micro Devices Inc, according to complaints. A complaint was filed before a U.S. court asking the court to pass orders to disgorge the alleged gains earned by way of insider trading, to restrain the accused from acting as officers or directors of any issuer of securities and to pay civil monetary penalties under U.S. securities laws. Rajaratnam is alleged to have made more than USD 20 million by using inside information from tipsters at companies ranging from chip-maker Intel to rating agency Moody's and consultancy firm McKinsey.

To cite some Indian cases, Rajiv Gandhi, the former company secretary and CFO of Wockhardt, and his immediate family members were alleged to have traded in the company's shares on the basis of unpublished financial results of the company. SEBI imposed a monetary penalty of INR 500,000 on Gandhi in 2006. The alleged party moved the Securities Appellate Tribunal (SAT) but the latter upheld the order passed by SEBI.

Another interesting case is that of ABS Industries. The promoter and MD, Rakesh Agrawal, was charged in 2001 with insider trading for allegedly purchasing his own company's shares from the market prior to a takeover deal between ABS and Bayer of Germany. SEBI directed Agrawal to deposit INR 3.4 million to compensate ABS' investors, besides initiating adjudication proceedings. Agrawal challenged the SEBI order before the SAT, which partially turned down the SEBI ruling of imposing the penalty on Agrawal and declined to issue any order related to adjudication. SEBI later contested the SAT order in the Supreme Court, which settled the case through a consent order, with Agrawal paying a monetary penalty.

In September 1996, even as Agrawal was negotiating with Bayer for a possible equity tie-up, he asked his brother-in-law, I.P. Kedia, to buy ABS shares from the market on his behalf. Agrawal's investment companies financed the purchases. The information on the strategic alliance was first given out to shareholders through a notice on the Bombay Stock Exchange on October 1, 1996.

In his affidavit filed before the SAT, Agrawal said that the acquisitions were made with the sole intention of helping Bayer with the takeover and not for making a profit for himself. A tie-up with Bayer was absolutely essential for ABS's survival. Since others were eyeing a relationship with the German company, quick action was also necessary. Further, he contended that the agreement reached with Bayer clearly stipulated that it would be binding only if Bayer acquired 51 per cent. This was reflected both in the shareholders' agreement and the share subscription agreement. There was ample reason to believe that if Bayer did not eventually have 51 per cent, the ABS had no agreement. This situation would have been extremely damaging for the future of the company. The structure approved by the boards indicated 51 per cent equity holding by Bayer and 26 per cent by ABS. Any sale of shares by Agrawal or his companies would have brought ABS's equity holding below 26 per cent, a situation Agrawal wanted to avoid particularly in the context of the agreement that he was to continue in the position of managing director or identical management capacity. Agrawal wanted to get as many shares for completing 51 per cent for Bayer for the success of the arrangement.

Accepting Agrawal's contention that he was acting in the interest of the company, the SAT's presiding officer, C. Achuthan, said he could not be considered to have violated Regulation 3(i) that says "no insider shall either on his own behalf or on behalf of any other person deal in securities of a company listed on any stock exchange on the basis of any unpublished price-sensitive information". The presiding officer further said that any gain Agrawal made by buying the shares from the market and tendering them in Bayer's open offer was incidental to the main objective of enhancing the interest of ABS. It is difficult to accept that the motive or intention of the person indulging in insider trading is irrelevant. Even though the regulations do not make a specific mention, if read with the objective of prohibiting insider trading, it is clear that the motive is built in and insider trading without establishing the motivating factor is not punishable, the tribunal observed. Delivering his last judgment, Achuthan, said "if it is established that the person who has indulged in insider trading has no intention of gaining any unfair advantage, the charge of insider trading warranting penalty cannot be sustained against him". Thus, the tribunal partially overturned the SEBI ruling imposing a penalty on Agrawal.

Another recent case is that of Reliance Industries Limited. On July 9, 2008, Amar Singh, then the general secretary of the Samajwadi Party, wrote to SEBI alleging insider trading in the shares of Reliance Petroleum Ltd (RPL). In his letter addressed to C.B. Bhave, the chairman of SEBI, Singh alleged that firms connected with Reliance Industries Ltd (RIL), which holds 70 per cent in RPL, had engaged in insider trading with prior knowledge of RIL's plan to sell 4.01 per cent in its subsidiary RPL in November 2007. It was alleged that firms related to RIL had made a profit of INR 10 billion from insider trading by entering into futures contracts in the first week of November 2007. The "RIL-connected entities" sold short 10.58 million shares in the futures and options market and made a profit of INR 4.01 billion in the first week of November 2007, the letter alleged. Because of these sales, the price of RPL shares quickly fell from a high of INR 295 to around INR 210. After the futures contracts were entered into, RIL sold RPL shares in the cash market. In an announcement to the BSE on November 26, 2007, RPL mentioned that RIL had sold 180 million shares representing 4.01 per cent of its share capital for INR 40.23 billion. The sale was made in two different periods. The first sale representing 2.54 per cent in RPL was undertaken between November 6–14, 2007, and the second sale of 1.47 per cent between November 15–23, 2007. The details (of the share sales) were not available in the block or bulk trade details of the BSE and NSE, nor were they put on the stock exchange notice board till November 24, 2007. This selling ensured that the price of RPL shares remained low and allowed an exit to the short-selling entities at a huge profit.

On its part, SEBI in April 2009 issued a show-cause notice to RIL and its associate entities following a probe into the insider trading charges. Again in November 2009, SEBI served an amended show-cause notice to RIL. RPL has since merged with RIL. In the show-cause notice, SEBI mentioned that it had noticed that between November 1–5, 2007, 12 entities acting on behalf of RIL had created short positions of around INR 76.5 million in RPL shares at INR 290 per share. This rose to nearly INR 100 million on November 6, 2007, accounting for 94 per cent of the total permissible open interest in RPL November futures. The 12 entities then heavily sold the RPL shares in the cash market, which depressed the futures prices and allowed the 12 entities to make a profit.

SEBI made the regulations more stringent to curb the misuse of price-sensitive information, especially by those working in senior positions in companies. The definition of an insider has been broadened to include any person who is and was connected with a company and is the recipient of price-sensitive information. SEBI norms also prohibit trades by certain categories of insiders for a period of six months. There is also an absolute prohibition on insiders from taking positions in derivative markets as far as the shares of the company are concerned at any time. In the case of subscription to initial public offerings, a designated insider will have to hold his investments for a minimum period of one month. In spite of such stringent measures, insider trading continues unabated. Since 1992–93, SEBI has undertaken more than 1,200 cases for investigation and called for punishment for some of them. The major hurdle is that it is very difficult to prove insider trading because of the evidentiary requirements in such cases.

Summary

1. The securities whose current market price is less than their intrinsic value are known as underpriced or undervalued securities, and the securities whose current market price is more than their intrinsic value are known as overpriced or overvalued securities.
2. When the current market price of a security equals the intrinsic value of the security, the price of the security is at equilibrium. Markets become efficient when the price of a security is at equilibrium.
3. As the markets become more developed and efficient, it is extremely difficult to make abnormal profits by buying and selling the securities. Markets differ in the degree of efficiency and offer opportunities to make even supernormal profits.
4. The disparities in the market prices and intrinsic values are noted by alert analysts and astute investors who will seek to take advantage of their discoveries.
5. Insider trading becomes unlawful when the insider, who is supposed to maintain the confidentiality of certain information, uses this price-sensitive information to his or her personal advantage (making profits or avoiding losses on securities trading) to the detriment of other investors who buy or sell their securities without the advantage of such information.
6. At the international level, following the stock market crash of 1929, the U.S. government enacted the Securities Act, 1933, and the Securities Exchange Act, 1934, which address insider trading directly.
7. SEBI has issued certain guidelines as disclosure norms that are aimed at controlling insider trading. In the recent past, SEBI has tightened insider trading norms. The stricter regulations are aimed at curbing the misuse of price-sensitive information.
8. According to SEBI, an insider is a person who is or was connected with a company or is deemed to have been connected with a company, and who is reasonably expected to have access to unpublished price-sensitive information in respect of the securities of a company, or

who has received or has had access to such unpublished price-sensitive information.

9. SEBI prescribes that no insider shall (a) either on his own behalf or on behalf of any other person deal in securities of a company listed on any stock exchange when in possession of any unpublished price-sensitive information, or (b) communicate, counsel or procure directly or indirectly any unpublished price-sensitive information to any person who, while in possession of such unpublished price-sensitive information, shall not deal in securities.

10. According to SEBI, employees/directors shall maintain the confidentiality of all price-sensitive information. Employees/directors shall not pass on such information to any person directly or indirectly by way of making a recommendation for the purchase or sale of securities.

11. SEBI regulations state that price-sensitive information shall be given by listed companies to stock exchanges and disseminated on a continuous and immediate basis. Listed companies may also consider ways of supplementing information released to stock exchanges by improving investor access to their public announcements.

12. SEBI made the regulations more stringent to curb the misuse of price-sensitive information, especially by those working in senior positions in the companies. The definition of an insider has been broadened to include any person who is and was connected with a company and is the recipient of price-sensitive information.

13. In spite of many stringent measures initiated by SEBI, insider trading continues unabated. The major hurdle is that it is very difficult to prove insider trading because of the evidentiary requirements in such cases.

Questions

1. What is the relationship between intrinsic value of a security and its market price?
2. What are the characteristics of an efficient market? What advantages can investors derive from efficient markets?
3. What is insider trading? Critically analyse some cases of insider trading.
4. Discuss the ill effects of insider trading.
5. What are the positive features of insider trading?
6. Examine the salient features of SEBI regulations with regard to insider trading.
7. What are the major problems of controlling insider trading?

Case Study

On March 25, 1996, the Unit Trust of India sold 800,000 shares of Brooke Bond Lipton India Limited (BBLIL) to Hindustan Lever Limited (HLL) at INR 350 per share when the ruling market price of BBLIL shares was INR 318. On April 19, 1996, HLL and BBLIL informed the stock exchanges of the proposal to merge. On April 22, 1996, the boards of the two companies approved the merger proposal in the ratio of 9 HLL shares for every 20 BBLIL shares. The market price of a BBLIL share was INR 390 on that day. Subsequently, BBLIL's share price increased to INR 410 and stabilized at INR 368. When there were complaints that HLL had indulged in insider trading, SEBI ordered an investigation into the case.

SEBI investigated the case for about two years. According to it, the objective in purchasing the shares of BBLIL was not to increase the stake of HLL in BBLIL but to help Unilever acquire a 51 per cent beneficial interest in BBLIL. Before the purchase of shares from UTI by HLL, Unilever had 50.74 per cent beneficial shareholding in BBLIL. Thus, HLL needed to buy 1.275 million shares of BBLIL to lift Unilever's shareholding in post-merger HLL to 51 per cent. Both BBLIL and HLL were subsidiaries of Unilever Plc, UK. Because HLL could purchase 800,000 shares of BBLIL from UTI, the parent company, Unilever, avoided bringing in foreign exchange equivalent to INR 500 million, thus cheating the country of that amount.

In the investigation, SEBI found that HLL had full knowledge of unpublished price-sensitive information at the time of purchase of shares, while UTI did not have any information of the impending merger and thus parted with the shares. Had UTI known of the information available with HLL before the sale of shares, it would have made at least INR 200 million more. Even otherwise, had the shares been sold after the prices stabilized, UTI would have got at least another INR 30 million. Thus, the deal deprived UTI of the increase in market price resulting from the merger. By this logic, SEBI on March 11, 1998, directed HLL to pay INR 30 million to UTI for purchasing 800,000 shares of BBLIL. SEBI also ordered that prosecution be launched against the company, its chairman Keki Dadiseth, his predecessor S.M. Datta and directors R. Gopalakrishnan, A. Lahiri and M.K. Sharma. But HLL contended that the information available with the company at the time of purchase did not constitute unpublished price-sensitive information, which is a prerequisite for indulging in the offence of insider trading.

HLL appealed against SEBI's order to the appellate authority in the finance ministry, Government of India, on April 2, 1998. On July 14, 1998, the appellate authority issued a 31-page judgment in which it stated that the SEBI order to award compensation, apart from suffering from procedural deficiencies, lacked in jurisdiction. According to the appellate authority, the order of prosecution should be based on conclusive determination of all aspects of insider trading and on specific justification in terms of the gravity of the offence. There was persuasive evidence pointing towards market knowledge and widespread speculation about the possibility of the merger before the purchase of shares in question by HLL from UTI, which weakens the crucial aspect of the charge of insider trading that the information involved should not be generally known. Thus, the appellate authority stated that SEBI had no power in the HLL case to take action under provisions of Section 11B of the SEBI Act and should have gone in for adjudication under Section 15G of the Act. The authority agreed that HLL did purchase shares before the merger was announced. It was an insider unto itself and information about the merger was price-sensitive. But corroborating the argument of HLL that the market knew about the impending merger of the two companies and that a newspaper had carried a report to that effect—which would constitute "published knowledge"—the appellate authority said that the information about the merger was not unpublished. The authority observed that the market price of the shares of BBLIL was not likely to have been impacted since the merger was generally known and therefore discounted. Although the appellate authority upheld the SEBI order on a number of grounds, it chose to differ on the crucial question of insider trading.

Questions

1. Analyse the case and bring out the facts that point to insider trading.
2. Did SEBI overreact? If so, how?
3. How would you defend the decision of the appellate authority?

Chapter 12

Credit Rating Services

LEARNING OBJECTIVES

After reading this chapter, you will be able to:

- Present a historical perspective of credit rating.
- Define the concept of credit rating.
- Explain the process of credit rating.
- Highlight the advantages and limitations of credit rating.
- Present the profile of credit rating agencies in India.
- Bring out the major features of SEBI regulations with regard to credit rating.
- Present some live cases in which credit rating is reviewed.

12.1 Introduction

Credit rating provides investors with information that helps them in making investment decisions. The rating indicates whether the issuer of securities will be able to meet their obligations with respect to those securities, that is, payment of interest and principal as per the terms and conditions stated in the certificates of the securities. **Credit rating** involves analysis and assessment of companies and governments that issue the financial securities. The rating agencies evaluate the issuer and the securities and assign a rating or grade according to the degree of relative creditworthiness of the issuer. The rating of debt securities ranges from "AAA" to "D" with some variation in notation by each agency.

***Credit rating** involves analysis and assessment of companies and countries that issue financial securities.*

Financial globalization has opened up several investment opportunities to the investors, but at the same time it presents challenges in choosing the right kind of investments. In the globalized financial markets, credit rating agencies play an important role in determining capital flows across the countries.

A credit rating agency, after assessing the issuer of securities or borrower of funds, indicates the likelihood of an issuer of securities making timely payments on a financial obligation. The credit rating agency collects data or information from a variety of sources regarding the issuer of securities, the market in which the issuer operates, the overall economy etc., and provides guidance to the investors in matters of credit risk associated with these securities so that the investors can take informed decisions. Thus, *credit rating agencies* are specialized institutions that analyse and evaluate the creditworthiness of an organization, which could be a government, which issues securities or borrows funds. A credit rating agency may assess an issuer of securities in two ways—assessment of the likelihood that the issuer will default on his financial obligations in general, or default on a particular security. The credit rating agency assigns a grade/rating to a capital issue or an organization and enables the investors and others concerned to identify the risk levels of that financial instrument or organization. The securities with higher credit rating command lower interest rate than the securities with lower credit rating. The securities with lower credit rating carry higher interest rate, embodying larger risk premium. Although investors in general are risk-averse, they do take risk provided there is commensurate premium for the risk taken. As a credit rating is an opinion on the relative degree of risk, an investor can use the credit rating to compare various investment options that are available and make a suitable investment decision.

***Information asymmetry** between investors and the issuer of securities is the driving force behind credit rating.*

The necessity of credit rating agencies arises because of **information asymmetry** between the issuer of securities (borrowers of funds) and the investors (lenders of funds) regarding the creditworthiness of the borrower. Information asymmetry arises because of non-availability or partial availability of information to the investors about the securities or the issuer of securities. Information asymmetry may also arise when the investors are not able to make sense of the vast amount of information available regarding an issuer or borrower, markets, and the economy. Credit rating helps bridge the information gap that may exist between the lenders and borrowers of funds. *Creditworthiness* may be understood as the ability and willingness of the borrower to pay the interest and repay the principal amount as per the terms and conditions of the loan.

In essence, credit rating agencies give investors and lenders a better understanding of the risks they face when lending to a particular borrower or when purchasing an issuer's securities. In fact, credit rating is the assessment of the relative degree of risk associated with the payment of interest and repayment of the principal associated with a loan or a debt security. Without credit rating, the investors may not be fully aware of the relative risk of various securities issued by corporate bodies or governments. This lack of information may result in investors demanding high or low risk premium or refusing to participate in the borrowing programme. Credit rating may enable the investors to demand the right amount of risk premium on their investment. This will also result in lower cost of capital for issuers of such securities.

12.1.2 A Historical Perspective of Credit Rating

Before the nineteenth century, business was mostly local and business transactions, particularly borrowing and lending, took place between people who knew each other. As economies opened up around the world, the scale and geographical scope of business transactions expanded. Resources, including human resources, became more mobile. Therefore, the need for information on suppliers, lenders, borrowers and customers increased. Earlier, the information given by a known person (for example, a banker or a lawyer) used to be adequate for taking decisions. Such informal sources of information sufficed for that time. But with the expansion of the scale and scope of business across countries, it was necessary to have a formal and professional source of information. In the 1800s, some merchants compiled information on the creditworthiness of their own customers and shared such information with others on commercial terms. In the mid-1800s, the U.S. railroad industry began to expand across the American continent and into underdeveloped territories. The expansion of railroads and other corporations necessitated the mobilization of funds on a large scale. As the demand for funds was beyond the capacity of the banks, the railroads and other corporations began raising capital by issuing bonds. The corporate bond market expanded as the investing public evinced increasing interest in the corporate bonds. At the same time, the need for better information about the debtors and debt securities increased. In response to this, Henry Varnum Poor published a manual called the *History of Railroads and Canals in the United States* in 1868. The manual contained operating and financial statistics for the major railroad companies and became an independent source of information on major corporate borrowers. It was considered to be a precursor of modern stock reporting and analysis. John Moody and Company first published *Moody's Manual* in 1900. It was a national publication that contained basic statistics and general information about stocks and bonds of financial institutions, government agencies, manufacturing, mining, utilities and food companies. Standard Statistics was formed in 1906, which published corporate bond, sovereign debt and municipal bond ratings. In 1909, Moody published *Moody's Analyses of Railroad Investments,* which contained analytical information on different kinds of industrial securities.

Moody's Investors' Service, established in 1914, is the first rating agency in the world.

In the later part of the nineteenth century, large-scale railroad development under the auspices of private companies in the United States had created a rapidly growing bond market. The sovereign bond market was also expanding. So investors needed bond ratings to choose from the great variety of bond issues. It was at this time that Moody initiated agency bond ratings in the United States in 1914 by setting up Moody's Investors' Service—the first rating agency in the world. Although the bond ratings initiated by Moody was an innovation of the twentieth century, it came late in the corporate history. Investors had been buying bonds for centuries, particularly in the Netherlands, England and the United States, on the basis of information provided by the financial press, credit reporting agencies and investment banks. Moody's Investors' Service started as a one–man crusade to provide knowledge to the ordinary investing public and later developed into a formidable global rating agency. The rating given by Moody could make or mar the prospects of even the mightiest of multinational corporations.

John Knowles Fitch founded Fitch Publishing Company in 1913, which published financial statistics in *The Fitch Stock and Bond Manual* and *The Fitch Bond Book* in 1924. For the first time, Fitch Publishing Company introduced the "AAA" to "D" rating scale. Standard Statistics merged with Poor's Publishing in 1941 to form Standard and Poor's Corporation, which was acquired by McGraw-Hill Companies Inc. in 1966. It may be noted that the Wall Street collapse in 1929, in which a very large number of U.S. investors lost their investments, and the Great Depression of the 1930s gave an added fillip to credit rating services.

All these rating agencies did not operate under the "issuer-pay" model. In other words, the ratings given by the rating agencies were purchased by subscribers and there was no charge on issuers of securities. But it was realized in the 1970s that the issuers of securities would get substantial benefits from the rating of capital issues. The cost of capital would decrease with rated capital issues, leading to an increase in the firm's value. Therefore, the rating agencies began the practice of charging issuers, usually a few basis points of the amount of the issue rated.

From the 1970s, the credit rating business expanded very rapidly because many companies increasingly sought access to the financial markets, especially bond markets. In the 1990s, the bond market surpassed bank lending as the dominant source of private capital. The importance of credit rating has increased tremendously with financial globalization. Regulatory changes have been brought about with regard to banks' capital requirements by the Basel Committee on Banking Supervision, giving a boost to the role of credit rating agencies. Basel II incorporates credit ratings into the rules for setting weights for credit risk. Thus, under Basel II, credit ratings can be used to assign risk weights determining minimum capital charges for different categories of borrowers.

The importance of credit rating has increased phenomenally following financial globalization.

In the United States, the Securities and Exchange Commission (SEC) permits the use of credit ratings given by certain credit rating agencies for regulatory purposes. The credit rating agencies whose ratings are permitted to be used for regulatory purposes are referred to as the Nationally Recognized Statistical Rating Organizations (NRSRO). The term NRSRO was first used in 1975 when the SEC promulgated rules regarding bank and broker-dealer net capital requirements. Some examples of NRSROs are Moody's Investors' Service Inc., Standard and Poor's Inc., Fitch Inc., Dominion Bond Rating Service Limited (DBRS) and A.M. Best Company Inc.

12.1.3 Credit Rating: The Indian Perspective

The Indian economy, particularly the financial market, entered a new era in the 1980s. Economic liberalization gave rise to several opportunities for investment. To cash in on the opportunities, entrepreneurs have taken up several projects involving a huge amount of funds. In other words, Companies have undertaken fund-raising programmes on a large scale. At the same time, business risks have increased with the liberalization of the economy. The success of industrial projects has become a gamble. As the industrial environment has become highly competitive and demanding, the companies has become jittery about their profitability. The earlier assurance of a protected environment has ceased to exist. It may be noted that one of the economic problems faced by a developing country such as India is the difficulty in mobilizing funds to meet the increasing needs of the industry. The levels of income of the people are not high enough to generate adequate savings. The financial markets are not developed enough to mobilize even the meagre savings generated and channelize them into capital formation. The industrial policy of the government, however, has encouraged rapid industrialization, which has resulted in a phenomenal increase in the number of investors and the amount of funds mobilized. The number of companies tapping the capital market directly has also increased. But the investors have realized that the company's name and size are no longer a sufficient guarantee of timely payment of interest and the principal amount. It is in this context that policymakers thought of introducing the credit rating system in India. Accordingly, the Industrial Credit and Investment Corporation of India Ltd (ICICI) and the Unit Trust of India (UTI) promoted the first rating agency, called the Credit Rating Information Services of India Ltd (CRISIL), in 1988. Although many developed nations such as the United States, the United Kingdom, France, Japan, Canada and Australia already had credit rating agencies by then, India was the first country in the developing world to set up a credit rating agency. With the integration of financial markets all over the world, credit ratings have become more important. As the financial markets have become highly competitive, the credit rating symbol has replaced the company's size and name. It is also said that the advent of the credit rating system reflects the capital market attaining a certain level of sophistication.

__Credit rating__ is the opinion of a rating agency on the ability and willingness of an issuer of a particular financial instrument or borrower of funds to honour on time the financial obligations attached to that financial instrument or borrowing.

12.1.4 The Concept of Credit Rating

Credit rating represents the current opinion of a rating agency on the ability and willingness of an issuer of a particular financial instrument or borrower of funds to honour on schedule the financial obligations attached to that financial instrument or borrowing. The opinion is formed on the basis of a thorough analysis and assessment of the present and prospective factors that may affect credit risk. The credit rating agency employs both qualitative and quantitative criteria for assessing the creditworthiness of the issuer and assigns a rating symbol. The rating symbol indicates in a summarized manner the current opinion of the rating agency about the relative safety of timely payment of interest/dividend and principal on a debenture, structured obligation, preference share, fixed deposit or a short-term instrument. The term "structured obligation" refers to securities in which the servicing of debt and related obligations is backed by some sort of financial assets. The main thrust of credit rating of a structured obligation is to ensure that the cash flows from the assets and the envisaged structure are capable of meeting the committed payments to the investors.

A credit rating of a particular capital issue relates to the assessment of that particular financial instrument and is not a rating for the issuer (company) as a whole in as much as it takes into account the specific terms of the capital issue. For example, an issuer may issue different types of securities and these securities may be assigned different ratings/grades depending on the risk profile of each security. Thus, the rating depends on the credit quality or risk profile of the securities and not the credit quality of the issuer alone. Further, the rating is neither a recommendation to invest or not to invest, to sell or not to sell a particular security, nor does it address the suitability of an investment for a particular investor. Rating also does not reflect the value of a given security. In other words, the rating process does not take into account many aspects that may influence an investment decision. For example, the possibilities for capital gains and liquidity in the secondary market are not considered in the rating process. The rating or grade assigned by a rating agency to a particular capital issue indicates the probability that the amount lent or invested will be returned with interest according to the terms and conditions agreed upon.

The scope of credit rating has widened to encompass the rating of companies engaged in the services sector.

12.1.5 The Scope of Credit Rating

Conventionally, credit rating is done for the following securities.

- Bonds
- Commercial paper
- Fixed deposits/certificates of deposit/inter-corporate deposits/term deposits
- Fully convertible debentures to be converted before 18 months of the issue
- Partly convertible debentures maturing before the 18th month of the issue
- Preference shares
- Structured obligation

However, of late, the scope of credit rating has increased tremendously. Credit rating is being undertaken for a variety of purposes. The rating of IPOs is a new phenomenon. In addition, credit rating agencies have expanded their business by undertaking the rating of real estate developers/projects, collective investment scheme rating, grading for healthcare institutions, corporate governance rating, claims paying ability rating, line of credit rating, rating of Indian states and rating of LPG/kerosene dealers/firms. Sovereign ratings (rating of countries), which enable governments to raise commercial loans or attract foreign investment, have also become common. Thus, credit rating is not just confined to rating capital issues but is applicable in a much broader sense.

Different credit rating agencies adopt different rating processes, depending on the nature of the financial instrument, the credit rating agency itself and the methodology used. Usually, both quantitative and qualitative factors are considered in the rating process.

12.2 The Process of Credit Rating

Different credit rating agencies adopt different rating processes depending on the nature of the instrument, the credit rating agency itself and the methodology used. Some credit rating agencies emphasize qualitative judgements in addition to quantitative models. But all credit rating agencies rely heavily on professional analysts to assess the degree of credit risk associated with a particular security or issuer.

The rating process begins at the request of a company. Rating agencies generally do not undertake unsolicited rating. On receipt of the request from the company, the credit rating agency constitutes different teams to carry out the assignment. The teams obtain the required data from the company and make suitable analyses in order to draw meaningful conclusions. The rating process may also include visits to factories and warehouses to get first-hand information about the company being rated. It may be noted that in certain situations, the credit rating agencies may conduct unsolicited ratings. Unsolicited ratings are ratings that the agencies may undertake without being formally engaged to do so by the issuer.

A rating agency generally assesses business risk as well as financial risk after taking into consideration several factors that could affect the creditworthiness of the issuer of securities. Various factors are analysed in order to determine the long-term fundamentals and probabilities of change in the fundamentals, which could affect the creditworthiness of the issuer. Besides quantitative factors, qualitative aspects like management capabilities and integrity play a very important role in determining the rating of a particular issue. The relative importance of qualitative and quantitative components of the analysis varies with the type of issuer. Thus, different credit rating agencies follow different criteria for assessing different kinds of capital issues or entities. However, the following are the broad and basic aspects that are covered in any evaluation process.

1. **Background and History:** The credit rating agency analyses the background and history that includes ownership, size, geographical spread, product spread and the organizational structure of the issuer of the securities. The history of the issuer could establish its expertise in certain products, and thus have a bearing on credit quality. Although, the history of the issuer is not a guide to its future performance, it certainly reveals why an organization performed the way it did, what problems it faced, the management's response to these problems and other such issues.
2. **Management:** The track record of the management, planning and control systems in the organization, depth of management talent, succession plans, management goals, philosophy and strategies, recruitment and training systems, attitude of the management towards risk, the management's tenacity and drive to overcome problems as they arise and shareholding pattern are factors seriously considered in the rating process. The quality of management is judged by the profile of operating executives, HR policies, organizational structure and the extent of delegation of authority among other factors.
3. **Business Analysis:** The rating process mainly focuses on business analysis under which the aspects covered are nature of the product, raw material, power and labour situation, nature and level of competition, key success factors, demand and supply position, structure of industry, cyclical/seasonal factors, government policies, market share, competitive advantages, selling and distribution arrangements, customer profiles, operating efficiency of the company (location advantages, cost structure, technological advantages) and legal position (terms of prospectus, trustees and their responsibilities).
4. **Financial Analysis:** Financial analysis starts with the assessment of the accounting quality in terms of the method of income recognition, inventory valuation, depreciation policies, off-balance sheet items and qualifications of auditors. Although accounting policies are mostly standardized, there are many areas where issuers have the freedom to adopt different policies. The sources of future earnings growth, profitability ratios, earnings in relation to fixed income charges, adequacy of cash flows in relation to debt and fixed and working capital needs, sustainability of cash flows, financial flexibility, the chances for the company to quickly raise funds in case of a crunch to meet debt servicing obligations, the ways to withhold the capital expenditure and disposal of investments are other aspects analysed in this regard.

For banks and finance companies, the assessment takes into consideration the following additional factors:

- Structure and regulatory framework of the financial system, trends in regulation/deregulation and their impact on the bank/financial institution.
- Relationship of the issuer with the government and RBI.
- Role and importance of the issuer (bank) in the economy, its position in the foreign markets.
- Capital adequacy (net worth of the organization, its adequacy in relation to the volume of business and the risk profile of the assets). The most important indicator in analysing the capital structure is the capital adequacy ratio. Based on capital requirement under Basel, the RBI has prescribed certain norms for both banks and finance companies with a schedule to attain the targeted ratio.
- Quality of the company's credit-risk management, systems for monitoring credit, sector risk, exposure to individual borrowers, management of NPAs, etc. The asset quality of investments is judged by analysing the type of investments, the internal system for management of investments, policies in respect of holding/divestment and policy for charging depreciation in the value of investments.

- Capital structure, term matching of assets and liabilities, policy on liquid assets in relation to financing commitments and maturing deposits. The maturity match between the sources and deployment of funds also indicates the liquidity of a bank. The liquidity is also understood with reference to quantity and quality of liquid assets, past trends in maintenance of SLR and CRR, unutilized refinance limits and the bank's standing in the financial market to raise resources quickly.
- Profits, spreads on fund deployment, revenues on non-fund based services and accretion to reserves. In analysing profitability, it is necessary to analyse the asset segment-wise spreads and their volatility. In analysing the total income, any extraordinary income is scrutinized to judge the probability of its recurrence. The operating expenses are considered not only in financial terms but also in terms of the basic operating efficiency indicators such as manpower utilization.
- Exposure to interest rate changes, tax law changes and hedge against interest rate.

12.3 Communicating the Rating

The rating assigned to a particular issue is communicated to the client along with a detailed rationale. The rating agencies may discuss with the management of a company any factors that the latter feels have not been considered. The rating agency may share with the company management the broad reasons for the rating it has assigned. Only ratings accepted by the clients are published and then monitored on a continuous basis over the life of the instrument. The client has the option of not accepting the final rating, in which case the rating arrived at by the rating agency will neither be published nor monitored. Although the rating process is transparent, any information provided by the company to the rating agency is kept confidential.

Once a rating is assigned and published, the rating agency keeps the rating under surveillance until the security is fully repaid. The surveillance process may result in rating changes from time to time. In other words, each rating is reviewed periodically. The review may be triggered by a major development in the company or in the industry, which may have a significant bearing on the creditworthiness of the issuer. A rating agency assigns a particular rating to a security based on certain expectations and assumptions about the factors that impact the company issuing the security. These factors are either company-specific or related to the business environment. As these factors can change significantly over time, especially in the fast-changing global economic environment, causing the company's performance to deviate materially from expectations, the rating agency may change the rating at its absolute discretion without concurrence of the client. However, a client may also ask for a review of the rating assigned and furnish additional information for the purpose. During the review the rating may be retained, upgraded or downgraded based on the changed prospects of the issuer. A change in rating indicates a change in the risk associated with the instrument. Thus, every rating assigned by a credit rating agency is current at all times and reflects all the available information that may impact the credit quality of the rated security.

Although there is no ideal time period for revising ratings, a rating is generally reviewed once a year unless there are material changes in the industry which necessitate an earlier review. The investors even blame credit rating agencies for being late in announcing the revised grades. But rating becomes difficult if a particular company shows trends contrary to industry trends. The rated instruments or institutions identified for possible changes in rating due to change in certain factors are first put on credit watch, pending completion of the rating review.

12.4 Advantages and Limitations of Credit Rating

Investors, issuers of securities, suppliers, customers and government regulators are the major users of credit ratings.

Credit ratings are used by different groups of people and organizations. Investors, issuers of securities, suppliers, customers and government regulators are the major groups that use credit ratings. Companies use credit ratings in raising funds for their business needs. As credit rating helps investors in assessing the degree of risk involved in a borrowing programme, the issuer or borrower can raise funds with cheaper cost of capital. Credit ratings are useful to foreign institutional investors in diversifying their portfolios. The suppliers particularly use issuer credit rating to assess the general creditworthiness of the companies. The credit rating enables customers to form correct opinions about the credibility of companies and their products. Government regulators may also use credit rating in formulating their monetary policy and fiscal policy.

The specific advantages of credit rating are as follows:

- Credit rating provides investors with convenient and readily identifiable symbols to make finer distinctions of risk.
- Credit rating sets a different corporate culture. A company whose securities are rated by an independent agency will have a wider participation of investors. Without credit rating, investors may not have the skills to undertake an assessment of the creditworthiness of an issuer, resulting in reluctance of such investors to subscribe to the capital issues. With credit rating, investors are fully informed about the relative risks of various securities, enabling them to participate in the fund-raising programmes of the companies. This also increases the size of the investing population. Thus, credit rating leads to the deepening and widening of the capital market and helps companies access a wider base of investors and a wider variety of financial products.
- By attracting investors, credit rating helps companies channelize the idle savings of the public into productive use.
- Credit rating also signifies the emergence of a certain sophistication in the capital market by supplanting the importance of the name or reputation of a company with an abstract rating or grading.
- In the globalized financial market, the advice of brokers/underwriters cannot be a sufficient guide for investors in choosing the right kind of capital issues for investment. Credit rating can provide the investor with information that will help determine if he is getting adequate return for the risk he will take in investing in a particular capital issue.
- Credit rating shifts the primary responsibility of establishing corporate credit quality from the broker/underwriter to the rating agency, thereby avoiding potential conflict of interest between brokers/underwriters and investors.
- Investors can have a choice of instruments based on graded risks and related returns. That is, credit rating enables investors to take a calculated risk in their investment decisions. It may be noted that there are investors in each grade of risk.
- Companies will have the advantage of reduction in interest rates besides easy market accessibility for fund mobilization when their capital issues are rated. It is said that the capability of a company to raise funds from the market depends mainly on the credit rating it gets for its issues. Thus, credit rating helps corporate bodies to enter the financial market confidently and raise funds at relatively cheaper rates.
- As the cost of borrowing is inversely related to the ratings received, companies with high growth potential will have greater advantage with credit rating.
- As the investors become aware of the utility of credit rating, it may become an effective tool for marketing capital issues.
- Credit rating plays an important role in protection of investors' interests without putting the burden of that responsibility on SEBI and other agencies.
- A sizeable portion of savings is garnered by institutional investors such as pension funds and insurance funds. These investors compulsorily seek credit rating for making their investment decisions.
- Credit rating may also help in benchmarking companies with respect to each other. A higher credit rating may mean that the company has implemented the best practices.
- Once an organization is assessed and given a rating by an outside agency, it will be under continuous surveillance by that agency. Therefore, the management of the rated company weighs all its options objectively before taking any administrative decision.
- The eligibility of some securities for portfolios of certain institutional investors is determined based on credit rating.

There are certain bottlenecks in the effective use of the rating system. Some of them are as follows.

- The average investor in India is not able to understand the significance of rating because of lack of awareness.
- Sometimes, ratings may create confusion in the minds of investors when different credit rating agencies give different ratings for the same instrument.

- There is no standardized fee structure. Therefore, different marketing endeavours are being carried out by credit rating agencies for developing their business.
- Rating agencies assign the rating based on information obtained from the issuer and other reliable sources, which are deemed to be accurate. Any distortion in the data may lead to wrong grading of the security.
- Although credit rating agencies are supposed to maintain appropriate independence from the issuer of securities, this is generally does not happen in practice.
- Credit rating agencies fail to adjust the ratings promptly as the performance of the issuer deteriorates.

12.5 Credit Rating Agencies in India

Despite the fact that credit rating is a new phenomenon in India, there are credit rating agencies of international repute in India.

Credit rating agencies are firms that analyse and evaluate a debtor or a debt instrument and assign a rate or grade according to its degree of credit risk or creditworthiness. Presently, there are seven credit rating agencies in India. They are:

1. Credit Rating Information Services of India Limited (CRISIL)
2. Investment Information and Credit Rating Agency of India Limited (ICRA)
3. Credit Analysis and Research Limited (CARE)
4. Fitch India Limited
5. Onicra Credit Rating Agency of India Limited
6. Brickwork Ratings India Pvt limited
7. SME Rating Agency of India Limited

Understanding the history and evolution of rating agencies gives investors and the others concerned insight into the methodology used to assign ratings and the quality of ratings given by them. With this insight, investors can take informed decisions about the countries, industries and classes of securities in which they can invest. With this objective, a profile of each credit rating agency in India is presented in the following paragraphs. It may be noted that some credit rating agencies offer ancillary business services in addition to credit rating services. The other services include risk management and consulting services extended on request to firms to manage their credit and operational risk.

12.5.1 Credit Rating Information Services of India Limited (CRISIL)

CRISIL, the first Indian rating company, has established guidelines and standards for credit rating in India.

CRISIL, established in 1987, started the rating of companies in India in 1988. In 1989, it started a credit assessment service for banks and also launched CRISIL Rating Scan to announce new and current ratings and disseminate the CRISIL ratings rationale. CRISIL was the first credit rating agency to be established in India. As part of its expansion programme, CRISIL established the Information Services Group in 1990. In 1995, it forged a strategic alliance with Standard & Poor's Rating Group and tied up with International Information Vendors for dissemination of CRISIL ratings.

For the first time in 1993, CRISIL made a public offer of 2,000,000 equity shares of INR 10 each at a premium of INR 40 per share. In 2004, the name of the company was changed from Credit Rating Information Services of India Limited to CRISIL Limited. In 2005, Standard & Poor, a division of the McGraw-Hill Company, made an open offer to the shareholders of CRISIL to acquire up to 3,534,488 fully paid-up equity shares of CRISIL representing 55.57 per cent of the company's voting equity capital as on December 31, 2004, subject to a minimum acceptance level of 2,643,983 shares (41.57 per cent of CRISIL's paid-up equity capital). Thus, Standard & Poor has since acquired a majority shareholding in CRISIL.

The main businesses of CRISIL are ratings and risk assessment, research and advisory. CRISIL is a pioneer in credit rating and the only credit rating agency in the country to operate on the basis of sectoral specialization. CRISIL provides rating and risk assessment services to manufacturing companies, banks, non-banking financial companies, financial institutions, housing finance companies, municipal bodies and companies in the infrastructure sector. It rates long-term instruments such as debentures, bonds, preference shares, structured obligations, fixed deposits, commercial paper and short-term deposits. It makes credit assessments of various entities including state governments and subsidiaries and joint ventures of multinationals. It also assigns ratings of financial strength to insurance companies. CRISIL has developed several structured ratings for multinational corporations based on guarantees and letters of comfort from the parent companies as well as standby letter of credit arrangements from bankers.

Through credit rating, CRISIL has played a leading role in the development of the debt market in the country. The Rating Criteria and Product Development Centre—which is responsible for policy research, new product development and ratings' quality assurance—has developed new rating methodologies for debt instruments and innovative structures across sectors. CRISIL has partnered with Standard & Poor (the world's foremost provider of independent credit ratings, indices, risk evaluation, investment research, data and valuations) on several projects in the United States and east Asia. It has developed a methodology and framework for rating foreign structured obligations, real estate developers' projects, single risk collateralized bond obligations backed by rated bonds, sales tax receivables securitization and personal loan securitization, brokers and developers. CRISIL has also launched grading of healthcare institutions and IPOs. IPO grading analyses the fundamental strengths of IPO issues.

CRISIL has also introduced CRISIL Governance and Value Creation (GVC) ratings. Under this, CRISIL makes an assessment of management quality, an indicator of value creation potential, and also the value created for various stakeholders. In other words, CRISIL evaluates the benefits of practising good governance. It is a genuine 360-degree evaluation rather than analysis of one aspect alone. The key parameters that CRISIL considers while analysing the value delivered to various categories of stakeholders are as follows.

- Shareholders: Return on invested capital compared to the weighted average cost of capital, dividend track record and payout ratio.
- Debt holders: Debt protection measures and credit ratings.
- Customer: Market share, assessment of customer satisfaction.
- Employee: Absolute salary levels, adjusted growth in average annual salaries, stock option programmes, attrition rates and intangible factors like work environment and facilities provided by employer.
- Supplier: Credit terms, support provided and transparent dealings.
- Society: Social projects taken up by the company, care for the environment and taxes paid to government.

CRISIL is a leading provider of fund evaluation services and risk solutions for the mutual fund industry. The fund services provided by CRISIL play an important role in shaping investor confidence and facilitating the introduction of best practices in the mutual fund industry.

CRISIL Research is the largest independent, integrated research house providing accurate and reliable research, analysis and forecasts on the Indian economy, industries and companies to several clients across the world. The Centre for Economic Research of CRISIL is uniquely positioned to provide benchmarks and analyses for India's policy and business decision makers. CRISIL has acquired Irevna, a leading global equity research and analytics company. Irevna provides high-end customized equity research and analytics and knowledge process outsourcing to the world's leading financial institutions, investment banks, private equity firms and consulting companies. CRISIL Research has also launched the CRISIL Commodity Views on gold, wheat, pepper, tur and soya and the CRISIL Agriculture Risk Monitor.

The financial data analysis business of CRISIL is supported by Global Data Services of India Limited. India Index Services and Products Limited (a joint venture of CRISIL and NSE) is dedicated to providing indices, index products and services to investors in Indian equities. Its main indices, licensed with Standard & Poor, are the S&P CNX Nifty and S&P CNX 500.

The CRISIL Infrastructure Advisory combines the best global practices with analytical excellence and a deep understanding of the local environment to provide policy, regulatory and transaction-level advice to governments and leading organizations across sectors. It has developed a methodology for assessing infrastructure development and partnered with Nordpool Consultants for a mandate from National Thermal Power Corporation Limited to set up the first power trading exchange in India.

CRISIL has also acquired the UK's leading gas advisory and information company, Gas Strategies Group Limited. With this, CRISIL has a significant presence in the international gas and LNG markets. Gas Strategies of CRISIL is a gas project finance adviser to international banks, export credit agencies and multilateral financial institutions such as the World Bank. CRISIL Risk Solutions provides integrated risk management solutions and advice to banks and corporate organizations. It also uses cutting edge research and methodologies.

CRISIL has spearheaded the formation of the world's first regional credit rating agency, known as the Caribbean Information and Credit Rating Services Limited (CariCRIS). CariCRIS, spanning 19 countries, has a diversified shareholding comprising some of the central banks in the region, U.S. and European commercial banks, development banks and financial institutions. CariCRIS has become a model for many countries in Europe, the Mediterranean and West Asia.

CRISIL Investment and Risk Management Services, set up in 2003, has developed a software tool, Corporate Risk Evaluator (CORE), to enable corporate organizations to comply with clause 49 of the listing guidelines with three distinct features. In 2007, CRISIL transferred its advisory business (CRISIL Infrastructure Advisory and CRISIL Investment and Risk Management Services) into a 100 per cent subsidiary called CRISIL Risk and Infrastructure Solutions Limited.

With many private and public sector banks directing resources towards and focusing on SME lending, the need has arisen for independent credit opinions. CRISIL offers its rating services to SMEs to meet this need.

The CRISIL rating for real estate developers is a measure of their past track record in executing real estate and their organizational and financial risk profiles. It is not a rating of the developer's credit quality. The important factors that are considered for assessing organizational and financial risk include quality systems, organizational structure, existing financial position and financial flexibility.

CRISIL has developed a framework for rating debt obligations of Indian corporate organizations supported by credit enhancements extended by entities based outside the country. The issues considered in this context include the creditworthiness of the offshore entity, the nature and structure of the credit enhancement mechanism to ensure timely payments on rated debt obligations and regulatory issues as regards transfer risk. The credit enhancements could be in the form of guarantees, letters of credit, asset backing or other suitable structures. The structured obligations ratings are based on the scale of CRISIL ratings for long-term instruments.

The ratings for insurance companies are broadly divided into two categories—secure and vulnerable. Rating categories from "AAA" to "BBB" are classified as secure ratings and are used to indicate insurance companies whose financial capacity to meet policyholder obligations is sound. Rating categories from "BB" to "D" are classified as vulnerable and are used to indicate insurance companies whose financial capacity to meet policyholder obligations is vulnerable to adverse economic and underwriting conditions. The ratings are not recommendations to purchase or discontinue a policy, contract or security issued by an insurance company, nor are they guarantees of financial strength.

Thus, CRISIL undertakes in-depth analysis and research on a sectoral basis. Within a span of 20 years, CRISIL has become the fourth-largest rating agency in the world. In spite of a competitive environment, it commands more than 60 per cent of the rating market.

12.5.2 Investment Information and Credit Rating Agency of India Limited (ICRA)

As a pioneer in the business of credit rating in India, CRISIL laid down the ground rules for credit rating in the country. It also set certain standards. However, by the early 1990s, the need for a second credit rating agency was felt in the country. Accordingly, the Investment Information and Credit Rating Agency of India Limited was incorporated in January 1991. It was promoted by leading financial institutions and banks in India. It launched credit rating services in September 1991. To provide information services to equity investors, ICRA launched EPRA (Earnings Prospects and Risk Analysis) and credit assessment for small and medium-scale industries in 1995. In 1996, ICRA signed an agreement with Financial Proformas Inc. (FPI), a Moody's company, to provide credit education, risk management software, credit research and consulting services to commercial banks, financial and investment institutions, financial services companies and mutual funds in India. It has launched Money and Finance, a research programme directed at the analysis of contemporary developments that characterize Indian money and finance. Moody's Investors' Service, the U.S.-based international credit rating agency, and ICRA entered into an agreement in 1998 to the effect that Moody's would take up minority stake in the equity capital of ICRA. According to the agreement, Moody's would also provide technical services to ICRA.

ICRA developed a rating methodology for the claims-paying ability of general insurance companies in India. By 1999, ICRA became the first Indian rating agency to rate all non-life insurance companies in the country. The rating of insurance companies enables purchasers of insurance policies and investors access to timely, authentic and dependable information about the fundamental capacity of an insurance company to service claims and obligations. At the same time, it helps the insurance company to increase its business.

In order to enable investors to take informed decisions on investing in mutual funds, ICRA has launched rating services for debt funds of Indian mutual funds. Similarly, it has launched grading services for entities involved in construction projects including contractors, consultants, project owners and the projects themselves.

In 2001, ICRA launched corporate governance rating with a focus on corporate organizations' business practices and quality of disclosure standards with respect to the requirements of regulators and interests of financial stakeholders. The grading system developed by ICRA for real estate developers helps buyers of property to assess the risks associated with the developer's ability to deliver in accordance with the terms and conditions. ICRA has also launched a grading scheme for healthcare institutions as well as maritime training institutes in India. The NSIC-ICRA performance and credit rating scheme provides a boost to the development of small scale enterprises in India.

The grading of initial public offerings aims at facilitating the assessment of equity issues offered to the public. ICRA assigns grades on a five-point scale, where IPO Grade-5 indicates the highest grading and IPO Grade-1 indicates the lowest grading. The grading is based on the fundamentals of the issuer company. The IPO grading methodology examines the following key variables.

- Business and competitive position, which includes industry prospects, market position and operating efficiency
- Financial position and prospects
- Management quality
- New project risks and prospects
- Management quality
- Corporate governance practices

ICRA assigns a grade to a particular IPO based on the detailed evaluation of each of the factors listed above. The assessment involves a combination of both quantitative factors as reflected in financial statements as well as qualitative factors such as risks associated with new projects and management ability. It is specifically mentioned that the IPO grade does not comment on the valuation or pricing of the issue that has been graded, nor does it indicate the likely returns to shareholders who subscribe to the IPO.

12.5.3 Credit Analysis and Research Ltd (CARE)

CARE was incorporated in April 1993 as a credit rating information and advisory services company. It was promoted by Industrial Development Bank of India, Canara Bank, Unit Trust of India and other leading banks and financial services companies. CARE has 14 shareholders.

CARE has been registered with SEBI under SEBI (Credit Rating Agencies) Regulations, 1999. It assigned its first rating in November 1993. Its rating coverage extends beyond industrial companies to include public utilities, financial institutions, infrastructure projects, special purpose vehicles, state governments and municipal bodies. Apart from credit rating, CARE prepares credit reports on specific requests from banks or business partners, conducts sector studies and provides advisory services in the areas of financial restructuring, valuation and credit appraisal systems. The government also seeks assistance from CARE in equity valuation of a number of state-owned companies and for suggesting divestment strategies for these companies. The clientele of CARE includes some of the largest private sector manufacturing and financial services companies.

CARE follows a different methodology for the following instruments and institutions.

- Municipal bonds
- Urban infrastructure projects
- Debt issues of toll road projects
- Residential mortgage-backed securities
- Non-banking finance companies/housing finance companies
- Manufacturing companies
- SMEs

- Private power projects
- State governments
- Port projects
- Banks
- Short-term instruments
- Issuer rating
- Shipping companies

Apart from rating services, CARE provides advisory services such as project advisory services and financial restructuring services. CARE also prepares confidential credit reports for companies, which may be useful in taking decisions with regard to financing options, joint ventures, acquisitions and collaborations. CARE conducts sector studies (for example, studies on the Indian power sector), which may be useful to industry participants, financial intermediaries and financial analysts. CARE helps banks and non-banking finance companies to set up or modify their credit appraisal systems.

12.5.4 Fitch India Limited

Duff and Phelps Credit Rating India Private Ltd was the first joint venture rating company promoted by JM Financials, Alliance Group and the international rating agency Duffs and Phelps. Established in 1995, Duff and Phelps offered a wide range of services including rating services and advisory services. With the acquisition of Duff and Phelps Credit Rating Company (headquartered in Chicago) in April 200 by Fitch Ratings, Duff and Phelps Credit Rating India Private Limited became Fitch India Limited.

Fitch Ratings was founded in 1913 as Fitch Publishing Company by John Knowles Fitch. Located in New York, Fitch Publishing Company began as a publisher of financial statistics, whose consumers included the New York Stock Exchange. In 1924, Fitch introduced a ratings scale to meet the growing demand for independent analysis of financial securities. Fitch was one of the three rating agencies that were first declared as nationally recognized statistical rating organizations by the Securities and Exchange Commission in 1975. In 1997, Fitch merged with IBCA Limited, headquartered in London. Through this merger, Fitch came to be owned by Fimalac SA, a holding company that acquired IBCA in 1992. The merger represented the first step in Fitch's plans to meet investors' need for an alternative global and complete service rating agency. As a result of its growth and acquisitions, Fitch now has 49 offices worldwide with coverage of more than 3,000 financial institutions, more than 1,200 corporate issuers and 89 sovereigns. The company has over 8,600 structured finance transactions under surveillance. Fitch also maintains surveillance of more than 1,200 European structured finance transactions and 200 Asian structured finance transactions.

Fitch India's corporate group rates securities of companies in various industries, including chemicals, steel, petroleum, automobiles, consumer goods, food and beverage, tobacco, textiles, fertilizers, healthcare, telecom and power. It rates public securities and private placements including investment grade or high yield securities. Specific issues include long-term debt, medium-term notes, commercial paper and preferred stock. Ratings are placed on a rating watch to indicate that there is a reasonable probability of a rating change and the likely direction of such a change. The directions are designated as positive, indicating a potential upgrade, negative for a potential downgrade or evolving if ratings may be raised, lowered or maintained. Fitch may also assign rating outlooks. A rating outlook indicates the direction in which a rating is likely to move over time. The rating outlook may be positive, negative or stable. A positive or negative rating outlook does not imply that a rating change is inevitable. Similarly, the firms whose outlooks are stable could be upgraded or downgraded before the outlook moves to positive or negative if circumstances warrant such an action.

Bond fund credit ratings provide a relative assessment of the combined credit quality of the fund's portfolio solely within the Indian context. The national rating assigned to a bond fund links its credit quality to the weighted average default probability of the portfolio of bonds. Thus, the credit quality of the fund is similar to that of a bond rated at the same level on the national credit rating scale.

National volatility ratings represent an opinion on the relative sensitivity of the total return (including price) on a fund's units to a broad array of assumed changes in interest rates, liquidity of the portfolio, spreads and other market conditions. Volatility ratings are expressed on a scale of V1+(Ind) (least volatile) through V10(Ind) (most volatile). V1+(Ind) is usually assigned to money market funds or similar investment pools that should not result in loss of principal value to participants even with severely adverse movements of market conditions. Volatility ratings, however, do not predict the magnitude or direction of these movements in such market conditions and hence do not predict whether, or the extent to which, any particular fund will perform favourably or adversely in the future.

The corporate group spends a significant amount of time and resources on developing relationships with investors. Services provided to investors include one-on-one visits, group meetings, conferences, conference calls and access to analysts by phone. The meetings with investors provide Fitch India with ideas for improving its products and services and can also provide useful feedback for issuers.

Fitch provides investors original research, clear explanations of complex credits and surveillance that is more rigorous than that in other rating agencies. The Fitch Ratings sovereigns group assigns ratings to foreign and local currency debt of sovereign governments. The sovereigns group, with offices in London, New York, Hong Kong and Singapore, is accessible to investors across the globe. The group provides informed analysis and commentary on key political and economic developments in the countries. This helps investors to holistically assess their risk exposure to financial institutions, corporate organizations or structured finance.

12.5.5 Onicra Credit Rating Agency of India Limited

Onicra is the first credit rating company established to provide individual credit assessment and scoring services.

The Onida Group floated in 1993 a separate rating agency, called Onicra Credit Rating Agency of India Limited, to provide individual credit assessment and scoring services. It is recognized by the Government of India for assessment of small-scale industries (SSI) and is the first rating agency in India to launch individual credit rating and reporting services business. The spectrum of services provided by Onicra includes credit rating, associate rating, employee screening, SSI/SME rating, customer verification, lifestyle analysis and royalty retention.

Individual credit rating is an objective assessment of the risks attached to a financial transaction with respect to an individual at a given point of time. Onicra conducts in-depth research into all aspects of the behaviour of individuals for various types of credit extension. The analysis takes into account a vast range of parameters that influence an individual's credit behaviour.

Individual credit rating helps individuals applying for a home mortgage, bank loan, car loan or any of the bank credit facilities including credit cards. The credit rating indicates whether or not a loan will be granted to an individual and influences the interest rate that will be charged. The credit report of an individual also helps him in getting an apartment or house on rent. A prospective employer may also check the credit report of an individual to gain insight into the character of the person. A good credit rating enables an individual to conduct business or purchase products easily in any part of the world.

Onicra offers associate rating services, which involve objective assessment of existing and potential associates of clients with reference to infrastructure, resources, adherence to a defined system and processes and commitment to their customers. Thus, associate rating is an objective assessment of the business relationship of the associates with the company. Associates include dealers, vendors, suppliers, franchises, C&F agents and outsourcing agents.

Onicra in collaboration with the National Small Industries Corporation Ltd offers the NSIC-ONICRA performance and credit rating scheme for small scale industries. The main objective of the scheme is to enhance the acceptability of SSI units with banks and financial institutions. The scheme is approved by the Indian Banks Association (IBA) and implemented through the NSIC, a nodal agency of the Government of India. The government offers a subsidy of 75 per cent on the rating fee to the SSI units. The rating given by Onicra through this scheme enables the SSI units to have quick access to institutional credit. It highlights the strengths and weaknesses of an SSI unit, which in turn enables the concerned unit to identify areas of improvement and focus on its strengths. The rating also highlights the parameters measuring operational, financial, business and management risks.

12.5.6 Brickwork Ratings India Pvt Limited

Brickwork Ratings India Pvt Ltd was founded in 2007 by a group of professionals to provide rating of public issues and others to help investors take informed decisions. The services provided by Brickwork are issuer rating (rating of issuers such as state governments, companies, financial institutions and banks), short-term rating (rating of short-term securities such as CDs and CPs), long-term rating (rating of long-term securities such as bonds, debentures and structured products), IPO rating, fixed deposit rating, mutual fund rating, SME rating, bank loan rating, facility rating, insurance company rating, corporate governance rating, real estate project rating and real estate developer rating. In addition, Brickwork provides training and research services.

Like other credit rating agencies, Brickwork undertakes rating assignments based on a direct request from the issuer. Once Brickwork decides to undertake the rating of a particular security issue or an organization, it asks for a rating mandate from the issuer. The rating mandate signifies that the issuer accepts the terms and conditions laid down by Brickwork in terms of cooperating with analysts and providing necessary information for carrying out the assignment. The mandate letter also contains information regarding fees, the nature of information required from the issuer, terms related to appeal and withdrawal. The Brickwork rating process is broadly classified as pre-rating, rating and post-rating processes. The rating process involves a number of steps, starting from the signing of the rating agreement. Each step in the process is subject to a strict timeline. Rating is done on well-defined and updated criteria, which are publicly available and consistently applied. The rating committees have the sole authority to assign ratings. Every rating assigned is kept under surveillance until it is withdrawn.

There are three functional groups involved in the rating process—the business development group, the analytical group and the criteria group. The business development group handles all business communication and finalizes the commercial terms of the rating assignment. The analytical group handles all analytical responsibilities for a rating assignment and for assessing credit risk for the relevant entity. It is also responsible for surveillance and review of ratings. The criteria group is responsible for formulating, maintaining and refining the criteria framework under which the various types of issuances are rated. These functional groups, though independent, are collectively responsible for the successful implementation of the rating process. Ratings are subjective credit opinions based on various qualitative and quantitative factors.

Brickwork broadly classifies the debt issuer segments as manufacturing sector, financial sector, infrastructure sector and government and local bodies. Within each segment, there could be further classifications. For example, the financial sector may be further classified into banks, insurance companies, mutual funds, NBFCs and micro-finance institutions.

Brickwork assigns two types of credit ratings—one to the issuers and the other to specific debt issues or other financial obligations. The rating of the issuer, which is called "Brickwork's counterparty credit rating", reflects the current opinion about an issuer's overall capacity to fulfill its financial obligations. In other words, the rating of the issuer is an opinion that focuses on the issuer's ability and willingness to meet its financial commitments on a timely basis. The other type of rating is the rating of issues, mainly the debt issues. Four types of analyses are broadly made in the credit rating process. They are business analysis, industry analysis, financial analysis and management analysis. In business analysis, the prospects of factors such as growth, stability or decline, pattern of business cycles are examined. Vulnerability to technological change, labour unrest or the impact of government intervention are also considered. Competition is given due importance in the assessment. In industry analysis, cyclical, competitive and technological changes that the industry is likely to experience are assessed because these factors affect the operating performance and financial condition of a company. Thus, the generic risk profile for the industry in which the company operates is also considered along with the business risk. The management's competency and integrity are very important factors in the success of any business. The ability of the entity's management to guide the company, exploit opportunities, develop and execute plans and react to market changes is extremely important for the financial well-being of the company. The rigorous analysis of financial statements is an important job in the credit rating process. The balance sheet, income statement, sources and uses of funds statements and financial projections provide essential information about the company's initial and ongoing repayment capacity. The accounting quality is also assessed to determine whether ratios and statistics derived from financial statements can be used accurately to measure a company's performance. Capitalization and liquidity of the company also warrant careful analysis because they indicate a borrower's ability to withstand an economic slowdown or unplanned events.

The criteria for rating an individual issuer/issue are different as compared to the rating of a pool for a structured product and the same may be observed in the attachments. The credit ratings of Brickwork are symbolic representations of its current opinion on the relative credit risks associated with the rated debt instruments. If the probability of default is extremely low, Brickwork assigns the highest rating of "AAA". If the probability of default is higher, Brickwork rates the instrument "AA", "A" or "BBB". Instruments rated below "BBB" belong to speculative grades. Box 12.1 lists some ratings provided by Brickwork, and Box 12.2 presents a specific case.

Box 12.1 Brickwork Ratings—Some Examples

Date	Title
1/1/2010	Brickwork Ratings assigns BWR AAA rating to Great Eastern Shipping Co. Ltd's proposed non-convertible debenture issue of INR 5000 million (in addition to the earlier two issues amounting to INR 4500 million)
1/1/2010	Brickwork Ratings assigns BWR A-(SO) for ABK Consultants Pvt. Ltd's secured non-convertible debt instruments issue up to INR 6000 million
1/1/2010	Brickwork Ratings assigns BWR A for Lakshmi Vilas Bank's lower tier II (subordinated) bonds issue of INR 1 billion
30/12/2009	Brickwork Ratings assigns BWR AA+ for Yes Bank Ltd's lower tier II bonds issue of INR 3 billion
30/12/2009	Brickwork Ratings reaffirms BWR AA+ for Andhra Bank's perpetual (tier I) bonds issue of INR 200 crore or INR 2 billion
24/12/2009	Brickwork Ratings, a credit rating agency, adopts standardization of rating symbols
23/12/2009	Brickwork Ratings assigns BWR IPO Grade 3 to the proposed initial public offer of Aqua Logistics Limited
19/12/2009	Brickwork Ratings assigns BWR BBB+ for Raghuleela Leasing and Real Estates Pvt Ltd's secured non-convertible debt instruments issue of INR 5 billion
14/12/2009	Brickwork Ratings assigns BWR AAA for Andhra Bank's lower tier II bonds issue of INR 5 billion
7/12/2009	Brickwork Ratings assigns BWR AAA+ for Indian Renewable Energy Development Agency Ltd's structured obligation rating
15/10/2009	Brickwork Ratings assigns BWR AAA+ (SO) for India Infrastructure Finance Company Limited's GoI guaranteed bonds issue of INR 20 billion
9/10/2009	Brickwork Ratings assigns BWR AAA+ for Punjab National Bank's innovative perpetual debt instrument (IPDI) issue of INR INR 7 billion
3/10/2009	Brickwork Ratings assigns BWR AA– for long-term debt and BWR P1+ for short-term debt (with maturity beyond 12 months and up to 18 months) for IFCI Limited's existing and proposed debt issues aggregating INR 100 billion
25/9/2009	Brickwork Ratings assigns BWR AA+ for Yes Bank Limited's hybrid tier I and upper/lower tier II bonds issue of INR 5.9 billion
25/9/2009	Brickwork Ratings assigns BWR AA– for Tulip Telecom Limited's long-term debt issue of INR1 billion
16/9/2009	Brickwork Ratings assigns BWR AA– for IFCI Limited's existing and proposed bonds issue of INR 100 billion
15/9/2009	Brickwork Ratings assigns BWR AA– for Tourism Finance Corporation of India Ltd's unsecured bonds issue of INR 500 million
9/9/2009	Brickwork Ratings assigns BWR AA for PTC India Financial Services Limited's non-convertible bonds issue of INR 1 billion
26/8/2009	Brickwork Ratings assigns BWR AAA+ for Great Eastern Shipping Co. Ltd's non-convertible debenture issue of INR 2.5 billion
13/8/2009	Brickwork Ratings assigns BWR AAA for Housing and Urban Development Corporation Ltd's (HUDCO) proposed unsecured non-convertible debentures issue of INR 10 billion with a 10-year tenure
11/8/2009	Brickwork Ratings assigns BWR P1+ for United Bank of India's certificate of deposits issue of INR 100 billion
6/8/2009	Brickwork Ratings assigns BWR A– for Development Credit Bank's subordinate bonds issue of INR 1 billion
31/7/2009	Brickwork Ratings assigns BWR AAA for Tata Chemicals Limited's unsecured non-convertible debenture issue of INR 2.5 billion
31/7/2009	Brickwork Ratings assigns BWR AA+ for Yes Bank Limited's hybrid tier I and upper/lower tier II bonds issue of INR 5.35 billion

Source: http://www.brickworkratings.com/ratingslist.html

Box 12.2 Reaffirmation of Ratings: Andhra Bank's Bond Issue

Brickwork Ratings has reaffirmed BWR AA+ (pronounced BWR double A plus) for Andhra Bank's perpetual (tier I) bonds issue of INR 2000 million. Brickwork Ratings' BWR AA+ signifies "high safety" and the rating outlook further signifies the direction of the rating being stable in the near term. Brickwork has relied upon the audited financial statements and information and clarifications provided by the issuer.

During FY '09, the bank adopted several business development initiatives to grow its business. One important initiative was to bring all the branches under core banking solution (CBS). With 100 per cent CBS branches, the bank competently managed the challenging economic conditions during the financial year to grow its total business by 23.6 per cent to reach INR 1038180 million in FY '09 as compared to INR 83,9930 million during FY '08. The bank's total income increased by 26.96 per cent to INR 4,8360 million during FY '09, reflecting the significant buoyancy in core banking operations, excellent fee-based income and focus on healthy earning assets which contributed to improvement in profitability. As a result, the bank's operating profit and net profit surged by 21.86 per cent and 13.46 per cent, respectively.

The bank's tier-I capital ratio stood at 8.67 per cent as on March 31, 2009, which was marginally higher than the previous year's figure of 8.54 per cent under Basel II. Overall, the bank has reported capital adequacy ratio of 13.22 per cent under Basel II as on March 31, 2009 (11.61 per cent in FY '08) while Basel I CRAR was at 12.37 per cent. As a special feature of its rating process, Brickwork calculates the leverage, which assesses the bank's net worth with reference to on and off-balance sheet items. During FY '09, the bank's leverage, though higher, was still comfortable at 18.31 in FY '09 as compared to 16.4 in FY '08.

The bank has continued its good performance in Q2 FY '10.Total deposits increased to INR 622790 million, while advances increased to INR 481820 million. The bank has been consistently reducing its non-performing assets. Gross and net NPAs stood at 0.83 per cent and 0.16 per cent, respectively, in Q2 FY '10. Further, the bank's net profit surged by 69.61 per cent quarter-to-quarter to reach INR 2730 million in Q2 FY '10. As result, the bank's return on assets improved to 1.53 per cent in Q2 FY '10 from 1.12 per cent in Q2 FY '09. The loan loss coverage improved to 83.66 per cent in Q2 FY '10 from 81.49 per cent in FY '09.

The bank was incorporated in 1923 and nationalized in 1980. The Government of India holds 51.55 per cent stake in the bank. The bank offers retail banking, small and medium enterprise (SME) banking and treasury and financial institutional services. During FY '09, the bank opened 66 branches and 70 ATMs. The bank's delivery network consists of 1,432 branches and 726 ATMs as of March 31, 2009.

The rating factored inter alia, the majority stake held by the Government of India, comfortable capital adequacy and tier I capital, lower term loan component in its loan assets, well diversified credit profile and prudential higher loan loss coverage.

Source: http://www.brickworkratings.com/press-pdf/andhra-bank_perpetual_2bn-rating_reaffirmation-press.pdf

12.5.7 SME Rating Agency of India Limited (SMERA)

The SME Rating Agency of India Limited, popularly known as SMERA, is a joint venture started by Small Industry Development Bank of India (SIDBI), Dun & Bradstreet Information Services India Private Limited (D&B) and several leading banks in India. SMERA is the country's first rating agency that focuses primarily on small and medium enterprises (SME) in India. The main objective of rating SMEs is to facilitate greater and easier flow of credit to SMEs from the banking sector. The SMERA rating categorizes SMEs according to size so as to enable fair evaluation. SMERA takes into consideration the overall financial as well as non-financial performance of the SME in its rating process. Financial performance is assessed by ratio analysis and important ratios considered are profitability ratios, growth ratios, gearing ratios and liquidity ratios among others. Management experience, qualifications, customer and supplier base are also considered to assess non-financial performance.

The rating process of SMERA consists of the following steps:

- Receipt of rating request/mandate

Table 12.1 NSIC-D&B SMERA rating scale

		Financial strength		
		High	*Moderate*	*Low*
Performance capability	Highest	SE1A	SE1B	SE1C
	High	SE2A	SE2B	SE2C
	Moderate	SE3A	SE3B	SE3C
	Weak	SE4A	SE4B	SE4C
	Poor	SE5A	SE5B	SE5C

Source: http://www.smera.in/ratingscale.aspx

- Enquiry placed with SMERA's correspondents located across India
- Dispatch of relevant documentation to SMERA's centralized office
- Draft report preparation
- Detailed analysis on both financial and non-financial information and rating assignment
- Dispatch and dissemination
- Request for rating review

SMERA follows different criteria for different industries. For this, it has divided the industries into eight categories. They are:

- Auto-ancillary industry
- Chemical industry
- Engineering industry
- Food and food processing industry
- IT and ITES industry
- Logistic land industry
- Steel industry
- Textile industry

In general, SMERA makes two types of analysis—business risk analysis and financial risk analysis. But the factors considered in each type of analysis are different for different types of industries. For example, the rating criteria (business risk analysis) for the auto ancillary industry include customer concentration risk, performance of the original equipment manufacturers (OEM), balance between direct sales to domestic OEM, export and aftermarket, position and significance in the value chain and technology and processes. Besides, SMERA follows the standard criteria used in all manufacturing companies for financial risk analysis of the auto ancillary industry.

The rating scale adopted by SMERA is presented in Table 12.1.

12.6 SEBI (Credit Rating Agencies) Regulations, 1999

The SEBI regulations and guidelines mainly focus on the protection of the interests of investors.

Government regulations for credit rating were introduced in January 1990 when the RBI issued guidelines for the issue of commercial paper (CP). The Controller of Capital Issues (CCI) had also insisted that all debentures and bonds be rated by a credit rating agency. With the Controller of Capital Issues (Repealed) Act, SEBI became the regulator of capital issues. In order to regulate the functioning of credit rating agencies and protect the interests of investors, SEBI issued comprehensive guidelines.

According to these guidelines, any organization proposing to commence any activity as a credit rating agency shall register with SEBI. The organization shall make an application to SEBI for the grant of a certificate of registration for the purpose. SEBI shall not consider an application unless the applicant is promoted by any one of the following organizations:

- A public financial institution
- A scheduled commercial bank
- A foreign bank operating in India with the approval of the RBI
- A foreign credit rating agency recognized by or under any law for the time being in force in the country of its incorporation, having at least five years' experience in rating securities
- Any company or a body corporate with continuous net worth of a minimum of INR 100 crore as per its audited annual accounts for the five years prior to the filing of the application with SEBI for the grant of the certificate under these regulations.

The applicant shall also fulfil certain eligibility conditions. The important ones are mentioned below.

- The applicant is set up and registered as a company under the Companies Act, 1956.
- The applicant has a minimum net worth of INR 5 crore, provided that a credit rating agency existing at the commencement of these regulations, with a net worth of less INR 5 crore, shall be deemed to have satisfied this condition if it increases its net worth to the said minimum within a period of three years of such commencement.
- The applicant has adequate infrastructure to enable it to provide rating services in accordance with the provisions of the SEBI Act and the relevant regulations.
- The applicant and the promoters of the applicant have professional competence, financial soundness and a general reputation of fairness and integrity in business transactions to the satisfaction of SEBI.

SEBI, on being satisfied that the applicant is eligible for the grant of a certificate of registration, shall grant the certificate subject to the condition that the credit rating agency shall comply with the provisions of the SEBI Act and the regulations made thereunder and the guidelines, directives, circulars and instructions issued by SEBI from time to time on the subject of credit rating.

The period of validity of the certificate of registration shall be three years. A credit rating agency, if it desires renewal of the certificate granted to it, shall make an application for the renewal of the certificate of registration.

Every credit rating agency shall enter into a written agreement with each client whose securities it proposes to rate. The agreement shall contain, among other things, the rights and obligations of each party with respect to rating of securities. Further, every credit rating agency shall, during the lifetime of the securities rated by it, continuously monitor and review the rating of such securities. If the client does not cooperate with the credit rating agency so as to enable the agency to comply with its obligations, the credit rating agency shall carry out the review on the basis of the best available information. A credit rating agency shall not withdraw a rating as long as the obligations under the security rated by it are outstanding, except where the company whose security is rated is wound up or merged or amalgamated with another company.

Every credit rating agency shall make public the definitions of the concerned rating, along with the symbol, and state that the ratings do not constitute recommendations to buy, hold or sell any security. Every credit rating agency shall make available to the general public information relating to the rationale of the ratings, which shall cover an analysis of the various factors justifying a favourable assessment as well as the factors constituting a risk.

Every credit rating agency shall specify the rating process and file a copy of the same with SEBI for record. Every credit rating agency shall, in all cases, follow a proper rating process and while rating a security, exercise due diligence in order to ensure that the rating given by the credit rating agency is fair and appropriate. Every rating agency shall have professional rating committees comprising members who are adequately qualified and knowledgeable to assign a rating.

SEBI may appoint one or more persons as inspecting officers to undertake inspection or investigation of the books of account, records and documents of the credit rating agencies. A credit rating agency that fails to comply with any condition subject to which a certificate has been granted, or contravenes any of the provisions of the SEBI Act or the regulations made under the act, shall be dealt with in the manner provided under the SEBI (Procedure for Holding Enquiry by Enquiry Officer and Imposing Penalty) Regulations, 2002.

As far as the code of conduct is concerned, a credit rating agency shall make all efforts to protect the interests of investors and observe high standards of integrity, dignity and fairness in the conduct of its business. A credit rating agency shall fulfil its obligations in a prompt, ethical and professional manner. It shall not make any untrue statement, suppress any material fact or make any misrepresentation in any documents, reports, papers or information furnished to SEBI, a stock exchange or the public at large. A credit rating agency shall ensure that there is no misuse of any privileged information including prior knowledge of rating decisions or changes. It shall not offer fee-based services to the rated entities, beyond credit ratings and research, and maintain an arm's-length relationship between its credit rating activity and any other activity. A credit rating agency shall not be party to or instrumental in the creation of a false market, price rigging or manipulation or dissemination of any unpublished price-sensitive information with respect to securities that are listed and proposed to be listed in any stock exchange, unless required, as part of the rationale for the rating accorded.

- **Restriction on rating of securities issued by promoters or by certain other persons:** SEBI has also laid down restrictions on the rating of securities issued by promoters or by certain other persons. A promoter is defined as a person who holds 10 per cent or more of the shares of the credit rating agency. An associate in relation to a promoter includes a body corporate in which the promoter holds 10 per cent or more of the share capital. No credit rating agency shall rate a security issued by its promoter. In case the promoter is a lending institution, its chairman, director or employee shall not be a chairman, director or employee of the credit rating agency or its rating committee. No credit agency shall rate a security issued by an entity which is:
    - A borrower of its promoter, or
    - A subsidiary of its promoter, or
    - An associate of its promoter, if there are common chairmen, directors between credit rating agency and these entities, if there are common employees or if there are common chairmen, directors or employees on the rating committee.

  No credit rating agency shall rate a security issued by its associate or subsidiary if the credit rating agency or its rating committee has a chairman, director or employee who is also a chairman, director or employee of any such entity.
- **IPO rating:** SEBI had in January 2007 permitted the grading of initial public offering (IPOs) by rating agencies like CRISIL, ICRA, FITCH and CARE. It was pointed out that acquiring a high grading symbol could make companies confident of commanding a better premium on their offer. SEBI has permitted IPO grading to enable investors to form an independent opinion from credible institutions on the fundamental strengths of the company. Though it is optional for companies to seek rating of their IPOs, it would be mandatory for them to mention the grading symbol on the offer document if they have opted to get themselves graded.

However, in March 2007, SEBI created an international precedent of sorts by asking the companies to get their initial public offerings graded by a rating agency. In other words, SEBI made grading of initial public offerings mandatory. The grading of an issue is based on business fundamentals of the company, the company's financial strengths, industry prospects, accounting strengths and management strength among other factors. The rating agency also takes into account the corporate governance practiced by the company. The grading exercise would be on a five-point scale with five indicating strong fundamentals and one indicating weak fundamentals. The rating agency would affix its name before the grading symbol.

The grading of an IPO is not a recommendation to buy or sell and does not comment on the pricing of the issue at all. Grading is an additional input available from an independent rating agency to help investors make informed decisions. Grading of IPOs particularly helps those companies that are not very well known to tap the markets.

12.7 Special Kinds of Ratings

Sovereign rating and rating of small and medium enterprises stand on a different footing. Hence they are highlighted in the following lines.

12.7.1 Sovereign Ratings

Sovereign ratings *help interested parties to assess country risk.*

Sovereign credit rating is the rating of the general creditworthiness of a country. The process of rating takes into account the overall economy of a country, which includes the balance of payments, foreign debt, foreign investment, public and private investment, foreign currency reserves, development of financial markets and capital market transparency. Political stability is also an important factor. In the rating process, the rating agencies use both quantitative and qualitative factors, the weight on each factor depending on whether the country has high income, a long history of institutional stability and whether it is in the midst of development. Specifically, the sovereign rating process covers GDP, inflation, unemployment, per capita income, import, export, government revenue, government expenditure, labour costs, exchange rate, current account balance, foreign currency debt, debt service ratio, short-term interest rates, internal debt, assets and liabilities of banks and foreign exchange reserves among other factors. Sovereign credit rating gives investors, particularly foreign institutional investors and those proposing foreign direct investment, insight into the level of risk associated with investing in a particular country. In sovereign credit rating, two types of risks are assessed—country risk and sovereign risk. *Country risk* is the risk caused by events in a particular country that are to some extent under the control of the government concerned. On the other hand, *sovereign risk* is the risk of lending to the government of a particular country. However, both kinds of risks are highly correlated and, therefore, they may be used interchangeably. It may be noted that the debt rating of a company cannot exceed the country's sovereign rating.

Thus, obtaining a good sovereign credit rating is essential for a country in order to access funding in international capital markets. In other words, a sovereign credit rating plays a major role in determining the cost and availability of foreign funds to a country. A weak sovereign rating may lead to domestic funds moving to foreign countries, a disruption of the financial system and an overall economic downturn. Many countries, especially developing countries and emerging economies, seek ratings from international credit rating agencies like Standard and Poor's, Moody's and Fitch in order to provide financial transparency and exhibit their credit standing to attract foreign capital, including foreign direct investment. It may be noted that it is only at the request of a country that a credit rating agency undertakes the rating process, in which the country's economic and political environment are duly assessed to determine a representative credit rating for the country.

12.7.2 Small and Medium Enterprises Rating

Small and medium enterprises (SMEs) play a vital role in the Indian economy. However, they are confronted with several problems such as fund-raising. Many SMEs have poor access to institutional credit. Credit institutions, particularly commercial banks, may be reluctant to lend to small-scale enterprises mainly because they lack adequate information to evaluate the risk in such firms. It is in this situation that credit rating of SMEs is necessary. Accordingly, the National Small Industries Corporation (NSIC) launched a programme where a micro or small enterprise with a maximum investment of INR 50 million in plant and machinery would receive a 75 per cent subsidy on rating fees (around INR 50,000) charged by any of the rating agencies. It is observed that rating by a recognized credit rating agency helps the SMEs command better terms with their buyers. On the basis of rating reports, banks are able to take faster decisions on project loans as well as on renewing and increasing credit limits for SMEs. Rating of SMEs is an independent third-party assessment of the overall condition of the enterprises, which helps the banks to take the right decision on lending to SMEs.

12.8 Review of Credit Rating

Surveillance of credit rating is necessary for review of the rating given to a particular issue.

Rating a capital issue involves projecting the future earning capacity of the issuer company. The perceptions about the future cash flows of a company could differ with a change of perspective. Besides, there are a host of factors that ought to be taken into consideration before arriving at an index for rating. Therefore, surveillance of credit rating is necessary for review of the rating given to a particular issue.

Downgrading or upgrading a given rating is a common phenomenon. For instance, in June 2007, CRISIL downgraded Aditya Birla flagship Hindalco to "AA" from "AAA". The reason was the USD 3.1-billion debt raised by the company to acquire Novelis, resulting in an increase in the overall debt burden of the company. In the same month of the same year, CRISIL downgraded Tata Steel to "AA" from "AAA" following the company's decision to acquire the Corus group. The acquisition of Corus for USD 12.9 billion, funded through a debt-to-equity mix of around 2:1, is expected to vitiate the consolidated entity's capital structure. CRISIL estimated that Tata Steel had a gearing (ratio of a company's level of long-term debt to its equity capital) in excess of four times in April 2007 (after the acquisition) compared with 0.3 times as on March 31, 2007. The Corus deal was a leveraged buyout (LBO)—where the acquisition was funded by loans taken against the security of assets (and cash flows) of the target company. Thus, the economic incentive and moral obligation on Tata Steel to make a success of Corus was very high.

In his budget speech on July 6, 2009, the Union finance minister said the government would continue to support public sector banks by retaining the majority stake of 51 per cent or more in all of them. This marked a change in the government's stance of reducing its minimum shareholding in public sector banks to 33 per cent while retaining management control, thus offering proactive support to the public sector banks. Further, the government stated that it would maintain the capitalization in public sector banks at about 12 per cent. In other words, the public sector banks would have an overall capital adequacy ratio (capital as a percentage of risk weighted assets) of 12 per cent. The government also infused INR 16,500 million in three public sector banks in the financial year 2009. Following these proactive measures of the government, CRISIL upgraded the rating on eight public sector banks. The ratings of Bank of India and Union Bank of India became "AAA" from the earlier "AA+". Canara Bank and Corporation Bank, which already enjoyed "AAA" rating, had their outlook revised to stable from negative. Allahabad Bank, Bank of Maharashtra, Dena Bank, IDBI Bank, Punjab and Sind Bank and UCO Bank had their rating outlook revised for the better. However, CRISIL stated that though there may not be much of a concern on the capital front, there could be pressure on profits of these public sector banks.

Rating agencies have made similar revisions before. For instance, in 1996, CRISIL downgraded the fixed deposit programmes of six companies and placed debenture ratings of two companies in the default grade. The ratings of non-convertible debentures (NCD) of Sandur Manganese and Iron Ore Ltd and the partly convertible debentures (PCD) programme of Indian Seamless Steel and Alloys Ltd were downgraded from "BBB" to "D" and "BB with rating watch" to "D", respectively. The revised rating indicated that the rated instrument was in default. CRISIL also downgraded the NCD of ASIL Industries Ltd from "BBB plus" to "BBB minus", the fixed deposit (FD) scheme of Instalment Supply Ltd from "FAA" to "FAA minus", the FD scheme of Integrated Finance Company Ltd from "FAA" to "FAA minus", the FD programme of Prakash Leasing Ltd from "FA plus" to "FA minus", the FD programme of Vardhan Properties and Investments Ltd from "FA minus" to "FB plus" and the PCD programme of VHEL Industries Ltd from "BBB with rating watch" to "B".

Sometimes, a credit rating may create a controversy. For instance, Mideast India Ltd, the flagship of the Mesco's group, was in default for at least INR 25 million in fixed deposits on February 23, 1996, the date on which CRISIL assigned "FAA" rating to its fixed deposit programme. The fixed deposits matured for repayment in January 1996. On February 10, 1996, Mideast expressed its inability to pay the amount and sought an extension of six months. When this request was refused by the authorities, the company sought a 90-day extension, which was also firmly refused as it was in contravention of company law. Besides, there had been widespread defaults in repayments of inter-corporate deposits, bill discounting obligations, lease rentals and fixed deposits. The company had also violated statutory provisions in payment of dividends for the fiscal 1994-95. In other words, the company had been facing a serious liquidity crunch. Nevertheless, the company had continued to enjoy a good rating as CRISIL failed to review the rating accorded by it. The issue became a subject of debate in investment circles. It was also said that the development of the capital market urgently required independent rating agencies of proven integrity and competence.

Companies that have been rated at or near the minimum investment grade may not cooperate with the rating agency and force them into suspending or withdrawing the ratings assigned. A company might anticipate that the outcome of a rating review is not likely to be favourable and seek to avoid the negative publicity that could result from a downgrade. On the other hand, rating agencies may feel deprived of the information required by them to make an informed judgment of a company's relative credit quality, and hence withdraw or suspend the ratings assigned. For instance, in 2000, ICRA withdrew the ratings of three NBFCs because they refused to share the required information. In the same year, CARE suspended the ratings of 11 companies and Duff and Phelps Credit Rating suspended the rating of one non-bank financial services company, both due to lack of cooperation. In the case of CRISIL, as many as 47 companies had to have their ratings withdrawn/suspended in 2000 because of lack of cooperation from the issuers. This despite the fact that a company, at the time of assigning the initial rating, signs a legally binding contract promising to share all the necessary information with the rating agency. Some companies, when they anticipate downgrading, may approach another credit rating agency to obtain an alternative rating and have the less favourable rating suspended. The credit rating agencies can arbitrarily change a rating if the issuer adopts a non-cooperative attitude. But this might lead to litigation or other controversies. The rating agencies can withdraw/suspend the rating in the case of non-cooperation not covered under SEBI regulations.

12.9 Credibility of Credit Rating Agencies

The standards of rating are the touchstone of the entire business of credit rating. The strength of a credit rating agency lies in its credibility. Credibility is built from the investors' perception about the fairness and impartiality of the credit rating agency. In other words, for a rating to have value, the rating agency must have credibility. Transparency, thoroughness, integrity and fairness are the important factors that influence the credibility of a credit rating institution. The credit rating institution should always keep in view the philosophy that it works as much for its client company as for investors.

Rating agencies may differ in rating the same company or instrument as the opinions on the future performance of the rated entity differ. For instance, in 1998, ICRA assigned "MAAA" rating to 20th Century Finance. For the same issue, CRISIL gave "FA". CARE assigned "BBB plus" for the fixed deposit scheme of BCL Financial Services but CRISIL gave "FB plus". ICRA assigned "MA" for the fixed deposit scheme of BCL Financial Services Ltd, while CARE assigned "BBB plus" to the same capital issue.

Taking another example, CRISIL originally gave a rating of "FA" to the FD programme of Llyods Finance in October 1991. It was reviewed in August 1992 but CRISIL decided to retain the same rating. In October 1993, CRISIL reviewed the rating again and upgraded it to "FA plus". But Llyods Finance was not satisfied as it thought it deserved a better rating. So the company decided to suspend that rating and approached CARE. CARE assigned "AA" rating to the FD programme of Llyods Finance in August 1994 and the subsequent review resulted in an upgradation to "AAA". Thus, the two rating agencies created confusion for the investors by assigning different ratings to the same capital issue.

It is said that lack of sufficient information is responsible for rating differentials. Ratings may also differ because of different methodologies adopted and different weightage assigned by rating agencies to present-versus-future performance. Some credit rating agencies follow lenient standards, while others (such as CRISIL) are very stringent. These may also cause difference in ratings.

After the global economic meltdown, the role of credit rating agencies came under public scrutiny. It is argued that credit rating agencies all over the world had not done their job with sincerity, seriousness and integrity. The laxity on the part of the credit rating agencies is clearly visible in the failure of several companies, especially finance companies, all over the world, particularly in the United States. Had their surveillance been up to the mark, the global economic meltdown could have been avoided, many experts believe. It is also argued that the overreaction of credit rating agencies to changes in the financial markets have aggravated the financial crisis in the recent past, leading to financial instability across the world. Therefore, ever since the global economic crisis, regulators have tightened the noose over credit rating agencies by hardening regulations and improving disclosure standards. Thus, the bankruptcies of big organizations have prompted legislative scrutiny of credit rating agencies. As a policy action, SEBI has asked the credit rating agencies to carry out internal audits. The International Organization of Securities Commission (IOSCO) has specified that the credit rating agencies should separate, operationally and legally, their credit rating business from their other businesses (such as consultancy and ancillary business operations) that may present a conflict of interest. It has also been stipulated that a credit rating agency should disclose if it receives 10 per cent or more of its annual revenue from a single issuer, originator, arranger, client or subscriber. Whether to retain the user-pays model in ratings or to go in for public funding of ratings remains a subject of debate. It is argued that the unsolicited rating model would sever the link between the rater and the issuer of securities, thereby make the credit rating agencies independent. Unsolicited ratings would ensure greater independence of credit rating agencies. The difference between the solicited rating model and unsolicited rating model is that in the former, the credit rating agency is requested and therefore paid for by the rated firm while the latter entails neither of the two.

Summary

1. Credit ratings provide investors with information that helps them in making investment decisions.
2. Credit rating agencies are specialized and professional institutions that analyse and evaluate the creditworthiness of an organization, including the government, which issues the securities or borrows the funds.
3. Credit rating represents the current opinion of the rating agency on the ability and willingness of an issuer of a particular financial instrument or borrower of funds to honour on schedule the financial obligations attached to that financial instrument or such borrowing.
4. The rating of debt securities ranges from "AAA" to "D" with some variation in notation of each agency.
5. The securities with higher credit rating command a lower interest rate than the securities with lower credit rating.
6. Moody's Investors' Service, established in 1914, is the first rating agency in the world.
7. Once a rating is assigned and published, the rating agency keeps the rating under surveillance until the security is fully repaid. The surveillance process may result in changes in the rating from time to time.
8. Credit rating agencies are firms that analyse and evaluate a debtor or a debt instrument and assign a rate or grade according to its degree of credit risk or creditworthiness. Presently, there are seven credit rating agencies in India.
9. CRISIL, the first credit rating agency in India, established certain procedures and standards of credit rating in India.
10. Onicra is the first credit rating company established in India to provide individual credit assessment and scoring services.
11. Credit ratings are used by different groups of people and different organizations. Investors, issuers of securities, suppliers, customers and government regulators are the major groups that use the credit ratings.
12. The uses of credit rating need to be popularized through investor education.
13. Transparency, thoroughness, integrity and fairness are important factors that influence the credibility of a credit rating institution.
14. According to SEBI regulations, any organization proposing to commence any activity as a credit rating agency shall register with SEBI by fulfilling certain conditions.
15. No credit rating agency shall rate a security issued by its promoter. No credit agency shall rate a security issued by an entity that is a borrower of its promoter or a subsidiary of its promoter or an associate of its promoter.
16. Every credit rating agency shall specify the rating process and file a copy of the same with SEBI for record.
17. Sovereign credit rating is the rating of the general creditworthiness of a country.
18. Rating agencies may differ in rating the same company or instrument as the opinions on the future performance of the rated entity differ.
19. After the global economic crisis, regulators have tightened the noose over credit rating agencies by hardening regulations and improving disclosure standards.

Questions

1. Present a historical perspective of the credit rating industry.
2. What is credit rating? Discuss the role of credit rating in the industrial development of a country.
3. What are the specific advantages of credit rating?
4. What are the main limitations of credit rating in a country like India?
5. What are the features of sovereign credit rating?
6. Discuss the credibility aspect of credit rating institutions in India.

7. Briefly explain the methodology adopted by credit rating agencies in India.
8. What is the necessity of review of credit rating?
9. Critically examine the SEBI regulations with regard to credit rating.
10. Compare and contrast the credit rating agencies in India.
11. Who are the main users of credit rating? How do they make use of credit rating?
12. What is the special significance of rating of SMEs? What could be the main problems in rating SMEs?
13. Does India require more credit rating agencies? Give reasons for your answer.

Appendix 12.1

Rating Symbols

1. CRISIL RATING SYMBOLS

The following is the rating scale adopted by CRISIL. CRISIL may apply "+" or "−" signs to ratings to reflect comparative standing within the category. The "r" attached to the rating indicates that the instrument (debenture for example) has an element of non-credit risk (such as market risk). CRISIL may also assign rating outlooks for ratings from "AAA" to "B". Ratings on the rating watch do not carry outlooks.

Long-term Instruments Rating Scale

i. High Investment Grades:

AAA: Highest safety. Instruments that are judged to offer the highest safety in timely payment of interest and/or principal.
AA: High safety

ii. Investment Grades:

A: Adequate safety
BBB: Moderate safety

iii. Speculative Grades:

BB: Inadequate safety
B: High risk
C: Substantial risk
D: Default

Short-term Instruments Rating Scale

P1: Degree of safety regarding timely payment is very strong
P2: Strong
P3: Adequate
P4: Degree of safety regarding timely payment is minimal
P5: Default on maturity or is in default

Healthcare Institutions Rating Scale

This has two components—hospital classification such as nursing home, general secondary care, speciality secondary care, single-speciality tertiary care and multi-speciality tertiary care; and hospital's grading within that classification on a four-point scale. The definition of various grades follows.

Grade A: Very good quality of delivered patient care.
Grade B: Good quality of delivered patient care.
Grade C: Average quality of delivered patient care.
Grade D: Poor quality of delivered patient care.

Fixed Deposit Rating Scale

FAAA: Highest safety in timely payment of interest and/or principal
FAA: High safety
FA: Adequate safety
FB: Inadequate safety
FC: High risk
FD: Default

Non-credit Risk Rating Scale

AAAr: Highest safety
AAr: High safety
Ar: Adequate safety
BBBr: Moderate safety

Speculative Grades

BBr: Inadequate safety
Br: High risk
Cr: Substantial risk
Dr: Default

2. ICRA RATING SYMBOLS

The following are the credit rating symbols used by ICRA.

Long-term Instruments Rating Scale

LAAA: Highest safety
LAA: High safety
LA: Adequate safety
LBBB: Moderate safety
LBB: Adequate safety
LB: Risk prone
LC: Substantial risk
LD: Default

Medium-term Instruments (Fixed Deposits, Certificates of Deposits, etc.) Rating Scale

MAAA: Highest safety
MAA: High safety
MA: Adequate safety
MB: Inadequate safety
MC: Risk prone
MD: Default

Short-term Instruments (Commercial Paper, etc.) Rating Scale

A1: Highest safety
A2: High safety
A3: Adequate safety
A4: Risk prone
A5: Default

Small-scale Industries Rating Scale

SS1: Very strong capacity for timely servicing of debt obligations
SS2: Strong capacity
SS3: Adequate capacity
SS4: Moderate capacity
SS5: Inadequate capacity
SS6: Poor capacity
SS7: Default

Insurance Companies (Claims-paying Capacity) Rating Scale

iAAA: Highest claims-paying ability
iAA: High claims-paying ability
iA: Adequate claims-paying ability
iBBB: Moderate claims-paying ability
iBB: Inadequate claims-paying ability
iB: Weak claims-paying ability
iC: Lowest claims-paying ability
ICRA may apply "+" or "−" signs to ratings to reflect comparative standing within the category.

IPO Grading

ICRA IPO Grade 5: Strong fundamentals
ICRA IPO Grade 4: Above average fundamentals
ICRA IPO Grade 3: Average fundamentals
ICRA IPO Grade 2: Below average fundamentals
ICRA IPO Grade 1: Poor fundamentals

3. CARE RATING SYMBOLS

The symbols and rating definitions followed by CARE are given below.

Long/Medium-term Instruments (Non-convertible Debentures/Fixed Deposits/ Certificates of Deposit/Structured Obligations/ Convertible Preference Shares/Redeemable Preference Shares) Rating Scale

CARE AAA: Best credit quality (minimal credit risk)
AA: High safety
A: Adequate safety
BBB: Moderate safety
BB: Inadequate safety
B: Instruments offer low safety in timely servicing of debt obligations and carry very high credit risk. Such instruments are susceptible to default
C: High likelihood of default
D: Default

Short-term Instruments Rating Scale

PR1: Lowest credit risk
PR2: Adequate capacity for timely repayment
PR3: Moderate capacity for timely repayment
PR4: Inadequate capacity for timely repayment
PR5: More likely to be in default on maturity

Issuer Rating Scale

AAA (Is): Best credit quality and the highest safety
AA (Is): High safety (very low credit risk)
A (Is): Adequate safety
BBB(Is): Moderate safety
BB(Is): Inadequate safety (high credit risk)
B (Is): Low safety (susceptible to default)
C (Is): High likelihood of default
D (Is): Default

Collective Investment Schemes Rating Scale

1 (CIS): Schemes to be very strong with high likelihood of achieving their objectives and meeting the obligations to investors.
2 (CIS): Schemes are strong with adequate likelihood of achieving their objectives and meeting the obligations to investors.
3 (CIS): Schemes have adequate strengths to achieve their objectives and meet the obligations to investors.
4 (CIS): Schemes inadequate capability to achieve their objectives and meet the obligations to investors.
5 (CIS): Schemes are weak and unlikely to achieve their objectives and meet the obligations to investors.

CARE assigns "+" or "−" signs after the assigned rating, wherever necessary, to indicate the relative position within the band covered by the rating symbol.

4. FITCH RATING SYMBOLS

Long-term Credit Rating Scale

i. Investment Grades:

AAA (Ind): This is the highest rating in the national rating scale. The rating is assigned to the lowest credit risk (highest credit quality) relative to all other issuers or issues in the country.
AA (Ind): It denotes very high credit quality.
A (Ind): It denotes high credit quality.
BBB(Ind): It denotes good credit quality.

ii. Speculative Grades:

BB(Ind): It denotes fairly weak credit risk.
B(Ind): It denotes significantly weak credit risk.
CCC (Ind): Substantial credit risk
CC (Ind): Very high level of credit risk
C(Ind): It denotes exceptionally high credit risk relative to other issuers or issues in the country.
RD (Ind): Restricted default
D (Ind); Default

Short-term Credit Rating Scale

F1 (Ind): Strongest capacity for timely payment of financial commitments (least credit risk).

F2 (Ind): Satisfactory capacity.
F3 (Ind): Adequate capacity
F4 (Ind): Highly uncertain capacity.
F5 (Ind): Actual or imminent payment default.

Within the band of rating symbols, the signs "+" or "–" may be appended to a rating to denote relative status within the rating category.

Bond Fund Rating Scale

AAA (Ind): Fnd portfolio provides the highest protection against loss from credit defaults.
AA (Ind): High protection against loss from credit defaults.
A (Ind): Adequate protection against loss from credit defaults.
BBB (Ind):Moderate protection against loss from credit defaults.
BB (Ind): Inadequate protection against loss from credit defaults.
B (Ind): High risk of loss from credit defaults.
C (Ind): Substantial risk of loss from credit defaults.

Fitch assigns ratings with the suffix "(Ind)", which indicates national ratings. National ratings provide a relative measure of creditworthiness for rated entities in countries with sub-investment or low investment-grade international sovereign ratings. The best risk within a country is rated "AAA" and other credits are rated only relative to this risk. National ratings are meant for local investors in local markets and signified by the addition of an identifier for the country concerned, such as "AAA (Ind)" for national ratings in India.

5. BRICKWORK RATING SYMBOLS

Long-term Debt Instruments Rating Scale

Long-term debt instruments include bonds, non-convertible debentures, certificate of deposits, fixed deposits, convertible preference shares, redeemable preference shares and structured obligations, all with original maturity exceeding one year.

i. Investment Grades:

BWR AAA (BWR triple A): Best credit quality in terms of timely servicing of debt obligations
BWR AA (BWR double A): High credit quality
BWR A: Adequate credit quality
BWR BBB (BWR triple B): Moderate credit quality

ii. Speculative Grades:

BWR BB (BWR Double B): Inadequate credit quality
BWR B: Low credit quality
BWR C: Very low credit quality
BWR D: Default or expected to default

Short-term Debt Instruments Rating Scale

Short-term debt instruments are those with original maturity up to one year.

BWR P1: Excellent credit quality
BWR P2: High credit quality
BWR P3: Moderate credit quality
BWR P4: Low credit quality
BWR P5: Default or expected to default

The modifier "+" is used only from P1 to P3 to reflect comparative higher stand within the categories. The mapping of long to short-term ratings has been explained elsewhere in the criteria

Issuer Rating Scale

BWR AAA (BWR triple A): Best creditworthiness
BWR AA (BWR double A): High creditworthiness
BWR A: Adequate creditworthiness
BWR BBB (BWR triple B): Moderate creditworthiness
BWR BB (BWR double B): Inadequate creditworthiness
BWR B: Low creditworthiness
BWR C: Very low creditworthiness
BWR D: Default or expected to default

IPO Rating Scale

BWR IPO Grade 5: Strong fundamentals
BWR IPO Grade 4: Above average fundamentals
BWR IPO Grade 3: Average fundamentals
BWR IPO Grade 2: Below average fundamentals
BWR IPO Grade 1: Poor fundamentals

Fixed Deposit Rating Scale

i. Investment Grades:

BWR FAAA (BWR F triple A): Deposits are considered to offer the best safety in terms of timely servicing of interest and principal.
BWR FAA (BWR F double A): High safety
BWR FA: Adequate safety

ii. Speculative Grades:

BWR FB: Low safety
BWR FC: Very low safety
BWR FD: Default or expected to default

Note:

1. Brickwork ratings for FD programme of PSUs, corporate bodies, banks, FIs and state government entities begin with the prefix "F" and the scale rating from "BWR FAAA" to "BWR FA" for investment grade ratings.
2. Brickwork uses modifiers ("+", "–") for ratings from "BWR FAA" to "BWR FC". The modifiers indicate the relative position of the instrument within the rating category.
3. Brickwork's speculative grade ratings are lower than "BWR FA". As such, "BWR FB", "BWR FC" and "BWR FD" are considered to have speculative characteristics. Brickwork's lowest rating category of "BWR FD" is normally event-specific.
4. In addition, certain issues that Brickwork considers good for offer only to qualified investors also receive speculative ratings. Brickwork believes that retail investors should never try to invest in speculative grade instruments.

Corporate Governance Rating Scale

BWR CG 1+: Quality of corporate governance is the best.
BWR CG 1: Quality of corporate governance is excellent.
BWR CG 2: Quality of corporate governance is high.
BWR CG 3: Quality of corporate governance is adequate.
BWR CG 4: Quality of corporate governance is moderate.
BWR CG 5: Quality of corporate governance is inadequate.
BWR CG 6: Quality of corporate governance is low.
BWR CG 7: Quality of corporate governance is very low.
BWR CG 8: Quality of corporate governance is the lowest.

SME Rating Scale

BWR aaa (BWR triple a):Best creditworthiness
BWR aa (BWR double a): High creditworthiness
BWR a : Adequate creditworthiness.
BWR bbb (BWR triple b): Moderate creditworthiness.
BWR bb (BWR double b): Inadequate creditworthiness.
BWR b: Low creditworthiness.
BWR c: Low creditworthiness.
BWR d: Default or expected to default.

Security Receipts Rating Scale

BW RR1+: Recovery value of the underlying assets is greater than 150 per cent of SR face value.

BW RR1: Recovery value of the underlying assets is in the range of 100–50 per cent of SR face value.

BW RR2: Recovery value of the underlying assets is in the range of 75–100 per cent of SR face value.

BW RR3: Recovery value of the underlying assets is in the range of 50–75 per cent of SR face value.

BW RR4: Recovery value of the underlying assets is in the range of 25–50 per cent of SR face value.

BW RR5: Recovery value of the underlying assets is less than 25 per cent of SR face value.

Insurance Companies Rating Scale

BWR In AAA: Best financial capability to meet policyholder's obligations.

BWR In AA: High financial capability to meet policyholder's obligations.

BWR In A: Adequate financial capability to meet policyholder's obligations.

BWR In BBB: Moderate financial capability to meet policyholder's obligations.

BWR In BB: Inadequate financial capability to meet policyholder's obligations.

BWR In B: Low financial capability to meet policyholder's obligations.

BWR In C: Very low financial capability to meet policyholder's obligations.

BWR In D: Default on current policyholder's obligations.

Mutual Funds Rating Scale

BWR MF AAA: Best credit quality of underlying debt portfolio.

BWR MF AA: High credit quality of underlying debt portfolio.

BWR MF A: Adequate credit quality of underlying debt portfolio.

BWR MF BBB: Moderate credit quality of underlying debt portfolio.

BWR MF BB: Inadequate credit quality of underlying debt portfolio.

BWR MF B: Low credit quality of underlying debt portfolio.

BWR MF C: Very low credit quality of underlying debt portfolio.

Real Estate Project Rating Scale

BWR RP 1+: Best project implementation.
BWR RP 1: Excellent project implementation.
BWR RP 2: Adequate project implementation.
BWR RP 3: Moderate project implementation.
BWR RP 4: Inadequate project implementation.
BWR RP 5: Low project implementation.

Real Estate Developer Rating Scale

BWR RD 1+: Best project implementation capability.
BWR RD 1: Excellent project implementation capability.
BWR RD 2: Adequate project implementation capability.
BWR RD 3: Moderate project implementation capability.
BWR RD 4: Inadequate project implementation capability.
BWR RD 5: Low project implementation capability.

Chapter 13

Mutual Funds

LEARNING OBJECTIVES

After reading this chapter, you will be able to:

- Explain the concept of mutual funds.
- Discuss the advantages and disadvantages of investing in mutual funds.
- Trace the origin of mutual funds in India.
- Outline the mutual fund guidelines issued by the Government of India and SEBI.
- Explain performance evaluation models for mutual funds.
- Present assets under management.

13.1 Introduction

A *collective investment vehicle* is an entity that pools the money of investors and invests the pooled money. Collective investment vehicles are classified as mutual funds, exchange traded funds, collective investment schemes and venture capital funds. A *mutual fund* is an entity that pools money from several investors and invests the pooled money in different kinds of securities or assets. An *exchange traded fund* is an investment company whose investment objective is to achieve similar returns as in the case of a particular market index. The International Organization of Securities Commission has defined the *collective investment scheme* (CIS) as an open-ended collective investment scheme that issues redeemable units and invests primarily in transferable securities or money market instruments. As a mutual fund, a collective investment management company that sponsors or launches a CIS shall seek registration with SEBI by fulfilling certain conditions. No entity can launch a CIS without obtaining a certificate of registration from SEBI. As per SEBI regulations, an entity proposing to operate as a collective investment management company (CIMC) shall register as a public limited company under the provisions of the Companies Act, 1956. The company shall have a minimum net worth of INR 50 million. Each CIS has to be rated by a recognized rating agency and the projects to be undertaken appraised by an appraising agency. The units of every CIS shall be listed on the stock exchange(s) immediately after allotment. A *venture capital fund* is an entity with a dedicated pool of capital to be invested in venture capital undertakings.

***Mutual funds** are financial intermediaries that play an important role in mobilizing savings, particularly household savings, and channelize them into the economy through the capital market route.*

Mutual funds are financial intermediaries that mobilize money from investors, particularly small investors, by selling their own shares or units of capital and using it to purchase financial assets or securities issued by others. Instead of making a direct purchase of shares or debt securities, investors can purchase those securities through mutual funds. Mutual funds provide a facility for small investors to obtain the benefits of portfolio investment under the aegis of professional management. They professionally manage the funds of individuals and institutions that may not have a high degree of expertise or sufficient time to cope with the complexities of investment. Mutual funds and investment companies have many things, including investment objectives, in common. Initially, mutual funds in India were not permitted to invest in physical assets. But, since 2006, mutual funds have been permitted to invest in gold by launching gold exchange traded fund schemes. Since 2008, mutual funds in India have also been permitted to invest in real estate by launching appropriate schemes.

Mutual funds are primarily helpful to investors with small or moderate financial resources. Such investors could individually buy only a few different securities and thus fail to get the benefits of owning a well-diversified portfolio. In order to get the benefits of diversification, they could invest in mutual funds. This provides diversification at a lower cost per unit of investment than would be incurred by a small investor. Further, a small investor investing directly in the stock or bond market would have to comply with many formalities or procedures of investing. In order to make the right investment decisions, investors would have to be continually on the lookout for mispriced securities. They would also have to assess risk levels of each security as well as that of the portfolio. By investing in mutual funds, individual investors can transfer all these tasks to the managers of mutual funds.

13.1.1 Mutual Funds in India

Unit Trust of India, established in 1963, was the first mutual fund in India and the first mutual fund scheme in India was US-64.

Mutual funds originated in the United States and moved to the United Kingdom in the 1930s. But the concept took root only in the 1960s. The Government of India, led by Jawaharlal Nehru as the prime minister, realized the need for an institution that would serve as a conduit for household savings to the capital market. Accordingly, the Unit Trust of India Bill was passed by Parliament in 1963, which gave a statutory life to the first mutual fund in India. The Unit Trust of India functioned under the regulatory and administrative control of the Reserve Bank of India till 1978, when the Industrial Development Bank of India took over the regulatory and administrative control of UTI in place of the RBI. UTI launched its first mutual fund scheme, called the Unit Scheme (US-64), in 1964. The US-64 had the distinction of being the largest open-end mutual fund scheme. Later, UTI launched many other mutual fund schemes. The first equity fund launched by UTI was the Mastershare (1986), which received overwhelming support from the investing public across the country. Investors in Mastershare multiplied their investment by more than 5.5 times over a period of just five years.

Non-UTI mutual funds debuted in India in 1987 with the establishment of SBI Mutual Fund. The State Bank of India was the first to set up a bank-run mutual fund, ending UTI's monopoly in this sector. It was followed by many other public sector mutual funds set up by public sector banks, LIC and GIC. The decision of the Government of India to allow institutions other than UTI to operate mutual funds represented a departure from its earlier position that only UTI, which was specifically formed for the purpose, should be allowed to operate mutual funds.

Private sector mutual funds started in 1993. Kothari Pioneer was the first private sector mutual fund in India, registered in July 1993. Subsequently, many other private sector mutual funds, including some multinational mutual funds, were established. India's first money market mutual fund scheme was the Kothari Pioneer Money Market Account Scheme floated by the Kothari Pioneer Mutual Fund in March 1997.

In February 2003, UTI was bifurcated into two separate entities. One is the Specified Undertaking of the Unit Trust of India that functions under rules framed by the Government of India and does not come under the purview of the SEBI Mutual Fund Regulations. It owned the US-64 scheme along with certain other schemes. The second is UTI Mutual Fund Ltd, sponsored by the State Bank of India, Punjab National Bank, Bank of Baroda and the Life Insurance Corporation of India. It is registered with SEBI and functions under its Mutual Fund Regulations.

13.1.2 The Structure of Mutual Funds

A mutual fund in India has the following constituents:

- Fund sponsor
- Trustees
- Asset management company
- Custodians
- Registrar and transfer agent
- Distributors/agents

A *fund sponsor* is a person or entity that establishes a mutual fund. A mutual fund can either be managed by a *board of trustees*, which is a body of individuals, or by a *trust company*, which is a corporate entity.

An *asset management company* is a company constituted by the sponsor of a mutual fund or the trustees that acts like the investment manager of the trust. A *custodian* is an organization established for safekeeping of securities and other assets of a mutual fund. The *registrar and transfer agent* maintains records of unit holders. A mutual fund may choose to hire an independent party registered with SEBI to provide such services or carry out these activities in-house. Communication between a mutual fund and its unit holders takes place through the registrar and transfer agent. Distributors/agents are banks, non-banking companies and other organizations that undertake to distribute the products of a mutual fund.

13.2 Classification of Mutual Funds

A typical small investor saves a part of his income to meet future expenses such as education, marriage, medical purposes and purchase of products. There may be some expenses that are unforeseen. These diverse needs are expressed in terms of investment objectives as safety, liquidity and high return. In order to meet the diverse needs of a multitude of investors, mutual funds have designed and offered a wide variety of mutual fund schemes. On the basis of their structure and objectives, mutual fund schemes are classified as the following:

- Closed-end funds
- Open-end funds
- Income funds
- Growth funds
- Balanced funds
- Money market funds
- Sector funds
- Index funds
- Fund of funds
- Value funds
- Offshore funds
- Load funds and no-load funds
- Mid-cap funds
- Large-cap funds
- Equity mutual funds

In **closed-end funds,** the size of the corpus of the fund and the number of shares/units is determined in advance. The shares/units of closed-end funds are initially offered to the public at a specified price. Once the subscription reaches the predetermined level, the entry of prospective investors to the fund is closed. The opening and closing dates of subscription are announced to the investing public. Thus, investors cannot participate in these schemes after the initial offer is over. Investors also have limited exit options. They might be allowed to exit at regular intervals but this comes at a cost in the form of a higher exit load. Consequently, the fund houses do not stand ready to purchase their own shares or units whenever any of their unit holders decides to sell them. But the units of closed-end schemes are traded either on an organized exchange or in the over-the-counter market. Thus, an investor who wants to buy or sell units of a closed-end fund would have to buy or sell the units either on an organized exchange or in the OTC market. Most of the closed-end funds are long-terms funds and the dividend, interest and capital gains received on investment in the fund shall be distributed to the unit holders.

> *In **closed-end mutual funds**, the size of the corpus of the fund and the number of shares/units is determined in advance. **Open-end funds** continuously offer new units to the public for a price at or near their net asset values and are ready at all times to purchase their own units at or near their net asset value.*

There is a distinction between closed-end debt schemes and closed-end equity schemes.

Closed-end debt schemes exist for a specific period. Investors are aware of the time period of the scheme and the amount that would be paid to the investor at the end of the period. On the other hand, *closed-end equity schemes* are structured in such a way that they are closed-ended for a certain period, say seven years, and then they are converted to open-ended schemes. This conversion is automatic and happens once the specified time period is over. In other words, a closed-ended equity scheme becomes an open-ended equity scheme after the completion of the initial time period.

The size of an **open-end fund** is not determined and entry to the fund is always open to investors. Open-end funds continuously offer new units to the public for a price at or near their net asset values and are also ready at all times to purchase their own units at or near their net asset value. Thus, the number of units and the unit capital of an open-end fund change every time investors purchase or redeem units. In the United Sates, which has a well-developed capital market, over 95 per cent of mutual funds are open-ended. Since investors can withdraw at any point of time, fund managers have to be on their toes to perform well.

Income funds offer average returns regularly to investors, but with lower capital appreciation than that in growth funds. To fulfill this objective, the fund invests mostly in fixed income-yielding securities such as non-convertible debentures and treasury bills.

Growth funds are mutual funds that aim at capital appreciation by investing in growth stocks. Growth funds build a portfolio of stocks that yields above-average returns. These funds do not offer/distribute income regularly but offer substantial capital appreciation in the long run. However, growth funds are more volatile than other types of funds and therefore only aggressive investors may invest in them.

Balanced funds are also known as hybrid funds. They invest in equity shares, preference shares, bonds and short-term securities that provide both income and capital appreciation without much risk. The fund balances its portfolio with equity shares (both listed and non-listed), debentures (both convertible and non-convertible), deposits and money market instruments at certain pre-indicated percentages. Such a portfolio is expected to strike a balance between risk, return, growth and liquidity. Balanced funds are ideal for investors who are a little risk averse.

A *money market mutual fund* is a fund that invests only in money market instruments such as treasury bills and commercial paper. Money market funds are generally very safe and liquid investments. Frequent realization of interest and redemption of the fund at short notice are the main advantages of the money market fund.

Sector mutual funds are funds that restrict their investments to a particular sector of the economy. Sector funds, also known as specialty funds, include sharply focused portfolios that might concentrate on a certain industry. For example, a sector fund may focus on infrastructure or utilities or pharmaceuticals that have strong growth potential. However, these funds are more volatile than funds holding a diversified portfolio of securities because the entire investment is concentrated in one industry.

An *index fund* is a type of mutual fund that invests in stocks that, in aggregate, are expected to move in line with a specific index and thereby replicate the performance of the index. Index funds may contain stocks comprising an index or a sample of stocks making up the index or derivatives that have the index as the underlying asset. Thus, the value of the fund depends on the performance of the chosen index. If the index rises, the value of the index fund rises and if the index falls, so does the value of the fund. Some examples of index funds are the Birla Sun Life Index Fund—dividend with Nifty 50 as the benchmark index; HDFC Index Fund—Nifty Plan with Nifty 50 as the benchmark index; ICICI Prudential Index Fund with Nifty 50 as the benchmark index; UTI Master Index Fund—growth with BSE Sensex as the benchmark index and LIC MF Index Fund—Sensex Plan—growth with BSE Sensex as the benchmark index. Most of the index funds in India attempt to replicate the performance of either the Nifty 50 or BSE Sensex. The benchmark S&P CNX 50 Fund was launched by Benchmark Mutual Fund in 2008. It is an open-end equity index fund replicating the S&P CNX 500 index giving investors a broad exposure to Indian equity. Index funds may tend to have very low expenses because index funds do not change the stocks in their portfolio as frequently as a typical mutual fund. In other words, index funds are passively managed. This reduces transaction costs. Index funds are useful to long-term investors looking at moderate risk and moderate return. Index funds are not appropriate or suitable for investors who expect the mutual funds to outperform a specific index.

Value funds are mutual funds that invest in companies that use their earnings to pay dividend. The stocks of these companies will have more conservative but less volatile returns. These stocks may have fallen out of favour with mainstream investors.

A *fund of funds* is a type of mutual fund that invests in other mutual funds. It is designed to achieve greater diversification than conventional mutual funds. Since a fund of funds buys many different funds, which themselves invest in many different stocks, it is possible for the fund of funds to own the same stock through several different funds.

Offshore funds invest in securities floated outside the country. They provide greater portfolio diversification by investing in international markets. If investments are chosen carefully by capitalizing on the world's best opportunities, offshore funds may provide very high returns. However, fund managers need to keep a close watch on foreign currencies and world markets as even profitable investments in a rising market can lose money if foreign currency rises against domestic currency. The Unit Trust of India was a pioneer in putting India on the international map by floating two offshore funds—the India Fund in UK in 1986 and the India Growth Fund, which was listed on the New York Stock Exchange in 1988. Offshore funds enable foreign investors to participate in the growth of the domestic capital market.

Mutual funds may sell their shares or units to the investing public by two methods—direct marketing and the use of sales force. In *direct marketing*, the mutual fund sells its shares or units directly to investors without the use of sales agents and, therefore, there are no up-front commission charges. Such funds are known as *no-load funds*. If the services of a *sales force* (brokers and commission agents) are used in selling the shares or units of a mutual fund, a commission is to be paid to the sales force. In other words, an investor who buys the units of a mutual fund may be subject to a one-time sales or commission charge. Such funds are known as *load funds* because the commission involves adding a load charge to the NAV of the fund. In order to discourage investors from selling their shares/units immediately after buying them, some mutual funds may charge a *redemption fee*.

13.3 Innovative Funds

In recent years, some innovative mutual funds have been launched in India to provide investors with greater access to markets like the gold market, art market and real estate. They are innovative in the sense that they are new to Indian investors. A brief profile of innovative funds is presented in the following sections.

13.3.1 Exchange Traded Funds

*An **exchange traded fund** is a diversified basket of securities that can be traded in real time like individual stocks on an exchange.*

An **exchange traded fund,** usually known as ETF, is a diversified basket of securities that can be traded in real time like individual stocks on an exchange. That is, the ETF can be bought and sold throughout the trading day like any stock. The ETF is similar to an index fund. An ETF can invest in either all of the stocks that comprise the chosen index in proportion to the weightage given to the stocks in the index or a representative sample of stocks that are included in the index. ETFs are highly flexible and appropriate for long-term investors who want instant exposure to the equity markets. They can also be used for arbitraging between the cash and futures markets. The units of an ETF are purchased or sold directly on the exchange. Therefore, the cost of distribution of units of an ETF is much lower but the reach is wider. Examples of ETFs are Nifty BeES, Junior BeES, Quantum Index and Reliance Bank ETF, Sensex Prudential ICICI ETF (SPIcE ETF), Kotak Sensex ETF and SUNDER (S&P CNX Nifty UTI Depository Receipts Scheme). The first ETF in India, Nifty BeES, was launched by Benchmark Mutual Fund in 2001. It was based on Nifty 50.

Although hundreds of ETFs are traded globally, only three kinds of ETFs are traded in India. They are equity index ETFs, liquid ETFs and gold ETFs. An *equity index ETF* tracks a particular index such as Sensex or Nifty. Generally, an equity index ETF is a better performer than an index fund. The expense of investing in an ETF is relatively low. The tracking error is also lower in an ETF as the fund tracks the equity index on a minute-to-minute basis whereas an index fund tracks it once a day. As the name implies, liquid ETFs aim at providing higher liquidity by tracking money market securities. Gold ETFs track gold and they are as liquid as gold. Buying and selling of gold ETFs can be done on the same day to book profits from intra-day movement in gold prices.

13.3.2 Gold ETFs

*A **gold ETF** is a mutual fund that invests in gold. As prices of gold increase, the gold mutual fund performs well.*

A **gold ETF** is a mutual fund that invests in gold. When an investor buys or invests in a gold mutual fund, fund managers invest that money in gold. Each unit of a gold ETF is representative of a certain quantity of pure gold and the traded price of the units moves in tandem with the price of the pure gold. Thus, when the price of gold increases, the gold mutual fund performs well. However, the exact performance and returns to the investor depend on how the fund managers manage the fund. Like any other mutual fund, when an investment is made in a gold mutual fund, the units of that mutual fund are allotted to the investor. The price of one unit is called NAV. When the mutual fund makes a profit, the NAV increases. If it makes a loss, the NAV decreases. Examples of gold funds are AIG World Gold Fund, DSP ML World Gold Fund, Kotak Gold ETF, Benchmark Gold ETF, UTI Gold ETF, Reliance Gold ETF and Quantum Gold ETF. The first gold ETF in India was the Gold Bees (Gold Benchmark Exchange Traded Scheme) launched in 2007 by the Benchmark Asset Management Company. Listed on the NSE, it offers investors a cost-effective opportunity to access the gold market.

There are three broad categories of gold ETFs—gold ETFs that own physical gold (for example, the SPDR Gold ETF and iShares Comex Gold Trust); gold ETFs that own gold mining stocks (for example, Market Vectors Gold Mining ETF); and gold ETFs that own futures contracts (for example, Powershares DB Gold Fund and E-Tracs CMCI Gold Total Return ETN).

The main advantage of a gold ETF is that it is very easy, particularly for small investors, to invest in the fund compared to buying physical gold themselves. Buying gold involves the verification of the purity of gold, storage and the safety of the gold that is purchased. Trading and investing in gold ETFs is a matter of a few clicks if an investor has a demat account and an online trading account. Gold ETFs eliminate the cost and hassle associated with the securing and storage of physical gold. Further, physical gold is an asset liable to wealth tax, but gold ETFs are exempt from wealth tax. In order to qualify for long-term capital gains in physical gold, one has to hold it for at least three years, whereas in the case of gold ETFs, it is only one year. It may be noted that mutual funds in India are not allowed to invest in commodities other than gold, but they can invest in global funds tracking any commodity.

13.3.3 Art Funds

*By investing in an **art fund,** one can become an owner of a particular art object(s) without actually spending large sums of money on that art object.*

Art funds are mutual funds in which people invest money and the fund manager buys art with the money. Investing in an art fund enables one to become an owner of a particular art object(s) without actually spending large sums of money on that art object. The main attraction of investing in art funds is the appreciation of the value of art over time. The fund managers make a periodic appraisal of each art object in the portfolio to ascertain the investment value of the art. The investors can thus reap the benefits of an appreciating art market. Art funds are usually managed by professionals who have good aesthetic sense. Some examples of established art funds in India are Osian's, Yatra, Copal Art, Crayon Capital and the Indian Fine Art Fund. All of them are close-ended funds with lock-in periods of three to five years. Osian Art Fund was the first art fund in India. It was launched in 2006 by Osian's Connoisseurs of Art Private Ltd, a leading archive and auction house. The fund was started with an initial corpus of INR 1,000 million. The purchase price per unit was INR 100 and the minimum investment was INR 10 million. All the units offered were oversubscribed within a few days. The Indian Fine Art Fund was launched by UK-based Philip Hoffman, the founder of the Fine Art Fund Group. It is the latest entrant in India with USD 25 million, the minimum subscription for which is USD 100,000. It raised funds through resident Indians, NRIs and other global investors and is a five-year closed-ended offshore fund.

The Indian art market has a vast potential because it currently accounts for only about 1 per cent of the global art market. As daily trading in art is very difficult for individual investors unless they are in the inner circle of the art fraternity, art funds have tremendous scope to grow. Art funds also benefit artists and collectors as the funds make pieces of art more popular through trading. Thus, art funds make art accessible to many people. But launching any art fund requires a certificate of registration from SEBI. Launching or floating of art funds or schemes without obtaining registration from SEBI would amount to violation of the SEBI Act and regulations.

13.4 Advantages and Limitations of Mutual Funds

The major advantages of mutual funds are professional portfolio management and diversification of risk.

There are many advantages of mutual funds, particularly for naïve and small investors. The advantages are as follows.

- ***Professional management:*** Mutual funds are professional fund managers, managing funds of individuals and institutions that may not have the time, knowledge and skills to cope with the complexities of buying and selling of securities and tax laws. The investment process basically involves identifying specific assets in which to invest and determining proportions of the fund to put into each asset. The selection of securities for the portfolios is an intellectual exercise involving a lot of equity research. Moreover, the timing of purchase and sale of securities is also very important. All these tricky issues are taken care of by the mutual funds with the help of security analysts and portfolio managers appointed for this purpose. Professional experts with considerable experience can handle investment matters easily and achieve superior or above-average returns for the investors.

- ***Diversification:*** Diversification refers to combining securities in a way that will reduce risk. However, even extensive diversification may not eliminate risk if the securities selected are perfectly positively correlated. The smaller the correlation between the returns of the securities, the greater the benefits of diversification. A negative correlation between the returns of the securities would be even better. The risk involved in holding a stock comprises systematic risk and unsystematic risk. Unsystematic risk is unique to a particular firm and independent of the factors that affect securities in a systematic manner. As the number of securities held in a portfolio is increased, the unsystematic risk is reduced. Efficient diversification can even eliminate unsystematic risk. In other words, all risk other than systematic risk can be diversified away. Mutual funds can minimize risk by investing in a large number of securities across companies and industries.
- ***Lower transaction costs:*** As mutual funds buy and sell securities in large quantities, transaction costs, particularly brokerage fees, and commissions are lower.
- ***Liquidity:*** Investment in mutual funds is highly liquid as the funds are listed on stock exchanges and trading of the units/shares of mutual funds takes place regularly. In certain cases, mutual funds also provide repurchase facility to investors.
- ***Flexibility and choice of schemes:*** Investments by mutual funds are more flexible, and depending upon changes, if any, in the investment objectives, the mutual funds can change their investment strategies. Investors can choose from a wide variety of mutual fund schemes according to their financial needs.
- ***Good regulation:*** The activities of mutual funds are always subject to SEBI/RBI guidelines and regulations. Therefore, the interests of the unit holders or investors are always protected. The regulations also ensure that there is greater transparency in the operations of mutual funds. This enables investors to monitor or keep track of the performance of the funds constantly and take appropriate timely decisions.
- ***High returns:*** In view of professional management taking the right investment decisions, economies of scale and efficiency in operations of mutual funds, investors expect superior returns on their investments.
- ***Pooling advantage:*** As savings are pooled and invested, even a small investor can reap the benefits of a large-sized investment.
- ***Better administration:*** Mutual funds are better administered compared to unmanaged funds. Investors need not be bothered about paperwork and switching between investments and investment of returns.
- ***Easy access to information:*** Mutual funds are well equipped to identify good investment opportunities since they have easy access to information related to companies, industries and the global scenario. Financial experts with the help of advanced financial models process this information and take informed decisions.

Mutual funds have certain drawbacks. When investors invest in a mutual fund, they depend on fund managers' capabilities to make the right investments and thereby earn good returns. If the fund managers fail to perform as well as the investors expected, the investors would not get the desired yield on their investments. Further, mutual funds account for different kinds of charges such as management fee, brokerage and commission, resulting in a lower NAV. In such cases, unmanaged funds may yield better returns than managed funds. When the stock market becomes extremely volatile, it is very difficult for investors to get an idea about the performance of mutual funds. The mutual funds, particularly closed-end funds, may not be the ideal investment vehicle for small retail investors if they trade at a discount to the NAV.

13.5 Guidelines for Mutual Funds

The Government of India issued guidelines for mutual funds on February 14, 1992. While issuing the guidelines, the government specifically mentioned that mutual funds had become a major vehicle for mobilization of savings, particularly from the small and household sectors, for investment in the stock market in view of their growing importance in the capital market and their expanding investor base. It was also felt necessary for the government to develop a comprehensive set of prudential guidelines for the all-round development and regulation of mutual funds and ensuring investor protection.

These guidelines are applicable to all mutual funds that invest primarily in the capital market and also partly in money market instruments subject to the following:

1. Money market mutual funds that would invest exclusively in money market instruments would be regulated by the Reserve Bank of India on the basis of specified guidelines to be laid down by the RBI. However, money market schemes of other mutual funds would be regulated by SEBI. These regulations will be in conformity with the guidelines to be issued by the RBI for money market mutual funds investing exclusively in money market instruments.
2. Offshore funds that have non-resident investors and are regulated by the provisions of the countries where they are registered shall be outside the purview of these guidelines. These funds shall continue to be governed by the rules and procedures laid down for the purpose of approving and monitoring their performance by the Government of India.
3. Mutual funds with special characteristics, for example funds dealing with assets other than securities, may be specifically exempted by the government from the purview of these guidelines.

The salient features of the guidelines are highlighted as follows:

Mutual funds shall be authorized for business by SEBI. The mutual funds shall be sponsored by registered companies with a sound track record, general reputation and fairness in all their business transactions. They shall be established in the form of trusts under the Indian Trusts Act. The sponsoring institution will be free to work out the details regarding the constitution of the trust. The trust will then be authorized to float one or several different schemes under which units shall be issued to the investors. Mutual funds shall be operated only by separately established asset management companies (AMCs).

13.5.1 Mutual Fund Schemes

Each trust is allowed to float different funds or schemes as long as the concerned AMC meets the required capital adequacy criteria and whose authorization has not been withdrawn by SEBI for any reason. Each scheme floated by a mutual fund should have prior registration with SEBI. The AMC should prepare a prospectus/letter of offer for each scheme and get it vetted by SEBI before inviting public participation. Mutual funds should be allowed to start and operate both closed-end and open-end schemes. For each closed-end scheme, the mutual fund should be required to raise at least INR 200 million and for each open-end scheme at least INR 500 million or 60 per cent of the targeted amount. Mutual funds should not be permitted to keep closed-end schemes open for subscription for more than 45 days. For open-end schemes, the first 45 days of the subscription period should be considered for determining the target figure or minimum size. Mutual funds should provide continuous liquidity. Closed-end schemes should be listed on exchanges. For open-end schemes, mutual funds shall sell and repurchase units at predetermined prices based on the NAV and such prices should be published at least once a week. Each fund under the same management should have a clearly identified and responsible fund manager.

13.5.2 Investment Limitations

Mutual funds will be allowed to invest only in transferable securities either in the money market or in the capital market, including any privately placed debentures or securitized debt. Privately placed debentures, securitized debt and other unquoted debt instruments holdings shall not exceed 10 per cent in the case of growth funds and 40 per cent in the case of income funds. All debt instruments should have been rated as investment grade by an approved credit rating agency. If not rated, the specific approval of the board of the AMC is required to become eligible for holding in the portfolio. Mutual funds should not be allowed to give term loans for any purpose.

No individual scheme of a mutual fund should invest more than 5 per cent of the corpus in any one company's shares. No mutual fund under all its schemes should own more than 5 per cent of any company's paid-up capital carrying voting rights. No mutual fund under all its schemes taken together should invest more than 10 per cent of its funds in the shares or debentures or other securities of a single company. No mutual fund under all its schemes taken together should invest more than 15 per cent of its funds in the shares and debentures of any specific industry. This provision will not, however, apply to a scheme that has been floated for investments in one or more specified industries and a declaration to that effect made in the offer letter. No scheme should invest in or lend to another scheme under the same AMC. The scrips purchased should be transferred to the fund's name and scheme, too. Transfers from one scheme to another in the same mutual fund should be allowed only if: (i) such transfers are done at the prevailing market price for quoted instruments on spot basis, (ii) the securities so transferred would be in accordance with the investment objective of the transferee scheme, (iii) transfer of unquoted instruments should be done only with specific approval of the board of trustees and (iv) the registration and accounting of the transaction is completed and ratified in the next meeting of the board of trustees.

13.5.3 Winding Up

Each closed-end scheme should have a fixed duration in terms of the number of years, at the end of which it should be wound up or extended with the permission of SEBI. An open-end scheme shall be wound up if the total number of units outstanding after repurchases at a point of time falls below 50 per cent of the originally issued number of units.

13.5.4 Expenses

The AMC may charge the mutual fund investment management and advisory fees, which should have been disclosed fully in the prospectus subject to the following ceiling:

(a) 1.25 per cent of the weekly average net assets outstanding in the current year for the scheme concerned as long as the net assets do not exceed INR 1 billion, and
(b) 1 per cent of the excess amount over INR 1 billion, where net assets so calculated exceed INR 1 billion.

In addition, the AMC may charge the mutual fund the following:

(a) Initial issue costs of sponsoring the fund and its schemes, and
(b) Recurring expenses including marketing and selling expenses, including agent's commission, if any, brokerage and transaction costs, and registrar services for transfer of shares sold or redeemed.

The fees payable to the trustees shall be charged to the mutual fund. The fees payable to the custodian for safekeeping of fund assets and related matters shall be charged to the mutual fund. The initial issue expenses should not exceed 6 per cent of the funds raised under each scheme. In any case, the total of all the expenses charged to the fund except the initial issue expenses should not exceed 3 per cent of the weekly average net assets outstanding during the current year and the same shall be disclosed through advertisements and accounts. All expenses should be clearly identified and appropriately attributed to individual schemes.

13.5.5 The Asset Management Company

The AMC shall be authorized for business by SEBI on the basis of certain criteria. The directors of an AMC should be persons of high repute and standing with at least 10 years of professional experience in relevant fields such as portfolio management, investment analysis and financial administration. At least 50 per cent of the board of an AMC should consist of independent directors not connected with the sponsoring organization. The AMC should at all times have a minimum net worth of INR 50 million. SEBI shall approve the memorandum and articles of association of the AMC.

The AMC can be changed by either the trustee company/board or by 75 per cent of the investors in the fund. If a change in the AMC is recommended by the trustee company/board, it should be subject to scrutiny and approval of SEBI. If the sponsor of a mutual fund recommends a change of the trustee, it should be subject to scrutiny and approval of SEBI.

13.5.6 Accounting Requirements

Mutual funds should be required to segregate their earnings as current income, short-term capital gains and long-term capital gains. Accounting for all the schemes should be required to be done for the same year-ending. For all quoted instruments, mutual funds must calculate the weekly NAV at the last available closing market prices. For unquoted investments, the valuation may be done once a week either at cost or by any other method authorized by SEBI. For investments considered doubtful, the directors' best estimate may be accepted, subject to scrutiny and certificate of reasonability.

13.6 SEBI (Mutual Funds) Regulations, 1996

After the setting up of SEBI, the government permitted SEBI to take over the task of regulating mutual funds in India. Accordingly, SEBI issued comprehensive regulations in 1996 and keeps updating the regulations as per changing requirements. The following are the important features of SEBI regulations.

1. Every mutual fund should get a certificate of registration from SEBI by fulfilling certain conditions, including that the sponsor of a mutual fund should have a sound track record and general reputation of fairness and integrity in all his business transactions. The sponsor should contribute at least 40 per cent to the net worth of the asset management company.
2. A mutual fund shall be constituted in the form of a trust and the instrument of trust shall be in the form of a deed, duly registered under the provisions of the Indian Registration Act, 1908, executed by the sponsor in favour of the trustees named in such an instrument.
3. The sponsor, or the trustee if authorized by the trust deed, shall appoint an asset management company, which has been approved by SEBI.
4. The asset management company has a net worth of not less than INR 10 crore.
5. Any director of the AMC shall not hold the office of director in another asset management company unless such a person is an independent director.
6. The AMC shall not act as a trustee of any mutual fund and not undertake any other business activities except in the nature of portfolio management services, management and advisory services to offshore funds, pension funds, provident funds, venture capital funds, management of insurance funds, financial consultancy and exchange of research on a commercial basis if any of these activities is not in conflict with the activities of the mutual fund.
7. The AMC shall exercise due diligence and care in all its investment decisions as would be exercised by other persons engaged in the same business.
8. The AMC shall be responsible for the acts of commission or omission by its employees or the persons whose services have been procured by the AMC.
9. An AMC shall not through any broker associated with the sponsor purchase or sell securities that are on an average 5 per cent or more of the aggregate purchases and sales of securities made by the mutual fund in all its schemes.
10. An AMC shall not purchase or sell securities through any broker, other than a broker referred above, that are an average of 5 per cent or more of the aggregate purchases and sales of securities made by the mutual fund in all its schemes unless the AMC has recorded in writing the justification for exceeding the limit of 5 per cent and reports of all such investments are sent to the trustees on a quarterly basis.
11. An AMC shall not utilize the services of the sponsor or any of its associates, employees or their relatives for the purpose of any securities transaction and distribution and sale of securities. Provided that an AMC may utilize such services if disclosure to that effect is made to the unit holders and the brokerage or commission paid is also disclosed in the half-yearly annual accounts of the mutual fund.
12. In case any company has invested more than 5 per cent of the net asset value of a scheme, the investment made by that scheme or by any other scheme of the same mutual fund in that company or its subsidiaries shall be brought to the notice of the trustees by the AMC and be disclosed in the half-yearly and annual accounts of the respective schemes with justification for such investment, provided the latter investment has been made within one year of the date of the former investment calculated on either side.
13. The mutual fund shall appoint a custodian to carry out custodial services for the schemes of the fund and send an intimation of the same to SEBI within 15 days of the appointment of the custodian.
14. No custodian in which the sponsor or its associates holds 50 per cent or more of the voting rights of the share capital of the custodian or where 50 per cent or more of the directors of the custodian represent the interest of the sponsor or its associates shall act as custodian for a mutual fund constituted by the same sponsor or any of its associates or subsidiary company.

15. No scheme shall be launched by the AMC unless the scheme is approved by the trustees and a copy of the offer document has been filed with SEBI. The offer document shall contain disclosures that are adequate in order to enable the investors to make informed investment decisions, including the disclosure on maximum investment proposed to be made by the scheme in the listed securities of the group companies of the sponsor.
16. Every closed-end scheme shall be listed in a recognized stock exchange within six months of the closure of the subscription. Provided that the listing of the closed-end scheme shall not be mandatory (i) if the said scheme provides for periodic repurchase facility to all the unit holders with restriction, if any, on the extent of such repurchase, or (ii) if the said scheme provides for monthly income or caters to special classes of persons like senior citizens, women, children, widows, physically challenged or any special class of persons providing for repurchase of units at regular intervals, or (iii) if the details of such repurchase facility are clearly disclosed in the offer document, or (iv) if the said scheme opens for repurchase within a period of six months from the closure of subscription.
17. The AMC may repurchase or reissue the repurchased units of a closed-end scheme at its discretion. The units of closed-end schemes may be open for sale or redemption at fixed predetermined intervals if the maximum and minimum amounts of sale or redemption of the units and the periodicity of such sale or redemption have been disclosed in the offer document. The units of a closed-end scheme may be converted into an open-end scheme if the offer document of such a scheme discloses the option and the period of such conversion or the unit holders are provided with an option to redeem their units in full and the initial issue expenses of the scheme have been amortized fully in accordance with the Tenth Schedule.
18. A closed-end scheme shall be fully redeemed at the end of the maturity period. Provided that a closed-end scheme may be allowed to be rolled over if the purpose, period and other terms of the rollover and all other material details of the scheme including the likely composition of assets immediately before the rollover, the net assets and net asset value of the scheme are disclosed to the unit holders and a copy of the same has been filed with SEBI. Provided further that such rollover will be permitted only in the case of those unit holders who express their consent in writing and the unit holders who do not opt for the rollover or have not given written consent shall be allowed to redeem their holdings in full at a net asset value-based price.
19. No guaranteed return shall be provided in a scheme (i) unless such returns are fully guaranteed by the sponsor or the AMC, (ii) unless a statement indicating the name of the person who will guarantee the return is made in the offer document, (iii) unless the manner in which the guarantee is to be met has been stated in the offer document.
20. A scheme of a mutual fund may be wound up after repaying the amount due to the unit holders (i) on the occurrence of any event which, in the opinion of the trustees, requires the scheme to be wound up, or (ii) if 75 per cent of the unit holders of a scheme pass a resolution that the scheme be wound up, or (iii) if SEBI so directs in the interests of the unit holders.
21. A mutual fund may invest the money collected under any of its schemes only in securities, money market instruments, privately placed debentures, securitized debt instruments, which are either asset-backed or mortgage-backed securities, or gold or gold-related instruments. The money collected under any money market scheme of a mutual fund shall be invested only in money market instruments. The money collected under any gold exchanged-traded fund scheme shall be invested only in gold or gold-related instruments.
22. Mutual funds shall not borrow except to meet temporary liquidity needs of the mutual funds for the purpose of repurchase, redemption of units or payment of interest or dividend to the unit holders. Provided that the mutual fund shall not borrow more than 20 per cent of the net asset of the scheme and the duration of such a borrowing shall not exceed a period of six months. The mutual fund shall not advance any loans for any purpose.
23. The funds of a scheme shall not in any manner be used in option trading or short selling or carry forward transactions. Provided that a mutual fund may enter into derivatives transactions in a recognized stock exchange, subject to such guidelines as may be specified by SEBI.
24. Every mutual fund shall compute the NAV of each scheme by dividing the net assets of the scheme by the number of units outstanding on the valuation date.

25. The price at which the units may be subscribed to or sold and the price at which such units may at any time be repurchased by the mutual fund shall be made available to the investors. While determining the prices of the units, the mutual fund shall ensure that the repurchase price is not lower than 93 per cent of the NAV and the sale price is not higher than 107 per cent of the NAV. Provided that the repurchase price of the units of a closed-end scheme shall not be lower than 95 per cent of the NAV. Provided further, the difference between the repurchase price and the sale price of the unit shall not exceed 7 per cent calculated on the sale price.
26. The AMC may charge the mutual fund investment and advisory fees, which are fully disclosed in the offer document subject to the condition that: (i) one and a quarter of one per cent of the weekly average net assets outstanding in each accounting year for the scheme concerned, as long as the net assets do not exceed INR 100 crore, and (ii) 1 per cent of the excess amount over INR 100 crore, where net assets so calculated exceed INR 100 crore. For schemes launched on a no-load basis, the AMC shall be entitled to collect an additional management fee not exceeding 1 per cent of the weekly average net assets outstanding in each financial year. In addition to the fees mentioned above, the AMC may charge the mutual fund marketing expenses, brokerage and transaction cost, audit fees, custodian fees, insurance premium, costs of statutory advertisements, costs related to investor communication, fees and expenses of trustees and initial expenses of launching closed-end schemes. The initial expenses of launching a closed-end scheme shall not exceed 6 per cent of initial resources raised.
27. The total expenses of the scheme excluding issue or redemption expenses, whether initially borne by the mutual fund or by the AMC, but including the investment management and advisory fee, shall be subject to the following limits.
    i. On the first INR 100 crore of the average weekly net assets 2.5 per cent.
    ii. On the next INR 300 crore of the average weekly net assets 2.25 per cent.
    iii. On the next INR 300 crore of the average weekly net assets 2.0 per cent and
    iv. On the balance of the assets 1.75 per cent.

    Provided that such recurring expenses shall be lesser by at least 0.25 per cent of the weekly average net assets outstanding in each financial year in respect of a scheme investing in bonds. Provided further that in case of a fund of funds scheme, the total expenses of the scheme including the management fees shall not exceed 0.75 per cent of the daily or weekly average net assets, depending on whether the NAV of the scheme is calculated on a daily or weekly basis. Any expenditure in excess of the limits specified above shall be borne by the AMC or by the trustees or sponsors.

    In a notification issued on November 16, 2007, SEBI put a limit on the annual expense charged by mutual funds for managing index schemes and exchange traded index schemes at 1.5 per cent. This is calculated on a weekly basis. In index schemes, fund managers replicate an index (Sensex or Nifty for example) by choosing stocks in the portfolio in proportion to their weightage in a particular index. As a result, the net asset value of such schemes would largely rise or fall with the movement of the particular index. In the case of exchange traded index funds, the units are like shares traded on stock exchanges. Since index schemes are managed passively, they should charge a lower fee compared to other schemes where fund managers actively buy and sell stocks to enhance portfolio returns. Thus, index schemes do not require any active fund management by fund managers and, therefore, the step (cap on the fees) is considered to be in the right direction.
28. A mutual fund may declare dividends in accordance with the offer document and subject to the guidelines as may be specified by SEBI.
29. The scheme-wise annual report of a mutual fund or an abridged summary thereof shall be maintained with all unit holders as soon as may be but not later than six months from the date of closure of the relevant accounts year.
30. The trustee shall be bound to make such disclosures to the unit holders as are essential in order to keep them informed about any information that may have an adverse bearing on their investments

Mutual funds are also strictly advised to desist from unhealthy and unethical practices like promising assured returns to a select group of investors and entering into clandestine deals with promoters and companies. It is stated that unethical practices of mutual funds go against the grain of the basic concept of mutual funds.

The regulations of SEBI also include 12 schedules covering various aspects such as trusteeship of the mutual fund, AMC, fees, contents of the investment management agreement, contents of the trust deed, code of conduct, advertisement code, restrictions on investments, investment valuation norms, accounting policies and standards, amortization of initial issue expenses, annual report and half-yearly financial results. As per a SEBI circular issued in April 2006, open-ended schemes of mutual funds are not permitted to charge initial expenses such as sales and marketing expenses. However, they could levy an entry load on investments. On the other hand, close-ended schemes are allowed to appropriate a maximum of 6 per cent of the corpus of the scheme towards initial expenses. But they should not levy an entry load.

13.6.1 Valuation Norms

SEBI has also prescribed investment valuation norms for mutual funds, the salient features of which are presented in the following paragraphs.

1. The traded securities shall be valued at the last quoted closing price on the stock exchange. When the securities are traded on more than one recognized stock exchange, the securities shall be valued at the last quoted closing price on the stock exchange where the security is principally traded. There should, however, be no objection for all scrips being valued at the prices quoted on the stock exchange where a majority in value of the investments is principally traded. When a security is not traded on any stock exchange on a particular valuation day, the value at which it was traded on the selected stock exchange or any other stock exchange, as the case may be, on the earliest previous day may be used, provided the date is not more than 30 days prior to the valuation date.

   SEBI has also defined thinly traded securities. When trading in an equity/equity-related security (such as convertible debentures, equity, warrants) in a month is less than INR 5 lakh or the total volume is less than 50,000 shares, it shall be considered as a thinly traded security and valued accordingly. A debt security, other than government securities, that has a trading volume of less than INR 5 in the previous calendar month shall be considered as a thinly traded security based on information provided by the relevant stock exchange on the volume of debt securities traded. A thinly traded debt security would be valued as per the norms set for non-traded debt securities.
2. When a security is not traded on any stock exchange for a period of 30 days prior to the valuation date, the scrip must be treated as a non-traded scrip. Non-traded/thinly traded securities shall be valued "in-good-faith" by the AMC on the basis of appropriate valuation methods based on the principles approved by the board of the AMC. For the purpose of valuation of non-traded/thinly traded securities, the following principles should be adopted.
   a. Equity instruments shall generally be valued on the basis of capitalization of earnings solely or in combination with the net asset value, using for the purposes of capitalization the price or earnings ratios of comparable traded securities and with an appropriate discount for lower liquidity.
   b. Debt instruments shall generally be valued on a yield-to-maturity basis, the capitalization factor being determined for comparable traded securities and with an appropriate discount for lower liquidity.
   c. While investments in call money, bills purchased under rediscounting scheme and short-term deposits with banks shall be valued at cost plus accrual, other money market instruments shall be valued at the yield at which they are currently traded. For this purpose, non-traded instruments (instruments not traded for a period of seven days) will be valued at cost plus interest accrued till the beginning of the day plus the difference between the redemption value and cost spread uniformly over the remaining maturity period of the instruments. Government securities will be valued at yield-to-maturity based on the prevailing market rate.
   d. With respect to convertible debentures and bonds, the non-convertible and convertible components shall be valued separately. The non-convertible component should be valued on the same basis as would be applicable to a debt instrument. The convertible component should be valued on the same basis as would be applicable to an equity instrument. If after conversion the resultant equity instrument would be traded *pari passu* with an existing instrument that is traded, the value of the latter instrument can be adopted after an appropriate discount of the non-tradability of the instrument during the period preceding the conversion while valuing such instruments, the fact whether the conversion is optional should also be factored in.
   e. With respect to warrants to subscribe for shares attached to instruments, the warrants can be valued at the value of the share that would be obtained on exercise of the warrant as reduced by the amount payable on exercise of the warrant. A discount similar to the discount to be determined in respect

of convertible debentures must be deducted to account for the period that must elapse before the warrant can be exercised.

f. Where instruments have been bought on "repo" basis, the instrument must be valued at the resale price after deduction of applicable interest up to the date of resale. Where an instrument has been sold on a "repo" basis, an adjustment must be made for the difference between the repurchase price (after deduction of applicable interest up to the date of repurchase) and the value of the instrument. If the repurchase price exceeds the value, depreciation must be provided for, and if the repurchase price is lower than the value, credit must be taken for the appreciation.

3. All expenses and income accrued up to the valuation date shall be considered for computation of the net asset value. For this purpose, while major expenses like management fees and other periodic expenses should be accrued on a day-to-day basis, other minor expenses and income need not be so accrued, provided the non-accrual does not affect the NAV calculation by more than 1 per cent.

13.6.2 Investment in Unlisted Equity Shares

SEBI has also issued guidelines for investment in unlisted equity shares, the highlights of which are presented as follows.

Unlisted equity shares of a company shall be valued "in good faith" on the basis of the following valuation principles.

Based on the latest available audited balance sheet, net worth shall be calculated as the lower of (i) and (ii):

i. Net worth per share (share capital plus free reserves, excluding revaluation reserves) minus (miscellaneous expenditure not written off or deferred revenue expenditure, intangible assets and accumulated losses) divided by the number of paid-up shares.
ii. After taking into account the outstanding warrants and options, net worth per share shall again be calculated as (share capital plus consideration on exercise of option/warrants received/receivable by the company plus free reserves, excluding revaluation reserves) minus (miscellaneous expenditure not written off or deferred revenue expenditure, intangible assets and accumulated losses) divided by the number of paid-up shares plus the number of shares that would be obtained on conversion/exercise of outstanding warrants and options.

Average capitalization rate (P/E ratio) for the industry based on either BSE or NSE data shall be taken and discounted by 75 per cent, i.e., only 25 per cent of the industry average P/E shall be taken as capitalization rate (P/E ratio). The EPS of the latest audited annual accounts will be considered for this purpose.

The value as per the net worth value per share and the capital earning value calculated as above shall be averaged and further discounted by 15 per cent for illiquidity so as to arrive at the fair value per share.

Mutual funds shall not make investment in unlisted equity shares at a price higher than that obtained by using the aforesaid methodology. However, this will not be applicable for investment made in initial public offers of companies or firm allotment in public issues where all the regulatory requirements and formalities pertaining to public issues have been complied with by the companies and where the mutual funds are required to pay just before the date of public issue.

13.7 Guidelines for Participation of Mutual Funds in Derivatives Trading

In view of several changes taking place in the structure of the cash market and a significant increase in retail participation in the derivatives market, SEBI has permitted mutual funds to participate in the derivatives market for the purpose of hedging and rebalancing their portfolio (SEBI circular dated December 31, 2002). Mutual funds are permitted to participate in the derivatives market on par with foreign institutional investors (FIIs). Accordingly, the mutual funds shall be treated on par with a registered FII with respect to position limits in index futures, index options, stock options and stock futures contracts. The mutual funds will be considered as trading members like registered FIIs and the schemes of mutual funds will be treated as clients like sub-accounts of FIIs.

Mutual funds shall be required to fully cover their positions in the derivatives market by holding underlying securities/cash or cash equivalent/option and/or obligation for acquiring underlying assets to honour the obligations contracted in the derivatives market. The securities held shall be marked to market by the AMC to ensure full coverage of investments made in derivative products at all times. The word "cash" shall include cash, money market instruments, deposits with scheduled commercial banks and net current assets.

The term "hedging" covers derivative market positions that are designed to offset potential losses from existing cash market positions. The use of derivatives for portfolio rebalancing covers situations where a particular desired portfolio position can be achieved more efficiently or at a lower cost using derivatives rather than cash market transactions. For example, if it is cheaper to buy stock futures rather than the stock itself, the mutual fund has a fiduciary obligation to use stock futures unless there are other tangible or intangible disadvantages in using derivatives.

The intention to trade in derivative products shall be disclosed in the offer document. The offer document of a scheme envisaging derivative trading shall state unambiguously and clearly the losses that may be suffered by the investors as a consequence of such investments. Mutual funds shall disclose as to how trading in derivatives will help in the furtherance of the investment objective of the scheme. They shall also lay down exposure limits for themselves and disclose the same in the scheme offer document.

In case the offer document of an existing scheme does not provide for trading in derivatives, the mutual fund, if it so desires, may trade in derivatives in accordance with these guidelines, provided it obtains approval from the trustees and informs the unit holders of its intention to trade in derivatives and making all disclosures. The participation of existing schemes of the mutual funds in the derivatives market shall be subject to the following conditions:

a. The extent and the manner of the proposed participation in derivatives shall be disclosed to the unit holders.
b. The risks associated with such participation shall be disclosed and explained by suitable numerical examples.
c. Positive consent shall be obtained from the majority of the unit holders.
d. An exit option shall be provided to the dissenting unit holders. This option shall be kept open for a period of one month prior to the scheme commencing trading in derivatives.
e. No exit load shall be charged to the unit holders exercising such exit options.

The position limits for mutual funds and its schemes shall be as follows:

1. Position limits for mutual funds in index option contracts
    a. INR 250 crore or 15 per cent of the total open interest of the market in index options, whichever is higher per stock exchange
    b. This limit would be applicable on open positions in all option contracts on a particular underlying index
2. Position limits for mutual funds in index futures contracts
    a. INR 250 crore or 15 per cent of the total open interest of the market in index futures, whichever is higher per stock exchange
    b. This limit would be applicable on open positions in all option contracts on a particular underlying index

In addition to the position limits stated above, mutual funds may take exposure in equity index derivatives subject to the following limits

a. Short positions in index derivatives (short futures, short calls and long pulls) shall not exceed (in notional value) the mutual fund's holding of stocks
b. Long positions in index derivatives (long futures, long calls and short puts) shall not exceed (in notional value) the mutual fund's holding of cash, government securities, T-bills and similar instruments

3. Position limit for mutual funds for stock-based derivative contracts
    a. For stocks in which the market-wise position limit is less than or equal to INR 250 crore, the mutual fund position limit in such stock shall be 20 per cent of the market-wise position limit
    b. For stocks in which the market-wise position limit is greater than INR 250 crore, the mutual fund position limit in such stock shall be INR 50 crore

4. Position limit for each scheme of a mutual fund
   a. For stock option and stock futures contracts, the gross open position across all derivatives contracts on a particular underlying stock of a scheme of a mutual fund shall not exceed the higher of:
      i. 1 per cent of the free float market capitalization (in terms of number of shares), or
      ii. 5 per cent of the open interest in the derivative contracts on a particular underlying stock (in terms of number of contracts)

These position limits shall be applicable to the combined position in all derivative contracts on an underlying stock at a stock exchange.

   b. For index based contracts, mutual funds shall disclose the total open interest held by its scheme or all schemes put together in a particular underlying index, if such open interest equals or exceeds 15 per cent of the open interests of all derivative contracts on that underlying index.

13.8 Entry Load and Exit Load

***Entry load** is an up-front (one-time) charge levied by a mutual fund on an investor on the purchase of units of a mutual fund and **exit load** is a charge levied as a percentage of the existing NAV at the time of exit.*

Entry load is an up-front (one-time) charge levied by a mutual fund on an investor on the purchase of units of a mutual fund. This entry load is usually passed on by the fund house, almost in its entirety, to the distributor who has marketed the fund. Thus, entry load effectively reduces the initial investment a person makes in a fund. It slices away the capital even before investors have gained anything. The rationale behind entry load is that the distributors of mutual funds offer a variety of services to investors of mutual funds apart from selling the units of the fund. They monitor the investments and regularly update the investor. They also ensure compliance with Know Your Customer (KYC) norms. KYC is an important documentation for both individuals and organizations. KYC norms prescribe that financial institutions and other organizations must perform due diligence to identify their clients and ascertain relevant information for doing business with them. For this purpose, distributors of mutual funds may have to visit the investor location. However, with effect from August 1, 2008, SEBI has done away with entry load on mutual funds. Instead, it is mandated that investors in mutual fund schemes must pay the commission directly to the distributors based on individual negotiations. SEBI clarified that distributors should disclose all the commissions payable to them for different competing schemes of various mutual funds, one or more of which they may be selling to the investor. Before this mandate by SEBI, mutual funds had levied a uniform 2.5 per cent entry load on the NAV for all equity funds sold to retail investors. This meant that for every INR 100 invested, only INR 97.5 would actually be deployed by the mutual fund, with the rest pocketed by the distributor.

With no entry load, it is up to the distributor to levy a separate commission for the services he renders to his clients. Distributors are free to compete with each other, offering lower commissions to attract investors. An investor has greater choice—either hunt for a bargain if he doesn't need advice or pay a higher commission if he values the quality of advice given. Earlier, neither the investor nor the distributor enjoyed this flexibility. Thus, the entry load waiver reduces costs for investors. While waiving the entry load, SEBI observed that "the present system of payment of commission has led to a lack of control by the investor over the quality of service vis-a-vis the commission being borne by him. This has led to a situation where advices rendered to the investors could be influenced by factors other than investor's interest. There appears to be a need to empower the investor in deciding the commission paid to the distributors and also to ensure transparency in commissions paid for mutual fund products." As investors would not be charged entry load by way of deduction from their investments, the entire amount would be invested and the investors would receive more units than they did earlier. However, there is nothing to stop mutual funds from paying distributors out of their own resources. So mutual funds, of late, are themselves bearing distributor commissions. The top fund houses are obliged to pay as much as 4–5 per cent for selling new fund offers.

Exit load is a charge levied as a percentage of the existing NAV at the time of exit if such exit is made within the time specified in the scheme. The primary objective of an exit load is to deter investors from exiting a fund within a short span of time, as frequent churning increases the cost incurred by the scheme. Exit loads are also charged to cover advertising and other expenses related to managing a scheme. There is no rule for utilization of such loads. Mutual funds may even use the load to pay distributors. However, SEBI has put a cap of 1 per cent on the maximum amount a mutual fund can retain from the exit load or the contingent deferred sales charges (CDSC) on mutual funds for marketing and selling expenses. As per the SEBI directives, of the exit load or CDSC charged to the investor, a maximum of 1 per cent of the redemption proceeds shall be maintained in a separate account that can be used by the mutual fund to take care of marketing and selling expenses.

While the entry load was waived, several mutual funds have announced changes in their exit load structure. They have hiked their exit load or increased the period of holding before which one would have to pay to exit. For example, UTI Mutual Fund charges an exit load of 1 per cent for most of its equity schemes if the investor sells his fund units within three years (one year for index funds) of purchase of such units. This cap was earlier one year. In UTI's Retirement Benefit Pension Fund, the holding period to avoid exit load is as high as five years. Similarly, in most equity schemes offered by other mutual funds such as Franklin Templeton India, Reliance, Fidelity and ING Vysya, the time limit for charging exit load is three years. For mutual fund schemes under Kotak Mutual Fund, the time frame is two years while HSBC charges a load of 2 per cent for exit before a year. Extended exit load time frames may make investors hold on to their funds longer. It may be noted that the exit load is a kind of deferred sales charge. The longer an investor holds the units, the lower his charges become; they may even be nil.

13.9 Benchmarks

*Comparison portfolios for mutual funds are known as **benchmarks.***

A fund manager may compare the returns obtained by a mutual fund with the returns that could have been obtained if one or more appropriate alternative portfolios had been chosen for investment. In other words, the performance of a mutual fund may be evaluated on a relative basis, not on an absolute basis. However, the performance of a mutual fund should be compared with returns on similar portfolios or indexes. Such comparison portfolios or indexes are referred to as **benchmark portfolios or indexes**. The benchmark portfolio or index should be relevant, feasible and represent alternative portfolios that could have been chosen for investment instead of the mutual fund being evaluated. In order to take care of the risk dimension of investment, the choice of benchmark portfolios or indices may be restricted to portfolios or indices perceived to have similar levels of risk so that a direct comparison of returns becomes meaningful.

According to SEBI guidelines, mutual funds are required to disclose their performance periodically (last six months, one year, three years, five years and since the date of launch of the mutual fund) while publishing half-yearly results in the prescribed format. In order to provide investors with an analysis of the performance of mutual funds in association with the rise or fall in the markets, SEBI has prescribed that the mutual funds should disclose the performance of benchmark indices also. Mutual funds may select any of the indices available—BSE Sensex, S&P CNX Nifty, BSE 100 or S&P CNX 500—depending on the investment objective and portfolio of the mutual fund scheme. In case of sector- or industry-specific schemes, the mutual funds may select any sectoral indices published by stock exchanges and other reputed agencies. These benchmark indices may be decided by the AMCs and trustees and any change at a later date shall be recorded and reasonably justified. As the purpose of benchmarks is to indicate the performance of the markets to investors, mutual funds may give the performance of more than one index if they so desire. They may also have the option of giving their management perception on their performance. The AMCs and trustees are required to review the performance of their schemes on a periodic basis. They may compare the performance of their schemes with benchmarks in all their meetings. They may also review the performance of their schemes in the light of the performance of the mutual funds industry as published from time to time by independent research agencies and financial newspapers and journals and take corrective action in case of unsatisfactory performance. Its compliance may be reported in the quarterly reports of AMCs and half-yearly reports of trustees to SEBI while reporting compliance with Regulation 25(2) on the exercise of due diligence in investment decisions. Mutual funds are also required to disclose the performance of benchmarks in case of various types of debt-oriented funds and balanced funds while publishing half-yearly results. These benchmarks shall be developed by research and rating agencies recommended by AMFI on a regular basis.

The three popular performance measures are Sharpe Performance Measure, Treynor's Performance Measure and Jensen's Performance Measure.

13.10 Methods of Performance Evaluation

An investor may have two alternative investment opportunities. One is that he can buy a large number of securities randomly (diversified portfolio) on his own and hold them for a certain period. Another is that he can invest in a mutual fund, which is known as a managed portfolio.

While taking a decision in this regard, the investor should know the relative performances of the various portfolios, managed as well as unmanaged, and he must also know whether a mutual fund is performing well or not.

One of the methods of measuring the performance of mutual funds involves comparison of the yields of different mutual funds, including an unmanaged portfolio. The popular holding-period-yield formula is given as follows:

$$\frac{NAV_t + D_t}{NAV_{t-1}} - 1$$

Where

NAV_t = Net asset value at the end of year t

D_t = Total distributions (income and capital gains) during year t

NAV_{t-1} = Net asset value at the end of the previous year

The yield as arrived at by the above formula for a mutual fund is compared with that of another mutual fund or benchmark fund, and accordingly the decisions are taken. While taking a decision or arriving at a conclusion, the investor should consider the additional expenditure incurred by him in subscribing to a mutual fund rather than purchasing a diversified portfolio on his own. He should also consider the relative riskiness of the portfolios, managed and unmanaged, under analysis. For example, a mutual fund could have achieved higher returns than another mutual fund or benchmark fund by taking on more risky investments. In such a case, the higher returns may be accompanied by higher risks. Unless the relative risks of mutual funds are considered, the comparison of returns is meaningless.

There are three popular performance measures that take into consideration the risk–return relationship of a mutual fund. They are Sharpe Performance Measure, Treynor's Performance Measure and Jensen's Performance Measure. A brief description of each of these measures is given in the following paragraphs.

13.10.1 Sharpe Performance Measure

Based on the capital asset pricing model, William Sharpe developed a summary measure of portfolio performance, known as the Sharpe Index. The Sharpe Index, designated as S_t, is stated as follows.

$$S_t = \frac{R_t - RFR}{\sigma_t}$$

Where

R_t = Average return on portfolio t during a specified period

RFR = Average risk-free rate of return during the same time period

σ_t = Standard deviation of the returns of portfolio t

The numerator in the model is the risk premium (the excess of return of a portfolio over the risk-free return) and the denominator is a measure of risk. The risk involved in a portfolio is measured by standard deviation. Thus, the Sharpe Index measures the risk premium earned per unit of total risk. It measures the performance of a mutual fund on a risk-adjusted basis. If the Sharpe Index value is low, it means that for a given level of risk, the additional return being earned is less. The investor should then go in for a mutual fund that has a higher Sharpe Index, which will ensure that the investor gets higher returns for the risk he has undertaken.

13.10.2 Treynor's Performance Measure

Treynor's model is a measure of performance of a mutual fund that applies to all types of investors regardless of their risk preferences. The model is as follows.

$$T_n = \frac{R_t - RFR}{\beta_t}$$

Where

R_t = Average return on portfolio t during a specified period
RFR = Average risk-free rate of return during the same time period
β_t = Beta coefficient of the returns of portfolio t

As in the Sharpe Index, the numerator measures the risk premium that is related to the amount of systematic risk as represented by beta of the returns of the portfolio. Treynor's model implicitly assumes that the portfolio under review is completely diversified and, therefore, the risk premium is only for the systematic part of the risk of the portfolio. A portfolio with a higher T_n value indicates superior risk-adjusted performance.

13.10.3 Jensen's Performance Measure

Jensen's model is a measure of absolute performance of a portfolio on a risk-adjusted basis. The model attempts to determine if more than expected returns are being earned for the portfolio's riskiness. Jensen's model is given as follows.

$$R_j - RFR = \alpha_t + \beta_j(R_m - RFR)$$

Where

R_j = Average return on portfolio j during a specified period
RFR = Average risk-free rate of return during the same time period
β_j = Beta coefficient of the returns of portfolio j
α_t = Measure of forecasting ability of the fund manager
β_j = Systematic risk of the portfolio j
R_m = Average return of a market portfolio for the specified period

In this model, the value of α_t indicates whether the fund manager is superior or inferior in stock selection. A positive value of α_t indicates the average superior extra return accruing to that particular portfolio, a negative value of α_t indicates inferior fund management performance and $\alpha_t = 0$ indicates neutral performance of the fund management. Thus, α_t represents how much of the rate of return on the fund is attributable to the fund manager's ability to get above-average returns adjusted for risk. Superior risk-adjusted returns indicate that the fund manager is good at managing the portfolio. If the value of α_t is negative, it would indicate that the fund manager has underperformed in the overall market.

Example 13.1

Given the following data (Table 13.1), rank the funds by using (i) Sharpe Index and (ii) Treynor's Measure. Has any fund outperformed the market? The risk-free rate of return is 8 per cent.

Table 13.1 The given data

Fund	*Average annual return (%)*	*Standard deviation (%)*	*Correlation with market*
P	22	15	0.75
Q	15	10	0.50
R	19	22	0.35
S	12	7	0.90
Market portfolio	12	10	

Solution

The Sharpe Index is given as follows.

$$S_t = \frac{R_t - RFR}{\sigma_t}$$

The Sharpe Index for each fund is calculated as follows.

(Continued)

Fund P:
(0.22 − 0.08)/0.15 = 0.93

Fund Q:
(0.15 − 0.08)/0.10 = 0.70

Fund R:
(0.19 − 0.08)/0.22 = 0.50

Fund S:
(0.12 − 0.08)/0.07 = 0.57

Treynor's Measure is given as follows.

$$T_n = \frac{R_t - RFR}{\beta_t}$$

As the model requires the β_t value, it is calculated as follows.

$$\beta = \frac{r_{jm}\sigma_j}{\sigma_m}$$

Where

r_{jm} = Correlation between returns for fund j and the market portfolio
σ_j = Standard deviation of the returns for fund j
σ_m = Standard deviation of the returns for the market portfolio

Thus, the beta for each of the funds is calculated as follows.

Fund P:

$$\beta = (0.75)\ (0.15)/0.10 = 1.125$$

Fund Q:

$$\beta = (0.50)\ (0.10)/0.10 = 0.50$$

Fund R:

$$\beta = (0.35)\ (0.22)/0.10 = 0.77$$

Fund S:

$$\beta = (0.9)\ (0.07)/0.10 = 0.63$$

The Treynor's Measure for each of the funds is calculated as follows.

Fund P:

$$T = (0.22 - 0.08)/1.125 = 0.124$$

Fund Q:

$$T = (0.15 - 0.08)/0.50 = 0.14$$

Fund R:

$$T = (0.19 - 0.08)/0.77 = 0.143$$

Fund S:

$$T = (0.12 - 0.08)/0.63 = 0.063$$

(Continued)

To determine whether any fund has outperformed the market, the following Jensen's model is used.

$$R_i - RFR = \alpha_t + \beta_i (R_m - RFR)$$

Fund P:

$$0.22 - 0.08 = \alpha + 1.125\,(0.12 - 0.08)$$
$$0.14 = \alpha + 0.045$$
$$\alpha = 0.095$$

Fund Q:

$$0.15 - 0.08 = \alpha + 0.50\,(0.12 - 0.08)$$
$$0.07 = \alpha + 0.02$$
$$\alpha = 0.05$$

Fund R:

$$0.19 - 0.08 = \alpha + 0.77\,(0.12 - 0.08)$$
$$0.11 = \alpha + 0.0308$$
$$\alpha = 0.0792$$

Fund S:

$$0.12 - 0.08 = \alpha + 0.63\,(0.12 - 0.08)$$
$$0.04 = \alpha + 0.0252$$
$$\alpha = 0.0148$$

Thus, as per Jensen's Measure, all the funds have outperformed the market.

The ranking of the funds is as shown in Table 13.2.

Table 13.2 Fund ranking

Sharpe's index	*Treynor's measure*
P	R
Q	Q
R	P
S	S

13.11 Funds Mobilized by Mutual Funds

The funds mobilized by mutual funds in India are presented in Table 13.3. As can be observed from the table, the net funds mobilized by mutual funds increased from INR 18 crore in 1970–71 to INR 183,998 crore in 2007–08. It can also be observed from the table that private sector mutual funds have become very active compared to public sector mutual funds in terms of the funds mobilized. For example, in 2007–08, the net funds mobilized by private sector mutual funds amounted to INR 163,356 crore as against INR 10,678 crore mobilized by UTI, INR 7,786 crore by bank-sponsored mutual funds and INR 2,178 crore by financial institutions-sponsored sector mutual funds.

Table 13.4 shows the scheme-wise mobilization of funds by mutual funds. As can be seen from the table, the number of schemes operated by mutual funds increased from 956 in 2007–08 to 1,001 in 2008–09. The net funds mobilized by mutual funds amounted to INR 153,801 crore in 2007–08. But in 2008–09, there was de-mobilization (outflow) of funds by mutual funds. This outflow was due to uncertain conditions in stock markets and redemption of units by banks and other firms. As a consequence of the global economic recession, the overseas financing of Indian industry became slow. Therefore, firms were forced to withdraw their investments from domestic money market mutual funds. It may be noted that a substantial proportion of funds raised by mutual funds is from banks and other firms, including big companies. In view of the substantial outflow of funds from mutual funds, the net assets of mutual funds declined from INR 505,152 crore as of March 2008 to INR 417,300 crore as of March 2009. The net assets include the funds mobilized during the year and increase in the market value of the portfolio. Income-oriented funds are more popular than other types of funds. They are often preferred because of their high liquidity with minimum risk. It may be further observed from the table that the number of funds mobilized with debt-oriented schemes exceeds the funds mobilized under equity-oriented schemes. This could be because of risk-averse investors and volatility in stock markets.

Table 13.3 Net resources mobilized by mutual funds

Year	*Unit Trust of India*	*Bank-sponsored mutual funds*	*Financial institution–sponsored mutual funds*	*Private sector mutual funds*	*Total*
1970–71	18	–	–	–	18
1971–72	15	–	–	–	15
1972–73	23	–	–	–	23
1973–74	31	–	–	–	31
1974–75	17	–	–	–	17
1975–76	29	–	–	–	29
1976–77	35	–	–	–	35
1977–78	73	–	–	–	73
1978–79	102	–	–	–	102
1979–80	58	–	–	–	58
1980–81	52	–	–	–	52
1981–82	157	–	–	–	157
1982–83	167	–	–	–	167
1983–84	330	–	–	–	330
1984–85	756	–	–	–	756
1985–86	892	–	–	–	892
1986–87	1,261	–	–	–	1,261
1987–88	2,059	250	–	–	2,309
1988–89	3,855	320	–	–	4,175
1989–90	5,584	889	315	–	6,788
1990–91	4,553	2,352	604	–	7,509
1991–92	8,685	2,140	428	–	11,253
1992–93	11,057	1,204	760	–	13,021
1993–94	9,297	148	238	1,560	11,243
1994–95	8,611	766	576	1,322	11,275
1995–96	−6,314	113	235	133	−5,833
1996–97	−3,043	7	137	864	−2,035
1997–98	2,875	237	204	749	4,065
1998–99	170	−89	547	2,067	2,695
1999–2000	4,548	336	296	16,938	22,118
2000–01	322	249	1,273	9,292	11,136
2001–02	−7,284	863	406	16,134	10,119
2002–03	−9,434	1,033	861	12,122	4,582
2003–04	1,050	4,526	787	41,510	47,873
2004–05	−2,467	706	−3,384	7,933	2,788
2005–06	3,424	5,365	2,112	41,581	52,482
2006–07	7,326	3,033	4,226	79,477	94,063
2007–08	10,678	7,786	2,178	163,356	183,998
2008–09	−4,112	4,489	5,954	−28,685	−22,355

Notes:

- Figures in INR crore.
- Data for 2008–09 are provisional.
- For Unit Trust of India, data are gross values (with premium) of net sales under all domestic schemes.
- Data for UTI for 2003–04 relate to UTI Mutual Fund for the period from February 1, 2003, to March 31, 2004, being the first year in operation after the bifurcation of the erstwhile UTI into UTI Mutual Fund and Specified Undertaking of the Unit Trust of India. Subsequent annual data (from 2004–05 onwards) pertain to UTI Mutual Fund only.

Source: Reserve Bank of India, Annual Report 2008–09

Table 13.4 Funds mobilized by mutual funds in India (scheme-wise)

Scheme	2007–08			2008–09		
	No. of schemes	Net mobilization	Net assets	No. of schemes	Net mobilization	Net assets
A. Income/debt-oriented schemes	593	103,867	312,997	599	(−)32,161	294,349
i. Liquid/money market	58	14,976	89,402	56	(−) 3,599	90,594
ii. Gilt	30	434	2,833	34	3606	6,413
iii. Debt (other than assured return)	505	88,457	220,762	509	(−)32,168	197,343
iv. Debt (assured return)	0	0	0	0	0	0
B. Growth/equity-oriented schemes	313	46,933	172,742	340	4,024	108,244
i. Equity-linked saving schemes	43	6,151	16,020	47	2,969	12,428
ii. Others	270	40,782	156,722	293	1,055	95,816
C. Balanced schemes	37	5,768	16,283	35	61	10,629
D. Exchange traded funds	13	(−)2,767	3,130	17	(−)998	1,396
i. Gold ETFs	5	276	483	5	84	736
ii. Other ETFs	8	(−)3,043	2,647	12	(−)1,083	660
E. Fund of funds	37	1,162	3,742	10	778	2,681
F. Total (excluding fund of funds)	956	153,801	505,152	1001	(−)28,296	417,300

Note: Figures in INR crore. Net assets at end-March.

Source: Reserve Bank of India, Annual Report 2008-09

13.12 Assets Under Management

"Assets under management" refer to the market value of assets which are managed by a mutual fund on behalf of investors. As evident from Table 13.5, all the mutual funds in the country managed assets to an extent of INR 5,218,990 million at the end of June 2008. Open-ended funds share a major chunk of total assets under management. Income schemes accounted for 49.07 per cent of assets under management, followed by growth schemes (26.28%) and money market schemes (17.67%).

Table 13.5 Assets under management at the end of June 2008

Scheme	Open ended	Close ended	Interval fund	Total	% to total
Income	1,502,830	775,320	282,610	2,560,760	49.07
Growth	1,087,360	282,690	1,490	1,371,540	26.28
Balanced	118,370	22,610	—	140,980	2.70
Liquid/Money market	922,390	—	—	922,390	17.67
Gilt	21,800	—	—	21,800	0.42
ELSS	119,750	24,680		144,430	2.77
Gold ETF	6,240	—		6,240	0.12
Other ETFs	20,330		—	20,330	0.39
Funds of funds investing overseas	30,520	—	—	30,520	0.58
Total	3,829,590	1,105,300	284,100	5,218,990	100.00

Source: NSE, *Indian Securities Market: A Review (2008)*

13.13 Tax Implications of Mutual Fund Investments

Mutual funds are broadly categorized as *equity-oriented funds* and *debt-oriented funds*. Equity-oriented funds invest a major part of their portfolio in equity shares, whereas debt-oriented funds invest a major part of their portfolio in interest-bearing securities. Income from equity-oriented investments has two facets—*dividend income* and *capital gains*. Presently, as per the provisions of the Income Tax Act, dividend income is exempted from tax in the hands of the investor. In other words, dividend income from equity-oriented funds is not subject to dividend distribution tax (DDT). However, debt funds, except liquid and money market funds, are subject to dividend distribution tax at 12.5 per cent plus surcharge at 10 per cent and education cess at 3 per cent. Liquid and money market funds are the funds that invest their money in very short-term debt instruments, ranging from one day to a few weeks. Liquid and money market funds are idle funds meant for investment for a short period. Such funds are subject to DDT at 25 per cent plus surcharge at 10 per cent and education cess at 3 per cent.

Capital gains arising on the redemption or sale of mutual fund units are subject to income tax. Depending on the period for which the mutual fund units are held by the investor, capital gains are classified as long-term capital gains and short-term capital gains. If the mutual fund units are sold within a period of one year from the date of purchase, the gains are treated as short-term capital gains and are subject to tax. In case of debt-oriented funds, short-term capital gains are taxed at the normal slab rates applicable to the individual. In case of equity-oriented funds, short-term capital gains are taxed at 10 per cent irrespective of the income tax slab to which the individual investor belongs.

Long-term capital gains arising from the sale of units after completion of one year are either exempt from tax or marginally taxed depending on the nature of the investment. In case of debt-oriented funds, long-term capital gains are taxed at the lower of 10 per cent without the benefit of indexation or 20 per cent with the benefit of indexation. In case of equity-oriented funds, long-term capital gains are exempt from income tax. The exit from equity-linked savings schemes that carry a lock-in period of three years is, however, tax-free and the initial investment in these funds is also eligible for deduction under the INR 100,000 threshold of Section 80C.

13.14 Trading of Mutual Funds

Mutual fund trading refers to buying and selling of mutual fund units on stock exchanges. The trading of mutual funds started after the National Stock Exchange launched the Mutual Fund Service System on November 30, 2009, and the Bombay Stock Exchange introduced the BSE Star MF Venture on December 4, 2009. These trading platforms were launched to increase retail participation in mutual funds. Therefore, investors are now able to trade mutual fund units through any member of the stock exchange who is registered as a mutual fund adviser with the Association of Mutual Funds of India. Investors can subscribe/redeem the mutual fund units through the members of the stock exchange (stockbroker) and opt for either the physical or the depository mode of delivery. The new trading platforms are order-routing systems and thus do not allow investors to trade with each other on the platform. Further, trading on the platforms is also subject to securities transaction tax. The transactions for buying mutual fund units are settled on a $T + 1$ basis while the transactions for redemption of units are done on a $T + 3$ basis for equity mutual funds and $T + 1$ for debt mutual funds. The main advantage of trading on the new platforms is that buying and selling of units are more efficient and transparent. But as in stock deals, investors have to pay brokerage for the service that involves buying or selling of mutual funds.

13.15 The Association of Mutual Funds of India (AMFI)

The Association of Mutual Funds of India is the apex body of all the registered asset management companies. It was incorporated as a non-profit organization on August 22, 1995. AMFI functions under the supervision and guidance of its board of directors. The association began its operations with creating awareness, followed by education, and then certification. As the next step to add value to the certification, AMFI introduced a process to register intermediaries who have passed the certification test as AMFI Registered Mutual Fund Advisers.

AMFI has taken the initiative of developing a cadre of trained professional intermediaries consisting of individual agents, brokers, distribution houses and banks engaged in selling mutual fund products. Mutual funds provide both basic services as well as value-added services to investors through their branches/offices and intermediaries. The basic services include providing basic information on schemes launched to investors, assisting them in filling application forms, submission of application forms along with cheques at the respective offices, delivering redemption proceeds and answering investors' scheme-related queries. The value-added services include product information and advice on financial planning and investment strategies. The advice encompasses analyzing an investor's financial goals depending on the segment of investor, assessing his/her resources, determining his/her risk-bearing capacity/preference and then using this information to recommend asset allocation/specific investments that are in tandem with the investor's needs. The investors may also receive information on taxation, estate planning and portfolio rebalancing to remain aware of the changes/developments in market conditions and adjust their portfolios from time to time according to their needs.

In order to ensure professional and healthy practices, AMFI has framed a broad set of guidelines along with a code of conduct. The code of conduct for intermediaries specifies that intermediaries should take necessary steps to ensure that the clients' interest is protected. The intermediaries should provide full and the latest information about schemes to investors in the form of offer documents, performance reports, fact sheets, portfolio disclosures and brochures, and recommend schemes appropriate for the client's situation and needs. They should avoid commission-driven malpractices such as recommending inappropriate products solely because the intermediary would get higher commission, and encouraging over-transacting and churning of mutual fund investments to earn higher commissions, even if they mean higher transaction costs and tax for investors.

The top 10 mutual funds in India in terms of their performance are presented in Box 13.1.

Box 13.1 Top 10 Mutual Funds in India

The top 10 mutual funds in India with their best performing schemes and assets under management (AUM) as on April 30, 2009, are as follows:

1. HDFC Mutual Fund established in June 2000 tops the list with the best performing schemes such as HDFC Top 200 (INR 23,380 million), HDFC Equity (INR 27,593 million) and HDFC MIP Long-Term (INR 8879 million). The HDFC Trustee Company Ltd is the trustee of HDFC Mutual Fund.
2. Tata Mutual Fund was established in June 1995 under the trusteeship of Tata Trustee Company Pvt Ltd. The top performing schemes of Tata Mutual Fund are Tata Pure Equity (INR 2699.5 million), Tata Index Nifty (INR 67.7 million) and Tata Short-Term Bond (INR 2920.8 million).
3. SBI Mutual Fund is one of the oldest mutual funds in India, established in 1987. The SBI Mutual Fund Trustee Company Pvt Ltd is the trustee of SBI Mutual Fund. The top performing schemes of SBI Mutual Fund are Magnum Contra (INR 19,585 million), Magnum Balanced (INR 3331.1 million) and Magnum Multiplier Plus (INR 6871.5 million).
4. Reliance Mutual Fund was established in June 1995 under the trusteeship of Reliance Capital Trustee Company Limited. The top performing schemes of Reliance Mutual Fund are Reliance MIP (INR 1685.2 million), Reliance Banking Retail (INR 6812.5 million) and Reliance Diversified Power Sector Fund (INR 38,095.7 million).
5. DSP BlackRock Mutual Fund was established in December 1996 under the trusteeship of DSP Merrill Lynch Trustee Company Pvt Ltd. The top performing schemes of the fund are DSPBR Top 100 Equity (INR 11,670.8 million), DSPBR Equity (INR 9197.7 million) and DSPBR GSF Longer Duration (INR 4256.7 million).
6. Kotak Mutual Fund was established in June 1998 and Kotak Mahindra Trustee Company Ltd is the trustee of the fund. The top performing schemes of the fund are Kotak Bond Regular (INR 4456.9 million), Kotak 30 (INR 6881.4 million) and Kotak Opportunities (INR 6585.0 million).
7. Principal Mutual Fund was established in November 1994 and Principal Trustee Company Pvt Ltd is the trustee of the company.

(Continued)

The top performing schemes of the fund are Principal Child Benefit (INR 198.1 million), Principal Index (INR 218.8 million) and Principal Personal Tax Saver (INR 3325.3 million).

8. Sundaram BNP Paribas Mutual Fund was set up in August 1996. The Sundaram BNP Paribas Trustee Company Limited is the trustee of the fund. The top performing schemes are Sundaram BNP Paribas Tax Saver (INR 7035.4 million), Sundaram BNP Paribas Select Focus Fund (INR 8807.8 million) and Sundaram BNP Paribas Bond Saver (INR 591.2 million).
9. Franklin Templeton Mutual Fund was established in February 1996 under the trusteeship of Franklin Templeton Trustee Services Pvt Ltd. The top performing schemes are Franklin India Blue Chip Fund (INR 16,428.7 million), Templeton IGSF PF (INR 326.8 million) and Franklin India Prima Plus (INR 11,532 million).
10. Birla Sun Life Mutual Fund started business in December 1994 and the Birla Sun Life Trustee Company Ltd is its trustee. The top performing schemes are Birla GSF Long-Term (INR 104.8 million), Birla Frontline Equity (INR 4811.4 million) and Birla '95 (INR 1271.2 million).

Source: http://www.itrust.in/forum/mutual-funds/list-of-top-10-mutual-fund-companies-in-india/2193.page.

Summary

1. Mutual funds are financial intermediaries that mobilize funds from investors by selling their own shares/units of capital and use it to purchase financial assets such as shares, debentures and government securities. Mutual funds are mainly helpful to investors with small or moderate financial resources.
2. The main advantages of mutual funds are professional management, diversification, lower transaction costs, flexibility and choice of schemes, high returns and better administration of funds. However, mutual funds have certain drawbacks like poor performance of funds in certain situations and high cost of administration.
3. Mutual funds are classified as open-ended and closed-ended funds. They are also classified as income funds, growth funds, balanced funds, money market funds, index funds, fund of funds, value funds, offshore funds, load funds and no-load funds.
4. In closed-ended funds, the size of the corpus of the fund and the number of shares/units is determined in advance and are initially offered to the public at a specified price. Once subscription reaches the predetermined level, the entry of prospective investors to the fund is closed. However, the units are traded either on an organized exchange or in the over-the-counter-market. The size of an open-ended fund is not determined and entry to the fund is always open to investors.
5. Mutual funds made an entry into India with the open-ended Unit Scheme (US-64) launched by Unit Trust of India in 1964. For a long time, no other mutual fund was operating in India. It was only in the late1980s that the State Bank of India established a mutual fund, followed by other banks like Punjab National Bank and Canara Bank. Kothari Pioneer was the first private sector mutual fund registered in July 1993. Subsequently, many other private sector mutual funds have come into existence.
6. The Government of India issued guidelines for mutual funds in February 1992. These guidelines are applicable to all mutual funds that invest primarily in the capital market and partly in money market instruments subject to certain conditions. According to the guidelines, mutual funds shall be sponsored by registered companies with a sound track record, general reputation and fairness in all their business transactions. They shall be established in the form of trusts. The trusts shall then be authorized to float one or several different mutual funds and they shall be operated by separately established asset management companies.
7. According to SEBI regulations, every mutual fund shall obtain a certificate of registration from SEBI by fulfilling certain conditions. The regulations shall also cover many aspects including net worth of the AMC, investment limits, expenses, valuation and trading in derivative products.
8. There are mainly three methods of performance evaluation—Sharpe Performance Measure, Treynor's Performance Measure and Jensen's Performance Measure. A fund manager may compare the returns obtained by a mutual fund with the returns that could have been obtained if one or more appropriate alternative portfolios had been chosen for investment.

9. Mutual funds in India have mobilized funds to the tune of INR 1,538,010 million in 2007–08 and the net assets of mutual funds stood at INR 5,051,520 million as on March 31, 2008. The year 2008–09 saw the outflow of funds from mutual funds due to redemption pressure from banks and other firms following the global liquidity squeeze. Mutual funds have also performed better than the benchmark index Sensex.

Questions and Problems

1. Explain the concept of mutual funds. Why should small investors prefer mutual funds to direct investment in the stock market?
2. What are the major advantages of mutual funds? Why would some investors avoid mutual funds?
3. What are the different types of mutual funds? What purpose(s) do they serve?
4. Trace the origin of mutual funds in India.
5. Examine the guidelines for mutual funds issued by the Government of India.
6. Discuss the salient features of SEBI (Mutual Funds) Regulations.
7. Explain the valuation norms prescribed by SEBI.
8. What is the rationale behind investment limits prescribed by SEBI for mutual funds?
9. Examine SEBI regulations with regard to derivatives trading by mutual funds.
10. Explain mutual funds performance evaluation measures.
11. What do you understand by benchmark portfolio?
12. How do you justify the removal of entry load?
13. Critically examine the role of SEBI in the development of the mutual fund industry.
14. What are the functions of AMFI? Does it really have a role in effective functioning of mutual funds in India?
15. What are the major ills of mutual funds in India?
16. Are the mutual funds in India serving small investors?
17. Table 13.6 shows the results recorded by five mutual funds. The market return is 20 per cent with 9 per cent standard deviation. The risk-free rate of return is 5 per cent. Rank the funds using Sharpe's method. Will the ranking be different if they are measured according to Treynor's method? Have any of these funds outperformed the market? If so, why?

Table 13.6 The performance of five mutual funds

Fund	*Average annual return (%)*	*Standard deviation (%)*	*Correlation with the market*
X	13.5	7	0.5
Y	15	9	0.7
Z	22	12	0.8
A	25	10	0.9
B	10	5	0.3

Chapter 14

Insurance Services

LEARNING OBJECTIVE

After reading this chapter, you will be able to:

- Trace the origin of insurance business in India.
- Describe the historical development of the insurance business in India.
- Highlight the objectives and functions of the Insurance Regulatory and Development Authority (IRDA).
- Explain the concept of reinsurance.
- Give an account of micro-insurance.
- Understand the regulatory measures pertaining to insurance in India.

14.1 Introduction

Though risk and uncertainty differ in a technical sense, risk is often referred to as uncertainty about the future outcome of an event. *Risk* is also described as the variability in outcomes around the expected value. Sometimes, risk is used to describe expected losses. Regardless of the specific meaning of risk, the higher the risk, the greater is the cost (expected losses). Risk may be business risk or personal risk. *Business risk* arises from possible reduction in the value of the business, whereas the risk faced by individuals and families is known as *personal risk.* There are many risk management methods, whether the risk is business risk or personal risk. In this context, three concepts are usually referred to. They are: risk reduction, risk mitigation and risk coping. *Risk reduction* and *risk mitigation* are strategies adopted before the risky event takes place. In other words, risk reduction and risk mitigation are ex-ante risk management strategies. On the other hand, *risk coping* is an ex-post strategy as it is used after the risky event has taken place. **Insurance** is a risk mitigation strategy. It is defined as a contract that requires the insurer to pay for specific losses in exchange for receiving a certain premium from the insured. The insurance policyholder (insured) pays a fixed premium to the insurer and in return the insurer promises to pay for the losses as specified under the terms of the insurance policy. Insurance acts as a protective shield against risk.

> ***Insurance** is a contract that requires the insurer to pay for specific losses in exchange for receiving a certain premium from the insured.*

Insurance not only plays a leading role within the financial system in a country but also has an important socio-economic function. The insurance and banking sectors together contribute about 7 per cent to the Indian GDP. After economic liberalization in the country, the insurance sector has been growing at the rate of 20–25 per cent per annum. The insurance industry facilitates economic development by mobilizing long-term savings for investment besides meeting the socio-economic needs of the people. Thus, insurance is a part of the country's economic and social infrastructure. The avowed objectives of insurance can be achieved when the country has strong insurers who are able to provide consumers with a wide range of world-class products and services at competitive prices, adopt international best practices, operate through various distribution channels for the convenience of consumers and maintain high professional standards. The insurance industry should also be productive, cost-efficient and financially resilient in the face of both market volatility and competitive pressure.

14.1.1 The History of Insurance in India

Insurance services have a deep-rooted history in India. There is a mention of pooling of resources that could be redistributed in times of calamities such as fire, floods, epidemics and famine in the writings of Manu (*Manusmriti*), Yagnavalkya (*Dharmasastra*) and Kautilya (*Arthasastra*). Early traces of insurance were also seen in marine trade loans and carriers' contracts.

History further reveals that the insurance of modern times started in India with the establishment of the Oriental Life Insurance Company in 1818. However, this company collapsed in 1834. Another life insurance company, the Madras Equitable Life Insurance Society, started its insurance operations in 1829 in the Madras presidency. The British Insurance Act was passed in 1870, which facilitated the establishment of Indian offices of foreign insurance companies such as Albert Life Assurance, Royal Insurance, Liverpool and London Globe Insurance. The foreign insurance companies gave stiff competition to Indian insurance companies like the Bombay Mutual Life Insurance Society and the Oriental Assurance Company.

*The modern concept of **life insurance** started in India with the establishment of the Oriental Life Insurance Company in 1818, and the Triton Insurance Company Limited was the first **general insurance** company, established in 1850 in Calcutta by the British.*

The Triton Insurance Company Limited was the first general insurance company. It was established in 1850 in Calcutta by the British. In fact, a few British insurance companies dominated the whole insurance market in India, serving mostly large urban centres. Initially, these insurance companies did not insure the lives of Indians; rather, they existed to meet the insurance needs of Europeans in India. It was only in later stages that insurance companies started providing insurance to Indians, but at a higher premium of 20 per cent or more. Indians were charged higher premium because Indian lives were considered to be riskier.

The Bombay Mutual Life Insurance Society, established in 1870, was the first company to charge the same premium for both Indians and non-Indians. The Indian Mercantile Insurance Company Limited was the first indigenous general insurance company, set up in Bombay in 1907. In view of the proliferation of insurance companies, the government wanted to regulate the insurance business. Therefore, the Indian Assurance Companies Act was passed in 1912. It was the first statutory measure to regulate the insurance business. In 1928, the Indian Insurance Companies Act was enacted to enable the government to collect statistical data about the insurance business in India. During 1920–30, a number of frauds took place in the insurance sector, which tainted the image of the insurance industry in India. With a view to effectively control the activities of insurance companies and protect the interests of the insured public, the Insurance Act was passed in 1938. The Insurance Act, 1938, was the first comprehensive legislation that provided strict state control over insurance business.

By 1956, after the collapse of many insurance companies, there remained 154 Indian insurance companies, 16 non-Indian insurance companies and 75 provident societies that were issuing insurance policies. The operations of the insurance companies were mostly confined to the cities. To promote insurance in towns and rural areas, and to channelize savings for its development programmes, the Government of India nationalized 245 Indian and foreign insurers and provident societies by an act of Parliament (Life Insurance Corporation of India Act, 1956) and brought into existence the Life Insurance Corporation of India (LIC). The main objectives of LIC were as follows:

i. To conduct business with the utmost economy and, in a spirit of trusteeship, to charge premiums no higher than warranted by strict actuarial considerations;
ii. To invest funds in order to obtain maximum yield for the policyholders, consistent with safety of the capital; and
iii. To render prompt and efficient service to policyholders, thereby making insurance widely popular.

The nationalization of life insurance was also justified on the ground that it would result in availability of much needed funds for rapid industrialization of the country, in conformity with the government's industrial policy.

The General Insurance Council, which was constituted in 1957, framed a code of conduct for the fair conduct of the insurance business. In 1968, the Insurance Act was amended to regulate investments and set minimum solvency margins. The Tariff Advisory Committee was also set up.

The general insurance business in India continued to thrive under the private sector till 1972. There were 107 private companies involved in the general insurance business in India but their operations were confined to organized trade and industry in large cities.

In 1972, the General Insurance Business (Nationalization) Act was passed and the Government of India, through nationalization, took over the shares of 55 Indian insurance companies and the undertakings of 52 insurers conducting general insurance business. Subsequently, they were amalgamated into four companies, namely, the National Insurance Company Limited, the New India Assurance Company Limited, the Oriental Insurance Company Limited and the United India Insurance Company Limited.

The General Insurance Corporation of India was formed in pursuance of Section 9(1) of the General Insurance Business (Nationalization) Act, 1972. It was incorporated on November 22, 1972, under the Companies

Act, 1956, as a private limited company by shares. The General Insurance Corporation of India was formed for the purpose of superintending, controlling and carrying on the business of general insurance. It also became the holding company of the four public sector general insurance companies.

The Malhotra committee dealt broadly with three topics, namely, (i) liberalization, restructuring and regulation of insurance; (ii) pricing of products and distribution of services; and (iii) surveyors, reinsurance and ombudsmen.

14.1.2 The Malhotra Committee

Although the Indian economy was opened up following economic reforms initiated in the early 1990s, insurance remained under the public sector. To complement the economic reforms, the Government of India constituted a committee headed by R.N. Malhotra, the governor of the Reserve Bank of India. The Malhotra committee was asked to suggest a suitable structure for the insurance industry, keeping in view the broader structural changes under way at the time and recognizing that insurance was an important part of the financial system. The committee submitted its report in 1994 and made a number of important and far-reaching recommendations. The report of the committee deals broadly with three topics: (i) liberalization, restructuring and regulation of insurance; (ii) pricing of products and distribution of services; and (iii) surveyors, reinsurance and ombudsmen. The specific recommendations of the committee included the following:

1. The government stake in insurance companies should be brought down to 50 per cent. The subsidiaries of the General Insurance Corporation of India should be made independent corporations so that they have greater freedom to operate.
2. Private companies with a minimum paid-up capital of INR 1 billion may be allowed to enter the insurance sector. No promoter group should own more than 40 per cent or less than 26 per cent, and no one else should own more than 1 per cent, of the equity. No company should deal in both life and general insurance through a single entity. Foreign companies may be allowed to enter the insurance industry in collaboration with domestic companies.
3. The Insurance Act should be modified to allow for the setting up of an insurance regulatory body.
4. LIC's mandatory investments in government securities should be reduced from 75 per cent to 50 per cent.
5. Settlement of claims should be done within a specific time frame. Insurance companies should pay interest on delay in payments beyond 30 days.
6. Insurance companies should pay special attention to the rural insurance business. Postal life insurance should be allowed to operate in rural areas.
7. All insurance companies should be given greater freedom to operate.
8. Insurance companies may be encouraged to set up unit linked pension plans.
9. Computerization of operations and updating of technology should be carried out.
10. Life insurance companies should be allowed to operate only at the state level in each state.

The Malhotra committee recommended the setting up of an insurance regulatory authority as a multi-member statutory body with a full-time chairperson, two full-time members and a few part-time members. The regulatory authority would have full functional autonomy and operational flexibility. It would be funded by a levy of 0.05 per cent on the premium income of Indian insurance companies.

Some of the principal functions of this insurance regulatory authority, as envisaged by the Malhotra committee, are to:

- set up capital adequacy, solvency and other prudential norms for insurance companies;
- decide on granting licences for conducting insurance business and function as a registering authority;
- set standards for insurance products and monitor and modify their rates, terms and conditions;
- ensure compliance with prescribed ceilings for management expenses of insurers and agency commissions;
- monitor the quality and performance of inward and outward reinsurances;
- ensure maintenance of adequate technical reserves by the insurers;
- review insurers' asset distribution and management;
- monitor compliance with prescribed prudential norms and patterns of investment;

- ensure, set and monitor accounting standards and transparency of reporting of accounts;
- accept annual accounts, valuation reports and solvency margin statements;
- detect sickness in the industry and take suitable corrective action;
- act as a dispute resolution forum for consumer grievances; and
- prepare and publish annual reports on the state of the insurance industry.

14.2 The Insurance Regulatory and Development Authority (IRDA)

The main objectives of IRDA are to protect the interests of policyholders and to regulate, promote and ensure orderly growth of the insurance industry.

Following the recommendations of the Malhotra committee, the Government of India enacted the Insurance Regulatory and Development Authority Act in 1999 and established the Insurance Regulatory and Development Authority (IRDA). The main objectives of IRDA are (a) to protect the interests of policyholders and (b) to regulate, promote and ensure orderly growth of the insurance industry. IRDA is a 10-member team consisting of a chairman, five full-time members and four part-time members, who are appointed by the Government of India. IRDA It strives to ensure that a sizable portion of the population, besides businesses enterprises, have adequate insurance against various risk exposures. IRDA aims at building a vibrant industry that will benefit all the stakeholders.

The powers, duties and functions of IRDA as specified in Section 14 of the IRDA Act include the following:

- Issuing certificates of registration to applicants, and renewing, modifying, withdrawing, suspending or cancelling such registration.
- Protecting the interests of policyholders in matters concerning assigning of policy, nomination by policyholders, insurable interest, settlement of insurance claims, surrender value of policy and other terms and conditions of contracts of insurance.
- Specifying requisite qualifications, codes of conduct and practical training for intermediary or insurance intermediaries and agents.
- Specifying the code of conduct for surveyors and loss assessors.
- Promoting efficiency in the conduct of the insurance business.
- Promoting and regulating professional organizations connected with the insurance and reinsurance businesses.
- Levying fees and other charges for carrying out the purposes of this act.
- Calling for information from, undertaking inspection of, and conducting enquiries and investigations, including audits, into the insurers, intermediaries, insurance intermediaries and other organizations connected with the insurance business.
- Controlling and regulating the rates, advantages, terms and conditions that may be offered by insurers with respect to the general insurance business not controlled and regulated by the Tariff Advisory Committee.
- Specifying the form and manner in which books of account shall be maintained and statement of accounts shall be rendered by insurers and other insurance intermediaries.
- Regulating investment of funds by insurance companies.
- Regulating maintenance of margins of solvency.
- Adjudicating disputes between insurers and intermediaries or insurance intermediaries.
- Supervising the functioning of the Tariff Advisory Committee.
- Specifying the percentage of insurers' premium incomes to be used to finance schemes for promoting and regulating professional organizations.
- Specifying the percentage of the life and general insurance businesses to be undertaken by the insurer in the rural or social sector.
- Exercising such other powers as may be prescribed.

Thus, IRDA has a specific development agenda besides consumer protection.

After the enactment of the IRDA Act, the Government of India has liberalized the insurance sector. Entry restrictions for private and foreign players have been lifted, with limits on direct foreign investment (FDI). FDI was restricted to 26 per cent of the total capital held by the insurance company. Foreign companies can enter the Indian insurance market through joint ventures with Indian companies.

14.3 The Post-liberalization Scenario

Insurance is a federal subject in India. The main legislative acts that deal with insurance in India are the Insurance Act of 1938 and the Insurance Regulatory and Development Authority Act of 1999. Till September 2000, there was only one life insurance company in India, that is, the Life Insurance Corporation of India (LIC). In the general insurance sector, the General Insurance Corporation of India (GIC) was a monolith with four subsidiary companies, namely, Oriental Insurance Company Ltd, New India Assurance Company Ltd, National Insurance Company Ltd and United India Insurance Company Ltd. These subsidiaries have been de-linked from the parent company and made independent insurance companies. With effect from December 2000, GIC has become a national reinsurer as well. As the sole reinsurer in the domestic reinsurance market, GIC provides reinsurance to general insurance companies in the Indian market.

The Indian insurance industry in the post-liberalization period witnessed a number of significant changes. The country now has a larger number of players in the market, greater competition, wider innovation, more products for consumers, additional channels of distribution and an increase in consumer awareness about the benefits and importance of insurance.

Due to the growing demand for insurance, more and more insurance companies have emerged in the Indian insurance sector. Several international leaders in the insurance sector have also ventured into the Indian insurance industry. The opening up of the insurance sector has led to greater spread and development of the insurance business in the country. The private companies that are in operation in India are listed in Box 14.1.

India has a total of 42 insurance companies—24 life insurance companies, 17 non-life insurance companies and one reinsurance company as on March 30, 2010. Many of these companies are in the private sector and have a joint venture partnership with foreign companies. Both public sector and private sector

Box 14.1 Private Insurance Companies in India

Life insurance

1. HDFC Standard Life Insurance Company Ltd
2. Max New York Life Insurance Company Ltd
3. ICICI Prudential Life Insurance Company Ltd
4. Kotak Mahindra Old Mutual Life Insurance Ltd
5. Birla Sun Life Insurance Company Ltd
6. Tata AIG Life Insurance Company Ltd
7. SBI Life Insurance Company Ltd
8. ING Vysya Life Insurance Company Pvt Ltd
9. Bajaj Allianz Life Insurance Company Ltd
10. Metlife India Insurance Company Ltd
11. Reliance Life Insurance Company Ltd
12. Aviva Life Insurance Company Ltd
13. Sahara India Insurance Company Ltd
14. Shriram Life Insurance Company Ltd
15. Bharti AXA Life Insurance Company Ltd
16. Future Generali India Life Insurance Company Ltd
17. IDBI Fortis Life Insurance Company Ltd
18. Canara HSBC Oriental Bank of Commerce Life Insurance Company Ltd
19. Aegon Religare Life Insurance Company Ltd
20. DLF Pramerica Life Insurance Company Ltd
21. Star Union Dai-ichi Life Insurance Company Ltd
22. India First Life Insurance Company Ltd
23. Royal Sundaram Alliance Insurance Company Ltd

General insurance

1. Reliance General Insurance Company Ltd
2. IFFCO Tokio General Insurance Company Ltd
3. Tata AIG General Insurance Company Ltd
4. Bajaj Allianz General Insurance Company Ltd
5. ICICI Lombard General Insurance Company Ltd
6. Cholamandalam General Insurance Company Ltd
7. Export Credit Guarantee Corporation Ltd
8. HDFC-Chubb General Insurance Company Ltd
9. Apollo Munich Health Insurance Company Ltd
10. Future Generali India Insurance Company Ltd
11. Universal Sompo General Insurance Company Ltd
12. Bharti Axa General Insurance Company Ltd
13. Raheja OBE General Insurance Company Ltd

companies are very strong players. The public sector companies have a long track record, while newer private players have Indian promoters who are highly regarded in their respective fields and foreign partners who have wide experience in both developed and emerging markets. Thus, the insurance sector in India has come full circle from being in the private sector to public sector and back to open competition over a period of almost two centuries. The monopoly of the state insurance companies has come to an end and state-controlled insurance companies like LIC and GIC are facing stiff competition from private insurance companies. Private insurance companies are able to take advantage of the shortcomings of the state-run insurance companies in India.

The insurance market in India has been expanding rapidly and the combined growth rate of both the life and non-life insurance sectors has crossed 20 per cent in the later part of 2000s. Although impressive, the insurance industry is relatively small by international standards. India constitutes 16 per cent of the world's population but accounts for only 1.68 per cent of the world insurance market. However, with the projected economic growth of about 9 percent in 2009–2010 and with reasonable chance of sustaining a high level of growth in the coming years, it is expected that a larger proportion of the population will reach per capita income levels that will result in increased demand for risk and savings-type products, thus increasing insurance penetration in the country. The potential for growth of the insurance industry in India is very high, as about 80 per cent of the Indian population still does not have life insurance or non-life insurance. Further, insurance premium as a percentage of GDP in India is only 4.1 per cent, against 13.1 per cent in the United Kingdom and 8.3 per cent in Japan. Thus, India's huge potential for insurance business growth is a result of a favourable demographic profile, rising incomes and growing investments in insurance and pensions.

14.4 Players in the Insurance Business

Insurance provides protection against financial losses resulting from a variety of perils or calamities. By purchasing insurance policies, individuals and organizations can get reimbursement for losses arising from accidents, theft of property, disability or death. The insurance business consists mainly of the insurers (insurance carriers), insurance brokers and insurance agencies. *Insurers* are the organizations that provide insurance and assume the risks covered by the policy. *Insurance agencies* sell insurance policies for the insurers. They may be directly affiliated with a particular insurer and sell only that insurer's policies or they may be independent agencies marketing the policies of a variety of insurers. There are also brokerages and other establishments that provide other insurance-related services.

The insurer clearly mentions in the insurance policy the terms and conditions of the agreement, particularly which losses it will provide compensation for and the amount that will be awarded. The policy also specifies the premium to be paid. The premium charged for a policy is based primarily on the amount to be awarded in case of loss and the probability (likelihood) of the insurer actually having to pay. In order to be able to pay policyholders for their losses, the insurers invest the money (premium) they receive from policyholders in a portfolio of financial and other assets. They use these income-generating assets to pay off any future claims that they may face.

14.5 Types of Insurance

The insurance business in India is classified as life insurance and general insurance. *Life insurance* covers the risk involved in a person's life, while *general insurance* provides protection against unforeseen events like accidents, floods, earthquake, and burglary. Fire insurance, marine insurance, and health insurance also come under general insurance. The companies that deal in life insurance are known as *life insurers* and other insurers are known as *general insurers*. No company is permitted to deal in both kinds of insurance.

Indian insurance companies offer a comprehensive range of insurance plans such as term life policies, endowment policies, joint life policies, whole life policies, unit linked insurance plans, group insurance policies, pension plans, annuities, and so on. More than 80 per cent of the life insurance business is from endowment policies and money-back policies. Linked products are a new variety of products launched by life insurers. General insurance plans cover motor insurance, home insurance, travel insurance, fire insurance, health insurance, cattle insurance and other related insurance. Motor vehicle insurance is compulsory. The Tariff Advisory Committee (TAC) lays down tariff rates for some of the general insurance products.

Life insurance provides financial protection to dependents on the death of the insured. *Disability insurance* provides a preset income to the insured if he or she is unable to work due to injury or illness. *Health insurance* pays expenses resulting from accidents and illness. *Property insurance* protects against loss or damage to property resulting from hazards such as fire, theft and natural disasters. *Liability insurance* shields the insured from financial responsibility for injuries to others or for damage to other people's property. An *annuity* is a contract between the insured and the insurer to provide a regular income to the insured during retirement for the remainder of his/her life. There are also special types of insurance such as medical malpractice insurance and property title insurance. Some insurance policies cover groups of people (*group insurance*). These policies are generally issued to employers for the benefit of their employees or other membership organizations for the benefit of their members.

14.5.1 Micro-insurance

> ***Micro-insurance*** *is a type of insurance for low-income individuals and households; it protects against specific perils like death, illness and weather catastrophes.*

Micro-insurance is a type of insurance for low-income individuals and households; it protects against specific perils like death, illness and weather catastrophes. Micro-insurance products are low-value products with low premiums and benefit packages, which sets them within the reach of low-income sections of society. Although such risks are common to any individual or family, economically disadvantaged people are more prone to their ill-effects because of their socio-economic condition. For instance, unless they sell their assets or take loans, they may not even be able to meet hospitalization charges. In view of this, all poverty alleviation programmes also aim at enhancing the ability of the economically disadvantaged to deal with various catastrophes or risks. Reducing poverty requires not just the generation of income among the underprivileged but also the protection of these incomes. The underprivileged, particularly in rural areas, not only want insurance to be affordable but also for it to protect against high-frequency risks such as serious illness, accidents, harvest failure and fire. However, insurance companies mostly offer standardized products for a clientele that is relatively better off and urban, with few insurance products for others.

In principle, micro-insurance works like any typical insurance. But there are certain differences between micro-insurance and other insurance. Micro-insurance products are cost-effective. Thus, they require different design and distribution strategies. Micro-insurance premiums are based on community risk ratings and not on individual risk ratings. Micro-insurance can be a group insurance that can cover thousands of customers under one contract. Further, micro-insurance requires an intermediary between the customer and the insurance company. Preferably, the intermediary is a non-government organization (NGO) or micro-finance institution.

The present reach of micro-insurance is around 5 million people, covering only 2 per cent of the economically disadvantaged in the country. Micro-insurance represents a huge untapped market. The factors contributing to emerging opportunities for micro-insurance in India include robust economic growth, increasing income among rural households, and rapidly expanding self-help groups comprising mostly women, which leads to more entrepreneurial activity in rural areas. Increased media exposure, which can boost marketing practices, is also another factor contributing to the growth of micro-insurance in India.

Micro-insurance is a win–win situation; insurers can increase commercial profit by servicing a hitherto untapped market with huge potential and, at the same time, low-income individuals or groups can avail themselves of insurance at affordable premiums to protect themselves against high-frequency risks. When designing and marketing micro-insurance products, insurers need to design products that suit the lifestyle and needs of the target population. For instance, health insurance, weather insurance, livestock insurance and insurance against natural disasters are more relevant than, say, insuring a house. The insurers also need to solve the challenges of reach and sustainability. The major challenge for insurers in reaching out to the disadvantaged is the high cost of providing coverage. Reaching people in rural areas and hinterlands is a challenge, as the cost of travel itself might exceed the transaction amount. Even if insurers can reach rural interiors, the processing of claims is also difficult. The claimant might not understand the policy conditions or the claim process and might not have a bank account to receive the claim money. Thus, to be successful in this space, an insurance company must design simple and flexible products and enable efficient administration. Technology can be a great enabler in this regard.

Micro-insurance is a new concept in India, introduced in the latter part of the twentieth century. The micro-finance institutions have also initiated negotiations with insurers for the purchase of customized group or standardized individual insurance schemes for people belonging to low-income groups. To cite an example, LIC has launched a micro-insurance product called Jeevan Madhur. Under this scheme, individuals can obtain life insurance coverage from a minimum of INR 5,000 to a maximum of INR 30,000. The product is customizable in that the customer can make minimum premium payments of INR 25 a week, INR 50 a fortnight, INR 100 a month and INR 250 over longer periods. The term of the policy ranges from 5 to 15 years. LIC has also tried to sell the Janashree Bima Yojana, a government-subsidized life insurance product, using microfinance institutions (MFIs) and NGOs as delivery channels. People in rural India, however, have few means of putting aside money for future investments. Realizing this, Bajaj Allianz started offering a savings life insurance, which works like a pension scheme, wherein the insured pays in a fixed amount of money every week. If the insured dies, his beneficiaries will receive the money. If he doesn't die, he will receive his savings plus interest after five years. Thus, micro-insurance also helps boost savings of low-income individuals.

Because interest in rural insurance has been building, IRDA issued regulations in November 2005 for the growth of the sector. To substantially increase the pool of permissible micro-insurance agents, the IRDA regulations have legally recognized NGOs, self-help groups and microfinance institutions as micro-insurance agents. The regulations also allow companies to provide both life and livelihood coverage, fix coverage limits and reduce procedural bottlenecks.

14.5.2 Reinsurance

Reinsurance is when an insurance company buys insurance from another company against potential losses. The insurers involved in such a transaction may be categorized as the direct insurer (ceding insurer) and the reinsurer (assuming insurer). The *direct insurer* is responsible for the initial underwriting of insurance policies and annuities, while the *reinsurer* assumes all or part of the risk associated with the existing insurance policies originally underwritten by the direct insurer. In the case of reinsurance, the original insurer retains only a part of the risk (usually less than 10 per cent), which can be safely borne by him, and the balance risk is reinsured. In other words, reinsurance is a process whereby the reinsurer takes on all or part of the risk covered under a policy issued by an insurance company in consideration of a premium payment. It is a form of insurance cover for direct insurers. The reinsurer absorbs and distributes the effects of unexpected catastrophes so that no single insurance company is overburdened. By providing a mechanism of reinsurance, the reinsurer enables insurance companies to offer coverage limits considerably higher than they could otherwise provide. As a result, the total sum insured by an insurance company would be several times its net worth. Through reinsurance, insurance companies can reduce fluctuations in loss and thereby ensure stability in their overall operating results. Thus, reinsurance forms the backbone of the insurance business as it provides a better spread of risk.

> **Reinsurance** *is a process whereby the reinsurer takes on all or part of the risk covered under a policy issued by an insurance company in consideration of a premium payment.*

In India, GIC is the national reinsurer; it reinsures amounts further with international companies. The reinsurers can also purchase their own reinsurance protection, called *retrocession*, in the same form and for the same reasons as the direct insurers.

There are two types of reinsurance agreements, namely, proportional and excess of loss. *Proportional reinsurance agreements* prorate all premiums, losses and expenses between the insurer and the reinsurer on a prearranged basis. They are used extensively in property insurance. *Excess of loss insurance agreements* require the primary insurer to bear all losses up to a predetermined amount (called the retention), while the reinsurer reimburses the insurance company for losses above that retention, up to the limit of the reinsurance contract.

14.5.3 Agricultural Insurance

Agriculture is a high-risk occupation as farm incomes are highly affected by natural disasters. With the commercialization of agriculture, the magnitude of loss due to unfavourable conditions is set to increase. Agricultural insurance is one method by which farmers can stabilize farm incomes. Management of risk in agriculture is one of the major concerns of the government. So, the Government of India has initiated agricultural insurance schemes, a recent one being the National Agricultural Insurance Scheme (NAIS). A brief profile of AIC is presented in Box 14.2.

14.6 Regulatory Measures

IRDA has issued guidelines or regulations pertaining to different aspects of insurance. These are the IRDA Guidelines on Unit Linked Insurance Products, the IRDA (Licensing of Corporate Agents) Regulations, the IRDA (Insurance Brokers) Regulations, the IRDA (Third Party Administrators-Health Services) Regulations and the IRDA (Protection of Policyholders Interests) Regulations. The highlights of these guidelines/regulations are stated in the following sections.

Box 14.2 Agricultural Insurance Company of India Limited (AIC)

In a country like India, where crop production has been subject to the vagaries of weather and large-scale damage due to attack of pests and diseases, crop insurance assumes a vital role in the stable growth of the sector. An All-Risk Comprehensive Crop Insurance Scheme (CCIS) for major crops was introduced in 1985, coinciding with the introduction of the seventh Five-Year Plan and subsequently replaced with the National Agricultural Insurance Scheme (NAIS) with effect from 1999–2000. These schemes have been preceded by years of preparation, studies, planning, experiments and trials on a pilot basis. In fact, the question of introduction of a crop insurance scheme was taken up for examination soon after Indian independence in 1947.

The Agricultural Insurance Company of India Limited (AIC) was set up to dispense insurance protection for agriculture and allied activities. AIC was incorporated under the Indian Companies Act, 1956, on December 20, 2002, with an authorized share capital of INR 15 billion and paid up capital of INR 2 billion. AIC commenced its business from April 1, 2003.

AIC was formed by the Government of India after a proposal by the Hon'ble Union Finance Minister in the general budget speech of FY 2002–03 to set up a new corporation for agriculture insurance to better serve the needs of farmers and to move towards a sustainable actuarial regime.

AIC has taken over the implementation of the National Agricultural Insurance Scheme (NAIS) which until FY 2003 was implemented by GIC. In the future, AIC would also be transacting other insurance businesses directly or indirectly concerning agriculture and its allied activities.

Share capital

AIC has an authorized share capital and paid-up share capital of INR 15,000 million and INR 2,000 million, respectively. The shareholding pattern is as follows:

Organization	*Shareholdings (%)*
General Insurance Corporation of India	35.00
National Bank for Agriculture And Rural Development (NABARD)	30.00
National Insurance Company Limited	8.75
New India Assurance Company Limited	8.75
Oriental Insurance Company Limited	8.75
United India Insurance Company Limited	8.75

The major insurance products offered by AIC are as follows:

- NAIS—National Agricultural Insurance Scheme
- WBCIS—Weather-Based Crop Insurance Scheme
- Wheat Insurance (Weather and Biomass)
- Rabi Weather Insurance
- Mango Insurance
- Poppy Insurance
- USBY—Uttarakhand Seb Bima Yojana (Apple Insurance)
- Potato Insurance
- Grapes Insurance
- Varsha Bima/Rainfall Insurance
- RISC—Rainfall Insurance Scheme for Coffee Growers (Coffee Insurance)
- Bio-Fuel Tree/Plant Insurance
- Pulpwood Tree Insurance
- Coconut Insurance
- Rubber Insurance

Source: http://www.aicofindia.org/

14.6.1 IRDA Guidelines on Unit Linked Insurance Policies

With the opening up of the insurance sector, unit linked insurance policies (ULIPs) have emerged as popular products. A ULIP is a life insurance policy which provides a combination of risk cover and investment. The premium paid by a policy holder on a ULIP is composed of two parts—premium for risk cover and investment. The investment portions of several ULIP holders are pooled to form a fund called unit fund. The unit fund will operate on the lines of a mutual fund. As in the case of mutual funds, unit funds may be of different types, such as income fund, growth fund, cash fund, or balanced fund. Each type of fund has its own objectives and time horizon. The risk profile of each fund is also different. The investment risk, if any, is borne by the investors (policy holders) themselves but not by the insurers.

The insurance sector has been witnessing significant growth in the ULIP business. Considering the several features differentiating ULIPs from traditional insurance products, IRDA issued certain guidelines on December 21, 2005, to protect the interests of policyholders by ensuring the following:

- Provision of fair insurance coverage
- Disclosures to facilitate informed decision-making by policyholders, who bear the investment risks
- Preservation of the long-term nature of these insurance products

The guidelines are intended to enhance transparency, provide a better understanding of the product design to potential investors/policyholders, enlarge the insurance cover in a consistent manner and conform to the medium- and long-term investment characteristics of insurance products.

The guidelines are applicable to all registered life insurers providing life insurance in India and registered in accordance with Section 3 of the Insurance Act, 1938, with respect to all life insurance products classified under linked business, including pension and annuity businesses.

The unit linked products and businesses should, at the minimum, satisfy the following features and criteria:

- Reasonable insurance cover with a linkage to the premium payment during the term of the contract
- Availability of greater part of a targeted sum at the longer end
- Basic features of life insurance contract including long-term nature.
- Avoid technical jargon
- Remain simple for the public to understand
- Complete transparency in all aspects of the product terms and conditions
- Despite the investment risk being borne by the policyholder, the investment strategy is aligned to the long-term nature of these contracts
- Adequate disclosure of information pertaining to investment of funds and the elements of risk involved
- A standard method, across the industry, with regard to computation of NAV (net asset value)

The following are the specific guidelines issued by IRDA as applicable to unit linked insurance products.

1. **Benefit payable on death:** Table 14.1 specifies the minimum sum assured with respect to death benefit under unit linked life insurance contracts, where:
   i. *T* is the policy term (*PT*) chosen by the policyholder (*T* shall be taken as 70 minus age at entry in case of whole life products).
   ii. *AP* is annualized premium selected by the policyholder at the inception of the policy.
   iii. *SP* is single premium chosen by the policyholder at the inception of the policy.

   With respect to products under pension and annuity business, the above is not mandatory.

Table 14.1 Minimum sum assured

Type of product	*Minimum sum assured*
Single premium products	125% of the *SP*
Non-single premium products	$0.5 \times T \times AP$ or $5 \times AP$, whichever is higher

The sum assured payable on death shall not be reduced at any point of time during the term of the policy except to the extent of the partial withdrawals made during the two-year period immediately preceding the death of the life assured. However, on attainment of 60 years of age of the life assured, all the partial withdrawals may be set off against the sum assured payable on death.

No cover should be extended after the expiry of the policy term and only settlement options (which are clearly outlined at the commencement of the contract) may be allowed.

2. **Minimum policy term:** The minimum policy term shall be five years.
3. **Guarantees on policy benefits:** A linked product must have a guaranteed sum assured payable on death and may have a guaranteed maturity value.

   Guarantees provided on death and/or on maturity shall be reasonable and consistent in relation to the current and long-term interest rate scenario. In this regard, demonstration of proper pricing, including the appropriateness through sensitivity and scenario testing, shall be required under the File and Use Procedure for all the guarantees provided for.
4. **Surrender value (SV):** Where a unit linked life insurance policy acquires a surrender value, it shall become payable only after the completion of the third policy anniversary.

   The surrender value or the surrender value formula must be published in the policy document and all other promotional materials of the life insurance contract.
5. **Options available on discontinuance of premiums:** The following are the options available on discontinuance of premiums:
   i. **Discontinuance of due premiums after paying at least three consecutive years' premiums:** If all the due premiums have been paid for at least three consecutive years and subsequent premiums are unpaid, life insurers shall give an opportunity to the policyholders to revive the contract within the limited period allowed for revival as per policy conditions. During this limited period for revival, the insurance cover under the unit linked life insurance contracts shall be continued levying appropriate charges.

      At the end of the allowed period for revival, if the contract is not revived, the contract shall be terminated by paying the surrender value. However, the life insurers can offer to continue the insurance cover under such contracts, if so opted by the policyholder, levying appropriate charges until the fund value does not fall below an amount equivalent to one full year's premium. When the fund value reaches an amount equivalent to one full year's premium, the contract shall be terminated by paying the fund value. It is clarified that the intention is to ensure payment of a minimum of one full year's premium to the policyholder.

   ii. **Discontinuance of due premiums within three years of inception of the policy:** If all the due premiums have not been paid for at least three consecutive years from inception, the insurance cover under the unit linked life insurance contracts shall cease immediately. Insurers shall give an opportunity to the policyholders to revive within the period allowed for revival as per policy conditions. In case the contract is not revived during this period, the contract shall be terminated and the surrender value, if any, shall be paid at the end of the third policy anniversary or at the end of the period allowed for revival, whichever is later.
6. **Loans:** No loans shall be granted under linked insurance products.
7. **Top-up premium:** A top-up premium is an amount of premium that is paid by the policyholders at irregular intervals besides basic regular premium payments specified in the contract and is treated as single premium. Top-up premiums can be remitted to the insurer during the period of contract only, where due basic regular premiums are paid up to date and if expressly stated in the terms and conditions of the contract. At any point of time during the term of the contract, so long as the total amount of top-up premiums remain within the 25 per cent of the total amount of the basic regular premiums paid up to that date, the top-up premium will not be required to have any insurance cover and the balance amount of such top-up premium shall have an insurance cover and shall remain constant during the period of the contract. The provisions in this paragraph shall not apply with respect to pensions and annuity business.
8. **Partial withdrawal:** The first partial withdrawal is allowed only after the third policy anniversary for all regular premium contracts and single premium contracts. Where partial withdrawals have been granted, in case of death during the term of the policy, the sum assured may be reduced to the extent

of the amount of partial withdrawals made during the two-year period immediately preceding the death of the life assured. However, on attainment of 60 years of age of the life assured, all the partial withdrawals may be set off against the sum assured payable on death. The provisions in this paragraph shall not apply with respect to pensions and annuity business. For the purpose of partial withdrawals, all top-up premiums, whether or not associated with insurance cover, shall be treated as single premium; for a top-up premium made during the period of the contract, a lock-in period of three years shall apply from the date of payment of that top-up premium (this condition will not apply if the top-up premiums are paid during the last three years of the contract).

9. **Settlement option:** There is no objection for an insurer providing to the policyholder settlement options, providing only periodical payments, in the contract so as to avoid the possibility of fluctuations affecting the maturity value. Settlement options should clearly indicate the inherent risk being borne by the policyholder during the period and should be explicitly understood by the policyholder. The period of settlement should not, in any case, be extended beyond a period of five years from the date of maturity. The provisions in this paragraph shall not apply with respect to pensions and annuity business.

10. **Unit pricing:** The basic equity principle of unit pricing for any unit linked fund offered by the life insurer shall be as follows. The interests of policyholders who have purchased units in that fund and not involved in a unit transaction should be unaffected by that transaction. The unit pricing shall be computed based on whether the company is purchasing (appropriation price) or selling (expropriation price) the assets in order to meet the day-to-day transactions of unit allocations and unit redemptions, i.e. the life insurer shall be required to sell/purchase the assets if unit redemptions/allocations exceed unit allocations/redemptions at the valuation date.

    The appropriation price shall apply in a situation when the company is required to purchase the assets to allocate the units at the valuation date as stated in 10.2. This shall be the amount of money that the company should put into the fund with respect to each unit it allocates in order to preserve the interests of the existing policyholders.

    The expropriation price shall apply in a situation when the company is required to sell assets to redeem the units at the valuation date. This shall be the amount of money that the company should take out of the fund with respect to each unit it cancels in order to preserve the interests of the continuing policyholders.

    - **Computation of NAV**
        - *When appropriation price is applied:* The NAV of a unit linked life insurance product shall be computed as the market value of the investment held by the fund plus expenses incurred in the purchase of the assets plus the value of any current assets plus any accrued income net of fund management charges less the value of any current liabilities less provisions, if any. This gives the net asset value of the fund. Dividing by the number of units existing at the valuation date (before any new units are allocated) gives the unit price of the fund under consideration.
        - *When expropriation price is applied:* The NAV of a unit linked life insurance product shall be computed as the market value of the investment held by the fund less the expenses incurred in the sale of the assets plus the value of any current assets plus any accrued income net of fund management charges less the value of any current liabilities less provisions, if any. This gives the net asset value of the fund. Dividing by the number of units existing at the valuation date (before any units are redeemed) gives the unit price of the fund under consideration.
    - **Uniform cut-off timings for applicability of net asset value:** The allotment of units to the policyholder should be done only after the receipt of premium proceeds as stated below.
    - **Allocations (premium allocations, switch in):** With respect to premiums/funds switched/received by 4.15 p.m. by the insurer along with a local cheque or demand draft payable at par at the place where the premium is received, the closing NAV of the day on which the premium is received shall be applicable.

        With respect to premiums/funds switched/ received after 4.15 p.m. by the insurer along with a local cheque or demand draft payable at par at the place where the premium is received, the closing NAV of the next business day shall be applicable. With respect to premiums received with outstation cheques/demand drafts at the place where the premium is received, the closing NAV of the day on which the cheque/demand draft is realized shall be applicable.

With regard to the above, the insurer shall ensure that each and every payment instrument is banked with utmost expedition at the first opportunity, given the constraints of banking hours, prudently utilizing every available banking facility (for example, high value clearing and account transfer). Any loss in NAV incurred on account of delays shall be made good by the insurer.

- **Redemptions:** With respect to valid applications received (surrender, maturity claim, switch out, for example) by 4.15 p.m. by the insurer, the same day's closing NAV shall be applicable. With respect to valid applications received (such as surrender, maturity claim, switch) after 4.15 p.m. by the insurer, the closing NAV of the next business day shall be applicable.

The NAV for each segregated fund provided under unit linked life insurance contracts shall be made available to the public in the print media on a daily basis. Also, the NAV shall be displayed in the respective web portals of the life insurer.

11. **Charges:** Life insurers shall use a uniform definition of charges under all their unit linked life insurance products in order to provide a better and clear understanding to the insuring public.
12. **Other conditions:** The other conditions are as follows:
    - All the riders to be attached to a unit linked life insurance contracts shall be filed separately with the authority. The rider premium shall be exclusive of expense loadings. The expenses shall be explicitly stated and levied separately in a transparent manner to the fund.
    - However, insurers have the option to continue the existing practice of appropriating the cost of the rider by cancellation of units, provided the rider cost including all the other charges on the fund, relating to the rider premium (such as allocation charge and fund management) does not exceed the actual rider premium filed with the authority.
    - Exposure to money market instruments under all linked products and to equities with respect to group gratuity and group superannuation shall be as per existing investment guidelines prescribed for other products.
13. **Furnishing statements of account**
    - Unit statement account shall form a part of the policy document.
    - Unit statement shall make a reference to the terms and conditions applicable under the respective policy document.
    - Unit statement shall be issued on every policy anniversary and also as and when a transaction takes place.

The insurance industry in India has come a long way from being a provider of tax planning instruments to offering plans for different purposes including wealth creation. In fact, life insurance is among the fastest growing industries in India. The total value of life insurance premiums (new and renewal) has increased from INR 99,360 crore in 2005–06 to INR 153,000 crore in 2006–07, an increase of 54 per cent. LIC has an overall market share of 75 per cent. Insurance products are designed to include features of life insurance as well as those of financial services. ULIPs, which have many similarities with mutual funds, have emerged as a preferred product. Insurance companies basically mobilize small savings for either retirement or other goals of policyholders. Therefore, policyholders should be assured that the funds they have placed with the insurance companies are deployed safely. IRDA has defined various investment guidelines to ensure security of the funds of policyholders. The insurance companies are expected to make investment decisions not to maximize potential gains by assuming any level of risk but to seek the best returns after adhering to predefined norms on risk. Thus, the investment policies of life insurance companies are designed to enable policyholders to meet their respective financial goals.

14.6.2 IRDA (Protection of Policyholders' Interests) Regulations, 2002

IRDA's regulations to protect the interests of insurance policyholders are highlighted in this section.

1. A prospectus of any insurance product shall clearly state the scope of benefits and the extent of insurance cover and in an explicit manner explain the warranties, exceptions and conditions of the insurance cover and, in the case of life insurance, whether the product is participating (with profits) or

non-participating (without profits). The allowable rider or riders on the product shall be clearly spelt out with regard to their scope of benefits, and in no case the premium relatable to all the riders put together shall exceed 30 per cent of the premium of the main product.

2. An insurer or its agent or other intermediary shall provide all material information with respect to a proposed cover to the prospect to enable the prospect to decide on the best cover that would be in his or her interest.
3. Where the prospect depends upon the advice of the insurer or his agent or an insurance intermediary, such a person must advise the prospect dispassionately.
4. Where, for any reason, the proposal and other connected papers are not filled by the prospect, a certificate may be incorporated at the end of proposal form from the prospect that the contents of the form and documents have been fully explained to him and that he has fully understood the significance of the proposed contract.
5. In the process of sale, the insurer or its agent or any intermediary shall act according to the code of conduct prescribed by:
   (i) The IRDA,
   (ii) The councils that have been established under Section 64C of the Insurance Act, 1938, and
   (iii) The recognized professional body or association of which the agent or intermediary or insurance intermediary is a member.

Proposal for insurance

1. Except in cases of marine insurance cover, where current market practices do not insist on a written proposal form, in all cases a proposal for grant of a cover, either for life business or for general business, must be evidenced by a written document. It is the duty of an insurer to furnish to the insured free of charge, within 30 days of the acceptance of a proposal, a copy of the proposal form.
2. Forms and documents used in the grant of cover may, depending on the circumstances of each case, be made available in languages recognized under the Constitution of India.
3. In filling the form of proposal, the prospect is to be guided by the provisions of Section 45 of the Insurance Act, 1938. Any proposal form seeking information for grant of life cover may prominently state therein the requirements of Section 45 of the act.
4. Where a proposal form is not used, the insurer shall record the information obtained orally or in writing and confirm it within a period of 15 days thereof with the proposer and incorporate the information in its cover note or policy. The onus of proof shall rest with the insurer with respect to any information not so recorded, where the insurer claims that the proposer suppressed any material information or provided misleading or false information on any matter material to the grant of a cover.
5. Wherever the benefit of nomination is available to the proposer, in terms of the act or the conditions of the policy, the insurer shall draw the attention of the proposer to it and encourage the prospect to avail himself of the facility.
6. Proposals shall be processed by the insurer with speed and efficiency and all decisions thereof shall be communicated by it in writing within a reasonable period not exceeding 15 days from the receipt of proposals by the insurer.

Grievance redressal procedure

Every insurer shall have in place proper procedures and an effective mechanism to address complaints and grievances of policyholders efficiently and with speed and the same along with the information with respect to Insurance Ombudsman shall be communicated to the policyholder along with the policy document as may be found necessary.

Matters to be stated in life insurance policy

1. A life insurance policy shall clearly state:
   i. The name of the plan governing the policy, its terms and conditions
   ii. Whether it is participating in profits or not

iii. The basis of participation in profits such as cash bonus, deferred bonus, simple or compound reversionary bonus
iv. The benefits payable and the contingencies upon which these are payable and the other terms and conditions of the insurance contract
v. The details of the riders attaching to the main policy
vi. The date of commencement of risk and the date of maturity or date(s) on which the benefits are payable
vii. The premiums payable, periodicity of payment, grace period allowed for payment of the premium, the date of the last installment of premium, the implication of discontinuing the payment of an installment(s) of premium and also the provisions of a guaranteed surrender value
viii. The age at entry and whether the same has been admitted
ix. The policy requirements for (a) conversion of the policy into paid-up policy, (b) surrender, (c) non-forfeiture and (d) revival of lapsed policies
x. Contingencies excluded from the scope of the cover, both with respect to the main policy and the riders
xi. The provisions for nomination, assignment and loans on security of the policy and a statement that the rate of interest payable on such loan amount shall be as prescribed by the insurer at the time of taking the loan
xii. Any special clauses or conditions, such as first pregnancy clause, suicide clause
xiii. The address of the insurer to which all communications with respect to the policy shall be sent
xiv. The documents that are normally required to be submitted by a claimant in support of a claim under the policy.

2. While acting under the above regulation in forwarding the policy to the insured, the insurer shall inform by the letter forwarding the policy that he has a period of 15 days from the date of receipt of the policy document to review the terms and conditions of the policy and where the insured disagrees to any of those terms or conditions, he has the option to return the policy stating the reasons for his objection, when he shall be entitled to a refund of the premium paid, subject only to a deduction of a proportionate risk premium for the period on cover and the expenses incurred by the insurer on the medical examination of the proposer and stamp duty charges.
3. With respect to a unit linked policy, in addition to the deductions under sub-regulation 2 of this regulation, the insurer shall also be entitled to repurchase the unit at the price of the unit on the date of cancellation.
4. With respect to a cover, where the premium charged is dependent on age, the insurer shall ensure that the age is admitted as far as possible before issuance of the policy document. In case the age has not been admitted by the time the policy is issued, the insurer shall make efforts to obtain proof of age and admit the same as soon as possible.

Matters to be stated in general insurance policy

1. A general insurance policy shall clearly state:
   i. The name(s) and address(es) of the insured and of any bank(s) or any other person having financial interest in the subject matter of insurance
   ii. Full description of the property or interest insured
   iii. The location or locations of the property or interest insured under the policy and, where appropriate, with respective insured values
   iv. Period of insurance
   v. Sums insured
   vi. Perils covered and not covered
   vii. Any franchise or deductible applicable
   viii. Premium payable and where the premium is provisional subject to adjustment, the basis of adjustment of premium be stated
   ix. Policy terms, conditions and warranties

x. Action to be taken by the insured on occurrence of a contingency likely to give rise to a claim under the policy
xi. The obligations of the insured in relation to the subject matter of insurance on occurrence of an event giving rise to a claim and the rights of the insurer in the circumstances
x. Any special conditions attaching to the policy
xi. Provision for cancellation of the policy on grounds of misrepresentation, fraud, non-disclosure of material facts or non-cooperation of the insured
xii. The address of the insurer to which all communications with respect to the insurance contract should be sent
xiii. The details of the riders attaching to the main policy
xiv. Proforma of any communication the insurer may seek from the policyholders to service the policy.

2. Every insurer shall inform and keep informed periodically the insured on the requirements to be fulfilled by the insured regarding lodging of a claim arising in terms of the policy and the procedures to be followed by him to enable the insurer to settle a claim early.

Claims procedure for a life insurance policy

1. A life insurance policy shall state the primary documents that are normally required to be submitted by a claimant in support of a claim.
2. A life insurance company, on receiving a claim, shall process the claim without delay. Any queries or requirement of additional documents, to the extent possible, shall be raised all at once and not in a piecemeal manner, within a period of 15 days of the receipt of the claim.
3. A claim under a life policy shall be paid or be disputed giving all the relevant reasons within 30 days from the date of receipt of all relevant papers and clarifications required. However, where the circumstances of a claim warrant an investigation in the opinion of the insurance company, it shall initiate and complete such investigation at the earliest. Where in the opinion of the insurance company the circumstances of a claim warrant an investigation, it shall initiate and complete such investigation at the earliest, in any case not later than six months from the time of lodging the claim.
4. Subject to the provisions of Section 47 of the Insurance Act, 1938, where a claim is ready for payment but the payment cannot be made due to any reasons for lack of a proper identification of the payee, the life insurer shall hold the amount for the benefit of the payee and such an amount shall earn interest at the rate applicable in a savings bank account with a scheduled bank (effective from 30 days following the submission of all papers and information).
5. Where there is a delay on the part of the insurer in processing a claim for a reason other than the one covered by sub-regulation 4, the life insurance company shall pay interest on the claim amount at a rate which is 2 per cent above the bank rate prevalent at the beginning of the financial year in which the claim was reviewed by it.

Claim procedure for a general insurance policy

1. An insured or the claimant shall give notice to the insurer of any loss arising under the contract of insurance at the earliest or within such extended time as may be allowed by the insurer. On receipt of such a communication, a general insurer shall respond immediately and give clear indication to the insured on the procedures that he should follow. In cases where a surveyor has to be appointed for assessing a loss/claim, it shall be so done within 72 hours of the receipt of intimation from the insured.
2. Where the insured is unable to furnish all the particulars required by the surveyor or where the surveyor does not receive the full cooperation of the insured, the insurer or the surveyor, as the case may be, shall inform in writing the insured about the delay that may result in the assessment of the claim. The surveyor shall be subjected to the code of conduct laid down by the authority while assessing the loss and shall communicate his findings to the insurer within 30 days of his appointment with a copy of the report being furnished to the insured, if he so desires. Where, in special circumstances of the case, either due to its special and complicated nature, the surveyor shall under intimation to the insured seek an extension from the insurer for submission of his report. In no case shall a surveyor take more than six months from the date of his appointment to furnish his report.

3. If an insurer, on the receipt of a survey report, finds that it is incomplete in any respect, he shall require the surveyor under intimation to the insured to furnish an additional report on certain specific issues as may be required by the insurer. Such a request may be made by the insurer within 15 days of the receipt of the original survey report.
4. The surveyor on receipt of this communication shall furnish an additional report within three weeks of the date of receipt of communication from the insurer.
5. On receipt of the survey report or the additional survey report, as the case may be, an insurer shall within a period of 30 days offer a settlement of the claim to the insured. If the insurer, for any reasons to be recorded in writing and communicated to the insured, decides to reject a claim under the policy, it shall do so within a period of 30 days from the receipt of the survey report or the additional survey report, as the case may be.
6. On acceptance of an offer of settlement as stated in sub-regulation 5 by the insured, the payment of the amount due shall be made within seven days from the date of acceptance of the offer by the insured. In cases of delay in payment, the insurer shall be liable to pay interest at a rate which is 2 per cent above the bank rate prevalent at the beginning of the financial year in which the claim was reviewed by it.

Policyholders' servicing

An insurer carrying on life or general business, as the case may be, shall at all times respond within 10 days of the receipt of any communication from its policyholders in all matters, such as:

(a) Recording change of address
(b) Noting a new nomination or change of nomination under a policy
(c) Noting an assignment on the policy
(d) Providing information on the current status of a policy indicating matters, such as accrued bonus, surrender value and entitlement to a loan
(e) Processing papers and disbursal of a loan on security of policy
(f) Issuance of duplicate policy
(g) Issuance of an endorsement under the policy, noting a change of interest or sum assured or perils insured, financial interest of a bank and other interests
(h) Guidance on the procedure for registering a claim and early settlement thereof.

Any breaches of the obligations cast on an insurer or insurance agent or insurance intermediary in terms of these regulations may enable IRDA to initiate action against each or all of them, jointly or severally, under the Insurance Act, 1938, and/or the Insurance Regulatory and Development Authority Act, 1999.

14.6.3 IRDA (Third Party Administrators—Health Services) Regulations, 2001

IRDA also issued certain regulations for third party administrators (TPA)—health services. Health services is defined by IRDA as all the services to be rendered by a TPA under an agreement with an insurance company in connection with health insurance business or "health cover", as defined in Regulation 2(f) of the IRDA (Registration of Indian Insurance Companies) Regulations, 2000, but does not include the business of an insurance company or the soliciting, directly or through an insurance intermediary including an insurance agent, of insurance business. TPA means a third party administrator who, for the time being, is licensed by IRDA and is engaged, for a fee or remuneration, by whatever name as may be specified in the agreement with an insurance company, for the provision of health services.

The main points of the regulations are stated in the following paragraphs.

Conditions of and procedure for licensing of TPAs

1. Only a company with share capital and registered under the Companies Act, 1956, can function as a TPA.
2. The main or primary object of the company shall be to carry on business in India as a TPA in health services and on being licensed by the authority, the company shall not engage itself in any other business.
3. The minimum paid-up capital of the company shall be in equity shares amounting to INR 1 crore.
4. At no point of time of its functioning shall the TPA have a working capital of less than INR 1 crore.

5. At least one of the directors of the TPA shall be a qualified medical doctor registered with the Medical Council of India.
6. The aggregate holdings of equity shares by a foreign company shall not at any time exceed 26 per cent of the paid-up equity capital of a third party administrator.
7. Any transfer of shares exceeding 5 per cent of the paid-up share capital shall be intimated by the TPA to the authority within 15 days of the transfer indicating the names and particulars of the transferor and transferee.

A. 1. The TPA shall obtain from the IRDA a licence to function as a TPA for rendering health services.
2. The application for licence shall be made in writing to the authority in Form TPA-1 and shall be accompanied by a non-refundable processing fee of INR 20,000 to IRDA by way of a crossed demand draft in favour of IRDA payable in Delhi.
3. IRDA may, in the course of examination of the application, call for such information or ask for production of such documents as it may deem fit and it shall be incumbent upon the applicant to furnish the same within the specified time.
4. IRDA, on examination of the application and details furnished by the applicant, may issue a licence if it is satisfied that the applicant TPA is eligible to function as a TPA.
5. Every TPA approved by IRDA shall pay a further sum of INR 30,000 to IRDA as licence fee before the licence is granted to it and the same shall be paid to the authority in the manner as stated in sub-regulation 2 of this regulation.
6. A TPA whose application has been rejected by IRDA shall not, for a period of two years from the date of such a rejection, apply again to IRDA for a licence.

B. A copy of the agreement entered into between the TPA and the insurance company, or any modification thereof, shall be filed within 15 days of its execution or modification, as the case may be, with IRDA.

C. More than one TPA may be engaged by an insurance company and, similarly, a TPA can serve more than one insurance company.

D. The parties to the agreement shall agree between themselves on the scope of the contract and the facilities that have to be provided. Such an agreement shall also prescribe the remuneration that may be payable to the TPA by the insurance company.

E. Every TPA shall appoint, with due intimation to IRDA, from among its directors or senior employees, a chief administrative officer (CAO) or chief executive officer (CEO) who shall be responsible for the proper day-to-day administration of the activities of the TPA.

F. 1. Every application received by IRDA pursuant to these regulations shall be considered by it within a reasonable time and its decision thereon communicated to the applicant.
2. On an examination of the material placed before it and on the basis of enquiries made by it, where the authority is of the opinion that the application does not deserve acceptance, it shall communicate its opinion to the applicant, who shall be given a reasonable opportunity to represent against the proposed rejection of the application.
3. Where on a complete examination of the materials, documents, information, etc., available to it, the authority finally comes to the conclusion that an application be rejected, it shall do so by making an order in writing, which shall be communicated to the applicant at the earliest.
4. Where the authority decides to issue a licence to the applicant to act as TPA, it shall issue the same in Form TPA-2.

G. Every licence granted by IRDA to a TPA or any renewal thereof, in terms of these regulations, shall remain in force for three years, unless the authority decides either to revoke or cancel it earlier, as provided in these regulations.

H. 1. A licence granted to a TPA may be renewed for a further period of three years on submission of the prescribed renewal application in Form TPA-3 along with a renewal fee of INR 30,000 at least 30 days prior to the date of expiry of the licence.
2. Any failure on the part of the TPA to get its licence renewed before its expiry has to be explained to the authority. A delayed application shall state the reasons for the delay and be accompanied by a late fee of INR 100.

3. IRDA after examining the reasons given in the application by the TPA may renew the licence if it is satisfied that the TPA was prevented by sufficient cause from applying for the renewal of its licence at least 30 days before the date on which the licence ceased to remain in force.
4. IRDA may, if it is satisfied that undue hardship would be caused otherwise, accept an application after the licence ceases to remain in force on payment by the applicant of INR 750.

I. Where a licence granted by IRDA is lost or mutilated, the authority may issue a duplicate licence on payment of a fee of INR 1,000 accompanied by an application in writing made by the TPA.

J. A licence granted to a TPA may after due notice be revoked or cancelled by the authority for one or more of the reasons as prescribed.

K. Before proceeding under regulation to revoke or cancel a licence granted to a TPA, IRDA shall grant a reasonable opportunity of being heard to the TPA.

L. A TPA whose licence has been revoked or cancelled in terms of these regulations may file a review application with the authority within 30 days of the receipt of the order cancelling or revoking the licence.

Code of conduct for TPAs

1. A TPA licensed under these regulations shall as far as possible act in the best professional manner.
2. In particular and without prejudice to the generality of the provisions contained above, it shall be the duty of every TPA, its chief administrative officer or chief executive officer and its employees or representatives to:
   a. Establish its or his or their identity to the public and the insured/policyholder and that of the insurance company with which it has entered into an agreement.
   b. Disclose its license to the insured/policyholder/prospect.
   c. Disclose the details of the services it is authorized to render with respect to health insurance products under an agreement with an insurance company.
   d. Bring to the notice of the insurance company with whom it has an agreement any adverse report or inconsistencies or any material fact that is relevant for the insurance company's business.
   e. Obtain all the requisite documents pertaining to the examination of an insurance claim arising out of the insurance contract concluded by the insurance company with the insured/policyholder.
   f. Render necessary assistance specified under the agreement and advice to policyholders or claimants or beneficiaries in complying with the requirements for settlement of claims with the insurance company.
   g. Conduct itself/himself in a courteous and professional manner.
   h. Refrain from acting in a manner which may influence directly or indirectly the insured/policyholder of a particular insurance company to shift the insurance portfolio from the existing insurance company to another insurance company.
   i. Refrain from trading on information and the records of its business.
   j. Maintain confidentiality of the data collected by it in the course of its agreement.
   k. Refrain from resorting to advertisements of its business or the services carried out by it on behalf of a particular insurance company without the prior written approval by the insurance company.
   l. Refrain from inducing an insured/policyholder to omit any material information or submit wrong information.
   m. Refrain from demanding or receiving a share of the proceeds or indemnity from the claimant under an insurance contract.
   n. Follow the guidelines/directions that may be issued by the authority from time to time.

Maintenance and confidentiality of information

1. A TPA shall maintain proper records, documents, evidence and books of all transactions carried out by it on behalf of an insurance company in terms of its agreement. These books and records shall be maintained by it in accordance with accepted professional standards of record-keeping and for a period of not less than three years. Such records, documents, evidence, books, etc., and the information contained

therein shall be available to the insurance company and the authority and access to them shall not be denied by the TPA on any ground.

2. Every TPA shall, in maintaining the records in terms of sub-regulation 1, follow strictly the professional confidentiality between the parties as required, but this does not prevent the TPA from sharing relevant information with any court of law/tribunal, the government or the authority in the case of any investigation carried out or proposed to be carried out by the authority against the insurance company, TPA or any other person or for any other reason.
3. If the licence granted to the TPA is either revoked or cancelled in terms of these regulations, the data collected by the TPA and all the books, records or documents, etc., relating to the business carried on by it with regard to an insurance company shall be handed over to that insurance company by the TPA forthwith, complete in all respects.

14.6.4 IRDA (Licensing of Corporate Agents) Regulations, 2002

IRDA has prescribed certain regulations for licensing of corporate agents. The highlights of these regulations are as follows:

Definitions

A composite corporate agent is a corporate agent who holds a licence to act as an insurance agent for a life insurer and a general insurer. A corporate agent is any person specified and licensed to act as such. A corporate insurance executive in the case of a company or firm is a director or partner or one or more of its officers or employees so designated by it, and in the case of any other person, the chief executive, by whatever name called, or one or more of his employees designated by him, who possesses the requisite qualifications and practical training and who have passed such an examination as required under clauses (e) and (f) of Section 42 of the Insurance Act.

Issue or renewal of licence

1. A person desiring to obtain or renew a licence (hereinafter referred to as "the applicant") to act as a corporate agent or a composite corporate agent shall proceed as follows:
   (a) The applicant shall make an application to a designated person in Form IRDA-Corporate Agents-A-1.
   (b) The fees payable by the applicant to the authority shall be as specified in the regulations.
2. The designated person may, on receipt of the application along with the evidence of payment of fees to the authority, and on being satisfied that the corporate insurance executive of the applicant:
   (i) possesses the qualifications as specified under Regulation 4,
   (ii) possesses the practical training as specified under Regulation 5,
   (iii) has passed the examination as specified under Regulation 6,
   (iv) has furnished an application complete in all respects,
   (v) has the requisite knowledge to solicit and procure insurance business and
   (vi) is capable of providing the necessary service to the policyholders, grant or renew, as the case may be, a licence in Form IRDA-Corporate Agents-L-1.

   Notwithstanding anything contained in the above, IRDA may refuse or reject, for reasons being recorded, an application if it feels that the grant of licence may be against public interest or when the application is from such a person or group of persons who is or are already engaged as insurance agents, brokers, etc.
3. The designated person shall grant or renew the licence within a period of three months from the date of application.
4. The designated person shall, if the consideration of the application is likely to get delayed, within 60 days of the receipt of the application inform the applicant about the reasons for such a delay, and the likely time it would take to do so.
5. If the designated person refuses to grant or renew a licence under this regulation, he shall give the reasons thereof to the applicant.

6. An individual desiring to become a specified person of a corporate agent/composite corporate agent shall apply through the corporate agent/composite corporate agent in Form IRDA-Corporate Agent-A-2 to the insurer.
7. The designated person of the insurer may, on receipt of such an application along with the evidence of payment of fees to the authority, grant or renew, as the case may be, a certificate in Form IRDA-Corporate Agents-L-2.

Qualifications

1. The applicant being a corporate agent shall ensure that depending on the nature of the entity, the partnership deed, memorandum of association or any other document evidencing the constitution of the entity shall contain as one of its main objects soliciting or procuring insurance business as a corporate agent.
2. The corporate insurance executive shall possess the minimum qualification of a pass in twelfth-standard or equivalent examination conducted by any recognized board/institution, where the applicant resides in a place with a population of 5,000 or more as per the last census, and a pass in 10th-standard or equivalent examination from a recognized board/institution if the applicant resides in any other place.
3. A specified person shall possess the minimum qualifications stipulated.
4. Every corporate insurance executive and each of the specified persons shall also not suffer from any of the disqualifications specified under Section 42D of the act.

Practical training

1. Where an applicant is seeking a licence for the first time to act as a corporate agent, a corporate insurance executive of such an applicant shall have completed from an approved institution at least 100 hours' practical training which may be spread over three to four weeks, in either life or general insurance business as the case may be. Provided that the corporate insurance executive of the applicant shall have completed from an approved institution at least 150 hours' practical training which may be spread over six to eight weeks, both in life and general insurance business, where such an applicant is seeking a licence for the first time to act as a composite corporate agent.
2. Where the corporate insurance executive of the applicant, referred to under sub-regulation (1), is:
   (a) an associate/fellow of the Insurance Institute of India, Mumbai;
   (b) an associate/fellow of the Institute of Chartered Accountants of India, New Delhi;
   (c) an associate/fellow of the Institute of Costs and Works Accountants of India, Calcutta;
   (d) an associate/fellow of the Institute of Company Secretaries of India, New Delhi;
   (e) an associate/fellow of the Actuarial Society of India, Mumbai;
   (f) a Master of Business Administration of any institution/ university recognized by any state government or the central government; or
   (g) possessing certified associateship of Indian Institute of Bankers (CAIIB); or
   (h) possessing any professional qualification in marketing from any institution/university recognized by any state government or the central government;

   he shall have completed at least 50 hours' practical training from an approved institution. Provided that such a corporate insurance executive of the applicant shall have completed from an approved institution at least 70 hours' practical training in life and general insurance business, where such an applicant is seeking a licence for the first time to act as a composite corporate agent.
3. A specified person shall undergo practical training of not less than 100 hours in life or general insurance business, as the case may be, from an approved institution. In case of training in both life and general insurance, the duration of practical training shall be not less than 150 hours. However, if he falls within one of the categories as given in sub-regulation 2 above, he shall have completed 50 hours from an approved institution. Provided that such a specified person of the corporate agent shall have completed from an approved institution at least 70 hours' practical training in life and general insurance business, where such a specified person of the corporate agent is seeking a certificate for the first time which will enable him to procure both life and general insurance business.

Examination

1. The corporate insurance executive of the applicant or a specified person shall have passed the pre-recruitment examination in life or general insurance business, or both, as the case may be, conducted by the Insurance Institute of India, Mumbai, or any other examination body duly recognized by the authority.
2. The examining body shall issue a certificate to every successful specified person, which shall enable him to procure insurance business on behalf of the corporate agent he is working for.

Fees payable

1. The fees payable to the authority for issue or renewal of the licence to act as a corporate agent shall be INR 250.
2. Every specified person of the corporate agent shall apply through the corporate agent to the designated person of the insurer to obtain the certificate, accompanied by a fee of INR 500 remitted to the authority.

Remuneration

1. Every corporate agent shall be paid a commission as per provisions of Section 40A of the act.
2. Every specified person shall be an employee of the corporate agent.

Code of conduct

1. Every licensed corporate agent shall abide by the code of conduct specified as follows.
   Every corporate agent shall:
   (a) be responsible for all acts of omission and commission of its corporate insurance executive and every specified person;
   (b) ensure that the corporate insurance executive and all specified persons are properly trained, skilled and knowledgeable in the insurance products they market;
   (c) ensure that the corporate insurance executive and the specified person do not make to the prospect any misrepresentation on policy benefits and returns available under the policy;
   (d) ensure that no prospect is forced to buy an insurance product;
   (e) give adequate pre-sales and post-sales advice to the insured with respect to the insurance product;
   (f) extend all possible help and cooperation to an insured in completion of all formalities and documentation in the event of a claim;
   (g) give due publicity to the fact that the corporate agent does not underwrite the risk or act as an insurer;
   (h) enter into service-level agreements with the insurer in which the duties and responsibilities of both are defined.
2. Every corporate agent or a corporate insurance executive or a specified person shall also follow the code of conduct as specified:
   (i) Every corporate agent/corporate insurance executive/specified person shall:
      (a) identify himself and the insurance company of which he is a representative;
      (b) disclose his licence/certificate to the prospect on demand;
      (c) disseminate the requisite information with respect to insurance products offered for sale by his insurer and take into account the needs of the prospect while recommending a specific insurance plan;
      (d) disclose the scales of commission with respect to the insurance product offered for sale, if asked by the prospect;
      (e) indicate the premium to be charged by the insurer for the insurance product offered for sale;
      (f) explain to the prospect the nature of information required in the proposal form by the insurer, and also the importance of disclosure of material information in the purchase of an insurance contract;

(g) bring to the notice of the insurer any adverse habits or income inconsistency of the prospect, in the form of a report (called "Insurance Agent's Confidential Report") along with every proposal submitted to the insurer, and any material fact that may adversely affect the underwriting decision of the insurer as regards acceptance of the proposal, by making all reasonable enquiries about the prospect;

(h) inform promptly the prospect about the acceptance or rejection of the proposal by the insurer;

(i) obtain the requisite documents at the time of filing the proposal form with the insurer and other documents subsequently asked for by the insurer for completion of the proposal;

(j) render necessary assistance to the policyholders or claimants or beneficiaries in complying with the requirements for settlement of claims by the insurer;

(k) advise every individual policyholder to effect nomination or assignment or change of address or exercise of options, as the case may be, and offer necessary assistance in this behalf, wherever necessary.

(ii) No corporate agent/corporate insurance executive/specified person shall:

(a) solicit or procure insurance business without holding a valid licence/ certificate;

(b) induce the prospect to omit any material information in the proposal form;

(c) induce the prospect to submit wrong information in the proposal form or documents submitted to the insurer for acceptance of the proposal;

(d) behave in a discourteous manner with the prospect;

(e) interfere with any proposal introduced by any other specified person or any insurance intermediary;

(f) offer different rates, advantages, terms and conditions other than those offered by his insurer;

(g) demand or receive a share of proceeds from the beneficiary under an insurance contract;

(h) force a policyholder to terminate the existing policy and to effect a new proposal from him within three years from the date of such termination;

(i) No corporate agent shall have a portfolio of insurance business from one person or one organization or one group of organizations under which the premium is in excess of 50 per cent of total premiums procured in any year;

(j) apply for fresh licence to act as an insurance agent, if his licence was earlier cancelled by the designated person, and a period of five years has not elapsed from the date of such cancellation;

(k) become or remain a director of any insurance company.

(iii) Every corporate agent shall, with a view to conserve the insurance business already procured through him, make every attempt to ensure remittance of the premiums by the policyholders within the stipulated time, by giving notice to the policyholder orally and in writing.

(iv) No director of a company or a partner of a firm or the chief executive or a corporate insurance executive or a specified person shall hold similar position with another corporate agent of any other insurance company.

Renewal of licence

1. Every licence granted by the authority to a corporate agent or any renewal thereof, in terms of these regulations, shall remain in force for three years.
2. A licence granted to a corporate agent may be renewed for a further period of three years on submission of the application form along with a renewal fee of INR 250, at least 30 days prior to the date of expiry of the licence.
3. The additional fees payable to the authority, under the circumstances mentioned in sub-section 3 of Section 42 of the act, shall be INR 100.
4. The authority may, if it is satisfied that undue hardship would be caused otherwise, accept any application after the licence ceased to remain in force, on the payment by the applicant of a payment of INR 750 as additional fee.

5. Every certificate granted to the specified person shall remain in force for a period of three years which can be renewed for a further period of three years on submission of an application form accompanied by fees of INR 100, provided that the licence of the corporate agent continues to be valid. The application form along with the fees shall be submitted at least 30 days prior to the date of expiry.
6. The specified person on ceasing to be an employee of the corporate agent shall surrender his certificate to the designated person. If he desires to become an individual insurance agent, then he shall follow the procedure as laid down in Insurance Regulatory and Development Authority (Licensing of Insurance Agents) Regulations, 2000. Such a person need not go through a further process of training and pass the examination within the period of licence granted to them.
7. Every corporate insurance executive or the specified person of the corporate agent shall have completed at least 25 hours' practical training in life or general insurance business, as the case may be, from an approved institution, for the purposes of renewal of licence to the corporate agent and/or renewal of certificate to the specified person. Provided that such an applicant before seeking renewal of the licence or certificate to act as a composite insurance agent shall have completed from an approved institution at least 50 hours' practical training in life and general insurance business

Cancellation of licence/certificate

The designated person may cancel a licence or a certificate of a corporate agent or a specified person if such a corporate agent or the corporate insurance executive or the specified person suffers, at any time during the currency of the licence, from any of the disqualifications mentioned in sub-section 4 of Section 42D of the Insurance Act and recover from him the licence or certificate granted to him.

14.6.5 IRDA (Insurance Brokers) Regulations, 2002

The main points of the regulations for insurance brokers are highlighted in the following paragraphs.

Functions of a direct broker

A direct broker is an insurance broker who, for the time being licensed by the authority to act as such, for a remuneration carries out the functions as specified under regulation 3 either in the field of life insurance or general insurance or both on behalf of his clients.

The functions of a direct broker shall include any one or more of the following:

(a) obtaining detailed information of the client's business and risk management philosophy;
(b) familiarizing himself with the client's business and underwriting information so that this can be explained to an insurer and others;
(c) rendering advice on appropriate insurance cover and terms;
(d) maintaining detailed knowledge of available insurance markets, as may be applicable;
(e) submitting quotation received from insurer/s for consideration of a client;
(f) providing requisite underwriting information as required by an insurer in assessing the risk to decide pricing terms and conditions for cover;
(g) acting promptly on instructions from a client and providing him written acknowledgements and progress reports;
(h) assisting clients in paying premium under Section 64VB of Insurance Act, 1938 (4 of 1938);
(i) providing services related to insurance consultancy and risk management;
(j) assisting in the negotiation of the claims; and
(k) maintaining proper records of claims.

Functions of a reinsurance broker

A reinsurance broker is an insurance broker who, for remuneration, arranges reinsurance for direct insurers with insurance and reinsurance companies.

The functions of a reinsurance broker shall include any one or more of the following:

(a) familiarizing himself with the client's business and risk retention philosophy;
(b) maintaining clear records of the insurer's business to assist the reinsurer(s) or others;
(c) rendering advice based on technical data on the reinsurance covers available in the international insurance and the reinsurance markets;
(d) maintaining a database of available reinsurance markets, including solvency ratings of individual reinsurers;
(e) rendering consultancy and risk management services for reinsurance;
(f) selecting and recommending a reinsurer or a group of reinsurers;
(g) negotiating with a reinsurer on the client's behalf;
(h) assisting in case of commutation of reinsurance contracts placed with them;
(i) acting promptly on instructions from a client and providing it written acknowledgements and progress reports;
(j) collecting and remitting premiums and claims within such time as agreed upon;
(k) assisting in the negotiation and settlement of claims;
(l) maintaining proper records of claims;
(m) exercising due care and diligence at the time of selection of reinsurers and international insurance brokers with regard to their respective security rating and establishing respective responsibilities at the time of engaging their services.

Application for grant of licence

1. An application by a person for grant of a licence as an insurance broker shall be made in Form A to IRDA. An insurance broker is a person for the time being licensed by IRDA, who for remuneration arranges insurance contracts with insurance companies and/or reinsurance companies on behalf of his clients.
2. The application shall be made for any one or more of the following categories:
   (a) direct broker;
   (b) reinsurance broker;
   (c) composite broker;
   along with the requisite fees as specified in the regulations.

A composite broker is an insurance broker who, for the time being licensed by the authority to act as such, for remuneration arranges insurance for his clients with insurance companies and/or reinsurance for his client/s.

Application to conform to the requirements

An application not complete in all respects and not conforming to the instructions specified in Form A and these regulations shall be rejected. Provided that before rejecting any such application, the applicant shall be given a reasonable opportunity to complete the application in all respects and rectify the errors, if any.

Furnishing information, clarification and personal representation

1. IRDA may require an applicant to furnish any further information or clarification for the purpose of disposal of the application and, thereafter, with regard to any other matter as may be deemed necessary by IRDA.
2. The applicant or its principal officer shall, if so required, appear before the authority for a personal representation in connection with an application.

Requirements of capital

1. Any applicant seeking to become an insurance broker under these regulations should satisfy the following conditions:
   (i) it shall have a minimum amount of capital as mentioned in Table 14.2.
   (ii) the capital in the case of a company limited by shares and a cooperative society shall be in the form of equity shares;

Table 14.2 Minimum amount of capital

Category	*Minimum amount*
Direct broker	INR 50 lakh
Reinsurance broker	INR 200 lakh
Composite broker	INR 250 lakh

(iii) the capital in the case of other applicants shall be brought in cash;

(iv) the applicant shall exclusively carry on the business of an insurance broker as licensed under these regulations.

2. No part of the capital of an applicant shall be held by a non-Indian interest beyond 26 per cent at any time. For the purposes of these regulations, the calculations of non-Indian interest shall be made in the same manner as specified in Insurance Regulatory and Development Authority (Registration of Indian Insurance Companies) Regulations, 2000, for an insurer.

Procedure for licensing

IRDA on being satisfied that the applicant fulfills all the conditions specified for the grant of licence shall grant a licence in Form B and send intimation thereof to the applicant mentioning the category for which the authority has granted the licence. The licence shall be issued subject to the insurance broker adhering to the conditions and the code of conduct as specified by the authority from time to time.

Validity of licence

A licence once issued shall be valid for a period of three years from the date of its issue, unless the same is suspended or cancelled pursuant to these regulations.

Renewal of licence

1. An insurance broker may, within 30 days before the expiry of the licence, make an application in Form A to IRDA for renewal of the licence. Provided, however, that if the application reaches IRDA later than that period but before the actual expiry of the current licence, an additional fee of INR 100 shall be payable by the applicant to IRDA. Provided further that the authority may for sufficient reasons, offered in writing by the applicant for a delay not covered by the previous proviso, accept an application for renewal after the date of the expiry of the licence on a payment of an additional fee of INR 750 only by the applicant.
2. An insurance broker before seeking a renewal of licence shall have completed at least 25 hours of theoretical and practical training imparted by an institution recognized by IRDA from time to time.
3. The application for a renewal under sub-regulation 1 shall be dealt with in the same manner as specified.
4. IRDA on being satisfied that the applicant fulfills all the conditions specified for a renewal of the licence shall renew the licence in Form B for a period of three years and send intimation to that effect to the applicant.
5. An insurance broker licensed under these regulations for a specified category may also apply for the grant of a licence by the authority for any other category by fulfilling the requirements of these regulations. However, such an application shall be made only after a lapse of one year from the grant of a licence in the first instance.

Procedure where a licence is not granted

1. Where an application for grant of a licence under regulations does not satisfy the conditions set out in regulations, IRDA may refuse to grant the licence.
2. The refusal to grant a licence shall be communicated by the authority within 30 days of such refusal to the applicant stating therein the grounds on which the application has been rejected.
3. Any applicant, if aggrieved by the decision of the authority, may apply within a period of 30 days from the date of receipt of such intimation to the chairman of the authority for a reconsideration of its decision.

4. The chairman of IRDA shall consider such an application and communicate his decision thereon to the applicant in writing within six weeks of the receipt thereof.

Effect of refusal to grant licence

Any applicant whose application for grant of a licence or of a renewal thereof has been refused by IRDA shall, on and from the date of the receipt of the communication, cease to act as an insurance broker. He, however, shall continue to be liable to provide services with respect to contracts already entered into through him. Such a service shall continue only up to the period of expiry of those current contracts, the details of which shall be disclosed to the authority on receipt of the communication.

Action against a person acting as an insurance broker without a valid licence

1. Notwithstanding and without prejudice to initiation of any criminal proceedings against any person who acts as an insurance broker without holding a valid licence issued under these regulations, IRDA may invoke against such a person penal action under the Insurance Act.
2. Where the person falling under sub-regulation 1 is a company or firm or body corporate, without prejudice to any other proceedings which may be taken by the authority against the company or firm or body corporate, every director, manager, secretary or other officer of the company or body corporate, and every partner of the firm, who is knowingly a party to such a contravention shall also be liable to be proceeded against.

Payment of fees and the consequences of failure to pay fees

1. Every applicant eligible for the grant of a licence shall pay such fees in such a manner and within such a period as specified in Schedule II.
2. Where an insurance broker fails to pay the annual fees payable, IRDA may suspend the licence, whereupon the insurance broker shall cease to carry on business for the period during which the suspension subsists.

Remuneration

1. No insurance broker shall be paid or contract to be paid by way of remuneration (including royalty or licence fees or administration charges or such other compensation), an amount exceeding:
   A. On direct general insurance business:
   (i) On tariff products:
      a. 10 per cent of the premium on that part of the business which is compulsory under any statute or any law in force
      b. 12.5 per cent of the premium on others
   (ii) on non- tariff products:
   17.5 per cent of the premium on direct business.
   B. On direct life insurance business:
   (i) individual insurance:
      a. 30 per cent of first year's premium
      b. 5 per cent of each renewal premium
   (ii) annuity:
      a. immediate annuity or a deferred annuity in consideration of a single premium, or where only one premium is payable on the policy:2 per cent of premium
      b. deferred annuity in consideration of more than one premium:
         (i) 7½ percent of first year's premium
         (ii) 2 percent of each renewal premium
   (iii) group insurance and pension schemes:
      a. one year renewable group term insurance, gratuity, superannuation, group savings linked insurance: 7.5 per cent of risk premium
      b. single premium: 2 per cent of risk premium

c. annual contributions, at new business procurement stage: 5 per cent of non risk premium with a ceiling of INR 3 lakh per scheme

d. single premium new business procurement stage: 0.5 per cent with a ceiling of INR 5 lakh per scheme

e. remuneration for subsequent servicing:

(i) one year renewable group term assurance: 2 per cent of risk premium with a ceiling of INR 50,000 per scheme.

C. On reinsurance business:

As per market practices prevalent from time to time.

2. The settlement of accounts by insurers with respect to remuneration of brokers shall be done on a monthly basis and it must be ensured that there is no cross settlement of outstanding balances.

Ceiling on business from single client

1. The business of the insurance broker shall be carried out in such a manner that not more than 50 per cent of the premium (quantum, receipts, etc. as the case may be) in the first year of business, 40 per cent of the premium in the second year of business, and 30 per cent of the premium from the third year of business onwards shall emanate from any one client.
2. The decision of IRDA as to whether a company, a business or an organization is under the same management shall be final.

Deposit requirements

1. Every insurance broker shall before the commencement of his business deposit and keep deposited with any scheduled bank a sum equivalent to 20 per cent of the initial capital in fixed deposit, which shall not be released to him unless the prior permission of the authority is obtained.
2. Every insurance broker shall furnish to IRDA as and when called upon to do so a statement certified by the bank in which such fixed deposit is kept.

Segregation of insurance money

1. The provisions of Section 64VB of the Insurance Act shall continue to determine the question of assumption of risk by an insurer.
2. In the case of reinsurance contracts, it may be agreed between the parties specifically or as part of international market practices that the licensed reinsurance broker or composite broker can collect the premium and remit to the reinsurer and/or collect the claims due from the reinsurer to be passed on to the insured. In these circumstances the money collected by the licensed insurance broker shall be dealt with in the following manner:

(a) he shall act as the trustee of the insurance money that he is required to handle in order to discharge his function as a reinsurance broker and for the purposes of this regulation it shall be deemed that a payment made to the reinsurance broker shall be considered as payment made to the reinsurer;

(b) ensure that "insurance money" is held in an "insurance bank account" with one or more of the scheduled banks or with such other institutions as may be approved by IRDA;

(c) give written notice to, and receive written confirmation from, a bank or other institution that he is not entitled to combine the account with any other account or to exercise any right of set-off, charge or lien against money in that account;

(d) ensure that all monies received from or on behalf of an insured is paid into the "insurance bank account" which remains in the "insurance bank account" to remain in deposit until it is transferred on to the reinsurer or to the direct insurer;

(e) ensure that any refund of premium which may become due to a direct insurer on account of the cancellation of a policy or alteration in its terms and conditions or otherwise shall be paid by the reinsurer directly to the direct insurer;

(f) interest on recovery/payment received shall be for the benefit of the direct insurer or reinsurer;

(g) only remove from the "insurance bank account" charges, fees or commission earned and interest received from any funds comprising the account;

(h) take immediate steps to restore the required position if at any time he becomes aware of any deficiency in the required "segregated amount".

Professional indemnity insurance

1. Every insurance broker shall take out and maintain and continue to maintain a professional indemnity insurance cover throughout the validity of the period of the licence granted to him by IRDA. Provided that IRDA shall in suitable cases allow a newly licensed insurance broker to produce such a guarantee within 15 months from the date of issue of the original licence.
2. The insurance cover must indemnify an insurance broker against:
   (a) any error or omission or negligence on his part or on the part of his employees and directors;
   (b) any loss of money or other property for which the broker is legally liable in consequence of any financial or fraudulent act or omission;
   (c) any loss of documents and costs and expenses incurred in replacing or restoring such documents;
   (d) dishonest or fraudulent acts or omissions by brokers' employees or former employees.
3. The indemnity cover:
   a. shall be on a yearly basis for the entire period of licence;
   b. shall not contain any terms to the effect that payments of claims depend upon the insurance broker having first met the liability;
   c. shall indemnify with respect to all claims made during the period of the insurance regardless of the time at which the event giving rise to the claim may have occurred. Provided that indemnity insurance cover not fully conforming to the above requirements shall be permitted by the authority in special cases for reasons to be recorded by it in writing.
4. Limit of indemnity for any one claim and in the aggregate for the year in the case of insurance brokers shall be as shown in Table 14.3.
5. The uninsured excess with respect to each claim shall not exceed 5 per cent of the capital employed by the insurance broker in the business.
6. The insurance policy shall be obtained from any registered insurer in India who has agreed to:
   (a) provide the insurance broker with an annual certificate containing the name and address, including the licence number of the insurance broker, the policy number, the limit of indemnity, the excess and the name of the insurer as evidence that the cover meets the requirements of the IRDA;
   (b) send a duplicate certificate to IRDA at the time the certificate is issued to the insurance broker;
   (c) inform the insurer immediately of any case of voidance, non-renewal or cancellation of the cover mid-term.
7. Every insurance broker shall:
   (a) inform IRDA immediately should any cover be cancelled or voided or if any policy is not renewed;
   (b) inform the insurer immediately in writing of any claim made by or against it;

Table 14.3 Limit of indemnity

Category of insurance broker	*Limit of indemnity*
Direct broker	Three times remuneration received at the end of every financial year subject to a minimum limit of INR 50 lakh
Reinsurance broker	Three times remuneration received at the end of every financial year subject to a minimum limit of INR 2.5 crore
Composite broker	Three times remuneration received at the end of every financial year subject to a minimum limit of INR 5 crore

(c) advise the insurer immediately of all circumstances or occurrences that may give rise to a claim under the policy;

(d) advise IRDA as soon as an insurer has notified that it intends to decline indemnity with respect to a claim under the policy.

Internal control and systems

Every insurance broker shall ensure that a proper system of internal audit is practised in business and that his internal controls and systems are adequate for the size, nature and complexity of his business.

Disclosures to IRDA

1. An insurance broker shall disclose to IRDA, as and when required by it, in any event not later than 30 days of a requisition, the following information:
   (i) his responsibilities with regard to the placement of an insurance contract;
   (ii) any change in the information or particulars previously furnished, which have a bearing on the licence granted to it;
   (iii) the names of the clients whose insurance portfolio he manages or has managed;
   (iv) any other requirement specified by IRDA from time to time.

Provided that in case of a person specified in Regulation 2(1)(j)(v) IRDA may call for and obtain such information as it deems fit.

Cancellation or suspension of licence with notice

1. The licence of an insurance broker may be cancelled or suspended after due notice and after giving him a reasonable opportunity of being heard if he:
   (a) violates the provisions of the Insurance Act, 1938 (4 of 1938), Insurance Regulatory And Development Authority Act, 1999 (41 of 1999), or rules or regulations made thereunder;
   (b) fails to furnish any information relating to his activities as an insurance broker as required by the authority;
   (c) furnishes wrong or false information, or conceals or fails to disclose material facts in the application submitted for obtaining a licence;
   (d) does not submit periodical returns as required by the authority;
   (e) does not cooperate with any inspection or inquiry conducted by the authority;
   (f) fails to resolve the complaints of the policyholders or fails to give a satisfactory reply to the authority in this behalf;
   (g) indulges in rebates or inducements in cash or kind to a client or any of the client's directors or other employees or any person acting as an introducer;
   (h) is found guilty of misconduct or his conduct is not in accordance with the code of conduct specified in Schedule III;
   (i) fails to maintain the capital requirements in accordance with the provisions of Regulation 10;
   (j) fails to pay the fees or the reimbursement of expenses under these regulations;
   (k) violates the conditions of licence;
   (l) does not carry out his obligations as specified in the regulations;
   (m) if the principal officer does not acquire practical training and pass the examination within the stipulated period as specified in Regulation 9.
2. In the circumstances where IRDA feels that the establishment of an insurance broker is only to divert funds within a group of companies or their associates, it can after due enquiries made by it cancel the licence granted to the insurance broker.

Cancellation or suspension of licence without notice

The licence of an insurance broker may be cancelled or suspended without notice if he:

(a) violates any one or more of the requirements under the code of conduct specified in Schedule III;

(b) is found guilty of fraud or is convicted of a criminal offence;

(c) commits such defaults which require immediate action in the opinion of IRDA, provided that IRDA has communicated the reasons for the cancellation in writing;

(d) the insurance broker has not commenced business within six months of being granted a licence.

Manner of holding enquiry before suspension or cancellation

1. For the purpose of holding an enquiry under the regulations, IRDA may appoint an enquiry officer.
2. The enquiry officer shall issue to the insurance broker a notice at the registered office or the principal place of business of the insurance broker, as the case may be, calling for such information as he considers necessary for the conduct of an enquiry;
3. The insurance broker may, within 15 days from the date of receipt of such a notice, furnish to the enquiry officer a reply together with copies of documentary or other evidence relied on by him or sought by the enquiry officer;
4. The enquiry officer shall give a reasonable opportunity of hearing to the insurance broker to enable him to make submissions in support of his reply;
5. The insurance broker may either appear in person or through any person duly authorized by him to present its case;
6. If it is considered necessary, the enquiry officer may require IRDA to present its case through one of its officers;
7. The enquiry officer shall, after taking into account all relevant facts and submissions made by the insurance broker, submit a report to IRDA within 90 days of the completion of the enquiry proceedings.

Show-cause notice and order

1. On receipt of the report from the enquiry officer, the authority shall consider it and issue a show-cause notice to the insurance broker if the contents of the report warrant a suspension or cancellation of the licence granted to him. Provided that no such notice is required, in case the provisions of Regulation 35 are attracted.
2. The insurance broker shall within 21 days of the date of receipt of the show-cause notice send a reply to the authority.
3. IRDA after considering the reply to the show-cause notice shall, as soon as possible, but not later than 30 days from the receipt of the reply, pass such an order as it deems fit. Provided, however, where the insurance broker on serving of the notice under this regulation fails to furnish any reply within the stated period, the authority may after the expiry of such time proceed to decide the case *ex parte*.
4. IRDA shall send a copy of the order made under Clause (3) to the insurance broker.

Effect of cancellation or suspension of licence

1. On and from the date of suspension or cancellation of the licence, the insurance broker shall cease to act as an insurance broker.
2. An insurance broker, however, shall continue to service the contracts already concluded through him for a period of six months within which suitable arrangements shall be made by him for having the contracts attended to by another licensed insurance broker.
3. IRDA in such an event may pass such an order as it thinks fit for the disposal of the deposit of the insurance broker.

Any disputes arising between an insurance broker and an insurer or any other person either in the course of his engagement as an insurance broker or otherwise may be referred to IRDA by the person so affected, and on receipt of the complaint or representation, the authority may examine the complaint and if found necessary proceed to conduct an enquiry or an inspection or an investigation in terms of these regulations.

Summary

1. Risk management methods include risk reduction, risk mitigation and risk coping.
2. An insurance policyholder (insured) pays a fixed premium to the insurer and in return the insurer promises to pay for the losses as specified under the terms of the insurance policy.
3. The Bombay Mutual Life Insurance Society, established in 1870, was the first company to charge the same premium for both Indians and non-Indians. The Indian Mercantile Insurance Company Limited was the first indigenous general insurance company set up in Bombay in 1907.
4. Reinsurance is a process whereby the reinsurer takes on all or part of the risk covered under a policy issued by an insurance company in consideration of a premium payment.
5. In 1994, the Malhotra committee recommended the setting up of the insurance regulatory authority as a multi-member statutory body with a full-time chairperson, two full-time and a few part-time members.
6. The main objectives of IRDA are to protect the interests of the policyholders and regulate, promote and ensure orderly growth of the insurance industry.
7. India has a total of 42 insurance companies—24 life insurance companies,17 non-life insurance companies and one reinsurance company as on March 30, 2010. Many of these companies are in the private sector, with joint venture partnership with foreign companies.
8. Indian insurance companies offer a comprehensive range of insurance plans. More than 80 per cent of the life insurance business consists of endowment policies and money-back policies. Linked products are a new variety of products launched by life insurers.
9. Micro-insurance products are low-value products with low premium and benefit packages to bring them within the reach of economically disadvantaged persons or groups.
10. IRDA has issued certain guidelines or regulations pertaining to different aspects of insurance. These are the IRDA Guidelines on Unit Linked Insurance Products, the IRDA (Licensing of Corporate Agents) Regulations, the IRDA (Insurance Brokers) Regulations, the IRDA (Third Party Administrators-Health Services) Regulations and the IRDA (Protection of Policyholders Interests) Regulations.

Questions

1. Trace the origins of the insurance business in India.
2. Bring out the changes that have taken place in the insurance business in India in the post-liberalization period.
3. How can reinsurance contribute to the development of the insurance sector?
4. Discuss the significance of micro-insurance in the Indian context.
5. Critically comment on the major recommendations of the Malhotra committee.
6. Explain the objectives and functions of IRDA.
7. What are the opportunities and challenges for the insurance sector in India?
8. Discuss the salient features of IRDA guidelines on unit linked insurance products.
9. Discuss the rationale behind the IRDA (Licensing of Corporate Agents) Regulations, the IRDA (Insurance Brokers) Regulations and the IRDA (Third Party Administrators-Health Services) Regulations.
10. To what extent will the IRDA (Protection of Policyholders Interests) Regulations solve the problems of insurance policyholders?

Chapter 15

Venture Capital Financing

LEARNING OBJECTIVES

After reading this chapter, you should be able to:

- Understand the concept of venture capital financing.
- Distinguish between venture capital and private equity.
- Describe the characteristics of venture capital financing.
- Highlight the methods used for valuation of projects.
- Examine the exit routes of venture capital financing.
- Highlight prominent venture capital funds.
- Bring out the salient features of SEBI regulations.

15.1 Introduction

The traditional sources of financing focus on projects with proven technology and clearly identifiable market demand. However, such projects cannot contribute to the development of an economy as fast and as much as desired. It is only innovation—in technology, products, management or any aspect of business—that can foster and accelerate the growth and development of an economy. In other words, innovation is the *mantra* or the key to the rapid economic development of a country. Therefore, it is necessary to promote and develop projects that involve new technology, new entrepreneurship or new management to produce and deliver innovative goods and services to society. Though such projects need to be encouraged and developed on a priority basis, the conventional sources of financing have not paid them much attention. Traditional credit institutions like commercial banks and term-lending institutions (development banks), being risk-averse and security-oriented, generally do not evince interest in financing untried technologies or innovative projects, which are high-risk businesses with high mortality rates. It is in this context that venture capital funds or firms have come into play. Venture capital financing began in the twentieth century to promote and develop innovative projects for faster economic development. **Venture capital financing** is an alternative source of financing business projects, particularly those that are high-technology, high-risk and high return-based. If a project is high-risk, the conventional sources of financing like bank credit and other institutional credit might not be available to it. The only source of financing that might be available to such projects is risk capital, which is known as venture capital.

***Venture capital financing** is an alternative source of financing business projects, particularly those that are high-technology, high-risk and high return-based.*

There are several people with new business ideas and entrepreneurial talent. They might come out with new or untried technology-based project proposals, but fail to attract the conventional sources of financing due to high risk factors. Such business ideas, though worth exploring, could die even before they are put forth. The problem of financing of new, high-risk business projects initiated by entrepreneurs who have business ideas but lack the necessary experience and funds to transform their ideas into reality has taken centre stage, particularly with liberalization of the economy. As the new and high technology-based projects are high-risk ventures, it would not be fair to involve the general investing public in such ventures initially. If common investors are involved in financing risky projects and if these projects fail, which is most likely, it would send a wrong message to the general investing public. Moreover, common investors do not have the business skills and knowledge to back such projects. Therefore, there is a need for a separate institutional setup that can take care of the interests of entrepreneurs who have business ideas but lack the required finance and managerial expertise. Such an organizational setup has come to be known as a venture capital firm, venture capital fund, venture capital team or simply venture capitalist. *Venture capitalists* finance innovation and ideas that lead to high-risk and high-return projects. They finance projects that have potential for high growth but also inherent uncertainties. Besides finance, venture capitalists might provide managerial expertise and skills to enterprises that are technology- and knowledge-based.

The projects, particularly new technology-based ones, are highly risk prone but, of course, have chances of yielding very high returns. As the probability of success of such projects is very low, the mortality rate is very high. Even in developed countries, where venture capital is well developed, it has been observed that more than 40 per cent of the firms promoted with the assistance of venture capitalists have failed with a loss of the entire capital. What motivates entrepreneurs to enter into such high-risk projects are the extraordinary profits. Venture capital firms that finance such projects also expect to make higher capital gains through appreciation of their investments if the projects prove successful. When a venture capital firm finances different projects, some of the projects might become successful and yield very high returns, which more than compensate the losses in others. As the untried technology-based projects might also require management expertise besides funds, venture capital firms often use their business development skills and expertise to make the project successful.

15.1.1 Definition of Venture Capital

The term venture capital has various meanings and definitions. Venture capital is generally understood as investment made in high-risk and high-reward industrial projects. Risk refers to a high degree of uncertainty with regard to generation of future cash flows and creation of profit by the project. Venture capital also refers to professional investment in risk capital of an enterprise and sharing of ownership as well as management responsibility with the entrepreneur. Thus, **venture capital** is an investment in equity share capital or long-term debt capital of an unlisted enterprise that is looking to start up, expand or buy out a business. The main attraction is the exceptional profitability of the enterprise. Venture capital investment is mostly in equity share capital of a company and, therefore, the return for the venture capital firm depends on the growth and profitability of the business of the investee. The venture capital firm generally acquires the equity shares of the investee company through private placement.

__Venture capital__ is an investment in equity share capital or long-term debt capital of an unlisted enterprise that is looking to start up, expand or buy out a business.

The organization that provides venture capital is called the venture capital firm or venture capitalist or venture capital fund. According to SEBI (Venture Capital Funds) Regulations, 1996, a *venture capital fund* is a fund established in the form of a trust or a company including a body corporate and registered under these regulations that has a dedicated pool of capital raised in a manner specified in the regulations and invests in accordance with these regulations.

15.1.2 Venture Capital Financing and Conventional Financing: A Comparison

Venture capital financing is not like conventional financing (such as equity financing and debt financing). If a company wants to raise funds by issuing equity shares, the company is required to have already reached a certain level of activity as well as regular public reporting as per SEBI and stock exchange regulations. Moreover, such shareholders might not be able to extend any managerial support to the company as they might not have such competence and expertise. As far as loan capital is concerned, banks and other institutions that provide loan capital to entrepreneurs are primarily interested in safeguarding their own interests. Accordingly, their prime considerations are the security and liquidity of their investment, which they assess by examining the track record of the entrepreneurs/promoters, quality of the management team, cash generating capacity of the project and other such factors. The lenders might demand guarantees, either personal or institutional. But the entrepreneurs might not be in a position to provide such guarantees. Moreover, the lenders might not be of any help to the entrepreneurs as far as management is concerned. Conventional credit institutions always remain passive in terms of providing managerial assistance. The entrepreneur is also expected to make periodic payments to the lending institution in the form of instalments of the principal and interest. But this might not be possible for the entrepreneur as cash flows to be generated by the project might not be enough to match the loan payments.

The main aim of venture capital financing is to promote and develop new technology, new products and new entrepreneurship and management, thereby getting high returns in the form of capital gains.

On the other hand, a venture capitalist has different considerations while making investment decisions. Venture capital funds mainly aim at promoting and developing new technology, new products and new entrepreneurship and management, thereby getting high returns in the form of capital gains on their investments. Even if the venture capital firm participates in the loan capital of a firm, it does not insist on periodic interest payments. Venture capital loans can be secured or unsecured. Such loans might have a provision for conversion into equity shares. The loans can have warrants attached, which gives the venture capital firm the option to subscribe to new equity shares on the terms fixed in the warrant. Venture capital loans typically carry a higher rate of interest than bank term loans but rank below bank loans in terms of payment of interest and repayment of the principal amount. The idea behind a venture capital firm is to profit if the enterprise grows. Accordingly, the venture capitalist focuses on business plans and chances of success of the project, which depend on several factors, including the quality and commitment of the entrepreneur.

15.1.3 Private Equity (PE)

***Venture capital** is an investment made in the early stage(s) of a business, whereas **private equity** is an investment made at the later stages of a company's life cycle.*

Private equity (PE) is the investment made by investors in equity capital of an unlisted company. Venture capital is a subset of private equity. But venture capital is an investment made at the launch or early expansion of an undertaking. In other words, **venture capital** is an investment made in the early stage(s) of a business, whereas private equity is an investment made in the later stages of a business (growth and maturity stages of a company's life cycle). However, both venture capital and private equity aim at developing the business or creating value by supporting entrepreneurial talent. Private equity firms not only provide capital to companies but also provide talent and strategy required for the success of a business. Companies seek private equity for launching new products, improving management capabilities, exploiting the creativity and innovation of management or strategically run their existing businesses. Private equity firms usually look for high growth, competitive products or services, solid business systems, quality and stable management team and transparent legal structure.

***Mezzanine financing** is provided to a company expected to go public, usually within a short period of time.*

Private equity funds are created with a specific purpose and their investments are normally in equity or quasi-equity securities through private placement. The number of private equity investors in any one firm is small but the investment size is large. The role of investors in the affairs of the investee firm is greater and active. Private equity funds can be government-owned, private partnerships or subsidiaries of financial firms. Asset reconstruction companies floated by governments are examples of government-owned private equity funds. Private partnerships are formed with limited partner(s) and general partner(s). Limited partners are the main investors in the fund, but they do not have management rights to the fund. Their liability is limited to the extent of their investment contribution. General partners are managers of a fund and have exclusive rights to the fund's investment decisions. Subsidiaries of commercial banks, investment banks or mutual funds can also act as general partners of a private equity fund. However, the major contributors to private equity funds are pension funds, funds of funds, insurance firms and high net worth individuals (HNIs). Private equity investments can take the form of financing leveraged buyouts, mezzanine financing, replacement funding (privatization or buyout of family-owned assets) and distress funding. Mezzanine financing is provided to a company expected to go public, usually within six to 12 months. Mezzanine financing is usually structured to be repaid from the proceeds of the IPO.

15.2 Characteristics of Venture Capital

The main objective of a venture capital firm is to get exceptional returns by participating in the long-term financing of business enterprises that have substantial growth opportunities. In line with the stated objective, venture capital financing has the following characteristics.

- A venture capital firm can participate in the equity, debt or a combination of debt and equity financing of a project. Since venture capital financing is by nature risk capital financing, it involves equity or quasi-equity participation, either actual or potential. That is, a venture capitalist assumes a considerable amount of risk by participating in equity or quasi-equity investment in a project.
- The venture capitalist assists the entrepreneur continuously till the project enters into commercial production or the venture capitalist liquidates its investment through an exit route.

- The venture capital firm has a long-term stake in the business of the investee firm.
- A venture capitalist can become a virtual partner in the business of the entrepreneur, sharing success and failure with the entrepreneur. The extent of involvement of the venture capital firm varies and usually depends on the circumstances and understanding between the venture capital firm and the investee firm.
- In order to safeguard its interests and help the entrepreneur, the venture capitalist might participate in the management of the client firm. A venture capital firm with its own team of experts can help the investee firm in the management of production, marketing and other functional areas including business planning.
- The main aim of venture capital funds is not to take control of the enterprise but to help the enterprise create value in order to realize a capital gain, shared with the entrepreneur, on exit. Thus, venture capital is "patient capital" as it seeks to profit from long-term capital gains rather than short-term and regular reimbursements.
- The venture capitalist involves itself in forming management teams, recruiting key executives and formulating production and marketing strategies of the enterprise in which it invests.
- The venture capital firm assists the investee firm in arranging strategic alliances and in the IPO.
- The venture capitalist and the entrepreneur work together closely in an enabling environment that allows the enterprises to become a powerful engine of economic growth and wealth creation for the nation.
- Venture capital financing is a long-term investment and, therefore, it is not easy to get back the invested funds on demand.
- Though venture capital financing was originally associated with financing high-technology-based projects, venture capitalists do assist the promotion and development of small- and medium-sized industries in their early stages of development. Thus, venture capital firms can also finance low-technology and service firms that have a potential market.
- The returns for the venture capitalist are in the form of substantial capital gains when the equity shares of the investee firm are listed on the stock exchange and the venture capitalist disinvests its shareholdings.
- Venture capital financing is an active form of investment with considerable degree of involvement in the management of the investee firm. This is a value-added function that distinguishes the venture capital financing from conventional financing.

15.3 Stages of Venture Capital Financing

The main difference between venture capital financing and conventional sources of financing lies in the nature and method of the financing. Conventional financing is mostly in the form of debt capital, which is usually made available at a later stage of the project, whereas venture capital financing is stage-wise financing. In other words, funds are made available by the venture capitalist at different stages of the growth and development of the project. The various stages of a company's life cycle and the participation of venture capital at each stage are discussed as follows.

The main stages of venture capital financing are seed capital, start-up, expansion and later-stage.

Seed-capital stage

The first stage of an enterprise is popularly known as seed-capital stage. This is the primary stage of a project involving research and development (R&D) activities. The typical activities involved are idea generation, idea screening, concept development and testing and marketing strategy. Financing the project at this time involves a lot of risk as the technology or the concept being developed might not succeed. The success of the fledgling project is unpredictable. However, the project at this stage needs strong and continuous financial backing. Therefore, the venture capitalist steps in and provides both equity capital and debt capital after assessing the technical and financial feasibility of the project. Making investment due diligence is important for the venture capital firm. In fact, entrepreneurs and their friends might contribute their personal funds to the seed capital in order to get the business off the ground.

Start-up stage

The second stage of a project's life cycle is known as the start-up stage. This means that the business is still in the creation phase and the company has not yet sold its product commercially. The start-up stage involves certain major activities including business analysis, product development, test marketing and commercialization. The risk of failure of the business at this stage is very high because the technology is untried at the commercial level, the market is undefined and potential competition is not known. At this stage, the project requires continuous financing besides proven managerial expertise and skills. The funding at this stage of the project is known as *first-round investment* and *follow-up investment*. The investors who provide capital at this stage of a company's life cycle are known as *angel investors*. Unlike venture capitalists, angel investors are rarely involved in the management of the client company. Further, angel investors provide relatively modest amounts of funds to the business of the client as compared to the venture capitalists who contribute relatively large sums.

Expansion stage

The third stage of a project's life cycle is called the expansion stage. At this stage, the entrepreneur seeks to expand the business, mainly the production and marketing of the product. Sometimes, there may be overruns in the project, which necessitate second-round financing. At this stage, it may be necessary to finance the additional working capital requirement in view of expansion of the business. By this stage, the project might not have reached the break-even level. Thus, it would require additional funding to further increase production and sales in order to achieve the cash break-even level. The venture capitalist will try to take the project towards profitability and sustain the business till the public issue is made. This stage of financing is also known as bridge financing. **Bridge financing** is short-term financing provided until long-term financing is arranged. The need for bridge financing arises when a company runs out of funds before it can obtain long-term funding. As the entrepreneur might not be able to get finance from conventional sources, the venture capitalist firm, which had earlier provided funding, might have to pump in additional doses of funding.

***Bridge financing** is short-term financing provided until long-term financing is arranged.*

Later stage

This is the stage at which the project has established itself and the business is set to expand further. At this stage, the technology has been tried commercially and the entrepreneur has acquired a track record. Funding might be required to finance diversification of business or/and acquire forward or backward integration. In other words, creation of additional production capacity and expansion of markets are the major activities at this time. This might necessitate additional doses of funding, which is known as later-stage financing or mezzanine financing or development financing. The venture capitalist can step in at this stage in order to realize short-term capital gains. The venture capitalist can also get tax relief or other incentives in addition to controlling interest by investing in later-stage projects.

The different stages of a company's life cycle are not standardized. The stages vary with industries and circumstances. A venture capitalist can participate in any or all the stages of financing. Normally, venture capital firms participate in seed capital financing only, and the venture capitalist can exit from a project before it breaks even.

However, there are cases in which venture capitalists have financed expansions, including mergers and acquisitions, and turnaround of distress firms. Entrepreneurs might seek to expand their business by mergers and acquisitions, which can also be financed by venture capitalists. In addition, venture capitalists can also finance turnarounds and buyouts. A *turnaround* is a situation in which a sick company recovers its ground. The term can also be used for a company that has been transformed from a poorly performing one to a profit-making venture (positive reversal of a company). To make a turnaround, a company might need a good amount of funds in addition to good management and leadership. Venture capitalists can provide the required funds as well as the managerial expertise to the sick firm in order to facilitate its turnaround. *Buyout* is a form of corporate restructuring. It involves the acquisition of an entire firm or a division/sub-unit of a firm by others, including the existing management of the firm. If the entire firm or the division of the firm is acquired (purchasing of controlling interest in the firm or the division) by the internal management of the firm, such a buyout is known as *management buyout*. If an external management team acquires the firm or division, it is known as *management buy-in*. When the potential acquiring management team does not have adequate funds to pay for the acquisition, it can seek financial support from others, such as a venture capitalist. This kind of buyout is known as leveraged buyout. Thus, a *leveraged buyout* is an acquisition that is financed principally with debt capital. Depending on the cash flow-generating capacity of the assets to be acquired, the management (acquirer) decides the amount of debt it can employ in a buyout. Thus, buyouts are an important source of business for venture capitalists.

15.4 Structure and Sources of Venture Capital Funds

Venture capital funds differ in their sources of funds and management structure. There are *independent venture capital funds* in which no investor holds a majority stake in the fund. On the other hand, there are venture capital funds in which one or a few investors contribute most of the capital of the fund. Such venture capital funds are known as *captive venture capital funds*. They can be subsidiaries or departments of banks, financial institutions or industrial organizations. There are also venture capital funds in which a few investors hold a large stake in the fund but a significant portion of the fund is raised from other investors. Venture capital funds also differ in their areas of specialization. Some companies float venture capital funds to invest in sectors relevant to their core activities. It may be noted that few venture capital funds are generalists (without sector or business specialization). In other words, the majority of venture capital funds specialize in financing certain industrial sectors or services or companies at a certain stage of development. Venture capital funds are also structured to operate within a specific geographical area (regional, national or international).

A venture capital firm can raise monies from any investor, whether Indian, foreign, or non-resident Indian, by issue of units.

A venture capital fund can be structured as a company or a trust and, accordingly, the finances can be raised through issue of securities/units, loans or donations.

A venture capital fund is administered by a fund manager called the asset management company. The asset management company is the investment execution and monitoring authority. An asset management company can manage more than one fund at one time. A venture capital fund can be structured as a company or a trust and, accordingly, the finances can be raised through issue of securities/units, loans or donations. Venture capital funds are also structured as limited partnerships with a fixed life. Within this period, the venture capital firm invests the money committed to it and returns the investors' money at the end of the period. The main sources of capital for venture capital firms worldwide are pension funds, endowments and foundations, angel investors and high net worth families and individuals. Venture capital firms can have commitments along with money from external investors.

According to SEBI regulations, a venture capital fund can raise monies from any investor, whether Indian, foreign or non-resident Indian, by issue of units. The investment from any investor should be not less than INR 500,000. But this condition is not applicable to the employees or the principal officer or directors of the venture capital fund or directors of the trustee company or trustees where the venture capital fund is established as a trust. The employees of the fund manager or asset management company are also exempted from this condition. Another condition prescribed by SEBI is that each scheme launched or fund set up by a venture capital fund shall have a firm commitment from the investors for contribution of at least INR 5 crore before the start of operations by the venture capital fund. A venture capital fund is not supposed to get its units listed on any stock exchange till the expiry of three years from the date of issuance of units.

15.5 Investments of Venture Capital Firms

Venture capital firms can invest in projects by subscribing to various kinds of securities to be issued by the client firms. The securities that the firms can issue to raise the funds include equity shares, non-voting equity shares, deferred ordinary shares, preference shares, cumulative convertible preferences shares, participating preference shares, preferred ordinary shares, cumulative convertible participatory preferred ordinary shares, convertible cumulative redeemable preference shares, equity warrants, conventional loans, secured premium notes, income notes, deep discount bonds, zero-interest debentures, partly convertible debentures and non-convertible debentures. The availability of different kinds of securities gives enough flexibility to the venture capitalists to structure their investment portfolios according to their investment goals and priorities.

Before making any investment, the venture capital firm can make a business analysis of the project by examining the following factors:

a. **The entrepreneur:** The venture capitalist primarily examines the background of the entrepreneur, which includes his qualifications, experience, training, technical competence, business ideas and leadership. The track record of the entrepreneur, including his fund-raising skills, is also a major consideration.

b. **The management:** The venture capital firm examines whether the investee firm has a quality management team. The quality of the management is assessed in terms of the capability of the management team in transforming business ideas into reality. Though the venture capital firm might not seek managerial control of the investee firm, it would like to ensure that the client firm has an experienced and competent management team. The venture capital firm seeks to identify the current and potential expertise of the management team at each level in order to assist the management of the enterprise with its own specialized experience and expertise. The venture capital firm can also look for good corporate governance in the investee firm and, accordingly, seek to be on the board of directors of the investee firm. However, the attitude of the entrepreneur is also very important in this regard. Some entrepreneurs prefer to retain total control of the firm and, therefore, oppose any move by the venture capitalist to dilute their control.

c. **Products:** The venture capitalist always looks for high-growth, competitive products and services. The venture capitalist can study the nature of the product/service being produced or proposed to be produced by the investee firm. It might analyse the market for the product/service by size, structure of competition, opportunities and challenges. Entry barriers and potential market leadership are also examined. The venture capitalist expects its client firm to be in the market where there is a rapidly growing need for the product.

d. **Financial structure:** The financial structure of the client firm is also examined by the venture capitalist. Financial structure refers to various means of financing of the assets of a firm. Liabilities plus equity constitute the financial structure of a firm. Financing decisions are important managerial decisions, which influence the return and risk of a firm. Therefore, the venture capitalist analyses the whole gamut of the financial structure before committing its resources to the client firm.

e. **Target return:** The venture capitalist always aims at a target return on its investment in the client firm and earns the return primarily in the form of capital gains. In other words, the venture capitalist would like to find the client's business growing into a big one. In view of the high risk of the project to be financed by it, the venture capitalist expects greater potential returns on its investment. The rule of thumb is to get at least 10 times the invested amount in five to 10 years.

15.5.1 Project Valuation Methods

Popular methods of valuation of projects are the conventional valuation method, the First Chicago method and the revenue multiplier method.

A venture capitalist has to value a project before investing in it. The valuation of the project is necessary for the venture capital firm to decide the proportion of its ownership of the project. The popularly used methods are conventional valuation method, First Chicago method and revenue multiplier method.

The conventional valuation method

This method involves the following steps.

- The venture capital firm assumes a fixed period for its investment in the project;
- The annual earnings from the project at the time of exit from the project are estimated by compounding the present annual earnings at an expected annual growth rate;
- The value of investment on the date of exit from the project is computed by multiplying future earnings as arrived at in Step 2 with the expected P/E ratio on the date of exit; and
- The present value of the project is then arrived at by discounting the value in the previous step.

Having obtained the value of the project, the venture capital firm decides how much it has to invest in order to have the target percentage of ownership in the project. The conventional method of valuation does not take into account the stream of earnings during the investment period, that is, from the date of investment to the date of exit.

The First Chicago method

This method was developed by Stanley Goldar of First Chicago Corporation, hence the name First Chicago method. Unlike the conventional valuation method, this method considers the earnings including losses, if any, of the project that can occur during the entire period of investment. This method involves the following steps.

- Three different situations—success, survival and failure—are assumed and each situation is assigned certain probabilities; and
- The stream of earnings including losses, if any, during the entire investment period under each situation is estimated and discounted by using an appropriate discount rate. The discounted values are then multiplied by the respective probabilities. The sum of these values gives the expected present value of the project.

Having obtained the value of the project, the venture capital firm invests accordingly. This method involves a lot of subjectivity in estimation of cash flows, probabilities and discount rate.

The revenue multiplier method

This method is based on the sales revenue to be generated by the project. At the first instance, the multiplier (*M*) is calculated by using the following equation:

$$M = \frac{(1+g)^n (PM)(PE)}{(1+r)^n}$$

where

g = Estimated annual growth rate of sales revenue
n = Number of years from the investment date to the exit date
PM = Expected after-tax profit margin percentage at the time of exit
r = Discount rate
PE = Expected P/E ratio at the exit date

The value of the project is thus arrived at by multiplying the estimated annual sales revenues with the multiplier. This method takes into account the project sales revenues but not project's earnings.

15.5.2 Valuation of Venture Capital Investments

Venture capitalists should value their investments in different projects from time to time in order to take appropriate and timely decisions. For this purpose, the investments are classified as unquoted venture investments, unquoted development investments and quoted investments.

Unquoted venture investments are investments in projects that are in seed stage, start-up stage or early stage. As the shares of such firms are not listed on a recognized stock exchange, there is no market value for the investments. However, such investments can be valued on the basis of their cost. Their original cost can be written up (higher than original cost) or written down (lower than original cost). The investments can be written up when the operating results of a project are significantly higher than those originally estimated. The investments can also be written up when a third party who is interested in investing in the project values the project independently at a significantly higher level compared to the original cost. The investment in a project is written down if the operating results of the project are lower than the results originally expected. If the project faces some serious long-term problems, then also the investment can be valued below the original cost. A third party valuation might also be a guide to valuing the investment at less than the original cost.

Unquoted development investments are investments in projects that have already passed their early stage and are making profits. As the shares have not been listed on the stock exchange, the investments in such projects have no market value. The valuation of such investments can be done on the same lines as that of unquoted venture investments. A suitable P/E ratio can be applied to the earnings of the project, discounted at an appropriate rate.

As far as *quoted investments* are concerned, there is a market price that can be taken as a benchmark for valuation of the investment in a project. If there are restrictions or limitations on the disposal of shares or buyback arrangements exist, the market value of the investment should be adjusted accordingly.

15.5.3 Monitoring the Investment

After investing in a project, a venture capitalist continuously monitors the functioning of the project. The main purpose of monitoring is to ensure good governance of the project and prevent or find solutions to problems the project faces. The venture capitalist is also interested in effective utilization of funds by the management team of the project.

The participation of venture capitalists in the management of an investee firm is of three kinds: hands-on, hands-off and hand-holding.

There are different ways in which a venture capitalist can monitor the progress of a project. The venture capitalist can call for periodic reports and carry out periodic inspections. It can also participate in the management of the investee firm. The participation of venture capitalists in the management of an investee firm is of three kinds: hands-on, hands-off and hand-holding. In the *hands-on* relationship, the venture capital firm gets involved in the management of the investee firm through its representative on the board of directors. By being on the board of the investee firm, the venture capitalist closely monitors the progress of the project and advises the entrepreneur on several aspects of the management of the firm. The venture capitalist thus makes a substantial contribution to the strategies, policies and programmes of the investee firm. In a *hands-off* relationship, the venture capitalist does not directly participate in the management of the investee firm. However, it occasionally gives suggestions to the management of the investee firm after analysing reports and the information that its gets periodically. The hands-off style relationship is more appropriate after the start-up stage of a project. The *hand-holding* relationship is in between the hands-on and hands-off styles. Though the venture capitalist has a right to have a representative on the board of the investee firm, it actively participates only in matters that are very crucial for the success of the project. The venture capitalist is consulted by the entrepreneur on key decisions. In other words, the venture capitalist assists the investee firm whenever it is asked to do so.

15.5.4 Exit Routes

A venture capitalist can plan to exit the investee firm after successful commencement of the business. Generally, a venture capital firm likes to exit a project when there is a substantial appreciation of the investment in the project. The firm might seek to liquidate its investment at its maximum liquidation value. The exit can be planned or unplanned.

The following are exit routes available to a venture capital firm.

- Initial public offering (IPO)
- Buyback by the investee firm
- Sale of the stake of the venture capitalist to another firm or another venture capitalist
- Liquidation of the project

Initial public offering (IPO)

An entrepreneur initially starts his project as a closely held company. When the project is successful, he might offer shares of the company to the investing public. The main idea behind going public is to find a value and liquidity for the equity stock of the firm. The move can also be prompted by the venture capital fund as it desires to realize the cash return on its investment. However, there are also cases in which firms remain private even after they have become successful ventures.

A company can enhance its image by going public. Offering shares to the public for subscription implies listing of shares on the stock exchange(s). Listing of shares has certain advantages both for the company as well as for investors. When the shares are issued to the public and listed on a recognized stock exchange, the shares of the investee firm can be traded in the stock market. Therefore, the venture capitalist firm can easily sell its shareholdings and realize cash. The venture capitalist firm can also sell its stock through private placement. The accountability to shareholders will also increase with the listing of shares on the stock exchange. A major constraint of going public is complying with the listing requirements. The cost of public issue can also be very high, resulting in a lower realizable value of the stock.

Buyback by the company

The investee firm can buy the shareholdings of the venture capitalist. The firm might have entered into a buyback agreement with the venture capitalist at the time of sealing their deal. The agreement can specify a particular time limit, which can be the commencement of commercial production of the product, for buyback of the shareholdings of the venture capitalist. The venture capitalist can also have a put option facility with a predetermined price. Alternatively, the price of the shareholdings of the venture capitalist can be negotiated at the time of offloading the stock.

Sale of the project

The entire investee firm can be sold to others. In this case, the shareholdings of both the entrepreneurs and the venture capitalist are disposed of to a third party. Sometimes, a venture capital firm gets a higher price for its shareholdings by this exit route. The venture capital firm can sell its shareholdings to another venture capitalist, thereby exiting the project. Another venture capitalist might enter into the project by buying the stake of the existing venture capitalist. This can happen at any stage of the project, but with the full consent of the entrepreneur of the investee firm.

Liquidation

Some projects can be liquidated as soon as the purpose for which they were established is over. Once the slated programme is completed, the assets of the projects are sold and the proceeds distributed to all the stakeholders according to their proportionate stake in the project. Alternatively, if the investee firm becomes insolvent, the venture capital firm shares with the entrepreneur the realized value of the investee firm.

Each venture capital firm follows its own exit route depending on the circumstances. The stage of the project at which a venture capital firm has entered or would seek to exit can influence the preference of a particular exit route. By taking into consideration several factors, including market conditions and performance of the project, the venture capitalist chooses an exit route that is appropriate and most beneficial. It is always better to have a planned exit strategy.

If the venture capital firm has taken to debt financing of the project, it can get back its principal amount with interest as per the terms and conditions of the loan. The venture capital firm realizes its debt investment, partly if not completely, on the liquidation of the investee firm. In the case of mixed financing—equity financing as well as debt financing—the venture capital firm can get back its investment with return, if any, in a mixed exit route. It is also possible to have a single exit route for both types of investment.

15.6 Venture Capital Financing in India

The Risk Capital Foundation (RCF), established in 1975 by the Industrial Financial Corporation of India, was the beginning of venture capital financing in India. The main aim of RCF was to encourage technocrats and professionals to promote new industries.

The concept of venture capital originated in the United States in the early 1950s and subsequently spread all over the world. It started in India as a solution to some financial problems faced by small- and medium-scale enterprises. While large-scale industries were able to raise funds from government-sponsored term-lending institutions, the small- and medium-scale industries were left high and dry. It was observed that the lack of organized financial support had hindered the technological development, particularly indigenous technology, in the country. The talent, skills and competitive advantage of local entrepreneurs remained unutilized due to lack of risk capital. It was also felt that the country could achieve technological self-reliance only if entrepreneurial talent was fully exploited. The efficient absorption of indigenous technology and adaptation of foreign technology to national priorities and resources would accelerate economic growth and development. Rapid industrialization could solve many problems, both economic and social, faced by the country. A Committee on Development of Small and Medium Enterprises, appointed in 1975, also stressed the need to develop venture capital as a source of funding for new technology and new entrepreneurs. Pursuant to the observations of the committee and other experts, the Risk Capital Foundation (RCF) was established in 1975 by the Industrial Financial Corporation of India. The main aim of RCF was to encourage technocrats and professionals to promote new industries. In fact, a rudimentary form of venture capital had existed even before the establishment of RCF. The Tata Group's Investment Corporation of India had entered the field and supported the promotion of enterprises such as Associated Bearings, National Rayon and CEAT Tyres. The World Bank started the Industrial Technology Development project in India in the 1980s and, as part of the project, made available a loan of USD 45 million to the Government of India. The loan was meant for financing innovative and growth-oriented small enterprises. Realizing the need and importance of risk capital, the Government of India established a venture capital fund in 1986 to be managed by the Industrial Development Bank of India (IDBI). The Industrial Credit and Investment Corporation of India Ltd (ICICI) also set up the Technology Development and Infrastructure Corporation of India (TDICI). RCF was converted into the Risk Capital and Technological Finance Corporation Ltd, which has a wider scope, in 1988. State-level industrial development corporations like the AP Industrial Infrastructure Development Corporation and Gujarat Industrial Investment Corporation and a number of commercial banks also established venture capital funds. ANZ Grindlays Bank launched the India Investment Fund with funds raised from abroad, particularly from non-resident Indians.

The first full-fledged private sector venture capital fund was the Credit Capital Venture Fund (India) Ltd sponsored by the Credit Capital Finance Corporation, a merchant bank, in 1989. Until then, venture capital financing had been the exclusive preserve of financial institutions and commercial banks. Later, a number of private sector organizations established venture capital funds. Some of the popular ones in India are IFCI Venture Capital Funds, SIDBI Venture Capital, IDBI's Venture Capital Fund, Technology Development and Information Company of India Ltd, Risk Capital and Technology Finance Corporation Ltd, SBI Capital Venture Capital Fund, Canbank Venture Capital Fund, 20th Century Venture Capital Fund, Indus Venture

Capital Fund, APIDC Venture Capital Ltd, India Investment Fund, IL&FS Venture Corporation Ltd, Indus Venture Management Ltd, IFB Venture Capital Finance Ltd, HSBC Private Equity Management Mauritius Ltd, Alliance Venture Capital Advisors Ltd, Walden Nikko India Management Company Ltd, Marigold Capital Management Ltd, Uttar Pradesh Venture Capital Fund, Orissa Venture Capital Fund and Gujarat Venture Capital Finance Ltd.

Private equity funds are also very active in India and have emerged as a very important investor class driving equity deals in India. Private equity is equity that is not publicly traded and mainly used to finance business start-ups. In 2006, the PE investment in India touched an all-time high of USD 7,460 million, spread over 299 deals, as against USD 2 billion in 124 companies in 2005 and USD 1.1 billion in 60 companies in 2004. Despite the fact that private equity investment in India is less than 2 per cent of the total public market investments, the PE route has been a key source of funding for Indian companies. Globally, private equity has contributed to economic growth by both providing smart capital and improving capital efficiency. It has encouraged entrepreneurship by supporting new ventures and promoting new industries such as business process outsourcing.

Private equity investments in India involve mostly late-stage funding of firms including public enterprises that are not listed on any recognized stock exchange. They typically control the management of companies in which they invest and often bring in new management teams with rich sector-specific experience to make the investee firms more valuable. Such active investment is superior to passive investing by mutual funds. In other words, private equity funds try to increase the productivity of the investee firms and thereby maximize the social wealth of the country.

Venture capital and private equity investments in India have recorded a phenomenal growth, both in terms of the amount invested and the number of deals. The amount invested increased from USD 1.8 billion in 2004 to USD 22 billion in 2007 but declined to USD 8.1 billion in 2008. Similarly, the number of deals increased from 80 in 2004 to 481 in 2007 but declined to 297 in 2008. In November 2009, SEBI relaxed the listing norms for small and medium enterprises (SMEs). The paid-up capital requirement for listing was reduced to INR 100 million for SMEs. SEBI also relaxed eligibility norms applicable to IPOs and allotted market makers for ensuring post-listing liquidity. These relaxed norms are expected to benefit venture capital funds, which are willing to make seed- and growth-stage investments in SMEs. The easier listing norms provide the venture capital firms good exit options.

15.6.1 Major Venture Capital Firms

As mentioned in the previous section, the Indian venture capital industry is highly progressive. The major players in the industry are briefly described in the following paragraphs.

IFCI Venture Capital Funds Ltd (IVCF)

The Industrial Finance Corporation of India established Risk Capital Foundation (RCF) as a society in 1975 to provide institutional support to first-generation professionals and technocrats setting up their own ventures in the medium-scale sector. In 1988, RCF was converted into a company—the Risk Capital and Technology Finance Corporation Ltd (RCTC)—for financing the development and commercialization of indigenous technology. In February 2000, RCTC was renamed IFCI Venture Capital Funds Ltd (IVCF) in order to reflect the shift in the company's activities. IVCF has formulated certain parameters for taking investment decisions. These parameters serve as a basis for effectively evaluating the profitability of a project, which is crucial for ensuring high returns. The parameters set as investment criteria are as follows.

1. Management team: The quality and depth of the management team is one of the most important criteria for considering investment. IVCF believes in backing the management team with industry expertise.
2. Investment instruments: Investment is considered in the form of equity and equity-linked instruments such as optionally and fully convertible debentures and preference shares. It adopts a flexible financing approach while structuring a deal to suit the financing requirements of individual projects.
3. Investment range: The investment range of IVCF is normally between INR 10 million and INR 40 million, while equity stake to be acquired in the companies ranges from 10 per cent to 40 per cent.
4. Exit option: IVCF looks for a time horizon of three to five years for exercising the exit option. The preferred exit routes are initial public offerings, strategic sale and buyback by company/promoters.

IVCF takes the following steps in the process of taking an investment decision:

- initial/preliminary discussions with promoters;
- presentation by promoters on the project;
- preparation of business plan;
- due diligence/investment appraisal; and
- investment decision/future direction.

IVCF takes about a week to complete the preliminary discussions and screening and the detailed investment process/due diligence is completed in 8–10 weeks.

IVCF aims at creating value by evolving a long-term relation with the entrepreneur. Besides, IVCF's pro-active responsive approach ensures the congruence of interests. IVCF is a firm believer in the hand-holding approach, which provides requisite support to management teams for effectively managing the affairs of the investee companies. It adds value to its investee companies by closely associating with entrepreneurs in upgrading management systems, formulating and implementing growth strategies, marketing tie-ups and facilitating technological upgradations without interfering in day-to-day operations. IVCF is sensitive to the needs of its investee firms and understands their specific requirements of multiple rounds of funding during the implementation and stabilization phases. It is always willing to support a venture more than once for optimizing its valuation.

SIDBI Venture Capital Ltd

The Small Industry Development Bank of India (SIDBI), as the apex financial institution for the small-scale sector, has played a very active role in the evolution of venture capital financing in India to support the risk capital requirements of small industries. The bank has been investing in several venture capital funds for onward investments in the SME sector. These include India Leverage Fund, India Advantage Fund and India Development Fund. It has partnered with US-based Small Enterprise Assistance Fund and Kotak Mahindra Bank Ltd in setting up the India Growth Fund. SIDBI has also invested in a number of state-level venture capital funds in collaboration with local institutions.

SIDBI established its own subsidiary, called SIDBI Venture Capital Ltd (SVCL), in July 1999. SVCL manages various venture capital funds launched by SIDBI. The mission of SVCL is to catalyse entrepreneurship by providing capital and other strategic inputs for building business around growth opportunities and maximize returns on investment. The important funds managed by SVCL are National Venture Fund for Software and Information Technology (NFSIT) and SME Growth Fund. NFSIT has been set up by SIDBI in association with the ministry of information technology, Government of India. It is a closed-ended 10-year fund with an initial corpus of INR 1,000 million. The main objective of the fund is to meet the total fund requirements of software and IT companies, particularly SMEs, to enable them to grow rapidly and maintain their competitive edge in domestic and international markets. The fund also considers funding innovative incubation projects and development of products in the IT sector.

The SME Growth Fund was set up by SIDBI in October 2004 in association with commercial banks such as Punjab National Bank, State Bank of India, Bank of Baroda, Bank of India, Central Bank of India, Union Bank of India, Oriental Bank of Commerce and Corporation bank. This eight-year life fund, dedicated to the SME sector, had an initial corpus of INR 5,000 million. It is the largest domestic VC fund dedicated to the SME. The main objective of the fund is to invest in companies in the early stage as well as in second-round financing for those with a track record of proven technology or business model and opportunities for growth and earnings. The fund attempts to develop international networking and enable assisted units to attract co-investment from international venture capitalists in subsequent rounds of financing.

In August 2005, SVCL exited from ECAD Technologies Ltd, an early-stage IT company funded by SVCL together with Karnataka IT Venture Capital Fund (KITVEN). The company, engaged mainly in design, simulation and testing of high-end printed circuit boards used in critical applications, was promoted by an ex-BEL executive and others in September 1997. It received venture capital funding from SVCL and KITVEN in March 2001. The exit of SVCL and KITVEN was facilitated by the acquisition of ECAD by Austria Technologies & Systemtechnik AG (AT&S), an Austrian company. AT&S acquired controlling interest in ECAD in August 2005. Pursuant to this acquisition, both the funds successfully exited from ECAD. SVCL and KITVEIN invested INR 20 million and INR 10 million, respectively, in ECAD and fully divested their investment for a total consideration of INR 75 million—a return of 150 per cent on their investment. While announcing the exit from ECAD, SVCL chairman N. Balasubramanian said, "We are delighted to announce our exit from ECAD. The most difficult part of the venture capital investment process is the exit and to have accomplished it smoothly is the ideal end result. The exit of our investment from ECAD vindicates our faith in the SME segment that it offers good investment and profit opportunities to venture capitalists."

ICICI Venture

ICICI Venture is one of the largest private equity firms in India with funds under management amounting to more than USD 2 billion. It is a subsidiary of ICICI Bank, the largest private sector bank in India. The focus areas of ICICI Venture include private equity, buyouts, real estate and mezzanine financing. Over the years, it has built an enviable portfolio of companies across sectors including pharmaceuticals, information technology, media, manufacturing, logistics, textiles and real estate. The investment philosophy is to pursue transactions with established firms that are leaders or potential leaders in their respective markets and where there is a clear proposition for value creation.

The funds under management are private equity funds, real estate funds and mezzanine funds. ICICI Venture manages USD 1.8 billion worth of private equity assets. These include India Advantage Fund Series 2 (USD 810 million), India Advantage Fund Series 1 (USD 267 million) and ICICI Emerging Sector Fund (USD 692 million). ICICI Venture manages a dedicated real estate fund with a corpus of USD 562 million. The fund invests in both domestic and foreign direct investment projects through equity, quasi-equity and equity-related instruments. ICICI Venture is a first mover in mezzanine financing in the Indian PE industry. The India Advantage Fund VII (Mezzanine Fund I) is conceptualized as a USD 51-million fund that would focus on mezzanine investment opportunities. Mezzanine finance is typically a structured debt with a component of cash income and benefits from potential upside returns from equity kickers. It bridges the gap in corporate capital structure between senior debt and equity. In other words, mezzanine finance provides medium- to long-term capital without significant ownership dilution.

ICICI Venture is a pioneer in buyout investing in India. It has a strong involvement in reorganizing, restructuring and re-strategizing the bought-out companies. It is also a pioneer in identifying unique scalable platforms that are ideal for investment in the form of roll-ups.

15.6.2 Government Initiatives

The World Bank had commissioned a study to examine the possibility of developing venture capital in the private sector. Following the observations of the study, the Union finance minister in his budget speech for 1988–89 referred to the problems of new entrepreneurs in raising equity capital and declared a scheme under which venture capital companies/funds would be able to invest in new companies and be eligible for concessional treatment of capital gains. Accordingly, in November 1988, the Government of India issued a set of guidelines to promote venture capital investment in new enterprises. The highlights of these guidelines are as follows.

1. The applications for the establishment of venture capital companies/funds should be submitted to the Controller of Capital Issues and the approvals will be given by the department of economic affairs, ministry of finance, Government of India, or such authority as notified by the Government of India.
2. The venture capital companies/funds should be managed by professionals such as bankers and persons with adequate experience in industry, finance, accounts, etc. If established by banks and other institutions, the venture capital companies/funds should maintain their independence.
3. Venture capital assistance should cover enterprises that fulfil the following parameters.
   a. **Size:** Total investment not exceeding INR 10 crore.
   b. **Technology:** New or relatively untried or very closely held or being taken from pilot to commercial stage, or which incorporates some significant improvement over the existing one in India.
   c. **Promoters/entrepreneurs:** Relatively new, professionally or technically qualified with adequate resources or backing to finance the project.

The venture capital fund (VCF)/venture capital company (VCC) should invest at least 75 per cent of its funds in the eligible enterprises. The 75 per cent level may be reached by the end of the fifth year of operations of the VCF/VCC. The balance amount may be invested in any new issue by an existing or a new company, of equity, CCPs, debentures, bonds or other securities approved for this purpose by the Controller of Capital Issues.

4. Investment in enterprises engaged in trading, broking, investment or financial services, agency or liaison work shall not be permitted. The recipient venture should be established as a limited company and must employ professionally qualified persons to maintain its accounts.
5. The minimum size of the VCF/VCC should be INR 10 crore. If it desires to raise funds from the public, the promoters' contributions should not be less than 40 per cent. The VCF/VCC can raise the funds through public issues and/or private placement. Foreign equity up to 25 per cent is permitted. NRI investment is permitted up to 74 per cent on a non-repatriable basis and up to 25 per cent/40 per cent on a repatriable basis.
6. Preferential tax treatment would be available to the approved VCF/VCC.

In the budget speech for 1995–96, the Union finance minister announced an exemption from tax on income by way of dividend and long-term capital gains from equity investment made by an approved VCF/VCC in unlisted companies in certain sectors. An amendment was also made to the SEBI Act providing powers to SEBI to regulate venture capital funds. Accordingly, the 1988 guidelines issued by the erstwhile office of the Controller of Capital Issues became defunct and were repealed with immediate effect. To operationalize the tax provisions, the Central Board of Direct Taxes (CBDT) issued its own guidelines in August 1995. Accordingly, the VCFs/VCCs are exempted from payment of income tax on dividend income and capital gains. This exemption, however, is available only in the case of income/capital gains from investment in unlisted companies engaged in manufacturing and software development. It was also stated that investment in a single company by a VCF/VCC should exceed 5 per cent of the paid-up corpus of the VCF/VCC and that the investment should be limited to 40 per cent of the paid-up capital of the company.

With the powers given by the act, SEBI framed guidelines notified as SEBI (Venture Capital Fund) Regulations, 1996, which were amended from time to time. The latest amended regulations—the SEBI (Venture Capital Fund) (Amendments) Regulations, 2006—came into effect on January 25, 2006. These regulations comprehensively cover various aspects such as registration of venture capital funds, investment conditions and restrictions, general obligations and responsibilities, inspection and investigation and procedure for action in case of default.

The highlights of the regulations are as follows.

1. A venture capital fund is a fund established in the form of a trust or a company including a body corporate and registered under these regulations, which has a dedicated pool of capital raised in a manner specified in the regulations, and invests in accordance with the regulations.
2. A venture capital undertaking is a domestic company whose shares are not listed in a recognized stock exchange in India, and which is engaged in the business of providing services, production or manufacture of articles or things, but does not include such activities or sectors that are specified in the negative list by SEBI, with the approval of the Union government, by notification in the official gazette in this behalf.
3. Any company or trust or a body corporate proposing to carry on any activity as a venture capital fund should obtain a certificate from SEBI by making an application to SEBI.
4. Any applicant whose application has been rejected shall not carry on any activity as a venture capital fund.
5. A venture capital fund may raise monies from any investor, whether Indian, foreign or non-resident Indian, by way of issue of units.
6. No venture capital fund set up as a company or any scheme of venture capital fund set up as a trust shall accept any investment from any investor that is less than INR 5 lakh. However, this condition is not applicable to investors who are employees or the principal officer or directors of the venture capital fund, or directors of the trustee company or trustees where the venture capital fund has been established as a trust, or the employees of the fund manager or asset management company.
7. Each scheme launched or fund set up by a venture capital fund shall have a firm commitment from the investors for contribution of an amount of at least INR 5 crore before the start of the operations by the venture capital fund.
8. The venture capital fund should disclose the investment strategy at the time of application for registration.

9. The venture capital fund should not invest more than 25 per cent of the corpus of the fund in one venture capital undertaking.
10. A venture capital fund may invest in securities of foreign companies subject to such conditions or guidelines that may be stipulated or issued by the RBI and SEBI from time to time.
11. A venture capital fund should not invest in associated companies.
12. A venture capital fund should invest at least 66.67 per cent of the investible funds in unlisted equity shares or equity-linked instruments of a venture capital undertaking.
13. A venture capital fund may invest not more than 33.33 per cent of the investible funds by way of subscription to the initial public offer of a venture capital undertaking whose shares are proposed to be listed, by way of subscription to debt or debt instruments of a venture capital undertaking in which the venture capital fund has already made an investment by way of equity, by way of subscribing to preferential allotment of equity shares of a listed company subject to a lock-in period of one year, by way of subscribing to the equity shares or equity-linked instruments of a financially weak company or a sick industrial undertaking whose shares are listed, or by way of subscribing to special-purpose vehicles that are created by a venture capital fund for the purpose of facilitating or promoting investment in accordance with these regulations.
14. The venture capital fund should disclose the duration of the life cycle of the fund.
15. No venture capital fund shall be entitled to get its units listed on any recognized stock exchange till the expiry of three years from the date of issuance of the units by the venture capital fund.
16. No venture capital fund shall issue any document or advertisement inviting offers from the public for the subscription or purchase of any of its units.
17. A venture capital fund may receive monies for investment in the venture capital fund only through private placement of its units.
18. SEBI may *suo motu* or upon receipt of information or complaint appoint one or more persons as inspecting or investigating officer to undertake inspection or investigation of the books of account, records and documents relating to a venture capital fund.
19. All the venture capital funds are required to provide information pertaining to their venture capital activity for every quarter.

The Chandrasekhar committee observed that India needed a large pool of risk capital, both from home and abroad, and this could happen only with the right regulatory, legal, tax and institutional environment, which play an enabling role.

SEBI (Chandrasekhar) Committee on Venture Capital, 2000

In order to identify impediments and suggest suitable measures to facilitate the growth of venture capital activity in the country, SEBI constituted a committee, known as the Chandrasekhar committee on venture capital, in July 1999. The committee consisted of industry participants and professionals. It made a thorough study of various aspects of venture capital and submitted its report in January 2000. The major observations and recommendations of the committee are as follows.

1. The committee observed that India needed a large pool of risk capital, both from home and abroad. However, this could happen only with the right regulatory, legal, tax and institutional environment, which play an enabling role. If the right environment is created by providing infrastructure and regulatory flexibility, large amounts of risk finance and venture capital money can flow into the country.
2. As venture capital plays a very important role in economic development, particularly in the context of increasing global integration, venture capital firms need to be financed by sophisticated investors and managed by professionals.
3. The committee observed that the venture capital industry comes under the purview of different sets of regulations. The multiple sets of guidelines and requirements create inconsistencies and detract from the overall objective of development of the venture capital industry in India. For example, a venture capital fund has to seek registration under the SEBI Act and approval under the income tax rules apart from seeking approval from the FIPB/RBI in the event of subscription to the fund by an overseas investor. This type of multiplicity of regulators creates an environment of conceptual inconsistencies and investment restrictions. The committee, therefore, recommended that since SEBI is responsible for the overall regulation and registration of venture capital funds, the need was to harmonize and consolidate all aspects within the SEBI regulations to provide a uniform, hassle-free, one-window

clearance. It also recommended that Section 10(23FA) of the Income Tax Act be amended in such a way that it provides complete exemption from income tax at the fund level on the basis of SEBI registration. Once registered with SEBI, a venture capital fund could be automatically entitled to tax exemption and CBDT guidelines would not be required.

4. SEBI regulations also need to be amended to provide for the registration of other entities such as limited liability companies (LLC) and limited liability partnerships (LLP). Foreign venture capital investors (FVCI) should be allowed the facility of registration with SEBI and the FVCIs bringing in foreign currency should be permitted to retain the same in foreign currency either with a bank in India or outside till it is actually invested. They may also be permitted to take forward cover as protection against currency and price fluctuation risk.
5. The current SEBI guidelines restrict investment by venture capital funds to unlisted equity or equity-related instruments and listed securities of financially weak or sick companies. The Government of India guidelines and income tax rules restrict investment only to unlisted equity of the investee company. Therefore, it was recommended that the investment, other than unlisted equity, may be permitted within an overall ceiling of 30 per cent of the investible fund and at least 70 per cent should be invested in unlisted equity only. Apart from equity investment, investment should be permitted in equity-related instruments and also other instruments convertible into equity.
6. In order to encourage domestic venture capital funds to go global, the domestic venture capital funds should be permitted to make investments abroad under transparent and automatic norms subject to ceilings. This would enable them to generate better returns globally and expose them to international market practices.
7. The existing guidelines for a buyback of equity shares by an unlisted company prohibit the company from making a fresh issue of capital for a period of 24 months. This is a major constraint for growth-oriented companies as they have to buy back their shares even if they have a cash surplus. The prohibition period for fresh issue of capital may be reduced to a period of six months as the investee firms are typically growing companies that need financing and should not be barred from making a fresh issue of capital for a long period of time. The present IPO guidelines of SEBI require a three-year track record of profit for a company to float a public issue. Therefore, IPO norms need to be reviewed in the cases of companies funded by venture capital funds to facilitate early exit from them. A provision may also be made for the listing of shares of the companies that are already listed on the stock exchanges outside the country.
8. If foreign employees invest in a venture capital fund, which in turn participates in the shares of the Indian employer company, the foreign employee should be allowed to invest without any limit in such a fund. Further, the venture capital fund's investment in the Indian employer company should not be regarded as foreign holding for the purposes of determining the overall ceiling of foreign share in such a company. It is also recommended that foreign employees be allowed to participate in employees' stock option plans (ESOP) so as to invest in shares of an Indian company with full repatriation benefits with a ceiling.

SEBI (Foreign Venture Capital Investors) Regulations, 2000

SEBI also issued separate regulations for foreign venture capital investors, called the Securities and Exchange Board of India (Foreign Venture Capital Investors) Regulations, 2000. The highlights of the regulations are as follows.

1. A foreign venture capital investor is an investor incorporated, established outside India, is registered under these regulations and proposes to make investments in accordance with these regulations.
2. A venture capital undertaking is a domestic company whose shares are not listed in a recognized stock exchange in India, and which is engaged in the business of providing services, production or manufacture of articles or things, but does not include such activities or sectors that are specified in the negative list by SEBI, with the approval of the Union government, by notification in the official gazette in this behalf.
3. Foreign venture capital investors should seek registration under these regulations by making an application in Form A to SEBI in order to carry on any activity as a foreign venture capital investor.
4. While examining the application for registration, SEBI will consider the following conditions for eligibility.

a. The applicant's track record, professional competence, financial soundness, experience, general reputation of fairness and integrity;
b. Whether the applicant has been granted necessary approval by the RBI for making investments in India;
c. Whether the applicant is an investment company, investment trust, investment partnership, pension fund, mutual fund, endowment fund, university fund, charitable institution or any other entity incorporated outside India;
d. Whether the applicant is an asset management company, investment manager or investment management company or any other investment vehicle incorporated outside India;
e. Whether the applicant is authorized to invest in a venture capital fund or carry on activity as a foreign venture capital investor; and
f. Whether the applicant is regulated by an appropriate foreign regulatory authority or is an income tax payer, or submits a certificate from its banker of its or its promoter's track record where the applicant is neither a regulated entity nor an income tax payer.

5. All investments to be made by a foreign venture capital investor shall be subject to the following conditions.

   a. It shall disclose to SEBI its investment strategy;
   b. It can invest its total funds committed in one venture;
   c. At least 66.67 per cent of the investible funds shall be invested in unlisted equity shares or equity-linked instruments of a venture capital undertaking;
   d. Not more than 33.33 per cent of the investible funds may be invested by way of subscription to an initial public offer or venture capital undertaking whose shares are proposed to be listed, and/or subscription to debt or debt instrument of a venture capital undertaking in which the foreign venture capital investor has already made an investment by way of equity, and/or subscription to preferential allotment of equity shares of a listed company subject to a lock-in period of one year, and/or special-purpose vehicles that are created for the purpose of facilitating or promoting investment in accordance with these regulations; and
   e. It shall disclose the duration of the life cycle of the fund.

6. A foreign venture capital investor or a global custodian acting on behalf of the foreign venture capital investor shall enter into an agreement with the domestic custodian to act as a custodian of securities for the foreign venture capital investor.

The other provisions in the SEBI (Foreign Venture Capital Investors) Regulations, 2000, are mostly on the lines of the corresponding provisions in SEBI (Venture Capital Funds) Regulations, 1996.

In July 2009, SEBI made it mandatory for foreign venture capital investors to obtain a firm commitment from their investors for at least USD 1 million of capital before seeking permission to invest in India. The foreign venture capital funds registered in India are also free to invest in almost any business in the country, barring a few sensitive sectors. However, the foreign venture capital funds will have to either approach the FIPB or invest directly in areas where FDI is permitted under the automatic route.

Summary

1. Innovation—in technology, products, management or any aspect of business—is key to fostering and accelerating the growth and development of an economy.
2. The traditional sources of financing, such as commercial banks and term-lending institutions (development banks), being risk-averse and security-oriented, do not evince interest in financing untried technologies or innovative projects.
3. Venture capital is referred to as professional investment in risk capital of an enterprise, sharing ownership as well as management responsibility with the entrepreneur.
4. Venture capital firms aim at promoting and developing new technologies, new products and new entrepreneurship and management, thereby getting high returns in the form of capital gain on their investments.

5. Venture capital is an investment made in the early stage(s) of a business, whereas private equity is an investment made in the later stages of a business.
6. A venture capitalist can become a virtual partner in the business of the entrepreneur, sharing both success and failure with the entrepreneur. The extent of involvement of the venture capital firm varies, usually depending on the circumstances and understanding between the venture capital firm and the investee firm.
7. According to SEBI regulations, a venture capital fund can raise monies from any investor, whether Indian, foreign or non-resident Indian, by issue of units.
8. Before making any investment, the venture capital firm may make a business analysis of the project by examining factors such as the entrepreneur, the management, the product, the technology, financial structure, target return and exit route.
9. The venture capitalist has to value the project before investing in it. The popularly used methods are conventional valuation method, First Chicago method and revenue multiplier method.
10. The exit routes available to a venture capital firm are IPOs, buyback by the investee firm, sale of the stake of the venture capitalist to another firm or to another venture capitalist and liquidation of the project.
11. The Risk Capital Foundation (RCF), established in 1975 by the Industrial Financial Corporation of India, marked the beginning of venture capital financing in India. The aim of RCF was to encourage technocrats and professionals to promote new industries.
12. The first private sector venture capital fund in a full-fledged form was the Credit Capital Venture Fund (India) Ltd, sponsored by the Credit Capital Finance Corporation, a merchant bank, in 1989.
13. In November 1988, the Government of India issued a set of guidelines to promote venture capital investment in new enterprises.
14. With the powers given by the act, SEBI framed guidelines and notified the SEBI (Venture Capital Fund) Regulations, 1996. These regulations comprehensively cover various aspects such as registration of venture capital funds, investment conditions and restrictions, general obligations and responsibilities, inspection and investigation and procedure for action in case of default.
15. SEBI also issued regulations separately for foreign venture capital investors as the Securities and Exchange Board of India (Foreign Venture Capital Investors) Regulations, 2000.

Questions

1. What factors have contributed to the origin of venture capital financing?
2. Define venture capital and distinguish between venture capital and private equity.
3. Examine the role of venture capital financing in the economic development of a country.
4. What are the factors that are analysed by venture capitalists while deciding on investments?
5. What are the exit routes available to a venture capitalist? What are the pros and cons of each one?
6. Discuss the methods of valuation of projects.
7. Bring out the salient features of SEBI regulations regarding venture capital funds.
8. Discuss the origin and development of venture capital financing in India.
9. Critically examine the working of Indian venture capital funds.
10. What are the main recommendations of the Chandrasekhar committee on venture capital?

Chapter 16

Securitization

LEARNING OBJECTIVES

After reading this chapter, you should be able to:

- Introduce the concept of securitization.
- Highlight the importance of securitization.
- Explain the process of securitization.
- Understand the advantages of securitization.
- Trace the origin and development of securitization in India.
- Bring out the salient features of the legal framework concerning securitization.

16.1 Introduction

The globalization of financial markets and services has resulted in many financial innovations across the world. In fact, the integration of financial markets has made such innovations necessary. One such innovation is securitization. *Securitization* is the process of transforming illiquid assets (receivables) into financial instruments that can be traded in the financial markets. Securitization can also be understood as a financial strategy to increase liquidity and accelerate the development of the financial markets.

Financial institutions, commercial banks and non-banking financial institutions of various kinds provide loans and advances to different customers, both individuals and institutions. Similarly, non-financial organizations such as manufacturing organizations, trading organizations and service organizations can sell goods and services on credit to their customers, resulting in bill receivables or sundry debtors. The loans and advances, bill receivables and sundry debtors are shown as assets in the balance sheet of the respective organization. However, these assets may be realized in trickles spread over a period of time, which may be even 10 years or more in the case of long-term assets (loans and advances). Therefore, the organizations that have such assets need to tap other sources of funds in order to continue or develop their operations. But other sources of funds might not be easy to tap; they might also be costly or they may have to be competed for. Further, the assets might eventually become non-performing or illiquid assets if the customers or borrowers fail to honour their commitments. So such financial assets might become risky assets for the organization holding them. Thus, there are two important issues involved in management of assets like loans and advances, bill receivables, sundry debtors and so on. One is the recycling of funds, and the other is credit risk. Securitization addresses these two issues.

Securitization is a recent financial innovation that has brought about revolutionary changes in the financial world. **Securitization** is a process that involves the conversion of receivables (loans and advances, for example) into marketable securities that can be sold to investors. *Receivables* refer to expected streams of cash flows. For example, in the case of loans and advances given by a bank, the borrowers are expected to pay back the principal amount (in instalments or in a lump sum) and make interest payments periodically on the borrowings. The expected cash flows of this nature are called receivables.

Securitization *is a process that involves the conversion of receivables into marketable securities that can be traded in the financial markets.*

Securitization is a structured process whereby financial assets like loans and advances, sundry debtors and other cash flow streams are packaged into pools of homogeneous assets (housing loans of similar maturity, for example) or homogeneous cash flows (such as credit card receivables). Following this, a type of marketable securities backed by these pools of receivables is created and marketed to the investing public. It may be noted that the pool of assets or stream of cash flows would become collateral to the securities issued. In other words, the receivables would become the security against which fresh funds are raised. For example, consider that a bank has INR 500 million worth of auto loans, on which it receives interest at the rate of 13 per cent per annum. It can securitize these loans into marketable securities that could carry a return of, say, 11 per cent and sell these securities to others. The principal and interest payments on the securitized financial instruments are met from the cash flows generated by the assets that are securitized (in this case, auto loans). Two important things may be noted in this context. One is that securitization allows the organization to recycle the funds much earlier than it could otherwise. Second, the credit risk involved in the financial assets is distributed among all the investors who have subscribed to the securitized financial instruments. The obvious advantage of faster recycling of funds is that the organization can acquire better or more productive assets or invest the funds into the business for further development. For example, a banking organization might be able to issue fresh loans to its customers with the sale proceeds of securitized financial instruments. In this way, securitization may become an alternate source of funds.

Securitization started with mortgage loans. Over time, the scope of securitization has extended to cover any predictable cash flow stream arising out of normal business transactions. The assets or cash flow streams that can be securitized include auto loans, auto leases, aircraft leases, computer leases, commercial loans, consumer loans, real estate loans, corporate loans, franchise loans, home loans, rentals, royalties, credit card receivables, property developers' receivables, toll fee receivables and trade receivables. For example, an organization having regular cash inflows by way of lease rentals can borrow funds by offering its future lease rentals as security. The lease rents will first be used to pay the loan, after which they can be used for other purposes.

If mortgage loans are converted into marketable securities, such securitization is known as *mortgage-backed securitization*; similarly, if financial assets such as sundry debtors are converted into marketable securities, such securitization is known as *asset-backed securitization*; and if cash flow streams (such as credit card receivables) are converted into marketable securities, it is known as *cash-flows securitization.* Securitization can also cover "future flows" of receivables to be generated in the future by the originator. This means that the originator can use the proceeds of the securitization to generate the future flow of receivables that are securitized. Thus, securitization involves packaging pools of assets with relatively predictable cash flow streams into marketable securities.

16.2 The Securitization Process

As mentioned in earlier paragraphs, securitization is a process of converting receivables into marketable securities. This process involves the following steps:

1. The first step is the identification of assets or cash flows that can be pooled for the purpose of securitization. That is, an organization that wants to go in for securitization will identify its loans, leases and other cash flow streams and organize or pool them into homogenous groups on a certain basis or criterion (such as type of credit, maturity, interest rate, risk profile). These assets/cash flows can be backed by the underlying mortgage, pledge, charge or guarantee. These credit enhancements may be built into the pooling of receivables so that the securitized financial instruments will have less chances of default. An organization that goes in for securitization is called the *originator*. The originator (for example, a commercial bank) generates receivables in the ordinary course of its business. The borrowers or customers (including potential customers) who owe money to the originator are called *obligors*. Although the originator can be any organization, it generally refers to banks, financial institutions, non-banking financial institutions or housing finance companies.
2. The assets or cash flow streams thus identified and pooled then pass through (are sold or assigned) to another institution called a **special purpose vehicle** (SPV). An SPV is an organization formed exclusively to deal with the securitization process. It is usually formed as a trust but can also be a company or a subsidiary of the originator company depending on the originator's objectives. The SPVs are generally constituted into trusts in order to avoid taxes because SPVs are usually tax-neutral entities. An SPV is also called an *issuer* because it ultimately issues the securities to investors. In other words, the SPV can also be owned by the originator.

*A **special purpose vehicle** (SPV) is an organization formed exclusively to deal with the securitization process.*

3. After acquisition of the assets or cash flow streams, the SPV notionally splits the pool of assets or cash flows into individual securities known as securitized financial instruments (such as notes or commercial paper). These securities are then offered to investors for subscription. It may be noted that

only one type of asset or cash flow stream is bundled together to create the securitized instrument. The securities are structured to synchronize, for redemption, with the maturities of the pooled assets or cash flows.

In mortgage-backed securitization (MBS), the banks (lenders) typically create mortgages against the loans provided by them to the purchasers of houses. These mortgages are assets to the bank and they generate cash flows represented by repayments of both principal and interest on the mortgage loans. In MBS, the mortgages are converted into marketable financial instruments and sold to the investors through an SPV. The cash flows that come as repayments from the borrowers are passed on to the investors by the SPV.

The originator can transfer the assets or cash flow streams to an SVP by ***novation, assignment*** *or* ***sub-participation.***

The originator can transfer the assets or cash flow streams to SVP by novation, assignment, or sub-participation. **Novation** refers to substitution of an SPV for the originator under an agreement. In other words, the originator gives all his rights to the SPV and the debtors of the originator become debtors of the SPV. This might require the assent of the debtors. Novation assumes writing off the assets from the balance sheet of the originator. The originator can also transfer his rights over the assets or cash flows by **assignment**, which may not require the consent of the debtors. In other words, the SPV gets full legal and beneficial interest in the assets assigned to it. **Sub-participation** involves an agreement with the SPV to deposit with the originator a sum of money representing an agreed proportion of the amount advanced by the originator. In return, the SPV acquires the right to receive from the originator the sum equal to the same proportion of the amount repaid by the debtors. The sub-participant relationship is only with the originator and the SPV acquires no interest in the underlying asset. Thus, the originator remains the lender of record to the debtors as there is no direct contractual relationship between the sub-participant and the debtors.

In some cases, a two-step structure is used whereby the receivables are first transferred to an intermediate SPV, which is permitted to engage in the business of acquiring the receivables, and then the intermediate SPV sells the receivables to the issuer of securities. The transaction between the intermediate SPV and the originator can be a true sale so that the originator gets the receivables off its balance sheet and books a profit or loss for accounting purposes. The actual securitization structure might involve many elements and participants depending on the objectives of the originator and classes of assets. An originator can sell receivables to an SPV that aggregates receivables from multiple originators. In other words, an SPV can aggregate receivables from multiple originators, even different forms of receivables, to create large pools that will reduce the cost of securitization.

Securitization can be structured in such a way that it has a bankruptcy-remote characteristic, which means that in the event of the bankruptcy of the originator the creditors of the originator cannot have any claim over the assets that are securitized. In other words, the bankruptcy of the originator will not affect the interests of the investors who have purchased the securitized financial instruments. The originator often does not want a true sale to occur and book a profit or loss, so it can structure the transaction as a secured loan. Fig. 16.1 presents a schematic diagram of securitization.

16.2.1 Parties Involved in Securitization

The main parties involved in securitization are obligors, the originator, the SPV, investors, administrators, credit rating agencies, underwriter or placement agents and structurers.

As shown in Figure 16.1, apart from obligors, originators, the SPV and investors, the other important parties involved in the securitization process are administrators, credit rating agencies, underwriters or placement agents and structurers. As stated earlier, obligors are the borrowers or customers who owe a certain amount to the originator. The dues from the obligors are the assets that are transferred to the SPV. Thus, the quality of the assets depends upon the credit standing of the obligors. The original underlying collateral assets as well as the securities to be issued by the SPV can be rated by credit rating agencies. Credit rating helps the investors select securities that suit their risk preferences. In certain cases of securitization, the administrator or servicer is also involved. The *administrator* or servicer helps the originator or SPV in collecting the amount due from the obligors. The administrator or servicer might follow up with delinquent parties and pursue legal remedies against defaulting parties. The servicer can actually deal with receivables on a day-to-day basis, collecting receivables and transferring funds to accounts controlled by the SPV. The originator can also act as the servicer. There might be backup servicers who can take over from the primary servicer, and also perform certain monitoring functions on a continuing basis. A typical securitization process involves a *structurer*. A financial institution can be involved in structuring the securitization deal. The *underwriter*

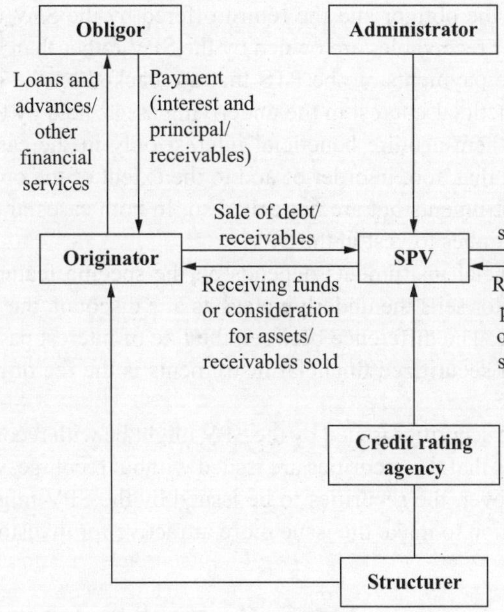

Figure 16.1 Schematic diagram of securitization

or *placement agents* sell or place the securitized financial instruments in a public offering or private placement. Expertise in the areas of securities law and tax law might be required in securitization.

16.2.2 Securitized Financial Instruments

Securitized financial instruments can be pass-through-certificates (PTC) or pay-through securities (PTS). A **pass-through certificate** is a conduit through which cash flows from the debtors (obligors) are passed on to the holders of securitized financial instruments. A PTC promises that the cash flow from the underlying receivables would be passed to the holders of the PTC in the form of periodic payments of interest and principal. The underlying assets or receivables are typically held in trust for the investors who have purchased the securitized financial instruments. The trust (SPV) receives the cash flows from the obligors with respect to the underlying collateral and then passes on such payments after deducting expenses and servicing fees on a pro-rata basis to the holders of the PTC. If the obligors make pre-payments, those are remitted to the PTC holders. Thus, the holders of the PTC acquire beneficial interest in the underlying receivables held by the SPV and, accordingly, all the risks and rewards on the underlying assets or cash flows are transferred to the PTC holders.

*A **pass-through certificate** is a conduit through which cash flows from the debtors (obligors) are passed on to the holders of securitized financial instruments.*

Mortgage-backed certificates are the most common type of PTC, where the borrowers' payments pass through an agency or investment bank to investors. The underlying assets of securitized financial instruments are self-amortizing, and by whatever amount they are amortized, they are passed on to the holders of the PTC. Surpluses, if any, generated by the securitized assets revert to the originator after all claims of investors and management fees of the SPV are taken care of. Thus, the PTC is evidence of the acquisition by its holder of an undivided right, title or interest in the assets or receivables involved in securitization. The term "undivided" in this context means that each holder of the security has a proportionate interest in each cash flow generated by the pooled assets or receivables. The PTC can be compared to securities like bonds and debentures that are issued by corporate organizations. The only difference is that they are issued against underlying securities.

Instead of providing undivided interest in the receivables, the SPV can create and issue **pay-through securities** (PTS) backed by the general credit of the SPV. The PTC can have different maturities, different yields and risks. In other words, the SPV owns the underlying financial assets and creates the PTS that is backed by the assets. The SPV is free to restructure the cash flows emanating from the underlying collateral assets into different payments to the holders of securitized financial instruments. There might be a difference between the rate of interest payable by the obligor and the return offered by the SPV to the holders of the PTS. In the case of the PTS, the assets or receivables are owned by the SPV rather than by the investors. But as a matter of law, the investors receive payments on the PTS that are backed by the general assets of the SPV. Investors holding PTC acquire beneficial interest in the underlying assets held by the SPV, whereas the in case of PTS, the investors holding them acquire beneficial interest only in the cash flows realized on the underlying assets or receivables and that, too, in order of and to the extent of the obligations contracted. Both PTC and PTS are derived debt instruments but are not called so. In both cases, the legal ownership of the underlying receivables or assets continues to vest in the SPV.

The pricing of the securitized financial instruments depends on the specific features of the respective underlying financial asset. If the originator sells the underlying assets at a discount, the SPV might issue the securities at a discount on the face value. The difference between the rate of interest payable by the obligors and the return payable to the holders of securitized financial instruments is the fee or remuneration for the services of the SPV.

Another important feature is that the securities issued by the SPV might be with recourse to the originator or without recourse. The usual practice is that the securities are issued without recourse, which means that the originator is free from credit risk. However, the securities to be issued by the SPV might be guaranteed by some reputed external guarantor-institution to make the issue more attractive for investors.

16.3 Credit Enhancement and Credit Rating

The risks in securitization are classified as default risk, delinquency risk, prepayment risk and commingling risk. *Default risk* arises on the non-repayment of underlying loans by the obligors. Temporary delays in payment from the underlying assets results in *delinquency risk.* High prepayments on underlying assets might lead to substantial reduction in future receivables, which leads to a cash flow deficiency. The originator in a securitized transaction collects receivables from the obligors and passes these receivables as per the payout schedule to those who are holding the securitized financial instruments. There may be a time lag between receivable collections and investor payouts. During this period, the originator or servicer holds in custody the monies that actually belong to the investors. Thus, *commingling risk* arises when these funds are temporarily used by the originator or servicer for its own operations.

Credit enhancement *occurs when the securitized financial instrument's credit quality is increased above that of the underlying receivables pool*

Securitization might require credit enhancement to reduce the overall credit risk of the securitized financial instruments. **Credit enhancement** occurs when the securitized financial instrument's credit quality is increased above that of the underlying receivables pool. The purpose of credit enhancement is to increase the likelihood that the investors will receive the cash flows to which they are entitled. There are a variety of credit enhancement techniques, which can be categorized as internal credit enhancement techniques and external credit enhancement techniques. Over-collateralization, subordination, excess servicing and turboing are examples of *internal credit enhancement techniques*. *External credit enhancement techniques* include surety bonds, third-party guarantee, letter of credit, cash collateral account and collateral invested account.

Over-collateralization is a technique of credit enhancement in which the face value of the underlying receivables exceeds the face value of the securitized financial instrument. In other words, the amounts of receivables are greater than the amount required to pay for the securities backed by the receivables. The amount of over-collateralization is usually determined by rating agencies, underwriters or placement agents depending on factors such as the quality of the receivables, nature of the industry and possibility of bankruptcy of the originator or servicer. In the case of foreign securitization, the sovereign risk is also taken into consideration while determining the amount of over-collateralization. A popular type of internal credit enhancement is the *senior/subordinated (or A/B) structure*. In this method, the securitized (or A-class) financial instruments are supported by subordinate or secondary (B-class) securities. The B-class securities function as protective layers for the A-class securities. In the event of problems (default on underlying assets), the loss incurred is absorbed by the subordinated securities. So the securitized financial instruments remain unaffected unless the losses in underlying assets exceed the amount of the subordinated tranches. There can be a number of classes of securities that are each subordinated to more highly rated securities.

There can be a *third-party credit enhancement,* which takes the form of a letter of credit or surety. The government can underwrite the securities so as to enhance their credit rating. A parent company or other third party might be contractually bound to meet the obligations to the investors. *Insurance policies* can be provided for compensation in the event of borrowers or customers failing to pay the receivables. Thus, insurance is a credit enhancement measure. It may be noted that credit enhancement improves credit rating. In other words, the incorporation of adequate credit enhancements usually implies a very high credit rating, which enhances the marketability and thus the liquidity of the securities to be issued by the SPV. A case of credit enhancement is given in Box 16.1.

All the major risks are considered in the evaluation of securitization by a credit rating agency. The credit rating of securitization is the rating of the securitized financial instruments at a particular credit enhancement. The basic assessment in rating a securitization transaction is to determine whether the credit enhancement is sufficient to cover the deficits in pooled cash flows even under stressed scenarios. The stressed scenarios relate to losses and delays in recovery from the underlying securitized pooled cash flows, which may lead to a loss or delay in payment on the securitized financial instrument if the credit enhancement is not sufficient. Thus, credit rating of a securitization transaction boils down to whether the credit enhancement is adequate to cover all the risks, particularly the credit risk, on the securitized financial instruments.

Box 16.1 Credit Enhancement to Residential Mortgage-backed Securities of Primary Lending Institutions by way of NHB Guarantee

Considering the need to promote the development of a secondary market for residential mortgage-backed securities (RMBS) in India, the RMBS Policy of National Housing Bank (NHB) envisages the introduction of specialized institutional measures to provide credit enhancements for promoting the development of the secondary market for residential mortgages. It may be mentioned that the presence of specialized forms of credit enhancements, such as guarantees of institutions like Fannie Mae, Freddie Mac and Ginnie Mae with respect to the RMBS issued by these institutions, have considerably contributed to the success of RMBS in developed nations such as the United States. Since such credit enhancements are presently absent in India, NHB introduced the scheme to guarantee the senior classes of residential mortgage-backed securities issued by NHB. This is expected to reduce credit enhancement costs, improving viability of RMBS transactions and encouraging housing finance companies (HFCs) and banks to take up securitization of their home loan portfolios.

Under the arrangement, NHB would offer to provide/furnish an irrevocable guarantee in its corporate capacity to the RMBS issues of eligible primary lending institutions (PLIs), that is, HFCs and banks, with the main intent to obtain a rating of investment grade indicating highest safety [AAA(So)] from an approved rating agency. At the same time, in order to ensure that the cash flows to the investors are sufficiently protected, it has been stipulated that there should be adequate subordination and/or adequate collateral levels to the guaranteed class of RMBS which are commensurate with high levels of the safety grade of rating [AA(So)] for the RMBS by an approved credit rating agency. Thus, the intent of the scheme is to enable HFCs to obtain AAA(So) benefits with collaterals equivalent to AA(So) requirements.

While the major objective of NHB's guarantee is to enable originator(s) to derive the pricing and other benefits of an AAA(So) RMBS at AA(So) terms, it has been stipulated that layer(s) of credit enhancements such as cash flows of subordinated-class RMBS (subscribed by originator) and cash collateral/reserve, etc. (as prescribed by the rating agency) shall act as the first-level credit supports for the senior classes of RMBS. The NHB guarantee shall be only in the event of exhaustion of the initial layer(s) of such credit enhancements. Therefore, in the event of any shortfalls in the collections for payments due on senior-class RMBS holders, NHB's guarantee shall be invokable as the last resort only after the residual income/principal of subordinate RMBS and all other forms of collaterals stipulated for the AA(So) rating have been exhausted/completed in a payout.

In a typical RMBS transaction, the size of credit enhancements would be considerably less. While the major objective of NHB's guarantee would be to enable originator(s) to derive the pricing and other benefits of an AAA(So) RMBS at AA(So) terms, it would be quite in order to ensure that NHB's guarantee is invoked in a transaction only in the event of non-availability of cash flows from the securitized pool to service the senior class of RMBS guaranteed by NHB. For the purpose, the following hierarchy of payments (payment waterfall) shall be built into the RMBS structure:

(Continued)

First in the sequence of payment	Service providers [trustees, guarantors, servicing and paying agencies, rating agency and other statutory dues (if any)]
Second in the sequence of payment	Interest to senior-class RMBS holders (Class-A PTCs)
Third in the sequence of payment	Principal to senior-class RMBS holders (Class-A PTCs)
Fourth in the sequence of payment	Replenishment of guarantee (to NHB) together with interest (at pass-through rate p.a.), if it had been invoked in the earlier payout(s)
Fifth in the sequence of payment	Replenishment of cash collateral/credit enhancement (provided/arranged by the originator) to obtain > targeted rating of AA(So) without interest
Sixth in the sequence of payment	Payment of principal to subordinate RMBS holders
Seventh in the sequence of payment	Payment of residual income to subordinate RMBS holders

In the event of any default on the part of the borrower(s) of the securitized pool of home loans in payment/repayment of any of the monies due on senior-class RMBS holders, NHB's guarantee can be invoked only after the residual income/principal of subordinate RMBS and all other forms of collaterals stipulated for the AA(So) rating have been exhausted/completed in a payout. With the credit risk component of the home loan market being very low, as also due to the cherry-picking exercise adopted for selection of the best quality home loans with excellent repayment track record for securitization, this would ensure sufficient safeguards for the transaction.

Source: www.nhb.org.in. This information is based on the extant Residential Mortgage-backed Securitization Policy of NHB.

16.4 A Case of Securitization of Export Receivables

Securitization of export receivables can be a good source of external funds for domestic companies. For example, consider an Indian firm that has a long-term export contract with a firm in England. In order to securitize its export receivables, the Indian firm creates a special purpose vehicle (SPV) overseas. SPVs are created preferably in a tax-haven country to avoid taxes such as withholding tax and stamp duty. The Indian firm assigns the SPV the right to collect all future export receivables from the importer British firm. Thus, there is a tripartite agreement between the Indian firm, the British firm and the SPV. On the basis of this tripartite agreement, the SPV issues debt securities to overseas investors and the sale proceeds are transferred to the Indian firm. The Indian firm gets funds in foreign currency, say pound sterling, worth all its future export commitments upfront at a discounted value, the discount being determined on the basis of certain factors including the rating obtained on the debt security issued by the SPV. The Indian firm will keep exporting to the British firm under the long-term contract. The payments by the British firm will be captured offshore and transferred to the SPV, which in turn will make payments, both principal and interest, to the holders of securitized financial instruments. Some important features may be noted in this example. Since the funds originate from overseas payers and are captured offshore, they are not constrained by the Indian country's sovereign rating. In other words, the cost of funds raised through securitization is cheaper. Thus, securitization of export receivables enables the Indian firm to get a higher credit rating than the rating in the country, which helps the Indian firm raise funds at a lower cost. If the Indian firm raises the overseas funds through the external commercial borrowings (ECB) route, the cost of funds may be higher as its credit rating would be constrained by the sovereign rating. Thus, securitization of export receivables opens up a new market for firms. However, securitization of export receivables is not free from risks. The exports are particularly subject to risk arising from changes in export prices and overseas demand for products. Such risks can be avoided if the exporter has a long-term export commitment or contract with overseas buyers. Another way of reducing the risk is by securitizing only a small portion of the expected exports in the beginning and subsequently, as things improve, particularly the credit rating, further securitization can be taken up. So securitization can be done in tranches to reduce risk. International banks or financial institutions can also be involved in the securitization process, particularly with regard to structuring of the deal. This can add value to securitization issues (issuing of securitized financial instruments). The experience and expertise of such institutions helps in reducing the risks involved in securitization of receivables.

16.5 Benefits of Securitization

Securitization confers several benefits on the parties involved in the securitization process.

1. For the originator, securitization converts illiquid assets or non-performing assets into liquid assets. Securitization thus leads to greater recycling of funds which, in turn, improves the business as well as profitability of the originator.
2. Securitization has a built-in risk reduction mechanism that lowers the cost of funds vis-à-vis other sources of funds for the originator.
3. Another great advantage of securitization is that it provides a flexible means of financing for the originator. The firm (originator) transforms or sells its illiquid assets depending on the financing needs of its business.
4. Once the non-performing assets are securitized, they can be removed from the balance sheet of the originator. This enhances the capital adequacy of the originator.
5. Cash inflows arising on the sale of illiquid assets can be used for repayment of borrowings of the originator, resulting in a better debt-equity ratio.
6. Securitization enables organizations, particularly banks, to convert the higher risk weighted assets to lower risk weighted ones.
7. Securitization is not affected by statutory pre-emption such as statutory liquid ratio and cash reserve ratio. This gives greater freedom to banks or other financial institutions to expand their volume of business, especially on the credit deployment side.
8. In the free interest-rate market, securitization eliminates interest rate risk.
9. By securitization, new kinds of securities are made available to investors, widening the choice of securities for the investing public.
10. Securitization helps organizations to diversify their funding base and reach out to new investors without increasing their financial leverage.
11. The securities issued by an SPV provide higher yield and liquidity compared to those of many other securities.
12. Being structured and asset-backed or mortgage-backed securities, the financial instruments originating from the securitization process have greater protection against default.
13. Securitization allows organizations to sell off their bad loans (non-performing assets) to an SPV, thereby helping them concentrate on their core business.
14. Securitization provides a source of fee-based income to many organizations.
15. Securitization offers a wide choice to potential investors in terms of risk-return profile, liquidity and maturity, yield and helps attract new investors into the capital market. In other words, securitization allows investors to invest in a variety of asset classes, enhancing the width and depth of the capital market.
16. Securitization leads to reallocation of risks in a planned and transparent manner.
17. Securitization helps in better management of the balance sheet. Banks and financial institutions can minimize the mismatch of their assets and liabilities through securitization.
18. Securitization upgrades the level of sophistication of banking and finance in the country.
19. Organizations benefit on account of possible gains arising from improvements in their credit and operating processes with securitization.
20. Securitized financial instruments are tradable in the secondary market, which enhances the broadening and deepening of financial markets in the country.

Despite several advantages, the development of the concept of securitization has been limited in India. This is mainly because of limited trading in the debt market and excessive stamp duty prevailing in most states. There is also a ceiling on the investment that can be made in securitized financial securities by qualified institutional buyers including banks, mutual funds and insurance companies. Further, there is no clarity on certain tax issues pertaining to securitization in India. Poorly managed securitization could also magnify the risks in the financial system, which will have a deleterious effect on the economy. In the event of a race for securitization, the quality of the assets could be undermined, leading to financial indiscipline in the market.

16.6 Securitization in India

Securitization took off in the United States with the buying of residential mortgage loans, making pools out of them and then issuing mortgage-backed securities. The U.S. government played an active role in promoting the residential mortgage market through the Federal National Mortgage Association (FNMA) and Government National Mortgage Association (GNMA). In the mid-1980s, securitization was extended to cover non-mortgage debts and it spread to other countries. Over the last few years, the concept of securitization has developed into an important financial innovation and means of fund-raising throughout the world, particularly in the United States, Canada, Europe, Latin America and South-East Asia. The market value of the outstanding global securitization volumes runs into some trillions of US dollars, of which more than 75 per cent is accounted for by the United States. U.S. investors, in fact, participate even in the securitization issues of other major markets such as Europe and Japan. The U.S. securitization market has grown at an astonishing rate over the period, particularly during the last decade (2000–2010), and it provides necessary liquidity to US financial institutions and their customers.

Securitization is relatively a new concept in the Indian financial market. The first deal in India was structured in 1991. Following the initiation of the economic liberalization process, commercial banks and other financial institutions deployed huge amounts of credit for projects, especially in the housing and infrastructure sectors. In order to offload their initial exposure and make room for financing new projects, the banks and financial institutions entered the securitization process. This resulted in the mortgage-backed securitization (MBS) market in India. Parallel to this, the NBFCs entered the retail business in a big way, generating large volumes of homogeneous classes of assets such as auto loans and lease financing. This led to the development of asset-backed securitization (ABS). However, securitization in India started off as a device for bilateral acquisitions of portfolios of finance companies. This means that the portfolios move from one originator to another. As there was no creation of any form of security, such securitization was called quasi-securitization. There were also provisions that provided recourse to the originator.

The main purpose of securitization in India is to avoid a mismatch between the assets and liabilities of banking institutions. So the SPV acquires illiquid assets from the banks and other financial assets by issuing debentures, bonds or entering into an arrangement with the originators. The SPV can then create and issue security receipts (SRs) to qualified institutional buyers (QIB) to invest in the securitization. The SRs represent undivided interest in the underlying receivables. The QIBs include foreign institutional investors, provident funds and pension funds. Public and private sector banks, mutual funds and insurance companies also participate in securitization transactions. The major originators in India are private sector banks, NBFCs and housing finance companies.

A formal deal between ICICI and Citibank to securitize the former's bill receivables under sellers' lines of credit in February 1991 marked the first securitization attempt in India. A sum of INR 150 million was raised in the transaction in which the Citibank acted as the agent of ICICI for the issue and redemption of PTCs. The PTC was in the form of a receipt and, therefore, it was not freely transferable. There was no secondary market for the PTCs. However, Citibank provided a premature redemption facility. Since then, many deals have been struck covering several kinds of debt and cash flows including auto loans, credit cards and other receivables of various organizations. Almost all the securitized debt pools have been privately placed with single investors who hold them till maturity.

Securitization of auto loans was the mainstay of the Indian securitization market in the 1990s, mainly because of factors such as perceived credit risk, higher volumes and homogenous nature of the receivables. Over time, the securitized market has spread into several asset classes such as housing loans, corporate loans, commercial mortgage receivables, project receivables, toll revenues, property rental receivables, power receivables, telecom receivables, lease receivables and medical equipment loan receivables. Asset-backed securitization is the largest product class because of the growing retail loan portfolio of banks and other financial institutions. The short maturity period of retail loans of banks and other financial institutions also drives the growth of ABS. ABS deals are mainly backed by assets such as car loans, commercial vehicle loans, construction equipment loans, two-wheeler loans and personal loans. The ABS market has grown substantially due to growth of bank retail lending. The MBS market has been rather slow in taking off in India despite a growing housing finance market due to lack of investor interest in long-term securities and lack of secondary market liquidity. Stamp duty issues have also adversely impacted the growth of the MBS market in India.

In 1994, National Housing Bank initiated a pilot mortgage-backed securitization programme that involved purchasing mortgage loans and issuing secondary market securities from pools of these loans. Five large housing finance companies were the originators of the mortgage-backed loans. Subsequently, a large number of hire purchase portfolios as well as bill receivables were securitized, and most of them originated from non-banking finance companies.

Cholamandalam Investment and Finance Company completed a first-of-its-kind securitization of INR 854 million of its auto loan portfolios in January 2005. The SPV—Asset Securitization Trust—issued six series of PTCs rated AAA (so) by Crisil. All the six series issued were parri passu senior PTCs. Senior PTCs are structured to receive semi-annual payments and have a door-to-door maturity of about two years with floating rate coupons linked to the local benchmark MIBOR (Mumbai Inter Bank Offer Rate). This was the first transaction in India in which a yield reserve was used to take care of interest rate mismatches. As the underlying receivables from the auto loans carried a fixed interest rate and the PTCs offered a floating rate to investors, the structure incorporated a yield reserve determined by the rating agency to cover the credit risk. Another innovation driven by investor demand was the staggered payment of prepayments on the pool to reduce unscheduled payments to investors.

16.6.1 Securitization by NHB

The Government of India announced the national housing and habitat policy in 1998 which enjoined upon NHB to play a lead role in starting mortgage-backed securitization and developing a secondary mortgage market in the country. Accordingly, the National Housing Bank Act was amended on June 12, 2000, to enable NHB to create an SPV for taking up mortgage-backed securitization. In terms of Section 14 (ea) of the NHB Act, the bank is authorized to purchase, sell or otherwise deal in any loans or advances secured by mortgage or charge on the immovable property relating to scheduled commercial banks or housing finance companies. As per Section 14 (eb) of the NHB Act, the bank can create one or more trusts and transfer loans or advances together with or without securities thereof to such trust(s) for consideration. Section 14 (ec) of the NHB Act authorizes the bank to set aside loans or advances and issue or sell mortgage-backed securities based on such loans or advances so set aside in the form of debt obligations, trust certificates of beneficial interest or other instruments, called by whatever name, and to act as trustee for the holders of such securities.

NHB launched a large-sized mortgage-backed securitization called RMBS in August 2000. The securitization transactions of NHB primarily involve assignment of retail housing loans from housing finance companies or banks to NHB. The loans, repayable in equated monthly instalments (EMIs), are packaged and offered to investors as PTCs by NHB, acting as the issuer and trustee. The housing loans, which constitute the receivables to be securitized, are held by an SPV in the nature of a trust declared by NHB. The PTCs are in the nature of trust certificates and represent proportionate undivided beneficial interest in the pool of housing loans.

NHB, in its corporate capacity as also in its capacity as sole trustee of the SPV, is the issuer of Class A and Class B PTCs. While Class A PTCs are allotted to investors, Class B PTCs are subscribed to entirely by originators. Class B PTCs are subordinated to Class A PTCs and act as credit enhancement for Class A PTC holders. The Class A PTCs of the MBS issues of NHB have been rated AAA(So). All the issues were fully subscribed by institutional investors including insurance companies, mutual funds, financial institutions and commercial banks. NHB has also been working towards the development of systems and building of institutions in order to make the MBS market sustainable in the long run. The securitization process of NHB is presented in Box 16.2.

16.6.2 The Regulatory Framework

There was no clear and specific regulatory framework for securitization in India until recently. The first legislative measure was the enactment of the Securitization and Reconstruction of Financial Assets and Enforcement of Security Interests Act, 2002 (SARFAESI Act, 2002). The act principally provides for the following:

- Enforcement of security interests by secured creditors;
- Transfer of non-performing loans to asset reconstruction companies (ARCs), which can then take measures for recovery as prescribed under the Securitization Act, 2002;
- A legal framework for securitization of assets.

Box 16.2 NHB: Securitization

The securitization process of NHB can be perceived as a two-stage process:

- First stage: Transfer of mortgage debt from the primary lending institution (originator) to a special-purpose vehicle (NHB SPV Trust set up by NHB through a declaration) with or without the underlying security.
- Second stage: The mortgage debt so acquired will be converted into tradable debt instruments (say, in the form of pass-through certificates) without any recourse to the originator or the SPV.

Securitization of mortgage debt: The NHB SPV can purchase and convert the housing loans into securities or PTCs concurrently and issue them in the capital market for investment by investing institutions.

Execution of memorandum of agreement with NHB: Based on the willingness to sell or securitize its portfolio of housing loans, the primary lending institution is required to enter into an umbrella agreement (called memorandum of agreement) with NHB to sell or securitize its portfolio of housing loans. The memorandum of agreement encapsulates the entire MBS transaction and entitles NHB to take necessary steps to purchase or securitize an identified pool of housing loans, including circulation of the information memorandum and collection of subscription amount from investors, as the case may be.

Selection of pool of housing loans: The pool of housing loans would be selected by the primary lending institution from its existing housing loans based on a pool selection criteria.

Eligibility criteria for home loans to qualify for securitization: The home loans should satisfy the following standards to be considered for selection in the mortgage pool offered for securitization:

- The borrower should be individual(s).
- The home loans should be current at the time of selection or securitization.
- The home loans should have a minimum seasoning of 12 months (excluding moratorium period).
- The maximum loan-to-value (LTV) ratio permissible is 85 per cent. Housing loans originally sanctioned with an LTV of more than 85 per cent but where the present outstanding is within 85 per cent of the value of the security will be eligible.
- The maximum installment (EMI) to gross income ratio permissible is 45 per cent.
- The loan should not have overdues outstanding for more than three months at any time throughout the period of the loan.
- The quantum of principal outstanding loan size should be in the range of INR 50,000 to INR 10 million.
- The pool of housing loans can comprise fixed and/or variable interest rates.
- The borrowers have only one loan contract with the primary lending institution (PLI).
- The loans should be free from any encumbrances or charge on the date of selection or securitization. The sole exception to this norm being loans refinanced by NHB (in such cases, the loans can be securitized subject to the originator substituting the same with other eligible housing loans conforming with the provisions of the refinance schemes of NHB).
- The loan agreement in each of the individual housing loans should have been duly executed and the security in respect thereof duly created by the borrower in favour of the PLI and all the documents should be legally valid and enforceable in accordance with the terms thereof.
- The bank or HFC has, with respect to each of the housing loans, valid and enforceable mortgage in the land/building/dwelling unit securing such housing loan and have full and absolute right to transfer and assign the same to NHB.

The pool selection criteria might be modified by NHB from time to time at its sole discretion.

Source: www.nhb.org.in. This information is based on the extant Residential Mortgage-backed Securitization Policy of NHB.

The main aim of the Securitization Act is to strengthen creditors' rights through foreclosure and enforcement of securities by banks and financial institutions by conferring on the creditors the right to seize the secured asset and sell the same in order to recover dues bypassing the time-consuming legal process through courts. Prior to this act, there was no provision for facilitating securitization of financial assets and the power to take possession of securitized assets and selling them off. The act came as a boon for the Indian banking industry at a time the industry was grappling with bad loans.

According to the act, **securitization** is the acquisition of financial assets by any securitization company or reconstruction company from any originator, whether by raising of funds by such a securitization company or reconstruction company from qualified institutional buyers by issue of security receipts representing undivided interest in such financial assets or otherwise. A *securitization company* is defined as any company formed and registered under the Companies Act, 1956, for the purpose of securitization. *Asset reconstruction* is acquisition by any securitization company or reconstruction company of any right or interest of any bank or financial institution in any financial assistance for the purpose of realization of such financial assistance. *Financial assistance* is any loan or advance granted or any debentures or bonds subscribed or any guarantees given or letters of credit established or any other credit facility extended by any bank or financial institution. An *originator* is the owner of a financial asset that is acquired by a securitization company or reconstruction company for the purpose of securitization or asset reconstruction. The *obligor* is defined as a person liable to the originator, whether under a contract or otherwise, to pay a financial asset or to discharge any obligation with respect to a financial asset, whether existing, future, conditional or contingent and includes the borrower.

According to the SARFAESI Act, 2002, ***securitization*** *is the acquisition of financial assets by any securitization company or reconstruction company from any originator.*

According to the act, any securitization company or reconstruction company can acquire financial assets of any bank or financial institution by issuing a debenture or bond or any other security in the nature of a debenture, for consideration agreed upon between such a company and the bank or financial institution, incorporating therein such terms and conditions as agreed upon between them or by entering into an agreement with such a bank or financial institution for the transfer of such financial assets to such a company on such terms and conditions as agreed upon between them. If the bank or financial institution is a lender in relation to any financial assets acquired by the securitization company or the reconstruction company, such a securitization company or reconstruction company shall, on such acquisition, be deemed to be the lender and all the rights of such a bank or financial institution shall vest in such a company in relation to such financial assets.

Any security interest created in favour of any secured creditor might be enforced, without the intervention of the court or tribunal, by such a creditor in accordance with the provisions of the act. A *secured creditor* is any bank or financial institution or any consortium or group of banks or financial institutions and includes the debenture trustee appointed by any bank or financial institution, or securitization company or reconstruction company or any other trustee holding securities on behalf of a bank or a financial institution in whose favour the security interest is created for due repayment by any borrower of any financial assistance.

Thus, the SARFAESI Act, 2002, enables securitization of non-performing assets of banks, which can sell off their NPAs to asset reconstruction companies registered with the RBI. The act has also set the framework for the constitution of ARCs specializing in securitizing distressed assets purchased from banks. The receivables are to be treated as NPAs if the same remain overdue for a period of 180 days or more. A brief profile of Asset Reconstruction Company of India Limited (ARCIL) is presented in Box 16.3.

Reserve Bank of India Guidelines and Directions, 2003

The Reserve Bank of India notified certain guidelines under the Securitization Act, known as the Securitization Companies and Reconstruction Companies (Reserve Bank) Guidelines and Directions, 2003. These guidelines provide for different aspects of securitization and asset reconstruction relating to registration, owned funds, permissible business, asset reconstruction, deployment of surplus funds, internal control systems, prudential norms and disclosure requirements.

The salient features of the guidelines and directions are as follows:

1. A securitization company or reconstruction company shall commence/undertake only the securitization and asset reconstruction activities and the functions provided for in Section 10 of the act. No securitization company or reconstruction company shall commence or carry on the business of securitization or reconstruction without obtaining a certificate of registration and having the owned fund of not less than INR 2 crore or such other amount not exceeding 15 per cent of total financial assets acquired or to be acquired by the securitization company or reconstruction company as the Reserve Bank of India by notification specifies. The amount of owned funds shall be continued to be held by the securitization company or reconstruction company until realization of assets and redemption of security receipts issued against such assets. The securitization company or reconstruction company shall invest in the security receipts issued by the trust set up for the purpose of securitization, an amount of not less than 5 per cent under each scheme.

Box 16.3 Asset Reconstruction Company of India Limited (ARCIL)

ARCIL was incorporated as a public limited company on February 11, 2002, and obtained its certificate of commencement of business on May 7, 2003. In pursuance of Section 3 of the Securitization Act, 2002, it holds a certificate of registration dated August 29, 2003, issued by the Reserve Bank of India and operates under powers conferred to it under the Securitization Act, 2002. ARCIL is also a financial institution within the meaning of Section 2 (h) (ia) of the Recovery of Debts due to Banks and Financial Institutions Act, 1993 (DRT Act).

The shareholders of ARCIL consist of State Bank of India, ICICI Bank Limited, Punjab National Bank, IDBI Bank Limited and some other prominent private sector banks. Punjab National Bank became the sponsor in October 2004 by virtue of its shareholding of 10 per cent.

The vision of the company is to be a major contributor to the Indian economy by enhancing velocity of capital.

Mission

- Maximize value through innovative resolution
- Establish fair and transparent business practices
- Facilitate development of market for distressed debt

Objectives

- Unlocking and recycling capital for the banking system and the economy
- Creating a vibrant market for distressed debt assets/securities in India by offering a trading platform for lenders
- Evolving and creating significant capacity in the system for quicker resolution of non-performing loans by optimal deployment of the assets

Organization structure

ARCIL is managed by a board of directors which comprises eminent personalities from the fields of banking, finance, management, taxation and private equity and who possess considerable experience and expertise therein. The board of directors lays down the policy framework for the overall functioning of the company. The supervisory role of the board is discharged through the committees of directors such as the executive committee, audit committee, capital and debt raising committee and the remuneration committee.

Corporate governance

ARCIL's corporate governance framework is based on the separation of the board's supervisory role from the executive management. The board of directors deliberates on matters relating to corporate policy, strategy and overall performance, whereas operational matters and other critical areas and functions are delegated to the committees of the board, comprising a majority of non-sponsor directors. The committees are chaired by a non-sponsor director.

The executive committee (EC) comprises only non-sponsor directors and has been empowered to take all decisions relating to operational matters, namely, proposals for acquisition of financial assets, investment in security receipts and resolution of financial assets (excluding those delegated to the committee of executives) and matters related thereto. In certain exceptional cases, the EC considers the proposals and recommends the same to the board of directors for approval. The EC also recommends policy matters to the board of directors.

ARCIL is the first asset reconstruction company in the country to commence the business of resolution of non-performing loans upon acquisition from Indian banks and financial institutions. As the first asset reconstruction company, ARCIL has not only participated in the process of framing guidelines by the RBI but also helped define the contours of the industry, claiming many of the firsts. ARCIL has meaningfully engaged the stakeholders in the asset reconstruction domain and established a business model conducive to Indian ecology.

Source: www.arcil.co.in

2. A securitization company or reconstruction company shall commence/undertake only the securitization and asset reconstruction activities and the functions provided for in Section 10 of the act.
3. A securitization company or reconstruction company shall not raise monies by way of deposits.
4. Every securitization company or reconstruction company shall frame with the approval of the board of directors a Financial Asset Acquisition Policy within 90 days of the grant of certificate of registration, which shall clearly lay down the policies and guidelines.

Table 16.1 Assets with risk-weights

On-balance-sheet items	*Percentage risk weight*
a. Cash and deposits with commercial banks	0
b. Investment in government securities	0
c. Other assets	100
Off-balance-sheet items	Percentage risk weight
All contingent liabilities	50

5. Every securitization company or reconstruction company shall frame a policy, duly approved by the board of directors, laying down the broad parameters for rescheduling or settlement of debts due from borrowers.
6. A securitization company or reconstruction company shall give effect to the provisions of Section 7 (1) and (2) of the act through one or more trusts set up exclusively for the purpose. The securitization company or reconstruction company shall transfer the assets to the said trusts at the price at which those were acquired from the originator. The trusts shall issue security receipts only to qualified institutional buyers, and hold and administer the financial assets for the benefit of the qualified institutional buyers. The trusteeship of such trusts shall vest with the securitization company or reconstruction company.
7. Every securitization company or reconstruction company shall maintain, on an ongoing basis, a capital adequacy ratio, which shall not be less than 15 per cent of its total risk weighted assets. The risk-weighted assets shall be calculated as the weighted aggregate of on-balance-sheet and off-balance-sheet items as detailed in Table 16.1. Shares held in other securitization company or reconstruction company shall not attract any risk weight.

8. A securitization company or reconstruction company may act as a sponsor and for the purpose of establishing a joint venture, invest in the equity share capital of a securitization company or reconstruction company formed for the purpose of asset securitization. It may deploy any surplus available with it only in government securities and deposits with scheduled commercial banks in terms of a policy framed in this regard by its board of directors. No securitization company or reconstruction company shall invest out of its owned funds in land and buildings, provided that this restriction will not apply to funds borrowed as also to owned fund in excess of the minimum prescribed.
9. Every securitization company or reconstruction company shall, after taking into account the degree of well-defined credit weaknesses and extent of dependence on collateral security for realization, classify the assets into the following categories.

   a. Standard assets
   b. Non-performing assets

   The non-performing assets shall be classified further as:

   (a) Sub-standard asset for a period not exceeding 12 months from the date it was classified as non-performing asset.
   (b) Doubtful asset if the asset remains a substantial asset for a period exceeding 12 months.
   (c) Loss asset if the asset is non-performing for a period exceeding 36 months or if the asset is adversely affected by a potential threat of non-recoverability due to either erosion in the value of security or non-availability of security if it has been identified as loss asset by the securitization company or reconstruction company or its internal or external auditor.

The asset may be upgraded as a standard asset only after satisfactory performance for a period of 12 months as per the renegotiated/rescheduled terms.

10. Every securitization company or reconstruction company shall make provision against non-performing assets, as shown in Table 16.2.
11. All investments shall be valued at lower of cost or realizable value. Where market rates are available, the market value would be presumed to be the realizable value and in cases where market rates are not

Table 16.2 Provisions against non-performing assets

Asset category	*Provision required*
Sub-standard assets	A general provision of 10% of the outstanding
Doubtful assets	(i) 100% provision to the extent the asset is not covered by the estimated realizable value of security (ii) In addition to (i), 50% of the remaining outstanding
Loss assets	The entire asset shall be written off. (If for any reason the asset is retained in the books, 100% thereof shall be provided for)

available, the realizable value should be the fair value. However, investments in other registered securitization company or reconstruction company shall be treated as long-term investments and valued in accordance with the accounting standards and guidance notes issued by the Institute of Chartered Accounts of India.

12. The income recognition shall be based on recognized accounting principles. Interest and any other changes in respect of all the NPAs shall be recognized only when they are actually realized. Any such unrealized income recognized by a securitization company or reconstruction company before the asset becomes non-performing and remaining unrealized shall be derecognized.
13. The accounting policies adopted in preparation and presentation of the financial statements shall be in conformity with the applicable prudential norms. Where any of the accounting policies is not in conformity with these directions, the particulars of departures shall be disclosed together with the reasons thereof and the financial impact on account thereof. Where such an effect is not ascertainable, the fact shall be so disclosed citing the reasons thereof.

Committee on Corporate Bonds and Securitization

In the budget 2005–06 speech, the Union finance minister announced the appointment of a high-level expert committee on corporate bonds and securitization to look into the legal, regulatory, tax and market design issues in the development of the corporate bond market. Pursuant to this announcement, a 12-member committee was constituted under the chairmanship of R.H. Patil on July 5, 2005. The key recommendations of the committee as applicable to securitization are as follows:

1. As stamp duty is a state subject, the government may coordinate with the state governments to bring uniformity in the application of stamp duties on corporate bonds.
2. To promote healthy growth of the securitization market, the government should consider establishing an appropriate institutional process to evolve a consensus across the states on the affordable rates and levels of stamp duty on debt assignment, PTCs and security receipts.
3. The government should provide an explicit tax pass through treatment to securitization SPVs and NPA securitization SPVs on a par with the tax pass through treatment applied under the tax law to SEBI-registered venture capital funds.
4. The government should consider notifying PTCs and other securities issued by securitization SPVs as securities under Securities Contract Regulation Act (SCRA).
5. There should be no withholding tax requirement on interest paid by the borrowers (whose credit exposure are securitized) to the securitization trust. Similarly, there should be no requirement of withholding tax on distribution made by the securitization trust to the holders of its PTC and/or security receipts.
6. The government may consider the possibility of proposing an appropriate amendment to the definition of security receipt in Section 2 (zg) of the SARFAESI Act. The amendment should enable the security receipts to also be an evidence of the right of its holder to the cash flows from realization of the financial asset involved in securitization (as differentiated from a right in the financial asset itself).
7. Large-sized NBFCs and non-NBFC corporate bodies established in India with net own funds in excess of, say INR 50 crore, may be permitted to invest in security receipts as QIBs. Similarly, private equity funds registered with SEBI as venture capital funds may also be permitted to invest in security receipts within the limits that are applied for investment by venture capital funds into corporate bonds.

Summary

1. The globalization of financial markets and services has witnessed many financial innovations across the world. Securitization is one of them.
2. Securitization is the process of transformation of illiquid assets (receivables) into financial instruments, which can be traded in financial markets.
3. Originally, securitization started with mortgage loans. Over time, the scope of securitization has increased to cover any predictable cash flow streams arising out of normal business transactions.
4. An organization that wants to go in for securitization may identify its loans, leases and other cash flow streams and organize or pool them into homogenous groups on a certain basis or criterion.
5. The special purpose vehicle (SPV) may be a trust formed exclusively to deal with the securitization process. The SPV can also be a company or a subsidiary of the originator company, depending on the originator's objectives.
6. The SPV is also called an issuer because it ultimately issues the securitized financial instruments to investors.
7. The originator can transfer the assets or cash flow streams to the SVP by novation, assignment or sub-participation.
8. The main parties involved in securitization are the obligor, originator, SPV, investors, administrators, credit rating agencies, underwriter/placement agents and structurers.
9. Securitized financial instruments may be pass-through certificates (PTC) or pay-through securities (PTS).
10. Internal credit enhancement techniques may be over-collateralization, subordination, excess servicing and turboing. External credit enhancement techniques are surety bonds, third-party guarantee, letter of credit, cash collateral account and collateral invested account.
11. The major benefit of securitization for the originator is that securitization converts illiquid or non-performing assets into liquid assets. Thus, securitization leads to greater recycling of funds, which in turn improves the business as well as the profitability of the originator.
12. Securitization is not affected by statutory pre-emption such as statutory liquid ratio and cash reserve ratio. This allows greater freedom for banks and other financial institutions to expand their volume of business, especially on the credit deployment side.
13. Securitization as a phenomenon took off in the United States, where it started with the buying of residential mortgage loans, making pools out of them and then issuing mortgage-backed securities.
14. Securitization is a relatively new concept in the Indian financial market and the first deal was structured in 1991.
15. Securitization of auto loans was the mainstay of the Indian securitization market in the 1990s mainly because of factors such as perceived credit risk, higher volumes and homogenous nature of receivables.
16. Over time, the securitized market in India has spread into several asset classes such as housing loans, corporate loans, commercial mortgage receivables, project receivables, toll fee receivables, property rental receivables, power receivables, telecom receivables, lease receivables and medical equipment loan receivables.
17. The Government of India announced the national housing and habitat policy in 1998, which enjoined upon the National Housing Bank to play a lead role in starting mortgage-backed securitization and the development of a secondary mortgage market in the country.
18. The first legislative measure in India was the enactment of the Securitization and Reconstruction of Financial Assets and Enforcement of Security Interests Act, 2002 (SARFAESI Act, 2002).
19. The guidelines and directions issued by the Reserve Bank of India provide for different aspects of securitization and asset reconstruction.
20. The recommendations of a high-level expert committee on corporate bonds and securitization have had far-reaching implications for the development of the debt market in India.

Questions

1. Trace the origin of securitization and bring out the significance of securitization.
2. Define and explain the scope of securitization.
3. Explain the process of securitization.
4. Discuss the role of each of the parties involved in securitization.
5. Distinguish between pass-through certificates and pay-through securities.
6. What are the specific advantages of securitization?
7. Trace the origin and development of securitization in India.
8. What are the salient features of the RBI Guidelines and Directions, 2003, with regard to securitization?
9. Discuss the recommendations of the R.H. Patil Committee with regard to securitization.
10. What are the impediments in the development of the securitization market in India?

Chapter 17

Corporate Restructuring

LEARNING OBJECTIVES

After reading this chapter, you should be able to:

- Explain the concept of restructuring.
- Explain types of mergers and their motives.
- Highlight the purposes of acquisition.
- Present methods of financing mergers and acquisitions.
- Discuss different kinds of divestitures.
- Present the salient features of SEBI regulations with regard to the acquisition of shares and takeovers.
- Discuss defensive takeover tactics.
- Discuss the implications of buyback of shares along with SEBI regulations.
- Present the accounting and tax aspects of mergers.
- Discuss the methods of evaluation of merger/acquisition.

17.1 Introduction

Corporate restructuring, a common phenomenon in the business world, involves restructuring of businesses, assets or ownership. **Corporate restructuring** refers to any change in operations, capital structure or ownership that occurs outside the normal course of business. *Restructuring of assets* refers to changes that are brought about in the asset mix of a company. *Restructuring of business* involves reorganization of business units, particularly strategic business units in a company, while *restructuring of ownership* is the change in the ownership of a company consequent to a merger or takeover. Thus, corporate restructuring can take different forms like mergers, acquisitions, spin-offs or divestitures in order to increase a firm's value. Corporate restructuring can also include business re-engineering. Restructuring may involve restating corporate goals, redesigning the organizational structure, revising the methods of production and changing the marketing and financial strategies. To put it differently, corporate restructuring can be brought about through a variety of mechanisms including mergers, acquisitions, divestitures and spin-offs. Corporate restructuring generally results in more efficient economic activity leading to more wealth for the shareholders. On the other hand, corporate restructuring can also lead to industrial concentration and exploitation of employees/workers, small investors and consumers.

***Corporate restructuring** refers to any change in operations, capital structure or ownership that occurs outside the normal course of business.*

17.1.1 The Concept of a Merger

A **merger** refers to the combination of two or more companies into one company. A **merger** is a strategy through which two firms agree to integrate their operations. The terms merger and amalgamation are used synonymously. There is no direct definition of merger in the legal literature of India. However, according to Section 2 (1B) of the Income Tax Act, "an amalgamation means the merger of one or more companies with another company or the merger of two or more companies to form one company in such a manner that (a) all the property of the amalgamating company or companies immediately before the amalgamation becomes the property of the amalgamated company by virtue of the amalgamation; (b) all the liabilities of the amalgamating company or companies immediately before the amalgamation become the liabilities of the amalgamated company by virtue of the amalgamation; and (c) shareholders holding not less than nine-tenths in the value of the shares in the amalgamating company or companies (other than shares already held therein immediately before the amalgamation by, or by a nominee for, the amalgamated company or its subsidiary) become shareholders of the amalgamated company by virtue of the amalgamation otherwise than as a result of the acquisition of the property of one company by another company pursuant to the purchase of such property by the other company or as a result of the distribution of such property to the other company after the winding-up of the first mentioned company". It is also stated that the company or companies that merge are referred to as the amalgamating company or companies and the company with which they merge or which is formed as a result of the merger is the amalgamated company.

17.1.2 Demerger and Reverse Merger

Demerger is the opposite of merger. It can be understood as the splitting of a conglomerate and creation of separate companies. For example, CEAT Tyres, an RPG group company, has demerged its tyre and investment portfolio business into two separate companies, CEAT Tyres and CHI Investments, in order to focus on core operations. According to the financial restructuring, the existing shareholders of CEAT Tyres got one share in CHI Investments and three shares in the new CEAT for every four shares held in CEAT Tyres. Essar Shipping Ports and Logistics Ltd has demerged its operations in shipping, logistics and oil fields into a separate entity, Essar Shipping.

Normally, a company that is less profitable or sick or small or young is absorbed by an established profit-making company. If a company that is less profitable or sick or relatively small absorbs an established and more profitable company, it is called a **reverse merger**. For example, ICICI Limited has merged with ICICI Bank. Reverse mergers are generally undertaken to get certain tax advantages or cash in on new opportunities available to a small or young company.

*A **merger** is a strategy through which two firms agree to integrate their operations. **Demerger** refers to splitting a conglomerate and forming separate companies. If a relatively small company absorbs an established and more profitable company, it is called a **reverse merger**.*

17.1.3 Merger Motives

The main motives behind corporate mergers are discussed here.

Synergy

Synergy is the principle motive for most mergers. It refers to the "two plus two equals five effect", which can be realized in a merger through increased revenues and/or reduced costs. Thus, mergers take place mainly to increase the value of the combined firm, which is the sum of the values of the individual firms plus any synergy that might be involved. There are different kinds of synergy such as managerial synergy, operating synergy and financial synergy.

- **Managerial synergy:** If a company has excess managerial capabilities, it might utilize the extra managerial resources by acquiring a company that is inefficiently managed due to the shortage of managerial resources. This kind of merger will be synergistic, since it combines the capabilities of the acquired company with the excess managerial resources of the acquiring company.
- **Operating synergy:** Before a merger, two firms operate at levels of activity that fall short of achieving economies of scale, which provide increasing returns. Therefore, if the two firms are merged, the combined firm might benefit from economies in management functions such as production, research, marketing and finance. For example, in production operations, the capacity of the plant and machinery can be utilized to increase the volume of production, leading to a reduction in the cost of production per unit. Economies of scale can also arise from other indivisibilities such as people (management) and equipment, which provide increasing returns if spread over a large number of units of production. A firm arising from a merger eliminates duplicate facilities and consolidates all the operations in the business. For example, the duplication of efforts of the sales force of two individual companies in a particular territory is eliminated when the two companies are merged. Thus, the combined firm with a larger size and capabilities can make the best use of resources and systems, resulting in economies of scale and increased profits.
- **Financial synergy:** A merger between a cash-rich company and a less liquid company can benefit the shareholders of both the companies. For example, a cash-rich company might not have enough internal opportunities to invest its surplus cash. On the other hand, a company that has greater internal investment opportunities might be starved of funds. If these two companies are merged, the combined firm can best utilize the surplus cash made available by the cash-rich company. The combined firm

might also have stable cash flows, which will reduce the risk of insolvency and thereby enhance the creditworthiness of the firm. This will increase the borrowing capacity of the firm and reduce borrowing costs. In other words, the merged firm will be able to borrow at a lower rate of interest. A merged firm might also be in a position to go in for a larger public issue, which will reduce the flotation or issue costs.

Pure diversification

A merger can reduce risk since the combination of resources strengthens the capabilities of the combined firm in facing unforeseen factors that could otherwise threaten the survival of the individual firms. A merger between firms engaged in different lines of businesses will reduce cyclical fluctuations in earnings and cash flows. A merger can thus result in diversification of products or services, which, in turn, helps the firm avoid violent fluctuations in the cash flows of the organization.

Market dominance

A merger can result in increased market share. The market share of the merged company might be bigger than the market shares of the two individual companies put together. This is because of lesser competition in the market or optimum utilization of resources. The merged firm might even become a market leader with attendant benefits. Thus, the increased market share can ultimately result in improved profitability of the merged company.

Tax benefits

When a profit-making company merges with a loss-making company, the merged firm reaps tax benefits. A firm with carry-forward losses might have little prospects of earning enough in future to utilize the tax benefits fully. By merging with a profitable firm, it might be possible for the combined company to utilize the carry-forward losses and thereby get tax benefits. For example, if a profitable company is merged with a sick company, the merged company can set off the carry-forward losses of the sick company against its profits and thereby save taxes. Thus, the firms with a large unused tax shield in the form of carry-forward losses can be good for mergers.

Sometimes, the motive for a merger or takeover has nothing to do with the benefits from combining the firms but is simply to replace the existing management.

17.2 Types of Mergers

Mergers are classified as horizontal merger, vertical merger and conglomerate merger. Each of them is briefly discussed in the following lines:

- **Horizontal merger:** A *horizontal merger* is a merger of two firms that are in the same industry and at the same stage of the industrial process. The main motive for horizontal mergers is to obtain economies of scale in production and marketing by eliminating duplication of facilities and operations. The firms can also undertake horizontal mergers in order to eliminate or reduce competition in the market. The merger of Tata Oil Mills Company Ltd (TOMCO) with Hindustan Lever Limited (HLL) is an example of a horizontal merger.
- **Vertical merger:** A *vertical merger* occurs between firms that are in different stages of production or distribution. Through a vertical merger, a firm expands its business either forward towards the ultimate consumer or backward towards the source of raw material. The acquiring company gains control over the production process on account of backward or forward integration. The merger of Tea Estate Ltd with Brooke Bond India Ltd is an example of a vertical merger.
- **Conglomerate merger:** A conglomerate merger involves firms engaged in unrelated lines of business. The merger between Lloyds Steel Ltd and Arron Investments Ltd is an example of a conglomerate merger. A conglomerate firm controls a range of activities in various industries that require different managerial skills. A firm can achieve diversification and thereby reduce business risk through a conglomerate merger. A conglomerate merger can be a product-extension merger, which broadens the product lines of a firm, or a pure conglomerate merger, which involves unrelated business activities.

17.3 Acquisitions

An **acquisition** is defined as the act of acquiring effective control over the assets or management of a firm by another firm. An acquisition is also a strategy through which one company buys a controlling or 100 per cent interest in another firm. A forced acquisition or unwilling acquisition is called a takeover. In other words, a *takeover* is a form of acquisition strategy where the target firm is not willing to be acquired. According to SEBI, "an acquirer means any person, who directly or indirectly, acquires or agrees to acquire shares or voting rights in the target company, or acquires or agrees to acquire control over the target company, either by himself or with any person acting in concert with the acquirer". The term control refers to the "right to appoint the majority of the directors or to control the management or policy decisions exercisable by a person or persons acting individually or in concert, directly or indirectly, including by virtue of their shareholding or management rights or shareholders agreements or voting agreements or in any other manner". The target company is a listed company whose shares or voting rights or control is directly or indirectly acquired or is being acquired.

*An **acquisition** is defined as the act of acquiring effective control over the assets or management of a firm by another firm.*

17.3.1 Acquisition Motives

There are many reasons for acquisitions. One is to achieve greater market power. For instance, a firm might have core competencies but lack sufficient market share to use its resources and capabilities. Therefore, it might seek to increase its market share by acquiring a competitor. Another reason for acquisition might be to overcome entry barriers. A firm might face difficulties in entering a particular market or product line. A firm also faces many entry barriers when it tries to enter international markets. Therefore, the firm can acquire an existing firm to overcome the barriers. Acquisitions are also a means by which a firm can get access to new products. Developing new products internally and successfully launching them require a lot of time. Moreover, the returns on new products are unpredictable. Therefore, acquisitions provide more predictable returns and faster market entry. Companies can also use acquisitions as a means to engage in product diversification or reduce competition in the market. To sum up, acquisitions are strategies used by firms to increase their competitiveness and earn above-average returns.

17.3.2 Methods of Acquisition

A firm can take over another firm by making offers directly to the shareholders of the target company. These offers may be tender offers, partial offers or any-or-all offers.

A *tender offer* is an offer to purchase shares of the target company at a fixed price, usually higher than the current market price, from shareholders who tender their shares. The incentive for the shareholders to tender their shares is the premium that is offered over the present market price. The offer can also be a two-tier tender offer, in which the acquiring company offers a first-tier price for a specified number of shares. At the same time, it announces its intention to acquire the remaining shares at a second-tier price. The acquiring company offers a higher price for the first tier of the stocks to motivate the shareholders to tender their shares early, so that it can successfully gain control over the target company. The purchase of shares might be made conditional on the receipt of a minimum number of shares sufficient to guarantee a controlling interest in the target firm.

Partial offers and any-or-all offers are also common means of takeovers. In a *partial offer*, the acquiring company specifies the maximum number of shares to be accepted without mentioning the plans with respect to the remaining shares. In *any-or-all offers*, the maximum number of shares is not specified and none will be purchased if the conditions of the offer are not met. All these offers can be *front-end loaded*, in which the offer price is greater than the price of any unpurchased shares. This means the shareholders of the target company get an incentive to tender their shares to receive the higher front-end price. Two-tier tender offers, partial offers and any-or-all offers are front-end loaded. The *back-end value* is the post-takeover price of the remaining (minority) shares and is typically lower than the bid price in all three types of offers. For example, the back-end value in a partial offer can simply be the market price of the remaining shares.

17.3.3 Creeping Acquisition

Creeping acquisition is a process through which a company gradually increases its stake in the target company in order to gain a controlling interest without making a public tender offer. As per SEBI's Takeover Code, if an acquirer, himself or with persons acting in concert with him, has acquired 15 per cent or more but less than 55 per cent of shares or voting rights (since changed to 75 per cent, vide a SEBI press release dated October 27, 2008), then limits are put on further acquisition. That person cannot acquire, either by himself or through persons acting in concert with him, additional shares or voting rights entitling him to exercise more than 5 per cent of the voting rights in any financial year, unless the acquirer makes a public announcement to acquire shares in accordance with the regulations. Thus, for an acquisition of more than 5 per cent of the shares or voting rights of the target company, a compulsory tender offer is required. There is an automatic exemption up to a 5 per cent increase in the shareholding of promoters after the buyback of shares by the company.

The increase in the creeping acquisition limit from 55 per cent to 75 per cent enables the promoters of a company to increase their stakes and also support the market price during market turbulence. As per the SEBI Substantial Acquisition of Shares and Takeovers (Amendment) Regulations of 2008, an acquirer (together with persons acting in concert with him) holding 55 per cent or more but less than 75 per cent of the shares or voting rights in a target company can acquire (either by himself or through or with persons acting in concert with him) additional shares or voting rights entitling him up to 5 per cent of the voting rights in the target company without making a public announcement. No acquirer shall acquire shares or voting rights, through market purchases and preferential allotment, which (taken together with shares or voting rights, if any, held by him or by persons acting in concert with him) entitle such an acquirer to exercise more than 75 per cent of the voting rights of the company. If the acquirer has acquired shares or voting rights through such market purchases or preferential allotment beyond 75 per cent of the voting rights in the company, he shall forthwith disinvest the shares acquired in excess of 75 per cent.

For example, Automobile Corporation of Goa (ACG) is one of the major suppliers of Tata Motors. Tata Motors increased its shareholding in ACG from 31.5 per cent in March 2007 to 37.7 per cent in March 2008. Further, Tata Motors scaled up shareholding by nearly 3 per cent to 40.6 per cent in as many months through open-market operations.

17.3.4 Tender Offer

A *tender offer* is a public bid or offer made by the potential acquirer to the existing shareholders of a firm to tender their shares at a fixed price, usually at a premium over the current market price, for a limited period of time. Tender offers can be successful only when the acquirer offers a price for the target firm's stock that is sufficiently high to induce a controlling fraction of the target's shareholders to tender. According to the SEBI Takeover Code, the public offer made by the acquirer to the shareholders of the target company shall be for a minimum of 20 per cent of the voting capital of the company. If any public offer is made pursuant to the SEBI Takeover Code, such an offer shall be for such a percentage of the voting capital of the target company so that the acquisition does not result in the public shareholding being reduced to a level below the limit specified in the listing agreement with the stock exchange for the purpose of listing on a continuous basis. If the promoters (acquirers or bidders) do not tender their shares, their ownership in terms of the number of shares would remain constant while the proportion of their shareholding in the company's capital would increase following the success of the tender offer. The rationale of a tender offer is to provide the minority shareholders (non-control shareholders) an option to sell out of the company.

Let us now consider an example of a tender offer. Satyam Computer Services Limited, renamed Mahindra Satyam by its new owner Tech Mahindra, was rocked by a USD 1.5-billion accounting scandal in 2008. In a revitalization process, Venturbay Consultants Private Limited, a wholly-owned subsidiary of Tech Mahindra Limited, was selected as the highest bidder in a competitive bidding process held on April 13, 2009, to acquire a controlling interest in Satyam Computers. Accordingly, Satyam Computers, Venturbay and Tech Mahindra entered into a share-subscription agreement. According to the agreement, Satyam Computers was required to issue to Venturbay, and Venturbay was required to purchase from Satyam Computers, 302,764,327 shares (initial allotment), representing 31 per cent of the enhanced share capital, at a purchase price of INR 58 per share in cash (purchase price). The total purchase price for all the shares purchased in the initial allotment was INR 17.56 billion (USD 351 million). The total purchase price for all the shares to be purchased in the initial allotment was required to be deposited by Venturbay into an escrow account by April 21, 2009. Satyam Computers and Venturbay entered into an escrow agreement with a mutually agreed upon escrow agent, following which Venturbay deposited the required funds into the account on April 20, 2009. On May 5, 2009, the initial allotment was completed. The enhanced share capital was 976,722,347 shares, which was equal to the number of shares outstanding as of April 22, 2009, and May 5, 2009, (673,958,020) plus the number of shares allotted in the initial allotment (302,764,327).

As of May 5, 2009, Satyam Computers had outstanding instruments convertible into 18,674,715 shares. Accordingly, for the purposes of open public offer, the enhanced share capital was 995,397,062, which was equal to the enhanced shares plus the number of shares issuable upon the conversion of outstanding convertible instruments.

The share subscription agreement provided that Venturbay would offer to purchase in the open public offer a minimum of 20 per cent of the share capital as required under the Takeover Regulations and a maximum of that percentage of the enhanced share capital that, when aggregated with the 31 per cent of the enhanced share capital acquired in the initial allotment and any other shares beneficially owned by Venturbay, would not exceed 70 per cent of the enhanced share capital of Satyam Computers.

Venturbay owned 302,764,327 shares, representing 31 per cent of the shares outstanding as of May 5, 2009. A public announcement was made on April 22, 2009, by Venturbay and Tech Mahindra to purchase 199,079,413 shares, representing 20 per cent of the shares outstanding as of May 5, 2009, on a fully diluted basis, or 20 per cent of the enhanced share capital at a purchase price of INR 58 (USD 1.16) per share payable in cash.

Kotak Mahindra Capital Company Limited (managers to the issue), on behalf of Venturbay (acquirer) and Tech Mahindra (person acting in concert), issued a post-offer public announcement to the shareholders of Satyam Computers (target company) to buy up to 199,079,413 fully paid-up equity shares of INR 2 each at a price of INR 58 per fully paid-up equity share, payable in cash. The offer opened on June 12, 2009, to close on July 1, 2009. But due to a surge in the share price of Satyam Computers (the share price hovered at INR 75, far higher than the offer price of INR 58), the tender offer evoked a poor response and only 420,915 shares were validly tendered, representing less than 0.1 per cent of the outstanding equity shares.

Under the agreement, if the public offer was not fully subscribed, then the acquirer could opt for a second preferential issue of shares to raise its stake to not more than 51 per cent of the expanded share capital. Satyam Computers received an approval from the Company Law Board for issuing 198.66 million new shares to the acquirer at INR 58 each, taking the latter's stake to 43 per cent of the share capital.

17.3.5 Proxy Fight

Instead of buying the equity stock of the target company by tender offer or otherwise, the acquirer might impress upon the shareholders of the target company to vote out the existing management in favour of a new management that will approve the takeover. Here, the acquirer votes for the new management by proxy. A proxy fight is a very effective technique used by a hostile bidder to rally a group of shareholders against the target company's incumbent management. In the proxy fight, the hostile bidder attempts to change the opinion of a group of existing shareholders in favour of the new management.

17.3.6 Defensive Tactics in Takeovers

Acquisitions can be friendly or hostile. Hostile acquisitions are generally known as takeovers. An acquisition can become hostile when the target company does not want to be acquired. There are many reasons why the target company might not want to be taken over. The existing management of the target company might want to retain control of the company or protect their jobs. The shareholders and/or management of the target company might feel that the proposed acquisition would reduce the value of the company or involve the risk of the company going out of business. On the other hand, the acquirer might think that the target company could generate more profit in future compared to the acquisition price. In strategic acquisitions, the acquirer wants access to distribution channels, customer base, brand name or technology.

Hostile takeovers have become an increasingly common means of corporate restructuring. Simultaneously, the targeted firms, actual or potential, have devised various ways to resist or prevent the hostile takeovers. The targeted firms initiate different defence tactics in order to discourage the raiders or make takeovers difficult. Takeover defences can be pre-emptive or post-facto. Pre-emptive defences are adopted prior to a takeover bid and post-facto defences are applied after a takeover bid has been announced.

Let us look at pre-emptive defences in a little more detail:

- Pre-emptive defences include promoters of the target company increasing their stake. If the promoters do not have controlling interest (at least 51 per cent of the equity stock) in the target company, they might plan to increase their stake in order to be insulated from takeover threats. The promoters can increase their stake through preferential allotment of shares, acquisition of shares (creeping) from the market and negotiated purchases from institutional shareholders.

- Hostile takeovers usually take place through tender offers. A tender offer is an offer made by the acquiring company to purchase shares of the target company at a fixed price from the shareholders who tender their shares. In order to prevent the raiders, the target company can convince its shareholders that the offer made by the raider is not in their best interests. The company can also increase the cash dividend or undertake a stock split to retain the shareholders.
- The company can move court to delay the process and frustrate the bidder.
- A company that does not want to be acquired can buy back its shares in the open market with an aim to push the price of the stock above that being offered by the potential acquirer.
- A popular defence tactic is known as *poison pill*, a term coined by Martin Lipton, an American business lawyer. It refers to a family of "shareholder rights" that can be triggered by or exercisable on an event of a hostile tender offer or accumulation of voting rights by an unfriendly buyer. These rights, which take several forms, would make it costly to acquire a controlling interest in the target firm. In other words, these rights would become poisonous to the raider if swallowed. For example, a target company can issue convertible preference shares on very favourable terms to the existing shareholders, which can be converted into equity when the company faces a takeover threat. When the convertible securities are converted into equity, the target company will become unattractive to the potential acquirer as the conversion dilutes the ownership of the hostile acquirer in the target company. It can also increase the cost of the takeover. A company can give its shareholders stock-purchase rights, which allow them to buy the stock of the target firm at a low price, should the acquirer accumulate shares of the target firm greater than a certain limit. As the discount is not available to the acquirer, it becomes extremely expensive for the acquirer to complete the takeover. This strategy, known as *flip in*, devalues the equity stock of the target firm and dilutes the percentage of the equity shares held by the hostile acquirer in the target company to the extent that it makes any further acquisition prohibitively expensive. Another poison-pill strategy is *flip over*, which allows shareholders of the target company to purchase equity shares of the new company (company formed after the takeover) at a substantial discount after the takeover.
- To make the target company's stock prohibitively expensive or otherwise unattractive, the target company, if acquired, can borrow on terms that require immediate repayment of all loans. This puts pressure on the acquiring firm to raise a large sum of money to pay off the loans.
- A firm can also grant golden parachutes to its management in case there is a change in the control of the management of the firm due to a hostile takeover. *Golden parachutes* may be incorporated as a clause in the employment contract between the employer and the employee, which calls for payment of certain benefits in case of a change of management of the company. Typical benefits in a golden parachute include a generous severance pay, bonus, stock options or a combination of these. The acquirer will either have to pay the associated increased costs when acquiring the target firm or back down from the takeover. Thus, a golden parachute discourages hostile takeovers.
- The target company can divest or spin off some of its divisions to reduce its attractiveness to the bidders.
- Sale of "crown jewels" is also an effective takeover defence. A *crown jewel* is a highly profitable business division owned by the target company that is especially sought-after by the acquiring company. With the sale of such division(s), the target company can become unattractive to the acquirer.
- Another takeover defence is the employee stock option scheme, which entitles the employees of the target company to an ownership stake in the company.
- In order to block a takeover, the target company might get a *white squire* (a friendly company) to buy an adequate number of its shares. As a last resort, the target company might seek a merger with another company that is friendly. This friendly company is known as a *white knight*.

17.4 Financing Mergers and Acquisitions

Once a merger deal is finalized and the value determined, the next step in the merging process is the method of payment. A merger or an acquisition can be financed either by cash or an exchange of shares, or a combination of cash, debt and shares.

Table 17.1 Pre-merger financial data for the two companies

	Company X	*Company Y*
Current earnings (INR million)	30	25
Number of equity shares (million)	7.5	7
Earnings per share (INR)	4	3.57
Market price of a share (INR)	100	80
Price-earnings ratio	25	22.4

17.4.1 Payment by Cash

Payment by cash is the easiest and quickest method of financing a merger or acquisition and the preferred route in many a case. If the acquiring firm has surplus cash, it can use that money to acquire the shares or assets of the target company straightaway. The acquiring company might prefer the cash payment route when it feels its equity stock is undervalued. Availability of easy and cheap institutional finance can also influence the decision of opting for the cash transaction. But employing more debt funds might increase the risk of the firm. Further, cash payment to the shareholders of the target company might increase their tax burden since the cash received by them is taxable. In case of cash payment for a merger or acquisition, the earnings per share (EPS) as well as ownership of the acquiring company are not diluted.

17.4.2 Stock Swaps

Recently, equity has been driving merger and acquisition deals. In other words, the acquiring company issues its shares to the shareholders of the target company at a negotiated exchange ratio. When the shares are issued, the acquiring company shares its ownership with the shareholders of the target company. Use of debt has become prominent in the United States and other countries because of tax considerations. If the shareholders of the target company receive stock in exchange for their existing stockholdings, it is not a taxable transaction till the time the shareholders sell the shares they have received.

Usually, a high P/E multiple stock is used to acquire a low P/E multiple stock—it is advantageous if the target firm has a low P/E multiple. Depending on the exchange ratio and the profitability of the combined company, the EPS of the acquiring company can change after the merger. For example, Company *Y* wishes to merge with Company *X* with a stock offer. Before the merger, the financial data for the two companies are as shown in Table 17.1.

Company *Y* has agreed to an offer of INR 85 a share to be paid in Company *X* shares. The exchange ratio is thus INR 85/100, or 0.85 share of Company *X* for each share of Company *Y*. Thus, Company *X* has to issue 5,950,000 shares to the shareholders of Company *Y*. Suppose the earnings of the two companies after the merger remain the same. Then the EPS of Company *X* will increase as shown in Table 17.2.

Suppose the ratio of exchange is changed. Company *X* has offered INR 90 per share of Company *Y*. Then the ratio of exchange is INR 90/100, or 0.9 share of Company *X* for each share of Company *Y*. Thus, Company *X* has to issue 6,300,000 shares to the shareholders of Company *Y*. The EPS of Company *X* after the merger would be as shown in Table 17.3. Thus, there is initial dilution in the EPS for Company *X* on account of the merger.

In this example, the P/E ratios are 85/3.57, or 23.8, and INR 90/3.57, or 25.2. Because the P/E ratio of Company *X* (before the merger) is 25, there is an increase in the EPS when it offers INR 85 for a share of Company *Y* and a decrease in the EPS when it offers INR 90 for a share of Company *Y*. In other words, a dilution in the EPS will occur when the P/E ratio paid for a company exceeds the P/E ratio of the acquiring company. Thus, the main emphasis in merger negotiations is on the market price of the acquired company. As the target company does not find one-to-one market to price ratio of exchange as enticing, the acquiring company must offer a price in excess

Table 17.2 Post-merger EPS

	Company X (after merger)
Earnings (INR million)	55
Number of shares (million)	13.45
Earnings per share (INR)	4.1

Table 17.3 EPS of Company *X* after the merger

	Company X (after merger)
Earnings (INR million)	55
Number of shares (million)	1.38
Earnings per share (INR)	3.98

of the current market price per share of the company it wishes to acquire. But, in the absence of synergism and improved management, the merger will not be in the interests of the shareholders of the acquiring company if it offers a price in excess of the target company's current market price.

In the example, the value of Company *X* before the merger is INR 750 million (7.5 million equity shares of INR 100 market price per share). Similarly, Company *Y* has a total market value of INR 560 million (7 million shares of INR 80 market price per share). After the merger, it is assumed that Company *X* will have a value of INR 1412.25 million. That means the economic advantage of the merger is INR 102.250 million, which is [INR 1412.250 million – (INR 750 million + INR 560 million)]. Suppose Company *X* is required to pay INR 50 million in cash to Company *Y* in addition to the shares to be issued to the shareholders of Company *Y*. Then the net economic advantage of the merger would be INR 52.25 million, which represents the benefit of the merger. This benefit would arise because of improved operating efficiency and synergy.

The shareholders of the acquiring company will be better off if their company's P/E ratio is higher than the acquired company's and the acquiring company after the merger is able to keep that higher P/E ratio. If a company with a higher P/E ratio is able to acquire another company with a lower P/E ratio, it would obtain an immediate increase in the earnings per share. If the higher P/E ratio continues after the merger, the market price of the shares of the acquired company will increase. This increase is not due to economies of scale or improved efficiency of the management after the merger but because of the bootstrap increase in EPS through the merger. The *bootstrap effect* occurs when there is no real gain created by the merger and no increase in the combined value of the two firms. In other words, the acquired company could increase its market value through the merger alone by acquiring a slowly growing firm with a lower P/E ratio. But in perfect market situations, acquisitions or mergers would not increase the shareholders' wealth without anticipating synergism and/or improved management after the merger.

17.4.3 Other Methods of Financing

The acquiring company can also issue debt securities like convertible debentures and preference shares to the shareholders of the target company. Financial institutions including investment banks and commercial banks can also come forward to finance mergers or acquisitions of the companies. They can offer financing packages to the target companies to finance stock repurchase plans or other defences against takeovers.

Another source of merger financing is junk bonds—bonds rated below the investment grade. An acquiring company can raise the required funds for the merger or acquisition by issuing junk bonds offering a rate of return several percentage points above the rate on more conservative investments. When a company uses debt financing, the debt-equity ratio of the acquiring company might change. The immediate EPS dilution can be avoided if the company issues debt securities. The shareholders of the acquiring company can also avoid dilution in their voting power if the debt or preference securities are issued to the shareholders of the target company. The issuing of convertible securities might be a better option to satisfy the shareholders of the target company when they need immediate protection of their incomes with the growth potential of equity shares. Some companies follow the deferred payment plan, according to which an initial payment is made to the shareholders of the target company with an undertaking that additional payments will be made or additional shares will be issued over a course of time in the event of the acquiring company being able to increase its earnings consequent to the merger. The advantage for the acquiring firm taking the deferred payment route is that the total payment is not made at the time of acquisition and further payment is contingent upon the realization of the projected earnings in the post-merger period.

***Divestiture** refers to the divesting of assets or business units by a firm in order to refocus on its core businesses.*

17.5 Divestitures

Mergers, acquisitions and divestitures are strategies of business firms to cope with their changing economic and political environments. **Divestiture** refers to the divesting of assets or business units by a firm in order to refocus on its core businesses. Divestitures can take place in order to improve efficiency and create more value. Following restructuring through a divestiture, a firm can be managed more efficiently and effectively. As the firm becomes less diversified, managerial effectiveness increases. With a divestiture, there may be reverse synergy, $(4 - 2 = 3)$. The assets or a business unit of a company could be more valuable to someone else in generating cash flows and net present value (NPV) than they are to the company. A company can undertake divestitures depending on its internal capabilities. For instance, a company might wish to concentrate on certain markets or products for competitive advantage. Therefore, it can divest its asset(s) or product line(s) or business unit(s). Tax considerations also influence the decision to divest. Some divestitures are attempts to correct earlier investment decisions. Further, the management of a firm might have acquired an undervalued firm. After increasing the value of the acquired segment, the management can use divestitures to realize the achieved gains. A divestiture can take the form of a sell-off or a spin-off or equity carve-out.

- **Sell-off:** A *sell-off* consists of the selling of the entire company or the selling of some business unit such as a subsidiary unit, a product line or a business segment. Unless it is in financial distress, a company might be sold completely in order to get a higher value than the present value of the expected cash flows emanating from the assets of the company. For instance, the assets of a company can be sold to multiple parties, resulting in a higher value than if they had been sold as a whole. In other words, the decision to sell a company in its entirety is taken to create more value for the stockholders. The sell-off can be a partial sell-off, where a part of the company is sold.
- **Spin-off:** A *spin-off* is divestiture of a business unit to existing shareholders. Unlike a sell-off, in which a business unit is sold for cash or securities, a spin-off involves the separation of a business unit from the company and distributing the shares of the business unit to the stockholders of the company on a pro rata basis. That is, in a spin-off, the existing shareholders maintain the same proportion of ownership in the newly created firm as they had in the original firm. After the spin-off, the business unit becomes a completely separate company with its own traded stock. As an independent firm with a different management, it can be run more efficiently. Thus, spin-offs can lead to improved productivity and more value for the shareholders.
- **Split-up:** If a firm has a number of divisions and if each division is carved out as a separate legal entity, the divestiture is called a *split-up*. A split-up of a firm consists of a number of spin-offs and the original firm ceases to exist once all the spin-offs come into existence.
- **Equity carve-out:** In an *equity carve-out*, a minority stock in a subsidiary is sold to the public while the parent company continues to retain controlling interest in the subsidiary. In other words, the parent company carves out a small proportion of the equity shares in its subsidiary and sells them in an IPO. Thus, the subsidiary has a separate stock price and public trading. An equity carve-out is different from a spin-off. In a spin-off, the shares in the subsidiary company are distributed pro rata to the shareholders of the parent firm as a form of non-cash payment, whereas in an equity carve-out, the stock of the subsidiary unit is sold in the primary market for cash that will be received by the parent firm. In a spin-off, the parent firm ceases to have control over the subsidiary unit. The equity carve-out, therefore, can attract and retain better managers. The carve-out is also a better means for financing a subsidiary than financing through the parent. The carve-out announcement might have a favourable impact on the market price of the shares of the parent company as well.

17.6 Leveraged Buyouts

A *leveraged buyout* commonly refers to transforming a public limited company into a private limited company. In a leveraged buyout, a party consisting of a few individuals or institutions, or some individuals and institutions, buy all the firm's assets with their own funds and a significant amount of debt. In some cases, mezzanine financing, which is a junior subordinated debt, might be involved in leveraged buyouts. That is, mezzanine financing fills the gap between what senior debt holders provide and what equity shareholders are able to bring in. Mezzanine financing is a speculative-grade investment. If a leveraged buyout is unsuccessful, the providers of mezzanine financing can lose everything.

Many leveraged buyouts involve the purchase of a division or a business unit of a company. There are also cases in which an entire company is acquired through a leveraged buyout. Another important feature of leveraged buyouts is that the buyouts are cash purchases and not stock purchases. Once the buyout is completed, the company's shares are no longer traded publicly. In other words, the business unit involved in a leveraged buyout becomes a privately held company. However, successful leveraged buyouts can go public again as soon as the operating performance of the company has been improved.

Leveraged buyouts can be management buyouts (MBOs) or employee buyouts (EBOs). In the case of *management buyouts*, the management of a company buys the company from its owners, while in *employee buyouts*, the employees of a company buy the company from its owners. As the experience and quality of the management are critical to the success of leveraged buyouts, lenders might have full confidence in the management/employees to make the best utilization of the resources of the company and create more value.

When companies are listed on stock exchanges, it leads to a wide dispersal of share ownership. On the other hand, leveraged buyouts tend to result in the reverse—a concentration of share ownership and economic power. As the shares are no longer traded on the stock exchanges, the owners have little liquidity of their shareholdings. Further, leveraged buyouts involve considerable debt financing. The high degree of financial leverage works both ways. If a company makes good operational profit, a high degree of financial leverage results in a high EPS. But when the operational profits are low, a high debt-equity ratio is not in the interests of the equity shareholders. In other words, leveraged buyouts usually result in a very high proportion of debt and, therefore, servicing of debt becomes a financial strain on the companies in the post-leveraged buyout period. Thus, the equity shareholders in leveraged buyouts play a high-risk game. However, the main advantage is that leveraged buyouts help professional managers run the companies without any fear of losing control due to a hostile takeover. Leveraged buyouts can lead to an increased equity ownership by the management, which acts as an incentive for the managers to work more efficiently.

17.7 Buyback of Securities

*A **buyback** is an arrangement through which a company purchases its own equity shares from its shareholders.*

The buying back of shares has assumed a lot of importance in recent years, particularly in the wake of many takeover bids. A **buyback** is an arrangement through which a company purchases its own equity shares from its shareholders. A company can purchase its shares on the floor of the stock exchange, or purchase its shares directly from its shareholders by making a tender offer, or buy its shares through negotiations with the concerned shareholders. The buyback of shares might not result in a reduction of the capital of the company, unless the shares are either cancelled or extinguished. A company can retain the repurchased shares as treasury capital to be reissued at a later date. In effect, the company holds its own shares as assets. In some cases, nominee trustees or a duly constituted trust acquire the shares from the shareholders. Subsequently, the company buys back those shares at an appropriate time. Thus, the buyback of shares results in a reduction in the floating stock.

17.7.1 Reasons for Buyback of Shares

There are many reasons for the buyback of shares.

- The buyback of shares is a defence mechanism available to a targeted company to ward off a takeover bid. The buyback provision enables the promoters to reduce the floating stock and simultaneously raise stakes in the company, thereby hedging against hostile takeover bids. Thus, in the face of a takeover bid, the buyback provision enables a company to take pre-emptive steps against raiders and predators.
- When a company has surplus funds from its operations but no profitable investment opportunities, it can reward its shareholders by repurchasing the shares at a high premium. In such a case, all the shareholders of the company will benefit. While the shareholders who sell the shares to the company get rewarded in the form of a higher price, the other shareholders, too, get the benefit of a higher EPS resulting from the reduced number of shares after the buyback. It can also encourage the management to improve its efficiency and performance. Thus, a buyback of shares is justifiable especially in the absence of worthwhile diversification opportunities.
- A buyback also gives an option to the shareholders either to offer their shares for sale or retain them, depending on their interests. In depressed market conditions, the share price could be below its intrinsic value. In such a situation, the buyback of shares would increase the value of the company's shares on two counts—by reducing the floating stock and by giving positive signals to the stock market, which would push up the prices of the shares of the company.

17.7.2 Advantages and Limitations of Buyback of Shares

The advantages of buybacks are:

- When the shares of a company are illiquid, it is advantageous, particularly for the shareholders, if the company buys back its shares at a good price.
- The buyback of shares is also beneficial to the company as it can substitute the equity capital with debt capital and thereby derive tax advantages.
- The buyback of shares can give a clear signal to the investors that the shares of the company are underpriced.
- The buyback provision enables the company to maintain share prices close to the intrinsic value of the shares. This helps the company raise funds, whenever needed, easily and at cheaper rates.
- The investors will be reassured that the company will buy their shares even in the absence of a good market for the shares.

The argument against the buyback of shares is as follows:

- The buyback of shares might not be in the interests of creditors, particularly when the buyback results in capital reduction. The net worth of the company is reduced to the extent that the reserves are used to mop up the company's shares. As a result, the debt-equity ratio deteriorates and the risk of the debt holders increases. Thus, the buyback of shares can make the debt holders, particularly financial institutions, recall their advances or refuse to lend further as they expect the company to always have a large net worth.
- As the buyback is extremely price sensitive, instances of insider trading and price manipulation are bound to increase. Some promoters keep the market depressed with a view to buy back the shares at a low price deliberately. The promoters can also divest their shareholdings by fixing a higher price and, thereby, derive an unfair advantage. In other words, the buyback can be programmed at a lower price level and the same can be manipulated for offloading the stock at a later stage. In all such situations, the shareholders lose heavily. The promoters of a company with a strong financial position can manipulate the buyback of the shares to their advantage. It gives a leeway to insider trading that can influence the price of the shares in the market.
- If the company buys back a substantial part of its shares from the market, the remaining stock might become illiquid. Further, if a company is not able to buy back the shares from all the shareholders who are willing to sell, then also the stock can become illiquid due to reduction in the floating stock once the buyback programme is over. Thus, the buyback can deprive some shareholders of an exit route.
- Contrary to the popular belief that buybacks improve share prices, in many cases the prices of the shares of companies that bought back their shares have fallen sharply below the buyback prices. In such situations, the shareholders who do not succeed in selling the shares under the buyback scheme may lose heavily.
- The buyback of shares can also be a stumbling block in the process of takeovers and the replacement of existing unprofessional management.

Thus, the buyback of shares is an important financial strategy with many facets. It is a double-edged sword, which can be used for the benefit of the shareholders or the benefit of the promoters alone. In view of the benefits of a buyback, both for the company as well as the investors, and the scope for manipulation and price rigging by unscrupulous promoters, the Government of India appointed a working group on the Companies Act in 1996. The recommendations of the working group also involved the buyback of shares. The legal position then was that a company was prohibited, under Section 77 of the Companies Act, 1956, to buy its own shares unless a reduction of capital is effected in pursuance of Section 100–104 or Section 402 of the act.

17.8 Mergers and Takeovers in India

Most of the mergers in India in earlier days were mainly undertaken for the purpose of revival of sick units and for utilizing tax benefits accruing under the Income Tax Act. Only a few mergers were forced by competitive pressures. In recent years, mergers have taken place for strategic business reasons, and they are carried out even in a hostile environment.

In India, two methods are essentially used for takeovers—(i) a takeover through direct negotiations with financial institutions (FIs) and/or the Board for Industrial and Financial Reconstruction (BIFR), or with promoters in consultation with FIs and/or BIFR to acquire the controlling interest in a sick company or to merge a sick company with a profit-making one in order to get tax benefits; and (ii) a takeover through direct negotiations with the promoter who owns a controlling interest in a company or through an open offer or market purchases of an adequate level of shareholdings to have a controlling interest in a company. In view of a strict industrial licensing policy of the government before economic liberalization in the country, many industrial groups acquired companies in diverse fields of activity. The enactment of the Foreign Exchange Regulation Act (FERA) in 1974 caused many companies, particularly foreign ones, to change hands. Financial institutions had a substantial stake in many companies and thus played an active role in mergers and takeovers in the country.

Following economic liberalization, there has been a discernible trend among promoters and established corporate groups towards consolidation of market share and diversification into new areas through acquisition of companies.

The first attempt to regulate takeovers was made in a limited way by incorporating a clause, known as Clause 40, in the listing agreement between the company and the stock exchange. This was amended in 1990 by incorporating Clause 40A and 40B in the listing agreement. But the SEBI Act, 1992, empowered SEBI to regulate the substantial acquisition of shares and takeovers and made substantial acquisition of shares and takeovers a regulated activity. Accordingly, SEBI notified its regulations for substantial acquisition of shares and takeovers in November 1994. The regulations preserved the basic framework of Clause 40 (A and B) by retaining the requirements of initial disclosure at the level of 5 per cent, threshold limit of 10 per cent for a public offer to acquire the minimum percentage of shares at a minimum offer price and making a public announcement by the acquirer followed by a letter of offer. But the regulations did involve a significant departure from Clause 40 (A and B) by dropping certain aspects and introducing several new provisions. SEBI gained considerable experience and insight into the complexities in this area through the administration of the regulations and Clause 40 (A and B) of the listing agreement. SEBI realized there were certain deficiencies in the existing provisions which needed to be specifically addressed. Therefore, it appointed a committee under the chairmanship of Justice P.N. Bhagavati to review the SEBI (Substantial Acquisition of Shares and Takeovers) Regulations, 1994. The committee was constituted with a wide representation from the chambers of commerce and industry, investors' associations, stock exchanges, merchant bankers, the Institute of Chartered Accountants of India, and legal experts. The terms of reference of the committee were to examine the areas of deficiencies in the existing regulations and suggest amendments in the regulations with a view to strengthening the regulations and make them more fair, transparent and unambiguous and protect the interest of investors and parties in the acquisition process. The committee deliberated extensively on all the provisions of the existing regulations and the issues that came up before SEBI in the course of administration of the regulations over the period. The preliminary report of the committee was made public and widely debated. By taking note of the comments made on the report by various sections of market participants, industrialists, academicians, investing public and the media, the committee prepared its final report and submitted it in September 1996. Based on these recommendations, SEBI issued the SEBI (Substantial Acquisition of Shares and Takeovers) Regulations, 1997, which have come into force from February 20, 1997. It may be noted that amalgamations and mergers, however, constitute a subject matter of the Companies Act, 1956, and the courts of law. SEBI's takeover regulations do not deal with mergers and amalgamations.

17.8.1 SEBI (Substantial Acquisition of Shares and Takeovers) Regulations, 1997

The salient features of the SEBI regulations are as follows:

1. An acquirer shall acquire shares or voting rights, which (taken together with shares or voting rights, if any, held by him or by persons acting in concert with him), entitle him to exercise 15 per cent or more of the voting rights in a company if a certain condition is true. That is that such an acquirer makes a public announcement to acquire shares of such companies in accordance with the regulations. Provided that no acquirer shall acquire shares or voting rights through market purchases and preferential allotment pursuance to a resolution passed under Section 81 of the Companies Act, 1956,

or any other applicable law, which (taken together with shares or voting rights, if any held by him or by persons acting in concert with him) entitle such an acquirer to exercise more than 55 per cent of the voting rights in the company. Provided further that if the acquirer has acquired shares or voting rights through such market purchases or preferential allotment beyond 75 per cent of the voting rights in the company, he shall forthwith disinvest the shares acquired in excess of 75 per cent and shall be liable for action under the regulations and the SEBI Act.

Thus, the percentage of shareholding/voting rights of the acquirer, together with persons acting in concert with him, in the target company shall not increase beyond 75 per cent. This limit is applicable irrespective of the level of minimum public shareholding required to be maintained by the target company in terms of Clause 40A of the listing agreement.

2. No acquirer who, together with persons acting in concert with him, has acquired in accordance with the provisions of law 15 per cent or more but less than 75 per cent of the shares or voting rights in a company shall acquire, either by himself or through persons acting in concert with him, additional shares or voting rights entitling him to exercise more than 5 per cent of the voting rights, unless such an acquirer makes a public announcement to acquire shares in accordance with the regulations.
3. The acquirer, together with persons acting in concert with him, holding shares or voting rights can acquire additional shares or voting rights up to a maximum of 5 per cent voting rights in the target company in one or more tranches, without any restriction on the time frame within which the same can be acquired. The acquisition of 5 per cent shall be calculated by aggregating all purchases, without netting the sales.
4. An acquirer who, together with persons acting in concert with him, has acquired, in accordance with the provisions of the law, 55 per cent or more but less than 75 per cent of the shares or voting rights in a target company can acquire, either by himself or through persons acting in concert with him, any additional shares or voting right, without making a public announcement under the SEBI regulations.

   An acquirer who has made a public offer and seeks to acquire further shares shall not acquire such shares during the period of six months from the date of closure of the public offer at a price higher than the offer price. However, it shall not apply where the acquisition is made through stock exchanges.

   The minimum public offer in this case shall be for such a percentage of the voting capital of the target company that the acquisition does not result in the public shareholding in such a company being reduced to a level below the limit specified in the listing agreement with the stock exchange for the purpose of listing on a continuous basis.
5. Irrespective of whether there has been any acquisition of shares or voting rights in a company, no acquirer shall acquire control over the target company, unless such a person makes a public announcement to acquire shares and acquires such shares in accordance with the regulations.
6. Any acquirer who acquires shares or voting rights that (taken together with shares or voting rights, if any, held by him) would entitle him to more than 5 per cent or 10 per cent or 14 per cent or 54 per cent or 74 per cent shares of voting rights in a company, in any manner whatsoever, shall disclose at every stage the aggregate of his shareholding or voting rights in that company to the company and to the stock exchanges where the shares of the target company are listed.
7. Before making any public announcement of the offer, the acquirer shall appoint a merchant banker who is not an associate or in the group of the acquirer of the target company.
8. Within 14 days from the date of public announcement, the acquirer shall, through its merchant banker, file with SEBI the draft of the letter of offer containing disclosures, as specified by SEBI.
9. The public offer made by the acquirer to the shareholders of the target company shall be for a minimum of 20 per cent of the voting capital of the company.
10. Where the number of shares offered for sale by the shareholders is more than the shares agreed to be acquired by the person making the offer, such a person shall accept the offers received from the shareholders on a proportional basis, in consultation with the merchant banker, taking care to ensure that the basis of acceptance is decided in a fair and equitable manner and does not result in non-marketable lots.
11. The public announcement of an offer to acquire the shares of the target company shall be made only when the acquirer is able to implement the offer.

12. The acquirer shall ensure that a firm financial arrangement has been made for fulfilling the obligations under the public offer and suitable disclosures in this regard shall be made in the public announcement of the offer.
13. The acquirer shall, within a period of 15 days from the date of the closure of the offer, complete all procedures relating to the offer including payment of consideration to the shareholders who have accepted the offer and for that purpose open a special account.
14. Any person, other than the acquirer who has made the first public announcement, who is desirous of making any offer shall, within 21 days of the public announcement of the first offer, make a public announcement of his offer for acquisition of the shares of the same target company. Such an offer shall be deemed to be a competitive bid.
15. No public announcement for an offer or a competitive bid shall be made after 21 days from the date of public announcement of the first offer.
16. Any competitive offer by an acquirer shall be for such a number of shares that, when taken together with the shares held by him along with the persons acting in concert with him, shall be at least equal to the holding of the first bidder including the number of shares for which the present offer by the first bidder has been made.
17. On the public announcement of a competitive bid or bids, the acquirer(s) who had made the public announcement(s) of the earlier offer(s) shall have the option to make an announcement revising the offer.
18. The acquirers who have made the public announcement of the offer(s) including the public announcement of competitive bid(s) shall have the option to make upward revisions in their offer(s), in the price and the number of shares to be acquired, at any time up to seven working days prior to the date of closure of the offer.
19. Where there is a competitive bid, the date of closure of the original bid as also the date of closure of all the subsequent competitive bids shall be the date of closure of the public offer under the last subsisting competitive bid and the public offers under all the subsisting bids shall close on the same date.
20. No public offer, once made, shall be withdrawn except under the following circumstances:
    a. the required statutory approval(s) have been refused;
    b. the sole acquirer, being a natural person, has died;
    c. such circumstances that in the opinion of SEBI merit withdrawal.
21. The offer to acquire shares shall be met at a price not lower than the price determined as follows:
    a. The negotiated price;
    b. The price paid by the acquirer or persons acting in concert with him for acquisition, if any, including by way of allotment in a public or rights or preferential issue during the 26-week period prior to the date of public announcement, whichever is higher;
    c. The average of the weekly high and low of the closing prices of the shares of the target company as quoted on the stock exchange where the shares of the company are the most frequently traded during the 26 weeks or the average of the daily high and low of the prices of the shares as quoted on the stock exchange where the shares of the company are the most frequently traded during the two weeks preceding the date of public announcements, whichever is higher.

Where the shares of the target company are infrequently traded, the offer price shall be determined by the acquirer and the merchant banker taking into account the following factors:

a. The negotiated price;
b. The price paid by the acquirer or persons acting in concert with him for acquisition, if any, including by way of allotment in a public or rights or preferential issue during the 26-week period prior to the date of public announcement, whichever is higher;
c. Other parameters include a return on the net worth, book value of the shares of the target company, earning per share and price earning multiple vis-à-vis the industry average.

The offer price for partly paid-up shares shall be calculated as the difference between the offer price and the amount due towards call-in arrears or calls remaining unpaid together with interest, if any, payable on the amount called up but remaining unpaid.

22. The offer price shall be payable in cash; by issue, exchange and/or transfer of shares (other than preference shares) of the acquirer company, if the person seeking to acquire the shares is a listed body corporate; or by issue, exchange and/or transfer of secured instruments of the acquirer company with a minimum "A" grade rating from a credit rating agency registered with SEBI. The offer price shall also be a combination of the above.
23. The acquirer shall, as and by way of security for performance of his obligations under the regulations, deposit in an escrow account such a sum as calculated in the following manner:
    a. For consideration payable under the public offer up to and including INR 1,000 million: 25 per cent; exceeding INR 1,000 million: 25 per cent up to INR 1,000 million and 10 per cent thereafter.
    b. For offers that are subject to a minimum level of acceptance, and the acquirer does not want to acquire a minimum of 20 per cent, then 50 per cent of the consideration payable under the public offer in cash shall be deposited in the escrow account.
24. Unless the approval of the general body of shareholders is obtained after the date of the public announcement of the offer, the board of directors of the target company shall not, during the offer period:
    a. sell, transfer, encumber or otherwise dispose of or enter into an agreement for sale, transfer, encumbrance or for disposal of assets otherwise, not being a sale or disposal of assets in the ordinary course of business of the company or its subsidiaries; or
    b. issue or allot any authorized but unissued securities carrying voting rights during the offer period; or
    c. enter into any material contracts.
25. On fulfilment of all obligations by the acquirers under the regulations as certified by the merchant banker, the board of directors of the target company shall transfer the securities acquired by the acquirer, whether under the agreement or from open market purchases, in the name of the acquirer and/or allow such changes in the board of directors as would give the acquirer representation on the board or control over the company.

17.8.2 Bail-out Takeovers

SEBI has also prescribed certain regulations for the substantial acquisition of shares in a financially weak company, which is not a sick company. It is in pursuance of the scheme of rehabilitation approved by a public financial institution or a scheduled bank (lead institution). The lead institution shall be responsible for ensuring compliance with the provisions. The main provisions of the regulations are as follows:

1. The lead institution shall appraise the financially weak company, taking into account the financial viability, and assess the requirement of funds for revival and draw up the rehabilitation package on the principle of protection of interests of minority shareholders, good management, effective revival and transparency.
2. The scheme can provide for acquisition of shares in the financially weak company by any of the following methods:
    a. Outright purchase of shares,
    b. Exchange of shares,
    c. A combination of (a) and (b).

    Provided that the scheme as far as possible ensures that after the proposed acquisition, the erstwhile promoters do not own any shares in case such an acquisition is made by the new promoters pursuant to such a scheme.
3. Before giving effect to any scheme of rehabilitation, the lead institution shall invite offers for the acquisition of shares from at least three parties. After receipt of the offers, the lead institution shall select one of the parties, keeping in mind the managerial competence, adequacy of financial resources and technical capability of the person acquiring the shares, to rehabilitate the financially weak company.

4. The person acquiring shares who has been identified by the lead institution shall on receipt of a communication in this behalf from the lead institution make a formal offer to acquire shares from the promoters or persons in charge of the affairs of the management of the financially weak company, financial institutions and also other shareholders of the company at a price determined by mutual negotiation between the person acquiring the shares and the lead institution.
5. The person acquiring shares from the promoters or the persons in charge of the management of the affairs of the financially weak company or the financial institution shall make a public announcement of his intention for acquisition of shares from the other shareholders of the company.
6. The letter of offer shall be forwarded to each of the shareholders, other than the promoters or the persons in charge of the management, of the financially weak company and the financial institutions.
7. If the offer results in the public shareholding being reduced to 10 per cent or less of the voting capital of the company, the acquirer shall either within a period of three months from the date of closure of the public offer make an offer to buy out the outstanding shares remaining with the shareholders at the same offer price, which may have the effect of delisting the target company, or undertake to disinvest through an offer for sale or by a fresh issue of capital to the public, which shall open within a period of six months from the date of closure of the public offer, such a number of shares that will satisfy the listing requirements.
8. While accepting the offer from shareholders other than the promoters or persons in charge of the financially weak company or the financial institutions, the person acquiring shares shall offer to acquire from the individual shareholder his entire holdings if such holding is up to 100 shares with face value of INR 10 each or 10 shares of face value of INR 100 each.

Sections 108A–108H of the Monopolies and Restrictive Trade Practices (MRTP) Act place restrictions on acquisitions and transfer of shares of a company under certain circumstances. These provisions apply when in substance:

a. the acquirer who is already an owner of a dominant undertaking increases his dominance,
b. the company whose shares are sought to be acquired is the owner of a dominant undertaking,
c. as a result of the acquisition, the acquirer becomes the owner of a dominant undertaking.

Section 108A provides that without the prior approval of the Government of India, the acquisition of equity shares, whose nominal value is more than 25 per cent of the paid-up value of the equity share capital of a public limited company or a private limited company that is a subsidiary of a public limited company, shall not be made. For the purpose of calculating the 25 per cent acquisition, the acquisition of the individual, firm, group, constituent of a group and body corporate (or bodies corporate) under the same management is required to be aggregated. The provisions apply not only to increase of holdings to beyond 25 per cent but even further acquisitions where the acquirer already holds more than 25 per cent. According to Section 108H, a body corporate (or bodies corporate) under the same management, which holds 10 per cent or more of the nominal value of the subscribed equity share capital of any other company, shall not transfer such shares without prior intimation to the Government of India.

17.8.3 SEBI (Buyback of Securities) Regulations

Based on the recommendations of the working group, SEBI has drawn up regulations for the buyback of securities, the important ones of which are as follows:

1. A company can buy back its shares and other specified securities by any one of the following methods:
    a. from the existing security holders on a proportionate basis through the tender offer;
    b. from the open market through:
        i. book-building process,
        ii. stock exchange.
    c. from odd-lot holders.
2. A company shall not buy back its shares or other specified securities from any person through negotiated deals, whether on or off the stock exchange or through spot transactions or through any private arrangement.

3. Any person or an insider shall not deal in securities of the company on the basis of unpublished information relating to buyback of shares or other specified securities of the company.

Buyback through a tender offer

1. A company can buy back its shares or other specified securities from its existing security holders on a proportionate basis in accordance with the SEBI regulations.
2. The company shall notify the maximum price at which the buyback of shares or other specified securities shall be made and whether the board of directors of the company is being authorized at the general body meeting to determine subsequently the specific price at which the buyback can be made at the appropriate time.
3. The company, which has been authorized by a special resolution or a resolution passed by the board of directors at its meeting, shall make a public announcement before the buyback of shares or other specified securities.
4. The company shall file with SEBI a draft letter of offer containing disclosures as specified by the regulations within seven working days of the public announcement. This will be through a merchant banker who is not associated with the company.
5. The offer for buyback shall remain open to the members for a period not less than 15 days and not exceeding 30 days.
6. In case the number of shares or other specified securities offered by the security holders is more than the total number of shares or other specified securities to be bought back by the company, the acceptances per security holder shall be equal to the acceptance tendered by the security holders divided by the total acceptances received and multiplied by the total number of shares or other specified securities to be bought back.
7. The company shall, as and by way of security for the performance of its obligations, under the regulations, on or before the opening of the offer deposit in an escrow account such a sum as specified.
8. The company shall immediately after the date of closure of the offer open a special account with a banker to an issue registered with SEBI and deposit therein such a sum as would, together with 90 per cent of the amount lying in the escrow account, make up the entire sum due and payable as consideration for buyback in terms of these regulations and for this purpose can transfer the funds from the escrow account.
9. The company shall within seven days of the time specified make the payment of consideration in cash to those security holders whose offer has been accepted or return the security certificates to the security holders.
10. The company shall extinguish and physically destroy the security certificates so bought back in the presence of a registrar to the issue or the merchant banker and the statutory auditor within 15 days of the date of acceptance of the shares or other specified securities.
11. The company shall furnish the particulars of the security certificates extinguished and destroyed to the stock exchanges where the shares of the company are listed on a monthly basis by the seventh day of the month succeeding the month in which the securities' certificates are extinguished and destroyed.

Buyback from the open market

1. A company can buy back its shares or other specified securities from the open market either through the stock exchange or through a book-building process.
2. A company shall buy back its shares or other specified securities through the stock exchange as given in the following.

   a. The special resolution passed by the board of directors at its meeting shall specify the maximum price at which the buyback shall be made.

   b. The buyback of the shares or other specified securities shall not be made from the promoters or persons in control of the company.

   c. The company shall appoint a merchant banker and make a public announcement at least seven days prior to the commencement of buyback.

d. The public announcement shall also contain disclosures regarding details of the brokers and stock exchanges through which the buyback of shares or other specified securities would be made.
e. The buyback of shares or other specified securities shall be made only through the order matching mechanism except the "all or none" order matching system.
f. The buyback shall be made only on stock exchanges with nationwide trading terminals.
g. The company and the merchant banker shall submit the information regarding the shares or other specified securities bought back to the stock exchange on a daily basis and publish the said information in a national daily on a fortnightly basis and every time an additional 5 per cent of the buyback has been completed.

3. A company can buy back its shares or other specified securities through the book-building process as provided below.
   a. The special resolution passed by the board of directors as its meeting shall specify the maximum price at which the buyback shall be made.
   b. The company shall appoint a merchant banker and make a public announcement at least seven days prior to the commencement of the buyback.
   c. The deposit in the escrow account shall be made before the date of the public announcement and the amount to be deposited in the escrow account shall be determined with reference to the maximum price as specified in the public announcement.
   d. The public announcement shall also contain the detailed methodology of the book- building process, the manner of acceptance, the format of acceptance to be sent by the security holders pursuant to the public announcement and the details of book-building centres.
   e. The book-building process shall be made through an electronically linked transparent facility.
   f. The offer for buyback shall remain open to the security holders for a period not less than 15 days and not exceeding 30 days.
   g. The merchant banker and the company shall determine the buyback price based on the acceptances received.
   h. The final buyback price, which shall be the highest price accepted, shall be paid to all holders whose shares or other specified securities have been accepted for buyback.

The company shall not buy back locked-in shares or other specified securities and non-transferable shares or other specified securities till the pendency of the lock-in or till the securities becomes transferable. The letter of offer, the public announcement of the offer or any other advertisement shall contain true, factual and material information and shall not contain any misleading information and must state that the directors of the company accept responsibility for the information contained in such documents. SEBI may, on failure of the merchant banker to comply with the obligations or failing to observe due diligence, initiate action against the merchant banker. SEBI can, on the failure of a registrar or a broker to comply with the provisions of these regulations or failing to observe due diligence, initiate action against the registrar or the broker.

SEBI rules for the buyback of securities by a private limited company/unlisted public limited company

1. A company can buy back its shares either from existing shareholders on a proportionate basis through private offers or by purchasing securities issued to the employees of the company pursuant to a scheme of stock option or sweat equity.
2. The company that has been authorized by a special resolution shall, before the buyback of shares, file with the registrar of companies a draft letter of offer containing the particulars.
3. The offer for a buyback shall remain open to the members for a period not less than 15 days and not exceeding 30 days from the date of dispatch of the letter of offer.
4. In case the number of shares offered by the shareholders is more than the total number of shares to be bought back by the company, the acceptance per shareholder shall be on a proportionate basis.
5. The company shall, immediately after the date of closure of the offer, open a special bank account and deposit therein such a sum as would make up the entire sum due and payable as consideration for the buyback in terms of these rules.

6. The company shall, within seven days of the time specified, make a payment of consideration in cash or a bank draft to those shareholders whose offer has been accepted or return the share certificates to the shareholders forthwith.
7. A company, after the completion of the buyback under these rules, shall file with the registrar a return in the prescribed format.
8. The company shall extinguish and physically destroy the share certificates so bought back in the presence of the company secretary in a whole-time practice within seven days from the date of acceptance of the shares.
9. The company shall maintain a record of share certificates that have been cancelled and destroyed within seven days of the buyback of shares.

17.9 Recommendations of the Takeover Regulations Advisory Committee

SEBI constituted a committee called the Takeover Regulations Advisory Committee in September 2009 to examine and review the Takeover Regulations of 1977 and to suggest suitable amendments as deemed fit. The committee, after a wide range of consultations and deliberations, submitted its report on July 19, 2010. The major recommendations of the committee are presented here:

1. Every open offer pursuant to a substantial acquisition of shares in, or change of control over, a target company under the Takeover Regulations ought to be for every share held by all the shareholders of the target company.
2. In the event the shares of the target company stand delisted pursuant to the open offer, every shareholder who has not tendered an acceptance of the tender offer shall be entitled to require the acquirer to acquire his shares at the offer price at any time within a period of 12 months from the fifteenth day from the date on which the shares are delisted from the stock exchanges. This exit window would also be available to the holders of all equity-linked instruments in the company.
3. The initial acquisition threshold for a mandatory open offer be raised to 25 percent of the voting capital of the target company.
4. Creeping acquisition limit of 5 per cent per financial year computed on a gross basis for all shareholders holding more than 25 per cent is recommended so long as the maximum non-public shareholding limit is not breached.
5. Acquirers collectively holding shares entitling them to exercise 25 per cent or more voting rights in the target company may voluntarily make an open offer to consolidate their shareholding. Voluntary offers should not, however, be of a size that could lead to breach of the maximum permissible non-public shareholding.
6. The definition of 'control' be modified to include 'ability' in addition to 'right' to appoint majority of the directors or to control the management or policy decisions.
7. The minimum offer price for direct acquisition should be the highest of:
   (a) the highest negotiated price per share of the target company for any acquisition under the agreement attracting the obligation to make a public announcement of an open offer;
   (b) the volume-weighted average price paid or payable for any acquisition, whether by the acquirer or by any person acting in concert with him during the 52 weeks immediately preceding the date of the public announcement;
   (c) the highest price paid or payable for any acquisition, whether by the acquirer or by any person acting in concert with him during the 26 weeks immediately preceding the date of the public announcement; and
   (d) the volume-weighted average market price, for frequently traded shares, during 60 trading days immediately preceding the date of the public announcement, computed on the basis of market prices on the stock exchanges where the shares of the company are most frequently traded during that period.

   Frequently traded shares should now be defined as shares which have a trading volume of 10 per cent or more of the total number of shares during a period of 12 months preceding the month in which the public announcement is made.

8. An open offer may be withdrawn where any condition stipulated in the agreement for acquisition attracting the obligation to make the open offer is not met for reasons outside the reasonable control of the acquirer, and such agreement is rescinded, subject to whether such conditions having been disclosed in the detailed public statement and the letter of offer.
9. An open offer made by a competing acquirer shall not be regarded as a voluntary open offer and therefore all provisions of Takeover Regulations shall apply accordingly.
10. An acquirer who has made a competing offer shall be entitled to acquire the shares acquired by the other competing acquirers in their respective competing open offers within 21 business days of the expiry of the offer period without attracting an obligation to make another open offer.
11. The acquirer or persons acting in concert with him may be represented on the board only after the expiry of a period of 15 business days from the date of the detailed public statement and provided the entire consideration payable under the open offer is deposited in cash in the escrow account and the offer is not subject to any conditions other than regulatory approvals.
12. The offer price may be paid (a) in cash; (b) by issue, exchange or transfer of frequently traded shares of the acquirer or of the persons acting in concert with the acquirer; (c) by issue, exchange or transfer of listed secured debt instruments issued by acquirer or the persons acting in concert with him with minimum rating of investment grade; (d) by issue, exchange or transfer of convertible debt securities entitling the holder to acquire listed shares of the acquirer or of the persons acting in concert with him; or (e) a combination of (a), (b), (c), and (d).
13. The merchant banker would be expected to demonstrate the application of due skill, care and diligence in the discharge of professional duties cast on him and the obligations of the merchant banker ought to be construed accordingly.
14. The acquirer promoter/shareholders shall be asked to disclose their acquisition on periodic as well as transaction-specific basis upon crossing the limits specified therein to the stock exchange.

17.10 Accounting for Mergers[1]

The Council of the Institute of Chartered Accountants of India has issued the Accounting Standard (AS) 14, which relates to accounting for amalgamations. The salient features of AS 14 are discussed here.

An amalgamation in the nature of merger satisfies the following conditions:

1. All the assets and liabilities of the transferor company become, after amalgamation, the assets and liabilities of the transferee company.
2. Shareholders holding not less than 90 per cent of the face value of the equity shares of the transferor company (other than the equity shares already held therein, immediately before the amalgamation, by the transferee company or its subsidiaries or their nominees) become equity shareholders of the transferee company by virtue of the amalgamation.
3. The consideration for the amalgamation receivable by those equity shareholders of the transferor company who agree to become equity shareholders of the transferee company is discharged by the transferee company wholly by the issue of equity shares in the transferee company, except that cash may be paid with respect to any fractional shares.
4. The business of the transferor company is intended to be carried on, after the amalgamation, by the transferee company.
5. No adjustment is intended to be made to the book values of the assets and liabilities of the transferor company when they are incorporated in the financial statements of the transferee company except to ensure uniformity of accounting policies.

According to this standard, there are two types of mergers:

- Case I: The amalgamations where there is a genuine pooling not merely of the assets and liabilities of the amalgamating companies but also of the shareholders' interests and the business of these companies. Such amalgamations are in the nature of a merger and the accounting treatment of such amalgamations should ensure that the resultant figures of assets, liabilities, capital and reserves more or less represent the sum of the relevant figures of the amalgamating companies.

- Case II: The amalgamations that are in effect a mode by which one company acquires another company and, as a consequence, the shareholders of the company that is acquired normally do not continue to have a proportionate share in the equity of the combined company, or the business of the company that is acquired is not intended to be continued. Such amalgamations are more in the nature of a purchase.

For Case I, accounting should be done according to the pooling-of-interests method. Accordingly, in preparing the transferee company's financial statements, the assets, liabilities and reserves (whether capital or revenue or arising on revaluation) of the transferor company should be recorded at their existing carrying amounts and in the same form as on the date of the amalgamation. The balance of the profit and loss account of the transferor company should be aggregated with the corresponding balance of the transferee company or transferred to the general reserve, if any. If, at the time of amalgamation, the transferor and the transferee companies have conflicting accounting policies, a uniform set of accounting policies should be adopted following the amalgamation. The effect of any changes in accounting policies on the financial statements should be reported in accordance with Accounting Standard 5. The difference between the amount recorded as the share capital issued (plus any additional consideration in the form of cash or other assets) and the amount of share capital of the transferor company should be adjusted in the reserves.

For Case II, the accounting should be done according to the purchase method. According to this, in preparing the transferee company's financial statements, the assets and liabilities of the transferor company should be incorporated at their existing carrying amounts or, alternatively, the consideration should be allocated to individual identifiable assets and liabilities on the basis of their fair values on the date of amalgamation. The reserves (whether capital or revenue or arising on revaluation) of the transferor company, other than the statutory reserves, should not be included in the financial statements of the transferee company, except as stated as follows:

1. Where the requirements of the relevant statute for recording the statutory reserves in the books of the transferee company are complied with, the statutory reserves of the transferor company should be recorded in the financial statements of the transferee company. The corresponding debit should be given to a suitable account head, for example, Amalgamation Adjustment Account, which should be disclosed as a part of "miscellaneous expenditure" or other similar category in the balance sheet. When the identity of the statutory reserves is no longer required to be maintained, both the reserves and the aforesaid account should be reversed.
2. Any excess of the amount of the consideration over the value of the net assets of the transferor company acquired by the transferee company should be recognized in the transferee company's financial statements as goodwill arising on amalgamation. If the amount of the consideration is lower than the value of the net assets acquired, the difference should be treated as capital reserve.
3. The goodwill arising on amalgamation should be amortized to the income on a systematic basis over its useful life. The amortization period should not exceed five years unless a somewhat longer period can be justified.

17.10.1 Common Procedures

The consideration for the amalgamation should include any non-cash element at fair value. In case of the issue of securities, the value fixed by the statutory authorities can be taken to be the fair value. In case of other assets, the fair value can be determined through a reference to the market value of the assets given up. Where the market value of the assets given up cannot be reliably assessed, such assets may be valued at their respective net book values.

Where the scheme of amalgamation provides for an adjustment to the consideration contingent on one or more future events, the amount of the additional payment should be included in the consideration if payment is probable and a reasonable estimate of the amount can be made. In all other cases, the adjustment should be recognized as soon as the amount is determinable.

17.10.2 Treatment of Reserves Specified in a Scheme of Amalgamation

Where the scheme of amalgamation sanctioned under a statute prescribes the treatment to be given, that scheme should be followed. Where the scheme of amalgamation sanctioned under a statute prescribes a different treatment, compared to the requirements of the statement that would have been followed had no treatment been prescribed by the scheme, the following disclosures should be made in the first financial statements following the amalgamation:

(a) A description of the accounting treatment given to the reserves and the reasons for following the treatment different from that prescribed in this statement.

(b) Deviations in the accounting treatment given to the reserves, as prescribed by the scheme of amalgamation sanctioned under the statute as compared to the requirements of this statement that would have been followed had no treatment been prescribed by the scheme.

(c) The financial effect, if any, arising due to such deviation.

17.10.3 Disclosure

For all amalgamations, the following disclosures should be made in the first financial statements following the amalgamation:

(a) The names and general nature of business of the amalgamating companies,

(b) The effective date of amalgamation for accounting purposes,

(c) The method of accounting used to reflect the amalgamation,

(d) The particulars of the scheme sanctioned under a statute.

For amalgamations for Case I, the following additional disclosures should be made in the first financial statements following the amalgamation:

(a) the description and number of shares issued, together with the percentage of each company's equity shares exchanged to effect the amalgamation.

(b) the amount of any difference between the consideration and the value of net identifiable assets acquired, and the treatment thereof.

For amalgamations for Case II, the following additional disclosures should be made in the first financial statements following the amalgamation:

(a) consideration for the amalgamation and a description of the consideration paid or contingently payable,

(b) the amount of any difference between the consideration and the value of net identifiable assets acquired, and the treatment thereof including the period of amortization of any goodwill arising on amalgamation.

17.10.4 Amalgamation after the Balance Sheet Date

When an amalgamation is effected after the balance sheet date but before the issuance of the financial statements of either party to the amalgamation, the disclosure should be made in accordance with AS 4, but the amalgamation should not be incorporated in the financial statements. In certain circumstances, the amalgamation can also provide additional information affecting the financial statements themselves, for instance, by allowing the going concern assumption to be maintained.

17.11 Tax Implications of Mergers

The important and relevant portion of the Income Tax Act, as applicable to mergers or demergers, is discussed here.

According to Section 2 (1B) of the Income Tax Act, a merger should satisfy the following conditions in order to qualify as an amalgamation:

1. All the properties of the amalgamating company immediately before the amalgamation should become the property of the amalgamated company by virtue of the amalgamation.
2. All liabilities of the amalgamating company immediately before the amalgamation should become the liabilities of the amalgamated company by virtue of the amalgamation.

3. Shareholders holding not less than three-fourths (in value) of the shares in the amalgamating company (other than shares already held by the amalgamated company or by its nominee) should become shareholders of the amalgamated company by virtue of the amalgamation.

It is also stated that there is no amalgamation for the purpose of the Income Tax Act in the following two cases though the element of merger exists.

a. Where the property of the company that merges is sold to the other company and the merger is a result of a transaction of sale; and
b. Where the company that merges is wound up in liquidation and the liquidator distributes its property to the other company.

Any gain arising on the transfer of capital assets is chargeable to tax U/S 45 of the Income Tax Act, if it is not eligible for exemption. Transfer in relation to a capital asset includes sale, exchange or relinquishment of the asset or the extinguishment of any rights therein or the compulsory acquisition thereof under the law. However, certain transactions, including the following that relate to amalgamation, are not included in transfer, provided they fulfil certain conditions as stated under Sections 47 (vi), 47 (vi a), 47 (vi aa), 47 (vi b), 47 (vi c), 47 (vi d) and 47 (vii):

a. Transfer of capital asset in a scheme of amalgamation
b. Transfer of shares in an Indian company held by a foreign company to another foreign company under a scheme of amalgamation of the two foreign companies
c. Transfer of capital asset in a scheme of amalgamation of a banking company with a banking institution
d. Transfer in demerger of a capital asset by the demerged company to the resulting company
e. Transfer of shares held in an Indian company by a demerged foreign company to the resulting foreign company
f. Transfer or issue of shares by the resulting company, in a scheme of demerger to the shareholders of the demerged company
g. Allotment of shares in the amalgamated company in lieu of shares held in amalgamating company

According to Section 49 (2) of the Income Tax Act, if a person holds shares in a company, which is merged with an Indian company, then in lieu of shares in the amalgamating company, he will get shares in the amalgamated company. In such a case, the cost of shares of the amalgamating company will become the cost of shares of the amalgamated company. To determine whether or not the shares in the amalgamated company are long-term capital assets, the period of holding shall be determined from the date of acquisition of shares in the amalgamating company. Further, as per Section 49 (2C)/(2D), the cost of acquisition of the shares in the resulting company shall be the amount that bears to the cost of acquisition of shares held by the assessee in the demerged company a certain proportion. This is the same proportion that the net book value of the assets transferred in a demerger bears to the net worth of the demerged company immediately before such a demerger. To determine whether or not the shares in the resulting company are long-term capital assets, the period of holding shall be determined from the date of acquisition of shares in the demerged company.

As per the provisions of the Income Tax Act, depreciation and business loss can be carried forward by a person who has incurred the loss. However, Section 72A of the act provides an exception to this rule in the following cases:

1. If the following conditions are satisfied, then the accumulated loss and the unabsorbed depreciation of the amalgamating company shall be deemed to be the loss/depreciation of the amalgamated company for the previous year in which the amalgamation was effected.
   (i) There has been an amalgamation of a company owning an industrial undertaking or a ship or a hotel with another company or an amalgamation of a banking company with the State Bank of India or any subsidiary of the State bank of India.
   (ii) The amalgamating company has been engaged in a business in which the accumulated loss incurred or depreciation remains unabsorbed for three years or more.
   (iii) The amalgamating company has held continuously as on the date of the amalgamation at least three-fourths of the book value of fixed assets held by it two years prior to the date of amalgamation.

(iv) The amalgamated company continues to hold at least three-fourths in the book value of fixed assets of the amalgamating company that it has acquired as a result of amalgamation for five years from the effective date of amalgamation.

(v) The amalgamated company continues the business of the amalgamating company for a minimum period of five years.

(vi) The amalgamated company that has acquired an industrial undertaking of the amalgamating company by way of amalgamation shall achieve a level of production that is at least 50 per cent of the installed capacity of the said undertaking before the end of four years from the date of amalgamation and continue to maintain the said minimum level of production till the end of five years from the date of the amalgamation.

(vii) The amalgamated company shall furnish to the assessing officer a certificate in Form No. 62, duly verified by an accountant, with reference to the books of income for the assessment year relevant to the previous year during which the prescribed level of production is achieved and for subsequent assessment years relevant to the previous years falling within five years of the date of amalgamation.

If the above conditions are satisfied, then the accumulated business loss and unabsorbed depreciation of the amalgamating company shall be deemed to be the loss and depreciation of the amalgamated company for the previous year in which amalgamation was effected. In case the above conditions are not fulfilled (after claiming adjustment of loss/depreciation), then that part of the brought-forward loss and unabsorbed depreciation that has been set off by the amalgamated company shall be treated as the income of the amalgamated company for the year in which the failure to fulfil the conditions occurs.

2. In the case of a demerger, the accumulated loss and unabsorbed depreciation of the demerged company will be allowed to be carried forward and set off in the hands of the resulting company.
3. In cases of succession of business, whereby a firm succeeded by a company fulfilling the conditions laid down under Section 47 (xiii) or a proprietary concern is succeeded by a company fulfilling the conditions laid down in Section 47 (xiv), the accumulated loss and unabsorbed depreciation of the predecessor firm or proprietary concern, as the case may be, shall be deemed to be the loss or, as the case may be, allowance for depreciation of the successor company for the previous year in which business reorganization was effected and the other provisions of the act relating to set off and carry forward loss and allowance for depreciation shall apply accordingly.

When conditions under Section 47 (xiii)/47 (xiv) are not satisfied, the setting off of loss or allowance for depreciation made in the previous year in the hands of the successor company shall be deemed to be the income of the company chargeable to tax in the year in which such conditions were not satisfied.

4. If there is an amalgamation of a banking company with any other banking institution under a scheme of amalgamation and that amalgamation is sanctioned and brought into force by the Government of India under Section 45 (7) of the Banking Regulation Act, 1949, the accumulated loss and unabsorbed depreciation of the amalgamating banking company shall be deemed to be the loss or the allowance for depreciation of the banking institution for the previous year in which the scheme for amalgamation was brought into force.

17.12 Evaluation of Mergers and Acquisitions: The DCF Approach

Before going in for a merger or acquisition, a firm should evaluate the target firm in terms of several aspects, both financial and non-financial. The non-financial aspects include organizational culture, competencies and skills of employees. The most important factor in mergers and acquisitions is financial evaluation, which involves assessing expected cash flows and potential risks. The acquiring company should also determine the maximum price payable or the number of shares to be issued to the shareholders of the target company. As a merger or acquisition involves both costs and benefits, the acquiring company should identify the various costs and benefits of the merger or acquisition and evaluate them by a suitable method in order to take a decision. It may be noted that the target firm might not accept an offer below the current value of its shares.

The acquiring firm might even have to pay a premium if it feels that the acquisition will create more value through synergy and other factors. Thus, the valuation of a merger or acquisition is an essential exercise involving consideration of several complex factors.

There are two types of values—book value and market value. The *book value* of a firm is determined by dividing the net worth by the number of equity shares outstanding. Though the book value, which is based on the historical costs of the assets, has limitations, it can reflect the revenue-generating capacity of the assets of the firm. It also serves as a useful guide in determining the exchange ratio of shares. The *market value* of a firm as determined by the market price of its shares, might reflect the true value of the firm. The market value reflects both the earnings potential as well as the corresponding risk of the firm. However, if the market price is influenced by speculative factors and market sentiments, it could fail to reflect the true value of the firm. In spite of this limitation, the market value is widely used in determining the exchange ratio of shares or the value to be paid to the shareholders of the target firm.

Although there are different approaches to the valuation of a merger or acquisition, the discounted cash flow (DCF) approach is most commonly followed. The DCF approach primarily involves the estimation of the incremental free cash flows to be generated by the target firm after the proposed merger or acquisition, determination of the cost of capital or discount rate and arriving at the NPV. The free cash flows are the after-tax operating earnings plus non-cash expenses like depreciation. The cost of acquisition includes the payment to be made to the shareholders and debt holders of the target firm, other payments to the target firm and expenses, if any, to be incurred in connection with the merger or acquisition less the amount, if any, to be realized on the sale of any of the assets of the target firm. The acquiring firm can also make certain assumptions about the profitability and future growth of the combined firm while estimating the free cash flows and determining the discount rate. A variant of the DCF approach is the adjusted present value (APV) approach. According to the APV approach, the target firm is valued in two components: (a) the value of the target firm if it were entirely equity-financed; and (b) the value of the impact of debt financing. In both the approaches (DCF and APV), the NPV is calculated. Depending on the NPV, the firm decides whether to go in for a merger/acquisition. If the NPV is positive, the firm usually decides to go ahead with the proposed merger or acquisition.

The impact of different sources of merger or acquisition financing on the EPS and P/E ratio is also assessed. Based on all such factors, including the NPV, the acquiring company decides how much it can offer or what should be the maximum exchange ratio of shares. It may be noted that the exchange ratio might not be in tandem with the prevailing stock price differentials of the two companies. This is because other factors like managerial quality and distribution network also influence merger or acquisition decisions. Thus, the price an acquirer pays does not necessarily reflect the firm's current realizable value since the ultimate value of the merger or acquisition can be proven over time. In the normal course, a company might go in for acquisition of a target company if the acquisition is expected to make a net contribution to shareholders' wealth.

Example 17.1

Company *A* wants to acquire Company *B*. The balance sheet of Company *B* as on March 31, 2007, is shown in Table 17.4:

Table 17.4 Balance sheet of Company B on March 31, 2007

Liabilities (INR million)		*Assets (INR million)*	
Equity share capital (.7 million shares of INR 100 each)	70	Cash	20
Retained earnings	20	Debtors	50
12 per cent debentures	30	Inventory	30
Current liabilities	80	Fixed assets (net)	100
Total	200		200

As per the negotiations, the shareholders of Company *B* will get two shares in Company *A* for every three shares. The shares of Company *A* would be issued at its current market price of INR 250 per share. The debenture holders and other creditors will get the same amount they have in Company *B*.

(Continued)

After acquisition of Company *B*, Company *A* is expected to have the incremental free cash flows shown in Table 17.5 for the next five years:

Table 17.5 Incremental free cash flows (INR million)

Year	*Incremental free cash flows (INR million)*
2007–08	50
2008–09	55
2009–10	62
2010–11	67
2011–12	75

The incremental free cash flows are expected to grow at 5 per cent per annum after five years. After the merger, the cost of capital for Company *A* is expected to be 12 per cent. Evaluate the acquisition.

Solution

Table 17.6 shows the present cost of acquisition.

Table 17.6 Present cost of acquisition (INR million)

Share capital (0.467 million shares at INR 250)	116.75
Debentures	30
Other liabilities	80
Total	226.75

The present value of incremental free cash flows are shown in Table 17.7.

Table 17.7 Present value of incremental free cash flows (INR million)

Year	*Cash flows*	*PV factor*	*Present value*
2007–08	500	0.893	44.65
2008–09	550	0.797	43.835
2009–10	620	0.712	44.144
2010–11	670	0.636	42.612
2011–12	750	0.567	42.525

Present value of incremental cash flow after five years
= Incremental free cash flows in the fifth year × $(1 + g)/(k_0 - g)$
= INR 750 (1 + 0.05)/(0.12–0.05)
= INR 1125 million
= INR 637.875 million

Present value of total incremental free cash flows
= INR 217.766 + INR 637.875
= INR 855.641 million
Cost of acquisition = INR 226.75 million
Net present value = INR 628.891 million
Since the net present value is positive, Company *A* can acquire Company *B*.

Example 17.2

M/S Rajeswari Constructions Ltd would like to take over M/S PLN Developers Ltd. The financial details of the two companies as on March 31, 2007, are as shown in Table 17.8.

(Continued)

Table 17.8 Financial details of the two companies as on March 31, 2007

	Rajeswari (INR)	*PLN (INR)*
Equity shares (INR 10 per share)	27,000,000	23,000,000
Reserves	13,000,000	17,000,000
Preference share capital	1,500,000	1,000,000
Debentures	8,000,000	6,000,000
Fixed assets	40,000,000	35,000,000
Net current assets	9,500,000	12,000,000
Profit available to equity shareholders (2007–08)	5,000,000	3,500,000
Current market price per share	25	30

Calculate the exchange ratio of shares based on (a) net asset value, (b) EPS and (c) current market price of the share.

Solution

Table 17.9 shows the net assets per share.

Table 17.9 Net assets per share

	Rajeswari	*PLN*
Fixed assets	40,000,000	35,000,000
Net current assets	9,500,000	12,000,000
Total assets	49,500,000	47,000,000
Less preference share capital	1,500,000	1,000,000
Less debentures	8,000,000	6,000,000
Net assets	40,000,000	40,000,000
Number of shares	2,700,000	2,300,000
Net assets per share	14.82	17.40

(a) Exchange ratio on net asset value = INR 17.40/14.82 = 1.17
The shareholders of PLN should get 1.17 shares of Rajeswari for every share held by them in PLN.
(b) Table 17.10 shows the EPS of two companies.

Table 17.10 Earnings per share

	Rajeswari	*PLN*
Profit available to equity shareholders (2007–08)	5,000,000	3,500,000
EPS	1.85	1.52

On the basis of EPS, the exchange ratio = 1.52/1.85 = 0.82
Thus, the shareholders of PLN should get 0.82 shares of Rajeswari for every share held by them in PLN.
(c) Table 17.11 shows the current market price.

Table 17.11 Current market price

	Rajeswari	*PLN*
Current market price per share	25	30

On the basis of market price, exchange ratio = 30/25 = 1.2
Thus, the shareholders of PLN should get 1.2 shares of Rajeswari for every share held by them in PLN.

M/S High Tech Systems Ltd wishes to acquire M/S Info Tech Ltd. The summary data available is as shown in Table 17.12.

Table 17.12 The summary data

	High Tech Systems Ltd	*Info Tech Ltd*
Net profit after tax (INR)	7,000,000	5,000,000
Number of shares outstanding	800,000	750,000
Price-earnings ratio	22	18

What is the market value per share? What is the maximum exchange ratio that High Tech Systems Ltd could offer to Info Tech Ltd without dilution of the EPS?

Solution

Market value per share is given as P/E ratio multiplied by EPS
EPS in the case of High Tech Systems = 7,000,000/800,000 = 8.75
EPS in the case of Info Tech Ltd = 5,000,000/750,000 = 6.67
Market value per share of High Tech Systems = 22 × 8.75 = INR 192.50
Market value per share of Info Tech Ltd = 18 × 6.67 = INR 138.40

Combined net profit after tax = INR 12 million
EPS of High Tech Systems = INR 8.75
Maximum number of shares in High Tech Systems after merger = 120/8.75= 1.37 million
Existing number of shares in High Tech Systems = 0.8 million
Maximum number of shares to be exchanged = 0.57 million
Existing number of shares in Info Tech Ltd = 0.75 million
Maximum share exchange ratio = 5.7/7.5 = 0.76

The maximum share exchange ratio can also be calculated alternatively.
Price-earnings ratio in the case of High Tech Systems = 22
EPS in the case of Info Tech Ltd = INR 6.67
High Tech Systems can offer up to INR 6.67 × 22 = INR 146.74 for every share of Info Tech Ltd without dilution in its EPS. Thus, the maximum exchange ratio can be INR 146.74/INR 192.50 = 0.76.

17.13 Mergers and Acquisitions: The Indian Scenario

Mergers and acquisitions are very common in the Indian corporate sector. Following the economic reforms initiated by the Government of India in the 1980s and accelerated in the subsequent decades, mergers and acquisitions have gained substantial importance in the Indian corporate world. They are very prominent in sectors such as telecom, finance, FMCG, construction materials, the automobile industry and the steel industry. Acquisition of foreign companies by Indian businesses has been the latest trend in the Indian corporate sector (Box 17.1). A merger case in the FMCG sector is discussed in Box 17.2.

Different factors have played a part in facilitating mergers and acquisitions in India. Favourable government policies, buoyancy in the economy, additional liquidity in the corporate sector, and dynamic attitudes of Indian entrepreneurs are the key factors behind the changing trends of mergers and acquisitions in India. Increased competition in the domestic as well as global markets has prompted companies to opt for mergers and acquisitions as an important strategic choice.

Box 17.1 Acquisition of Corus by Tata Steel

At USD 12.1 billion, the acquisition of Anglo-Dutch steelmaker Corus by Tata Steel is the biggest acquisition in the history of Indian business and the second-largest in the global steel industry. With this acquisition, Tata Steel became the world's fifth-largest steelmaker in terms of turnover as well as capacity (24 million tonnes). The other steel majors in the world are ArcelorMittal, Nippon Steel, JFE Holdings and Posco.

(Continued)

In the auction that lasted nine rounds, Tata Steel beat Companhia Siderurgica Nacional (CSN), a Brazilian company, by 5 pence per share. Tata Steel's final offer was 608 pence per share as against CSN's bid of 603 pence. Although Corus was valued at USD 13.6 billion, nine times its EBIT for 2005–06, the Tata Steel share price crashed by 10.6 per cent to INR 463.9 after the deal was announced on January 31, 2007. On the other hand, the share price of Corus increased to 608 pence, up by 6.7 per cent. However, the management of Tata Steel asserted that the buy price (USD 12.1 billion) was much lower than what it would have incurred in setting up a greenfield project of the same magnitude.

With the acquisition, Tata Steel was supposed to be vested with bargaining power over its financial suppliers as well as commodity suppliers. It was also expected that Tata Steel would get better prices for its finished products. Corus would have made it easy for Tata Steel to enter the European market, which is expanding due to high industrial growth, particularly in the construction, auto and packaging industries. In fact, the taking over of Corus was part of the global strategy of Tata Steel, as it had also acquired Millennium Steel, the largest steel company in Thailand (2003), and the Singapore-based NatSteel Asia (2004). Moreover, the steel industry at the global level was in a consolidation phase and there was a pressure on individual steelmakers to grow in order to compete with the global steel giant, ArcelorMittal. The steel industry is in an increasingly flattening global market and, therefore, competitiveness can be achieved by synergy.

With the acquisition of Corus, Tata Steel has become a truly global company with a significant presence in 25 countries, including the United States and Latin American nations. Before the acquisition, Tata Steel ranked around 1,000 among the global steelmakers. As Corus is a bigger company—more than thrice the size of Tata Steel—the Tata Steel–Corus combine ranked about 250 in the Fortune Global 500 list. Tata Steel also became the second-largest company in India after IndianOil.

Corus had been bogged down by the highest production costs in the world and was on the brink of bankruptcy. With the acquisition, Corus was expected to save about USD 350 million per annum in costs as it would have access to Tata Steel's low-cost and efficient production facilities. Further, Corus could enter easily the South-east Asian market, which has a high demand for its products. In other words, the acquisition by Tata Steel was expected to be a turnaround for Corus. It was also claimed that the acquisition was in the best long-term interests of the employees.

Box 17.2 Merger of BBIL with HLL

Following economic liberalization in the early 1990s, Unilever raised its stake in three group companies, Brooke Bond, Lipton and HLL, to 51 per cent. While the stake in Brooke Bond was raised by merging it with Tea Estates and Doom Dooma Tea, in which Unilever had a 74 per cent stake, Unilever picked up an additional 11 per cent equity in both Lipton and HLL (Hindustan Lever Limited, since renamed as Hindustan Unilever Limited). Once Unilever had 51 per cent in all the three companies, it effected the first of the mergers—Brooke Bond and Lipton—to create BBLIL (Brooke Bond Lipton India Limited), a premier foods company. Subsequently, BBIL acquired Kothari General Foods, Kissan, Dollops, Kwality, Milk Food and Pepsi's tomato ketchup facilities. HLL bought Tomco and claimed part ownership of the Lakme brand equity through a joint venture with Lakme.

BBLIL then amalgamated with HLL in 1996. The financial results of the two companies for the year ending 1995 are as shown in Table 17.13.

Table 17.13 Financial results of the two companies for FY 1995 (INR million)

	BBIL	*HLL*
Gross sales	21,080	33,670
Other income	641	667
Interest	237	201
PBIT	1,772	3,921
Depreciation	206.3	236.1
Tax	270	1,330
Net profit	1265	2,390
Reserves	2,912.5	4,924.4
Equity	1,204.8	1,458.4

(Continued)

The shareholding pattern in both the companies as on the date of merger was as shown in Table 17.14.

Table 17.14 The shareholding pattern

	BBIL	*HLL*
Foreign holdings	50.59%	51.71%
Corporate bodies	2.77%	2.43%
FIs	20.44%	16.72%
Others	26.20%	29.14%

The basic purpose of the merger was to enable the high-cash generating potential of HLL to be channelled into the capital-intensive investment plans of the high-growth foods business of BBLIL. The merger would have a common treasury, which would not only give HLL more muscle power but also provide tremendous leverage while raising debt. There was very little synergy expected.

The merger was effected with a swap ratio of nine shares of HLL for every 20 shares of BBLIL. The valuation process for the merger was carried out by ICICI Securities and Finance Company Ltd, ANZ Grindlays Bank, YH Malegam of S.B. Billimoria and Arun Gandhi of NM Raiji and Co.

The announcement of the merger had a marginal impact on the share prices of the two companies. On the NSE, the share price of HLL touched a high of INR 780 on April 19, 1996, up from its previous day's close of INR 778.25, before closing at INR 770. The BBLIL stock touched a high of INR 410.9 on April 19, 1996, before closing at INR 405.95 against the previous closing of INR 399.35. Both BBLIL and HLL shares had been rising steadily in the few months before the merger. The BBLIL stock price, which touched a low of INR 217 in January 1996, climbed to INR 405 the day before the announcement of the merger. On the other hand, the HLL price moved up from INR 622 in January 1996 to touch INR 772.85 the day before the announcement of the merger.

Summary

1. Corporate restructuring takes different forms like mergers, acquisitions and divestitures in order to increase value for the shareholders. A merger is a strategy through which two firms agree to integrate their operations, whereas an acquisition is an act of acquiring effective control over the assets or management of a firm by another firm.
2. The organization can go in for horizontal mergers, vertical mergers or conglomerate mergers for synergy, pure diversification and/or tax benefits.
3. Acquisitions are strategies used by firms to increase their effectiveness and earn above-average returns. A forced acquisition or unwilling acquisition is called a takeover. In other words, a takeover is a form of acquisition strategy where the target firm is not willing to be acquired.
4. A divestiture refers to divesting of its assets or business units by a firm in order to refocus on its core businesses. A divestiture can take the form of a sell-off or spin-off or equity carve-out.
5. There are many methods of financing mergers and acquisitions. Stock swapping is one such method, in which the acquiring company issues its shares to the shareholders of the target company at a negotiated exchange ratio.
6. A leveraged buyout refers to transforming a public limited company into a private limited company. In a leveraged buyout, a party consisting of a few individuals or institutions, or some individuals and institutions, buy all of a firm's assets with their own funds and significant amounts of debt.
7. SEBI has prescribed a takeover code, according to which no acquirer shall acquire shares or voting rights in a company unless such an acquirer complies with the regulations incorporated therein.
8. The targeted firms might initiate different defence mechanisms in order to discourage the raiders or make takeovers difficult. The takeover defences can be preemptive or post-facto.
9. Hostile takeovers usually take place through tender offers. A tender offer is an offer made by the acquiring company to purchase shares of the target company at a fixed price from the shareholders who tender their shares.
10. A popular defence tactic is a poison pill, which refers to the creation of securities that provide the holders with special rights exercisable after some time. These rights, which take several forms, would make it costly to acquire controlling interest in the target firm.
11. Buyback of shares is an arrangement by which a company purchases its own equity shares from its shareholders. The company can purchase its shares on the floor of the stock exchange or directly purchase its shares from its shareholders by making a tender offer, or buy its shares through negotiations with the concerned shareholders.
12. There are different approaches to the valuation of a merger or acquisition. The discounted cash flow approach, which is most commonly followed, primarily involves an estimation of incremental free cash flows to be generated by the target firm after the proposed merger or acquisition, determination of cost of capital or discount rate, and arriving at the NPV.

Questions and Problems

1. What are the different forms of corporate restructuring? What purpose(s) do they serve?
2. Discuss merger motives.
3. What are the different types of mergers? Give examples of each type.
4. What do you understand by acquisitions? When does an acquisition become a takeover? Discuss the reasons for takeovers.
5. What is the role of price-earnings ratio in stock swapping? Illustrate your answer.
6. Discuss different methods of financing mergers and acquisitions.
7. What is a divestiture? What are different forms of divestitures? Why do companies undertake divestitures?
8. What is a leveraged buyout? What are the implications of a leveraged buyout?
9. Discuss the salient features of the SEBI takeover code.
10. What is a bailout takeover? What are the SEBI regulations in this regard?
11. Discuss takeover defensive tactics.
12. What are the motives for buying back of shares?
13. Discuss the SEBI regulations pertaining to buyback of shares.
14. Explain a buyback through tender offer.
15. Discuss the salient features of AS 14.
15. Explain the tax implications of mergers and acquisitions.
16. Explain the DCF approach to the evaluation of a merger/acquisition.
17. Company *ABC* wants to acquire company *PQR* on a share-exchange basis. The relevant financial data of the two companies are as shown in Table 17.15.

Table 17.15 Financial data of the two companies

	ABC	*PQR*
Number of shares outstanding (in millions)	10	7.14
Profit after tax (INR million)	100	50
Earnings per share (INR)	10	7
Price-earnings ratio	15	10

Based on the above data, determine: (i) the pre-merger market price of a share of each company; and (ii) the maximum exchange ratio *ABC* can offer without dilution of EPS and market price per share.

18. A summary balance sheet of M/S Srinivas Enterprises is provided in Table 17.16.

Table 17.16 Summary balance sheet of M/S Srinivas Enterprises (INR million)

Liabilities		*Assets*	
Paid-up equity share capital (10 million shares at INR 10)	100	Net fixed assets	150
Reserves and surplus	50	Investments	30
12% debentures	80	Sundry debtors	5
Sundry creditors	7	Inventory	15
Other current liabilities	3	Cash	40
Total	240	Total	240

Another company, Ketan Products Limited, wants to acquire M/S Srinivas Enterprises by offering the following.

a. 12 per cent preference shares of INR 80 million for paying 12 per cent debentures of Srinivas Enterprises. The sundry creditors and other current liabilities would be paid off by Ketan Products at 110 per cent of their book value.

b. Cash of INR 800 million.

Ketan Products Limited expects to realize INR 31 million, INR 13.5 million and INR 4.5 million, respectively, on the sale of investments, inventory and book debts of Srinivas Enterprises if the acquisition takes place.

Calculate the total cost of acquisition of M/S Srinivas Enterprises. How much annual after-tax cash flows should Ketan Products Limited generate in the post-acquisition period (10 years) to get a required rate of return of 25 per cent on the investment to be made in the acquisition?

Case Study

Ballarpur Industries Limited (BIL) is a public limited company established under the Companies Act, 1956. It is primarily engaged in the business of manufacture and sale of paper, both in India and overseas. The equity shares of the company are listed on Indian stock exchanges. It has two subsidiaries in the Netherlands, namely, Ballarpur International Holdings BV (direct subsidiary) and Ballarpur Paper Holdings BV (wholly owned step-down subsidiary, referred to as BPH). These subsidiaries were established with the object of acquiring Sabah Forest Industries Sdn Bhd, an integrated pulp and paper manufacturing company based in Malaysia. BPH holds 97.8 per cent of the paid-up capital of Sabah. BIL has two undertakings engaged in the manufacture and sale of printing quality paper at Bhigwan and Ballarpur and one undertaking engaged in the manufacture and sale of pulp at Kamalapuram. These undertakings are referred to as BILT New Undertaking.

BILT Graphic Paper Products Limited (referred to as BILT) is also a public limited company engaged in the business of manufacture and sale of paper. The entire share capital of BILT is held by BIL.

In July 2007, BIL came out with a proposal known as Scheme of Arrangement and Reorganization. The scheme envisaged the following:

i. A slump exchange of the BILT New Undertaking for shares and debentures of BILT;
ii. The transfer of the shares and debentures of BILT held by BIL to BPH for cash consideration of INR 19,500,000,000; and
iii. A reorganization of the capital of BIL through stock split and buyback.

Upon the scheme coming into effect, the authorized share capital of BILT of INR 1,000,000 divided into 100,000 equity shares of INR 10 each will stand enhanced by an amount of INR 45,000,00,000 divided into 4,500,00,000 equity shares of INR 10 each.

BIL would utilize the consideration of INR 19,500,000,000 towards the following:

(a) Retiring wholly or partially of its debts owed to creditors which would be undertaken by part repayment/ prepayment of debts, aggregating to between INR 70 million and INR 90 million;
(b) Buyback of 40 per cent of the paid-up equity capital and additional equity shares of small shareholders, i.e., those holding 1,000 equity shares (pre-split) or less, desiring to sell all their shareholdings in BIL in terms of the scheme; and
(c) The residue of the funds received will be utilized for other purposes as may be decided by the board of directors of BIL.

As part of the scheme, every issued, subscribed and fully paid-up equity share of face value of INR 10 each of BIL shall be reorganized and subdivided into five fully paid-up equity shares of INR 2 each. Further, BIL would buy back from every equity shareholder two equity shares of INR 2 each, whether held in physical or dematerialized form, at a price of INR 25 per equity share. The equity shareholders holding 1,000 equity shares pre-split, or 5,000 equity shares post-split, or less in BIL, shall have the option to tender in the manner prescribed in the scheme the balance equity shareholding in BIL after buyback at a price of INR 30 per equity share and BIL shall be bound to purchase the same. The equity shareholders of BIL, who continue to hold their equity shares in physical form as on the record date, shall be issued fresh share certificates with new and distinctive numbers consequent upon the reorganization of capital, and after accounting for the buyback of shares.

Shareholding Pattern of BIL

Prior to implementation of the scheme:

Promoter holding: 72,199,234 equity shares of INR 10 each (38.88 per cent)

Public holdings: 113,508,196 equity shares of INR 10 each (61.12 per cent)

After implementation of the scheme (post-split and buyback of shares):

Promoter holding: 216,597,702 equity shares of INR 2 each (38.88 per cent)

Public holding: 340,524,588 equity shares of INR 2 each (61.12 per cent)

Shareholding Pattern of BILT

Prior to implementation of the scheme:

BIL holding (along with its six individual nominees): 50,000 equity shares of INR 10 each (100 per cent)

After implementation of the scheme (post-split and buyback of shares):

BPH holding: 450,000,000 equity shares of INR 10 each (99.99 per cent)

BIL holding (along with its six individual nominees): 50,000 equity shares of INR 10 each (0.01 per cent)

After implementation of the scheme, 75 per cent of the total issued capital of BPH shall continue to be held indirectly by BIL through BIH, which is its wholly owned subsidiary.

Question

Analyse the case and list out the major benefits for BIL after implementation of the scheme of reorganization.

Endnote

1 This section is taken from data taken from The Institute of Chartered Accountants of India, accessed at http://www.icai .org/resource_file/256accounting_standards_as14new.pdf, July 2010.

Chapter 18

Leasing and Hire Purchase

LEARNING OBJECTIVES

After reading this chapter, you should be able to:

- Explain the concepts of leasing and hire purchase.
- Present historical developments in leasing.
- Explain types of leasing.
- Discuss different methods of lease evaluation.
- State the advantages and limitations of leasing.
- Present a sketch of the leasing industry in India.
- Explain the method of evaluation of hire purchase.
- Discuss the accounting treatment of leases.

18.1 Introduction

Leasing is an age-old concept all over the world. The first leasing transaction is believed to have occurred in 1066, when William the conqueror rented ships for intrusion into Britain. During World War II, many factors contributed to the evolution of equipment leasing. Machinery was required for arms production that would be unnecessary during peace time after the war, increasing the demand for leasing. Continuing into the twenty-first century, economic reforms generated an increased attraction towards equipment leasing. Traditionally, land, animals—particularly horses—and agricultural tools were the assets mostly involved in leasing. But over time, the range of leasing has increased to include high-value items like ships, aircraft, cars, and railroad equipment, and low-value items like small transport vehicles, computers and office equipment. Leasing is suitable for financing investments in productive assets and is used by a variety of businesses and organizations such as hospitals, educational institutions, associations and government agencies.

In the ancient times, leasing was the last-resort financing option. Over time, it has become a primary method of financing assets. Although several financing options are available for present-day businesses, leasing has a role to be reckoned with in industrial financing. Leasing is particularly used as an alternative to debt financing.

When an asset is acquired, either by purchasing or by leasing, it is used for productive operations of the firm. It is the service rendered or use from the asset that is critical to the firm and not the title to the asset. Legal ownership would give the owner the right to use the asset. But it is not necessary for a person to own an asset in order to use it. Thus, leasing can be an alternative to buying.

Although there are two principal parties directly involved in leasing—the leasing company (lessor) and the lessee firm—the manufacturer or supplier of the asset or equipment also has an interest or stake in leasing. In some leasing arrangements, banks or financial institutions provide funds to the leasing firm and secure a direct charge over the lease revenues and collateral over the leased asset. The leasing company acquires the equipment from the manufacturer or supplier, arranges for the insurance, prices the lease transactions and passes on the equipment to the lessee under an agreement. Thus, the lessee provides the business for both the manufacturer or supplier of the equipment and the leasing company.

18.2 Leasing: Concept and Operations

A **lease** is a transaction in which a party owning an asset provides the asset for use over a certain period of time to another for consideration either in the form of periodic rent and/or in form of a down payment.

The Transfer of Property Act defines a **lease** as a transaction in which a party owning an asset provides the asset for use over a certain period of time to another for consideration either in the form of periodic rent and/or in the form of a down payment. A lease can also be defined as a contract between two parties for the hire of a specific asset where the lessor retains ownership of the asset while the lessee has possession and use of the asset upon payment of the specified rentals over a period of time. A lease is also defined as a contract in which one party (the owner of an asset or the lesser), grants to another party (the lessee) a right to use the asset in return for payment of a certain amount, which is known as *lease rent*. According to Accounting Standard (AS) 19 (see Appendix 18.1), a lease is an agreement whereby the lessor conveys to the lessee the right to use an asset for an agreed period of time in return for a payment or series of payments. Thus, under a lease contract, the lessee acquires the right to use an asset without acquiring ownership of the same by paying the fee towards the use that is called a lease rental. The payment of lease rentals can be in advance (paid at the beginning of the lease period) or in arrears (paid at the end of the lease period).

18.2.1 Classification of Leases

A lease can be an operating lease or a financial lease. An **operating lease** is a short-term lease whereas a **financial lease** is a long-term lease.

Leases are broadly classified into an operating lease and a financial lease. An **operating lease** is a relatively short-term lease. According to AS 19, an operating lease is a lease other than a financial lease. Generally an operating lease requires the lessor to maintain and service the leased asset. That is, unless otherwise stated, the lesser pays for the maintenance, repairs, taxes and insurance of the asset. As the term of the operating lease is shorter than the asset's economic life, the lease rentals paid under the lease arrangement are not sufficient for the lessor to recover the full cost of the asset. Therefore, the lessor recovers the full cost of the asset by subsequent re-leasing of the asset or by selling the asset. An operating lease might contain a cancellation clause according to which the lessee will have the right to cancel the lease and return the asset to the lessor before the expiration of the lease agreement. The cancellation clause of the lease facilitates the lessee to return the asset when it is no longer needed because of changing circumstances. An operating lease, also known as a short-term lease, is typically for assets that have high depreciation potential like computers and windmills. Operating leases are for a period of two to three years and they tend to be useful to companies that have a high taxable income in the near future.

A **financial lease** is a long-term lease, the period of which generally coincides with the economic life of the asset. Financial leases are fully amortized. That is, the lessor receives the total amount (the cost of the asset and a return thereon) from the lessee. Ordinarily, the financial lease cannot be cancelled unless the lesser is paid in full. Further, the lessee is expected to maintain and service the leased asset.

As per IAS 19, a lease is classified as a finance lease if it transfers all the risks and rewards incident to ownership substantially. The situations that would normally lead to a lease being classified as a finance lease are as follows:

- The lesser transfers ownership of the asset to the lessee by the end of the lease term;
- The lessee has the option to purchase the asset at a price that is expected to be substantially lower than the fair value at the date the option becomes exercisable such that, at the inception of the lease, it is reasonably certain that the option will be exercised;
- The lease term is for the major part of the economic life of the asset even if the title is not transferred;
- At the inception of the lease, the present value of the minimum lease payments amounts to at least substantially all of the fair value of the leased asset; and
- The leased asset is of a specialized nature such that only the lessee can use it without major modifications.

Financial leases, also known as long-term leases, are suitable for assets that have low depreciation eligibility, such as plant and machinery, cars, furniture and fixtures, and have a long economic life. Companies that are interested in leveraging the balance sheet to achieve a higher operational profit prefer financial leases.

Leases can also be categorized as sales-type lease, direct financing lease, leveraged lease and cross-border lease. In a *sales-type lease*, the lessor, usually the manufacturer or dealer of the asset, leases the asset in lieu of selling it. A sales-type lease is structured so that the lessor not only earns an interest income but also earns a profit on the transaction. In a *direct financing lease*, the lessor (usually a bank or financial institution) buys an asset from the manufacturer or vendor and then leases it to the lessee. A direct financing lease is the functional equivalent of a loan. In other words, a direct financing lease is an alternative to the commercial loan in which a borrower uses the bank loan proceeds to purchase an asset.

In the case of *leveraged leasing*, there are three parties involved—the lessee, the lessor (equity participant) and the lender (debt participant). The lessor purchases the asset by providing only a percentage, say 30 percent, of the capital needed and takes out a non-recourse loan from a creditor for the balance of the purchase price of the asset. The lessor thus partly finances the leased asset with the borrowed funds. The loan is usually secured by a first lien on the asset, assignment of the lease and assignment of the lease rental payments. The lessor, as the owner of the asset, is entitled to a depreciation allowance and can claim any available investment allowance based on the total cost of the asset. The lessor also retains the residual value rights to the property at the end of the lease period. When the cost of the asset is large, a leveraged lease might involve several lessors and debt participants. In such cases, one party generally holds a title to the property and represents the lessors.

Cross-border leasing takes place between a lessor and a lessee who are in two different countries. Cross-border leasing, also known as international leasing, is more complex and has more tax implications than domestic leases. It enables the parties to take advantage of tax concessions and incentives offered by different countries. Moreover, the lessee might get access to cross-country equipment and technology.

18.2.2 Sale-and-Lease-Back

A **sale-and-lease-back** is a type of lease agreement whereby a party that owns an asset sells it to another party and then takes back the asset on lease for a fixed period. There is no physical transfer of the asset. There are two separate transactions in a sale-and-lease-back. The owner of the asset sells the asset and then leases it back. When the party sells the asset, it receives the sale proceeds and the asset is leased back, the original owner of the asset gets the right to use the asset. In a sale-and-lease-back, the lessor buys the asset from the lessee instead of from the vendor. Under this lease arrangement, the lessee gets the funds (sale proceeds of the asset) immediately for its other uses and at the same time enjoys the economic use of the asset. The sale-and-lease-back can bring down the debt-equity ratio, thereby creating additional borrowing capacity for the lessee. Thus, sale-and-lease-back is a special type of leasing that provides liquidity to the lessee. This arrangement might also result in substantial tax gains.

*In a **sale-and-lease-back,** a firm that owns an asset sells it to another party and then takes it back on lease.*

18.2.3 Banks as Lessors

Banks and financial institutions are widely involved in lease transactions. Banks can engage in net leases for different kinds of assets and properties. In a *net lease*, a bank as a lessor is not directly or indirectly obligated to assume the expenses of maintaining the asset or property that is leased out. A bank generally acquires the asset to be leased only after it enters into a legally enforceable agreement with the lessee indemnifying the bank against a loss in connection with the acquisition of the leased asset. Banks engage in leasing in order to diversify their business or to increase their sources of revenue. Leasing is thus a bank product that can satisfy the needs of its customers. However, leasing is safer than other bank products (commercial loans, for example) because leasing transactions are more secure. Also, banks leases are more profitable than commercial loans because of tax advantages inherent in the lease structure. At the same time, the cost of lease (lease rental) will be less if banks are the lessors because banks can mobilize the funds required for leasing at a lower cost compared to other leasing companies. However, banks also face certain risks in lease financing. These risks are credit risk, interest rate risk, liquidity risk, compliance risk and transaction risk. *Credit risk* is the risk to earnings or capital arising from the failure of lessee to honour the terms of the lease. Of course, if the lessee defaults, the bank as the lessor can recover the asset expeditiously. *Interest rate risk* is the risk to earnings or capital arising from fluctuations in interest rates in the economy. Fixed interest rates expose the banks to interest rate risk when interest rates change. Like commercial bank loans, leases are also subject to interest rate risk. Unlike commercial bank loans, the interest on which is explicit, lease transactions are negotiated and underwritten based on an implicit interest rate. Interest rate risk can also arise from prepayments or early termination of leases. *Liquidity risk* is the risk to income or principal amount arising from a bank's inability to liquidate its assets quickly and

Banks face certain risks such as credit risk, interest rate risk, liquidity risk, compliance risk and transaction risk in lease financing.

without minimal loss in value. An asset's liquidity risk is assessed in terms of the expected life of the asset and the ease with which it can be converted into cash. *Compliance risk* is the risk to income or capital arising from non-compliance with laws, rules, regulations and ethical standards. *Transaction risk* is the risk to income and capital arising from problems with servicing of the lease transaction.

18.3 Economic Evaluation of a Lease

To buy an asset, a firm requires an amount of funds equivalent to the cost of the asset at the time of buying. In case the asset is used on lease, the firm has to pay lease rentals periodically during the lease period. Both buying and leasing have tax implications. In case of a lease, the total amount of lease rentals is a charge on the profits of the lessee's business. That is, lease rentals are tax-deductible expenses for the lessee. But the same lease rentals are subject to tax in the hands of the lessor.

Alternatively, if the asset is purchased, the amount of depreciation is a charge in computing taxable income. Thus, a firm will lose a series of depreciation tax shields when it acquires the asset on lease. If an asset is purchased with borrowed funds, the interest on such funds is also a tax-deductible expense. Further, with an asset purchase, the purchaser can realize the salvage value of the asset, whereas with a lease, the lessor enjoys the benefit of salvage value, which is also subject to tax.

Both the lessor and the lessee evaluate a lease from their own perspective. The user of an asset has the option of either buying the asset or taking the asset on lease. Before taking the decision, the user must determine whether leasing the asset involves a lower cost than buying it. Similarly, the supplier of an asset has two alternatives— to lease the asset or not lease the asset. Therefore, the supplier of the asset should know whether lease payments could provide the required return on the capital invested in the asset to be leased or not and accordingly take the decision.

A lease transaction starts with the identification of an asset, its supplier and price, among other things, by the lessee. Then the lessor and the lessee negotiate various terms of the lease, which might culminate in a lease contract. A typical lease analysis is simply concerned with whether to obtain the use of the asset by a lease or by a purchase. Before taking such a decision, a firm might have to decide whether to acquire the economic use of an asset. In other words, a leasing decision primarily involves an investment decision by a firm. Depending on the cash flows associated with the asset as well as the required rate of return, the lessee decides whether or not to go in for the asset. So the financial viability of the project should be determined apart from the specific method of financing the asset. A decision to acquire the use of an asset is an investment decision, which involves a capital budgeting process. By applying the discounted cash flow (DCF) technique, a firm can decide whether or not to accept the asset. Once the decision to use an asset is taken, the firm then decides how it is to be financed.

An asset can be purchased with borrowed funds or it can be acquired by a lease. If the asset is acquired by a lease, the lease is comparable to a loan as the firm is required to make a specified series of payments. Leasing is thus a substitute for debt financing because lease financing has the same capital structure effect as that of debt financing.

A lease decision can be taken by applying an appropriate model. The most popular models are as follows.

- Weingartner's model
- The equivalent loan model
- The Bower–Herringer–Williamson model
- Bower's model

These models are described in the following sections.

18.3.1 Weingartner's Model

This model involves the following steps:

- Compute the net present value (*NPV*) of the lease alternative or NPV_l;
- Compute the *NPV* of the purchase alternative or NPV_p;
- Select the best alternative.

$$NPV_p = -I_0 = \sum_{i=1}^{n} \frac{X_i(1-T)}{(1+K)^i} + \sum_{i=1}^{n} \frac{D_i T}{(1+K)^i} + \frac{SV}{(1+K)^n}$$

Where

I_0 = Initial purchase price of the asset including incidental expenses, if any
X_i= Net operating income at the end of period i
T = Tax rate
D_i= Amount of depreciation at the end of period i
SV = Salvage value of the asset (post-tax)
K = Weighted average cost of capital
n = Number of periods to the end of the lease

$$NPV_l = -L - \sum_{i=1}^{n-1} \frac{L}{(1+K)^i} + \sum_{i=1}^{n} \frac{LT}{(1+K)^i} + \sum_{i=1}^{n} \frac{X_i(1-T)}{(1+K)^i}$$

Where

L = Lease rentals

In the NPV_l model, the first factor, that is $-L$, represents advance lease rentals, if any, paid by the lessee. If advance lease rentals are paid, then the regular lease rentals are required to be paid only for $n-1$ periods. Further, the payment of lease rentals and tax shield on them can occur at different points of time. The stream of operating incomes (X_i) would be identical to those in the NPV_P assuming that the lessor bears the maintenance and other related expenses. In some cases, the lessor allows the lessee to acquire the leased asset by paying a nominal amount. In such cases, the lessee might have the salvage value of the net asset of the amount paid to the lessor at the end of the lease period and this can appropriately be incorporated in the NPV_l model.

The two alternatives—NPV_l and NPV_p—are mutually exclusive, which means that only one of them can be accepted. The alternative with a higher positive NPV is the obvious choice. The lessee can go in for leasing of the asset if the net advantage of leasing (NAL) is positive. That is, the lessee can go in for lease of the asset if the $NPV_l > NPV_p > 0$. Alternatively, a firm can go in for buying of the asset if $NPV_p > NPV_l > 0$. The difference between NPV_l and NPV_p is the NAL.

Example 18.1

KK Industries Limited plans to acquire automated assembly line equipment with a five-year life at a cost of INR 55 million. The company can borrow the required INR 55 million at a simple interest rate of 10 per cent per annum. The equipment is expected to have a scrap value of zero after five years of use.

The company can lease the equipment for five years at a rental charge of INR 12 million payable at the beginning of each year. The lease contract stipulates that the lessor will maintain the equipment at no additional charge to the company. However, if the company borrows and buys, it will have to bear the cost of maintenance, which will be done by the equipment manufacturer at a fixed contract rate of INR 0.25 million per year, payable at the beginning of each year. The company's tax rate is 30 per cent. Advise the company on acquiring the equipment.

Solution

Table 18.1 shows the cash flows under the borrowing and leasing options.

Table 18.1 Cash flows under borrowing and lease options (figures in INR million)

	Year 0	*Year 1*	*Year 2*	*Year 3*	*Year 4*	*Year 5*
1. After-tax loan payments	—	(3.85)	(3.85)	(3.85)	(3.85)	(58.85)
2. Maintenance cost	(0.25)	(0.25)	(0.25)	(0.25)	(0.25)	(0.25)

(Continued)

3. Tax saving on maintenance cost	0.075	0.075	0.075	0.075	0.075	0.075
4. Depreciation tax shield	—	3.3	3.3	3.3	3.3	3.3
Net cash flows	(0.175)	(0.725)	(0.725)	(0.725)	(0.725)	(55.55)
Present values*	(0.175)	(0.6778)	(0.6329)	(0.5916)	(0.5532)	(39.607)
5. Lease payments	(12)	(12)	(12)	(12)	(12)	—
6. Tax saving due to lease payments	3.6	3.6	3.6	3.6	3.6	—
Net cash flows	(8.4)	(8.4)	(8.4)	(8.4)	(8.4)	—
Present values*	(8.4)	(7.85)	(7.33)	(6.85)	(6.41)	—

Note:* Discounted at after-tax cost of debt

Present value of cost of borrowing and buying: INR 42.24 million

Present value of cost of leasing: INR 36.84 million

Net advantage of leasing = Present value of cost of owning – Present value of cost of leasing
= INR 42.24 million – INR 36.84 million
= INR 5.4 million

Thus the company is advised to go in for leasing of the asset.

Example 18.2

Royal Industries Ltd is considering investment in equipment, the details of which are as follows:

The equipment costs INR 30 million and is expected to have a five-year effective life with zero salvage value. The company follows the straight-line method of depreciation. The company can buy the equipment through a term loan and its own funds in the ratio 2:1. The loan carries a simple rate of interest of 10 per cent and is repayable in five equal annual instalments. The equipment is expected to generate an incremental EBDIT (earnings before depreciation, interest and taxes) of INR 20 million per year. The company has received an offer from a leasing company. The offer details are as follows.

Primary lease period: 5 years

Management fee: 0.5 per cent of cost of equipment

Annual lease rentals: INR 300/INR 1,000

The lease rentals are payable annually in arrears but the management fee is payable immediately on signing the lease. The corporate tax rate is 30 per cent and the marginal cost of capital for Royal Industries is 12 per cent. Which alternative is better for the company?

Solution

Net present value of the net cash flows associated with the buying option can be calculated as follows.

After-tax EBIT stream of cash flows = INR 20 million (1– 0.3) = INR 14 million per annum. The present value of EBIT for five-year period is as follows.

$$PV = \frac{14}{(1+0.12)} + \frac{14}{(1+0.12)^2} + \frac{14}{(1+0.12)^3} + \frac{14}{(1+0.12)^4} + \frac{14}{(1+0.12)^5}$$

= INR 50.47 million

Depreciation tax-shield = Annual depreciation × tax rate
= INR 5 million × 0.3
= INR 1.5 million each year

(Continued)

Present value of depreciation tax shield (discounted at 12%) for five years = INR 5.41 million

Interest tax shield:

Loan amount = INR 20 million

Interest amount at the rate of 10% = INR 2 million per annum

Tax shield = INR 2 million × 0.30 (tax rate) = INR 0.6 million per annum

PV of interest tax shield (discounted at 12%) for five years = INR 2.16 million

Net present value of purchase option denoted by NPV (B) = (–) Initial investment + *PV* of EBIT + *PV* of depreciation tax shield – *PV* of interest + *PV* of interest tax shield – *PV* of salvage value

NPV(B) = (–) INR 30 million + INR 50.47 million + INR 5.41 million – INR 7.21 million + INR 2.16 million + 0 million = INR 20.83 million.

Net present value of the net cash flows associated with the leasing option can be calculated as follows:

Annual lease rentals at the rate of INR 300/INR 1,000 for the asset cost of INR 30 million = INR 9 million per annum

PV of lease rentals for the five year period = INR 32.45 million

PV of tax shield on lease rentals = INR 9 million × 0.30 (tax rate) × 3.605(PVFA) = INR 9.73 million

Management fee = INR 0.3 million per annum

Tax shield on management fee = INR 0.3 million × 0.3 (tax rate)
= INR 0.09 million *PV* of tax shield on management fee
= INR 0.09 million (as paid immediately on agreement).

The net present value of leasing denoted by NPV (L) is calculated as follows:

NPV (L) = (–) PV of lease rentals + *PV* of EBIDT + *PV* of tax shield on lease rentals – *PV* of management fee + *PV* of tax shield on management fee
= (–) INR 32.45 million + INR 50.47 million + INR 9.73 million – INR 0.3 million + INR 0.09 million
= INR 27.54 million

Since *NPV (L)* > *NPV (B)*, the equipment may be leased.

18.3.2 The Equivalent Loan Model

As the name indicates, an equivalent loan is the loan amount which requires debt servicing (stream of fixed commitments) as equivalent to the financial obligations of the firm under the lease option. How much of loan amount can be serviced with the proposed lease liability is the focal point of this method. Example 18.3 explains the step-by-step calculations under the equivalent loan model.

Example 18.3

Ramco Ceramics Limited is contemplating investing in equipment costing INR 20 million. The company can purchase the equipment by raising additional debt at a simple interest rate of 10 per cent per annum. The equipment has an effective life of five years with zero salvage value. The company follows the straight-line method of depreciation and is in the 30 per cent tax bracket. Alternatively, the company can take the equipment on a finance lease with a five-year primary period at INR 5 million payable annually in arrears. Should the company use the asset on lease?

Solution

Table 18.2 shows the cash flows of lease financing.

Table 18.2 Cash flows of lease financing (figures in INR million)

	Year 0	*Year 1*	*Year 2*	*Year 3*	*Year 4*	*Year 5*
1. Purchase price avoided	20	—	—	—	—	—
2. Depreciation	—	(4)	(4)	(4)	(4)	(4)
3. Depreciation tax shield	—	(1.2)	(1.2)	(1.2)	(1.2)	(1.2)
4. Before-tax lease rentals	—	(5)	(5)	(5)	(5)	(5)

(Continued)

Table 18.2 (Cont.)

	Year 0	Year 1	Year 2	Year 3	Year 4	Year 5
5. After-tax lease rentals	—	(3.5)	(3.5)	(3.5)	(3.5)	(3.5)
6. Net cash flows	20	(4.7)	(4.7)	(4.7)	(4.7)	(4.7)

With leasing, the purchase price of the asset is avoided. But at the same time, the lessee loses the depreciation tax shield as well as the net salvage value of the asset. The lease rentals paid by the lessee are tax-deductible expenses.

The equivalent loan method involves determining the amount of loan that can be serviced with these cash flows.

In the last year (fifth year), there is a net cash flow of INR 4.7 million, which can service the principal amount at the beginning of the fifth year and after-tax interest for the fifth year. By applying the capital recovery factor, the amount of INR 4.7 million can be apportioned as principal amount and interest.

The after-tax interest rate is 7 per cent, [i.e., 0.10/(1 − 0.30)]. Let the outstanding loan amount at the beginning of the year be *P*.

Thus, the outstanding loan amount (principal) at the beginning of the fifth year can be calculated as follows:

$$1.07P = \text{INR } 4.7 \text{ million}$$
$$P = \text{INR } 4.39 \text{ million}$$

The after-tax interest for the fifth year is INR 0.31 (i.e., INR 4.7 million – INR 4.39 million). Thus, before-tax interest paid is INR 0.44 million [i.e., INR 0.31 million/0.70].

The outstanding loan amount at the beginning of the fourth year would be equal to principal repayments in the fourth and fifth years. The principal amount repaid in the fifth year is INR 4.39 million and the principal amount repaid in the fourth year is calculated as follows:

The after-tax interest in the fourth year would be:

$$0.07(P + \text{INR } 4.39 \text{ million}) = 0.07P + \text{INR } 0.307 \text{ million}$$

The total amount paid in the fourth year is INR 4.7 million. This includes the repayment of the principal amount and after-tax interest. To find the principal amount for the fourth year, the following equation can be used:

$$1.07P + \text{INR } 0.307 \text{ million} = \text{INR } 4.7 \text{ million}$$
$$P = \text{INR } 4.1 \text{ million}$$

Thus, in the fourth year, the principal amount repaid is INR 4.1 million and the after-tax interest paid is INR 0.595 million (i.e., INR 4.7 million – INR 4.1 million). The before-tax interest paid in the fourth year is INR 0.85 million [i.e., INR 0.595 million/0.70].

The outstanding loan at the beginning of the third year would be equal to the principal repayments in the third, fourth and fifth years. The principal amount repaid in the fourth and fifth years are INR 4.1 million and INR 4.39 million, respectively.

$$0.07(P + \text{INR } 4.39 \text{ million} + \text{INR } 4.1 \text{ million}) = \text{INR } 4.7 \text{ million}$$
$$0.07P + \text{INR } 0.3073 \text{ million} + \text{INR } 0.2874 \text{ million} = \text{INR } 4.7 \text{ million}$$
$$1.07P = \text{INR } 4.7 \text{ million} - \text{INR } 0.3073 \text{ million} - \text{INR } 0.2874 \text{ million}$$
$$P = \text{INR } 3.84 \text{ million}$$

Thus, P = INR 3.84 million. This is the principal amount repaid in the third year. The after-tax interest paid in the third year is INR 0.86 million and the before-tax interest paid is INR 1.23 million (i.e., INR 0.86 million/0.70).

The outstanding loan at the beginning of the second year would be equal to principal repayments in the second, third, fourth and fifth years. The principal amount repaid in the third, fourth and fifth years are INR 3.84 million, INR 4.1 million and INR 4.39 million, respectively.

$$0.07(P + \text{INR } 4.39 \text{ million} + \text{INR } 4.10 \text{ million} + \text{INR } 3.84 \text{ million}) = 0.07P$$
$$+ \text{INR } 0.3073 \text{ million} + \text{INR } 0.2874 \text{ million} + \text{INR } 0.2688 \text{ million}$$
$$1.07P = \text{INR } 4.7 \text{ million} - \text{INR } 0.3073 \text{ million} - \text{INR } 0.2874 \text{ million} - \text{INR } 0.2688 \text{ million}$$
$$P = \text{INR } 3.59 \text{ million}$$

Thus, in the second year, the principal amount repaid is INR 3.59 million. The after-tax interest is INR 1.11 million (i.e., INR 4.7 million – INR 3.59 million) and before-tax interest paid is INR 1.59 million (i.e., INR 1.11 million/0.70).

(Continued)

The outstanding loan at the beginning of the first year would be equal to principal repayments in the second, third, fourth and fifth years. The principal amount repaid in the second, third, fourth and fifth years are INR 3.59 million, INR 3.84 million, INR 4.1 million and INR 4.39 million, respectively.

$$0.07\ (P + \text{INR } 4.39 \text{ million} + \text{INR } 4.1 \text{ million} + \text{INR } 3.84 \text{ million} + \text{INR } 3.59 \text{ million})$$
$$1.07P = \text{INR } 4.7 \text{ million} - \text{INR } 0.3073 \text{ million} - \text{INR } 0.2874 \text{ million} - \text{INR } 0.2688 \text{ million} - \text{INR } 0.2513 \text{ million}$$
$$P = \text{INR } 3.35 \text{ million.}$$

This is the principal amount repaid in the first year. The after-tax interest is INR 1.35 million (i.e., INR 4.7 million – INR 3.35 million) and before-tax interest paid is INR 1.93 million (i.e., INR 1.35 million/0.70).

Table 18.3 shows the details of the debt servicing.

Table 18.3 Debt servicing (cash flows in INR million)

Year	*Net cash flows*	*Before-tax interest*	*After-tax interest*	*Principal repaid*	*Amount of loan outstanding*
0	—	—	—	—	19.27
1	4.7	1.93	1.35	3.35	15.92
2	4.7	1.59	1.11	3.59	12.33
3	4.7	1.23	0.86	3.84	8.49
4	4.7	0.85	0.6	4.1	4.39
5	4.7	0.44	0.31	4.39	0

Thus, the lease cash flows can service an equivalent loan of INR 19.27 million while the available lease finance for the same cash flows is INR 20 million. Thus, lease financing is advantageous and, therefore, the company can go in for using the asset on lease.

18.3.3 The Bower–Herringer–Williamson (BHW) Model

According to the BHW model, the lease-related cash flow stream is divided into two parts—financing and tax shields. The cash flow stream related to financing is called the financial advantage (*FA*) of leasing, which can be defined as follows:

FA(L) = Initial investment – *PV* of lease payments

The cash flow stream related to tax shields and residual value is called the operating advantage (*OA*) of leasing, which is defined as follows:

OA(L) = *PV* of tax-shields – residual value of the asset

If *FA(L)* plus *OA(L)* is positive, the asset can be leased. Otherwise, the asset can be purchased. A negative *FA(L)* signifies financial disadvantage of leasing and a negative *OA(L)* indicates operating disadvantage of leasing. If *FA(L)* plus *OA(L)* is negative, leasing is not beneficial.

Example 18.4

A company is considering acquiring an asset costing INR 10 million. The company can purchase the asset by raising an additional loan at a cost of 10 per cent per annum, which can be repaid in equated annual instalments.

Alternatively, the company can acquire the asset on a finance lease with a five-year primary period at a rate of INR 300/INR 1,000 payable annually in arrears. The company's tax rate is 30 per cent.

The asset will have a five-year life with a salvage value of INR 1 million.

Should the company use the asset on lease?

Solution

The amount of each instalment of the loan is calculated as follows.

$$\frac{10}{PVIFA(10,5)} = \frac{10}{3.791} = \text{INR } 2.64 \text{ million}$$

(Continued)

The cash flows for servicing the debt are shown in Table 18.4.

Table 18.4 Cash flows for servicing of debt (figures in INR million)

Year	*Loan outstanding at the beginning*	*Rate of interest*	*Interest component*	*Capital component*	*Instalment*
1	10	10%	1	1.64	2.64
2	8.36	10%	0.84	1.8	2.64
3	6.56	10%	0.66	1.98	2.64
4	4.58	10%	0.46	2.18	2.64
5	2.40	10%	0.24	2.4	2.64

PV of interest tax shield (discounted at after-tax cost of debt) = INR 0.82 million
PV of interest amounts (at a discount rate of 10%) = INR 2.56 million
Depreciation tax shield = INR 0.54 million
PV of depreciation tax shield (discounted at 7%) = INR 2.21 million
Lease rentals = INR 3 million per annum (at INR 300/INR 1,000)
PV of lease rentals (at a discount rate of 10%) = INR 11.37 million
Tax shield on lease rentals = INR 0.9 million per annum
PV of tax shield on lease rentals (discounted at after-tax cost of debt) = INR 3.69 million
Financial advantage of leasing = INR 10 million – INR 11.37 million = (–) INR 1.37 million
Operating advantage of leasing = *PV* of tax shield on lease rentals – *PV* of tax shield on interest – *PV* of tax shield on depreciation – *PV* of salvage value
= INR 3.69 million – INR 0.82 million – INR 2.21 million – INR 0.713 million
= (–) INR 0.053 million
Overall advantage = INR (–) 1.37 million – INR 0.021 million
= (–) INR 1.423 million
Since there is an overall disadvantage, the asset cannot be used on lease.

18.3.4 Bower's Model

According to Bower's model, the cost of purchase (*COP*) is defined as follows.

COP = Initial Investment – *PV* of depreciation tax shield – *PV* of the net salvage value

Similarly, the cost of leasing (*COL*) is defined as follows.

COL = *PV* of lease rentals – *PV* of tax shield on lease rentals + *PV* of tax shield on interest

If *COL* > *COP*, it is better to purchase the asset and if *COP* > *COL*, the asset may be leased.

18.3.5 Evaluation of a Lease: The Lessor's Point of View

The lessor generally considers leasing as a business proposition to earn profit. So the lessor tries to evaluate a lease to determine the possible rate of return on the amount invested in the asset to be leased out. In other words, the lessor tries to find out how much his lease rentals should be in order to break even and, accordingly, he negotiates with the lessee on the suitable terms and conditions of the lease. The evaluation process involves the following steps.

- Determining the initial investment in the asset;
- Identification of periodic cash flows (such as lease payments, maintenance expenses);
- Estimation of the salvage value of the asset; and
- Finding the *NPV* by applying a suitable cost of capital.

Example 18.5

A firm is engaged in the business of leasing. There is a request from a manufacturing company for equipment on lease. The details of the equipment are as follows.

(Continued)

Equipment cost: INR 20 million
Expected salvage value of the equipment after five years: INR 2 million
The firm is in the 30 per cent tax bracket and its marginal cost of capital is 12 per cent. Calculate the break-even rental for the firm.

Solution

Let L = Annual break-even lease rental
Cost of equipment = INR 20 million
PV of lease rentals = $L \times PVIFA$ (12,5)
= $3.605L$
PV of tax on lease rentals = $3.605L \times 0.3$
= $1.0815L$
Annual depreciation = INR 3.6 million
Depreciation tax shield per annum = INR 1.08 million
PV of depreciation tax shield = INR 3.8934 million
PV of salvage value = INR 2 million × 0.567
= INR 1.134 million
The value of L can be obtained as follows:
$- 20 + 3.605L - 1.0815L + 3.8934 + 1.134 = 0$
L = INR 5.94 million
Thus, the firm should receive INR 5.94 million annually as lease rentals for five years in order to break even.

Example 18.6

ABC Ltd is considering acquiring machinery. The cost of the machinery is INR 10 million. The machinery will have an effective life of five years with no salvage value. The company's tax rate is 30 per cent. The marginal cost of capital for the company is 12 per cent.

ABC Ltd has received a lease proposal from First Leasing Company at a lease rental of INR 300/INR 1,000 payable every year in arrears. First Leasing Company expects to get at least 8 per cent on the lease. Determine the break-even rentals for ABC and also for First Leasing Company.

Solution

Cost of the machinery = INR 10 million
PV of lease rentals = $L \times PVIFA(12,5)$
= $3.605L$
PV of tax shield on lease rentals = $1.082L$
PV of tax shield foregone on depreciation
Annual depreciation = INR 2 million
Depreciation tax shield = INR 0.6 million
PV of depreciation tax shield = INR 0.6 million × 3.605 = INR 2.16 million
Table 18.5 presents the displaced debt repayment schedule.

Table 18.5 Displaced debt repayment schedule

Year	*Amount outstanding at the beginning*	*Capital component*	*Interest component*	*Instalment*
1	$3.605L$	$0.567L$	$0.433L$	$1L$
2	$3.038L$	$0.635L$	$0.365L$	$1L$
3	$2.403L$	$0.712L$	$0.288L$	$1L$
4	$1.691L$	$0.797L$	$0.203L$	$1L$
5	$0.894L$	$0.894L$	$0.106L$	$1L$

(Continued)

PV of interest tax shield on displaced debt = 0.322*L*

Setting the *NAL* of the lease proposal equal to zero,

$$10 - 3.605L + 1.082L - 2.16 - 0.322L = 0$$
$$L = \text{INR 2.76 million per year}$$

Thus, the maximum lease rental that the lessee will be prepared to pay is INR 2.76 million per annum.

The break-even rentals for First Leasing Company would be as follows.

Cost of the asset = INR 10 million

PV of lease rentals (at 8% minimum required return) = 3.993*L*

PV of tax on lease rentals = 1.2*L*

PV of depreciation tax shield = 0.6 × 3.993 = INR 2.4 million

By putting the values in equation form,

$$-10 + 3.993L - 1.2L + 2.4 = 0$$
$$L = \text{INR 2.72 million}$$

The minimum lease rental that First Leasing Company should charge to earn 8 per cent return is INR 2.72 million per annum, while the maximum lease rental ABC Ltd will be prepared to pay is INR 2.76 million per annum. The difference in the break-even lease rentals of the lessor and the lessee will give scope for negotiations. The benefit from leasing mainly comes from the lower cost of capital of the lessor.

18.3.6 The Internal Rate of Return (IRR) Method

A lease can also be evaluated by using the IRR method. The IRR of a lease contract can be defined as follows:

$$I_0 - \sum_{t=1}^{n} \frac{(L_t - MC_t)(1-T) + DTS_t}{(1+r)^t} - \frac{SV_n}{(1+r)^n} = 0$$

Where

I_0 = Initial cost of the leased asset

L_t = Lease rentals paid at the end of the period t

DTS_t = Depreciation tax shield in period t

T = Corporate tax rate

MC_t = Maintenance cost for period t

SV_n = After-tax net salvage value

r = Internal rate of return (IRR)

n = Number of periods to the end of the lease

By trial and error, the IRR can be found. Thus, the IRR is the rate of discount that equates the cost of the asset with the present value of the after-tax lease payments, the present value of after-tax maintenance cost (assumed to be borne by the lessor), the present value of the depreciation tax shield and the present value of the net salvage value. Thus, the cost of leasing includes lease payments and depreciation tax shield and net salvage value foregone by virtue of leasing the asset instead of purchasing it. The present value of the maintenance cost—if it is to be borne by the lessor—should also form part of the equation. It may be noted that the equation implicitly includes the loss of the interest tax shield on debt displaced by leasing.

The after-tax cost of leasing (IRR) is compared with the after-tax cost of borrowing alternative. The alternative with the lowest rate is chosen.

The popular methods of structuring lease rentals are the equated, stepped-up, ballooned, deferred and bell-shaped methods.

18.4 Structuring of Lease Rentals

One of the advantages of lease financing is the flexibility of the process. Lease financing, being flexible, allows both the lessor and the lessee to structure the lease payments according to their convenience. The lease rentals can be structured in such a way as to synchronize with the cash flow pattern of the leased asset. For example, if the cash flows to be generated by the leased asset are to increase steadily over the life of the asset, the lease rentals can be structured accordingly.

If the leased asset requires a gestation period to generate cash flows, the lease rentals can be structured with a deferment period.

There are four popular methods of structuring lease rentals—equated, stepped-up, ballooned, deferred and bell-shaped. Each of these methods is explained with a numerical example here.

Example 18.7

M/S Chennai Financial Services Ltd is engaged in equipment leasing. In a particular case, it expects to get a gross yield of 20 per cent on leasing equipment costing INR 1 million for a period of five years. The company does not expect any residual value of the equipment after five years.

Calculate the lease rentals per INR 1,000 so as to get a return of 20 per cent per annum according to: (i) equated rentals (rentals will be collected annually in arrears); (ii) stepped-up rentals (rentals will be stepped up by 10 per cent every year); (iii) deferred rentals (deferment period of two years); (iv) bell-shaped rentals (lease rentals will be stepped up by 20 per cent and then by 30 per cent and subsequently stepped down in the reverse order in the fourth and fifth years); and (v) ballooned rentals (annual lease rentals of INR 0.18 million for years 1 to 4).

Solution

(i) Table 18.6 presents the calculation of lease rentals using equated rentals.

Table 18.6 Equated rentals

Year	*Lease rental*	*PV factor at 20%*	*Present value*
1	L	0.833	$0.833L$
2	L	0.694	$0.694L$
3	L	0.579	$0.579L$
4	L	0.482	$0.482L$
5	L	0.402	$0.402L$
Total			$2.99L$

Lease rentals per annum and per INR 1,000 will be:

$$L = \frac{1000}{2.99} = \text{INR } 334.45$$

(ii) Table 18.7 shows the calculation of lease rentals using stepped-up rentals.

Table 18.7 Stepped-up rentals

(1) Year	*(2) Lease rental*	*(3) PVIF at 20% as multiplied by (2)*	*(4) Present value of lease rentals*
1	$L(1.00)$	$0.833 \times 1L$	$0.833L$
2	$L(1.10)$	$0.694 \times 1.1L$	$0.763L$
3	$L(1.10)^2$	$0.579 \times 1.21L$	$0.701L$
4	$L(1.10)^3$	$0.482 \times 1.331L$	$0.642L$
5	$L(1.10)^4$	$0.402 \times 1.4641L$	$0.589L$
Total			$3.528L$

Lease rentals to be charged in the first year per INR 1,000:

$$L = \frac{1000}{3.528} = \text{INR } 283.45$$

(Continued)

Lease rentals in the subsequent years are as shown in Table 18.8.

Table 18.8 Lease rentals in the subsequent years

Year	*Lease rentals (INR)*
2	311.8
3	342.98
4	376.99
5	414.97

(iii) The calculation of lease rentals using deferred rentals will be as follows:

Lease rentals are deferred for the first two years and, therefore, the lease rentals for the first two years will be zero. For years 3–5, the present value of lease rentals will be 1.463*L*. Therefore, the lease rentals per INR 1,000 for years three through five are as follows.

$$L = \frac{1000}{1.463} = \text{INR } 683.53$$

(iv) The calculation of lease rentals using bell-shaped rentals will be as follows:

The lease rentals will be stepped up by 20 per cent and then by 30 per cent. Subsequently, they will be stepped down in the reverse order in the fourth and fifth years.

Table 18.9 shows the present value of lease rentals.

Table 18.9 Present value of lease rentals

(1) Year	*(2) Lease rental*	*(3) PVIF at 20% as multiplied by (2)*	*(4) Present value of lease rentals*
1	$L(1)$	$0.833 \times 1L$	0.833L
2	$L(1.2)$	$0.694 \times 1.2L$	0.8328L
3	$L(1.3)$	$0.579 \times 1.3L$	0.7527L
4	$L(1.2)$	$0.482 \times 1.2L$	0.5784L
5	$L(1.3)$	$0.402 \times 1.3L$	0.5226L
Total			3.5195L

Lease rentals to be charged in the first year per INR 1,000:

$$L = \frac{1000}{3.5195} = \text{INR } 284.13$$

Lease rentals in the subsequent years are as shown in Table 18.10.

Table 18.10 Lease rentals in the subsequent years

Year	*Lease rentals (INR)*
2	340.96
3	369.37
4	340.96
5	369.37

(v) The calculation of lease rentals using ballooned rentals will be as follows:

Annual lease rental of INR 0.18 million will be paid for years 1–4. The lease rentals to be paid in the fifth year for the equipment will be as follows:

$$0.18 \text{ million} \times PVIFA(20,4) + L \times PVIF(20,5) = \text{INR 1 million}$$
$$0.18 \text{ million} \times 2.589 + 0.402L = \text{INR 1 million}$$
$$L = 1.328 \text{ million}$$

18.5 Discount Rate

In the evaluation of leasing, the **discount rate** plays an important role. The acceptance of lease or otherwise also depends on the discount rate. Usually, the weighted average cost of capital is taken as the discount rate. The weighted average cost of capital is defined as follows:

*The **discount rate** is the rate at which future cash flows are discounted to arrive at their present values.*

$$K = K_e \frac{E}{D+E} + r(1-T)\frac{D}{D+E}$$

Where

K_e = Cost of equity

r = Interest rate

D = Debt capital in the firm

E = Equity capital in the firm

K = Weighted average cost of capital

There are also cases in which lease payments are treated as debt payments, and, accordingly, the lease payments are discounted at the lessee's after-tax borrowing rate. The after-tax lease rentals and depreciation tax shields can also be discounted at the after-tax borrowing rate of the lessee. However, the net salvage value of the asset is always discounted at the lessee's overall cost of capital. A discount rate higher or lower than the marginal cost of capital can be used in cases where the risk associated with the cash flows is significantly higher or lower than the risk of existing investments. Thus, the discount rate reflects the riskiness of the cash flows being discounted. The discount rate used by the lessor might be different because of the difference in the cost of capital. Generally, the cost of capital for the lessor is lower than that of the lessee because leasing companies can raise funds at cheaper rates. Further, the debt-equity ratio of the lessor is normally much higher than that of the lessee.

18.6 Advantages and Limitations of Leasing

The main reason for the popularity of leasing is its off-balance sheet funding of assets. Leasing is better than straightforward lending, particularly during a recession. It is also said that leasing is anti-recession because the lessee can keep his investment low and reserve the cancellation option of lease in an environment of uncertainty. The lessor also finds himself in a better situation with a title over the asset and a remarketing opportunity. More specifically, the advantages of leasing are as follows.

- Leasing provides complete financing for the asset as the user of the asset can avoid payment for the cost of the asset. It is only in some cases that advance payments are made towards lease rentals.
- The lessee of the asset is not obliged to show the leased asset on the balance sheet if it is an operating lease. So the asset acquired on the lease can be off-the-balance-sheet. The leased asset, being owned by the lessor, is not shown by the lessee firm in its balance sheet. The lease payments are also not shown as loan obligations on the liabilities side of the balance sheet. This helps in maintaining a favourable set of financial ratios. Thus, leasing provides off-the-balance-sheet financing. Nevertheless, the debt servicing capacity of the firm is reduced by its lease payments obligations.
- Leasing offers flexibility to both the lessor and the lessee. The lessor and the lessee can negotiate the terms and conditions of leasing in such a way as to benefit both the parties.
- Leasing is a convenient method of financing. Buying an asset and disposing of it after use might be cumbersome, whereas acquiring the asset on a lease is relatively simple.
- No doubt, leasing is a substitute for debt financing. But borrowing, particularly from institutional agencies, involves long and complicated procedures and formalities. Leasing is thus a relatively easy method of financing assets.
- The risk of obsolescence, which arises due to rapid technological changes, is usually borne by the lessor. But the lessor, being a specialized agency in lease financing, can manage such risks effectively.
- The lessor, being an expert in maintenance and specialized services, can provide better services to the lessee at a lower cost.

- The lessee might be required to pay lower lease rentals when the lessor is benefited with investment-related tax shields.
- Leasing is not always a zero-sum-game. Sometimes, particularly when the lessor and the lessee are in different tax brackets, a lease contract can provide net benefits to both the lessor and the lessee. How much benefit each party is able to get depends on the supply and demand conditions in the leasing market.
- In buying an asset, the lessor can enjoy economies of scale that might not be available to the lessee. The lessor might pass on some of these benefits to the lessee in the form of lower lease rentals.
- If a lessee goes bankrupt, the lessor can get back his asset. However, in the case of borrowing, if the borrower liquidates, the lender finds it more difficult and costly to gain possession of the secured asset.
- A firm can go in for leasing when it is uncertain about the demand for its products or services and thus about how long the asset will be needed.
- Leasing can enable a lessee to use the services of an asset that he otherwise cannot acquire.
- Leasing, particularly cross-border leasing, facilitates transfer of foreign technology to domestic industry.

The main limitations of leasing are as follows:

- It is generally difficult to estimate the cash flows-generating capacity of the leased assets.
- The residual value of the asset is seldom known with certainty.
- Different parties use different rates in determining the present value of the cash flows. This might result in different conclusions about the leasing alternative.
- Lease financing is generally attractive only to those in low or zero tax brackets who are unable to enjoy the full tax benefits associated with owning an asset.
- Although debt financing and lease financing are alternative methods of financing, in certain cases debt payment is higher at the beginning and declines with successive payments. The tax benefits associated with these payments follow the same pattern over time. Therefore, from the point of view of present values, this pattern of debt payments benefits the lessee relative to the lease payments, which are usually constant over time.
- Some lease contracts contain restrictive covenants relating to the utilization of the leased assets. This can put the lessee in a disadvantage position.
- The non-cancellable feature of the financial lease can become a serious disadvantage, particularly when the technology is changing fast.
- Lease financing is relatively costly because the funding costs of leasing companies are generally higher. Banks or financial institutions that provide finance to the leasing companies generally quote higher rates of interest than for a direct-term loan for the same asset.

18.7 The Leasing Industry in India

The leasing industry has played an important role in the Indian economy. It has become a source of financial strength to the consumer goods industry, small scale industries, heavy industries, automobiles, railways and electricity boards. Despite many upheavals, the leasing industry in India has achieved an average annual growth rate of more than 30 per cent, and has become the twelfth to thirteenth largest leasing industry in the world and third largest in Asia after Japan and Korea. The annual leasing business in India is estimated at USD 3.67 billion.

The leasing industry in an organized form came into existence with the establishment of First Leasing Company of India Ltd on September 10, 1973 (see Box 18.1). For several years, First Leasing Company was the only leasing company in India until 20th Century Finance Corporation Ltd, Jayabharat Credit Ltd (formerly known as Jaybharat Credit and Investment Ltd), Motor and General Finance Ltd and Sundaram Finance Ltd entered the industry in the 1980s. There has been an appreciable entry of first-generation entrepreneurs into leasing. Thus, it was only in the 1980s that the leasing industry in India picked up a significant momentum. The Railway Wagon Leasing Scheme is presented in Box 18.2 as an example.

Box 18.1 First Leasing Company of India Ltd

First Leasing Company of India Ltd was incorporated on September 10, 1973. In fact, it was First Leasing that pioneered organized leasing in India. It started leasing operations in 1973, added hire purchase financing in 1986 and diversified into consumer finance in 1988. The company's operations are primarily focused on corporate financing. The product range of the company includes leases, short-term leases, long-term leases, operating leases, sale-and-lease-back, hire purchase, consumer credit, inter-corporate deposit and fixed deposits. The company provides services like syndication, securitization and debt placement. Its activity also involves wind power generation. The major clients are Citibank, Johnson & Johnson, Volvo, Siemens Public Communications, ABB, ANZ Grindlays, IDBI Bank, TELCO, Knoll Pharmaceuticals and Bayer among others. The company head office is located in Chennai, and has 13 branches in various parts of the country. It was appointed as a financial consultant to the financial wing of Indian Railways, namely, the Indian Railway Finance Corporation (IRFC). It has been the chairperson of the Association of Leasing and Financial Services Companies for several years. The income from operations and profit after tax for the year ending March 31, 2009, was INR 19101.7 million and INR 3354.9 million, respectively. With equity capital of INR 2279.1 million, the company's earnings per share (EPS) was INR 14.72 as on March 31, 2009. First Leasing was invited to address the World Leasing Conference in Washington, Sydney, San Francisco, Istanbul, Mexico, Dublin and Hong Kong in 1985, 1988, 1995, 1997, 1998, 2000 and 2001, respectively. The product offerings include vendor leasing, software leasing, green energy and windmills leasing, cross-border leasing, leasing of telecom towers, corporate loans, hire purchase and refinancing of hire purchase. First Leasing is authorized by the Reserve Bank of India to collect fixed deposits from the public. First Leasing has also been rated Ind AA+ (FD), signifying high credit quality, by FITCH Ratings India Private Limited.

In the rest of the world, banks are the frontrunners in the leasing market. But in India, only a few banks like State Bank of India and Canara Bank are in the leasing business through their subsidiaries. Specialized financial institutions are also active in the leasing business. ICICI was one of the pioneers in the leasing business in India.

The post-liberalization era has witnessed a slow but steady increase in foreign investment in Indian leasing. Starting with GE Capital's entry, an increasing number of foreign-owned financial firms and banks are currently engaged or interested in leasing in India. In view of the fierce competition in the industry with the entry of several multinational players, many leasing companies reported heavy losses with a decline in their business. Some leasing companies have announced their plans of quitting the business. Nevertheless, there has been significant growth in the leasing business assisted by funding from banks and financial institutions. Presently, there are more than 400 leasing players in India; about 10 per cent of them operate on a large scale from more than one location and offer funding against a variety of assets. Some of the firms are specialized leasing firms and others are diversified industrial groups with a leasing division. It may be noted that the

Box 18.2 Railway Wagon Leasing Scheme (WLS)

For a long time, the Indian Railway Finance Corporation (IRFC) had complete monopoly in providing wagons for Indian Railways. But it was realized that the IRFC could not attend to the growing infrastructure requirement adequately. Therefore, the government has allowed private players into wagon leasing by the Railway Wagon Leasing Scheme (WLS). The scheme is reserved for companies with a net worth of INR 2,500 million and the minimum relevant experience of five years. The leasing company participant needs to pay a one-time registration fee of INR 50 million (non-refundable) to Indian Railways. This initial fee holds good for 20 years and can be extended for 10 years based on performance. Under the WLS, high-capacity wagons with a payload of at least 2 tonne more than the prevalent 25 tonne and 22.9 tonne axle-load wagons or special-purpose wagons for specific commodities can be owned and leased out to private companies. The wagon leasing contract is a bipartite agreement between the wagon owner and the end user. The wagon lessors pay a maintenance fee to the railways. Companies from sectors like coal, automobiles, steel and cement will be the major beneficiaries as they able to take wagons on lease depending on their requirements.

Source: Based on irfc.nic.in

number of lessors in India exceeds the total number of leasing players in the United States, which is the largest leasing market in the world. Another significant phase in the development of Indian leasing was the Dahotre Committee's recommendations, based on which the RBI formed guidelines on commercial bank funding to leasing companies. Leasing companies are categorized under the non-banking finance companies (NBFCs) as per the RBI classification.

The factors that have facilitated the growth of the leasing industry in India are mentioned here.

- There were no entry barriers to the leasing business till 1996. It was only in 1997 that the RBI made it mandatory for any NBFC to have prior registration with the apex bank.
- The liberalization measures initiated by the Government of India have encouraged a spate of new ventures and fresh investments by existing ventures. Most of these ventures relied on leasing companies for additional funding.
- Tax concessions are also motivators of leasing. The lessee is allowed to claim lease rentals as expense. The lessors are allowed a depreciation allowance. Items such as pollution control devices, energy saving devices, renewable energy devices, rollers in flour mills and gas cylinders are eligible for 100 per cent depreciation. So the companies engaged in other businesses that give them taxable profits have entered the leasing business for tax gains.
- The rapid development in technology is also responsible for many firms increasingly resorting to leasing.

The major problems of the leasing industry are as follows:

- Many of the leasing companies rely extensively on public deposits, which are mostly one-year deposits. But their funds are mostly deployed for longer tenures. Thus, the leasing companies suffer from asset-liability mismatch.
- The major problem of the leasing industry is sales tax on lease transactions. State governments have been allowed to enact a legislation to treat a lease as a deemed sale and thereby subject lease rentals to sales tax. Many state governments have enacted the legislations and included plant and machinery leasing and equipment leasing in the definition of sale. The consequent imposition of sales tax on lease rentals has increased the cost of leasing.
- There is no separate act that governs lease transactions exclusively. Therefore, any dispute arising from lease transactions is dealt under the provisions of the Indian Contract Act, 1872.
- Another problem of leasing is the stamp duty payable on lease agreements in some states. A lease is treated on a par with sale of immovable property and charged ad valorem stamp duty, which works out to a significant amount.

18.8 Hire Purchase

***Hire purchase** is an agreement according to which the hire-purchaser (hirer) agrees to take goods on hire at a stated rental with an option to purchase the goods.*

Hire purchase is a type of instalment credit under which the hire-purchaser (hirer) agrees to take goods on hire at a stated rental with an option to purchase the goods. That is, hire purchase is a form of financial arrangement whereby the owner (hiree) provides an asset to the hirer on hire for a consideration of payment (hire charges) in instalments for a specified period. The ownership of the asset is transferred to the hirer on payment of the last instalment. However, the hirer gets possession of the asset as soon as the hire purchase agreement is signed. The hirer has the right to terminate the agreement at any time before the transfer of ownership of the asset. In other words, the hirer has the option to purchase the asset. If the hirer decides to terminate the agreement, the hirer has to either (i) return the asset and avoid payment of instalments due thereafter, the amounts already paid by the hirer being deemed to be the hire charges of the asset; or (ii) pay the future instalments either fully or at a discount as mutually agreed and take ownership of the asset.

In case a finance company is the hiree, the finance company purchases the equipment from the manufacturer or supplier before it lets it out on hire to the hirer. It is the usual practice for the hirer to make a down payment of a certain percentage of the cost of the equipment and pay the balance with interest in instalments either in advance or in arrears.

Although the ownership of the asset is passed on to the hirer on payment of the last instalment, the hirer is entitled to claim depreciation. When the hirer gets the ownership of the asset, he can also claim the salvage value of the asset. The hire purchase payments are bifurcated into interest payments and principal repayments. The hirer gets tax relief on the interest paid.

A hire purchase is different from an instalment sale. In an *instalment sale*, the legal ownership of the asset is transferred to the buyer as soon as the agreement is made and after payment of the first instalment. The balance amount (instalments) is treated as a secured loan. It may be noted that instalment sale and hire purchase are similar in nature except for the timing of the transfer of ownership.

Essentially, both leasing and hire-purchasing are asset-based financing and similar in many respects. The main distinction is in the nature of assets being financed. Leasing has been used mostly for plants and machinery, while hire purchase has commonly been used for vehicles. In fact, hire purchase in India has thrived as almost the only form of external finance available for commercial vehicles. The hire purchase industry has become synonymous with truck financing. This is mainly because motor vehicle laws give the surest legal protection any law can give to the financier of motor vehicles. Thus, the financier would not have to carry any of the operational risks of a motor vehicle. Any transfer of the vehicle would not be possible without the financier's assent. On the other hand, in the earlier days, the motivation for leasing was investment allowance available for industrial plant and machinery but not for transport vehicles. Hence, leasing has historically clung to industrial plants and machinery. But the factors for which leasing was used mostly for plant and machinery and hire purchase for vehicles have vanished over time. Investment allowance has since been abolished and there are no tax preferences on a lease. The RBI treats lease and hire purchase on a par and has stopped the distinctive classification of leasing and hire-purchase companies. Accounting norms have the same effect on pre-tax income as also balance sheet values, be it a lease or a hire-purchase transaction. Further, motor vehicle laws now treat leases and hire purchases on a par from the viewpoint of financier-protection. However, leasing and hire purchase are subject to different treatment under tax laws, such as income tax and sales tax. The choice between leasing and hire purchase depends on tax consequences.

18.8.1 Evaluation of Hire Purchase

A hirer is required to make payments in equated periodical instalments spread over a certain period. The interest component of each instalment is determined with reference to a specified flat rate of interest. But the equivalent effective rate of interest will be different and can be calculated by different methods.

On the lines of defining the cost of lease, the cost of hire purchase (COHP) is defined as follows.

COHP = Immediate payment (down payment) + *PV* of hiring charges (instalments)
+ *PV* of service charges – *PV* of depreciation tax shield – *PV* of net salvage value

From a hiree's angle, the *NPV* of a hire purchase (NPV(HP)) is as follows:

NPV(HP) = (–) Cost of the asset – initial costs + *PV* of HP instalments
– *PV* of tax on interest component of the HP instalments + *PV* of tax shield on initial costs

As far as accounting is concerned, the cash purchase price of the asset is capitalized and the unpaid instalments are recorded as a secured loan in the books of the hirer. In other words, the hirer shows all HP assets as fixed assets in the balance sheet (without any note thereto) even when he is not the owner of such an asset till the HP period is over. In the books of the hiree, the hire purchase instalments are shown as current asset under the head "stock on hire" and the unearned finance component of the hire purchase instalments is shown as current liability under the head "unmatured finance charges".

Example 18.8

First Leasing Company offers an asset on hire purchase to Indian Breweries on the following terms:
Cost of the asset = INR 0.1 million
Rate of interest = 10% (flat)
Hire purchase period = 4 years
Payment in yearly instalments in arrear
Down payment = 20 per cent
Indian Breweries is in the 30 per cent tax bracket. The asset will have a four-year life with zero salvage value.
What is the effective rate of interest?

(Continued)

Solution

Amount of loan = Cost of the asset – down payment
= INR 0.1 million – INR 0.02 million
= INR 0.8 million

Interest at flat rate = INR 320,000

Annual equated instalments = INR (800000 + 320000)/4
= INR 280,000

There are different methods of distributing the interest amount of INR 320,000 over the hire purchase period. The most commonly used method is the sum-of-years-digit (SYD) method. According to this method, first, the sum of the years of the hiring period is calculated. For a four-year period, the sum is 10. Accordingly, the amount of interest each year is as shown in Table 18.11.

Table 18.11 Amount of interest each year

Year	*Interest*
1	INR 320,000 × 4/10 = INR 128,000
2	INR 320,000 × 3/10 = INR 96,000
3	INR 320,000 × 2/10 = INR 64,000
4	INR 320,000 × 1/10 = INR 32,000

The implied interest rates will be as shown in Table 18.12.

Table 18.12 Implied interest rates

Year	*Principal amount (INR)*	*Instalment amount (INR)*	*Interest paid (INR)*	*Principal amount repaid (INR)*	*Outstanding amount (INR)*	*Implied interest rate (%)*
0	1,000,000			200,000	800,000	
1		280,000	128,000	152,000	648,000	16
2		280,000	96,000	184,000	464,000	14.8
3		280,000	64,000	216,000	248,000	13.8
4		280,000	32,000	248,000	—	12.9

The implied interest rate for the whole period is as follows:

$$800{,}000 = \frac{280{,}000}{(1+r)} + \frac{280{,}000}{(1+r)^2} + \frac{280{,}000}{(1+r)^3} + \frac{280{,}000}{(1+r)^4}$$

Therefore, r = 15% (approximately)

Example 18.9

Sriram Leasing & Hire Purchase Company offers equipment costing about INR 1.5 million on hire purchase to Britannia Industries. The hire purchase instalments will be paid annually for five years. The hiree calculates interest at a flat rate of 18 per cent. Britannia Industries will depreciate the asset for five years and the asset has no salvage value. The corporate tax rate is 35 per cent. Evaluate the hire purchase offer. Britannia Industries is also offered the same asset on lease. How much lease rental is the company prepared to pay?

Solution

Interest for five years at 18% per annum = INR 1,350,000

$$\text{Instalment} = \text{INR}\ \frac{1{,}500{,}000 + 1{,}350{,}000}{5}$$

= INR 570,000

The amount of interest is distributed according to the sum-of-years-digit method and accordingly, the interest amount in each year is as shown in Table 18.13.

(Continued)

Table 18.13 Interest amount in each year

Year	Interest (INR)
1	450,000
2	360,000
3	270,000
4	180,000
5	90,000

Table 18.14 shows the yearly cash flows and the outstanding amount.

Table 18.14 Year-wise cash flows and outstanding amount

Year	Principal amount (INR)	Instalment amount (INR)	Interest paid (INR)	Principal amount repaid (INR)	Outstanding amount (INR)
0	1,500,000				1,500,000
1		570,000	450,000	120,000	1,380,000
2		570,000	360,000	210,000	1,170,000
3		570,000	270,000	300,000	870,000
4		570,000	180,000	390,000	480,000
5		570,000	90,000	480,000	—

$$1{,}500{,}000 = \frac{570{,}000}{(1+r)} + \frac{570{,}000}{(1+r)^2} + \frac{570{,}000}{(1+r)^3} + \frac{570{,}000}{(1+r)^4} + \frac{570{,}000}{(1+r)^5}$$

r = 25 % (approximately)

The after-tax cost of hire purchase financing is shown in Table 18.15.

Table 18.15 After-tax cost of hire purchase financing

1. Year	2. Purchase price avoided (INR)	3. Instalment amount (INR)	4. Principal repaid (INR)	5. After-tax interest (INR)	6. Dep. tax shield (INR)	7. Net cash flows (4 + 5 − 6) (INR)
0	1,500,000					1,500,000
1		570,000	120,000	292,500	105,000	307,500
2		570,000	210,000	234,000	105,000	339,000
3		570,000	300,000	175,500	105,000	370,500
4		570,000	390,000	117,000	105,000	402,000
5		570,000	480,000	58,500	105,000	433,000

$$1{,}500{,}000 = \frac{307{,}500}{(1+r)} + \frac{339{,}000}{(1+r)^2} + \frac{370{,}500}{(1+r)^3} + \frac{402{,}000}{(1+r)^4} + \frac{433{,}000}{(1+r)^5}$$

r = 7% (approximately)

Thus, the after-tax cost of hire purchase financing is about 7 per cent.

Given the after-tax cost of 7 per cent (hire purchase financing), the lease rentals that Britannia Industries is prepared to pay are calculated as follows:

$$1{,}500{,}000 = \frac{\sum_{t=1}^{n}(1-T)L_t}{(1+0.07)^t}$$

$$1{,}500{,}000 = 4.1\ (1 - 0.35)\ L_t;\ (\text{PVIFA } 7, 5 = 4.1)$$
$$= 2.665L_t$$
$$L_t, \text{ or lease rentals} = \text{INR } 562{,}852$$

Thus, Britannia Industries will be indifferent between lease financing and hire purchase financing if the lease rentals are INR 562,852. If the lease rentals are higher than INR 562,852, hire purchase will be preferable.

18.8.2 Tax Implications of Hire Purchase

According to the Income Tax Act, the hirer is entitled to tax shields on depreciation calculated with reference to the cash purchase price of the asset and tax shield on the "consideration for hire". From the hiree's (owner's) angle, the consideration for hire received from the hirer is liable to tax.

Hire purchase transactions are subject to sales tax. For the purpose of levying sales tax, a sale is deemed to take place only when the hirer exercises the option to purchase. The amount of sales tax is determined with reference to the depreciated value of the goods at the time when the hirer exercises the purchase option. The state in which the goods have been delivered to the hirer is the state entitled to levy and collect sales tax. Since the inter-state movement of goods would have occurred before the hirer exercises the option to buy, no hire purchase transaction is likely to be subject to central sales tax.

18.9 Accounting Treatment of Leases

According to IAS 19, the lessee should recognize the lease at the inception of a finance lease as an asset and a liability. Such recognition should be of an amount equal to the fair value of the leased asset at the inception of the lease. However, if the fair value of the leased asset exceeds the present value of the minimum lease payments from the standpoint of the lessee, the amount recorded as an asset and a liability should be the present value of the minimum lease payments from the standpoint of the lessee. In other words, at the inception of the lease, the asset and the liability for the future lease payments are recognized in the balance sheet at the same amounts. The liability for a leased asset should be presented separately in the balance sheet as a current liability or a long-term liability as the case may be. It is rightly observed that if lease transactions are not reflected in the lessee's balance sheet, the economic resources and the level of obligations of an enterprise are understated, thereby distorting financial ratios.

Finance lease payments should be apportioned between the finance charge and the reduction of the outstanding liability. The finance charge should be allocated to periods during the lease term so as to produce a constant periodic rate of interest on the remaining balance of the liability for each period.

Operating lease payments should be recognized as an expense in the statement of profit and loss on a straight-line basis over the lease term unless another systematic basis is more representative of the time pattern of the user's benefit.

The lessor should recognize assets given under a finance lease in its balance sheet as a receivable at an amount equal to the net investment in the lease. The recognition of finance income should be based on a pattern reflecting a constant periodic rate of return on the net investment of the lessor outstanding with respect to the finance lease. The manufacturer or dealer should recognize the transaction of sale in the statement of profit and loss for the period, in accordance with the policy followed by the enterprise for outright sales. If artificially low rates of interest are quoted, profit on sale should be restricted to that which would apply if a commercial rate of interest were charged. Initial direct costs should be recognized as an expense in the statement of profit and loss at the inception of the lease.

The lessor should present an asset given under operating lease in the balance sheet under fixed assets. The lease income from operating leases should be recognized in the statement of profit and loss on a straight-line basis over the lease term, unless another systematic basis is more representative of the time pattern in which the benefit derived from the use of the leased asset diminishes.

The accounting treatment of a sale-and-lease-back transaction depends on the type of lease involved. If a sale-and-lease-back transaction results in a finance lease, any excess or deficiency of sales proceeds over the carrying amount should not be immediately recognized as income or loss in the financial statements of a seller-lessee. Instead, it should be deferred and amortized over the lease term in proportion to the depreciation of the leased asset. If a sale-and-lease-back transaction results in an operating lease, and it is clear that the transaction is established at fair value, any profit or loss should be recognized immediately. If the sale price is below the fair value, any profit or loss should be recognized immediately except that if the loss is compensated by future lease payments below the market price, it should be deferred and amortized in proportion to the lease payments over the period for which the asset is expected to be used. If the sale price is above the fair value, the excess over the fair value should be deferred and amortized over the period for which the asset is expected to be used. For operating leases, if the fair value at the time of a sale-and-lease-back transaction is less than the carrying amount of the asset, a loss equal to the amount of the difference between the carrying amount and fair value should be recognized immediately.

According to IAS 19, the definition of a lease includes agreements for the hire of an asset which contain a provision giving the hirer the option to acquire the title of the asset on fulfilment of agreed conditions. These agreements are commonly known as hire purchase agreements.

Summary

1. A lease is an agreement in which one party (the owner of an asset or the lessor) grants to another party (the lessee) the right to use an asset in return for payment of a certain amount, which is known as the lease rent.
2. Leases are classified as financial lease and operating lease. A financial lease is a long-term lease and the period of the lease generally coincides with the economic life of the asset. An operating lease is a short-term lease and is a lease other than a financial lease. An operating lease might contain a cancellation clause according to which the lesee will have the right to cancel the lease and return the asset to the lessor before the expiration of the lease agreement. Generally, an operating lease requires the lessor to maintain and service the leased asset. Sale-and-lease-back and cross-border leasing are other types of leasing.
3. The user of an asset has the option of either buying the asset or taking the asset on lease. Depending on the comparative costs of leasing the asset and buying it, the user of an asset takes a decision. Similarly, the supplier of an asset has two alternatives—to lease the asset or not to lease the asset. Depending on whether the lease payments can provide the required rate of return on the capital invested in the asset to be leased, the lessor takes a decision.
4. The popular lease evaluation models are Weingartner's model, the equivalent loan model, the Bower–Herringer–Williamson model and Bower's model.
5. There are many advantages of leasing. As a substitute for debt financing, leasing offers more flexibility to both the lessor and lessee and they can negotiate the terms and conditions of leasing in such a way as to benefit both the parties. However, lease financing is relatively costly.
6. The leasing industry has played a significant role in the Indian economy. It is a source of financial strength to many industries, especially small- and medium-scale enterprises. In spite of many upheavals, the leasing industry in India has recorded an annual growth rate of more than 30 per cent and is the third largest leasing industry in Asia after Japan and Korea.
7. Hire purchase is a form of financial arrangement whereby the owner (hiree) provides an asset to the hirer on hire for a consideration of payment (hire charges) in instalments for a specific period. The ownership of the asset is transferred to the hirer on payment of the last instalment.
8. According to the Income Tax Act, the hirer is entitled to a tax shield on depreciation calculated with reference to the cash purchase price of the asset and on the consideration for hire. From the hiree's angle, the consideration for hire received from the hirer is liable to tax. Hire purchase transactions are also subject to sales tax.
9. IAS 19 specifies the manner in which lease transactions should be accounted for in the books of the lessee as well as those of the lessor. According to IAS 19, the definition of a lease includes agreements for the hire of an asset, and contains a provision giving the hirer the option to acquire the title of the asset on fulfilment of agreed conditions. These agreements are known as hire purchase agreements.

Questions and Problems

1. Trace the origin of leasing and give a historical perspective of lease financing.
2. Define lease financing. How is it different from debt financing?
3. Distinguish between financial lease and operating lease.
4. How does sale-and-lease-back benefit the lessee?
5. Discuss the economic aspects of lease financing.
6. How can a lease be evaluated using the IRR method?
7. Discuss the advantages and limitations of lease financing.
8. Trace the factors that have facilitated the growth of the leasing industry in India.
9. How is hire purchase financing different from lease financing?
10. Explain the tax implications of hire purchase financing.
11. Discuss the salient features of IAS 19.
12. Sriram Polymer Company Ltd wants to acquire machinery costing INR 5 million, which has an economic life of eight years with zero salvage value. The company is considering two alternatives—taking the machinery on lease and purchasing the asset outright by raising a loan. If the company acquires the asset on lease, it has to pay INR 0.7 million every year as lease rental. The company can borrow INR 5 million at an interest rate of 13 per cent per annum. The loan has to be repaid in eight equal annual instalments.

The company follows the straight-line method of depreciation. The corporate tax rate is 35 per cent. Which alternative is better for the company?

13. M/S Symphony Limited is considering investment in a project. The cost of the equipment is estimated to be INR 15 million. The equipment has a 10-year life and it will have a salvage value of INR 0.1 million. The company follows the straight-line method of depreciation.

    The company has two ways of financing— lease financing and debt financing. The lease rental for a 10-year non-cancellable lease is INR 25 per month per INR 1,000 payable in arrears (at the end of every year). The company can borrow and buy the equipment. The borrowing cost is 18 per cent per annum and the debt is repayable in 10 equal instalments. The corporate tax rate is 35 per cent. Should the company buy or lease the equipment?

14. A manufacturing company wants to acquire an asset costing INR 1 million. A non-banking finance company (NBFC) offers hire purchase financing to the manufacturing company. The hire purchase instalments will be paid annually for 6 years and the NBFC will calculate interest at a flat rate of 15 per cent. The principal amount and the interest will be paid in equal instalments due at the end of every year. For its internal calculation (total interest distribution over 10 years), the manufacturing company can follow the sum-of-years-digit method. What is the compound rate of return the NBFC would get?

    Suppose the manufacturing company is in the 35 per cent tax bracket. The company follows the straight-line method of depreciation and the asset will not have any salvage value. What is the after-tax cost of the hire purchase financing to the manufacturing company? Further, suppose the manufacturing company is offered the asset on lease. Given the after-tax cost of the hire purchase financing, how much lease rental is the manufacturing company prepared to pay?

Appendix 18.1

Accounting Standard (AS) 19 (issued in 2001)

Accounting Standard (AS) 19, Leases, issued by the Council of the Institute of Chartered Accountants of India, comes into effect in respect of all assets leased during accounting periods commencing on or after April 1, 2001, and is mandatory in nature from that date. Accordingly, the Guidance Note on Accounting for Leases issued by the Institute in 1995 is not applicable in respect of such assets. Earlier application of this Standard is, however, encouraged.

In respect of accounting periods commencing on or after April 1, 2004, an enterprise that does not fall in any of the following categories need not disclose the information required by paragraphs 22(c), (e) and (f); 25(a), (b) and (e); 37(a), (f) and (g); and 46(b), (d) and (e), of this Standard:

i. Enterprises whose equity or debt securities are listed, whether in India or outside India.
ii. Enterprises that are in the process of listing their equity or debt securities as evidenced by the board of directors' resolution in this regard.
iii. Banks including cooperative banks.
iv. Financial institutions.
v. Enterprises carrying on insurance business.
vi. All commercial, industrial and business reporting enterprises, whose turnover for the immediately preceding accounting period on the basis of audited financial statements exceeds INR 50 crore. Turnover does not include "other income".
vii. All commercial, industrial and business reporting enterprises having borrowings, including public deposits, in excess of INR 10 crore at any time during the accounting period.
viii. Holding and subsidiary enterprises of any one of the above at any time during the accounting period.
ix. In respect of an enterprise which falls in any one or more of the above categories, at any time during the accounting period, the Standard is applicable in its entirety.

Where an enterprise has been covered in any one or more of the above categories and subsequently, ceases to be so covered, the enterprise will not qualify for exemption from paragraphs 22(c), (e) and (f); 25(a), (b) and (e); 37(a), (f) and (g); and 46(b), (d) and (e), of this Standard, until the enterprise ceases to be covered in any of the above categories for two consecutive years.

Where an enterprise has previously qualified for exemption from paragraphs 22(c), (e) and (f); 25(a), (b) and (e); 37(a), (f) and (g); and 46(b), (d) and (e), of this Standard (being not covered by any of the above categories) but no longer qualifies for exemption in the current accounting period, this Standard becomes applicable, in its entirety, from the current period. However, the corresponding previous period figures in respect of above paragraphs need not be disclosed.

An enterprise, which, pursuant to the above provisions, does not disclose the information required by paragraphs 22(c), (e) and (f); 25(a), (b) and (e); 37(a), (f) and (g); and 46(b), (d) and (e) should disclose the fact.

The details of AS 19 are as follows:

Objective

The objective of this Statement is to prescribe, for lessees and lessors, the appropriate accounting policies and disclosures in relation to finance leases and operating leases.

Scope

1. This Statement should be applied in accounting for all leases other than:

   a. lease agreements to explore for or use natural resources, such as oil, gas, timber, metals and other mineral rights;
   b. licensing agreements for items such as motion picture films, video recordings, plays, manuscripts, patents and copyrights; and
   c. lease agreements to use lands.

2. This Statement applies to agreements that transfer the right to use assets even though substantial services by the lessor may be called for in connection with the operation or maintenance of such assets. On the other hand, this Statement does not apply to agreements that are contracts for services that do not transfer the right to use assets from one contracting party to the other.

Definitions

3. The following terms are used in this Statement with the meanings specified:

   A *lease* is an agreement whereby the lessor conveys to the lessee in return for a payment or series of payments the right to use an asset for an agreed period of time.

   A *finance lease* is a lease that transfers substantially all the risks and rewards incident to ownership of an asset.

   An *operating lease* is a lease other than a finance lease.

   A *non-cancellable lease* is a lease that is cancellable only:

   - upon the occurrence of some remote contingency; or
   - with the permission of the lessor; or

- if the lessee enters into a new lease for the same or an equivalent asset with the same lessor; or
- upon payment by the lessee of an additional amount such that, at inception, continuation of the lease is reasonably certain.

The inception of the lease is the earlier of the date of the lease agreement and the date of a commitment by the parties to the principal provisions of the lease.

The *lease term* is the non-cancellable period for which the lessee has agreed to take on lease the asset together with any further periods for which the lessee has the option to continue the lease of the asset, with or without further payment, which option at the inception of the lease it is reasonably certain that the lessee will exercise.

Minimum lease payments are the payments over the lease term that the lessee is, or can be, required to make excluding contingent rent, costs for services and taxes to be paid by and reimbursed to the lessor, together with:

a. in the case of the lessee, any residual value guaranteed by or on behalf of the lessee; or
b. in the case of the lessor, any residual value guaranteed to the lessor:
    i. by or on behalf of the lessee; or
    ii. by an independent third party financially capable of meeting this guarantee.

However, if the lessee has an option to purchase the asset at a price which is expected to be sufficiently lower than the fair value at the date the option becomes exercisable that, at the inception of the lease, is reasonably certain to be exercised, the minimum lease payments comprise minimum payments payable over the lease term and the payment required to exercise this purchase option.

Fair value is the amount for which an asset could be exchanged or a liability settled between knowledgeable, willing parties in an arm's length transaction.

Economic life is either:

a. the period over which an asset is expected to be economically usable by one or more users; or
b. the number of production or similar units expected to be obtained from the asset by one or more users.

Useful life of a leased asset is either:

a. the period over which the leased asset is expected to be used by the lessee; or
b. the number of production or similar units expected to be obtained from the use of the asset by the lessee.

Residual value of a leased asset is the estimated fair value of the asset at the end of the lease term.

Guaranteed residual value is:

a. in the case of the lessee, that part of the residual value which is guaranteed by the lessee or by a party on behalf of the lessee (the amount of the guarantee being the maximum amount that could, in any event, become payable); and
b. in the case of the lessor, that part of the residual value which is guaranteed by or on behalf of the lessee, or by an independent third party who is financially capable of discharging the obligations under the guarantee.

Unguaranteed residual value of a leased asset is the amount by which the residual value of the asset exceeds its guaranteed residual value.

Gross investment in the lease is the aggregate of the minimum lease payments under a finance lease from the standpoint of the lessor and any unguaranteed residual value accruing to the lessor.

Unearned finance income is the difference between:

a. the gross investment in the lease; and
b. the present value of:
    i. the minimum lease payments under a finance lease from the standpoint of the lessor; and
    ii. any unguaranteed residual value accruing to the lessor at the interest rate implicit in the lease. Net investment in the lease is the gross investment in the lease less unearned finance income.

The *interest rate implicit in the lease* is the discount rate that, at the inception of the lease, causes the aggregate present value of:

a. the minimum lease payments under a finance lease from the standpoint of the lessor; and
b. any unguaranteed residual value accruing to the lessor, to be equal to the fair value of the leased asset.

The *lessee's incremental borrowing rate of interest* is the rate of interest the lessee would have to pay on a similar lease or, if that is not determinable, the rate that, at the inception of the lease, the lessee would incur to borrow over a similar term, and with a similar security, the funds necessary to purchase the asset.

Contingent rent is that portion of the lease payments that is not fixed in amount but is based on a factor other than just the passage of time (such as percentage of sales, amount of usage, price indices and market rates of interest).

4. The definition of a lease includes agreements for the hire of an asset which contain a provision giving the hirer an option to acquire title to the asset upon the fulfillment of agreed conditions. These agreements are commonly known as hire purchase agreements. Hire purchase agreements include agreements under which the property in the asset is to pass to the hirer on the payment of the last installment and the hirer has a right to terminate the agreement at any time before the property so passes.

Classification of Leases

5. The classification of leases adopted in this Statement is based on the extent to which risks and rewards incident to ownership of a leased asset lie with the lessor or the lessee. Risks include the possibilities of losses

from idle capacity or technological obsolescence and of variations in return due to changing economic conditions. Rewards may be represented by the expectation of profitable operation over the economic life of the asset and of gain from appreciation in value or realization of residual value.

6. A lease is classified as a finance lease if it transfers substantially all the risks and rewards incident to ownership. The title may or may not eventually be transferred. A lease is classified as an operating lease if it does not transfer substantially all the risks and rewards incident to ownership.

7. Since the transaction between a lessor and a lessee is based on a lease agreement common to both parties, it is appropriate to use consistent definitions. The application of these definitions to the differing circumstances of the two parties may sometimes result in the same lease being classified differently by the lessor and the lessee.

8. Whether a lease is a finance lease or an operating lease depends on the substance of the transaction rather than its form. Examples of situations that would normally lead to a lease being classified as a finance lease are:

    a. the lease transfers ownership of the asset to the lessee by the end of the lease term;
    b. the lessee has the option to purchase the asset at a price which is expected to be sufficiently lower than the fair value at the date the option becomes exercisable such that, at the inception of the lease, it is reasonably certain that the option will be exercised;
    c. the lease term is for the major part of the economic life of the asset even if title is not transferred;
    d. at the inception of the lease the present value of the minimum lease payments amounts to at least substantially all of the fair value of the leased asset; and
    e. the leased asset is of a specialized nature such that only the lessee can use it without major modifications being made.

9. Indicators of situations that individually or in combination could also lead to a lease being classified as a finance lease are:

    a. if the lessee can cancel the lease, the lessor's losses associated with the cancellation are borne by the lessee;
    b. gains or losses from the fluctuation in the fair value of the residual fall to the lessee (for example in the form of a rent rebate equalling most of the sales proceeds at the end of the lease); and
    c. the lessee can continue the lease for a secondary period at a rent that is substantially lower than market rent.

10. Lease classification is made at the inception of the lease. If at any time the lessee and the lessor agree to change the provisions of the lease, other than by renewing the lease, in a manner that would have resulted in a different classification of the lease under the criteria in Paragraphs 5 to 9 had the changed terms been in effect at the inception of the lease, the revised agreement is considered as a new agreement over its revised term. Changes in estimates (for example, changes in estimates of the economic life or of the residual value of the leased asset) or changes in circumstances (for example, default by the lessee), however, do not give rise to a new classification of a lease for accounting purposes.

Leases in the Financial Statements of Lessees

Finance leases

11. At the inception of a finance lease, the lessee should recognize the lease as an asset and a liability. Such recognition should be at an amount equal to the fair value of the leased asset at the inception of the lease. However, if the fair value of the leased asset exceeds the present value of the minimum lease payments from the standpoint of the lessee, the amount recorded as an asset and a liability should be the present value of the minimum lease payments from the standpoint of the lessee. In calculating the present value of the minimum lease payments the discount rate is the interest rate implicit in the lease, if this is practicable to determine; if not, the lessee's incremental borrowing rate should be used.

    In case the interest rate implicit in the lease is not known to the lessee, the present value of the minimum lease payments from the standpoint of the lessee would be computed using the lessee's incremental borrowing rate.

12. Transactions and other events are accounted for and presented in accordance with their substance and financial reality and not merely with their legal form. While the legal form of a lease agreement is that the lessee may acquire no legal title to the leased asset, in the case of finance leases the substance and financial reality are that the lessee acquires the economic benefits of the use of the leased asset for the major part of its economic life in return for entering into an obligation to pay for that right an amount approximating to the fair value of the asset and the related finance charge.

13. If such lease transactions are not reflected in the lessee's balance sheet, the economic resources and the level of obligations of an enterprise are understated, thereby distorting financial ratios. It is therefore appropriate that a finance lease be recognized in the lessee's balance sheet both as an asset and as an obligation to pay future lease payments. At the inception of the lease, the asset and the liability for the future lease payments are recognized in the balance sheet at the same amounts.

14. It is not appropriate to present the liability for a leased asset as a deduction from the leased asset in the financial statements. The liability for a leased asset should be presented separately in the balance sheet as a current liability or a long-term liability as the case may be.

15. Initial direct costs are often incurred in connection with specific leasing Year Finance Payment activities, as in

negotiating and securing leasing arrangements. The costs identified as directly attributable to activities performed by the lessee for a finance lease are included as part of the amount recognized as an asset under the lease.

16. Lease payments should be apportioned between the finance charge and the reduction of the outstanding liability. The finance charge should be allocated to periods during the lease term so as to produce a constant periodic rate of interest on the remaining balance of the liability for each period.

17. In practice, in allocating the finance charge to periods during the lease term, some form of approximation may be used to simplify the calculation.

18. A finance lease gives rise to a depreciation expense for the asset as well as a finance expense for each accounting period. The depreciation policy for a leased asset should be consistent with that for depreciable assets which are owned, and the depreciation recognized should be calculated on the basis set out in Accounting Standard (AS) 6, Depreciation Accounting. If there is no reasonable certainty that the lessee will obtain ownership by the end of the lease term, the asset should be fully depreciated over the lease term or its useful life, whichever is shorter.

19. The depreciable amount of a leased asset is allocated to each accounting period during the period of expected use on a systematic basis consistent with the depreciation policy the lessee adopts for depreciable assets that are owned. If there is reasonable certainty that the lessee will obtain ownership by the end of the lease term, the period of expected use is the useful life of the asset; otherwise the asset is depreciated over the lease term or its useful life, whichever is shorter.

20. The sum of the depreciation expense for the asset and the finance expense for the period is rarely the same as the lease payments payable for the period, and it is, therefore, inappropriate simply to recognize the lease payments payable as an expense in the statement of profit and loss. Accordingly, the asset and the related liability are unlikely to be equal in amount after the inception of the lease.

21. To determine whether a leased asset has become impaired, an enterprise applies the Accounting Standard dealing with impairment of assets, that sets out the requirements as to how an enterprise should perform the review of the carrying amount of an asset, how it should determine the recoverable amount of an asset and when it should recognize, or reverse, an impairment loss.

22. The lessee should, in addition to the requirements of AS 10, Accounting for Fixed Assets, AS 6, Depreciation Accounting, and the governing statute, make the following disclosures for finance leases:

a. assets acquired under finance lease as segregated from the assets owned;

b. for each class of assets, the net carrying amount at the balance sheet date;

c. a reconciliation between the total of minimum lease payments at the balance sheet date and their present value.

In addition, an enterprise should disclose the total of minimum lease payments at the balance sheet date, and their present value, for each of the following periods:

i. not later than one year;

Accounting Standard (AS) 28, Impairment of Assets, specifies the requirements relating to impairment of assets.

ii. later than one year and not later than five years;

iii. later than five years;

d. contingent rents recognized as expense in the statement of profit and loss for the period;

e. the total of future minimum sublease payments expected to be received under non-cancellable subleases at the balance sheet date; and

f. a general description of the lessee's significant leasing arrangements including, but not limited to, the following:

i. the basis on which contingent rent payments are determined;

ii. the existence and terms of renewal or purchase options and escalation clauses; and

iii. restrictions imposed by lease arrangements, such as those concerning dividends, additional debt, and further leasing.

Operating leases

23. Lease payments under an operating lease should be recognized as an expense in the statement of profit and loss on a straight-line basis over the lease term unless another systematic basis is more representative of the time pattern of the user's benefit.

24. For operating leases, lease payments (excluding costs for services such as insurance and maintenance) are recognized as an expense in the statement of profit and loss on a straight-line basis unless another systematic basis is more representative of the time pattern of the user's benefit, even if the payments are not on that basis.

25. The lessee should make the following disclosures for operating leases:

a. the total of future minimum lease payments under non-cancellable operating leases for each of the following periods:

i. not later than one year;

ii. later than one year and not later than five years;

iii. later than five years;

b. the total of future minimum sublease payments expected to be received under non-cancellable subleases at the balance sheet date;

c. lease payments recognized in the statement of profit and loss for the period, with separate amounts for minimum lease payments and contingent rents;

d. sub-lease payments received (or receivable) recognized in the statement of profit and loss for the period;

e. a general description of the lessee's significant leasing arrangements including, but not limited to, the following:

   i. the basis on which contingent rent payments are determined;

   ii. the existence and terms of renewal or purchase options and escalation clauses; and

   iii. restrictions imposed by lease arrangements, such as those concerning dividends, additional debt, and further leasing.

Leases in the Financial Statements of Lessors

Finance leases

26. The lessor should recognize assets given under a finance lease in its balance sheet as a receivable at an amount equal to the net investment in the lease.

27. Under a finance lease, substantially all the risks and rewards incident to legal ownership are transferred by the lessor, and thus the lease payment receivable is treated by the lessor as repayment of principal, i.e., net investment in the lease, and finance income to reimburse and reward the lessor for its investment and services.

28. The recognition of finance income should be based on a pattern reflecting a constant periodic rate of return on the net investment of the lessor outstanding in respect of the finance lease.

29. A lessor aims to allocate finance income over the lease term on a systematic and rational basis. This income allocation is based on a pattern reflecting a constant periodic return on the net investment of the lessor outstanding in respect of the finance lease. Lease payments relating to the accounting period, excluding costs for services, are reduced from both the principal and the unearned finance income.

30. Estimated unguaranteed residual values used in computing the lessor's gross investment in a lease are reviewed regularly. If there has been a reduction in the estimated unguaranteed residual value, the income allocation over the remaining lease term is revised and any reduction in respect of amounts already accrued is recognized immediately. An upward adjustment of the estimated residual value is not made.

31. Initial direct costs, such as commissions and legal fees, are often incurred by lessors in negotiating and arranging a lease. For finance leases, these initial direct costs are incurred to produce finance income and are either recognized immediately in the statement of profit and loss or allocated against the finance income over the lease term.

32. The manufacturer or dealer lessor should recognize the transaction of sale in the statement of profit and loss for the period, in accordance with the policy followed by the enterprise for outright sales. If artificially low rates of interest are quoted, profit on sale should be restricted to that which would apply if a commercial rate of interest were charged. Initial direct costs should be recognized as an expense in the statement of profit and loss at the inception of the lease.

33. Manufacturers or dealers may offer to customers the choice of either buying or leasing an asset. A finance lease of an asset by a manufacturer or dealer lessor gives rise to two types of income:

   a. the profit or loss equivalent to the profit or loss resulting from an outright sale of the asset being leased, at normal selling prices, reflecting any applicable volume or trade discounts; and

   b. the finance income over the lease term.

34. The sales revenue recorded at the commencement of a finance lease term by a manufacturer or dealer lessor is the fair value of the asset. However, if the present value of the minimum lease payments accruing to the lessor computed at a commercial rate of interest is lower than the fair value, the amount recorded as sales revenue is the present value so computed. The cost of sale recognized at the commencement of the lease term is the cost, or carrying amount if different, of the leased asset less the present value of the unguaranteed residual value. The difference between the sales revenue and the cost of sale is the selling profit, which is recognized in accordance with the policy followed by the enterprise for sales.

35. Manufacturer or dealer lessors sometimes quote artificially low rates of interest in order to attract customers. The use of such a rate would result in an excessive portion of the total income from the transaction being recognized at the time of sale. If artificially low rates of interest are quoted, selling profit would be restricted to that which would apply if a commercial rate of interest were charged.

36. Initial direct costs are recognized as an expense at the commencement of the lease term because they are mainly related to earning the manufacturer's or dealer's selling profit.

37. The lessor should make the following disclosures for finance leases:

   a. A reconciliation between the total gross investment in the lease at the balance sheet date, and the present value of minimum lease payments receivable at the balance sheet date. In addition, an enterprise should disclose the total gross investment in the lease and the present value of minimum lease payments receivable at the balance sheet date, for each of the following periods:

      i. not later than one year;

      ii. later than one year and not later than five years;

      iii. later than five years;

   b. unearned finance income;

   c. the unguaranteed residual values accruing to the benefit of the lessor;

d. the accumulated provision for uncollectible minimum lease payments receivable;

e. contingent rents recognized in the statement of profit and loss for the period;

f. a general description of the significant leasing arrangements of the lessor; and

g. accounting policy adopted in respect of initial direct costs.

38. As an indicator of growth it is often useful to also disclose the gross investment less unearned income in new business added during the accounting period, after deducting the relevant amounts for cancelled leases.

Operating leases

39. The lessor should present an asset given under operating lease in its balance sheet under fixed assets.

40. Lease income from operating leases should be recognized in the statement of profit and loss on a straight line basis over the lease term, unless another systematic basis is more representative of the time pattern in which benefit derived from the use of the leased asset is diminished.

41. Costs, including depreciation, incurred in earning the lease income are recognized as an expense. Lease income (excluding receipts for services provided such as insurance and maintenance) is recognized in the statement of profit and loss on a straight line basis over the lease term even if the receipts are not on such a basis, unless another systematic basis is more representative of the time pattern in which benefit derived from the use of sale-and-lease-back the leased asset is diminished.

42. Initial direct costs incurred specifically to earn revenues from an operating lease are either deferred and allocated to income over the lease term in proportion to the recognition of rent income, or are recognized as an expense in the statement of profit and loss in the period in which they are incurred.

43. The depreciation of leased assets should be on a basis consistent with the normal depreciation policy of the lessor for similar assets, and the depreciation charge should be calculated on the basis set out in AS 6, Depreciation Accounting.

44. To determine whether a leased asset has become impaired, an enterprise applies the Accounting Standard dealing with impairment of assets that sets out the requirements for how an enterprise should perform the review of the carrying amount of an asset, how it should determine the recoverable amount of an asset and when it should recognize, or reverse, an impairment loss.

45. A manufacturer or dealer lessor does not recognize any selling profit on entering into an operating lease because it is not the equivalent of a sale.

46. The lessor should, in addition to the requirements of AS 6, Depreciation Accounting, and AS 10, Accounting for Fixed Assets, and the governing statute, make the following disclosures for operating leases:

a. for each class of assets, the gross carrying amount, the accumulated depreciation and accumulated impairment losses at the balance sheet date; and

i. the depreciation recognized in the statement of profit and loss for the period;

ii. impairment losses recognized in the statement of profit and loss for the period;

iii. impairment losses reversed in the statement of profit and loss for the period;

Accounting Standard (AS) 28, Impairment of Assets, specifies the requirements relating to impairment of assets.

b. the future minimum lease payments under non-cancellable operating leases in the aggregate and for each of the following periods:

i. not later than one year;

ii. later than one year and not later than five years;

iii. later than five years;

c. total contingent rents recognized as income in the statement of profit and loss for the period;

d. a general description of the lessor's significant leasing arrangements; and

e. accounting policy adopted in respect of initial direct costs.

Sale-and-lease-back transactions

47. A sale-and-lease-back transaction involves the sale of an asset by the vendor and the leasing of the same asset back to the vendor. The lease payments and the sale price are usually interdependent as they are negotiated as a package. The accounting treatment of a sale-and-lease-back transaction depends upon the type of lease involved.

48. If a sale-and-lease-back transaction results in a finance lease, any excess or deficiency of sales proceeds over the carrying amount should not be immediately recognized as income or loss in the financial statements of a seller-lessee. Instead, it should be deferred and amortized over the lease term in proportion to the depreciation of the leased asset.

49. If the lease-back is a finance lease, it is not appropriate to regard an excess of sales proceeds over the carrying amount as income. Such excess is deferred and amortized over the lease term in proportion to the depreciation of the leased asset. Similarly, it is not appropriate to regard a deficiency as loss. Such deficiency is deferred and amortized over the lease term.

50. If a sale-and-lease-back transaction results in an operating lease, and it is clear that the transaction is established at fair value, any profit or loss should be recognized immediately. If the sale price is below fair value, any profit or loss should be recognized immediately except that, if the loss is compensated by future lease payments at below market price, it should be deferred and amortized in proportion to the lease payments over the period for which the asset is expected to be

used. If the sale price is above fair value, the excess over fair value should be deferred and amortized over the period for which the asset is expected to be used.

51. If the lease-back is an operating lease, and the lease payments and the sale price are established at fair value, there has in effect been a normal sale transaction and any profit or loss is recognized immediately.

52. For operating leases, if the fair value at the time of a sale-and-lease-back transaction is less than the carrying amount of the asset, a loss equal to the amount of the difference between the carrying amount and fair value should be recognized immediately.

53. For finance leases, no such adjustment is necessary unless there has been impairment in value, in which case the carrying amount is reduced to recoverable amount in accordance with the Accounting Standard dealing with impairment of assets.

54. Disclosure requirements for lessees and lessors apply equally to sale-and-lease-back transactions. The required description of the significant leasing arrangements leads to disclosure of unique or unusual provisions of the agreement or terms of the sale-and-lease-back transactions.

55. Sale-and-lease-back transactions may meet the separate disclosure criteria set out in Paragraph 12 of Accounting Standard (AS) 5, Net Profit or Loss for the Period, Prior Period Items and Changes in Accounting Policies.

Source: The Institute of Chartered Accountants of India, accessed at http://www.icai.org/resource_file/263accounting_standards_as19new.pdf, July 2010.

Chapter 19

Non-banking Finance Companies

LEARNING OBJECTIVE

After reading this chapter, you should be able to:

- Define and classify non-banking finance companies (NBFCs)
- Discuss the role of NBFCs
- Present prudential norms governing NBFCs
- Highlight how corporate governance relates to NBFCs
- Look at the Know-Your-Customer guidelines

19.1 Introduction

Financial sector reforms in India aim at integrating various segments of the financial market, thereby increasing its efficiency, besides broadening and deepening the market. Accordingly, the financial sector has witnessed many initiatives, particularly in the first decade of the twenty-first century. One such initiative aims at strengthening the non-banking finance companies (NBFCs) in the country. NBFCs, which evolved to cater to the needs of small investors and borrowers, have come a long way. They have grown both in magnitude and depth. That is, the number of NBFCs has grown very significantly and their operations have broadened and deepened. There are several reasons for the upsurge in the number of finance companies. As there is no technology involved, it is not difficult to start an NBFC. Also, there are no barriers to entry and exit, so any organization can easily enter and exit the industry. The success of a few NBFCs has also given rise to a herd mentality, leading to several firms being set up irrespective of their feasibility.

NBFCs in India are an integral part of the country's financial system. They are able to mobilize substantial amounts of deposits and provide credit to certain sectors, especially where a credit gap exists. Trading firms, unregistered manufacturing firms and non-corporate private construction firms are the major clients of NBFCs. Thus, NBFCs in India operate mostly in the unorganized and under-serviced segments of the economy. The chief characteristics of an NBFC are:

- Very close customer interaction and relationship;
- A deep and clear understanding of customer needs;
- Wide and specialized branch network; and
- Low-cost operations.

NBFCs have the ability to take quicker decisions, assume greater risks and customize their services according to the needs of their customers (by providing tailor-made services). Quick treatment of cases is a unique feature of NBFCs and this is possible because of fewer pre- and post-sanction requirements. NBFCs' customers have the advantage of quicker response to their demands with fewer documentation difficulties. Another special feature of NBFCs is that that they offer a wide range of financial services to cover the financial needs of all sectors of the economy with a special focus on the informal sector. Thus, NBFCs have extreme customer focus with extensive financial product portfolios. It may be noted that the NBFCs have a loyal clientele notwithstanding the higher cost of borrowing from NBFCs.

NBFCs supplement the services provided by commercial banks and their services are both fund-based and fee-based.

NBFCs provide both fund-based services such as leasing, hire purchase, bill discounting and promoter funding, and fee-based services such as merchant banking, advisory services, syndication of loans, portfolio management, stock-broking and underwriting. Many NBFCs have launched mutual funds and obtained corporate membership on the stock exchange. Some of them have set up commercial banks and also entered the insurance sector. The activities of NBFCs have undergone qualitative changes over the years through functional specialization.

Despite the widespread growth of commercial bank branches and large-scale credit deployment in the country, credit penetration levels and access to financial services remain low in India. NBFCs play an important role in broadening and deepening the financial services in the country. Though they are called non-banking institutions, NBFCs are very much recognized as a complementary setup in the banking system. As financial institutions, they mobilize the savings of the people, particularly those with small means, and deploy them in productive activities. NBFCs can accept deposits from the public, but not demand deposits. Demand deposits (such as savings account deposits and current account deposits) are deposits that are payable on demand (that is, immediately). Deposits with NBFCs are not covered by deposit insurance of the Deposit Insurance and Credit Guarantee Corporation (DICGC). Further, NBFCs cannot provide the cheque facility to its customers as they are not participants in the payment and settlement system of banks.

NBFCs are popularly known for their effective deposit mobilization strategies or techniques. They practically dominate the fixed or public deposit market by offering very attractive returns. The saving schemes offered by NBFCs are flexible enough to be suitable even to small investors and fixed-income groups. In view of the volatile performance of the stock markets, these categories of investors can bank upon the fixed deposit market largely consisting of schemes launched by NBFCs. NBFCs offer returns to the depositors on their deposits in the form of upfront incentives, redemption bonus and sharing of commission by the depositors with their marketing brokers. NBFCs also offer a variety of loan schemes under one roof to suit to the variegated needs of the borrowing public.

19.1.1 Definition and Classification of NBFCs

A **non-banking finance company (NBFC)** is a company registered under the Companies Act, 1956, and engaged in the business of loans and advances, acquisition of shares/stocks/bonds/debentures/securities, leasing, hire purchase, insurance business and chit business but does not include any institution whose principal business is that of agricultural activity, industrial activity and sale/purchase/construction of immovable property. It is further clarified by the Reserve Bank of India (RBI) that a company will be treated as a non-banking financial company if its financial assets are more than 50 per cent of its total assets (netted off by intangible assets) and the income from financial assets is more than 50 per cent of the gross income. Both these conditions must be satisfied. Any company that carries on the principal business of agricultural activities, industrial activities, trading in commodities or dealing in immovable properties is, however, not a financial institution.

*A **non-banking finance company (NBFC)** is a company registered under the Companies Act, 1956, to provide the services as specified by the Reserve Bank of India.*

For regulatory purposes, the RBI has classified NBFCs as:

- NBFCs comprising equipment leasing companies, hire purchase finance companies, loan companies, investment companies including primary dealers and residuary non-banking companies;
- Mutual benefit financial companies such as nidhi companies; and
- Miscellaneous non-banking companies such as chit fund companies.

The principal business of NBFCs, in terms of Section 45 l(f) read with Section 45 i(c) of the RBI Act, 1934, as amended in 1997, is that of receiving deposits or that of a financial institution, such as lending, investment in securities, hire purchase finance or equipment leasing. The principal business of investment companies is acquisition of securities. These include primary dealers who deal in underwriting and market-making for government securities. Loan companies provide finance by giving loans or advances or otherwise for any activity other than its own. Residuary non-banking companies receive deposits under any scheme or arrangement in one lump sum or in instalments by way of contributions or subscriptions or by sale of units or certificates or other instruments, or in any manner.

With effect from December 6, 2006, NBFCs registered with the RBI have been reclassified as asset finance companies (AFC), investment companies (IC), loan companies (LC) and residuary non-banking companies (RNBCs). An *asset finance company* is any company that is a financial institution carrying on as its principal business the financing of physical assets supporting productive or economic activity. An *investment company* is defined as any company that is a financial institution carrying on as its principal business the acquisition of securities. A *loan company* refers to any company that is a financial institution carrying on as its principal business the providing of finance, whether by giving loans or advances or otherwise, for any activity other than its own but does not include an equipment leasing company or a hire purchase finance company. A *residuary non-banking company* is a type of NBFC whose principal business is receiving deposits under any scheme or arrangement or in any other manner and is not an investment/asset financing/loan company. The functioning of RNBCs is different from that of NBFCs in terms of the method of mobilization of deposits and the requirement of deployment of depositors' funds.

NBFCs can be further classified into three categories—(i) those accepting public deposits; (ii) those not accepting public deposits but engaged in financial business; and (iii) core investment companies with 90 per cent of their total assets as investments in the securities of their group/holding/subsidiary companies.

19.1.2 Registration of NBFCs

No NBFC is allowed to commence the business of financial activities without obtaining a certificate of registration from the RBI.

It is mandatory for every NBFC to register with the RBI, irrespective of whether the company holds public deposits or not, by fulfilling prescribed norms. A company incorporated under the Companies Act, 1956, and desirous of conducting NBFC business must have a minimum net owned fund of INR 25 lakh (raised to INR 200 lakh with effect from April 2, 1999). The company is required to submit an application for registration in the prescribed form, along with necessary documents, for consideration by the RBI. The RBI issues a certificate of registration after being satisfied that the conditions enumerated in Section 45 IA of the RBI Act, 1934, have been complied with. According to the RBI Act, NBFCs are not permitted to accept public deposits unless they hold a valid certificate of registration with authorization to accept public deposits.

Although housing finance companies, merchant banking companies, stock exchanges, companies engaged in the business of stockbroking or sub-broking, venture capital fund companies, nidhi companies, insurance companies and chit fund companies are NBFCs according to the definition, they are exempted from the requirement of registration under Section 45 IA of the RBI Act, 1934, subject to certain conditions. Nevertheless, housing finance companies are regulated by the National Housing Bank; merchant banks/venture capital fund companies/stock exchanges/stockbroking companies/sub-broking companies are registered with SEBI and regulated by SEBI; insurance companies obtain a certificate of registration from the Insurance Regulatory and Development Authority (IRDA) and are regulated by IRDA; chit fund companies are regulated by the respective state governments under the Chit Funds Act, 1982; and nidhi companies are regulated by Ministry of Company Affairs, Government of India, under Section 620A of the Companies Act, 1956. In brief, it is mandatory that every NBFC be registered with the RBI to commence or carry on any business of non-banking financial institutions. However, the mandatory requirement that every NBFC should be registered with the RBI is waived for companies that are regulated by other regulatory agencies in order to obviate dual regulation.

19.2 The Regulatory Framework

NBFCs have mushroomed in the 1990s. They have varying business interests and, accordingly, offer a variety of savings and loan schemes to attract both depositors and borrowers. Many NBFCs perform several functions of commercial banks and, therefore, the distinction between NBFCs and commercial banks is very thin. In fact, NBFCs can pose a serious challenge to commercial banks, compelling them to improve their business operations, particularly on the customer service front. On one hand, NBFCs and commercial banks are complementary to each other, and on the other hand, both are serious competitors in mobilization of deposits and credit deployment. Therefore, it is necessary to ensure the healthy growth of the banking industry as a whole so that the country has a vibrant and resilient banking system. In view of this, the regulatory authority, particularly the RBI, has initiated several measures to improve the functioning of NBFCs. The regulatory framework also attempts to ensure orderly development of NBFCs in the country. In effect, the measures provide a level playing field and bring convergence between commercial banks and NBFCs.

19.2.1 RBI Guidelines

In 1992, the RBI set up a committee headed by A.C. Shah to suggest regulatory and control measures to ensure the healthy growth and operations of NBFCs. In pursuance of the recommendations of the Shah committee, the RBI issued guidelines in April 1993; the salient features of these guidelines are as follows:

- NBFCs with net owned funds of INR 50 lakh and above are required to register with the RBI. The registered companies are to submit the necessary information to the RBI in the prescribed format.
- Inter-corporate deposits, borrowings and monies received from the directors/shareholders of private limited companies are to be treated as regulated deposits.
- Hire purchase companies and equipment leasing companies are required to maintain liquid assets at 10 per cent on the revised definition of deposits, which include inter-corporate deposits/borrowings.
- Loans and investment companies are required to maintain liquid assets to the extent of 5 per cent of deposits. At least half of the liquid assets will have to be in the form of government securities or/and government guaranteed bonds.
- For residuary NBFCs, the minimum period of deposit will be 12 months and maximum period of deposit 84 months.
- All accounting standards and guidance noted issued by the Institute of Chartered Accountants of India dealing with lease accounting, depreciation, etc. may be followed.

19.2.2 Prudential Norms for NBFCs

The Reserve Bank of India Act, 1935, was amended in 1997 in order to entrust the RBI with the responsibility of regulating and supervising NBFCs. Accordingly, the objectives of the RBI with regard to NBFCs are as follows:[1]

- To ensure healthy growth of financial companies;
- To ensure that these companies function as a part of the financial system within the policy framework in such a manner that their existence and functioning do not lead to systemic aberrations; and
- To sustain the quality of surveillance and supervision over NBFCs by keeping pace with the developments in the financial sector.

Prudential norms are guidelines for NBFCs on their income recognition, asset classification and provisioning requirements with the main objective of protecting the interests of depositors.

Many NBFCs mushroomed following the liberalization of the economy, particularly in the early 1990s. Subsequently, a number of NBFCs, including CRB Limited and ITC Classic, went into the red mainly because of severe competition in the market and improper management of funds. Therefore, the need was felt to regulate the business of NBFCs at the entry stage itself. Accordingly, the RBI issued Non-Banking Financial Companies Prudential Norms (Reserve Bank of India) Directions, 1998. The prudential norms, *inter alia*, prescribe guidelines on income recognition, asset classification and provisioning requirements applicable to NBFCs, exposure norms, constitution of audit committee, disclosure in the balance sheet, requirement of capital adequacy and restrictions on investment in land, buildings and unquoted shares. The norms mainly focus on "deposit-taking NBFCs" so as to protect the interests of the depositors. "Non-deposit taking NBFCs" are subject to minimal regulations.

The highlights of the prudential norms directions issued by the RBI on January 31, 1998, and duly updated are given here. All the provisions of these directions shall apply to:

- A non-banking financial company (referred to in these directions as "NBFC"), except a mutual benefit financial company and a mutual benefit company as defined in the Non-Banking Financial Companies Acceptance of Public Deposits (Reserve Bank) Directions, 1998, which has net owned fund (referred to in these directions as "NOF") of INR 25 lakh and above and accepting/holding public deposit; and
- A residuary non-banking company (referred to in these directions as "RNBC") as defined in the Residuary Non-Banking Companies (Reserve Bank) Directions, 1987.

These directions shall apply to infrastructure loans as well. However, these directions shall not apply to an NBFC which is an investment company; provided that it:

- Holds investments in securities of its group/holding/subsidiary companies and the book value of such holding is not less than 90 per cent of its total assets and it is not trading in such securities; and
- Does not accept/hold public deposits.

Further, these directions, except the provisions of information with regard to the change of address, directors, auditors, etc. to be submitted by NBFCs not accepting/holding public deposit, shall not apply to an NBFC being a government company as defined under Section 617 of the Companies Act, 1956 (1 of 1956).

Definitions

For the purpose of these directions, unless the context otherwise requires:

(i) Break-up value is the equity capital and reserves as reduced by intangible assets and revaluation reserves, divided by the number of equity shares of the investee company;

(ii) Carrying cost is the book value of the assets and interest accrued thereon but not received;

(iii) Current investment is an investment which is by its nature readily realizable and is intended to be held for not more than one year from the date on which such investment is made;

(iv) Doubtful asset is:

(a) a term loan, or
(b) a lease asset, or
(c) a hire purchase asset, or
(d) any other asset, which remains a substandard asset for a period exceeding 18 months.

(v) Earning value is the value of an equity share computed by taking the average of profits after tax as reduced by the preference dividend and adjusted for extraordinary and non-recurring items, for the immediately preceding three years and further divided by the number of equity shares of the investee company and capitalized at the following rate:

(a) in case of predominantly manufacturing company, 8 per cent;
(b) in case of predominantly trading company, 10 per cent; and
(c) in case of any other company, including an NBFC, 12 per cent;

If, an investee company is a loss-making company, the earning value will be taken to be zero.

(vi) Fair value is the mean of the earning value and the break-up value;

(vii) Hybrid debt is a capital instrument that possesses certain characteristics of equity as well as of debt;

(viii) Infrastructure loan is a credit facility extended by NBFCs to a borrower by way of a term loan, project loan subscription to bonds/debentures/ preference shares/equity shares in a project company acquired as a part of the project finance package such that such subscription amounts to be "in the nature of advance" or any other form of long-term funded facility provided to a borrower company engaged in:

- Developing, or
- Operating and maintaining, or
- Developing, operating and maintaining any infrastructure facility that is a project in any of the following sectors:

(a) a road, including toll road, bridge or rail system;
(b) a highway project including other activities being an integral part of the highway project;
(c) a port, airport, inland waterway or inland port;
(d) a water supply project, irrigation project, water treatment system, sanitation and sewerage system or solid waste management system;
(e) telecommunication services, whether basic or cellular, including radio paging, domestic satellite service (i.e., a satellite owned and operated by an Indian company for providing telecommunication service), broadband network and internet services;

(f) an industrial park or special economic zone;

(g) generation or generation and distribution of power;

(h) transmission or distribution of power by laying a network of new transmission or distribution lines:

- construction relating to projects involving agro-processing and supply of inputs to agriculture;
- construction for preservation and storage of processed agro-products, perishable goods such as fruits, vegetables and flowers, including testing facilities for quality;
- construction of educational institutions and hospitals; and

(i) any other infrastructure facility of similar nature.

(ix) Loss asset is:

(a) an asset that has been identified as loss asset by the NBFC or its internal or external auditor or by the Reserve Bank of India during the inspection of the NBFC, to the extent that it is not written off by the NBFC; and

(b) an asset that is adversely affected by a potential threat of non-recoverability due to either erosion in the value of the security or non-availability of the security or due to any fraudulent act or omission on the part of the borrower;

(x) Long-term investment is an investment other than a current investment;

(xi) Net asset value is the latest declared net asset value by the concerned mutual fund with respect to that particular scheme;

(xii) Net book value is:

(a) in the case of hire purchase asset, the aggregate of overdue and future instalments receivable as reduced by the balance of unmatured finance charges and further reduced by the provisions made as per these directions;

(b) in the case of leased asset, aggregate of the capital portion of overdue lease rentals accounted as receivable and depreciated book value of the lease asset as adjusted by the balance of lease adjustment account;

(xiii) With effect from March 31, 2003, non-performing asset (referred to in these directions as NPA) means:

(a) an asset with respect to which interest has remained overdue for a period of six months or more;

(b) a term loan inclusive of unpaid interest, when the instalment is overdue for a period of six months or more or on which interest amount remained overdue for a period of six months or more;

(c) a demand or call loan that remained overdue for a period of six months or more from the date of demand or call or on which the interest amount remained overdue for a period of six months or more;

(d) a bill that remains overdue for a period of six months or more;

(e) the interest with respect to a debt or the income on receivables under the head "other current assets" in the nature of short term loans/advances, which facility has remained overdue for a period of six months or more;

(f) any dues on account of sale of assets or services rendered or reimbursement of expenses incurred, which has remained overdue for a period of six months or more;

(g) the lease rental and hire purchase instalment that has become overdue for a period of 12 months or more;

(h) with respect to loans, advances and other credit facilities (including bills purchased and discounted), the balance outstanding under the credit facilities (including accrued interest) made available to the same borrower/beneficiary when any of the above credit facilities becomes a non-performing asset.

Provided that in the case of lease and hire purchase transactions, an NBFC may classify each such account on the basis of its record of recovery.

Non-performing asset (referred to in these directions as "NPA") means:

(a) an asset with respect to which interest has remained due for six months;

(b) a term loan inclusive of unpaid interest, when the instalment is overdue for more than six months or on which interest amount has remained due for six months;

(ba) a demand or call loan that has remained overdue for six months from the date of demand or call or on which interest amount remained due for a period of six months;

(c) a bill that remains overdue for six months;

(d) the interest with respect to a debt or the income on receivables under the head "other current assets" in the nature of short-term loans/advances, which facility has remained overdue for a period of six months;

(e) any dues on account of sale of assets or services rendered or reimbursement of expenses incurred, which remain overdue for a period of six months;

(f) the lease rental and hire purchase instalment, which has become overdue for a period of more than 12 months;

(g) with respect to loans, advances and other credit facilities (including bills purchased and discounted), the balance outstanding under the credit facilities (including accrued interest) made available to the same borrower/beneficiary when any of the above credit facilities becomes a non-performing asset. Provided that in the case of lease and hire purchase transactions, an NBFC can classify each such account on the basis of its record of recovery;

(xiv) Owned fund is paid-up equity capital, preference shares that are compulsorily convertible into equity, free reserves, balance in share premium account and capital reserves representing surplus arising out of sale proceeds of asset, excluding reserves created by revaluation of asset, as reduced by accumulated loss balance, book value of intangible assets and deferred revenue expenditure, if any;

(xv) Past due is an amount of income or interest that remains unpaid for a period of 30 days beyond the due date;

(xvi) Standard asset is an asset with respect to which no default in repayment of principal or payment of interest is perceived and which does not disclose any problem nor carry more than normal risk attached to the business;

(xvii) Substandard asset is:

(a) an asset that has been classified as non-performing asset for a period not exceeding 18 months;

(b) an asset where the terms of the agreement regarding interest and/or principal have been renegotiated or rescheduled or restructured after commencement of operations until the expiry of one year of satisfactory performance under the renegotiated or rescheduled or restructured terms. Provided that the classification of infrastructure loan as a substandard asset shall be in accordance with the provisions of Paragraph 13C of these directions;

(xviii) Subordinated debt is a fully paid-up capital instrument, which is unsecured and subordinated to the claims of other creditors and free from restrictive clauses and not redeemable at the instance of the holder or without the consent of the supervisory authority of the NBFC. The book value of such an instrument shall be subjected to discounting as provided hereunder:

Remaining maturity of the instruments and rate of discount

(a) Up to one year: 100 per cent

(b) More than one year but up to two years: 80 per cent

(c) More than two years but up to three years: 60 per cent

(d) More than three years but up to four years: 40 per cent

(e) More than four years but up to five years: 20 per cent to the extent that such discounted value does not exceed 50 per cent of Tier I capital;

(xix) Substantial interest is the holding of a beneficial interest by an individual or his spouse or minor child, whether singly or taken together, in the shares of a company, the amount paid up on which exceeds 10 per cent of the paid-up capital of the company; or the capital subscribed by all the partners of a partnership firm;

(xx) Tier-I capital means owned fund as reduced by investment in shares of other NBFCs and in shares, debentures, bonds, outstanding loans and advances including hire purchase and lease finance made to and deposits with subsidiaries and companies in the same group exceeding, in aggregate, 10 per cent of the owned fund;

(xxi) Tier-II capital includes the following:

(a) preference shares other than those which are compulsorily convertible into equity;
(b) revaluation reserves at discounted rate of 55 per cent;
(c) general provisions and loss reserves to the extent these are not attributable to actual diminution in value or identifiable potential loss in any specific asset and are available to meet unexpected losses, to the extent of one-and-one-fourth per cent of risk weighted assets;
(d) hybrid debt capital instruments; and
(e) subordinated debt to the extent the aggregate does not exceed Tier-I capital.

Other words or expressions used but not defined herein and defined in the Reserve Bank of India Act, 1934 (2 of 1934), or the Non-Banking Financial Companies Acceptance of Public Deposits (Reserve Bank) Directions, 1998, or the Residuary Non-Banking Companies (Reserve Bank) Directions, 1987, shall have the same meaning as assigned to them under that act or those directions. Any other words or expressions not defined in that act or those directions shall have the same meaning assigned to them in the Companies Act, 1956 (1 of 1956).

1. Income recognition

The income recognition shall be based on recognized accounting principles. Income including interest/discount or any other charges on NPAs shall be recognized only when it is actually realized. Any such income recognized before the asset became non-performing and remaining unrealized shall be reversed.

With respect to hire purchase assets, where instalments are overdue for more than 12 months, income shall be recognized only when hire charges are actually received. Any such income taken to the credit of profit and loss account before the asset became non-performing and remaining unrealized shall be reversed.

With respect to lease assets, where lease rentals are overdue for more than 12 months, the income shall be recognized only when lease rentals are actually received. The net lease rentals taken to the credit of profit and loss account before the asset became non-performing and remaining unrealized shall be reversed. Net lease rentals mean gross lease rentals as adjusted by the lease adjustment account debited/credited to the profit and loss account and as reduced by depreciation at the rate applicable.

2. Income from investments

Income from dividend on shares of corporate bodies and units of mutual funds shall be taken into account on cash basis. Provided that the income from the dividend on shares of corporate bodies may be taken into account on an accrual basis when such dividend has been declared by the corporate body in its annual general meeting and the NBFC's right to receive payment is established.

Income from bonds and debentures of corporate bodies and from government securities/bonds may be taken into account on an accrual basis. Provided that the interest rate on these instruments is pre-determined and interest is serviced regularly and is not in arrears. Income on securities of corporate bodies or public sector undertakings, the payment of interest and repayment of principal of which have been guaranteed by the central government or a state government may be taken into account on an accrual basis.

3. Accounting of investments

Investments in securities shall be classified into current and long-term at the time of making each investment. The investments shall be transferred scrip-wise from current to long-term or vice-versa at book-value or market-value, whichever is lower. The depreciation in one scrip shall not be set off against appreciation in another scrip at the time of such inter-class transfer, even with respect to scrips of the same category.

Quoted current investments shall be grouped into the following categories—equity shares, preference shares, debentures and bonds, government securities including treasury bills, units of mutual funds and others. Quoted current investments for each category shall be valued at cost or market value, whichever is lower. Unquoted equity shares in the nature of current investments shall be valued at cost or break-up value, whichever is lower. The fair value may be substituted for break-up value of the shares, if considered necessary. Unquoted preference shares in the nature of current investments shall be valued at cost or face value, whichever is lower. Investments in unquoted government securities or government guaranteed bonds shall be valued at carrying cost. Unquoted investments in the units of mutual funds in the nature of current investments shall be valued at the net asset value declared by the mutual fund with respect to each particular scheme. Commercial papers shall be valued at carrying cost. A long-term investment shall be valued in accordance with the Accounting Standard issued by ICAI.

4. Need for policy on demand/call loans

1. The board of directors of every NBFC granting/intending to grant demand/call loans shall frame a policy for the company and implement the same.
2. Such policy shall, *inter alia*, stipulate the following:
   - (i) A cut-off date within which the repayment of demand or call loan shall be demanded or called up;
   - (ii) The sanctioning authority shall record specific reasons in writing at the time of sanctioning the demand or call loan, if the cut-off date for demanding or calling up such loan is stipulated beyond a period of one year from the date of sanction;
   - (iii) The rate of interest which shall be payable on such loans;
   - (iv) Interest on such loans as stipulated shall be payable either at monthly or quarterly rests;
   - (v) The sanctioning authority shall record specific reasons in writing at the time of sanctioning the demand or call loan if no interest is stipulated or a moratorium is granted for any period;
   - (vi) A cut-off date for review of the performance of the loan, not exceeding six months commencing from the date of sanction;
   - (vii) Such demand or call loans shall not be renewed unless the periodical review has shown satisfactory compliance with the terms of sanction.

5. Asset classification

1. Every NBFC shall, after taking into account the degree of well-defined credit weaknesses and extent of dependence on collateral security for realization, classify its lease/hire purchase assets, loans and advances and any other forms of credit into the following classes:
   - (i) Standard assets;
   - (ii) Substandard assets;
   - (iii) Doubtful assets; and
   - (iv) Loss assets.
2. The class of assets referred to above shall not be upgraded merely as a result of rescheduling, unless it satisfies the conditions required for the upgradation.

6. Provisioning requirements

1. Every NBFC shall, after taking into account the time lag between an account becoming non-performing, its recognition as such, the realization of the security and the erosion over time in the value of security charged, make provision against substandard assets, doubtful assets and loss assets as provided hereunder:

The provisioning requirement with respect to loans, advances and other credit facilities including bills purchased and discounted shall be as shown in Table 19.1.

Lease and hire purchase assets:
The provisioning requirements with respect to hire purchase and leased assets shall be as follows:

Hire purchase assets:

(i) The total dues (overdue and future instalments taken together) as reduced by:
   - (a) the finance charges not credited to the profit and loss account and carried forward as unmatured finance charges; and
   - (b) the depreciated value of the underlying asset shall be provided for.

Table 19.1 Provisioning requirements

1. Loss assets	The entire asset shall be written off. If the assets are permitted to remain in the books for any reason, 100% of the outstandings should be provided for.
2. Doubtful assets	(a) 100% provision to the extent advance is not covered by the realizable value of the security to which the NBFC has a valid recourse shall be made. The realizable value is to be estimated on a realistic basis. (b) In addition to (a) above, depending on the period for which the asset has remained doubtful, provision to the extent of 20% to 50% of the secured portion (i.e. estimated realizable value of the outstandings) shall be made on the following basis: *Period for which asset has been considered doubtful* — *% of provision* Up to one year — 20 One to three years — 30 More than three years — 50
3. Substandard assets	A general provision of 10% of total outstandings shall be made.

Additional provision for hire purchase and leased assets:

(ii) With respect to hire purchase and leased assets, additional provision shall be made as shown in Table 19.2.

(iii) On expiry of a period of 12 months after the due date of the last instalment of the hire purchase/leased asset, the entire net book value shall be fully provided for.

7. Disclosure in the balance sheet

1. Every NBFC shall separately disclose in its balance sheet the provisions made as per the paragraph above without netting them from the income or against the value of assets.
2. The provisions shall be distinctly indicated under separate heads of accounts as follows:
   (i) provisions for bad and doubtful debts; and
   (ii) provisions for depreciation in investments.

Table 19.2 Additional provisions

a. Where any amounts of hire charges or lease rentals are overdue up to 12 months	Nil
Substandard assets:	
b. Where any amounts of hire charges or lease rentals are overdue for more than 12 months but up to 24 months	10 per cent of the net book value
Doubtful assets:	
c. Where any amounts of hire charges or lease rentals are overdue for more than 24 months but up to 36 months	40 per cent of the net book value
d. Where any amounts of hire charges or lease rentals are overdue for more than 36 months but up to 48 months	70 per cent of the net book value
Loss assets:	
e. Where any amounts of hire charges or lease rentals are overdue for more than 48 months	100 per cent of the net book value

3. Such provisions shall not be appropriated from the general provisions and loss reserves held, if any, by the NBFC.
4. Such provisions for each year shall be debited to the profit and loss account. The excess of provisions, if any, held under the heads general provisions and loss reserves may be written back without making adjustment against them.

Constitution of audit committee by NBFCs:

An NBFC with assets of INR 50 crore and above as per its last audited balance sheet shall constitute an audit committee consisting of not less than three members of its board of directors.

Accounting year:

Every NBFC shall prepare its balance sheet and profit and loss account as on March 31 every year with effect from its accounting year ending March 31, 2001. Provided that if the accounting year of any NBFC ends on any date other than March 31, 2001, such an NBFC shall prepare its balance sheet and profit and loss account for any fraction of the year ending on March 31, 2001.

Transactions in government securities:

1. Every NBFC:
   (i) shall hold its investments in approved securities in a Constituent's Subsidiary General Ledger (CSGL) account opened with a scheduled commercial bank or the Stock Holding Corporation of India Ltd or in a dematerialized account opened with a depository through a depository participant registered with the Securities and Exchange Board of India; and
   (ii) shall transact in these securities only through its CSGL account or its dematerialized account.
2. No NBFC shall undertake transactions in these securities in physical form with any broker.

8. Requirement as to capital adequacy

(Not applicable to a loan company, an investment company, a hire purchase finance company and an equipment leasing company, which has net owned funds of INR 25 lakh and above but not accepting/holding public deposit.)

Every NBFC shall maintain a minimum capital ratio consisting of Tier I and Tier II capital which shall not be less than:

(i) 1 per cent on or before March 31, 1998; and

(ii) 12 per cent on or before March 31, 1999, of its aggregate risk weighted assets and of risk adjusted value of off-balance sheet items.

The total of Tier II capital, at any point of time, shall not exceed 100 per cent of Tier I capital.

Explanations:

On balance sheet assets:

In these directions, degrees of credit risk expressed as percentage weightages have been assigned to balance sheet assets. Hence, the value of each asset/item requires to be multiplied by the relevant risk weights to arrive at the risk adjusted value of assets. The aggregate shall be taken into account for reckoning the minimum capital ratio. The risk-weighted asset shall be calculated as the weighted aggregate of funded items as detailed in Table 19.3.

Netting may be done only with respect to assets where provisions for depreciation or for bad and doubtful debts have been made. Assets that have been deducted from owned funds to arrive at net owned fund shall have a weightage of zero.

Off-balance sheet items:

In these directions, degrees of credit risk exposure attached to off-balance sheet items have been expressed as a percentage of the credit conversion factor. Hence, the face value of each item is to be first multiplied by the relevant conversion factor to arrive at the risk adjusted value of off-balance sheet items. The aggregate shall be taken into account for reckoning the minimum capital ratio. This shall have to be again multiplied by the risk weight of 100. The risk-adjusted value of the off-balance sheet items shall be calculated as per the credit conversion factors of non-funded items as detailed in Table 19.4.

Table 19.3 Risk-weighted assets

Weighted risk assets (balance sheet items)	*Percentage weight*
1. Cash and bank balances including fixed deposits and certificates of deposits with banks	0
2. Investments	
a. Approved securities	0
b. Bonds of public sector banks and fixed deposits/certificates of deposits/bonds of public financial institutions	20
c. Units of Unit Trust of India	20
d. Shares of all companies and debentures/bonds/commercial papers of companies other than in (b) above/units of mutual funds other than in (c) above	100
3. Investments	
a. Approved securities (except at (c) below)	0
b. Bonds of public sector banks	20
c. Fixed deposits/certificates of deposits/bonds of public financial institutions	100
d. Shares of all companies and debentures/bonds/commercial papers of all companies and units of all mutual funds	100
4. Current assets	
a. Stock on hire (net book value)	100
b. Inter-corporate loans/deposits	100
c. Loans and advances fully secured against deposits held by the company itself	0
d. Loans to staff	0
e. Other secured loans and advances considered good	100
f. Bills purchased/discounted	100
g. Others (to be specified)	100
5. Fixed assets (net of depreciation)	
a. Assets leased out (net book value)	100
b. Premises	100
c. Furniture and fixtures	100
6. Other assets	
a. Income tax deducted at source (net of provision)	0
b. Advance tax paid (net of provision)	0
c. Interest due on government securities	0
d. Others (to be specified)	100

Table 19.4 Credit conversion factors

Nature of item	*Credit conversion factor (%)*
1. Financial and other guarantees	100
2. Share/debenture underwriting obligations	50
3. Partly paid shares/debentures	100
4. Bills discounted/rediscounted	100
5. Lease contracts entered into but yet to be executed	100
6. Other contingent liabilities (to be specified)	50

Cash margins/deposits shall be deducted before applying the conversion factor. Loans against the NBFC's own shares are prohibited. No NBFC shall lend against its own shares. Any outstanding loan granted by an NBFC against its own shares on the date of commencement of these directions shall be recovered by the NBFC as per the repayment schedule.

9. NBFC failing to repay public deposit prohibited from making loans and investments

An NBFC that has failed to repay any public deposit or part thereof in accordance with the terms and conditions of such deposit, as provided in Section 45QA(1) of the Reserve Bank of India Act, 1934 (2 of 1934), shall not grant any loan or other credit facility by whatever name called or make any investment or create any other asset as long as the default exists.

No equipment leasing company or hire purchase finance company, which is accepting a public deposit, shall invest in:

(a) land or building, except for its own use, an amount exceeding 10 per cent of its owned fund;
(b) unquoted shares of another company, which is not a subsidiary company or a company in the same group of the NBFC, an amount exceeding 10 per cent of its owned fund.

No loan company or investment company that is accepting a public deposit shall invest in:

(a) land or building, except for its own use, an amount exceeding 10 per cent of its owned fund;
(b) unquoted shares of another company, which is not a subsidiary company or a company in the same group of the NBFC, an amount exceeding 20 per cent of its owned fund.

Provided that the land or building or unquoted shares acquired in satisfaction of its debts shall be disposed of by the NBFC within a period of three years or within such period as extended by the bank, from the date of such acquisition if the investment in these assets together with such assets already held by the NBFC exceeds the above ceiling. Provided further that the land or building or unquoted shares held by the company in excess of the ceiling specified hereinabove on the date of commencement of these directions shall be disposed of so as to bring down such holding within the said ceiling by the NBFC within three years or within such period as extended by the Reserve Bank of India from the date of coming into force of these directions.

While calculating the ceiling on investment in unquoted shares, investments in such shares of all companies shall be aggregated. Provided further that the above ceiling on the investment in unquoted shares shall not be applicable to an equipment leasing company or a hire purchase finance company or a loan company or an investment company with respect to investment in the equity capital of an insurance company up to the extent specifically permitted, in writing, by the Reserve Bank of India.

10. Concentration of credit/investment

(Not applicable to a loan company, an investment company, a hire purchase finance company and an equipment leasing company, which has net owned funds of INR 25 lakh and above but not accepting/holding public deposit.)

1. No NBFC shall:

   (i) lend to

      (a) any single borrower exceeding 15 per cent of its owned fund; and
      (b) any single group of borrowers exceeding 25 per cent of its owned fund;

   (ii) invest in

      (a) the shares of another company exceeding 15 per cent of its owned fund; and
      (b) the shares of a single group of companies exceeding 25 per cent of its owned fund;

   (iii) lend and invest (loans/investments taken together) exceeding

      (a) 25 per cent of its owned fund to a single party; and
      (b) 40 per cent of its owned fund to a single group of parties.

Provided that the above ceilings on credit/investment concentration shall not be applicable to an RNBC with respect to investments in approved securities, bonds, debentures and other securities issued by a government company or a public financial institution or a scheduled commercial bank under the provisions of paragraph 6(1) (a) and 6(1) (b) of the Residuary Non-Banking Companies (Reserve Bank) Directions, 1987. Provided further that the above ceiling on the investment in shares of another company shall not be applicable to an NBFC with respect to investment in the equity capital of an insurance company up to the extent specifically permitted, in writing, by the Reserve Bank of India.

2. Any loan granted and investment made by the NBFC in excess of the ceilings specified hereinabove and existing on the date of commencement of these directions shall be brought down by the NBFC as per the repayment schedule in due course.

For determining the above mentioned limits, off-balance sheet exposures shall be converted into credit risk by applying the conversion factors explained hereinabove.

The investments in debentures for the above purpose shall be treated as credit and not investment. The above ceilings on credit/investments shall be applicable to the own group of the NBFC as well as to the other group of borrowers/investee companies.

Submission of half-yearly return:

NBFCs including RNBCs referred to in paragraph 1(3)(i)(a) and (b) shall submit a half-yearly return within three months of the expiry of the relative half-year as on September and March every year, commencing from the half-year ending March 31, 1998, in the format (NBS-2) to the regional office of the department of non-banking supervision of the Reserve Bank of India under whose jurisdiction the registered office of the company is located as per the Second Schedule to the Non-Banking Financial Companies Acceptance of Public Deposits (Reserve Bank) Directions, 1998, and Schedule B to Residuary Non-Banking Companies (Reserve Bank) Directions, 1987.

11. Information with regard to change of address, directors, auditors, etc. to be submitted by NBFCs not accepting/holding public deposits

Every NBFC not accepting/holding public deposits shall, not later than one month from the occurrence of any change in the following matters, intimate:

(a) the complete postal address, telephone number/s and fax number/s of the registered/corporate office;
(b) the names and residential addresses of the directors of the company;
(c) the names and the official designations of its principal officers; and
(d) the names and office address of the auditors of the company; and furnish the specimen signatures of the officers authorized to sign on behalf of the company to the regional office of the department of non-banking supervision of the Reserve Bank of India as indicated in the Second Schedule to the Non-Banking Financial Companies Acceptance of Public Deposits (Reserve Bank) Directions, 1998.

12. Exposure to capital market

Every NBFC holding public deposits of INR 50 crore and above and RNBC with aggregate liabilities to the depositors of INR 50 crore and above as on March 31, 2002, or thereafter, shall submit a quarterly return within one month of the expiry of the relative quarter commencing from the quarter ending December 31, 2002, in the format NBS-6 annexed hereto to the regional office of the department of non-banking supervision of the Reserve Bank of India as indicated in the Second Schedule to the Non-Banking Financial Companies Acceptance of Public Deposits (Reserve Bank) Directions, 1998, and Schedule B to the Residuary Non-Banking Companies (Reserve Bank) Directions, 1987.

13. Norms relating to infrastructure loan

1. Applicability:

   (i) These norms shall be applicable to restructuring and/or rescheduling and/or renegotiation of the terms of agreement relating to infrastructure loan which is fully or partly secured standard and sub standard asset and to the loan, which is subjected to restructuring and/or rescheduling and/or renegotiation of terms with effect from the financial year 2003–04.

   (ii) Where the asset is partly secured, a provision to the extent of shortfall in the security available shall be made while restructuring and/or rescheduling and/or renegotiation of the loans, apart from the provision required on present value basis and as per prudential norms.

2. Restructuring, rescheduling or renegotiation of terms of infrastructure loan: NBFCs may, not more than once, restructure or reschedule or renegotiate the terms of the infrastructure loan agreement as per the policy framework laid down by the board of directors of the company in the following stages:

   (a) before commencement of commercial production;

   (b) after commencement of commercial production but before the asset has been classified as substandard;

   (c) after commencement of commercial production and the asset has been classified as substandard:

   Provided that in each of the above three stages, the restructuring and/or rescheduling and/or renegotiation of principal and/or interest may take place, with or without sacrifice, as part of the restructuring or rescheduling or renegotiating package evolved.

3. Treatment of restructured standard loan:

   The rescheduling or restructuring or renegotiation of the instalments of the principal alone at any of the aforesaid first two stages shall not cause a standard asset to be reclassified in the substandard category if the project is reexamined and found to be viable by the board of directors of the company or by a functionary at least one step senior to the functionary who sanctioned the initial loan for the project, within the policy framework laid down by the board. Provided that rescheduling or renegotiation or restructuring of the interest element at any of the foregoing first two stages shall not cause an asset to be downgraded to the substandard category subject to the condition that the amount of interest foregone, if any, on account of adjustment in the element of interest as specified later is either written off or 100 per cent provision is made against it.

4. Treatment of restructured substandard asset:

   A substandard asset shall continue to remain in the same category in case of restructuring or rescheduling or renegotiation of the instalments of the principal until the expiry of one year and the amount of interest foregone, if any, on account of adjustment, including adjustment by way of write-off of the past interest dues, in the element of interest as specified later, shall be written off or 100 per cent provision made thereagainst.

5. Adjustment of interest:

   Where rescheduling or renegotiation or restructuring involves a reduction in the rate of interest, the interest adjustment shall be computed by taking the difference between the rate of interest as currently applicable to the infrastructure loan (as adjusted for the risk rating applicable to the borrower) and the reduced rate and aggregating the present value (discounted at the rate currently applicable to the infrastructure loan, adjusted for risk enhancement) of the future interest payable so stipulated in the restructuring rescheduling or renegotiation proposal.

6. Funded interest:

   In the case of funding of interest with respect to NPAs, where the interest funded is recognized as income, the interest funded shall be fully provided for.

7. Income recognition norms:

   The income recognition with respect to infrastructure loan shall be governed by the provisions of paragraph 3 of these directions.

8. Treatment of provisions held:

   The provisions held by NBFCs against a non-performing infrastructure loan, which may be classified as standard after the coming into effect of these norms, shall continue to be held and not be reversed until full recovery of the loan is made.

9. Eligibility for upgradation of restructured substandard infrastructure loan:

   The substandard asset subjected to rescheduling and/or renegotiation and/or restructuring, whether with respect to instalments of principal amount or interest amount, by whatever modality, shall not be upgraded to the standard category until the expiry of one year of satisfactory performance under the restructuring and/or rescheduling and/or renegotiation terms.

10. Conversion of debt into equity:

    Where the amount due as interest is converted into equity or any other instrument, and income is recognized in consequence, full provision shall be made for the amount of income so recognized to offset the effect of such income recognition. Provided that no provision is required to be made if the conversion of interest is into equity which is quoted. Provided further that in such cases, interest income may be recognized at market value of the equity, as on the date of conversion, not exceeding the amount of interest converted to equity.

11. Conversion of debt into debentures:

Where principal amount and/or interest amount with respect to NPAs is converted into debentures, such debentures shall be treated as NPA, *ab initio*, in the same asset classification as was applicable to the loan just before conversion and provision shall be made as per norms.

12. Increase in exposure limits for infrastructure-related loan and investment:

NBFCs may exceed the concentration of credit/investment norms, as provided in paragraph 12 of these directions, by 5 per cent for any single party and by 10 per cent for a single group of parties, if the additional exposure is on account of infrastructure loan and/ or investment.

13. Risk weight for investment in AAA rated securitized paper:

The investment in AAA rated securitized paper pertaining to the infrastructure facility shall attract a risk weight of 50 per cent for capital adequacy purposes subject to the fulfillment of the following conditions:

(i) The infrastructure facility generates income/cash flows, which ensure servicing/repayment of the securitized paper.

(ii) The rating by one of the approved credit rating agencies is current and valid.

The rating relied upon shall be deemed to be current and valid if the rating is not more than one month old on the date of opening of the issue and the rating rationale from the rating agency is not more than one year old on the date of opening of the issue, and the rating letter and the rating rationale form part of the offer document.

(iii) In the case of secondary market acquisition, the AAA rating of the issue is in force and confirmed from the monthly bulletin published by the respective rating agency;

(iv) The securitized paper is a performing asset.

14. Exemptions

The Reserve Bank of India may, if it considers it necessary for avoiding any hardship or for any other just and sufficient reason, grant extension of time to comply with or exempt any NBFC or class of NBFCs from all or any of the provisions of these directions either generally or for any specified period, subject to such conditions as the Reserve Bank of India may impose.

19.2.3 NBFC's Acceptance of Public Deposits (Reserve Bank of India) Directions, 1998

The Government of India set up a committee, known as the Vasudev Committee, to review the regulatory framework for NBFCs. Based on the recommendations of the committee, the RBI issued guidelines in 1998 to regulate the acceptance of deposits by NBFCs. The salient features of these guidelines are as follows.[2]

- NBFCs with net owned funds of less than INR 25 lakh (with or without credit rating) are not permitted to accept public deposits.
- Unrated and underrated (rating below the minimum investment grade) NBFCs in the category of equipment leasing and hire purchase finance companies with net owned funds of INR 25 lakh and above are allowed to accept public deposits up to 1.5 times of their net owned funds or INR 10 crore, whichever is less, provided their capital to risk-weighted assets ratio (CRAR) is 15 per cent or above as per their last audited balance sheet.
- The unrated and underrated NBFCs in the category of loan and investment companies, irrespective of their net owned funds and CRAR, are not permitted to accept public deposits.
- NBFCs in the category of equipment leasing and hire purchase finance companies with net owned funds of INR 25 lakh and above as well as minimum investment-grade credit rating can accept public deposits four times the net owned funds provided they have a CRAR of not less than 10 per cent as on March 31, 1998, and shall have a CRAR of not less than 12 per cent as on March 31, 1999.

- NBFCs in the category of loan and investment companies with net owned funds of INR 25 lakh and above as well as minimum investment-grade credit rating can accept public deposits not exceeding 1.5 times the net owned funds provided they have a CRAR of 15 per cent or above with immediate effect.
- NBFCs in the category of equipment and hire purchase companies should endeavour to increase their CRAR to 15 per cent as early as possible.
- NBFCs in the category of loan and investment companies that do not have minimum CRAR of 15 per cent as on the date but otherwise comply with all the prudential norms and (a) have a credit rating of AAA may accept or renew public deposits up to the level outstanding as at the close of business on December 18, 1998, or 1.5 times the net owned funds, whichever is more, subject to the condition that they should attain a CRAR of 15 per cent by March 31, 2000, and bring down the excess deposits, if any, by December 31, 2001, and (b) have credit rating of AA/A may accept or renew public deposits as per the existing provisions of the directions (0.5/1.0 times their net owned funds) but they should attain a minimum CRAR of 15 per cent on or before March 31, 2000, as per their audited balance sheet, failing which they should regularize their position by repayment or otherwise by December 31, 2001.
- The above benefit will not be available to those companies whose CRAR is presently 15 per cent and above but slips down below the minimum level of 15 per cent subsequently.
- The disclosure norms for NBFCs accepting public deposits have been widened so as to enable depositors to make informed decisions.
- Stipulations on prudential norms, ceiling on interest rates, payment of brokerage on public deposits, etc. remain unchanged.
- NBFCs have been advised not to invest more than 10 per cent of their owned funds in land and buildings except for their own use. The ceiling on investment in unquoted shares of companies other than their group/subsidiary companies has been fixed at 10 per cent of their owned fund for equipment leasing and hire purchase finance companies and 20 per cent of the owned fund for loan and investment companies. A time limit of three years has been set for NBFCs to dispose of the excess of such assets, including the assets acquired in satisfaction of their debts, wherever a company surpasses the ceiling indicated above.
- The unincorporated bodies engaged in the business of a non-banking financial institution are not allowed to accept deposits except from relatives specified and in the manner prescribed in the provision of Section 45-S of the RBI Act. However, such entities are now allowed to access loans from bodies with a corporate identity, including NBFCs. Accordingly, the deposits from (a) the companies incorporated under the Companies Act, (b) corporations established under any statute, and (c) cooperative societies registered under any state law have been exempted from the definition of "deposit" under the RBI Act. Individuals, firms, associations of persons, Hindu undivided family (HUF) and partnership firms may accept deposits from the above mentioned corporate entities also for the purpose of their financial business.

In terms of Section 45-IB of the RBI Act, 1934, the minimum level of liquid assets to be maintained by NBFCs is 15 per cent of public deposits outstanding as on the last working day of the second preceding quarter. Of the 15 per cent, NBFCs are required to invest not less than 10 per cent in approved securities and the remaining 5 per cent can be in unencumbered term deposits with any scheduled commercial bank. The liquid assets can consist of government securities, government guaranteed bonds and term deposits with any scheduled commercial banks.

NBFCs accepting public deposits should furnish to RBI the audited balance sheet of each financial year and audited profit and loss account with respect to that year as passed in the general body meeting together with a copy of the report of the board of directors and a copy of the report and notes on accounts furnished by auditors, statutory annual return on deposits, certificate from the auditors that the company is in a position to repay the deposits as and when the claims arise, quarterly return on liquid assets, half-yearly return on prudential norms, half-yearly asset-liability management (ALM) returns by companies with public deposits of INR 20 crore and above or with assets of INR 100 crore and above, irrespective of the size of deposits, monthly return on exposure to capital market by companies with public deposits of INR 50 crore and above, and a copy of the credit rating obtained once a year along with one of the half-yearly returns on prudential norms. NBFCs with size of INR 100 crore and above but not accepting public deposits are required to submit a monthly return on important financial parameters of the company. All companies not accepting public deposits have to pass a board resolution to the effect that they have neither accepted public deposits nor will accept any public deposit during the year.

All NBFCs are not allowed to accept public deposits. Only those NBFCs holding a valid certificate of registration with authorization to accept public deposits can accept/hold public deposits. NBFCs are allowed to accept/renew public deposits for a minimum period of 12 months and maximum period of 60 months. They cannot accept deposits repayable on demand. NBFCs cannot offer interest rates higher than the ceiling rate prescribed by the RBI from time to time. The present ceiling is 12.5 per cent per annum from April 24, 2007. This is the maximum permissible rate an NBFC can pay on its public deposits but they can offer lower rates. The interest can be paid or compounded at rests not shorter than monthly rests. NBFCs should not offer gifts/incentives or any other additional benefit to depositors. NBFCs (except certain AFCs) should have the minimum investment-grade credit rating. The repayment of deposits by NBFCs is not guaranteed by the RBI. The deposits with NBFCs are not insured. An unrated NBFC, except certain asset finance companies, cannot accept public deposits. An exception is made in case of unrated asset finance companies with a CRAR of 15 per cent, which can accept public deposits up to 1.5 times of the net owned funds or INR 10 crore, whichever is lower, without having a credit rating.

Where an NBFC fails to repay any deposit or part thereof in accordance with the terms and conditions of such deposit, the Company Law Board (CLB), either on its own motion or on an application from the depositor directs, by order, the NBFC to make repayment of such deposit or a part thereof forthwith or within such time and subject to such conditions as may be specified in the order.

19.2.4 NBFCs and the Insurance Business

NBFCs registered with the RBI are permitted to set up insurance joint ventures for undertaking insurance business with risk participation. Before entering into the insurance business, NBFCs are required to obtain prior approval of IRDA and the RBI. However, they can take up insurance agency business on a fee basis and without risk participation without the approval of the RBI subject to the following conditions:

i. NBFCs should obtain requisite permission from IRDA and comply with IRDA regulations for acting as a composite corporate agent with insurance companies.
ii. NBFCs should not adopt any restrictive practice of forcing its customers to go in only for a particular insurance company with respect to assets financed by the NBFC. The customers should be allowed to exercise their own choice.
iii. As the participation by an NBFC's customers in insurance products is purely on a voluntary basis, it should be stated in all publicity material distributed by the NBFC in a prominent way. There should be no linkage, either direct or indirect, between the provision of financial services offered by the NBFC to its customers and use of the insurance products.
iv. The premium should be paid by the insured directly to the insurance company without routing through the NBFC.
v. The risks, if any, involved in insurance agency should not get transferred to the business of the NBFC.

19.2.5 Distribution of Mutual Fund Products by NBFCs

In order to strengthen the financial position of NBFCs by allowing diversification in their business, the RBI has allowed NBFCs, selectively, to market and distribute mutual fund products as agents of mutual funds. NBFCs fulfilling the following minimum requirements are eligible to apply to the RBI for permission.

- Minimum net owned funds of INR 100 crore;
- The company should have made net profit as per the last two years' audited balance sheet;
- The percentage of net NPAs to net advances of the NBFC as per the last audited balance sheet should not be more than 3 per cent; and
- The non-deposit-taking NBFCs should have a CRAR of 10 per cent and deposit-taking NBFCs should have a CRAR of 12 per cent or 15 per cent, as applicable to the company.

In addition, NBFCs seeking approval from the RBI to market and distribute mutual fund products should adhere to the following stipulations.

a. The NBFC should comply with the SEBI guidelines/regulations, including their code of conduct, for distribution of mutual fund products.
b. The company should not adopt any restrictive practice of forcing its customers to go in for a particular mutual fund product sponsored by it. The customers should be allowed to exercise their own choice.
c. The participation by a company's customer in mutual fund products is purely on a voluntary basis and this information should be stated in all publicity material distributed by the company in a prominent way. There should be no linkage, either direct or indirect, between the provisions of financial services offered by the company to its customers and distribution of the mutual fund products.
d. The company should only act as an agent of the customers, forwarding the investor's application for purchase/sale of mutual fund units together with the payment instruments, to the mutual fund/registrars/transfer agents. The purchase of units should be at the customers' risk and without the company guaranteeing any assured return.
e. The company should neither acquire units of mutual funds from the secondary market for sale to customers, nor should it buy back units of mutual funds from its customers.
f. In case the company has custody of mutual fund units on behalf of the customers, it should ensure that its own investments and the investments belonging to its customers are kept distinct from each other.
g. The risks, if any, involved in the mutual fund agency business should not get transferred to the business of the NBFC.
h. The company should be adhering to Know-Your-Customer guidelines and provisions of Prevention of Money Laundering Act.
i. The NBFC should comply with other terms and conditions as the RBI may specify on this behalf from time to time.

The permission given to an NBFC to market and distribute mutual fund products as agents of mutual funds is liable to be withdrawn with a notice period of three months in the event of any undesirable/unhealthy operations coming to the notice of the RBI.

19.2.6 Corporate Governance

__Corporate governance__ deals with how companies are directed and controlled with a focus on wealth creation.

In order to enable NBFCs to adopt best practices and greater transparency in their operations, the RBI has issued the following guidelines:

- Audit committee: An NBFC with assets of INR 50 crore and above, as per its last audited balance sheet, is required to constitute an audit committee consisting of not less than three members of its board of directors. In addition, all deposit-taking NBFCs with deposit size of INR 20 crore may also consider constituting an audit committee on similar lines.
- Nomination committee: The deposit-taking NBFCs with deposit size of INR 20 crore and above and non-deposit-taking NBFCs with asset size of INR 100 crore and above may form a nomination committee to ensure "fit and proper" status of proposed/existing directors.
- Risk management committee: The market risk for NBFCs with public deposits of INR 20 crore and above or having an asset size of INR 100 crore of above as on the date of last audited balance sheet is addressed by the asset liability management committee (ALCO) constituted to monitor the asset liability gap and strategize action to mitigate the associated risk. To manage the integrated risk, a risk management committee may be formed in addition to the ALCO in case of the above category of NBFCs.
- Disclosure and transparency: The following information should be put up by the NBFC to the board of directors at regular intervals as may be prescribed by the board in this regard.
    - Progress made in putting in place a progressive risk management system, and risk management policy and strategy followed.
    - Conformity with corporate governance standards, viz. in composition of various committees, their role and functions, periodicity of the meetings and compliance with coverage and review functions, etc.
    - Connected lending: In order to obviate conflict of interest in the lending operations of the NBFC, it should not grant any loan, advance or non-fund based facility or any other financial accommodation/facility to:

a. its directors or their relatives;
b. to any firm in which any of its directors is interested as partner, manager, employee or guarantor;
c. any individual with respect to whom any of its directors is a guarantor;
d. any company of which, or the subsidiary or the holding company of which, any of the directors of the NBFC is a director, managing agent, manager, employee or any firm in which he holds substantial interest; and
e. any entity, whether incorporated or not, which uses as a part of its name or in connection with its business the name of the NBFC or any such word as would show its association with the NBFC.

NBFCs are required to submit information pertaining to loans and advances granted to their directors, relatives and other entities referred to above for each quarter-end in the prescribed proforma to the regional office concerned of the department of non-banking supervision within 15 days from the close of the respective quarter.

NBFCs shall frame their internal guidelines on corporate governance, enhancing the scope of the guidelines without sacrificing the spirit underlying the above guidelines and it shall be published on the company's website, if any, for the information of various stakeholders.

19.2.7 Regulations for Systemically Important NBFCs

The RBI has also issued guidelines for the overall regulation of systemically important NBFCs. These guidelines are issued in the light of the divergent regulatory requirements for various aspects of the functioning of banks and NBFCs. The salient features of these guidelines, issued in December 2006, are as follows:

1. Regulatory framework for systematically important NBFCs (non-deposit taking NBFCs with an asset size of INR 100 crore and more):
   - They shall maintain a minimum CRAR of 10 per cent.
   - No NBFC shall lend to any single borrower exceeding 15 per cent of its owned fund and to any single group of borrowers exceeding 25 per cent of its owned funds.
   - No NBFC shall invest in the shares of another company exceeding 15 per cent of its owned funds and in the shares of a single group of companies exceeding 25 per cent of its owned funds.
   - No NBFC shall lend and invest (loans/investments taken together) exceeding 25 per cent of its owned funds to a single party and 40 per cent of its owned funds to a single group of parties.

   The above ceiling on the investment in shares of another company shall not be applicable to an NBFC with respect to investment in the equity capital of an insurance company to the extent specifically permitted by the RBI. For determining the above mentioned limits, off-balance sheet exposures be converted into credit risk by applying the conversion factors. Investments in debentures will be treated as lending and not investment. The NBFCs may exceed the concentration of credit/investment norms, as above, by 5 per cent for any single party and by 10 per cent for a single group of parties, if the additional exposure is on account of infrastructure loan and/or investment. NBFCs not accessing public funds both directly and indirectly may apply to the RBI for an appropriate dispensation consistent with the spirit of the exposure limits.
2. The companies financing real/physical assets for productive/economic activity are classified as asset finance companies (AFCs). They are permitted to exceed the exposure to a single party and single group of parties up to a further 5 per cent of their owned funds in exceptional circumstances with the approval of their boards.
3. NBFCs set up under the automatic route will be permitted to undertake only those 19 activities that are permitted under the automatic route. Diversification into any other activity would require the prior approval of the Foreign Investment Promotion Board (FIPB). Similarly, a company that has entered into an area permitted under the FDI policy (such as software) and seeks to diversify into the NBFC sector subsequently would also have to ensure compliance with the minimum capitalization norms and other regulations as applicable.

The objective of KYC guidelines is to prevent NBFCs from being used, intentionally or unintentionally, by criminal elements for money laundering activities.

19.2.8 Know-Your-Customer (KYC) Guidelines

Following the terrorist attack on the World Trade Center in New York on September 11, 2001, the global financial community was alerted and supervisors in many countries took steps to eliminate money laundering. The G7 countries set up the Financial Action Task Force (FATF), with 26 countries as members, to monitor money laundering trends and techniques and suggest counter measures. The FATF suggested several measures and the International Monetary Fund (IMF) recommended that the suggestions be implemented by February 1, 2002. The countries that fail to implement them could face financial sanctions and their banks could be excluded from international financial markets. This has led to banks focusing more on knowing their customers and ensuring that they have strong internal controls. Based on the recommendations of the FATF and the paper issued on Customer Due Diligence (CDD) for banks by the Basel Committee on Banking Supervision, the RBI has issued detailed guidelines to the banks. These guidelines are equally applicable to NBFCs. NBFCs are advised to adopt the same with suitable modifications depending on the activity undertaken by them and ensure that a proper policy framework on Know-Your-Customer and anti-money laundering measures are formulated and put in place. NBFCs had to comply with the provisions of the RBI circular dated February 21, 2005, before December 31, 2005.

The objective of KYC guidelines is to prevent NBFCs from being used, intentionally or unintentionally, by criminal elements for money laundering activities. The KYC procedures also enable NBFCs to know and understand their customers and their financial dealings better, which in turn help them manage their risks prudently. NBFCs should frame their KYC policies incorporating the following four key elements.

1. Customer acceptance policy: NBFCs should develop a clear customer acceptance policy laying down explicit criteria for acceptance of customers. The customer acceptance policy must ensure that explicit guidelines are in place.
2. Customer identification procedures: NBFCs should clearly spell out the customer identification procedure to be carried out at different stages—while establishing a banking relationship, carrying out a financial transaction or when the NBFC has a doubt about the authenticity/veracity or the adequacy of previously obtained customer identification data.
3. Monitoring of transactions: Ongoing monitoring is an essential element of effective KYC procedures. NBFCs can effectively control and reduce risk only if they have an understanding of the normal and reasonable activity of the customer so that they have the means of identifying transactions that fall outside the regular pattern of activity.
4. Risk management: NBFCs should ensure that an effective KYC programme is put in place by establishing appropriate procedures and ensuring their effective implementation. It should cover proper management oversight, systems and controls, segregation of duties, training and other related matters. Responsibility should be explicitly allocated within the NBFC for ensuring that the NBFC's policies and procedures are implemented effectively.

NBFCs are advised to apply the KYC norms to all the existing customers in a time-bound manner on the basis of materiality and risk. Transactions in existing accounts should be continuously monitored and any unusual pattern in the operation of the account should trigger a review of the CDD measures. Where the NBFC is unable to apply appropriate KYC measures due to non-furnishing of information and/or non-cooperation by the customer, the NBFC may consider closing the account or terminating the banking/business relationship after issuing due notice to the customer explaining the reasons for taking such a decision.

Box 19.1 provides a brief profile of one of the oldest NBFCs.

Box 19.1 The Peerless General Finance and Investment Company Ltd

Incorporated in 1932 as The Peerless Insurance Co Ltd, a leading indigenous insurance company, the company is now known as The Peerless General Finance and Investment Co Ltd. The vision of PGFI is to emerge as the country's most trusted doorstep financial services provider in the private sector with the lowest servicing cost to the customers.

PGFI mission

- To be a premier financial services company helping people build their security by providing them with innovative financial products and quality investment solutions through dedicated service.

(Continued)

- To create livelihood solutions across the length and breadth of the country.
- To fulfil its role as a responsible corporate citizen.
- To provide a supportive and rewarding environment for employees

Unique distinctions

- The country's premier financial service provider in the private sector with over 77 years of experience.
- A wide variety of tailor-made, co-branded, insurance-linked financial products.
- Technology-based, prompt and personalized service, right at the customer's doorstep.
- Helping people build regular saving habit and offering assured return with total security.
- Set a spotless record of maturity payment—over INR 158 billion already disbursed.
- Safe and risk-less—secured approved investments
- Tapping the untapped areas—mopping up huge unsurfaced resources and injecting the same into the mainstream of the country's economy.
- Generating excellent, enormous self-employment opportunities through Smart Rojgar Yojna, which is the source of livelihood for teeming millions across the country.

Smart solutions in financial products

- Irrespective of whether a customer is a high net worth individual or a professional, or has a modest monthly earning, he/she can choose from a variety of fixed deposits to invest in depending on his/her investible surplus and its duration.
- Among recurring deposit schemes, a customer can save convenient amounts at chosen intervals, i.e., daily or monthly. With the power of compounding, watch the customer's savings grow to a sizeable amount at the end of the tenure.
- Through its vast network of branches, agents and financial advisers, Peerless offers free investment advice at the customer's doorstep, keeping the customer's interest in mind. That's what makes Peerless a trusted household name in India.

Doorstep customer service

Through a vast network of agents, financial advisers and branches, Peerless provides personalized doorstep service to depositors.

A responsible corporate citizen

- Promoting different worthy causes for the welfare of society is an integral part of the company's corporate ethos.
- To ensure greater good of a greater number and enrich the quality of life, Peerless has been contributing generously towards various social welfare projects. Peerless Brachy Therapy unit at Thakurpukur Cancer Centre and Welfare Home, Peerless Yatrinivas and Free Soil Testing Laboratory in collaboration with Ramakrishna Mission at Kamarpukur, Peerless Polyclinics, Milan Tirtha—a unique old age home at Baranagore, Kolkata, Peerless Pedestrian Overbridge at VIP Road and Ultadanga Crossing, Kolkata, are some of the prominent examples of the company's social welfare projects.
- For the underprivileged tribal people of Ghatsila and its adjoining areas, two extraordinary welfare projects were taken up in collaboration with Bharat Sevashram Sangha. A charitable dispensary in the name of Peerless Diamond Jubilee Charitable Dispensary was set up in Ghatsila with a view to imparting training to the tribal people for grooming them for self-employment.
- What is more, the company has always reached out to the people in distress, offering aid, succour and relief to the victims of natural calamities like flood or earthquake across the country.

Source: www.**peerless.co**.in

Summary

1. NBFCs evolved to cater to the needs of small investors and borrowers. Following the economic reforms initiatives in India, NBFCs have grown in both magnitude and depth.
2. NBFCs are characterized by close customer interaction and relationships, deep understanding of customer needs, wider and specialized branch networks and low-cost operations.

3. Equipment leasing companies, hire purchase finance companies, loan companies, investment companies, residuary non-banking companies, mutual benefit financial companies or nidhi companies, miscellaneous non-banking companies or chit fund companies are examples of NBFCs.
4. NBFCs provide both fund-based services (such as leasing, hire purchase, bill discounting, promoter funding) and fee-based services (such as merchant banking, advisory services, syndication of loans, portfolio management, stockbroking and underwriting).
5. On the one hand, NBFCs and commercial banks are complementary to each other, but on the other hand, both are serious competitors in mobilization of deposits and credit deployment.
6. The Non-Banking Financial Companies Prudential Norms (Reserve Bank) Directions, 1998, prescribe guidelines on income recognition, asset classification and provisioning requirements applicable to NBFCs, exposure norms, constitution of audit committee, disclosure in the balance sheet and requirement of capital adequacy.
7. Based on the recommendations of the Vasudev Committee, the Reserve Bank of India issued guidelines in 1998 to regulate the acceptance of deposits by NBFCs.
8. NBFCs registered with the RBI are also permitted to set up insurance joint ventures for undertaking insurance business with risk participation.
9. The Reserve Bank of India has also permitted NBFCs, though selectively, to market and distribute mutual fund products as agents of mutual funds.
10. In order to enable NBFCs to adopt best practices and encourage greater transparency in their operations, the Reserve Bank of India has issued certain guidelines on corporate governance.
11. The Reserve Bank of India has also issued guidelines for the overall regulation of systemically important NBFCs.
12. NBFCs are advised to adopt Know-Your-Customer guidelines issued by the Reserve Bank of India.

Questions

1. What are the special characteristics of NBFCs?
2. How are NBFCs classified?
3. Discuss the implications of prudential norms with respect to income recognition.
4. Explain the salient features of prudential norms with respect to capital adequacy.
5. What are the norms to be followed by NBFCs to sanction infrastructure loans?
6. What are the provisioning requirements as per the prudential norms of the RBI?
7. What are the minimum requirements for NBFCs to be eligible to distribute mutual fund products?
8. What are the regulations with regard to acceptance of deposits by NBFCs?
9. Discuss the corporate governance guidelines. How are they relevant for the customers of NBFCs?
10. Can banking frauds be reduced with the implementation of Know-Your-Customer guidelines? If so, how?
11. What are the conditions to be fulfilled by NBFCs to take up insurance business?

Endnotes

1. This section is based on The Reserve Bank of India Act, 1935 (amended in 1997), accessed at http://www.rbi.org.in/home.aspx, July 2010.
2. This section is based on data taken from the Reserve Bank of India.

Chapter 20

Chit Funds

LEARNING OBJECTIVES

After reading this chapter, you should be able to:

- Trace the origin of chit funds.
- Explain the modus operandi of chit funds.
- Highlight the role and responsibilities of the foreman.
- Present the legal framework of chit funds.

20.1 Introduction

The concept of chit funds originated in India before commercial banks came into being, thus filling a large credit gap in the economy. It started with farmers pooling in periodically a certain quantity of food grains so that a farmer could draw on the pool when in need. Eventually, people in villages and small towns without banking facilities started contributing a certain amount of money periodically. The pooled amount would be given to a person in the group who was in urgent need of money. There was no discount or interest involved. The major benefit was that the person could get a lump sum though he contributed to the pool in instalments. As time passed, competition grew among members of the group to draw on the pooled amount. The members were even willing to forgo a certain portion of the pooled amount to get an earlier chance to draw on it. This eventually led to bidding and the concept of discount. Thus, the chit fund business developed to satisfy the smaller money-needs of people.

The chit fund industry had a humble beginning in the households of Kerala. It has now become popular throughout the country. In every state, people are attracted to chit funds in large numbers. It has spread to other countries as well. Chit funds developed parallel to the organized banking system in India. Despite the enormous expansion in the banking system in recent decades, chit funds continue to fill the credit gap in the economy. Today, chit funds, with their vast network of operations, are recognized as important credit and investment agencies.

The term "chit" came from the Tamil word chitty meaning a piece of paper on which something is written.

Colloquially, chits are known as "chitty" or "kuri", and internationally as ROSCA, or rotating savings and credit associations. It is believed that the term "chit" came from the Tamil word *chitty* meaning a piece of paper on which something is written. The word could also indicate pieces of papers used in the conventional lottery method to determine the winner of the chit. Primarily, chits are committed savings and contingency insurance for low-income groups, self-employed (particularly small traders) and salaried classes. The motto of chit funds is "save for a rainy day". People from different strata of society can converge to meet their financial needs—to invest their savings or borrow for their immediate financial requirements.

Before it was organized, the chit fund business was confined to households and close-knit neighbourhoods. The business was based on personal faith. The principle of mutual interest governed chit funds. Subsequently, small firms and wealthy individuals entered the business.

In recent years, corporate organizations including public sector companies (such as Kerala State Financial Enterprises Limited) have entered the chit fund business. A chit company forms different chit fund schemes, also called groups. Each group consists of a certain number of subscribers, who agree to contribute a specific amount as instalment for a certain number of months.

Many chit fund companies in India are small and medium enterprises (SMEs) and are important sources of finance for SMEs operating in other sectors of the economy. There were about 9,900 chit fund companies in India as of March 2009. The leading players include Shriram Chits, Margadarsi Chit Fund and Balussery Benefit Chit Fund.

20.1.1 Definition of Chit Fund

According to the Chit Fund Act, 1982, a *chit fund* is an indigenous financial institution involving regular periodical subscriptions by a group of persons. It is, in law, a contract between the subscribers and the foreman that provides that the subscribers shall subscribe a certain sum by periodical instalments for a definite period. Each subscriber shall, in turn, as determined by lot or by auction or in such other agreed manner be entitled to the prized amount.

20.1.2 Modus Operandi of Chit Funds

*A **chit fund** is a mutual benefit fund wherein a group of people voluntarily agrees to contribute to a common fund such that each one is entitled to certain benefits.*

A **chit fund** can be called a mutual benefit fund wherein a group of people voluntarily agree to contribute to a common fund and thereby get certain benefits. Each and every subscriber, also known as a member, contributes periodically (monthly or daily for a certain period) a predetermined amount to a common pool, which is known as *chit value* or the *pot*. There shall be as many periodical instalments as there are members. The pot is auctioned periodically on a particular date. The members who wish to participate in the auction assemble at a particular place and call out their bids (for the chit value). Any member who is unable to be physically present at the bidding can send his/her bid in a sealed cover to the manager/foreman of the chit well before the auction commences.

To illustrate, consider a chit fund scheme that has the following characteristics:

Chit value: INR 100,000
Period: 25 months
Number of subscribers: 25
Monthly subscription: INR 4,000

Every month, each member pays INR 4,000, totalling to INR 100,000. This amount, called the pot, is auctioned out. On a specific day of every month, the members assemble at a particular place to bid for the pot (INR 100,000). The manager of the chit fund starts the bid with a small amount, say INR 5,000, after which the members can bid for any amount above INR 5,000. Suppose, a member bids for INR 10,000 and some other member wants to challenge his bid. So, he or she will bid above INR 10,000. The auction continues thus. Suppose a member bids for INR 20,000, and the deal is closed at that level of discount as there is no challenger. There is a fixed time frame for the entire auction, which is usually five minutes. Thus, the highest bid on completion of the fixed time is declared successful by the manager. The highest bidder is awarded INR 80,000 (i.e., INR 100,000 – INR 20,000), which is known as the prized amount. The *prized amount* is the amount for which the chit is prized or auctioned. The bid amount (INR 20,000) is known as the *discount*, and it is distributed equally among all the members. Thus, every member is entitled to a dividend of INR 800 (INR 20,000/25). For the next instalment, each member is expected to pay INR 3,200 (INR 4,000 – INR 800). In other words, a member saves INR 800 for that month. The discount amount can also be divided among the members as cash payout. Also, all the bid amounts (discounts) can be collected and made available to the members to bid, so that the time period for which the members pay the subscription gets reduced. The process of bidding and dividing the bid amount among the members is repeated every month till the end of the scheme (25 months). Once a member wins the bid, he is called the *prized subscriber*. Prized subscribers are not allowed to participate in future biddings. In other words, as time passes, the number of bidders (non-prized subscribers) lessens until in the last month, only one member is eligible to receive the chit value. Therefore, after the first month, there will be 24 members eligible to bid, in the second month there will be 23 members, and so on. On the twenty-fifth month, only one member will be eligible to participate in the bidding, hence he will be awarded the chit amount in full. It may be noted that every member of the chit fund gets an opportunity to receive the chit amount once during the tenure of that particular scheme. However, a member is allowed to win the bid only once during the chit period. A chit fund completes its cycle when all the agreed number of instalments are paid and distributed to all the members. Another notable feature is that the members are entitled to bid at the auction even if only one instalment has been paid, that is, the first instalment. Also, every member contributes to the chit fund by paying the instalments till the end of the duration of the chit fund and the contribution to be made each time by the members is also the same. But the amount taken out from the chit fund by each member varies depending on the competition among the bidders and the period left for the completion of the chit scheme. A chit fund combines saving and borrowing as each member can simultaneously be a saver and a borrower.

Bid amounts (discounts) vary from auction to auction and from scheme to scheme. Although multiple factors influence the bid amounts, it is mainly the cost of carry that determines the bid amount. **Cost of carry** is the annualized interest cost the bidder decides to pay on the prized amount. A higher cost of carry is indicative of competition to bid and vice versa. In some chit fund schemes, there may not be any bidder towards the end of the term of the scheme. Therefore, the prized amount is decided by the minimum (base) bid amount and the amount is allotted by lottery and paid to the member who wins the lottery.

A member who wins the bid is known as prized subscriber.

***Cost of carry** is the annualized interest cost the bidder decides to pay on the prized amount.*

The bid amounts are usually greater in the initial periods of the chit and keep decreasing as time passes. Thus, the discount to the face value of the chit fund is higher in the initial period (months/days) of the chit fund as compared to later periods. The earlier the bid during the period of the chit fund scheme, the greater the discount and lesser the amount to be received by the member. For instance, in a 25-month chit fund scheme, the amount to be received by the prized subscriber in the second month will be less than that in, say, the twentieth month. The higher bid amounts (discount) in the initial stages of the chit fund scheme correspond to the higher interest amount on the money borrowed (prized amount). For example, consider a chit value of INR 100,000. In the second month, a member wins the bid at INR 40,000. This means he will receive INR 60,000. The amount of INR 40,000 can be understood as the interest payable on the loan amount of INR 60,000. In other words, the subscription amount that the member pays periodically (instalments) is composed of the principle and interest components of the loan.

If the chit fund is a registered one, the provisions of the relevant act apply to the operations of the chit. For example, according to the Chit Fund Act, 1982, there is a minimum (5 per cent of the chit amount) and a maximum (45 per cent of the chit amount) limit of the bid. That is, there is a 45 per cent cap on the bidding amount. The minimum bid of 5 per cent is normally the manager's commission. Thus, out of the discount amount, 5 per cent of the chit value (the total contribution collected from all the subscribers each time) goes to the manager as commission for conducting the chit and meeting other expenses, if any, and the balance of the discount amount is distributed equally among the members of the chit scheme. The manager is also a subscriber of a particular chit scheme and he is entitled to obtain the chit amount once and, of course, without any discount. The chit manager has to deposit an amount equal to the chit value with the Registrar of Chits. Normally, the first auction of the chit goes to the manager of the chit and it is deposited with the Registrar of Chits. There is also a minimum tick for every chit scheme. That is, the members have to bid in multiples of, say, INR 10.

20.1.3 Role and Responsibilities of the Foreman

The organizer of a chit fund is called **foreman** or **manager**. The foreman can be an individual or individuals representing, by some designation(s), a public limited company, a private limited company, a public sector organization, a cooperative organization or a trust. A large part of the chit fund market in India is unorganized, and the individual who initiates and organizes a chit fund becomes the foreman. The agreement between the foreman and the chit holders is based on the trusteeship assumed by the foreman. The foreman underwrites the regular subscriptions of each chit holder. If there are defaulters on any instalments, it is the foreman who must substitute the cash flow from his own funds. Although the public can subscribe to a chit fund, the foreman reserves the right to reject applications. It is the usual practice that the manager screens the applications (of those who wish to join the chit fund) before admission.

*The **foreman**, otherwise known as **manager**, is one who manages the chit.*

If any of the subscribers defaults in paying any of the periodical subscriptions, the foreman has the responsibility of demanding and securing the payment of instalments on behalf of the other members. The foreman is also obliged to make good that amount to the other subscribers pending realization from the defaulting subscriber. Generally, the successful bidders will be paid the amount on furnishing a security or surety (personal surety or guarantee). If the successful bidder fails to provide the security or surety, the amount may not be paid to him.

Chit funds are severely affected by default in subscriptions. The chit fund manager has to pump in money to keep the business going. In case of continued default by many members in big amounts, a chit fund can collapse. To meet such exigencies, the foreman should maintain adequate capital base. The financial solvency of the foreman is required to take care of all the infrastructural needs as well as meet the shortfall in periodical subscriptions should some members delay their payments. The Chit Fund Act has also stipulated that the foreman has to create a fixed deposit with a bank for an amount equivalent to the face value of the chit group/scheme and keep the fixed deposit receipt with the Registrar of Chits. The amount will be released only after satisfactory evidence is produced by the company that all the subscribers of the group have been paid off. It is also prescribed that a firm engaged in the business of chit funds should have a paid-up capital equivalent to 10 per cent of the total value of the chit groups in operation at any point of time.

In order to safeguard their interests against defaults, the chit fund firm can insist on sureties to be submitted by the members while drawing the money on winning the bid. The sureties include personal surety (such as any salaried person or companies), bank guarantee, property pledge and fixed deposit pledge. The type of surety depends on the future liability of the chit fund. When a member fails to make his periodical contribution, he is appropriately informed and after a continuous period, of say three months (if it is monthly scheme) of default, he can be removed from the subscriber list.

As far as legal immunity for the managers is concerned, there is also a provision under the Chit Fund Act that provides for immediate redressal of losses suffered by the manager. A case can also be filed with the Registrar of Chit Funds or in the court of law. The registrar or the court may attach the salary, collateral and sometimes even the personal property of the defaulter. The guarantor or surety can also be asked to make the payment. In case of delay in payment of subscriptions, as per the provisions of the act, interest can be charged on the delayed payment and the dividends can be forfeited if the delay is substantial.

20.2 Chit Fund as an Avenue for Savings and Source of Loan

A chit fund can be an avenue for saving for future needs or a source of loan for emergency needs.

A chit fund is a mechanism for saving (investment) and a source of loan for different purposes, including consumption. The periodical contributions made by a member of the chit fund are both savings and investment. When a member enters into an agreement with a chit fund, he compulsorily saves the instalment amount from his income and contributes to the chit fund. But for the compulsory payment of subscriptions to the chit fund, the member would have spent that amount elsewhere. The subscriber is forced to save small amounts periodically, which eventually grow into a large amount that he can use to buy assets or property or meet family commitments such as marriages and children's education. Thus, the periodical payments made by the member automatically become investments and the dividend a member is entitled to every month (periodically) is the return on the investment. Depending on the composition of the membership of the chit fund and the market interest rates, the return on investment for each member varies. For example, if a group consists of mostly business people who seek short-term funding for their businesses, the discount rates tend to be higher compared to salaried income groups.

Any member of a chit fund can bid in the periodical auctions and get the prized amount. This is nothing but borrowing from the chit fund out of the amounts already contributed and the contributions to be made in future. It can be said that the prized amount that a member gets through bidding is a loan against his own investment (accumulated savings). The bid amount (discount) is the cost of funds or cost of borrowing. Once the loan (prized amount) is received by a member, he continues to pay the periodic instalments, which cover both the interest and principal repayment. The periodic instalments get reduced because of the dividend a member is entitled to in every period. Thus, the interest and principal amount payable by a member get reduced over time. While bidding, the members decide their own interest rates depending on the need or urgency of the money and also the market interest rates. A member has two options—to invest or to borrow. If he opts for investment, he will not participate in the auctions, thereby allowing his contributions to accumulate. At the end of the chit fund, he will get the chit value minus the minimum discount. If he decides to borrow, he will participate in the periodic auctions and bid for the amount. Before participating in the auctions, the member must be convinced about investing in the chit fund or borrowing from it. Whether it is investment or borrowing, an implied interest rate is involved. Whether to invest or to borrow depends mainly on the rate of return to be yielded by the investment and the market interest rates. The main advantage of chit funds vis-à-vis other sources of borrowings is that chit funds enable subscribers to choose the timing and interest rate while borrowing.

The main advantage of a chit fund is that it pools the scattered savings of people and invests them in the form of loans to the members.

20.3 Advantages and Limitations of Chit Funds

A chit fund provides an option to members to borrow as and when they require the loan amount during the chit fund period at an interest rate suitable to them. Thus, a chit fund is a savings-cum-borrowing instrument. Moreover, chit funds are available in geographical areas that have little or no access to banking facilities. The specific advantages of chit funds are as follows.

- Easy accessibility and flexibility are the hallmarks of chit fund financing. Members can conveniently participate in periodic auctions and draw on the chit fund. Borrowing from chit funds is not only easy because of less documentation and procedures but also flexible as members can participate in the auctions and draw the money when needed.
- Members can draw on their chit fund for any purpose including family functions, festivals, education, housing, medical and other domestic expenses. Money can be readily drawn in an emergency. Chit funds are also used to pay off costlier loans from other agencies like moneylenders.
- Chit funds are also valuable to the business community, particularly sole traders and small and medium enterprises. These business groups are not favoured by commercial banks and, therefore, they have to fall back on their own savings for their financial needs. Banks generally avoid small businesses because of their poor accounting practices and record-keeping. It can be said that chit funds are a boon to such firms that would otherwise have to choose between moneylenders, who generally charge a very high rate of interest, and the organized banking sector, which stipulates stringent operational procedures.
- Chit funds provide an opportunity to businesses, particularly small businesses, to save their surplus cash on a daily or monthly basis and, at the same time, have access to easy financing.
- Interest rates on borrowings are determined by the subscribers (members) themselves, based on mutual decisions.
- The money that is borrowed by a member from the chit fund comes out of the funds already contributed and to be contributed by him in future.
- There is no need for a tangible security if a member wants to borrow from the chit fund, unlike banks and other financial institutions, which demand such a security.
- Organization of chit funds is easy because of very low capital requirement.
- Cost of intermediation is low in the case of chit fund financing.
- A chit fund normally gives a higher return compared to recurring deposit schemes of banks.

Chit funds also have certain limitations. The main drawback is that members cannot be sure whether they will get the loan whenever needed because only one member wins the pot in each auction. In other words, chit funds might not be advantageous to those members who cannot postpone their fund requirement. When two or more members are desperately in need of money, the auctions might end up with heavy discounts on the face value of the chits, which means that the borrowing rate would be very high. That is, a member who needs money urgently might be successful in winning in the auction for the pot, but end up with an extremely high discount (high interest rate). Some members might have several loans from varied sources. Such members run the risk of defaulting in their periodic subscriptions as they might be caught in a debt trap (vicious circle of debt). The integrity and financial soundness of the manager or foreman is also very important for the success of the chit funds. Due diligence must be carried out by the prospective members not only on the chit fund manager but also on other members of the group before entering into an agreement with the chit fund. A right blend of savers (investors) and borrowers is necessary for any chit fund to be rewarding to the members.

20.4 Legislative Framework

The first enactment on chit funds was made by the government of Travancore in 1914. Subsequently, many state governments formulated and enacted laws governing chit funds. Following the collapse of some big chit funds in the early 1970s, the Government of India asked the Banking Commission to study the functioning of chit funds. In the wider context of examining the activities of non-banking financial intermediaries, the Banking Commission (1972) recommended *inter alia* that there should be a uniform chit fund legislation applicable to the whole country and, as such, either an all-India Chit Funds Act be enacted or a model law be prepared for adoption by all the states. The commission also observed that it would be desirable to provide in the legislation that only public limited companies can run chit funds.

The Government of India examined the recommendations of the Banking Commission and asked the Reserve Bank of India (RBI) to prepare a model bill to regulate the conduct of chit funds for adoption by all the state governments. Accordingly, the RBI prepared and referred the draft bill to the Study Group on Non-Banking Companies, constituted by it in June 1974 under the chairmanship of James S. Raj. The study group recommended that the bill be enacted as a central legislation to ensure uniformity in the provisions applicable to chit funds throughout the country. The draft bill was sent to the state governments for their comments. The repeal of the existing state legislations on the subject was also provided for in the bill. After taking into account the views of all the state governments, the bill was introduced in Parliament, which came to be known as the Chit Fund Act, 1982. The act extends to the whole of India except the state of Jammu and Kashmir and it came into force on such date as the central government, by notification in the official gazette, announced and different dates could be notified for different states. The provisions under the Chit Fund Act, 1982, are applicable to chit funds run in different parts of the country.

As per a notification issued on August 28, 2009, by the RBI, chit funds are prohibited from accepting deposits from the public with immediate effect. However, they can accept deposits from their shareholders. Any deposits accepted and held by chit funds other than from their shareholders as on that date was required to be repaid on maturity and not be renewed. The notification was issued in public interest, particularly to regulate the credit system of the country.

Despite several legal and regulatory measures, the unorganized chit fund market remains a major challenge for the regulators, particularly the RBI. The large and expanding chit fund market has caused problems not only for the industry but also for the government. In the unorganized chit fund market, persons with inadequate means might start a chit fund with an aim of making quick profits, thus cheating many gullible investors.

20.4.1 The Chit Funds Act, 1982

According to the Chit Funds Act, a chit (or chit fund, chitty or kuri) is a transaction under which a person enters into an agreement with a specified number of persons that every one of them shall subscribe a certain sum of money (or a certain quantity of grain instead) by way of periodic instalments over a definite period and that each such subscriber shall, in his turn, as determined by lot or by auction or by tender or in such other manner as may be specified in the chit agreement, be entitled to the prize amount.

The main and important provisions of the Chit Funds Act, 1982, are as follows:

1. No chit shall be commenced or conducted without obtaining the previous sanction of the state government within whose jurisdiction the chit is to be commenced or conducted or of such officer as may be empowered by that government in this behalf, and unless the chit is registered in that state in accordance with the provisions of this act. Further, except with the general or special permission of the state government, no company carrying on chit business shall conduct any other business.
2. No person shall issue or cause to be issued any notice, circular, prospectus, proposal or other document inviting the public to subscribe for tickets in any chit unless such notice, circular, prospectus, proposal or document contains a statement that the previous sanction required under Section 4 has been obtained and the particulars of such sanction. No person shall carry on a chit business unless he uses as part of the name any of the words "chit", "chit fund", "chitty" or "kuri" and no person other than a person carrying on chit business shall use as part of his name any such word.
3. Notwithstanding anything contained in the Companies Act, 1956 (1 of 1956), but subject to the provisions of this act, a company shall not commence or carry on chit business unless it has a paid-up capital of not less than INR 1 lakh. Every company having paid-up capital of less than INR 1 lakh and carrying on chit business on the commencement of this act shall, before the expiry of a period of three years from such commencement, increase its paid-up capital to not less than INR 1 lakh.
4. Every company carrying on chit business shall create and maintain a reserve fund and shall, out of the balance of profit of each year as disclosed in its profit and loss account and before any dividend on its shares is declared, transfer to such reserve fund a sum equal to not less than 10 per cent of such profit. No company shall appropriate any sum or sums from the reserve fund except with the prior approval of the registrar and, for the purpose of obtaining such approval, it shall make an application in the prescribed form to the registrar explaining the circumstances relating to such appropriation.
5. Every foreman shall, after all the tickets specified in the chit agreement are fully subscribed, file a declaration to that effect with the registrar. A ticket is the share of a subscriber in a chit. The registrar shall, after satisfying himself that all the requirements relating to sanction, registration of chit and other matters have been duly complied with, grant a certificate of commencement to the foreman. No

foreman shall commence any auction or the draw of any chit or appropriate any chit amount unless a certificate of commencement is obtained by him.

6. No foreman, other than a firm or other association of individuals or company or cooperative society, shall commence or conduct chits, the aggregate chit amount of which at any time exceeds INR 25,000. Where the foreman is a firm or other association of individuals, the aggregate chit amount of the chits conducted by the firm or other association shall not at any time exceed:

   (a) Where the number of partners of the firm or the individuals constituting the association is not less than four, a sum of INR 1 lakh.

   (b) In any other case, a sum calculated on the basis of INR 25,000 with respect to each such partner or individual.

   Where the foreman is a company or cooperative society, the aggregate amount of the chits conducted by it shall not at any time exceed 10 times the net owned funds of the company or the cooperative society, as the case may be.

7. No person carrying on chit business shall utilize the moneys collected with respect to such business other than commission or remuneration payable to such person or interest or penalty, if any, received from a defaulting subscriber, except for:

   (a) Carrying on chit business; or

   (b) Giving loans and advances to non-prized subscribers on the security of subscriptions paid by them; or

   (c) Investing in trustee securities within the meaning of Section 20 of the Indian Trusts Act, 1882 (2 of 1882); or

   (d) Making deposits with approved banks mentioned in the chit agreement.

8. Every draw in a chit shall be held on the date at the time and place mentioned in the chit agreement and notice therefore in such form and in such manner as may be prescribed shall be issued by the foreman to all the subscribers. Every such draw shall be conducted in accordance with the provisions of the chit agreement and in the presence of not less than two subscribers. Where any draw was not conducted on the ground that two subscribers required to be present at a draw were not present or on any other ground, the registrar may, on his own motion or on an application made by the foreman or any of the subscribers, direct that the draw be conducted in his presence or in the presence of any person deputed by him.

9. No person carrying on chit business shall open a new place of business without obtaining the prior approval of the registrar within whose territorial jurisdiction his registered office or, as the case may be, the place or the principal place of business is situated. Where a person carrying on chit business opens a new place of business in a state other than the state (hereinafter referred to as the state of origin) in which his registered office or the place or the principal place of his business is situated, the registrar of the state in which such new place of business is opened may also exercise and perform any of the powers and functions which the registrar of the state of origin may exercise and perform with respect to the chit business carried on at such new place of business.

10. For the proper conduct of the chit, every foreman shall, before applying for a previous sanction:

    (a) deposit in an approved bank an amount equal to the chit amount in the name of the registrar, or

    (b) transfer government securities of the face value or market value (whichever) of not less than one-and-a-half times the chit amount in favor of the registrar; or

    (c) transfer in favour of the registrar such other securities, being securities in which a trustee may invest money under Section 20 of the Indian Trusts Act, 1882 (2 of 1882) of such value as may be prescribed by the state government from time of time.

    Provided that the value of the securities referred to in Cl (c) shall not in any case be less than one-and-a-half times the value of the chit amount.

    Where a foreman conducts more than one chit, he shall furnish security in accordance with the above provisions with respect to each chit. Provided that the face value or market value (whichever is less) of the substituted security shall not be less than one-and-a-half times the value of the chit amounts.

The security given by the foreman or any security substituted shall not be liable to be attached in execution of a decree or otherwise until the chit is terminated and the claims of all the subscribers are fully satisfied.

Where the chit is terminated and the registrar has satisfied himself that the claims of all the subscribers have been fully satisfied, he shall order the release of the security furnished by the foreman or the security substituted as the case may be, and in doing so, he shall follow such procedure as may be prescribed.

Notwithstanding anything to the contrary contained in any other law for the time being in force, the security furnished under this section shall not be dealt with by the foreman during the currency of the chit to which it relates and any dealing by the foreman with respect thereto by way of transfer or other encumbrances shall be null and void.

11. The foreman shall be entitled:

(a) in the absence of any provision in the chit agreement to the contrary, to obtain the chit amount at the first instalment without deduction of the discount specified in the chit agreement, subject to the condition that he shall subscribe to a ticket in the chit.

Provided that in case the foreman has subscribed to more than one ticket, he shall not be eligible to obtain more than one chit amount in a chit without discount.

(b) to such amount not exceeding 5 per cent of the chit amount as may be fixed in the chit agreement, by way of commission, remuneration or for meeting the expenses of running the chit.

(c) to interest and penalty, if any, payable on any default in the payment of instalments and to such other amounts as may be payable to him under the provisions of the chit agreement;

(d) to receive and realize all subscriptions from the subscribers and to distribute the prize amounts to the prized subscribers;

(e) to demand sufficient security from any prized subscriber for the due payment of future subscriptions payable by him.

12. The foreman shall, on the prized subscriber furnishing sufficient security for the due payment of future subscriptions, be bound to pay him the prize amount. Provided that the prized subscriber shall be entitled to the payment of the prize amount without any security whatsoever if he agrees to the deduction therefrom of the amount of all future subscriptions and in such a case, the foreman shall pay the prize amount to the prized subscriber within seven days after the date of the draw or before the date of the next succeeding instalment, whichever is earlier. Provided further that where the prize amount has been paid to the prized subscriber under the first proviso, the amount deducted shall be deposited by the foreman in an approved bank mentioned in the chit agreement and he shall not withdraw the amount so deposited except for the payment of future subscriptions.

If, owing to the default of the prized subscriber, the prize amount due with respect to any draw remains unpaid until the date of the next succeeding instalment, the foreman shall deposit the prize amount forthwith in a separated account in an approved bank mentioned in the chit agreement and intimate in writing the fact of such deposit and the reasons therefore to the prized subscriber and the registrar.

Provided that where any prized subscriber does not collect the prize amount with respect to any instalment of a chit within a period of two months from the date of the draw, it shall be open to the foreman to hold another draw with respect to such instalment.

Every payment of the prize amount or the amount of future subscriptions and the deposit of the prize amount shall be intimated to the subscribers at the next succeeding draw and the particulars of such payment or deposit shall be entered in the minutes of the proceedings of that draw.

The foreman shall not appropriate to himself any amount in excess of what he is entitled to. Provided that where the foreman is himself a prized subscriber, he shall be entitled to appropriate to himself the prize amount subject to his complying with provisions of Section 31. Provided further, the foreman may appropriate to himself the interest accruing on the amount deposited.

The foreman shall not admit any person as a subscriber to a chit if, by such admission, the total number of tickets mentioned in the chit agreement is increased.

The foreman shall distribute among the subscribers in accordance with the chit agreement the dividend either in cash, grain or by way of adjustment towards the subscriptions payable for the next instalment, if any.

13. The foreman shall maintain in the registered office or, as the case may be, in the place or the principal place of his business, or where the foreman has any branch office, sub-office or any place of business for the conduct of chit business in a state other than the state in which his registered office or the principal place of his business is situated, in such branch office, sub-office or place of business in respect of the business conducted in that state:

(a) a register containing:

(i) the names and full particulars of the subscribers in each chit together with the number of tickets held by each subscriber;

(ii) the dates on which the subscribers signed the chit agreement; and

(iii) in the case of an assignment of a ticket by a subscriber, the name and full address of the assignee with the date of assignment and the date on which the assignment had been recognized by the foreman.

(b) a book containing the minutes of the proceedings of each draw;

(c) a ledger containing:

(i) the amounts paid to the prized subscribers in each chit and the dates of such payments;

(ii) the amounts paid to the prized subscribers and the dates of such payments; and

(iii) in the case of any deposit in an approved bank mentioned in the chit agreement, the date and the amount of such deposit;

(d) a register in the prescribed form showing the amounts deposited in approved banks as required under the provisions of this act with respect to all chits conducted by the foreman at his office; and

(e) such other registers and books in such form as may be prescribed by the state government within whose jurisdiction the chit is conducted.

14. Without prejudice to the provisions of the Companies Act, 1956 (1 of 1956), every foreman shall prepare and file with the registrar within such time as may be prescribed, a balance sheet as on the last date of each calendar year, or, as the case may be, the financial year of the foreman and a profit and loss account relating to the year of account, in the forms set out in Parts I and II of the Schedule, or as near thereto as circumstances admit, with respect to the chit business and audited by auditors qualified to act as auditors under the Companies Act, 1956, or by a chit auditor appointed under Section 61;

Provided that where a balance sheet is audited by an auditor qualified to act as auditor under the Companies Act, 1956 (1 of 1956), a chit auditor appointed under Section 61 shall have the right to audit the balance sheet at any time if so authorized by the registrar in this behalf.

15. Every foreman shall be liable to account to the subscribers for the amounts due to them. Where there is more than one foreman in a chit, each one of them jointly and severally and, if the foreman is a firm or other association of individuals, each one of the partners or individuals thereof jointly and severally and, if the foreman is a company, the company as such, shall be liable to the subscribers with respect to the obligations arising out of the chit.

16. No foreman, or where there is more than one foreman in a chit, none of them shall withdraw from the chit until its termination unless such withdrawal is assented to in writing by all the non-prized and unpaid prized subscribers and a copy of such assent has been filed with the registrar under Section 41.

17. A non-prized subscriber who defaults in paying his subscription in accordance with the terms of the chit agreement shall be liable to have his name removed from the list of subscribers and a written notice of such removal shall be given by the foreman to the defaulting subscriber within 14 days of the date of such removal.

Provided that if the defaulter pays the defaulted instalment with interest at such rate as may be prescribed within seven days of the date of receipt of such notice, his name shall be re-entered in the list of such subscribers.

Every such removal shall, with the date thereof, be entered in the relevant book maintained by the foreman.

Any defaulting subscriber aggrieved by the removal of his name from the list of subscribers may, within seven days of the date of receipt of the notice of removal, refer the matter to the registrar for arbitration under Section 64.

18. A foreman may substitute in the list of subscribers any person (hereinafter in this chapter referred to as the substituted subscriber) in place of the defaulting subscriber whose name has been removed under sub-section (1) of Section 28.

Every substitution with the date thereof be entered in the relevant book maintained by the foreman and a true copy of every such entry shall be filed by the foreman with the registrar within 14 days from the date of substitution.

19. A foreman shall, out of the amounts payable by and realized from the substituted subscriber towards the instalment relatable to the period before the date of the substitution (including the arrears due from the defaulting subscriber), deposit, before the date of the next succeeding instalment, in a separate identifiable account in an approved bank mentioned in the chit agreement, an amount equal to the contributions made by the defaulting subscriber less such deductions as may be provided for in the chit agreement, and shall inform the defaulting subscriber as well as the registrar of the fact of such deposit and shall not withdraw the amount so deposited except for payment of the defaulting subscriber.

The amount so deposited shall be paid to the defaulting subscriber as and when he claims the amount and the amount so deposited shall not be withdrawn by the foreman for any purpose other than for such payment.

The contributions of any defaulting subscriber, who has not been substituted till the termination of the chit, shall be paid to him within 15 days from the date of termination of the chit subject to such deduction as may be provided for in the chit agreement.

20. Every prized subscriber shall, if he has not offered to deduct the amount of all future subscriptions from the prize amount due to him, furnish, and a foreman shall take, sufficient security for the due payment of all future subscriptions and, if the foreman is a prized subscriber, he shall give security for the due payment of all the future subscriptions to the satisfaction of the registrar.

21. Every prized subscriber shall pay his subscriptions regularly on the dates and times and at the place mentioned in the chit agreement and, on his failure to do so, he shall be liable to make a consolidated payment of all the future subscriptions forthwith.

22. A foreman shall not be entitled to claim a consolidated payment from a defaulting prized subscriber under Section 32 unless he makes a demand to that effect in writing. Where a dispute is raised under this act by a foreman for a consolidated payment of future subscriptions from a defaulting prize subscriber and if the subscriber pays to the foreman on or before the date on which the dispute is posted for hearing the arrears of subscriptions till that date together with the interest thereon at the rate provided for in the chit agreement and the cost of adjudication of the dispute, the registrar or his nominee hearing the dispute shall, notwithstanding any contract to the contrary, make an order directing the subscriber to pay to the foreman the future subscriptions on or before the dates on which they fall due, and that, in case of any default of such payments, by the subscriber, the foreman shall be at liberty to realize, in execution of that order, all future subscriptions and interest together with the costs, if any, less the amount, if any, already paid by the subscriber with respect thereof.

Provided that if any such dispute is on a promissory note, no order shall be passed under this sub-section unless such a promissory note expressly states that the amount due under the promissory note is towards the payment of subscriptions to the chit.

Any person who holds any interest in the property furnished as security or part thereof shall be entitled to make the payment.

All consolidated payment of future subscriptions realized by a foreman shall be deposited by him in an approved bank mentioned in the chit agreement before the date of the succeeding instalment and the amount so deposited shall not be withdrawn except for payment of future subscriptions.

Where any property is obtained as security in lieu of the consolidated payment of future subscriptions, it shall remain as security for the due payment of future subscription.

23. No transfer of the rights of a foreman to receive subscriptions from the prized subscribers shall be made without the previous sanction in writing of the registrar.

Any transfer of the rights of a foreman to receive subscriptions from the prized subscribers shall, if it is likely to defeat or delay the interests of a non-prized or unpaid prized subscriber, be voidable at the instance of such subscriber.

When a transfer is disputed by a subscriber, the burden of providing that the foreman was in solvent circumstances at the time of the transfer and that the transfer does not defeat or delay the interests of such subscriber is on the transferee.

24. Every transfer under Section 35 shall, within a period of 14 days from the date of receipt of the proposal for transfer by the foreman, be recognized by him unless the transferee is not solvent or the transfer was effected with a view to defeating the provisions of any law including this act and the decision of the foreman to recognize the transfer or not shall forthwith be communicated to the parties concerned.

25. The foreman may, on his own motion, convene a special meeting of the general body of subscribers for considering any proposal to pass a special resolution.

The foreman shall convene such a meeting on the requisition in writing of not less than 25 per cent of the number of non-prized and unpaid prized subscribers, and the meeting so convened shall be held within 30 days of the date of receipt of the requisition and if the foreman refuses or fails to call such a meeting within 14 days of the date of receipt of such requisition, not less than 25 per cent of the number of non-prized and unpaid prized subscribers may give notice of the fact to the registrar.

The registrar shall, within 21 days of the receipt of the notice, convene or direct the convening of a special meeting of the general body of the subscribers and on receipt of such a direction, it shall be the duty of the foreman to comply with such direction.

Notice of not less than 14 days shall be given to all the subscribers of a meeting under this section specifying the object, date, hour and place of meeting and a copy of the special resolution shall be sent along with the notice of the meeting.

26. Where a foreman dies or becomes of unsound mind or is otherwise incapacitated, the chit may continue in accordance with the provisions of the chit agreement.

Where a foreman is adjudicated an insolvent, or withdraws from the chit under Section 26, or fails to conduct the chit at any instalment or on any other date before the next succeeding instalment as may have been agreed upon by a special resolution, any one or more of such subscribers authorized by such resolution may, in the absence of any provision in the chit agreement for the future conduct of the chit, take the place of the foreman and continue the chit or make other arrangements for the further conduct the chit.

27. A chit shall be deemed to have terminated:

(a) when the period specified in the chit agreement has expired provided the payment of dues to all the subscribers has been completed; or

(b) when all the non-prized and unpaid prized subscribers and the foreman consent in writing to the termination of the chit and a copy of such consent is filed with the registrar as required under Section 41; or

(c) where a foreman dies or becomes of unsound mind or is otherwise incapacitated and the chit is not continued in accordance with the provisions of the chit agreement;

Provided that, in a case where the foreman is a firm, if a partner thereof dies or becomes of unsound mind or is otherwise incapacitated, the chit shall not be deemed to have terminated and the surviving partner or partners shall conduct the chit in the absence of any provision to the contrary in the chit agreement.

28. Every non-prized subscriber shall, unless otherwise provided for in this act or in the chit agreement, be entitled to get back his subscriptions at the termination of the chit without any deduction for dividend, if any, earned by him. Provided that any person to whom the rights of a non-prized subscriber are transferred in accordance with the provisions of Section 35 shall, in addition to his own subscription, be entitled to get back the subscriptions paid by such non-prized subscriber, subject to the conditions specified in this section.

29. Every foreman shall, on payment of such fee not exceeding INR 5 as may be specified in the chit agreement, allow the non-prized subscribers and unpaid prized subscribers reasonable facilities on all the dates of draw or on such other dates and within such hours as may be provided for in the chit agreement, for the inspection of security bonds and documents, receipts and other records taken from the prized subscribers, or furnished by the foreman as a subscriber and all the chit records, including books of accounts, pass books, balance sheet and profit and loss accounts and such other records as may show the actual financial position of the chit.
30. A chit may be wound up by the registrar within whose territorial jurisdiction the chit has been registered, either on his own motion or on an application made by any non-prized or unpaid-prized subscriber:
   (a) if the chit has terminated under Cl. (c) of Section 40; or
   (b) if the foreman commits any such act with respect to the security specified in Section 20 as is calculated to impair materially the nature of the security or the value thereof; or
   (c) if he fails to deposit any amount required to be deposited under any of the provisions of this act; or
   (d) if it is proved to the satisfaction of the registrar that the foreman is unable to pay the amounts due to the subscribers; or
   (e) if the execution or other process issued on an order passed by the registrar in favor of any subscriber with respect to amounts due to him from the foreman in relation to the chit business is returned unsatisfied in whole or in part; or if it is proved that there has been a fraud or collusion on the part of the foreman in the matter of taking securities from any prized subscriber; or if the foreman has appropriated the prize amount in his capacity as a subscriber without furnishing sufficient security for future subscriptions; or if the registrar is satisfied that the affairs of the chit are being conducted in a manner prejudicial to the interests of the subscribers; or if it is just and equitable that the chit should be wound up.
31. Where during the pendency of the proceedings for the winding up of a chit, the foreman is adjudicated an insolvent, or where the foreman is a firm, all the partners or all the partners except one thereof are adjudicated insolvents, or where the foreman is a company, the company has been ordered to be wound up by the court, the winding-up proceeding under this chapter shall cease and the distribution of the chit assets shall, subject of the provisions of Sections 43 and 52, be made by all the insolvency court or the court winding up the company, as the case may be.

    Where an application for the winding up of a chit is dismissed and the registrar is satisfied that the petition is frivolous or vexatious, he may, on the application of the foreman, award against the petitioner such amount, not exceeding INR 1,000, as he deems reasonable as compensation to the foreman for the expenses or injury caused to him by the presentation of the application and the proceedings thereon, and such amount may be realized as if the award were a decree of a civil court.

    On the making of an award under sub-section (1), no suit for compensation with respect to an application for any winding up of the chit shall be entertained.
32. The foreman or any subscriber or any other person aggrieved by a decision or order of the registrar in any proceedings for the winding up a chit may, within 60 days from the date of such decision or order, appeal to the state government.
33. Where an order refusing to wind up a chit has been made under this act, the chit shall be deemed to have been under suspension from the date of presentation of the application to the date of such order with respect to non-prized subscribers; and notwithstanding anything contained in the chit agreement, no non-prized subscriber who was not a defaulter on the date of the presentation of the petition for winding up shall be deemed to be a defaulter on the date of such order.

    Where an order refusing to wind up a chit has been made under this act, in computing a period of limitation prescribed for any suit or other legal proceedings (other than a suit or application with respect to which the leave of the court had been obtained) which might have been brought or instituted, but for the presentation of the application for the winding up of the chit, the period from the date of the presentation of the application to the date of the order refusing to wind up a chit shall be excluded.

    Nothing contained in this chapter shall effect the rights of a subscriber to proceed against the foreman personally for the balance, if any, of the amount due to him after the declaration of the final dividend in the proceedings for the winding up of the chit and in computing the period of limitation prescribed for any such proceedings, the period from the date of the presentation of the application for the winding up the chit to the date of the declaration of the final dividend

34. Notwithstanding anything contained in any other law for the time being in force, any dispute touching the management of a chit business shall be referred by any of the parties to the dispute to the registrar for arbitration if each party thereto is one or the other of the following, namely:

    (a) a foreman, a prized subscriber or a non-prized subscriber, including a defaulting subscriber, past subscriber or a person claiming through a subscriber, or a deceased subscriber to a chit;

    (b) a surety of a subscriber, past subscriber, or a deceased subscriber.

    Where any question arises as to whether any matter referred to for the award of the registrar is a dispute or not, the same shall be decided by the registrar whose decision thereon shall be final.

    No civil court shall have jurisdiction to entertain any suit or other proceedings with respect to any dispute. Notwithstanding anything contained in the sub-sections above, the registrar may admit a dispute after the expiry of the period of limitation specified therein if the applicant satisfies the registrar that he had sufficient cause for not referring the dispute within such period.

35. If the registrar is satisfied that any matter referred to him or brought to his notice is a dispute within the meaning of Section 64, he shall, subject to such rules as may be prescribed, settle the dispute himself or refer it for disposal to a person appointed by him.

    Where any dispute is referred for settlement of the nominee, the registrar may, at any time for reasons to be recorded in writing, withdraw such dispute from the nominee and may settle the dispute himself, or refer it again for settlement to any other nominee appointed by him.

36. The Reserve Bank of India may tender to any state government such advice on questions of policy with respect to this act as it thinks fit either on its own motion or on a request made by the state government.

37. Any foreman aggrieved by the decision of the registrar:

    (a) refusing to register the chit agreement under Section7;

    (b) refusing to grant a certificate of commencement under sub-section (2) of Section 9;

    (c) refusing to accept any security under sub-section (1) of Section 20 or Section 31; or

    (d) refusing to release the security charged under Section 20 or Section 31; may, within 30 days of the communication to him of such decision, appeal to the state government or to such officer or authority as may be empowered by notification in the official gazette by the state government in that behalf.

    Any foreman or other person aggrieved by the order of the registrar as under sub-section (1) of Section 34 may, within 30 days of the communication to him of such decision, appeal to the state government or to such officer or authority as may be empowered by notification in the official gazette by the state government in that behalf.

    The state government or such officer or authority aforesaid may, after giving the appellant an opportunity of making his representation, pass such order on the appeal as it or he thinks fit and such order shall be final.

38. Whoever contravenes or abets the contravention of any of the provisions of Sections 4, 5, 8, 9, 11, 12, 13, 14, 19, 20, 22, 24, 30 and 31, sub-section (4) of Section 33, Sections 46 and 47 or sub-section (5) of Section 61 shall, on conviction be punishable with imprisonment for a term which may extend to two years or with fine which may extend to INR 5,000 or both.

    Any foreman:

    (a) who fails to file any document required to be filed under this act within the period specified or within such further time as may be allowed; or

    (b) who fails to comply with the requirements of the chit agreement regarding the date, time and place at which the chit is to be drawn or who fails to comply with the requirements of any direction given under sub-section (3) of Section 38; or

    (c) who contravenes or fails to comply with any other requirement under this act shall, on conviction, be punishable with fine which may extend to INR 3,000.

Whoever willfully makes a statement in any document required to be filed under this act which is false in any material particular shall, on conviction, be punishable with imprisonment for a term which may extend to two years or with fine which may extend to INR 5,000 or both.

39. If any person convicted of an offence under sub-section (1) or sub-section (3) of Section 76 is again convicted of an offence under any of the said sub-sections, he shall be punishable for the second and for every subsequent offence with imprisonment for a term which may extend to two years and shall also be liable to fine.

40. Where an offence under this act has been committed by a company, every person who, at the time the offence was committed, was in charge of and responsible for the company for the conduct of the business of the company, as well as the company, shall be deemed to be guilty of the offence and be liable to be proceeded against and punished accordingly.

Provided that nothing contained in this sub-section shall render any such person liable to any punishment provided in this act if he proves that the offence was committed without his knowledge or that he exercised all due diligence to prevent the commission of such offence.

Notwithstanding anything contained in the sub-section above, where an offence under this act has been committed with the consent or connivance of, or is attributable to, any neglect on the part of any director, manager, secretary or other officer shall also be deemed to be guilty of that offence and be liable to be proceeded against and punished accordingly.

41. Nothing in this act shall apply with respect to:

(a) any chit started before the commencement of this act; or

(b) any chit the amount of which, or where two or more chits were started or conducted simultaneously by the same foreman, the aggregate amount does not exceed INR 100.

42. Notwithstanding anything contained in this act, no bank shall commence or carry on chit business after the commencement of this act.

Where a chit had been started by any bank before such commencement, such chit may be continued after such commencement until it is completed, and the provisions of the chit agreement and such laws, if any, as were applicable to it immediately before the commencement of this act shall apply to such chit.

43. The state government may, in consultation with the Reserve Bank of India, by notification in the official gazette and subject to such conditions as may be specified in the notification, exempt any person or class of persons or any chit or class of chits from all or any of the provisions of this act.

44. No suit, prosecution or other legal proceedings shall lie against the state government, the registrar or other officer of the state government or the Reserve Bank of India or any of its officers exercising any powers or discharging any functions under this act with respect to anything which is in good faith done or intended to be done in pursuance of this act or the rules made thereunder.

45. The state government may, in consultation with the Reserve Bank of India, by notification in the official gazette, make rules for giving effect to the provisions of this act.

Every rule made under this section shall be laid, as soon as may be after it is made, before each house of the state legislature where it consists of two houses, or, where such legislature consists of one house, before that house.

46. The Andhra Pradesh Chit Funds Act, 1971 (Act of 1971), the Kerala Chitties Act, 1975 (Act 23 of 1975), the Maharashtra Chit Funds Act, 1974 (Act 55 of 1974), the Tamil Nadu Chit Funds Act, 1961 (Act 24 of 1961), as in force in the state of Tamil Nadu and in the Union territories of Chandigarh and Delhi, the Uttar Pradesh Chit Funds Act, 1975 (Act 53 of 1975), the Goa, Daman and Diu Chit funds Act, 1973 (Act 16 of 1973) and the Pondicherry Chit Funds Act, 1966 (Act 18 of 1966) are hereby repealed and the provisions of Section 6 of the General Clauses Act, 1897 (10 of 1897) shall apply to such repeal as if each such act so repealed were a central act.

20.4.2 Prize Chits and Money Circulation Schemes (Banning) Act, 1978

Money circulation schemes are rampant throughout the country, particularly in the southern states. The gullible public is often lured with the promise of easy money and cheated of large amounts of funds. To check this menace, the Government of India introduced an act called the Prize Chits and Money Circulation

Schemes (Banning) Act, 1978. The act provides that all prize chit schemes run by jewellery shops are illegal except the chits registered with the Registrar of Chits and schemes run by non-banking finance companies registered with the RBI. Under this act, the penalty for promoting or conducting such schemes or prize chits or participating in them is imprisonment for a term of up to three years. Anyone who prints, sells, distributes or advertises tickets or coupons for such schemes is punishable with imprisonment of up to two years. The same applies to those in possession of such material and anyone who induces or invites any person to send any ticket or coupon. The penalty is the same for renting out premises for such schemes.

The main provisions of the act are:

1. No person shall promote or conduct any prize chit or money circulation scheme, or enroll as a member of any such chit or scheme, or participate in it otherwise, or receive or remit any money in pursuance of such chit or scheme.
2. Whoever contravenes the provisions of Section 3 shall be punishable with imprisonment for a term which may extend to three years or fine which may extend to INR 5,000 or both. Provided that in the absence of special and adequate reasons to the contrary to be mentioned in the judgment of the court, the imprisonment shall not be less than one year and the fine shall not be less than INR 1,000.
3. Whoever, with a view to promotion or conduct of any prize chit or money circulation scheme in contravention of the provisions of this act or in connection with any chit or scheme promoted or conducted as aforesaid:

   (a) prints or publishes any ticket, coupon or other document for use in the prize chit or money circulation scheme; or

   (b) sells or distributes or offers or advertises for sale or distribution, or has in his possession for the purpose of sale or distribution any ticket, coupon or other document for use in the prize chit or money circulation scheme; or

   (c) prints, publishes or distributes, or has in his possession for the purpose of publication or distribution:

      (i) any advertisement of the prize chit or money circulation scheme; or

      (ii) any list, whether complete or not, of members in the prize chit or money circulation scheme; or

      (iii) any such matter descriptive of, or otherwise relating to the prize chit or money circulation scheme as is calculated to act as an inducement to persons to participate in that prize chit or money circulation scheme or any other prize chit or money circulation scheme; or

   (d) brings or invites any person to send, for the purpose of sale of distribution, any ticket, coupon or other document for use in a prize chit or money circulation scheme or any advertisement of such prize chit or money circulation scheme; or

   (e) uses any premises, or causes or knowingly permits any premises to be used for purposes connected with the promotion or conduct of the prize chit or money circulation scheme; or

   (f) causes or procures or attempts to procure any person to do any of the above mentioned acts, shall be punishable with imprisonment for a term which may extend to two years or fine which may extend to INR 3,000 or both. Provided that in the absence of special and adequate reasons to the contrary to be mentioned in the judgment of the court, the imprisonment shall not be less than one year and the fine shall not be less than INR 1,000.
4. Where an offence under this act has been committed by a company, every person who, at the time the offence was committed, was in charge of and responsible for the company for the conduct of the business of the company, as well as the company, shall be deemed to be guilty of the offence and be liable to be proceeded against and punished accordingly. Provided that nothing contained in this sub-section shall render any such person liable to any punishment provided in this act if he proves that the offence was committed without his knowledge or that he exercised all due diligence to prevent the commission of such offence.

   Notwithstanding anything contained in the sub-section above, where an offence under this act has been committed by a company and it is proved that the offence has been committed with the consent or connivance of, or is attributable to, any neglect on the part of any director, manager, secretary or other officer of the company, such director, manager, secretary or other officer shall also be deemed to be guilty of that offence and be liable to be proceeded against and punished accordingly.

5. It shall be lawful for any police officer not below the rank of an officer in charge of a police station:
   (a) to enter, if necessary by force, whether by day or night, with such assistance as he considers necessary, any premises which he has reason to suspect is being used for purposes connected with the promotion or conduct of any prize chit or money circulation scheme in contravention of the provisions of this act;
   (b) to search the said premises and the persons whom he may find therein;
   (c) to take into custody and produce before any judicial magistrate all such persons as are concerned or against whom a complaint has been made or credible information has been received or a reasonable suspicion exists of their having been concerned with the use of the said premises for purpose connected with, or with the promotion or conduct of any such prize chit or money circulation scheme as aforesaid;
   (d) to seize all things found in the said premises which are intended to be used, or reasonably suspected to have been used, in connection with any such prize chit or money circulation scheme as aforesaid.

   Any officer authorized by the state government in this behalf may:
   (a) at all reasonable times, enter into and search any premises which he has reason to suspect is being used for the purpose connected with, or conduct of, any prize chit or money circulation scheme in contravention of the provisions of this act;
   (b) examine any person having control of, or employed in connection with, any such prize chit or money circulation scheme;
   (c) order the production of any documents, books or records in the possession or power of any person having the control of, or employed in connection with, any such prize chit or money circulation scheme, and inspect and seize any register, books of accounts, documents or any other literature found in the said premises.

   All searches under this section shall be made in accordance with the provisions of the Code of Criminal Procedure, 1973 (2 of 1974).
6. Where any newspaper or other publication contains any material connected with any prize chit or money circulation scheme promoted or conducted in contravention to the provisions of this act or any advertisement in relation thereto, the state government may, by notification in the official gazette, declare every copy of the newspaper and every copy of the publication containing such material or the advertisement to be forfeited to the state government.
7. No court inferior to that of a chief metropolitan magistrate, or as the case may be, chief judicial magistrate, shall try any offence punishable under this act.
8. All offences punishable under this act shall be cognizable.
9. Nothing contained in this act shall apply to any prize chit or money circulation scheme promoted by:
   (a) a state government or any officer or authority on its behalf; or
   (b) a company wholly owned by a state government which does not carry on any business other than the conducting of a prize chit or money circulation scheme, whether it is in the nature of a conventional chit or otherwise; or
   (c) a banking company as defined in clause (c) of Section 5 of the Banking Regulation Act, 1949 (10 of 1949), or a banking institution notified by the central government under Section 51 of that act or the State Bank of India constituted under Section 3 of the State Bank of India Act, 1955 (23 of 1955), or a subsidiary bank constituted under Section 3 of the Banking Companies (Acquisition and Transfer of Undertakings) Act, 1970 (5 of 1970), or a Regional Rural Bank established under Section 3 of the Regional Rural Banks Act, 1976 (21 of 1976) or a co-operative bank as defined in clause (bii) of Section 2 of the Reserve Bank of India Act, 1934 (2 of 1934); or
   (d) any charitable or educational institution notified in this behalf by the state government in consultation with the Reserve Bank of India.
10. The state government may, by notification in the official gazette and in consultation with the Reserve Bank of India, make rules for the purpose of carrying out the provisions of this act.

In particular and without prejudice to the generality of the foregoing power, such rules may provide for:

(a) the office of the Reserve Bank of India to whom full information regarding any prize chit or money circulation scheme may be furnished under the first proviso to sub-section (1) of Section 12 and the form in which and the period within which such information may be furnished;

(b) the particulars relating to the winding-up plan of the business relating to prize chits or money circulation schemes.

11. The Andhra Pradesh Money Circulation Scheme (Prohibition) Act, 1965 (Andhra Pradesh Act 30 of 1965), as in force in the state of Andhra Pradesh, and in the Union territory of Chandigarh and the Madhya Pradesh Dhan Parichalan Skeem (Pratishedh) Adhiniyam, 1975 (Madhya Pradesh Act of 19 of 1975), are hereby repealed.

Notwithstanding the repeal of any act referred to in sub-section (1), anything done or any action taken under the provisions of any such act shall, in so far as such thing or action is not inconsistent with the provisions of this act, be deemed to have been done or taken under the provisions of this act as if the said provisions were in force when such thing was done or such action was taken and shall continue in force accordingly until superseded by anything done or any action taken under this act.

20.5 The All India Association of Chit Funds (AIACF)

The All India Association of Chit Funds (AIACF) is the national apex body committed to the welfare of the chit fund industry. Confederating all the chit fund associations in the country, the apex body aims at promoting healthy and efficient functioning of the chit fund business, propagating and uplifting the image of the chit fund system and extending help to the chit fund fraternity in times of need.

Besides being a unifying force of the chit fund fraternity, the AIACF serves as a bridge between the industry and the government. The rapport with the government is said to be highly rewarding. Whenever regulation-related problems threaten the industry, the AIACF can ably present them before the government and bring about redress. The AIACF also conducts seminars, conferences and workshops across the country to educate the members on the chit fund business. It also holds executive meetings periodically in different parts of the country to find solutions to regional problems. The AIACF has come to be recognized by the government as the representative and spokesman of the chit fund industry. The RBI extends due recognition by consulting the AIACF on policy decisions on chit funds.

Box 20.1 presents a brief account of a leading chit fund company.

Box 20.1 Margadarsi Chit Fund Private Limited

Over three decades ago, the Margadarsi Chit Fund showed the people of Andhra Pradesh the way to a happier life. Guided by the vision and determination of Sri Ramoji Rao, Margadarsi made its humble beginning in October 1962 in a small office with just two people. To him can be credited the pioneering of the concept of chit funds in the state. Now it has become a household name in Andhra Pradesh. Far from being a popular form of planning that it is today, a chit fund was a little known concept when Margadarsi unfolded in Andhra Pradesh. With the passage of time and experience, chit funds became popular as people discovered in it an ideal way to save profitably and raise money at short notice to meet contingencies. Many companies followed suit and chit fund companies sprung up like mushrooms. In this changing scenario, Margadarsi's unchanging values like honesty of performance, professional integrity, high quality of service and absolute financial discipline helped in retaining its leadership position.

Margadarsi enjoyed exponential growth over the years and today employs 3,700 employees, has 8,000 agents, 99 branches, over 370,000 subscribers and a turnover of over INR 50 billion. Margadarsi is not only the No.1 chit fund company but also a household name in Andhra Pradesh.

The hallmark of Margadarsi's success is its meticulous planning, coupled with hard work and deep commitment to serve its customers in the best possible manner. New schemes are introduced from time to time to meet the financial needs of the customers and fulfill their aspirations. At present, the company offers schemes as shown in Table 20.1.

(Continued)

Table 20.1 Schemes offered by Margadarsi Chit Fund

Sl. no.	*Monthly subscription*	*No. of months*	*Chit value*	*Total members*	*Scheme*
1.	400	25	10,000	25	STF
2.	1,000	25	25,000	25	STG
3.	2,000	25	50,000	25	STM
4.	4,000	25	100,000	25	STP
5.	6,000	25	150,000	25	STS
6.	10,000	25	250,000	25	STT
7.	20,000	25	500,000	25	STX
8.	1,000	30	30,000	30	TTG
9.	5,000	30	150,000	30	TTB
10.	10,000	30	300,000	30	TTT
11.	20,000	30	600,000	30	TTX
12.	30,000	30	900,000	30	TTC
13.	100,000	30	3,000,000	30	TTV
14.	1,250	40	50,000	40	FTQ
15.	2,500	40	100,000	40	FTW
16.	5,000	40	200,000	40	FTB
17.	7,500	40	300,000	40	FTU
18.	10,000	40	400,000	40	FTT
19.	12,500	40	500,000	40	FTN
20.	25,000	40	1,000,000	40	FTZ
21.	50,000	40	2,000,000	40	FTD
22.	75,000	40	3,000,000	40	FTKK
23.	100,000	40	4,000,000	40	FTV
24.	500	50	25,000	50	LTH
25.	1,000	50	50,000	50	LTG
26.	1,500	50	75,000	50	LTY
27.	2,000	50	100,000	50	LTM
28.	3,000	50	150,000	50	LTA
29.	4,000	50	200,000	50	LTP
30.	5,000	50	250,000	50	LTB
31.	6,000	50	300,000	50	LTS
32.	10,000	50	500,000	50	LTT
33.	20,000	50	1,000,000	50	LTX
34.	30,000	50	1,500,000	50	LTC
35.	50,000	50	2,500,000	50	LTD
36.	60,000	50	3,000,000	50	LTCC
37.	80,000	50	4,000,000	50	LTII
38.	100,000	50	5,000,000	50	LTV

Efficient and prompt services are available to customers at all times. Subscribers can rest assured that the company will serve its customers with the same zeal throughout the association, right up to the termination of the chit. In keeping with its promise of providing high-quality professional and personalized service, Margadarsi started the unique 72-hour response facility. This facility of quick disbursement of money (subject to documentation) is unique to Margadarsi and currently not offered by any other chit fund company.

Source: www.margadarsi.com

Summary

1. Chit funds evolved at a time when banking facilities had not developed, thus filling an important credit gap in the economy.
2. A chit fund is an indigenous financial institution involving regular periodic subscriptions by a group of persons.
3. Before it was organized, the chit fund business was based on the personal faith each member (subscriber) of the chit fund had in others.
4. Each and every subscriber, also known as member, contributes periodically a predetermined amount to a common pool, which is known as chit value or the pot. The pot is auctioned periodically on a particular date.
5. A member is allowed to win the bid only once during the chit period, so that every member gets a chance to win the bid
6. The periodic payments made by a member automatically become investments and the dividend a member is entitled to every period (such as a month) is the return on the investment.
7. The bid amounts are usually greater in the initial periods of the chit and keep decreasing as time passes. Although multiple factors influence the bid amounts, it is mainly the cost of carry that determines the bid amount.
8. Easy accessibility and flexibility are the hallmarks of chit fund financing.
9. The main limitation of chit funds is that the members are not sure whether they will get the loan whenever needed because only one member wins the pot in every auction.
10. The Banking Commission has recommended that it is essential to have a uniform chit fund legislation applicable to the whole country.
11. As per the provisions under the Chit Fund Act, 1982, no chit shall be commenced or conducted without obtaining previous sanction of the state government within whose jurisdiction the chit is to be commenced or conducted or of such officer as may be empowered by that government in this behalf.
12. It is also prescribed that a firm engaged in the business of chit funds should have a paid-up capital equivalent to 10 per cent of the total value of the chit groups in operation at any point of time.
13. Every prized subscriber shall pay his subscriptions regularly on the dates and times and at the place mentioned in the chit agreement and on his failure to do so, he shall be liable to make a consolidated payment of all the future subscriptions forthwith.
14. As per the provisions under the Prize Chits and Money Circulation Schemes (Banning) Act, 1978, no person shall promote or conduct any prize chit or money circulation scheme, or enroll as a member to any such chit or scheme, or participate in it otherwise, or receive or remit any money in pursuance of such chit or scheme.
15. Except the chits registered with Registrar of Chits and schemes run by non-banking finance companies registered with the RBI, all the prize chit schemes run by jewellery shops are illegal.
16. Confederating all chit fund associations in the country, the AIACF aims at promoting healthy and efficient functioning of the chit fund business, propagating and uplifting the image of chit fund system and extending help to the chit fund fraternity in times of need.

Questions

1. Trace the origin of chit funds in India.
2. What are the important features of chit funds?
3. Define chit funds.
4. Explain the modus operandi of chit fund financing.
5. Discuss the role and responsibilities of the foreman of a chit fund as per the Chit Funds Act, 1982.
6. What are the important provisions under the Chit Funds Act that prevent default in chit funds?
7. How can the grievances of a subscriber of a chit be redressed as per the provisions of the Chit Fund Act, 1982?
8. Does the Chit Fund Act constrain the development of the chit fund business in the country? Explain.
9. Bring out the salient features of the Prize Chits and Money Circulation Schemes (Banning) Act, 1978.

Chapter 21

Nidhis

LEARNING OBJECTIVES

After reading this chapter, you should be able to:

- Trace the origin of the concept of Nidhi.
- Define a Nidhi.
- Describe the regulating authority of Nidhis.
- Present the recommendations underlying the norms prescribed by committees for Nidhis.
- Highlight the prudential norms governing Nidhis.
- Give an account of the Chamber of Nidhis.

21.1 Introduction

The concept of Nidhis is more than a century old and it has a chequered history. The origin of Nidhis can be traced to the beginning of the twentieth century when some people conceived an idea to provide relief to the "have-nots" of society. When people, particularly those in the lower-middle income group, were in dire financial need, they would invariably pawn their jewels and other assets to borrow from moneylenders at very high rates of interest. The plight of such people prompted some philanthropic persons to start mutual benefit institutions without any profit motive. The modus operandi was that the "haves" of society provided the needed funds in the form of deposits to be given away at reasonable and affordable interest rates to the "have-nots" through an informal organizational setup. In promoting these institutions, the only reward the founders of such institutions sought was recognition and goodwill from society. Thus, Nidhis are socially evolved institutions governed by self-regulation. As time passed, even people with moderate means started coming together to form such institutions, each one contributing to the share capital and benefiting either as depositor or borrower. The area of operation of such organizations was small—within a town or a village, or a locality in a city. In other words, the concept of Nidhi envisages the coming together of people who know each other for mutual benefit. The principle of mutual benefit is fundamental—to lend to members from the savings mobilized (deposits) from members. Nidhis never have dealing with non-members.

It is said that the Nidhis are an innovation of southern India, particularly the state of Tamil Nadu, and are hence colloquially called "dhoti-clad" financial institutions.

The primary object of **Nidhis** has been to carry on the business of accepting deposits and lending money to member-borrowers only against fixed deposit receipts, jewels, house property, etc. at reasonable rates of interest. Nidhis thus enable members to invest their savings and secure loans at favourable rates of interest. Members of Nidhis are individuals only. Firms, corporate bodies or trusts are never admitted as members. Even though a large number of Nidhis operate under principles as pronounced by the founding fathers, a few of them have been organized as an entrepreneurial effort to earn private profit. Nevertheless, Nidhis play a very important role in the lives of millions of people, particularly from lower-middle income groups, by providing need-based financial services, particularly credit facility, with minimum formalities.

> ***Nidhis** are financial institutions that mobilize the savings (acceptance of deposits) of members and give loans to the members only.*

The business of Nidhis is carried out by companies under different names such as Nidhi, permanent fund, benefit fund, mutual benefit fund and mutual benefit company. The word Nidhi shall not form part of the name of any company, firm or individual engaged in borrowing and lending money without incorporation by the Department of Company Affairs. No company can borrow or lend without obtaining the certificate of commencement of business and without notification as Nidhi under Section 620A of the Companies Act, 1956. All companies, unless and until they are notified as Nidhis under Section 620A of the Companies Act, despite having been working on the Nidhi pattern, would be treated as loan companies.

21.1.1 Definition

"Nidhi" is a Sanskrit term meaning "treasure". However, there is no precise definition of Nidhis. According to the Sabanayagam Committee, Nidhi is "a company formed with the exclusive object of cultivating the habit of thrift, savings and functioning for the mutual benefit of members by receiving deposits only from individuals enrolled as members and by lending only to individuals, also enrolled as members, and which functions as per notifications and guidelines prescribed by the Department of Company Affairs (DCA). The word Nidhi shall not form part of the name of any company, firm or individual engaged in borrowing and lending money without incorporation by DCA and such contravention will attract penal action."

The distinguishing features of Nidhis are as follows:

- Nidhis are a kind of non-banking financial institution evolved on the principle of mutual benefit.
- Transactions of Nidhis are only with members.
- Only individuals can become members of a Nidhi.
- Deposits are mobilized from the members to lend to members only.
- Nidhis perform geography-specific financial services.
- Both the lenders and borrowers are from the same locale. In other words, all the members of a Nidhi are known to each other.
- Nidhis inculcate the habit of thrift.
- Loans are generally taken to meet family requirements such as marriage of children, education of children, house building, purchase of properties and medical expenses.
- Loans are fully secured as they are backed by certain tangible assets (such as jewellery). So the incidence of delinquency is less.
- Loans are mostly hassle-free with minimum formalities.
- Shares of Nidhis are not publicly traded.
- Nidhis are characterized by highly personalized operations.

21.1.2 Regulatory and Supervisory Authority

Nidhis are regulated and supervised by both the Reserve Bank of India and the Ministry of Corporate Affairs.

Nidhis are companies governed by Section 620A of the Companies Act, 1956. Accordingly, Nidhis come under the supervision of the Ministry of Corporate Affairs (MCA), Government of India. The MCA is primarily concerned with administration of the Companies Act, 1956, other allied acts and rules and regulations framed thereunder, mainly for regulating the functioning of the corporate sector in accordance with law. However, Nidhis are different from other companies as they are classified as a kind of non-banking finance companies (NBFCs). Being finance companies, Nidhis perform quasi-banking functions. Hence, they come under the supervision of the Reserve Bank of India. Thus, there is dual control over Nidhis: the power to supervise and regulate the administration of Nidhis is with the MCA whereas their financial activities (deposit acceptance and lending) are governed by the RBI Act and guidelines thereunder. Although the core provisions under the RBI Act are applicable to all NBFCs, Nidhis stand on a different footing, particularly in matters relating to their deposit acceptance. Nidhis are barred from payment of brokerage on deposits and issuing advertisements in any manner.

A finance company desirous of availing itself of exemptions provided by the government under Section 620A of the Companies Act would have to apply to the MCA. For that purpose, the information required by the MCA has to be furnished. After getting the declaration, the company gets the status of Nidhi, is exempted from many provisions of the Companies Act, 1956, and enjoys certain special privileges under the act. Once it is exempted from Section 53 (1) of the Companies Act, it is not required to send individual notices of general meetings. Similarly, it is exempted from sending copies of audited balance sheet to individual shareholders, except those holding 100 or more shares. In turn, it has to display the balance sheets on the notice boards of its office, apart from getting them published in two newspapers, one in English and another in a local language. It may be noted that companies do not automatically become Nidhis eligible for exemptions and privileges until they are notified in the Central Government gazette as Nidhis. Until so notified, they are regarded as loan companies subject to RBI supervision.

21.2 Legal Framework

Over time, Nidhis, on account of their financial and administrative strength, opened branches outside the local territory even as the concept of mutual benefit remained fundamental. Once they started branching out, monitoring and supervision became difficult. Some Nidhis, even though they were localized, became wayward in their operations, leading to failures. Several depositors were left in the lurch. These failures compelled the government to introduce strict prudential norms for Nidhis.

21.2.1 Norms for Nidhis

Nidhis have a deposit cap of INR 20 crore. Once this limit is crossed, a Nidhi becomes a non-banking finance company.

The MCA rationalized the norms relating to Nidhis to reinforce the confidence of small investors following large-scale defaults in refund of deposits by some Nidhi companies. The following are the highlights of the norms issued by the MCA, vide Notification GSR 737 dated November 1, 1999.

- All Nidhis will have a deposit cap of INR 20 crore. Once this limit is crossed, a Nidhi will become a non-banking finance company. Nidhis with a deposit of over INR 20 crore (up to November 1, 1999) will not be allowed to increase the deposit beyond this limit.
- No Nidhi will be allowed to accept deposits for a period of less than six months.
- Nidhis will not be allowed to give loans to its directors beyond INR 15 lakh. If loans are given to directors beyond this limit, they would be bound to bring it down to INR 15 lakh within one year.
- Each Nidhi will be required to maintain a contingency fund that will be built up by transferring 0.5 per cent of each deposit to this fund, which will be kept in deposit form with a nationalized bank.
- Nidhis are not allowed to enter into any arrangement for change of management without the approval of the MCA.
- The directors appointed to the board of Nidhis cannot hold the post beyond a period of 10 years. Such directors can be reappointed only after a gap of two years.
- The Nidhis that have branches outside the state in which they are registered will be given three years' time to shut down their branches outside the state.
- Nidhis with more than three branches in the state or district will be given five years' time to bring them down to the ceiling of three branches over and above the registered headquarters.
- The MCA will have the right to appoint a special officer to monitor the working of the Nidhis in case a default in repayment of deposits is alleged by more than 10 depositors. The directions given by the officer will be binding on the Nidhis.
- The MCA will also have the right for special audit of the company and its accounts if the auditors are found giving vague certificate relating to companies.

21.2.2 The Sabanayagam Committee

Any company desirous of doing Nidhi business should have the word "Nidhi" added to its name.

The government appointed different committees at different points of time to examine various issues related to the functioning of Nidhis. These committees were the Viswanatha Shastri Committee (1965), Banking Commission (1972), James Raj Committee (1975), Chakravarthy Committee (1987) and A.C. Shah Committee (1992). However, none of these committees was exclusively appointed to study the functioning of Nidhis. The first committee appointed exclusively to study the functioning of Nidhis and make recommendations was the Sabanayagam Committee. This was a nine-member expert committee appointed consequent to the failure of a number of Nidhis. The committee was constituted on April 23, 2000, by the Government of India to suggest an appropriate policy framework for the overall improvement of Nidhis, instill and restore the confidence of the investing public, especially small depositors, and facilitate the healthy functioning of Nidhi companies. More particularly, the committee was constituted to:

- Evaluate the present mechanism for monitoring the activities of Nidhi companies and suggest improved mechanisms to sustain and strengthen them.
- Suggest prudential norms for deployment of funds of Nidhis on the lines of NBFCs and develop guidelines for adoption.

- Suggest a supervisory framework to track non-compliance of such norms and examine the feasibility of bringing in deposit insurance cover and some sort of rating that can be imposed on these Nidhis.
- Develop a future long-term growth plan for Nidhis for their development and proper functioning so that they can play a role in the context of financial reforms, inter alia, technological developments, emerging needs of stakeholders and national imperatives.

The committee made a thorough study and gave recommendations for the effective functioning of Nidhis in the country. The major recommendations are as follows:

1. Any company desirous of doing Nidhi business should have the word "Nidhi" added to the company's name so that the public and the authorities have no confusion as to whether a company is a Nidhi or not.
2. Nidhis can issue only rights shares and the unsubscribed portion of the rights issue can be apportioned by the board of directors as per the existing law. Nidhis should not be allowed to issue any new preference shares at any time. In case Nidhis have already issued preference shares, they shall not be permitted to issue fresh preference shares once the preference shares already issued are redeemed.
3. No member shall exercise voting rights in excess of 10 per cent of the total voting rights of the equity shareholders.
4. Considering the purchasing power of the rupee, the committee recommended that for new companies to function as Nidhis, the share value should be INR 10 with the proviso that the company shall not levy service charges.
5. Nidhis may be permitted to privately circulate to their members their loan and deposit schemes and abstract of the balance sheet. No advertisement shall be made for mobilization of resources. No brokerage or incentives will be allowed to be paid for mobilizing deposits or granting loans.
6. Fixed deposits shall be for a minimum period of 12 months and a maximum period of 84 months.
7. Nidhis can operate recurring deposit schemes with its members ranging for a period of 12 months to 84 months.
8. The net owned funds to deposits shall be in the ratio of 1:20. Net owned funds would mean the aggregate of paid-up equity capital and free reserves as reduced by accumulated losses and intangible assets.
9. Nidhis should be permitted to increase deposits subject to the prudential norms. The restrictions on incremental deposits become redundant and may, therefore, be removed.
10. Considering the fact that Nidhis are not supposed to perform normal banking functions, savings deposit accounts may be permitted with a limit of INR 20,000 and the rate of interest shall be not more than 2 per cent above the savings bank interest rate of nationalized commercial banks. No interest shall be paid by Nidhis if the limit of INR 20,000 is exceeded. There is no case for permitting Nidhis to maintain current accounts as this would amount to normal banking business.
11. Not less than 10 per cent of the funds deposited in Nidhis should be deposited in a nationalized commercial bank in the form of unencumbered fixed deposit receipts and only 90 per cent should be used for business.
12. Nidhis should earmark 0.5 per cent of their deposits towards a contingency fund. The purpose of setting up this fund is to have sufficient resources to help Nidhis that may face a financial crunch on account of unexpected withdrawal of deposits or delayed recovery/realization of dues from loanees.
13. In order to strengthen the Nidhi and to give the loanee a sense of participation, all loanees should be required to hold equity shares of face value of at least 5 per cent of the loan amount with respect to loans up to INR 1 lakh, 3 per cent with respect to loans exceeding INR 1 lakh but less than INR 5 lakh and 2 per cent with respect to loans above INR 5 lakh.
14. Loans shall be given only to individuals against the following securities.
    - Jewellery, gold and silver;
    - Immovable property;
    - Kisan Vikas Patra (KVP) / National Savings Certificate (NSC) / National Savings Scheme (NSS) / insurance policies and other government securities; and
    - Fixed deposit receipts.

In the case of loans against the security of jewellery, gold and silver, the loan amount shall not exceed 60 per cent of the estimated value of the security offered. The period of loan shall be not more than 12 months.

15. For loans against immovable property, the loan amount shall not be more than 33.3 per cent of the value of the property offered as security. Since loans against property are long-term loans, the following ceiling on loans is to be observed.

    (a) Not more than INR 2 lakh per individual where the total amount of deposits held by the Nidhi is INR 2 crore or less and the sum total of all individual loans of INR 50,000 and above should not exceed 15 per cent of the total deposits.
    (b) Not more than INR 750,000 per individual where the deposits held by the Nidhi is more than INR 2 crore but not exceeding INR 20 crore and the sum total of all individual loans of INR 2 lakh and above should not exceed 15 per cent of the total deposits.
    (c) Not more than INR 12 lakh per individual where the deposits held by the Nidhi is more than INR 20 crore but not exceeding INR 50 crore and the sum total of all individual loans of INR 3 lakh and above should not exceed 15 per cent of the total deposits.
    (d) Not more than INR 15 lakh per individual where the deposits held by the Nidhi exceed INR 50 crore and the sum total of all individual loans of INR 4 lakh and above should not exceed 15 per cent of the total deposits.
    (e) The sum total of such mortgage loans should not exceed 40 per cent of the amount of overall loans outstanding on the date of approval by the board of directors.

16. Loans against property shall be permitted only if the loanee executes a mortgage with power to the mortgagee to sell without intervention of the court and is properly registered with the department of registration.
17. While granting loans against KVP, NSC, etc., Nidhis should take adequate precautions by having the certificates discharged by the holders and an undertaking from the holders that on maturity, the loan would be repaid by them to the Nidhi or earlier by premature encashment.
18. Investing in the stock market is not favoured because the very object of Nidhis would be fractured if trading in shares is permitted.
19. Nidhis may advance credit to self-help groups (SHGs) by observing the following condition:

    A group should have a minimum of 10 members. Each member may be entitled to a loan of INR 500 and no one SHG can be given more than INR 10,000. These loans shall be secured by the guarantee of all the members of the group. There shall, however, be a ceiling—the sum total of all such loans shall not exceed 5 per cent of the value of all loans.

20. The sum total of all loans given against the security of property shall not be more than 40 per cent; with respect to loans against jewels and gold not more than 50 per cent; and with respect to SHGs, the ceiling shall be 5 per cent. The balance of loans may be spread over to loans against KVP, NSC, etc.
21. The rate of interest on fixed deposits shall not exceed the rate prescribed by the regulatory authority. The rate of interest on loans shall not exceed 5 per cent of the highest rate of interest offered on deposits by the Nidhis based on reducing balance method.
22. The ceiling on dividend shall be pegged at 25 per cent subject to the condition that an equal amount is transferred to general reserves and there has been no default in repayment of matured deposits and interest thereon.
23. Nidhis shall be managed by a board of directors with due representation for depositors and women. No director shall continue beyond 10 continuous years except with the approval of the regulatory authority. A person can be a director in only one Nidhi. No loan shall be given in future to a director. A person who has a loan subsisting with a Nidhi shall be debarred from becoming a director of that Nidhi. The maximum amount that may be paid to a director for attending board meetings shall not be more than INR 10,000 a year.
24. Any Nidhi can open branches only if it has earned operating profits for at least three continuous years and its projections reveal that it would be able to recover the capital expenditure within a period of three years. A Nidhi can open three branches without requiring any approval so long as they are within

Table 21.1 Provisions for bad and doubtful debts

Assets	Provision
Standard assets	No provision
Substandard assets	10% of the aggregate outstanding
Doubtful assets	50% of the aggregate outstanding
Loss assets	100% of the outstanding

the revenue district. If, however, a Nidhi wants to open a branch outside the district but within close proximity, it should obtain the approval of the regulatory authority. Nidhis that already have three branches within or outside the district and desirous of opening new branches shall apply to the regulatory authority. No Nidhi can open any branch outside the state. For Nidhis with branches outside the state, such a branch or branches in one state should be constituted as a separate entity. For every five years of completed service, one branch can be allowed to be opened in the district in which the company is registered or outside the district, but not outside the state.

25. Nidhis should not be allowed to borrow from or lend money to any body corporate or invest in any body corporate. In other words, the Nidhi's dealings should be only with members.
26. A Nidhi with 10,000 members or INR 2 crore by way of deposits shall publish its balance sheet in two dailies, one in English and the other in the local vernacular. Others need only publish the abstract of the balance sheet by way of pasting it on the notice board of the Nidhi and sending such abstract to members holding 10 or more shares.
27. Income should not be taken to the profit and loss account on accrual basis on any borrowal account if it is a non-performing asset. Non-performing assets are those borrowal accounts where interest income and/or instalment of loan towards repayment of principal amount have remained unrealized fully for 12 months. Part receipt of interest income, during or after the amount becomes non-performing, would not be reckoned as complete discharge of the liability by the borrower and hence the aforementioned principle would be applicable.
28. The provisioning for bad and doubtful debts are as shown in Table 21.1.

Substandard assets are those borrowal accounts that are non-performing assets. Doubtful assets are those borrowal accounts that remained non-performing for more than one year but up to two years. Loss assets are those borrowal accounts that remained non-performing asset for more than two years or the documents executed may become invalid if subjected to legal processes.

21.2.3 Revised Norms

Following the recommendations of the Sabanayagam Committee, the Ministry of Corporate Affairs, revised its norms for Nidhis on May 1, 2000. The highlights of the revised norms are as follows.

1. Nidhis with deposits of INR 50 crore and above shall be allowed incremental deposits of 2 per cent per annum of the deposits as on the date of the last balance sheet for the next 10 years.
2. Nidhis were earlier asked to shut down their branches situated outside the state in which they were registered within a period of three years and bring down the number of branches situated within the state or district in which they were registered to not more than three by five years. Now, Nidhis that have completed 25 years as on November 1, 1999, should not increase the number of branches as existed on that date and other Nidhi companies should bring down the number of branches as existed on November 1, 1999, within a period of 10 years from the date of publication of this notification.
3. Nidhis were earlier not allowed to accept deposits for a period of less than six months. This shall not include savings deposits earmarked by members for the limited purposes of crediting the loan and interest amounts and periodically withdrawn.
4. In case of retirement of two-thirds of the directors or more in any one year, one-third of the total number of directors shall vacate office in the ensuing annual general meeting immediately due and the balance number of directors shall retire at the two subsequent annual general meetings due later.

21.2.4 Expert Group Recommendations

Pursuant to the implementation of the recommendations of the Sabanayagam Committee, representations were received by the MCA, particularly from the Chamber of Nidhis and several Nidhis. To examine these representations, the Government of India constituted a six-member expert group under the chairmanship of A.R. Rao on February 13, 2002.

The group endeavoured to make an objective assessment of the implications of the Notifications GSR.555 (E) & 556(E) dated July 26, 2001, on the existing and potential Nidhis. The various representations received by the group were examined in detail and the recommendations were made taking into account the positive role played by Nidhis.

Increase in face value of shares

After deliberations, the group came to the conclusion that the existing Nidhis notified under Section 620A of the Companies Act, as well as potential Nidhis awaiting declaration under Section 620A, which are already functioning may be allowed to continue with the existing capital structure without any variation in the face value of the equity shares. In other words, status quo may be maintained so far as existing Nidhis and potential Nidhis are concerned. However, the group found that the new companies, which were to be incorporated after the notification, may be insisted upon to have equity shares of face value of INR 10 each as contemplated therein. These new companies, which would be incorporated after the issue of the notification, would not face any difficulties in having equity shares of face value of INR 10 each.

Preferential allotment of shares

As per Clause 1(a) (v) of the notification, no company declared as Nidhi under Section 620A of the Companies Act shall make any preferential allotment of shares to any persons or group of persons but shall make only rights issue and the unsubscribed portion can be apportioned by the board of directors in terms of Section 81 of the act. The group considered the difficulties faced by the Nidhis and came to the conclusion that the existing Clause 1(a) (v) needed to be modified with a suitable proviso that the restriction shall not apply to allotment of shares with face value up to INR 100 to new deposit holders and borrowers, and with respect to qualifying shares to be held by the directors.

Prepaid interest warrants

According to Clause 1(a) (xiv) of the notification, no company declared as Nidhi under Section 620A of the act shall issue prepaid interest warrants. The group recommended that the existing restriction relating to issue of prepaid interest warrants may be retained.

Exclusion of preference share capital from net owned funds

In Clause 1(b) (iii) of the notification, it is provided that the proceeds of preference share capital will not be considered for arriving at the net owned fund of a Nidhi. The group heard representations of the management of various Nidhis and understood that preference share capital can be either redeemed by issuing fresh equity share capital or the preference share capital can be converted into equity share capital by following necessary legal procedures under the Companies Act, 1956.

Ratio of net owned funds to deposits

In Clause 1(d) (i) of the notification, it is prescribed that a Nidhi may accept deposits not exceeding 20 times its net owned funds as per the last audited balance sheet. Provided that in the case of existing Nidhis with deposits in excess of the aforesaid limits, the same shall be brought to the prescribed limit by increasing the net owned fund position or alternatively by reducing the deposit within two years from the date of the notification. Provided further that the ratio will apply to incremental deposits immediately.

As Nidhis should be ultimately regulated by the prescribed norms, and what is required for the present is that they should be given sufficient time to adhere to the norms, the group, therefore, came to the conclusion that the norms should be achieved by the companies within the extended period mentioned below:

(a) Companies with deposits below 25 times the net owned funds as on March 31, 2001: by March 31, 2004

(b) Companies with deposits between 26 times and 40 times the net owned funds as on March 31, 2001: by March 31, 2005

(c) Companies with deposits between 41 times and 80 times the net owned funds as on March 31, 2001: by March 31, 2006

(d) Companies with deposits exceeding 80 times the net owned funds as on March 31, 2001: by March 31, 2007

Period of fixed deposits/recurring deposits

Clause 1(d) (ii) (A) (B) provides that recurring deposits/fixed deposit accounts can be opened for a minimum period of 12 months and a maximum period of 60 months. The group recommended a minor modification of the existing clause to provide that in the case of recurring deposits related to mortgage loans, the maximum period of recurring deposits may exceed 60 months if it corresponds to the repayment period of the loan disbursed by the company.

Saving deposit account

Clause 1(d) (ii) (C) of the notification provides that the maximum balance at any given time qualifying for interest in savings deposit accounts shall not exceed INR 20,000. The rate of interest shall not be more than 2 per cent of the rate of interest payable on savings bank accounts by nationalized banks. The group considered the representations of the Nidhis and, after due deliberations, came to the conclusion that there was no justification for enhancing the existing limit of INR 20,000 qualifying for interest in savings deposit accounts. The group found that there was no ceiling on the amount that can be retained in savings bank accounts, but the restriction was only in relation to the amount qualifying for interest. The savings deposit account holder always has the freedom or choice of transferring the amount in excess of INR 20,000 to a fixed deposit account. Moreover, as Nidhis cater to people in the lower economic groups, members with such huge balances may be very few. The group also found that the restriction on the rate of interest at 2 per cent above the rate of interest offered by nationalized banks was reasonable. The group, therefore, recommended the retention of the existing provision with the benchmark rate being reckoned on the rate on savings bank accounts offered by the State Bank of India, if the rates offered by nationalized banks vary.

Format of application form to contain various details about the company

Clause 1(e) (A) (i) to (xii) and (B) (i) to (v) of the notification prescribes various items of information to be incorporated in the application forms for accepting deposits from the members. The group was of the opinion that the deposit application forms should also carry an abridged version of the latest balance sheet of the company as an additional disclosure.

Issue of minimum INR 100 worth of shares to every member

Clause 1(f) (i) (A) of the notification specifies that every Nidhi shall allot to every deposit holder a minimum of 10 equity shares or shares equivalent to INR 100, whichever is higher. The group discussed the issue with various Nidhis and came to the conclusion that the existing companies should be permitted to continue with their present setup in so far as present depositors are concerned, subject to their allotting a minimum number of shares with a total face value of INR 100 to all newly opened deposits and renewed deposits. The group also felt that it was necessary to exempt savings bank account holders and recurring deposit account holders from this provision since they would be mostly very poor depositors or borrowers who repay the loans in instalments.

Foreclosure of deposits

Clause 1(f) C(ii) to (iv) of the notification provides that every Nidhi shall permit fixed deposit accounts to be foreclosed by the depositors only on the following conditions:

(i) A Nidhi shall not repay any deposit within a period of three months from the date of its acceptance;

(ii) Where a Nidhi at the request of the depositor repays any deposit after a period of three months, the depositor shall not be entitled to any interest up to six months from the date of deposit;

(iii) Where a Nidhi at the request of the depositor makes repayment of the deposit before the expiry of the period for which such deposit was accepted, the rate of interest payable on such deposit shall be reduced by 2 per cent from the rate the Nidhi would have ordinarily paid had the deposit been accepted for the period for which such deposit had run.

However, it has been provided that in the event of death of a depositor, the deposit may be repaid prematurely to the surviving depositor in case of joint holding with survivor clause, or to the nominee or legal heir, with interest at the rate which the company would have ordinarily paid had such deposit been accepted for the period for which such deposit had run, up to the date of repayment.

The group felt that any lenience in this regard would encourage Nidhis to accept fixed deposits for shorter duration through the back door and, thereby, the restrictions provided in Paragraph 1(d)(ii)(A) relating to the minimum period of fixed deposits and recurring deposits would be defeated. Therefore, the group recommended the continuation of the existing restrictions relating to foreclosure of deposits as these were reasonable restrictions and did not warrant any relaxation.

Investment of 10% of the Nidhi's deposits with a scheduled bank

Clause 1(g) of the notification provides that every Nidhi shall invest and continue to invest, with effect from September 1, 2001, in unencumbered term deposits with a scheduled commercial bank, other than a co-operative bank or a regional rural bank, an amount which shall not be less than 10 per cent of the deposits outstanding at the close of business on the last working day of the second preceding month. The group was of the view that there should be a provision for regulating the withdrawals from the deposit accounts in cases of unforeseen commitments in the matter of repayment of the deposits.

Loan against immovable properties

Clause 1(h) of the notification deals with various loans that can be advanced by Nidhis to its members. In sub-clause (i) (B), it is provided as follows:

"Provided that the loan against immovable property shall not exceed 50 per cent of the overall loan outstanding on the date of approval by the board and the individual loan shall not exceed 50 per cent of the value of property offered as security. The period of such loan shall not exceed five years. Existing Nidhis shall bring down the ratio of loan against immovable property to 50 per cent of the overall loan outstanding within two years from the date of this notification."

The group found that the representations made by the various Nidhis had merit. The requirement that mortgage loans should not exceed 50 per cent was very restrictive, especially when it was seen that many of these companies could lend only on immovable properties and not jewellery. It was represented to the group that these companies lent only on registered mortgage of properties and as per the provisions of Section 69 of the Transfer of Property Act, it was possible for the companies to sell the mortgaged property without the intervention of the court in specified towns like Chennai, Mumbai and Kolkata. The experience of these companies has been that the borrowers invariably settle their dues when they are threatened with the auction of the mortgaged property, with resort to recovery action through courts being exceptional. Therefore, the group was of the view that the immovable property loans were good assets from the angle of recovery. Considering the practical experience of these companies, the group recommended that registered mortgage loans may be exempted from the limit of 50 per cent. Loans on immovable properties by any other type of mortgage would alone be considered for the purposes of Clause 1(h)(i)(B) of the notification. While making this recommendation, the group took due note of the fact that liquidity problems that may arise on account of mortgage loans are minimized by the liquidity regime mentioned in the recommendation on Issue No. 11.

A have higher ceiling of a seven-year period for mortgage loans is in the interest of the borrowers as well as of the company, and the group recommended the extension of the time limit of immovable property loans to seven years. The group took note of the fact that these loans were generally given to persons in the lower-income bracket for fulfilling social obligations and the limit of five years for repayment would be unrealistic.

Loans on own FD, KVP, NSC, etc.

Clause 1(h) (i) (C) of the notification provides that every Nidhi may give loans to its shareholders or members against securities such as fixed deposit receipts, Kisan Vikas Patras, National Saving Schemes, insurance policies and other government securities provided that such securities are pledged to the company duly discharged and the lock-in period of such securities does not fall beyond the loan period or one year, whichever is earlier.

The group considered the representations and found that the reasons adduced for relaxation of this provision were valid. The group came to the conclusion that the existing clause may be relaxed as far as loans against fixed deposits were concerned and the tenure restriction need not apply to loans against fixed deposits.

Accordingly, the group recommended that the tenure of loans against fixed deposits may correspond to the remainder period of fixed deposits.

Margin of interest charged on loans

In Clause 1(hI) (ii) of the notification, it is provided that the rate of interest charged on loans given by a Nidhi shall not exceed 5 per cent of the highest rate of interest offered on deposits accepted by them and shall be based on reducing balance method. The group examined the representations as well as the need to control the spread so that the borrowers are not squeezed heavily. The group concluded that the spread of interest rates should not exceed 7.5 per cent. Accordingly, it recommended that the spread may be increased from 5 per cent to 7.5 per cent in Clause 1(h) (ii).

Tenure of directors

Clause 1(h) (second h)(i) (A) provides that no company declared as Nidhi after the publication of the notification shall have any person as director for a continuous period of more than 10 years except with the approval of the regulatory authority. The group considered representations against this restriction and found that the grounds adduced for relaxation of this restriction were not very convincing. The group took note of the causes for the failure of leading Nidhis such as Royapettah Benefit Fund and Alwarpet Benefit Fund, which accepted the dominance of the management by a few directors who functioned with vested interest. The group was of the view that the existing restriction was reasonable, particularly in view of the provision for continuation in office beyond 10 years with the approval of the regulatory authority. Therefore, the group recommended continuation of the existing restriction without any alteration.

Press publication of annual accounts

Clause 1(h) (second h) (ii) of the notification provides that every Nidhi with membership of 10,000 and above, or deposits of INR 2 crore or above as at the end of each financial year, shall publish the audited accounts in two dailies, one in English and one in the vernacular, within six months from the closure of the financial year.

The group recommended that Clause 1(h) (second (h) (ii) may be deleted. To protect the interest of potential depositors of Nidhis, the group recommended the inclusion of an abridged version of the latest balance sheet of the company in the application form.

Undisbursed dividend

Clause 1(h) (second(h)(v) of the notification provides that any dividend remaining unclaimed for a period beyond seven years shall be transferred to the central government account in terms of Section 205C of the Companies Act, 1956.

The group considered the representations of Nidhis against this provision and found that the grounds for its relaxation were not tenable and any modification would require amendment of the Companies Act, 1956, which may not be warranted. Therefore, the group recommended that the existing restriction may continue and Nidhis be treated on a par with other companies in the matter of transfer of unclaimed dividend to the Investors' Protection Fund as contemplated in Section 205C of the act.

Prudential norms

GSR 556 (E) dated July 26, 2001 (hereafter referred to as the second notification) deals with prudential norms for income recognition and asset classification and has come into force from the date of the notification. Separate norms have been prescribed for mortgage loans and loans against jewellery, government securities and own deposits.

Assets are classified as ***standard assets, substandard assets, doubtful assets, non-performing assets and loss assets.***

The group felt that certain relaxations in the norms for classification of assets and also extension of adequate lead time were required. The group recommended that the explanation for classification of assets in Paragraph 1(ii)a be restated as follows.

1) *Standard asset* means the asset with respect to which no default in repayment of principal or payment of interest is perceived and which does not disclose any problem nor carry more than normal risk attached to the business;
2) *Substandard asset* will be that borrowal account which is a non performing asset.

Table 21.2 Recommended changes

Nature of asset	*Provision required*
Standard asset	No provision
Substandard asset	10% of the aggregate outstanding amount
Doubtful asset	25% of the aggregate outstanding amount
Loss asset	100% of the aggregate outstanding amount

3) *Doubtful asset* will be that borrowal account which remained non-performing for more than two years but up to three years.
4) *Loss asset* will be that borrowal account which remained non-performing for more than three years or where, as per the opinion of the Nidhi or its internal auditor or by the inspecting authority during the course of its inspection, a shortfall in the recovery of the loan account is expected because the documents executed may become invalid if subjected to legal processes or for any other reason,
5) *Non-performing asset* will be that borrowal account where interest income and/or instalment of loan towards repayment of principal amount remained unrealized for 12 months.

The group also recommended that the provision required against the assets classified be changed as shown in Table 21.2.

As regards loans against jewellery, etc., the aggregate outstanding amount of loan granted against such security should be either recovered or renewed within the next three months after the due date of repayment specified at the time of grant of such loans. If not recovered or not sold, it should make 100 per cent provision against the current year's profit and loss account to the extent of the unrealized amount or aggregate outstanding amount of loan as applicable. No income shall be recognized on such loans outstanding after the expiry of three months' period or sale of jewellery, whichever is earlier.

21.2.5 Prudential Norms for Income Recognition

Prudential norms *pertain to revenue recognition and classification of assets with respect to mortgage loans or jewel loans.*

Following the recommendations of the expert group, the Ministry of Corporate Affairs issued a notification on April 30, 2002. Accordingly, every Nidhi shall adhere to the prudential norms stated therein. These norms pertain to revenue recognition and classification of assets with respect to mortgage loans or jewel loans.

Income including interest or any other charges on non-performing assets shall be recognized only when it is actually realized. Any such income recognized before the asset became non-performing and remaining unrealized shall be reversed in the current year's profit and loss account.

The classification of assets and the provision required as prescribed are shown in Table 21.3.

Provided that Nidhis incorporated on or before July 26, 2001, shall make a provision with respect to loans disbursed and outstanding as on March 31, 2002, for income reversal and non-performing assets as per Table 21.4.

Provided further that a Nidhi company or mutual benefit society may make the provision exceeding the above limits. Provided also that the accounts for the year ending March 31, 2006, and the account for succeeding years should clearly indicate the total amount of provision to be made on account of income reversal and non-performing assets remaining unrealized by notes on accounts and the amount provided in that year and the balance amount to be provided, till the entire amount of income recognized without providing for non-performing assets and the amount remain unprovided for non-performing assets as on March 31, 2002.

Table 21.3 Classification of assets

Nature of asset	*Provision required*
Standard asset	No provision
Substandard asset	10% of the aggregate outstanding amount
Doubtful asset	25% of the aggregate outstanding amount
Loss asset	100% of the aggregate outstanding amount

Table 21.4 Provision required for loans

For the year ended	*Extent of provision*
31-03-2006	50% of pre-tax profit as per published accounts
31-03-2007	50% of pre-tax profit as per published accounts
31-03-2008 31-03-2009 31-03-2010 31-03-2011	Unprovided balance on an equal basis over the balance 4 years

Provided also that it shall be the duty of the statutory auditor to certify that the note exhibit true and fair view of the same.

As per the notification issued by the MCA, standard asset means the asset with respect to which no default in repayment of principal or payment of interest is perceived and which does not disclose any problem nor carry more than normal risk attached to the business. Substandard asset is that borrowal account which is a non-performing asset. Reschedulement or renegotiation or rephasement of the loan instalment or interest payment would not change the classification of assets unless the borrowal account has satisfactorily performed for at least 12 months after such reschedulement or renegotiation or rephasement. Doubtful asset is a borrowal account that remained non-performing for more than two years but up to three years. Loss asset is the borrowal account that remained non-performing for more than three years or where, as per the opinion of the Nidhi or its internal auditor or by the inspecting authority during the course of its inspection, a shortfall in the recovery of the loan account is expected because the documents executed may become invalid if subjected to legal process or for any other reason. Non-performing asset refers to a borrowal account where interest income and/or instalment of the loan towards repayment of principal amount remained unrealized for 12 months.

The aggregate outstanding amount of loan granted against the security of gold, jewellery etc. should be either recovered or renewed within the next three months after the due date of repayment specified at the time of grant of such loans. If the loan is not recovered or the security is not sold within the given time, the company should make 100 per cent provision against the current year's profit and loss account to the extent of the unrealized amount or aggregate outstanding amount of the loan as applicable. No income shall be recognized on such loans outstanding after the expiry of three months' period or sale of jewellery, whichever is earlier.

The above prudential norms for revenue recognition and classification of assets shall be applicable to all Nidhis notified under Section 620A of the Companies Act, 1956, before or after the publication of this notification. The government, if satisfied that the circumstances have arisen and if found in public interest, after recording the reasons in writing, may relax any of the directions mentioned above either generally or for any specified period, subject to such terms and conditions as the government may specify for avoiding any hardship to any Nidhi or class of Nidhis.

Despite stringent parameters set by it, the government continues to receive depositor complaints against defaulting entities. The major problem Nidhis generally face is the mismatch between assets and liabilities when mature deposits are not offered for renewal. The situation worsens when there are foreclosures of deposits. No Nidhi would be able to service a large number of foreclosures all of a sudden, more so those with low net owned funds. Since Nidhis are conceived and formed without any separate class of investors as shareholders, they never feel the need to keep aside a part of their profits as reserves and surplus. Hence, the net owned funds of Nidhis are low due to low share capital and hardly any reserves and surplus.

The history of Nidhis includes a number of failures. However, what hit the headlines recently was the failure of leading Nidhis involving millions of rupees and depositors, caused by imprudent lending and mismanagement by those in control. On account of these startling failures, there was a tendency to condemn Nidhis as a whole. The fact is that a large number of Nidhis has been functioning without any problems or inconvenience to the people and serving the larger interests of society.

21.3 The Chamber of Nidhis

The Chamber of Nidhis has been in the forefront of championing the cause of its member institutions and in getting their grievances redressed. Established on April 23, 1986, under Section 25 of the Companies Act, 1956, the Chamber of Nidhis has the following objectives.

1. To aid, stimulate and promote the concept of Nidhis.
2. To bring about friendly relationship, feeling, understanding and unanimity among the member Nidhis.
3. To consider and formulate opinion on all matters affecting the member Nidhis and to represent them to the concerned authorities to seek remedy and relief.
4. To collect, classify and circulate information and statistics relating to the activities and functioning of member Nidhis in a periodical bulletin.
5. To maintain a library of books and publications of interest and use to Nidhis to provide information and guidance to members.
6. To start chapters affiliated to the Chamber of Nidhis anywhere in the country to motivate and propagate the concept of Nidhis and further the cause of the chamber with a functionary nominated or elected, as deemed necessary, by the executive committee of the chamber under the given circumstances.

The affairs of the chamber are looked after by a committee consisting of the president, two vice-presidents, honorary secretary, honorary joint secretary, honorary treasurer and a few members. Only Nidhis recognized by the government as such under Section 620A of the Companies Act are entitled to become members of the chamber on payment of a prescribed admission and annual membership fees. However, the rules have been subsequently amended to admit all benefit funds, whether notified under Section 620A or not, as associate members on payment of the prescribed fees, pending their recognition as Nidhi.

Summary

1. The concept of Nidhi envisages the coming together of people who know each other for mutual benefit. The principle of mutual benefit is fundamental—to lend to the members from the savings mobilized (deposits) from the members.
2. The primary object of Nidhis is to carry on the business of accepting deposits and lending money to member borrowers only against fixed deposit receipts, jewels, house property, etc. at reasonable rates of interest.
3. All companies, unless and until they are notified as Nidhis under Section 620A of the Companies Act, despite having been working on the Nidhi pattern, would be treated as loan companies.
4. Nidhis with deposits of INR 50 crore and above shall be allowed incremental deposits of 2 per cent per annum of the deposits as on the date of the last balance sheet for the next 10 years.
5. The Sabanayagam Committee recommends that no member shall exercise voting rights in excess of 10 per cent of the total voting rights of the equity shareholders. It is also recommended by the committee that for new companies to function as Nidhis, the share value should be INR 10 with the proviso that the company shall not levy service charges.
6. The expert group came to the conclusion that existing Nidhis notified under Section 620A of the Companies Act, as well as potential Nidhis awaiting declaration under Section 620A, which are already functioning may be allowed to continue with the existing capital structure without any variation in the face value of the equity shares. However, new companies will have equity shares of face value of INR 10 each.
7. Following the recommendations of the expert group, the Ministry of Corporate Affairs issued a notification on April 30, 2002. Accordingly, every Nidhi shall adhere to the prudential norms stated therein. These norms pertain to revenue recognition and classification of assets with respect to mortgage loans or jewel loans.
8. The Chamber of Nidhis was established on April 23, 1986, under Section 25 of the Companies Act, 1956, to champion the cause of the member institutions and get their grievances redressed.

Questions

1. Outline the evolution of Nidhis.
2. Define a Nidhi and discuss its salient features.
3. Distinguish between Nidhis and NBFCs.
4. What could be the reasons for failure of some Nidhis in the recent past?
5. Discuss the major recommendations of the Sabanayagam Committee.
6. Discuss the implications of dual control over Nidhis.
7. Discuss the prudential norms for Nidhis.
8. Elucidate the major recommendations of the expert group on Nidhis.
9. Write a brief note on the Chamber of Nidhis.

Chapter 22

Housing Finance

LEARNING OBJECTIVES

After reading this chapter, you should be able to:

- Explain the importance of housing and housing finance.
- Present the sources of housing finance.
- Describe the National Housing Bank.
- Highlight the National Housing and Habitat Policy.
- State the RBI's directives for scheduled commercial banks.
- Present the directives of the NHB for housing finance companies.

22.1 Introduction

After food and clothing, shelter is an essential requirement of human life. A house, besides being a place of dwelling, is an important social need for a family. Housing and quality of life are intimately related. Good housing, along with other facilities like safe drinking water, sanitation, electricity and clean surroundings, tend to increase people's productivity. The lifestyle and culture of people are also reflected in the type of houses they live in.

Housing is both a social and economic need for a human family. Housing also reflects the culture and customs of the people.

During the last 50 years (1951–2001), India's population has more than doubled. The urban population has increased by more than five times, but the decennial growth rates of population have declined during the last two decades. The geometric increase in population and migration of people from rural to urban areas have put tremendous pressure on urban housing, infrastructure and services. This has led to unorganized settlements and many social problems (the mafia, for example).

Although the growth trends in housing and household formation have more or less followed the growth trends in population, the housing problem continues to be alarming. The useable housing stock is much smaller than the number of households both in rural and urban areas. It is observed that the growth rate of useable dwelling units continues to be lower than the required rate in spite of several initiatives by the government to augment the housing stock. The housing problem is more acute in urban areas than in rural areas.

Housing shortage is estimated on the basis of the number of households and available and acceptable housing stock. *Congestion* and *overcrowding* are assessed on the basis of the number of rooms in a house, number of members in a family and number of married couples in the family. These factors are also considered in estimating housing shortage. It is heartening to note that the tendency to own a house has shown an increasing trend, particularly in recent years, in both rural and urban areas. Along with the aspirations of people to own a house, the unit cost of housing has increased many times due to various factors including inflation. The increasing cost of housing also makes it difficult for many people to afford a dwelling.

Congestion and overcrowding characterize the Indian housing system.

The housing finance sector in India has undergone unprecedented change, especially over the past two decades. Traditionally, the chief source of finance for housing was individual personal savings. The personal savings were supplemented by borrowings from moneylenders. Many households remained houseless for several years, mainly because of lack of funds. Gradually, the government realized the importance of housing and, accordingly, initiated several measures to improve housing conditions. Housing not only serves a social need of the people but also creates employment, both directly and indirectly. Presently, the construction industry is one of the major sources of employment. It is reported that the real estate sector is the second largest employment generator in the country.

The housing financial system has undergone a tremendous change from being dominated by non-institutional sources to institutional sources.

There is a distinct recognition by the government of the need to move away from the role of being a provider of finance to a facilitator.

Over the years, there has been a distinct recognition by the government, both state and central, of the need to shift from being a provider of finance to facilitator by creating required institutional infrastructure to meet the housing needs of the people. Realizing that state-owned corporations were not efficient and cost-effective, the government initiated measures to foster private-public partnerships in providing housing finance. Accordingly, the government encouraged the private sector to enter the housing finance sector. Established in 1977, the Housing Development Finance Corporation (HDFC) Limited is India's first private sector housing finance company. The government also permitted commercial banks and regional rural banks to finance the housing and real estate sectors. Thus, there has been a considerable shift in the method of financing—from the unorganized to the organized sector. Presently, housing finance can be sourced from scheduled commercial banks, housing finance companies, cooperative housing societies, cooperative banks, Housing and Urban Development Corporation (HUDCO) and state housing boards besides the unorganized sector (such as moneylenders). Some companies, especially large companies and governments (state and central) finance the housing needs of their respective employees. Growing competition in the housing finance sector has brought down the lending rates of interest. Thus, accessibility to housing finance has increased. The easy accessibility and lower cost of loans have in turn increased the number of borrowers willing to take loans and make houses. In view of the lending rates being brought down by severe competition, financing agencies work on lesser margins. To improve their profit margins, they may have to improve their volume of business, increase efficiency and reduce cost of funds. Since they have found good value in funding the housing sector, all housing finance institutions have, of late, come up with a variety of schemes to finance housing and real estate in a big way. Housing finance institutions have also customized their lending policies and procedures to be customer-friendly and thereby increased their business.

Housing finance institutions provide different kinds of loans such as home equity loans, home extension loans, home improvement loans, home purchase loans and land purchase loans.

Housing finance institutions provide different kinds of loans such as home equity loans, home extension loans, home improvement loans, home purchase loans and land purchase loans. *Home equity loans* are loans availed of by the borrowers on mortgage of their house property but the purpose of the loan may be something other than housing. All other kinds (terms) of loans mentioned here are self-explanatory. Housing finance institutions including commercial banks have adopted aggressive sales promotion strategies to attract customers. These include intensive advertising campaigns, waivers of processing and administration fees, gift offers and other incentives, on-the-spot loan approvals and loan-to-value ratios that exceed 100 per cent.

22.2 Suppliers of Housing Finance

Banks have become more responsive to social needs, including housing needs, of the community since the nationalization of major commercial banks in 1969.

The *cooperative sector* is a pioneer in providing housing finance, particularly in rural and semi-urban areas. The cooperative housing finance sector essentially has a two-tier structure, comprising the apex cooperative housing finance society at the state level and the primary cooperative housing finance society at the retail level. Several different types of cooperative housing societies operate at the primary level. They include tenant ownership housing societies, tenant co-partnership housing societies, house construction or housing building societies and house mortgage societies. Although many other institutions, particularly housing finance companies and commercial banks, have come up in a big way with innovative loan products, the cooperative sector continues to play an important role as it is well entrenched and stabilized in rural and semi-urban areas.

Traditionally, banks were reluctant to lend for housing as they preferred financing working capital needs of commerce, industry and trade. The banks had a valid reason for their reluctance to extend credit for housing as a regular part of their business. Banks are primarily mobilizers of short-term funds in the form of savings account deposits and current account deposits. So bankers think it risky to tie up such short-term funds with long-term housing loans. In other words, there is an asset-liability mismatch if banks undertake housing loans. But this thinking changed after the nationalization of major commercial banks. Banks have become more responsive to the social needs of the community after 1969. The government has also asked banks to lend to the housing sector by prescribing certain mandatory requirements. For example, scheduled commercial banks are required to earmark a minimum of 3 per cent of their incremental deposits for extending credit to the housing sector. To encourage institutional housing finance, loans up to INR 15 lakh have also been brought under priority sector lending of banks. Over the years, commercial banks have realized that the demand for housing loans is tremendous and, therefore, housing finance could be one of the lucrative diversified businesses of banking. Their large branch network has also helped them expand their business in housing finance. Thus, commercial banks have emerged as major players in the housing finance sector. Despite being late entrants in the business, banks have overtaken established housing finance companies over the past 10 years or so. Several commercial banks have also set up housing finance subsidiaries which function as independent units.

The Housing Development Finance Corporation Limited (HDFC) is the largest private sector housing finance company in the country. Its dominant presence and high credit rating have enabled HDFC to achieve sustainable market leadership.

Recognizing that housing is a constitutional right of the people, the Government of India enunciated the national housing policy, which stresses the importance of public-private partnership. The government has realized that the vacuum in institutional finance for housing and other construction activities is due to inadequate flow of funds for such activities from existing institutions. So the government has initiated certain measures to encourage specialized credit institutions to provide funds for the housing and real estate sector. In response, many specialized housing finance institutions have been established, both in the private sector and public sector. They include Can Fin Homes Ltd, Cent Bank Home Finance Ltd, Deutsche Postbank Home Finance Ltd, Dewan Housing Finance Corporation Ltd, DHFL Vysya Housing Finance Ltd, GIC Housing Finance Ltd, GRUH Finance Ltd, Housing and Urban Development Corporation Ltd, Housing Development Finance Corporation Ltd, ICICI Home Finance Company Ltd, IDBI Homefinance Ltd, Ind Bank Housing Ltd, LIC Housing Finance Ltd, Manipal Housing Finance Syndicate Ltd, National Trust Housing Finance Ltd, PNB Housing Finance Ltd, REPCO Home Finance Ltd, Sundaram BNP Paribas Home Finance Ltd, Vishwakriya Housing Finance Ltd and AIG Home Finance India Ltd. The Housing Development Finance Corporation Limited (HDFC) is the largest private sector housing finance company. Its dominant presence and high credit rating have enabled HDFC to achieve sustainable market leadership. The housing finance sector is always capital-deficient as the housing shortage in the country has grown alarmingly. The purpose of setting up more specialized institutions is to have dedicated outlets for supply of housing credit. Housing finance companies are basically non-banking finance companies. An NBFC is classified as a housing finance company if providing housing finance is the principal object of the company or where there are more than one principal object as per the memorandum and articles of association, housing finance should form a major share of the company's asset pattern as revealed in the latest balance sheet.

Apart from the various financial institutions which act as retail lenders, the central and state governments also indirectly support the house-building efforts of the people. Besides laying down broad principles of social housing schemes, the Government of India provides financial assistance in the form of loans and subsidies to state governments. The central government has also set up the Housing and Urban Development Corporation (HUDCO) to finance and undertake housing and urban development programmes, development of land for satellite townships and setting up of building centres. The Government of India also provides house-building loans to certain categories of its own employees. The state governments, besides supporting state housing boards, provide finances to cooperative institutions that are engaged in financing the housing sector.

The Life Insurance Corporation of India (LIC) and General Insurance Corporation of India (GIC) also support housing activity. LIC is statutorily required to invest 25 per cent of its net annual accretion in socially-oriented schemes including housing. GIC and its subsidiaries are required to invest 35 per cent of their annual accretion by way of loans to socially-oriented sectors. They also provide loans to state governments for their rural housing programmes and to state-level apex cooperative housing finance societies. These corporations may also subscribe to bonds floated by HUDCO and the state housing boards. They provide loans to individuals who are policy holders. LIC has promoted a housing finance subsidiary called LIC Housing Finance Ltd and provides funds to it. GIC has established a separate subsidiary, GIC Housing Finance Ltd, particularly to finance housing finance requirements and it provides funds for the subsidiary's operations.

The government's support to housing had traditionally been centralized and directed through the state housing boards. The state housing boards have been set up in most of the state governments with the following objectives.

- To provide housing accommodation to needy citizens at reasonable prices
- To construct houses and allot them under the categories of high income group, middle income group and low income group
- To select sites for housing and decide the services to be provided

- To formulate schemes for self-financing that help the middle- and high-income groups
- To construct commercial complexes, multi-storied buildings and shops and then to lease them out so as to secure financial resources for the boards.

HUDCO was incorporated on April 25, 1970, under the Companies Act, 1956, as a fully owned enterprise of the Government of India. The establishment of HUDCO was the first major initiative of the government to finance housing and urban infrastructure. The main objectives of HUDCO are as follows.

- To provide long-term finance for construction of houses for residential purposes or finance or undertake housing and urban development programmes in the country.
- To finance or undertake, wholly or partly, the setting up of new or satellite towns.
- To subscribe to debentures and bonds to be issued by the state housing (and urban development) boards, improvement trusts and development authorities, specifically for the purpose of financing housing and urban development programmes.
- To finance or undertake the setting up of industrial enterprises for building material.
- To administer the moneys received from time to time from the Government of India and other sources as grants or otherwise for the purposes of financing or undertaking housing and urban development programmes.
- To promote, establish, assist, collaborate and provide consultancy services for the projects of designing and planning works related to housing and urban development programmes in India and abroad.

22.3 National Housing Bank

The sub-group on housing finance during the Seventh Five-Year Plan (1985-90) identified the vacuum in the availability of long-term housing finance, particularly for individual households, and recommended the setting up of a national-level institution. To examine the recommendations of the sub-group, a high-level group under the chairmanship of Dr C. Rangarajan, the then deputy governor of the Reserve Bank of India (RBI), was constituted. The group recommended the setting up of National Housing Bank (NHB) as an autonomous housing finance institution. The Government of India accepted the recommendations and introduced the National Housing Bank Bill in the winter session (1987) of Parliament. The bill was passed in Parliament and, with the assent of the President of India on December 23, 1987, it became an act of Parliament. The act provides the legislative framework for the establishment of the NHB. According to the act, the NHB was set up on July 9, 1988, as a wholly owned institution by the RBI, which contributed the entire paid-up capital of the NHB. The general superintendence, direction and management of the affairs and business of the NHB vest, under the act, in a board of directors. The basic functions of the NHB are to operate as a principal agency to promote housing finance institutions both at local and regional levels and provide financial and other support to such institutions and for matters connected therewith or incidental thereto. The vision statement states that "NHB ensures a sound and healthy housing finance system in India through effective regulation and supervision of housing finance institutions. As a financial institution, NHB is known for its commitment, innovation and quality of service, offering a broad spectrum of financial products to address the needs of the housing sector with motivated employees working in a congenial and participative work environment."

The principal objectives of the NHB are:

a. To promote a sound, healthy, viable and cost-effective housing finance system to cater to all segments of the population and to integrate the housing finance system with the overall financial system.
b. To promote a network of dedicated housing finance institutions to adequately serve various regions and different income groups.
c. To augment resources for the sector and channelize them for housing.
d. To make housing credit more affordable.
e. To regulate the activities of housing finance companies based on regulatory and supervisory authority derived under the act.
f. To encourage augmentation of supply of buildable land and also building materials for housing and to upgrade the housing stock in the country.

The NHB supports the housing finance sector by extending refinance to different primary lenders with respect to eligible housing loans extended by them, lending directly with respect to projects undertaken by public housing agencies for housing construction and development of housing-related infrastructure, guaranteeing the repayment of principal and payment of interest on bonds issued by housing finance companies and acting as a special-purpose vehicle for securitizing the housing loan receivables.

The categories of institutions that are eligible to take refinance from the NHB are housing finance companies (HFC), scheduled commercial banks, regional rural banks, state-level apex cooperative housing finance societies and state cooperative agriculture and rural development banks.

Institutions seeking refinance from the NHB are required to fulfill certain basic criteria. The terms and conditions for refinancing of housing loans are discussed here.

22.3.1 Refinance Scheme for Housing Finance Companies

Refinance assistance is extended to HFCs with respect to their direct lending up to INR 1 crore to individuals for purchase/construction/repair and upgradation of housing units. The financial assistance can be drawn by the HFCs with respect to loans already advanced by them as also towards their prospective disbursements. The HFCs fulfilling certain criteria are eligible to draw refinance from the NHB. The criteria include the following.

- The HFC should be registered with the NHB to carry out housing finance activity in the country.
- The HFC should provide long-term finance for construction/purchase/repair/ upgradation of dwelling units by home-seekers.
- The HFC should invest at least 75 per cent of capital employed by way of long-term finance for housing.
- The HFC should have net owned fund (NOF) of not less than INR 10 crore. The NOF will carry the same meaning as per Housing Finance Companies (NHB) Directions, 2001.
- The HFC should comply with the provisions of the National Housing Bank Act, 1987, and Housing Finance Companies (NHB) Directions, 2001, as amended from time to time.
- The net non-performing assets of the HFC should not be more than 5 per cent of the net advances.
- The HFC will have to attain the minimum stipulated rating to be eligible for financial assistance from the NHB. For this purpose, the NHB has developed an internal credit rating model to determine the eligibility for financial assistance for HFCs.

Financial assistance will be provided either at fixed or floating rates of interest. The HFC would have the option to choose either floating or fixed interest rate depending on its requirement. The interest rate charged to the HFC will be as prevailing on the date of disbursement and will depend on the internal credit rating assigned to it by the NHB, slab of housing loans and repayment period sought under refinance. There will be a levy of 0.5 per cent of the loan outstanding on conversion from fixed to floating rate of interest. The applicable interest rate will be the then prevailing floating rate of interest for the term equivalent to the residual repayment period of that loan, as applicable. The HFCs opting to convert loans from floating to fixed rate of interest will have to pay levy as that stipulated with respect to prepayment of floating rate refinance. The applicable interest rate will be the then prevailing fixed rate of interest for the term equivalent to the residual repayment period of that loan.

In case of refinance extended at fixed rates of interest, the NHB will have the option to revise the rates on outstanding loans on completion of three years. The revised rate will be effective from the quarter immediately following the quarter in which three years was completed. The applicable interest rate will be the then prevailing fixed rate of interest for the term equivalent to the original repayment period of that loan. In the case of upward revision, HFCs will have the option to either continue with the outstanding balance on the revised rates or to prepay the same without any prepayment levy. However, in case of downward revision, if the HFC so desires, it would be allowed to prepay the amount only on payments of applicable prepayment levy.

The refinance will be repayable within a period of not less than two years and not exceeding 15 years. HFCs will have the option to choose the repayment period as per their requirement. Repayment of principal and payment of interest will be on a quarterly basis. Repayment of principal will start after one clear calendar quarter from the date of release while payment of interest will start from the immediate quarter.

The HFC, after getting refinance from the NHB, may repay the whole or any part of the amount earlier than the due date by giving two months' notice to the NHB of its intention to effect such repayment before the due date. The NHB will levy a prepayment charge at prescribed rates on such prepayments. The prepayment levy payable by HFCs to the NHB would be independent of whether prepayment levy is being charged by HFCs from their borrowers.

Security to be obtained from individual beneficiaries: An HFC should generally obtain mortgage of property as security for the loan advanced by it. Where it is not feasible, the HFC may accept, at its discretion, security of adequate value in the form of life insurance policies, promissory notes, shares and debentures, or such other security, as it may deem appropriate to fully secure the loan, with the charge properly created in its favour. The credit risk of the primary loan will be fully taken by the HFC and the refinance sought from the NHB is repayable irrespective of the primary loan account remaining regular or otherwise.

Refinance from the NHB may generally be secured by charge on the book debts of the HFC. Additional security such as charge on immovable properties/movable properties and guarantee of promoter may be stipulated at the NHB's discretion. If at any time the NHB is of the opinion that the security provided by the HFC has become inadequate to cover the outstanding refinance, it may advise the HFC to provide and furnish to the satisfaction of the NHB such additional security as may be acceptable to the NHB to cover such deficiency.

22.3.2 Refinance Scheme for Scheduled Banks

The objective of the scheme is to provide refinance assistance to scheduled banks (SBs) with respect to direct/indirect loans already advanced by them for purchase/construction/repairs and upgradation of housing units. All housing loans covered/to be covered under refinance should be standard assets as per RBI guidelines.

The following categories of SBs are eligible to draw refinance from the NHB under the scheme:

(a) Scheduled commercial banks (public sector banks, private sector banks and foreign banks in India) [SCB];
(b) Scheduled state cooperative banks [SCOB]; and
(c) Scheduled primary (urban) cooperative banks [UCB].

SBs fulfilling the following criteria will be eligible to draw refinance from the NHB:

(a) The net non-performing assets of the bank as a percentage of the net advances should not exceed 10 per cent for the entire portfolio of the bank.
(b) The capital adequacy ratio of the banks should be as per the norms prescribed by Reserve Bank of India.
(c) The SB should be making profit for the last two years.
(d) It should be permissible for the SCOB and UCB to borrow from the NHB under the concerned cooperative societies act and their registered bylaws.

The following direct and indirect loans would be eligible for refinance from the NHB:

(a) Direct housing loans up to INR 1 crore disbursed by SBs to individuals.
(b) Indirect term loans disbursed by the SCB to HFCs registered with NHB covering housing loans given to individuals by the HFCs.

Scheduled primary urban cooperative banks (UCBs) shall fulfill the following criteria to be eligible to draw refinance from NHB:

- The net non-performing assets as a percentage of the net advances should not exceed 5 per cent for the entire portfolio of the bank.
- The capital adequacy ratio should be as per the norms prescribed by Reserve Bank of India.
- The bank should be making profit for the last two years.

Direct housing loans up to INR 40 lakh disbursed by the UCB to individuals would be eligible for refinance from the NHB.

Financial assistance under the scheme will be provided either at fixed or floating rates of interest. The SB would have the option to choose either the floating or fixed interest rate depending on its requirement. The interest rate charged to the SB shall be as prevailing on the date of disbursement and will depend on the slab of housing loan and repayment period opted by the SB. The rate of interest is subject to periodic revision by the NHB and this will be informed from time to time. An SB can convert the outstanding loans from fixed rate structure to floating or vice versa in certain conditions.

The refinance will be repayable within a period of not less than two years and not exceeding 15 years. The SBs will have the option to choose the repayment period as per their requirement. Repayment of principal and payment of interest will be on a quarterly basis. The principal along with accumulated interest can be repaid in one bullet instalment after expiry of a fixed term opted by the SB varying from two to five years. In this option, the bullet repayment and the accumulated interest will be paid in one instalment at the end of the desired maturity. The repayment period for refinance to the SB with respect to its indirect loans will not exceed the weighted average unexpired maturity of such indirect loans.

The SB, after availing itself of refinance from the NHB, may repay the whole or any part of the amount earlier than the due date by giving two months' notice to the NHB of its intention to effect such repayment before the due date. The NHB will levy a prepayment charge as prescribed by the NHB.

The SB should generally obtain mortgage of property as security for the loan advanced by it. Where it is not feasible, the SB may accept, at its discretion, security of adequate value in the form of life insurance policies, promissory notes, shares and debentures, or such other security, as it may deem appropriate to fully secure the loan, with the charge properly created in its favour. The credit risk of the primary loan will be fully taken by the SB and the refinance sought from the NHB is repayable irrespective of the primary loan account remaining regular or otherwise. The SB will have to execute a one-time memorandum of agreement in favour of the NHB.

22.3.3 NHB's Project Finance Policy

NHB's project finance policy envisages extending financial assistance to public housing agencies like housing boards, development authorities, municipal bodies, state slum clearance boards/authorities, public private partnership entities, community-based organizations such as MFIs/NGOs constituted as societies/trusts and private sector agencies. The NHB has a four-fold strategy in this initiative. First, it actively markets project finance through suitable MFIs/NGOs. Second, it develops refinance products. Third, it offers financing as top-up on government schemes such as Jawaharlal Nehru National Urban Renewal Mission (JNNURM). Fourth, it uses technical assistance either with the NHB's own funds or from any other national/international agency for capacity building and borrower education.

22.3.4 NHB's Equity Participation in HFCs

A housing finance company that seeks equity participation from the NHB under one of its schemes shall, among others:

- Be a public limited company.
- Provide long-term finance for construction or purchase of houses in India for residential purposes.
- Invest 75 per cent of capital employed by way of long-term finance for housing.

Capital employed means and includes the following:

- Paid-up capital of the company and its free reserves less intangibles;
- Long-term borrowings;
- Deposits with maturity period of five years and above collected from the public and others, excluding the amount required to be kept or maintained in specified assets as stipulated in Section 29B of the National Housing Act, 1987, as amended from time to time.

An HFC should have a minimum paid-up capital of not less than INR 10 crore inclusive of equity support of the NHB or such other amount as may be stipulated from time to time by the NHB and/or the Securities and Exchange Board of India (SEBI) for listing shares on recognized stock exchanges, whichever is higher. Minimum promoters' contribution in the share capital will always be the same as applicable to a company making an issue to the public.

The NHB's participation in equity shall be on a par and restricted to 25 per cent of the paid-up capital of the housing finance company. However, where the housing financing company is promoted with the main object of catering to the home loan requirements of EWS/LIG/rural segments of society, the NHB's participation can be up to 50 per cent of the paid up capital.

22.4 Government Policy Initiatives

Housing holds the key to accelerating the economic development of a country. Investment in housing, like any other industry, has a multiplier effect on income and employment.

The government has viewed housing as a social need rather than a development activity with many spin-offs for the economic development of the country.

The state governments, besides implementing social housing schemes formulated by the central government, may also formulate their own schemes for providing houses to the economically disadvantaged and backward classes. Besides extending loans to their own employees for construction of houses, state governments also provide funds for rental houses to their employees and to various housing boards and development authorities for constructing houses for different income groups.

The Union Government has realized that state governments alone cannot support and develop the housing sector. Therefore, the Government of India has initiated several measures to develop the housing sector, which includes dwelling units and other amenities required for human habitation. These policy initiatives focus on public–private partnerships for sustainable development of human settlements. The important policy initiatives are presented in the following paragraphs.

22.4.1 National Urban Housing and Habitat Policy, 2005

The Government of India announced the National Urban Housing and Habitat Policy in 1998 with the main aim of facilitating an investment environment for housing. But it was revisited on September 6, 2005. The new policy took note of the government's special focus on shelter for all and development of related infrastructure with particular reference to the economically disadvantaged. The policy mainly aims at the following.

- Creation of adequate housing stock both on rental and ownership basis.
- Facilitating accelerated supply of serviced land and housing with particular focus on EWS and LIG categories.
- Facilitating upgradation of infrastructure of towns and cities and to make these comparable with the needs of the times.
- Ensuring that all dwelling units have easy access to basic sanitation facilities and drinking water.
- Promotion of larger flow of funds to meet revenue requirements of housing and infrastructure using innovative tools.
- Providing quality and cost-effective housing and shelter options to citizens, especially vulnerable groups and economically disadvantaged.
- Using technology for modernizing the housing sector to increase productivity, energy efficiency and quality.
- Guiding urban and rural settlements so that planned and balanced growth is achieved with the help of innovative methods.
- Development of cities and towns in a manner that provides for healthy environment, increased use of renewable energy sources and pollution-free atmosphere with a concern for solid waste disposal and drainage.
- Using the housing sector to generate more employment and achieve skill upgradation in housing and building activity, which continue to depend on unskilled and low-wage employment to a large extent.
- Removing legal, financial and administrative barriers for facilitating access to tenure, land, finance and technology.
- Facilitating, restructuring and empowering institutions in state and local governments to mobilize land and planning and financing for housing and basic amenities.
- Forging strong partnerships between private, public and cooperative sectors to enhance the capacity of the construction industry to participate in every sphere of housing and urban infrastructure.
- Meeting the special needs of SC/ST/disabled/freed bonded labourers/slum dwellers, elderly, women, street vendors and other weaker and vulnerable sections of society.

- Involving disabled, vulnerable sections of society, women and weaker sections in formulation, design and implementation of the housing schemes.
- Protecting and promoting cultural heritage, architecture and traditional skills. Establishing a management information system in the housing sector to strengthen monitoring of building activity in the country.

The objectives of the policy would be carried out through action-oriented initiatives at all levels of the government.

The central government would:

- take steps to bring in planning, housing, financial, regulatory institutional and legal reforms.
- devise macroeconomic policies to enable flow of resources to the housing and infrastructure sector.
- evolve plans, strategies and parameters for optimal use of available resources including land for sustainable development.
- devise action plans for the provision and creation of adequate infrastructure facilities like water sources, connectivity and power supply.
- develop and enforce appropriate ecological standards to protect the environment and provide a better quality of life in human settlements.
- continue and pursue urban reforms with focus on revision of bylaws, municipal laws, simplification of legal and procedural framework, initiation of partnership, reduction of municipal manpower, introduction of property title, introduction of regulators, implementation of urban street vendor policy, etc.
- provide fiscal concessions for housing, infrastructure, regulatory and monitoring mechanism to ensure that the concessions are correctly targeted and utilized.
- develop convergence and integration between urban sector initiatives and financial sector reforms.
- mobilize global resources (including FDI) in housing and urban infrastructure sectors.
- advise and guide respective state governments to adopt and implement the National Urban Housing and Habitat Policy 2005 in a time-bound manner.
- strengthen a nationwide management information system (MIS) on house-building activities to help in designing and developing housing programmes and also assist in decision-making.
- promote research and development, innovative building material, transfer of technology and energy-efficient construction to these sectors.

The state government is required to do the following:

- prepare the state urban housing and habitat policy.
- prepare long-term programmes and short-term strategies to tackle problems in housing and basic services and synergize the provision of adequate infrastructure facilities like water sources, connectivity, drainage, sewerage, sanitation, solid waste management and power supply.
- review the legal and regulatory regime to give a boost to housing and supporting infrastructure.
- facilitate, restructure and empower local bodies in regulatory and development functions.
- amend the existing laws and procedures or promulgate legislation for the effective implementation of the State Urban Housing and Habitat Policy (SUHHP) with particular reference to easy and affordable access to land by government/private sector.
- promote and incentivize the private sector and cooperatives in undertaking housing and infrastructure projects for all segments in urban areas.
- Encourage NGOs/CBOs and partnership with ULGs/government bodies in housing, micro-finance and infrastructure activities.
- facilitate training of construction workers by converging other development programmes.
- promote and incentivize decentralized production and availability of building material.
- develop MIS at state and local levels.
- Research and development activities in the field of housing through appropriate capacity-building programmes.

In the same way, the urban local government authorities, housing finance institutions, and public, private and cooperative agencies have been assigned important roles in the implementation of the policy.

22.4.2 National Urban Housing and Habitat Policy 2007 (NUHHP 2007)

The Government of India announced the National Urban Housing and Habitat Policy 2007 (NUHHP 2007) to meet the growing requirements of shelter and related infrastructure in urban areas. The goal of the policy is "affordable housing for all". Accordingly, the policy seeks to promote various types of public-private partnership to realize the goal with emphasis on the urban poor. In view of the severity of housing shortage and budgetary constraints of the government, both central and states, the policy seeks to involve the private sector, the cooperative sector and the industrial sector in housing development.

According to the action plan of the NUHHP 2007, the Government of India encourages and supports the states in preparing a state urban housing and concomitant state urban housing and habitat action plan. These action plans may include passing of specific acts to realize the policy objectives through legal and regulatory reforms, fiscal concessions, financial sector reforms and introduction of innovative instruments for mobilizing recourses for housing and related infrastructure development at the state/Union territory level.

The policy envisages specific roles for the central government, state governments, local bodies, banks and housing finance companies and other agencies. The roles of these agencies are briefly discussed as follows.

The Government of India will:

- Act as a facilitator and enabler
- Advise and guide respective state governments to adopt and implement the National Urban Housing and Habitat Policy in a time-bound manner
- Promote balanced regional development in the country by suitably decentralizing functions relating to development of the housing sector and promotion of an ecologically sound habitat
- Develop suitable financial instruments for promotion of housing for the EWS and LIG groups serviced by basic amenities
- Promote action plans for creation of adequate infrastructure facilities relating to water, drainage, sanitation, sewerage, power supply and transport connectivity
- Develop economically viable housing promotion models and standards for provision of physical, social and economic services
- Develop suitable fiscal concessions in collaboration with the ministry of finance for promotion of housing and urban infrastructure with special focus on EWS/LIG beneficiaries.

The state government will:

- Prepare the state urban housing and habitat policy
- Act as a facilitator and enabler in collaboration with ULBs/private sector/cooperative sector/NGOs with regard to integrated slum development projects as well as integrated township development projects
- Ensure suitable flow of financial resources to potential EWS/LIG beneficiaries as well as undertake viability gap funding of large housing and habitat development projects
- Prepare medium- and long-term strategies for tackling problems relating to provision of adequate water supply, drainage, sewerage, sanitation, solid waste management, power supply and transport connectivity
- Promote and incentivize decentralized production and availability of local building materials
- Prepare and update master plans along with zonal plans, metropolitan plans, district plans and state-level regional plan by respective agencies with provision of adequate land for the urban poor
- Promote well-designed public-private partnerships to undertake housing and infrastructure projects
- Encourage cooperative group housing societies, employees' organizations, labour housing promotion organizations, non-government organizations (NGO) and community-based organizations (CBO) to enter into partnerships with urban local bodies/parastatals in relation to housing related microfinance and housing development
- Promote in-situ slum upgradation with partnership between the central government, state government, urban local bodies, banks/MFIs and potential beneficiaries.

Banks and housing finance institutions will:

- Reassess their strategies to make them more inclusive in terms of EWS and LIG segments
- Promote innovative financial instruments like development of mortgage-backed securitization market (MBSM) and secondary mortgage market

- Enhance/strengthen the income spread of housing loans portfolio to increasingly cover BPL and EWS beneficiaries
- Adopt a more flexible and innovative approach in relation to credit appraisal norms
- Develop financial products that encourage EWS and LIG beneficiaries to take insurance cover
- Ploughing part of their resources towards financing slum improvement and upgradation programmes
- Devise innovative housing finance schemes for targeting the EWS and LIG segments, with suitable subsidy support from the government
- Promote MFIs and SHGs for mobilizing savings and playing a significant role in housing finance sector.

22.4.3 Indira Awaas Yojana (IAY)

The National Rural Employment Programme (NREP), 1980, and the Rural Landless Employment Guarantee Programme (RLEGP), 1983, were aimed at creating rural employment through various activities including construction of houses in rural areas. But the various states in the country did not have a uniform policy with regard to rural housing. For example, some states allowed only part of the construction cost to be borne by NREP/RLEGP funds and the balance was met by beneficiaries from savings or loans obtained by them. Other states permitted the entire expenditure to be borne by NREP/RLEGP funds. Further, while some states allowed construction of only new dwellings, others permitted renovation of existing houses of beneficiaries. To bring about uniformity, the Government of India launched the Indira Awaas Yojana (IAY) in 1985–86 as a sub-scheme of the RLEGP. Subsequently, the IAY became a sub-scheme of the Jawahar Rozgar Yojana (JRY) when it was launched in April 1989. The scope of lAY has also been extended to cover below-poverty-line (BPL) non-Scheduled Caste/Scheduled Tribe families in rural areas. Simultaneously, the allocation of funds for implementing the scheme was raised from 6 per cent to 10 per cent of the total resources available under JRY at the national level, subject to the condition that the benefits to non-Scheduled Caste/Scheduled Tribe poor should not exceed 4 per cent of the total JRY allocation. Since January 1, 1996, the IAY has been delinked from the JRY and made an independent scheme.

The IAY is a cash subsidy based programme under which assistance is provided to rural BPL families for constructing dwelling units on their own using their own design and technology. Selection of IAY beneficiaries is carried out by Gram Sabhas. Sixty per cent of the funds provided under IAY are meant for SC and ST beneficiaries and the subsidy is sanctioned either in the name of the female member of the household or jointly in the names of both spouses. The present per unit assistance is INR 35,000 in plains and INR 37,500 in hilly and difficult terrain. Funding under IAY is provided by the Government of India and the state government in the ratio of 3:1. However, in the case of Union territories, the entire funds under IAY are provided by the Government of India. Public sector banks have been advised to include IAY houses under the differential rate of interest (DRI) scheme and lend up to INR 20,000 per unit at an interest rate of 4 per cent per annum.

22.4.4 Golden Jubilee Rural Housing Finance Scheme

The objective of the scheme is to address the problem of rural housing through improved access to housing credit, which would enable an individual to build a modest new house or improve or add to his old dwelling in rural areas. The scheme envisages the provision of institutional credit at normal rates of interest to individuals desirous of constructing/acquiring new dwelling units and improving or adding to existing dwelling units in rural areas. The scheme has two channels. The first channel comprises commercial banks and the second channel comprises institutions like the ARDBs, ACHFS, RRBs and HFCs. At the time of formation of the scheme, it was envisaged that commercial banks, being the largest mobilizers of savings in the economy and having a vast network of branches, including in rural areas, would play an important and extensive role in the successful implementation of the scheme. It was, therefore, envisaged that they would take a major share of the proposed disbursements under the scheme. The National Housing Bank also provides refinance of loans under the scheme for loans up to INR 15 lakh. The NHB also provides necessary professional/specialist inputs by way of guidelines on technical, financial and legal appraisal, construction methodologies including design options and cost estimates thereof and training. The performance of the scheme is being closely monitored by the NHB. Primary lending institutions (PLIs) were required to report the progress on a quarterly basis to the NHB in the prescribed format.

22.4.5 Scheme of 1% Interest Subvention

The Government of India has approved a Scheme of Interest Subvention on Housing Loan up to INR 10 lakh, provided the cost of units does not exceed INR 20 lakh. An allocation of INR 1,000 crore was announced for the purpose. The objective of the scheme is to provide interest subsidy on housing loans as a measure to increase affordability of housing for eligible borrowers and generate additional demand for credit. The scheme, to be implemented throughout the country, was to be in operation for one year beginning October 1, 2009, up to September 30, 2010. Interest subsidy of 1 per cent will be applicable for the first 12 months of eligible loans sanctioned and disbursed during the currency of the scheme.

The scheme is being implemented through scheduled commercial banks and housing finance companies registered with the National Housing Bank. The RBI and NHB are the nodal agencies for the scheme for SCBs and HFCs, respectively. After sanctioning and disbursing the eligible loans, the implementing agencies claim disbursement of subsidy from respective nodal agency on a monthly basis.

22.5 Legal Framework for Housing Finance Institutions

The major players in housing finance are scheduled commercial banks and housing finance companies. Scheduled commercial banks are governed and supervised by the Reserve Bank of India, whereas housing finance companies are regulated by the National Housing Bank. So the regulations or directives for these institutions come from these two regulatory bodies.

22.5.1 RBI Directives for Scheduled Commercial Banks, 2009

Scheduled commercial banks can deploy their funds under the housing finance allocation in any of three categories—direct finance, indirect finance and investment in bonds of NHB/HUDCO, or a combination thereof.

In the past decade, housing has emerged as one of the sectors attracting a large quantum of institutional finance, particularly bank finance. Keeping in view the credit requirements of the housing sector and the national housing policy of the Government of India, the Reserve Bank of India has made attempts to ensure orderly growth of housing loan portfolios of banks. Towards this end and under the powers conferred by Sections 21 and 35A of the Banking Regulation Act, 1949, the Reserve Bank of India issued statutory directives on July 1, 2009, as updated up to June 30, 2009. These directives are applicable to all scheduled commercial banks excluding regional rural banks. The salient features of these directives are presented in the following paragraphs.[1]

Banks can deploy their funds under the housing finance allocation in any of three categories:

(i) Direct finance
(ii) Indirect finance
(iii) Investment in bonds of NHB/HUDCO, or a combination thereof.

Direct finance

Direct housing finance refers to finance provided to individuals or groups of individuals including cooperative societies. Banks are free to evolve their own guidelines with the approval of their boards on aspects such as security, margin, age of dwelling units and repayment schedule. The following types of bank finance may be included under direct housing finance.

(i) Bank finance extended to a person who already owns a house in a town/village where he resides, for buying/constructing a second house in the same or other town/village for the purpose of self-occupation.

(ii) Bank finance extended for purchase of a house by a borrower who proposes to let it out on rental basis on account of his posting outside the headquarters or because he has been provided accommodation by his employer.

(iii) Bank finance extended to a person who proposes to buy an old house where he is presently residing as a tenant.

(iv) Bank finance granted only for purchase of a plot, provided a declaration is obtained from the borrower that he intends to construct a house on the said plot, with the help of bank finance or otherwise, within such period as may be laid down by the banks themselves.

(v) Supplementary finance.

(a) Banks may consider requests for additional finance within the overall ceiling for carrying out alterations/additions/repairs to the house/flat already financed by them.

(b) In the case of individuals who might have raised funds for construction/ acquisition of accommodation from other sources and need supplementary finance, banks may extend such finance after obtaining *pari passu* or second mortgage charge over the property mortgaged in favour of other lenders and/or against such other security, as they may deem appropriate.

Indirect housing finance

Banks should ensure that their *indirect housing finance* is channeled by way of term loans to housing finance institutions, housing boards and other public housing agencies, primarily for augmenting the supply of serviced land and constructed units. It should also be ensured that the supply of plots/houses is time-bound and public agencies do not utilize the bank loans merely for acquisition of land. Similarly, serviced plots should be sold by these agencies to cooperative societies, professional developers and individuals with a stipulation that the houses should be constructed thereon within a reasonable time, not exceeding three years. For this purpose, banks may take advantage of various guidelines issued by the NHB for augmenting the supply of serviced land and constructed units.

Lending to housing finance institutions:

(i) Banks may grant term loans to housing finance institutions taking into account (long-term) debt-equity ratio, track record, recovery performance and other relevant factors.

(ii) In terms of NHB guidelines, housing finance companies' total borrowings, whether by way of deposits, issue of debentures/ bonds, loans and advances from banks or from financial institutions including any loans obtained from the NHB, should not exceed 16 times their net owned funds (paid-up capital and free reserves less accumulated balance of loss, deferred revenue expenditure and intangible assets).

(iii) All housing finance companies registered with the NHB are eligible to apply for refinance from the NHB and will be eligible subject to the refinance policy. The quantum of term loan to be sanctioned to them will not be linked to the net owned fund as the NHB has already prescribed the above referred ceiling on total borrowings of housing finance companies.

Lending to housing boards and other agencies:

Banks may extend term loans to state-level housing boards and other public agencies. However, in order to develop a healthy housing finance system, while doing so, the banks must not only keep in view the past performance of these agencies in the matter of recovery from the beneficiaries but should also stipulate that the boards will ensure prompt and regular recovery of loan instalments from the beneficiaries.

Financing of land acquisition:

In view of the need to increase the availability of land and house sites for increasing the housing stock in the country, banks may extend finance to public agencies and not private builders for acquisition and development of land, provided it is a part of the complete project, including development of infrastructure such as water systems, drainage, roads and provision of electricity. Such credit may be extended by way of term loans. The project should be completed as early as possible and, in any case, within three years so as to ensure quick recycling of bank funds for optimum results. If the project covers construction of houses, credit extended therefore with respect to individual beneficiaries should be on the same terms and conditions as stipulated for direct finance.

It has been observed that while financing real estate developers, certain banks were found to be valuing the land for the purpose of security, on the basis of the discounted value of the property after it is developed, less the cost of development. This is not in conformity with established norms. In this connection, it is advised that banks should have a board-approved policy in place for valuation of properties, including collaterals accepted for their exposures, and that valuation should be done by professionally qualified independent valuers. As regards the valuation of land for the purpose of financing of land acquisition as also land secured as collateral, banks may be guided as follows:

(a) Banks may extend finance to public agencies and not to private builders for acquisition and development of land, provided it is a part of the complete project, including development of infrastructure such as water systems, drainage, roads and provision of electricity. In such limited cases in which land acquisition can be financed, the finance is to be limited to the acquisition price (current price) plus development cost. The valuation of such land as prime security should be limited to the current market price.

(b) Wherever land is accepted as collateral, valuation of such land should be at the current market price only.

Terms and conditions for lending to housing intermediary agencies

Banks have the freedom to charge interest rates to housing intermediary agencies without reference to the benchmark prime lending rates (BPLR).

(i) In order to enhance the flow of resources to the housing sector, term loans may be granted by banks to housing intermediary agencies against the direct loans sanctioned/ proposed to be sanctioned by the latter, irrespective of the per borrower size of the loan extended by these agencies, and such term loans would be reckoned for the purpose of achievement of their housing finance allocation.

(ii) Banks can grant term loans to housing intermediary agencies against the direct loans sanctioned/proposed to be sanctioned by them to non-resident Indians also. However, banks should ensure that housing finance intermediary agencies being financed by them are authorized by the RBI to grant housing loans to NRIs as all housing finance intermediaries are not authorized by the RBI to provide housing finance to NRIs. Further, such finance granted by banks to housing finance intermediary agencies against the agencies' lending to NRIs will not be treated as housing finance for the purpose of the scheme of yearly allocation of housing finance applicable to banks.

(iii) Banks have the freedom to charge interest rates to housing intermediary agencies without reference to benchmark prime lending rates (BPLR).

Term loans to private builders

In view of the important role played by professional builders as providers of construction services in the housing field, especially where land is acquired and developed by state housing boards and other public agencies, commercial banks may extend credit to private builders on commercial terms by way of loans linked to each specific project. However, banks are not permitted to extend fund-based or non-fund-based facilities to private builders for acquisition of land even as part of a housing project. The period of credit for loans extended by banks to private builders may be decided by banks themselves based on their commercial judgement subject to usual safeguards and after obtaining such security as banks may deem appropriate. Such credit may be extended to builders of repute, employing professionally qualified personnel. It should be ensured, through close monitoring, that no part of such funds is used for any speculation in land.

Care should also be taken to see that prices charged from the ultimate beneficiaries do not include any speculative element, that is, prices should be based only on the documented price of land, the actual cost of construction and a reasonable profit margin.

It is advised that banks adhere to the National Building Code (NBC) formulated by the Bureau of Indian Standards (BIS) to ensure the safety of buildings, especially in case of natural disasters. Banks may consider this aspect for incorporation in their loan policies.

Construction activities eligible for bank credit as housing finance

The following types of bank credit will be eligible to be treated as housing finance.

(i) Loans to individuals for purchase/construction of dwelling unit per family and loans given for repairs to the damaged dwelling units of families.

(ii) Finance provided for construction of residential houses to be constructed by public housing agencies like HUDCO, housing boards, local bodies, individuals, cooperative societies and employers, priority being accorded to financing construction of houses meant for economically weaker sections, low income groups and middle income groups.

(iii) Finance for construction of educational, health, social, cultural or other institutions/centres, which are part of a housing project and which are necessary for the development of settlements or townships.

(iv) Finance for shopping complexes, markets and such other centres catering to the day-to-day needs of residents of the housing colonies and forming part of a housing project.

(v) Finance for construction meant for improving conditions in slum areas, for which credit may be extended directly to the slum dwellers on the guarantee of the government or indirectly to them through state governments.

(vi) Bank credit given for slum improvement schemes to be implemented by slum clearance boards and other public agencies.

(vii) Finance provided to:

(a) the bodies constituted for undertaking repairs for houses, and

(b) the owners of building/house/flat, whether occupied by themselves or by tenants, to meet need-based requirements for their repairs/additions, after satisfying themselves regarding the estimated cost (for which the requisite certificate should be obtained from an engineer/architect, wherever necessary) and obtaining such security as deemed appropriate.

(viii) Housing finance provided by banks for which refinance is provided by the NHB.

(ix) Investment in guarantee/non-guaranteed bonds and debentures of NHB/HUDCO in the primary market, provided investment in non-guaranteed bonds is made only if guaranteed bonds are not available.

Construction activities not eligible for bank credit

Banks should not grant finance for construction of buildings meant purely for government/semi-government offices, including municipal and panchayat offices. However, banks may grant loans for activities that will be refinanced by institutions like NABARD.

Projects undertaken by public sector entities that are not corporate bodies (public sector undertakings not registered under the Companies Act or which are not corporations established under the relevant statute) may not be financed by banks. Even with respect to projects undertaken by corporate bodies, as defined above, banks should satisfy themselves that the project is run on commercial lines and that bank finance is not in lieu of or to substitute budgetary resources envisaged for the project. The loan could, however, supplement budgetary resources if such supplementing was contemplated in the project design. Thus, in the case of a housing project, where the project is run on commercial lines, and the government is interested in promoting the project either for the benefit of the weaker sections of society or otherwise, and a part of the project cost is met by the government through subsidies made available and/or contributions to the capital of the institutions taking up the project, bank finance should be restricted to an amount arrived at after reducing from the total project cost the amount of subsidy/capital contribution receivable from the government and any other resources proposed to be made available by the government.

Banks had, in the past, sanctioned term loans to corporations set up by government, like the State Police Housing Corporation, for construction of residential quarters for allotment to employees, where the loans were envisaged to be repaid out of budgetary allocations. As these projects cannot be considered to be run on commercial lines, it would not be in order for banks to grant loans for such projects.

Home loan account scheme (HLAS) of NHB

The NHB also operates the home loan account scheme, the details of which are provided in the following paragraphs.

- **Foreclosure of loans:** A member of the HLAS is eligible for a loan after subscription to the scheme for a minimum period of five years. The member has to declare while joining the scheme/taking a loan that he/ she does not own a house/flat. However, a member may acquire a house or a flat from a public agency/cooperative/private builder by obtaining a loan from a bank at the normal rate of interest or from friends and relatives or through a hire-purchase scheme of the housing board/development authority. Thereafter, when the member becomes eligible for a loan under HLAS, he/she may approach the bank for such a loan to repay the loan(s) raised earlier from other sources. There is no objection to bank loans under HLAS being utilized for foreclosing loans secured earlier from other sources, as a special case.
- **Classification of deposits/loans:** Under HLAS, the participating bank is required to accept deposits on behalf of the NHB and make use of these deposits by way of refinance under any scheme approved by the NHB from time to time. The surplus funds, if any, not so utilized (that is, excess of deposits

over refinance) can either be remitted by the participating bank to the NHB or retained by it, subject to compliance with the statutory reserve requirements as follows:

(i) The deposits under the HLA Scheme are on a recurring basis; they should be treated as "time" liabilities subject to reserve requirements under Section 42(1) of the Reserve Bank of India Act, 1934, as also under Section 24 of the Banking Regulation Act, 1949, and included under Item II (a) (ii) of Form A.

(ii) In terms of sub-clause (ii) of Clause (c) of the explanation to sub-section (1) of Section 42 of the RBI Act, as amended by Clause 3 of the Second Schedule to the National Housing Bank Act, 1987, "liabilities" will not include any loan taken from the NHB. Hence, the deposits utilized as refinance from the NHB should be deducted from the total deposits received under the HLA Scheme while including the amount under Item II (a) (ii) of Form A.

Banks' exposure to the real estate sector

While the development of real estate is welcome, banks need to curb excessively risky lending by exercising selectivity and strengthening the loan approval process. Banks should ensure that borrowers have obtained prior permission from the government/local governments/other statutory authorities for the project, wherever required. While the proposals could be sanctioned in the normal course, disbursements should be made only after the borrower has obtained requisite clearances from the government authorities.

Terms and conditions for banks' investment in mortgage-backed securities (MBS)

Banks' investments in MBS should satisfy the following terms and conditions:

(i) The right, title and interest of an HFC in securitized housing loans and receivables thereunder should irrevocably be assigned in favour of a special purpose vehicle (SPV)/trust.

(ii) Mortgaged securities underlying the securitized housing loans should be held exclusively on behalf of and for the benefit of the investors by the SPV/trust.

(iii) The SPV or trust should be entitled to the receivables under the securitized loans with an arrangement for distribution of the same to the investors as per the terms of issue of the MBS. Such an arrangement may provide for appointment of the originating HFC as the servicing and paying agent. However, the originating HFC participating in a securitization transaction as a seller, manager, servicer or provider of credit enhancement of liquidity facilities:

- shall not own any share capital in the SPV or be the beneficiary of the trust used as a vehicle for the purchase and securitization of assets. Share capital for this purpose shall include all classes of common and preferred share capital.
- shall not name the SPV in such manner as to imply any connection with the bank.
- shall not have any directors, officers or employees on the board of the SPV unless the board is made of at least three members and where there is a majority of independent directors. In addition, the official(s) representing the bank will not have veto powers.
- shall not directly or indirectly control the SPV.
- shall not support any losses arising from the securitization transaction or by investors involved in it or bear any of the recurring expenses of the transaction.

(iv) The loans to be securitized should be loans advanced to individuals for acquiring/constructing residential houses that should have been mortgaged to the HFC by way of exclusive first charge.

(v) The loans to be securitized should be accorded an investment grade credit rating by any of the credit rating agencies at the time of assignment to the SPV.

(vi) The investors should be entitled to call upon the issuer SPV to take steps for recovery in the event of default and distribute the net proceeds to the investors as per the terms of issue of the MBS.

(vii) The SPV undertaking the issue of the MBS should not be engaged in any business other than the business of issue and administration of MBS of individual housing loans.

(viii) The SPV or trustees appointed to manage the issue of MBS have to be governed by the provisions of Indian Trust Act, 1882.

If the issue of MBS is in accordance with the terms and conditions stated above and includes irrevocable transfer of risk and reward of housing loan assets to the SPV/trust, investment in such MBS by any bank would not be reckoned as an exposure on the HFC originating the securitized housing loan. However, it would be treated as an exposure on the underlying assets of the SPV/trust.

Home loans for non-resident Indians

Non-resident Indians (NRIs) can also acquire immovable property in India other than agricultural property, plantation or farmhouse. The RBI has issued certain directive for home loans for NRIs. According to these directives, the home loan amount for NRIs should not exceed 85 per cent of the cost of the dwelling unit, as the remaining amount (that is 15 per cent) needs to be provided as own contribution towards the cost of the unit financed. The cost of the dwelling unit, which is own contribution financed less the loan amount, can be met from direct remittances from abroad through normal banking channels, a non-resident external account or non-resident ordinary account in India.

However, repayment of the loan, comprising the principal and interest including all the charges, are to be remitted to the housing finance company from abroad through normal banking channels, the non-resident external account or non-resident ordinary account in India.

22.5.2 National Housing Bank (NHB)–Housing Finance Companies Directions, 2001

The NHB issued certain directions to housing finance companies on September 27, 2001, the salient features of which are presented here.

Restriction on acceptance of deposits

(1) No housing finance company with net owned fund (hereinafter referred to as NOF) of less than INR 25 lakh shall accept public deposits.

(2) No housing finance company having NOF of INR 25 lakh and above shall accept or renew public deposits except to the extent specified below:

(i) not exceeding five times its NOF where the housing finance company has obtained credit rating for fixed deposits not below "A" from any one of the approved rating agencies at least once a year and a copy of the rating is sent to the National Housing Bank and it complies with all the prudential norms; and

(ii) in the absence of credit rating as specified in (i), not exceeding two times its NOF or INR 10 crore, whichever is lower, including any amount remaining outstanding in its books as on the date of acceptance or renewal of such deposit, provided: (a) it complies all the prudential norms and (b) has capital adequacy ratio of not less than 15 per cent as per the last audited balance sheet.

(3) No housing finance company shall have deposits inclusive of public deposits, the aggregate amount of which together with the amounts, if any, held by it which are referred in Clauses (iii) to (vii) of sub-section (bb) of Section 45 I of the Reserve Bank of India Act, 1934 (2 of 1934), as also loans or other assistance from the National Housing Bank, is in excess of 16 times its NOF.

(4) Where a housing finance company holds as on the date of commencement of these directions public deposits in excess of the limits specified in (2) and as applicable to it or deposits inclusive of the items mentioned in (3) in excess of the limits specified in (3), it shall:

(a) not accept fresh deposit or open new deposit account; or

(b) not renew the existing deposit or where the deposits are received under any recurring scheme, receive instalments under such scheme after the expiry of the scheme period;

(c) reduce such excess deposit by repayment on maturity.

(5) in the event of downgradation of the credit rating to any level below "A" from the level earlier held by the housing finance company, it shall:

- report the position within 15 working days to the National Housing Bank;
- with immediate effect stop accepting fresh public deposit if the public deposit held by it is in excess of the limit specified under Clause (ii) of Paragraph 3(2) above; and

- reduce within three years from the date of downgrading of credit rating the amount of excess public deposit to nil or the appropriate extent permissible under Clause (ii) of Paragraph 3(2) above as the case may be, to which it is entitled to accept, by repayment as and when such deposit falls due or otherwise.

Period of deposits

No housing finance company shall accept or renew any public deposit:

(a) which is repayable on demand or on notice; or

(b) unless such deposit is repayable after a period of 12 months or more but not later than 84 months from the date of acceptance or renewal of such deposits.

Where a public deposit is in instalments, the period of such deposit shall be computed from the date of receipt of the first instalment.

Where so desired, deposits may be accepted in joint names with or without any of the clauses, namely, "Either or Survivor", "Number One or Survivor/s", "Anyone or Survivor/s".

Particulars to be specified in application form soliciting public deposits

(i) No housing finance company shall accept or renew any public deposit except on a written application from the depositors in the form to be supplied by the housing finance company, which form shall contain all the particulars specified in the Non-Banking Financial Companies and Miscellaneous Non-Banking Companies (Advertisement) Rules, 1977, made under Section 58A of the Companies Act, 1956 (1 of 1956), and also contain the particulars of the specific category of the depositors, i.e. whether the depositor is a shareholder or a director or a promoter of the housing finance company or a member of public or a relative of a director of the company.

(ii) The application form shall also contain:

(a) the credit rating assigned for its deposits and the name of the credit rating agency that rated the housing finance company;

(b) a statement to the effect that in case of any deficiency of the housing finance company in servicing its deposits, the depositor may approach the national consumers disputes redressal forum, the state-level consumers disputes redressal forum or the district-level consumers disputes redressal forum for relief;

(c) a statement to the effect that in case of non-repayment of the deposit or part thereof in accordance with the terms and conditions of the deposit, the depositor may make an application to authorized officer of the National Housing Bank;

(d) a statement to the effect that the financial position of the housing finance company as disclosed and the representations made in the application form are true and correct and that the housing finance company and its board of directors are responsible for the correctness and veracity thereof;

- a statement to the effect that the housing finance company is within the regulatory framework of the National Housing Bank. It must, however, be distinctly understood that the National Housing Bank does not undertake any responsibility for the financial soundness of the housing finance company or for the correctness of any of the statements or the representations made or opinions expressed by the housing finance company, and for repayment of deposit/discharge of liabilities by the housing finance company;
- the information relating to and the aggregate dues from the facilities, both fund and non-fund based, extended to, and the aggregate dues from companies in the same group or other entities or business ventures in which the directors and/or the housing finance company are/is holding substantial interest and the total amount of exposure to such entities;
- at the end of application form but before the signature of the depositor, the following verification clause by the depositor shall be appended. "I have gone through the financial and other statements/particulars/representations furnished/made by the housing finance company and after careful consideration I am making the deposit with the housing finance company at my own risk and volition."

Introduction of depositors

Every housing finance company shall obtain proper introduction of new depositors before opening their accounts and accepting the deposits, and shall keep on its record the evidence on which it has relied for the purpose of such introduction.

Introduction shall mean identification of the prospective depositor and it may be done either by one of the existing depositors or on the basis of any one of income tax permanent account number (PAN), election identity card, passport or ration card.

Furnishing of receipts to depositors

(1) Every housing finance company shall furnish to every depositor or his agent, unless it has done so already, a receipt for every amount that has been or may be received by the housing finance company by way of deposit before or after the date of commencement of these directions.

(2) The said receipt should be duly signed by an officer entitled to act for the housing finance company in this behalf and shall state the date of deposit, the name of depositor, the amount in words and figures received by the housing finance company by way of deposit, rate of interest payable thereon and the date on which the deposit is repayable.

Provided that if such receipts pertain to instalments subsequent to the first instalment of a recurring deposit, it may contain only name of the depositor/s, date and amount of deposit.

Register of deposits

(1) Every housing finance company shall keep one or more registers in which shall be entered separately in the case of each depositor or group of joint depositors the following particulars:

- name and address of the depositor or group of joint depositors, their nominees,
- date and amount of each deposit,
- duration and due date of each deposit,
- date and amount of accrued interest or premium on each deposit,
- date and amount of each repayment, whether of principal, interest or premium,
- date of claim made by the depositor,
- the reasons for delay in repayment beyond five working days, and
- any other particulars relating to the deposits.

(2) The register or registers aforesaid shall be kept at each branch with respect to the deposit accounts opened by that branch of the housing finance company and a consolidated register for all the branches taken together at the registered office of the housing finance company and shall be preserved in good order for a period of not less than eight years following the financial year in which the latest entry is made of the repayment or renewal of any deposit of which particulars are contained in the register.

Provided that, if the housing finance company keeps the books of account referred to in sub-section (1) of Section 209 of the Companies Act, 1956 (1 of 1956), at any place other than its registered office in accordance with the provisions to that sub-section, it shall be sufficient compliance with this sub-paragraph if the register aforesaid is kept at such other place subject to the condition that the housing finance company delivers to the National Housing Bank a copy of the notice filed with the registrar under the proviso to the said sub-section within seven days of such filing.

Information to be included in the board's report

(1) In every report of the board of directors laid before the housing finance company in a general meeting under sub-section (1) of Section 217 of the Companies Act, 1956 (1 of 1956), after the date of commencement of these directions, the following particulars or information shall be included:

- the total number of accounts of public deposit of the housing finance company that have not been claimed by the depositors or not paid by the housing finance company after the date on which the deposit became due for repayment; and

- the total amounts due under such accounts remaining unclaimed or unpaid beyond the dates referred to in clause (a) as aforesaid.

(2) The said particulars or information shall be furnished with reference to the position as on the last date of the financial year to which the report relates and if the amounts remaining unclaimed or undisbursed as referred to in clause (b) of the preceding sub-paragraph exceed in the aggregate the sum of INR 5 lakh, there shall also be included in the report a statement on the steps taken or proposed to be taken by the board of directors for the repayment of the amounts due to the depositors or group of joint depositors and remaining unclaimed or undisbursed.

Ceiling on the rate of interest and brokerage and interest on overdue public deposits

1(a) On and from March 27, 2003, no housing finance company shall invite or accept or renew any public deposit at a rate of interest exceeding 11 per cent per annum. Interest may be paid or compounded at rests which shall not be shorter than monthly rests.

1(aa) On and from September 20, 2003, no housing finance company shall invite or accept or renew repatriable deposits from non-resident Indians in terms of Notification No. FEMA.5/2000-RB dated May 3, 2000, under Non-Resident (External) Account Scheme at a rate exceeding the rates specified by the Reserve Bank of India for such deposits with scheduled commercial banks. The period of deposits shall not be less than one year and not more than three years.

(b) No housing finance company shall pay to any broker on public deposit collected by or through him (i) brokerage, commission, incentive or any other benefit by whatever name called, in excess of 2 per cent of the deposit so collected; (ii) expenses by way of reimbursement on the basis of relative vouchers/bills produced by him, in excess of 0.5 per cent of the deposit so collected.

Payment of interest on overdue deposit:

A housing finance company may, at its discretion, allow interest on an overdue public deposit or a portion of the said overdue deposit from the date of maturity of the deposit subject to the conditions that:

- the total amount of overdue deposit or a part thereof is renewed in accordance with other relevant provisions of these directions from the date of its maturity till some future date, and
- the interest allowed shall be at the appropriate rate operative on the date of maturity of such overdue deposit, which shall be payable only on the amount of deposit so renewed.

Provided that where a housing finance company fails to repay the deposit along with interest on maturity on the claim made by the depositor, the housing finance company shall pay interest from the date of claim till the date of repayment at the rate as applicable to the deposit.

General provisions regarding repayment of deposits

(i) No housing finance company shall repay any public deposit within a period of three months from the date of its acceptance.

(ii) Where a housing finance company at the request of depositor/s repays a public deposit after the period indicated in Clause (i) above but before its maturity, it shall pay interest at the rate given in Table 22.1.

Table 22.1 Interest rates

Tenure	*Rate*
Minimum lock-in period	Three months
After three months but before six months	No interest
After six months but before the date of maturity.	The interest payable shall be 2 per cent lower than the interest rate applicable to a public deposit for the period for which the deposit has run or if no rate has been specified for that period, then 3 per cent lower than the minimum rate at which the public deposits are accepted by that housing finance company.

(iii) A housing finance company may grant a loan up to 75 per cent of the amount of public deposits to a depositor after the expiry of three months from the date of public deposit at an interest rate of 2 percentage points above the interest rate payable on the public deposit.

(iv) It is obligatory on the part of an HFC to intimate the details of maturity of the deposit to the depositor at least two months before the date of maturity of the deposit.

(v) All deposit accounts standing to the credit of sole/first-named depositor in the same capacity shall be clubbed and treated as one deposit account for the purpose of premature repayment.

(vi) Provided that in the event of death of a depositor, the public deposit may be paid prematurely to the surviving depositor/s in the case of joint holding with the survivor clause, or to the nominee or legal heir/s with interest at the contracted rate up to the date of repayment.

(vii) For the purpose, HFCs are classified into two categories—a problem HFC and a normally run HFC. An HFC, which is normally run-HFC, with effect from the date of this notification, can permit premature repayment of a public deposit after the lock-in period at its sole discretion only and premature closure cannot be claimed as a matter of right by the depositors. Problem HFCs have been prohibited from making premature repayment of any public deposits or granting any loan against public deposits except in the case of death of the depositor or in the case of tiny deposit up to INR 10,000 in entirety or to enable the depositor to meet expenses of an emergent nature up to an amount not exceeding INR 10,000.

A problem HFC is one that:

- has refused or failed to meet within five working days any lawful demand for repayment of the matured public deposits; or
- intimates the CLB under Section 58AA of the Companies Act, 1956, about its default to a small depositor in repayment of any public deposit or part thereof or any interest thereupon; or
- approaches the bank for withdrawal of liquid asset securities to meet its deposit obligations; or
- approaches the bank for any relief or relaxation or exemption from the provisions of Housing Finance Companies (NHB) Directions, 2001, or from that of prudential norms for avoiding default in meeting public deposit or other obligations; or
- has been identified by the NHB as a problem HFC either *suo motu* or based on complaints from depositors about non-repayment of public deposits or on complaints from the company's lenders about non-payment of dues.

Provided that in the event of death of a depositor, the public deposit may be paid prematurely to the surviving depositor/s in the case of joint holding with the survivor clause, or to nominee or legal heir/s with interest at the contracted rate up to the date of repayment.

(viii) A housing finance company may grant a loan up to 75 per cent of the amount of public deposit to a depositor after the expiry of three months from the date of public deposit at a rate of interest two percentage points above the interest rate payable on the public deposit.

Renewal of public deposit before maturity

Where any housing finance company permits an existing depositor to renew his public deposit before maturity for availing himself of the benefit of higher rate of interest, such company shall pay the depositor the increase in the rate of interest provided,

(i) the public deposit is renewed in accordance with the other provisions of these directions and for a period longer than the remaining period of the original contract; and

(ii) the interest on the expired period of the public deposit is reduced by one percentage point from the rate at which the housing finance company would have ordinarily paid, had the deposit been accepted for the period for which such public deposit had run; any interest paid earlier in excess of such reduced rate is recovered/adjusted.

Safe custody of approved securities

(1) Every housing finance company shall entrust to one of the scheduled commercial banks designated by it on that behalf, in the place where the registered office of the housing finance company is situated,

the unencumbered approved securities required to be maintained by it in pursuance of Section 29B of the National Housing Bank Act, 1987.

Provided that where a housing finance company intends to entrust these securities to the Stock Holding Corporation of India Ltd or to its designated banker at a place other than the place at which its registered office is located or to keep them in the form of constituent's subsidiary general ledger account with a scheduled commercial bank, or with a depository participant registered with the Securities and Exchange Board of India under the Securities and Exchange Board of India Act, 1992 (15 of 1992), it shall obtain prior approval, in writing, of the National Housing Bank.

(2) The securities mentioned in sub-paragraph (1) above shall continue to be entrusted with such designated banker or the Stock Holding Corporation of India Ltd or the depository participant or held in the constituent's subsidiary general ledger account with the scheduled commercial bank for the benefit of the depositors and shall not be withdrawn or encashed or otherwise dealt with by the housing finance company except for repayment to the depositors.

Provided that,

- a housing finance company shall be entitled to withdraw a portion of such securities proportionate to the reduction of its deposits duly certified to that effect by its auditors;
- where the housing finance company intends to substitute such securities, it may do so by entrusting substitute securities of equal value to the designated bank before such withdrawal.

Employee security deposit

A housing finance company receiving any amount in the ordinary course of its business as security deposit from any of its employees for due performance of his duties shall keep such amount in an account with a scheduled commercial bank or in a post office in the joint names of the employee and the housing finance company on the following conditions:

- it shall not withdraw the amount without the consent, in writing, of the employee; and
- the amount shall be repayable to the employee along with interest payable on such deposit account unless such amount or any part thereof is liable to be appropriated by the housing finance company for the failure on the part of the employee for due performance of his duties.

Advertisement and statement in lieu of advertisement

(1) Every housing finance company soliciting public deposits shall comply with the provisions of the Non-Banking Financial Companies and Miscellaneous Non-Banking Companies (Advertisement) Rules, 1977, and shall also specify in every advertisement to be issued thereunder the following:

(a) the actual rate of return by way of interest, premium, bonus or other advantage to the depositors;
(b) the mode of payment to the depositors;
(c) maturity period of deposits;
(d) the interest payable on a specified deposit;

- the rate of interest that will be payable to the depositor in case the depositor withdraws the deposit prematurely;
- the terms and conditions subject to which a deposit will be renewed;
- any other special features relating to the terms and conditions subject to which the deposits are accepted/renewed; and
- information relating to the aggregate dues (including the non-fund-based facilities) provided to/from companies in the same group or other entities or business ventures in which the directors and/or the housing finance company hold substantial interest and the total amount of exposure to such entities.

(2) Where a housing finance company intends to accept public deposits without inviting or allowing or causing any other person to invite such deposits, it shall, before accepting deposits, deliver to the office of the National Housing Bank at New Delhi for registration, a statement in lieu of advertisement containing all the particulars required to be included in the advertisement pursuant to the

Non-Banking Financial Companies and Miscellaneous Non-Banking Companies (Advertisement) Rules, 1977, as also the particulars stated in sub-paragraph (1) hereinabove, duly signed in the manner provided in the aforesaid rules.

(3) A statement, delivered under sub-paragraph (2), shall be valid till the expiry of six months from the date of closure of the financial year in which it is so delivered, or until the date on which the balance sheet is laid before the housing finance company in the general meeting, or where the annual general meeting for any year has not been held, the latest day on which that meeting should have been held in accordance with the provisions of the Companies Act, 1956 (1 of 1956), whichever is earlier, and a fresh statement shall be delivered in each succeeding financial year before accepting deposits in that financial year.

Opening and closure of branches

A housing finance company shall, before opening a branch or an office, inform the National Housing Bank in writing of its intention to open the branch or office. No housing finance company accepting deposits shall close its branch/office without publishing such intention in any one national-level newspaper and one vernacular newspaper in circulation in the relevant place and without advising the National Housing Bank, before 90 days of the proposed closure.

Income recognition

(1) Income recognition shall be based on recognized accounting principles.

(2) Income including interest/discount or any other charges on NPA shall be recognized only when it is actually realized. Any such income recognized before the asset became non-performing and remaining unrealized shall be reversed.

(3) With respect to hire purchase assets, where instalments are overdue for more than 12 months, income shall be recognized only when hire charges are actually received. Any such income taken to the credit of profit and loss account before the asset becoming non-performing and remaining unrealized shall be reversed.

(4) With respect to lease assets where lease rentals are overdue for more than 12 months, the income shall be recognized only when lease rentals are actually received. The net lease rentals taken to the credit of the profit and loss account before the asset became non-performing and remaining unrealized shall be reversed.

Net lease rentals are the gross lease rentals as adjusted by the lease adjustment account debited/credited to the profit and loss account and as reduced by depreciation at the rate applicable under Schedule XIV of the Companies Act, 1956.

Income from investments

(1) Income from dividend on shares of corporate bodies and units of mutual funds shall be taken into account on cash basis, provided that the income from dividend on shares of corporate bodies may be taken into account on accrual basis when such dividend has been declared by the corporate body in its annual general meeting and the housing finance company's right to receive payment is established.

(2) Income from bonds and debentures of corporate bodies and government securities/bonds may be taken into account on accrual basis, provided that the interest rate on these instruments is predetermined and interest is serviced regularly and is not in arrears.

(3) Income on securities of corporate bodies or public sector undertakings, the payment of interest and repayment of principal of which have been guaranteed by the central government or a state government, may be taken into account on accrual basis.

Accounting standards

Accounting Standards and Guidance Notes issued by the Institute of Chartered Accountants of India (referred to in these directions as ICAI) shall be followed insofar as they are not inconsistent with any of these directions.

Accounting for investments

(1) (a) The board of directors of every housing finance company shall frame investment policy for the company and implement the same;

(b) The criteria to classify the investments into current and long-term investments shall be spelt out by the board of the company in the investment policy;

(c) Investments in securities shall be classified into current and long-term at the time of making each investment;

(d) (i) There shall be no inter-class transfer on ad-hoc basis;

(ii) The inter-class transfer, if warranted, shall be effected only at the beginning of each half-year, on April 1 or October 1, with the approval of the board;

(iii) The investments shall be transferred scrip-wise, from current to long-term or vice-versa, at book value or market value, whichever is lower;

(iv) Depreciation, if any, in each scrip shall be fully provided for and appreciation, if any, shall be ignored;

(v) The depreciation in one scrip shall not be set off against appreciation in another scrip at the time of such inter-class transfer, even with respect to the scrips of the same category.

(2) A long-term investment shall be valued in accordance with the accounting standard issued by the ICAI.

(3) Quoted current investments shall, for the purpose of valuation, be grouped into the following categories:

- Equity shares,
- Preference shares,
- Debentures and bonds,
- Government securities including treasury bills,
- Units of mutual fund, and
- Others.

Quoted current investments for each category shall be valued at cost or market value, whichever is lower. For this purpose, the investments in each category shall be considered scrip-wise and the cost and market value aggregated for all investments in each category. If the aggregate market value for the category is less than the aggregate cost for that category, the net depreciation shall be provided for or charged to the profit and loss account. If the aggregate market value for the category exceeds the aggregate cost for the category, the net appreciation shall be ignored. Depreciation in one category of investments shall not be set off against appreciation in another category.

(4) Unquoted equity shares in the nature of current investments shall be valued at cost or break-up value, whichever is lower. Where the balance sheet of the investee company is not available for two years, such shares shall be valued at INR 1 per company.

(5) Unquoted preference shares in the nature of current investments shall be valued at cost or face value or the net asset value, whichever is less. In case the net asset value is negative or the balance sheet of the investee company is not available for two years, it should be valued at INR 1 per company.

(6) Investments in unquoted government securities or government guaranteed bonds shall be valued at carrying cost.

(7) Unquoted investments in the units of mutual funds in the nature of current investments shall be valued at the net asset value declared by the mutual fund with respect to each particular scheme.

(8) Commercial papers shall be valued at carrying cost.

Unquoted debentures shall be treated as term loans or other type of credit facilities depending upon the tenure of such debentures for the purpose of income recognition and asset classification.

Need for policy on demand/call loans

(1) The board of directors of every housing finance company granting/intending to grant demand/call loans shall frame a policy for the company and implement the same.

(2) Such policy shall, *inter alia*, stipulate the following:

- A cut-off date within which the repayment of demand or call loan shall be demanded or called up;
- The sanctioning authority shall record specific reasons in writing at the time of sanctioning demand or call loan, if the cut-off date for demanding or calling up such loan is stipulated beyond a period of one year from the date of sanction;
- The rate of interest that shall be payable on such loans;
- Interest on such loans as stipulated shall be payable either at monthly or quarterly rests;
- The sanctioning authority shall record specific reasons in writing at the time of sanctioning demand or call loan, if no interest is stipulated or a moratorium is granted for any period;
- A cut-off date for review of performance of the loan, not exceeding six months commencing from the date of sanction;
- Such demand or call loans shall not be renewed unless the periodical review has shown satisfactory compliance with the terms of sanction.

Asset classification

(1) Every housing finance company shall, after taking into account the degree of well-defined credit weaknesses and extent of dependence on collateral security for realization, classify its lease/hire purchase assets, loans and advances and any other forms of credit into the following classes, namely:

- Standard assets;
- Substandard assets;
- Doubtful assets; and
- Loss assets.

(2) The class of assets referred to above shall not be upgraded merely as a result of rescheduling unless it satisfies the conditions required for the upgradation.

Provisioning requirement

Every housing finance company shall, after taking into account the time lag between an account becoming non-performing, its recognition as such, the realization of the security and the erosion over time in the value of security charged, make provision against substandard assets, doubtful assets and loss assets as provided hereunder:

Loans, advances and other credit facilities including bills purchased and discounted:

(1) The provisioning requirement with respect to loans, advances and other credit facilities including bills purchased and discounted shall be as shown in Table 22.2.

Table 22.2 Provisioning requirement with respect to loans, advances and other credit facilities

1. Loss assets	The entire assets shall be written off. If the assets are permitted to remain in the books for any reason, 100% of the outstandings should be provided for.
2. Doubtful assets	(a) 100% provision to the extent to which the advance is not covered by the realizable value of the security to which the housing finance company has a valid recourse shall be made. The realizable value is to be estimated on a realistic basis; (b) in addition to item (a) above, depending upon the period for which the asset has remained doubtful, provision to the extent of 20% to 50% of the secured portion (i.e., estimated realizable value of the outstandings) shall be made on the following basis:
Period for which the asset has been considered doubtful	*Percentage of provision*
Up to one year	20
One to three years	30
More than three years	50
3. Substandard assets	A general provision of 10% of total outstanding should be made.

Table 22.3 Additional provision with respect to hire purchase and leased assets

(a) Where any amounts of hire charges or lease rentals are overdue up to 12 months	Nil
(b) Where any amounts of hire charges or lease rentals are overdue for more than 12 months but up to 24 months	10% of the net book value
(c) Where any amounts of hire charges or lease rentals are overdue for more than 24 months but up to 36 months	40% of the net book value
(d) Where any amounts of hire charges or lease rentals are overdue for more than 36 months but up to 48 months	70% of the net book value
(e) Where any amounts of hire charges or lease rentals are overdue for more than 48 months	100% of the net book value

(2) The provisioning requirements with respect to hire purchase and leased assets shall be as follows:

(i) With respect to hire purchase assets, the total dues (overdue and future installments taken together) as reduced by the finance charges not credited to the profit and loss account and carried forward as unmatured finance charges and the depreciated value of the underlying asset shall be notionally computed as the original cost of the asset to be reduced by depreciation at the rate of 20 per cent per annum on a straight-line method. In the case of a second-hand asset, the original cost shall be the actual cost incurred for acquisition of such second hand asset.

(ii) With respect to hire purchase and leased assets, additional provision shall be made as shown in Table 22.3.

(iii) On expiry of a period of 12 months after the due date of the last instalment of the hire purchase/ leased asset, the entire net book value shall be fully provided for.

Disclosure in balance sheet

(1) Every housing finance company shall separately disclose in its balance sheet the provisions made without netting them from the income or against the value of assets.

(2) The provisions shall be distinctly indicated under separate heads of accounts separately for housing and non-housing finance business and individually for each type of assets as follows:

- provisions for substandard, doubtful and loss assets; and
- provisions for depreciation in investments.

(3) Such provisions shall not be appropriated from the general provisions and loss reserves held, if any, by the housing finance company.

(4) Such provision for each year shall be debited to the profit and loss account. The excess of provisions, if any, held under the heads general provisions and loss reserves may be written back without making adjustment against them.

(5) Every housing finance company shall separately disclose in the notes on accounts to the balance sheet in its next annual report:

- the details of the levy of penalty, if any, imposed on the housing finance company by the National Housing Bank, and
- adverse comments, if any, on the housing finance company made in writing by the National Housing Bank on regulatory compliances, with a specific communication to the housing finance company to disclose the same to the public.

Requirement as to capital adequacy

(1) Every housing finance company shall maintain a minimum capital ratio consisting of tier-I and tier-II capital, which shall not be less than:

- 10 per cent on or before March 31, 2001, and
- 12 per cent (on or before March 31, 2002) and thereafter, of its aggregate risk-weighted assets and of risk-adjusted value of off-balance sheet items.

(2) The total tier-II capital, at any point of time, shall not exceed 100 per cent of aggregate risk-weighted assets and of risk-adjusted value of off-balance sheet items.

Table 22.4 Risk-weighted assets

		Weighted risk assets – on-balance sheet items	*% weight*
(1)		Cash and bank balances including fixed deposits and certificates of deposits with banks	0
(2)		Investments:	
	(a)	Approved securities as defined in the National Housing Bank Act, 1987	0
	(b)	Bonds of public sector banks and fixed deposits/certificates of deposits/bonds of public financial institutions	20
	(c)	Units of Unit Trust of India	20
	(ca)	Mortgage-backed security, receipt or other security evidencing the purchase or acquisition by a housing finance company of an undivided right, title or interest in any debt or receivable originated by a housing finance company recognized and supervised by National Housing Bank or a scheduled commercial bank and secured by mortgage of residential immovable property, provided the conditions specified below in Note (4) are fulfilled	50
	(d)	Shares of all companies and debentures/bonds/commercial papers of companies other than in (b) above/units of mutual funds other than in (c) above	100
(3)	(a)	Housing/project loans guaranteed by central/state governments **Note:** *Where guarantee has been invoked and the concerned government has remained in default for a period of more than 90 days after the invocation of the guarantee, a risk weight of 100% should be assigned*	01
	(b)	Housing loans to individuals secured by mortgage of immovable property, which are classified as standard assets	75
	(c)	Other housing loans	100
	(d)	(i) Fund-based and non-fund-based exposures secured by mortgages on commercial real estate (office buildings, retail space, multipurpose commercial premises, multi-family residential buildings, multi-tenanted commercial premises, industrial or warehouse space, hotels, land acquisition, development and construction, etc.). (ii) Investments in mortgage-backed securities and other securitized exposures backed by exposures as at (i) above.	125
(4)		Current assets:	
	(a)	Stock on hire (please see note 2 below)	100
	(b)	Inter-corporate loans/deposits	100
	(c)	Loans and advances fully secured by company's own deposits	0
	(d)	Loan to staff	0
	(e)	Other secured loans and advance considered good	100
	(f)	Bills purchased/discounted	100
	(g)	Others (to be specified)	100
(5)		Fixed assets (net of depreciation)	
	(a)	Assets leased out (net book value)	100
	(b)	Premises	100
	(c)	Furniture and fixtures	100
	(d)	Other fixed assets (to be specified)	100
(6)		Other assets:	
	(a)	Income tax deducted at source (net of provision)	0
	(b)	Advance tax paid (net of provision)	0
	(c)	Interest due on government securities and approved securities	0
	(d)	Others (to be specified)	100

Degree of credit risk expressed as percentage weightages have been assigned to balance sheet assets. Hence, the value of each asset/item requires to be multiplied by the relevant risk weights to arrive at the risk-adjusted value of assets. The aggregate shall be taken into account for reckoning the minimum capital ratio. The risk-weighted asset shall be calculated as the weighted aggregate of funded items as detailed in Table 22.4.

Netting may be done only with respect to assets where provisions for depreciation or for bad and doubtful debts have been made. Stock on hire should be shown net of finance charges, that is, interest and other charges recoverable. Assets that have been deducted from owned fund to arrive at tier-I capital pursuant to Paragraph 2(1)(zd) will have a weightage of zero.

(4) For being eligible for risk weight of 50 per cent, investments in mortgage-backed security, receipt or other security referred to in item (ca) of sub-explanation (2) should fulfill the following terms and conditions:

- The assignment of debt together with the securities thereof and the receivables thereunder by the originating housing finance company or scheduled commercial bank in favour of the trust or the securitization company as defined in Clause (za) of sub-section (1) of Section 2 of the Securitization and Reconstruction of Financial Assets and Enforcement of Security Interest Act, 2002 (54 of 2002), issuing such receipt or other security is complete and irrevocable.
- The trust or the securitization company holds the debt together with the securities thereof exclusively for the benefit of the investors in such receipt or other security.
- The originating housing finance company or scheduled commercial bank participating in the securitization transaction, in which such mortgage-backed security, receipt or other security has been issued, as a seller, manager, servicer or provider of credit enhancement or liquidity facilities:

  (i) does not own any equity or preference share in the capital of the securitization;
  (ii) company or is the beneficiary of the trust;
  (iii) has not named the trust or the securitization company in such manner which implies any communication with it;
  (iv) does not have any of its directors, officers or employees on the board of the securitization company unless the board is made up of at least three members and there is a majority of independent directors and the official representing the originating institution in the board of the securitization company does not have veto powers;
  (v) does not directly or indirectly control the trust or the securitization company; and
  (vi) has not agreed to support any losses arising out of the securitization transaction or to be suffered by investors involved in it or agreed to bear recurring expenses of the transaction.

- Each debt securitized is a loan advanced to an individual for the acquisition/construction of residential immovable property which has been mortgaged in favour of the originating housing finance company or scheduled commercial bank on exclusive basis.
- Securitized debt had investment grade credit rating by any of the credit rating agencies at the time of assignment to the trust/securitization company.
- The investors are entitled to call upon the issuer—the trust/securitization company—to take steps for recovery in the event of default and distribute the net proceeds to the investors as per the terms of issue of receipt or other security.
- The trust or the securitization company undertaking the issue in which investment has been made is not engaged in any business other than the business of issue and administration of securitization of housing loans.
- The trustees appointed to manage the issue are governed by the provisions of Indian Trusts Act, 1882 (2 of 1882).

Degrees of credit risk exposure attached to off-balance sheet items have been expressed as a percentage of credit conversion factor. Hence, the face value of each item requires to be first multiplied by the relevant conversion factor to arrive at the risk-adjusted value of the off-balance sheet item. The aggregate shall be taken into account for reckoning the minimum capital ratio. This shall have to be again multiplied by the risk weight of 100. The risk-weighted value of the off-balance sheet items shall be calculated as per the credit conversion factors of non-funded items as detailed in Table 22.5.

Provided that in item (i) above, in those cases where no documents are executed, no disbursement has taken place and in case sanction lapses in course of time and notice to that effect is served on the prospective borrower, the credit conversion factor shall be taken as 0 per cent, and in the case of partly disbursed housing loans, the credit conversion factor shall be taken as 50 per cent.

Table 22.5 Credit conversion factor

	Nature of items	*Credit conversion factor (%)*
(i)	Undisbursed amounts of housing loans sanctioned	50
(ii)	Financial and other guarantees	100
(iii)	Shares/debentures underwriting obligations	50
(iv)	Partly paid shares/debentures	100
(v)	Bills discounted/rediscounted	100
(vi)	Lease contracts entered into but yet to be executed	100
(vii)	Other contingent liabilities (to be specified)	50

Restrictions on exposure to capital market, investment in real estate and engagement of brokers

(1) No housing finance company shall:

(a) invest in land or building, except for its own use, an amount exceeding 20 per cent of its capital fund, provided that such investment over and above 10 per cent of its owned fund shall be made only in residential units.

Capital fund means the aggregate of tier-I capital and tier-II capital.

(b) acquire shares, convertible debentures of corporate bodies and units of equity-oriented mutual funds in excess of a ceiling of 5 per cent of the total outstanding advances (including commercial paper) as on March 31 of the previous year. Within the overall ceiling of 5 per cent for total exposure to the capital market, the total investment in shares, convertible bonds and debentures and units of equity-oriented mutual funds by a housing finance company should not exceed 20 per cent of its net worth.

Provided that the land or building or shares, convertible bonds or debentures of corporate organizations or units of equity-oriented mutual funds acquired in satisfaction of its debts shall be disposed of by the housing finance company within a period of three years or within such a period as extended by the National Housing Bank, from the date of such acquisition, if the investment in these assets together with such assets already held by the housing finance company exceeds the above ceiling. Provided further that the land or building or shares, convertible bonds or debentures of corporate organizations or units of equity-oriented mutual funds held by the company in excess of the ceiling specified hereinabove on the date of coming into force of the above provisions shall be disposed of so as to bring down such holding within the said ceiling by the housing finance company within three years or within such period as extended by the National Housing Bank from the date of coming into force of these directions.

(2) For engagement of brokers to deal in investment transactions, the housing finance companies should observe the following:

- Transactions should not be put through the brokers' accounts. The brokerage on the deal payable to the broker, if any (if the deal was put through with the help of a broker), should be clearly indicated on the notes/memorandum put up to the top management seeking approval for putting through the transaction and separate account of brokerage paid, broker-wise, should be maintained.
- If a deal is put through with the help of a broker, the role of the broker should be restricted to that of bringing the two parties to the deal together.
- While negotiating the deal, the broker is not obliged to disclose the identity of the counterparty to the deal. On conclusion of the deal, he should disclose the counterparty and his contract note should clearly indicate the name of the counterparty.
- On the basis of the contract note disclosing the name of the counterparty, settlement of deals—both fund settlement and delivery of security—should be directly between the parties and the broker should have no role to play in the process.

- With the approval of their top managements, housing finance companies should prepare a panel of approved authorized brokers who should be reviewed annually, or more often if so warranted. Clear-cut criteria should be laid down for empanelment of brokers, including verification of their creditworthiness and market reputation. A record of broker-wise details of deals put through and brokerage paid should be maintained.
- A disproportionate part of the business should not be transacted through only one or a few brokers. Housing finance companies should fix aggregate contract limits for each of the approved brokers. A limit of 5 per cent of total transactions (both purchase and sales) entered into by a housing finance company during a year should be treated as the aggregate upper contract limit for each of the approved brokers. This limit should cover both, the business initiated by a housing finance company and the business offered/brought to the housing finance company by a broker. Housing finance companies should ensure that the transactions entered into through individual brokers during a year normally do not exceed this limit. However, if for any reason it becomes necessary to exceed the aggregate limit for any broker, the specific reasons thereof should be recorded, in writing, by the authority empowered to put through the deals. Further, the board should be informed of this post facto. However, the norm of 5 per cent would not be applicable to (i) a housing finance company whose total transactions in a year do not exceed INR 20 crore; and (ii) housing finance companies' dealings through primary dealers.
- (g) The auditors who audit the treasury operations should scrutinize the business done through brokers also and include it in their monthly report to the chief executive officer of the housing finance company. Besides, the business put through any individual broker or brokers in excess of the limit, with the reasons thereof, should be covered in the half-yearly review to the board of directors.
- Housing finance companies may undertake securities transactions through stockbrokers only on the NSE, BSE or OTCEI.

Concentration of credit investment

(1) No housing finance company shall:

(i) lend to:

- any single borrower exceeding 15 per cent of its owned fund; and
- any single group of borrowers exceeding 25 per cent of its owned fund;

(ii) invest in:

- shares of another company exceeding 15 per cent of its owned fund; and
- the shares of a single group of companies exceeding 25 per cent of its owned fund;

(iii) lend and invest (loans/investments together) exceeding:

- 25 per cent of its owned fund to a single party; and
- 40 per cent of its owned fund to a single group of parties.

(2) Any loan granted and investment made by the housing finance company in excess of the ceilings specified hereinabove and existing on the date of commencement of these directions shall be brought down by the housing finance company as per the repayment schedule in due course.

For determining the above mentioned limits, off-balance sheet exposures be converted into credit risk by applying the conversion factors explained hereinabove. The investment in debentures for the above purpose be treated as credit and not investment. The above ceilings on credit/investments shall be applicable to the own group of the housing finance company as well as to the other group of borrowers/investee companies.

Auditor's report

In addition to the report made by the auditor under Section 227 of the Companies Act, 1956, on the accounts of a housing finance company after the commencement of these directions, the auditor shall make a report to the board of directors of the company on the matters specified in Paragraphs 30 and 31 below.

The auditor's report on the accounts of a housing finance company shall include a statement on the following:

- where the housing finance company was incorporated before June 12, 2000, whether it has applied for registration as required under Section 29A of the National Housing Bank Act, 1987, and whether it has received any communication from the National Housing Bank about grant or refusal of certificate of registration to it;
- where the housing finance company was incorporated on or after June 12, 2000, whether it has obtained a certificate of registration from the National Housing Bank;
- whether the housing finance company has complied with the liquidity requirements as specified under Section 29B of the National Housing Bank Act, 1987, and kept the securities with the designated bank;
- whether the housing finance company has complied with Section 29C of the National Housing Bank Act, 1987;
- whether the housing finance company has complied with provisions of these directions;
- whether the capital adequacy ratio as disclosed in the return submitted to the National Housing Bank has been correctly determined and whether such ratio is in compliance with the minimum capital to risk-weighted asset ratio as prescribed by the National Housing Bank in these directions;
- whether the housing finance company has accepted/holds public deposits;
- where the housing finance company has not accepted public deposits, whether (a) the board of directors has passed a resolution for non-acceptance of any public deposits; (b) the company has accepted any public deposits during the relevant period/year; and (c) the company has complied with prudential norms.

Where, in the auditor's report, the statement regarding any of the items referred to in Paragraph 30 above is unfavourable or qualified, the auditor's report shall also state the reasons for such unfavourable or qualified statement, as the case may be. Where the auditor is unable to express any opinion on any of the items referred to in Paragraph 30, the auditor's report shall indicate such fact together with reasons thereof.

Where, in the case of a housing finance company, the statement regarding any of the items referred to in Paragraph 30 is unfavourable or qualified or in the opinion of the auditor the company has not complied with the provisions of these directions or the provisions of Chapter V of the National Housing Bank Act, 1987, it shall be the obligation of the auditor to make a report containing the details of such unfavourable or qualified statements and/or about the non-compliance, as the case may be, with respect to the company to the head office of the National Housing Bank in New Delhi.

Loans against housing finance company's own shares

(1) No housing finance company shall lend against its own shares.

(2) Any outstanding loan granted by a housing finance company against its own shares on the date of commencement of these directions shall be recovered by the housing finance company as per the repayment schedule.

Housing finance companies failing to repay public deposit

A housing finance company that has failed to repay any public deposit or part thereof in accordance with the terms and conditions of such deposit as provided in Section 36A(1) of the National Housing Bank Act, 1987, shall not grant any loan or other credit facility, by whatever name called, or make any investment or create any other asset as long as the default exists.

Constitution of audit committee

A housing finance company with assets of INR 50 crore and above as per its last audited balance sheet shall constitute an audit committee consisting of not less than three non-executive directors of the board. The audit committee constituted under this paragraph shall have the same powers, functions and duties as laid down in Section 292A of the Companies Act, 1956.

Accounting year and submission of accounting reports

Every housing finance company shall prepare its balance sheet and profit and loss account as on March 31 every year with effect from the accounting year ending March 31, 2002. Provided that if the accounting year of any housing finance company ends on any date other than March 31, 2002, such housing finance company shall prepare its balance sheet and profit and loss account for any fraction of the year ending on March 31, 2002.

Every housing finance company shall deliver to the National Housing Bank an audited balance sheet as on the last date of each financial year and audited profit and loss account with respect to that year as passed by the housing finance company in the general meeting together with a copy of the report of the board of directors laid before the housing finance company in such meeting in terms of Section 217(1) of the Companies Act, 1956 (1 of 1956) within 15 days of such meeting as also a copy of the report and the notes on accounts furnished by its auditors.

Every housing finance company shall submit to the National Housing Bank:

- an annual return furnishing the information specified in Schedule I to these directions with reference to its position as on March 31 every year and a half-yearly return furnishing the information specified in Schedule II to these directions with reference to its position as on September 30 and March 31 every year,
- housing finance companies accepting/holding public deposits, housing finance companies not accepting/ holding public deposits but with an asset size of INR 100 crore and more shall submit to the National Housing Bank a quarterly return furnishing the information specified in Schedule III with reference to its position as at the end of every calendar quarter.

Every housing finance company shall, within one month from the commencement of business, deliver to the National Housing Bank a written statement containing:

- the names and official designations of its principal officers;
- the complete postal address, telephone number/s and fax number/s of the registered/corporate office;
- the names and office addresses of the auditors of the company;
- the names and the residential addresses of the directors of the housing finance company; and
- the specimen signatures of the officers authorized to sign on behalf of the housing finance company returns specified in sub-paragraph (1).

Auditor's certificate

Every housing finance company holding/accepting public deposits shall furnish to the National Housing Bank, along with a copy of the audited balance sheet as provided under Paragraph 37, a copy of the auditor's report to the board of directors and a certificate from its auditors to the effect that the full amount of liabilities to the depositors of the company, including interest payable thereon, are properly reflected in the balance sheet and that the company is in a position to meet the amount of such liabilities to the depositors.

Full cover for public deposits

HFCs should ensure that at all times there is full cover available for public deposits accepted by them. While calculating this cover, the value of all debentures (secured and unsecured) and outside liabilities other than the aggregate liabilities to depositors may be deducted from the total assets. Further, the assets should be evaluated at their book value or realizable/market value, whichever is lower, for this purpose.

In addition to the above, the powers, functions and duties of audit committees of HFCs have been made similar to those laid down in Section 292A of the Companies Act, 1956.

22.6 Impediments in Housing Finance

Foreign direct investments have helped finance the housing sector besides bringing in the professional expertise of international developers along with new technology to the sector.

The major problem in the housing finance sector is paucity of funds. The available funds for the sector are not sufficient to meet the growing needs of housing and real estate. To meet the increasing requirement of funds, the Government of India introduced a scheme in 1993 for NRI investment in housing and real estate development. The government also permitted 100 per cent foreign direct investment (FDI) in housing development. FDI is permitted in integrated development of townships, housing, built-up infrastructure and construction development projects. The FDI is subject to a stipulation of minimum land holding of 100 acres and has a minimum lock-in period of three years with respect to repatriation of profit on the original capital invested. It is expected that with FDI, the housing sector will benefit from the professional expertise of international developers along with new technology. The government also introduced a scheme for NRI investment in housing. The scheme envisages investment by NRIs/OCBs/PIOs in the development of serviced plots and construction of built-up residential premises, development of townships, investment in manufacturing of building materials and investment in housing finance institutions.

The housing finance sector has three markets—primary mortgage market, secondary mortgage market and capital market. *Primary mortgage market* is the market in which mortgages are created and funds are loaned directly to the borrowers. The *secondary mortgage market* is the market for existing mortgage loans and mortgage-based securities. *Capital market* is the market for stocks, bonds and other long-term securities issued by organizations (such as HUDCO and HDFC) involved in housing finance. The development of these markets will help increase the flow of funds into the housing and real estate sector.

The problems of rural housing are varied. Fluctuation in the incomes of rural households, difficulty in assessing the repaying capacity of rural borrowers and non-availability of title deeds are major bottlenecks in the financing of rural houses. High operational costs also prevent housing finance companies from being active in the rural housing sector. Nevertheless, commercial banks, especially public sector banks, have been financing the rural housing sector. The widespread network of branches in rural and semi-urban areas may facilitate banks in undertaking housing finance against many odds (such as fluctuating earnings of borrowers, absence of land titles and collateral). As affordable rural housing is the focal point of every housing policy initiative, rural housing has picked up momentum in recent years, particularly with increasing budgetary allocations by the government. Efforts have also been made to involve microfinance institutions in rural housing finance. With well-developed credit and recovery mechanisms as well as a wide client base, microfinance institutions have proved to be an appropriate and effective channel for ensuring flow of housing credit to rural households.

Summary

1. Housing and quality of human life are intimately related. Good housing along with other domestic facilities tends to increase productivity of the people. Housing also reflects the culture and customs of a community.
2. Housing not only serves a social need but also creates employment, both directly and indirectly.
3. Over the years, the housing financial system has changed from unorganized to organized.
4. Recognizing that state-owned corporations were not very efficient and cost-effective, the government initiated measures to foster private-public partnership in providing housing finance.
5. Housing finance can be sourced from scheduled commercial banks, housing finance companies, cooperative housing societies, cooperative banks, HUDCO and state housing boards, besides indigenous moneylenders.
6. The cooperative housing finance sector essentially has a two-tier structure comprising the apex cooperative housing finance society at the state level and the primary cooperative housing finance society at the retail level.
7. Scheduled commercial banks are required to earmark a minimum of 3 per cent of their incremental deposits for extending credit to the housing sector. To encourage institutional housing finance, loans up to INR 15 lakh have been brought under priority sector lending of banks.
8. State housing boards have been set up to provide housing accommodation to needy citizens at reasonable prices.
9. The Government of India announced the National Urban Housing and Habitat Policy to meet the growing requirement for shelter and related infrastructure in urban areas.
10. One of the principal objectives of the National Housing Bank is to promote a sound, healthy, viable and cost-effective housing finance system to cater to all segments of the population.
11. The institutions that are eligible to take refinance from the NHB are housing finance companies, scheduled commercial banks, regional rural banks, state-level apex cooperative housing finance societies and state cooperative agriculture and rural development banks.
12. The Indira Awaas Yojana is a cash subsidy-based programme, under which assistance is provided to rural BPL families to construct dwelling units on their own using their own design and technology
13. The objective of the Golden Jubilee Rural Housing Finance Scheme is to address the problem of rural housing through improved access to housing credit, which would enable an individual to build a modest new house or improve or add to his old dwelling in rural areas.
14. Direct housing finance refers to finance provided to individuals or groups of individuals, including cooperative societies, whereas indirect housing finance is channeled by way of term loans to housing finance institutions, housing boards and other public housing agencies.

15. As per NHB directives, no housing finance company with net owned fund of less than INR 25 lakh shall accept public deposits and no housing finance company with NOF of INR 25 lakh and above shall accept or renew public deposits.
16. Every housing finance company shall maintain a minimum capital ratio consisting of tier-I and tier-II capital.
17. The major problem of the housing finance sector is paucity of funds. The available funds for the housing sector are not sufficient to meet the growing needs of housing and real estate.
18. Foreign direct investments are permitted in the integrated development of townships, housing, built-up infrastructure and construction of development projects.

Questions

1. What are the socio-economic benefits of housing in India?
2. What are the drawbacks of traditional sources of housing finance?
3. Explain the objectives of HUDCO.
4. Discuss the refinancing policy of the National Housing Bank.
5. Discuss the salient features of the National Housing and Habitat Policy of 2007.
6. Critically examine the RBI directives for scheduled commercial banks with regard to housing finance.
7. Bring out the salient features of the NHB's directions to housing finance companies.
8. Discuss the prudential norms to be followed by housing finance companies.
9. What are the impediments in rural housing finance?

Endnote

1. This section is based on data taken from the Reserve Bank of India. Reproduced with permission.

Chapter 23

Factoring and Forfaiting Services

LEARNING OBJECTIVES

After reading this chapter, you should be able to:

- Trace the evolution of factoring and forfaiting.
- Highlight the importance of factoring and forfaiting.
- Explain the concept and mechanism of factoring.
- Classify factoring services.
- Discuss the benefits of factoring.
- Present a brief sketch of factoring service providers.
- Evaluate the performance of the global factoring business.
- Explain the need and importance of forfaiting.

23.1 Introduction

Most countries have adopted an economic growth strategy involving trade development. Trade development is the *sine qua non* of a country's economic development. Therefore, all the barriers to trade, in whatever form they exist, need to be removed or eased to accelerate the economic growth of a country. The absence of adequate trade financing, limited access to trade financing and high costs of trade financing are, in effect, equivalent to trade barriers.

A paradoxical situation arises in trade—the buyer expects to pay only after the goods are received and not in advance, whereas the seller expects the buyer to pay before the goods are lifted, if not well in advance. In international trade, exporters face the same problem, where buyers insist on being granted trade credit on *open account terms*. This means that the exporter would receive payment from the importer only after some days or months after delivery of the goods or services. Extending trade credit on open account terms can affect the liquidity position of the seller. It is in this context that trade financing has assumed importance. **Trade financing** refers to the provision of finance to facilitate selling or buying of goods and services pending actual payment for the same.

Trade financing *refers to the provision of finance to facilitate selling or buying of goods and services pending actual payment for the same.*

Instruments of trade finance include letters of credit (LC), bank guarantees, buyer's credit, seller's credit, bills acceptance and avalization, structured finance, countertrade, factoring and forfaiting. Providing trade-related information to the concerned parties also amounts to trade financing. A *letter of credit* is a document issued by a bank stating its commitment to pay a seller a specified amount on behalf of a buyer, on certain conditions. There are different kinds of letters of credit, such as revocable letter of credit, irrevocable letter of credit, revolving letter of credit, standby letter of credit, red clause letter of credit, transferable letter of credit and back-to-back letter of credit. A letter of credit allows the buyer to delay payment to the seller and at the same time allows the seller to access credit by presenting the letter of credit to a bank. A *bank guarantee* is a written promise given by a bank to compensate the seller in the event that the buyer (obligor) fails to honour his/her obligations. *Countertrade* involves the exchange of goods or services at an agreed value without cash or credit terms. That is, in a countertrade, the seller accepts goods or services in partial or whole payment for the products he has sold. Countertrade, also known as reciprocal or compensatory trade, is an umbrella term that covers barter, counterpurchase, buyback, switch trading and tolling. *Seller's credit,* also known as *supplier credit*, is a trade instrument under which an exporter allows credit terms to a buyer. *Buyer's credit* is the provision of direct credit to a buyer so that the seller can be paid immediately when the goods are shipped. *Bill acceptance* refers to the offering of trade credit to the buyer by the seller against bills of exchange. *Avalization* refers to a payment undertaking given by a bank with respect to a bill of exchange. *Structured finance* is a technique by which the risks in trade financing are transferred from parties that are less able to bear the risks to those more equipped to bear them. The faster and easier the process of financing trade transactions, the more trade will be facilitated. Any hindrance in financing trade may result in substantial reduction in the movement of goods between the producer and the consumer, leading to a low rate of economic growth.

23.1.1 The Open Account System

A very large proportion of trade is transacted on an open account basis. Open account transactions are also described as "buy now, pay later" transactions. In *open account deals*, the payment is made by the buyer only after taking possession of the goods. The entire risk in the transaction, particularly default risk or delayed payment risk, is borne by the seller. In the open account system, the seller enters in his books of accounts a debit against the account of the buyer, which implies that the buyer owes the seller the amount debited. Open accounts are also known as book debts or receivables. The only evidence of the buyer's debt to the seller is the seller's books of accounts. As there are regular payments for a continual flow of goods rather than specific transactions, open account trade is much cheaper for corporations and has been adopted by several firms, especially smaller corporate organizations that have comfortable relations with their buyers.

The open account system has many disadvantages, too, especially for the seller. For instance, if a seller needs a loan, he must use his own securities as he does not have his customers' notes (such as bills of exchange and promissory notes) to discount at his bank. The open account system might limit the business activities of the seller in that he must wait until he realizes sale proceeds upon his accounts. As a result, the seller might have to borrow on his own account, possibly at a higher interest rate. As the open account system permits the buyer to hold off payment, it also results in the loss of interest charges for the seller. Further, the seller has to bear the risk of default or delayed payment as the open account system might result in slow collection, bad debts and unnecessary losses.

Another serious problem a seller faces is that of liquidity. If it remains unaddressed, the liquidity problem might threaten the very survival of the business. The liquidity crunch has driven many a company, particularly small and medium enterprises, to liquidation.

23.1.2 Receivables Management

The main motive for selling goods on credit is to absorb the shocks of changing demand for the product.

Receivables, also known as accounts receivables, arise when a firm sells its products on credit. The main motives for credit sales are:

- To absorb the shocks of changing demand for the product. When the demand for a product declines, the seller can extend credit to the buyer to boost the sales of the product.
- To enter new market(s). The seller can sell goods on an open account basis in order to penetrate new market(s).
- To increase market share. The seller can attempt to increase market share by offering sales on credit to customers.
- To place investable funds for a short period. A firm may expect some economic value by lending liquid resources to customers as trade credit (i.e., selling goods on credit).

On the other hand, trade credit might result in a sizeable portion of the working funds of an organization being locked up in receivables. Receivables also involve default risk. The volume of funds and the period for which the amount is locked up in receivables are a function of trade credit policy as well as management of receivables in an organization. An optimal trade credit policy and good receivables management increase the value of the firm.

__Factoring__ is defined as buying at a discount the debts owed to another in order to profit by collecting them. Factoring can be considered as an alternative to in-house management of receivables.

23.2 Factoring

One of the techniques of managing receivables is factoring. There is no precise and comprehensive definition of the term because the concept of factoring has become broad and is used to describe a number of related financial services.

The *Concise Oxford English Dictionary* defines factoring as "to buy at a discount the debts owed to another, in order to profit by collecting them". More elaborately, **factoring** is an agreement between a firm (client) and factoring organization (factor) under which the sales ledger administration and receivables collection of the firm (client-firm) are entrusted to an external agency called the factor. The agreement governs the legal relationship between the factor and the client-firm. The legal status of the factor is that of an assignee. Factoring is also defined as a specialized financial service that involves working capital financing, credit risk protection, sales ledger administration and accounts receivables collection. The UNIDROIT Convention on International Factoring has defined factoring as "the assignment by a supplier of receivables arising from contracts of sale of goods made between the supplier and its customers (debtors) to a factor, in which the factor is to perform at least two of the following functions:

- Finance for the supplier, including loans and advance payments;
- Maintenance of accounts (ledgering) relating to the receivables;
- Collection of receivables;
- Protection against default in payment by debtors."

Therefore, a typical factoring arrangement involves sales ledger administration (accounting and maintenance of sales ledger including collection of receivables), financing (prepayments) and risk control (credit appraisal and credit control). Factoring is also known as invoice financing and sales financing.

23.2.1 The Origin of Factoring

Although the concept of factoring has been formally defined only recently, factoring as a financial service has been in use since the dawn of trade and commerce. The origin of factoring as a financial service can be traced to rich manufacturers and merchants in ancient Rome who used mercantile agents (factor) to administer the sales of their merchandise. Sometime after the sixteenth century, exporters of consumer goods from Europe sought the help of mercantile agents to promote their trade, particularly with regard to collecting payments from buyers. In the United States, factoring began with merchant bankers providing funds to suppliers of raw materials like timber, fur and cotton while their raw materials were in transit to buyers. This enabled the suppliers of raw materials to continue their operations without waiting for the money to be received from the purchasers. In such cases, the factor only advances money at a discount on the invoice price. In other words, the factor bears the risk of non-payment by the buyers.

After the industrial revolution, the main focus of factoring was buying receivables arising on extending credit to the customers. Factors also helped client-firms determine which of their customers were most creditworthy, thus helping them reduce their credit risk or bad debts. In recent times, factoring has become a multifarious financial services business, and the factoring industry has become a sunrise industry with an annual turnover of billions of dollars.

23.2.2 The Process of Factoring

A typical factoring arrangement consists of a factor agreeing to purchase the invoices of the client as they arise in the normal course of trading. Once a firm receives an order from its customers, it transmits the order to the factor for approval; if approved by the factor, the firm sells the goods on credit to the customers. The factor advances a part of the invoice amount; the customer pays the dues to the factor; the factor remits the balance amount, less the factoring commission and other charges to the firm. Although credit rating is not required for a firm to avail itself of factoring services, each credit proposal is subject to credit risk analysis by the factor before sanctioning credit limits.

In addition to purchasing the book debts, the factor takes on the administration of the client's sales ledger and collects book debts from the customers. The factor also maintains regular documentation detailing the receipt of invoices from the client, advances, and payments by customers and other reports relating to sales ledger activity.

The typical mechanism of factoring is presented in Figure 23.1. The figure depicts the interrelationships between different parties involved in factoring. It also shows the role of the factor in receivables management of a firm. The steps involved in factoring are:

1. Customer places orders for goods or services with the client-firm and requests trade credit.
2. In certain cases, the factor approves credit sale to the customer.

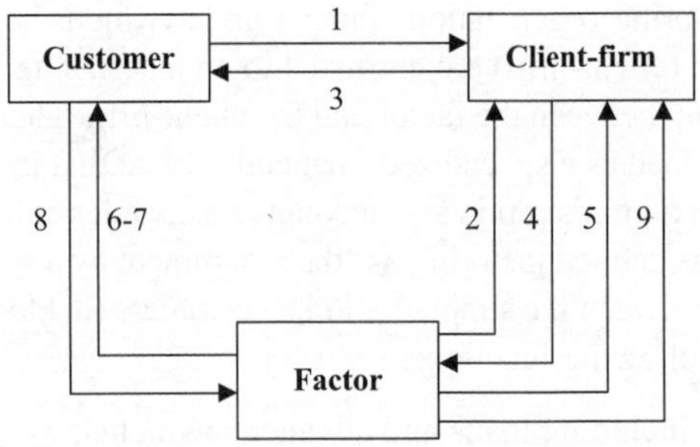

Figure 23.1 The process of factoring

3. Client-firm sells goods or services to the customer and sends invoice with notice to pay the factor.
4. Client-firm sends a copy of invoice to the factor as well.
5. Factor pays advance up to 80–90 per cent of the amount of invoice.
6. Factor sends periodical statements to the customers.
7. Factor follows up the unpaid book debts.
8. Customers make payment to factor.
9. Factor settles the balance amount with the client-firm.

23.2.3 Functions of the Factor

Factoring is a comprehensive term that incorporates many functions; the important functions are:

1. **To undertake credit evaluation:** Credit evaluation is the assessment of the creditworthiness of a customer or debtor, which implies assessing the credit risk involved in sanctioning trade credit to a particular customer. A factor, usually a bank with a network of branches, is likely to have access to credit intelligence to help assess the credit risk of a particular customer. Once the creditworthiness of a customer is assessed and detailed by the factor, and the trade credit is sanctioned, it becomes easy to monitor and collect the money from such accounts either by the client-firm or by the factor.
2. **To undertake sales ledger administration:** Sales ledger administration involves recording all credit sale transactions, analysis of credit sales data and preparing reports for monitoring and management of credit collection. Dues and repayments are recorded in such a way that there is easy access to and monitoring of credit transactions. As the factor undertakes sales ledger administration, the client-firm can concentrate on its core business activities.
3. **To collect book debts:** The factor undertakes collection of accounts receivables from the customers as and when they become due. This involves several activities such as:
   - Sending statements of accounts to the customer
   - Initiating personal collection efforts (such as sending letters, telephonic reminders, visiting the customers personally)
   - Collecting money from the customer on maturity of the debts or when the customer is able to pay
   - Taking legal action if the dues are not recoverable
4. **To assume the risk of default:** The factor assumes the responsibility of collecting the receivables from the customers, thereby relieving the client-firm of credit risk or bad debt losses. Essentially, the factor buys the factored receivables from the client-firm and provides full protection to the client-firm against bad debts.
5. **To provide finance:** The factor can provide finance to the client-firm against book debts, usually up to 90 per cent of the invoice value of the factored receivables. The maximum advance a factor provides can be equal to the amount of factored receivables less the factoring commission and other charges. Thus, the client-firm gets funds immediately upon signing the agreement. This helps the client-firm in managing its working capital effectively.

6. **To provide information:** The factor can also provide business information such as sales analysis and invoice analysis. Because the factor is a professional with expertise, it can also provide information to the firm on various topics like export and import potential, implications of government trade policy and market trends. It offers advisory services on marketing strategies and foreign collaborations. As the factor is constantly in contact with customers, it can gather a fund of information about the customers, including their perceptions, attitudes and general buying behaviour. With such knowledge and experience, the factor is in a good position to guide and help the client in adopting suitable business strategies.
7. **To provide insurance:** The factor can provide debt insurance to the client-firm against possible losses arising from insolvency or bankruptcy of a customer.

23.2.4 Classification of Factoring Services

There are several forms of factoring. The important ones are as follows:

> *In **non-recourse factoring**, the factor assumes full responsibility of collecting dues from the debtors, whereas in **recourse factoring**, the risk of non-payment of dues is borne by the client.*

- **Recourse factoring and non-recourse factoring:** In recourse factoring, the factor buys the receivables of the client-firm on the condition that the loss arising due to bad debts will be borne by the client-firm. That is, the factor does not provide protection against bad debts. This is less risky from the factor's point of view, but from the client's point of view, there is no protection against the risk of bad debts. Recourse factoring is the most common type of factoring and is often used when a firm has high-risk customers and credit information is scarce.

  Under non-recourse factoring, the factor bears the risk of bad debts arising from non-payment of dues by the customers. The factor has no claim on the client-firm if the receivables turn out to be bad debts. Once the receivables are sold to the factor, the client-firm does not bear any risk whatsoever. For bearing this risk, the factor charges an additional commission, which is called a *del credere commission*. The factor also assumes the responsibility of maintaining the sales ledger. Although non-recourse factoring is expensive for the client-firm, it is used when the firm has a very large number of customers and it is difficult for it to monitor and control the credit collection. Moreover, non-recourse factoring provides 100 per cent financing of receivables. However, the factor might set credit limits for customers while undertaking non-recourse factoring. Although the factor is supposed to absorb the losses arising from insolvency or bankruptcy of the customers, the factor might expect the client-firm to absorb a part of the losses. While undertaking non-recourse factoring, the smaller independent factors might arrange for bad-debt protection through a trade credit insurance company. In some countries, non-recourse factoring is also known as old-line factoring.
- **Advance factoring and maturity factoring:** In advance factoring, the factor agrees to pay the client-firm, as an advance, a certain proportion of the amount involved in the factored receivables. The balance amount is paid on the collection of factored receivables or on a date specified in the agreement. Of course, the factor can charge interest on the amount paid as advance. In the case of maturity factoring, the factor does not pay any amount upfront (i.e., advance). Instead, the factor pays an amount to the client on a specified date in the future, regardless of whether customers have settled their dues, or on the collection of receivables.
- **Bank participation factoring:** This is a form of factoring wherein a bank can participate to the extent of financing the receivables of a client against the reserves maintained by the factor. For example, suppose that a factor has advanced 80 per cent of the invoice value. A bank can provide finance to the client-firm against the remaining 20 per cent of the value of the factored receivables.
- **Non-notification factoring:** In a usual factoring arrangement, the client-firm notifies the customers that it must pay the dues to the factor. But in non-notification factoring, the customers of the client are not informed about the factoring arrangement. The factor does not deal with the customers directly. In this type of factoring, the factor performs all the same functions, but its identity is not known to the customers. Firms use this type of factoring when they are financially strong and therefore may not need any advance payments from the factor but need certain services from it.
- **Agency factoring:** Agency factoring, also known as bulk factoring, refers to an arrangement in which customers are informed that all debt payments should go to the factor, but the client takes on

the responsibility of collecting the debts, effectively acting as an agent for the factor. Sales ledger administration is also carried out by the client-firm itself. This type of factoring is used when there are many small accounts and full factoring is expensive because of a large number of low-value debts. It is also used when the client-firm is not well established.

- **Channel financing factoring:** A factor can set up lines of credit to each of the dealers of the client-firm and fund the client-firm against book debts within the limits. In general, *line of credit* is an arrangement between a bank and a firm (customer) that establishes the maximum loan the bank will provide the customer. The borrower can draw on the line of credit at any time, as long as the borrowing is within the maximum limit set by the bank. The same principle is applied in this context. Channel financing ensures the immediate availability of sales proceeds for the client, effectively making its transactions cash sales. On the other hand, the dealer gets trade credit for a pre-decided tenor sanctioned by the factor. Thus, factoring enables smooth liquidity management both at the client-firm's end and at the dealer's end. The factor can also provide protection against credit risk by arranging insurance cover.
- **Invoice discounting:** Invoice discounting, also known as invoice financing, is a form of factoring in which the factor provides finance to the client-firm against its receivables while allowing the client-firm full control over sales ledger administration and collection of debts from the debtors. Under invoice financing, the factor agrees to purchase the client-firm's outstanding invoices (debtors) that are payable over time on an ongoing basis and provides finance by way of prepayment of the invoice values. Normally, the factor provides funds to the client-firm up to 80–90 per cent of the amount of the invoice depending on the creditworthiness of the debtors, historical bad debt levels and the client-firm's financial strength. Before providing funds, the factor approves the list of invoices that it is prepared to finance. The factor has the right to disapprove of any invoice (debtor) and make it ineligible for financing under this factoring arrangement. As the responsibility of debt collection remains with the client-firm, the payments from the debtors are received by the client-firm directly and passed on to the factor. The client-firm is obliged to make payments to the factor on the due dates of the invoices, irrespective of whether the debtors have paid. The factor can also have the right to stop further financing of invoices of a particular debtor who has failed to make payments by the due date.

  Invoice financing is provided on a non-disclosed basis, which means that the client-firm does not notify its customers (debtors) about the factoring arrangement. In many cases, the identity of the factor is kept confidential. This form of factoring is more often provided by larger factoring organizations because of the greater sums of money involved. The firms can go in for invoice discounting when they need immediate finances despite the fact that they have sound receivables management. But for the finances, the firm may not need the services of the factor.
- **Reverse factoring:** In reverse factoring, a factor and a buyer enter into a contract according to which the buyer provides the factor a list of invoices to be paid by the buyer to suppliers in due course. Then the factor offers each supplier an option to discount, without recourse, its invoices. If the supplier accepts this, the factor will make an advance payment, of say 80 per cent, to the supplier. Thus, with reverse factoring, the supplier gets immediate funds and the buyer outsources his payments.

23.2.5 International Factoring

International trade has assumed importance in the globalization era. The growth and development of economies of countries largely depend on their international business transactions. International trade is even the bread and butter for some countries. However, international trade is a challenge for many enterprises and countries because of numerous barriers, particularly in customs, currency systems, laws and languages.

It is but natural for importers to insist that the trade be conducted on open account terms. But extending trade credit on open account terms can cause severe cash flow problems for exporters. Further, exporters can face liquidity problems if there are unusual delays in payments by the importers. The dues may exceed the risk-bearing capacity of the exporter if the importer becomes insolvent or bankrupt.

It is also very difficult for the exporters to evaluate the creditworthiness of customers domiciled in other countries. This poses a serious credit risk for the exporters. It is in this context that factoring services come in handy.

International factoring, also called cross-border factoring, encompasses financing, credit protection, collection and sales ledger management for exports on open account terms. International factoring services are offered to exporters (clients) who sell their products to customers (importers) in other countries on open account terms. The credit period usually ranges between 60 days and 180 days. The mechanism or process of international factoring is similar to that of domestic factoring except that in international factoring, the client (exporter) and the customer (importer) are in two different countries. As domestic factors are often unwilling to finance export receivables because of their own limitations, international factoring has become an alternative and possibly better solution to the problems faced by exporters.

***International factoring** is an overseas receivables management service provided by a factor.*

In international factoring, it is customary to use a *two-factor system*; accordingly, there is an export factor in the exporter's country and an import factor in the importer's country. The same organization can act as both export factor and import factor. The functions of the factor are distributed between the export factor and the import factor.

The steps involved in typical international factoring are as follows.

1. A firm (exporter) approaches an international factoring agency through its local bank and seeks factoring services.
2. The international factoring agency (export factor) assesses the financial strength of the exporter.
3. On being satisfied with the financial strength of the exporter, the export factor enters into a factoring agreement with the exporter.
4. The exporter seeks to set a credit limit for the overseas importer.
5. The export factor appoints an import factor and requests for a credit check on the importer.
6. After due diligence, the import factor can grant a credit limit based on the assessment of the creditworthiness of the importer. This means that the import factor will take on the importer's credit risk.
7. The export factor issues a letter of undertaking of the credit risk—original copy to the exporter's bank and duplicate copy to the exporter.
8. Once the credit limit of the importer is approved, shipment of goods and invoicing of the importer are carried out by the exporter. A copy of the invoice is sent to the export factor, who in turn forwards the invoice to the import factor for collection of receivables.
9. The exporter receives an advance amount from the export factor on delivery of the documents through his bank.
10. The import factor ensures the transfer of the money paid minus his commission and costs to the exporter through the export factor.

In international factoring, there are two linked agreements: one between the exporter and the export factor, and the other between the export factor and the import factor. However, the client (exporter) is required to deal with only one factor—the one residing in his own country. International factoring formalities are also similar to those governing domestic operations. As with domestic factoring, international factoring encompasses services such as advance payments, sales ledger administration, credit protection and debt collection. However, the main limitation of international factoring is the cost, since two factor firms are involved. The exporter might also need to meet minimum factor volume levels.

The tangible benefits of factoring are in the form of savings in the cost of sales ledger administration and reduction in bad debt losses. A firm can also reduce investment in receivables, thereby reducing opportunity cost (interest cost) thereon. As far as costs are concerned, the firm has to pay service charges to the factor, besides interest on prepayments.

23.2.6 Benefits of Factoring

The benefits of factoring are:

- The firm receives most of the sale proceeds upfront without waiting for the buyer to pay. The firm can receive payment from the factor faster than a bank loan.
- A firm is relieved of receivables management if it utilizes the services of a factor. It need not maintain an administrative setup to collect dues from customers and, thereby, it can reduce the cost of collection of receivables. The firm is no longer bogged down with bad and doubtful debts as the factor undertakes the collection of receivables from all the customers.

- By outsourcing its credit function, a firm can convert the fixed cost of operating a credit department into a variable expense by paying a commission to the factor based on the sales volume.
- As the firm gets the funds from the factor as advance immediately after the sale of goods, the funds of the firm are no longer locked up in receivables. This facilitates the use of funds in better investment opportunities. With improved liquidity, the client can reduce or avoid many problems of funds management.
- Factoring enhances the borrowing capacity of the client-firm.
- As the firm is relieved of the responsibility of collection of receivables, it can concentrate on its main business activities like planning, production and marketing, thereby improving its profitability.
- Administration of sales ledgers is a difficult task, particularly when the firm has operations overseas. In such cases, the factor provides a multi-currency sales ledgering system that enables the firm to keep track of its sales in various currencies.
- Since the factor is a professional and specialized agency, it can reduce the expenditure on sales ledger administration and collection of debts. It can even pass on a part of the savings to the client in the form of lower factoring costs.
- As the factor operates independent of its client-firms, it can collect even the doubtful debts, thereby improving the funds position of the client-firm.
- The incidence of bad debts comes down due to more accurate credit limits. With the involvement of the factor in the credit granting process, credit risk is reduced. Firms utilizing factoring services are likely to have a healthier customer portfolio.
- Firms utilizing factoring services might have an edge over their competitors as they can offer quality products with better credit terms.
- Factoring can also be viewed as a flexible form of financing. As the working capital needs of the firm increase with the increase in the value of its receivables, the factor increases the advance to be extended to the firm, and vice versa.
- Factoring is a very simple method of financing. It allows the client-firm to access instant cash against credit sales. Once the factoring agreement is signed, the client-firm can sell its invoices to the factor again and again without getting it approved each time. On the other hand, for a bank loan, the firm has to seek approval for every loan every time, which is inconvenient.
- In the case of international factoring, the exporter needs to deal with only one factor (the export factor) regardless of the location of his/her sales, which saves a lot of factoring costs besides avoiding delays.
- The client-firm gets information about the customers from the factor. In international factoring, the import factors in different countries can provide customer information to the exporter. Such information enables the client-firm to design appropriate marketing strategies. Factoring also helps the client-firm in designing effective management information systems.
- International factoring is a better option for an exporter in terms of costs, delays and credit protection as compared to other options such as letters of credit and documents against acceptance. Moreover, it allows the client-firm (exporter) to increase its market share in the international market by offering competitive open account terms.
- International factors can arrange factoring services for exports to a wide range of countries, including countries that may be considered high-risk. International factoring allows exporters to offer extended credit terms even to such countries.
- In international factoring, the factor bears currency risk and interest rate risk besides credit risk.
- The client-firm (exporter) can seek expert advice from the factor(s) on international trade documentation and logistics.
- In order to take advantage of factoring services, the client-firm should maintain certain standards, particularly with regard to the quality of the products. It might also have to maintain minimum volume levels according to the terms of factoring. Thus, business systems and performance levels in the client-firm generally improve with factoring, especially with international factoring.
- Factoring, particularly international factoring, enables the importer to purchase goods from overseas suppliers on short-term credit on open account terms without the need for opening a letter of credit.

- Today, international trade has increased in countries where factors are very active. This implies that factoring facilitates world trade.
- Customers (buyers) can be assured of the quality of sellers as factors carry out a complete review of the seller (client-firm) before entering into a factoring arrangement with it.
- The customers (buyers) need not go through the cumbersome process of opening letters of credit as they can buy the products under an open account supported by a factor. In other words, factoring allows the buyer to save on the additional cost (opening charges, negotiation charges) involved in opening an LC.

23.2.7 Cost of Factoring

The benefits of factoring described in the previous section do not come free of cost. The client-firm has to pay charges, which may take two forms: service charge and interest (discount). A *service charge* is levied for the administrative services provided by the factor and is based on the work involved and services offered. The *service charge* is calculated as a percentage of the gross value of invoices factored. This is usually collected by the factor upfront from the client-firm. The factor can buy the receivables at a discount on the invoice value. In other words, the factor collects interest on prepayments made to the client-firm. The rate of interest is arrived at by taking into consideration various aspects including cost of funds, credit rating of the client and quality of transactions. The interest can be collected periodically, usually on a monthly basis, on the actual drawings by the client from his prepayment account. Another hidden cost for the client-firm is a potentially strained relationship between the client-firm and its customers. As the factor takes over sales ledger management and collection of receivables, the client-firm loses its relationship with its customers. Any disagreement between customers and the factor might result in strained relations between the client-firm and its customers. Thus, there is a potential loss of control over customer relationship management.

Factoring services are not easily available to many firms. This is because factors insist on certain prerequisites for factoring. Mainly, firms should have a strong track record of profitable sales along with a proven track record of management. The firm should have creditworthy customers who must also be loyal to the firm and its products. The factor must be able to obtain a priority collateral position on the financed receivables. The firm should also make a minimum size deals as prescribed by the factoring agency. These are some of the limitations of factoring, in view of which many firms, especially small and medium enterprises, are not able to access factoring services.

Generally, receivables arising on sale of capital goods are not accepted for factoring as the sales realization period is very long. Further, there are elements like advance payment, part payment, retention money, guarantees and warranties associated with the sale of capital goods like equipment. This makes it difficult to track collection, control and monitor book debts arising on the sale of capital goods. However, consumer durables or capital goods that are in the form of small components or accessories may be amenable to factoring if there are no warranties.

23.2.8 Evaluation of Factoring

A firm should take into account the tangible costs and benefits while assessing the feasibility or desirability of factoring. It may be noted that factoring is an alternative to in-house management of receivables. Further, financing by a factor is an alternative to bill discounting or bank overdraft. So it is also important for financing to be at competitive rates.

Example 23.1

The marketing manager of M/s Srikrishna Industries Ltd has met the chief manager of SBI Factors for factoring receivables. After a preliminary study of the firm, the chief manager has agreed to extend recourse factoring services to the firm and quoted the following rates:

Discount charges payable upfront: 13 per cent per annum
Other charges payable upfront: 0.5 per cent

(Continued)

The chief manager has also consented to pay advance to the extent of 80 per cent of the factored receivables and take up sales ledger administration and monitoring of receivables.

The firm sells on terms 2/15 net 60. On an average, 40 per cent of the customers pay on the 15th day and avail themselves of the discount of 2 per cent; and the remaining customers pay, on average, 90 days after the invoice date. The bad debts are expected to be 1 per cent of the sales turnover. The expected sales turnover in the coming years is INR 1,000 million. The gross margin on sales is 20 per cent.

At present, the firm maintains a sales department and three executives of the sales department look after the collection of receivables. A careful look at their effort reveals that the firm can increase its annual turnover by at least 10 per cent if they concentrate on sales promotion without having the responsibility of receivables collection. The firm can also save administrative overhead up to INR 2 million per annum if sales ledger administration and credit monitoring are hived off.

Presently, the firm borrows from the State Bank of India for its working capital requirement at 15 per cent interest per annum.

Evaluate the factoring proposal.

Solution

In-house management of receivables:

Average collection period: (15 × 0.4) + (90 × 0.6) = 60 days
Cash discount: INR 1,000 million × 0.02 × 0.4 = INR 8 million
Cost of funds invested in receivables: INR 1,000 million × 60/360 × 0.15 = INR 25 million
Bad debt loss: INR 1,000 million × 0.01 = INR 10 million
Gross margin on otherwise increase in sales: 10% of INR 1,000 million × 20% = INR 20 million
Savings in administrative overhead: INR 2 million

Relevant costs of recourse factoring:

Amount of advance: 80% of INR 1,100 million (INR 1,000 million + INR 100 million increase in sales) = INR 880 million
Discount charges: INR 880 million × 0.13 × 60/360 = INR 19.1 million
Other charges: INR 1,100 million × 0.005 = INR 5.5 million
Cost of funds to be locked up in receivables: INR 220 million (110 – 88) × 0.15 × 60/360 = INR 5.5 million

Cost-benefit analysis of factoring:

Benefits:

Cash discount: INR 8 million
Cost of funds invested in receivables: INR 25 million
Gross margin on extra sales: INR 20 million
Savings in administrative overhead: INR 2 million

Total benefit: INR 55 million

Costs:

Discount charges: INR 19.1 million
Other charges: INR 5.5 million
Cost of funds locked up in receivables: INR 5.5 million
Total costs: INR 30.1 million

Net benefit = INR 24.9 million

Thus, the firm is advised to go in for factoring services offered by SBI Factors.

23.2.9 Factoring Versus Bill Discounting

Bill financing or bill discounting is another form of trade financing. Under bill financing, the seller of the goods writes (draws) a bill of exchange (similar to a promissory note) on the buyer. The buyer then accepts (signs) the bill and returns it to the seller. By signing the bill, the buyer (drawee) assumes the legal obligation to pay the bill at maturity. Subsequently, the seller (drawer or maker of the bill) can discount the bill with a bank or financial institution and avail himself of the finance for his working capital needs. A bill can be rediscounted several times before maturity. On the due date, the bill is again presented to the drawee for the payment stated in the bill. The drawer is responsible for compensating the holder of the bill if it is dishonoured. In legal terminology, a *bill of exchange* is a negotiable instrument containing an unconditional order signed by the maker directing a certain person to pay a certain sum of money only to, or to the order of, a certain person or to the bearer of the instrument.

Bill financing and factoring are, thus, alternative forms of trade financing or commercial finance that firms can use to meet their working capital needs. However, bill financing is not the same as factoring. Under bill discounting, a firm can get only finance (advance against bills). In factoring, a firm can get a package of services, which includes prepayments, sales ledger maintenance, advisory services, receivables collection, credit protection and credit monitoring. In bill discounting, the drawer of the bill (seller) can get an advance against the bill by discounting with a bank but in factoring, the receivables can be purchased by the factor with or without recourse. The prepayments made by a factor to the client-firm are not considered as loans for assessing the borrowing capacity (or debt servicing capacity) of the client-firm, whereas bill discounting is treated as a loan from the bank and, accordingly, it reduces the borrowing capacity of the firm.

23.2.10 Factors Chain International (FCI)

Factors Chain International is a network of leading factoring companies across the world.

Factors Chain International (FCI) is a network of leading factoring companies across the world. Established in 1968, FCI has become the largest factoring network in the world. FCI has its headquarters in Amsterdam (The Netherlands) and had 247 factoring companies in 66 countries at the end of 2009. The constitution of FCI lays down the basic requirements of membership and rules of conduct. One basic requirement is that a factoring organization should be sponsored by a commercial bank and that it should have a minimum equity of USD 1 million.

The main objectives of FCI are:

- To introduce the concept of factoring in countries where factoring services are not yet available; and
- To develop a framework for international factoring that would allow factors in the country of both the exporter and the importer to work closely together.

The FCI helps its members achieve competitive advantage in international trade finance services through:

- A global network of first-class factoring companies.
- Modern and effective communication systems to enable them to conduct their businesses in a cost-efficient way.
- A reliable legal framework to protect exporters and importers.
- Standard procedures aimed at maintaining a universal quality.
- A package of training programmes.
- Worldwide promotion aimed at positioning international factoring as the preferred method of trade finance.

FCI has played a major role in bringing factoring into many countries in the world. Factors in each country operate in their own way in accordance with local customs and culture. However, each factor-member operates according to a standard communication system and a global code of conduct.

23.2.11 EU Federation for the Factoring and Commercial Finance Industry

The EU Federation for the Factoring and Commercial Finance Industry (EUF) is the representative body for the factoring and commercial finance industry in the European Union (EU). It is composed of national and international industry associations that are active in the European Union. The objectives of EUF are as follows.

- To represent the industry with EU policymakers and promote harmonization in the EU's legal, fiscal and regulation environment.
- To promote an understanding of the benefits of factoring, receivables financing and asset-based lending (ABL) as an appropriate and flexible form of growth finance from companies.
- To gather information and publish papers and statistics on industry-related subjects.
- To observe law and EU policy initiatives affecting the industry.
- To lobby in favour of policy decisions that can increase the growth and effectiveness of the industry or lobby against policy initiatives that would put barriers in the industry's growth.
- To encourage the establishment of factoring and commercial finance activities in EU countries.

The members of EUF are as follows:

1. The Asset Based Finance Association (UK and Ireland)
2. Asociacion Espanola de Factoring (Spain)
3. I'Association Francaise de Societes financiers (France)
4. Associazione Italiana per il Factoring (Italy)
5. Deutscher Factoring-Verband (Germany)
6. Factors Chain International (EU countries)
7. International Factors Group (EU Countries)
8. Polski Zwiazek Faktorow (Poland)
9. Finans og Leasing (Denmark)

Thus, EUF brings together all major national associations in the EU as well as two global factoring associations, representing about 250 factoring and commercial finance companies within the EU.

23.3 Factoring in India

In view of the many benefits that factoring offers, especially to SMEs, the Reserve Bank of India (RBI) appointed a study group in 1988 under the chairmanship of C.S. Kalyanasundaram to study the feasibility of introducing factoring in India. The group observed that there was sufficient scope for introducing factoring services that would be complementary to the services provided by banks. It also felt that the introduction of factoring services would provide an additional facility to exporters. The group, after examining several aspects of commercial finance, made certain recommendations encompassing aspects such as promotion of factoring organizations, funding of factoring organizations, pricing of factoring services, linkages between banks and factoring organizations and competition. As a follow-up on the recommendations, the Banking Regulation Act, 1949, was amended to enable commercial banks in the country to undertake factoring services. Based on the recommendations of the study group, the RBI also issued guidelines in 1990, according to which banks can set up separate subsidiaries or invest in factoring companies jointly with other banks. A factoring subsidiary is not permitted to finance other factoring companies.

To start with, the RBI permitted two major commercial banks, the State Bank of India and Canara Bank, to set up subsidiaries to undertake factoring. Accordingly, the State Bank of India established SBI Factors and Commercial Services Pvt Ltd (SBI Factors) and Canara Bank set up Canbank Factors Ltd (Canbank Factors) in 1991. Subsequently, the RBI also permitted other commercial banks to take up factoring either departmentally or through a subsidiary setup. Other organizations like EXIM Bank, in partnership with other finance companies, established independent factoring organizations. In addition to SBI Factors and Canbank Factors, the other organizations providing factoring services in India now are Citibank, Export Credit Guarantee Corporation of India Ltd, Foremost Factor Limited, Global Trade Finance Limited, Hong Kong and Shanghai Banking Corporation Ltd and Small Industries Development Bank of India.

With the establishment of independent factoring organizations, the factoring market in India has grown phenomenally over the past 10 years. However, only a minuscule proportion of firms in India have access to factoring facilities. Bills of exchange and letters of credit continue to play a dominant role in the credit market. The problem with domestic factoring is that, unlike international factoring, no due diligence is performed on the buyer and no default insurance is provided. If a customer delays payment beyond the due date, the client-firm is required to pay off the accumulated debt to the factor. Moreover, factoring in India also works out to be rather expensive because of additional stamp duty. Factoring charges in addition to interest include a fee that is calculated on the agreed volume of trade, which can be quite significant.

Adding to these barriers, particularly for SMEs, is the fact that the choice of factors in India is limited. Though there are eight factoring organizations in India, Canbank Factors Limited and SBI Factors are the only full-fledged Indian factoring companies. Export factoring works out cheaper than conventional methods of financing. For example, the charges to open an LC abroad could be 3–4 per cent of the trade volume, significantly more than the factor charge. Thus, export factoring in India has picked up because firms consider the LC route expensive.

A brief sketch of the dominant players in the Indian factoring market is given in the following paragraphs.

23.3.1 SBI Factors and Commercial Services Pvt Ltd (SBI Factors)

SBI Factors was established in February 1991 by the State Bank of India. The State Bank of India and its two associate banks have a 70 per cent stake in SBI Factors, while 20 per cent is held by SIDBI and 10 per cent by Union Bank of India. SBI Factors, a subsidiary of the State Bank of India, was the first factoring company to be set up in India.

SBI Factors' mission is:

- To become a premier factoring and commercial services company with the motto "profit with prudent business growth";
- To add maximum value to clients by enhancing their cash flows by converting their accounts receivables to immediate cash, thereby providing liquidity and improving profitability of their enterprises;
- To ensure excellence in customer service with the help of state-of-the-art technology and ensuring the highest employee satisfaction and development; and
- To give maximum value to shareholders by reasonable profits and increased dividends.

SBI Factors offers domestic factoring (with or without recourse), export factoring (with recourse), purchase bill factoring and factoring of domestic or export bills drawn under LC or bank guarantee. Its factoring products include Bill 2 Cash, a receivables factoring facility, Cash 4 Purchase, a type of purchase bill factoring, and Vishwavyapaar, an export factoring facility.

Bill 2 Cash is a domestic factoring facility in which the seller invoices the goods to the buyer, assigns the same to SBI Factors and receives prepayment up to 90 per cent of the invoice value immediately. The balance amount is paid to the client when the customer pays to the factor. This facility can be with recourse or non-recourse. Cash 4 Purchase is an attractive avenue of finance that facilitates instant payment for purchases made. Generally sanctioned in conjunction with the receivables factoring facility or export factoring facility, Cash 4 Purchase empowers the purchaser to bargain for cash terms, the best quality and immediate delivery. It is a form of purchase bill factoring, which is a financing facility for making instant payments to the suppliers of clients for purchase of raw materials, stores, spares, etc. on cash terms. This facility enables the clients to bargain for the best terms on price, quality and delivery schedule.

Vishwavypaar is a colloquial term for export factoring. The export factoring service offers a complete package to help the clients develop their overseas business profitably and with confidence. Under export factoring, the factor invoices drawn on overseas buyers and makes a prepayment of up to 90 per cent of the invoice amount immediately. The benefits accruing to the client-firm from export factoring are:

- 100 per cent credit cover as against 80 per cent offered by export credit agencies.
- Claims are settled in invoice currency, as against domestic currency in the case of bank finance.
- Import factor is located in the importer's country, which ensures better due diligence on the latter.

In May 2008, ICRA assigned A1+ rating for the INR 5,000 million short-term debt programme of SBI Factors. This rating indicates the highest credit-quality rating assigned by ICRA to short-term debt instruments. ICRA has retained the LAAA rating for the INR 400 million long-term debt programme of the company. The LAAA rating is the highest credit-quality rating. Further, CARE reaffirmed in January 2006 its rating of CARE AAA to outstanding subordinated debt in the form of promissory note aggregating to INR 400 million issued by the company. Instruments carrying this rating are supposed to be of the best quality, carrying negligible investment risk.

Table 23.1 Business performance of SBI Factors (Figures in INR lakh)

Parameter	*2005–06*	*2006–07*	*2007–08*	*2008–09*
Turnover	365,197	467,581	64,7869	597,900
Total income	6,130	9,563	14,589	16,425
Expenses	4,550	7,527	10,273	9,933
Profit before tax	1,580	2,036	4,317	6,493
Profit after tax	1,067	1,317	2,838	4,279
Paid-up capital	4,500	4,500	4,500	8,500
Reserves and surplus	4,118	4,804	6,796	9,145
Debt purchase outstanding	10,2571	129,749	202,083	160,361
Prepayment outstanding	91,936	122,001	190,764	149,664

Source: SBI Global Factors Ltd.

The product portfolio of SBI Factors includes instant cash, sales ledger administration, credit protection and advisory services. SBI Factors provides prepayment to the client up to 80 per cent of the invoice value. The maximum debt period permitted under factoring is 150 days inclusive of a maximum grace period of 60 days.

In order to keep the client informed of the factored invoices, SBI Factors sends monthly statement of account to the supplier. Various MIS reports such as *Debtors Ageing Analysis*, weekly statements of accounts, sales analysis and statements of outstanding invoices are given to clients or customers free of charge.

As can be observed from Table 23.1, SBI Factors registered a turnover of INR 597,900 lakh in 2008–09 as against INR 647,869 lakh in 2007–08 and INR 365,197 lakh in 2005–06. The profit after tax increased from INR 1,067 lakh in 2005–06 to INR 4,279 lakh in 2008–09. The net worth of the company also increased from INR 8,618 lakh in 2005–06 to INR 17,645 lakh in 2008–09. The outstanding prepayments increased from INR 91,936 lakh in 2005–06 to INR 149,664 lakh in 2008–09.

23.3.2 Canbank Factors Limited

Canbank Factors Limited (CBF) is a subsidiary of Canara Bank, a leading public sector bank in India. It was established in 1991 with the Small Industries Development Bank of India (SIDBI) and Andhra Bank as co-promoters. It is a member of Factors Chain International. CBF offers a package of factoring services that includes sales ledger administration, debt collection services, credit information services and advisory services. It has also launched invoice discounting and export factoring. Under this, CBF provides finance against invoices backed by LCs/hundis/tripartite agreements. This enhances the liquidity of the firm as it converts credit sales into cash sales. Recourse factoring with prepayment facility is the most popular product of CBF. CBF considers undisclosed factoring for companies of very high repute and sound financial base. Under undisclosed factoring, the client's customers are not notified about the factoring arrangement and they continue to make payments to the client. The client has the responsibility of making payments to the factor on the due date, irrespective of whether its customers make the payments or not.

To be considered by CBF for extending factoring services, a firm should be in the line of manufacturing or trading or services, have a sound financial base and a turnover of not less than INR 5 million per annum. CBF also expects the client-firm to have a strong customer base that is prompt in payment. "Factorability" is the underlying principle to entertain a proposal.

CBF also accepts public deposits and inter-corporate deposits. They have been rated FAA+ by Crisil, indicating a high degree of safety. The commercial paper issue of CBF has been rated P+ by Crisil, indicating the highest safety. CBF has been accredited with an ISO certificate—DIN EN ISO 9901:2000 by TUV CERT of Germany.

CBF levies two types of charges—service charge and discount charge—on its clients.

- Service charge is levied based on the work involved and services offered, such as sales ledger maintenance, and calculated as a percentage of the gross value of invoices factored. It can vary from 0.1 per cent to 1 per cent depending on various factors. This is collected upfront from clients.

Table 23.2 Business performance of Canbank Factors (Figures in INR crore)

SL. NO.	*Parameter*	*2007–08*	*2008–09*	*2009–10*
1	Capital	20.00	20.00	20.00
2	Reserves and surplus (USD)	85.82	101.85	119.13
3	Loan funds	623.49	483.73	734.97
4	Factored turnover	3483.24	3178.54	3734.57
5	Total income	78.07	85.08	84.56
6	Funds in use	739.34	619.73	902.83
7	Average funds in use	597.6	608.92	715.11
8	Profit before tax	30.34	31.26	36.55
9	Profit after tax	20.19	19.69	24.37
10	Dividend	3.51	3.51	3.74
11	Return on equity (%)	19.08	16.16	17.52
12	Net owned funds	105.82	121.84	139.13
13	NPA (Absolute figure)	5.07	24.31	25.65
14	NPA as % of FIU	0.69	3.92	2.84
15	Net NPA	Nil	2.62	0.87

Source: Canbank Factors Ltd

- Discount charges are levied for providing instant credit to the client-firm by way of prepayment. Various aspects are taken into account, such as cost of funds, credit rating of the client and quality of transactions while fixing the rate. This is collected on a monthly basis on the actual drawings by the client from its pre-payment account.

In addition, a nominal processing charge for the work related to processing of the proposal is also collected from the client-firm.

CBF recorded a factoring services turnover of INR 3734.57 crore in 2009–10 as against INR 3178.54 crore in 2008–09 and INR 3483.24 crore in 2007–08. It can also be observed from Table 23.2 that the profit after tax was INR 24.37 crore, INR 19.69 crore and INR 20.19 crore in 2009–10, 2008–09 and 2007–08, respectively. The net owned funds of CBF increased from INR 105.82 crore in 2007–08 to INR 121.84 crore in 2008–09 and INR 139.13 crore in 2009–2010. The return on equity declined from INR 19.08 crore in 2007–08 to INR 16.16 crore in 2008–09 but increased to INR 17.52 crore in 2009–10. Although the non-performing assets (NPA) increased from INR 24.31 core in 2008–09 to INR 25.65 crore in 2009–10, the NPA as percentage of funds in use declined from 3.92 in 2008-09 to 2.84 in 2010.

23.3.3 Global Trade Finance Limited

Global Trade Finance Limited (GTF) was established in September 2001 as a joint venture between West LB, Germany (40%), Export-Import Bank of India (35%) and International Finance Corporation, Washington (25%). From December 24, 2004, the shareholding of GTF changed to Export-Import Bank of India (40%), FIM Bank (38.5%), IFC (12.5%) and Bank of Maharashtra (9%). GTF has received a license and authorized dealer status from the RBI for conducting export and import factoring and forfaiting business and foreign currency operations in India.

The services provided by GTF include international factoring, forfaiting, domestic factoring, channel financing, LC discounting and import factoring. GTF is the only provider of international factoring, domestic factoring and forfaiting services under one roof in India. It has established itself as a market leader in international factoring, providing value added services to its clients. GTF is a member of Factors Chain International.

The financing provided by GTF is flexible and directly linked to the clients' sales. Financing for up to 95 per cent of the invoice value is made available. GTF provides credit protection against payment default of buyers. GTF assumes responsibility for collection of receivables under the factoring agreement. It has systems in place for tracking receivables on an invoice-to-invoice basis and has an effective correspondent network in more than 80 countries for follow-up of receivables. GTF manages complete sales ledger maintenance for its clients. It has now provided web access to its clients for accessing their accounts online via its GTF Client Access module, becoming the first factoring company in India to provide online access to its clients. GTF extends an automatic revolving line to every buyer. The limit is automatically renewed on receipt of payment from the buyer on the due date. GTF discounts the LCs of prime banks acceptable to GTF. It offers this facility in combination with its basic factoring facility. Under the LC discounting scheme, GTF finances the seller up to 100 per cent of the LC value. It also maintains accounts related to accounts receivables. The company also undertakes reverse factoring or purchase bill discounting. Reverse factoring is the discounting of suppliers' bills in respect of the client's regular purchases from them. GTF assesses and considers only regular suppliers of clients who have a relationship of a minimum of six months. Suppliers have to be pre-approved by GTF. Under this scheme, GTF finances the supplier by prepaying up to 100 per cent of the invoice value or bill value. The period of credit is up to 120 days. Another product scheme offered by GTF is channel financing, which enables clients to discount their receivables on account of supplies made to all their dealers. GTF sets up a line of credit aggregating sub-limit for each dealer and funds the clients within the set limits for supplies to the dealer. Channel finance ensures the immediate realization of sales proceeds, making it practically a cash sale. On the other hand, the dealer gets credit for a pre-decided tenor sanctioned by GTF, enabling smooth liquidity management.

Box 23.1 gives a bird's-eye view of factoring services offered by HSBC.

Box 23.1 HSBC Factoring Solutions

HSBC offers factoring solutions for small and medium businesses. The structured working capital finance solution includes finance against domestic or export receivables, collection of receivables on the due date, credit protection and credit advisory services. It is an internationally accepted financing solution that converts the accounts receivables into cash, thereby releasing the cash generation potential of a business.

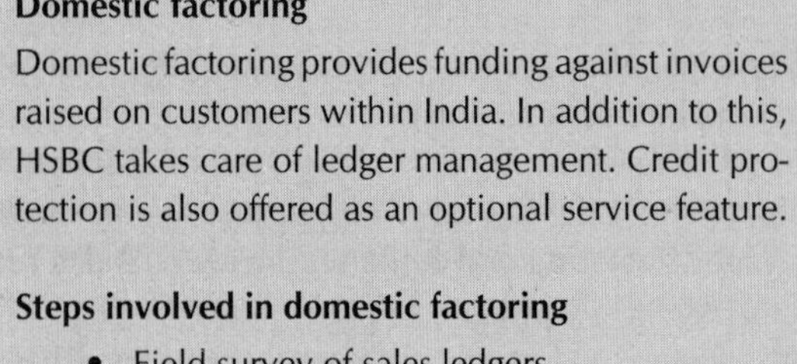

Domestic factoring

Domestic factoring provides funding against invoices raised on customers within India. In addition to this, HSBC takes care of ledger management. Credit protection is also offered as an optional service feature.

Steps involved in domestic factoring

- Field survey of sales ledgers
- Credit assessment of the company
- Setting of credit limits for each customer
- Signing of factoring agreement between the client and HSBC
- Customers accept to route all payments through HSBC
- Post delivery of goods, forward copies of invoices and supporting documents to HSBC
- Client can draw prepayments up to the agreed limit

Invoice factoring

Invoice factoring is an alternate solution to domestic factoring if the client wants to avail itself of financing against accounts receivables but would like to continue managing collections. The steps involved are the same as those of domestic factoring, except that the client need not inform its customers about the arrangement with HSBC. The customers continue to pay directly to the client. HSBC is not responsible for collection of the proceeds. As soon as the customers make the payments, the client remits the payment to HSBC.

Export factoring

Export factoring provides immediate financing against export receivables. Financing can be in rupees or in foreign currency. HSBC offers credit protection for export receivables. As part of the full service package, HSBC also offers sales ledger management, wherein it handles all the ledger administration and collection jobs through overseas factor partners, saving the client's time and overhead costs.

(Continued)

Steps involved in export factoring

- Field survey of sales ledgers
- Credit assessment of the company
- Setting of credit limits for each of client's overseas customers
- Signing of factoring agreement between client and HSBC
- Post shipping of goods, forward copies of invoices and supporting documents to HSBC
- Client can draw prepayments up to the agreed limit
- Under HSBC's supervision, an overseas factor partner collects and transfers payments to HSBC
- HSBC credits client's account, less prepayments and/or charges

Factoring solutions are offered to the following types of concerns

- Sole proprietorships
- Partnerships
- Private limited companies

Other criteria

- The entity should be in operation for the past three years
- The entity should have generated profits during the last two years and satisfy HSBC's internal credit parameters
- The concern must have a positive tangible net worth

Source: http://www.hsbc.co.in/1/2/business/factoring-solutions

23.3.4 Bank Finance to Factoring Companies

The RBI issued a master circular dated July 1, 2008, wherein it is stated that banks that satisfy the following criteria can extend financial assistance to support the factoring business of factoring companies:

- The companies carry out all the components of standard factoring activity such as financing of receivables, sales ledger management and collection of receivables.
- They derive at least 80 per cent of their income from factoring activity.
- The receivables purchased or financed, whether on with recourse or without recourse basis, form at least 80 per cent of the assets of the factoring company.
- The assets or income referred to above would not include the assets or income relating to any bill discounting facility extended by the factoring company.
- The financial assistance extended by the factoring companies is secured by hypothecation or assignment of receivables in their favour.

23.3.5 Factoring Turnover

Factoring has assumed international importance and become established even in developing economies. Today, it is accepted that almost every business firm can profit from factoring. Service companies have also become clients of factoring organizations in increasing numbers. All the fast-growing and sales-driven organizations have realized the importance of factoring services, particularly in improving cash flows and profitability. The global factoring turnover has increased phenomenally. As can be observed from Table 23.3, the world factoring turnover has increased from EUR 623,840 million in 2000 to EUR 1,325,111 million in 2008 but came down to EUR 1,283,559 million. Many countries have registered a very high increase in factoring turnover over 2000–08 but a decline in 2009. For example, Taiwan's factoring turnover increased from EUR 3,650 million in 2000 to EUR 48,750 million in 2008 but came down to EUR 33,800 million in 2009. India's turnover increased from EUR 470 million in 2000 to EUR 5,200 million in 2008 but declined to EUR 2650 million in 2009. The United States recorded a decline in factoring turnover from EUR 102,268 million in 2000 to EUR 100,000 million in 2008 and further to EUR 88,500 million in 2009. However, China's factoring turnover increased from EUR 212 million in 2000 to EUR 55,000 million in 2008 and further to EUR 67,300 million in 2009. Notwithstanding the increase in the number of factoring companies in the world from 1809 in 2008 to 1909 in 2009, there had been a significant fall in the factoring turnover around the world. The main reason for the decline in the global factoring turnover in 2009 could be because of global economic downturn. Brazil had the highest number of factoring companies with 590 in 2009, followed by the United States (350). It is the single digit figure of number of factoring companies in many of the countries.

Table 23.3 Factoring turnover in select countries

Country	Number of factoring companies (2008)	Number of factoring companies (2009)	Turnover in 2000 (EUR million)	Turnover in 2006 (EUR million)	Turnover in 2008 (EUR million)	Turnover in 2009 (EUR million)
Global	1,809	1,909	623,840	1,134,288	1,325,111	1,283,559
France	19	15	52,450	100,009	135,000	128,182
Germany	50	55	23,483	72,000	106,000	96,200
Italy	45	45	110,000	120,435	128,200	124,250
Belgium	6	7	8,000	16,700	22,500	23,921
Netherlands	5	5	15,900	25,500	30,000	30,000
Spain	24	24	19,500	66,772	100,000	104,222
UK	90	50	123,770	248,769	188,000	195,613
Brazil	674	590	12,012	20,054	22,055	29,640
Canada	61	57	2,256	3,386	3,000	3,250
USA	120	350	102,268	96,000	100,000	88,500
China	16	18	212	14,300	55,000	67,300
Hong Kong	11	13	2,400	9,710	8,500	8,079
India	8	10	470	3,560	5,200	2,650
Japan	13	7	58,473	74,530	106,500	83,700
Singapore	10	10	2,100	2,955	4,000	4,700
Taiwan	24	20	3,650	40,000	48,750	33,800

Source: http://www.factors-chain.com

As it can be observed from Table 23.4, all the factoring companies across the world in 2009 generated a total turnover of EUR 1,283,559 million, of which domestic factoring turnover accounted for EUR 1,118,100 million. Europe accounts for a large share in the world factoring turnover, followed by Asia and the Americas. The United Kingdom recorded the highest domestic factoring turnover of EUR 182,863 million, followed by France (EUR 109,581 million), Italy (EUR 113,250 million) and the United States with domestic factoring turnover of EUR 80,000 million. Thus, in all the countries, the domestic factoring turnover accounted for a lion's share in their respective total factoring turnover.

Table 23.4 Domestic and international factoring turnover in 2009 in select countries

Country	Domestic turnover (EUR million)	International turnover (EUR million)	Total turnover (EUR million)
World	**1,118,100**	**165,459**	**1,283,559**
Europe	**760,699**	**115,950**	**876,649**
Americas	**132,278**	**9735**	**142,013**
Africa	**14,335**	**461**	**14,796**
Asia	**170,743**	**39,279**	**209,991**
Australasia	**40,075**	**35**	**40,110**
France	109,581	18,601	128,182
Germany	70,400	25,800	96,200
Italy	113,250	11,000	124,250
Belgium	14,592	9389	23,921
Netherlands	20,000	10,000	30,000

(Continued)

Table 23.4 (Cont.)

Spain	94,634	9588	104,222
UK	182,863	12750	195,613
Brazil	29,600	40	29,640
Canada	2,700	550	3,250
USA	80,000	8500	88,500
China	52,200	15,100	67,300
Hong Kong	3152	4,927	8,079
India	2,500	150	2,650
Japan	83,000	700	83,700
Singapore	3,200	1500	4,700
Taiwan	20,600	13,200	33,800

Source: http://www.factors-chain.com

23.4 Forfaiting

***Forfaiting** allows an exporter to convert a credit-based trade transaction into a cash transaction.*

Exporters are often faced with the situation of having to extend trade credit to importers for longer periods, say, beyond 180 days. Consequently, the exporters are exposed to risks such as credit risk and currency risk. The intensity of the risks depends on factors like the importer's country and period of trade credit. Moreover, it is difficult to appraise the creditworthiness of the importer because the importer is in a foreign country and the factors that govern the importer's credit-worthiness are not known to the exporter. As part of credit appraisal, it is also necessary to take into account the sovereign risk of the country in which the importer is domiciled. It is in this backdrop that the concept of forfaiting has gained importance. The term "forfait" is a French term meaning to relinquish a right. In this context, *forfait* refers to the exporter (seller of goods or services) relinquishing his right to receivables from the buyer of his products in exchange for immediate cash payment on agreed terms. The exporter thereby transfers all risks and responsibilities for collecting the receivables to the forfaiter. Thus, the forfaiter is a bank or specialized financial institution that provides supplier credit to the exporter in order to enable him to extend trade credit (medium-term) to the importers. An importer can pay a portion of the invoice value of the goods that he purchased in cash and issue a promissory note or accept a bill of exchange in an international format avalized by a bank. These instruments are issued as evidence of the importer's obligation to pay the balance of the invoice value. So the exporter accepts deferred payment from the importer for the goods sold. The forfaiter usually provides credit to the exporter by discounting the bills of exchange or promissory notes. The letters of credit are also used in obtaining finance from the forfaiter. In sum, forfaiting is a method of financing exporters through the buying of medium-term foreign account receivables at a discount on a non-recourse basis.

Forfaiting is a European concept that originated in the 1960s. With the growth in world trade, the concept spread to other countries, including developing countries such as India and China. It has also changed from post-shipment finance to pre-export finance. Traditionally, forfaiting was a fixed-interest-rate and medium-term (3–5 years) financing. Now it is structured for longer periods up to 10 years or shorter periods around 90 days. Forfaiting is generally used for high-value exports like capital goods, bulk commodities and project exports. Promissory notes, bills of exchange, drafts drawn under time letters of credit or other freely negotiable instruments can also be purchased or discounted under forfaiting.

Forfaiting has thus become an effective and alternative method of financing firms, particularly small and medium enterprises (SME) that are capital-scarce and cannot provide their foreign customers (importers) with credit. The SMEs are often faced with financial problems in view of high market interest rates and limited sources of funds. They also have a heavy commitment of capital for modernizing and merchandizing their business. In view of these problems, they find it difficult to attract foreign buyers by providing credit terms. The conventional methods of short-term financing, including factoring, are not suitable for the SMEs that are engaged in selling capital goods in international markets. Thus, a forfaiter provides supplier credit in the form of non-recourse, medium-term (for a period beyond the traditional 90 or 180 days) financing to the firms, particularly SMEs, and free them from the risks associated with their receivables.

In India, forfaiting as an export financing option has been approved by the RBI. The forfaiting facility is provided by an international forfaiting agency through an authorized dealer in India. The authorized dealer who, apart from handling documentation, also provides customs certification. Forfaiting proceeds, on a without-recourse basis, are to be received as soon as possible after shipment but definitely within a 180-day period specified by the RBI for all exports.

23.4.1 The Mechanism of Forfaiting

The mechanism of forfaiting is as follows.

1. After negotiations between the exporter and importer on the proposed sale contract, the exporter approaches a forfaiter for discounting of accounts receivables that would arise on the sale of goods on credit to an importer.
2. The forfaiter then collects information about the importer and details of the sale. The information might pertain to the type of goods to be sold, value of the goods, expected shipment date, repayment terms, guarantees, business of the importer, domicile of the importer and invoice currency. Such information is sought by the forfaiter to assess the amount of credit involved and also the associated risk.
3. Once the risk appraisal is completed, the forfaiter indicates the discount rate (interest rate) as well as other charges like commitment fee, if any. The discount rate is usually quoted as a margin over the benchmark rate (LIBOR for example). The discount rate usually comprises the cost of funds plus cost of covering the risks such as credit risk, country risk, currency risk and interest rate risk. The degree of risk varies based on where the importer is domiciled, length of the credit period, repayment structure and currency of invoice. The higher the risk, the higher the margin and thus the discount rate. The discount rate essentially depends on the market situation.
4. The exporter incorporates the discount rate into the selling price of the goods to be sold. If such a price is acceptable to the importer, the exporter signs a commercial contract with the importer. Simultaneously, he executes a forfaiting contract with the forfaiter.
5. The exporter ships the goods to the importer and obtains the documents such as promissory notes, bills of exchanges and letter of credit, if any,
6. The exporter then submits to the forfaiter the documents such as copy of commercial invoice, copy of shipping documents (bill of lading), confirmed copy of the letter of credit (if any), letter of assignment of proceeds in favour of the forfaiter and letter of guarantee.
7. The forfaiter makes the payment to the exporter as agreed in the commitment. Since the payment is without recourse, the exporter has no further interest in the transaction. In other words, the exporter is free from sales ledger administration and collection of receivables. The non-recourse feature of forfaiting transforms the credit sale into a cash sale for the exporter.
8. The forfaiter then holds the credit instrument until maturity or sells it to another investor on a non-recourse basis. As the credit instrument is due, the holder of the instrument presents the same to the guaranteeing bank or importer's bank, which remits the payment as specified. The bank, in turn, collects the payments due from the importer.

23.4.2 Factoring Versus Forfaiting

Although forfaiting combines several features of traditional methods of short-term financing such as bill financing, it is a special form of financing especially suitable for small and medium enterprises.

Forfaiting is the purchase of claims from the exporter as in international factoring. However, there are some differences between the two.

- Forfaiting is related to financing of the export of capital goods, commodities and projects, whereas factoring covers mostly smaller claims for consumer goods and services.
- A factor can undertake sales ledger administration and provide other advisory services besides financing receivables, whereas a forfaiter provides only trade credit financing.

- Factoring can be either domestic factoring or international factoring, whereas forfaiting is international as it covers only international trade transactions.
- Factoring is a method of short-term financing whereas forfaiting is used for financing the claims of terms between a few months and several years.
- Forfaiting is on a one-contract basis (one-time deal), whereas factoring covers the ongoing volume of business or a certain volume of the seller's yearly sales.
- Factoring covers only credit risk if it is not international factoring, whereas forfaiting covers several risks such as credit risk, exchange rate risk, interest rate risk and sovereign risk.
- Factoring usually follows already negotiated or established sale contracts, whereas sale contracts are negotiated on the basis of prior commitment from a forfaiter.
- High-risk countries are usually avoided in international factoring, whereas forfaiting does not avoid even high-risk countries in purchasing foreign accounts receivables.

23.4.3 Benefits of Forfaiting

There are many benefits of forfaiting; the important ones are as follows.

- Forfaiting allows an exporter to convert a credit-based trade transaction into a cash transaction. It enables the exporter to substitute medium-term claims into cash.
- The exporter is freed from all sorts of risks (such as credit risk, currency risk, interest rate risk) by selling his foreign accounts receivables on a non-recourse basis. This can enable the exporter to extend his market to other unknown countries (riskier countries) as well.
- The exporter is freed from maintenance of sales ledgers and the onerous task of collecting foreign accounts receivables.
- Forfaiting allows the exporter greater flexibility in structuring a financial deal with a forfaiter. The forfaiter might grant an option to the exporter for some time that entitles the exporter to withdraw from the forfaiting agreement, but against payment of an option fee. The option provision can provide a leeway to the exporter to negotiate with the importer for better trading terms.
- As the exporter is free from the risks associated with accounts receivables, he can concentrate on his core business and thereby improve his business at a faster rate.
- Documentation is very simple, requiring evidence of underlying transactions and certain confirmations from the obligor or guaranteeing bank. Settlement of forfaiting transactions is simple and quick.
- The forfaiter aids the industrial development of a country by buying risk-related claims of SMEs and thereby enabling them to participate more intensely in the industrialization process.
- Forfaiting can be considered as an innovative form of risk capital financing.
- Forfaiting is both a method of financing and a means of investment. The forfaiter can assign payments due to him to a special purpose vehicle that can then issue investment-grade bonds. So the investors can invest in such bonds (forfaiting papers) and diversify their portfolios besides getting a good return. There is also a possibility of resale of forfaited claims.

23.4.4 Forfaiting Costs

The cost of forfaiting includes the discount rate and other charges. The forfaiter provides finance to the exporter at the face value of the receivables minus the discount for the total term of the credit. This means that the discount is an upfront cost to the exporter. The other charges include option fee, special charges, collection costs and commitment fee. The option fee is charged for providing a right to the exporter to withdraw unilaterally from the forfaiting contract. Special charges are levied on each forfaiting transaction as a one-time cost. The forfaiter can also charge the exporter collection costs when the receivables mature. The commitment fee is charged for the period between the signing of the forfaiting agreement and the payment to the exporter. The commitment fee is calculated as a certain percentage per month on the financing sum for the duration of the commitment period. Besides, a penalty might be imposed when the exporter unilaterally fails to honour the forfaiting contract.

23.5 Forfaiting Bodies

Forfaiting has grown with international trade. Accordingly, many organizations have come up across the world to provide forfaiting services. In order to provide common rules and standards for the conduct of the forfaiting business, some association bodies have been constituted. These bodies also facilitate the growth and development of the forfaiting business.

23.5.1 International Forfaiting Association (IFA)

The International Forfaiting Association (IFA), founded in August 1999, is an association of financial institutions and intermediaries actively engaged in the forfaiting business. Organizations that do not conduct forfaiting transactions can become associate members of the association, provided they have a strong link with the forfaiting market. The main activities of the IFA include organizing annual forfaiting conferences, recommending the use of standardized documentation by introducing market practice guidelines, offering conciliation and arbitration in cases of disputes in which a member is involved, and providing a website for sharing ideas, information, opinions and concerns with professionals who have mutual interests.

23.5.2 Association of Trade and Forfaiting in the Americas Inc (ATFA)

The Association of Trade and Forfaiting in the Americas Inc (ATFA), with its headquarters in New York, is an association of financial institutions involved in forfaiting. The main objectives of the ATFA are as follows.

- To serve as a medium of exchange of information between organizations interested in forfaiting and international trade finance;
- To organize seminars, lectures and convocations on topics of international trade finance in order to educate its members;
- To serve as a specialized trade association offering advice and counsel to interested parties involved in trade finance;
- To foster national and international communication, cooperation and understanding by encouraging contact with similar trade organizations overseas and complementary organizations in the Americas; and
- To promote the highest degree of ethical and professional standards among its members.

23.5.3 South Asian Forfaiting Facility (SAFF)

The South Asian Forfaiting Facility (SAFF) was launched as a project in 2000 by the International Finance Corporation (IFC). The project's primary sponsor was West LB, a leading European bank and the third largest in Germany. IFC and West LB worked together on this project. The SAFF comprises three country-specific forfaiting facilities covering India, Bangladesh and Sri Lanka. It is part of the larger Asian Forfaiting Facility (AFF), which also includes the China, Indonesia, Malaysia, Korea, Philippines and Thailand. The objective of the SAFF is to support trade between the project countries within the South Asia region as well as imports from other countries. For each country facility—that is, India, Bangladesh and Sri Lanka—West LB has set up a revolving forfaiting facility with a final two-year term. IFC provides a partial guarantee of 40 per cent of the exposure of each forfaiting transaction for the first 185 to 365 days depending on the credit quality of the respective local bank. The IFC's total exposure is capped at USD 28 million. The SAFF is therefore part of a regional initiative that can provide a new product to a number of markets in an effective, efficient and coordinated fashion.

Summary

1. With the growing importance of international trade accompanied by intense global competition, sellers face a major problem of insistence by buyers to grant trade credit on open account terms. This means that the sellers could receive payment from the buyers only after some days or months after delivery of the goods or services.
2. Trade financing refers to the provision of finance to facilitate selling or buying of goods and services, pending actual payment for the same.
3. In open account deals, the seller bears the risks as the payment for the trade is made by the buyer only after the latter has taken possession of the goods.

4. Factoring is an agreement between a firm and a factoring organization (factor) under which the sales ledger administration and receivables collection of the firm are entrusted to an external agency called the factor.
5. The major functions of a factor are credit evaluation, financing of receivables and sales ledger administration.
6. Factoring can be classified as recourse factoring, non-recourse factoring, agency factoring, non-notification factoring, reverse factoring, domestic factoring, international factoring, bank participation factoring and channel financing factoring.
6. In recourse factoring, bad debt losses are borne by the seller himself and in non-recourse factoring, the factor assumes the full responsibility of collecting dues from the debtors.
7. International factoring services are offered to exporters who sell their products to customers domiciled in other countries on open account terms.
8. In international factoring, there are two agreements that are linked: one between the exporter and the export factor and the other between the export factor and the import factor. But the client-firm deals with only one factor.
9. The main benefit of factoring is that the client-firm can receive most of the sale proceeds upfront without waiting for the buyer to pay. Further, a firm can be relieved of receivables management if it utilizes the services of a factor.
10. A firm should take into account both the tangible costs and benefits while assessing the feasibility or desirability of factoring.
11. Factors Chain International, established in 1968, is a global network of leading factoring companies in the world.
12. The institutions that offer factoring services in India include SBI Factors and Canbank Factors, Citibank, Export Credit Guarantee Corporation of India Ltd, Foremost Factor Limited, Global Trade Finance Limited, Hong Kong and Shanghai Banking Corporation Ltd and Small Industries Development Bank of India.
13. The world factoring turnover has increased from EUR 623,840 million in 2000 to EUR 1,325,111 million in 2008.
14. Forfaiting has become an effective and alternative method of financing for firms, particularly small and medium enterprises, which are capital-scarce and cannot provide their foreign customers with credit.
15. Although forfaiting combines several features of traditional methods of short-term financing, it is a special form of financing especially suitable for small and medium enterprises.
16. Forfaiting is related to financing of export of capital goods, commodities and projects, whereas factoring covers mostly smaller claims for consumer goods and services.

Questions

1. Discuss the need and importance of factoring with special reference to India.
2. What is receivables management?
3. What is the open credit system?
4. What are the different types of factoring?
5. Distinguish between recourse factoring and non-recourse factoring.
6. What are the functions of a factor?
7. Explain the factoring mechanism.
8. What do you understand by sales ledger administration?
9. How is international factoring different from domestic factoring?
10. What are the specific advantages of factoring?
11. What are the costs of factoring?
12. What are the benefits of forfaiting? Mention the forfaiting costs.
13. What are the objectives of International Factoring Chain?
14. Distinguish between factoring and forfaiting.

Index

N

O

P

Q

R

S

T

U

V

W

Z